OpenVMS AXP Internals and Data Structures

VERSION 1.5

VERSION 1.5

OpenVMS AXP Internals and Data Structures

Ruth E. Goldenberg

Saro Saravanan

Digital Press

Digital Press™ is an imprint of Butterworth-Heinemann, Publisher for Digital Equipment Corporation.

 In recognition of the importance of preserving what has been written, Butterworth-Heinemann prints its books on acid-free paper whenever possible.

Cover designer: Hannus Design Associates
Interior designer: David Ford
Copy editor: Alice Cheyer
Art editor: Carol Keller
Composition: Sarah Lemaire; Paul C. Anagnostopoulos, Marsha Finley,
    Caroline McCarley using ZzTeX
Index: Sarah Lemaire, Rosemary Simpson, John Mann
Proofreader: Cecilia Thurlow
Production: Superscript Editorial Production Services

Quotations from the following works appear as epigraphs in this book: Edgar A. Guest, "The Package of Seeds," *Collected Verse of Edgar A. Guest*, copyright 1934 by Contemporary Books, Chicago, Illinois 60601, reprinted by permission of Contemporary Books; excerpt from "The Hollow Men," in *Collected Poems 1909–1962* by T. S. Eliot, copyright 1936 by Harcourt Brace Jovanovich, Inc., copyright © 1964, 1963 by T. S. Eliot, reprinted by permission of Harcourt Brace Jovanovich and Faber and Faber Ltd.

Jacket painting: Paul Klee, 1930, Solomon R. Guggenheim Museum, New York; photo: David Heald © The Solomon R. Guggenheim Foundation, New York.

Trademarks appear on page 1523, which constitutes an extension of the copyright page.

Library of Congress Cataloging-in-Publication Data

Goldenberg, Ruth E.
    OpenVMS AXP Internals and Data Structures : version 1.5 / Ruth E.
Goldenberg, Saro Saravanan.
        p. cm.
    Includes index.
    ISBN 1-55558-120-X
    1. Operating systems (Computers)   2. Open VMS AXP.   I. Saravanan,
Saro.   II. Title.
QA76.76.O63G6385   1994
005.4'469–dc20   94-11874
                                                                            CIP

The publisher offers discounts on bulk orders of this book. For information, please write:
Manager of Special Sales, Digital Press
Butterworth-Heinemann
313 Washington St.
Newton, MA 02158

Order number: EY-Q770E-DP.

10 9 8 7 6 5 4 3 2 1

Printed in the United States of America.

To
our parents,

to
Lucas Sorn Anagnostopoulos
Daniel Keller Franc
Eric Hosmer Lemaire
Nikila Saravanan,
new arrivals to the families
of the makers of this book
during the course of its creation,

and to
Chase Duffy,
guide and friend.

Preface

Digital Equipment Corporation has introduced a new 64-bit RISC architecture—Alpha AXP—and OpenVMS support for it.

The Alpha AXP architecture is a load/store architecture, with all operations done between registers. There are 32 integer registers and 32 floating-point registers, each 64 bits wide. A load or store instruction moves a longword or quadword between a register and memory. A memory operand is specified as a 16-bit signed displacement from the contents of an integer register.

Complex functions, such as interrupt and exception initiation, implemented in microcode on a VAX processor, are implemented in privileged architecture library (PALcode) routines. Written in Alpha AXP instructions, these routines run in kernel mode with interrupts disabled. They extend the CPU architecture to provide a more complete environment for the operating system than the CPU alone could.

The subject of this book is the OpenVMS operating system that supports this RISC architecture. Its formal name is the OpenVMS AXP operating system.

Version 1.0 of the OpenVMS AXP operating system was ported from VAX VMS Version 5.4-2. A majority of its source modules are based upon VAX VMS Version 5.4-2 source modules. OpenVMS AXP Version 1.5 is based upon VAX VMS Version 5.4-3.

A typical VAX VMS source module is slightly modified, compiled by a compiler that produces Alpha AXP instructions, and linked to produce an OpenVMS AXP image. Because much of the OpenVMS executive is closely connected to specific architectural and hardware features, many executive modules have been more than slightly changed. Modules that interface directly with architectural features, for example, the scheduling code that swaps process contexts and the service routine for asynchronous system trap (AST) interrupts, have been entirely rewritten.

Just as the OpenVMS AXP operating system has been ported from VAX VMS Version 5.4-2, this book has been ported from *VAX/VMS Internals and Data Structures: Version 5.2*, by Ruth E. Goldenberg and Lawrence J. Kenah (Digital Press, 1991).

ORGANIZATION OF THIS PUBLICATION

This book is divided into nine parts, each of which describes a different aspect of the operating system.

▶ Part 1 presents an overview of the operating system and reviews those concepts that are basic to its workings.

▶ Part 2 describes the mechanisms used to pass control between user programs and the operating system, and within the system itself.

▶ Part 3 describes OpenVMS synchronization methods.

▶ Part 4 describes scheduling, time support, and process control.

▶ Part 5 discusses memory management, with emphasis on system data structures and their manipulation by paging and swapping routines. It also describes management of dynamic memory, such as nonpaged pool.

▶ Part 6 contains an overview of the I/O subsystem, paying particular attention to the I/O-related system services.

▶ Part 7 describes the life cycle of a process: its creation, the activation and termination of images within its context, and its deletion.

▶ Part 8 describes the life of the system: its organization, initialization, error handling, and shutdown. It also explains symmetric multiprocessing support.

▶ Part 9 discusses the implementation of logical names and the internals of several miscellaneous system services.

▶ The appendixes include a summary of OpenVMS data structures and of Alpha AXP systems, layouts of system and P1 virtual address spaces, information on the use of listings and map files, the conventions used in naming symbols, and information about lock and resource use by various OpenVMS components.

CONVENTIONS

A number of conventions are used throughout the text and figures of this book.

During the life of the VAX VMS operating system, the exact form of its name has changed several times: from VAX/VMS Version 1.0 to VAX VMS Version 5.0 to OpenVMS VAX Version 5.5. In describing the evolution of VMS algorithms and discussing the foundation of the OpenVMS AXP operating system, this book refers to the OpenVMS VAX operating system by whichever name is appropriate for the version referenced.

The term *executive* refers to those parts of the operating system that are loaded into and that execute from system space. The executive includes the system base images, SYS$BASE_IMAGE.EXE and SYS$PUBLIC_VECTORS.EXE, and a number of other loadable executive images. Unlike OpenVMS VAX executive images, all images loaded into OpenVMS AXP system space have the form of a loadable executive image. Because there is no longer a need to distinguish different types of executive image, this book generally shortens the term *loadable executive image* to *executive image*.

The terms *system* and *OpenVMS system* describe the entire OpenVMS software package, including privileged processes, utilities, and other support software as well as the executive itself. The OpenVMS system consists of many different components, each a different file. One component is the system base image, SYS$BASE_IMAGE.EXE. Others are executive images, device drivers, command language interpreters, and utility programs.

The source modules from which these components are built and their listings are divided into facilities. Each facility is a directory on a source or listing medium containing sources and command procedures to build one or more components. The facility [DRIVER], for example, contains sources for most of the device drivers. The facility [SYSBOOT] contains sources for the secondary bootstrap program, SYSBOOT. The facility [SYS] contains the sources that make up the base images and many executive images.

This book identifies a [SYS] facility source module only by its file name. It identifies a module from any other facility by facility directory name and file name. For example, [SYSGEN]SYSGEN refers to the source for the system generation utility (SYSGEN).

Almost all source modules are built so as to produce object modules and listing files of the same file name as the source module. Thus, a reference in the book to a source module name identifies the file name of the listing file as well. In a case where the two names differ, the book explicitly identifies the name of the listing file. Appendix B discusses how to locate a module in the source listings.

This book identifies a macro from SYS$LIBRARY:LIB.MLB by only its name, for instance, WFIKPCH. The macro library of all other macros is specified.

The unmodified terms *process control block* and *PCB* refer to the software data structure used by the scheduler. The data structure that contains a process's hardware context, the hardware privileged context block (HWPCB), is always called the HWPCB.

The term *inner access modes* means those access modes with more privilege. The term *outer access modes* means those with less privilege. Thus, the innermost access mode is kernel and the outermost mode is user.

SYSGEN parameters include both the dynamic parameters, which can be changed on the running system, and the static parameters, whose changes do not take effect until the next system boot. These parameters are referred to by their parameter names rather than by the global locations where their values are stored. Appendix C relates parameter names to their corresponding global locations.

The terms *byte index, word index, longword index,* and *quadword index* derive from methods of VAX operand access that use context-indexed addressing modes. That is, the index value is multiplied by 1, 2, 4, or 8 (for bytes, words, longwords, or quadwords, respectively) as part of operand evaluation, to calculate the effective address of the operand. Although the Alpha AXP architecture does not include these addressing modes, the concept of context indexing is relevant to various OpenVMS AXP data structures and tables.

A term in small capital letters refers to the formal name of an argument to an OpenVMS system service, for example, the LOGNAM argument.

A bit field is sometimes described by its starting and ending bit numbers within angle brackets; for example, the interrupt priority level of the processor, in the processor status bits $\langle 12:8 \rangle$, is contained in bits 8 through 12.

Three conventions are observed for lists:

▶ In lists like this one, where no order or hierarchy exists, list elements are indicated by leading triangular bullets. Sublists without hierarchy are indicated by round bullets.

▶ Lists that indicate an ordered set of operations are numbered. Sublists that indicate an ordered set of operations are lettered.

▶ Numbered lists with the numbers enclosed in circles indicate a correspondence between the list elements and numbered items in a figure or example.

Several conventions are observed for figures. In all diagrams of memory, the lowest virtual address appears at the top of the page and addresses increase toward the bottom of the page. Thus, the direction of stack growth is depicted upward from the bottom of the page. In diagrams that display more detail, such as bytes within longwords, addresses increase from right to left. That is, the lowest addressed byte (or bit) in a longword is on the right-hand side of a figure and the most significant byte (or bit) is on the left-hand side.

Each field in a data structure layout is represented by a rectangle. In many figures, the rectangle contains the last part of the name of the field, excluding the structure name, data type designator, and leading underscore. A rectangle the full width of the diagram generally represents a longword regardless of its depth. A field smaller than a longword is represented in proportion to its size; for example, bytes and words are quarter- and half-width rectangles. A quadword is generally represented by a full-width rectangle with a short horizontal line segment midway down each side. In some figures, a rectangle the full width of the diagram represents a quadword. In these figures, bit position numbers above the top rectangle show numbers from 0 to 63 to indicate that the rectangle represents a quadword.

For example, Figure 9.7 shows the layout of a spinlock control block. The rectangle labeled SPINLOCK represents the longword SPL$L_SPINLOCK; the rectangle labeled OWN_CPU, the longword SPL$L_OWN_CPU; and the rectangle labeled ACQ_COUNT, the quadword SPL$Q_ACQ_COUNT.

In almost all data structures, the data structure's full-width rectangles represent longwords aligned on longword boundaries. In a few data structures, a horizontal row of boxes represents fields whose sizes do not total a longword. Without this practice, most of the fields in this kind of structure would be split into two part-width rectangles in adjoining rows, because they are unaligned longwords.

Some data structures have alternative definitions for fields or areas within them. A field with multiple names is represented by a box combining the names separated by slash (/) characters. An area with multiple layouts is shown as a rectangle with a dashed line separating the alternative definitions. For example, in Figure E.7, fields PCB$L_EFWM and PCB$L_PQB are two names for the same field. Figure E.7 also shows an example of alternative definitions for an area; the longword at PCB$L_EFC2P is also divided into the word PCB$W_PGFLCHAR, byte PCB$B_PGFLINDEX, and an unused byte.

A data structure field containing the address of another data structure in the same figure is represented by a bullet connected to an arrow pointing to the other structure. Where possible, the arrow points to the rightmost end of the field, that is, to bit 0. A field containing a value used as an index into that or another data structure is represented by an x connected to an arrow pointing to the indexed location.

Two conventions indicate elisions in a data structure layout. A specific amount of space is shown as a rectangle whose sides contain dots. Text within the rectangle indicates the amount of space it represents.

Field SPL$L_OWN_PC_VEC in Figure 9.7, for example, represents 16 longwords.

An indeterminate amount of space, often unnamed, representing omitted and undescribed fields, is indicated by a rectangle whose sides are intersected by short parallel horizontal lines.

For example, Figure 16.1, which identifies only the PCB fields related to memory management, contains five sets of omitted fields among the labeled fields.

JACKET ILLUSTRATION

For the jacket of this edition of the book, the author has chosen the painting "Open Book," by Paul Klee. In it, the pages of an open book communicate the sense of varying levels of depth and complexity.

It was selected not only for its esthetic qualities but also as a commentary on this book. Our goal has been to illuminate the OpenVMS executive. Where feasible, we provide different depths of discourse, from an overview at the beginning of a chapter to the detailed code descriptions at the end. The ultimate answers, however, are in the source code, for which this book is a road map.

ACKNOWLEDGMENTS

In addition to acknowledging the work of the many contributors to *VAX/VMS Internals and Data Structures: Version 5.2*, the precursor of the present book, we would like to acknowledge the contributors to the present book.

First and foremost, we would like to thank the OpenVMS AXP developers, especially Nancy Kronenberg and Vince Orgovan. As technical director, Nancy was the backbone and guiding spirit of the OpenVMS AXP development project. Her clarity and energy provided inspiration for this book. Vince was the project manager of OpenVMS AXP Version 1.0. We appreciated his cheerful willingness to answer our questions about project schedules, logistics, and politics.

Sarah Lemaire made significant and varied contributions to the creation of the current and preliminary editions of this book. She painstakingly and skillfully applied the figure and text edits, and updated the index, all of Appendix C and much of Appendix E. We were very glad of her help.

A number of people reviewed most or all of the book, contributing greatly to its quality: Dick Buttlar, Wayne Cardoza, Jim Fraser, Mike Harvey, Robert Hoffman, and Ben Thomas. Dick Buttlar made suggestions that improved the writing and advised us on VAX DOCUMENT and OpenVMS documentation. Wayne Cardoza answered many questions, especially on architectural issues and motivations. Jim Fraser reviewed multiple drafts of many chapters, pointed out omitted explanations, wrote several subsections, and helped with phrasing. Mike Harvey provided many detailed explanations and was especially helpful in areas related to memory management. Robert Hoffman provided much help, in particular with CPU-specific material and the console subsystem. Ben Thomas was helpful in many areas, particularly in matters related to the I/O subsystem.

A number of others reviewed substantial portions of the book and made suggestions that improved its quality: Dave Bernardo, Paul Blaney, Denise Dumas, Hai Huang, Nitin Karkhanis, Jim Kauffman, Karen Noel, Thomas Siebold, and Larry Stewart.

Chase Duffy of Digital Press managed the production of the preliminary edition and masterminded the publication of this one with exceptional forethought. She assembled a fine book production team, several of whose members are veterans of the VAX VMS editions of the book.

Alice Cheyer did her utmost to ensure the consistency, accuracy, and readability of the book. Carol Keller applied her esthetic sense and talent for precision to the preparation of the figures. We were glad to work again with these experienced book producers.

Paul Anagnostopoulos converted our VAX DOCUMENT chapter files into TEX, translating David Ford's masterful design into type with an original program, ZzTEX. Maintaining their sangfroid under pressure, Marsha Finley and Caroline McCarley composed the pages and Ann Knight provided production management services. Cecilia Thurlow proofread the book with a good eye for deviations from correctness.

Beth French of Digital Press oversaw the manufacture of the volumes of the preliminary edition.

John Osborn of Digital Press initiated the program by which we published new and revised chapters of this book in the preliminary edition. Frank Satlow, Technical Director of Butterworth-Heinemann, publisher of this book, took over the process.

Howard Hayakawa, our manager, made this book possible when he chose to fund its creation and gave us continuing encouragement and support during our work on it.

Ruth E. Goldenberg
Saro Saravanan
March 1994

Contents

Contents

III / Synchronization   215

Contents

Contents

VI / Input/Output 749

Contents

VIII / Life of the System   1091

Contents

Contents

PART I / Introduction

1 System Overview

For the fashion of Minas Tirith was such that it was built on
seven levels, each delved into a hill, and about each was set a
wall, and in each wall was a gate.

J.R.R. Tolkien, *The Return of the King*

The subject of this book is the OpenVMS AXP operating system. This version of the OpenVMS operating system supports the Alpha AXP architecture, Digital Equipment Corporation's 64-bit RISC architecture.

The architecture is a load/store architecture, with all operations done between registers. There are 32 integer registers and 32 floating-point registers, each 64 bits wide. A load or store instruction moves a longword or quadword between a register and memory. A memory operand is specified as a 16-bit signed displacement from the contents of an integer register. Complex functions, such as interrupt and exception initiation, implemented in microcode on a VAX processor, are implemented in privileged architecture library (PAL-code) routines.

Version 1.0 of the OpenVMS AXP operating system was ported from VAX VMS Version 5.4-2. OpenVMS AXP Version 1.5 is based upon VAX VMS Version 5.4-3 and contains some features from more recent releases.

This chapter introduces some basic OpenVMS concepts and components. It also introduces some of the features of the Alpha AXP architecture that are used by the operating system.

1.1 PROCESS, JOB, IMAGE, AND THREAD

The fundamental unit of scheduling, the entity that is selected for execution, is the process. A process can create subprocesses. The collection of the creator process, all the subprocesses created by it, if any, and all subprocesses created by its descendants is called a job. The programs executed in the context of a process are called images.

The term *thread of execution* as used in this book refers to a computational entity, an agent of execution. In the environment provided by a single process there can be many threads of execution, some of which may coexist. For example, execution of the mainline code in an image is one thread, and execution of an asynchronous system trap (AST) procedure in the same image is another. A DECthreads application could have multiple threads of execution.

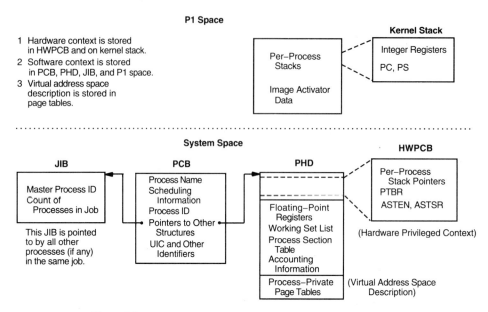

Figure 1.1
Data Structures That Describe Process Context

1.1.1 Process

A process is described by data structures that specify its hardware and software context and virtual address space. This information is stored in several different places in the virtual address space. The data structures that contain the various pieces of process context are pictured in Figure 1.1.

1.1.1.1 Hardware Context.

When a process is executing, its hardware context consists of integer registers, the program counter (PC), the processor status (PS), and the process-specific processor registers: for example, the page table base (PTBR) register, the asynchronous system trap enable (ASTEN) register, and the AST summary register (ASTSR). If the process is performing floating-point arithmetic, its hardware context includes the floating-point registers.

A process can be executing in any of four access modes: user, supervisor, executive, and kernel. The PS identifies the process's current access mode. There are four per-process access mode stacks and stack pointers, one for each of the four access modes. The stack pointers are also part of a process's hardware context. Code executing in the context of a process uses the stack associated with the process's current access mode.

When a process is not current, a subset of its hardware context, called hardware privileged context, is stored in a data structure called a hardware privileged context block (HWPCB). Figure 13.6 shows the layout of the HWPCB.

4

When a process is removed from execution, some of its nonprivileged hardware context (the integer registers, PC, and PS) is saved on its kernel stack and its privileged context is saved in its HWPCB. If the process is performing floating-point arithmetic, the contents of the floating-point registers are saved in its process header (PHD). When the process is placed back into execution, its privileged context is restored from the HWPCB and its nonprivileged context from the kernel stack. If appropriate, floating-point registers are restored from the PHD.

1.1.1.2   **Software Context.** Software context consists of all the data required by various parts of the operating system to control that portion of common resources allocated to a given process. This context includes the process software priority, its scheduling state, process privileges and identifiers, quotas and limits, process page file assignments and reservations, and miscellaneous information, such as process name and process identification.

The information about a process that must be in memory at all times is stored in a data structure called the process control block (PCB). This information includes the software priority of the process, its unique process identification (PID), and the particular scheduling state that the process is in at a given point in time. When a process is outswapped, its location in a swap file on a mass storage device is recorded in its PCB. The PCB also records some process quotas and limits. Other quotas and limits are recorded in the job information block (JIB).

The PCB incorporates another data structure called an access rights block (ARB), which lists the identifiers that the process holds. Identifiers are names that specify to what groups a process belongs for purposes of determining access to files and other protected objects. Identifiers are described briefly in Section 1.5.1.4.

Some information about a process that does not have to be permanently resident is contained in its PHD. This information is needed when the process is resident and consists mainly of information used by memory management when page faults occur. The swapper uses the data in the PHD when it removes the process from memory (outswaps) or brings the process back into memory (inswaps). The HWPCB is a part of the PHD.

Other process-specific information is stored in the P1 portion of the process virtual address space. This includes information about the image that is currently executing. Information that is stored in P1 space is only accessible when the process is executing (is current on some CPU), because P1 space is process-private.

1.1.1.3   **Virtual Address Space Description.** OpenVMS AXP virtual address space is largely based upon OpenVMS VAX address space:

▶ Each process has a process-private P0 space to run programs.

▸ Each process has a process-private P1 space for its process stacks, permanent process control information maintained by the operating system, and a command language interpreter (CLI) if one is being used.

▸ Each process accesses a shared region called system space, occupied by operating system components and systemwide data.

The virtual address space of a process is described by a three-level page table hierarchy, much of which is in the PHD of that process.

Section 1.6 provides a brief introduction to the organization and use of virtual address space.

1.1.2   Image

An image is a file that contains binary code and data and that can be executed on an OpenVMS AXP system. The linker processes one or more object modules produced by a language processor such as a compiler and builds an image. When the user initiates image execution (as part of process creation or through a Digital command language (DCL) command in an interactive or batch job), an operating system component called the image activator reads the image header and sets up the process-private page tables to point to the appropriate sections of the image file. The OpenVMS paging mechanism reads image pages into memory as they are referenced.

Chapter 28 discusses the image activator.

1.1.3   Job

A collection of subprocesses with their common root process is called a job. The concept of a job exists for the purpose of sharing resources. Processes in the same job can share jobwide logical names and mass storage volumes. Some quotas and limits are shared among all processes in the same job. The current values of these quotas are contained in the JIB, which is shared by all processes in the same job. Figure E.5 shows this structure.

1.2   OPENVMS AXP COMPONENTS

There are several names for different subsets of the OpenVMS AXP system. The terms *system* and *OpenVMS AXP system* describe the entire OpenVMS AXP software package, whose components include

▸ Utilities
▸ Program development tools
▸ Run-time libraries
▸ System processes such as the job controller
▸ DCL interpreter
▸ Record Management Services (RMS)
▸ Files-11 Extended QIO Processor (XQP)
▸ The executive

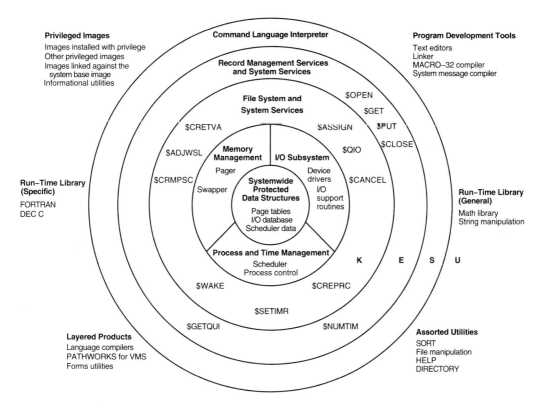

Figure 1.2
Layered Design of the OpenVMS AXP Operating System

The system provides services at several levels so that user applications may execute easily and effectively. Its layered structure is pictured in Figure 1.2. In general, components in a given layer can make use of the facilities in the same layer and in all inner layers.

1.2.1   OpenVMS AXP Executive

The term *executive* refers to a subset of the components that reside in system space. The subset excludes shareable and executable images installed permanently resident in system space. (The term *executive* is distinct from the term *executive access mode*, although the executive typically executes in kernel or executive access mode.) In Figure 1.2, the OpenVMS AXP executive is shown as the center circle and three surrounding rings, including the one labeled Record Management Services and System Services. It is implemented as a number of separately loadable executive images. Some of these images are loaded on all systems, while others support features specific to particular system configurations.

An executive image is built from source modules performing related functions and from data and initialization code specific to those functions. The image PROCESS_MANAGEMENT.EXE, for example, includes the rescheduling interrupt service routine, process creation and deletion system services, and the subroutine for reporting scheduler events.

Two of the executive images, called base images, connect requests for system services and other system functions with the routines that provide them. These routines are located in other executive images. The base image SYS$PUBLIC_VECTORS.EXE resolves calls to system service procedures and is linked by default with any image that requests a system service.

The base image SYS$BASE_IMAGE.EXE resolves calls to executive routines and contains static executive data. An image that calls executive routines or references executive data must be explicitly linked with SYS$BASE_IMAGE.EXE. To resolve references to routines in other executive images, an executive image links against SYS$BASE_IMAGE.EXE. Appendix A lists OpenVMS components that are linked with SYS$BASE_IMAGE.EXE.

Each executive image is linked independently of the others and mapped into system space allocated for it. This separation makes it possible for one image to be replaced at system initialization by an enhanced or corrected version with no impact on other executive images or the base images. Furthermore, there is not necessarily an impact on any other images linked with SYS$BASE_IMAGE.EXE.

The executive is divided into conceptual categories, such as MEMORY_MANAGEMENT, each with its own version number. The version number of a category changes when an interface in that category changes. Each data cell or routine identified in SYS$BASE_IMAGE.EXE specifies the categories with which it is associated. When an OpenVMS release contains an incompatible change in a category, the version number of that category changes, and an image referencing a system data cell or routine affected by the change must relink.

Chapter 32 discusses the organization and loading of executive images, as well as their conceptual categories.

1.2.2 OpenVMS AXP Kernel

The OpenVMS AXP kernel is a subset of the executive. (The term *kernel* is distinct from the term *kernel access mode*, although kernel routines typically execute in kernel mode.) In Figure 1.2, the kernel is shown as the innermost three layers. The main topic of this book is the OpenVMS AXP kernel: the I/O subsystem, memory management, the scheduling subsystem, and the system services that support and complement these components.

The discussion of these three components and other miscellaneous parts of the operating system kernel focuses on the data structures that are manipulated by a given component. In describing what each major data structure represents and how that structure is altered by different sequences of events in the system, this chapter summarizes the operations of each major piece of the kernel.

The I/O subsystem consists of device drivers and their associated data structures; device-independent routines within the executive; and several system services, the most important of which is the Queue I/O Request ($QIO) system service. All forms of I/O request made by outer layers of the system are transformed into $QIO requests.

The I/O subsystem is described in detail from the point of view of adding a device driver in the manual *OpenVMS AXP Device Support: Creating a Step 1 Driver from an OpenVMS VAX Device Driver*. Chapters 23 and 24 of this book describe some aspects of the I/O subsystem that are not described in that manual.

The memory management subsystem consists largely of the page fault handler, which implements OpenVMS AXP virtual memory support, and the working set swapper, which allows the system to utilize more fully the amount of physical memory that is available. The data structures used and manipulated by the page fault handler and swapper include the page frame number (PFN) database and the page tables of each process. The PFN database describes each page of physical memory. A virtual address space description of each currently resident process is contained in its process-private page tables. The system page table describes the system space portion of virtual address space, which is shared among all processes.

System services enable a user (or the system on behalf of the user) to create or delete specific portions of virtual address space or to map a file into a specified virtual address range.

Chapters 15 through 20 describe the memory management subsystem in detail.

The scheduling subsystem is the third major component of the kernel. It selects processes for execution and removes from execution processes that can no longer execute. Chapter 13 describes these operations. The scheduling subsystem also services the hardware clocks and includes timer-related system services (see Chapter 12). System services are available to allow a process to create or delete other processes. Other services provide one process the ability to obtain information about another and control its execution (see Chapter 14).

One area of the operating system kernel that is not pictured in Figure 1.2 involves the many miscellaneous services that are available in the operating system kernel. Some of these services for such tasks as logical name creation or string formatting are available to the user in the form of system services. Others, such as pool manipulation routines and certain synchronization techniques, are only used by the kernel and privileged utilities. Still others, such as the lock management system services, are used throughout the system—by users' programs, system services, RMS, the file system, and privileged utilities.

1.2.3   Interface among Kernel Subsystems

The connection among the three major subsystems pictured in Figure 1.2 is somewhat misleading because there is relatively little interaction between the three components. In addition, each component has its own data structures for which it is responsible. When one of the other pieces of the system needs to access such data structures, it does so through some controlled interface. Figure 1.3 shows the interactions between the three major subsystems in the operating system kernel.

The I/O subsystem makes a request to memory management to lock down specified pages for a direct I/O request. The page fault handler or swapper is notified directly when the I/O request that just completed was initiated by either one of them.

I/O requests can result in the requesting process's being placed in a wait state until the request completes. This change of state requires that the scheduling subsystem be notified. In addition, at I/O completion, the I/O subsystem notifies the scheduling subsystem that the event flag associated with the I/O request has been set, possibly causing the process's scheduling state to change to computable.

Both the page fault handler and the swapper require input and output operations to fulfill their functions. They use special entry points into the I/O subsystem rather than requesting the $QIO system service. These entry points queue prebuilt I/O packets directly to the driver, bypassing unnecessary protection checks and preventing irrelevant attempts to lock pages associated with these direct I/O requests.

If a process incurs a page fault resulting in a read from disk or if a process requires physical memory and none is available, the process is put into one of the memory management wait states by the scheduling subsystem. When the page read completes or physical memory becomes available, the process is made computable again.

The scheduling state of a process may affect its treatment by the swapper. When the swapper detects that free memory is becoming scarce, it can reclaim physical pages from the working sets of resident processes. Processes in certain wait states are more likely to be subject to memory reclamation than others. Processes in certain long-lasting wait states are more likely to be outswapped than computable processes. When an outswapped process becomes computable, it is eventually inswapped.

The scheduling subsystem interacts very little with the rest of the system. It plays a more passive role when cooperation with memory management or the I/O subsystem is required. One exception is that the scheduling sub-

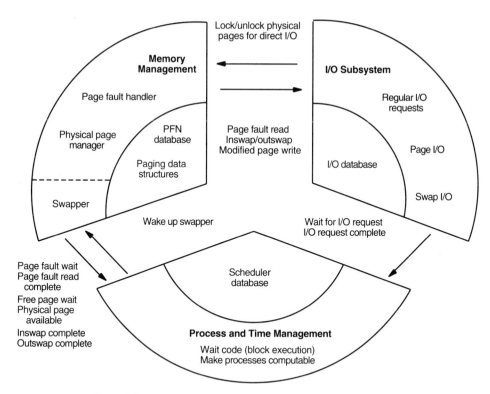

Figure 1.3
Interaction Between Components of OpenVMS AXP
Kernel

system awakens the swapper when a process that is not currently memory-resident becomes computable.

1.2.4   Data Management

The OpenVMS AXP system provides data management facilities at two levels. The record structure that exists within a file is implemented by RMS, which is in the layer just outside the kernel. RMS consists of a set of system service procedures located in an executive image. Most of the procedures in RMS execute in executive access mode, providing a thin wall of protection between RMS and the kernel itself.

Access to files on mass storage volumes is controlled by the Files-11 XQP or one of the disk or tape ancillary control processes (ACPs). ACPs and the Files-11 XQP interact with the kernel both through the system service interface and by the use of utility routines not accessible to the general user.

The Files-11 XQP controls the on-disk structure employed on almost all block-structured mass storage volumes. (The placement of files on a block-

11

structured medium, such as a disk volume or a block-structured tape, is referred to as on-disk structure.) The XQP is implemented as an extension to the $QIO system service and runs in process context. A process's XQP file operations are serialized with those of other processes and processors through lock management system services.

The magtape ACP (MTAAACP.EXE) controls the placement of files on a magtape. Two ACPs (F11CACP.EXE and F11DACP.EXE) support the CD-ROM volume and file structure defined by the International Standards Organization (ISO) 9660 standard.

1.2.5   User Interface

The interface presented to the user (as distinct from the application programmer who is using system services and Run-Time Library procedures) is a command language interpreter. The DCL CLI is available on all OpenVMS AXP systems. Currently, it is the only CLI that is shipped as part of the OpenVMS AXP system.

Some of the services performed by a CLI call RMS or the system services directly; others result in the execution of external images. These images are generally no different from user-written applications because their only interface to the executive is through system service and RMS requests.

A Portable Operating System Interface (POSIX) command interface is available as part of the layered optional software product POSIX for Open-VMS AXP, Version 1.0.

In addition, a graphical user interface is available through the layered product DECwindows Motif for OpenVMS AXP.

1.2.6   Images That Run with Privilege

Some of the informational utilities and disk and tape volume manipulation utilities require that selected portions of protected data structures be read or written in a controlled fashion. Images that require privilege to perform specific functions can be installed (made known to the operating system) with built-in privilege by a system manager so that nonprivileged users can execute them and have them perform their functions. Such images include AUTHORIZE, LOGINOUT, MONITOR, SET, and SHOW. Appendix A lists images that are installed with privilege in a typical OpenVMS AXP system.

Other images that perform privileged functions are not installed with built-in privilege because their functions are inherently sensitive and more varied. These images could reveal security information or destroy the system if executed by naive or malicious users. Thus, in effect, they can only be executed by privileged users. (Although a nonprivileged user could execute them, such images running in a nonprivileged process would be unable to perform their functions.) Examples include the system generation (SYSGEN) utility, for modifying SYSGEN parameters; the System Dump Analyzer (SDA), for examining the contents of memory; or the network control program (NCP), for network management. Other images that require privilege to execute but are not installed with privilege in a typical OpenVMS AXP system are listed in Appendix A.

1.3   OPENVMS AXP CALLING STANDARD

The OpenVMS AXP calling standard defines the data structures, conventions, and methods by which a native procedure calls other procedures and is itself called. (A procedure is a closed sequence of instructions that is entered from a caller and that returns control to its caller.) The standard defines attributes of the interface between modules, such as the calling sequence, argument list, register use, and condition handling conventions.

The standard was created with the following goals:

- ▸ To provide a high degree of compatibility with existing OpenVMS VAX programs
- ▸ To simplify coexistence with VAX procedures that execute in the Translated Image Environment
- ▸ To minimize the cost of procedure calls
- ▸ To provide an efficient mechanism for calling procedures that do not need the overhead of setting up a stack call frame
- ▸ To enable one procedure to call another using the same interface regardless of the type of target procedure

Any procedure that adheres to this standard can be called from any native language, an advantage for a large application that uses the features of several languages. The OpenVMS AXP operating system adheres to this standard in its interfaces to system and RMS services, Run-Time Library procedures, and other utility procedures.

This section introduces calling standard terms and concepts. The *Open-VMS Calling Standard* manual provides a more complete description.

1.3.1   Procedure Descriptor and Procedure Frame

Each procedure is described by a data structure called a procedure descriptor. When a language compiler processes a source module, it identifies the procedures within the module and adds to the object module a procedure descriptor for each procedure. A procedure descriptor defines the procedure's type, describes its register and stack use, and identifies its code entry point. A procedure descriptor is typically not accessed during run time. It is, however, used in interpreting the chain of nested procedures when exceptions occur, when the call chain is being unwound, and when the image is being debugged.

A particular procedure is identified by a procedure value, that is, the value of the symbol that names the procedure. The procedure value of an Open-VMS AXP procedure is the address of its procedure descriptor.

A procedure is characterized by the type of its procedure frame, the information that it must save to enable it to return properly to its caller. There are three types of procedures:

▸ A stack frame procedure maintains its caller's context on the stack.
▸ A register frame procedure maintains its caller's context in registers.
▸ A null frame procedure does not establish a context and is said to execute in the context of the procedure that called it.

In OpenVMS AXP executive code, stack frame and null frame procedures predominate.

1.3.2   Calling Conventions

Calling conventions are the rules and methods used for communicating information between a caller and a called procedure. OpenVMS AXP calling conventions include the following:

▸ The caller passes to a called procedure the procedure value of the called procedure in R27, the procedure value (PV) register. Section 1.3.3 describes the use of the PV as linkage pointer.
▸ When a called procedure is entered, R26, the return address (RA) register, contains the address in the caller to which control must be returned.
▸ The caller loads R25, the argument information (AI) register, with information about the arguments being passed, in particular, the number of the arguments and the types of the first six arguments. The first six arguments, which can be a mix of integer and floating-point, are passed in registers, R16 through R21 if they are integer, or F16 through F21 if floating-point. Additional arguments are stored as quadwords on the stack.
▸ The caller must align the stack to an octaword boundary before calling another procedure.
▸ A called procedure returns an integer value in R0.
▸ A called procedure is required to save the contents of R2 through R15 before modifying them. By convention, R1, R22–R24, and R28 are scratch registers and need not be saved before use. The PV, RA, AI, and argument registers may be modified and not restored by the called procedure.
▸ R29, the frame pointer (FP) register, defines the current procedure. It always contains either the procedure value of the current procedure or the address of an aligned quadword that contains the procedure value.

The Alpha AXP architecture is a RISC architecture and has no instructions resembling the VAX CALLG, CALLS, and RET instructions, which provide a foundation for the OpenVMS VAX calling standard. Instead, compiler-generated AXP instructions implement the OpenVMS AXP calling standard and provide functions similar to those of the VAX instructions. Prologue code executes at the beginning of each procedure to save the caller's context and build a procedure frame. Epilogue code executes at the end of each procedure to restore the caller's context and return to it. For a stack or register frame procedure, prologue code also loads FP, thereby formally establishing that procedure's context; epilogue code restores the FP of the calling procedure, switching back to its context.

Appendix B gives examples of prologue and epilogue code.

1.3.3 Linkage Section and Linkage Pointer

The architecture specifies a fixed instruction length of 32 bits and a memory address length of 64 bits. Consequently, an instruction cannot contain a full address. The architecture is described as a base register architecture, one in which memory references within a limited range from a given address are expressed as displacements from the contents of a register that contains the base address of the memory area.

When compiling a source module, an OpenVMS AXP compiler creates a program section called a linkage section, which contains descriptors of the module's procedures and address constants that a procedure uses to access static storage, external procedures, and variables. The compiler generates references to the linkage section as positive or negative displacements from a base register called the linkage section pointer. When a procedure is entered, R27 contains its procedure value and can thus be used as a linkage pointer. Most compilers generate references to linkage section data as offsets from the procedure value. A procedure that calls another procedure copies its own procedure value to another register, often R13.

1.3.4 Linkage Pair

A linkage to an external procedure is represented in the calling procedure's linkage section as a two-quadword data structure called a linkage pair. By the time a call using a linkage pair is executed, the first quadword of the linkage pair must contain the external procedure's code entry address, and the second quadword must contain the address of its procedure descriptor. When the linker links an object module containing a call with the object module containing the called procedure, the linker fills in the linkage pair in the calling object module.

The instruction most commonly used to transfer control is the JSR instruction. It passes control to the address in a designated register and loads the address of the instruction that follows it in another designated register. The instruction saves no state except the return address. A typical OpenVMS AXP call sequence resembles the following generated code excerpt, which loads a linkage pair from the linkage section, pointed to by R13:

```
                          ;R13 = address of linkage section
    LDQ     R26, x(R13)   ;Load code entry address of procedure
    LDQ     R27, x+8(R13) ;Load its procedure value
    JSR     R26, R26      ;Transfer control and save
                          ; return address in R26
```

15

When the linker links an executable image containing a call to an external procedure in a shareable image, the linker cannot resolve the contents of the linkage pair because a shareable image is not assigned address space until it is activated. Instead, the linker records in the image the need for the image activator to resolve the contents. Chapter 28 describes image activation, fixup, and relocation.

Example 1.1 is an excerpt from a MACRO-32 listing, showing linkage section data and references to it, as well as a transfer of control to a system service. Most comments in the generated code have been added to the excerpt to document it.

1.3.5   Symbol Vector

The global symbols from object modules in a shareable image that are to be visible externally are called universal symbols. All universal symbols must be identified to the linker by means of options specified when the shareable image is linked. The linker creates a universal symbol for each global symbol identified in the SYMBOL_VECTOR option. To describe the universal symbols, the linker creates within the shareable image both a symbol vector and a global symbol table.

A symbol vector contains two quadwords for each universal symbol. For a universal symbol that is the name of a procedure, the two quadwords hold addresses of the procedure's code entry point and its procedure descriptor. That is, they form replacement contents for a linkage pair. A global symbol table lists the shareable image's universal symbols and their values. The value of a universal symbol, as recorded in a global symbol table, is the offset of its two quadwords from the beginning of the symbol vector. In contrast, the value of an OpenVMS VAX universal symbol is its offset in the shareable image.

During image activation address space is assigned to a shareable image, and its symbol vector entries are updated to contain actual addresses of the procedure descriptors and code entry points. Subsequently, for any image that is activated with a shareable image and that contains a call to a procedure in the shareable image, the image activator resolves the linkage pair for the call by replacing the linkage pair's contents with the corresponding contents from the symbol vector of the shareable image.

1.4   ARCHITECTURE ASSISTANCE TO THE OPERATING SYSTEM

The Alpha AXP architecture was designed for high performance and with OpenVMS software migration in mind. The VAX features most critical to the OpenVMS system are four access modes, protection at the page level, 32 interrupt priority levels (IPLs), the interrupt and exception mechanism, the AST mechanism, and the ability to request software interrupts. The Alpha AXP architecture provides much of this support through PALcode routines.

16

Example 1.1

References to Linkage Section Data

```
; MACRO-32 statements
;
            .
            .
            .
        .PSECT  $DATA$,EXE,WRT
KERNEL_ARGS:
        .LONG   1
        .LONG   10
;
        .PSECT  $CODE$,EXE,NOWRT
;
        .ENTRY  MAIN,^M<>
        .SHOW   BINARY
        $CMKRNL_S  ROUTIN=KERNEL_ROUTINE, ARGLST=KERNEL_ARGS
                PUSHAB  KERNEL_ARGS
                PUSHAB  KERNEL_ROUTINE
                CALLS   #2,G^SYS$CMKRNL
        .NOSHOW BINARY
        $EXIT_S RO
        .END    MAIN
;
; Generated code - note that these displacements are decimal
;
        .PSECT  $CODE$, OCTA, NOPIC, CON, REL, LCL,-
                NOSHR, EXE, RD, NOWRT
 MAIN:
            .
            .                       ;Prologue code that builds stack frame
            .
        MOV     R27, R13        ;Copy PV to R13
        LDQ     R26, 56(R13)    ;Load code entry point of SYS$CMKRNL
        LDQ     R16, 40(R13)    ;Load first system service argument
        LDQ     R27, 64(R13)    ;Load procedure value of SYS$CMKRNL
        LDQ     R17, 24(R13)    ;Load second system service argument
        BIS     R31, 2, R25     ;Load AI register
        JSR     R26, R26        ;Transfer control to SYS$CMKRNL
            .
            .
;
; Linkage section - note that these PSECT offsets are hexadecimal
;
        .PSECT  $LINKAGE, OCTA, NOPIC, CON, REL, LCL,-
                NOSHR, NOEXE, RD, NOWRT

0000    ; Heavyweight Frame invocation descriptor
                Entry point:        MAIN
                Registers saved:    R13, FP
                Fixed Stack Size:   48
            .
            .
0040    .ADDRESS $PSECT_BASE7
0048    .LONG   286331153       ;Large instruction stream constant
```

(continued)

Example 1.1 *(continued)*
References to Linkage Section Data

```
0050      .ADDRESS  KERNEL_ROUTINE
0058      .LONG   572662306       ;Large instruction stream constant
0060      .LINKAGE  SYS$CMKRNL
             .
             .
             .

0078      ; Heavyweight Frame invocation descriptor
                  Entry point:          KERNEL_ROUTINE
                  Registers saved:      R2-R4, FP
                  Fixed Stack Size:     48
                  Call Signature:       0020


             .
             .
             .
          .PSECT  $DATA$, OCTA, NOPIC, CON, REL, LCL,-
                  NOSHR, EXE, RD, WRT
             .LONG   1
             .LONG   10
```

These routines insulate the operating system from the underlying hardware by abstracting certain architectural features such as interrupt and exception initiation, return from interrupt and exception, and context swap. They extend the CPU architecture to provide a more complete environment for an operating system.

There are different versions of PALcode for the different operating systems supported on Alpha AXP CPUs. This enables a better match in the interface between hardware and operating system and reduces bias in the Alpha AXP architecture toward a particular style of computing.

Written in Alpha AXP instructions, these PALcode routines run in kernel mode with interrupts disabled. Some circumstances, such as an interrupt request from an external device, cause the CPU to trap to a PALcode routine. Other PALcode routines are invoked explicitly under program control through the CALL_PAL instruction.

Several features of the architecture are used for specific purposes by the operating system:

▶ The memory management protection scheme protects code and data used by more privileged access modes from access by less privileged modes.
▶ The architecture provides several mechanisms for transferring between access modes (see Figure 1.4).

The change mode instructions (CALL_PAL CHME and CALL_PAL CHMK) increase access mode. In addition, most exceptions and all interrupts result in changing mode to kernel. Section 1.4.2 introduces exceptions and interrupts.

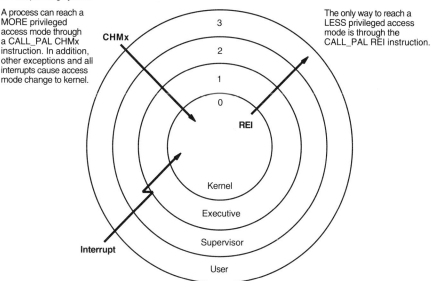

The current access mode field in the PS is not directly accessible to the programmer or to the operating system.

A process can reach a MORE privileged access mode through a CALL_PAL CHMx instruction. In addition, other exceptions and all interrupts cause access mode change to kernel.

The only way to reach a LESS privileged access mode is through the CALL_PAL REI instruction.

The boundaries between the access modes are nearly identical to the layer boundaries pictured in Figure 1.2.
Nearly all system services execute in kernel mode.
RMS and some system services execute in executive mode.

Command language interpreters normally execute in supervisor mode.
Utilities, application programs, Run–Time Library procedures normally execute in user mode.
Privileged utilities sometimes execute in kernel or executive mode.

Figure 1.4
Methods for Altering Access Mode

Only one mechanism can be used to decrease access mode: the CALL_ PAL REI instruction, the common exception and interrupt exit path. It prevents a less privileged mode from entering a more privileged mode. It also includes checks for pending interrupts.

▶ Code running in kernel mode can request a software interrupt to cause execution of an interrupt service routine that performs a particular function.

▶ Implicit protection is built into special instructions that can only be executed from kernel mode. Because only the executive and suitably privileged process-based code execute in kernel mode, such instructions as CALL_PAL MTPR, CALL_PAL SWPCTX, and CALL_PAL HALT are protected from execution by nonprivileged users.

▶ The architecture supports a mechanism called the load-locked/store-conditional mechanism for atomic modification of memory shared among multiple threads of execution. A memory modification is not atomic (a single indivisible act), but is, in fact, a read followed by a write. When multiple threads of execution modify the same memory at the same time, it is possible for each to read the same initial data but for one to overwrite the other's change. When all processors use the load-locked/store-conditional mechanism to modify shared memory, their modifications are atomic.

The mechanism is the basis of atomic forms of queue manipulation, addition, and bit manipulation. With this mechanism, the executive implements spinlocks, structures that describe the state of a particular set of shared data and that enable a set of processors to serialize their access to the data. Chapter 9 provides more information on multiprocessor synchronization and spinlocks.

▶ The operating system uses IPL for several purposes, for example, to block interrupts. An interrupt can be blocked by elevating IPL to a value at or above the IPL associated with the interrupt.

IPL is also used as a synchronization tool. For example, any routine that accesses certain systemwide data structures, such as the scheduler database, must raise IPL to the level at which the data structures are synchronized. On a uniprocessor, this is sufficient to protect the data. On a symmetric multiprocessing (SMP) system, additional synchronization is required (see Section 1.5.2.1).

The assignment of various hardware and software interrupts to specific IPL values establishes an order of importance to the hardware and software interrupt services that the OpenVMS AXP operating system performs.

▶ The architecture provides privileged hardware context and the instruction CALL_PAL SWPCTX to swap the privileged hardware context of one process with that of another.

▶ The Alpha AXP architecture specifies a standard form for representing 32-bit data loaded into 64-bit registers. When a 32-bit value is loaded into an integer register, the high-order 32 bits of the register are made equal to bit 31. This feature, in combination with the OpenVMS placement of system space at FFFFFFFF 80000000_{16}, enables addresses to be stored in memory as longwords and simplifies porting VAX code to AXP code.

1.4.1 Memory Management and Access Modes

The address translation mechanism is described in Chapter 15. When a reference is made to a page that is not valid, a translation-not-valid exception is generated. Control is transferred to a software exception service routine, the page fault handler, which takes the steps required to make the page valid. This mechanism enables the OpenVMS kernel to gain control on address translation failures to map pages dynamically while a program is executing.

Before the address translation mechanism checks the valid bit in the page table entry, it checks whether the requested access is allowable. The check is based on the current access mode in the PS, a protection code that is defined for each virtual page, and the type of access (read, write, or execute). This protection check allows the operating system to make read-only portions of the executive write-inaccessible to any access mode, preventing corruption of operating system code. In addition, privileged data structures can be protected from even read access by nonprivileged users, preserving system integrity.

1.4.2 Exceptions, Interrupts, and REI

The exception and interrupt mechanism is very important to the executive. The following sections compare exceptions and interrupts and briefly describe features of the mechanism used by the executive.

1.4.2.1

Comparison of Exceptions and Interrupts. An interrupt occurs asynchronously to the currently executing instruction stream. An exception occurs synchronously as a direct effect of the execution of an instruction. In response to either type of condition, the initiate exception, interrupt, or machine check (IEI) PALcode routine selects a specific system control block (SCB) entry and passes control to the service routine identified by the entry. Service routines perform exception-specific or interrupt-specific processing.

Exceptions are generally a part of the currently executing process. Their servicing is an extension of the instruction stream that is currently executing on behalf of that process. Interrupts are generally systemwide events, and their service routines cannot rely on executing in process context.

The IEI PALcode routine switches stacks, if necessary, usually to kernel mode, and saves R2 through R7, the PC, and the PS on the new stack. It passes interrupt- or exception-specific information to the service routine in R2 through R7. It forms a new PS that specifies the new IPL and current access mode (usually kernel).

Initiating an interrupt raises IPL, whereas initiating an exception does not. An interrupt can be blocked by elevating IPL to a value at or above the IPL associated with the interrupt. Exceptions cannot.

Chapter 3 describes the architectural interrupt and exception mechanisms in more detail.

1.4.2.2

Some Uses of Exceptions and Interrupts. In addition to the translation-not-valid fault used by memory management software, the operating system also uses the CHMK and CHME exceptions as entry paths to the executive. System services that must execute in a more privileged access mode use either the CALL_PAL CHMK or the CALL_PAL CHME instruction to increase access mode (see Figure 1.4). The system handles most other exceptions by dispatching to user-defined condition handlers, as described in Chapter 6.

Hardware interrupts temporarily suspend code that is executing so that an interrupt-specific routine can service the interrupt. Each interrupt has an IPL associated with it. The CPU raises IPL when it grants the interrupt. High-level interrupt service routines thus prevent the recognition of low-level interrupts. Low-level interrupt service routines can be interrupted by subsequent high-level interrupts. Kernel mode routines can also block interrupts by explicitly raising the IPL.

The architecture also defines a set of software interrupt levels. The executive uses them for scheduling, I/O postprocessing, and synchronizing access to certain classes of data structures.

Chapter 4 summarizes hardware interrupts and their service routines. Chapter 5 describes the software interrupt mechanism and its use.

1.4.2.3 **The CALL_PAL REI Instruction.** The CALL_PAL REI instruction is the common exit path for interrupt and exception service routines. Some protection and privilege checks are incorporated into this instruction. Because the current mode field in the PS cannot be written under program control, the CALL_PAL REI instruction provides the only means for changing access mode to a less privileged one (see Figure 1.4).

Although the IPL field of the PS is accessible through the IPL processor register, execution of a CALL_PAL REI instruction is a common way to lower IPL during normal execution. Because a change in IPL can alter the deliverability of pending interrupts, many hardware and software interrupts are delivered after a CALL_PAL REI instruction is executed.

Chapter 3 further describes this instruction and the PALcode routine that implements it.

1.4.3 **Implementation of OpenVMS AXP Kernel Routines**

In Section 1.2.2, the OpenVMS AXP kernel was discussed as three functional parts and an external system service interface. Alternatively, the kernel can be considered with respect to the method used to gain access to each part. The three classes of routines within the kernel are procedure-based code, exception service routines, and interrupt service routines. Other systemwide functions, the working set swapping and modified page writing performed by the swapper, are implemented in a separate process that resides in system space.

Figure 1.5 shows some of the entry paths into the three subsystems of the kernel.

1.4.3.1 **Process Context and System Context.** The first section of this chapter summarizes the description of a process. Process context includes a complete address space description, quotas, privileges, scheduling data, and any other private data. Any executive routine that executes in the context of a process has all these process attributes available.

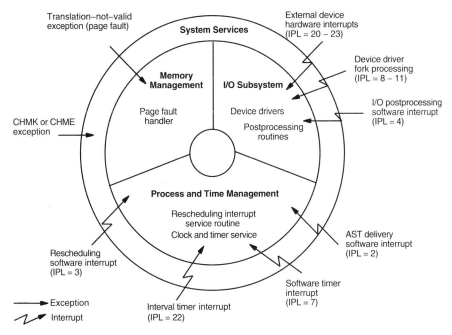

Figure 1.5
Paths into Components of OpenVMS AXP Kernel

The Alpha AXP architecture requires that there always be a valid HWPCB to define a context for CPU execution, minimally to specify the address of a kernel stack and contents for the PTBR. During system initialization OpenVMS AXP builds a HWPCB and allocates a kernel stack to define a context in which the system can execute the scheduling idle loop when there is no computable process to be placed into execution. On an SMP system, each CPU has its own HWPCB and kernel stack.

This HWPCB does not represent a process that can be scheduled. It merely provides a limited environment for the execution of kernel mode code in system space. To avoid confusion of this context with that of a normal process, this book refers to this HWPCB as the system HWPCB and this context as system context, also known as the null context.

While a processor executes the scheduling idle loop in system context, if an interrupt with an IPL higher than the current IPL is requested, the interrupt would be granted. Its interrupt service routine would execute in system context and would be constrained by the characteristics of that limited environment. If the same interrupt were requested while a process was executing, the service routine would run on the process's kernel stack and in process context. However, because the context is unpredictable when an interrupt is granted, an interrupt service routine must be coded to meet the constraints of the more limited environment, namely, system context.

System context can be characterized in the following ways:

- ▶ All stack operations take place on a kernel stack.
- ▶ The current access mode is kernel mode, and the IPL is higher than 2.
- ▶ If an interrupt service routine is executing, bit 2, the interrupt-in-progress bit, in the PS is likely to be set.
- ▶ The SCB, the data structure that controls the dispatching of interrupts and exceptions, can be thought of as a secondary structure that describes system context.
- ▶ Code that executes in system context can only refer to system virtual addresses. In particular, no P1 space is available, so the system context kernel stack must be located in system space.
- ▶ No page faults are allowed. The page fault handler generates a fatal bugcheck if a page fault occurs at an IPL above 2.
- ▶ No exceptions are allowed, other than unaligned access exceptions. Exceptions such as page faults are associated with a process. The exception dispatcher generates a fatal bugcheck if an exception occurs at an IPL above 2.
- ▶ Floating-point arithmetic operations are not allowed. Floating-point arithmetic operations are assumed to be in process context.
- ▶ ASTs, asynchronous events by which a process receives notification of external events, are not allowed. The AST delivery interrupt is not requested when IPL is 2 or above.
- ▶ System services may not be requested from system context.

1.4.3.2 **Process Context Routines.** Procedure-based code (RMS services, Files-11 XQP, and system services) and exception service routines usually execute in the context of the current process.

System services are implemented as procedures and are available to programs written in any language. The system service dispatchers, actually the dispatchers for the CHMK and CHME exceptions, are exception service routines. Chapter 7 details their operation.

System services must be requested from process context. They are not available to system context code. One reason for requiring process context is that the various services assume the existence of a process whose privileges can be checked and quotas charged as part of the normal operation of the service. Some system services reference locations in P1 space, a portion of address space only accessible from process context.

The page fault handler is the service routine for translation-not-valid exceptions. It resolves a page fault in the context of the process that incurred the fault. Because page faults are associated with a process, the system cannot tolerate page faults incurred by interrupt service routines or other routines that execute in system context. The actual restriction imposed by the page fault handler is even more stringent. Page faults are not allowed above

IPL 2. This restriction applies to process-based code executing at elevated IPL as well as to system context code.

1.4.3.3   **Interrupt Service Routines.** All OpenVMS AXP interrupt service routines except AST delivery interrupt service routines, must be able to execute in the limited environment of system context.

- ▸ I/O requests are initiated through the $QIO system service, which can be requested directly by the user or by some intermediary, such as RMS or the Files-11 XQP, on the user's behalf. Once an I/O request has been placed into a device queue, it remains there until the driver is triggered, usually by an interrupt generated by the external device.

  Two classes of software interrupt support the I/O subsystem: fork level interrupts and the I/O postprocessing interrupt. Fork level interrupts enable a device driver to stall a driver code thread and resume it at a lower IPL, thus lowering IPL in a controlled fashion. The I/O postprocessing interrupt enters a software interrupt service routine for final processing of I/O requests.
- ▸ Time support in the operating system requires both the interval timer interrupt service routine and a lower IPL software interrupt service routine to service individual time-based requests.
- ▸ Another software interrupt performs rescheduling, by which one process is removed from execution and another selected and placed into execution.

1.4.3.4   **The Swapper Process.** Some OpenVMS AXP functions are best performed from process context. The swapper process performs the most significant of these. As the inswapper of all newly created processes, the swapper process cannot be created in the conventional way. Its code and process data structures are therefore built into the executive. During system initialization its PCB is inserted into the scheduler database compute queues so that it can be the first process selected to execute.

Other characteristics of the swapper process include the following:

- ▸ Its PHD is static and contains no working set list and no process section table. It does not support page faults. All code executed by the swapper must be locked into memory in some way. In fact, the swapper code is contained in a nonpageable section of an executive image.
- ▸ The swapper executes entirely in kernel mode, thereby eliminating the need for stacks for the other three access modes.
- ▸ Its limited P1 space includes only the P1 pointer area, containing the location CTL$GL_PCB. Its kernel stack is located in system space.
- ▸ The swapper process temporarily maps P0 space to transform disjoint pages into a virtually contiguous I/O buffer, for example, to outswap a process working set.

Despite its limited context, the swapper process behaves in a normal fashion in every other way. It is selected for execution by the scheduling subsystem just like any other process in the system. It spends its idle time in the hibernate state until some component in the system recognizes a need for one of the swapper functions and awakens it. Chapter 20 discusses the swapper in detail.

1.4.3.5   **The Null Process.** Prior to VAX VMS Version 5.0, the system included a null process with a context similar to that of the swapper process. All CPU time not used by any other process in the system was used executing the null process. In subsequent versions on both VAX and AXP platforms, there is no longer a null process to schedule for execution. Instead, a per-processor null PCB and PHD are defined as placeholders. This change was made because SMP support necessitated a different form of idle loop.

1.4.3.6   **Special Subroutines.** There are several utility subroutines within the operating system related to scheduling and resource allocation that are called from both process context code, such as system services, and from software interrupt service routines. These subroutines are constrained to execute within the limited environment of system context. An example of such a routine is SCH$QAST, which is invoked to queue an AST to a process. It may be invoked from the I/O postprocessing and software timer interrupt service routines as well as from various system services.

1.5   **OTHER SYSTEM CONCEPTS**

This chapter began by discussing the most important concepts in the Open-VMS AXP operating system: process and image. Several other fundamental ideas should be mentioned before beginning a detailed description of the internals.

1.5.1   **Resource Control**

The system protects itself and other processes in the system from careless or malicious users with hardware and software protection mechanisms, software privileges, and software quotas and limits.

1.5.1.1   **Hardware Protection.** The memory management protection mechanism that is related to access mode prevents unauthorized users from modifying or even reading privileged data structures. Access mode protection also protects system and user code and read-only data structures from modifications resulting from programming errors.

A more subtle but perhaps more important aspect of protection provided by the memory management architecture is that the process-private address space of one process (P0 space or P1 space) is not accessible to code running in the context of another process. When such accessibility is desired to share common routines or data, the operating system provides controlled access through global sections. System virtual address space is addressable by all processes, although page-by-page protection may deny read or write access to specific system virtual pages by certain access modes.

1.5.1.2   **Process Privileges.** Many operations that are performed by system services could destroy operating system code or data or could corrupt existing files if performed carelessly. Other services allow a process to adversely affect other processes in the system. Processes executing these potentially damaging operations must be suitably privileged. Process privileges are assigned when a process is created, either by the creator or through the user's entry in the authorization file.

These privileges are described in the *OpenVMS System Manager's Manual* and the *OpenVMS System Services Reference Manual*. The privileges themselves are specific bits in a quadword that is stored in the PCB. When a system service that requires privilege executes, it checks whether the associated bit in the process privilege mask is set. The locations and manipulations of the several process privilege masks maintained by the operating system are discussed in Chapter 28.

1.5.1.3   **Quotas and Limits.** The executive also controls allocation of its systemwide resources, such as nonpaged dynamic memory and page file space, through the use of quotas and limits. Like privilege, these process attributes are assigned when the process is created. By restricting such items as the number of concurrent I/O requests or pending ASTs, the executive exercises control over the resource drain that a single process can exert on system resources, such as nonpaged dynamic memory. In general, a process cannot perform certain operations, such as queuing an AST, unless it has sufficient quota (nonzero PCB$L_ASTCNT in this case). The locations and values of the various quotas and limits are described in Chapter 27.

1.5.1.4   **User Access Control.** The OpenVMS AXP system uses a user identification code (UIC) for two different protection purposes. To perform some control operation (Suspend, Wake, Delete, and so on) on any other process, a process requires WORLD privilege. A process with GROUP privilege can affect only other processes with the same group number. A process with neither WORLD nor GROUP privilege can affect only other processes with the same UIC.

The system also uses UIC as a basis for protection of various system objects, such as files, global sections, logical names, and mailboxes. The owner of a file, for example, specifies what access to the file she grants to herself, to other processes in the same group, and to other processes in the system.

Access control lists (ACLs) provide more selective levels of sharing. An

ACL lists individual users or groupings of users who are to be allowed or denied access to a system object. ACLs specify sharing on the basis of UIC, as well as other groupings, known as identifiers, that can be associated with a process. ACLs can be specified for files, directories, devices, global sections, queues, and shareable logical name tables.

1.5.2 Other System Primitives

Several other mechanisms used by the system are mentioned throughout this book. They are introduced in the sections that follow and described in more detail in other chapters.

1.5.2.1

Synchronization. Any multiprogramming system must take measures to coordinate concurrent access to system data structures. The problem is further complicated by multiprocessing, where several CPUs have independent access to shared memory. The executive implements four synchronization techniques: elevated IPL, spinlocks, mutexes, and locks.

On a uniprocessor, elevating IPL is sufficient to synchronize access to systemwide data structures. By elevating IPL, the processor can block a subset of interrupts, allowing unrestricted and uncontested access to the data structures. The most common synchronization IPL used by the executive is IPL 8.

To extend the uniprocessor synchronization provided by IPL to a multiprocessing environment, the executive uses spinlocks. A spinlock describes the state of a particular set of shared data and enables a set of processors to serialize their access to the data. A resource synchronized by elevated IPL on a uniprocessor is synchronized by the ordered combination of elevated IPL and spinlock on an SMP system.

A section of code that accesses shared data in a synchronized way first raises IPL and, in an SMP system, acquires a spinlock. When finished, the code lowers IPL and, in an SMP system, releases the spinlock. The OpenVMS AXP system provides macros to implement these IPL-raising/spinlock acquisition and spinlock release/IPL-lowering operations. The macros acquire and release spinlocks only on SMP systems; otherwise, they only elevate and restore IPL. For simplicity, this book refers to this combined type of synchronization as acquiring and releasing spinlocks. That the macros merely alter IPL on a uniprocessor is implicit; that they also alter IPL on an SMP member often goes without saying.

The use of a spinlock to synchronize access to certain types of data structures is sometimes undesirable or even potentially harmful to system performance. For example, a process that has acquired a spinlock must execute at or above IPL 3, blocking process rescheduling on that CPU until it releases the spinlock. In addition, because page faults are not allowed above IPL 2, any pageable data structure cannot be synchronized with a spinlock.

Thus, the executive requires a third synchronization tool to allow synchronized access to pageable data structures. This tool must also allow a process to be removed from execution while it maintains ownership of the structure in question. One synchronization tool that fulfills these requirements is called a mutual exclusion semaphore (mutex).

Synchronization, including the use of mutexes, is discussed in Chapter 9.

The executive and other system components, such as the Files-11 XQP, RMS, and the job controller, use a fourth tool, the lock management system services, for more flexible sharing of resources among processes. These services provide a waiting mechanism for processes whose desired access to a resource is blocked. They also provide notification to a process whose use of a resource blocks another process. Most important, the lock management system services provide sharing of clusterwide resources. Chapter 11 describes the lock management system services.

1.5.2.2   **Dynamic Memory Allocation.** The system maintains several dynamic memory areas from which blocks of memory can be allocated and deallocated. Nonpaged pool contains those systemwide structures that might be manipulated by (hardware or software) interrupt service routines or process context code executing above IPL 2. Paged pool contains systemwide structures that do not have to be kept memory-resident. The process allocation region and the kernel request packet (KRP) lookaside list, both in process P1 space, are used for pageable data structures that will not be shared by any other process. Dynamic memory allocation and deallocation are discussed in detail in Chapter 21.

1.5.2.3   **Logical Names.** The system uses logical names for many purposes, including a transparent way of implementing a device-independent I/O system. The use of logical names as a programming tool is discussed in the *OpenVMS System Services Reference Manual*. The internal operations of the logical name system services, as well as the internal organization of the logical name tables, are described in Chapter 38.

1.6   **VIRTUAL ADDRESS SPACE**

The sections that follow provide brief introductions to the regions of virtual address space. Chapter 15 provides more details.

1.6.1   **System Virtual Address Space**

Figure 1.6 shows a simplified layout of system space. A more detailed layout is shown in Figure F.2 and further described in Tables F.2 and F.3.

Appendix F describes system space in detail.

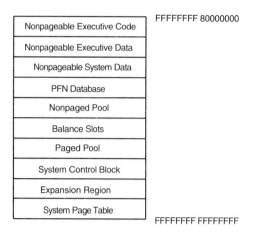

FFFFFFFF 80000000

Nonpageable Executive Code
Nonpageable Executive Data
Nonpageable System Data
PFN Database
Nonpaged Pool
Balance Slots
Paged Pool
System Control Block
Expansion Region
System Page Table

FFFFFFFF FFFFFFFF

Figure 1.6
Layout of System Space

1.6.2 P1 Space

Figure 1.7 shows a simplified layout of P1 space, which is sometimes referred to as the control region.

Some of the pieces of P1 space are created dynamically when the process is created. These include a CLI if one is being used, command tables and data for that CLI, and the process I/O segment. In addition, the Files-11 XQP stack and data area are mapped at process creation.

The low-address end of P1 space (for example, the user stack) is created dynamically each time an image executes and is deleted as part of image rundown.

Chapters 27 and 28 contain more information on process creation and image activation and exit.

Appendix F contains a more detailed layout of P1 space and a description of the different pieces of P1 space, including their sizes and memory management page protection and the name of the system component that maps a given portion.

1.6.3 P0 Space

Figure 1.8 shows simplified layouts of P0 space both for a native image produced by the linker and for an image translated from an OpenVMS VAX image by the DECmigrate for OpenVMS AXP layered product.

The exact layout of P0 space for a native image depends upon the image being run, the shareable images with which it was linked, and the page boundary to which the image was linked. P0 space is sometimes referred to as the program region.

By default, the first part of P0 space is not mapped (protection set to No Access). This no-access space allows easy detection of two common program-

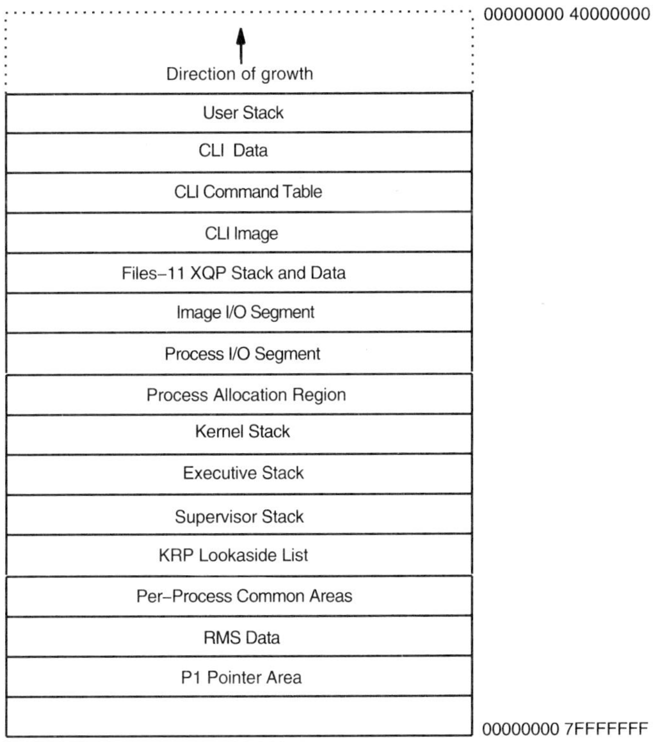

```
                                            ·· 00000000 40000000
                  ↑
          Direction of growth
  ┌─────────────────────────────┐
  │         User Stack          │
  ├─────────────────────────────┤
  │          CLI  Data          │
  ├─────────────────────────────┤
  │      CLI Command Table      │
  ├─────────────────────────────┤
  │          CLI Image          │
  ├─────────────────────────────┤
  │  Files–11 XQP Stack and Data│
  ├─────────────────────────────┤
  │      Image I/O Segment      │
  ├─────────────────────────────┤
  │     Process I/O Segment     │
  ├─────────────────────────────┤
  │   Process Allocation Region │
  ├─────────────────────────────┤
  │         Kernel Stack        │
  ├─────────────────────────────┤
  │       Executive Stack       │
  ├─────────────────────────────┤
  │       Supervisor Stack      │
  ├─────────────────────────────┤
  │      KRP Lookaside List     │
  ├─────────────────────────────┤
  │    Per–Process Common Areas │
  ├─────────────────────────────┤
  │          RMS Data           │
  ├─────────────────────────────┤
  │       P1 Pointer Area       │
  └─────────────────────────────┘
                                            ·· 00000000 7FFFFFFF
```

Figure 1.7
Layout of P1 Space

ming errors, using zero or a small number as the address of a data location or using such a small number as the destination of a control transfer. (A link-time request or system service call can alter the protection of this page or pages.) The size of the no-access part is determined by the value specified for the BPAGE qualifier to the LINK command. Most executable images that ship with the OpenVMS AXP system have been linked with a value of 16. Its image sections thus begin on 64-KB boundaries, with the first image section based at 64 KB.

The main native image is mapped in P0 space, after the no-access space. Shareable images it was linked with (for example, LIBRTL) are generally mapped following the main image. The order in which these shareable images are mapped is determined during image activation. The code sections of any shareable images that have been installed resident are accessed through their system space addresses.

If the debugger or the traceback facility is required, these images are mapped at image activation or run time (even if /DEBUG was selected at link time). This mapping is described in detail in Chapter 28.

A translated image is mapped in P0 space starting at location 0. Most VAX

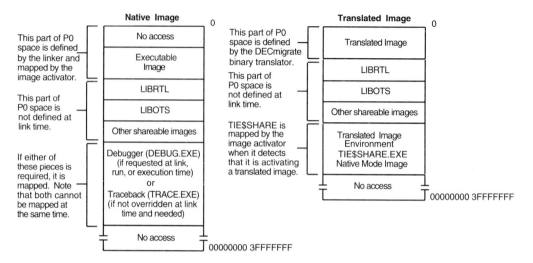

Figure 1.8
P0 Space Allocation

images are linked to a base of 200_{16} and thus require virtual page 0 on an AXP system to be mapped. During translation, a shareable image entry is added to the image that specifies the Translated Image Environment (TIE) shareable image, under whose control the translated image will execute. When the image activator activates a translated image, it also activates any shareable images it was linked with, mapping them following the translated image.

2 | I/O Architecture

Always design a thing by considering it in its next larger
context—a chair in a room, a room in a house, a house in an
environment, an environment in a city plan.

Eero Saarinen

This chapter outlines a model of a generic AXP I/O system and defines the
basic terms used to describe its components. It also outlines other architectural aspects of I/O on an AXP system.

2.1 THE GENERIC AXP I/O SYSTEM

This section presents a generic AXP I/O system and introduces the terms
that describe various system components. Only a functional description of
system components is provided.

The functional building blocks of an AXP system are hardware blocks and
interconnects.

▶ A hardware block is an assembly of hardware components that implements a specific function.

A hardware block can be a part of a hardware module, a whole hardware
module, or more than one hardware module. The term *hardware module*
refers to a *physical* entity—it is a board with hardware components assembled on it.

▶ An interconnect is a physical medium that carries address, data, and control signals between various hardware blocks. A bus is one form of interconnect; a crossbar switch is another.

A hardware block connected to an interconnect is called a node on that
interconnect.

Figure 2.1 shows a generic AXP system, and Figure 2.2 shows the AXP I/O
hardware blocks and interconnects. The major hardware blocks and interconnects shown are the following:

▶ Central processing unit (CPU). This hardware block consists of an AXP
processor and cache memory along with cache management and addressing logic. Except where stated otherwise, the terms *processor* and *CPU* are
used interchangeably in this book.

There can be more than one CPU in some configurations.

▶ Memory. This hardware block contains random access memory (RAM)
chips along with interface and control logic. If there are multiple CPUs,
memory is shared by all of them.

33

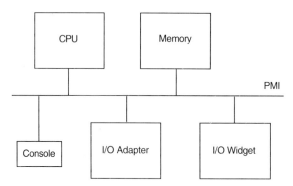

Figure 2.1
A Generic AXP System

▶ Console. The console subsystem enables a human operator to monitor and
control the system. It also supports system transitions such as power on,
power failure, and bootstrap. Chapter 33 provides more information on
consoles.

▶ Processor-memory interconnect (PMI). CPUs and memory communicate
on this interconnect. I/O widgets and I/O adapters (defined later in this list)
can also connect to the PMI.

▶ I/O interconnect. This is an interconnect whose primary purpose is I/O.
There are two classes of I/O interconnect: tightly coupled and loosely coupled. Historically, *I/O bus* has referred to both classes, but this book usually specifies which class of interconnect is meant.

A tightly coupled I/O interconnect has an address space that is accessible to the CPU through direct or mailbox access, whereas a loosely coupled I/O interconnect does not. The terms *address space, direct access,*
and *mailbox access* are defined in Section 2.2, and further distinctions between tightly coupled and loosely coupled I/O interconnects are given in
Section 2.3.

Tightly coupled I/O interconnects include the following:

• Extended Memory Interconnect (XMI)
• TURBOchannel
• The DEC 4000 system family local I/O bus (L-bus)

Loosely coupled I/O interconnects include the following:

• Small Computer System Interconnect (SCSI)
• Digital Storage Systems Interconnect (DSSI)
• Network interconnect (NI)
• Fiber Distributed Data Interconnect (FDDI)
• Computer interconnect (CI)
• Storage interconnect (SI)
• Serial (EIA-232) lines

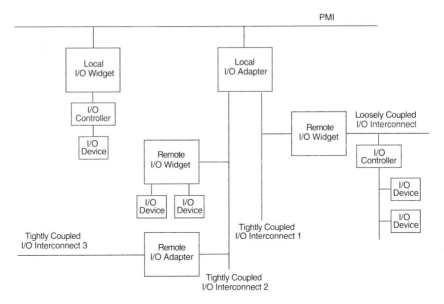

Figure 2.2
AXP I/O Hardware Blocks and Interconnects

▶ I/O adapter. This hardware block connects one or more tightly coupled I/O interconnects to the PMI or to another tightly coupled I/O interconnect. Its primary purpose is to transform one interconnect protocol to another. An I/O adapter is also sometimes called a bridge.

▶ I/O widget. This hardware block connects one or more loosely coupled I/O interconnects to the PMI or to a tightly coupled I/O interconnect. The term *multichannel I/O widget* refers to an I/O widget to which multiple loosely coupled I/O interconnects are connected.

The terminology that describes VAX systems does not differentiate tightly coupled from loosely coupled interconnects or adapters from widgets; *adapter* has referred to both types of hardware block, and *I/O bus* has referred to both types of interconnect. The terminology used here is a change from that tradition.

The adjective *local* describes an I/O adapter or I/O widget that connects directly to the PMI. *Remote* describes an I/O adapter or I/O widget connected to a tightly coupled I/O interconnect. In descriptions of the components of an I/O adapter, *local* refers to a component that is electrically closer to the PMI than a *remote* one.

Figure 2.3 shows the components of an I/O adapter. Minimally, an I/O adapter has a local side and a remote side connected by a hose. In this context, *side* refers to a hardware block that implements an interconnect protocol. The term *hose* refers to the data path between the local side and the remote side. An I/O adapter can have one or more local sides and one or

35

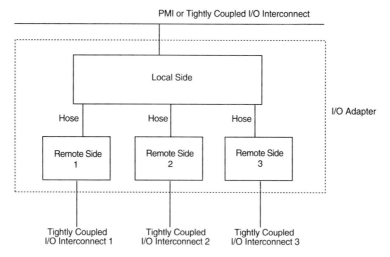

Figure 2.3
Components of an I/O Adapter

more remote sides; each remote-local pair must be connected by a separate hose.

▶ I/O device (also called I/O device unit). This is the target of an I/O operation. It can be a physical device, such as a disk or tape, or a pseudo device. A pseudo device is one with no physical embodiment that is simulated by the operating system.

▶ I/O device controller. This hardware block provides control logic with interface registers to enable software to control the operation of one or more devices.

An I/O device controller can be implemented as an integral part of a device or as part of an I/O widget that connects the device(s) to a tightly coupled I/O interconnect.

2.2 PHYSICAL ADDRESS SPACE

The collection of all physical locations addressable by a PMI node is its physical address space. The extent of this address space is defined by the number of physical address bits that the PMI node implements.

The Alpha AXP architecture specifies that a processor can implement up to 48 physical address bits. Specific implementations can implement subsets of this range. A DEC 4000 system CPU, for example, supports 34 address bits. Consequently, it can address byte locations 0 through $2^{34} - 1$.

Architecturally, a processor's physical address space is divided into four areas of equal size, as shown in Figure 2.4. A processor can use an area either for memory references or for I/O location references, but not both. Area 0

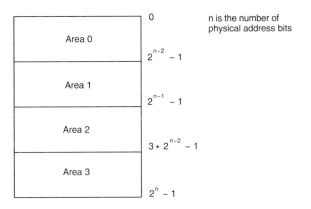

Figure 2.4
Physical Address Space of an AXP Processor

must be used for memory references only. There is no such restriction on areas 1, 2, and 3; however, all areas used for memory references must be contiguous. See the *Alpha AXP Architecture Reference Manual* for more information on these areas. Appendix G presents the physical address space layout for some AXP systems.

When a processor executes a load or store instruction, the source or target of the data can be either a memory space or an I/O space address.

2.2.1 Memory Space

The portion of a processor's physical address space through which it accesses memory is called its memory space.

A memory module is typically available in a standard size such as 32 MB, 64 MB, 128 MB, or 256 MB. Depending on system, configuration, and other factors, each memory module implements a unique portion of the memory space of the system.

AXP systems vary in the way address ranges are assigned to the memory modules. In one system, a hardware attribute such as its PMI slot number determines the address range that a memory module implements; in another system, console software assigns the address ranges during system initialization.

2.2.2 I/O Space

The portion of a processor's physical address space through which it accesses hardware interface registers is known as its I/O space.

A hardware interface register, or interface register for short, is the place where software interfaces with a hardware block. Every hardware block on an AXP system, including CPU and memory, has a set of interface registers. The term *control/status register* (CSR) is sometimes used instead of the generic term *interface register*. In this book, *CSR* refers to a specific type of interface register that allows status determination and control of a hardware block.

A processor's I/O space is sometimes known as local I/O space to distinguish it from remote I/O space. The term *remote I/O space* describes the address space of any tightly coupled I/O interconnect on an AXP system. The processor accesses remote I/O space through a hardware mailbox operation or by using mapped access, as described in Section 2.2.4. On a multiprocessor system, a given remote I/O space location is uniformly accessible to all processors.

A processor's I/O space is subdivided into smaller regions. A common subdivision, called node space, describes the part of physical address space through which a node's interface registers are accessed. For some details on other possible regions of I/O space, see Appendix G.

2.2.3   **Device Driver I/O**

A device driver typically interacts with an I/O device controller in the following manner to accomplish I/O:

1. The driver requests and initiates a device function.
2. The controller carries out the requested function.
3. The controller informs the driver of request completion.
4. The driver determines the status of the completed operation.

How each of these steps is actually accomplished depends on the design of the driver-controller interface. A simple interface consists of a set of interface registers that allows the driver to request and determine the status of I/O operations. In this model, driver-controller interaction is as follows:

1. The driver writes one or more interface registers to request and initiate a device function.
2. The controller carries out the requested function.
3. The controller generates an interrupt to inform the driver of request completion.
4. The driver reads one or more interface registers to determine the status of the completed operation.

A more sophisticated interface includes command and response buffers in addition to interface registers. The command and response buffers are allocated in memory and managed by the driver. In this model, driver-controller interaction is as follows:

1. The driver initializes a command buffer to request a device function; it can use multiple command buffers at one time. To initiate controller action, the driver writes to a controller interface register, notifying the controller that one or more command buffers are available.
2. The controller carries out the requested functions.

3. The controller records completion status in one or more response buffers and generates an interrupt to notify the driver of one or more request completions.

4. The driver determines the status of completed operations from the response buffers.

The latter model of I/O provides better performance for the following reasons:

▶ An interrupt disrupts the processor's instruction pipeline, thus affecting system performance. This model minimizes interrupts because one interrupt can signal the completion of multiple I/O operations.

▶ Interface register access is typically slower than access to memory or to the processor's cache. Read operations to interface registers usually take longer to complete than write operations (see Section 2.2.4). This model minimizes interface register access by having the controller write completion status to memory instead.

Chapter 4 describes device interrupts.

2.2.4   Interface Register Access

There are two types of interface register: those a processor accesses directly and those it accesses only through a hardware mailbox operation.

2.2.4.1   Direct Access.
An interface register with an address in local I/O space is directly accessible; it can be accessed with a load or store instruction. Software can directly access the interface register of a PMI node such as CPU, memory, local I/O adapter, or local I/O widget.

Software can directly access interface registers for remote I/O widgets only if the system implementation maps their addresses into the processor's I/O space. This special form of direct access is sometimes known as memory-mapped access, or simply, mapped access. The DEC 3000 system, for example, uses mapped access.

2.2.4.2   Hardware Mailbox Access.
Some systems do not support mapped access but instead support a mechanism called a hardware mailbox for accessing remote interface registers.

By this method, software creates a data structure in memory called a hardware mailbox and stores a command in it; this command, when issued over a remote interconnect, accesses a location on that interconnect. To initiate the access, software writes the hardware mailbox's physical address to a local I/O adapter's interface register. The local I/O adapter fetches the command from the mailbox and delivers it to the remote interconnect.

Hardware mailbox access overcomes the following disadvantages of mapped access.

▶ A tightly coupled I/O interconnect can have an address space that exceeds the maximum architecture-specified physical address space. All the address space of such an interconnect cannot be mapped into the processor's physical address space.

▶ The Alpha AXP architecture supports only aligned quadword and longword accesses. Some I/O devices and interconnects require byte and word accesses.

▶ The PMI can be kept busy for the duration of a mapped access, thus delaying other PMI operations.

Hardware mailbox allocation and initialization can occur at any time, depending on how the structure is defined and used by the driver. A driver can use a unique hardware mailbox for each type of access it requires, or it can reuse the same mailbox for each access. The usage model and OpenVMS AXP support for mailbox access are discussed in Chapter 26.

The Alpha AXP architecture defines the layout of the hardware mailbox structure, which is shown in Figure 2.5. To access a remote interface register using this method, a driver initializes the hardware mailbox as follows:

1. It deposits a remote interconnect command in the CMD field that specifies an I/O operation such as a read or a write. This is the command that the local I/O adapter must deliver to the remote interconnect to which the target I/O widget is connected.
2. It writes a mask in the MASK field that specifies the size (byte, word, tribyte, longword, or quadword) of the target location.
3. If the local I/O adapter connects to multiple tightly coupled I/O interconnects, the driver selects the appropriate tightly coupled I/O interconnect by entering a value in the HOSE field.
4. It writes the tightly coupled I/O interconnect address of the target interface register in the RBADR field.
5. If the remote interconnect command is a write, the driver initializes the WDATA field with data that is to be written to the target interface register.
6. It zeros all other fields of the hardware mailbox.

After initializing the hardware mailbox, the driver initiates the mailbox operation by writing the physical address of the hardware mailbox to the mailbox pointer register (MBPR), an interface register on a local I/O adapter. This action triggers the local I/O adapter to read the hardware mailbox and perform the requested remote access.

After writing to the MBPR, the driver polls the DON bit in the STATUS field. For a write operation, a local I/O adapter can set the DON bit immediately after it has read the hardware mailbox or only after the remote write operation has actually completed, depending on I/O adapter implementation; the former scheme results in increased performance. For a read operation,

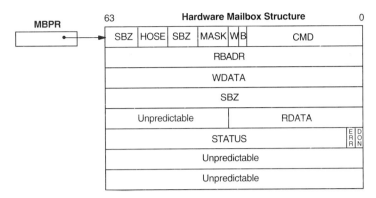

Figure 2.5
Layout of an AXP Hardware Mailbox

however, the local I/O adapter can set the DON bit only after it has written the requested data to the RDATA field of the hardware mailbox.

The local I/O adapter can set the ERR bit to indicate an error. The ERR bit is valid only when the DON bit is set. For a write operation, success is not ensured even if the ERR bit is clear when the DON bit is set. If ERR is set, however, additional error status is contained in the STATUS field.

2.2.5 **Direct Memory Access**

During an I/O operation, a controller can access data, command, and response buffers in memory without the intervention or assistance of the processor. Such an access is called direct memory access (DMA). If the controller is associated with a local I/O widget, DMA is a simple PMI operation.

A controller associated with a remote I/O widget requires the assistance of one or more intervening I/O adapters to access memory. Consider, for example, the remote I/O widget connected to tightly coupled I/O interconnect 1 in Figure 2.2. Tightly coupled I/O interconnect 1 connects to the local I/O adapter and there is no intervening I/O adapter. To assist in DMA, the local I/O adapter must transform the controller's request to access a location in the tightly coupled I/O interconnect's address space into a PMI request to access a memory location.

In other words, the local I/O adapter must map a portion of the tightly coupled I/O interconnect's address space into the processor's memory space.

2.3 **TIGHTLY COUPLED AND LOOSELY COUPLED I/O INTERCONNECTS**

The distinctions between tightly coupled and loosely coupled I/O interconnects are not obvious or precise. Refer to the lists in Section 2.1, where a number of I/O interconnects are classified. The following are general guidelines for classification.

▶ A tightly coupled I/O interconnect has an address space that is accessible to the CPU through direct or mailbox access, whereas a loosely coupled I/O interconnect does not.

A loosely coupled I/O interconnect always has an associated I/O widget that connects it to a tightly coupled I/O interconnect or to the PMI. The CPU has direct or mailbox access to the I/O widget's interface registers.

▶ A tightly coupled I/O interconnect is typically limited in range to a system cabinet, whereas a loosely coupled I/O interconnect generally extends beyond the boundary of the system cabinet.

PART II / Control Mechanisms

3 Interrupts, Exceptions, and Machine Checks

By indirections find directions out.

Shakespeare, *Hamlet*, 2, i

This chapter describes the Alpha AXP architectural mechanisms for initiation of and return from an interrupt, exception, or machine check. It summarizes OpenVMS use of the mechanisms.

3.1 OVERVIEW

During system operation, events occur that require the execution of software other than the current thread of execution. The processor responds to such events by altering the control flow from the current thread of execution. Where control is transferred is determined by the system control block (SCB). The SCB contains an entry for each event specifying the address to which control is to be transferred.

Some of these events are unrelated to the current thread of execution and are asynchronous to it. Other events are triggered by the current thread and are typically synchronous to it. The three types of events are interrupts, exceptions, and machine checks.

Interrupts are unrelated to the current thread and asynchronous to it. Interrupts are requested by hardware and software components. Most hardware interrupts are requested by signals from devices external to the processor when they need attention from the operating system. The hardware interrupt capability makes it unnecessary for the processor to poll the device to determine whether its state has changed. A few types of hardware interrupt are requested by signals from components within the processor, such as the interval timer.

A software interrupt is an interrupt requested by kernel mode code rather than by an external device. The OpenVMS AXP executive is interrupt-driven and requests software interrupts to schedule operating system functions.

To enable arbitration among concurrent interrupt requests and their servicing, each interrupt request has an associated interrupt priority level (IPL). When an interrupt is granted, processor IPL is raised to that of the interrupt. When the processor IPL is at or above that of the interrupt request, the interrupt is blocked. A processor executing a privileged architecture library (PALcode) routine cannot be interrupted.

When an interrupt is requested, the processor determines whether its associated IPL permits it to interrupt:

▶ If the processor is running at an IPL equal to or higher than that of the interrupt request, the interrupt request is deferred until processor IPL drops below the IPL of the request.

▶ If the processor is running at a lower IPL than that of the interrupt request, the interrupt is granted.

To grant the interrupt, a typical AXP processor may drain the instruction pipeline and complete any outstanding load instructions (these are CPU-specific steps). It then transfers control to a PALcode routine that saves processor state and dispatches to the interrupt's service routine through the SCB entry associated with the interrupt. Chapter 1 briefly describes PALcode.

An exception is the processor's response to an anomaly or error it encounters while fetching or executing an instruction, for example, an access violation in a load or store instruction. Synchronous to the current thread, an exception occurs in direct response to a particular instruction sequence and would occur again if the instruction were repeated under the same circumstances. (Note, however, that arithmetic exceptions are imprecise; there can be a delay between execution of the instruction that incurs the exception and initiation of the exception.) When an exception is initiated, the processor transfers control to a PALcode routine that saves processor state and dispatches to the exception's service routine through the SCB entry associated with the exception.

An AXP processor indicates that a hardware error has occurred through a machine check. Like interrupts and exceptions, a machine check involves a transition from the control flow being executed to a service routine identified by a particular SCB entry.

Interrupts are asynchronous and unrelated to the current control flow, whereas exceptions are synchronous to and triggered by the current control flow. Machine checks, however, include both asynchronous and synchronous errors. A synchronous machine check is always initiated immediately. The initiation of an asynchronous machine check, also called a maskable machine check, is deferred until IPL is less than the IPL associated with that kind of machine check.

In general, each type of exception, interrupt, and machine check has its own PALcode entry point. Most converge to common code, which this chapter calls the initiate exception, interrupt, or machine check (IEI) PALcode routine. The IEI PALcode dispatches to a service routine specified by the operating system for that type of event. The service routine returns control to the previous thread of execution by executing the instruction CALL_PAL REI.

3.2   **SYSTEM CONTROL BLOCK**

Operating system software initializes the SCB, and the IEI PALcode routine dispatches all interrupts and exceptions through it. Each exception, interrupt, and type of machine check has a unique entry, identified by its offset from the beginning of the SCB. Figure 3.1 shows the layout of an SCB entry.

Each entry consists of two quadwords. The first quadword, called the vector, contains the virtual address of a service routine for that exception, interrupt, or machine check. Because no mapping context is switched at interrupt and exception initiation, the architecture requires that a particular service routine exist at the same virtual address in every process context. The OpenVMS AXP operating system deals with this requirement by placing all interrupt, exception, and machine check service routines in system space.

The second quadword, called the parameter, is passed in R3 as an argument to the service routine. The Alpha AXP architecture does not define its contents. Except for parameters of I/O interrupt entries, each parameter contains an address that can serve as a linkage section pointer for the service routine. (A service routine written in anything other than MACRO-64 assembly language begins with a compiler directive describing this linkage, which differs from that specified by the OpenVMS AXP calling standard.)

Typically, the OpenVMS AXP executive stores the address of the service routine's procedure descriptor, thereby creating a standard linkage pair in the SCB entry. For an I/O interrupt, the executive stores information that enables the common I/O interrupt service routine to dispatch to a device-specific routine.

The SCB is page-aligned. Its size is platform-dependent and can be from one to four pages. The system control block base (SCBB) processor register contains the page frame number of the first page of the SCB. The IEI PALcode routine calculates the address of a particular entry using the contents of the SCBB processor register and the offset into the SCB of the entry. This design enables executive software to place the SCB in memory known to be good at system initialization. If the SCB were required to be at a fixed location, and if that memory had uncorrectable errors, the system would be unable to run. During system initialization the operating system allocates physically

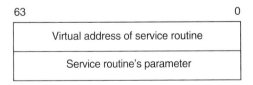

Figure 3.1
System Control Block (SCB) Entry

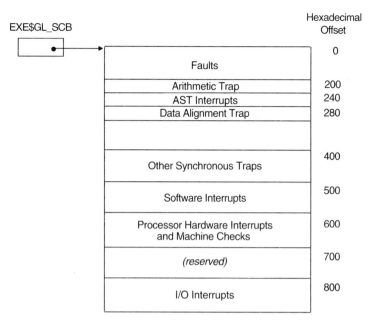

Figure 3.2
System Control Block Organization

contiguous memory for the SCB and one or more system page table entries (SPTEs) to map it, initializes the SCBB and the SPTEs, and stores its starting virtual address in global location EXE$GL_SCB.

Figure 3.2 shows the general organization of the SCB. It contains entries for faults and traps (which are types of exceptions), software interrupts, asynchronous system trap (AST) interrupts, processor hardware interrupts, machine checks, and I/O interrupts. The macro $HWSCBDEF defines symbolic offsets for its entries. The *Alpha AXP Architecture Reference Manual* contains the detailed SCB layout.

The executive handles most exceptions in a uniform way. Some exceptions, however, result in special action. Chapter 6 lists the exception SCB entries, describes the executive's handling of most exceptions, and summarizes responses to special exceptions.

Chapter 5 contains more details about software and AST interrupts and summarizes their service routines.

Chapter 4 summarizes processor hardware interrupts, machine checks, and their service routines.

Chapters 4 and 24 describe the assignment of I/O interrupt SCB entries and I/O interrupt service routines.

3.3 INTERRUPTS

The Alpha AXP architecture provides 16 hardware IPLs, from IPL 31 down to IPL 16. Interrupts at the higher levels are primarily for processor errors and power failure. The middle levels are for interrupts from external adapters, I/O devices, and the interval timer. The lower levels are unused.

There is no one-to-one correspondence between IPL and hardware interrupt vector. The SCB contains multiple entries whose interrupts are at the same hardware IPL.

There is, however, a one-to-one correspondence between IPL and software interrupt entry. The architecture provides 15 entries in the SCB for software interrupts at IPLs 1 through 15. It provides four entries in the SCB for AST interrupts, one for each access mode.

3.3.1 Interrupt Requests

The architecture provides a means for kernel mode code and system console commands to request software interrupts.

Kernel mode code requests a software interrupt at a particular IPL by invoking a PALcode routine to write that IPL into the software interrupt request register (SIRR). MACRO-32 code generally uses the SOFTINT macro, which expands into the following statement:

```
MTPR    ipl,S^#PR$_SIRR
```

When compiled, that statement generates instructions that load R16 with the IPL and perform a CALL_PAL MTPR whose destination is the SIRR processor register. The following CPU console command can also write the SIRR processor register:

```
D SIRR ipl
```

Writing to the SIRR processor register causes the bit with the same number as the IPL to be set in another processor register, the software interrupt summary register (SISR). Figure 3.3 shows the layouts of these two registers. At any given time, the SISR processor register contains a bit set for each level at which a software interrupt has been requested but not yet granted. The processor reads the SISR processor register to test for pending software interrupts. When the processor grants a software interrupt request, it clears the corresponding bit in the SISR processor register.

An AST interrupt is requested by each of the following PALcode routines whenever it detects that a pending AST is deliverable: the REI, SWASTEN, MTPR_IPL, MTPR_ASTSR, and MTPR_ASTEN routines.

To block interrupts of any type, kernel mode code can raise IPL to that of the highest interrupt to be blocked. The architectural concept of an interrupt includes the idea that an interrupt request is expected to persist until serviced or until the device withdraws the request.

3.3.2 Interrupt Dispatching

When an interrupt is requested and granted, the IEI PALcode routine takes the following steps.

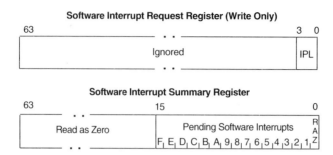

Figure 3.3
Layouts of Software Interrupt Request Register (SIRR) and
Software Interrupt Summary Register (SISR)

1. The IEI PALcode routine switches to the kernel stack, if not already there. If the system was running on an outer access mode stack, the routine saves the contents of the stack pointer (SP) register in the stack pointer internal processor register for that mode. On an AXP CPU type that does not implement these processor registers, the IEI PALcode routine instead stores SP in a save area in the process's hardware privileged context block (HWPCB). It loads the SP from the HWPCB save area for the kernel stack because there is no kernel SP processor register on any AXP processor.

2. It aligns the kernel stack to a 64-byte boundary.

3. It saves the access mode and IPL that were current prior to the interrupt by pushing onto the stack the processor status (PS) register. It records the previous alignment of the kernel stack in the quadword containing the saved PS. It also pushes onto the stack the program counter (PC) current at the time of the interrupt, that is, the address of the next instruction to be executed in the interrupted thread.

   Saving the PC and PS preserves state so that the interrupted thread of execution can continue after the interrupt is dismissed. Saving the alignment enables the SP to be restored to its previous value when the interrupt is dismissed.

   If the kernel stack is invalid when the IEI PALcode routine tries to push the interrupt frame onto the stack, the processor enters the kernel-stack-not-valid restart sequence. Chapter 36 gives a description of error restart processing.

4. The IEI PALcode routine saves R2 through R7 on the stack, freeing them to pass information to the interrupt service routine. The 64-byte set of information saved on the stack, shown in Figure 3.4, is called an interrupt, exception, or machine check stack frame. This chapter refers to it as an interrupt/exception stack frame. The macro $INTSTKDEF defines symbolic offsets for its fields.

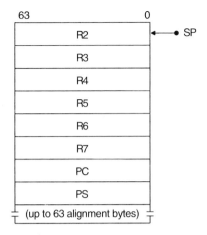

63   0

R2	←—• SP
R3	
R4	
R5	
R6	
R7	
PC	
PS	
(up to 63 alignment bytes)	

Figure 3.4
Layout of an Interrupt, Exception, or Machine Check
Stack Frame

As a result of the 64-byte alignment performed in step 2, the 64-byte interrupt/exception stack frame resides within one page, simplifying the IEI and REI PALcode routines.

5. The IEI PALcode routine determines the offset into the SCB of the entry corresponding to the interrupt it is servicing.

6. It loads the address of the service routine from the first quadword of the SCB entry into R2 and loads R3 from the second quadword.

7. The IEI PALcode routine constructs a new PS whose IPL is that associated with the interrupt. Its current mode is kernel, the mode in which the interrupt will be serviced. Its software bits are zero. Unless the interrupt is an AST delivery interrupt, the IEI PALcode sets bit 2 in the PS. When set, this bit means an interrupt is in progress.

8. When a software interrupt is dispatched, the IEI PALcode routine clears the bit in the SISR processor register corresponding to the IPL of the interrupt.

9. The IEI PALcode routine transfers control to the interrupt service routine, whose address is in R2.

The interrupt service routine executes. An interrupt service routine written in MACRO-64 assembly language uses R3 as a linkage section pointer. The prologue code for a MACRO-32 or BLISS interrupt service routine assumes R3 contains a procedure descriptor address and copies it to another register for use as a linkage section pointer.

The interrupt service routine exits with the instruction CALL_PAL REI. (REI stands for return from exception or interrupt.) The REI PALcode routine, described in Section 3.7, restores the registers from the interrupt/exception stack frame, restores the previous SP, and resumes the interrupted thread of execution (a process or lower priority interrupt service routine) at the restored PC and with the restored PS.

3.3.3   Restrictions Imposed on Interrupt Service Routines

An interrupt service routine runs at elevated IPL on the kernel stack of the current process. Which process is current at the time of an interrupt is indeterminate. Consequently, an interrupt service routine must be capable of executing in the most constrained possible environment, system context. Chapter 1 describes this limited environment.

Several restrictions are imposed on interrupt service routines by either the architecture or the OpenVMS AXP executive. Many of these result from the limitations of system context and execution at elevated IPL. The following list indicates some of the constraints placed on an interrupt service routine. The description of system context in Chapter 1 contains a more general list of these and other restrictions. Chapter 9 describes synchronization rules applicable to an interrupt service routine.

- To reduce overhead, no context switch occurs with an interrupt. Therefore, the executive requires that instructions executed and data referenced by an interrupt service routine be in system space. An interrupt service routine may not refer to process address space: it could be executing in system context, which has no process-private address space, or the target address could be in a page not currently part of the process's working set. Either case would cause a system crash.
- An interrupt service routine should be brief and do as little processing as possible at elevated IPL to minimize the length of time the servicing of other interrupts is blocked.
- An interrupt service routine must save any registers it uses other than R2 through R7, which are saved by the IEI PALcode routine; otherwise, the contents of registers in use by the interrupted thread of execution could be overwritten and thus corrupted. An interrupt service routine written in a language other than MACRO-64 assembly language generally leaves this detail to the compiler.
- Prior to exiting, an interrupt service routine must remove anything it pushed onto the stack and restore any additional saved registers. Otherwise, the REI PALcode routine would be unable to restore correctly the interrupt stack frame registers and to resume the interrupted thread of execution. An interrupt service routine written in a language other than MACRO-64 assembly language leaves this detail to the compiler.
- An interrupt service routine should be conservative in its use of stack space to minimize the chance of overflowing the kernel stack, which could be quite full at the time of the interrupt.
- The executive does not allow an interrupt service routine (or any other code) that executes above IPL 2 to access pageable routines or data struc-

tures. The page fault exception service routine generates a fatal bugcheck if a page fault occurs while IPL is above 2.

▸ The executive generates a fatal bugcheck if an interrupt service routine (or any other code) that executes above IPL 2 incurs an exception that would otherwise be dispatched to a condition handler.

▸ Although an interrupt service routine can raise IPL, it may not lower IPL below the level at which the original interrupt occurred. An interrupt service routine that lowers IPL below that of its interrupt enables itself to be reentered by another interrupt and breaks its own synchronization.

3.4   **EXCEPTIONS**

When an exception is detected, the IEI PALcode routine takes the following steps:

1. It determines on which stack the exception is to be serviced. Which stack depends on the access mode in which the exception occurred and the type of exception. A change mode exception is generally serviced on the stack of its target mode. All other exceptions are serviced on the kernel stack.

   Use of the kernel stack for most exceptions avoids the possibility of attempting to report an exception on, for example, the user stack, only to find that it is corrupted in some way (invalid or otherwise inaccessible), resulting in another exception. If the kernel stack is invalid when IEI PALcode tries to push the interrupt/exception frame onto the new stack, the processor enters the kernel-stack-not-valid restart sequence (see Chapter 36).

2. If necessary, the IEI PALcode routine switches stacks, saving the previous SP in a processor register or the HWPCB, as described in Section 3.3.2. It aligns the stack to a 64-byte boundary.

3. It pushes the PC and PS onto the new stack. The exception PC that it pushes depends on whether the exception is a fault or a trap:

   • For a fault, the IEI PALcode routine pushes the address of the faulting instruction onto the stack. When a fault is dismissed through the REI PALcode routine, the faulting instruction reexecutes. A fault is triggered, for example, by an attempt to access a location in a way prohibited to the current access mode (access violation), an attempt to access a location whose page table entry is not valid (translation-not-valid), or an attempt to execute a floating-point instruction when floating-point is disabled.

   • For a trap, the IEI PALcode routine pushes the address of the next instruction onto the new stack. An instruction that causes a trap does not reexecute when the exception is dismissed. Illegal instructions, unaligned data, and change mode to kernel are examples of traps. These are called synchronous traps to distinguish them from arithmetic traps.

53

• An arithmetic trap occurs as the result of performing an arithmetic or conversion operation that incurs one of several possible errors. When an arithmetic exception condition is detected, several other instructions can be in various stages of execution. These instructions must complete executing before the arithmetic exception is initiated and can generate more arithmetic errors, possibly as the result of erroneous data forwarded from the instruction incurring the first trap. Consequently, arithmetic traps are imprecise, and a particular trap can represent multiple arithmetic exceptions. The IEI PALcode routine passes information in R5 summarizing the multiple arithmetic exceptions represented by the trap.

The IEI PALcode pushes the address of the instruction that was the next to be executed when the trap was detected rather than the instruction following the one that incurred the exception.

4. The IEI PALcode routine saves R2 through R7 on the stack, forming the rest of the interrupt/exception frame.
5. It loads the address of the service routine from the first quadword of the SCB entry into R2 and loads R3 from the second quadword.
6. The IEI PALcode routine constructs a new PS whose IPL is unchanged. Its current mode is set to the mode in which the exception will be serviced. Its software bits are zero.
7. Depending on the exception type, it loads exception-specific information into R4 and R5.
8. The IEI PALcode routine transfers control to the exception service routine, whose address is in R2.

The exception service routine executes. It eventually exits by executing a CALL_PAL REI instruction to dismiss the exception.

The REI PALcode routine, described in Section 3.7, restores the registers saved in the exception frame, including the PC and PS, restores the previous SP, and resumes the thread of execution that incurred the exception.

3.5   COMPARISON OF EXCEPTIONS AND INTERRUPTS

The following list contrasts exceptions and interrupts.

▶ An interrupt occurs asynchronously to the currently executing instruction stream and is serviced between individual instructions. An exception occurs synchronously as a direct effect of the execution of an instruction. Except for imprecise arithmetic exceptions, an exception is serviced before the next instruction.

▶ Interrupts are generally systemwide events that cannot rely on support of a process in their service routines. Exceptions are generally a part of the currently executing process. Exception servicing is an extension of the instruction stream that is currently executing on behalf of that process.

▸ Interrupts cause an IPL change. Other than machine check exceptions, exceptions do not cause an IPL change.

▸ An interrupt is blocked while the processor executes at an IPL at or above the IPL associated with the interrupt. Exceptions cannot be blocked by elevated IPL.

▸ Certain exception service routines (for example, those for exceptions that can be passed to user-written condition handlers) record the previous access mode in bits ⟨1 : 0⟩ of the new PS. (Unlike the VAX processor status longword register, the Alpha AXP PS does not include an architecturally defined previous mode field. The Alpha AXP architecture does, however, leave the definition of the low two bits of the PS to software.) No interrupt service routine sets these bits. This difference between exceptions and interrupts reflects the fact that interrupts are not related to the interrupted instruction stream.

▸ At initiation of an interrupt other than AST delivery, the IEI PALcode sets bit 2 in the PS to indicate that an interrupt is in progress.

3.6   **MACHINE CHECKS**

Machine checks are generally caused by some sort of hardware condition, although some can be triggered by software. In particular, software can cause machine checks by accessing nonexistent local I/O space locations to determine what devices are present. Some hardware conditions are transient and disappear after reinitialization of the hardware in which the error occurred; others are persistent.

Errors reported through the machine check mechanism are categorized in two different ways:

▸ Whether they have been corrected or are uncorrectable

The OpenVMS AXP executive is notified that hardware or PALcode has detected and corrected a hardware error so that error statistics can be kept and errors logged. The executive is notified that an uncorrectable error has occurred so that it can log the error and determine how to proceed.

▸ Whether they are system or processor errors

A system error is one that is detected by a hardware module external to the CPU module. A processor error is one that is detected by the CPU module itself.

Whether a machine check is maskable and the IPL associated with it depend on the type of machine check:

▸ A system uncorrectable machine check is maskable and deferred until IPL drops below 31.

▸ A system corrected error machine check is maskable and deferred until IPL drops below 20.

► A processor uncorrectable machine check can be maskable or nonmaskable, depending on how the hardware handles that particular kind of error. If nonmaskable, a processor uncorrectable machine check is initiated immediately. If maskable, it is deferred until IPL drops below 31.

► A processor corrected error machine check is maskable and deferred until IPL drops below 31.

Regardless of the type of machine check, the IEI PALcode routine switches to the kernel stack and takes most of the steps described in Section 3.3.2. It builds an interrupt/exception stack frame whose saved PC is that of the next instruction that would have been issued if the error that triggered the machine check had not occurred.

The IEI PALcode constructs a new PS whose IPL is either 20 or 31, depending on the type of machine check. Its current mode is kernel, and its software bits and bit 2 are clear.

The constraints described in Section 3.3.3 apply to machine check service routines.

PALcode provides a flag that a machine check service routine can test to determine whether the hardware state makes returning from the machine check feasible. If it is feasible, the service routine dismisses the machine check by executing a CALL_PAL REI instruction. Chapter 4 describes this flag and its use by the service routine in more detail.

3.7 THE REI PALCODE ROUTINE

An interrupt, exception, or machine check service routine exits by executing a CALL_PAL REI instruction, which causes dispatch to the REI PALcode routine. The architecture limits the types of transitions from one access mode to another; the CALL_PAL REI instruction is the only way to change access mode to a less privileged one (see Figure 1.4). This property of CALL_PAL REI, in conjunction with the architectural constraint that code running in an inner access mode will not be interrupted to deliver an AST to an outer mode, makes the REI PALcode routine a logical place to test whether an AST delivery interrupt should be requested.

Execution of a CALL_PAL REI instruction is a common way for IPL to be lowered. Because lowering IPL can make a pending interrupt deliverable, hardware and software interrupts are often delivered after a CALL_PAL REI instruction is executed.

Some protection and privilege checks are incorporated into the REI PALcode routine to prevent the system from entering illegal or inconsistent states. CALL_PAL REI is not a privileged instruction, and these checks prevent, for example, an attempt to enter a more privileged access mode.

The REI PALcode routine takes the following steps.

1. It checks that the stack is aligned to a 64-byte boundary, generating an illegal PALcode operand trap if it is not.

2. The REI PALcode routine checks that, if the mode is not kernel, the saved PS IPL and must-be-zero bits are zero. If the bits are not zero, the routine generates an illegal PALcode operand trap. This test prevents any mode other than kernel from raising IPL and also detects some forms of stack corruption.

   Note that, unlike VAX REI microcode, the REI PALcode routine does not prevent kernel mode code from executing an REI to a higher IPL; kernel mode code is assumed to be written correctly in this regard.

3. On some AXP implementations, the REI PALcode routine executes a STQ_C instruction (writing the contents of a stack frame quadword back to itself) to clear the lock flag register in case it was set. As described in Chapter 9, the architecture requires that the lock flag register be cleared at return from an interrupt, exception, or machine check by either hardware or PALcode. Clearing the flag enables a STx_C instruction within an interrupted LDx_L/STx_C instruction sequence to detect that the sequence has been interrupted and that the store would not be atomic and should not occur.

4. It checks that the saved PS current mode is no more privileged than the current PS current mode. If the attempted mode transition is illegal, the routine generates an illegal PALcode operand trap. This test prevents an attempt to REI to a more privileged mode.

5. It stores the interrupt/exception stack frame contents into temporary internal registers and restores SP to its value prior to the IEI alignment and push of the interrupt/exception stack frame.

6. The REI PALcode routine saves the contents of the updated SP register in a processor register (ESP, SSP, or USP) or, for kernel mode or any mode on a processor without stack pointer processor registers, in the HWPCB. This step records the pointer into the current access mode's stack.

   The routine loads SP from the appropriate xSP processor register. This step restores the pointer into the now-current stack. On an AXP CPU type that does not implement these processor registers, the REI PALcode routine instead loads SP from the appropriate quadword in the process's HWPCB.

7. It restores R2 through R7, PC, and PS from the temporary locations in which it placed them in step 5.

8. It tests for a pending interrupt of high enough priority to interrupt the thread about to be resumed or an AST that could be delivered, given the IPL and access mode being restored. If any exists, it occurs before the next instruction.

9. Unless another interrupt occurs, execution resumes with the instruction being executed at the time of the interrupt or exception.

4 Hardware Interrupts and Machine Checks

While I nodded, nearly napping, suddenly there came a tapping,
As of someone gently rapping, rapping at my chamber door.
Edgar Allan Poe, *The Raven*

The OpenVMS AXP operating system is often described as interrupt-driven and nonmonolithic. Hardware interrupts notify the executive of such important events as device operation completion, hardware error and alert conditions, power failure, and work requests from one processor to another in a symmetric multiprocessing (SMP) system. In addition, the interval timer interrupt allows the executive to keep system time. Machine checks inform the operating system of serious hardware error conditions.

This chapter provides an overview of hardware interrupts, hardware interrupt priority levels (IPLs), and machine checks.

4.1 OVERVIEW

As described in Chapter 3, many hardware interrupts are requested by signals from devices external to the CPU module when they need attention from the operating system. Hardware interrupts are requested by controllers, widgets, adapters, or other processors in an SMP system. In addition, the processor itself can request some hardware interrupts.

The Alpha AXP architecture provides 16 priority levels, 16 through 31, for hardware interrupts and 15 priority levels, 1 through 15, for software interrupts. Chapter 5 describes software IPLs.

When a hardware interrupt occurs, the interrupted processor raises its priority to the IPL associated with the interrupt. Table 4.1 provides a summary of hardware IPLs and their use by the executive. IPLs 16 through 19 are unused. Corrected errors are reported at IPL 20. Device interrupts occur at IPLs 20 through 23. Interval timer and interprocessor interrupts occur at IPL 22. Urgent conditions such as machine checks and power failure are reported at the highest priority levels, IPLs 24 through 31. A power failure is reported at IPL 30. IPL 31 blocks all interrupts.

Software running in kernel mode can raise and lower the priority of the processor by executing the CALL_PAL MTPR_IPL instruction, as described in Chapter 3. Thus, software has the ability to block hardware interrupts as necessary. For example, a device driver raises IPL to 31 to block the powerfail interrupt and synchronize with powerfail recovery.

A processor's response to any interrupt request, hardware or software, is always the same. If the processor's priority and state permit the requested

Table 4.1   Hardware Interrupt Priority Levels and Their Use

IPL	Name	Use
31	IPL$_POWER	Block all interrupts
	IPL$_EMB	Synchronize error logging
	IPL$_MCHECK	Synchronize machine check processing
	IPL$_MEGA	Synchronize miscellaneous structures
30	—	Powerfail interrupt
30–24	—	System- and processor-specific error interrupts
23–20	—	I/O interrupts
22	IPL$_HWCLK	Interval timer interrupt
	IPL$_IPINTR	Interprocessor interrupt
21	IPL$_INVALIDATE	Synchronize translation buffer (TB) invalidation
20	—	Corrected error machine checks
19–16	—	Unused

interrupt to be granted, the processor transfers control to a privileged architecture library (PALcode) routine. This routine saves the processor state on the current process's kernel stack and dispatches through the system control block (SCB) entry associated with the interrupt to its service routine.

Table 4.2 summarizes hardware interrupts and machine checks and their service routines. The following sections provide brief descriptions.

4.2   POWERFAIL INTERRUPT

CPU hardware requests a powerfail interrupt at IPL 30 when operating voltage drops. EXE$POWERFAIL, in module POWERFAIL, is the powerfail interrupt service routine.

The powerfail interrupt is not initiated until processor IPL drops below 30. Critical code sequences can block the powerfail interrupt by raising IPL to 31. Chapter 36 describes power failure and recovery. Some AXP systems have an uninterruptible power supply. No existing systems generate powerfail interrupts.

4.3   PROCESSOR-SPECIFIC INTERRUPTS

The architecture reserves SCB entries at offsets 680_{16} to $6B0_{16}$ for processor-specific interrupts. For more information, see the appropriate hardware manuals.

4.4   INTERVAL TIMER INTERRUPT

The interval timer enables the OpenVMS AXP executive to keep system time. It requests at least 1,000 interrupts every second; the number varies depending on system implementation. Console software records the frequency of interval timer interrupts in the hardware restart parameter block (HWRPB) (see Chapter 33).

Table 4.2   Summary of Hardware Interrupts and Machine Checks

SCB Entry Offset	*IPL*	*Description*	*Service Routine*
		HARDWARE INTERRUPTS	
600_{16}	22	Interval timer interrupt	EXE$HWCLKINT
610_{16}	22	Interprocessor interrupt	SMP$INTSR
640_{16}	30	Powerfail interrupt	EXE$POWERFAIL
680_{16}–$6B0_{16}$	—	Processor-specific interrupts	Processor-specific
800_{16}–$7FF0_{16}$	20–23	I/O interrupts	Device-specific
		MACHINE CHECKS	
620_{16}	20	System corrected error machine check	EXE$SYSTEM_ CORRECTED_ERROR [1]
630_{16}	20	Processor corrected error machine check	EXE$PROCESSOR_ CORRECTED_ERROR [1]
660_{16}	31	System uncorrectable error machine check	EXE$SYSTEM_ MACHINE_CHECK [1]
670_{16}	31	Processor uncorrectable error machine check	EXE$PROCESSOR_ MACHINE_CHECK [1]

[1] The service routines for corrected and uncorrected machine checks have different names for each AXP system and are found in different system-specific modules. The routine names shown in the table are used for a majority of the systems. These routines are in facility [CPU*xxyy*], in module ERROR_ROUTINES_*xxyy* or CPU_SUPPORT_*xxyy*, where *xx* is the system type designator and *yy* is the processor type designator. Appendix G lists system and processor designations.

Specifically, the routines are in the following modules (and have the names shown in the table unless otherwise stated):

- Module [CPU0202]ERROR_ROUTINES_0202 (DEC 4000 Model 600 series)
- Module [CPU0302]ERROR_ROUTINES_0302 (DEC 7000 Model 600 series and DEC 10000 Model 600 series): EXE$PROC_CORRECTED_ERROR, EXE$SYSTEM_CORRECTED_ERROR, EXE$SYSTEM_MCHK_ABORT, EXE$PROCESSOR_MCHK_ABORT
- Module [CPU0402]CPU_SUPPORT_0402 (DEC 3000 Models 500 and 400 series)

Interval timer interrupts are serviced by EXE$HWCLKINT, in module TIMESCHDL, at IPL 22. Chapter 12 describes EXE$HWCLKINT in detail.

4.5   INTERPROCESSOR INTERRUPT

On an SMP system, the executive uses the interprocessor interrupt mechanism to interrupt a specific processor for a specific task or to interrupt all processors or a subset of all processors to perform tasks as required. To request an interprocessor interrupt, a processor can write to the interprocessor interrupt request (IPIR) internal register using the CALL_PAL MTPR_IPIR instruction. An interprocessor interrupt is serviced by SMP$INTSR, in module SMPINT_COMMON. Chapter 37 describes SMP$INTSR in detail.

4.6   **I/O INTERRUPTS**

The architecture reserves SCB entries at offsets 800_{16} through $7FF0_{16}$ for I/O interrupts. Interrupts from I/O adapters, I/O widgets, and I/O controllers are all vectored through these SCB offsets; which SCB offset is used for a specific interrupt source depends on the system implementation.

Regardless of SCB offset, all I/O interrupts are serviced by a single interrupt service routine, IO_INTERRUPT, in module IOCINTDISP. IO_INTERRUPT locates and calls the appropriate service routine for the interrupt. Chapter 24 provides information about IO_INTERRUPT and I/O interrupt dispatching.

4.7   **UNEXPECTED INTERRUPTS AND EXCEPTIONS**

ERL$UNEXP, in module UNEXPINT, is the default service routine for all SCB entries. An entry for an interrupt or exception of interest to the executive is reinitialized when the executive image containing its service routine is loaded. ERL$UNEXP saves registers R0 through R29 on the stack, loads the offset of the associated SCB vector from the high-order longword of the second quadword of the SCB entry into R18, and generates the non-fatal bugcheck UNEXINTEXC. When control returns to ERL$UNEXP, it dismisses the unexpected interrupt or exception. Chapter 35 describes bugcheck processing.

4.8   **MACHINE CHECKS**

An AXP processor generates a machine check in response to a hardware error condition. In the case of a recoverable error, the processor generates a corrected error machine check to notify the operating system of potential hardware problems. When hardware recovery is impossible, the processor generates an uncorrectable error machine check. Software recovery from a condition that causes an uncorrectable error machine check may or may not be possible.

Some machine checks can be triggered by software. In particular, the OpenVMS AXP executive can cause machine checks by accessing nonexistent local I/O space locations to determine what devices are present.

A machine check error is processor- or system-specific. Examples of uncorrectable error system machine checks include processor-memory interconnect protocol and parity errors and multiple-bit memory errors. An example of a corrected error system machine check is a single-bit memory error generated by a read reference to memory from an I/O device.

Examples of uncorrectable error processor machine checks include accesses to nonexistent local I/O space and translation buffer parity errors. An example of a corrected error processor machine check is a single-bit memory error generated by an instruction-stream reference.

PALcode typically informs the executive of the details of a particular machine check through data recorded in a structure called a logout frame. During bootstrap, the console subsystem allocates physical memory for a logout area that can accommodate a number of logout frames and stores its starting address and length in the per-CPU slot of the HWRPB. During system initialization the executive maps the logout area and stores its system virtual address in the per-CPU database field CPU$L_LOGOUT_AREA_VA_L. On an SMP system, each processor can react to its own internal errors as well as to errors in common hardware blocks or interconnects. Each processor has its own set of logout frames.

A particular logout frame is identified by its offset from the start of this area. Before dispatching to a machine check service routine, PALcode records data about the error in a logout frame and loads R4 with its offset. If no logout frame was filled out, PALcode initializes R4 to –1. It then initiates a machine check. If the machine check is maskable, it is deferred until IPL drops below 31 or 20, depending on the type. If the machine check is not maskable, it is initiated immediately.

For either type of machine check, the machine check mechanism includes raising IPL to 31 or 20, depending on the type of machine check; switching to the kernel stack; and building an interrupt/exception stack frame to record the state of the previous control flow. The PALcode routine then dispatches to a service routine through one of the four SCB entries listed in Table 4.2.

A machine check service routine gets the starting virtual address of the logout frame area and calculates the virtual address of the particular logout frame whose offset is in R4.

Figure 4.1 shows the layout of a logout frame, which has three optional areas. The first longword contains the size in bytes of the entire frame.

Bit 31 in the second longword, when set, indicates that after logging the error the service routine should continue executing the previous control flow. If the bit is clear, the error has left the system in a state from which resumption is not possible. This bit is always set in a logout frame that describes a corrected error.

Bit 30 is always clear in a logout frame that describes an uncorrectable error. When set, it indicates that the logout frame describes a corrected error and another one occurred before a previous one of the same type was serviced.

The third longword contains the offset in bytes from the base of the logout frame to the CPU-specific data. If its contents are equal to the contents of the fourth longword, the frame has no CPU-specific data. If it contains 10_{16}, the frame contains no PALcode-specific information.

The fourth longword contains the offset in bytes from the base of the logout frame to the system-specific data. If its contents are equal to the frame size in bytes, the logout frame contains no system-specific information.

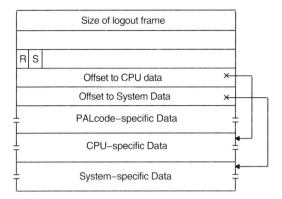

Figure 4.1
Layout of a Machine Check Logout Frame

PALcode and machine check service routines communicate through a processor register called the machine check error summary (MCES) register. It contains five bits. The low-order three bits identify the type of machine check that occurred: bit 0 is set by the hardware or PALcode when an uncorrectable machine check occurs; bit 1 is set if the machine check is a system corrected error; and bit 2 is set for a processor corrected error. As the executive completes the servicing of a machine check, it writes a 1 to the appropriate bit to clear it.

The purpose of the bit for uncorrectable error machine checks is to permit detection of nested uncorrectable error machine checks. If one occurs when that bit is already set, PALcode generates a double-error processor restart (see Chapter 36). Each of the other two bits indicates whether the logout frame corresponding to that type of corrected machine check is in use.

Bits 3 and 4 in the MCES register are set to disable the reporting of corrected processor and system errors. If, for example, bit 3 is set, and a correctable error occurs, the error is corrected but no machine check is initiated.

4.9   RELEVANT SOURCE MODULES

The source modules described in this chapter include

    [CPU0202]ERROR_ROUTINES_0202.B64
    [CPU0302]ERROR_ROUTINES_0302.BLI
    [CPU0402]CPU_SUPPORT_0402.BLI
    [CPU0602]ERROR_ROUTINES_0602.B64
    [CPU0702]CPU_SUPPORT_0702.BLI
    [SYS]UNEXPINT.M64

5 Software Interrupts

And now I see with eye serene
The very pulse of the machine.

William Wordsworth, *She Was a Phantom of Delight*

The Alpha AXP architecture provides the capability for kernel mode software to request interrupts at any interrupt priority level (IPL) from 1 to 15. Requested by software rather than hardware, these are called software interrupts. In addition, the architecture provides four interrupts to signal asynchronous system trap (AST) delivery to each of the access modes.

Software interrupts are fundamental to the OpenVMS AXP operating system. Software interrupt service routines perform many of the most important OpenVMS system functions. These include scheduling (IPL 3), I/O postprocessing (IPL 4), checking whether the current process has reached quantum end (IPL 7), and dispatching fork processes (IPLs 6 and 8 through 11). This chapter summarizes how the operating system uses software interrupts and discusses fork processing in detail.

5.1 AST DELIVERY INTERRUPTS

An AST is a mechanism for signaling an asynchronous event to a process. An AST delivery interrupt signals that there is an AST for the current process to execute. An AST interrupt is always requested on behalf of the current process and must be serviced in its context.

An AST delivery interrupt service routine delivers an AST by transferring control to the designated AST routine at the specified access mode. Some ASTs are requested by the process, for example, as notification of I/O request completion. Others are queued to the process by the executive as part of normal system operations, such as automatic working set limit adjustment.

On a VAX processor, AST delivery to all modes is initiated through an IPL 2 software interrupt and handled by a common interrupt service routine. On an AXP processor, there are four different AST interrupts, one for each access mode. These interrupts occur at IPL 2 but are not requested through the software interrupt request register (SIRR) and are not dispatched through the IPL 2 software interrupt system control block (SCB) entry.

These interrupts are mentioned here for completeness; the details of their request mechanism and delivery are given in Chapter 8.

5.2   OVERVIEW

The OpenVMS AXP executive requests a software interrupt to cause an interrupt service routine to execute and perform its designated function. It does this by executing a `CALL_PAL MTPR_SIRR` instruction to write a particular IPL into the SIRR processor register. Sometime later, when the interrupt request is granted, the initiate exception, interrupt, or machine check (IEI) PALcode routine dispatches through the appropriate SCB vector to the software interrupt service routine associated with that IPL. Chapter 3 describes the processor registers involved in software interrupts and the IEI PALcode routine.

The executive uses software interrupts to schedule operating system functions. Using software interrupts is more efficient than periodically checking whether these functions need to be done. IPLs are assigned to the different operating system functions, in part as an indication of their relative importance.

The executive also uses specific IPLs and interrupt requests at those IPLs to synchronize access to shared data structures. Chapter 9 discusses synchronization through raising IPL.

It requests the software interrupt service routines for IPLs 3, 4, 6, 7, 8, and 11 from within a hardware interrupt service routine or another software interrupt service routine. Software interrupts at 12 and 14 are requested only as the result of a person's entering a CPU console command. Although fork dispatching is provided at IPLs 9 and 10, OpenVMS components make little or no use of them. The executive does not use the software interrupt vectors for IPLs 1, 2, 5, 13, and 15.

The architecture constrains software interrupt service routines by providing only one bit to indicate that a software interrupt has been requested at a particular IPL. The service routine is thus unable to determine how many requests for it were outstanding when the interrupt request was granted. As a result, either the software must supply some protocol for determining this number or it must be irrelevant to the execution of the service routine. The scheduling interrupt service routine is an example of a routine that has one function to do, regardless of how many times that function has been requested.

Other interrupt service routines use queues to keep track of their work. Each element in the queue represents a specific item of work for the interrupt service routine and an instance of the interrupt's having been requested.

A queue-driven interrupt service routine generally performs each work item in its queue before dismissing the interrupt. It removes an item from the queue, if one is present; processes that item; and tries to remove another. If no item was removed because the queue is empty, the interrupt service routine's work is complete; it then exits through a `CALL_PAL REI` instruction. Such a software interrupt service routine reacts gracefully to a no longer necessary interrupt, one granted when there is no work left for the service routine to do.

5.3 SOFTWARE INTERRUPT SERVICE ROUTINES

No central OpenVMS monitor routine controls the sequence of operating system functions. Instead, any executive thread that identifies the need for a particular function performed within a software interrupt service routine can request the associated interrupt. Scheduling operating system functions as software interrupts eliminates any requirement for polling whether these functions need to be done. It also enables more important functions to interrupt less important ones.

Table 5.1 shows the software interrupt service routine functions and their associated IPLs. In some cases, the assigned IPL only indicates the relative importance of the interrupt, and the interrupt service routine runs primarily at a higher IPL for synchronization. The table also shows the common symbolic names for these IPLs, defined by the macro $IPLDEF.

The executive interprets software interrupts, except the AST delivery and rescheduling interrupts, as systemwide events that are serviced independently of the context of a specific process. These higher IPL software interrupt service routines are said to run in system context. Chapter 1 compares system context and process context.

Some software interrupt service routines perform the same functions every time they execute, while others perform more varied functions. The

---

Table 5.1   Software Interrupt Levels Used by the Executive

IPL	IPL Names	Software Interrupt Use
1		Unused
2	IPL$_ASTDEL	Unused [1]
3	IPL$_RESCHED	Rescheduling
4	IPL$_IOPOST	I/O postprocessing
5		Unused
6	IPL$_QUEUEAST	Fork dispatching
7	IPL$_TIMERFORK	Software timer
8	IPL$_SYNCH, IPL$_IOLOCK8, IPL$_SCHED, IPL$_SCS, IPL$_TIMER, IPL$_MMG	Fork dispatching
9	IPL$_IOLOCK9	Fork dispatching
10	IPL$_IOLOCK10	Fork dispatching
11	IPL$_MAILBOX, IPL$_IOLOCK11	Fork dispatching
12		IPC intervention
13		Unused
14		XDELTA
15		Unused

---

[1] AST interrupts are IPL 2 interrupts; they are distinct, however, from the IPL 2 software interrupt, which is currently unused.

rescheduling interrupt service routine, for example, takes the current process out of execution, selects another to run, and places it into execution. The I/O postprocessing interrupt service routine has a specific function to perform but is data-driven by the I/O request packets (IRPs) in its work queue. A fork dispatching interrupt exists solely to dispatch to system routines running as fork processes, but which routines and fork processes execute varies with system operation.

The software interrupts used by the executive are described briefly in the following sections. Some are described at more length in subsequent chapters. The following sections are in order by interrupt level except that the fork dispatching interrupts are discussed last.

Each of the interrupt service routines for unused software interrupts merely logs an error and dismisses the interrupt.

5.3.1   **Rescheduling Interrupt (IPL 3)**

The executive requests a rescheduling interrupt at IPL 3 whenever a resident process of high enough priority to preempt the current process becomes computable. (Although this statement is true for a uniprocessor system, it is a simplification of what happens on a symmetric multiprocessing (SMP) system.)

SCH$INTERRUPT, in module SCHEDULER, which is the IPL 3 interrupt service routine, begins execution at IPL 3 on the kernel stack of the current process. It acquires the SCHED spinlock, raising IPL to IPL$_SCHED, and changes the state of the current process from current (CUR) to computable (COM). It selects the highest priority resident computable process and executes a CALL_PAL SWPCTX instruction, switching from the context of the previous process to that of the new process. The new process's scheduling state is changed to CUR. (On an SMP system, selecting the next process to execute is somewhat more complex.)

Many of the events that make a process computable occur as part of servicing software interrupts between IPL$_IOPOST and IPL$_SCHED. That the scheduler database is modified from these software interrupts has the following implications:

▸ To block any other accesses to the scheduler database while it takes one process out of execution and selects another to run, SCH$INTERRUPT must raise IPL to IPL$_SCHED and acquire the SCHED spinlock.
▸ The IPL 3 interrupt can be requested a number of times before it is granted. The number of times the interrupt has been requested is not recorded but is irrelevant, since the interrupt service routine always does the same task.
▸ When the IPL 3 interrupt is granted, all events that might affect the choice of which process to run have been serviced. That is, the higher priority software interrupt service routines that affect the scheduler database have completed their work. Thus, the interrupt service routine can make

the best possible choice at the time it blocks further alterations to the database.

Chapter 13 discusses the scheduler database, events that affect the scheduler database, the rescheduling interrupt, and the additional complexities of scheduling on an SMP system.

5.3.2 I/O Postprocessing (IPL 4)

When a device driver has completed an I/O request, it invokes a routine that places the IRP associated with the request at the tail of the I/O postprocessing queue. If the queue was empty, the routine requests a software interrupt at IPL$_IOPOST (IPL 4). If the queue was not empty, a software interrupt has already been requested; requesting another would impose additional overhead and serve no purpose.

There is one per-CPU queue for each member of an SMP system and one systemwide I/O postprocessing queue to which most IRPs are queued. An IRP for a request completed in process context (that is, by a driver's preprocessing function decision table action routine) is typically queued to a postprocessing queue in the per-CPU database. The I/O postprocessing interrupt service routine, running on a uniprocessor or on the primary processor of an SMP system, services the systemwide queue and its own per-CPU queue. The I/O postprocessing interrupt service routine, running on each secondary, services only that processor's per-CPU queue. Chapters 24 and 37 give further details.

The I/O postprocessing interrupt service routine, IOC$IOPOST in module IOCIOPOST, runs on each member of an SMP system. Running on the primary processor or on a uniprocessor, it removes each IRP in turn from the beginning of the systemwide queue and processes it. The details of the processing vary with the type of IRP. For example, IOC$IOPOST distinguishes between buffered and direct I/O requests. When a direct I/O request completes, IOC$IOPOST unlocks the buffer pages from memory. When a buffered output request completes, IOC$IOPOST deallocates the buffer to nonpaged pool and returns process byte count quota.

IOC$IOPOST, running on a uniprocessor or on any member of an SMP system, then services the per-CPU I/O postprocessing queue for that processor. After processing all IRPs in the queue, it dismisses the interrupt with an REI statement. Example 5.1, a slightly simplified extract from module IOCIO-POST, shows this sequence.

Chapter 23 contains further general information about I/O postprocessing, and Chapter 18 gives specific information about postprocessing of memory management requests.

5.3.3 Software Timer (IPL 7)

The executive includes both a hardware interrupt service routine to service the hardware clock and a software timer interrupt service routine. Together

Example 5.1
IOC$IOPOST Interrupt Service Routine Extract

```
;IOC$IOPOST::                        ;I/O postprocessing interrupt
IOPOST:
        EVAX_MFPR_PRBR               ;Get per-CPU data address into R0
        CMPL    CPU$L_PHY_CPUID(R0),SMP$GL_PRIMID ;Are we the primary?
        BNEQ    5$                   ;If NEQ, no
        TSTL    IOC$GQ_POSTIQ        ;Is systemwide queue empty?
        BEQL    5$                   ;Branch if yes, service per-CPU queue
        $REMQHI IOC$GQ_POSTIQ,R5     ;Get IRP from systemwide queue
        BVC     60$                  ;If VC, got one
5$:     REMQUE  @CPU$L_PSFL(R0),R5   ;Get IRP from per-CPU queue
        BVC     60$                  ;If VC, got one
        REI                          ;No more IRPs to postprocess.  Exit
60$:    .                            ;Postprocess this
        .                            ; I/O request packet
        BRW     IOPOST               ;Get next I/O request packet
```

these routines service time-dependent requests. Chapter 12 describes them in detail; this section summarizes some of their interaction.

The hardware interrupt service routine is EXE$HWCLKINT in module TIMESCHDL. (TIMESCHDL is conditionally compiled. Its listing and object modules are named TIMESCHDL_MIN and TIMESCHDL_MON. The latter version performs additional sanity checks.) EXE$HWCLKINT runs in response to a hardware clock interrupt at IPL 22. Some of its duties are to update the system time, perform CPU time accounting, check for quantum expiration of the current process, and check whether the first timer queue entry (TQE) has come due.

A TQE describes a time-dependent request, which is typically made through the Schedule Wakeup ($SCHDWK) or Set Timer ($SETIMR) system service. The queue of TQEs is kept ordered by expiration time, with the soonest due first. Quantum-end processing and TQE servicing require lengthier execution than is appropriate at high IPL and require modification to the scheduler database, which is synchronized with the SCHED spinlock.

If the current process has run out of quantum, EXE$HWCLKINT requests an IPL$_TIMERFORK (IPL 7) interrupt. The IPL$_TIMERFORK interrupt service routine, EXE$SWTIMINT in module TIMESCHDL, checks whether the current process's quantum has expired. If it has, EXE$SWTIMINT invokes the routine that performs quantum-end processing.

If the first TQE has come due, EXE$HWCLKINT requests execution of an IPL 8 fork process to service the timer queue. In early VAX/VMS versions, such servicing was performed by EXE$SWTIMINT. This change reduces the latency to service timer requests on a system with substantial I/O activity.

The IPL 8 fork process executes routine EXE$SWTIMINT_FORK, in module TIMESCHDL. Its fork lock is the TIMER spinlock. EXE$SWTIMINT_FORK acquires the HWCLK spinlock, raising IPL to IPL$_HWCLK, to synchronize its access to the queue of TQEs and, in particular, the first TQE.

It removes the first TQE if its expiration time is the same as or earlier than the current system time. It releases the two spinlocks, lowering IPL to IPL$_ TIMER (IPL 8). EXE$SWTIMINT_FORK then processes the TQE.

It reacquires the TIMER and HWCLK spinlocks and checks the TQE that is now first in the queue. EXE$SWTIMINT_FORK continues in this manner until it reaches a TQE that has not yet expired. Leaving unexpired TQEs in the queue, it then releases the HWCLK spinlock and returns to the fork dispatcher, which releases the TIMER spinlock.

5.3.4   IPC (IPL 12)

The IPL 12 interrupt is only requested by a person depositing 12 into the software interrupt request register at the CPU console terminal.

The IPL 12 interrupt service routine, EXE$IPCONTROL in module IP-CONTROL, facilitates certain types of human intervention when the system might otherwise have to be crashed.

When the IPL 12 interrupt request is granted, the interrupt service routine first checks if it is running on either a uniprocessor or the primary processor of an SMP system. If not, the routine does not have access to the console and exits. If it is running on the primary processor, it temporarily disables SMP sanity and spinlock wait timeouts (see Chapter 37) so that operations below IPL 12 can be stalled on this CPU without adverse consequences.

It then prompts on the console for human input with the following text: IPC>. (IPC is a shortened form of IPL C, where C_{16} is 12.) The IPL 12 interrupt service routine accepts the following commands:

Command	Meaning
C *ddcu:*	Cancel mount verification in progress
Q	Recalculate quorum for the VMScluster
X	Activate XDELTA (if it is resident)
CTRL/Z	Return the system to normal operation

The C command is issued with a device specification to cancel mount verification on the specified disk or tape. Mount verification is a mechanism that enables the system to recover gracefully from certain kinds of transient device failures by stalling I/O requests to a device while it is offline or inaccessible. If the device comes back on line, the system confirms that this is the same device as was previously mounted and resumes normal I/O processing on the volume. If SYSGEN parameter MVTIMEOUT seconds elapse before a disk comes back on line, mount verification times out and the system aborts I/O requests in progress to that disk. For a tape, the SYSGEN parameter TAPE_MVTIMEOUT specifies the length of the mount verification timeout period.

While a device is in a state of mount verification in progress, all users' I/O requests to it are stalled until the mount verification times out or the device comes back on line. An impatient user can type CTRL/C or CTRL/Y and STOP to abort the image and cancel its I/O requests. However, the user cannot cancel any I/O request the file system might have made on the user's behalf, and subsequent file system activity in the process will be blocked until mount verification times out or is canceled.

Therefore, if the device failure is known to be permanent, it may be appropriate to cancel mount verification before the mount verification timeout period has elapsed. In most cases, the DISMOUNT/ABORT command is the preferred way to cancel mount verification. (The *OpenVMS DCL Dictionary* gives further information on this command.) However, if the state of the system prevents that command from being entered, the C command to the IPL 12 interrupt service routine may be entered instead.

For additional information on mount verification, see the *OpenVMS System Manager's Manual*.

In response to a Q command, EXE$IPCONTROL requests the VMScluster system connection manager to recalculate dynamic quorum based on the current cluster configuration. The Q command can be issued when a VMS-cluster system hangs because of quorum loss, after a node crashes and fails to reboot.

Running as an IPL 12 interrupt service routine, EXE$IPCONTROL cannot acquire the SCS spinlock in order to synchronize its access to the connection manager. The IPL associated with the SCS spinlock is IPL$_SCS, or IPL 8. EXE$IPCONTROL therefore creates an IPL 8 fork process whose fork lock is the SCS spinlock. Section 5.4 provides more information about fork processing.

The fork process calls a connection manager routine to recompute quorum. If any error occurs, the fork process issues a fork and wait request (see Section 5.4.5), retrying its call whenever it is reentered. Once the call to the routine is successful, the fork process exits.

In response to an X command, EXE$IPCONTROL invokes INI$BRK to activate XDELTA, as described in Section 5.3.5. Note, however, that this method is not commonly used because XDELTA can be activated directly through a higher priority IPL 14 interrupt.

In response to CTRL/Z, EXE$IPCONTROL restores the previous state of the SMP sanity and spinlock wait timeouts and exits, dismissing the IPL 12 interrupt with a CALL_PAL REI instruction.

5.3.5   XDELTA (IPL 14)

XDELTA, the executive debugger, can optionally be loaded at system initialization. If XDELTA is resident, the SCB vector for the breakpoint exception points to a service routine within XDELTA. XDELTA remains quiescent, transferring control to the usual exception service routine when breakpoints occur, until a breakpoint is executed whose address is contained in XDELTA's breakpoint table. Initially, the only such breakpoint is at routine INI$BRK, in module SYSTEM_ROUTINES.

When such a breakpoint instruction is executed, XDELTA accepts command input from the CPU console terminal. User-entered commands can include setting other breakpoints, setting single-step mode, and examining system space. Often programmers debugging kernel mode code that runs above IPL 0, such as a device driver, invoke INI$BRK from their code to activate XDELTA. The *OpenVMS Delta/XDelta Debugger Manual* provides further information about XDELTA (and DELTA) commands.

OpenVMS uses the IPL 14 software interrupt to enable a person to activate XDELTA by depositing 14 in the software interrupt request register at the CPU console terminal. The interrupt service routine to activate XDELTA is INI$MASTERWAKE, in module SYSTEM_ROUTINES. This interrupt service routine consists of a call to INI$BRK and a CALL_PAL REI instruction. When XDELTA is entered through its BPT exception service routine, it raises IPL and executes at IPL 31. When XDELTA is dismissed through a ;P or ;G command, it returns to INI$MASTERWAKE, which dismisses the interrupt.

When XDELTA is not resident, the instruction at INI$BRK is a NOP rather than a CALL_PAL BPT. Thus, a system without XDELTA reacts gracefully to an XDELTA interrupt or a JSB to INI$BRK.

5.4 FORK PROCESSING

Five software interrupts (IPLs 6 and 8 to 11) exist solely to dispatch to fork processes. Although called a process, a fork process bears little resemblance to a normal process. A fork process is simply a routine invoked by one of these interrupt service routines. The routine's code and any data it accesses must be in nonpageable system space. A fork process and its context are described by a fork block (FKB).

Each of the interrupt service routines has its own work queue of fork blocks. When one of these interrupts is granted, the interrupt service routine removes from its queue each fork block in turn and dispatches to the fork process it describes. The fork process mechanism essentially creates a list of routines to be executed based on current system needs.

The following sections describe fork process data structures and service routines in more detail.

5.4.1 Fork Process Data Structures

A fork block describes a routine to be called by a fork dispatching interrupt service routine and some context for that routine. The macro $FKBDEF defines symbolic names for the fields in a fork block. A minimal fork block, shown in Figure 5.1, includes the procedure value of the fork process entry point (FKB$L_FPC) and the contents of R3 and R4. (Note that the field name FKB$L_FPC stands for fork program counter (PC) on OpenVMS VAX. The field name is unchanged for OpenVMS AXP, although the exact meaning of its contents has changed.) The first two longwords of a fork block link

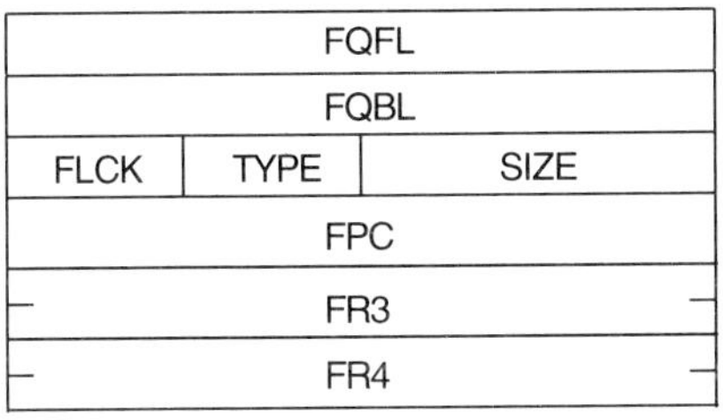

FQFL		
FQBL		
FLCK	TYPE	SIZE
FPC		
FR3		
FR4		

Figure 5.1
Layout of a Fork Block (FKB)

it into a queue. The fields FKB$W_SIZE and FKB$B_TYPE complete the standard dynamic data structure header.

The field FKB$B_FLCK identifies the spinlock associated with the fork process. It is an index into a table of static spinlocks, pointed to by SMP$AR_SPNLKVEC, and also into a table of spinlock IPLs, at SMP$AL_IPLVEC. The indexed value in the spinlock IPL table specifies into which fork block queue the fork block is inserted and at what IPL its routine will run. (In contrast, on OpenVMS VAX the field FKB$B_FLCK, also known as FKB$B_FIPL, can contain an actual fork IPL.) Chapter 9 describes spinlocks in detail.

A fork block must be in nonpageable system space. Most often, it is part of a larger data structure, such as a unit control block or class driver request packet, which contains additional data. The combination of standard fork block fields, additional fork block data, and the routine that is to be executed is called a fork process.

Figure 5.2 shows the array of fork block queue listheads. The array is in the per-CPU database so that each CPU in an SMP system has its own fork block queues. (Chapter 37 contains more information on the per-CPU database.) The listheads of these queues are ordered in an array that includes a placeholder listhead for IPL 7. Since the IPL 7 interrupt is serviced by the software timer routine, there is no fork process dispatching at IPL 7. However, having the placeholder listhead simplifies the fork process creation code.

5.4.2 Reasons for Creating a Fork Process

Fork processing exists, in part, so that device drivers do not have to execute at high IPLs for long periods of time, blocking other device interrupts. Device interrupt service routines run at device IPLs between 20 and 23. Often, servicing an interrupt requires lengthy processing but not high-IPL execution. Typically, a device interrupt service routine switches to a lower IPL as soon as possible. However, it may not simply lower IPL directly; that could interfere with the synchronization of code already running at the lower IPL. Instead, it creates a fork process that will run at the lower IPL when its turn comes.

A driver or any high-IPL thread of execution might also create a fork

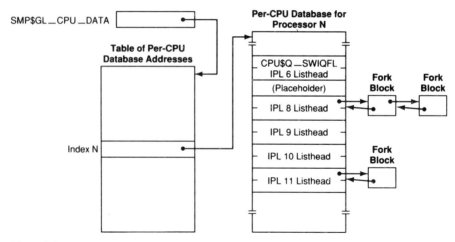

Figure 5.2
Fork Block Queues

process at a lower IPL to access a system database synchronized at that lower IPL, for example, if the driver needed to queue an AST to a process. Another example is the routine that allocates nonpaged pool. It can be invoked from process context code and from interrupt threads of execution at IPLs up to 11. If the routine determines that pool must be expanded before any can be allocated, but IPL is above IPL$_MMG or the processor holds a higher ranking spinlock than MMG, the routine creates an IPL 6 fork process to perform the expansion. Chapter 21 gives more information on pool allocation.

5.4.3 Creating a Fork Process

To fork, a driver invokes routine EXE$PRIMITIVE_FORK, or EXE$QUEUE_FORK, in module FORKCNTRL, specifying the address of the fork block, the contents of R3 and R4, and the procedure value of the fork process entry point. (FORKCNTRL is conditionally compiled. Its listing and object modules are named FORKCNTRL_MIN and FORKCNTRL_MON. The latter version performs additional sanity checks.)

Generally a driver routine forks by invoking the macro FORK or IOFORK, either of which generates code that performs the following steps:

1. It stores the procedure value of the fork process entry point in the fork block field FKB$L_FPC.
2. It invokes EXE$PRIMITIVE_FORK.
3. When the routine returns, it returns to code generated by the macro that returns to the invoker of the driver routine (the default) or transfers to a specified place within the driver routine containing the macro.

Example 5.2 shows the MACRO-32 statements generated by a simple invocation of the FORK macro.

Example 5.2
FORK Macro and Generated Statements

```
; The macro invocation
      FORK
; The generated statements
      $FKBDEF
      MOVAB   L1,FKB$L_FPC(R5)
      JSB     G^EXE$PRIMITIVE_FORK
      RSB
L1:   .JSB_ENTRY  -
         INPUT=<R3,R4,R5>,SCRATCH=<R0,R1,R2>
```

Example 5.3
EXE$PRIMITIVE_FORK Routine Extract

```
      UNIVERSAL_JSB   EXE$PRIMITIVE_FORK,INPUT=<R3,R4,R5>,OUTPUT=<R3,R4>
;EXE$PRIMITIVE_FORK::
      EVAX_STQ-                         ;Save R3 and R4 in fork block
            R3,FKB$Q_FR3(R5)            ;Use a built-in to store all
      EVAX_STQ-                         ; 64 bits of the register
            R4,FKB$Q_FR4(R5)
                                        ;Fall through into EXE$QUEUE_FORK
      UNIVERSAL_JSB   EXE$QUEUE_FORK,INPUT=<R5>,OUTPUT=<R3,R4>
;EXE$QUEUE_FORK::
      MOVZBL  FKB$B_FLCK(R5),R4         ;Get fork lock index
      MOVL    SMP$AL_IPLVEC[R4],R4      ;Get fork IPL from spinlock database
      FIND_CPU_DATA R3                  ;Get base of CPU data area
      ASSUME  FQH_SIZE EQ 8             ;Assumption required for use of MOVAQ
      MOVAQ   -                         ;Get address of fork queue listhead
            CPU$Q_SWIQFL-<6*FQH_SIZE>(R3)[R4],R3
      INSQUE  (R5),@4(R3)               ;Insert fork block in fork queue
      BNEQ    10$                       ;If queue already populated
                                        ; avoid extra interrupt
      SOFTINT R4                        ;Request software interrupt
10$:  RSB                               ;Return
```

The IOFORK macro first generates a statement that clears a bit to disable an I/O timeout on the device, and then the IOFORK macro invokes the FORK macro.

EXE$PRIMITIVE_FORK stores R3 and R4 in the fork block. At subentry point EXE$QUEUE_FORK, it converts the spinlock index in FKB$B_FLCK to an IPL by indexing the array at SMP$AL_IPLVEC with it. EXE$PRIMITIVE_FORK inserts the fork block at the tail of the fork block queue for that IPL and requests a software interrupt at that IPL if the queue was empty.

EXE$PRIMITIVE_FORK then returns to the macro-generated code, which returns as previously described.

The instructions in EXE$PRIMITIVE_FORK that perform these functions are listed in Example 5.3. Figure 5.3 shows the general flow of the creation of a fork process and dispatch into it.

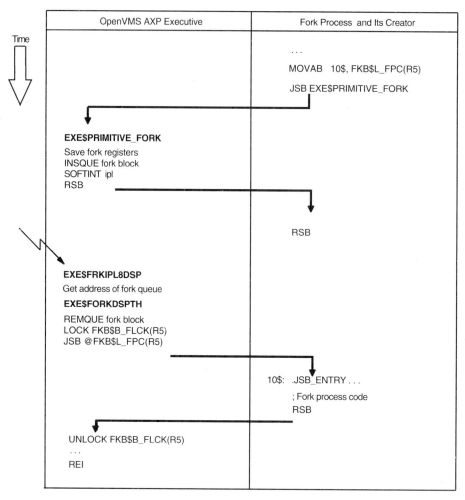

Figure 5.3
Creating and Dispatching to a Fork Process

When IPL drops below that of the requested fork interrupt, the fork dispatching interrupt will be granted and serviced on the CPU on which it was requested. The fork process will execute on that CPU as well.

The steps to create a fork process are different from those in OpenVMS VAX. An OpenVMS VAX driver executes a JSB to EXE$FORK, which pops the return address off the stack and stores it in FKB$L_FPC as the fork process entry point. When EXE$FORK returns, it returns to the invoker of the driver routine; that is, it returns to "its caller's caller." OpenVMS AXP does not support that form of return and instead requires nested returns.

Requiring explicit control of the stack, the caller's caller form of return is not feasible for code written in anything but an assembler language. A typical

MACRO-32 routine compiled for AXP execution, for example, begins with compiler-generated register saves and ends with compiler-generated register restores. To ensure that saved registers and the state of the stack are restored, a routine must execute its own return code.

For a fork process routine that must maintain context on the stack across stalls, OpenVMS AXP provides a mechanism called a kernel process, described in Section 5.5.

5.4.4   Dispatching a Fork Process

When a fork interrupt is granted, the IEI PALcode routine dispatches to its interrupt service routine. Each fork IPL has a unique interrupt service routine that performs setup for common fork dispatching code. The interrupt service routine stores the offset of the corresponding fork queue listhead in R6 and branches to the common fork dispatching code. The interrupt service routines for IPLs 6 and 8 and the common fork dispatching code, EXE$FORKDSPTH, are listed in Example 5.4. These routines are in module FORKCNTRL.

EXE$FORKDSPTH loads R6 with the address of the fork block queue specified by the sum of R6 and the address of the per-CPU database for this processor. It removes the first fork block from the queue. It loads R3 and R4 from the fork block. It acquires the spinlock whose index is in FKB$B_FLCK. It then initiates the fork process by invoking the routine whose procedure value address is in FKB$L_FPC.

When the fork process returns, EXE$FORKDSPTH releases the spinlock whose index is in FKB$B_FLCK. The fork process itself must not release the spinlock before returning; if it does, EXE$FORKDSPTH's attempted release will cause the system to crash. Note that even though all the fork processes EXE$FORKDSPTH initiates as the consequence of a particular interrupt execute at the same IPL, they do not necessarily acquire the same fork lock; each fork block identifies the fork lock that must be acquired by the associated fork process.

EXE$FORKDSPTH then removes the next fork block and processes it in the same manner as the first. The removal and processing continue until the queue is empty, when the dispatcher dismisses the interrupt with an REI statement. Note that, to improve performance, EXE$FORKDSPTH detects removal of the last entry in the queue and avoids a subsequent fruitless REMQUE by dispatching the last entry in a separate code path.

Figure 5.3 shows a simplified form of this flow.

Since a fork process routine runs in system context as the result of an interrupt above IPL 2, it cannot rely on any particular process context. It may access no per-process address space except the stack on which it runs (which can be a kernel stack in some process's P1 space). Its code and data

Example 5.4
Fork Dispatching Interrupt Service Routine Extract

```
EXE$FRKIPL6DSP:                          ;Fork IPL 6 entry point
        .EXCEPTION_ENTRY PRESERVE=<R0,R1>
                                         ;Tell compiler to save R0, R1
        CLRL    R6                       ;Get offset to fork queue listhead
        BRB     EXE$FORKDSPTH            ;Branch to common code



           .
           :


    EXE$FRKIPL8DSP:                      ;Fork IPL 8 entry point
        MOVZBL  #<<8-6>*FQH_SIZE>,R6     ;Get offset to fork queue listhead
;
; Drop through to common code
;
EXE$FORKDSPTH:                           ;Software interrupt fork dispatcher
        FIND_CPU_DATA   R7               ;Get base of CPU-specific database
        MOVAB   CPU$Q_SWIQFL(R7)[R6],R6  ;Get address of fork queue listhead
10$:    REMQUE  @(R6),R5                 ;Remove next entry from fork queue
        BVS     90$                      ;Branch if none to remove
        BNEQ    20$                      ;Branch if more follow the REMQUEd entry
        CLRL    R6                       ;Otherwise, this is last, so clear R6
;
; Obtain fork level spinlock and dispatch to fork routine with
;
;   R0,R1,R2     available as scratch registers
;   R3,R4        restored from the FORK block
;   R5           pointing to the FORK block
;
; On return from the fork routine, release the spinlock
;
20$:    EVAX_LDQ-               ;Restore R3 and R4 for fork routine
                FKB$Q_FR3(R5),R3
        EVAX_LDQ-               ;Use built-in to load all 64 bits
                FKB$Q_FR4(R5),R4
        MOVZBL  FKB$B_FLCK(R5),R7        ;Get fork lock number
        FORKLOCK -                       ;Acquire spinlock
                LOCK    =R7,-            ; using fork lock index
                PRESERVE=NO              ; destroying R0
        JSB     @FKB$L_FPC(R5)           ;Execute fork routine
        FORKUNLOCK -                     ;Release the spinlock
                LOCK    =R7,-            ; using fork lock index
                PRESERVE=NO              ; destroying R0
        TSTL    R6                       ;If this was not the last entry
        BNEQ    10$                      ; then go back and REMQUE next

90$:    REI                             ;Restore registers, dismiss interrupt
```

must be in nonpageable system space; it must not incur page faults, execute change mode instructions, or incur any exceptions that are dispatched to user-defined condition handlers (see Chapter 6). While a fork process is executing, it may use R0 through R5 and, if saved and restored, the other general registers. A fork process may also use the stack. However, when a fork process returns control to the fork dispatcher, the stack must be in the same state as when the fork process was entered.

5.4.5   **Stalling a Fork Process**

A fork process can be stalled for various reasons and have to wait. When a fork process waits, its context is saved in the FKB: R3, R4, and the procedure value corresponding to where it should be reentered. The FKB is then placed in a queue of FKBs.

An example of such a wait is a driver fork process that tries to obtain exclusive access to its device's controller. The fork process is stalled until another fork process that has previously obtained exclusive access releases the controller. The routine called to release the controller restores the context of the waiting fork process so that it can repeat its attempt to obtain the controller. Note that all fork processes that can stall waiting for a particular resource must use the same spinlock.

OpenVMS also implements a fork and wait wakeup mechanism so that a fork process can stall itself for a short while and be awakened automatically. To fork and wait, a fork process invokes the macro FORK_WAIT.

The disk and tape class drivers use this mechanism after an unsuccessful attempt to allocate nonpaged pool, assuming that nonpaged pool will become available. When the fork process is reentered, it repeats its attempt to allocate nonpaged pool. In this example, the fork and wait mechanism is used in lieu of nonpaged pool availability reporting, the mechanism used by full processes (see Chapters 13 and 21).

The fork and wait mechanism is also used by the IPL 12 interrupt service routine when it recomputes quorum, following an unsuccessful attempt to force the VMScluster connection manager to recalculate quorum (see Section 5.3.4).

The FORK_WAIT macro generates code that performs the following steps:

1. It stores the procedure value of the fork process entry point in the fork block field FKB$L_FPC.
2. It invokes EXE$PRIMITIVE_FORK_WAIT, in module FORKCNTRL.
3. EXE$PRIMITIVE_FORK_WAIT returns to code generated by the macro that returns to the invoker of the driver routine (the default) or transfers to a specified place within the driver routine containing the macro. Typically the macro generates a return to the fork dispatcher, which releases the fork lock and dispatches the next fork process.

EXE$PRIMITIVE_FORK_WAIT saves the fork process's context in the fork block. Raising IPL to 31, it acquires the MEGA spinlock, which serializes access to the systemwide fork and wait queue, and inserts the fork block at the tail of the queue. EXE$PRIMITIVE_FORK_WAIT then releases the MEGA spinlock, restoring the IPL at entry, and returns to its invoker.

The fork and wait queue is serviced once every second by the routine EXE$TIMEOUT, in module TIMESCHDL. Thus, on average, the fork process waits for half a second. EXE$TIMEOUT and fork processes stalled in this manner run on the primary processor of an SMP system. EXE$TIMEOUT acquires the MEGA spinlock to serialize its access to the fork and wait queue. It copies the queue listhead, whose address is in EXE$AR_FORK_WAIT_QUEUE, initializes the listhead to represent an empty queue, and releases the MEGA spinlock.

EXE$TIMEOUT removes each fork block in turn from its copy of the listhead and restores its R3 and R4. EXE$TIMEOUT acquires the spinlock whose index is in FKB$B_FLCK, raising to the IPL associated with the spinlock. EXE$TIMEOUT then dispatches to the fork process. When the fork process returns, EXE$TIMEOUT releases the spinlock. When the copied listhead is empty, EXE$TIMEOUT is done servicing the queue and continues with other processing.

Part of the restoration of fork process context involves changing IPL from IPL$_TIMER to the IPL indirectly specified by FKB$B_FLCK. Because lowering IPL would violate the interrupt nesting scheme, use of the fork and wait mechanism is limited to fork processes with fork IPLs at or above IPL$_TIMER.

Chapter 12 contains further information about EXE$TIMEOUT.

5.4.6 Use of Fork IPLs

There are five different fork IPLs; three are used by most device drivers supplied as part of OpenVMS:

► IPL 6 is for drivers that support attention ASTs or that otherwise need access to the scheduler database or any other data synchronized at a lower IPL or with a lower ranked spinlock than that of the driver fork process. Chapter 9 discusses the need for IPL 6 fork processing in somewhat more detail.

► IPL 11 is for the mailbox driver. The mailbox driver runs at the highest fork IPL so that any driver fork process can write mailbox messages without the need to fork to a lower IPL. A driver fork process, for example, may write a device-offline message to the OPCOM process's mailbox.

► IPL 8 is the most common driver fork IPL.

The following considerations affect the choice of fork lock and IPL for any particular driver:

► Higher fork IPLs are serviced first.

► All device drivers on a particular bus or adapter competing for bus or adapter resources, such as map registers, must use the same fork lock and thus run at the same fork IPL. When one fork process deallocates a resource for which another fork process is waiting, the waiting fork process is resumed. The resource routine assumes that both fork processes use the same spinlock; it does not release the deallocator's fork lock, nor does it acquire the waiting fork process's fork lock. If the two fork processes were to use different fork locks, the waiting fork process would fail to synchronize its accesses to data structures protected by its fork lock.

Any direct memory access (DMA) drivers servicing devices on a bus or adapter one of whose DMA devices is serviced by a OpenVMS driver must use the IOLOCK8 spinlock.

▶ All device drivers that compete for exclusive access to the same controller must use the same fork lock for the reason just described.

▶ All system communication services (SCS) class and port drivers must use the IOLOCK8 spinlock, partly for the reason previously described and additionally because SCS routines invoked by these drivers assume that the IOLOCK8 spinlock (also known as the SCS spinlock) is held.

▶ A disk driver must use the IOLOCK8 spinlock in order to synchronize clusterwide mount verification.

▶ A driver that accesses a systemwide database synchronized with a spinlock whose associated IPL is IPL$_SYNCH can do so from fork level if the following conditions are met:

• Its fork IPL is 8, the value of IPL$_SYNCH.

• The driver's fork lock is either the same one that synchronizes the database of interest or is one of lower rank so that the fork process can acquire the needed spinlock.

5.5   KERNEL PROCESSES

As previously described, the OpenVMS AXP operating system requests software interrupts to schedule operating system functions. Some software interrupt service routines perform the same function and execute the same routines each time they execute. Others, most notably the fork dispatchers, dispatch to the routines specified by the data structures in their work queues. Various executive components that identify the need to execute a particular system context thread of execution at a particular IPL create a work queue data structure to represent the thread. Creating a fork process is the most common way to do this. Other possibilities are timer queue entry system subroutines dispatched by EXE$SWTIMINT and end action routines dispatched by IOC$IOPOST.

The essential characteristics of such a system context thread of execution are as follows:

▶ The constraint that it access only system space (and, in OpenVMS AXP, possibly a P1 space kernel stack)

▶ A particular routine to execute

▶ A data structure containing information for the routine

▶ Execution at elevated IPL (commonly 6 or 8 through 11, the fork IPLs)

Typically, such a system context thread of execution is short-lived; once dequeued and initiated, it completes its task immediately and exits. Sometimes, however, a thread cannot complete its task immediately and instead must stall itself to restart later. Such a system context thread of execution can use the stack on which it runs but cannot leave information on the stack between a stall and a restart.

The kernel process mechanism, new with OpenVMS AXP, enables a system context thread of execution to run on its own private stack. While a kernel process is stalled, it can leave execution state on the stack, such as nested stack frames and saved registers. This ability to save execution state across a stall is the primary motivation for kernel processes. It simplifies driver algorithms that are naturally expressed as nested subroutine calls and that would otherwise require complex state descriptions. Also, this ability is a prerequisite to supporting device drivers written in a high-level language.

To run as a kernel process, a system context thread of execution, such as a fork process, calls a set of OpenVMS-provided routines that preserve register context and switch stacks. Entry into and exit from a kernel process always involves a stack switch:

- At initiation, a switch from the current kernel stack to that of the kernel process
- At a stall, a switch from the kernel process's stack to the one current when the kernel process was entered
- At restart, a switch from the current kernel stack to that of the kernel process
- At termination, a switch from the kernel process's stack to the one current when the kernel process was most recently entered

Basically, calling these OpenVMS-provided routines maintains the environment of a kernel process. Any system context thread of execution that calls these routines to run on its own stack is a kernel process. That the thread of execution runs on a private stack is transparent to the rest of the system. The thread of execution must be entered through a standard mechanism and then call the appropriate executive routine to begin or resume execution as a kernel process on a private stack. Once executing as a kernel process, in order to stall, the thread must call a routine that can switch stacks and then save the thread's state in such a way that it can restart when the stall ends.

Currently, routines are provided that transform driver fork processes back and forth into kernel processes; only driver fork processes currently use the kernel process mechanism.

Section 5.5.1 describes the data structures associated with kernel processes; and Section 5.5.2, the routines that support them. Section 5.5.3 discusses an example kernel process flow.

5.5.1   **Kernel Process Data Structures**

Two data structures are associated with each kernel process:

▶ A kernel process block (KPB) describes the context and state of a kernel process.

▶ A stack records the current state of the kernel process's execution.

The data structures are created when a kernel process is initiated and deleted when it ends. However, it is possible for the data structures to be preallocated and used by many kernel processes. Typically, when a KPB allocated for I/O is no longer needed, it is inserted into a lookaside list. The stack associated with that KPB remains in existence. Later, when the executive initiates another kernel process for an I/O operation, it reuses that KPB and its associated stack. Moreover, a set of kernel process data structures is preallocated for each possible concurrent modified page write. Chapter 18 discusses the modified page writer.

A KPB is a nonpaged pool data structure of type DYN$C_MISC and subtype DYN$C_KPB. The data structure is variable-length, consisting of one mandatory and several optional areas. The KPBs created for use by the OpenVMS AXP executive (referred to in code comments as VMS executive software type KPBs, or VEST KPBs) have a standard form, shown in Figure 5.4.

The macro $KPBDEF defines symbolic names for the fields in a KPB. KPBIW_SIZE, KPBIB_TYPE, and KPB$IB_SUBTYPE are the standard dynamic data structure header fields.

The areas of a KPB are

▶ The base area, present in all KPBs
▶ The scheduling and executive special parameters areas, present in all KPBs
▶ A spinlock area, present in OpenVMS AXP executive KPBs
▶ A debug area, not used in any production software
▶ A general parameters area, not used by OpenVMS AXP executive KPBs

All but the general parameters area have a fixed size; KPB$IS_PRM_LENGTH contains the size in bytes of the general parameters area, if it is present. Fields KPBPS_SPL_PTR, KPBPS_DBG_PTR, and KPB$PS_PRM_PTR point to optional areas; each area has a bit in KPB$IS_FLAGS that, when set, indicates the area's presence in the KPB. Because each KPB has scheduling and executive special parameters areas whose fields can be accessed through fixed offsets, KPB$PS_SCH_PTR is not used. Currently all KPBs have the standard form shown in Figure 5.4.

KPBIS_STACK_SIZE, KPBPS_STACK_BASE, and KPB$PS_STACK_SP, shown in Figure 5.5, describe the kernel process's stack. KPB$PS_SAVED_SP contains the stack pointer on the stack current when the kernel process was initiated or restarted. That pointer is restored when the kernel process stalls or terminates.

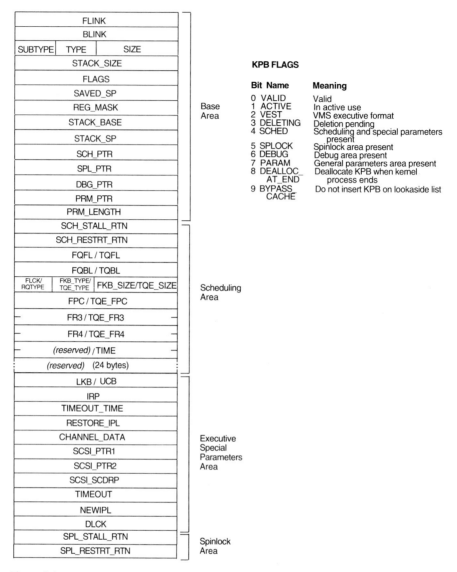

Figure 5.4
Layout of an OpenVMS AXP Executive Kernel Process
Block

The scheduling area can contain either a fork block (see Figure 5.1) or a timer queue entry (see Figure 12.1). In order to use the fork block, the code that creates a kernel process must initialize KPB$IB_FLCK with a spinlock index.

KPB$PS_SCH_STALL_RTN and KPB$PS_SCH_RESTRT_RTN contain procedure values of routines to be called when a kernel process is stalled or

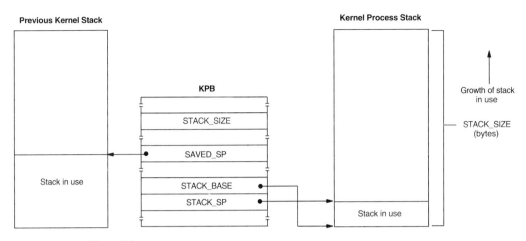

Figure 5.5
Kernel Process Stack

restarted. The scheduling stall routine takes whatever steps are necessary to guarantee eventual rescheduling of the kernel process. In current use, these steps include saving fork process context. The scheduling restart routine is currently unused.

The executive special parameters area contains fields to support device driver fork processes.

KPB$PS_SPL_STALL_RTN and KPB$PS_SPL_RESTRT_RTN can contain procedure values of routines to be called when a kernel process is stalled or restarted. The routines release or reacquire spinlocks needed by the kernel process. These routines are currently not necessary: the fork dispatcher acquires and releases the fork spinlock for a kernel process that is entered as a fork routine. However, they would be useful for a kernel process entered through a means other than a fork interrupt.

A kernel process's stack occupies one or more pages of system space allocated for that purpose when the kernel process is created. The stack has a no-access guard page at each end so that stack underflow and overflow can be detected immediately. Creating a kernel process's stack from one or more pages of virtual memory rather than from nonpaged pool simplifies guard page creation. A typical kernel process's stack is one page long, not counting the guard pages.

Figure 5.5 shows the stack and the fields in the KPB related to it.

The lookaside list of I/O KPBs is at IOC$GQ_KPBLAL, in module KERNEL_PROCESS. When an I/O KPB with a standard stack size is deallocated, it is inserted into the lookaside list. The KPB retains its connection to the associated stack, which is not deallocated. The list grows as I/O kernel processes are deleted and shrinks as new ones are created. When nonpaged pool

85

reclamation is initiated (see Chapter 21), KPBs are removed from the lookaside list, their associated stacks are deleted, and the KPBs are deallocated to nonpaged pool.

5.5.2 Kernel Process Routines

Routines that support and implement kernel processes include the following:

- ► EXE$KP_ALLOCATE_KPB and EXE$KP_DEALLOCATE_KPB, to allocate and deallocate the KPB and stack
- ► EXE$KP_START, to initiate a kernel process
- ► EXE$KP_STALL_GENERAL, to stall a kernel process
- ► EXE$KP_RESTART, to restart a kernel process
- ► EXE$KP_END, to end a kernel process

The sections that follow describe them in detail.

In addition, alternative versions of several routines are provided that enable a kernel process to take typical driver fork process actions, such as fork, I/O fork, wait for interrupt, and request channel. Section 5.5.3 describes the routine that implements fork. The others are described in Chapter 24.

5.5.2.1 Routines to Create and Delete Data Structures.
Routines that create and delete kernel process data structures are in module KERNEL_PROCESS, which is conditionally compiled. Its listing and object modules are named KERNEL_PROCESS_MIN and KERNEL_PROCESS_MON. The latter version records performance statistics.

EXE$KP_ALLOCATE_KPB, in module KERNEL_PROCESS, is called with arguments specifying the size of the stack, which KPB areas to include, whether the KPB is for an I/O request, and whether to deallocate the KPB when the kernel process ends. Its most frequent caller is routine EXE$KP_STARTIO, in module KERNEL_PROCESS, a routine used by drivers whose start I/O routines run as kernel processes.

EXE$KP_ALLOCATE_KPB takes the following steps:

1. After validating its argument count, it calculates how big the KPB is to be.
2. If the KPB is for an I/O request and if the requested stack size is the standard I/O request stack size, EXE$KP_ALLOCATE_KPB tries to remove a KPB from the lookaside list. If successful, it returns the status SS$_NORMAL and the address of the KPB to its caller.
3. Otherwise, EXE$KP_ALLOCATE_KPB allocates and zeros nonpaged pool for the KPB.
4. It initializes the KPB header, the pointers to its areas, and KPB$IS_FLAGS.
5. To calculate the stack size, EXE$KP_ALLOCATE_KPB rounds up the requested size to the next integral number of pages, based on the proces-

sor's page size, and stores the corresponding number of bytes in KPB$IS_STACK_SIZE.

6. It allocates enough system page table entries (SPTEs) to map each page of stack, plus two to serve as guard pages. It stores the address of the high end of stack (excluding the guard pages) in KPB$PS_STACK_BASE.

7. EXE$KP_ALLOCATE_KPB acquires the MMG spinlock, raising IPL to IPL$_MMG, and calls MMG$ALLOC_PFN_MAP_SVA, in module ALLOCPFN, to allocate physical pages for the stack and map them with the allocated SPTEs.

   - If MMG$ALLOC_PFN_MAP_SVA can allocate the stack page or pages, it initializes the page frame number (PFN) database record for each page to show the page as an active system page with a reference count of 1. (Chapter 16 describes the PFN database.) It initializes each SPTE that maps a physical page of stack with a protection of KW, valid and address space match bits set, and owner of kernel mode, and inserts the PFN.

     EXE$KP_ALLOCATE_KPB clears the guard pages' SPTEs. It returns the status SS$_NORMAL and the address of the KPB to its caller.

   - If MMG$ALLOC_PFN_MAP_SVA is unable to allocate enough physical pages, it deallocates any allocated, reinitializes any related memory management data structures, and returns an error status.

     EXE$KP_ALLOCATE_KPB deallocates the KPB to nonpaged pool and returns the error status SS$_INSFRPGS to its caller.

EXE$KP_DEALLOCATE_KPB, in module KERNEL_PROCESS, is called with the address of a KPB. It takes the following steps to delete the kernel process data structures:

1. After validating its argument count and checking the structure type of the KPB, it checks whether the KPB is one used for I/O with a standard stack size. If both are true, it inserts the KPB into the lookaside list and returns.

2. Otherwise, it sets the KPB$V_DELETING bit in KPB$IS_FLAGS.

3. It initializes the fork block in the KPB to describe an IPL 6 fork process that is to execute the routine CLEANUP_KPB, in module KERNEL_PROCESS.

4. It returns.

Sometime later, when the fork interrupt is granted, CLEANUP_KPB executes. It takes the following steps:

1. It calculates the address of the SPTE that maps the first (and possibly only) page of the kernel process's stack.

2. It acquires the MMG spinlock, raising IPL to IPL$_MMG.

3. CLEANUP_KPB deallocates the physical page mapped by the SPTE and

clears its PFN database record. It clears the SPTE and invokes TBI_SINGLE to invalidate any cached translation buffer entry for that page. It repeats these actions for any additional stack pages.

4. It deallocates the SPTEs that mapped stack pages and the guard pages' SPTEs and releases the MMG spinlock.
5. It deallocates the KPB to nonpaged pool.
6. CLEANUP_KPB returns to the fork dispatcher.

5.5.2.2   **Routines to Enter and Leave a Kernel Process.** EXE$KP_START, in module KERNEL_PROCESS_MAGIC, is called with the address of the KPB, the procedure value of the target kernel process routine, and optionally a register save mask. Initially it runs on the stack of its invoker but then switches to the kernel process stack.

EXE$KP_START takes the following steps to initiate a kernel process:

1. It validates its argument count.
2. If a register save mask argument was supplied, EXE$KP_START confirms that it contains no scratch registers (R0, R1, R16–R25, R28, R30, R31) and merges in those that the kernel process routines need saved (R12–R15, R26, R29).

   If one was not supplied, EXE$KP_START stores a default register save mask designating the minimum required registers.
3. It aligns the stack to a quadword boundary so that it can do quadword stores without incurring unaligned data traps. It saves the previous contents of the SP register (that is, the original unaligned stack pointer) and then pushes onto the stack each of the registers specified by the mask, from low register number to high. It saves the value of the updated SP in KPB$PS_SAVED_SP. As a result, R26, the return address in the routine that called EXE$KP_START, is now saved on the current kernel stack.
4. EXE$KP_START loads SP from KPB$PS_STACK_BASE, switching to the kernel process's stack. It initializes KPB$PS_STACK_SP to the contents of KPB$PS_STACK_BASE to reflect a currently empty stack.
5. It sets the active and valid bits in KPB$IS_FLAGS, indicating that the KPB is valid and describes an active kernel process.
6. It stores the address of the KPB at the high end of the new stack, followed by a quadword containing the value DEADDEADDEADDEAD$_{16}$, and two quadwords of zero.
7. It pushes onto the stack the return address from the call to EXE$KP_START, its own linkage section pointer, and the address of the KPB. These are on the stack to ensure that when the kernel process returns to EXEKP_START, EXEKP_START has enough information to call EXE$KP_END to end the kernel process. (Typically, control should return to EXE$KP_START's caller when the fork process stalls and the stall routine switches back to the caller's stack and returns.)

8. It calls the target kernel process routine with one argument, the address of the KPB.

EXE$KP_STALL_GENERAL, in module KERNEL_PROCESS_MAGIC, is called from a routine running on that kernel process's stack. It performs the register context save, stack switch, and register context restore necessary to stall a kernel process for any reason. It has one argument, the address of the KPB.

Typically, EXE$KP_STALL_GENERAL is called by a more specific stall routine, which first stores the procedure value of a callback routine in KPB$PS_SCH_STALL_RTN. For example, IOC$KP_WFIKPCH, in module KERNEL_PROCESS, which stalls a fork process to wait for an interrupt or I/O timeout, stores the procedure value of the stall routine STALL_WFIKPCH and then calls EXE$KP_STALL_GENERAL. After performing the steps just summarized, EXE$KP_STALL_GENERAL calls STALL_WFIKPCH, which performs a standard WFIKPCH. Chapter 24 details the sequence by which a fork process waits for an interrupt and is reentered when the interrupt occurs or after the wait time has elapsed.

EXE$KP_STALL_GENERAL takes the following steps to stall a kernel process:

1. It validates its argument count.
2. It aligns the stack to a quadword boundary so that it can do quadword stores without incurring unaligned data traps. It saves the previous contents of the SP register (that is, the original unaligned stack pointer) and then pushes each of the registers specified by the mask, from low register number to high. It saves the value of the updated SP in KPB$PS_STACK_SP. As a result, R26, the return address in the routine that called EXE$KP_STALL_GENERAL, is now saved on the current kernel stack.
3. EXE$KP_STALL_GENERAL loads SP from KPB$PS_SAVED_SP, switching to the stack current when the kernel process was entered.
4. It restores the register context saved on that stack at the time of the stack switch onto the kernel process's stack, including the return address in the routine that caused entry to the kernel process and the original unaligned stack pointer.
5. It clears the active bit in KPB$IS_FLAGS, leaving the valid bit set, to indicate that the KPB is valid and describes a stalled kernel process.
6. Passing two arguments, EXE$KP_STALL_GENERAL calls the scheduling stall routine whose procedure value is in KPB$PS_SCH_STALL_RTN. Such a routine performs only those actions that require the kernel process's registers and state to have been saved. The existing scheduling stall routines are driver-related; each inserts a fork block into a queue specific to its stall. STALL_FORK, in module KERNEL_PROCESS, for example, inserts the fork block on a fork queue, from which it will be

removed eventually by the fork dispatching interrupt service routine associated with that queue. A scheduling stall routine is called with the address of the KPB and the contents, which can be zero, of KPB$PS_SPL_STALL_RTN. Thus, a scheduling stall routine can call the specified spinlock stall routine, if any.

The scheduling stall routine saves R3 and R4 in the fork block. It stores in FKB$L_FPC a procedure value within the scheduling stall routine. It queues the fork block and returns to EXE$KP_STALL_GENERAL.

7. When control returns to EXE$KP_STALL_GENERAL, it returns to the routine whose return address was saved on the original kernel stack, the one that caused the most recent entry to the kernel process.

When the fork process is reentered sometime later, the scheduling stall routine will call EXE$KP_RESTART.

EXE$KP_RESTART, in module KERNEL_PROCESS_MAGIC, is called from a routine running on a stack other than that of the kernel process, typically from the restarted fork process. Its function is to restore the kernel process context and stack. It is called with the address of the KPB and optionally a status to return to the kernel process routine that is being restarted.

EXE$KP_RESTART takes the following steps to restart a kernel process:

1. It validates its argument count.
2. It aligns the stack to a quadword boundary so that it can do quadword stores without incurring unaligned data traps. It saves the previous contents of the SP register (that is, the original unaligned stack pointer) and then pushes each of the registers specified by the mask, from low register number to high. It saves the value of the updated SP in KPB$PS_SAVED_SP. As a result, R26, the return address in the routine that called EXE$KP_RESTART, is now saved on the current kernel stack.
3. EXE$KP_RESTART loads SP from KPB$PS_STACK_SP, switching to the kernel process's stack.
4. It restores the register context saved on that stack at the time of the stack switch from the kernel process's stack, including the return address in the routine that stalled the kernel process and the original unaligned stack pointer.
5. It sets the active bit in KPB$IS_FLAGS to indicate that the KPB describes an active kernel process.
6. EXE$KP_RESTART tests the field KPB$PS_SCH_RESTRT_RTN and, if it is zero, continues with the next step. Currently, all kernel process stall routines clear this KPB field.

If the field is nonzero, EXE$KP_RESTART calls the routine whose procedure value is in KPB$PS_SCH_RESTRT_RTN, passing it three arguments: the address of the KPB, the status to be passed back to the kernel process, and the contents of KPB$PS_SPL_RESTRT_RTN. Thus, a scheduling restart routine can call the specified spinlock restart routine, if any.

7. EXE$KP_RESTART returns to the kernel process routine that stalled, the one that called EXE$KP_STALL_GENERAL.

EXE$KP_END, in module KERNEL_PROCESS_MAGIC, is called with the address of the KPB from a routine running on that kernel process's stack. Its function is to terminate the kernel process and return to the routine that most recently caused entry into the kernel process.

EXE$KP_END takes the following steps to terminate a kernel process:

1. After validating its argument count, it switches back to the stack whose pointer was saved in KPB$PS_SAVED_SP and zeros that field to prevent its reuse.
2. It restores the context saved on that stack, namely, the registers specified by KPB$IS_REG_MASK, and then restores the original value of the stack pointer, popping off any alignment bytes.
3. It clears the active and valid bits in KPB$IS_FLAGS.
4. If KPB$V_DEALLOC_AT_END is set, its typical state, EXE$KP_END calls EXE$KP_DEALLOCATE_KPB, which deallocates the KPB and kernel process stack.
5. It then returns to the routine that had most recently caused entry to the kernel process. Its return address was restored to R26 in step 2.

5.5.3   Example Kernel Process Flow

Figure 5.6 shows a partial possible flow of a kernel process that runs as a fork process. Some kernel mode thread of execution is running and enters the kernel process, perhaps by calling EXE$KP_START. EXE$KP_START switches to the kernel process's stack.

The figure shows the interaction between the kernel process and the standard fork routines as well as the flow among some of the kernel process routines previously described. The rightmost column in the figure shows the stack switches. Each vertical bar in the column represents stack execution: the right-hand ones, execution on the kernel process's stack, and the left-hand ones, execution on another kernel stack.

After the kernel process has been entered, the flow proceeds as follows:

1. The kernel process calls EXE$KP_FORK, in module KERNEL_PROCESS, to fork. EXE$KP_FORK is called with the address of a KPB and optionally the address of a fork block.
2. EXE$KP_FORK takes the following steps:
   a. EXE$KP_FORK determines whether the second argument was passed to it and, if not, gets the address of the fork block in the KPB.
   b. It stores the procedure value of its routine STALL_FORK in KPB$PS_SCH_STALL_RTN and clears KPB$PS_RESTRT_RTN.

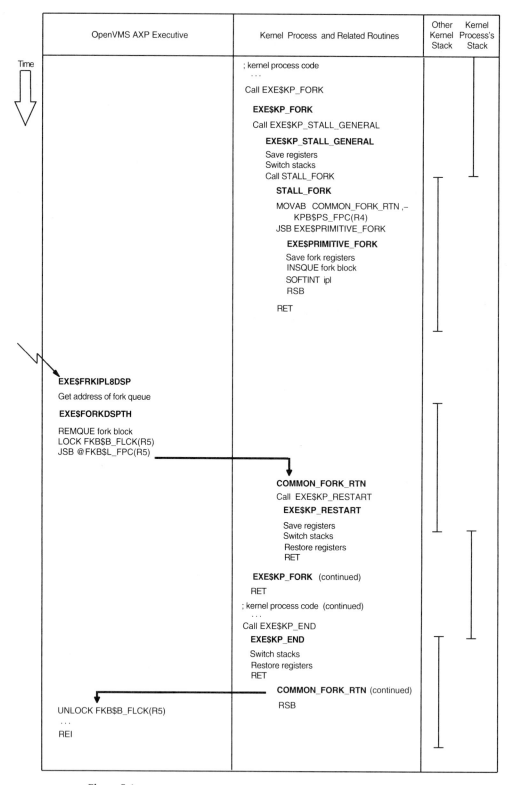

Figure 5.6
Example Kernel Process Flow

c. It calls EXE$KP_STALL_GENERAL to stall the kernel process using the routine STALL_FORK.

Control will return to EXE$KP_FORK when the requested fork process executes.

3. EXE$KP_STALL_GENERAL saves the register context of the kernel process, including the return address of EXE$KP_FORK, and switches stacks. EXE$KP_STALL_GENERAL calls STALL_FORK.

4. STALL_FORK stores the procedure value of the local routine COMMON_FORK_RTN in FKB$L_FPC. It invokes the FORK macro, described in Section 5.4.3, which transfers control to EXE$PRIMITIVE_FORK.

5. EXE$PRIMITIVE_FORK, in module FORKCNTRL, saves the fork registers, inserts the KPB's fork block into the fork queue corresponding to its spinlock's IPL, and requests a software interrupt at that IPL (in this example, the IPL 8 queue). It returns to STALL_FORK.

6. STALL_FORK returns to EXE$KP_STALL_GENERAL, which returns to the routine that entered the kernel process, that is, the routine that called EXE$KP_START or EXE$KP_RESTART. (The latter part of this step is not shown in the figure.)

7. Sometime later, the fork interrupt is granted. The interrupt service routine executes on whichever kernel stack is current. It could be the kernel stack of any process, the system process's stack, or a different kernel process's stack.

   EXE$FORKDSPTH removes the KPB's fork block from the queue, acquires the specified spinlock, and dispatches to the routine whose procedure value is stored in FKB$L_FPC, COMMON_FORK_RTN.

8. COMMON_FORK_RTN calls EXE$KP_RESTART. Control will return to COMMON_FORK_RTN when the kernel process either stalls again or ends.

9. EXE$KP_RESTART saves the register context, switches stacks to that of the kernel process, and restores its register context. It returns to EXE$KP_STALL_GENERAL's caller, EXE$KP_FORK.

10. EXE$KP_FORK returns to its caller, the kernel process routine.

11. If the kernel process has completed its task, it can either call EXE$KP_END itself or return to EXE$KP_START, which will call EXE$KP_END. If the kernel process has not completed its task but has to wait before proceeding further, it can stall again.

12. Whether called by the kernel process or by EXEKP_START, EXEKP_END switches stacks to the stack on which the fork interrupt occurred and optionally deallocates the KPB and kernel stack. It returns to the routine that entered the kernel process, COMMON_FORK_RTN.

13. COMMON_FORK_RTN returns to the fork dispatcher.

5.6   **RELEVANT SOURCE MODULES**

The source modules described in this chapter include

[LIB]FKBDEF.SDL
[LIB]KPBDEF.SDL
[SYS]FORKCNTRL.MAR
[SYS]IPCONTROL.MAR
[SYS]KERNEL_PROCESS.MAR
[SYS]KERNEL_PROCESS_MAGIC.M64
[SYS]SYSTEM_ROUTINES.M64

6 Condition Handling

"Would you tell me, please, which way I ought to go from here?"
"That depends a good deal on where you want to get to," said
the Cat.

Lewis Carroll, *Alice's Adventures in Wonderland*

Like its VAX counterpart, the OpenVMS AXP operating system defines a generalized uniform condition handling facility for the following classes of conditions:

▶ Conditions detected and generated by the processor, called exceptions
▶ Conditions detected and generated by user mode software, called software conditions
▶ Conditions detected and generated by the OpenVMS AXP executive, called special conditions

The executive provides this facility for users and also uses the facility for its own purposes.

This chapter describes exceptions, software conditions, and special conditions. It describes how the executive dispatches most conditions to user-specified procedures called condition handlers and how it handles those it does not dispatch. It describes condition handler actions and summarizes default condition handlers provided by the executive.

6.1 OVERVIEW

When an AXP processor detects an anomaly or error such as an access violation fault or a bugcheck trap, it generates an exception. The term *processor* as used in this chapter includes both hardware and the privileged architecture library code (PALcode); hardware generates some exceptions, PALcode others. In either case, generating an exception begins with the transfer of control to an exception-handling PALcode routine. Each exception typically has its own PALcode routine; most such routines converge to common code, the initiate exception, interrupt, or machine check (IEI) PALcode routine.

The IEI PALcode routine determines the mode in which the exception will be serviced; typically, this is kernel mode. It saves on that mode's stack the processor status (PS), the program counter (PC), and registers R2 through R7. The stack area in which this information is saved is called an exception stack frame. The IEI PALcode routine then transfers control to the OpenVMS AXP exception service routine (ESR) identified by the exception's system control block (SCB) entry. Chapter 3 describes the exception mechanism in more detail.

An ESR's action depends on the type of exception and the mode in which it occurred. The exception must be handled before the processor can proceed any further with the thread of execution that incurred the exception. The ESR either handles the exception itself or uses the condition handling facility to report the exception to a condition handler. Section 6.3 outlines the salient features of the condition handling facility, which encompasses the declaration of a condition handler, the search for a condition handler, and the responses available to a condition handler.

As a normal part of its operation, the OpenVMS AXP executive expects and handles many exceptions itself, transparently to application software. Examples of such exceptions include the translation-not-valid fault and the change-mode-to-kernel trap. Section 6.5.1 outlines exceptions that the executive always handles itself.

In response to an exception that the executive does not handle itself, such as an arithmetic trap or an illegal instruction trap, the ESR saves additional exception context on the stack and calls the condition dispatcher. The condition dispatcher locates and calls condition handlers declared by outer levels of software. This method of handling exceptions is called reporting or signaling. A condition reported in this manner is sometimes called a signal. (Note that the term *signal* has a different connotation when used in the context of POSIX for OpenVMS.) Section 6.5.2 outlines exceptions that the executive reports to a condition handler.

When software detects an anomaly or error, it can report the error to a condition handler by simulating an exception and calling the condition dispatcher. Software simulates an exception by building exception context on the stack similar to that which PALcode builds when an exception occurs. Reporting processor-detected and software-detected errors in a similar manner allows user mode software to deal with all errors using the same mechanisms.

A software-detected error reported in this fashion is called a software condition. User mode software can report a software error as a software condition by calling one of two Run-Time Library procedures, LIB$SIGNAL or LIB$STOP, described in the *OpenVMS RTL Library (LIB$) Manual*. The executive reports some special conditions in a similar manner, although it uses an internal procedure rather than LIB$SIGNAL or LIB$STOP. Section 6.6 outlines software conditions. Section 6.7 describes special conditions.

A condition handler is established for a specific access mode. The search for a condition handler encompasses only those handlers that were established in the access mode in which the condition occurred. A condition handler is classified as frame-based or software-vectored depending on how it is established and entered. Section 6.4 discusses condition handlers and how they are established.

The executive handles all conditions uniformly regardless of whether the condition was the result of an exception or a software-detected error. The condition dispatcher searches for condition handlers and calls any that it finds with two arguments: the addresses of two arrays, called the signal array and the mechanism array. The signal array consists of a status value that identifies the condition type and condition-specific parameters. The mechanism array has a save area for saving register context, a work area for the condition dispatcher, and an area through which the condition dispatcher communicates with a condition handler. With the exception stack frame and additional exception context saved by the ESR, the signal and mechanism arrays make up a compound structure called the exception context area. Section 6.8 describes the exception context area and the condition dispatcher's actions.

Based on the contents of the signal array, a condition handler decides which of three actions to take:

▶ If the handler can fix the condition, it returns the status SS$_CONTINUE to the condition dispatcher, which terminates the search and resumes the thread of execution that incurred the exception.
▶ If the handler cannot fix the condition, it can alter the flow of control by returning control to a previous point of execution.
▶ Alternatively, if the handler cannot fix the condition, it can resignal the condition. If a handler resignals, the condition dispatcher continues its search.

Section 6.10 describes possible condition handler actions. Section 6.11 summarizes default condition handlers provided by the executive.

6.2   **OPENVMS AXP CALLING STANDARD TERMS**

Chapter 1 provides a brief overview of OpenVMS AXP calling standard terms used in this chapter. These include *procedure, procedure frame, stack frame procedure, register frame procedure, null frame procedure,* and *procedure descriptor.* The meanings of a few other terms are outlined here.

The current procedure invocation, or current procedure for short, is the one in whose context the thread of execution is currently executing. At any instant, a thread of execution has exactly one current procedure. If code in the current procedure calls another procedure, then the called procedure becomes the current procedure. When a stack frame or register frame procedure is called, its invocation context is recorded in a procedure frame. The invocation context is mainly a snapshot of process registers at procedure invocation; it is used during return from the called procedure to restore the calling procedure's state. Note that a null frame procedure does not have a procedure frame.

The chain of all procedure frames starting with the current procedure and going all the way back to the first procedure invocation for the thread is named the call chain. While a procedure is part of the call chain, it is called an active procedure.

6.3   THE CONDITION HANDLING FACILITY

The condition handling facility is defined by the OpenVMS AXP calling standard. It encompasses the declaration of a condition handler, the search for a condition handler, and the responses available to a condition handler. The condition handling facility provides that software conditions be directed to the same condition handlers as exceptions. Thus, user mode software can centralize its handling of exceptions and software conditions.

The *OpenVMS Programming Concepts* manual describes the declaration and coding of condition handlers.

The major goal of the condition handling facility is to provide an easy-to-use, general-purpose mechanism for handling errors. User mode software and layered products can use this mechanism rather than inventing application-specific tools. The condition handling facility supports this goal with the following features:

▶ A procedure can declare a frame-based condition handler using a language-specific statement if one is available for that language. For example, the BLISS language statement ENABLE can be used to declare a frame-based condition handler.

▶ Condition handling can be specific to a procedure, a processwide facility, or both.

Each procedure can establish its own condition handler. This enables condition handlers to be nested with the procedures that establish them. A nested inner handler can either service a detected exception or pass it along to some outer handler established by an earlier procedure.

▶ Because a condition handler is itself a procedure, it can establish its own condition handler to field errors that it might cause. The semantics of the programming languages used to code an application determine whether a condition handler can be called recursively to service conditions incurred by its own execution. Typically, a handler does not deal with its own errors.

If a programming language supports it, however, a handler can be called recursively to handle conditions that it itself incurs.

▶ As far as the user mode programmer is concerned, there is no difference in the handling of exceptions and software conditions.

▶ Some languages such as Ada specify signaling and error handling as part of the language. The general mechanism supports their needs.

Because condition handling can be specific to a procedure, software written in a high-level language can establish a handler that examines its arguments to determine whether the signal was generated as a part of that language's support library. If so, the handler can attempt to fix the error in the manner defined by the language. If not, the handler can resignal the error.

6.4   **CONDITION HANDLERS AND HOW THEY ARE ESTABLISHED**

A condition handler is classified as frame-based or software-vectored, depending on how it is established and entered.

6.4.1   **Frame-Based Condition Handlers**

A frame-based condition handler is one that has been declared as being associated with a specific procedure.

In OpenVMS VAX, every procedure has a stack frame, and if the procedure has an associated condition handler, its address is moved into the highest addressed longword of the stack frame, typically as the first step in procedure execution.

In OpenVMS AXP, by contrast, a procedure can have a stack frame, a register frame, or no frame at all. A stack frame or register frame procedure can declare a frame-based handler provided the language in which it is written supports it. A null frame procedure cannot declare a frame-based handler. The association between a procedure and its frame-based condition handler is typically established statically during compilation. If a language implementation permits it, however, a frame-based handler can be dynamically associated with a procedure at run time. For example, the BLISS language statement ESTABLISH associates a frame-based handler with its establishing procedure at run time.

A frame-based condition handler is located at run time via its declaring procedure's procedure descriptor. The PDSC$V_HANDLER_VALID flag in the PDSC$W_FLAGS field of a procedure descriptor is set for a procedure that has declared a handler. Depending on whether the declaring procedure is a register frame procedure or a stack frame procedure, the handler's procedure value is in PDSC$Q_REG_HANDLER or PDSC$Q_STACK_HANDLER.

The OpenVMS VAX Run-Time Library procedure LIB$ESTABLISH is used to declare an OpenVMS VAX frame-based condition handler dynamically. LIB$ESTABLISH is not available in the OpenVMS AXP Run-Time Library because the OpenVMS AXP calling standard only provides for static association between a procedure and its condition handler. To facilitate the porting of OpenVMS VAX programs, however, OpenVMS AXP compilers for certain languages, such as BLISS, DEC C, and FORTRAN, convert a call to LIB$ESTABLISH into a call to an internal procedure that provides an equivalent function through an additional level of indirection. The DEC C compiler treats a call to VAXC$ESTABLISH in the same manner. Also, the Translated Image Environment (TIE) facility provides a translated version of LIB$ESTABLISH, usable only in that environment.

6.4.2 **Software-Vectored Condition Handlers**

Software-vectored condition handlers are located through predefined P1 space locations. There are three types of software-vectored condition handlers. They differ primarily in the order in which the condition dispatcher calls them:

▶ Primary vectored handler, called before any other handler

▶ Secondary vectored handler, called after the primary vectored handler but before any frame-based handler

▶ Last chance handler, called after all frame-based handlers have been called

One of each of these handlers can be established for each access mode.

A quadword array at CTL$AQ_EXCVEC, indexed by access mode, identifies the process's primary and secondary vectored handlers. The first longword in each quadword contains zero or the procedure value of the primary vectored handler for that mode. The second longword contains zero or the procedure value of the secondary vectored handler. A longword array at CTL$AL_FINALEXC, also indexed by access mode, contains the procedure values of the last chance handlers.

By default, the executive provides no primary or secondary vectored handlers. The executive does, however, establish last chance handlers for kernel, executive, and user access modes.

An image can request the Set Exception Vector ($SETEXV) system service to establish or remove a software-vectored condition handler. The *OpenVMS System Services Reference Manual* provides further information.

The system service has four arguments, all of which are optional:

▶ The VECTOR argument identifies the type of handler. If this argument is omitted or if the value is zero, the handler is the primary vectored handler.

▶ The ADDRES argument contains the procedure value of a handler or the address of a catch-all extension block if the VECTOR argument indicates that the handler is a catch-all extension (see Section 6.11.2). Note that the use of catch-all extensions is reserved to Digital and otherwise completely unsupported. If this argument is omitted or if the address is zero, the existing handler is to be removed.

▶ The ACMODE argument specifies the access mode of the handler. If this argument is omitted, its default value is the mode from which the service was requested. If it is present, the less privileged of the requesting mode and ACMODE is used, preventing a process from declaring a handler for a more privileged mode.

▶ The PRVHND argument specifies the address of a longword to receive the procedure value of the previously established handler, if appropriate.

The system service procedure EXE$SETEXV, in module SYSSETEXV, runs in kernel mode. It determines the access mode of the handler and the type of handler to be established, and stores the procedure value of the specified handler (or a longword containing zero) in the specified software vector. EXE$SETEXV rejects any attempt to establish a procedure in a translated VAX image as a handler by returning the error status SS$_IVSSRQ.

User mode software-vectored condition handlers are automatically removed at image rundown, when the address space that contains them is being deleted. All others must be explicitly removed.

6.5   TYPES OF EXCEPTIONS

Table 6.1 lists each exception defined by the Alpha AXP architecture and the ESR that services it. The table distinguishes the exceptions that the executive always handles itself from those it reports to a condition handler.

The executive always handles

▸ Exceptions used in the course of normal system operations, for example, page faults and CHMK exceptions
▸ Exceptions indicating fatal software errors, namely bugchecks

It reports all others to a condition handler.

Section 6.5.1 summarizes the exceptions that the executive always handles itself, and Section 6.5.2, those it reports to a condition handler.

The Alpha AXP architecture defines two categories of exceptions:

▸ Faults
▸ Traps

A fault represents an error that prevents successful instruction execution. If the circumstances that led to a fault are corrected, the instruction can reexecute successfully. To simplify reexecuting the instruction, the IEI PALcode routine pushes the instruction's address onto the stack as the saved PC. The most common fault is the translation-not-valid fault, usually known as page fault. An instruction referencing a page not in memory incurs a page fault. After the page fault handler makes the page valid, the instruction can reexecute successfully.

Traps are varied. Some traps represent errors in instruction execution, while others are deliberately triggered. One example of an error trap is an illegal instruction trap. Change-mode-to-executive and change-mode-to-kernel traps, by contrast, are deliberately induced to request operating system services.

For all traps except arithmetic traps, the IEI PALcode routine pushes onto the stack as the saved PC the address of the instruction following the one that incurred the trap.

For an arithmetic trap, the IEI PALcode routine pushes onto the stack as the saved PC the address of an instruction that would have been issued had the trapping condition not occurred. Under normal operation, a pipelined processor can be executing several instructions in various stages at any given instant; one or more of these instructions can trigger an arithmetic trap. The

Table 6.1   Exceptions and Their Service Routines

SCB Entry Offset [1]	Exception Name	Mode of ESR [2]	Service Routine
		FAULTS	
010	Floating-point disabled [3]	K	SCH$FLOAT_DISABLE in module SCHEDULER
080	Access violation	K	EXE$ACVIOLAT_EXCEPTION_ENTRY in module EXCEPTION
090	Translation-not-valid, also known as page fault [3]	K	SCH$PAGEFAULT in module SCHEDULER
0A0	Fault-on-read [4]	K	SCH$FAULT_ON_READ in module SCHEDULER
0B0	Fault-on-write [3]	K	MMG$FAULT_ON_WRITE in module MODIFY_FAULT
0C0	Fault-on-execute [4]	K	SCH$FAULT_ON_EXECUTE in module SCHEDULER
		TRAPS	
200	Arithmetic	K	EXE$ARITH_EXCEPTION_ENTRY in module EXCEPTION
280	Unaligned access [4]	K	EXE$REPORT_ALIGN_FAULT in module ALIGN
400	Breakpoint	K	EXE$BREAK_EXCEPTION_ENTRY in module EXCEPTION
410	Bugcheck [3]	K	EXE$BUGCHECK in module BUGCHECK_SAVE
420	Illegal instruction	K	EXE$OPCDEC_EXCEPTION_ENTRY in module EXCEPTION
430	Illegal CALL_PAL operand	K	EXE$ROPRAND_EXCEPTION_ENTRY in module EXCEPTION
440	Software trap, also known as GENTRAP	K	EXE$GENTRAP_EXCEPTION_ENTRY in module EXCEPTION
480	Change-mode-to-kernel [3]	K	EXE$CMODKRNL in module SYSTEM_SERVICE_DISPATCHER
490	Change-mode-to-executive [3]	E	EXE$CMODEXEC in module SYSTEM_SERVICE_DISPATCHER
4A0	Change-mode-to-supervisor	S	EXE$CMODSUPR_EXCEPTION_ENTRY in module EXCEPTION
4B0	Change-mode-to-user	U	EXE$CMODUSER_EXCEPTION_ENTRY in module EXCEPTION

[1] Hexadecimal byte offset of SCB entry from SCB base.
[2] K = Kernel, E = Executive, S = Supervisor, U = User.
[3] This exception is always handled by the OpenVMS AXP executive.
[4] This exception is generally handled by the OpenVMS AXP executive but may sometimes be reported as a condition (see Section 6.5.2).

saved PC does not precisely identify the instruction that generated the exception; for this reason, an arithmetic trap is sometimes called an *imprecise* exception. All other exceptions are precise.

The TRAPB instruction allows software to guarantee that all previous arithmetic instructions will complete before any instructions following the TRAPB instruction are issued. Thus, any arithmetic traps incurred by instructions that execute before the TRAPB instruction can be handled before any instructions that follow the TRAPB instruction are issued. The TRAPB instruction enables software to request generation of more precise arithmetic exceptions. Support for this feature is available in some high-level languages. The BLISS language compiler, for example, appropriately uses instances of the TRAPB instruction in a procedure that has established a condition handler to ensure that any arithmetic traps that occur in that procedure are handled before control returns to the procedure's caller.

6.5.1 Exceptions That the Executive Handles Itself

This section briefly outlines exceptions that the executive handles itself and never reports to user mode software.

Change-mode-to-executive and change-mode-to-kernel traps occur when the processor executes CALL_PAL CHME and CALL_PAL CHMK instructions. The executive uses these exceptions to provide controlled paths into inner access mode code. The service routines for these exceptions, known as the change mode dispatchers, transfer control to Record Management Services (RMS) and system services, as described in Chapter 7.

A fault-on-write exception occurs when an instruction attempts to write to a page whose page table entry (PTE) has the fault-on-write bit set. The ESR clears the fault-on-write bit and sets the modify bit in the PTE to indicate that the page's contents have been changed. The Alpha AXP architecture provides this mechanism so that the operating system, rather than the processor, can maintain the modify bit. The state of the modify bit will determine what the executive does with the page when it is removed from the working set. Chapter 18 provides more information.

A translation-not-valid exception occurs when a reference is made to a virtual address not currently mapped to physical memory. This exception is the entry path into the page fault handler, described in detail in Chapter 18.

A floating-point-disabled fault occurs when a process whose floating-point enable register (FEN) contains zero executes any floating-point instruction. The ESR sets the FEN to 1, sets the PHD$V_SW_FEN bit in PHD$L_FLAGS2, and zeros all floating-point registers. The Alpha AXP architecture provides this mechanism to inform the operating system when a process begins using floating-point instructions. Saving and restoring floating-point registers for a process that has not executed any floating-point instructions is unnecessary overhead. The value of bit PHD$V_SW_FEN determines

103

whether the executive saves and restores a process's floating-point registers, for example, when the process's context is being swapped.

The processor generates a bugcheck trap when it executes a CALL_PAL BUGCHK instruction. When the executive detects an inconsistency in system state, it executes the CALL_PAL BUGCHK instruction. The mode in which the trap occurs and the parameter to the CALL_PAL BUGCHK instruction determine the bugcheck ESR's course of action. If the trap occurs in user or supervisor mode, the bugcheck ESR can log an error and exit the current image; otherwise, the ESR can log an error and crash the system. Chapter 35 describes the bugcheck ESR in detail.

6.5.2   Exceptions That the Executive Reports to Condition Handlers

The executive reports most exceptions other than the ones outlined in Section 6.5.1 to condition handlers (see Table 6.1). The ESRs for most of these exceptions are in module EXCEPTION. Each ESR performs approximately the same actions in preparing for the execution of a condition handler: it builds an exception record and a signal array on the stack (see Section 6.8.1) and transfers control to EXE$EXCEPTION. This section describes the actions each ESR takes.

The processor generates an arithmetic exception when any one of the arithmetic conditions listed in Table 6.2 arises during instruction execution. The arithmetic ESR builds the signal array and reports the SS$_HPARITH condition. The SS$_HPARITH status value indicates a general arithmetic condition; the exception summary parameter in the signal array (see Section 6.8.1) has bits set to indicate the specific type of arithmetic condition that occurred. If the exception is not handled by user mode software, the Put Message ($PUTMSG) system service, which is eventually requested by the catch-all condition handler (see Section 6.11.2), determines the condition value corresponding to the exception summary parameter based on an internal table and prints the appropriate error message. This condition value is one listed in Table 6.2. Note that user mode software will never see the status values listed in Table 6.2.

Table 6.2   Summary of Arithmetic Conditions

Status Value	*Meaning*
SS$_FLTINV	Invalid floating-point arithmetic, conversion, or comparison
SS$_FLTDIV	Floating-point divide by zero
SS$_FLTOVF	Floating-point overflow
SS$_FLTUND	Floating-point underflow
SS$_FLTINE	Floating-point inexact result
SS$_INTOVF	Integer overflow

The processor generates an access control violation fault when it attempts to access a virtual address whose access is not allowed in the current mode. Most access violations reported back to the user signify programming errors. User stack overflow is also detected as an access violation at the low-address end of P1 space. The access control violation ESR tests whether the faulting virtual address is at the low end of P1 space. If it is, the ESR attempts to expand the user stack by creating additional virtual address space. If the attempt is successful, the ESR dismisses the exception; otherwise, it reports the SS$_ACCVIO condition.

The processor generates a fault-on-read or fault-on-execute exception when it attempts to read or execute an instruction from a page whose corresponding PTE fault-on bit is set. The corresponding ESR might clear the fault-on bit and reexecute the instruction, or it might report the fault as an access violation (SS$_ACCVIO). The executive uses the fault-on-read bit as part of the implementation of granularity hint regions; it uses the fault-on-execute bit to optimize translation buffer invalidation. Chapter 32 contains more details. The TIE facility uses the fault-on-execute bit to identify pages containing VAX instructions, as described in Chapter 29.

An unaligned access occurs when an attempt is made to load or store a longword or quadword to or from a memory location that does not have a naturally aligned address. The processor transfers control to PALcode in such an event. (To be naturally aligned, a longword must be on a longword boundary, and a quadword must be on a quadword boundary.) PALcode automatically executes a sequence of instructions that perform the desired access; then it checks whether unaligned access reporting is enabled. If so, it generates an unaligned access trap. Performing the access in PALcode is slower than performing an equivalent aligned access. The unaligned access trap provides a way for the executive to report the unaligned access to the process so that software accessing the unaligned data can be improved to eliminate or minimize such access. The unaligned access ESR executes in kernel mode. The ESR's actions depend on several factors related to data alignment reporting system services, described in Chapter 39. One possible action of the ESR is to report the SS$_ALIGN condition.

The processor generates a breakpoint trap when it executes the CALL_PAL BPT instruction. EXE$BREAK_EXCEPTION_ENTRY, the usual breakpoint ESR, reports the SS$_BREAK condition. If, however, XDELTA, the system debugger, is loaded, the SCB entry for the breakpoint trap points to XDELTA's own breakpoint ESR. XDELTA's breakpoint ESR determines whether a breakpoint trap is one that it requested. If so, it handles the trap; otherwise, the ESR transfers control to EXE$BREAK_EXCEPTION_ENTRY as though the routine were entered directly as a result of the trap. A user mode breakpoint trap is typically serviced by the debugger's SS$_BREAK condition handler.

The processor generates a change-mode-to-supervisor trap when it executes the CALL_PAL CHMS instruction. The change-mode-to-supervisor ESR builds the signal array and determines the mode in which the exception occurred. If it occurred in kernel or executive mode, the ESR reports the SS$_CMODSUPR condition. If the exception occurred in user or supervisor mode, the ESR determines whether the process has declared a change-mode-to-supervisor handler using the Declare Change Mode Handler ($DCLCMH) system service. If so, the ESR calls that handler; otherwise, it reports the SS$_CMODSUPR condition.

The processor generates a change-mode-to-user trap when it executes the CALL_PAL CHMU instruction. The change-mode-to-user ESR is functionally similar to the change-mode-to-supervisor ESR. If the exception occurred in any mode other than user, it reports the SS$_CMODUSER condition. If the exception occurred in user mode and a change-mode-to-user handler was declared, it calls that handler; otherwise, it reports the SS$_CMODUSER condition.

The processor generates an illegal instruction trap when it attempts to execute an instruction reserved to Digital or one that requires emulation. It also generates the trap when it attempts to execute a privileged instruction while in an access mode other than kernel mode. The ESR simply reports the SS$_OPCDEC condition.

The processor generates an illegal CALL_PAL operand trap when it attempts to execute a CALL_PAL instruction whose operand it does not recognize. The ESR simply reports the SS$_ROPRAND condition.

The processor generates a software trap (also called GENTRAP) when it executes the CALL_PAL GENTRAP instruction. The GENTRAP exception is used primarily by low-level support routines for compilers. For example, OTS$DIV_I, a low-level compiler routine that performs integer division, uses the GENTRAP exception to signal an integer divide-by-zero condition that it detects. Note that there is no AXP instruction to perform integer division. The GENTRAP ESR examines the GENTRAP code, which is passed to it by PALcode. If the code is outside a predefined range of values, the ESR builds a signal array with SS$_GENTRAP as the status value and includes the GEN-TRAP code as an additional parameter in the signal array. Otherwise, the ESR indexes an array of status values with the code. It substitutes that status value for SS$_GENTRAP, builds a signal array with just the three basic parameters, and reports that condition.

6.6   SOFTWARE CONDITIONS

A software condition can be considered a software-simulated exception. The mechanism used to report a software condition is similar to that used to report an exception; the only difference is that PALcode builds the exception stack frame in the case of an exception, whereas software builds the exception stack frame in the case of a software condition.

An exception is generated by the processor in response to an error or anomaly in instruction execution, whereas a software condition is generated by user mode software in response to a software error or anomaly not necessarily related to instruction execution.

One of the choices in the design of a modular procedure is the method for reporting error conditions back to the caller. There are two common methods: returning a status in the procedure's return value (typically in R0 or F0), and signaling the error by calling one of the Run-Time Library procedures LIB$SIGNAL or LIB$STOP.

In some cases, signaling is preferable to returning status. Some procedures may return a value other than a status condition. For example, the string manipulation Run-Time Library procedure STR$POSITION returns the relative position of a substring within a source string. The procedure must therefore use the signaling mechanism to indicate an error condition, for example, an illegal source string.

Another common use of signaling occurs in an application using an indeterminate number of procedure calls to perform some action, such as a recursive procedure that parses a command line. In such a case, the use of a return status is often cumbersome and difficult to code. The signaling mechanism provides a graceful way not only to indicate that an error has occurred but also to return control (through the Unwind Call Chain ($UNWIND) system service) to a known alternative return point in the calling hierarchy.

Section 6.8.3 describes how user mode software reports a software condition.

6.7   SPECIAL CONDITIONS

The OpenVMS AXP executive reports certain special conditions that are not directly related to exceptions; these conditions can occur in the context of an exception, an interrupt, a machine check, or other processing performed by the executive. The mechanism used to report these conditions is similar to that used for software conditions. A brief description of each of these special conditions follows.

Most access control violations are detected by the processor and reported by the executive to a condition handler. The executive can also report an access violation condition detected by software rather than by the processor. This special condition is generated by the translation-not-valid ESR when it detects a process faulting a page in the process header of another process. The ESR calls EXE$ACVIOLAT, in module EXCEPTION, to report an access control violation. EXE$ACVIOLAT joins EXE$ACVIOLAT_EXCEPTION_ENTRY. This is an unusual error, typically the result of a software failure in executive or kernel mode code. The fault-on-read and fault-on-execute ESRs, outlined in Section 6.5.2, also may signal an access violation.

When an asynchronous system trap (AST) delivery interrupt service routine detects an inaccessible stack while attempting to deliver an AST to a process, it reports the AST delivery stack fault (SS$_ASTFLT) special condition by jumping to EXE$ASTFLT, in module EXCEPTION (see Chapter 8). EXE$ASTFLT is entered with current and previous modes both kernel, since it runs as part of an interrupt service routine. The special condition must be reported to the mode at which the AST would have been delivered. Therefore EXE$ASTFLT adjusts the saved PC and saved PS in the interrupt stack frame to be the PC and PS of the failed AST before transferring control to EXE$EXCEPTION.

The Digital command language (DCL) interpreter generates the debug (SS$_DEBUG) special condition in response to a DEBUG DCL command entered by a user when image execution has been interrupted with a CTRL/C or CTRL/Y or through a call to the Run-Time Library procedure LIB$PAUSE. The DEBUG DCL command processor builds a signal array on the supervisor stack and calls EXE$REFLECT to report the special condition. DCL calls EXE$REFLECT rather than LIB$SIGNAL to generate this software condition, because the DEBUG DCL command is processed in supervisor mode but the condition must be reported back to user mode. Section 6.11.1 gives more details.

If system service filtering is enabled, the SCB entries for the CHMK and CHME exceptions are loaded with the procedure values of alternative dispatchers EXE$CMODKRNLX and EXE$CMODEXECX rather than the normal dispatchers. The alternative dispatchers include a test of CTL$GB_SSFILTER, the per-process system service filter mask. A process can request the Set System Service Filter ($SETSSF) system service to alter this mask. If CTL$GB_SSFILTER contains zero, its default value, an alternative dispatcher branches to the standard change mode dispatcher. Otherwise, depending on the value in CTL$GB_SSFILTER, the dispatcher may deny a kernel or executive mode system service request by reporting the inhibit CHMK (SS$_INHCHMK) or inhibit CHME (SS$_INHCHME) special condition. The dispatcher generates the condition by jumping to EXE$INHCHMK or EXE$INHCHME in module EXCEPTION; either routine builds additional exception context and the signal array, and joins EXE$REFLECT at the RE-FLECT_ANY_MODE entry point. Chapter 7 contains more information on system service filtering.

A machine check is a processor-specific error condition that is potentially the result of serious, nonrecoverable hardware failure. Chapter 4 provides an overview of machine checks. Chapter 35 describes the machine check service routine. When a nonrecoverable machine check occurs in kernel or executive mode, the machine check service routine generates a fatal bugcheck. When a nonrecoverable machine check occurs in supervisor or user mode, the service routine calls EXE$MCHECK, in module EXCEPTION, to report the machine check (SS$_MCHECK) special condition. (Note that supervisor mode and user mode nonrecoverable machine check support is not fully implemented in OpenVMS AXP Version 1.5.) EXE$MCHECK builds additional exception context and the signal array, and transfers control to EXE$EXCEPTION.

When a process incurs a second page fault for a page on which a read error occurred during a previous fault for the same page, the translation-not-valid ESR reports either the page fault read error (SS$_PAGRDERR) special condition or the cross-mode page fault read error (SS$_PAGRDERRXM) special condition by jumping to EXE$PAGRDERR, in module EXCEPTION. EXE$PAGRDERR builds additional exception context and the signal array, and transfers control to EXE$EXCEPTION.

If the second page fault occurred in user or supervisor mode, or in kernel or executive mode for a page owned by kernel or executive mode, the executive reports the SS$_PAGRDERR special condition. If the second page fault occurred in kernel or executive mode for a page owned by user or supervisor mode, the executive reports the SS$_PAGRDERRXM special condition. Chapter 18 describes the page fault handler and these special conditions. As described in Section 6.11.3.1, the kernel and executive mode last chance handlers force process rundown for the SS$_PAGRDERRXM special condition.

When a process has enabled signaling of system service failures through the Set System Service Failure Mode ($SETSFM) system service, and a system or RMS service returns unsuccessfully with an error or severe error status, the change mode dispatcher (see Chapter 7) reports the system service failure (SS$_SSFAIL) special condition by jumping to EXE$SSFAIL, in module EXCEPTION. EXE$SSFAIL builds additional exception context and the signal array, and joins EXE$REFLECT at the REFLECT_ANY_MODE entry point.

6.8   SEARCHING FOR AND DISPATCHING TO CONDITION HANDLERS

Before any condition is reported to a condition handler, the code path that reports the condition builds an exception context area on the stack for the exception mode. This section describes the exception context area. It outlines the steps taken to report exceptions, software conditions, and special conditions. It also describes condition handler dispatching.

6.8.1   Exception Context Area

The exception context area, shown in Figure 6.1, consists of the exception stack frame, the exception record, the OpenVMS VAX-style signal array, the mechanism array, and the condition handling facility (CHF) context area. The exception stack frame, exception record, and signal array serve as input to EXE$SRCHANDLER; the rest of the exception context area is a work area for EXE$SRCHANDLER.

At the high-address end of the exception context area is the exception stack frame, outlined in Section 6.1 and described in Chapter 3.

An exception record describes an exception. For example, the exception

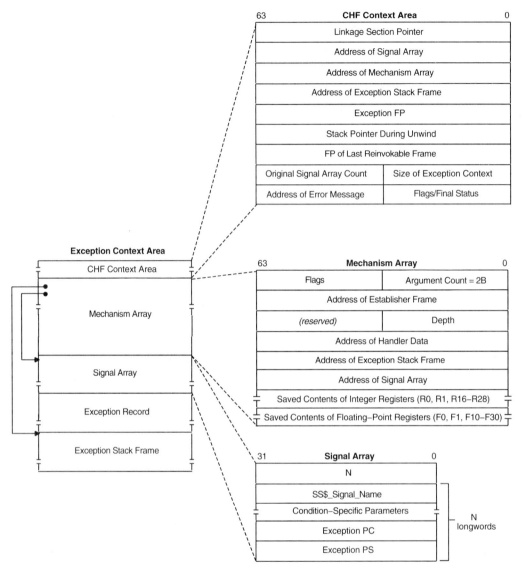

Figure 6.1
Exception Context Area

record for an access violation fault contains the status value identifying the condition (symbolically represented as SS$_ACCVIO) and the condition-specific parameters, namely, the faulting virtual address and the reason mask. Although the executive builds an exception record as part of the exception context area, OpenVMS AXP condition handlers never use the exception record; rather, they use the functionally equivalent OpenVMS VAX-style signal array.

A signal array also describes an exception. Although similar in content to an exception record, it has a different format. It contains the following information:

▶ The number of longwords in the signal array
▶ The status value identifying the exception condition, symbolically represented as SS$_*signal-name*
▶ Condition-specific parameters, if any
▶ Exception PC, copied from the exception stack frame
▶ Exception PS, copied from the exception stack frame

Note that the signal array contains longword entries to be compatible with an OpenVMS VAX signal array. A signal array always includes at least four longwords: a count of the number of longwords in the array, the status value, the saved PC, and the saved PS. If the signal array contains an odd number of longwords, an extra longword of padding is added to keep the stack quadword-aligned.

Information in the exception record, though unused for the most part by the executive, can be useful in some situations, for example, when it is necessary to determine the value in the high longword of an exception parameter, or when it is necessary to find the original value of an exception parameter and the signal array has been changed.

Table 6.3 lists the exceptions that the executive reports to condition handlers and the condition-specific information in the signal array for each exception. Table 6.4 lists the special conditions that the executive generates and the condition-specific information in the signal array for each condition.

The mechanism array is used partly by EXE$EXCEPTION to save integer and floating-point registers that could potentially be used in condition handling and partly as a work area for EXE$SRCHANDLER. It contains the following information:

▶ Contextual information that is useful to the condition handler about to be called, such as the address of the establisher frame and the depth of the search
▶ Saved contents of integer registers R0, R1, and R16 through R28
▶ Saved contents of floating-point registers F0, F1, and F10 through F30, if the process is using floating-point instructions

The CHF context area is an extension of the mechanism array. It is a scratch area built by EXE$SRCHANDLER and used by various exception processing routines including EXE$SRCHANDLER, EXE$REFLECT, and EXE$UNWIND. The macro $CHFCTXDEF defines the offsets into the CHF context area. The STARLET macro $CHFDEF defines the offsets into the signal and mechanism arrays.

Table 6.3   Signal Array Parameters for Exceptions That the Executive Reports to Condition Handlers

Exception Name	Status Value	Array Size	Additional Parameters
Arithmetic	SS$_HPARITH	6	Integer register write mask, Floating-point register write mask, Exception summary
Access violation	SS$_ACCVIO	5	Reason mask, Faulting virtual address
Alignment	SS$_ALIGN	5	Faulting virtual address, Read/write indicator
Breakpoint	SS$_BREAK	3	None
Change-mode-to-supervisor	SS$_CMODSUPR	4	Change mode code
Change-mode-to-user	SS$_CMODUSER	4	Change mode code
Illegal instruction	SS$_OPCDEC	3	None
Illegal CALL_PAL operand	SS$_ROPRAND	3	None
Software (GENTRAP)	SS$_GENTRAP or specific signal	3 or 4	Parameter [1]

[1] If the GENTRAP parameter is one that the OpenVMS AXP executive recognizes, the signal array has three parameters; otherwise it has four (see Section 6.5.2).

6.8.2   How the Executive Reports an Exception

Figure 6.2 outlines the steps involved in reporting exceptions, software conditions, and special conditions. The numbers in the figure correspond to the numbered steps in the following list. (Other steps are described in Sections 6.8.3 and 6.8.4.) All the code paths that report conditions converge at step 15, which dispatches the condition to a condition handler.

① In response to an exception, the processor normally changes mode to kernel and transfers control to a PALcode routine. The PALcode routine builds an exception stack frame on the appropriate stack and dispatches to an ESR.

② If the exception is one that the executive handles itself (see Table 6.1), then the ESR handles the exception and, if appropriate, resumes program execution.

  If the exception is not one that the executive handles itself, then the ESR prepares to report the exception to a condition handler.

③ As its first step in reporting the exception, the ESR builds an exception record and a signal array describing the exception. It then transfers control to EXE$EXCEPTION, the common ESR exit path.

④ EXE$EXCEPTION builds a mechanism array.

⑤ If the exception occurred at an interrupt priority level (IPL) greater than

Table 6.4   Signal Array Parameters for Special Conditions Generated by the Executive

Condition Name	Status Value	Array Size	Additional Parameters
Access violation	SS$_ACCVIO [1]	5	Reason mask, Faulting virtual address
AST delivery fault	SS$_ASTFLT	7	SP preventing delivery, AST parameter, Interrupt PC, [2,3] Interrupt PS [2]
Debug	SS$_DEBUG	Signal-specific	Signal-specific
Inhibit CHME	SS$_INHCHME	4	Exception parameter
Inhibit CHMK	SS$_INHCHMK	4	Exception parameter
Machine check	SS$_MCHECK	3	None
Page read error	SS$_PAGRDERR or SS$_PAGRDERRXM	5	Reason mask, Faulting virtual address
System service failure	SS$_SSFAIL	4	Exception parameter
Unaligned SP load	SS$_UNALIGN_ SP_LOAD	4	Faulting virtual address

[1] This condition can also be reported as the result of an exception (see Table 6.3).

[2] The AST delivery code exchanges the interrupt PC/PS pair and the PC/PS pair of the failed AST.

[3] When the AST delivery code cannot deliver an AST because of an invalid AST procedure code address, this longword contains the procedure value of the AST procedure.

2, EXE$EXCEPTION generates the fatal bugcheck INVEXCEPTN. Otherwise, it proceeds to the next step.

⑥ If the exception occurred in kernel mode, EXE$EXCEPTION proceeds to step 15; otherwise, it proceeds with the next step.

⑬ EXE$EXCEPTION allocates space on the outer mode stack for the exception context area, as described in Section 6.8.4.

⑭ If space was successfully allocated, EXE$EXCEPTION copies the exception context area to the stack of the mode in which the exception occurred. (If there is not enough room for building the exception context area on the target stack, EXE$EXCEPTION performs the actions outlined in Section 6.8.4.)

EXE$EXCEPTION calls EXE$REI_INIT_STACK_ALT, in module REI, to remove the exception context area from the current stack, change access mode to the mode of the exception, and continue execution with the code at step 15.

⑮ Running in the mode of the exception, EXE$EXCEPTION initiates the search for a condition handler by calling EXE$SRCHANDLER, whose actions are described in Section 6.8.5.

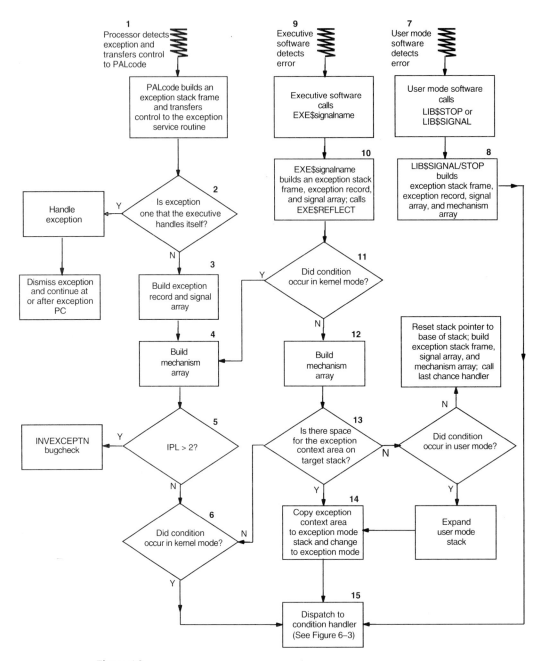

Figure 6.2
Condition Handling Overview

EXE$REI_INIT_STACK_ALT enables an inner mode caller to change to a specified outer mode and transfer control to a specified procedure. EXE$REI_INIT_STACK_ALT resets the SP to a specified location (by default, the base of the current mode's stack) and fabricates an exception frame on the stack with a PC and PS based on the caller's arguments. It then executes the CALL_PAL REI instruction to change mode and transfer control.

6.8.3   **How User Mode Software Reports a Software Condition**

This section describes how user mode software reports a software condition. The numbers in the following list correspond to the numbers in Figure 6.2.

⑦ A procedure calls LIB$SIGNAL or LIB$STOP with the name of the condition to be signaled and whatever additional parameters are to be passed to a condition handler. LIB$STOP is an alternative entry point to LIB$SIGNAL. This chapter collectively refers to these procedures as LIB$SIGNAL/STOP.

   LIB$SIGNAL and LIB$STOP differ in whether normal execution may be resumed after the condition handler for the signaled error returns. Use of LIB$SIGNAL enables the image to continue if the condition handler returns the status SS$_CONTINUE. Use of LIB$STOP does not. The two entry points store different values in the CHF context area flags longword, which is tested by the condition dispatcher.

⑧ Before LIB$SIGNAL/STOP can initiate the search for a condition handler, it must transform the stack to one resembling an exception stack.

   LIB$SIGNAL/STOP fabricates an exception context area on the stack similar to the one created by an ESR for an exception that the executive reports to a condition handler. The signal array includes any arguments from the call to LIB$SIGNAL/STOP.

   LIB$SIGNAL/STOP next builds a mechanism array and enters the same condition handler search code as exception handling, albeit through a jacket routine called SYS$SRCHANDLER. LIB$SIGNAL/STOP jumps to SYS$SRCHANDLER, a system service vector that contains a jump to EXE$SRCHANDLER. The indirection gives the Run-Time Library a constant procedure value through which to dispatch to EXE$SRCHANDLER.

The search for a condition handler takes place on the stack of the caller of LIB$SIGNAL/STOP (see Section 6.8.5).

6.8.4   **How the Executive Reports a Special Condition**

The following steps outline how the executive reports a special condition. The step numbers correspond to the numbers in Figure 6.2.

⑨ Running in an inner mode, the OpenVMS AXP executive detects an error that must be reported; it calls procedure EXE$*signal-name*, in module EXCEPTION, where *signal-name* is the abbreviated condition name.

⑩ EXE$*signal-name* simulates an exception by building an exception stack frame on the stack. Additionally, it builds an exception record and a signal array, and calls EXE$REFLECT, also in module EXCEPTION.

⑪ If the error was detected in kernel mode, EXE$REFLECT transfers control to EXE$EXCEPTION, and the error is treated just like an exception from that point onward. Section 6.8.2 describes EXE$EXCEPTION's flow.

⑫ If the error was detected in any other mode, EXE$REFLECT builds a mechanism array on the stack. (This step corresponds to the REFLECT_ANY_MODE entry point of EXE$REFLECT.)

⑬ If the condition must be reported to an outer mode, EXE$REFLECT allocates space for the exception context area on the outer mode stack.

⑭ If the space was successfully allocated, EXE$REFLECT copies the exception context area to the outer mode stack. Next, it calls EXE$REI_INIT_STACK_ALT to remove the exception context area from the current stack and change access mode to the mode of the exception.

⑮ Running in the mode to which the error must be reported, EXE$REFLECT calls EXE$SRCHANDLER to dispatch to a condition handler. The actions taken by EXE$SRCHANDLER are described in Section 6.8.5.

When EXE$EXCEPTION or EXE$REFLECT must report a condition to an outer mode condition handler, either procedure must build an exception context area on the outer mode stack.

Running in an inner mode, the procedure must ensure that there is room on the target mode stack for the exception context area. It requests the Adjust Outer Mode Stack Pointer ($ADJSTK) system service to check that there is room and, if so, to modify the stack pointer accordingly.

EXE$ADJSTK, the $ADJSTK system service procedure, returns the error status SS$_ACCVIO if there is no room on the target stack unless the target is the user mode stack. If the target is the user mode stack and there is no room, EXE$ADJSTK expands the stack transparently. If the $ADJSTK system service request is successful, EXE$EXCEPTION/EXE$REFLECT proceeds to copy the exception context area to the outer mode stack.

The $ADJSTK system service also returns the SS$_ACCVIO status if the target mode stack overflowed, if the target mode stack pointer is corrupted, or if the address space of the target mode stack is nonexistent. In response to an SS$_ACCVIO status, EXE$EXCEPTION/EXE$REFLECT resets the outer mode SP to its base, the contents of the CTL$AL_STACK array element for that mode. If there is no address space at that address, the procedure attempts to create it. If the address space cannot be created, the procedure takes one of the following actions:

▶ If the target mode is user or supervisor, it requests the Delete Process ($DELPRC) system service to delete the process.

▶ If the target mode is executive, it generates the nonfatal UNABLCREVA bugcheck.

▶ In the unlikely event that the target mode is kernel, it generates the fatal
UNABLCREVA bugcheck.

6.8.5   **Condition Handler Dispatching**

Once the exception context area has been built on the stack of the access
mode to which a condition is to be reported, and control has been passed
to EXE$SRCHANDLER, exceptions, software conditions, and special condi-
tions are processed identically. Figure 6.3 outlines the major steps performed
by EXE$SRCHANDLER. It uses a part of the mechanism array as a work area
to contain useful information for both itself and any condition handlers it
calls. In particular, it uses the flags and the depth fields to communicate with
the condition handlers it calls.

The numbers in Figure 6.3 correspond to the numbered steps in the following list:

① EXE$SRCHANDLER begins its search with the primary vectored handler
of the access mode to which the condition is to be reported. If the vector contains the procedure value of a condition handler (if it contains a
nonzero value), EXE$SRCHANDLER sets the depth to –2 and calls the
handler.

The primary handler, like any other handler, can resignal the condition,
alter the flow of program execution, or fix the error and continue (see Section 6.10). In Figure 6.3, the three possible actions of a condition handler
are labeled RESIGNAL, UNWIND, and CONTINUE.

② If the primary handler does not exist, or if it resignals, EXE$SRCHAN-
DLER looks for a secondary vectored handler for that access mode. If one
exists, EXE$SRCHANDLER sets the depth to –1 and calls it.

③ If the secondary handler does not exist, or if it resignals, the routine
begins its search for frame-based condition handlers. If the procedure descriptor associated with the current procedure frame has a valid handler
field, EXE$SRCHANDLER calls that handler with the depth set to 0.

If the procedure descriptor does not have an associated handler, or if
that handler resignals, EXE$SRCHANDLER examines the next earlier
procedure frame by using the saved FP in the current procedure frame.
As it examines each earlier procedure frame, it increments the depth to
record the number of frames already examined and places that frame's
address in the saved FP field in the mechanism array.

EXE$SRCHANDLER continues the search until one of the following
occurs:

• A handler fixes the error and returns the status SS$_CONTINUE, re-
questing resumption of the thread that incurred the exception.

• EXE$SRCHANDLER finds a saved FP whose value is zero or is not
within the bounds of that access mode's stack. A saved FP of zero indicates the end of the call chain.

117

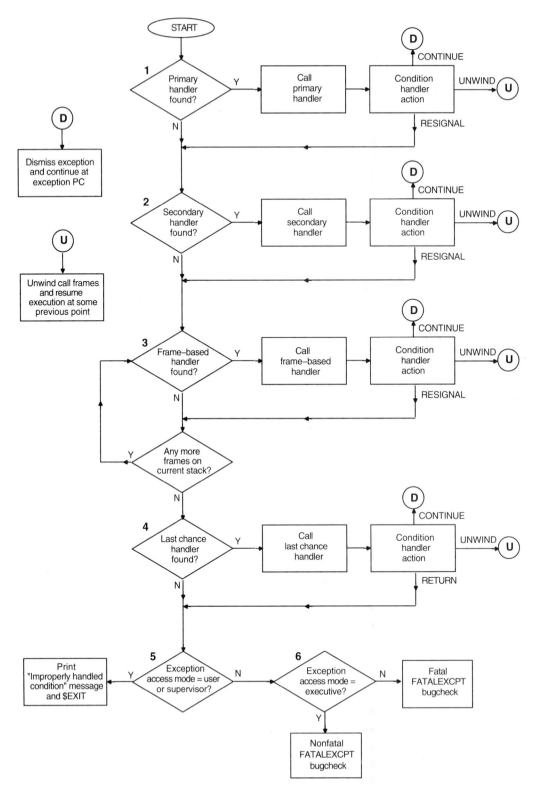

Figure 6.3
Dispatching to Condition Handlers

118

A saved FP may be out of range as a result of stack corruption, or it can also indicate the end of the call chain.

- EXE$SRCHANDLER finds either a change mode dispatcher procedure frame, described in Chapter 7, or an AST delivery procedure frame, described in Chapter 8, indicating that an access mode change occurred and thus terminating the call chain for that mode.

④ If all frame-based handlers resignal, or if no frame-based handlers are found, EXE$SRCHANDLER calls the last chance handler for the exception's access mode with the depth set at −3. This handler is also called if an error occurs during the search for a condition handler. The usual last chance handler is the catch-all condition handler, established as part of image startup. Section 6.11.2 describes this handler.

⑤ If the last chance handler returns, or if there is none, and the exception occurred in user or supervisor mode, EXE$SRCHANDLER calls the executive procedure EXE$EXCMSG, in module EXCEPTMSG. Its two input parameters are the address of an ASCII string containing message text and an OpenVMS VAX-style argument list with two arguments: the addresses of the signal array and the mechanism array. EXE$EXCMSG writes a message like the one shown in Example 6.1 to the process's SYS$OUTPUT device.

Following the call to EXE$EXCMSG, EXE$SRCHANDLER requests the Exit ($EXIT) system service with a status indicating either that no handler was found or that a bad stack was detected while searching for a condition handler.

Example 6.1
Example of Message Written by EXE$EXCMSG

```
Improperly handled condition, image exit forced.
  Signal arguments:   Number = 00000005
                      Name   = 0000000C
                               00000004
                               00000000
                               0002001C
                               0000001B

Register dump:
R0  = 0000000000000000  R1  = 0000000000030000  R2  = 0000000000000004
R3  = 000000007FF48610  R4  = 000000007FFBF80C  R5  = 000000007FFBF960
R6  = 000000007FFA0D34  R7  = 000000007FFA0D34  R8  = 000000007FFA05F8
R9  = 000000007FFA0800  R10 = 000000007FFA1380  R11 = 000000007FFBE3E0
R12 = 0000000000000007  R13 = 000000007FEEA790  R14 = 0000000000000000
R15 = 0000000000000000  R16 = 000000007FFBF874  R17 = 000000007FEEDF80
R18 = 000000007FFBF80C  R19 = 000000007FFBF960  R20 = 0000000000000028
R21 = 0000000000000000  R22 = 000000000000000D  R23 = 0000000000000000
R24 = 0000000000010000  R25 = 0000000000000006  R26 = 000000007FF2432C
R27 = 0000000000010000  R28 = 0000000000000000  R29 = 000000007FE73B80
PC  = 000000000002001C  PS  = 000000000000001B
```

⑥ If the exception occurred in executive or kernel mode, EXE$SRCHAN-
DLER generates a FATALEXCPT bugcheck, nonfatal for executive mode
and fatal for kernel mode.

If a handler returns the SS$_CONTINUE status, EXE$SRCHANDLER restores all scratch registers from the mechanism array. It removes from the
stack all of the exception context except the exception stack frame and executes a CALL_PAL REI instruction. This step, which corresponds to the label
D in Figure 6.3, resumes the thread of execution that incurred the exception.

Note that EXE$SRCHANDLER executes the CALL_PAL REI instruction
even for a software condition generated by LIB$SIGNAL. This is valid
because LIB$SIGNAL fabricated an exception stack frame, simulating an
exception.

Section 6.10.1 describes in more detail what happens when a handler returns the SS$_CONTINUE status. Section 6.10.2 describes what happens
when a handler does not return and instead unwinds the call chain.

6.9   MULTIPLE ACTIVE CONDITIONS

It is possible for multiple conditions to be active at the same time. This
happens when a condition handler or some procedure called by a condition
handler incurs an exception.

An OpenVMS VAX condition handler is not reinvokable, that is, a condition handler cannot service an exception that it itself incurs. An Open-
VMS AXP condition handler can be declared reinvokable. The OpenVMS
AXP calling standard provides a flag in the procedure descriptor, PDSC$V_
HANDLER_REINVOKABLE, which, when set, indicates that a procedure's
handler is reinvokable. Certain high-level languages such as BLISS do not allow handlers to be reinvokable; others allow the declaration of reinvokable
handlers.

EXE$SRCHANDLER calls CHF_SEARCH, in module EXCEPTION_ROU-
TINES, to locate and dispatch to a condition handler. CHF_SEARCH needs
to take special action when it services a condition while it is already servicing one or more other conditions. If a condition handler is not a reinvokable
one, CHF_SEARCH skips the handler's frame. For this skipping to work correctly, procedure frames of condition handlers must be distinguishable from
other procedure frames. CHF_SEARCH arranges this by calling all handlers
from a common call site, so that the return address of the condition handler
procedure frame is readily identifiable.

6.9.1   Common Call Site for Condition Handlers

To dispatch to any condition handler, CHF_SEARCH calls SYS$CALL_
HANDL, in module EXCEPTION_ROUTINES, with the procedure value of
the handler in R1. SYS$CALL_HANDL merely calls the condition handler
and, when the handler returns, returns to its caller.

The global location SYS$GL_CALL_HANDL contains the address of the procedure descriptor for SYS$CALL_HANDL. While traversing the call chain, EXE$UNWIND, the $UNWIND system service procedure, and CHF_SEARCH compare the value in this global location to the address of the procedure descriptor associated with each procedure frame. When they match, a condition handler's procedure frame has been identified.

6.9.2 Reinvokable Handlers and Multiple Active Conditions

Each time it is called to dispatch a condition, CHF_SEARCH traverses the call chain, examining every procedure frame regardless of the number of conditions that are active. If only one condition is currently active, CHF_SEARCH calls each condition handler in the call chain until the condition is handled or there are no more frames. If multiple conditions are currently active and a condition handler was previously called, CHF_SEARCH calls the handler only if it is reinvokable. (If there are more than two active conditions, CHF_SEARCH uses a more complex algorithm; its description is beyond the scope of this book.)

Section 6.12 describes an example in which two conditions are active and the handlers are nonreinvokable.

6.10 CONDITION HANDLER ACTIONS

A condition handler first determines the nature of the condition by examining the signal name longword in the signal array (see Figure 6.1). It then decides which action to take:

- ▶ It can pass the condition along to another handler by resignaling.
- ▶ It can fix the condition and allow execution to continue at the point in the thread of execution that incurred the exception.
- ▶ It can also allow execution to resume at a previous place in the calling hierarchy by removing a number of procedure frames from the call chain, a mechanism called unwinding.

A condition handler can also return the condition value as a return status to the caller of the procedure that established the handler (the establisher). This implicitly involves unwinding. A special Run-Time Library procedure, LIB$SIG_TO_RET, exists for this purpose. An application can declare this procedure as a condition handler, or a condition handler can call it. LIB$SIG_TO_RET unwinds the call chain as necessary and returns to the caller of its establisher with the condition value as the return status.

An executive procedure that must return the condition value as a return status to its establisher's caller uses EXE$SIGTORET, in module EXCEPTION_ROUTINES, as its condition handler. EXE$SIGTORET is functionally similar to LIB$SIG_TO_RET. Use of EXE$SIGTORET is reserved to Digital and otherwise completely unsupported.

The Run-Time Library procedure LIB$SIG_TO_STOP can be used as a condition handler by a user mode procedure that must terminate execution when it encounters a condition.

6.10.1   Resignal or Continue

If a condition handler cannot deal with the type of condition signaled, it returns the status SS$_RESIGNAL to inform EXE$SRCHANDLER that the search for a handler must proceed. A condition handler, like any other procedure, returns a status in R0.

If, however, a condition handler can resolve the condition, it does so and then returns the status SS$_CONTINUE to EXE$SRCHANDLER. This status means that the thread of execution that incurred the condition can continue.

When EXE$SRCHANDLER receives the status SS$_CONTINUE, it first checks if this was a condition signaled through LIB$STOP. If so, normal execution cannot continue, and EXE$SRCHANDLER calls the last chance handler, if it has not already been called, and proceeds with the actions described in Section 6.8.5.

If the condition was not signaled through LIB$STOP, EXE$SRCHANDLER restores all saved registers from the mechanism array and removes from the stack all of the exception context area except the exception stack frame. Finally, it removes the exception stack frame by executing a CALL_PAL REI instruction to dismiss the exception and return to the thread of execution that incurred the condition.

Where control returns depends on what sort of condition occurred:

▶ If the condition was a fault type of exception, such as an access violation, control returns to the instruction that caused the exception.
▶ If the condition was a trap type of exception, such as a CHMU trap, or if it was an executive-generated special condition, control returns to the instruction following the one that caused the exception.
▶ If the condition was an application-generated software condition, control returns to user mode software at the point following the call to LIB$SIGNAL. Note that control does not return from a call to LIB$STOP.

Because EXE$SRCHANDLER copies the saved PC field in the signal array to the exception stack frame, it is possible for a condition handler to alter the flow of control by altering the saved PC field in the signal array. Condition handlers established by the debugger and the Delta utility use this mechanism to alter the flow of control. Note that control cannot be transferred unless the target PC and the saved PC share the same linkage section. Use of this feature is reserved to Digital and otherwise completely unsupported.

6.10.2   **Unwinding Procedure Frames from the Call Chain**

Instead of resignaling or continuing, a condition handler can also alter the flow of control by requesting the $UNWIND system service.

Normally, when a current procedure returns to its calling procedure, the most recent procedure frame is removed from the call chain and used to restore the calling procedure's state. As each current procedure returns to its calling procedure, its associated procedure frame is removed from the call chain. This is the process by which a call chain is normally unwound.

It is possible to unwind the call chain forcibly, bypassing the normal return path. The $UNWIND system service allows a condition handler to transfer control from a series of nested procedure invocations to a previous point of execution, bypassing the normal return path. The $UNWIND system service procedure restores saved register context for each nested procedure invocation, calling the condition handler, if any, for each procedure frame that it unwinds. Restoring saved register context from each procedure frame from the most recent one to the target procedure frame ensures that the register context is correct when the target procedure gains control. Also, each condition handler called during unwind can release any resources acquired by its establishing procedure.

The $UNWIND system service has two arguments, both of which are optional:

▶ The DEPADR argument specifies the number of frames to be removed from the call chain. If it is omitted, its default is for all the procedure frames to be unwound from the frame that incurred the condition up to and including the frame whose condition handler is executing. This argument should be used with extreme caution (see Section 6.10.5).

▶ The NEWPC argument specifies the address to which control should be returned after the unwind is complete. If it is omitted, its default is for control to return to the return address saved in the procedure frame next outermost to the unwound ones.

The $UNWIND system service procedure, EXE$UNWIND in module SYSUNWIND, runs in the mode from which it is requested. It uses two routines, CHF_STARTUNWIND and CHF_LOOPUNWIND, both in module EXCEPTION. EXE$UNWIND does not actually remove frames from the stack. Rather, it replaces the saved return address in the specified number of frames. In all frames except the most recent one, EXE$UNWIND replaces the saved return address with the code address of CHF_LOOPUNWIND; in the most recent frame, it replaces the saved return address with the code address of CHF_STARTUNWIND. CHF_STARTUNWIND, entered when the first procedure whose frame is unwound attempts to return to its caller, starts the unwinding process. CHF_LOOPUNWIND performs the actual unwinding of the frame.

Unwinding a VAX call frame is accomplished through the MACRO-32 RET instruction. The RET instruction restores saved registers based on the register save mask in the call frame and resets the stack pointer to its value at procedure entry. In contrast, OpenVMS AXP procedure calls and returns are implemented in software rather than hardware. Consequently, unwinding procedure frames must be performed by software.

If the NEWPC argument was present, EXE$UNWIND replaces the saved return address in the procedure frame just earlier than the unwound ones (at higher addresses) with the specified value.

As each procedure returns, the registers saved in its procedure frame are restored and control is passed to CHF_LOOPUNWIND. If the current frame has an associated frame-based condition handler, CHF_LOOPUNWIND signals it with the condition name SS$_UNWIND so that it can perform procedure-specific cleanup. When the condition handler returns, or if there is none, CHF_LOOPUNWIND restores the registers saved by the procedure and calculates the stack pointer upon entry to the procedure. It does not set the stack pointer to this value, however; that is done at the end of the unwinding operation.

If a handler called in this way requests the $UNWIND system service rather than returning, the $UNWIND system service returns the error status SS$_UNWINDING to indicate that an unwind is already in progress. The technique of calling handlers as a part of the unwind sequence enables a handler that previously resignaled a condition to regain control and perform procedure-specific cleanup and also ensures correct restoration of registers saved within each procedure frame.

This sequence continues until the required number of procedure frames have been discarded. At the end of this sequence, EXE$UNWIND resets the stack pointer to the most recently calculated value. Section 6.10.3 provides an example that describes the unwinding of the call chain.

6.10.3 Example of Unwinding the Call Chain

Figure 6.4 illustrates an example of an unwind sequence. The example, in which all procedures are assumed to be stack frame procedures, begins with the following sequence of events. Procedure A calls procedure B, which calls procedure C. Procedure C generates signal S. The primary and secondary handlers (if they exist) simply resignal. Handlers CH and BH also resignal.

Finally, handler AH is called. To unwind the call chain back to its establisher frame, AH requests the $UNWIND system service with the DEPADR argument equal to the value contained in the mechanism array, in this example, 2. After the call to $UNWIND, but before the frame modification occurs, the stack has the form pictured on the left-hand side of Figure 6.4.

EXE$UNWIND's frame modification proceeds as follows:

1. EXE$UNWIND scans the stack for a condition handler procedure frame. Recall that a condition handler procedure frame is one whose return ad-

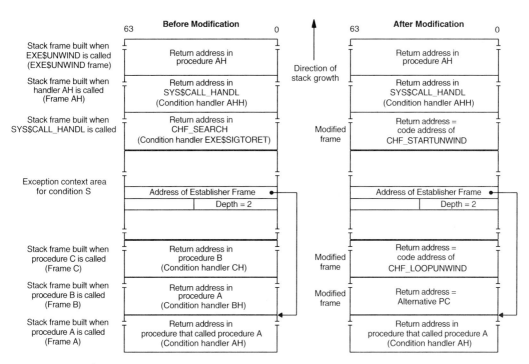

Figure 6.4
Procedure Frame Modification by EXE$UNWIND

dress field has the same contents as the SYS$GL_CALL_HANDL long-word.

2. EXE$UNWIND does not modify its own frame. Later, when it returns to its caller, control will return to handler AH.

3. The first frame that is modified by EXE$UNWIND is the one built when SYS$CALL_HANDL is called. EXE$UNWIND replaces its saved return address with the code entry point of CHF_STARTUNWIND.

   When SYS$CALL_HANDL later attempts to return to its caller, control will return to CHF_STARTUNWIND rather than to EXE$SRC-HANDLER. Consequently, control will not return to procedure C, the one that incurred the exception.

4. EXE$UNWIND continues to modify the saved return address in successive frames in the call chain until the number of frames specified (or implied) in its DEPADR argument have been modified. In all frames except the first, it replaces the saved return address with the code entry point of CHF_LOOPUNWIND.

5. If the NEWPC argument was present, the procedure frame in which it would be inserted is the next frame beyond the last frame specified (or implied) in the DEPADR argument. In this example, the value of the NEWPC argument would be stored in the procedure frame for procedure B.

125

At this point, all frames have been modified and the stack looks as shown on the right-hand side of Figure 6.4. Actual unwinding occurs as follows:

1. EXE$UNWIND returns control to handler AH.
2. Handler AH does whatever else it needs to do to service the condition. When it is done, it returns to the saved return address, passing control to SYS$CALL_HANDL.
3. SYS$CALL_HANDL returns to its modified return address, thus passing control to CHF_STARTUNWIND.
4. CHF_STARTUNWIND performs the following setup:
   a. It converts the original signal name to SS$_UNWIND.
   b. It sets the STOP flag in the CHF context area to prevent the signal from being continued.
   c. It calculates the value of the stack pointer before the exception. CHF_STARTUNWIND then falls through to CHF_LOOPUNWIND.
5. CHF_LOOPUNWIND performs the following steps:
   a. If a handler was established for this frame, CHF_LOOPUNWIND calls it with the signal name SS$_UNWIND. A handler called with the SS$_UNWIND signal is expected to release any resources acquired by its establisher and perform any other cleanup necessary.
   b. It restores all registers saved in the current procedure frame. Integer registers R0, R1, and R16 through R28 and, if they were saved, the floating-point registers F0, F1, and F10 through F30 are restored into the mechanism array. Registers R2 through R7 are restored into the exception stack frame. Registers R8 through R15 are restored into themselves.
   c. It calculates the stack pointer on entry to the procedure.

   CHF_LOOPUNWIND repeats these three steps for each frame to be unwound. At the end of the call chain, CHF_LOOPUNWIND restores all scratch registers from the mechanism array. It restores registers R2 through R7 from the exception stack frame. It sets the SP to the value it had on entry to the last procedure unwound. It restores the previous FP from the last frame unwound and returns control to the saved return address in the last frame.

In effect, CHF_LOOPUNWIND simulates returns from each nested procedure that it unwinds. These procedures never receive control again, although the outermost procedures receive control as if all the nested procedures had returned normally.

6.10.4 Potential Infinite Loop

One possible problem can occur with this implementation. Section 6.9 pointed out that EXE$SRCHANDLER takes care (when multiple conditions are active) not to search frames for the second condition that were examined on the first pass. Unless it establishes itself as its own handler, a condition handler is not called in response to a condition that it generates.

EXE$UNWIND cannot perform such a check, however. It must call each condition handler that it encounters as it removes frames from the stack. Thus, a poorly written condition handler (one that generates an exception) could result in an infinite loop of exceptions if a handler higher up in the calling hierarchy unwinds the frame in which this poorly written handler is declared. This loop has no effect on the system beyond that of any compute-bound process but will prevent any further useful work by that image.

6.10.5 Correct Use of Default Depth in $UNWIND

If the DEPADR argument is not specified, or if it is specified as the address 0, the $UNWIND system service unwinds the call chain back to the caller of the handler's establisher. A handler can specify a depth other than the default depth but must do so with extreme caution. To unwind to the establisher frame, a handler should specify as the depth argument the address of the depth field of the mechanism array (CHF$IS_MCH_DEPTH) rather than an explicit value. An explicit value could be wrong for any of the following reasons:

▸ The presence of the condition dispatcher procedure frame
▸ The presence of jacket frames, if there are any translated procedures in the call chain (see Section 6.13)
▸ The presence of multiple active software conditions
▸ Potential compiler optimization, with the compiler substituting inline code for a procedure call

6.10.6 Unwinding ASTs

EXE$UNWIND must perform special processing to unwind out of ASTs. Simply removing the procedure frames would ignore the presence of the AST and fail to dismiss the AST properly. CHF_LOOPUNWIND recognizes an AST dispatcher procedure frame and takes special action when it encounters one. The procedure value of either SCH$ASTDEL or SCH$ASTDEL_K can be found in the AST dispatcher's procedure frame. The AST stack area, described in Chapter 8, can be found at immediately higher addresses on the stack.

This situation is shown in Figure 6.5. All procedures are assumed to be stack frame procedures. Handler XH can unwind to its establisher, procedure X, or to its establisher's caller, the AST dispatcher. If handler XH resignals the condition, handler BH is called. Handler BH can unwind to its establisher, procedure B, or to its establisher's caller, procedure A.

If handler XH unwinds to the AST dispatcher, the AST is dismissed as it would normally be dismissed. If handler XH resignals, however, EXE$UNWIND must call handler BH after the AST is properly dismissed. In this

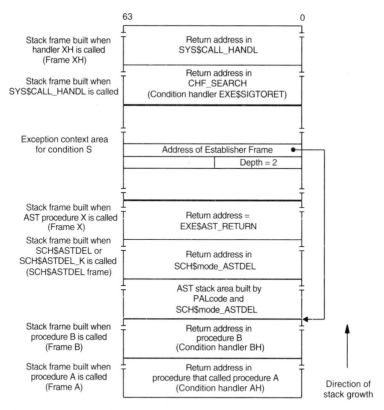

Figure 6.5
Unwinding ASTs

case, control is actually not returned to the AST dispatcher. Instead, CHF_ LOOPUNWIND simulates a return to the AST dispatcher, cleaning up the stack and restoring registers appropriately.

Unwinding out of an AST requires some caution. If the AST procedure has any sort of side effects, it is essential to have a condition handler declared by the AST procedure to clean up the side effects when the AST is unwound. Note that issuing an I/O request is a side effect of the highest order!

6.11 DEFAULT CONDITION HANDLERS

The OpenVMS AXP executive establishes some default condition handlers as a part of process creation or image activation. Chapters 27 and 28 point out exactly when and how each of the handlers described in this section is established. The following sections outline the actions each handler takes when it is called.

6.11.1 Traceback Handler Established by Image Startup

When an image includes either the debugger or the traceback handler, another procedure frame is built before the image itself is called (see Chapter 28). EXE$IMGSTA, in module SYSIMGSTA, is the procedure that executes before the image is called. It has an associated condition handler that will be entered for any subsequent condition not handled by an intervening condition handler.

This handler first checks whether the condition that occurred is SS$_DEBUG. If so, it maps the debugger into P0 space (if not already mapped) and passes control to it. The condition SS$_DEBUG is signaled by a command language interpreter (CLI) in response to a DEBUG command. This feature allows an image that was not linked or run with debugger support to be interrupted and have a debugger invoked.

For all other errors, if the severity level of the error is warning, error, or severe (fatal) error, the handler maps the traceback facility above the end of defined P0 space and passes control to it. The traceback facility terminates the image after writing information about the exception to the process's SYS$OUTPUT device. The information resembles the following:

```
%SYSTEM-F-ACCVIO, access violation, reason mask=04,
 virtual address=00000000, PC=0002001C, PS=0000001B
%TRACE-F-TRACEBACK, symbolic stack dump follows
 Image Name  Module Name  Routine Name  Line Number  rel PC    abs PC
    TEST                                          0  0001001C  0002001C
                                                  0  80126F08  80126F08
                                                  0  7FF2432C  7FF2432C
```

If the condition is actually a successful one, and not an error condition, the traceback condition handler resignals the condition, which usually means that the condition is being reported to the catch-all condition handler.

6.11.2 **Catch-All Condition Handler**

EXE$CATCH_ALL, in module PROCSTRT, is the catch-all condition handler. It is always established for the initial procedure frame on the user stack and in the last chance vector for user mode by either EXE$PROCSTRT when the process is created or by a CLI before an image is called. This handler is always called if no other handlers exist or if all other handlers resignal. Because the handler is also declared as a last chance handler, it is also called in the event of an error in the search through the user stack.

The first step that EXE$CATCH_ALL takes is to call EXE$CATCHALL_EXTENSION, in module PROCSTRT, which calls all catch-all condition handler extensions. Next, EXE$CATCH_ALL calls SYS$PUTMSG (see Chapter 39), which results in output of the following form on the process's SYS$OUTPUT device:

```
%SYSTEM-F-ACCVIO, access violation, reason mask=04,
 virtual address=00000000, PC=0002001C, PS=0000001B
```

If the handler was called through the last chance vector (the depth argument in the mechanism array is −3) or if the severity level of the condition name in the signal array indicates severe (condition-name ⟨2 : 0⟩ GEQU 4), then EXE$EXCMSG (see Chapter 39) is called to output a summary message of the form shown in Example 6.1, and the image is terminated; otherwise, the image is continued.

Catch-all condition handler extensions provide a language-independent mechanism to declare a handler that must be called before the catch-all condition handler executes but after all other condition handlers have been called. A layered product, such as the DEC C language Run-Time Library or the Performance Coverage Analyzer, can establish a catch-all condition handler extension by requesting the $SETEXV system service, described in Section 6.4.2. The DEC C language Run-Time Library, for example, establishes a catch-all condition handler extension to convert an OpenVMS AXP condition to a POSIX-style signal. Use of this feature is reserved to Digital and otherwise completely unsupported.

An image constructs a catch-all extension block to describe its catch-all extension procedure and requests the $SETEXV system service, passing it the address of the block. EXE$SETEXV, the $SETEXV system service procedure, maintains the process's list of catch-all extension blocks. Its list head is at CTL$GL_CATCHALL_EXTENSION, and the number of blocks in the list is in CTL$GL_CATCHALL_EXTENSION_CNT.

Later, when a condition occurs and the condition dispatcher reports it to the catch-all condition handler, EXE$CATCH_ALL calls EXE$CATCHALL_EXTENSION. For each block in the list of catch-all extensions, the latter calls the catch-all condition handler extension procedure. If that procedure fields the condition and returns the status SS$_CONTINUE, EXE$CATCH-ALL_EXTENSION returns to its caller. If, instead, the procedure returns the status SS$_RESIGNAL, EXE$CATCHALL_EXTENSION calls the next catch-all condition handler extension. If all procedures resignal the error, EXE$CATCHALL_EXTENSION resignals the error also.

EXE$SIGTORET, EXE$CATCHALL_EXTENSION's procedure frame condition handler, protects it from any condition that could potentially be caused by corruption of catch-all extension blocks, which are in process-private space and writable from user mode.

6.11.3   Non–User Mode Handlers

In addition to the handlers that the executive supplies for user mode conditions, it sets up handlers for the other three access modes.

6.11.3.1   Exceptions in Kernel or Executive Mode.

When a kernel mode exception occurs, EXE$EXCEPTION checks that the IPL was at or below 2. If this is not true, the dispatcher generates a fatal INVEXCEPTN bugcheck. Routines whose exceptions can cause this bugcheck include interrupt service routines, device drivers (except for their function decision table action routines), process-based code executing above IPL 2 (such as portions of various system services), and any code running in the context of the swapper process.

If IPL is 2 or lower, EXE$EXCEPTION dispatches the exception in the normal manner. If no primary, secondary, or procedure frame condition handlers service the exception, the condition dispatcher calls the last chance condition handler.

The last chance exception vectors for both kernel and executive modes are initialized at process creation in module SHELL*xx*K, where *xx* is 8, 16, 32, or 64, depending on the system's page size in kilobytes (see Chapter 27).

The kernel mode last chance handler, EXE$EXCPTN, in module SYSTEM_ROUTINES, checks whether the dispatched condition is the SS$_PAGRDERRXM special condition. If so, EXE$EXCPTN requests the $EXIT system service to run down the process that incurred the special condition. Otherwise, it generates a fatal SSRVEXCEPT bugcheck. Routines whose exceptions can result in this bugcheck include portions of many system services, many exception service routines, device driver function decision table action routines, user-written system services, and procedures that are entered through the Change to Kernel Mode ($CMKRNL) system service.

The executive mode last chance handler, EXE$EXCPTNE, in module SYSTEM_ROUTINES, checks whether the dispatched condition is the SS$_PAGRDERRXM special condition. If not, it generates a nonfatal SSRVEXCEPT bugcheck, causing an error to be logged. Whether or not it generated the bugcheck, EXE$EXCPTNE exits the image from executive mode, causing the process to be deleted. Routines that execute in executive mode include RMS, parts of the executive, user-written system services, and procedures that are entered through the Change to Executive Mode ($CMEXEC) system service. Note that if the SYSGEN parameter BUGCHECKFATAL is 1, a nonfatal SSRVEXCEPT bugcheck is treated as a fatal bugcheck and results in a crash.

Chapter 35 describes bugcheck processing in detail.

6.11.3.2 **DCL's Condition Handler.** The LOGINOUT image activates the DCL CLI and calls DCL's main procedure. This procedure is the earliest one on the supervisor mode call chain and has an associated supervisor mode condition handler that performs two tasks when it is called:

1. It cancels any exit handlers that have been established.
2. It resignals the error.

There are no other condition handlers. When the search ends, the image is exited in supervisor mode, resulting in process deletion.

6.12 **NONREINVOKABLE HANDLERS AND TWO ACTIVE CONDITIONS**

The modified flow of control when EXE$SRCHANDLER encounters a condition handler procedure frame can best be illustrated through an example. The following example assumes that the primary and secondary vectored handlers (if they exist) have resignaled, that all condition handlers are non-reinvokable, and that all procedures are stack frame procedures.

The numbers in Figure 6.6 correspond to the following steps:

①　Procedure A calls procedure B, which calls procedure C.

②　Procedure C generates condition S. Handler CH resignals the condition. The depth argument is 1, and the establisher frame argument points to the procedure frame for procedure B, when BH is called.

③　The procedure frame for handler BH is located later in time on the stack, at lower virtual addresses than the signal and mechanism arrays for condition S. The saved FP in the procedure frame for BH points to the frame of the condition dispatcher.

④　Handler BH now calls procedure X, which calls procedure Y.

⑤　Procedure Y generates condition T. The desired sequence of frames to be examined is frame Y, frame X, frame BH, and then frame A. Frames B and C are skipped because they were examined while condition S was being serviced.

EXE$SRCHANDLER proceeds in its normal fashion. The primary and secondary vectors are examined first (no skipping here). Then frames Y, X, and BH are examined, resulting in handlers YH, XH, and BHH being called in turn. Assume that all these handlers resignal. After handler BHH returns to EXE$SRCHANDLER with a status of SS$_RESIGNAL, EXE$SRCHANDLER notes that the previous frame of BH is that of the condition dispatcher because its procedure value is identical to the contents of the SYS$GL_CALL_HANDL longword.

EXE$SRCHANDLER locates the exception context for condition S by calculating the SP before entry to the condition dispatcher using the condition dispatcher procedure frame. From the exception context, EXE$SRCHANDLER locates the address of the mechanism array, which contains the address of the frame that established handler BH.

The frame pointed to by the establisher FP in the mechanism array, which is the procedure frame for B, has already been searched. Any frame already searched while servicing condition S (namely, those for procedures C and B) would not have its handler called unless the procedure has the PDSC$V_HANDLER_REINVOKABLE bit set in its procedure descriptor. The next frame examined by the search procedure is the procedure frame of A, which is pointed to by the saved FP in the procedure frame of B.

The depths that are passed to handlers are 0 for YH, 1 for XH, 2 for BHH, and 6 for AH. Figure 6.6 shows the state of the stack when handler AH is called.

6.13　CONDITION HANDLING IN THE TIE FACILITY

The Translated Image Environment facility supports the execution of user mode OpenVMS VAX images that have been translated by the VAX En-

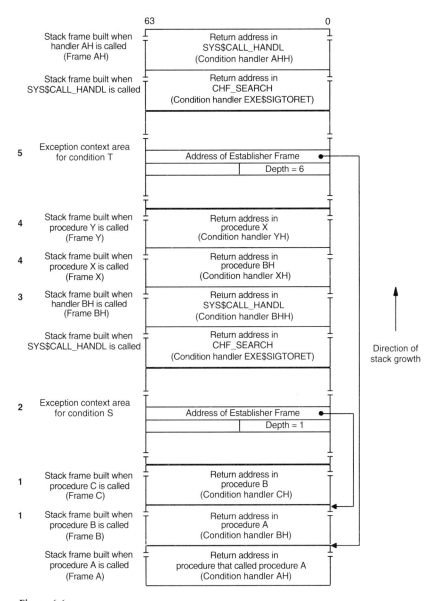

Figure 6.6
Frame Skipping with Multiple Active Conditions

vironment Software Translator. Procedure calls between native AXP procedures and translated OpenVMS VAX procedures are performed through
jacket procedures. Dispatching to condition handlers in this environment is
complicated because the dispatcher has to deal with OpenVMS VAX-style
call frames, AXP procedure frames, and frames left by calls to jacket procedures in both environments.

Chapter 29 discusses condition handling in this environment.

6.14   **$GOTO_UNWIND SYSTEM SERVICE**

The $UNWIND system service, briefly described in Section 6.10.2, allows a condition handler to transfer control from a series of nested procedure invocations to a previous point of execution, bypassing the normal return path. New for OpenVMS AXP Version 1.0, the Goto Unwind ($GOTO_UNWIND) system service allows any procedure, even one that is not a condition handler, to achieve the same effect.

The $GOTO_UNWIND system service allows compilers and Run-Time Library procedures for languages such as Ada and C to implement nonlocal GOTO statements through a supported interface. A nonlocal GOTO statement is one whose target destination is outside the scope of the current procedure but within the scope of some procedure in the call chain. The C language functions setjmp() and longjmp(), for example, can be implemented using the $GOTO_UNWIND system service.

The $GOTO_UNWIND system service procedure restores saved register context for each nested procedure invocation, calling the condition handler, if any, for each procedure frame that it unwinds. Restoring saved register context for each procedure frame from the most recent one to the target procedure frame ensures that the register context is correct when the target procedure gains control. Also, each condition handler called during unwind can release any resources acquired by its establishing procedure.

The $GOTO_UNWIND system service defines two types of unwind operation: goto unwind and exit unwind. A goto unwind operation unwinds procedure frames and transfers control to a specified target location within a procedure in the call chain. The specified target procedure is identified by a value called an invocation handle.

An invocation handle uniquely identifies a procedure invocation in the call chain. It is constructed from bits $\langle 62 : 4 \rangle$ of either the SP or the FP (whichever is the procedure frame base register) at procedure invocation, shifted left by one bit, and ORed with one of the following:

▸ 31, for a stack frame procedure
▸ The register number that contains the calling procedure's return address, for a register frame procedure

User mode software should not attempt to construct an invocation handle. Instead, a user mode procedure should call the Run-Time Library procedure LIB$GET_CURRENT_INVO_HANDLE to get its own invocation handle. To get the invocation handle of another active procedure, a procedure should call the Run-Time Library procedure LIB$GET_PREVIOUS_INVO_HANDLE. The *OpenVMS RTL Library (LIB$) Manual* gives more information on these procedures.

An exit unwind operation unwinds procedure frames and returns control to the saved return address in the oldest procedure frame in the call chain.

The oldest procedure frame on the user stack, that is, the very first one built on it, has the PDSC$V_BASE_FRAME bit set.

For a process that is not using the DECthreads Run-Time Library, the oldest procedure frame is the one built by the process startup procedure, EXE$PROCSTART (see Chapter 27); the Image Startup system service procedure, EXE$IMGSTA; or a DCL interpreter procedure, like DCLRUN, DCLMCR, or DCL$EXTIMAGE, that runs user images. Returning control to this procedure results in image exit.

For a process that is using the DECthreads Run-Time Library, the oldest procedure frame on a thread's stack is one built by the Run-Time Library. Returning control to this procedure results in the thread's termination.

The $GOTO_UNWIND system service has the following arguments, all of which are optional:

▶ The TARGET_INVO argument is the address of the invocation handle of the active procedure to which control should return. If the TARGET_INVO argument is omitted or is zero, then an exit unwind operation is initiated; otherwise, a goto unwind operation is initiated to the location specified by the TARGET_PC argument.

▶ The TARGET_PC argument is the address of a location that contains the address at which execution should resume. The return address should be a location within the procedure specified by the TARGET_INVO argument. If the TARGET_PC argument is omitted or is zero, control returns to the target procedure's saved return address.

▶ The NEW_R0 argument is the address of the value to be placed in R0 when execution begins at the target location. If it is omitted, the value of R0 at the time of the $GOTO_UNWIND request is used.

▶ The NEW_R1 argument is the address of the value to be placed in R1 when execution begins at the target location. If it is omitted, the value of R1 at the time of the $GOTO_UNWIND request is used.

6.14.1   Flow of the $GOTO_UNWIND System Service

EXE$GOTO_UNWIND, the $GOTO_UNWIND system service procedure, in module SYSUNWIND, runs in the requestor's access mode. It performs the following operations:

1. As its first step, it calls GOTO_UNWIND_INT, a local procedure. For reasons outside the scope of this description, EXE$GOTO_UNWIND performs all its operations within this local procedure. This description does not distinguish between GOTO_UNWIND_INT and EXE$GOTO_UNWIND except to note that the call to GOTO_UNWIND_INT has resulted in a stack frame that is currently at the low-address end of the stack.

2. EXE$GOTO_UNWIND allocates and initializes a work area on the

135

stack. This work area has the same format as the exception context area described in Section 6.8.1. EXE$GOTO_UNWIND creates a signal array in the work area. The three-longword signal array contains the status value SS$_UNWIND and either the status value SS$_EXIT_UNWIND or SS$_GOTO_UNWIND, depending on whether an exit unwind or a goto unwind operation was requested.

3. It establishes EXE$SIGTORET, in module EXCEPTION_ROUTINES, as its own frame-based condition handler. EXE$SIGTORET is a general-purpose condition handler used by many executive condition handling support procedures. It converts any condition within its establishing procedure to a return status.

4. If a goto unwind operation was requested, EXE$GOTO_UNWIND copies the TARGET_INVO argument to the work area at CHFCTX$L_UNWIND_TARGET. If a TARGET_PC argument was specified, EXE$GOTO_UNWIND copies it to the CHFCTX$L_UNWIND_TARGET_PC field in the work area.

5. If either or both of the NEW_R0 and NEW_R1 arguments were specified, EXE$GOTO_UNWIND records their new values in the mechanism array fields CHF$IH_MCH_SAVR0 and CHF$IH_MCH_SAVR1.

6. It replaces EXE$SIGTORET, the current frame-based condition handler, with the local procedure GOTO_UNWIND_HANDLER. If called to handle a condition generated within its establishing procedure, GOTO_UNWIND_HANDLER writes an error message to the process's SYS$OUTPUT device and forces an image exit with the SS$_UNWIND status.

7. The current frame, identified by the value in the FP, is the one built when EXE$GOTO_UNWIND called GOTO_UNWIND_INT. EXE$GOTO_UNWIND uses two fields in this procedure frame, the saved return address (RA) field and the saved previous FP field, to keep track of the saved RA and the saved previous FP for each procedure frame that it unwinds.

   EXE$GOTO_UNWIND calls CHF_RESTORE_REGS, in module EXCEPTION_ROUTINES, to restore saved integer and floating-point registers based on the respective register save masks from the current frame into the work area as follows:

   • Registers R2 through R7 are restored into the exception stack frame in the work area.
   • Registers R16 through R27 and the FP are restored into the mechanism array.
   • Registers R8 through R15 are restored into themselves.

   EXE$GOTO_UNWIND calls CHF_GET_PREVIOUS_FP, in module EXCEPTION_ROUTINES, to get the previous FP value into the FP register.

8. Next, EXE$GOTO_UNWIND loops to unwind as many previous procedure frames as necessary to service the request.

a. It stores the FP in its own stack frame as well as in the mechanism array.

b. It copies the saved value of register R26 from the mechanism array to the saved RA field on its own stack frame.

c. It constructs the invocation handle for the current procedure frame (the one pointed to by the FP) and compares it to the TARGET_INVO argument of the $GOTO_UNWIND request. If there is a match, it proceeds to step 9. (In the case of an exit unwind request, the value of this argument is zero and thus there is never a match.)

d. If there is no handler associated with that frame, it proceeds to the next step. Otherwise, it calls the handler associated with that frame. A handler called at this step, that is, with the SS$_UNWIND signal, is expected to release any resources allocated by the procedure and return.

e. It calls CHF_RESTORE_REGS to restore registers that were saved in the current frame.

f. It calls CHF_GET_PREVIOUS_FP to get the previous FP. If there is no previous frame, that is, the previous FP contains zero, or the procedure descriptor associated with the previous frame has the PDSC$V_BASE_FRAME bit set in PDSCW_FLAGS, EXEGOTO_UNWIND proceeds to step 9. Otherwise, it continues with step 8a.

EXE$GOTO_UNWIND can handle any of the following conditions during its unwind operation:

- If the frame being processed is one built by entry to SYS$CALL_HANDL, then the $GOTO_UNWIND system service was requested in the context of an active condition; in this case EXE$GOTO_UNWIND takes special care to restore registers from the condition dispatcher stack frame.

- If EXE$GOTO_UNWIND was called in the context of an active call to EXE$UNWIND or EXE$GOTO_UNWIND, an unwind collision has occurred. If so, EXE$GOTO_UNWIND returns control to the outermost return address requested.

- If EXE$GOTO_UNWIND reaches the end of the call chain without finding a procedure frame whose invocation handle matches the TARGET_INVO argument, EXE$GOTO_UNWIND treats the request as an exit unwind request.

9. EXE$GOTO_UNWIND restores all saved registers from the work area, including the saved FP and SP, making the target procedure the current procedure and resuming execution at TARGET_PC. If an exit unwind was requested, this step restores the procedure that built the oldest procedure frame in the call chain. This ensures that any necessary exit processing is performed by the initiator of the thread of execution.

If the unwind operation failed for any reason, EXE$GOTO_UNWIND writes an error message to the process's SYS$OUTPUT device and requests the $EXIT system service with the error status SS$_UNWIND.

6.14.2 Exit Unwind Operation Example

This section outlines steps 7, 8, and 9 of EXE$GOTO_UNWIND for an example exit unwind operation.

Figure 6.7 shows the layout of the stack in this example as EXE$GOTO_UNWIND enters step 7. Frame A is the oldest procedure frame, built when procedure A was called. Procedure A called procedure B, which called procedure C. Procedure C requested the $GOTO_UNWIND system service, as a result of which the newest procedure frame and the work area built by EXE$GOTO_UNWIND were added at the high-address end of the stack.

EXE$GOTO_UNWIND performs the following steps:

1. It restores saved registers from frame E into the work area.
2. It gets the previous FP, which points to frame D, and saves the previous FP into frame E and the mechanism array. It initializes frame E's saved RA field from the saved R26 field of the mechanism array.

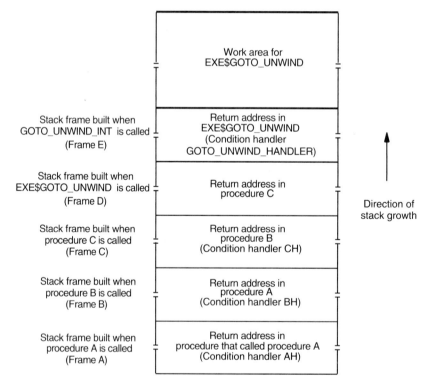

Figure 6.7
$GOTO_UNWIND Procedure Frame Processing

3. EXE$GOTO_UNWIND restores the saved registers from frame D into the work area.

4. It gets the previous FP, which points to frame C, and saves the previous FP into frame E and the mechanism array. It initializes frame E's saved RA field from the saved R26 field of the mechanism array.

5. It calls handler CH with the signal SS$_UNWIND.

6. EXE$GOTO_UNWIND restores the saved registers from frame C into the work area and saves the previous FP into frame E and the mechanism array. It initializes frame E's saved RA field from the saved R26 field of the mechanism array.

7. The routine calls handler BH with the signal SS$_UNWIND.

8. It restores the saved registers from frame B into the work area and saves the previous FP into frame E and the mechanism array. It initializes frame E's saved RA field from the saved R26 field of the mechanism array.

9. It calls handler AH with the signal SS$_UNWIND.

10. It restores the saved registers from frame A into the work area. Since the PDSC$V_BASE_FRAME bit is set in A's procedure descriptor, it restores all registers from the work area, including the FP and SP. It resumes execution at the saved RA in frame A.

6.15   RELEVANT SOURCE MODULES

The source modules described in this chapter include

[SYS]EXCEPTION.M64
[SYS]EXCEPTION_ROUTINES.MAR
[SYS]SYSSETEXV.MAR
[SYS]SYSUNWIND.MAR

7 System Service Dispatching

Between the idea
And the reality
Between the motion
And the act
Falls the Shadow.
T. S. Eliot, *The Hollow Men*

Many of the operations that the OpenVMS AXP operating system performs on behalf of a user are implemented as procedures called system services. A user application requests system services directly, and components such as the file system request system services on behalf of the user.

Most system service procedures are contained in executive images and reside in system space; others are contained in privileged shareable images.

System services typically execute in kernel or executive access mode so that they can read and write data structures protected from access by outer modes.

This chapter describes how control is passed from an image to a procedure that executes service-specific code and back to the image.

7.1 OVERVIEW

A system service is a procedure, typically in the OpenVMS AXP executive, that performs a function for a process, usually at the process's request. An image running in the process requests a particular service by calling the associated procedure.

A major distinction between system service procedures and other procedures is that system services are generally provided by the executive, although some are provided by privileged shareable images. Section 7.2 describes system services in executive images, and Section 7.7, system services in privileged shareable images.

Another important distinction between a system service procedure and, for example, a Run-Time Library procedure, is access mode. Most system service procedures execute in kernel or executive mode and may be requested from any mode equally or less privileged. (Some system services, however, known as mode of caller services, execute in the same mode as their requestor and can be requested from any mode.) Run-Time and other library procedures generally execute in user mode and may only be requested from user mode.

The implementation of inner mode system services is based on a controlled change of access mode. Although an unprivileged process can enter an inner access mode to execute code in that mode, it can only execute pro-

140

cedures that are part of the executive or that have been specifically installed by the system manager. Only a process with suitable privilege may change to an inner access mode and execute a procedure of its own designation (see Section 7.8.2).

When a process requests an inner mode system service, it executes a system service transfer routine that serves as a bridge between the requestor's mode and the inner mode in which the service procedure executes. A system service transfer routine contains an instruction that loads R0 with a number identifying the system service and either a CALL_PAL CHMK or a CALL_PAL CHME instruction. Executing one of these instructions causes a CHMK or CHME exception; the CHMK and CHME exception service routines are called change mode dispatchers. A change mode dispatcher transfers control to a procedure that is identified by the number in R0 and that actually implements the service. Section 7.2.3 describes system service transfer routines; Section 7.4, change mode instructions; and Sections 7.5.2 and 7.5.3, the operations of the change mode dispatchers.

A key goal for the implementation of system services has been that an image requesting system services need not be relinked from one version of the operating system to the next. On VAX systems, this constraint was initially met by forever reserving the lowest pages of system space for system service transfer routines (called system service vectors). Each system service transfer routine was given a global name whose value was an address within the reserved pages. In VAX/VMS Version 3 and subsequent versions, a region of P1 space was also reserved for this purpose.

The OpenVMS AXP implementation of system services has the same goal: that an image requesting a system service need not be relinked from one version of the system to the next. The goal, however, is satisfied differently. System service transfer routine names are resolved using the same mechanisms that apply to externally visible names in a shareable image. Section 7.2.1 briefly summarizes the concept of a shareable image symbol vector and explains its use in resolving system service transfer routine names.

Section 7.8 describes several system services related to change mode dispatching.

7.2   TRANSFER ROUTINES FOR SYSTEM SERVICES IN EXECUTIVE IMAGES

This section discusses transfer routines for system services in executive images: the resolution of their externally visible names, their initialization, and their contents. Section 7.7 contains similar information about transfer routines for system services in privileged shareable images.

The external name of a system service transfer routine generally has the form SYS$*service*. A transfer routine executes in the mode of the caller and serves as a bridge between the caller and the procedure that actually implements the service request. That procedure is typically part of an executive image and typically executes in an inner access mode. The name of a procedure that performs the actual work of the system service is usually of the form EXE$*service* or RMS$*service*. For a mode of caller system service, the name SYS$*service* is also the name of the service-specific procedure.

7.2.1 Resolving System Service Transfer Routine Names

Every OpenVMS AXP procedure is described by a data structure called a procedure descriptor, which contains the address of the procedure's code entry point and information about its type and characteristics. As described in Chapter 1, a compiler generates a procedure descriptor for each procedure in a module and places them together in a program section called a linkage section. Executive image system service transfer routines and their associated procedure descriptors are defined in the module SYSTEM_SERVICES.

Chapter 1 describes how a universal symbol in a shareable image is represented by both a global symbol table entry and a symbol vector entry. The global symbol table entry gives the offset of the symbol vector entry. When a shareable image is activated, each symbol vector entry representing a routine is updated to contain the actual addresses of the procedure descriptor and code entry point. The module SYSTEM_SERVICES is linked to create the shareable image SYS$PUBLIC_VECTORS.EXE. Its global symbol table lists all the system service transfer routine names and their offsets in the image's symbol vector.

When an image that requests a system service is linked, the linker must resolve the system service transfer routine name. By default, it searches the file SYS$LIBRARY:SYS$PUBLIC_VECTORS.EXE to resolve any still unresolved symbols after it searches STARLET.OLB. The linker stores the symbol vector offset corresponding to the system service transfer routine into the linkage section of the image making the service request. It stores information about the need to update that linkage pair in the fixup section of the image.

Unlike other shareable images, SYS$PUBLIC_VECTORS.EXE is not activated with an executable image. Instead, as part of the executive, it is loaded into system space during system initialization. Because all processes map system space, SYS$PUBLIC_VECTORS.EXE is shared. The addresses in its symbol vector are updated as system services are loaded (see Section 7.2.2 and Chapter 32).

When an image that requests a system service is activated, the image activator sees that the image has been linked with SYS$PUBLIC_VECTORS.EXE, which it treats as a shareable image that has already been activated. The image activator replaces the contents of the linkage pair representing the system service transfer routine with the two quadwords of information in the loaded SYS$PUBLIC_VECTORS.EXE symbol vector.

Figure 7.1 shows how references to system services are resolved in a linked user image and how they are fixed up after the image is activated. After the

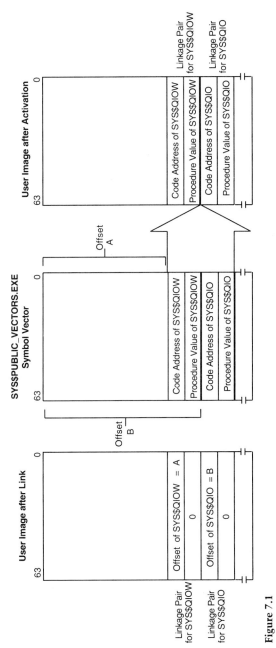

Figure 7.1
System Service Name Resolution

image is linked, its linkage pairs that refer to system services contain the offsets of those symbols in the SYS$PUBLIC_VECTORS.EXE symbol vector. For simplicity, the figure places the symbol vector entries for SYS$QIO and SYS$QIOW in adjacent positions and omits the user image's fixup section, which contains a linkage pair type of fixup for each of these references. Section 7.2.2 explains the difference between the symbol vector entries for SYS$QIO (an inner mode service) and SYS$QIOW (a mode of caller service). When the image is activated, the linkage pairs are fixed up to contain the replacement linkage pair contents at those offsets in the loaded SYS$PUBLIC_VECTORS.EXE symbol vector.

The order of the entries in a symbol vector is determined by the order in which global symbols are listed in the SYMBOL_VECTOR link option. To ensure upward compatibility of images linked with a shareable image, the SYMBOL_VECTOR link option symbols must remain in the same order from one version of the shareable image to the next. New symbols may be added at the end, and a deleted symbol must be replaced by a new symbol or the name of a placeholder procedure. To ensure that an OpenVMS AXP image that references system services can run without relinking on a new version of OpenVMS AXP, the order of the symbols defined in SYS$PUBLIC_VECTORS.EXE is guaranteed.

7.2.2   Initialization of System Service Transfer Routines and Procedure Descriptors

SYS$PUBLIC_VECTORS.EXE contains not only the symbol vector for system service transfer routine names but also their procedure descriptors and the system service transfer routines themselves. During system initialization, SYS$PUBLIC_VECTORS.EXE is loaded into system space. The base image cells EXE$GL_PUBLIC_VECTOR_SYMVEC and EXE$GL_PUBLIC_VECTOR_SYMVEC_END contain the beginning and end addresses of the symbol vector within SYS$PUBLIC_VECTORS.EXE.

The procedure descriptor for a system service transfer routine is a particular type called a bound procedure descriptor. A bound procedure descriptor contains the address of a second procedure descriptor to which the first is bound. This provides a mechanism by which the target of a procedure call can be resolved at run time.

Each system service transfer routine procedure descriptor contains the code entry point of a transfer routine in module SYSTEM_SERVICES. At assembly time, each transfer routine is defined as a call to the procedure to which its procedure descriptor is currently bound. Initially the procedure descriptor is bound to SYS$LOAD_ERROR, in module SYSTEM_SERVICES. SYS$LOAD_ERROR simply returns the error status SS$_ILLSER to the system service requestor.

An executive image module that contains system services procedures contains one invocation of the SYSTEM_SERVICE macro for each of them. This macro labels the procedure and, for an inner mode system service, creates a system service descriptor block that describes the system service: the address of its own system service transfer routine, access mode, and other characteristics (see Figure 32.7).

When an executive image containing one or more inner mode services is loaded, the routine EXE$CONNECT_SERVICES, in module SYSTEM_SERVICE_LOADER, uses the system service descriptor block to determine the modifications to be made to the system service transfer routine in the loaded SYS$PUBLIC_VECTORS.EXE. It leaves the system service transfer routine procedure descriptor alone, assigns a change mode number, and replaces the transfer routine's procedure call with a CALL_PAL CHMx. Section 7.2.3 shows the resulting transfer routine.

When an executive image containing a mode of caller service is loaded, the executive image loader leaves the transfer routine alone. If the executive image is one that may not be unloaded, the loader modifies the system service's linkage pair replacement contents in the symbol vector. If the executive image is removable, one that may be unloaded, the loader does not change the linkage pair replacement contents in the symbol vector entry. In either case, it binds the transfer routine's procedure descriptor in SYS$PUBLIC_VECTORS.EXE to the newly loaded procedure in the executive image.

When an image is activated that requests a mode of caller service, its linkage pair is fixed up with the contents of the symbol vector entry. Because most mode of caller services are in executive images that may not be unloaded, typically the linkage pair for a mode of caller service is fixed up with the addresses of the procedure descriptor and code entry point of the procedure in the executive image rather than those of the transfer routine.

Figure 7.2 shows the relations among system service transfer routines, their procedure descriptors, and the system service symbol vector after system services are connected. It contrasts the structures and routine for the kernel mode service Queue I/O Request ($QIO), on the left side of the figure, with those for the mode of caller service Queue I/O Request and Wait ($QIOW), on the right. The executive image containing these services is one that may not be unloaded.

Chapter 32 contains more details about system service initialization.

7.2.3   Flow of System Service Transfer Routines

A system service transfer routine is generally identified by a universal name of the form SYS$*service*. The routine consists of instructions that cause a transfer of control to a service-specific procedure in the executive.

Many system services execute in kernel mode; after the services are loaded, their system service transfer routines contain a CALL_PAL CHMK instruction. The transfer routines for a few system services and many RMS services contain a CALL_PAL CHME instruction. Some services, such as the

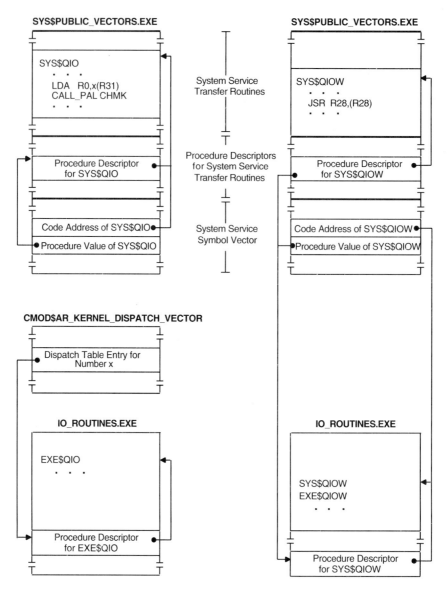

Figure 7.2
System Service Transfer Routines

text-formatting services, execute in the access mode of the caller. When an image calls such a service, it dispatches directly to the service-specific procedure in the executive that implements the service.

Following are the three sets of instructions found in system service transfer routines. Table 7.1 lists the OpenVMS AXP system services that use each of these three methods of initial dispatch.

A transfer routine for a system service that changes mode to kernel consists of the following code:

```
SYS$service::               ;Entry point
    BIS     SP,R31,R28       ;Copy stack pointer
    LDA     R0,chmk_code(R31)
                             ;Load service-specific value
    CALL_PAL CHMK            ;Change mode to kernel
    RET     R31,(R26)        ;Return to service caller
    NOP                      ;No-op for padding
    NOP                      ;No-op for padding
```

A transfer routine for a system service that changes mode to executive consists of the following code:

```
SYS$service::               ;Entry point
    BIS     SP,R31,R28       ;Copy stack pointer
    LDA     R0,chme_code(R31)
                             ;Load service-specific value
    CALL_PAL CHME            ;Change mode to executive
    RET     R31,(R26)        ;Return to service caller
    NOP                      ;No-op for padding
    NOP                      ;No-op for padding
```

A transfer routine for a mode of caller system service consists of the following code:

```
SYS$service::               ;Entry point
    LDQ     R27,16(R27)      ;Load procedure value
    LDQ     R28,8(R27)       ;Load code entry address
    JSR     R28,(R28)        ;Transfer to procedure
    NOP                      ;No-op for padding
    NOP                      ;No-op for padding
    NOP                      ;No-op for padding
```

An image requesting a mode of caller service in a nonremovable executive image dispatches directly to the mode of caller service without going through the system service transfer routine. An image requesting a mode of caller service in a removable executive image executes the transfer routine to dispatch to the service-specific procedure.

7.2.4 System Service Requests from Translated Images

An OpenVMS VAX image that executes on an OpenVMS VAX system can call a system service through either the P1 or system space address of its vector, although use of system space vector addresses is rare. To be translatable, an OpenVMS VAX image must restrict itself to the default P1 space resolution of system service vector addresses.

The translated version of an OpenVMS VAX system service request is a call to a jacket routine provided by the Translated Image Environment. The

Table 7.1   System Services and RMS Services That Use Each Form of System Service Transfer Routine

The following services execute initially in kernel mode.

EXE$GETSPI [1,3]	SYS$DELETE_BUFOBJ [3]	SYS$REMOVE_REF [3]
IPC$SERVICE [1,3]	SYS$DELLNM	SYS$RESCHED
PTD$CANCEL [1]	SYS$DELMBX	SYS$RESUME
PTD$CREATE [1]	SYS$DELPRC	SYS$SAVE_ALIGN_ FAULT_DATA
PTD$DECTERM_SET_ PAGE_SIZE [1,3]	SYS$DELTVA	SYS$SAVE_SYS_ ALIGN_FAULT_ DATA
PTD$DELETE [1]	SYS$DEQ	SYS$SCHDWK
PTD$READ [1]	SYS$DERLMB [3]	SYS$SET_COPY [3]
PTD$SET_EVENT_ NOTIFICATION [1]	SYS$DEVICE_SCAN	SYS$SETEF
PTD$WRITE [1]	SYS$DGBLSC	SYS$SETENV [3]
SPI$DSKINI [1,3]	SYS$DIAGNOSE [3]	SYS$SETEXV
SPI$RMSMAP [1,3]	SYS$DLCEFC	SYS$SETFLT [3]
SYS$ABORT_TRANS	SYS$DTI [1,3]	SYS$SETIME
SYS$ADD_BRANCH [3]	SYS$END_BRANCH [3]	SYS$SETIMR
SYS$ADJSTK	SYS$END_TRANS	SYS$SETPFM [3]
SYS$ADJWSL	SYS$ENQ	SYS$SETPRA
SYS$ALLOC	SYS$ERAPAT	SYS$SETPRI
SYS$ASCEFC	SYS$EXIT	SYS$SETPRN
SYS$ASSIGN_LOCAL [3]	SYS$EXPREG	SYS$SETPRT
SYS$BRKTHRU	SYS$FINISH_RMOP [3]	SYS$SETPRV
SYS$CANCEL	SYS$FORCEX	SYS$SETRWM
SYS$CANCEL_ SELECTIVE [3]	SYS$FORGET_RM [3]	SYS$SETSFM
SYS$CANEXH	SYS$GET_ALIGN_ FAULT_DATA	SYS$SETSSF [3]
SYS$CANTIM	SYS$GET_SYS_ ALIGN_FAULT_ DATA	SYS$SETSTK
SYS$CANWAK	SYS$GETCHN [2]	SYS$SETSWM
SYS$CHKPRO	SYS$GETDEV [2]	SYS$SIGPRC [3]
SYS$CLRAST [3]	SYS$GETDVI	SYS$SNDERR [3]
SYS$CLRAST_MODE [3]	SYS$GETENV [3]	SYS$START_ALIGN_ FAULT_REPORT
SYS$CLREF	SYS$GETJPI	SYS$START_ BRANCH [3]
SYS$CMKRNL	SYS$GETLKI	SYS$START_TRANS
SYS$CNTREG	SYS$GETSYI	SYS$STOP_ALIGN_ FAULT_REPORT
SYS$COPY_FOR_ PAGE [3]	SYS$GETTIM	SYS$STOP_SYS_ ALIGN_FAULT_ REPORT
SYS$CREATE_ BUFOBJ [3]	SYS$HIBER	SYS$SUSPND

Table 7.1   System Services and RMS Services That Use Each Form of System Service Transfer Routine *(continued)*

The following services execute initially in kernel mode.

SYS$CREATE_UID[3]	SYS$INIT_SYS_ ALIGN_FAULT_ REPORT	SYS$TOGGLE_ALIGN_ FAULT_REPORT
SYS$CRELNM	SYS$JOIN_RM[3]	SYS$TRNLNM
SYS$CRELNT	SYS$KRNDWN[3]	SYS$ULKPAG
SYS$CREMBX	SYS$LCKPAG	SYS$ULWSET
SYS$CREPRC	SYS$LKWSET	SYS$UPDSEC
SYS$CRETVA	SYS$MAKE_REF[3]	SYS$WAITFR_ COMMON[3]
SYS$CRMPSC	SYS$MGBLSC	SYS$WAITFR_INT[3]
SYS$DACEFC	SYS$MTACCESS	SYS$WAKE
SYS$DALLOC	SYS$PROCESS_SCAN	SYS$WFLAND_ COMMON[3]
SYS$DASSGN	SYS$PERM_DIS_ ALIGN_FAULT_ REPORT	SYS$WFLAND_INT[3]
SYS$DCLAST	SYS$PERM_REPORT_ ALIGN_FAULT	SYS$WFLOR_ COMMON[3]
SYS$DCLCMH	SYS$PURGWS	SYS$WFLOR_INT[3]
SYS$DCLEXH	SYS$QIO	
SYS$DECLARE_RM[3]	SYS$READEF	

The following system services execute initially in executive mode.

$CHANGE_PROT[1,3]	SYS$DISMOU[1]	SYS$MOD_IDENT[1]
$INIT_VOL_ CLEANUP[1,3]	SYS$END_RU[2]	SYS$NUMTIM
$INIT_VOL_EXEC[1,3]	SYS$ERNDWN[3]	SYS$PREPARE_RU[2]
SYS$ABORT_RU[2]	SYS$FIND_HELD[1]	SYS$REM_HOLDER[1]
SYS$ADD_HOLDER[1]	SYS$FIND_HOLDER[1]	SYS$REM_IDENT[1]
SYS$ADD_IDENT[1]	SYS$FINISH_RDB	SYS$SETUAI[1]
SYS$ASCTOID	SYS$FORGE_WORD[1,3]	SYS$SNDACC[2]
SYS$CHANGE_ACL[1]	SYS$GETQUI	SYS$SNDJBC
SYS$CHANGE_ CLASS[1,3]	SYS$GETRUID[2]	SYS$SNDOPR
SYS$CHECK_ACCESS[1]	SYS$GETUAI[1]	SYS$SNDSMB[2,3]
SYS$CMEXEC	SYS$IDTOASC	SYS$START_RU[2]
SYS$COMMIT_RU[2]	SYS$IMGACT[3]	SYS$VMOUNT[1,3]
SYS$CREATE_RDB[1]	SYS$MOD_HOLDER[1]	

The following system services execute initially in the mode of the caller.
Several of them change to a more privileged mode during execution.

SYS$ASCTIM	SYS$FORMAT_ AUDIT[1]	SYS$PUTMSG[4]
SYS$ASSIGN	SYS$FORMAT_ CLASS[1,3]	SYS$READ_THREAD_ UNQ[3]
SYS$BINTIM	SYS$GETMSG[5]	SYS$REVOKID[5]
SYS$BRDCST[2]	SYS$GOTO_UNWIND	SYS$RUNDWN[3]

(continued)

149

Table 7.1   System Services and RMS Services That Use Each Form of System Service
Transfer Routine *(continued)*

The following system services execute initially in the mode of the caller.
Several of them change to a more privileged mode during execution.

SYS$CHECK_FEN	SYS$GRANTID [5]	SYS$SETAST
SYS$CLI [3]	SYS$HASH_ PASSWORD	SYS$TRNLOG [2]
SYS$CRELOG [2]	SYS$IMGFIX [3]	SYS$UNWIND
SYS$DELLOG [2]	SYS$IMGSTA [3,4]	SYS$WAITFR
SYS$EXCMSG [3,5]	SYS$INIT_VOL [1,5]	SYS$WFLAND
SYS$FAO	SYS$MOUNT [1,5]	SYS$WFLOR
SYS$FAOL	SYS$PARSE_ACL [1]	SYS$WRITE_THREAD_ UNQ
SYS$FORMAT_ACL [1]	SYS$PARSE_CLASS [1,3]	

The following mode of caller system services are synchronous services.
Each requests the asynchronous form of the service and then a wait-for
service.

PTD$READW [1]	SYS$FINISH_RMOPW [3]	SYS$QIOW
SYS$ABORT_TRANSW	SYS$FORGET_RMW [3]	SYS$SNDJBCW
SYS$ADD_BRANCHW [3]	SYS$GETDVIW	SYS$START_ BRANCHW
SYS$BRKTHRUW	SYS$GETJPIW	SYS$START_TRANSW
SYS$DECLARE_RMW [3]	SYS$GETLKIW	SYS$SYNCH
SYS$END_BRANCHW [3]	SYS$GETQUIW	SYS$UPDSECW
SYS$END_TRANSW	SYS$GETSYIW	
SYS$ENQW	SYS$JOIN_RMW [3]	

The following RMS services execute in executive mode.

SYS$FILESCAN	SYS$RMS_FREE [3]	SYS$RMS_SEARCH [3]
SYS$RMS_CLOSE [3]	SYS$RMS_GET [3]	SYS$RMS_SPACE [3]
SYS$RMS_CONNECT [3]	SYS$RMS_MODIFY [3]	SYS$RMS_ TRUNCATE [3]
SYS$RMS_CREATE [3]	SYS$RMS_NXTVOL [3]	SYS$RMS_UPDATE [3]
SYS$RMS_DELETE [3]	SYS$RMS_OPEN [3]	SYS$RMS_WAIT [3]
SYS$RMS_ DISCONNECT [3]	SYS$RMS_PARSE [3]	SYS$RMS_WRITE [3]
SYS$RMS_DISPLAY [3]	SYS$RMS_PUT [3]	SYS$RMSRUNDWN
SYS$RMS_ENTER [3]	SYS$RMS_READ [3]	SYS$SETDDIR
SYS$RMS_ERASE [3]	SYS$RMS_RELEASE [3]	SYS$SETDFPROT
SYS$RMS_EXTEND [3]	SYS$RMS_REMOVE [3]	SYS$SSVEXC
SYS$RMS_FIND [3]	SYS$RMS_RENAME [3]	
SYS$RMS_FLUSH [3]	SYS$RMS_REWIND [3]	

The following RMS services are mode of caller services. Each requests
the executive mode form of the service and then optionally waits.

SYS$CLOSE	SYS$FLUSH	SYS$REMOVE
SYS$CONNECT	SYS$FREE	SYS$RENAME
SYS$CREATE	SYS$GET	SYS$REWIND
SYS$DELETE	SYS$MODIFY	SYS$SEARCH
SYS$DISCONNECT	SYS$NXTVOL	SYS$SPACE

Table 7.1   System Services and RMS Services That Use Each Form of System Service Transfer Routine *(continued)*

The following RMS services are mode of caller services. Each requests
the executive mode form of the service and then optionally waits.

SYS$DISPLAY	SYS$OPEN	SYS$TRUNCATE
SYS$ENTER	SYS$PARSE	SYS$UPDATE
SYS$ERASE	SYS$PUT	SYS$WAIT
SYS$EXTEND	SYS$READ	SYS$WRITE
SYS$FIND	SYS$RELEASE	

[1] This service is implemented in a privileged shareable image.
[2] This service has been superseded.
[3] Use of this service is reserved to Digital.
[4] This system service can be called only from supervisor and user modes.
[5] This system service can be called only from executive and less privileged access modes.

jacket routine makes any necessary argument list transformations and calls the corresponding OpenVMS system service. Chapter 29 provides more details on support for translated images.

7.3   SYSTEM SERVICES THAT DO NOT CHANGE MODE

Some system services do not change to a more privileged access mode and instead execute in the mode from which they were requested. The system service transfer routine for one of these mode of caller services transfers control directly to the service procedure (unless, as previously described, the service is in a removable executive image).

When the service-specific procedure has completed its operation, it loads a status into R0 and returns control to the requestor of the service at the instruction following the system service request. Table 7.1 lists the mode of caller system services.

Figure 7.3 shows the control flow from a user image to a mode of caller service procedure.

7.4   CHANGE MODE INSTRUCTIONS

There are four change mode instructions: CALL_PAL CHMU, CALL_PAL CHMS, CALL_PAL CHME, and CALL_PAL CHMK. Unlike a VAX CHMx instruction, an Alpha AXP CALL_PAL CHMx instruction does not have an operand to identify the change mode number. Instead, a register must be loaded with a change mode number before the instruction is executed. The OpenVMS AXP change mode dispatchers expect the number to have been loaded into R0 before a CALL_PAL CHME or CALL_PAL CHMK instruction is executed.

Executing any of the CALL_PAL CHMx instructions generates an exception. The privileged architecture library (PALcode) routine that initiates exceptions, interrupts, and machine checks, the IEI PALcode routine, alters the

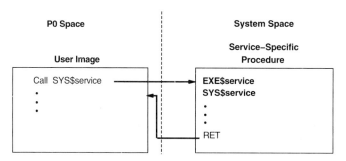

Figure 7.3
Control Flow of System Services That Do Not Change
Mode

access mode, if necessary, and switches to that mode's stack. The actual access mode used is the innermost of the access mode indicated by the instruction and the current access mode. The IEI PALcode routine pushes onto that stack the processor status (PS), the program counter (PC) of the next instruction, and R7 through R2, forming an interrupt/exception frame (shortened in this chapter to exception frame). It then dispatches through the system control block (SCB) entry for that CHMx exception to its exception service routine.

The OpenVMS AXP system uses the CALL_PAL CHME and CALL_PAL CHMK instructions exclusively to request system services. Their exception service routines are known as the change mode dispatchers.

CHMS and CHMU exceptions are treated much like other exceptions that the executive passes to a user-declared condition handler (see Chapter 6).

7.5 CHANGE MODE DISPATCHING

Each change mode dispatcher processes the argument list and, using the CHMx number, indexes into a dispatch table. From the entry in the dispatch table, it gets the address of the system service procedure descriptor and the code entry address and calls the procedure.

7.5.1 Change Mode Dispatcher Data Structures

Each change mode dispatcher has its own dispatch table to describe loaded services and a cell representing the number of loaded services. These tables and cells are defined in module CHANGE_MODE_DATA. Each dispatch table has a maximum of 256 entries. The executive mode dispatch table begins at CMOD$AR_EXEC_DISPATCH_VECTOR, and the kernel mode table at CMOD$AR_KERNEL_DISPATCH_VECTOR. The cells containing counts of loaded services are CMOD$GL_CHMK_LIMIT and CMOD$GL_CHME_LIMIT. Each is initialized to 1.

SERVICE_ROUTINE	
ENTRY_POINT	
(reserved)	FLAGS
(reserved)	

Figure 7.4
Change Mode Dispatch Table Entry

Figure 7.4 shows the format of a dispatch table entry. The macro $DISP-DEF defines symbolic names for its fields:

▶ The service routine procedure value field contains the address of the procedure descriptor for the service-specific procedure. The name of a service-specific procedure in an executive image is generally of the form EXE$*service* or RMS$*service.*

▶ The entry point field contains the address of the entry point for the service-specific procedure. Getting this address from the table entry, which would already be in memory cache, is faster than getting it from the procedure descriptor.

▶ The flags field has four flags, whose symbolic names are defined by the $SSDESCRDEF macro:

• SSFLAG_K_WCM, when set, means the service can return the status SS$_WAIT_CALLERS_MODE (see Section 7.5.3).

• SSFLAG_K_WCM_NO_REEXEC, when set, means the service can return the status SS$_WAIT_CALLERS_MODE but should not reexecute the service (see Section 7.5.3).

• SSFLAG_K_CLRREG, when set, means the change mode dispatcher should clear scratch integer registers before returning to the system service requestor. A security-related service sets this flag to ensure that any sensitive information left in scratch registers cannot be passed to the requestor.

• SSFLAG_K_RETURN_ANY, when set, means the service can return arbitrary values in R0, including ones that otherwise would be taken to mean SS$_WAIT_CALLERS_MODE or SS$_QIO_CROCK.

Use of these flags is reserved to kernel mode services.

When an executive image containing one or more system services is loaded, it is assigned a unique change mode number equal to the contents of CMOD$GL_CHMx_LIMIT. The lowest legal change mode number is 1. The dispatch table entry indexed by that change mode number is initialized and CMOD$GL_CHMx_LIMIT is incremented. Section 7.2.2 describes the modifications that are made to the system service transfer routine or its procedure descriptor. Chapter 32 describes the actual image loading and address space assignment.

7.5.2   **Operations of the Change Mode Dispatchers**

Module SYSTEM_SERVICE_DISPATCHER contains the change mode dispatchers: EXE$CMODKRNL for CHMK exceptions and EXE$CMODEXEC
for CHME exceptions. Their operations are almost identical. The following
description applies to both dispatchers, unless otherwise specified:

1. Each dispatcher extracts the access mode from the PS in the exception
   frame and records it in the current PS's software bits as the previous
   mode.
2. It compares the contents of R0, the service-specific change mode number, with those of CMOD$GL_CHMK_LIMIT or CMOD$GL_CHME_
   LIMIT. If the change mode number is equal to or greater than the appropriate limit, the dispatcher checks whether the service is supplied as
   part of a privileged shareable image, as described in Section 7.7.

   If the change mode number is less than the limit, the service procedure
   is part of an executive image.
3. Each dispatcher indexes its dispatch table with the change mode number. Examining the dispatch table entry, the kernel mode dispatcher,
   EXE$CMODKRNL, tests whether SSFLAG_K_WCM is set. (This mech-
   anism is only supported for kernel mode services.) If so, the service can
   return the status SS$_WAIT_CALLERS_MODE with the intent that the
   service reexecute. If the flag is set, EXE$CMODKRNL copies the argu-
   ment information (AI) register and the argument registers (R16 through
   R21) to the kernel stack. Later, EXE$CMODKRNL will be able to restore
   them from the stack if the service returns a status indicating that the
   process should be placed into a wait state.

   Thus, the service can be rerequested after the wait with the same arguments even if the service procedure overwrote those registers. (Because
   no floating-point argument registers are saved, a service that uses this
   mechanism cannot rely on restored floating-point argument registers and
   must refrain from overwriting them.)
4. Each dispatcher tests the low byte of the AI register to determine the
   number of arguments being passed to the system service. If there are
   more than six, the seventh and subsequent arguments are currently on
   the previous mode stack. Each dispatcher executes a CALL_PAL PROBER
   instruction to confirm that the previous mode has read access to the list.
   If not, it dismisses the change mode exception, returning the error status
   SS$_ACCVIO to the system service requestor.

   Each dispatcher copies the seventh and subsequent arguments from
   the outer mode stack to the inner mode stack, where the calling standard
   requires them to be at entry to the service procedure.
5. EXE$CMODKRNL loads the address of the process's process control
   block (PCB) into R4.

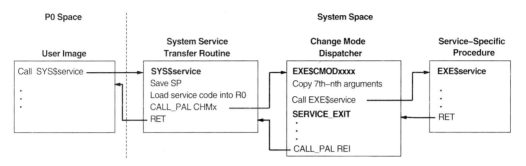

Figure 7.5
Control Flow of System Services That Change Mode

6. Each dispatcher saves the return address (RA) register contents so that later it can return to the system service requestor.
7. Each dispatcher gets the procedure value of the service-specific procedure from the dispatch table entry associated with the change mode number and calls it.

Figure 7.5 illustrates the control flow from the user program to the service-specific procedure. This flow is the same for both kernel and executive access modes.

The first code in each executive image service-specific procedure, apart from compiler-generated prologue code, is code generated by the SYSTEM_SERVICE macro to check that the service has been called with at least the required number of arguments. If not, the code loads the status SS$_INSFARG into R0 and immediately returns to the change mode dispatcher.

7.5.3 Change Mode Dispatcher Common Exit Path

When a service-specific procedure has completed its operation, it loads a status into R0 and returns to the change mode dispatcher at SERVICE_EXIT. SERVICE_EXIT takes the following steps:

1. It tests the status returned in R0. If the status is a success or warning, the routine resets the stack pointer, leaving only the exception frame. If the dispatch table entry for this service indicates that the scratch registers should be cleared, SERVICE_EXIT clears R16 through R25, R27, and R28. It restores the saved RA contents to R26. It executes a CALL_PAL REI instruction, changing access mode to the mode from which the service request was made and transferring control to the RET instruction in the system service transfer routine. Execution of the RET instruction returns control to the address in R26, the instruction following the system service request.

2. If the service-specific procedure returned a status other than SS$_WAIT_CALLERS_MODE or SS$_QIO_CROCK, SERVICE_EXIT continues with step 6.

3. If the service-specific procedure returned one of those statuses, SERVICE_EXIT tests the dispatch table entry to see if this service is permitted to return that status. If not, SERVICE_EXIT also checks whether the service is one permitted to return any error status value. If so, SERVICE_EXIT continues with step 6. (This additional test permits a service such as $CMKRNL to return arbitrary data in R0 instead of a status return.) Otherwise, SERVICE_EXIT generates the fatal bugcheck IVSSRVRQST.

4. If the status returned is SS$_WAIT_CALLERS_MODE, SERVICE_EXIT must cause the process to be taken out of execution. (The service-specific procedure has changed the process's state and placed its PCB in the corresponding wait queue, but the process is, in fact, still current and provides the context in which SERVICE_EXIT executes.) Some system services must be reexecuted after the process's wait ends, whereas others must not. SERVICE_EXIT tests the service's dispatch table entry flag SSFLAG_K_WCM_NO_REEXEC to determine which type this service is.

   - If the flag is clear, the service must be reexecuted, and SERVICE_EXIT restores the argument registers from the kernel stack, leaving only the exception frame on the kernel stack. It subtracts 12 from the PC saved in the exception frame, so that it contains the address of the beginning of the system service transfer routine. The process will wait in the access mode from which the service was requested.

     If the dispatch table entry for this service indicates that the scratch registers should be cleared, SERVICE_EXIT clears R22 through R24, R27, and R28. (The contents of the AI and argument registers are preserved for subsequent system service reexecution.) SERVICE_EXIT invokes SCH$WAIT_ANY_MODE, in module SCHEDULER, to take the process out of execution and select a new one to execute.

     Later, when the process becomes current again, it will reexecute the transfer routine and reenter the change mode dispatcher, which will call the service-specific procedure. The Hibernate ($HIBER) system service, for example, uses this mechanism so that a hibernating process can receive asynchronous system traps (ASTs). Chapter 13 contains details related to process waits, and Chapter 14 describes hibernation.

   - If the flag is set, the service should not reexecute, and SERVICE_EXIT simply invokes SCH$WAIT_ANY_MODE. The process will be placed back into execution at the address following the CALL_PAL CHMK instruction. This mechanism is used only by certain forms of the event flag wait system services.

5. The SS$_QIO_CROCK status is returned only from EXE$QIO, which is the service-specific procedure for the $QIO system service. It returns that status when a direct I/O buffer page must be faulted into the process's working set. So that outer mode ASTs can be delivered to the process during a potential page fault wait, the page fault must occur in the access mode from which the $QIO service was requested.

   SERVICE_EXIT restores the argument registers from the kernel stack, leaving only the exception frame on the kernel stack. It restores the saved RA. It replaces the PC saved in the exception frame with the address of routine FAULTY$TOWERS, in module SYSTEM_SERVICE_DISPATCHER. It executes a `CALL_PAL REI` instruction, transferring control to FAULTY$TOWERS in the access mode from which the $QIO system service was requested.

   FAULTY$TOWERS accesses the direct I/O buffer page, causing a page fault for that page; any resulting page fault wait occurs in the mode of the $QIO system service requestor. Later, after the page fault completes, the SERVICE_EXIT routine jumps to the $QIO system service transfer routine, which causes reentry to the change mode dispatcher.

6. If the status in R0 is an error or a severe error, SERVICE_EXIT checks whether the process owns any mutexes (see Chapter 9). In general, a service-specific procedure should release any mutexes that it has acquired before returning to SERVICE_EXIT. To minimize overhead, SERVICE_EXIT only performs the check for mutexes when a service returns an error or a severe error status.

   - If the process owns a mutex, SERVICE_EXIT tests whether the interrupt priority level (IPL) is 2. If so, the assumption is that one system service has acquired a mutex and then requested another system service, which is returning an error status. In this case, SERVICE_EXIT merely dismisses the exception as described in step 1, returning control to the presumed original service.
   - If the process owns a mutex but is running at IPL 0, SERVICE_EXIT generates a fatal MTXCNTNONZ bugcheck.
   - If the process does not own a mutex, SERVICE_EXIT continues.

7. If system service exceptions are disabled for the access mode in which the system service was requested, SERVICE_EXIT dismisses the CHMx exception as described in step 1.

8. Otherwise, the process has enabled system service exceptions for the access mode in which the service was requested. (Section 7.8.1 describes the means by which a process requests that errors be signaled as software conditions.) Since the exception code must be entered at IPL 0, SERVICE_EXIT explicitly lowers IPL if the process is running in kernel

mode. Executive mode services do not need a similar check because elevated IPL requires kernel mode operation. (Lowering IPL is unnecessary unless the process has enabled system service failure exceptions, because the CALL_PAL REI instruction that dismisses the CHMK exception lowers the IPL.)

9. To signal the system service exception, SERVICE_EXIT transfers control to EXE$SSFAIL, in module EXCEPTION. It signals the condition SS$_SSFAIL to the caller.

Chapter 6 describes condition handling and system service failures.

7.6   SYNCHRONOUS SYSTEM AND RMS SERVICES

Some system services perform their requested function and always return immediately to their requestor. Others, called asynchronous system services, initiate some system activity on behalf of the requestor and return before the activity is complete. To synchronize with completion of the initiated activity, the requestor can wait for an event flag associated with the system service request. A synchronous service initiates the activity, just as its asynchronous counterpart does, but waits for completion of the activity before returning to its requestor.

A synchronous system service is generally named for the asynchronous system service it requests. A trailing "W" in the name of the synchronous service distinguishes the two: $QIO and $QIOW, for example. Many RMS services also have both synchronous and asynchronous forms. The two forms, however, are not distinct services with different names. Instead, an image requests either asynchronous or synchronous return from a particular RMS service through a bit in the file or record stream data structure associated with the request.

An OpenVMS AXP synchronous service is implemented as a mode of caller service that requests the asynchronous service, tests the return status to ensure that the service was initiated, and then waits for the activity initiated by the service to complete. The process waits in the access mode from which it requested the system service. The sections that follow describe both synchronous system services and synchronous returns from RMS services. Although their implementations differ slightly in structure, they are similar in purpose and algorithm.

7.6.1   Synchronous System Services

An OpenVMS VAX synchronous system service is an inner mode service whose system service vector potentially requests multiple system services—the asynchronous form of the service and, minimally, a wait service. OpenVMS AXP system service transfer routines are more limited, and the method used to construct a synchronous OpenVMS VAX system service at service load time is not viable.

Example 7.1
MACRO-32 Code for the $QIOW System Service

```
EXE$QIOW::
        MOVL    QIO$_EFN(AP),R7     ;Save event flag number for $SYNCH
        MOVL    QIO$_IOSB(AP),R8    ;Save IOSB address, if specified,
                                    ; for $SYNCH
        ASSUME  QIO$_NARGS EQ 12    ;Push arguments on stack for $QIO
        PUSHL   QIO$_P6(AP)
          .
          .
          .
        PUSHL   QIO$_CHAN(AP)
        PUSHL   R7                  ;Event flag number
        CALLS   #QIO$_NARGS,SYS$QIO
                                    ;Request the $QIO system service
        BLBC    R0,1000$            ;Branch if error queuing request
        BSBW    EXE$SYNCH_LOOP      ;Invoke $SYNCH internal routine
1000$:
        RET                         ;Return to caller
```

Instead, an OpenVMS AXP synchronous system service is implemented as a mode of caller service that performs the same steps as its OpenVMS VAX counterpart:

1. It requests the asynchronous form of the service.
2. If the asynchronous service returns an error status, the synchronous service returns the error immediately to the service requestor.
3. Otherwise, it branches to a synchronization routine that waits the process in the mode of the system service requestor.

To guarantee completion of a synchronous system service request, the service requestor must specify both an event flag and a status block (I/O status block or lock status block). The asynchronous service-specific procedure clears the event flag and status block associated with the request. The synchronization routine tests the combination of event flag and status block for request completion, placing the process into event flag wait if the request is not complete.

Testing the combination prevents a premature return to the synchronous service requestor as the result of concurrent uses of the same event flag. If the service requestor omits the optional status block, the mechanism reverts to being a simple wait for event flag. The mechanism is requested explicitly as the Synchronize ($SYNCH) system service and implicitly as part of each synchronous system service. Table 7.1 lists the synchronous system services.

The MACRO-32 code for the synchronous service $QIOW is shown in Example 7.1 in a slightly simplified form.

Figure 7.6 illustrates the control flow from a user image, through a service-specific procedure, to the synchronization routine.

The $SYNCH system service procedure, EXE$SYNCH in module SYS-SYNCH, executes in the mode of its requestor. It is typically requested with

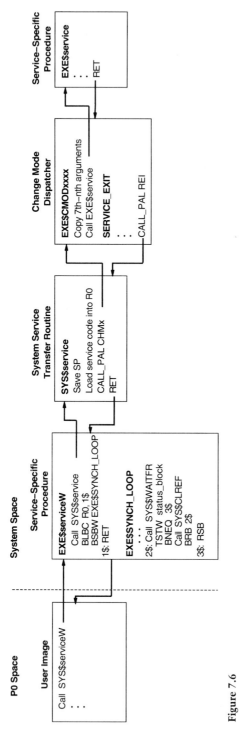

Figure 7.6
Control Flow of Synchronous Services

the number of an event flag and the address of a status block. It simply invokes the routine EXE$SYNCH_LOOP, the same routine invoked by synchronous system services such as $QIOW and $ENQW.

EXE$SYNCH_LOOP takes the following steps to determine whether the requested operation is complete:

1. It first tests whether a status block was specified by the requestor. For $GETLKIW and $ENQW, the lock status block serves this purpose; in all other cases, an I/O status block is used.

   If no status block was specified, EXE$SYNCH_LOOP requests the Wait for Single Event Flag ($WAITFR) system service to place the process into an event flag wait state until the specified flag is set. When the flag is set, the process is taken out of its wait state, and EXE$SYNCH_LOOP returns to its invoker, either EXE$SYNCH or a synchronous system service.

2. If a status block was specified, EXE$SYNCH_LOOP tests the status word of the status block. A nonzero status indicates that the asynchronous service has completed, and EXE$SYNCH_LOOP returns to its invoker. Note that if the status block is being used concurrently for multiple requests, one or both of the requested services can complete prematurely; the $SYNCH service assumes that nonzero contents imply asynchronous service completion and does not test whether the event flag is set.

   A zero status indicates that the asynchronous service has not yet completed.

3. EXE$SYNCH_LOOP requests the $WAITFR system service to wait for the specified event flag.

4. Later, when the event flag is set and the process is placed into execution, EXE$SYNCH_LOOP tests the low word of the status block. If it is nonzero, EXE$SYNCH_LOOP returns to its invoker.

5. If the low word of the status block is zero, then the flag has been set spuriously, perhaps by another concurrent use. EXE$SYNCH_LOOP requests the Clear Event Flag ($CLREF) system service to clear the flag and retests the low word of the status block in case the request has completed in the meantime. If the word contents are nonzero, EXE$SYNCH_LOOP requests the Set Event Flag ($SETEF) system service to set the flag that it just cleared and returns to its invoker.

   If the status is still zero, EXE$SYNCH_LOOP proceeds with step 3.

A crucial point in this implementation is that the process waits at the access mode associated with the original synchronous system service request, thus allowing AST delivery to all access modes at least as privileged as that of the synchronous service request. In the usual case where a synchronous system service is requested from user mode, an AST of any access mode can be delivered while the process is waiting for the service to complete.

7.6.2   **Synchronous Returns from RMS Services**

Often, an RMS service-specific procedure cannot complete an RMS operation until the completion of an I/O or lock request it has made. When an image requests such an RMS service, it can specify that the service procedure not return until the RMS operation is complete. Alternatively, the image can specify that the service return after the I/O or lock request is initiated so that the image can continue execution. Table 7.1 lists the RMS services that can perform synchronous returns.

By setting the asynchronous (ASY) bit in the file access block (FAB) or record access block (RAB), an image indicates that the service should return even though the RMS operation is not complete. When the image can no longer execute without the RMS operation's having been completed, the image requests the $WAIT RMS service. By default, the ASY bit is clear, and an image requests a synchronous return from an RMS service.

This section describes the mechanism by which an RMS service-specific procedure waits for completion of an I/O or lock request when the ASY bit in the FAB or RAB is clear. It also describes the $WAIT service.

7.6.2.1   **RMS Synchronization.** When the OpenVMS VAX change mode dispatcher REIs after dispatching an RMS service that may have to wait, it returns to a stall routine rather than to the RMS service vector. That is, the exception PC has been overwritten with the address of a stall routine.

Because OpenVMS AXP requires nested calls and returns, this method is not viable. Instead, each RMS service that may need to stall the process is implemented as a mode of caller service. The mode of caller service requests an executive mode RMS service. When the mode of caller service returns, it invokes a synchronization routine if a stall is necessary. Although a detailed description of the implementation of RMS services is beyond the scope of this book, the following example illustrates what happens when a process requests an RMS operation and must wait for its completion.

1. RMS$READ in module [RMS]RMS0SERVICES, the $READ service procedure, is a mode of caller service that requests the executive mode service $RMS_READ.
2. RMS$RMS_READ in module [RMS]RMS0BLKIO, the $RMS_READ procedure, requests the $QIO system service on behalf of its caller. It specifies the number of an event flag to be set (one of the flags permanently allocated to RMS) and the address of an executive mode AST procedure to be executed when the I/O operation completes. The AST procedure it specifies is RM$STALLAST, in module [RMS]RM0THDMGR.

    After the $QIO system service returns, the RMS procedure calls RM$STALL, in module [RMS]RM0THDMGR. RM$STALL tests the ASY bit in the FAB or RAB associated with the request. If the bit is clear, RM$STALL saves the state and context of this RMS request in an RMS data structure and returns to the change mode dispatcher with the status RMS$_STALL and the number of the associated event flag.

3. The change mode dispatcher dismisses the CHME exception and returns to the mode of caller RMS service procedure, in this example, RMS$READ.

4. The mode of caller service procedure tests the return status. If the status is anything other than RMS$_STALL, it returns to its caller.

   If the status is RMS$_STALL, it invokes WAIT_IO_DONE, in module [RMS]RMS0SERVICES, to place the process into a wait for the event flag associated with the $QIO request.

5. Executing in the caller's mode, WAIT_IO_DONE sets a "busy" bit in the FAB or RAB associated with the request to ensure that another request cannot lead to the structure's reuse before the wait is over. It then takes steps that parallel those listed for EXE$SYNCH_LOOP in Section 7.6.1. The main difference is that the status tested is in the FAB or RAB associated with the RMS operation.

6. When the I/O request completes, the associated event flag is set and RM$STALLAST is entered. It restores the saved state and context of the RMS request and reenters the original RMS executive mode procedure, in this example, RMS$RMS_READ.

7. RMS$RMS_READ continues execution from the point at which it invoked RM$STALL. If it determines that the RMS operation is not complete, it requests the next service and stalls using the technique just described.

   Otherwise, if the RMS operation is complete, RMS$RMS_READ calls RM$EXRMS, in module [RMS]RM0EXTRMS, to set the final status in the associated FAB or RAB and to exit from the executive mode AST procedure.

8. AST exit code returns control to WAIT_IO_DONE, whose event flag wait is now over. Executing in the requestor's access mode, WAIT_IO_DONE checks whether the RAB or FAB status field is zero. If so, it again places the requestor into an event flag wait state. In other words, a nonzero value in the status field of the FAB or RAB is the actual indication that the RMS operation is complete.

   When the status field indicates successful completion or a warning, WAIT_IO_DONE returns to the mode of caller service. Otherwise, when WAIT_IO_DONE discovers an error or the status field indicates an error, it performs the error processing described in Section 7.6.2.3.

A crucial point in this implementation is that the requestor waits at the access mode associated with the original RMS service request and not in executive mode, thus allowing AST delivery to all access modes at least as privileged as that of the service request. In the usual case where an RMS service is requested from user mode, an AST of any access mode can be delivered while the process is waiting for the RMS operation to complete.

7.6.2.2   **$WAIT Service.** An image requests the $WAIT service to synchronize with completion of an outstanding RMS operation that was requested with an asynchronous return. The service has one argument, the address of the FAB or RAB associated with the outstanding RMS request.

The $WAIT procedure, RMS$WAIT in module [RMS]RMS0SERVICES, executes in the mode of its caller. If, through its actions, the process is placed in a wait state, the process will be able to receive ASTs for its current mode and inner modes. RMS$WAIT requests the executive mode service $RMS_WAIT, passing it the associated structure address.

The $RMS_WAIT service-specific procedure, RMS$RMS_WAIT, in module [RMS]RMS0WAIT, performs several sanity checks on the RMS structure and tests whether the related RMS operation is actually complete. If it is, RMS$RMS_WAIT returns the status of the operation to RMS$WAIT. If not, it clears the event flag associated with the request and returns the status RMS$_STALL to RMS$WAIT along with a flag indicating how the process should be stalled.

If R0 contains the status RMS$_STALL, RMS$WAIT stalls process execution until an asynchronous RMS operation completes. An action flag argument returned by the $RMS_WAIT service determines the method used to decide whether the operation is complete. If the action flag is clear, the completion of the RMS operation is indicated by the status field in the RAB, so RMS$WAIT invokes WAIT_IO_DONE to stall in the normal manner. Otherwise, RMS$WAIT alone cannot determine completion of the operation. It requests the $WAITFR system service to wait for the event flag specified by the $RMS_WAIT service procedure. When the event flag is set, RMS$WAIT rerequests the $RMS_WAIT service to allow it to decide whether the operation is complete.

7.6.2.3   **RMS Error Detection.** WAIT_IO_DONE, executing as part of the mode of caller RMS service procedure, reports an error or a severe error by requesting the executive mode RMS service $SSVEXC. The service has one argument, an error status.

Running in executive mode, RMS$SSVEXC in module [RMS]RMS0-SERVICES, the $SSVEXC service procedure, simply returns to the change mode dispatcher, passing its one argument as return status.

The change mode dispatcher, whose actions are described in Sections 7.5.2 and 7.5.3, can signal the error as a software condition or simply return it to the image. (Section 7.8.1 describes the means by which a process requests that errors be signaled as software conditions.) The reason for this somewhat roundabout way of returning the error is that it can be signaled as a system service failure software condition only from an inner access mode.

7.7   **SYSTEM SERVICES IN PRIVILEGED SHAREABLE IMAGES**

Not all system services are part of an executive image. A user can write system services as part of a privileged shareable image. Moreover, a number of OpenVMS system services are supplied in privileged shareable images, including the following:

▸ $MOUNT, in SYS$SHARE:MOUNTSHR.EXE

▸ $DISMOU, in SYS$SHARE:DISMNTSHR.EXE

▸ Services relating to system security, in SYS$SHARE:SECURESHR.EXE and SYS$SHARE:SECURESHRP.EXE

▸ Services for pseudo terminal support, in SYS$SHARE:PTD$SERVICES_ SHR.EXE

Implementing these less frequently used services as privileged shareable images means that they are resident only when explicitly requested and are mapped in process-private space rather than system space. Thus, they page in process working sets rather than in the system working set. Note, however, that if the system manager installs a privileged shareable image as a resident library, it is permanently resident and mapped in system space.

This section examines how control is passed to a system service that is part of a privileged shareable image. The *OpenVMS Programming Concepts* manual and the *OpenVMS Linker Utility Manual* describe how privileged shareable images are created.

Dispatching to system services in privileged shareable images resembles dispatching to system services in executive images. The basic steps are as follows:

1. An image calls a transfer routine associated with a system service within a privileged shareable image.
2. The transfer routine loads a change mode number into R0 and executes a `CALL_PAL CHMx` instruction.
3. The change mode dispatcher attempts to dispatch to a privileged shareable image whenever R0 contains a value outside the range of those for services in executive images.
4. The change mode dispatcher searches a P1 space data structure to determine which privileged shareable image implements that system service.
5. It then indexes a dispatch table in the privileged shareable image to get the procedure value of the associated service-specific procedure and calls it.

The OpenVMS AXP implementation of privileged shareable images differs from that of OpenVMS VAX in the following ways:

▸ The instructions that make up the system service transfer routines associated with an OpenVMS AXP privileged shareable image are written by the image activator rather than by the user.

▸ An OpenVMS AXP privileged shareable image contains a user-written dispatch table, called a privileged library vector, rather than a dispatching routine.

▸ OpenVMS AXP change mode numbers are assigned dynamically by the

TYPE = PLV$C_TYP_CMOD
(reserved)
KERNEL_ROUTINE_COUNT
EXEC_ROUTINE_COUNT
KERNEL_ROUTINE_LIST
EXEC_ROUTINE_LIST
KERNEL_RUNDOWN_HANDLER
EXEC_RUNDOWN_HANDLER
RMS_DISPATCHER
KERNEL_ROUTINE_FLAGS
EXEC_ROUTINE_FLAGS

Figure 7.7
Layout of a Privileged Library Vector (PLV)

image activator as a privileged shareable image is activated rather than determined by values specified in the image source.

A change mode number for a system service in a privileged shareable image serves only to connect the system service transfer routine's name with a particular dispatch table entry. Change mode numbers in one activated privileged shareable image are independent from those in another and therefore need not be unique within a process. Ambiguity of change mode number values from one privileged shareable image to the next is not a problem, as it is for OpenVMS VAX privileged shareable images.

7.7.1   **Data Structures Related to Privileged Shareable Images**

A privileged shareable image is an image that contains one or more kernel and executive mode system services. Each such privileged shareable image contains a data structure called a privileged library vector (PLV). The macro $PLVDEF defines symbolic offsets for this structure. The programmer codes the PLV to describe the services within the image and constructs tables containing the addresses of the service-specific procedures. The PLV must be the only contribution to a program section defined with the VEC attribute. Figure 7.7 shows the layout of a PLV.

PLV$L_TYPE identifies the PLV as one that describes inner access mode routines rather than, for example, a message vector. Chapter 39 describes the layout and use of message vector PLVs. This section describes the fields in this type of PLV that are related to system services in a privileged shareable image; Chapter 28 discusses rundown routines.

PLV$L_KERNEL_ROUTINE_COUNT contains the number of kernel

mode services in the privileged shareable image, and PLV$L_EXEC_ROU-TINE_COUNT, the number of executive mode system services. PLV$PS_KERNEL_ROUTINE_LIST and PLV$PS_EXEC_ROUTINE_LIST each point to an array of addresses of service-specific procedure descriptors.

PLV$PS_KERNEL_ROUTINE_FLAGS contains zero or the address of an array of quadwords containing the defined flags associated with each kernel system service. Currently, only two flags are defined, PLV$V_WAIT_CALLERS_MODE and PLV$V_WAIT_CALLERS_NO_REEXEC. When either is set, it means that the kernel mode service may return the status SS$_WAIT_CALLERS_MODE. As described in Section 7.5.1, the two flags differ in specifying whether the system service should be reexecuted after the process's wait ends. Section 7.5.3 describes the change mode dispatcher's reaction to this status. Because there are no defined flags for executive mode, PLV$PS_EXEC_ROUTINE_FLAGS should always contain zero.

Figure 7.8 shows the relations among some of the parts of a privileged shareable image with two kernel mode system services. PLV$PS_KERNEL_ROUTINE_LIST points to the array of kernel service-specific procedure values. Because neither of the services returns SS$_WAIT_CALLERS_MODE, there is no need for a flags table, and PLV$PS_KERNEL_ROUTINE_FLAGS contains zero. Each procedure descriptor contains the address of the code entry point for its service.

After creating one or more modules containing system services and a PLV, the programmer links them to create a privileged shareable image. A privileged shareable image must be linked with the /SHAREABLE qualifier; its image sections that contain inner mode code and data must be protected, through use of either the PROTECT option or the /PROTECT qualifier. In addition, it must be linked with the SYMBOL_VECTOR option to force the creation of a symbol vector. The option must specify all global symbols that are to be universal. In particular, it must identify each system service. Each system service must be identified in that option as a procedure.

The format of the SYMBOL_VECTOR option, for example, to describe the procedures in the example of Figure 7.8 is as follows:

```
SYMBOL_VECTOR = (-
             K_RTN1_EXT/K_RTN1_INT = PROCEDURE,-
             K_RTN2_EXT/K_RTN2_INT = PROCEDURE)
```

In this example, each procedure is identified by both an externally visible name, which is the universal alias name, and the internal name of the service-specific procedure. Code within the privileged shareable image can call the procedure through its internal name or its external name. It must use the external name if the transfer routine must be executed to change access mode. Otherwise, if no access mode change is required, the internal name may be used for a more direct transfer of control.

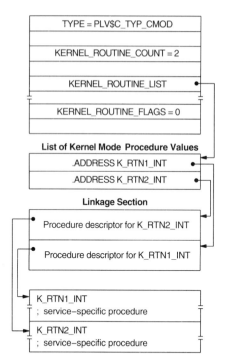

Figure 7.8
Privileged Shareable Image

The shareable image must be installed with the qualifiers /PROTECTED and /SHARED.

An executable image can be linked with multiple privileged shareable images. A compound data structure called the activated privileged library dispatch vector contains information about the privileged shareable images that are active in the process. Figure 7.9 shows some of the fields in this data structure, whose starting address is contained in P1 space location CTL$A_DISPVEC. The macro $APLDDEF defines symbolic offsets for fields in this structure.

The structure includes two tables, one for executive mode and one for kernel mode. The executive mode table begins at offset APLD$R_EXEC_APLD_VECTOR, and the kernel mode, at offset APLD$R_KERN_APLD_VECTOR. When a privileged shareable image is activated that contains inner mode system services, a substructure called an activated privileged library dispatch vector entry (APLD) is initialized in the executive or kernel mode table. If the image contains both executive and kernel mode services, an APLD is initialized in both tables. Each table can accommodate up to 42 APLDs. The image activator initializes an APLD from information in the PLV of the privileged shareable image being activated.

An individual APLD describes the set of executive mode or kernel mode system services within one activated privileged shareable image. APLD$PS_

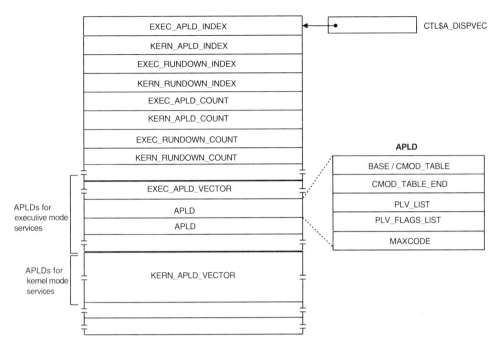

Figure 7.9
Layout of an Activated Privileged Library Dispatch Vector

CMOD_TABLE contains the address of the beginning of the system service transfer routines associated with the image, and APLD$PS_CMOD_TABLE_END contains the address of the end of the transfer routines. If this APLD describes executive mode services, APLD$PS_PLV_LIST contains the address of the list of executive mode service-specific procedures; otherwise, it contains the address of the list of kernel mode service-specific procedures. APLD$PS_PLV_FLAGS_LIST contains the address of the flags quadwords for the services. APLD$L_MAXCODE contains the value of the highest change mode number assigned to a service of that particular mode.

APLD$L_EXEC_APLD_INDEX contains the number of executive mode APLDs that have been initialized, and APLD$L_KERN_APLD_INDEX, the number of kernel mode APLDs. As the image activator performs fixup and relocation on a privileged shareable image, it increments APLD$L_EXEC_APLD_COUNT, APLD$L_KERN_APLD_COUNT, or both.

The structure also describes rundown routines and message vectors associated with activated privileged shareable images. Chapter 28 describes the image activator and the use of rundown routines, and Chapter 39, the use of message vectors.

When a user runs an executable image that has been linked with a privileged shareable image like the one shown in Figure 7.8, the image activator activates both images. The presence of the VEC image section in the

169

privileged shareable image causes the image activator to perform additional processing for the privileged shareable image.

The image activator takes the following additional steps:

1. It initializes an APLD in the kernel mode table in the activated privileged library dispatch vector, copying information from the PLV to the APLD.

2. It allocates additional P0 space to build a system service transfer routine and procedure descriptor for each system service in the privileged shareable image and stores the low and high addresses of the transfer routines in APLD$PS_CMOD_TABLE and APLD$PS_CMOD_TABLE_END.

   The transfer routine for each system service resembles those discussed in Section 7.2.3. One key difference is that the image activator rather than EXE$CONNECT_SERVICES assigns the change mode number. The image activator assigns the number 65,536 * 1 (equal to 1 in the high-order word of a longword) to the first kernel mode service and the first executive mode service in each privileged shareable image it activates. The next number in the sequence is 65,536 * 2. The sequence continues with increasing multiples of 65,536.

   The other key difference between this transfer routine and those previously discussed is the instruction that loads the change mode number into R0. A multiple n of 65,536 is the integer n shifted into the high-order word of the longword; such a number can be loaded into R0 with the instruction LDAH R0,n(R31). Thus, system service transfer routines are the same length whether the service is part of an executive image or a privileged shareable image.

3. The image activator searches the privileged shareable image's symbol vector to locate each linkage pair that contains one of the procedure values in APLD$PS_PLV_LIST. It modifies the linkage pair so that it describes the procedure descriptor and code entry point addresses of the corresponding system service transfer routine.

4. It establishes a more restrictive protection, user read and executive write (UREW), on protected image section pages, namely, the pages that contain the privileged shareable image, its system service transfer routines, and their procedure descriptors.

Figure 7.10 shows the activated form of the privileged shareable image of Figure 7.8. Chapter 28 contains details on image activation.

7.7.2   Dispatching to System Services in a Privileged Shareable Image

When an image requesting a system service in a privileged shareable image is activated, the image activator updates its linkage pair that represents the service procedure with information from the shareable image's symbol vector.

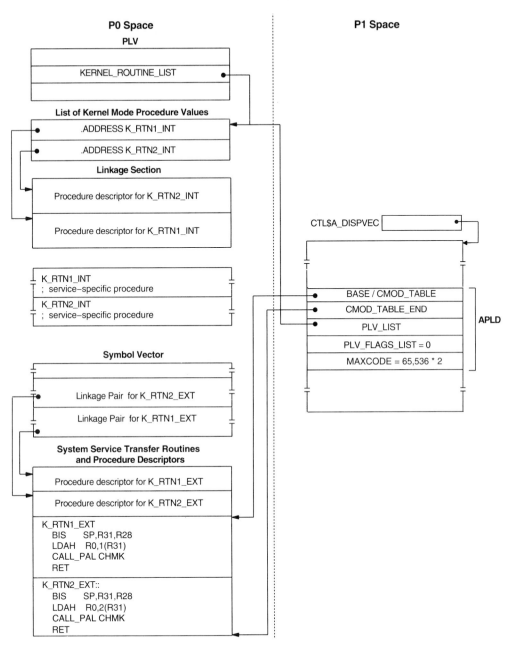

Figure 7.10
Activated Privileged Shareable Image

The linkage pair is updated to contain the addresses of the transfer routine code entry and procedure descriptor.

When the image calls the procedure, it transfers control to the corresponding system service transfer routine, which loads the corresponding change mode number into R0 and executes a CALL_PAL CHMx instruction. Executing that instruction causes an exception, which is dispatched to the appropriate change mode dispatcher. The PC saved in the exception frame is an address within the system service transfer routine.

For any CHMK or CHME exception, each change mode dispatcher performs some initial operations, such as checking the accessibility of arguments in memory, and, for kernel mode system services, storing the PCB address in R4 (see Section 7.5.2). When a change mode dispatcher detects that the change mode number is equal to or greater than the value in CMOD$GL_CHMx_LIMIT, it tries to dispatch to a system service in a privileged shareable image. The following description applies to both the executive and kernel mode dispatchers unless otherwise noted.

1. The change mode dispatcher checks that the change mode number is 65,536 or larger, returning the error status SS$_ILLSER if not.

2. From the exception frame on the stack, it gets the PC, the address of the instruction following the CALL_PAL CHMx instruction in the system service transfer routine.

3. It examines the initialized APLDs in either the executive or kernel mode part of the process's activated privileged library dispatch vector. It scans until it reaches the end or finds one whose set of system service transfer routines contains the address of the change mode instruction that triggered this exception. APLD$PS_CMOD_TABLE and APLD$PS_CMOD_TABLE_END point to the low- and high-address ends of these transfer routines.

   If it reaches the end without finding such an APLD, the change mode dispatcher returns the error status SS$_ILLSER.

4. If the change mode dispatcher finds an APLD whose transfer routines contain the exception PC, it compares the change mode number to the contents of APLD$L_MAXCODE. If the change mode number is larger, the dispatcher returns the error status SS$_ILLSER.

5. It transforms the change mode number into a number suitable for use as a longword index into the list of procedure descriptors in the PLV. This requires the combination of shifting it 14 bits to the right (to divide by 65,536 and then to multiply by 4) and then subtracting 4, since the list of procedure descriptors is zero-based.

6. The kernel mode dispatcher indexes into the PLV flags table, pointed to by APLD$PS_PLV_FLAGS_LIST, to test whether this service can return SS$_WAIT_CALLERS_MODE. If so, it copies the AI and argument registers (up through the first six arguments) to the kernel stack. Each

dispatcher performs the same argument list processing that it does for a system service in an executive image. Section 7.5.2 describes processing of the argument list.

7. The change mode dispatcher indexes into the PLV list of procedure values, pointed to by APLD$PS_PLV_LIST, to get the address of the procedure descriptor for this service.

8. The kernel mode dispatcher loads the address of the process's PCB into R4.

9. The change mode dispatcher calls the service-specific procedure.

10. When the service-specific procedure returns, the change mode dispatcher jumps to SERVICE_EXIT.

7.8 **RELATED SYSTEM SERVICES**

Several system services are closely related to system service dispatching and the change mode instructions. Chapter 6 describes the Declare Change Mode Handler ($DCLCMH) system service. This section describes the Set System Service Failure Exception Mode ($SETSFM) system service, the change mode system services, and the Set System Service Filter ($SETSSF) system service.

7.8.1 **$SETSFM System Service**

The $SETSFM system service enables or disables the signaling of errors and severe errors returned by an inner mode service-specific procedure. (A mode of caller service always simply returns to its requestor.) By default, an error or severe status is merely returned to the system service requestor in R0. If system service failure exception mode is enabled, SERVICE_EXIT instead signals an error or severe error as a software condition. The condition is signaled in the mode from which the system service was requested. Chapter 6 contains more details on condition signaling and handling.

   System service failure exception mode is controlled by four bits, one for each access mode, in PCB$L_STS. The bits begin at bit position PCB$V_SSFEXC. A bit, when set, enables signaling of an error or severe error. By default, all four bits are clear.

   The $SETSFM procedure, EXE$SETSFM in module SYSSETMOD, simply sets or clears the bit in PCB$L_STS corresponding to the access mode from which the system service was requested and returns the status SS$_WASSET or SS$_WASCLR to describe the previous state of the bit.

7.8.2 **Change Mode System Services**

The Change to Kernel Mode ($CMKRNL) and Change to Executive Mode ($CMEXEC) system services provide a simple path for privileged processes to execute code in kernel or executive mode. Their service-specific procedures are EXE$CMKRNL, which runs in kernel mode, and EXE$CMEXEC, which runs in executive mode, both in module SYSCHGMOD. Each procedure checks that the process has the necessary privilege (CMKRNL or CMEXEC) and, if not, returns the status SS$_NOPRIV. Note that if $CMKRNL is requested from executive mode, no privilege check is made.

Each of these system services has one required argument, the address of a user-specified procedure, and one optional argument, the address of a list of arguments for that procedure. If the second argument is nonzero, it must be the address of an argument list that begins with an argument count. (Note that this interpretation of the second argument is more strict than the OpenVMS VAX interpretation.) EXE$CMKRNL and EXE$CMEXEC call the user-specified procedure, which must load a status into R0 before returning. EXE$CMKRNL and EXE$CMEXEC return R0 unchanged to the change mode dispatcher, which uses its contents to determine whether an error occurred.

When the user-specified procedure returns, the system service procedure returns to SERVICE_EXIT. Section 7.5.3 describes the actions taken by the change mode dispatcher when control returns to it.

7.8.3 System Service Filtering

Some applications (especially user-written command language interpreters) require that images running in user mode have no direct access to system and RMS services. A mechanism is provided whereby code running in an inner mode can prevent user mode code in that process from directly requesting certain services. The mechanism is known as system service filtering. It includes alternative system service dispatchers, a SYSGEN parameter to enable system service filtering systemwide, and the system service $SETSSF to enable filtering of a particular process's user mode system service requests.

Each OpenVMS AXP system service in an executive image specifies an inhibit mask at compile time as a parameter to the SYSTEM_SERVICE macro. The inhibit mask indicates whether execution of the system service can be blocked by the $SETSSF system service. If the service can be blocked, the mask also indicates the system service filter groups for which the service is blocked. Group 0 specifies all services except $EXIT; group 1 specifies most services, with the exception of $EXIT and those services required for condition handling or image rundown. The *OpenVMS System Services Reference Manual* lists the services that are not blocked by $SETSSF.

The mask is stored in the system service descriptor block for the service. As a service is loaded, its inhibit mask is copied from its descriptor block into one of two tables, depending on the mode of the service. CMOD$AB_KERNEL_INHIBIT_MASK is the table for kernel mode services, and CMOD$AB_EXEC_INHIBIT_MASK for executive mode. Each table is indexed by change mode number; for example, the kernel mode system service assigned change mode number x stores its inhibit mask at offset x from the address in CMOD$AB_KERNEL_INHIBIT_MASK.

The byte at offset CTL$GB_SSFILTER in the per-process control region contains the system service filter mask for a particular process. Usually this mask contains the value zero. The $SETSSF system service procedure, EXE$SETSSF in module SYSSETSSF, confirms that it was requested from a mode other than user and, if not, returns the error status SS$_NOPRIV. Otherwise, it writes the mask value specified as its argument into CTL$GB_SSFILTER.

The bit EXE$V_SSINHIBIT at global location EXE$GL_DEFFLAGS corresponds to the SYSGEN parameter SSINHIBIT, which, when set, enables system service filtering. If system initialization code discovers that the inhibit bit is set, it loads the SCB entries for CHME and CHMK exceptions with the addresses of the alternative dispatchers EXE$CMODEXECX and EXE$CMODKRNLX, in module SYSTEM_SERVICE_DISPATCHER.

The processor dispatches to these alternative change mode dispatchers when CHME and CHMK exceptions occur. They branch to the standard change mode dispatchers for CALL_PAL CHMx instructions executed in inner modes. However, for a CALL_PAL CHMx instruction executed in user mode, the alternative dispatcher ANDs the value in CTL$GB_SSFILTER with the value in the appropriate system service filter table (CMOD$AB_EXEC_INHIBIT_MASK or CMOD$AB_KERNEL_INHIBIT_MASK) entry indexed by the CHMx number. If the result of the AND is zero, the dispatcher branches to the standard change mode dispatcher. If the result of the AND is nonzero, the dispatcher returns the error status SS$_INHCHME or SS$_INHCHMK, depending on the mode of the system service.

If CTL$GB_SSFILTER is nonzero, the dispatcher also denies access to services in privileged shareable images. An attempt to request those services results in the error SS$_INHCHME or SS$_INHCHMK, depending on the mode of the service.

7.9   RELEVANT SOURCE MODULES

Source modules described in this chapter include

[LIB]APLDDEF.SDL
[LIB]PLVDEF.SDL
[LIB]VECTORS.SDL
[RMS]RMS0SERVICES.B32
[SYS]CHANGE_MODE_DATA.MAR
[SYS]SYSCHGMOD.MAR
[SYS]SYSSETMOD.MAR
[SYS]SYSSETSSF.MAR
[SYS]SYSSYNCH.MAR
[SYS]SYSTEM_SERVICES.M64
[SYS]SYSTEM_SERVICE_DISPATCHER.M64

8 ASTs

What you want, what you're hanging around in the world
waiting for, is for something to occur to you.
Robert Frost

An asynchronous system trap (AST) is a mechanism that enables an asynchronous event to trigger a change in the control flow within a process. Specifically, as soon as possible after the asynchronous event occurs, a procedure or routine designated by either the process or the system executes in the context of the process.

A process can request an AST as notification that an asynchronous system service has completed. ASTs requested by the system result from operations such as I/O postprocessing, process suspension, and process deletion. These require that executive code execute in the context of a specific process. ASTs fulfill this need.

When the asynchronous event occurs, the executive inserts an AST control block (ACB) that describes the AST on a process-specific queue. The process eventually becomes current, and an AST delivery interrupt is triggered. Executing in the context of that process, an AST delivery interrupt service routine removes the ACB from the queue and dispatches into the AST procedure it describes.

This chapter discusses the architectural support for ASTs and the Open-VMS AXP implementation of ASTs, in particular the queuing of ACBs and delivery of ASTs. Based on the OpenVMS VAX implementation of ASTs, the OpenVMS AXP implementation preserves documented external interfaces. The chapter also describes AST-related system services and some examples of the executive's use of ASTs.

8.1 CHARACTERISTICS OF ASTS

An AST is ranked by its access mode, the mode in which the AST procedure executes. In general, within a process, inner access mode activity is higher priority than outer access mode activity. For ASTs in particular, delivery of an inner mode AST is more important than delivery of an outer mode AST. Moreover, an inner access mode thread of execution is never interrupted for delivery of an AST to a less privileged mode.

Within an access mode, ASTs are serialized. The first queued is the first delivered. Only one AST of a particular access mode is active at one time; the executive does not interrupt an AST thread to deliver another AST to the same mode. This serialization limits the number of concurrent threads of execution within a process and helps ensure that AST procedures are not

176

entered recursively, thus simplifying synchronization among the different threads in an access mode.

Running in a particular access mode, a process can enable or disable AST delivery to that mode. Temporarily disabling AST delivery enables a non-AST thread of execution to synchronize access to a data structure shared with an AST thread by blocking AST execution. The concept of AST re-entrancy and ways of achieving it are described in the *Guide to Creating OpenVMS Modular Procedures*.

Kernel mode ASTs are further divided into normal and special. A special kernel mode AST is one requested by the system, and its execution is considered more critical than the execution of a normal kernel mode AST. Thus, its delivery cannot be disabled, although its delivery can be blocked temporarily while the process executes at interrupt priority level (IPL) 2 or above.

8.2 ARCHITECTURAL SUPPORT FOR ASTS

Alpha AXP hardware and privileged architecture library (PALcode) instructions and routines assist the executive in the queuing and delivery of ASTs by providing the following:

▶ The AST summary (ASTSR) and AST enable (ASTEN) processor registers, and their save areas in the hardware privileged context block (HWPCB)

▶ The AST enable (CALL_PAL SWASTEN) instruction

▶ Support in several PALcode routines to detect that an AST interrupt should be requested

▶ The four IPL 2 AST interrupts, whose service routines are described in Section 8.7.1

The hardware context of an Alpha AXP process includes four AST summary bits in the ASTSR processor register and four AST enable bits in the ASTEN processor register. Each register has a bit for each access mode; the lowest order bit corresponds to kernel mode. The registers have a combined save area in the HWPCB, at field PHD$Q_ASTSR_ASTEN. The SWPCTX PALcode routine stores these registers in the HWPCB of the process being taken out of execution and loads them from the HWPCB of the process being placed into execution. Chapter 13 contains more information on the HWPCB and swapping of process context.

The ASTSR register summarizes the state of the process's AST queues. An AST summary bit, when set, means that at least one AST at that mode is pending; a pending AST is an ACB representing a particular AST queued to the process. Running in kernel mode, the executive can read and modify the process's summary bits through the CALL_PAL MFPR_ASTSR and CALL_PAL MTPR_ASTSR instructions.

An AST enable bit, when set, means that AST delivery to that access mode is enabled. When a process is created, all four bits are set to enable delivery to all modes. A process can set or clear the enable bit for the current mode by executing the CALL_PAL SWASTEN instruction. Section 8.4 provides more details on enabling and disabling AST delivery. Running in kernel mode, the executive can read and modify the process's enable bits through the CALL_PAL MFPR_ASTEN and CALL_PAL MTPR_ASTEN instructions. The executive executes the CALL_PAL MTPR_ASTEN instruction when an image is run down, to enable AST delivery to the mode of the rundown and less privileged modes. Chapter 28 describes image rundown.

An AST interrupt is requested for a particular access mode when all the following conditions are true:

▶ The bit corresponding to the mode is set in the ASTSR register, indicating that an AST of that mode is pending.

▶ The bit corresponding to the mode is set in the ASTEN register, indicating that AST delivery to that mode is enabled.

▶ The process is executing in a mode equal to or less privileged than that of the pending AST.

▶ IPL is less than 2.

AST interrupt requests are triggered by the PALcode routines that implement instructions altering one or more of these conditions. These instructions are CALL_PAL REI (decreasing access mode and IPL), CALL_PAL MTPR_IPL (decreasing IPL), CALL_PAL SWASTEN (enabling AST delivery), CALL_PAL MTPR_ASTEN (enabling AST delivery), and CALL_PAL MTPR_ASTSR (declaring a pending AST). Each of these routines, when otherwise complete, checks the previously listed conditions to determine whether there is a deliverable AST. If so, the routine triggers an AST interrupt request. AXP hardware or PALcode, depending on the implementation, clears the ASTSR bit and requests the AST interrupt.

Typically, the ASTSR register is modified several times during the queuing and delivery of an AST:

▶ When an AST is queued to a current process, the bit corresponding to the AST's mode is set.

▶ When an AST interrupt is initiated for a particular access mode, the bit corresponding to the mode has been cleared by the hardware or PALcode that requested the interrupt. Otherwise, executing any of the previously mentioned PALcode instructions while the AST is active would result in a redundant AST interrupt to the same access mode.

▶ When an AST procedure exits, the register is updated to reflect other potential pending ASTs for the same access mode. Section 8.3.2 describes the algorithm for updating the register.

The PALcode routines that modify the ASTSR and ASTEN registers accept an argument composed of two masks: one containing the bits to be left unchanged and the other the bits to be explicitly set or cleared. This enables kernel mode code to specify that certain bits be changed and others simply preserved without having to read the state of the register first.

The STARLET macro $PRDEF defines symbolic values for the bit positions in each register and symbols for values to load into them. For example, the symbol PR$M_ASTSR_KPD can be ORed with PR$M_ASTSR_PRSRV_ALL to form an eight-bit mask that sets kernel mode pending and preserves any other set pending bits.

8.3   AST DATA STRUCTURES

The principal data structure related to ASTs is the ACB, described in Section 8.3.1. The executive queues ACBs to a process as the corresponding asynchronous events (for example, I/O completion and timer expiration) occur.

The ACB listheads for a process are in its software process control block (PCB), which also contains several other fields related to ASTs. Section 8.3.2 contains further information.

In addition to the PHD$Q_ASTSR_ASTEN field already described, the process header (PHD) has other AST-related information. The field PHD$L_ASTLM contains the process's authorized AST quota, typically taken from the user authorization file. The PHD$L_FLAGS2 bit PHD$V_AST_PENDING, when set, means that a deliverable AST has been queued to the process. The scheduler tests the flag when it places a process into execution to optimize delivery of the AST (see Section 8.7).

8.3.1   AST Control Block

An ACB describes a pending AST request and identifies the target process, the procedure to be executed, and the access mode of the procedure. Figure 8.1 shows the layout of an ACB. The macro $ACBDEF defines symbolic names for the fields in an ACB.

An ACB is allocated from nonpaged pool, often as part of a larger structure associated with the requested asynchronous event. An ACB is included as the first section of an I/O request packet (IRP), lock block (LKB), and timer queue entry (TQE). In fact, the two reserved longwords in an ACB provide space necessary to accommodate IRP fields.

Compare the ACB format pictured in Figure 8.1 with the TQE format shown in Figure 12.1, the LKB format shown in Figure 11.4, or the IRP format shown in Figure 22.16.

ACB$L_ASTQFL and ACB$L_ASTQBL link the ACB into one of the AST queues in the PCB.

The field ACB$B_RMOD contains five bit fields:

▶ Bits ⟨1 : 0⟩ (ACB$V_MODE) specify the access mode at which the AST procedure is to execute.

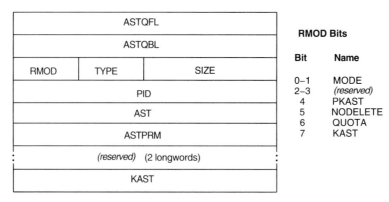

Figure 8.1
Layout of an AST Control Block (ACB)

▶ Bit ⟨4⟩ (ACB$V_PKAST), when set, indicates the presence of a piggyback special kernel mode AST (see Section 8.8.5).

▶ Bit ⟨5⟩ (ACB$V_NODELETE), when set, indicates that the ACB should not be deallocated after the AST is delivered.

▶ Bit ⟨6⟩ (ACB$V_QUOTA), when set, indicates that the process AST quota has been charged for this ACB.

▶ Bit ⟨7⟩ (ACB$V_KAST), when set, indicates the presence of a system-requested special kernel mode AST (see Section 8.8). If ACB$V_KAST is clear, the ACB describes a normal AST.

ACB$L_PID contains the internal process ID of the process to receive the AST.

ACB$L_AST and ACB$L_ASTPRM contain the procedure value of the designated AST procedure and its optional argument.

ACB$L_KAST contains the procedure value of a system-requested special kernel mode AST routine if the ACB$V_PKAST or ACB$V_KAST bit is set.

8.3.2 PCB Fields Related to ASTs

Figure 8.2 shows the PCB fields related to AST queuing and delivery.

Each process has five absolute queues of pending ASTs: one for each access mode and one for special kernel mode ASTs. The listheads of these queues are in the PCB. The ACBs in each queue are in the chronological order in which the ASTs were queued to the process. The fields PCB$L_ASTQFL_SPK and PCB$L_ASTQBL_SPK are the listheads for special kernel mode ACBs queued to the process. The other listheads are PCB$L_ASTQFL_*x* and PCB$L_ASTQBL_*x*, where *x* is a letter indicating the access mode.

Because executive routines access these queues holding the SCHED spinlock, they have no need to perform atomic INSQUEs and REMQUEs. Instead, some of them insert and remove ACBs through sequences of instructions

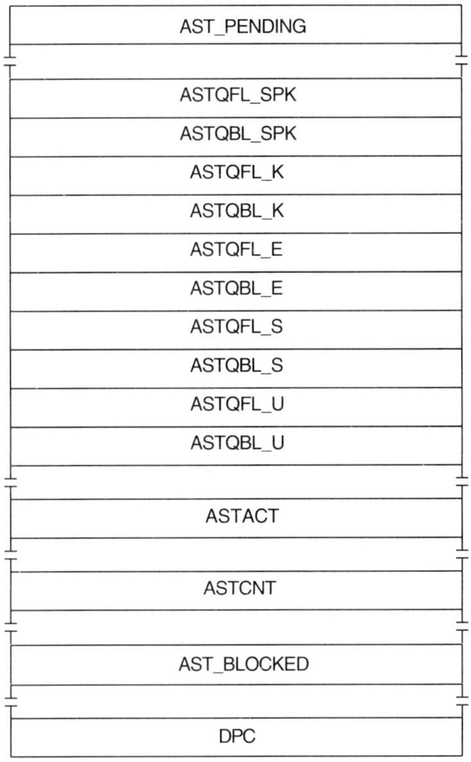

AST_PENDING

ASTQFL_SPK
ASTQBL_SPK
ASTQFL_K
ASTQBL_K
ASTQFL_E
ASTQBL_E
ASTQFL_S
ASTQBL_S
ASTQFL_U
ASTQBL_U

ASTACT

ASTCNT

AST_BLOCKED

DPC

Figure 8.2
AST-Related Fields in the Software PCB

that outperform the equivalent PALcode routines. Entering PALcode would flush the instruction pipeline. Moreover, the PALcode routines take extra steps to provide atomicity guarantees that are unnecessary under these circumstances.

The condition (empty or not) of each of these queues is summarized by one of the low-order four bits in PCB$L_AST_PENDING. If the queue contains one or more ACBs, the bit is set; if the queue is empty, the bit is clear. Bit 0 represents both the special kernel and kernel queues. The appropriate bit in PCB$L_AST_PENDING is set by SCH$QAST, in module ASTDEL, when it queues an AST to a process. When the AST delivery interrupt service routine removes the last AST from a PCB queue during AST delivery, it clears the corresponding bit in PCB$L_AST_PENDING. When the AST procedure is complete, AST exit code copies this longword to update the ASTSR register rather than acquiring the SCHED spinlock and examining each ACB queue to determine which bits to set. Section 8.2 lists circumstances under which the ASTSR register is updated.

The field PCB$L_ASTCNT specifies how many concurrent ASTs the process can request at the moment. It is initialized to the process's AST quota from PHD$L_ASTLM. When a process requests an asynchronous system service with AST notification or when a process declares an AST by requesting the Declare AST ($DCLAST) system service, the system service confirms that PCB$L_ASTCNT is greater than zero and then decrements it, to charge the process AST quota. If the count is not greater than zero, the service returns the error SS$_EXQUOTA. PCB$L_ASTCNT is incremented and decremented atomically with the load-locked/store-conditional mechanism described in Chapter 9.

It is the responsibility of the system service and of any other code charging AST quota to set the ACB$V_QUOTA bit in the ACB (see Section 8.3.1) as a flag that quota must be restored when this AST is delivered. When such an AST is delivered, the AST delivery routine increments PCB$L_ASTCNT. The difference between the contents of PHD$L_ASTLM and PCB$L_ASTCNT is the number of outstanding ASTs the process has requested.

The process delete pending count, PCB$L_DPC, is incremented for every reason the process should not be deleted or suspended. It is incremented by the Files-11 Extended QIO Processor (XQP) to indicate that an XQP operation is in progress and that the process should not be deleted or suspended until the operation completes. This field is modified and tested only within process context. Section 8.9 discusses the use of this field and its significance to ASTs in more detail.

The low-order four bits of PCB$L_ASTACT specify in which modes ASTs are active. One bit corresponds to each access mode, with bit 0 for kernel mode. Each PCB$L_ASTACT bit, when set, indicates that an AST is active at that access mode in the process. Note that these bits describe only normal ASTs; that is, the low bit of PCB$L_ASTACT does not describe special kernel mode AST activity.

The executive uses these bits to serialize ASTs for each access mode. The AST delivery routine tests and sets the bit corresponding to the mode of the interrupt to guarantee that only one AST for a given access mode executes at one time. When the AST is complete, AST exit code clears the bit. It is possible, though not usual, for an AST procedure itself to clear a PCB$L_ASTACT bit using the Clear AST ($CLRAST) system service (see Section 8.7.3).

The low-order bit in PCB$L_AST_BLOCKED temporarily records the state of the kernel mode AST enable bit. The Alpha AXP architecture does not distinguish between normal kernel mode ASTs and special kernel mode ASTs; in particular, there is only one kernel mode enable bit. Nonetheless, when a process disables delivery of normal kernel mode ASTs, special kernel mode ASTs must still be deliverable. Therefore, when a special kernel mode AST is queued to a process that has disabled kernel mode delivery, the executive reenables kernel mode delivery and sets the low-order bit of PCB$L_AST_BLOCKED. After the last special kernel mode AST is delivered, the disabled state of the kernel mode enable bit will be restored.

Accesses to the ACB queues and to the fields PCB$L_AST_PENDING and PCB$L_AST_BLOCKED are synchronized with the SCHED spinlock. PCB$L_ASTACT is accessed only from within process context: bits in it are tested and set at IPL 2 in the AST delivery interrupt service routine and cleared at IPL 0 by AST exit code.

8.4   ENABLING AND DISABLING AST DELIVERY

OpenVMS VAX support for enabling and disabling ASTs is implemented entirely in software. A process sets or clears AST enable bits in the PCB by requesting the Set AST Enable ($SETAST) system service. Before dispatching to an AST procedure, the AST delivery interrupt service routine must check that delivery to that mode is currently enabled and, if it is not, dismiss the interrupt.

In contrast, AST enable bits are part of Alpha AXP hardware process context. A process running in any access mode can simply execute the CALL_PAL SWASTEN instruction; this instruction provides a fast way to enable or disable delivery to the current mode. Code running in kernel mode can execute the CALL_PAL MTPR_ASTEN instruction to affect any modes. A PALcode routine that detects the need to request an AST interrupt itself tests the enable bit for that mode; AST delivery interrupts are not requested for disabled modes.

For OpenVMS VAX compatibility, OpenVMS AXP supports the $SETAST system service, implementing it as a mode of caller service.

EXE$SETAST, the $SETAST system service procedure, simply executes a CALL_PAL SWASTEN instruction with the contents of the ENBFLG argument. It then returns either the status SS$_WASCLR or SS$_WASSET to reflect the original state of the AST enable bit. Enabling delivery of ASTs to a mode for which one or more ASTs are pending results in an immediate IPL 2 AST delivery interrupt request. That is, the AST is delivered before control returns to the instruction following the CALL_PAL SWASTEN instruction in the system service.

Temporarily disabling AST delivery enables a non-AST thread of execution to synchronize access to a data structure shared with an AST thread at the same access mode by blocking execution of the AST.

8.5   CREATING AN AST

ASTs can be created in three ways. The first is a process request for AST notification of the completion of an asynchronous system service, such as Queue I/O Request ($QIO) or Enqueue Lock Request ($ENQ). The arguments for these system services include an AST procedure value and an argument to be passed to the AST procedure. The system service charges the process AST quota and allocates an ACB. When the asynchronous part of the service is complete, the service queues the ACB to the process.

The second is the system's queuing an AST to execute code in the context of the selected process. An ACB used in this situation is not deducted from the AST quota of the target process because of its involuntary nature; the ACB$V_QUOTA bit is clear to indicate this.

The system's ability to initiate the execution of code in a particular process context is crucial to OpenVMS operations. Only the AST mechanism provides this capability. The executive employs this mechanism primarily to access the process's virtual address space.

In a virtual memory operating system, resolving a process-private address outside its process context is difficult at best. The process's pages, as well as page table pages, might not be resident; they can be in a page file, swap file, or in transition. Rather than attempt to locate the relevant page table page(s) and process page(s), the executive references the address in process context through the AST mechanism so that standard memory management mechanisms can be used.

Examples of the system's queuing an AST include the following:

- I/O postprocessing
- The Force Exit ($FORCEX) system service
- Expiration of CPU time quota
- Working set limit adjustment performed at quantum end (see Chapter 13)
- The Get Job/Process Information ($GETJPI) system service

These and other examples are described in Sections 8.8 and 8.9.

The third way to create an AST is an explicit declaration of an AST by a process through the $DCLAST system service.

The $DCLAST system service procedure, EXE$DCLAST in module SYS-ASTCON, runs in kernel mode. It simply allocates an ACB, initializes it with information from the system service arguments, and invokes the routine SCH$QUEUE_AST_CURRENT, in module ASTDEL, to queue the ACB. The access mode in which the AST is to execute can be no more privileged than the mode from which $DCLAST was requested. The system service charges the process AST quota.

8.6 QUEUING AN AST TO A PROCESS

The routine SCH$QAST, in module ASTDEL, queues an AST to a process. It can be invoked from any kernel mode thread of execution running at an IPL less than or equal to IPL$_SCHED and holding no spinlock of rank greater than SCHED. Basically, SCH$QAST inserts the ACB into one of the queues in the process's PCB.

SCH$QAST performs the following steps:

1. It acquires the SCHED spinlock, raising IPL to IPL$_SCHED, to synchronize access to the scheduler database and the process's AST-related data.
2. If the process is nonexistent, SCH$QAST releases the SCHED spinlock

and returns the error status SS$_NONEXPR. If bit ACB$V_NODELETE in ACB$B_RMOD is clear, its usual state, SCH$QAST deallocates the ACB before returning.

If the process exists, SCH$QAST gets the address of its software PCB.

3. It determines in which AST queue this ACB should go, based on ACB$V_KAST and the access mode bits in ACB$B_RMOD, and inserts the ACB at the tail of that queue:

    - It inserts a special kernel mode AST in the special kernel mode AST queue.
    - It inserts a normal AST in the queue corresponding to the mode bits.
    - It inserts a piggyback special kernel mode AST in the queue corresponding to the mode of the normal AST whose ACB it shares.

4. It sets the bit corresponding to the AST mode in PCB$L_AST_PENDING.

5. It determines new contents for the ASTSR processor register or PHD$Q_ASTSR_ASTEN as a function of the old contents plus a set bit that corresponds to the mode of the newly queued ACB. It stores the contents as follows:

    - If the target process and SCH$QAST are currently executing on the same CPU, SCH$QAST stores the new ASTSR value in the processor register. (The Alpha AXP architecture prohibits software from modifying the HWPCB of a current process.) If the process is currently executing on a different member of a symmetric multiprocessing system, SCH$QAST stores the new value in SMP$GL_ASTSR_ACK and requests an interprocessor interrupt of the other CPU to update its ASTSR register. Still holding the SCHED spinlock, SCH$QAST busy waits until the other processor responds to ensure that the target process remains current on the other processor until the interprocessor interrupt is serviced. Chapter 37 gives further details.

    - If the process is not currently executing, but its PHD is memory-resident, SCH$QAST stores the new value for ASTSR in PHD$Q_ASTSR_ASTEN but not in the processor register, which represents some other process's state. In addition, if delivery to that mode is enabled, SCH$QAST sets bit PHD$V_AST_PENDING in PHD$L_FLAGS2. Sometime later, when the process becomes current, if the flag is set, scheduling code may dispatch directly to an AST delivery interrupt service routine (see Section 8.7).

    - If the process and its PHD are outswapped, PHD$Q_ASTSR_ASTEN cannot be updated because the PHD is not available. When the process later becomes resident, the swapper reinitializes the summary bits in PHD$Q_ASTSR_ASTEN, based on the state of the process's AST queues.

When queuing a special kernel mode AST, SCH$QAST tests whether the process has disabled delivery of normal kernel mode ASTs. If so, SCH$QAST sets the low-order bit of PCB$L_AST_BLOCKED and reenables delivery to kernel mode to ensure that the special kernel mode AST will be delivered.

SCH$QAST does not check whether delivery to the mode of the AST is disabled or whether there is an AST already active at that mode. If AST delivery is disabled for that mode, no AST interrupt will be requested. It is thus not necessary for SCH$QAST to make that check. If an AST is already active at that mode, an unnecessary AST interrupt for delivery to that mode will be requested, but the AST delivery interrupt service routine will dismiss it as blocked and undeliverable.

6. Unless the process is currently executing, SCH$QAST invokes the routine SCH$RSE, in module RSE, to report that an AST has been queued to the process. SCH$RSE makes the process computable if it is not current, already computable, or suspended in kernel mode.

7. SCH$QAST releases the SCHED spinlock, restoring the previous IPL, and returns to its invoker.

SCH$QUEUE_AST_CURRENT, in module ASTDEL, provides a faster way for code running in process context to queue an AST to that process. The routine acquires the SCHED spinlock, inserts the ACB at the tail of the appropriate queue, sets the appropriate bit in PCB$L_AST_PENDING, updates the ASTSR processor register, releases the spinlock, and returns.

8.7   DELIVERING AN AST

AST delivery is initiated when a pending AST is deliverable and IPL is less than 2. For a pending AST to be deliverable, AST delivery to the access mode of the AST must be enabled and the access mode to be interrupted (or the mode being restored by the REI PALcode routine) must be less than or equally privileged to that of the AST. This test prevents a process running in an inner mode from being interrupted to deliver an AST to an outer mode. AST delivery is initiated indirectly through one of the AST delivery interrupts.

It can also be initiated directly by the rescheduling interrupt service routine, SCH$INTERRUPT, in module SCHEDULER. After swapping process context, but before returning to the interrupted thread of execution in the newly current process, SCH$INTERRUPT tests the process's PHD$V_AST_PENDING bit. As previously described, SCH$QAST sets this bit when it queues an AST for a mode to which delivery is enabled. If the bit is set, SCH$INTERRUPT clears it, releases the SCHED spinlock it acquired at entry, and makes some tests to determine whether an AST interrupt would be appropriate.

▶ It checks that the IPL to be restored is less than 2.

▶ It checks that the mode of the most privileged pending AST is equally or more privileged than the mode being restored.

▶ It checks that delivery to that mode is enabled.

If the process's AST state is such that an AST interrupt would be requested if SCH$INTERRUPT executed a CALL_PAL REI instruction to resume the interrupted thread, SCH$INTERRUPT itself initiates AST delivery. It clears the ASTSR bit corresponding to that mode, lowers IPL to 2, clears the software bits in the PS, and jumps directly to the appropriate AST interrupt service routine just as though an interrupt had occurred. This shortcut improves performance in cases where a waiting process is made computable by the queuing of a deliverable AST and then selected for execution. Because PHD$V_AST_PENDING is in a PHD field the scheduler accesses for other reasons, the cost of testing the bit is minimal.

8.7.1   AST Delivery Interrupt Service Routines

As described in Chapter 3, there is a separate AST delivery interrupt for each access mode. When an AST delivery interrupt request is triggered and granted, the IEI PALcode routine, which initiates an exception, interrupt, or machine check, executes. The routine transfers control through the appropriate system control block (SCB) entry to an interrupt service routine. The functions of each interrupt service routine are to remove the first pending AST from the queue associated with that mode, determine that the interrupt is not a spurious one, and dispatch to the specified AST routine at the specified access mode.

OpenVMS AXP implements these interrupt service routines in a combination of MACRO-32 and MACRO-64 code. Stack manipulation necessary for AST delivery and exit must be written in MACRO-64.

Figure 8.3 shows the major steps in delivering an AST to an outer mode.

The MACRO-64 AST delivery interrupt service routine entry points, in module ASTDEL_STACK, are

▶ SCH$USER_ASTDEL, for user mode ASTs

▶ SCH$SUPER_ASTDEL, for supervisor mode ASTs

▶ SCH$EXEC_ASTDEL, for executive mode ASTs

▶ SCH$KERNEL_ASTDEL, for both normal and special kernel mode ASTs

Each is entered in kernel mode at IPL 2 with the bit in ASTSR that corresponds to the AST mode already cleared. Each stores the AST access mode in a register and creates a stack save area in which it saves the integer registers that might otherwise be overwritten as a result of the AST procedure call or the service routine's actions. The macro $ASTSTKDEF defines symbolic offsets for this stack save area. The registers that compiler-generated

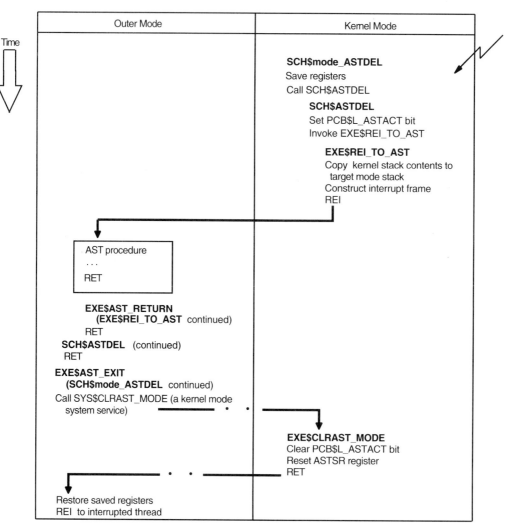

Figure 8.3
Outer Mode AST Delivery Flow

code would not save and restore include the function value, argument passing, and scratch registers.

Figure 8.4 shows the contents of the stack during AST delivery: the interrupt stack frame, the stack save area, and the procedure stack frame built during a later step. Initially, all this information is on the kernel stack. Later it is copied to the stack of the AST access mode. Dispatch into the AST procedure adds another procedure stack frame.

These interrupt service routines all converge in common code, but the path for kernel mode AST delivery differs in a number of ways, one of which is the delivery of special kernel mode ASTs.

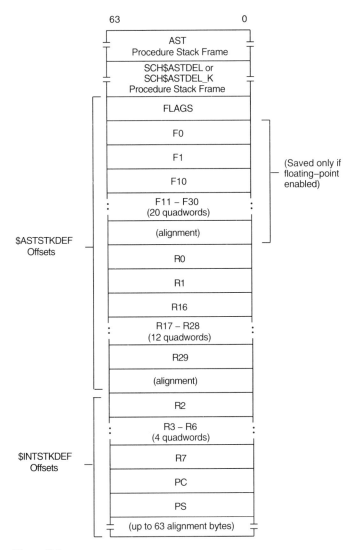

Figure 8.4
AST Stack Contents

This section first describes outer mode delivery and then the differences in kernel mode delivery.

8.7.1.1   **Outer Mode AST Delivery.** The key concerns in delivering an AST to an outer mode are as follows:

▶ Making a mode transition from kernel to the outer access mode to call the AST procedure
▶ Returning from the AST procedure to the interrupted thread of execution with all its state restored

189

After creating the stack save area, each outer mode service routine tests the low bit of PHD$L_FLAGS (the software copy of the floating-point enable, FEN, register) to determine whether the process is using floating-point. If so, the scratch floating-point registers must be saved. An AXP processor has both a set of integer registers for addressing and integer arithmetic and a set of floating-point registers. Compiler-generated code for a routine that executes floating-point instructions is responsible for saving and restoring floating-point registers used by the routine, other than the scratch registers.

If floating-point is not enabled for this process, each routine clears the stack quadword that represents the floating-point state. If it is enabled, each sets two flags in the quadword: ASTSTK$V_FEN, to indicate that floating-point is enabled, and ASTSTK$V_FP_SAVE_DELAYED, to indicate that the scratch floating-point registers have not yet been saved. These registers are not saved now because they would only have to be copied to the AST access mode stack later. AST delivery code does not use them, so they can be saved later (see steps 8 and 15 of the list that follows).

Each outer mode service routine then calls SCH$ASTDEL, in module AST-DEL, specifying a return address of EXE$AST_EXIT.

SCH$ASTDEL, in combination with the MACRO-64 routine EXE$REI_TO_AST, in module ASTDEL_STACK, takes the following steps:

1. SCH$ASTDEL acquires the SCHED spinlock, raising IPL to IPL$_SCHED, to synchronize access to the process's AST queues.
2. If an AST of that mode is already active (the corresponding PCB$L_ASTACT bit is set), it releases the SCHED spinlock and returns to EXE$AST_EXIT with a status indicating that no AST was delivered. (SCH$ASTDEL leaves the access mode bit in ASTSR clear to prevent further spurious interrupts. When the AST procedure exits, the ASTSR bit will be reset.) AST exit code is described further in Section 8.7.3.

   If no AST of that mode is active, SCH$ASTDEL removes the first ACB from the appropriate PCB queue. If the queue was empty or is empty after the removal, SCH$ASTDEL clears the bit in PCB$L_AST_PENDING corresponding to the mode of the interrupt.
3. If the queue was empty, SCH$ASTDEL releases the SCHED spinlock, updates ASTSR, and returns to EXE$AST_EXIT with a status indicating no AST was delivered.
4. Otherwise, SCH$ASTDEL sets the bit corresponding to the AST access mode in PCB$L_ASTACT to indicate that there is an active AST at this mode and to block concurrent delivery of another AST.
5. If ACB$V_QUOTA is set in the ACB, SCH$ASTDEL returns process AST quota.
6. It releases the SCHED spinlock, lowering IPL to 2.
7. It copies the AST parameter from the ACB for use as an argument to the AST procedure.

8. If a piggyback special kernel mode AST is associated with this AST, SCH$ASTDEL tests whether the process is using floating-point. If so, it saves the scratch floating-point registers on the stack in case the piggyback kernel mode AST routine uses them and clears the ASTSTK$V_FP_SAVE_DELAYED bit.

   SCH$ASTDEL invokes the piggyback special kernel mode routine at IPL 2. When it returns, SCH$ASTDEL continues with step 10.

9. If the ACB$V_NODELETE bit is clear (its usual state), SCH$ASTDEL deallocates the ACB to nonpaged pool.

10. It initializes the other argument registers (see Section 8.7.2).

11. The code that actually calls an AST procedure must execute in the access mode of the AST. Before leaving kernel mode, however, AST delivery code must copy the kernel stack contents to the stack of the AST access mode so that the information is accessible from the outer mode at AST exit. SCH$ASTDEL invokes EXE$REI_TO_AST to perform that step and the rest of AST delivery.

12. EXE$REI_TO_AST first checks the accessibility of the AST procedure descriptor. If it cannot be read by the AST access mode, EXE$REI_TO_AST returns an error status to SCH$ASTDEL.

   In response to that error status, SCH$ASTDEL clears the PCB$L_ASTACT bit, lowers IPL to 0, and returns to EXE$AST_EXIT with information about the failure. As described in Section 8.7.3, EXE$AST_EXIT signals the error SS$_ASTFLT.

13. If the AST procedure descriptor can be read, EXE$REI_TO_AST aligns the target access mode stack to a 64-byte boundary in preparation for copying the kernel stack contents, which include the interrupt stack frame. Later, after the AST procedure exits, control will be returned to the interrupted thread of execution through a CALL_PAL REI instruction, which requires the stack to be aligned.

14. EXE$REI_TO_AST probes the target mode stack to confirm that the contents of the kernel stack can be copied to it. If not, it returns an error status to SCH$ASTDEL. As described in Section 8.7.3, if the target mode stack cannot be expanded, SCH$ASTDEL clears the PCB$L_ASTACT bit, lowers IPL to 0, and returns to EXE$AST_EXIT. EXE$AST_EXIT signals the error SS$_ASTFLT.

15. If the target stack is accessible, EXE$REI_TO_AST modifies the target mode stack pointer to reflect its position after the copy and updates the frame pointer (FP) register to point to the location on the target mode stack of the moved stack frame from the entry to SCH$ASTDEL.

   It copies the information pushed onto the kernel stack by SCH$ASTDEL's prologue code, namely, SCH$ASTDEL's procedure stack frame.

   It tests ASTSTK$V_FEN to determine whether the process is using floating-point. If not, it continues with the next step. If so, it tests whether the scratch floating-point registers have been saved already, perhaps prior to the execution of a piggyback special kernel mode AST routine. If they have, EXE$REI_TO_AST reloads them from the kernel stack save area and clears its ASTSTK$V_FP_SAVE_DELAYED flag. It stores the scratch floating-point registers on the target access mode stack.

16. It copies the kernel stack save area and the interrupt stack frame to the target stack. It adjusts the stack alignment bits in the saved processor status (PS) in the copied interrupt stack frame to reflect the target mode stack alignment described in step 13.

17. It modifies the interrupt stack frame on the kernel stack so that it can REI to the target mode and enter the AST procedure: it inserts the target mode as previous and current in the PS to be restored; it saves its own caller's return address (in SCH$ASTDEL) in the R2 contents to be restored from the interrupt stack frame and loads R26 with the address of EXE$AST_RETURN, a return address within EXE$REI_TO_AST.

18. EXE$REI_TO_AST examines the AST's procedure descriptor to determine whether it is a native procedure or a translated procedure.

    If it is a native procedure, EXE$REI_TO_AST stores its entry point address in the program counter (PC) to be restored, loads its procedure value into R27, and executes a CALL_PAL REI instruction, entering the AST procedure in its access mode.

    If the AST procedure is translated, EXE$REI_TO_AST instead stores the entry point address of SYS$NATIVE_TO_TRANSLATED and loads its procedure value. The jacket routine SYS$NATIVE_TO_TRANS-LATED will call the AST procedure itself. Chapter 29 provides more information on the Translated Image Environment.

8.7.1.2 **Kernel Mode AST Delivery.** The kernel mode AST delivery interrupt service routine is concerned with

- ▶ Delivering all queued special kernel mode ASTs in response to one interrupt
- ▶ Delivering one normal AST as well, if possible

SCH$KERNEL_ASTDEL performs the same actions as the other AST delivery interrupt service routines except that, if floating-point is enabled, it saves the floating-point registers, since the current stack is the AST access mode stack. It then calls SCH$ASTDEL_K, in module ASTDEL, specifying a return address of EXE$AST_EXIT.

SCH$ASTDEL_K takes the following steps:

1. It checks whether SMP is enabled and, if so, continues with step 2. Otherwise, it checks for the relatively common case of a special kernel mode AST queue that contains exactly one ACB. If the queue contains exactly

one ACB, SCH$ASTDEL_K removes it and updates the listhead using the load-locked/store-conditional mechanism, described in Chapter 9, without the overhead of acquiring and releasing the SCHED spinlock. It continues with step 5 to deliver the special kernel mode AST.

If the queue is empty or contains more than one ACB, SCH$ASTDEL_K continues with step 2.

2. It acquires the SCHED spinlock, raising IPL to IPL$_SCHED.

3. It removes the ACB from the head of the special kernel mode AST queue or, if the queue is empty, continues with step 7.

4. It releases the SCHED spinlock, lowering IPL to 2.

5. It clears the ACB$V_KAST bit in ACB$B_RMOD.

6. It invokes the special kernel mode AST routine, passing it the addresses of the PCB and ACB in R4 and R5.

When the special kernel mode AST routine returns, SCH$ASTDEL_K continues with step 2, delivering all pending special kernel mode ASTs.

7. When the special kernel mode AST queue is empty, SCH$ASTDEL_K tests and clears the low bit of PCB$L_AST_BLOCKED.

8. If the bit was set, indicating that kernel mode AST delivery should be disabled, SCH$ASTDEL_K disables kernel mode delivery by executing a CALL_PAL SWASTEN. It releases the SCHED spinlock, updates the ASTSR register with the contents of PCB$L_AST_PENDING, and returns to EXE$AST_EXIT with a status indicating no normal AST was delivered.

9. If the low bit of PCB$L_AST_BLOCKED was clear, SCH$ASTDEL_K tests the kernel mode PCB$L_ASTACT bit. If the bit is set, indicating a kernel mode AST already active, it releases the SCHED spinlock and returns to EXE$AST_EXIT with a status indicating no normal AST was delivered.

10. If the PCB$L_ASTACT bit was clear, SCH$ASTDEL_K removes the first ACB from the kernel mode PCB queue. If the queue was or is now empty, it clears the kernel mode bit in PCB$L_AST_PENDING. If SCH$ASTDEL_K did remove an ACB, its flow converges with that of SCH$ASTDEL, at step 4. (Note, however, that because no access mode change is necessary, the stack is already set up for calling the AST procedure; much of the stack manipulation in EXE$REI_TO_AST is bypassed.)

11. If the queue was empty, SCH$ASTDEL_K examines the pending ASTs to determine whether there is one whose mode is enabled and whose mode is equal to or more privileged than that of the interrupted thread.

If there is none, SCH$ASTDEL_K releases the SCHED spinlock and returns to EXE$AST_EXIT with a status indicating no normal AST was delivered.

12. If there is an appropriate pending AST, SCH$ASTDEL_K updates the ASTSR register by clearing the bit corresponding to the mode of the AST, as PALcode or hardware-initiated delivery would have done, and merges with SCH$ASTDEL at step 2.

8.7.2   AST Arguments

An AST procedure is called with the following arguments:

▸ AST parameter
▸ Contents of R0 at the time of the interrupt
▸ Contents of R1 at the time of the interrupt
▸ The PC of the interrupted thread of execution
▸ The PS of that thread

The only argument directly intended for the AST procedure is the AST parameter, which was originally an argument to a system service such as $QIO, $ENQ, or $DCLAST. SCH$ASTDEL copies the AST parameter from the ACB where it was initially stored by the system service. Its meaning is application-specific.

Although the other arguments are present for OpenVMS VAX compatibility, they have no subsequent use after the AST procedure exits; modifying them therefore has no effect on the thread of execution to be resumed at AST exit.

8.7.3   AST Exit Path

After an AST procedure has executed, its associated PCB$L_ASTACT bit must be cleared and ASTSR must be recomputed. Requiring kernel mode, these steps are performed by the $CLRAST and $CLRAST_MODE system services. (The distinction between the two forms of this service is that the latter is passed an argument containing the access mode.) In most cases, the AST procedure implicitly requests the $CLRAST_MODE system service by simply returning. Direct request of these system services is discussed later in this section.

When the AST procedure returns, the following steps occur:

1. By returning, the AST procedure transfers control to EXE$AST_RE-TURN, in module ASTDEL_STACK, which simply loads a success status into R0 and returns to SCH$ASTDEL.
2. SCH$ASTDEL tests R0 to distinguish successful AST execution from bad stack and inaccessible procedure descriptor errors.
3. If R0 contains a success status, SCH$ASTDEL continues with the actions in step 7.
4. If R0 contains an error status, SCH$ASTDEL, still in kernel mode because no AST was delivered, determines which error occurred. If the target access mode stack could not accommodate the kernel stack contents, SCH$ASTDEL tests whether the target mode is user. If so, it invokes EXE$EXPANDSTK, in module EXCEPTION, to expand the user stack. Chapter 17 contains further details. If the expansion succeeds, SCH$ASTDEL invokes EXE$REI_TO_AST again to deliver the AST (see step 11 and subsequent steps in the description of SCH$ASTDEL in Section 8.7.1.1).

If the expansion fails or the target mode is not user, SCH$ASTDEL loads registers with information about the error and continues with step 6.

5. If the AST procedure descriptor is inaccessible, SCH$ASTDEL loads registers with information about the error.

6. It clears the PCB$L_ASTACT bit for the AST mode, lowers IPL to 0, and returns to EXE$AST_EXIT, in module ASTDEL_STACK, with an error status. Returning, SCH$ASTDEL's epilogue code removes the procedure stack frame and restores the registers saved by SCH$ASTDEL's prologue code.

   EXE$AST_EXIT restores the registers from the stack save area and removes the stack save area from the stack, leaving only the interrupt stack frame. It jumps to EXE$ASTFLT. Chapter 6 describes EXE$AST-FLT's actions to signal the error.

7. If R0 contains a success status, the AST executed successfully. Running in the access mode of the AST, SCH$ASTDEL returns to its caller, the AST delivery interrupt service routine, at EXE$AST_EXIT. Returning, SCH$ASTDEL's epilogue code removes the procedure stack frame and restores the registers saved by SCH$ASTDEL's prologue code.

8. EXE$AST_EXIT, still running in the mode of the AST, temporarily disables AST delivery to that mode to block a possible AST interrupt until step 10b. It determines the current access mode. If it is an outer mode, EXE$AST_EXIT requests the $CLRAST_MODE system service. If it is kernel mode, EXE$AST_EXIT simply invokes EXE$CLRAST_KERNEL, an alternative entry point of EXE$CLRAST, bypassing the unnecessary system service dispatch.

9. EXE$CLRAST and EXE$CLRAST_MODE, in module ASTDEL, the $CLRAST and $CLRAST_MODE system service procedures, perform the following steps:

   a. EXE$CLRAST extracts the previous mode bits from the PS to determine the relevant access mode; EXE$CLRAST_MODE uses the mode passed.

   b. Each clears the corresponding PCB$L_ASTACT bit to indicate that no AST procedure is active in that mode.

   c. Each invokes SCH$RESET_ASTSR, in module ASTDEL, to update the ASTSR register.

   d. Each returns.

10. EXE$AST_EXIT resumes at the previous access mode, the mode of the AST. (If EXE$AST_EXIT had not disabled AST delivery, the REI from the system service dispatch return could have triggered an AST interrupt for a pending AST at this access mode.)

    a. It restores the general registers and, if saved, the floating-point registers from the stack save area.

b. It restores the previous state of the AST enable for this mode by executing a CALL_PAL SWASTEN. Typically, this reenables delivery to the current mode, enabling delivery of another AST to this mode.

c. EXE$AST_EXIT executes a CALL_PAL REI instruction to dismiss the interrupt and remove the interrupt stack frame from the stack. This returns control to the access mode and instruction originally interrupted by AST delivery.

The CALL_PAL SWASTEN instruction in EXE$AST_EXIT, at step 10b, can cause another AST delivery interrupt to occur, depending upon the ASTSR contents and the access mode transitions.

If another AST delivery interrupt does occur before the CALL_PAL REI in step 10c dismisses the current one, the interrupt stack frame of the nearly completed current AST is still on the stack. Allowing subsequent AST interrupts to nest within the current one could potentially fill the stack with interrupt stack frames. SCH$ASTDEL attempts to avoid both the nesting and the CALL_PAL REI. It checks whether an AST interrupt occurred at the CALL_PAL SWASTEN instruction by examining the PC in the newer interrupt stack frame. If it did, SCH$ASTDEL checks further whether the current AST and the previous AST are for the same access mode. If they are, SCH$ASTDEL invokes EXE$REI_TO_AST with a flag indicating that the newer interrupt stack frame should not be saved. For an outer mode AST, this means it is not copied to the target stack; for a kernel mode AST, it means that the AST-STK save area and SCH$ASTDEL procedure stack frame overlay the newer interrupt stack frame.

If an AST procedure requests the $CLRAST or $CLRAST_MODE system service directly rather than simply returning, the appropriate PCB$L_ASTACT bit is cleared and ASTSR register is updated. This has the effect that another AST can be delivered to the same mode; the current procedure is now an ordinary thread interruptible by ASTs. The procedure stack frame built by the call to SCH$ASTDEL remains on the stack, as do the stack save area and interrupt stack frame. The former AST procedure must return in order to remove this information from the stack and restore saved registers before returning to the code interrupted by the AST delivery. Furthermore, the former AST procedure is now responsible for any synchronization with another AST thread of execution.

Note that the $CLRAST and $CLRAST_MODE system services are not supported by Digital, except for use within Digital software, and are not documented in the *OpenVMS System Services Reference Manual*.

8.8 SPECIAL KERNEL MODE ASTS

Special kernel mode ASTs differ from normal ASTs in several ways:

▶ A special kernel mode AST routine is dispatched at IPL 2 and executes at that level or higher. Synchronization is provided by the interrupt mechanism itself rather than requiring an additional PCB$L_ASTACT bit. Only one special kernel mode AST can be active at any time because the kernel mode AST delivery interrupt is blocked.

▶ Special kernel mode ASTs cannot be disabled by clearing the kernel mode ASTEN bit. Delivery of a special kernel mode AST can only be blocked by raising IPL to 2 or above.

▶ All special kernel mode ASTs result from the operations of kernel mode code. That is, a user cannot directly request special kernel mode AST notification of an asynchronous event.

▶ A special kernel mode AST routine is identified as a .JSB_ENTRY entry point rather than as a .CALL_ENTRY entry point.

   The arguments passed to a special kernel mode AST routine are the PCB address in R4 and the ACB address in R5. When the routine exits, the stack must be in the same state as when the routine was entered. The routine may use R0 through R5 but must save other registers defined to be nonscratch by the OpenVMS AXP calling standard before use and restore them before exiting. A special kernel mode AST routine written in a language other than MACRO-64 leaves this detail to the compiler.

▶ As the result of one interrupt, all pending special kernel mode ASTs are delivered as well as possibly one other pending deliverable AST.

▶ A special kernel mode AST routine is responsible for the deallocation of the ACB to nonpaged pool. For normal ASTs, this deallocation is done by the AST delivery routine.

The next several sections briefly describe examples of the special kernel mode AST mechanism.

8.8.1   I/O Postprocessing in Process Context

Completing an I/O request requires the delivery of a special kernel mode AST to the process whose I/O completed. The I/O postprocessing interrupt service routine queues a former IRP as an ACB to the process whose I/O completed. The ACB specifies the special kernel mode AST routine BUFPOST or DIRPOST, in module IOCIOPOST. (DIRPOST is actually a subentry point of BUFPOST.)

The operations performed by the I/O completion AST routine are those that must execute in process context, particularly those that reference process virtual addresses. These include the following:

1. For buffered read I/O operations only, BUFPOST copies the data from the system buffer to the user buffer in process address space and deallocates the system buffer to nonpaged pool.

2. If a user diagnostic buffer was associated with the I/O request, DIRPOST copies the diagnostic information from the system diagnostic buffer to the user's buffer and deallocates the system buffer.

3. DIRPOST decrements the channel control block field CCB$L_IOC, the

number of I/O requests in progress on this channel. Channel control blocks are in P1 space.

4. If the I/O request specified an I/O status block (IOSB), the routine copies information from the IRP to the IOSB, which is in process address space.

5. If ACB$V_QUOTA was set in IRP$B_RMOD (the same offset as ACB$B_RMOD), AST notification of I/O completion was requested. The AST procedure value and the optional AST argument were originally stored in the IRP (now an ACB). DIRPOST invokes SCH$QAST to requeue the former IRP as an ACB. This time the IRP/ACB represents a normal AST in the access mode at which the I/O request was made.

6. Otherwise, if ACB$V_QUOTA is clear, DIRPOST deallocates the IRP/ACB to nonpaged pool.

I/O postprocessing is described in more detail in Chapter 23.

8.8.2 $GETJPI System Service

A process requests the $GETJPI system service to obtain information about itself or another process. If the request is for information in the virtual address space of another process on the same VMScluster node, the $GETJPI system service queues an AST to the target process. Running in the context of the target process, $GETJPI's special kernel mode AST routine can easily examine process-private address space. Chapter 14 describes the $GETJPI system service in detail and discusses the additional steps necessary to obtain information from the virtual address space of a process running on another VMScluster node.

The $GETJPI system service procedure, EXE$GETJPI in module SYSGETJPI, performs the following steps:

1. It allocates and fills in an extended ACB to describe a special kernel mode AST and the desired items of information. The ACB includes a buffer to return the data.

2. It queues the AST to the target process.

3. The special kernel mode AST routine, executing in the context of the target process, moves the requested information into the buffer. It modifies the ACB so that it can be used to queue a second special kernel mode AST back to the requesting process.

4. The second special kernel mode AST routine copies data from the extended ACB buffer to buffers in the requesting process. It also sets the event flag associated with this request.

5. If the process has requested AST notification of request completion, the extended ACB is used for the third time. The special kernel mode AST routine uses it to cause delivery of a normal AST in the access mode from which the system service was requested.

   If the process has not requested AST notification, the extended ACB is deallocated to nonpaged pool.

8.8.3   **Reading and Writing Process-Private Address Space**

An image running in the context of one process can call EXE$READ_PROCESS or EXE$WRITE_PROCESS, in module PROC_READ_WRITE, to read or write the process-private address space or registers of another process. Note that these routines are not system services and can only be called from code already running in kernel mode. These routines are used by the DELTA debugger and, when analyzing the running system, the System Dump Analyzer (SDA).

The arguments to either routine include a starting address or register, a number of bytes, and a target process ID. The routines can also be used to access system space. The *OpenVMS AXP Version 1.5 Release Notes* describe the interface to these routines. This section briefly describes their operation, which resembles that of the $GETJPI system service procedure.

In the absence of errors, the sequence is as follows:

1. The kernel mode code calls EXE$READ_PROCESS or EXE$WRITE_PROCESS.
2. EXE$READ_PROCESS or EXE$WRITE_PROCESS validates the request, checking that IPL at entry is 0, that the target process exists, that the user's input or output (depending on whether this is a write or read) buffer is accessible, and that its arguments are correct.
3. The routine allocates and fills in an extended ACB to describe a special kernel mode AST, the address or registers in the target process, and if this is a write, the new contents for the address or registers. The extended ACB also contains the current contents of the process's image counter, PHD$L_IMGCNT.

   When the special kernel mode AST routine later returns information to the requesting process, the routine compares the current image counter value to the one saved as a sanity check before writing information to the process's address space. PHD$L_IMGCNT is always incremented at image rundown, so the test detects the possibility that the image invoking EXE$READ_PROCESS or EXE$WRITE_PROCESS exited before the AST returned. The field is also incremented by EXE$READ_PROCESS or EXE$WRITE_PROCESS if the AST does not return within 3 seconds.

   The specified special kernel mode AST routine is one of the following:

   - EXE$READ_PROCESS_AST, in module PROC_READ_WRITE, which reads another process's virtual address space
   - EXE$WRITE_PROCESS_AST, in module PROC_READ_WRITE, which writes another process's virtual address space
   - EXE$READ_PROCESS_REG_AST, in module PROC_READ_WRITE_REG, which reads another process's registers
   - EXE$WRITE_PROCESS_REG_AST, in module PROC_READ_WRITE_REG, which writes another process's registers

4. The routine queues the AST to the target process, resuming the target process if necessary.

5. It requests the Set Timer ($SETIMR) system service in order to receive AST notification when 3 seconds have elapsed and then hibernates.

6. The specified special kernel mode AST routine executes in the context of the target process:

   • EXE$READ_PROCESS_REG_AST builds a stack data structure that contains the original contents of all the integer registers and, if the process is using floating-point, the floating-point registers. It calls EXE$READ_PROCESS_AST, which copies data from the stack data structure into the extended ACB and requeues the ACB to the originating process. It then returns.

   • EXE$WRITE_PROCESS_REG_AST builds a stack data structure that contains the original contents of all the integer registers and, if the process is using floating-point, the floating-point registers. It calls EXE$WRITE_PROCESS_AST to copy data from the extended ACB into the stack data structure and requeue the ACB to the originating process. When EXE$WRITE_PROCESS_AST returns, EXE$WRITE_PROCESS_REG_AST copies information from the stack data structure either to the target registers or to the save area from which they will be restored and then returns.

   • EXE$READ_PROCESS_AST confirms that kernel mode has read access to the specified address and then copies it to the extended ACB. It requeues the ACB to the originating process and returns.

   • EXE$WRITE_PROCESS_AST confirms that kernel mode has write access to the specified address and copies data from the extended ACB to the address. It requeues the ACB to the originating process and returns.

7. In the case of a read request, the second special kernel mode AST routine, running in the context of the originating process, checks that the same image is running as when the first AST was queued, checks that the output buffer in the current process is writable, and copies data from the extended ACB buffer to the output buffer.

   In either case, the second special kernel mode AST routine awakens the originating process from its hibernation and deallocates the extended ACB.

8. EXE$READ_PROCESS or EXE$WRITE_PROCESS cancels the timer request and returns to its caller.

8.8.4 Power Recovery ASTs

The implementation of power recovery ASTs relies on special kernel mode ASTs. A power recovery AST enables a process to receive notification that a power failure and successful restart have occurred. Chapter 36 describes this feature in more detail.

When a power recovery occurs, the executive queues a special kernel mode AST to each process that has requested power recovery AST notification. The special kernel mode AST routine copies the procedure value of the user-requested AST procedure, which is stored in P1 space, to ACB$L_AST and requeues the ACB as a normal AST. The special kernel mode AST routine is necessary for accessing the process's P1 space.

8.8.5   Piggyback Special Kernel Mode ASTs

Piggyback special kernel mode ASTs (PKASTs) enable a special kernel mode AST to ride piggyback in the ACB$L_KAST field of a normal AST. The normal access mode determines the order of enqueuing and delivery. If delivery to that access mode is disabled or blocked, the piggyback special kernel mode AST cannot be delivered.

The AST delivery interrupt service routine invokes the piggyback special kernel mode AST routine just before calling the normal AST. When the special kernel mode AST returns, the normal AST is called.

There are several reasons for using piggyback special kernel mode ASTs:

▸ It is faster to deliver two ASTs together than to deliver two ASTs separately.

▸ There are times when delivering an AST requires some additional work in kernel mode in the context of the target process. Piggyback special kernel mode ASTs facilitate this work.

  The $ENQ system service uses a piggyback special kernel mode AST to write to the requestor's lock status block and lock value block. To copy the information from the lock database to the requestor's process space, a piggyback special kernel mode AST is required.

  Piggyback special kernel mode ASTs are also used in terminal out-of-band ASTs (see Section 8.10.2.3).

▸ A piggyback special kernel mode AST can queue other normal ASTs to a process. The $ENQ system service uses this feature to deliver both blocking and completion ASTs to a process through one ACB. Chapter 11 contains further information.

8.9   SYSTEM USE OF NORMAL ASTS

Several other executive features are implemented through normal ASTs. For example, the automatic working set limit adjustment that takes place at quantum end is implemented with a normal kernel mode AST. Chapter 13 discusses quantum-end activities, and Chapter 19 provides a detailed description of automatic working set limit adjustment.

CPU time limit expiration is implemented with potentially multiple ASTs. Beginning in user mode, the AST procedure requests the Exit ($EXIT) system service. If the process is not deleted, a supervisor mode time expiration AST is queued. This loop continues with higher access modes until the process is deleted.

The executive also uses the AST mechanism for the $FORCEX, Suspend Process ($SUSPND), and Delete Process ($DELPRC) system services. These services can affect a process running on another VMScluster node. If the target process is executing on the same VMScluster node as the system service requestor, the system service queues an AST directly to the target process. Chapter 14 discusses the additional steps required to affect a process running on another VMScluster node.

The $FORCEX system service, detailed in Chapter 14, queues a user mode AST that requests the $EXIT system service from the context of the target process. The $SUSPND and $DELPRC system services queue an AST to the target process to implement suspension or deletion through code running in the context of the target process.

The $SUSPND system service queues either a supervisor or kernel mode AST to its target process, depending on the access mode of the suspension. A process suspended through a supervisor mode AST (the default) can execute kernel and executive mode ASTs. A process suspended through a kernel mode AST can become computable only when it is resumed through another process.

Process deletion and kernel mode suspension must take care to synchronize their actions with the activities of the Files-11 XQP. The Files-11 XQP runs in process context as a kernel mode AST thread, taking out locks and making I/O requests in response to the process's file system requests. The XQP indicates that it is active by incrementing the PCB field PCB$L_DPC. When the XQP must wait for a lock to be granted or an I/O request to complete, it returns from the AST procedure so that the process can wait at the access mode in which the file system request originated.

Waiting in the outer mode allows delivery of ASTs to that mode and more privileged modes. While the XQP is executing or waiting, kernel mode suspension of the process would risk blocking other processes with interests in the same locks. Deletion of the process would risk relatively minor on-disk corruption, such as dangling directory entries and lost files.

Therefore, the kernel mode suspension and process deletion services queue normal kernel mode ASTs, which cannot be delivered until the XQP AST completes. Furthermore, these AST procedures check that PCB$L_DPC is zero before proceeding with actual process suspension or deletion.

If PCB$L_DPC is not zero, these AST procedures place the process into a wait. They clear bit 0 of PCB$L_ASTACT so that another kernel mode AST can be delivered, invoke SCH$RESET_ASTSR to reset the ASTSR register, and place the process into the resource wait RSN$_ASTWAIT. The process waits in kernel mode at IPL 0. Thus, special and normal kernel mode ASTs can be delivered to it. The resource wait PC is an address within the AST procedure, so after the XQP AST completes, the suspend or delete AST procedure will be reentered to finish its job.

Some time later, queuing of an AST makes the process computable, and delivery of an XQP completion AST causes the XQP to be reentered. When the XQP is done, it decrements PCB$L_DPC and returns from its AST procedure. The suspend or delete AST procedure is reentered and can proceed, now that PCB$L_DPC is zero.

8.9.1 Process Suspension

The $SUSPND system service causes a target process to be placed into a suspended state. After checking the capability of the initiating process to affect the target process, the system service procedure determines whether a supervisor or kernel mode suspension has been requested. Supervisor mode is the default. Kernel mode suspension, specified in the optional FLAGS argument, can only be requested from executive or kernel mode. The system service procedure queues either a kernel or a supervisor mode AST to the target process so that the suspension and waiting will occur in that process's context. The wait mechanism requires that a process be placed into a wait from its own context.

When the kernel mode AST is delivered to a process undergoing kernel mode suspension, the SUSPND AST procedure tests whether a Resume Process ($RESUME) system service has been requested for this process. If so, the SUSPND AST procedure returns, leaving the process unsuspended. If not, SUSPND tests PCB$L_DPC to determine whether an XQP operation is in progress.

If PCB$L_DPC is greater than zero, SUSPND places the process into a resource wait. If PCB$L_DPC is zero, SUSPND places the process into a suspended wait state. The process waits in kernel mode at IPL 0. Its saved PC is an address within SUSPND, so when the process is later placed into execution, it again tests whether a $RESUME has been requested.

When the supervisor mode AST is delivered to a process undergoing supervisor mode suspension, the SUSPEND_SOFT AST procedure requests the $SUSPND system service. Running in kernel mode in the context of the target process, the $SUSPND system service procedure tests whether a $RESUME has been requested for the process. If not, the $SUSPND system service procedure cleans up the kernel stack and places the process into a suspended wait state. These actions can only be done from kernel mode.

The process waits in supervisor mode with the supervisor mode PCB$L_ASTACT bit set. Its saved PC is an address within the SUSPEND_SOFT AST procedure, so when the process is placed back into execution, it again requests the $SUSPND system service to test whether a $RESUME has been requested. Waiting in this manner, the process can execute kernel and executive mode ASTs.

Chapter 14 provides further details.

8.9.2 Process Deletion

The $DELPRC system service causes a target process to be deleted. After checking the capability of the initiating process to affect the target process, the system service procedure queues a normal kernel mode AST to the target process so that the deletion will occur in the context of that process. Chapter 31 provides a detailed explanation of process deletion.

The use of the AST mechanism provides the following advantages:

▶ Queuing the AST makes the process computable, regardless of its wait state, unless the process is suspended. The $DELPRC system service ensures the deletion of a suspended process by requesting the $RESUME system service before queuing the AST.

▶ The process must be resident for the AST to be delivered. Therefore, special cases, such as the deletion of a process that is outswapped, simply do not exist.

▶ The DELETE AST procedure, running in process context, is able to request standard system services, such as Deassign Channel ($DASSGN), Deallocate Device ($DALLOC), and Delete Virtual Address Space ($DELTVA), to implement process deletion. These system services and the AST procedure reference process-private address space, and thus they must run in process context.

8.10 ATTENTION AND OUT-OF-BAND ASTS

Several OpenVMS AXP device drivers queue an AST to notify a process that a particular attention condition has occurred on a device. The terminal driver, for example, queues an attention AST to notify an interested process that CTRL/C or CTRL/Y has been typed on its terminal. The terminal driver can also queue an out-of-band AST as notification that a control character other than CTRL/C and CTRL/Y has been typed. The mailbox driver can queue an attention AST as notification that an unsolicited message has been put in a mailbox or that an attempt to read an empty mailbox is in progress.

The basic sequence for both attention ASTs and out-of-band ASTs follows:

1. A process assigns a channel and requests the $QIO system service, specifying that it should receive AST notification of an attention condition on that device.

2. The device driver builds a data structure to describe the attention AST request, inserts it on a list connected to the device unit control block (UCB), and completes the I/O request.

3. If the attention condition occurs, the device interrupt service routine delivers the attention AST by queuing an AST to the process.

The major distinction between the attention AST and the out-of-band AST mechanisms is that out-of-band ASTs automatically repeat, whereas attention ASTs must be "rearmed." That is, a process must repeat its $QIO request for each attention notification.

8.10.1 Attention ASTs

The sections that follow describe aspects of attention AST support.

8.10.1.1 Requesting Attention ASTs.
To request an attention AST for a particular device whose driver supports this feature, the user requests the $QIO system service with the I/O function IO$_SETMODE or, for some devices, IO$_SETCHAR. The kind of attention AST requested is indicated by a function modifier.

The relevant function decision table (FDT) action routine for such a driver invokes COM$SETATTNAST, in module COMDRVSUB, which performs the following actions:

1. If the user AST procedure value (the $QIO P1 parameter) is zero, the request is interpreted as a flush attention AST list request (see Section 8.10.1.3).
2. Otherwise, COM$SETATTNAST allocates an expanded ACB from non-paged pool and charges it against the process AST quota. The expanded ACB will be used both as a fork block (FKB) and as an ACB and is referred to as a FKB/ACB.
3. COM$SETATTNAST copies information into the FKB/ACB, such as the AST procedure value, AST argument, channel number, and PID.
4. It acquires the device lock, raising IPL to UCB$B_DIPL, to synchronize access to the attention AST list. An attention AST list is a singly linked, last-in/first-out (LIFO) list of FKB/ACBs connected to the UCB of a device. The location of the FKB/ACB listhead is driver-specific; some UCBs have multiple listheads, one for each attention condition the driver supports. The FDT action routine passes the address of the listhead in a register to COM$SETATTNAST.

   COM$SETATTNAST inserts the FKB/ACB into the attention AST list.
5. COM$SETATTNAST then releases the device lock, restoring the previous IPL, and returns to the FDT action routine.

8.10.1.2 Queuing Attention ASTs.
When the driver (typically the device interrupt service routine) determines that the attention condition has occurred, it invokes COM$DELATTNAST with the address of the FKB/ACB listhead.

COM$DELATTNAST queues every FKB/ACB on the list to its target process. A driver invokes an alternative entry point, COM$DELATTNASTP, to specify that only ASTs requested by a particular process be queued. Each process that has assigned a channel to the device can request AST notification of an attention condition.

Although COM$DELATTNAST is entered at device IPL, the queuing of ASTs must occur at IPL$_SCHED with the SCHED spinlock held to synchronize access to the scheduler database (see Chapter 9). Specifically, IPL must not be lowered to IPL$_SCHED. To accomplish correct synchronization and not block activities at IPL 7 and IPL 8, COM$DELATTNAST creates an IPL$_QUEUEAST (6) fork process to queue each AST.

The following steps summarize queuing of attention ASTs:

1. COM$DELATTNAST acquires the device lock to synchronize access to the attention AST list.
2. It scans each FKB/ACB in the list.
   In the case of entry through COM$DELATTNASTP, the routine compares the PID in the FKB/ACB to the requested PID. If they are not equal, the routine leaves the data structure in the queue and goes on to the next entry. If the PIDs match, the routine continues with the next step.
3. The routine removes the FKB/ACB from its list, stores the procedure value of a fork routine in FKB$L_FPC of the FKB/ACB, and dispatches to EXE$PRIMITIVE_FORK. EXE$PRIMITIVE_FORK queues the fork block to the fork IPL 6 listhead and requests an interrupt at that IPL.
4. When IPL drops below 6, the fork interrupt is granted. The IPL 6 fork dispatcher removes the FKB/ACB from the IPL 6 fork block queue and dispatches to COM$DELATTNAST's fork process routine.
5. At IPL 6, COM$DELATTNAST's fork process routine reformats the fork block into an ACB, describing the AST procedure and the access mode of the original attention AST request.
6. The fork process routine invokes SCH$QAST to acquire the SCHED spinlock and queue the ACB to the process requesting the attention AST.

8.10.1.3   **Flushing an Attention AST List.** The list of attention ASTs is flushed as the result of an explicit user request, a Cancel I/O on Channel ($CANCEL), or a $DASSGN system service request for the associated device.

A user explicitly requests that the attention AST list be flushed by requesting the $QIO system service with an I/O function code and modifier for establishing an attention AST but with an AST procedure value of zero (see Section 8.10.1.1). Invoked this way, COM$SETATTNAST branches to COM$FLUSHATTNS.

COM$FLUSHATTNS is entered with the PID and channel number of the attention ASTs to be deleted. COM$FLUSHATTNS performs the following operations.

1. It acquires the device lock, raising IPL to UCB$B_DIPL of the device.
2. It scans the FKB/ACB list looking for all FKB/ACBs with a PID and channel number that match those of the requested flush operation.
3. COM$FLUSHATTNS removes each FKB/ACB with matching PID and channel number from the attention AST list. It increments the process AST quota and deallocates the FKB/ACB to nonpaged pool.
4. It continues its scan of the list with step 1. Reaching the end of the list, COM$FLUSHATTNS releases the device lock, restoring the IPL at which it was entered, and returns to its invoker.

8.10.1.4 **Examples in the OpenVMS AXP Executive.** Brief descriptions follow of the terminal and mailbox drivers' support of attention ASTs.

Notification of CTRL/C and CTRL/Y is requested through a $QIO to the terminal driver with a function code of IO$_SETMODE or IO$_SETCHAR and function modifier of IO$M_CTRLCAST or IO$M_CTRLYAST. There is a separate listhead for each condition in each terminal UCB.

When the Digital command language (DCL) is first entered in a process, it requests CTRL/Y notification; because it executes in supervisor mode, its attention AST will be a supervisor mode AST. A user image, running in the same process, can also request CTRL/C and CTRL/Y notification. Typically, the image's attention ASTs will be user mode ASTs. Note that DCL's supervisor mode AST would be entered first if CTRL/Y is typed. If an application is to receive control in response to CTRL/Y, DCL must cancel its request. Typically, such an application calls the Run-Time Library procedure LIB$DISABLE_CTRL; alternatively, the application could run in a process in which the DCL command SET NOCONTROL=Y had been issued.

When an interactive user (or the running image) spawns a subprocess, DCL, running in the context of the spawned subprocess, requests CTRL/Y notification. The image running in the spawned subprocess can also request CTRL/C and CTRL/Y notification. All the attention AST requests, because they are associated with the same terminal, are queued to the same CTRL/C and CTRL/Y listheads. As the user spawns a new subprocess or attaches to an already created process, DCL, running in the context of that process, tells the terminal driver the PID of the process currently associated with the terminal.

When CTRL/C is typed, the terminal driver invokes COM$DELATTN-ASTP to deliver only those CTRL/C attention ASTs requested by the process currently associated with the terminal. If no CTRL/C attention AST has been requested, the terminal driver interprets CTRL/C as CTRL/Y and searches the CTRL/Y AST list instead. When a CTRL/Y is typed, the driver searches only the CTRL/Y attention AST list. For more information on spawn and attach, see Chapter 30.

Because the FKB/ACB data structures are not reused, CTRL/C and CTRL/Y attention ASTs must be reenabled each time they are delivered to a process.

The CTRL/Y attention AST list is flushed by a $DASSGN request. The CTRL/C attention AST list is flushed by $CANCEL as well as by $DASSGN. Both lists can be flushed by an explicit user request.

A process requests a mailbox attention AST by requesting the $QIO system service with the function code IO$_SETMODE or IO$_SETCHAR. The possible function modifiers are IO$M_READATTN, IO$M_WRTATTN, and IO$M_MB_ROOM_NOTIFY. IO$M_WRTATTN requests notification of an unsolicited message written to that mailbox. An unsolicited message is one written to a mailbox that has no outstanding read request. IO$M_READATTN requests notification when any process requests a read from that mailbox and there is no message in it. IO$M_MB_ROOM_NOTIFY requests notification when room becomes available in the mailbox.

Attention ASTs of each type can be declared by multiple processes for the same mailbox. When a condition corresponding to an attention AST occurs, all ASTs of the appropriate type are delivered. Only the first process to make a corresponding I/O request will be able to complete the transfer of data signaled by a read or write attention AST.

These attention ASTs must be reenabled after delivery because the entire attention AST list is delivered and removed after each occurrence of the specified condition.

Chapter 30 describes how DCL uses mailbox attention ASTs to communicate among spawned subprocesses and the top-level process.

8.10.2 Out-of-Band ASTs

The OpenVMS AXP terminal driver uses a newer form of AST mechanism to notify a process that an out-of-band character has been received from its terminal. (Out-of-band characters are control characters, the ASCII codes 00 to 20_{16}.) However, for compatibility with earlier VAX/VMS versions, the OpenVMS AXP terminal driver, like its OpenVMS VAX counterpart, provides the attention AST mechanism described previously to notify a process of the receipt of the out-of-band characters CTRL/C and CTRL/Y.

Out-of-band ASTs are similar to attention ASTs in that the terminal driver forks down to IPL$_QUEUEAST to queue an ACB to the process.

The most significant difference between the attention AST mechanism and the out-of-band AST mechanism is that, once declared, out-of-band ASTs are delivered to the process for its lifetime or until the $CANCEL system service is requested to flush the AST list. Another difference is that the out-of-band AST mechanism employs a piggyback special kernel mode AST routine.

8.10.2.1 The Terminal AST Block.
The terminal driver builds a data structure called a terminal AST block (TAST) to describe an out-of-band AST request. Figure 8.5 illustrates the TAST. The TAST can be in two lists at once because

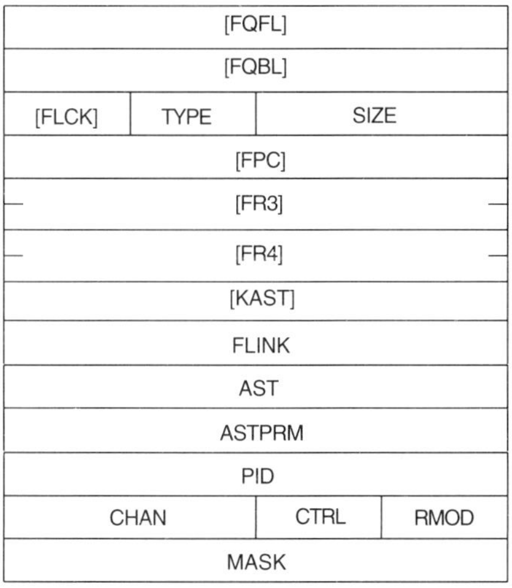

[FQFL]		
[FQBL]		
[FLCK]	TYPE	SIZE
[FPC]		
[FR3]		
[FR4]		
[KAST]		
FLINK		
AST		
ASTPRM		
PID		
CHAN	CTRL	RMOD
MASK		

Figure 8.5
Layout of a Terminal AST Block (TAST)

of its structure. Through TAST$L_FLINK, the TAST is always queued to the terminal UCB in a singly linked list. Through the first two longwords of the TAST, it can be inserted into a fork queue or a process's ACB queue. The terminal driver sets the bit TAST$V_BUSY in TAST$B_CTRL when the TAST is in use as a fork block or ACB. The TAST includes space for fork process context (that is, procedure value of a fork process routine, fork R3, and fork R4) and the AST information (procedure value of the AST procedure and its argument, PID, and RMOD fields).

8.10.2.2   **Set Out-of-Band AST Mechanism.** A process requests out-of-band notification by requesting the $QIO system service, specifying IO$_SETMODE (or IO$_SETCHAR) with the function modifier IO$M_OUTBAND.

The terminal driver's FDT action routine invokes COM$SETCTRLAST, in module COMDRVSUB, which performs the following steps:

1. If the user AST procedure address ($QIO P1 parameter) is zero or the character mask ($QIO P2 parameter) is zero, COM$SETCTRLAST interprets the request as a flush out-of-band AST list request (see Section 8.10.2.4).
2. Otherwise, COM$SETCTRLAST allocates a TAST from nonpaged pool.
3. It then acquires the device lock, raising IPL to UCB$B_DIPL, to synchronize access to the TAST list.
4. COM$SETCTRLAST next scans the list of out-of-band TASTs, searching for one with the same characteristics as the $QIO request. The following items are checked.

209

- The PID. Out-of-band ASTs can be requested for the same terminal device from a process and its subprocesses (which will have different PIDs).
- The channel number.

5. If COM$SETCTRLAST finds a TAST with the same characteristics that is not in use, it modifies the existing TAST by replacing the AST procedure value and the control mask. It then invokes COM$DRVDEALMEM, in module COMDRVSUB, to create a fork process to deallocate the just-allocated TAST. This unusual sequence is required because COM$SET-CTRLAST must hold the device lock while scanning the TAST list. During that time, it cannot allocate pool, synchronization to which is controlled at a lower IPL.

   If the TAST is in use (perhaps queued as an ACB to the process), COM$SETCTRLAST marks it as "lost" and removes it from the list. COM$SETCTRLAST charges the process AST quota and initializes the just-allocated TAST to describe the request. It copies information from the IRP (the AST procedure address, channel number, and PID) and the $QIO character mask into the TAST. It inserts the TAST into the queue position of the lost TAST.

6. If it does not find a similar TAST, it initializes the just-allocated TAST and charges the process AST quota. It places the TAST at the tail of the list.

7. COM$SETCTRLAST ORs the $QIO character mask into the terminal's out-of-band AST summary mask, the field UCB$L_TL_OUTBAND. This mask represents all the control characters for which the terminal driver must deliver an out-of-band AST. It then releases the device lock, restoring the previous IPL.

8.10.2.3 **Delivery of Out-of-Band ASTs.** When a control key is typed at a terminal, the terminal driver checks whether that control character is represented in the terminal's out-of-band AST summary mask. If the bit in the summary mask is set, an out-of-band AST has been requested for that control character. The terminal driver interrupt service routine invokes COM$DELCTRLAST, in module COMDRVSUB, to deliver the out-of-band AST. The terminal driver uses an alternative entry point, COM$DELCTRLASTP, to specify that only ASTs requested by a particular process be delivered.

The following steps summarize the delivery of out-of-band ASTs:

1. COM$DELCTRLAST is entered at device IPL. It acquires the device lock to synchronize access to the TAST list. It scans the list of TASTs for one whose character mask contains the character typed at the terminal.

   When it finds one with a matching character mask, it checks the busy bit to see whether the control block is already in use. In the case of entry through COM$DELCTRLASTP, the routine also compares the PID in

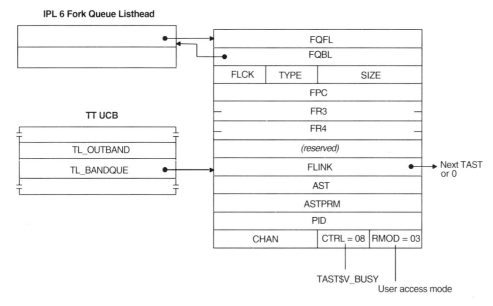

IPL 6 Fork Queue Listhead

FQFL		
FQBL		
FLCK	TYPE	SIZE
FPC		
FR3		
FR4		
(reserved)		
FLINK		
AST		
ASTPRM		
PID		
CHAN	CTRL = 08	RMOD = 03

TT UCB

TL_OUTBAND

TL_BANDQUE

Next TAST or 0

TAST$V_BUSY

User access mode

Figure 8.6
TAST Used as a Fork Block

the TAST to the requested PID. If they are not equal, the routine goes on to the next TAST in the queue.

If TAST$V_BUSY is set, COM$DELCTRLAST skips that TAST. If TAST$V_BUSY is clear, COM$DELCTRLAST sets it, marking the TAST in use, and records in TAST$L_ASTPRM the control character that was received.

2. The synchronization considerations previously described for COM$DEL-ATTNAST apply to COM$DELCTRLAST as well. It creates an IPL 6 fork process, using the TAST as an FKB, to queue each AST. The TAST also remains linked to the terminal UCB list of TASTs. Figure 8.6 shows the TAST in the terminal UCB's TAST list and in the fork block queue.

3. When IPL drops below 6, the fork interrupt is granted. The IPL 6 fork dispatcher removes the TAST from the IPL 6 fork block queue and dispatches to COM$DELCTRLAST's fork process.

4. At IPL 6, COM$DELCTRLAST's fork process routine reformats the fork block into an ACB describing the AST procedure and the access mode of the original out-of-band AST request. The no-delete and piggyback special kernel mode AST flags are set in the ACB, and the special kernel mode AST field is loaded with the procedure value of COM$DELCTRLAST's piggyback special kernel mode AST.

5. The fork process routine invokes SCH$QAST to acquire the SCHED spinlock and queue the ACB to the process that requested the attention AST. Figure 8.7 shows the TAST in use as an ACB.

211

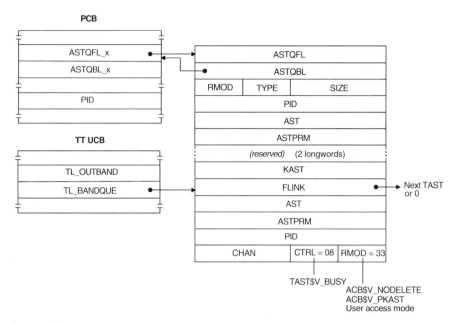

Figure 8.7
TAST Used as an ACB

6. When the process receives the AST, the piggyback special kernel mode AST routine is executed first. The piggyback special kernel mode AST performs two functions:

   a. It clears TAST$V_BUSY.

   b. If the TAST is marked as "lost," the piggyback special kernel mode AST routine deallocates it and returns AST quota to the process. A TAST is "lost" when COM$FLUSHCTRLS is unable to deallocate it because its busy bit is set (see Section 8.10.2.4). Once the AST has been delivered, the TAST is no longer needed.

8.10.2.4   **Flushing an Out-of-Band AST List.** The list of out-of-band ASTs is flushed as the result of an explicit user request, a $CANCEL, or a $DASSGN request for the associated device.

A user explicitly requests that the out-of-band AST list be flushed by requesting a $QIO set out-of-band AST with an AST procedure value of zero or a character mask of zero (see Section 8.10.2.2). When COM$SETCTRLAST receives such a request, it branches to COM$FLUSHCTRLS.

COM$FLUSHCTRLS is entered with the PID and channel number of the attention ASTs to be deleted. COM$FLUSHCTRLS performs the following operations:

1. It acquires the device lock, raising IPL to UCB$B_DIPL of the device.
2. It scans the out-of-band AST list and compares the PID and channel

number in the TAST with those of the requested flush operation. As it scans the list, it builds a new out-of-band AST summary mask. If COM$FLUSHCTRLS finds a TAST that does not match, COM$FLUSH-CTRLS ORs its control characters into the summary mask being built and goes on to the next TAST.

3. If the PIDs and channel numbers match, COM$FLUSHCTRLS removes the AST from the list. It checks TAST$V_BUSY to see whether the TAST is in use as a FKB or ACB.

   If TAST$V_BUSY is set, COM$FLUSHCTRLS sets the "lost" bit so that the TAST will be deallocated once its AST is delivered.

   If the TAST is not busy, COM$FLUSHCTRLS returns the process AST quota and deallocates the TAST to nonpaged pool.

4. COM$FLUSHCTRLS continues processing until it has scanned the entire list. It then replaces the old summary mask with the one just built.

5. COM$FLUSHCTRLS releases the device lock, restoring the IPL at which it was entered.

8.11   RELEVANT SOURCE MODULES

Source modules described in this chapter include

[LIB]ASTSTKDEF.SDL
[LIB]ACBDEF.SDL
[LIB]PCBDEF.SDL
[LIB]TASTDEF.SDL
[SYS]ASTDEL.MAR
[SYS]ASTDEL_STACK.M64
[SYS]COMDRVSUB.MAR
[SYS]SCHEDULER.M64
[SYS]SYSASTCON.MAR

PART III / Synchronization

9   Synchronization Techniques

"Time," said George, "why I can give you a definition of time.
It's what keeps everything from happening at once."
Ray Cummings, *The Man Who Mastered Time*

In an operating system that allows interrupts, the interrupting code must coordinate, or synchronize, with the code being interrupted to ensure correct behavior. Routines sharing data structures must synchronize modifications to shared data; a thread of execution modifying shared data must synchronize with both read and write accesses by other threads.

A thread of execution sharing data with an I/O processor must synchronize its accesses to the data with the I/O processor's. Similarly, when an operating system runs on multiple processors sharing the same memory, an executive code thread running on one processor must synchronize its accesses to shared data with those of executive code threads running on the others. Also, a process running on one processor must synchronize its accesses to shared data with those of other processes running on the other processors.

The OpenVMS AXP operating system uses a combination of the following Alpha AXP mechanisms and software techniques to synchronize the actions of code threads that might otherwise interfere with each other:

▶ Atomic memory accesses to aligned longwords and quadwords
▶ Load-locked (LDx_L) and store-conditional (STx_C) instructions
▶ Interrupt priority level (IPL)
▶ Memory barriers to enforce order on reads and writes of data accessed by multiple processors (CPUs and I/O processors)
▶ Queue support, provided by privileged architecture library (PALcode) routines
▶ Spinlocks to synchronize access to executive data shared by multiple processors
▶ Mutual exclusion semaphores (mutexes)
▶ Lock management system services
▶ Event flags
▶ Parallel processing Run-Time Library routines

Because many of the executive synchronization techniques used by the OpenVMS AXP system were originally based upon the VAX architecture, this chapter discusses VAX synchronization mechanisms as background for explaining Alpha AXP mechanisms and contrasts VAX and Alpha AXP mechanisms.

This chapter deals primarily with synchronizing access to memory. Although access to other types of storage must be synchronized, for example,

217

to shared hardware resources or data in files, the techniques for such synchronization are based upon synchronizing access to memory.

9.1   OVERVIEW

Synchronization is a term commonly used to refer to the simultaneous occurrence of two or more events. In a computer context, however, the word is used to refer to the coordination of events. The coordination can still be as specific as the simultaneous occurrence of events; this use of the term occurs most often in descriptions of hardware mechanisms. In descriptions of software, *synchronization* usually refers to the coordination of events in such a way that only one event happens at a time. This specialized kind of synchronization is known as serialization. Serialized events are assigned an order and processed one at a time in that order. While a serialized event is being processed, no other event in the series is allowed to disrupt it.

Atomicity and mutual exclusion are frequently described as different types of serialization, although the two concepts overlap. *Atomicity* refers to the indivisibility of a small number of actions, such as those occurring during the execution of a single instruction or a small number of instructions. *Mutual exclusion* refers to serializing the execution of groups of instructions so that one group completes before another starts.

Algorithms requiring synchronization take many forms and arise in many contexts. Most of them reduce to solving a small number of fundamental problems.

One such problem is the requirement that a thread of execution read or write multiple data items as an atomic operation. If a thread has written some but not all of the items when another thread interrupts and reads the data, the interrupting thread obtains an inconsistent view of the data. If, on the other hand, a thread has read some but not all of the items when another thread interrupts and writes them all, the interrupted thread gets the inconsistent view.

Another closely related synchronization problem is the requirement that a thread of execution read a data item and write an updated value into the same location. If another thread with the same intent toward that location can intervene after the read and before the write, so that both threads read the same value and both write the location, the change to that location is not atomic: the change made by one of the threads overlays the change made by the other.

The selection of a synchronization method for threads of execution that access a shared data item depends upon issues like the following:

▶ Which threads of execution can interrupt a thread accessing the data, and which threads can it interrupt?

- Do all the threads execute within the same process context?
- In which access mode do the threads execute?

218

- Do all the threads execute in process context?
- At which IPL do the threads execute?
- Do all the threads run on the same processor?

▸ What are the characteristics of the shared data item?

- In which address space is it?
- What is its size and alignment?
- What is the protection of the pages that it occupies?

The sections that follow discuss synchronization issues in more detail: the types of threads of execution, the kinds of memory accesses, Alpha AXP synchronization mechanisms, the software synchronization techniques based on those mechanisms, and the software techniques appropriate to different types of threads of execution.

9.1.1   Threads of Execution

Code threads that can execute within one process include the following:

▸ Mainline code in an image being executed

▸ Asynchronous system traps (ASTs) that interrupt the image

▸ Condition handlers established by the image and entered after exceptions occur

▸ Inner access mode threads of execution entered as a result of system service, Record Management Services (RMS) service, and command language interpreter (CLI) callback requests

Process-based threads of execution can potentially share any data in P0 and P1 address space and must synchronize access to any data they share. A thread of execution can incur an exception, as a result of which control passes to a condition handler, or receive an AST, as a result of which control passes to an AST procedure. Moreover, an AST procedure can incur an exception, and a condition handler's execution can be interrupted by AST delivery. If a thread of execution requests a system or RMS service, control passes to an inner access mode thread of execution. Code executing in the inner mode can also incur exceptions, receive ASTs, and request services.

Multiple processes, each with its own threads of execution, can execute concurrently. Although each process has private P0 and P1 address space, processes can share data in a global section mapped into each process's address spaces. Synchronizing access to global section data is required because a thread of execution accessing the data in one process can be blocked or preempted; as a result, a thread of execution in another process can access the same data.

Although processes access the same system address space, the protection on system space pages usually prevents outer mode access. However, process-based code threads running in inner access modes can concurrently access data in system space and must synchronize access to it.

Interrupt service routines access only system space. They must synchronize access to shared system space data among themselves and with process-based inner mode threads of execution.

An I/O processor and a thread of execution running on a CPU must synchronize their accesses to shared data structures, for example, structures containing descriptions of I/O operations to be performed. (The term *I/O processor* includes I/O adapters and I/O widgets, described in Chapter 2.)

Multiprocessor execution adds synchronization requirements when the threads that must synchronize can run concurrently on different processors. Because a process executes on only one processor at a time, synchronization among threads of execution within a process is unaffected by whether the process runs on a uniprocessor (one with only one CPU) or on a symmetric multiprocessing (SMP) system. However, multiple processes can execute simultaneously on different processors. As a result, processes sharing data in a global section may require additional synchronization for SMP system execution. Furthermore, process-based inner mode and interrupt-based threads can execute simultaneously on different processors and thus may require synchronization of access to system space beyond what would suffice on a uniprocessor.

9.1.2   Reading and Writing Memory

The term *alignment* refers to the placement of a data item in memory. For a data item to be naturally aligned, its lowest addressed byte must reside at an address that is a multiple of the size of the data item in bytes. For example, a naturally aligned longword has an address that is a multiple of 4. An unaligned data item is one whose address is not naturally aligned. Usually, the term *naturally aligned* is shortened to *aligned.*

The term *atomicity* means the indivisibility of one or more actions. When there is more than one action, one of the actions cannot occur by itself; if one occurs, they all occur. The term must be qualified by the viewpoint from which the actions appear indivisible; an operation that is atomic for threads running on the same processor can appear as multiple actions to a thread of execution running on a different processor.

An atomic memory reference is one that results in one indivisible read or write of a data item in memory; no other access to any part of that data can occur during the course of the atomic reference. Atomic memory references are important for synchronizing access to a data item shared by multiple writers or by one writer and multiple readers. References need not be atomic to a data item that is not shared or to one that is shared but only read.

Given a thread of execution trying to write atomically to memory, the basic synchronization issues are as follows:

1. Based on the size and alignment of the data item, can the write be performed as a single memory operation indivisible from any viewpoint? If

it can, there is no synchronization issue. If the data item is unaligned, larger than the maximum size of memory access, or smaller than the minimum size of memory access, the write must be performed as multiple memory operations.

2. If multiple memory operations are required to write the data item, are there any other threads of execution that share it? If the data item is not shared, there is no synchronization issue. If the data item is shared, an intermediate state of memory might be visible, or multiple threads might each write part of the data item, resulting in inconsistent data.

3. If other threads of execution share the memory, can each such thread successfully prevent all other threads from accessing the data item during its own access?

   In other words, if the other threads execute on the same CPU, can interrupts or exceptions intervene so that one or more of these threads execute while the data item is in an intermediate state? Can the interrupts or exceptions be blocked, or can the other threads somehow be prevented from accessing the data item in an intermediate state?

4. If the threads accessing the data item execute on multiple CPUs, can each thread prevent the others from accessing the data item in an intermediate state? Also, how can a thread ensure that the others see its writes in order? That is, if they see the last write, does that imply that they see the earlier ones as well? If they write to the same memory locations, can each block the others until its writes complete?

The VAX architecture requires a VAX CPU to read or write the following memory operands in a single memory operation that is indivisible from the viewpoint of any other thread of execution:

▸ Byte operand
▸ Aligned word operand
▸ Aligned longword operand
▸ Bit field contained in one byte
▸ Aligned longword address used in a displacement deferred mode or auto-increment deferred mode operand specifier. For example, in the instruction BICL R0,@88(R7), if the longword at 88(R7) is aligned, its fetch is atomic.

A VAX CPU is not required to implement access to any other operand types as a single operation. For example, to write to an unaligned longword that crosses a quadword boundary, most VAX CPUs would perform two separate memory operations. Nonetheless, the VAX architecture requires that such an access be atomic with respect to other threads of execution on the same processor, if the instruction causing the access is uninterruptible.

The access is not, however, atomic with respect to processes executing on other processors. Another memory command from a different CPU could be

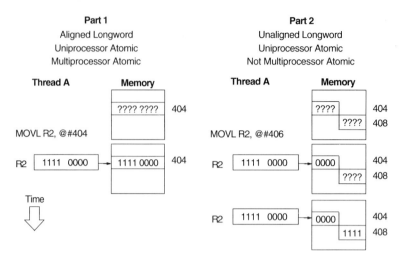

Figure 9.1
Writing Aligned and Unaligned Data on a VAX CPU

issued and carried out between the two commands issued by the first CPU. As a result, another process could read the longword and receive half old contents and half new. This type of inconsistency is known as data incoherency or word tearing, where *word* refers not necessarily to a 16-bit quantity but to any unit in which the memory is accessed.

Figure 9.1 contrasts writing to aligned and unaligned longwords on a VAX CPU. In Figures 9.1 through 9.4, each hexadecimal digit represents a nibble, that is, half a byte. The string ?? represents the initial indeterminate value of a byte.

Part 1 of Figure 9.1 shows a simple aligned longword write by thread A running on a VAX CPU. Part 2 shows the two successive memory operations required for a write to an unaligned longword that crosses a quadword boundary. Figure 9.2 shows how thread B, running on a different processor, can read the unaligned longword after it has been only partially updated by thread A. Because the unaligned longword cannot be written in a single memory operation, thread B can read it while it is in an intermediate, inconsistent state, half written by thread A and half still the initial contents.

In contrast to the variety of memory accesses allowed by the VAX architecture, the Alpha AXP architecture allows access only to an aligned longword or an aligned quadword. Reading or writing an aligned longword or quadword of memory is atomic with respect to any other thread of execution on the same or other processors. Part 1 of Figure 9.3 shows a simple aligned longword read from memory.

Reading or writing unaligned longwords and unaligned quadwords is possible only through a sequence of instructions. An instruction sequence that stores an unaligned longword, for example, requires the following steps.

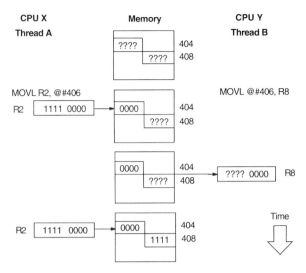

Figure 9.2
Word Tearing on a VAX System

1. Read each quadword in which part of the longword resides.
2. Insert the longword's bytes into each quadword.
3. Write each quadword back to memory.

Example 9.1 shows a sequence of AXP instructions that stores the low 32 bits of data from a register into an unaligned longword occupying two quadwords. Assuming that the longword is unaligned, the sequence uses load-unaligned and store-unaligned instructions. These instructions transform unaligned addresses into aligned ones by clearing the low-order bits and then loading from or storing to the aligned addresses. The numbers in Example 9.1 correspond to numbered steps in Part 2 of Figure 9.3, which illustrates the effects of load-unaligned and store-unaligned instructions.

When a load or store instruction other than a load-unaligned or store-unaligned one references an unaligned longword or quadword, the processor traps to a PALcode routine. The PALcode routine executes an instruction sequence analogous to that shown in Example 9.1.

The instruction sequence to access unaligned data is not atomic, whether executed under program control or by the PALcode routine. Although the PALcode routine's accesses are atomic with respect to threads on the same processor under some circumstances, they are not guaranteed to be atomic. In particular, if the data crosses a page boundary, one access could succeed and the next trigger a translation-not-valid or other memory management fault.

The VAX and Alpha AXP architectures differ in granularity of data access. The phrase *granularity of data access* refers to the size of neighboring units of memory that can be written independently and atomically by multiple

Example 9.1

Instructions for Storing Data into an Unaligned Longword

```
; At this point:
; R2    bits <31:0> contain the new data to be stored;
;       bits <63:32> are not relevant.
; R28   contains the address of the longword to receive the data;
;       the longword can be unaligned and cross a quadword boundary.
;
; Calculate the address of the high-order byte of the longword and
; load the aligned quadword that contains it and possibly other bytes.
        LDQ_U   R25, 3(R28)   (1)  ;Load quadword containing the
                                   ; high-order bytes of target
        INSLH   R2, R28, R26       ;Position/isolate the high-order
                                   ; bytes of the new data
        MSKLH   R25, R28, R25      ;Zero the corresponding
                                   ; destination bytes
        BIS     R25, R26, R25      ;Replace them with the new data
        STQ_U   R25, 3(R28)   (2)  ;Store the quadword with updated
                                   ; high-order bytes
;
; Calculate the address of the low-order byte of the longword and
; load the aligned quadword that contains it and possibly other bytes.
        LDQ_U   R25, (R28)    (3)  ;Load quadword containing the
                                   ; low-order bytes of target
        INSLL   R2, R28, R26       ;Position/isolate the low-order
                                   ; bytes of the new data
        MSKLL   R25, R28, R25      ;Zero the corresponding
                                   ; destination bytes
        BIS     R25, R26, R25      ;Replace them with the new data
        STQ_U   R25, (R28)    (4)  ;Store the quadword with updated
                                   ; low-order bytes
```

processors. Regardless of the order in which the two units are written, the results must be identical. The VAX architecture provides byte granularity: individual adjacent bytes within the same longword can be written by multiple threads of execution on one or more processors, as can aligned words and longwords.

The Alpha AXP architecture provides only longword and quadword granularity; that is, only adjacent aligned longwords or quadwords can be written independently. Writing a word or a byte requires loading a register with the aligned longword or quadword that it occupies, inserting the word or byte into the register, and writing the register to memory. This multi-instruction sequence is not atomic. Section 9.2.2 shows a method by which the sequence can be made atomic from any viewpoint for data within a single aligned longword or quadword.

The absence of byte and word granularity on AXP CPUs improves CPU performance but has significant implications for access to shared data. In effect, any memory write of a data item other than an aligned longword or quadword must be done as a read-modify-write operation. Furthermore, because the amount of data read and written is an entire longword or quadword,

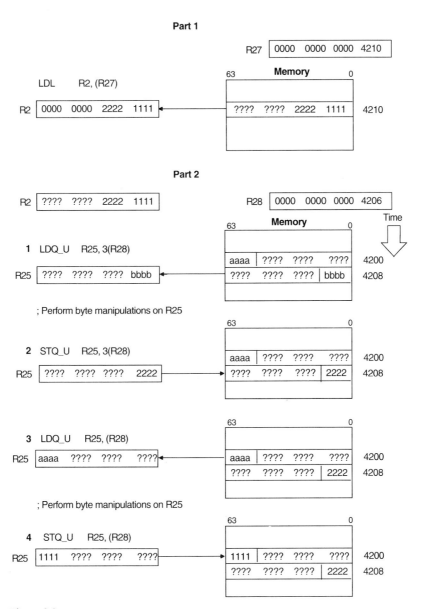

Figure 9.3
Accessing Aligned and Unaligned Data on an AXP CPU

programmers must take particular care to ensure that all accesses to all fields within the longword or quadword are synchronized with each other.

Figure 9.4 shows how two threads of execution writing to adjacent words in the same longword can interfere with one another.

Thread A reads the longword containing the word from memory into a register, inserts 2222 into the low-order word in the register, and writes a

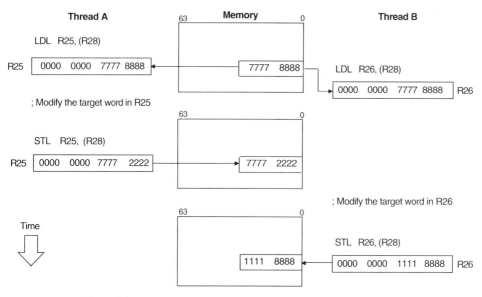

Figure 9.4
Interfering Word Accesses on an AXP CPU

longword from the register to memory. If thread B interrupted that sequence and concurrently attempted to write 1111 to the other word in the longword, its write or thread A's write would be lost. Whether the end result includes both threads' writes or only one depends on the timing of their loads and stores. Section 9.2.2 shows how the two load and store sequences can be serialized, enabling both writes to have effect.

9.1.3   Read-Modify-Write Memory Operations

A fundamental synchronization primitive for accessing shared data is an atomic read-modify-write operation. This operation consists of reading the contents of a memory location and replacing them with new contents based on the old; any intermediate memory state is not visible to other threads. The VAX and Alpha AXP architectures both provide this synchronization primitive but implement it in markedly different ways.

The VAX architecture provides a number of uninterruptible instructions, each of which both reads and writes memory within one instruction. Each provides a read-modify-write sequence that is atomic with respect to threads of execution on the same VAX processor but not atomic to threads on other processors. For example, when a VAX CPU executes the instruction INCL X, it issues two separate commands to memory: a read, followed by a write of the incremented value. Another thread of execution running concurrently on another processor could issue a command to memory that reads or writes location X between the INCL's read and write. Section 9.2.4 describes read-modify-write sequences that are atomic with respect to threads on all VAX CPUs in an SMP system.

The Alpha AXP architecture provides no single instruction that both reads and writes memory. An atomic read-modify-write operation is only possible through a sequence that includes load-locked and store-conditional instructions, described in Section 9.2.2. Use of these instructions provides a read-modify-write operation on data within one aligned longword or quadword that is atomic with respect to threads on all CPUs in an SMP system.

9.1.4   **Cache and Memory Coherency**

Thus far, memory has been treated as a single unit connected to the processor-memory interconnect (PMI). More typically, however, a system has a hierarchy of memory that includes one or more levels of cache. This section provides background information about caches, but not an exhaustive survey of cache protocols or a detailed description of any particular cache protocol.

A cache is a relatively small amount of relatively fast memory that the CPU can access without the delay inherent in sending a command to memory over the PMI. The alternative, requiring the CPU to wait for all memory accesses to complete before proceeding, slows overall system performance dramatically.

Using a cache is an effective strategy for dealing with the speed difference between CPU access and memory access. Some systems have multiple levels of cache. For example, a processor might have a first-level cache on the same chip as the CPU with a minimal access time and a larger, second-level cache on a different chip with an access time longer than that of the first-level cache but still considerably shorter than memory access time.

A cache generally includes the contents of memory locations recently accessed by the CPU and those of adjacent locations. Ideally, at any given time, the cache includes the contents of memory locations that the CPU is about to access. The principle is that memory accesses are generally not random but are often related to preceding accesses. For example, an image might access successive elements of an array, or it might execute successive instructions or a loop of instructions.

Before the CPU reads a memory location, it checks whether the target location's contents are in the cache. If not, it reads that location and adjoining ones from memory and loads them into cache; this is called a cache miss. Whenever the CPU references a location whose contents are in cache (a cache hit), the CPU gets them from the cache, thus accessing them more quickly.

The set of adjoining locations transferred together on a cache miss is called a cache block or cache line. A cache is characterized by the size of its cache blocks, the number of cache blocks it contains, and the mechanism by which the CPU determines whether a particular location's contents are in the cache.

Because cache is considerably smaller than memory, a one-to-one mapping between them is impossible. Instead, a subset of the bits in a memory address identifies a specific cache block (or set of cache blocks, in some cache organizations). Thus, all the memory addresses that have the same value in the subset bits map to the same cache block. Each cache block has an associated valid bit; when the bit is set, the block contains valid data that the CPU can use. Each valid cache block identifies the specific addresses whose contents it includes.

The problem of keeping the contents of cache and memory up-to-date is called cache coherency.

On a typical system, the CPU is not the only reader and writer of memory. Even on a uniprocessor system, direct memory access (DMA) I/O operations are performed concurrently with instruction execution. When an I/O processor writes directly to memory locations whose previous contents had been cached, the data that the CPU has cached becomes out-of-date, or stale. On an SMP system, each CPU has its own cache and shares physical memory with the other CPUs. Keeping multiple processors' caches and memory consistent is more complex than uniprocessor cache coherency.

Basic cache coherency issues include the following:

▶ How is a cache notified that a modification has been made to a location whose contents it holds?

▶ How does it respond to such notification?

▶ How does a cache coordinate a write to a location whose contents may be held in other CPUs' caches?

Caches are categorized by the way in which they handle memory writes. On a system with write-through caches, every CPU write to cache goes to memory at the same time. Thus, memory always has a valid copy of the data. In some cache protocols, memory plays an active role in coordinating writes, by sending messages to CPUs to invalidate their cached, stale copies of the data. In others, the writes are broadcast on the PMI, and each cache watches the PMI for invalidates it must perform. An alternative to a simple invalidate message is one that includes the new contents of the modified location so that each cache holding the location can update itself.

On a system with write-back caches, every CPU write goes to its cache. If the data is not in cache, it is first read from memory. The cache is updated, but the new contents are not necessarily written back to memory immediately. Each cache block has an associated "dirty" bit. When the dirty bit is set, it means that the cache block contains modified data not yet written to memory. On a CPU with a write-back cache, when a memory reference results in a cache miss and the address maps to a cache block whose dirty bit is set, the block will be reused but its contents must first be written to memory. Also, because a write-back cache may contain the most up-to-date version of the locations in its cache, it must monitor the PMI for other processors' reads of memory locations it has cached so that it can supply the data.

Write-back caches improve performance by minimizing writes of frequently modified locations. They also reduce PMI traffic, making it possible to connect more processors to the same PMI.

In some protocols, the cache obtains exclusive ownership of the block before updating it by broadcasting a message to any other cache that holds that location; in response, each such cache writes any modified data to memory and invalidates its cache block. In other protocols, the cache monitors the PMI and records whether any of its blocks' contents are cached by other CPUs. The cache can then treat a shared block as though it were write-through and always write the new contents to memory. Other cache protocols offer additional alternatives.

On an SMP system, processors execute concurrently and read and write memory asynchronously. Caches increase the possibility of delay between the time one processor writes a location and the time the change is propagated and visible to all other processors needing to reference that location. For example, on a system with a write-back cache, there can be a delay between the time a cache inserts a dirty block's contents into a write buffer in preparation for reusing the block and the time the write buffer contents are visible on the PMI as they are written to memory. Furthermore, a PMI write from one processor may not result in an immediate invalidate in a second processor's cache.

A hardware synchronization mechanism that ensures a processor exclusive access to a data item must also ensure that previous changes to it have been processed by the cache and have reached the coherency point.

On an AXP system with multiple processors, there is no common time signal for all processors. Therefore, a term like *most recent* is not meaningful when comparing events on multiple processors. Instead, the *order* in which events (such as reads, writes, interrupt requests) occur is significant. The term *coherency point* refers to the place in a system's memory hierarchy where an order is imposed on reads and writes to a location. The synchronization instructions on an AXP system (LDx_L, STx_C, and memory barriers) operate at the coherency point. On current AXP systems, the coherency point is the PMI.

9.1.5   **Order of Reads and Writes**

Another strategy for dealing with the difference between memory controller speed and CPU speed is for memory reads and writes to be asynchronous to other steps of instruction execution. On some types of CPU, memory reads and writes are sufficiently asynchronous so that they do not occur in the same order in which they were issued. Although the lack of order does not affect uniprocessor operation, it is significant for any system with more than one processor, even a system with one CPU and one I/O processor. VAX and AXP CPUs differ in the extent to which they perform asynchronous memory reads and writes. More important, the architectures differ in whether ordering of reads and writes is required.

VAX CPUs perform reads asynchronously; if the necessary data is not in cache, a command is sent to memory, and processing continues, if possible, on other operands of the instruction. (On a pipelined CPU, operand fetch and evaluation for other instructions may continue.) At the point where instruction execution absolutely requires the read data, instruction processing stalls until the memory operation completes.

Many types of VAX CPU perform memory writes asynchronously, so that while the command and data are being sent to memory, instruction execution can continue. On a VAX CPU that allows only a single asynchronous memory write, a subsequent instruction that attempts another write is stalled until the outstanding write completes. Other types of VAX CPU maximize use of the PMI bandwidth by buffering memory writes, for example, to bytes within an octaword. The assumption behind this approach is that successive writes, for example, to the stack, are often to adjacent memory locations.

Despite the asynchronicity, VAX multiprocessors are required to implement ordering of reads and ordering of writes. That is, if one processor in a multiprocessing system executes instructions that issue writes of multiple data items, the writes must be made to memory in the same order in which the CPU issued them. This means, for example, that when CPU A writes location X and then writes location Y, if CPU B reads Y and gets its new value, it is guaranteed to be able to read the new value in X.

The VAX architecture requires only that reads be ordered with respect to other reads, and writes be ordered with respect to other writes. Some processors make every read and write access to memory in the order in which they were issued, but the architecture does not require it. It permits reads and writes to be disordered with respect to each other.

VAX interlocked instructions, described in Section 9.2.4, order the read and write streams with each other.

Without interlocked instructions, certain synchronization algorithms cannot work. A traditional mutual exclusion algorithm, as described by E. Dijkstra, involves two processes running on different processors; each writes its own variable and each reads the other's variable:

Processor A	*Processor B*
Write X	Write Y
Read Y	Read X

Each processor can read either the old or the new contents of the other's variable. Such an algorithm relies on both processors' having the same view of the lock variables; it can work on a VAX processor only if the accesses are done with interlocked instructions.

Strict ordering of reads and writes impedes the improvement of CPU performance. To improve hardware performance, therefore, the Alpha AXP architecture does not require strict ordering. Instead, an AXP CPU can reorder memory reads and writes.

Reordering can occur if there are unequal delays for different pieces of data to be written to or read from memory. A pipelined machine can have multiple pipes or unequal pipe lengths. Data traveling through different pipes can have different delay times as a result of different pipe lengths, I/O loading, or memory interference from other processors. A cache can also cause unequal delays if some data stays in the cache longer than other data.

The reordering done by an AXP CPU is transparent to threads running on that CPU; processes that execute on a single processor can rely on writes from that processor becoming visible in the order in which they are issued. However, multiprocessing applications cannot rely on the order in which writes to memory become visible throughout the system.

For example, writes issued by a CPU can become visible to an I/O processor or another CPU in an order different from that in which they were issued. One common reason is that many types of CPU contain write buffers in which the CPU merges data to be written to adjacent memory locations. When the write buffer is full, the CPU flushes its contents to memory. Consider an instruction sequence that contains a write to location A followed by a write to location B. If location A is within the address range of a partially full write buffer, the CPU may merge the data intended for location A in the write buffer but write location B to memory immediately. In that case, the write to location B completes before the write to location A.

Another way in which writes can complete out of order is when location A is not in cache, but location B is. Because location A is not in cache, it must be read into cache before being written. In the meantime, the write to location B completes. This is called a write hit under a miss.

Yet another way in which writes can be disordered is when an error occurs. Consider an instruction sequence that contains a write to location A followed by a write to location B. The data written to A is received at the memory controller with an error, but the write of B completes. The CPU resends the write to A, but in the meantime an I/O processor or other CPU reads A and B, getting an old value of A and a new value of B. To guarantee strictly ordered memory writes, a CPU must delay writing buffers to memory until a previously written buffer has been accepted by memory without parity error. Because such delays decrease performance, AXP CPUs are not required to delay a subsequent write until the first has been received correctly.

Reads issued by a CPU can complete out of order. Consider an instruction sequence that contains a read from location A followed by a read from location B. Location A is not in the cache, but location B is. This is called a read hit under a miss. After the read of B completes, but before A is read from memory, an I/O processor or other CPU writes both A and B. Although the CPU's cache is invalidated, it has already loaded the old value of B into a register. As a result, after the read of A completes, the CPU has an old value of B and a new value of A.

A multiprocessing application that assumes read-write ordering and that works on a uniprocessor can fail if it runs on an SMP system. The following example shows two processes, A and B, that share two pieces of data, X and FLAG. Process A calculates a new value for X and then sets FLAG as a signal to process B that it can read the new value of X.

Process A	*Process B*
Clear FLAG	Read FLAG and test for nonzero
Calculate new value of X	Read FLAG and test for nonzero
Store new value of X	. . .
Store 1 in FLAG	
	If nonzero, read X

If A's writes are visible in the wrong order to process B, then B can read a nonzero FLAG and an old value of X, contrary to the intent of the algorithm.

Care must be taken with application or executive code that shares data with an I/O processor or with another process or thread of execution that can run concurrently on a different CPU. Where strict ordering is required for correct execution, the code must explicitly specify the necessary ordering. Section 9.2.3 describes memory barriers, which provide the basic ordering mechanism.

9.1.6 Instruction Execution

VAX instructions are quite varied—in length, number of operands, number of memory references, operand size, and addressing modes. Some instructions read from memory, some write to memory, and some do both.

The VAX architecture is based on a model of instruction stream processing in which one instruction executes at a time. Basically, an instruction consists of an opcode and all its operand specifiers. Additionally, for certain types of operands, an instruction can include short literals, immediate mode operands, absolute addresses used in absolute mode addressing, branch displacements, and so on.

In processing an instruction, a VAX CPU takes the following steps:

1. Translate the virtual instruction address.
2. Fetch the instruction from memory.

3. Decode the instruction.
4. Fetch the required operands.
5. Execute the instruction.
6. Store results, if any, in the specified locations.
7. Update the program counter (PC).

The CPU completes the execution of each instruction, including all memory accesses, before starting the execution of any part of the next instruction.

Because a strict interpretation of this model yields poor performance, many VAX CPUs overlap the steps of instruction processing. For example, most have instruction lookahead logic that prefetches and decodes one or more instructions from memory during the execution of other instructions. As a result, whenever a thread of execution alters the instruction stream, it must synchronize its alterations with the CPU's execution. Section 9.2.5 describes how this is done.

Whether an instruction's memory references are atomic or not depends on whether the operands are types to which atomic references are possible, whether the CPU permits interrupts during the instruction's execution, and whether more than one thread can execute concurrently.

When only one thread can execute at a time (as in a system with only one CPU and no intelligent I/O processors or controllers), memory references are atomic with respect to other threads of execution on that CPU if interrupts are prevented. For example, the absolute queue instructions INSQUE and REMQUE each make several memory references in manipulating a queue. A VAX CPU allows no interrupts during the execution of these instructions. Thus, the insertion or removal of an element at the head or tail of an absolute queue is atomic with respect to threads of execution on the same processor.

The VAX architecture allows interrupts in only one category of instructions, called first-part-done (FPD) instructions. FPD instructions, MOVC3, for example, can be interrupted at well-defined points during their execution; sufficient status is saved in general registers to permit instruction restart at the point of interruption. The VAX architecture specifies that all other instructions are to be uninterruptible in the following sense. If an instruction is interrupted, the microcode must save the software-visible state of the CPU, so that when the interrupt is dismissed, the instruction can restart and execute correctly. This guarantee of restartability for non-FPD instructions generally means that their execution is effectively uninterrupted.

An exception can result from the attempted execution of most types of instruction. A VAX exception is synchronous with attempted instruction execution and is incurred immediately; that is, VAX exceptions are precise. If the exception is one from which recovery is possible, for example, a page fault, the architecture specifies that the software-visible state of the CPU be restored so that the instruction can be restarted from the beginning after the exception is dismissed.

AXP instructions are simpler than VAX instructions. Each AXP instruction has a fixed form and a fixed length, and can make at most one memory reference, either a load into a register or a store from one. As previously described, no single AXP instruction performs a read-modify-write operation, and memory references can only be made to aligned longwords and quadwords. (PALcode routines implement several key functions, such as queue support and process context switch, that require multiple memory references. A PALcode routine is invoked with one instruction, runs with interrupts disabled, and may not incur exceptions; its memory references thus appear atomic with respect to any threads of execution on the same processor.)

In processing an instruction, an AXP CPU takes the following steps:

1. Translate the virtual instruction address.
2. Fetch the instruction from memory.
3. Decode the instruction.
4. Execute the instruction, loading or storing a memory operand, if present.
5. Update the PC.

Unlike the VAX architecture, the Alpha AXP architecture permits multiple non-conflicting instructions to be executed concurrently, with results forwarded from one instruction to another. Compilers schedule code sequences that maximize concurrency, with memory accesses separated from one another where possible.

AXP CPUs have instruction lookahead. As on a VAX CPU, alterations to the instruction stream must be synchronized with the CPU's lookahead and concurrent execution of multiple instructions. Section 9.2.5 describes how this is done.

AXP instructions are not interruptible.

Exceptions, other than arithmetic ones, are synchronous with attempted instruction execution and are incurred immediately. However, to increase performance, the Alpha AXP architecture permits imprecise arithmetic exceptions. When an arithmetic exception is detected, the PC may have been updated an indeterminate number of instructions past the one whose execution triggered the exception. In other words, an arithmetic exception does not uniquely identify the PC of the instruction that incurred the exception. A thread of execution can force the generation of a pending exception by executing a TRAPB or CALL_PAL DRAINA instruction. All other exceptions are precise. Chapter 6 discusses the imprecision of arithmetic exceptions in more detail.

As previously described, the order in which memory writes from one processor are visible to another, such as an I/O processor, is not necessarily the order in which they were originally written. Software must provide explicit ordering, when necessary, by executing a memory barrier instruction, described in Section 9.2.3.

9.2   SYNCHRONIZATION AT THE HARDWARE LEVEL

To assist with synchronization, the VAX architecture provides atomic memory references, uninterruptible instructions, IPL, and interlocked memory accesses. Many read-modify-write instructions, including queue manipulation instructions, are uninterruptible and thus provide an atomic update capability on a uniprocessor. A kernel mode code thread can block interrupt and process-based threads of execution on the same CPU by raising IPL. It can thereby execute a sequence of instructions atomically with respect to the blocked threads. Threads of execution that run on multiple processors of an SMP system synchronize access to shared data with read-modify-write instructions that interlock memory.

These synchronization mechanisms are of particular interest because the OpenVMS AXP executive has been ported from MACRO-32 and BLISS code that uses them. Some of these mechanisms are present in AXP hardware; others have been implemented in PALcode routines.

An AXP processor provides several mechanisms to assist with synchronization. Although all instructions that access memory are uninterruptible, no single one performs an atomic read-modify-write. A kernel mode thread of execution can raise IPL to block other threads on that processor while it performs a read-modify-write sequence or executes any other group of instructions. Code running in any access mode can execute a sequence of instructions containing load-locked (LD*x*_L) and store-conditional (ST*x*_C) instructions to perform a read-modify-write sequence that appears atomic to any other thread of execution. Memory barrier instructions order a CPU's memory reads and writes from the viewpoint of other CPUs and I/O processors. Additional synchronization mechanisms are provided by PALcode routines that emulate VAX queue and interlocked queue instructions.

The sections that follow describe these mechanisms in more detail. The mechanisms are discussed in complete detail in the *VAX Architecture Reference Manual* and the *Alpha AXP Architecture Reference Manual*.

9.2.1   Interrupt Priority Level

On a uniprocessor system, accesses to systemwide data structures are synchronized when all threads sharing data run at the IPL of the highest priority interrupt that causes any of them to execute. Thus a thread's accessing of data cannot be interrupted by any other thread that would access the same data. Section 9.4 describes the use of elevated IPL.

IPL is a processor-specific mechanism; raising IPL on one processor has no effect on another. On an SMP system, code threads running concurrently on different CPUs must synchronize access to shared system data by some method in addition to raising IPL.

On a VAX system, code threads running concurrently on different processors synchronize through instructions that interlock memory. Memory interlock instructions also synchronize access to data shared by an I/O processor and a code thread.

On an AXP system, code threads running concurrently on different processors synchronize through a load-locked/store-conditional sequence. Such a sequence can also synchronize access to data shared by an I/O processor and a code thread.

9.2.2   LDx_L and STx_C AXP Instructions

Together the LDx_L and STx_C AXP instructions enable the construction of a code sequence that performs an atomic read-modify-write to an aligned longword or quadword. Rather than blocking other threads' modifications of the target memory, the code sequence determines whether the memory locked by the LDx_L instruction could have been written by another thread during the sequence. If so, the entire sequence is repeated. If not, the store is performed, with the new memory contents moved to the coherency point. If the store succeeds, the sequence is atomic with respect to other threads on the same processor and other processors. These instructions can be executed in any access mode.

To implement these instructions, a processor has two internal registers: one contains a lock flag, and the other, a physical address that identifies the target memory location. These registers describe per-processor state; each member of an SMP system has its own lock flag and locked physical address register. The amount of memory locked by a LDx_L instruction (called the locked range) is implementation-dependent. The minimum is an aligned quadword. Typically, the amount locked is the size of a cache block, for example, 128 bytes aligned on a 128-byte boundary.

Executing a LDx_L instruction, the processor records the locked physical address and sets the lock flag to indicate that a load-locked/store-conditional sequence is in progress. If an event occurs that could alter a memory location in the locked range after the processor reads it with the LDx_L instruction, the lock flag is cleared. Executing a STx_C instruction, the processor confirms that the lock flag is still set before performing the store; these steps happen atomically to block any event that could alter the state of the flag. The processor copies the lock flag value to the first operand of the STx_C instruction. The code sequence tests the register specified by that operand to determine whether the write occurred.

Example 9.2 shows a typical sequence of code that contains these instruc-

Example 9.2
Code Sequence Containing Load-Locked/
Store-Conditional Instructions

```
; R27 contains the target address.
;
RETRY:  LDQ_L   R1,(R27)    (1)      ;Get current contents
          .                          ;Modify R1
          .
        STQ_C   R1,(R27)    (2)      ;Try to store the new value
        BEQ     R1,FAILED   (3)      ;Branch if R1 is zero; the store
                                     ; attempt failed
SUCCESS:                             ;The store was successful
          .
          .
FAILED:                              ;Test for too many failed attempts
        BR      RETRY                ;Repeat attempt
```

tions. The numbers in the example correspond to numbered steps in the following list:

(1) If no exception occurs in the execution of the LDQ_L instruction, the processor loads R1 with the quadword whose address is in R27, records the locked physical address, and sets the lock flag.

(2) Executing the STQ_C instruction, the processor tests whether the lock flag is still set.

- If so, it writes to memory and clears the lock flag. The test and store are atomic.
- If the flag was already clear, the processor does not perform the store.

In either case, it records in R1 the state of the lock flag at the time of testing.

(3) The code sequence tests R1 to determine what the state of the lock flag was. If the lock flag was set, then the store has succeeded.

If the lock flag was clear, the code sequence must be repeated. The conditional test to initiate the repeat is a branch "forward" in the instruction stream to improve performance for the more likely successful store: on an AXP processor, backward branches are predicted to be taken, and forward branches are predicted not to be taken.

The code sequence must be coded so as to generate correct results when reexecuted. To avoid infinite loops, the code sequence can keep a count of failed attempts to perform the store and stop trying after a finite number. Executive code, however, typically continues to retry on the assumption that the sequence will eventually complete.

The lock flag is cleared by a store to the locked location that originates from outside the processor. To prevent interference by another code thread on the same processor, the architecture also requires that the lock flag be cleared at execution of a CALL_PAL REI instruction. Otherwise, the following sequence could occur:

1. Thread A executes a load-locked instruction to lock location X.
2. Thread B, running as the result of an interrupt, stores to location X; does a load-locked from location X, resetting the locked flag and lock address register; and dismisses the interrupt by executing a CALL_PAL REI instruction.
3. Thread A executes a store-conditional to location X and is successful, although it should not be.

The Alpha AXP architecture also permits a CPU implementation to clear the lock flag under the following two circumstances:

▶ If the processor performs another memory access between executing the LDx_L and STx_C instructions
▶ If the processor branches or otherwise transfers control between executing the two instructions

A load-locked/store-conditional code sequence should not include any sub-settable instructions, that is, instructions whose implementation on a particular CPU can be through software emulation rather than in hardware. If a particular CPU does not implement some subsettable instructions, executing one causes an exception whose service routine emulates the instruction. This exception and its subsequent dismissal would clear the lock flag and prevent the LDx_L/STx_C sequence from ever storing successfully.

Furthermore, the code sequence should not be so long that it can incur a timer interrupt at every repeat and thus never be able to complete the store.

Frequently referenced data items, such as spinlocks or semaphores, whose accesses are synchronized through this mechanism should not be located within the same lock range. Concurrent stores by different threads of execution to different data items within the same lock range will lead to failures caused by contention. Optimally, a spinlock or semaphore is located within a lock range containing primarily data that is mostly read and whose access is correlated with ownership of the spinlock or semaphore.

Because the load-locked/store-conditional mechanism can construct read-modify-write sequences that are atomic with respect to threads of execution on all members of an SMP system, it serves several important needs:

▶ Because the lock flag is cleared by return from an interrupt or exception, the mechanism can perform an atomic read-modify-write of memory data shared between a mainline thread of execution and an AST procedure or a condition handler.
▶ The mechanism enables a read-modify-write operation on an aligned long-word or quadword that is atomic with respect to writes or read-modify-writes by threads of execution on all processors in the system.

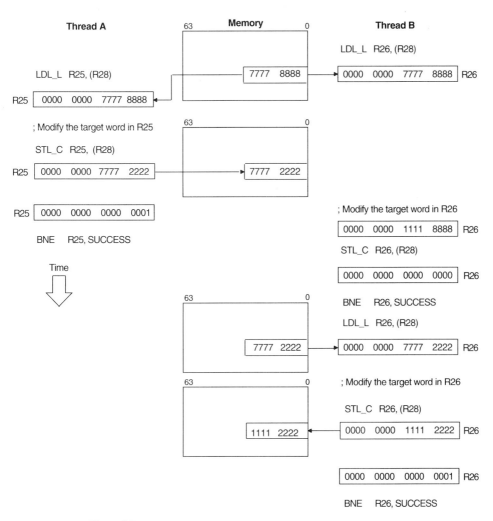

Figure 9.5
Alpha AXP Load-Locked/Store-Conditional Mechanism

▶ Furthermore, it enables the sequence of instructions necessary for writing a byte or word of data (within one quadword) to be atomic with respect to writes from threads of execution on the same or other processors in the system.

▶ It makes possible AXP emulation of the VAX interlocked instructions, described in Section 9.2.4.

Figure 9.4 showed how two threads of execution trying to write adjacent words in the same quadword can interfere with one another. Figure 9.5 demonstrates how the two writes can be serialized with the use of the load-locked/store-conditional mechanism.

Note that all threads performing read-modify-write operations within the same aligned longword or quadword must use the load-locked/store-conditional mechanism for proper synchronization. Although a thread using this mechanism can detect a concurrent store to the target location, it cannot defend against a second thread that omits load-locked and store-conditional instructions while it does an explicit read-modify-write operation or an implicit one resulting from writing a piece of a longword or quadword. Depending on the timing of the two threads' loads and stores, the memory write of the store-conditional can be overwritten.

Figure 9.6 shows an example of the possible consequences when some threads do not use this mechanism. Thread A executes a load-locked/store-conditional sequence to modify a word within a quadword, the word at location 400, and thread B reads and then writes an unaligned longword, the longword at 402, within the same quadword. As shown, if thread B's load happens before A's store and B's store happens after A's store, A's store is lost. With both threads executing on the same processor, once thread A's load-locked occurs, any interrupt or exception that results in entry to another thread will cause thread A's store to fail; as a result, some of the sequences that might otherwise lead to problems will result in A's repeating its load-locked/store-conditional sequence.

On an SMP system, thread B can execute independently of thread A, and a problem could occur if thread B's load happens before A's store and its store happens after A's store.

To prevent problems caused by desynchronized access to fields within a longword or quadword, Digital recommends aligning data on natural boundaries and unpacking shared fields into individual aligned longwords or quadwords. In principle, one shared field that makes up part of a longword or quadword can be accessed without synchronization problems. However, in practice, a compiler can generate unsynchronized read-modify-write operations on data in other fields in the longword or quadword, affecting the shared field as well. If unpacking shared fields is not possible, an alternative is to add appropriate compiler directives to force atomic access to both the shared and nonshared fields.

9.2.3   Memory Barriers

There are no implied memory barriers in the Alpha AXP architecture except those performed by the PALcode routines that emulate the interlocked queue instructions. Explicit memory barriers must be inserted into code wherever necessary to impose an order on memory references.

On a uniprocessor an instruction's read of a memory location always returns the data from the most recent write access to the same location (unless the memory has been overwritten by DMA I/O). However, as described in Section 9.1.5, reads and writes issued by a processor can complete out of order from the viewpoint of an I/O processor or another SMP member. Memory

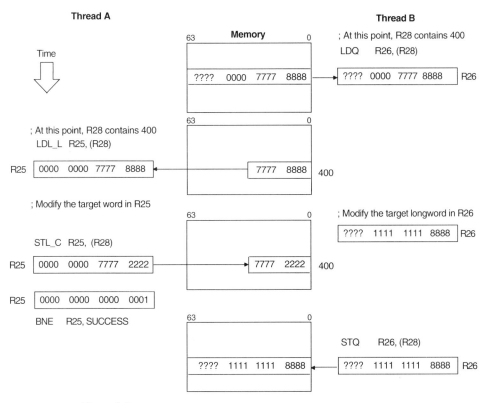

Figure 9.6
Desynchronized Access to Fields in a Quadword

barriers are required for ensuring the order in which other members of an SMP system or an I/O processor see writes to shared data and the order in which reads of shared data complete.

Memory barriers include the following:

▶ The MB instruction
▶ The instruction memory barrier (IMB) PALcode routine, which also flushes prefetched instructions that may have been overwritten by a write of the instruction stream (see Section 9.2.5)

Executing either of those memory barriers forces every preceding write issued by the CPU to reach its coherency point. This does not mean that the memory writes have actually been done when the instruction execution completes; it means that the order of the eventual writes is committed. For example, it may mean that the write commands and data are acknowledged as having been received with good parity at a queue to the memory board; the actual writes may happen later.

Executing either of those memory barriers also orders reads. It forces all queued cache invalidates to be delivered to the cache before any subsequent read or write is started. Otherwise, a read could be satisfied from cache with stale data, or a write could modify cache only to be effectively overwritten by a later-delivered invalidate. Executing a memory barrier prevents cache hits under misses; the processor waits for an earlier miss to complete before a later hit, thus ensuring that the invalidates have occurred.

Note that any type of memory barrier only affects the order of the memory accesses of the CPU that executes it.

The executive and device drivers must access a memory-resident data structure shared with an I/O processor as though it were shared with another CPU. In particular, a memory barrier is necessary in the following cases:

▶ After updating a data structure and before setting a flag to indicate that the data structure is valid

▶ After observing a newly updated flag set by an I/O processor or other CPU and before accessing the data structure whose state the flag represents

Following are several examples of the use of memory barriers to order access to data shared with an I/O processor:

▶ After updating a memory data structure, a driver executes an MB instruction before writing to an I/O processor's interface register to inform it that the structure has been updated.

▶ A driver separates multiple consecutive accesses to I/O processor interface registers with MB instructions if the register accesses must be seen by the I/O processor in order.

▶ To access a remote I/O processor's interface registers through an I/O mailbox (see Chapter 2), a driver initializes fields in a hardware mailbox data structure and executes an MB instruction to ensure that the data structure writes complete before the driver initiates the hardware mailbox operation.

▶ When a driver and an I/O processor share a command ring buffer with a pointer, the driver must execute an MB instruction after writing a new command in the ring buffer and before updating the pointer.

9.2.4 Interlocked Instructions

The VAX architecture provides seven instructions that interlock memory. A memory interlock enables a VAX CPU or I/O processor to make an atomic read-modify-write to a location in memory shared by multiple processors. The instructions, whose operations are described in detail in the *VAX Architecture Reference Manual*, are the following:

▶ ADAWI—Add aligned word, interlocked
▶ BBCCI—Branch on bit clear and clear, interlocked
▶ BBSSI—Branch on bit set and set, interlocked
▶ INSQHI—Insert entry into queue at head, interlocked
▶ INSQTI—Insert entry into queue at tail, interlocked
▶ REMQHI—Remove entry from queue at head, interlocked
▶ REMQTI—Remove entry from queue at tail, interlocked

(For simplicity, the description of the interlocked instruction mechanism that follows assumes that the interlock is implemented by the memory controller, as it is in many, but not all, VAX systems and that the cache is write-through so that memory has up-to-date contents.) When a VAX CPU executes an interlocked instruction, it first issues an interlock-read command to the memory controller, bypassing cache. The memory controller sets an internal flag and responds with the requested data. While the flag is set, the memory controller stalls any subsequent interlock-read commands for that same aligned longword from other CPUs and I/O processors, although it continues to process ordinary reads and writes. Because interlocked instructions are noninterruptible, they are atomic with respect to threads of execution on the same processor.

When the VAX processor executing the interlocked instruction issues a write-unlock command, the memory controller writes the modified data back and clears its internal flag. The memory interlock persists for the duration of only one instruction. That is, execution of an interlocked instruction includes paired interlock-read and write-unlock memory controller commands.

Synchronizing data with interlocks requires that all accessors of that data use them. In other words, the memory references of an interlocked instruction are atomic only with respect to other interlocked memory references.

The granularity of the interlock is VAX-implementation-dependent. For example, on some processors, while an interlocked access to a location is in progress, no interlocked access to any other location in memory is allowed. The VAX architecture guarantees only aligned longword granularity.

An interlocked queue instruction does its interlocking in two stages. In the first stage, the VAX processor issues an interlock-read command to read the forward link. It then makes a bit test and issues a write-unlock command, setting and checking the low-order bit of the forward link. (Self-relative queue elements are constrained to be quadword-aligned; the low-order three address bits are thus available for other uses.) If the low-order bit was clear, the processor continues with the second stage of the instruction.

During execution of the interlocked queue instruction, the queue itself is interlocked by the low-order bit in the forward link, but only the queue is interlocked; the rest of the memory that would otherwise be interlocked is free. The use of this "secondary interlock" reduces memory interlock contention.

If the low-order bit of the forward link was already set, the processor sets the C condition code bit and completes instruction execution without performing any queue manipulations. The code containing the interlocked queue instruction is expected to test the C bit and, if it is set, try to execute the instruction again. After a number of failures, the queue is presumed corrupt.

The Alpha AXP architecture provides no single instruction that both reads from and writes to memory nor does it include a mechanism to interlock

Example 9.3

A MACRO-32 BBSSI Code Sequence

```
; The MACRO-32 statement

        BBSSI    #0,FKB$Q_FR3(R5),100$    ;Lock access to fork block
                                          ;Branch if fork in progress
        MOVZWL   #1,R3                    ;Set fork-in-progress bit
        FORK                              ;Queue fork
          .
          .
          .

100$:
;
; An annotated extract from the generated AXP instructions
; (Instructions that transform the bit number into an
; address offset and bit mask are omitted.)
          .
          .
          .

; In the sequence that follows,
; 16(R25) is the address of the quadword containing the bit.
; R26 has a mask with only the target bit set.
;
        MB                               ;Memory barrier
$L45:   LDQ_L   R26, 16(R5)              ;Load quadword containing spinlock bit
        AND     R26, R27, R25            ;Test if target bit is already set
        BNE     R25, $L18                ;Branch if bit is already set
        BIS     R26, R27, R26            ;OR the target bit with the rest
                                         ; of the quadword
        STQ_C   R26, 16(R5)              ;Conditionally store the quadword
        BEQ     R26, $L46                ;Branch to retry if the store failed
                                         ; (forward branch is predicted to fail)
        MB                               ;Memory barrier
          .
          .
          .

$L18:                                    ;100$:
          .
          .
          .

$L46:   BR      $L45
```

memory against other interlocked accesses. Instead, the load-locked/store-conditional mechanism, described in Section 9.2.2, makes possible a sequence of instructions that performs an atomic read-modify-write. The MACRO-32 compiler generates load-locked/store-conditional sequences for ADAWI, BBSSI, and BBCCI statements. Each sequence begins and ends with an MB instruction.

Example 9.3 shows a BBSSI, extracted from the module IPCONTROL, and its generated code. This instruction sequence continues to retry until it is successful. Similar code is generated for the MACRO-32 statement ADAWI.

Note that the generated code includes two memory barriers. The first MB ensures that the quadword containing the bit is not read or changed until memory reads and writes issued earlier by this processor have occurred and that any pending cache invalidates have been processed. The second MB ensures that the quadword containing the bit is written back to memory before any subsequent memory reads or writes are issued, for example, of fields in data structures protected by the bit.

On a VAX CPU, an interlocked instruction is the only way to perform an atomic read-modify-write on a shared piece of data. On an AXP CPU, the load-locked/store-conditional mechanism serves that need. Some interlocked instructions in the OpenVMS AXP executive have been replaced by code sequences that generate only the load-locked/store-conditional sequence without the MB instructions. The MB instructions are not necessary in cases where the atomic read-modify-write is an end in itself rather than a means to implement a semaphore.

A sequence to implement an interlocked queue instruction, however, requires more than a load-locked/store-conditional sequence. Although testing and setting the secondary interlock bit could be done with a load-locked/store-conditional sequence, once a thread of execution has set the bit, its insertion or removal of an element from the queue must complete without interruption to prevent deadlocks. Consider, for example, a thread that succeeds in setting the secondary interlock bit and that is then interrupted by a higher priority thread that loops trying to acquire the secondary interlock itself: the two threads would deadlock. The interlocked queue instructions are therefore emulated by PALcode routines that execute with all interrupts blocked. Furthermore, these PALcode routines begin and end with MB instructions to order reads and writes.

Typically, OpenVMS AXP executive code written in MACRO-32 performs interlocked queue manipulations through invocation of one of the following macros: $INSQHI, $INSQTI, $REMQHI, and $REMQTI. The macros include a retry loop in case an access to the queue is already in progress. A sample invocation of $INSQTI and its expanded MACRO-32 code follows:

```
; The MACRO-32 macro invocation
        $INSQTI (R3),G^IOC$GQ_POSTIQ ;Insert packet on queue

; Its expanded code
        CLRL    R0
30000$: INSQTI  (R3),G^IOC$GQ_POSTIQ
        BCC     30001$
        AOBLSS  #900000,R0,30000$
        BUG_CHECK BADQHDR,FATAL
30001$:
```

9.2.5 Synchronizing Access to the Instruction Stream

As described in Section 9.1.6, one part of a CPU prefetches and evaluates instructions while another part executes previously fetched instructions. As a result, any write to memory locations containing instructions must be synchronized with the execution of the instructions. Otherwise, it is indeterminate which instructions are executed: old ones, new ones, or a mix. Basically, the prefetched instructions must be discarded, or flushed, and refetched to ensure that the instruction modifications take effect. Both the VAX and Alpha AXP architectures provide a way to flush instruction prefetch.

On a VAX processor, a write to the instruction stream must be followed by an REI instruction. For example, when the debugger sets a breakpoint at an instruction by replacing the opcode with a BPT instruction, it must execute an REI instruction to flush instruction prefetch. Similarly, when it removes the breakpoint by replacing it with the original instruction, it must also execute an REI. When XDELTA executes on a processor in an SMP system, the other processors execute an idle loop waiting for XDELTA to complete. When it does, they each must execute an REI instruction to flush possible prefetch of instructions and operands altered as a result of the XDELTA activity.

On an AXP processor, a write to the instruction stream must be followed by a CALL_PAL IMB. The IMB PALcode routine ensures coherency between prefetched instructions and modifications of the instruction stream. In addition, it provides the same ordering effects as the MB instruction, described in Section 9.2.3.

For example, a debugger running on an AXP processor executes a CALL_PAL IMB instruction after setting a breakpoint by overwriting an instruction with a CALL_PAL BPT. The loader routine that reads nonpageable portions of executive images must also execute a CALL_PAL IMB instruction before it returns to its invoker. OpenVMS AXP executive code written in MACRO-32 invokes the INSTRUCTION_MB macro to perform the CALL_PAL IMB. If SMP support is enabled, the macro also requests an interprocessor interrupt for the other members to execute a CALL_PAL IMB instruction.

9.3   SYNCHRONIZATION AT THE SOFTWARE LEVEL

The synchronization primitives provided by the hardware are the basis for several different synchronization techniques. The following sections summarize OpenVMS AXP synchronization techniques, both those available to application software and those used by the executive.

9.3.1   Synchronization Within a Process

Process-private space data is typically accessible only to threads of execution running within process context. Because only one thread of execution can execute within a process at a time, synchronization of threads executing simultaneously is not an issue. However, delivery of an AST or the occurrence of an exception can intervene in a sequence of instructions in one thread of execution. Therefore, application design must take into account the need for synchronization with condition handlers and AST procedures.

As described in Sections 9.1.2 and 9.1.3, accessing unaligned data, writing bytes or words, or performing a read-modify-write operation each requires a sequence of AXP instructions. If the sequence incurs an exception or is interrupted by AST delivery, another process code thread can run. If that thread accesses the same data, it can read incompletely written data or cause data corruption. Aligning data on natural boundaries and unpacking word and byte data reduces this risk.

An application written in a language other than MACRO-32 must identify to the compiler data accessed by any combination of mainline code, AST procedures, and condition handlers to ensure that the compiler generates code atomic with respect to other threads. Similarly, data shared with other processes must be identified.

Furthermore, as described in Section 9.2.2, it is possible for a compiler inadvertently to desynchronize access to a piece of shared data through the code it generates for access to other fields in the same quadword. It may therefore be advisable to unpack shared longwords into quadwords or to identify as shared those data fields in the same quadword as other shared data.

A related requirement, not unique to AXP programs, is identifying variables that are modified by routines external to the source module.

Synchronizing access to multiple pieces of data or to one piece of data that occupies multiple quadwords requires use of a higher level technique, such as acquiring ownership of a semaphore during access to the data.

In the case of process-private data accessed from both AST and non-AST threads of execution, the non-AST thread can block AST delivery through the Set AST Enable ($SETAST) system service. Code running in kernel mode can also raise IPL to block AST delivery. The concept of AST reentrancy and other ways of achieving it are described in the *Guide to Creating OpenVMS Modular Procedures*.

Data accessed by an inner mode thread of execution is usually in pages whose protection prohibits access by any outer mode.

9.3.2   Multiprocess Application Synchronization

Multiprocess applications can be synchronized through common event flags, lock management system services, and the parallel processing Run-Time Library procedures. Basic event synchronization is provided through event flags. Common event flags can be shared among cooperating processes running on a uniprocessor or an SMP system. The processes must be in the same UIC group. A shared, or common, event flag can represent any event detectable and agreed upon by the cooperating processes. Chapter 10 describes the implementation of event flags and a technique for using them in multiprocess synchronization.

The lock management system services (Enqueue Lock Request, $ENQ, and Dequeue Lock Request, $DEQ) provide multiprocess synchronization tools that can be requested from all access modes. Furthermore, lock management is the fundamental VMScluster-wide synchronization primitive.

The parallel processing Run-Time Library procedures provide support for a number of different synchronization techniques suitable for user access mode applications. These techniques include

▶ Mutual exclusion implemented through an application-created semaphore or spinlock
▶ Event synchronization, by which one or more processes can wait for the occurrence of a user-defined event that is triggered by another process
▶ Barrier synchronization, by which multiple processes wait until a specified number of them have all reached a designated point in their execution

The *OpenVMS RTL Parallel Processing (PPL$) Manual* describes these procedures and their use.

Synchronization of access to shared data by a multiprocess application should be designed to support processes executing concurrently on different members of an SMP system. Applications that share a global section can use MACRO-32 statements, such as BBCCI and BBSSI, or their equivalent in other languages to synchronize access to data in the global section. They can also use the lock management system services for synchronization.

9.3.3   Executive Synchronization Techniques

Table 9.1 contrasts the synchronization techniques most commonly used by the executive. These techniques are based upon the synchronization primitives described in earlier sections; in some cases, the executive simply uses the synchronization primitives provided by the architecture.

The techniques listed in the table are intended for synchronizing the accesses of process-based threads executing in multiple processes or of process-based threads and interrupt-based threads. Synchronization based on lock management system services is the only method available to any access mode other than kernel.

The VAX/VMS operating system was originally designed to run on a uniprocessor and traditionally synchronized access to system data structures using IPL. However, IPL alone is insufficient to synchronize access to data structures in memory shared by the CPUs of an SMP system. To extend to an SMP system the uniprocessor synchronization provided by IPL, VAX VMS Version 5 introduced a mechanism called a spinlock. In that and subsequent versions, a thread of execution not only raises IPL to block interrupts on the same processor but also acquires a spinlock to block concurrent access by other processors. Each systemwide database that could be accessed concurrently has an associated spinlock.

Derived from VAX VMS Version 5.4-3, OpenVMS AXP code also invokes macros that lock and unlock a spinlock to synchronize access to the database protected by the spinlock. Section 9.5 describes spinlocks in detail.

Accesses to shared system data structures by multiple processes from IPLs

Table 9.1 Characteristics of Executive Synchronization Methods

Characteristic	IPL	Spinlocks	Mutexes	Locks
VMScluster-wide	No	No	No	Yes
SMP systemwide	No	Yes	Yes	Yes
Available to outer modes	No	No	No	Yes
Usable from process context	Yes	Yes	Yes	Yes
Usable from system context	Yes	Yes	Yes [1]	Yes
Kinds of sharing	Exclusive	Exclusive	Multiple readers or one writer	Varied modes
Creation	n/a	Most fixed; some dynamic	Most fixed; some dynamic [2]	Dynamic

[1] Mutexes are used almost entirely for process context synchronization. The I/O database mutex is the only one currently locked from system context.

[2] Most mutexes are fixed. Several data structures, however, have a field containing a mutex to synchronize access to other fields in the data structure. These mutexes are created dynamically with the data structures that contain them.

below 3 can be synchronized by mutexes. Section 9.7 describes mutexes. The executive uses lock management system services to provide clusterwide multiprocess synchronization for components like RMS, the file system, the job controller, the device allocation routines, and the Mount utility. Appendix H describes some of these uses. The lock management system services are described in the *OpenVMS System Services Reference Manual*. Chapter 11 in this book describes their internal workings.

Another important synchronization issue involves disk storage. Data structures on a shared disk (for example, files and records within files and the actual disk structure) are protected by lock management system services. This form of synchronization serves whether the disk is accessed by multiple processes on a single system or by multiple processes on multiple nodes of a VMScluster system.

9.4 ELEVATED IPL

Raising IPL on a processor blocks all interrupts on that processor at the specified IPL value and all lower values of IPL. The traditional method of synchronizing access to system data is to raise IPL to a high enough level to block all interrupts whose service routines read or write that data. For example, access to the variable-length nonpaged pool list is synchronized at

IPL 11, the IPL of the highest interrupt thread from which nonpaged pool allocation is permitted. At IPL 11, all fork process interrupts are blocked, but higher priority software and hardware interrupts can still be granted.

The IPL, stored in the processor status (PS) register bits $\langle 12:8 \rangle$, is altered when the IPL processor register is altered. The register can be altered through the MTPR PALcode routine, which is usually invoked through the MACRO-32 statement MTPR or through a compiler built-in. Typically, executive code alters IPL by invoking the SETIPL or DSBINT macro. Their macro definitions, somewhat simplified, follow:

```
.MACRO  SETIPL  IPL = #31
        MTPR    IPL,S^#PR$_IPL
.ENDM SETIPL


.MACRO  DSBINT  IPL = #31, DST = -(SP)
        MFPR    S^#PR$_IPL,DST
        MTPR    IPL,S^#PR$_IPL
.ENDM   DSBINT
```

The SETIPL macro changes IPL to the specified value. If no argument is present, IPL is elevated to 31. This macro is invoked when the IPL will later be explicitly lowered with another SETIPL or simply as a result of executing a CALL_PAL REI instruction. That is, the value of the saved IPL is not important to the routine that is using the SETIPL macro.

The DSBINT macro saves the current IPL before elevating IPL to the specified value. If no argument is present, IPL is elevated to 31. If no alternative destination is specified, the old IPL is saved on the stack. This macro is usually invoked when a later sequence of code must restore the IPL to the saved value with the ENBINT macro. ENBINT, the counterpart to the DSBINT macro, restores the IPL to the value in the designated source argument.

The successful use of IPL as a synchronization tool requires that IPL be raised (not lowered) to the appropriate synchronization level. Lowering IPL defeats any attempt at synchronization. Note, however, that a thread of execution may raise and then lower its IPL as long as it does not lower IPL below that of its entry or below that associated with any spinlocks it holds.

Suppose a thread of execution modifying more than one location in a shared database raises IPL to x to block interrupts from other accessors of the database. The first thread of execution is interrupted, after partly making its modifications, by a second thread running in response to a higher priority interrupt. The shared database is now in an inconsistent state. If the second thread were to lower IPL to x in a mistaken attempt to synchronize access to the database, it could receive incorrect data or corrupt the database.

Integrity of the database would, however, be maintained if the second thread of execution were to reschedule itself to run as the result of an interrupt at or below x and access the database from the rescheduled thread. In that case, the first thread could complete its modifications before the second thread is reentered to access the database. Forking is the primary way in which an interrupt thread of execution reschedules itself to run at a lower IPL. Chapter 5 describes forking in more detail.

The following sections briefly describe the synchronization use of various IPLs. Note, however, that most of the SETIPL, DSBINT, and ENBINT macro invocations in the executive have been replaced by invocations of macros that acquire and release spinlocks. Each of the IPLs traditionally used for synchronizing access to shared data now has one or more spinlocks associated with it. On a uniprocessor system, the act of acquiring a spinlock is transparently reduced to raising IPL to that of the spinlock. Section 9.5.6 describes the use of each spinlock. From the perspective of a uniprocessor system, those sections can be interpreted as describing the synchronization use of the spinlocks' IPLs.

The macro $IPLDEF defines symbolic names for IPL values.

9.4.1 IPL$_POWER (31)

Kernel mode code raises IPL to IPL$_POWER, or 31, to block all interrupts, including power failure, an IPL 30 interrupt, and maskable IPL 31 machine checks. IPL is raised to this level only for a short period of time once the system has been initialized. IPL$_EMB and IPL$_MCHECK are synonyms for IPL$_POWER; they are two different names for the same spinlock.

- A device driver raises IPL to 31 to prevent a powerfail interrupt from occurring, just before it stalls, waiting for an interrupt.
- The entire bootstrap sequence operates at IPL 31 to put the system into a known state before allowing interrupts to occur.
- As described in Section 9.5.6.16, error log buffer allocation and deallocation occur at this IPL.
- As described in Section 9.5.6.15, certain machine check service routines and parts of the CPU-specific error interrupt service routines execute at IPL 31.
- XDELTA, the executive debugger, runs at IPL 31.

9.4.2 IPL$_HWCLK and IPL$_IPINTR (22)

When IPL is raised to IPL$_HWCLK or IPL$_IPINTR, interval timer and interprocessor interrupts are blocked. Section 9.5.6.13 describes the use of the spinlock associated with IPL$_HWCLK.

9.4.3 Device IPLs (20–23)

A device driver raises IPL to the level at which its associated device interrupts. Raising IPL prevents the grant of an interrupt request from the device while its device registers are being read or written (see Section 9.5.4).

9.4.4   IPL$_PERFMON (15)

IPL$_PERFMON is the IPL associated with the PERFMON spinlock, which synchronizes access to performance monitoring data (see Section 9.5.6.11).

9.4.5   Fork IPLs (6, 8–11)

The executive uses fork IPLs to synchronize access to unit control blocks (UCBs). UCBs are accessed by device drivers and by process-based code, such as the Queue I/O ($QIO) and Cancel I/O on Channel ($CANCEL) system services.

A device driver also uses its associated fork IPL as a synchronization level when accessing data structures that control shared resources, such as multiunit controllers. For this synchronization to work properly, all devices sharing a given resource must use the same fork IPL.

Fork processing, the technique whereby a device driver lowers IPL below device interrupt level in a manner consistent with the interrupt nesting scheme, also uses the serialization technique described in Section 9.6.

9.4.6   IPL 8

IPL 8 is the IPL at which the software timer fork routine executes. This routine services timer queue entries (TQEs). Chapter 12 gives further details.

This is the level to which IPL must be raised for any routine to access several systemwide data structures, for example, the scheduler database. By raising IPL to 8, all other interrupt service routines on that processor that might access the same systemwide data structure are blocked from execution until IPL is lowered.

This is also the IPL at which most driver fork processing occurs. While the processor is executing at this IPL, certain systemwide events, such as scheduling and I/O postprocessing, are blocked. However, other more important operations, such as hardware interrupt servicing, can continue.

Traditionally IPL$_SYNCH is the symbolic VAX/VMS name for this IPL. OpenVMS AXP synonyms for IPL$_SYNCH with the same numeric value are more commonly used. Each of the following synonyms is associated with its own spinlock: IPL$_MMG, IPL$_SCHED, IPL$_FILSYS, IPL$_TIMER, and IPL$_IO_MISC. IPL$_SCS and IPL$_IOLOCK8, which are also synonyms of IPL$_SYNCH, are two different names for the same spinlock.

In early VAX/VMS versions the value of IPL$_SYNCH was 7. In VAX/VMS Version 4, its value was changed to 8 to enable three executive components to run at the same IPL: the distributed lock manager system application (SYSAP), system communication services (SCS), and the computer interconnect (CI) port driver.

On a VMScluster system, the distributed lock manager SYSAP must communicate clusterwide with its counterparts on other nodes to perform locking. They communicate using the message services of SCS. SCS is also used heavily by class and port drivers and runs at the same IPL as they do, IPL$_SCS, or 8. The SCS port drivers must run at IPL 8 because some of them need to synchronize access to shared resources and data structures such as buffer and response descriptor tables and synchronize with mount verification activity.

In addition to having to communicate with SCS at IPL$_SCS, the lock manager SYSAP also requires access to the scheduler database, which was historically synchronized by raising IPL to IPL$_SYNCH. To simplify the interactions among the lock manager, SCS, and other threads of execution modifying the scheduler database, IPL$_SYNCH and IPL$_SCS were made the same value by changing the value of IPL$_SYNCH.

9.4.7   IPL$_QUEUEAST (6)

When IPL$_SYNCH had a value of 7, to access data such as the scheduler database, device drivers and other high IPL threads of execution forked to IPL 6 so that they could raise IPL to IPL$_SYNCH.

The terminal driver, for example, might notify a requesting process of unsolicited input or a CTRL/Y through an AST (see Chapter 8). Queuing an AST to a process requires scheduler database modifications, which had to be made at IPL$_SYNCH. The IPL 7 interrupt could not have been used to achieve the same result because it is reserved for software timer interrupts. Thus, this synchronization technique used the first free IPL below 7, the IPL 6 software interrupt. IPL 6 was named IPL$_QUEUEAST, since its primary use as a fork IPL was AST enqueuing.

As a result of changing IPL$_SYNCH to 8, IPL$_QUEUEAST forking is generally unnecessary for serializing access to databases synchronized at IPL$_SYNCH. Fork processes running at IPL 8 can remain at 8; device interrupt service routines and fork processes running at IPLs above 8 can fork to 8. However, many instances of IPL$_QUEUEAST fork processing remain in OpenVMS, unchanged from earlier versions. Executing these operations at IPL$_QUEUEAST rather than at IPL 8 results in placing a somewhat higher priority on IPL 8 fork processing, which is typically I/O processing.

9.4.8   IPL$_RESCHED (3)

IPL$_RESCHED is the IPL of the rescheduling interrupt, whose service routine removes the current process from execution and selects another process to execute. Kernel mode code running in process context raises IPL to IPL$_RESCHED to block this interrupt. For example, the System Generation (SYSGEN) utility raises to this IPL while performing a WRITE ACTIVE command.

This is one of the two IPLs used for synchronization that do not have an associated spinlock.

9.4.9   IPL$_ASTDEL (2)

The IPL of AST interrupts is architecturally defined and cannot be changed by operating system software. Throughout the book, therefore, this IPL is referred to explicitly as 2 rather than symbolically as IPL$_ASTDEL.

IPL 2 execution blocks AST interrupts within a process. When system service procedures raise IPL to 2, they are blocking the delivery of all ASTs, but often particularly a kernel AST that causes process deletion or suspension. In other words, if a process is executing at IPL 2 or above, it cannot be deleted or suspended. It is also possible to block process deletion and suspension by disabling AST delivery to kernel mode.

Raising IPL to 2 prevents process deletion between the time that some system resource (such as system dynamic memory) is allocated and the time that ownership of that resource is recorded (such as the insertion of a data structure into a list). For example, the $QIO system service executes at IPL 2 from the time that an I/O request packet is allocated from nonpaged dynamic memory until that packet is queued to a UCB or placed into the I/O postprocessing queue.

IPL 2 is also significant in that it is the highest IPL at which page faults are permitted. If a page fault occurs above IPL 2, the page fault exception service routine generates the fatal bugcheck PGFIPLHI. If there is any possibility that a page fault can occur, because either the code executing or the data being referenced is pageable, then that code cannot execute above IPL 2. The converse of this constraint is that any code that executes above IPL 2, its linkage section, any routines it invokes, and all data referenced by such code, must be locked into memory in some way. Appendix B shows some of the techniques that the executive uses dynamically to lock into memory code or data referenced from IPLs above 2.

This is one of the two IPLs used for synchronization that do not have an associated spinlock. Because the IPL associated with a spinlock must be at least 3, to block rescheduling, there could not be a spinlock with this IPL.

9.5   SPINLOCKS

A spinlock is acquired by a processor to synchronize access to data shared by members of an SMP system. On a VAX system, the most basic form of spinlock is a bit describing the state of a particular set of shared data; the bit is set to indicate that a processor is accessing the data. The bit can be tested and set, or tested and cleared, atomically with respect to any other threads of execution on the same or other processors. A spinlock enables a set of processors to serialize their accesses to shared data.

A processor that needs to access some shared data can test and set the spinlock associated with that data using an interlocked bit test and set instruction. If the bit was clear, the processor is allowed to access the data. This is known as locking or acquiring the spinlock. If the bit was already set, the processor must wait, because another processor is accessing the data. A waiting processor essentially spins in a tight loop, repeatedly testing the state of the spinlock. This is known as a busy wait. It is from this spinning that the term *spinlock* derives. The busy wait ends when the processor accessing the data releases the spinlock and changes its state to unowned.

The OpenVMS AXP implementation of spinlocks uses the load-locked/store-conditional mechanism. Its basic spinlock form is a quadword consisting of an owner count and owner CPU identification. To lock a spinlock, a processor tests whether the spinlock is owned and, if not, records the address of its per-CPU database to identify itself as owner and increments the spinlock owner count. To unlock or release the spinlock, the owner clears the owner ID and sets the owner count to –1.

A resource synchronized through elevated IPL on a uniprocessor is synchronized through a combination of spinlock and elevated IPL on an SMP system. A thread of execution running on one processor acquires a spinlock to serialize access to the data with threads of execution running on other processors. Before acquiring the spinlock, the thread of execution raises IPL to block access by other threads of execution running on the same processor. The IPL value is determined by the spinlock being locked.

The use of spinlocks extends the blocking effect of raising IPL on a uniprocessor to all members of an SMP system. It is not equivalent to simply raising IPL simultaneously across all processors, however, because only those threads of execution that try to acquire a spinlock owned by another processor are blocked. Thus, work by other SMP members can continue, which would not be the case with a (hypothetical) trans-system IPL raise. Furthermore, because some IPLs, like IPL 8, are now represented by multiple spinlocks, the granularity of locking is finer, which also facilitates parallel processing.

To adapt more easily from uniprocessor IPL-based synchronization to the needs of symmetric multiprocessing, the implementation of spinlocks permits nested acquisitions of a spinlock. For example, many routines that manipulate the scheduler database raised IPL to IPL$_SCHED in earlier versions of VAX/VMS. If one routine already at IPL$_SCHED invoked another routine that raised IPL to IPL$_SCHED to access the same database, no harm was done. On a system that supports SMP, this sequence results in multiple concurrent, or nested, acquisitions of the SCHED spinlock by the same processor.

A quadword containing the owner count and owner ID that is used as a spinlock is actually part of a larger data structure called a spinlock control block. Some spinlock control blocks are defined in the executive; these are called static spinlocks. Others, created during system operation, are called dynamic. Section 9.5.1 describes the spinlock control block; Section 9.5.3, static spinlocks; and Section 9.5.4, dynamic spinlocks.

To acquire or release a spinlock, MACRO-32 kernel mode code invokes one of several macros, identifying the spinlock in a macro argument. (Description of comparable mechanisms for use by other languages is beyond the scope of this chapter.) The macros generate code that dispatches to executive routines that perform the actual spinlock operations.

There are actually three different versions of these routines, conditionally assembled from one source module and built into three loadable executive images:

▸ Module SPINLOCKS, in SYSTEM_SYNCHRONIZATION_MIN.EXE, is the default version on an SMP system. It is optimized for performance and is referred to as the minimum or streamlined version.
▸ Module SPINLOCKS_MON, in SYSTEM_SYNCHRONIZATION.EXE, is the full-checking version, which monitors spinlock activity. It is designed to facilitate troubleshooting of synchronization problems.
▸ Module SPINLOCKS_UNI, in SYSTEM_SYNCHRONIZATION_UNI.EXE, runs on a uniprocessor, a processor that is not a member of an SMP system.

The SYSGEN parameter MULTIPROCESSING dictates which of these is loaded at system initialization. Its possible values are

▸ 0—Load the uniprocessor image.
▸ 1—Load the full-checking multiprocessing version if the CPU type is capable of symmetric multiprocessing and if two or more CPUs are present; otherwise, load the uniprocessing version.
▸ 2—Always load the full-checking version, regardless of CPU configuration.
▸ 3—Load the streamlined multiprocessing version if the CPU type is capable of symmetric multiprocessing and if two or more CPUs are present; otherwise, load the uniprocessing version.
▸ 4—Always load the streamlined version, regardless of CPU configuration.

The default value for this parameter is 3.

Section 9.5.8 summarizes the spinlock routines. Section 9.5.9 describes the streamlined versions of the spinlock routines, and Section 9.5.10, the full-checking versions, which implement a more complex form of spinlock than the streamlined ones do.

9.5.1 Spinlock Control Block

Figure 9.7 shows the layout of a spinlock control block. The macro $SPLDEF defines symbolic names for its fields.

SPL$L_OWN_CPU contains the address of the per-CPU database of the processor that has acquired the spinlock. The address is recorded when a processor acquires the spinlock. The field is cleared when a processor releases its last nested acquisition of the lock.

SPL$L_OWN_CNT records how many concurrent and nested times a processor has locked the spinlock. This field is initialized to –1 to indicate that a spinlock is unowned. With an owner count biased by –1, the acquire code can more easily distinguish increments that cause a transition between unowned

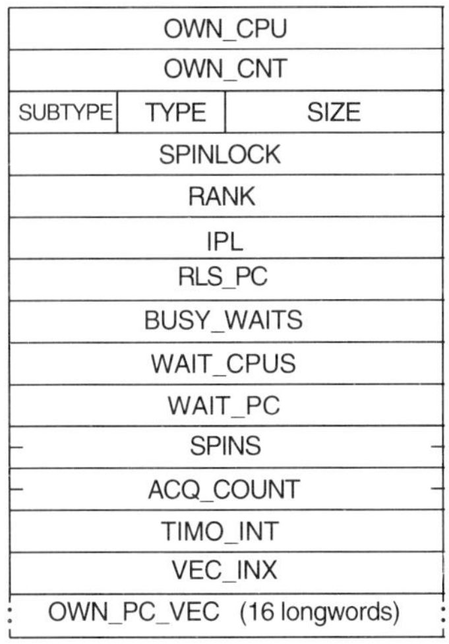

OWN_CPU		
OWN_CNT		
SUBTYPE	TYPE	SIZE
SPINLOCK		
RANK		
IPL		
RLS_PC		
BUSY_WAITS		
WAIT_CPUS		
WAIT_PC		
SPINS		
ACQ_COUNT		
TIMO_INT		
VEC_INX		
OWN_PC_VEC (16 longwords)		

Figure 9.7
Layout of a Spinlock Control Block

and owned from those that do not. When a processor first acquires a spinlock, the value is incremented to 0. If a thread of execution invokes another routine that acquires the same spinlock, the owner count is incremented to 1.

The fields SPL$L_OWN_CNT and SPL$L_OWN_CPU are the actual lock.

SPL$W_SIZE and SPL$B_TYPE contain the spinlock control block's size and type. SPL$B_SUBTYPE indicates the type of spinlock: static spinlock, fork spinlock, or device spinlock. These types are described further in the sections that follow.

The field SPL$L_SPINLOCK is only used by the full-checking routines to serialize access to the spinlock control block.

SPL$L_RANK defines the rank of the spinlock. Spinlock rank is stored in an inverted form. Its possible values range from 0 to 31, with 0 being the highest rank. That is, rank increases from 31 to 30 to 29, and so on. This chapter uses the inverted form in its descriptions. Each static spinlock has a unique rank; all dynamic spinlocks have the same rank, which is 31. A thread of execution that acquires multiple static spinlocks must acquire them in increasing rank (see Section 9.5.5).

SPL$L_IPL specifies the IPL associated with the spinlock, the minimum IPL at which a processor runs while holding the spinlock.

SPL$L_TIMO_INT is the maximum amount of time a processor can wait for the spinlock. After this interval has elapsed, the attempted spinlock acquisition times out. During system initialization the timeout value is initialized to one of two values: if the spinlock IPL is less than or equal to 8, the value of the SYSGEN parameter SMP_LNGSPINWAIT is used; otherwise, the value of the SYSGEN parameter SMP_SPINWAIT is used. There are two different values because the MMG and SCHED spinlocks are occasionally held longer than would be reasonable for spinlocks with higher IPLs.

The spinlock control block fields that follow are used only by the full-checking version of the spinlock routines.

SPL$L_WAIT_CPUS contains the number of processors waiting to acquire the spinlock.

The 16 longwords beginning at SPL$L_OWN_PC_VEC form a ring buffer that records the most recent PCs from which an owner CPU acquired and released the spinlock. SPL$L_VEC_INX contains the index of the next entry to be written in the ring buffer.

SPL$L_WAIT_PC contains the address of the most recent busy wait for the spinlock.

SPL$Q_ACQ_COUNT is the cumulative number of successful acquisitions of the spinlock. SPL$L_BUSY_WAITS is the cumulative number of failed acquisitions. It is incremented once when a processor fails to acquire a spinlock on its first attempt. SPL$Q_SPINS is the cumulative number of spins. It is incremented when a processor fails to acquire a spinlock on its first attempt and again at each unsuccessful attempt during the processor's spinwait.

SPL$L_RLS_PC is the most recent return PC of a thread of execution that releases all nested acquisitions at once.

9.5.2   Spinlock-Related Per-CPU Database Fields

In an SMP system, all processors map to the same system space. Each processor, however, has a system space data structure for its own use, called the per-CPU database. The area contains, for example, the processor's fork queues, the hardware privileged context blocks of its dedicated system process and termination process, and space to store the registers of the process current at the time of a fatal bugcheck. Chapter 37 contains more information on the organization and use of the per-CPU database.

Executive code invokes the FIND_CPU_DATA macro to determine the address of the processor's data structure, which is stored in the processor base register (PRBR). The macro $CPUDEF defines symbolic names for the fields in the per-CPU database.

There are several fields in the per-CPU database whose use is related to spinlocks:

▶ CPU$L_PHY_CPUID—Processor physical ID number
▶ CPU$L_RANK_VEC—Summary of spinlocks that are currently held by the processor
▶ CPU$L_IPL_VEC—Summary of IPLs at which spinlocks are currently held
▶ CPU$L_IPL_ARRAY—Array of elements that count the number of spinlocks currently held at each IPL

When a processor is trying to acquire a spinlock, it tests whether it has

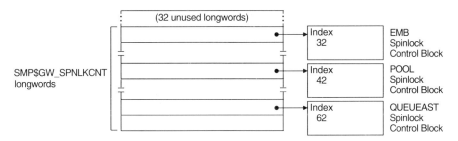

Figure 9.8
Static Spinlock Table

bugchecked by examining the bit number of its CPU ID in the cell that describes such CPUs. It also compares its ID to that of the primary to test whether it is the primary CPU.

The other three per-CPU database fields previously listed are used primarily by the full-checking spinlock routines.

Each bit, excluding bit 31, set in the per-CPU database field CPU$L_RANK_VEC corresponds to a static spinlock held by the processor; its bit position identifies the spinlock rank. As a processor acquires and releases a spinlock, the bit corresponding to the spinlock's rank is set and cleared. Since each spinlock has a unique rank, the number of bits set in the longword are the number of different spinlocks held by the processor. Bit 31 is not used in this way because the rank 31 is for all dynamic spinlocks, more than one of which can be held concurrently.

Each bit set in the field CPU$L_IPL_VEC corresponds to an IPL at which the processor holds one or more spinlocks. The IPL representation is inverted. When a processor acquires a spinlock, the IPL of the spinlock is subtracted from 31. The bit in CPU$L_IPL_VEC corresponding to that number is set. The field thus represents the current set of (inverted) spinlock IPLs active on the processor.

The inverted number is also used as an index into the 32-longword array at CPU$L_IPL_ARRAY. It counts the number of different spinlocks held at each IPL. There is no one-to-one mapping of spinlock to IPL: each IPL does not have a unique spinlock associated with it; some IPLs have more than one associated spinlock.

9.5.3   Static Spinlocks

All static spinlock control blocks are defined in module LDAT, which also contains a table listing their addresses. The global SMP$AR_SPNLKVEC contains the address of the table, and SMP$GW_SPNLKCNT contains the number of spinlocks in the table. Figure 9.8 shows this table and several representative spinlocks.

A static spinlock is identified by an index that locates its address in the table. The index is a longword index into the table. The macro $SPLCODDEF defines symbolic names for these indexes; for example, SPL$C_SCHED is the index of the SCHED spinlock. The lowest index used is 32. Having index values of 32 or greater makes it easy to distinguish a spinlock index from an IPL value. (When spinlocks were first introduced in VAX VMS Version 5, it was necessary to make this distinction: some fork blocks contained an IPL and others a fork spinlock index. Now, however, all OpenVMS AXP fork blocks contain a fork spinlock index.)

Each static spinlock is aligned on a 128-byte boundary to prevent unnecessary failures accessing the spinlock using the load-locked/store-conditional mechanism described in Section 9.2.2. If two spinlocks were located in the same lock range, writing to fields in one could cause a concurrent store-conditional attempt in the other to fail.

Table 9.2 lists the static spinlocks with a brief description of what each synchronizes and its associated IPL. The spinlocks are listed in order by rank, with lower ranking spinlocks first. Section 9.5.6 describes their use in more detail.

A static spinlock that synchronizes fork processing is called a fork spinlock, often shortened to fork lock. A device UCB and any other type of fork block (FKB) identify the driver's fork lock, and indirectly its fork IPL, by specifying the spinlock index in the field UCB$B_FLCK or FKB$B_FLCK. Some static spinlocks are never used as fork locks; their associated IPLs are not in the fork IPL range. Some static spinlocks are only used as fork locks, for example, the IOLOCK8 spinlock, and some are sometimes used as fork locks, for example, the MAILBOX spinlock.

The SPL$B_SUBTYPE field of a spinlock used only as a fork lock contains the value SPL$C_SPL_FORKLOCK; all other static spinlocks are identified simply as spinlocks, with the value SPL$C_SPL_SPINLOCK. The main distinction between fork locks and other static spinlocks is that fork locks are typically acquired and released through different macros. Kernel mode code acquires and releases a static spinlock by invoking the LOCK and UNLOCK macros; the FORKLOCK and FORKUNLOCK macros are used for fork locks. Section 9.5.7 describes these macros.

Another table with information about static spinlocks is the spinlock IPL table, at global symbol SMP$AL_IPLVEC. The table is indexed by static spinlock index and contains the IPL corresponding to that spinlock. This table is referenced by the routine EXE$PRIMITIVE_FORK (see Chapter 5).

9.5.4　Dynamic Spinlocks

A dynamic spinlock is not listed in the spinlock table and has no index. A dynamic spinlock control block is allocated from nonpaged pool and is identified by its address. Currently, the only type of dynamic spinlock used is a device spinlock, usually called a device lock. The SPL$B_SUBTYPE field

Table 9.2 Static Spinlocks

Name	IPL	Synchronizes
QUEUEAST	6	IPL 6 fork processing
FILSYS	8	File system data structures such as file control blocks
IOLOCK8/SCS [1]	8	IPL 8 fork processing; SCS-related code
TX_SYNCH	8	DECdtm transactions
TIMER	8	Timer queue entries
IO_MISC	8	Controller register access mailbox allocation and deallocation
MMG/CACHE [1]	8	Memory management data structures; virtual I/O cache
SCHED	8	Scheduler database
IOLOCK9	9	IPL 9 fork processing
IOLOCK10	10	IPL 10 fork processing
IOLOCK11	11	IPL 11 fork processing
MAILBOX	11	Writing mailbox messages
POOL	11	Nonpaged pool lists and related data
PERFMON	15	Performance monitoring
INVALIDATE	21	Translation buffer invalidation
HWCLK	22	Hardware clock database
MEGA	31	Miscellaneous data structures such as the fork and wait queue
MCHECK/EMB [1]	31	Machine check serialization; error log buffers

[1] These two names are synonyms for the same spinlock.

of a device lock's spinlock control block contains the value SPL$C_SPL_DEVICELOCK.

All dynamic spinlocks have the same rank, 31. However, the field SPL$L_RANK in a dynamic spinlock control block is initialized to –1 for quick identification in the routines that acquire and release spinlocks.

As the [IOGEN]SYS$LOAD_DRIVER procedure configures devices, it creates device locks. It invokes the routine SMP$ALLOC_SPL to create a device lock and SMP$INIT_SPL to initialize it. Both routines are in module SPINLOCKS.

In general, there is one device lock for each unique device controller. SYS$LOAD_DRIVER stores its address in the controller's channel request block field CRB$L_DLCK and in the field UCB$L_DLCK for each unit on that controller.

A device driver acquires and releases the device lock by invoking the DEVICELOCK and DEVICEUNLOCK macros (see Section 9.5.7). The device lock synchronizes access to the controller's registers and to fields in the UCB that describe the controller's state.

9.5.5   **Rules for Acquiring and Releasing Spinlocks**

For synchronization with spinlocks to be successful, threads of execution that use spinlocks must follow certain rules.

All threads of execution that access shared data must first acquire the spinlock associated with it. A thread of execution that acquires a spinlock to serialize access to shared data is guaranteed exclusive access to the data while it holds the spinlock. Thus, all its modifications to the data can be considered atomic with respect to another thread trying to acquire the same spinlock to access the same data. To ensure this degree of atomicity, the implementation of spinlocks does not include breaking spinlock deadlocks. Rather, deadlocks are prevented by requiring threads of execution that use spinlocks to acquire spinlocks in a particular order.

The rank values of static spinlocks reflect code paths and interdependence among the shared data structures protected by spinlocks. A thread of execution that acquires multiple spinlocks must acquire them in order by increasing rank. This rule prevents a deadlock such as the following: One processor has acquired spinlock A and is busy waiting to acquire spinlock B to complete its task; a second processor has acquired spinlock B and is busy waiting to acquire spinlock A to complete its task.

All device locks share the same rank, 31, which is lower than that of any static spinlock. However, a processor holding a static spinlock may acquire a device lock; the rule previously listed does not apply to acquisition of a device lock. The assumption is that the shared resource protected by a device lock is not dependent on the resources protected by the static spinlocks. Furthermore, each device lock is assumed to be independent of others, and a processor is permitted to hold more than one device lock at a time. All code acquiring multiple device locks concurrently must be written to prevent deadlocks; all threads must acquire such device locks in the same order.

A thread of execution about to acquire a spinlock must be running at an IPL less than or equal to that of the spinlock. This is analogous to the principle of raising IPL to synchronize on a uniprocessor system. This rule prevents the following type of synchronization failure:

1. Thread A, running at IPL x, acquires a spinlock and begins to manipulate the database it protects.
2. An interrupt at IPL $x + 1$ is requested and granted on the same processor, and thread B begins execution, interrupting thread A.
3. To access the same database, thread B tries to acquire its spinlock. Because threads A and B are running on the same processor, the nested acquisition is successful, and thread B begins to manipulate the database left in an inconsistent state by the interruption to thread A.

A thread of execution that has acquired a spinlock may raise IPL but must not lower it below the value associated with the spinlock. Lowering IPL could lead to the synchronization failure just described.

9.5.6 **Use of Static Spinlocks**

The sections that follow describe the use of each of the static spinlocks.

9.5.6.1 **Use of the QUEUEAST Spinlock.** The QUEUEAST spinlock synchronizes fork processing at IPL 6. The need for IPL 6 fork processing is largely historical, based on constraints from VAX/VMS Version 3 and earlier versions, as described in Section 9.4.7. IPL 6 is also used for fork processing that is lower priority than I/O fork processing and can be deferred. For example, the control block and stack associated with a deleted kernel process (see Chapter 5) are deallocated within an IPL 6 fork process.

9.5.6.2 **Use of the FILSYS Spinlock.** The file system database consists of data structures that describe the mount state of a volume and the condition of open files on the volume. The FILSYS spinlock synchronizes access to pieces of the file system database that are accessed by routines external to the file system. (As described in Appendix H, lock management system services synchronize access to much of the file system database.)

For example, each open file is described by one or more window control blocks (WCBs). A WCB contains retrieval pointers that map the virtual blocks of a file to logical blocks on a device. As part of processing an I/O request to a file, IOC$MAPVBLK, in module IOSUBRAMS, uses WCB contents to convert virtual block numbers to their equivalent logical block numbers. IOC$MAPVBLK and the file system routines that alter WCBs synchronize their access to WCBs by acquiring the FILSYS spinlock.

9.5.6.3 **Use of the IOLOCK8/SCS Spinlock.** A driver can specify one of the IOLOCK*x* spinlocks as its fork lock. A device UCB, which is also used as a fork block, contains the fork spinlock index in the field UCB$B_FLCK. The fork lock synchronizes access to data structures modified by the fork process, in particular, its UCB.

To synchronize access to UCB fields manipulated at fork level, an executive routine or the driver fork process itself acquires the spinlock specified in UCB$B_FLCK.

IOLOCK8 is the fork lock most commonly used by device driver fork processes. It is used by all standard drivers that compete for shared resources like a device controller. On a VMScluster system that supports remote I/O, the Mass Storage Control Protocol (MSCP) server uses the IOLOCK8 spinlock.

IOLOCK8 and SCS are two names for the same spinlock. SCS routines and lock manager routines coordinate access to VMScluster and lock management data structures using the SCS spinlock. An SCS routine that executes as a fork process uses the SCS spinlock as its fork lock. The $ENQ and $DEQ system services acquire the SCS spinlock before altering the lock database.

9.5.6.4 **Use of the TIMER Spinlock.** The TIMER spinlock is the fork lock for the software timer fork routine. It holds the TIMER and HWCLK spinlocks while it tests whether the first entry in the time-ordered queue of TQEs has expired and removes the entry if it has expired.

The routines that insert and remove TQEs from the timer queue hold the TIMER spinlock while they manipulate the queue. The Set Time ($SETIME) system service acquires the TIMER spinlock when it resets the system time and reorders the timer queue as a result of recalibrating pending TQEs with delta times. Chapter 12 provides more information on these routines and the timer queue.

9.5.6.5 **Use of the IO_MISC Spinlock.** The IO_MISC spinlock synchronizes access to the data structures that describe the collection of controller register access mailbox (CRAM) data structures but does not synchronize access to each individual CRAM. Prior to accessing a controller register, a device driver allocates and initializes a CRAM with the address of a particular I/O space register. The routines that a driver calls to allocate and deallocate a CRAM acquire this spinlock. Chapters 22 and 24 describe accessing controller registers through hardware mailboxes.

9.5.6.6 **Use of the MMG Spinlock.** The MMG spinlock synchronizes access to the memory management database. This includes the page frame number database, section tables, page and swap file bitmaps, list of available system page table entries, and working set lists. It also synchronizes access to the data structures that describe the virtual I/O cache.

Its main users are the page fault exception service routine, the swapper, memory management system services, and routines that lock and unlock direct I/O buffer pages into memory.

9.5.6.7 **Use of the SCHED Spinlock.** The SCHED spinlock synchronizes access to the scheduler database, the set of software process control blocks and their state queues, and mutex data structures. It also synchronizes access to a process's AST data, such as the PCB$L_ASTACT bits and the queues of pending AST control blocks.

9.5.6.8 **Use of the IOLOCK*n* Fork Spinlocks.** The spinlocks IOLOCK9, IOLOCK10, and IOLOCK11 are fork locks intended for use on any processor. Their use is similar to that of IOLOCK8, although they are not as commonly used.

9.5.6.9 **Use of the MAILBOX Spinlock.** The MAILBOX spinlock synchronizes access to mailboxes. It is the fork lock for the mailbox driver. The mailbox driver's internal routines EXE$SNDEVMSG and EXE$WRTMAILBOX, invoked by device drivers to write messages to a mailbox, acquire this spinlock to synchronize access to the mailbox.

9.5.6.10 **Use of the POOL Spinlock.** The POOL spinlock synchronizes access to the nonpaged variable-length list. The spinlock's main users are routines such

as EXE$ALONONPAGED and EXE$DEANONPAGED, in module MEMO-
RYALC. It also synchronizes access to the performance monitoring statistics
kept on nonpaged variable-length pool allocation failures. Access to the nonpaged lookaside lists is synchronized with the load-locked/store-conditional
mechanism rather than with the POOL spinlock.

The code that implements the DCL SHOW MEMORY command acquires
the POOL spinlock while it scans the list to collect information for its display.

9.5.6.11   **Use of the PERFMON Spinlock.** The PERFMON spinlock synchronizes access to the I/O performance database. Its main users are routines such as
PMS$START_REQ, in module IOPERFORM.

9.5.6.12   **Use of the INVALIDATE Spinlock.** Routines such as MMG$TBI_SINGLE, in
module PAGEFAULT, are invoked to flush a stale entry from the translation
buffer when a valid page table entry is made invalid. If the address is a system
space address in an SMP system, multiple processors might have the translation cached in their translation buffers. To invalidate a cached system space
address translation, a member of an SMP system acquires the INVALIDATE
spinlock. The spinlock prevents more than one processor at a time from initiating the sequence required for all SMP members to invalidate the entry in
their translation buffers (see Chapter 37).

9.5.6.13   **Use of the HWCLK Spinlock.** The HWCLK spinlock synchronizes access
to the cell EXE$GQ_1ST_TIME, which contains the expiration time of the
first TQE in the list, and various other time-related cells, such as EXE$GQ_
SYSTIME, the current system time.

The interval timer interrupt service routine, running on the primary processor in an SMP system or on a uniprocessor, acquires the HWCLK spinlock
to update EXE$GQ_SYSTIME and to test whether the first TQE has expired.
If it has, the interrupt service routine queues the software timer fork process.

The software timer fork routine acquires the HWCLK spinlock while it
tests whether the first TQE has expired and, if so, removes the TQE from
the queue.

The routines that insert and remove TQEs from the timer queue acquire
the HWCLK spinlock if they have to manipulate the first TQE in the list.
Chapter 12 gives more information on the timer routines and the timer
queue.

9.5.6.14   **Use of the MEGA Spinlock.** The MEGA spinlock synchronizes access to the
fork and wait queue, used by fork processes to stall themselves for approximately half a second (see Chapter 5). It also synchronizes the entry of SMP
members into the benign state (see Chapter 37).

9.5.6.15   **Use of the MCHECK Spinlock.** The machine check exception service routines for CPUs that can be members of an SMP system acquire the MCHECK spinlock as needed.

9.5.6.16   **Use of the EMB Spinlock.** The EMB spinlock synchronizes access to the error log allocation buffers (see Chapter 35). The routines that reserve and release pieces of error log allocation buffer for error messages acquire the EMB spinlock.

The ERRFMT process acquires the EMB spinlock when it is altering data structures that describe the state of the error log allocation buffer. As Chapter 35 describes, ERRFMT copies an error log allocation buffer in several stages. It examines the error log buffer status flags and message counts with the spinlock held. If it can copy the buffer, it sets a flag in the buffer to inhibit further allocations in it and then releases the spinlock. At IPL 0, ERRFMT copies the error log allocation buffer to its P0 space, and formats and writes the messages to the error log file.

This spinlock also synchronizes access to a buffer pool used by SMP code. A fork block is allocated from the buffer pool to create a thread of execution that runs on the primary SMP processor.

9.5.7   **MACRO-32 Macros for Acquiring and Releasing Spinlocks**

There are three sets of MACRO-32 macros for acquiring and releasing spinlocks:

- LOCK and UNLOCK for static spinlocks
- FORKLOCK and FORKUNLOCK for static spinlocks used to synchronize fork processing
- DEVICELOCK and DEVICEUNLOCK for dynamic spinlocks

These macros facilitate writing code that can synchronize properly whether it executes on a uniprocessor or a member of an SMP system. Each of these macros has a number of arguments, only a few of which are described here. The manual *OpenVMS AXP Device Support: Creating a Step 1 Driver from an OpenVMS VAX Device Driver* describes the use of these macros and their arguments in more detail.

These macros differ primarily in the way their arguments identify the spinlock of interest:

- An argument to LOCK and UNLOCK specifies the symbolic index of a static spinlock.
- In a typical use of FORKLOCK or FORKUNLOCK, R5 contains the address of a UCB in which the field UCB$B_FLCK has a static spinlock index.
- In a typical use of DEVICELOCK or DEVICEUNLOCK, R5 contains the address of a UCB in which the field UCB$L_DLCK has the address of the device lock.

The lock macros generate the following approximate sequence:

1. Optionally (determined by macro argument SAVIPL), save the current IPL.
2. If SMP is not enabled, set IPL as requested and branch around the rest of the instructions. The low bit of global SMP$GL_FLAGS is set when SMP is enabled.
3. Optionally (determined by macro argument PRESERVE, whose default value is the string YES), save all 64 bits of R0.
4. Store the static spinlock index or the address of a dynamic spinlock in R0.
5. Invoke SMP$ACQNOIPL in the case of a static spinlock with macro argument CONDITION=NOSETIPL; SMP$ACQUIRE in any other case of a static spinlock; or SMP$ACQUIREL or SMP$ACQNOIPL in the case of a dynamic spinlock.
6. If R0 was saved, restore it.

A sample invocation of LOCK with its expansion follows:

```
;The macro invocation
;locks spinlock with index SPL$C_MMG
        LOCK    LOCKNAME=MMG,-      ;Lock MMG database
                PRESERVE=NO         ;Don't preserve R0

;Its expansion
        ASSUME  SMP$V_ENABLED EQ 0
        BLBC    SMP$GL_FLAGS,30002$
        MOVL    S^#SPL$C_MMG,R0
        JSB     G^SMP$ACQUIRE
        BRB     30003$
30002$: MTPR    #IPL$_MMG,#PR$_IPL
30003$:
```

A sample invocation of FORKLOCK with its expansion follows:

```
;The macro invocation
;locks spinlock whose index is in UCB$B_FLCK
        FORKLOCK -
                UCB$B_FLCK(R5),-    ;Lock fork access
                SAVIPL=-(SP)        ;Save current IPL

;Its expansion
        MFPR    S^#PR$_IPL,-(SP)
        $PUSH64 R0
        MOVZBL  UCB$B_FLCK(R5),R0
        ASSUME  SMP$V_ENABLED EQ 0
        BLBC    SMP$GL_FLAGS,30002$
        JSB     G^SMP$ACQUIRE
        BRB     30003$
30002$: MTPR    SMP$AL_IPLVEC[R0],S^#PR$_IPL
30003$: $POP64  R0
```

A sample invocation of DEVICELOCK with its expansion follows:

```
;The macro invocation
;locks spinlock whose address is in UCB$L_DLCK
        DEVICELOCK -
                LOCKADDR=UCB$L_DLCK(R5),- ;Lock device interrupts
                CONDITION=NOSETIPL,-      ;Don't alter IPL
                PRESERVE=NO               ;Don't preserve R0

;Its expansion
        ASSUME  SMP$V_ENABLED EQ 0
        BLBC    SMP$GL_FLAGS,30002$
        MOVL    UCB$L_DLCK(R5),R0
        JSB     G^SMP$ACQNOIPL
30002$:
```

The unlock macros generate the following approximate code sequence:

1. If SMP is not enabled, go to step 6.
2. Optionally (determined by macro argument PRESERVE, whose default value is the string YES), save all 64 bits of R0.
3. Store the static spinlock index or the address of a dynamic spinlock in R0.
4. If the macro argument CONDITION=RESTORE is present, invoke either SMP$RESTORE to relinquish one acquisition of a static spinlock or SMP$RESTOREL for a dynamic spinlock.

   If the macro argument is not present, invoke either SMP$RELEASE to relinquish all nested acquisitions of a static spinlock or SMP$RELEASEL for a dynamic spinlock.
5. If R0 was saved, restore it.
6. Optionally (determined by macro argument NEWIPL), set the IPL as requested.

A sample invocation of UNLOCK with its expansion follows:

```
;The macro invocation
        UNLOCK  LOCKNAME=INVALIDATE,-
                PRESERVE=NO,-            ;Don't save R0
                NEWIPL=(SP)+            ;Restore IPL from stack

;Its expansion
        ASSUME  SMP$V_ENABLED EQ 0
        BLBC    SMP$GL_FLAGS,30002$
        MOVL    S^#SPL$C_INVALIDATE,R0
        JSB     G^SMP$RELEASE
30002$: MTPR    (SP)+,S^#PR$_IPL
```

A sample invocation of FORKUNLOCK with its expansion follows:

```
;The macro invocation
        FORKUNLOCK -
```

```
                UCB$B_FLCK(R5),-  ;Release fork access
                NEWIPL=(SP)+      ;Restore IPL from stack

;Its expansion
        ASSUME   SMP$V_ENABLED EQ 0
        BLBC     SMP$GL_FLAGS,30002$
        $PUSH64  R0
        MOVZBL   UCB$B_FLCK(R5),R0
        JSB      G^SMP$RELEASE
        $POP64   R0
30002$: MTPR     (SP)+,S^#PR$_IPL
```

A sample invocation of DEVICEUNLOCK with its expansion follows. This example results in dispatch to SMP$RESTOREL rather than to SMP$RELEASEL.

```
;The macro invocation
        DEVICEUNLOCK -
                LOCKADDR=UCB$L_DLCK(R5),-
                                  ;Release device interrupts
                NEWIPL=(SP)+,-    ;Restore IPL
                CONDITION=RESTORE ;Conditionally release spinlock

;Its expansion
        ASSUME   SMP$V_ENABLED EQ 0
        BLBC     SMP$GL_FLAGS,30002$
        $PUSH64  R0
        MOVL     UCB$L_DLCK(R5),R0
        JSB      G^SMP$RESTOREL
        $POP64   R0
30002$: MTPR     (SP)+,S^#PR$_IPL
```

9.5.8   **Spinlock Routines**

As described in Section 9.5, there are three versions of the spinlock routines, conditionally assembled from one source. Having different versions of the routines hides the details of the actual synchronization method used. It enables code requiring synchronization to invoke the same macros and routines regardless of the CPU configuration. This section summarizes the spinlock routines. Section 9.5.9 describes the streamlined multiprocessor versions of these routines, and Section 9.5.10, the full-checking versions of these routines.

The following spinlock routines run in kernel mode at IPL 3 and above:

▶ SMP$ACQUIRE—Acquire a static spinlock

▶ SMP$ACQUIREL—Acquire a dynamic spinlock

▶ SMP$ACQNOIPL—Acquire a static or dynamic spinlock without altering IPL

▶ SMP$RESTORE—Relinquish one acquisition of a static spinlock

▶ SMP$RESTOREL—Relinquish one acquisition of a dynamic spinlock

> ▸ SMP$RELEASE—Relinquish all nested acquisitions of a static spinlock
> ▸ SMP$RELEASEL—Relinquish all nested acquisitions of a dynamic spin-lock

The spinlock lock macros dispatch to SMP$ACQUIRE or to one of its alternative entry points, SMP$ACQNOIPL or SMP$ACQUIREL.

The default spinlock unlock macro invocations dispatch to SMP$RE-LEASE or its alternative entry point SMP$RELEASEL. The spinlock un-lock macro invocations that request a restore (relinquish one acquisition of a spinlock) dispatch to SMP$RESTORE or to its alternative entry point SMP$RESTOREL.

Because the macros all test whether SMP is enabled, it is unlikely that control would ever be transferred to the uniprocessor versions of the spinlock routines, in module SPINLOCKS_UNI.

9.5.9 Streamlined Spinlock Routines

This section describes the streamlined version of the spinlock routines, in module SPINLOCKS.

Following is a description of the actions of the spinlock lock routines, with some details of SMP operations omitted for simplicity:

1. At entry to SMP$ACQUIRE, R0 contains the index of a static spinlock. Indexing into the static spinlock table, SMP$ACQUIRE obtains the ad-dress of the spinlock and stores it in R0. (Entry points SMP$ACQUIREL and SMP$ACQNOIPL are entered with the address of a spinlock already in R0.)

2. The routine raises IPL to that of the spinlock, SPL$L_IPL. (Entry point SMP$ACQNOIPL is entered with an IPL that is known to be correct and thus not to be altered.)

3. SMP$ACQUIRE gets the address of the processor's per-CPU database.

4. It executes a LDQ_L instruction to load the spinlock owner count and owner ID fields in one memory reference and increments the register-held owner count.

   If the resulting owner count is nonzero, the spinlock is already owned, possibly by another CPU. SMP$ACQUIRE continues with step 7.

5. If the resulting owner count is zero, the spinlock is unowned. SMP$AC-QUIRE stores the address of the processor's per-CPU database in the low longword of the register and executes a STQ_C instruction to store the owner count and owner ID fields.

   If the conditional store fails, SMP$ACQUIRE repeats the sequence beginning at step 4.

6. If the store succeeds, this CPU owns the spinlock. SMP$ACQUIRE exe-cutes an MB instruction to order the spinlock acquisition with any sub-

sequent accesses to the data structures the spinlock synchronizes and returns to its invoker.

7. If the resulting owner count is nonzero, the spinlock has already been acquired, possibly by the processor trying to acquire it now. SMP$ACQUIRE compares the address of this processor's per-CPU database with that stored in SPL$L_OWN_CPU. If the two are equal, this attempted lock is a nested acquisition. SMP$ACQUIRE stores the updated owner count and returns to its invoker.

8. If the two addresses are not equal, another processor owns the spinlock and this processor must spinwait until it is released. The spinwait consists of the steps described in the following paragraphs, through step 14.

   SMP$ACQUIRE sets to a nonzero value the field CPU$L_BUSYWAIT in the per-CPU database as a signal to the interval timer interrupt service routine. When this field is nonzero, the interrupt service routine does not charge soft ticks against process quantum (see Chapter 12).

9. SMP$ACQUIRE loops, testing whether the spinlock owner count has reached –1, indicating that it has been released. When the count reaches –1, SMP$ACQUIRE repeats its attempt to acquire the spinlock by executing LDQ_L and STQ_C instructions to increment the owner count to 0 and store its per-CPU database address.

   If the conditional store fails, SMP$ACQUIRE continues its spin.

10. If the store succeeds, this CPU owns the spinlock. SMP$ACQUIRE executes an MB instruction to order the spinlock acquisition with any subsequent accesses to the data structures the spinlock synchronizes and returns to its invoker.

11. The waiting processor does more than repeatedly test whether the spinlock is available. If the IPL at which it spins is higher than or equal to that of an interprocessor interrupt, the processor cannot receive interrupts requesting that it perform various SMP functions (see Chapter 37). Under such circumstances, SMP$ACQUIRE must make explicit tests for these requests and perform them as necessary.

12. Also, while SMP$ACQUIRE is spinning, it performs a countdown and times out the attempted acquisition if its wait time exceeds the spinlock timeout value stored in SPL$L_TIMO_INT. At the end of the interval, SMP$ACQUIRE tests whether the spinlock's current owner is the same as the processor that owned it at the beginning of the interval.

13. If the owners are not the same, the original owner released the spinlock and some other processor acquired it before this one was able to. SMP$ACQUIRE repeats the countdown, attempting to acquire the spinlock.

14. If the owners are the same, something is interfering with the proper operation of the owning processor. SMP$ACQUIRE invokes SMP$TIMEOUT, in module SMPROUT (see Chapter 37). If it is possible that a recoverable condition led to the timeout, SMP$TIMEOUT returns, and

SMP$ACQUIRE repeats the countdown. If it is not possible, SMP$TIME-OUT generates the fatal bugcheck CPUSPINWAIT.

The spinlock unlock macro invocations that request a restore (relinquish one acquisition of a spinlock) dispatch to SMP$RESTORE or to its alternative entry point, SMP$RESTOREL. Those that request a release (relinquish all nested acquisitions) dispatch to SMP$RELEASE or to SMP$RELEASEL.

These routines run in kernel mode at IPL 3 and above. They do not alter IPL but run at the IPL at which they were entered. Following is a description of their typical actions.

1. At entry to SMP$RESTORE, R0 contains the index of a static spinlock. Indexing into the static spinlock table, SMP$RESTORE obtains the address of the spinlock and stores it in R0.

   (Entry point SMP$RESTOREL is entered with the address of a dynamic spinlock already in R0.)

2. SMP$RESTORE executes a LDQ_L instruction to load the owner count and owner ID fields. If the count is negative, indicating that the spinlock is not owned, SMP$RESTORE generates the fatal bugcheck SPLRELERR on the presumption that a serious failure has occurred.

3. Otherwise, it decrements the register-held spinlock owner count. If the count is zero or positive, indicating that the spinlock is still owned by this processor, the routine stores the updated count in the spinlock and returns to its invoker.

4. If the spinlock is now free, SMP$RESTORE executes an MB instruction to order any preceding accesses to the database synchronized by the spinlock with the release of the spinlock, stores the updated owner count of –1, and clears the ID field.

SMP$RELEASE and SMP$RELEASEL take the following steps:

1. At entry to SMP$RELEASE, R0 contains the index of a static spinlock. Indexing into the static spinlock table, SMP$RELEASE obtains the address of the spinlock and stores it in R0. (Entry point SMP$RELEASEL is entered with the address of a dynamic spinlock in R0.)

2. The routine executes a MB instruction to order any preceding accesses to the database synchronized by the spinlock with the release of the spinlock.

3. It loads the fields containing the owner count and owner ID.

4. If the spinlock has already been released, the routine generates the fatal bugcheck SPLRELERR on the presumption that a serious failure has occurred.

   Otherwise, it sets the owner count to –1, clears SPL$L_OWN_CPU, and returns to its invoker.

9.5.10 **Full-Checking Spinlock Routines**

The full-checking version of the spinlock routines is in module SPIN-LOCKS_MON. This module includes the same entry points as the stream-lined version. The entry points are invoked from the same lock and unlock macros.

Following is a description of the full-checking version of the acquire routines, with some details of SMP operations omitted for simplicity:

1. When SMP$ACQUIRE is entered, R0 contains the index of a static spinlock. Indexing into the static spinlock table, SMP$ACQUIRE obtains the address of the spinlock and stores it in R0. (Entry points SMP$ACQUIREL and SMP$ACQNOIPL are entered with the address of a spinlock already in R0.)

2. The routine confirms that the spinlock address is valid (that is, nonzero) rather than a reference to a reserved spinlock index. If the address is zero, the routine generates the fatal bugcheck INCONSTATE. It also checks whether the IPL at entry is higher than that of the spinlock, indicating a possible synchronization failure. If it is, the routine makes several additional sanity checks and, if appropriate, generates the fatal bugcheck SPLIPLHIGH.

   If the IPL is not higher, SMP$ACQUIRE sets the IPL to that of the spinlock. (Entry point SMP$ACQNOIPL is entered with an IPL already known to be correct and thus not to be altered.)

3. SMP$ACQUIRE gets the address of the processor's per-CPU database.

4. It tests whether the target spinlock is a device lock. If it is, SMP$ACQUIRE skips the next step; a processor may acquire multiple device locks, and the spinlock acquisition rule does not apply.

5. If the target lock is not a device lock, SMP$ACQUIRE tests whether the attempted lock would violate the spinlock acquisition rule (see Section 9.5.5). It examines CPU$L_RANK_VEC to determine if the processor already holds a higher ranking spinlock. If the processor does, the routine generates the fatal bugcheck SPLACQERR.

6. SMP$ACQUIRE raises IPL to 31 and executes the MACRO-32 statement BBSSI to test and set the low bit of SPL$L_SPINLOCK. If the bit is already set, some other processor has exclusive access to the spinlock control block and this processor must wait. SMP$ACQUIRE restores the previous IPL and spinwaits, as described in Section 9.5.9, simply retesting the state of the bit with a noninterlocked instruction.

   When the bit becomes clear, the routine raises IPL to 31 and repeats its attempt to acquire exclusive access to the spinlock control block. The processor runs at IPL 31 to block all interrupts while it has exclusive access to the spinlock control block. This avoids potential delays and deadlocks that could occur if another processor, the owner of the spinlock, were unable to release it while the processor with exclusive access to the control block was executing some interrupt service routine.

7. When the processor obtains exclusive access to the spinlock control block, SMP$ACQUIRE examines the spinlock owner count and, if necessary, owner ID, to determine whether this processor may acquire the spinlock.

8. If some other processor owns the spinlock, SMP$ACQUIRE takes the following steps:

   a. It sets to a nonzero value the field CPU$L_BUSYWAIT in the per-CPU database as a signal to the interval timer interrupt service routine. When this field is nonzero, the interrupt service routine does not charge soft ticks against process quantum (see Chapter 12).

   b. It increments SPL$L_WAIT_CPUS, the number of processors waiting for the spinlock, and SPL$L_BUSY_WAITS, the cumulative number of acquisitions that had to wait. The quotient of SPL$Q_SPINS, the number of cumulative spins by all processors waiting for the spinlock during its current use, and SPL$L_BUSY_WAITS is the basis of the Monitor utility statistic "spins per failed acquisition."

   c. It executes the MACRO-32 statement BBCCI to clear the low bit of SPL$L_SPINLOCK to release its exclusive access to the spinlock control block and lowers IPL to the larger of the invoker's IPL and IPL$_RESCHED. This prevents any rescheduling during the spinwait.

   d. It zeros a register to serve as its own spin counter.

   e. It then spins, incrementing the spin counter each time and testing the spinlock owner count to see whether the spinlock has been released. While it spins, it performs a countdown and tests whether it must perform SMP functions, as described in Section 9.5.9.

   f. When the owner count indicates no owner, SMP$ACQUIRE raises IPL to 31 and executes the MACRO-32 statement BBSSI to acquire exclusive access to the spinlock control block, as described in step 6.

   g. When SMP$ACQUIRE has exclusive access to the spinlock control block, it adds its spin count to the total in SPL$Q_SPINS. It decrements SPL$L_WAIT_CPUS to indicate one less processor waiting for the spinlock. It decrements CPU$L_BUSYWAIT.

   h. Reentering the main flow at step 7, SMP$ACQUIRE repeats its attempt to acquire the spinlock.

9. If the spinlock is already owned by this processor, SMP$ACQUIRE increments the owner count. It continues with step 11.

10. If the owner count is −1, indicating no owners, SMP$ACQUIRE increments the count and stores the address of the processor's per-CPU database in SPL$L_OWN_CPU. It sets the bit corresponding to the spinlock's rank in the per-CPU database field CPU$L_RANK_VEC.

It inverts the IPL of the spinlock and sets the corresponding bit in CPU$L_IPL_VEC. It increments the corresponding longword in CPU$L_IPL_ARRAY.

11. At each successful acquisition, it saves the invoking thread's return PC at the next position in the spinlock ring buffer at SPL$L_OWN_PC_VEC and updates the index to point to the next entry. It increments SPL$Q_ACQ_COUNT to indicate one more successful acquisition.

12. It executes the MACRO-32 statement BBCCI to release its exclusive access to the spinlock control block, lowers IPL to that associated with the spinlock, and returns to its invoker with the spinlock held.

Following is a description of the full-checking version of the restore/release routines, with some details of SMP operations omitted for simplicity. These routines do not alter IPL but run at the IPL at which they were entered.

1. At entry to SMP$RESTORE, R0 contains the index of a static spinlock. Indexing into the static spinlock table, SMP$RESTORE obtains the address of the spinlock and stores it in R0. (Entry point SMP$RESTOREL is entered with the address of a dynamic spinlock in R0.)

2. SMP$RESTORE compares the IPL at entry to the spinlock IPL. If the IPL is lower than that of the spinlock, the routine generates the fatal bugcheck SPLIPLLOW.

3. SMP$RESTORE gets the address of the processor's per-CPU database.

4. It executes the MACRO-32 statement BBSSI to obtain exclusive access to the spinlock control block, spinwaiting (see step 6 in the preceding SMP$ACQUIRE description) until the block is available.

5. It checks whether the spinlock is indeed owned by this processor. If not, the routine generates the fatal bugcheck SPLRSTERR.

6. SMP$RESTORE decrements the spinlock owner count.

   - If the count is zero or positive, indicating that the spinlock is still owned, the routine saves the invoking thread's return PC at the next position in the spinlock ring buffer at SPL$L_OWN_PC_VEC and updates the pointer to the next entry.

     It executes the MACRO-32 statement BBCCI to release its exclusive access to the spinlock control block and returns to its invoker.

   - If the owner count is –1, indicating that the spinlock is now free, SMP$RESTORE's path joins that of SMP$RELEASE, at step 11, below.

7. At entry to SMP$RELEASE, R0 contains the index of a static spinlock. Indexing into the static spinlock table, SMP$RELEASE obtains the address of the spinlock and stores it in R0. (Entry point SMP$RELEASEL is entered with the address of a dynamic spinlock already in R0.)

8. SMP$RELEASE makes the check against entry IPL (described in step 2) and, if it is too low, generates the fatal bugcheck SPLIPLLOW.

9. It tests that the processor is indeed the spinlock owner and, if it is not, generates the fatal bugcheck SPLRELERR.

10. It decrements the spinlock owner count. If the resulting count is non-negative, it sets the count to –1 and records the invoking thread's return PC in SPL$L_RLS_PC as the most recent thread to relinquish multiple nested acquisitions of the spinlock.

11. It inverts the IPL associated with the spinlock and decrements the corresponding longword in CPU$L_IPL_ARRAY to indicate one less spinlock held at that IPL. If the count becomes zero, SMP$RELEASE clears the corresponding bit in CPU$L_IPL_VEC.

12. It clears the bit corresponding to the spinlock's rank in CPU$L_RANK_VEC.

13. It clears the spinlock owner field.

14. It saves the invoking thread's return PC at the next position in the spinlock ring buffer at SPL$L_OWN_PC_VEC and updates the pointer to the next entry.

15. It executes the MACRO-32 statement BBCCI to release its exclusive access to the spinlock control block and returns to its invoker.

9.6 SERIALIZED ACCESS

The OpenVMS AXP executive combines software interrupts and queues to serialize several requests for the same data structure or procedure. An example of this serialization is the use of fork processes by device drivers and other parts of the executive.

Fork processing is the technique that allows a device driver to lower IPL in a manner consistent with the interrupt nesting scheme defined by the Alpha AXP architecture. When a device driver receives control in response to a device interrupt, it performs whatever steps are necessary to service the interrupt at device IPL. For example, before dismissing the device interrupt, it reads any device registers whose contents would be destroyed by another interrupt.

Usually, some processing can be deferred. For DMA devices, an interrupt signifies either completion of the operation or an error. The code that distinguishes these two cases and performs error processing is usually lengthy. If it executed at device IPL for extended periods of time, it would reduce response to high-priority interrupts.

To delay further processing until IPL drops below the fork IPL associated with this driver, the device driver interrupt service code records the procedure value of the routine in the driver to which control should return when IPL drops and invokes an executive routine, EXE$PRIMITIVE_FORK, in module FORKCNTRL. EXE$PRIMITIVE_FORK saves some minimal context, namely, two integer registers, in a fork block. (The layout of a fork block is shown in Figure 5.1.)

EXE$PRIMITIVE_FORK extracts the fork block field FKB$B_FLCK, which contains a static spinlock index, and indexes the static spinlock IPL table with it to obtain the IPL value associated with that spinlock. The routine inserts the fork block at the end of the fork queue for that IPL and requests a software interrupt at that IPL if the queue was previously empty.

A thread of execution that creates a fork process can use any appropriate static spinlock as its fork lock. The only requirement is that the spinlock IPL be one at which fork processing is performed: 6, 8, 9, 10, or 11.

Chapter 5 describes fork processing in further detail.

9.7	**MUTUAL EXCLUSION SEMAPHORES (MUTEXES)**

The synchronization techniques described so far all execute at elevated IPL, thus blocking certain operations, such as a rescheduling request. However, in some situations requiring synchronization, elevated IPL is an unacceptable technique. One reason elevated IPL might be unacceptable is that the processor would have to remain at an elevated IPL for an indeterminately long time because of the structure of the data. For example, associating to a common event block cluster requires a search of the list of common event blocks (CEBs) for the specified CEB. This might be a lengthy operation on a system with many CEBs.

Furthermore, elevated IPL is unacceptable for synchronizing access to pageable data. The executive bugchecks if a page fault occurs at an IPL above 2. Thus, a pageable data structure cannot be protected by elevating IPL.

One synchronization mechanism that does not require elevated IPL is a mutual exclusion semaphore, or mutex. The executive uses mutexes for synchronizing kernel mode accesses to certain shared data structures. A mutex is essentially a counter that controls read or write access to a given data structure or database. With this mechanism either multiple readers or one writer can access a data structure or database synchronized through mutex acquisition. Typically, the threads of execution whose accesses are synchronized through a mutex are process context threads.

Access to a mutex itself must be gained at elevated IPL with the SCHED spinlock held. However, once a mutex is acquired, elevated IPL is not required to access the database represented by the mutex.

Table 9.3 lists the executive data structures protected by mutexes and the names of the corresponding mutexes. (The "CPU mutex," used in SMP code, is discussed in Chapter 37.)

A mutex is a data structure consisting of an owner count and status bits. The owner count is the number of processes accessing the data, that is, the number of processes that have locked the mutex. The owner count value is initialized to -1 to indicate no owners. Thus, a mutex with a 0 in the owner count field has one owner. Biasing the owner count by -1 simplifies the code

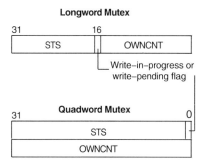

Figure 9.9
Layout of a Mutex

that tests for the transition between unowned and owned. Only one status flag is currently implemented. The flag is set to indicate that a write is either in progress or pending for this mutex.

All OpenVMS VAX mutexes and some OpenVMS AXP mutexes consist of a single longword. OpenVMS AXP adds support for quadword mutexes, which can be locked and unlocked with fewer memory operations than longword mutexes. The macro $MTXDEF defines symbolic names for the fields in the longword mutex, and $MUTEXDEF, for the fields in the quadword mutex. Figure 9.9 shows their layouts. Some mutexes remain longwords; others have been converted to quadwords. Module MUTEX contains two sets of routines, one for each form of mutex:

- SCH$LOCKR and SCH$LOCKR_QUAD—Lock a mutex for read access to the data structures it synchronizes
- SCH$LOCKW and SCH$LOCKW_QUAD—Lock a mutex for write access
- SCH$UNLOCK and SCH$UNLOCK_QUAD—Unlock a mutex

The process control block (PCB) field PCB$L_MTXCNT contains the number of mutexes a process currently owns. This field is initialized to zero and incremented each time a process acquires a mutex.

Typically, executive code invokes the routines described in the following sections to lock or unlock a mutex whose address is specified in R0. Some subsystems, however, use routines such as SCH$IOLOCKR, SCH$IO-LOCKW, and SCH$IOUNLOCK, which load the address of the I/O database mutex into R0 and transfer to their more general counterparts.

9.7.1 Locking a Mutex for Read Access

When a process needs read access to a data structure protected by a mutex, it invokes routine SCH$LOCKR or SCH$LOCKR_QUAD with the address of the mutex. Each routine takes the following steps.

Table 9.3   List of Data Structures Protected by Mutexes

Data Structure	*Global Name of Mutex*
Shared logical name data structures	LNM$AQ_MUTEX
I/O database	IOC$GQ_MUTEX [1]
Common event block list	EXE$GL_CEBMTX
Paged dynamic memory list	EXE$GL_PGDYNMTX
Global section descriptor list	EXE$GL_GSDMTX
Not currently used	EXE$GL_ENQMTX
Line printer unit control block	UCB$L_LR_MUTEX [2]
Audio device unit control block	UCB$L_SO_MUTEX [2]
Not currently used	EXE$GL_ACLMTX
System intruder lists	CIA$GL_MUTEX
Object rights block access control list	ORB$L_ACL_MUTEX [3]
System service database	CHANGE_MODE_MUTEX [4]
Terminal fallback database	TFF$L_VEC_MUTEX [5]
Executive image data structures	EXE$GQ_BASIMGMTX
Not currently used	QMAN$GL_MUTEX

[1] This mutex is used by the Assign Channel and Allocate Device system services during a search through the linked list of device data blocks and UCBs for a device. It is also used when UCBs are added or deleted, for example, during the creation of mailbox, disk, and network devices.

[2] This mutex does not have a fixed address. As a field in a device UCB, its location depends on that of the UCB.

[3] This mutex does not have a fixed address. As a field in an ORB, its location depends on that of the ORB.

[4] This mutex is local to the EXCEPTION.EXE executive image.

[5] This mutex is local to the fallback driver.

1. It acquires the SCHED spinlock, raising IPL to IPL$_SCHED.

2. It tests whether the mutex's write flag is set. If so, no further readers are allowed to acquire the mutex. It transparently stalls the process (see Section 9.7.3) until the mutex is available.

3. If the write flag is clear, indicating that no write operation is in progress or pending, it grants the process read ownership of the mutex – it increments the mutex's owner count and increments the count of mutexes owned by this process.

4. If this mutex is the first that the process currently has locked and if the process is not a real-time process, its current and base priorities are saved in the PCB fields PCB$L_PRISAV and PCB$L_PRIBSAV and then both are elevated to 16. The process receives a priority boost to minimize the time during which it holds the mutex and blocks other processes that require the mutex. To alter the current priority, the routine invokes SCH$CHANGE_CUR_PRIORITY, in module RSE, which is described in Chapter 13. The check on the number of owned mutexes prevents a

process that gains ownership of two or more mutexes from receiving a permanent priority elevation to 16.

5. SCH$LOCKR or SCH$LOCKR_QUAD releases the SCHED spinlock and returns control to its invoker with IPL at 2.

The process is expected to remain at IPL 2 or above while it owns the mutex to prevent its own deletion or suspension. Neither the Delete Process ($DELPRC) system service nor the Suspend Process ($SUSPND) system service checks whether the target process owns any mutexes. If the process deletion or suspension were to succeed, the locked mutex would no longer be lockable and thus the locked data structure would be inaccessible.

9.7.2   Locking a Mutex for Write Access

When a process needs write access to a data structure that is protected by a mutex, it invokes routine SCH$LOCKW or SCH$LOCKW_QUAD with the address of the mutex. Each routine takes the following steps:

1. It acquires the SCHED spinlock, raising IPL to IPL$_SCHED.
2. It tests the mutex's write flag.
3. If the flag is set, no further readers or writers are allowed to acquire the mutex. It transparently stalls the process (see Section 9.7.3) until the mutex is available.
4. If the write flag is clear, it tests whether there are any current owners of the mutex. If there are, it sets the write flag and transparently stalls the process.
5. If the write flag is clear and there are no owners of the mutex, the routine grants the process write ownership of the mutex: it increments the mutex owner count and PCB$L_MTXCNT, and it can alter the process's software priority, as previously described. It releases the SCHED spinlock and returns to its invoker at IPL 2.

When SCH$LOCKW or SCH$LOCKW_QUAD stalls the process, the mutex write flag is set so that future requests for read access will also be denied. This prevents a stream of read accesses from continuously locking the mutex. When the last current owner of the mutex releases it, the write flag is cleared. At that point, the highest priority process waiting for the mutex gets first access to it, whether the process is requesting a read or a write access.

If a reader acquires the mutex, other previously waiting would-be readers whose priority is greater than that of the highest priority would-be writer can also acquire read access, as a result of standard scheduling operations. The higher priority would-be readers execute first, and their read accesses are granted. If readers still own the mutex when the would-be writer executes, its attempted write access is blocked again.

Alternative entry points, SCH$LOCKWNOWAIT and SCH$LOCKWNO-

WAIT_QUAD, return control to the invoker with R0⟨0⟩ cleared to indicate failure if the requested mutex is already owned.

9.7.3   Mutex Wait State

The mutex lock routines transparently stall a process when its requested mutex acquisition cannot be granted. Each stores the address of the mutex being requested in the PCB field PCB$L_EFWM. Because the process is not waiting for an event flag, the field is available for this purpose. Each places the process into the miscellaneous wait state (MWAIT). Each calls the routine that selects a new process to place into execution and that releases the SCHED spinlock. Chapter 13 describes miscellaneous waits and rescheduling in more detail.

   The saved PC of such a process is an address within EXE$KERNEL_WAIT_PS, in module MUTEX. On the stack is a return address within one of the mutex lock routines. The process's saved PS has a current mode of kernel and IPL 2. When the mutex becomes available, the process becomes computable again. When the process is placed into execution, it reattempts its mutex lock.

9.7.4   Unlocking a Mutex

A process releases a mutex by invoking SCH$UNLOCK or SCH$UNLOCK_QUAD with the address of the mutex to be released. Each routine takes the following steps:

1. It acquires the SCHED spinlock, raising IPL to IPL$_SCHED.
2. It decrements the process's PCB$L_MTXCNT. If this process does not own any more mutexes, SCH$UNLOCK restores the saved base priority from PCB$L_PRIBSAV and invokes SCH$CHANGE_CUR_PRIORITY to restore the current priority from PCB$L_PRISAV.

   If there is a computable resident process with a higher priority than this process's restored priority, SCH$CHANGE_CUR_PRIORITY requests a rescheduling interrupt. This situation is known as delayed preemption of the current process.
3. SCH$UNLOCK or SCH$UNLOCK_QUAD also decrements the mutex owner count. If the mutex owner count is greater than –1, there are other outstanding owners of this mutex; the routine simply releases the SCHED spinlock, restoring the IPL at entry, and returns to its invoker.
4. If the mutex count is decremented to –1, the mutex is now unowned. The routine tests its write flag. If the bit is clear, the routine releases the SCHED spinlock, restoring the IPL at entry, and returns to its invoker.
5. If the bit is set, there may be processes waiting to acquire this mutex. (A waiting or owning writer would have set this bit, blocking any new potential readers and any writers.) The routine clears the bit and calls EXE$WAIT_QUEUE_RELEASE, in module MUTEX.

EXE$WAIT_QUEUE_RELEASE scans the miscellaneous resource wait queue to locate any process whose PCB$L_EFWM field contains the address of the unlocked mutex. For each such process, it reports the availability of the mutex by invoking a scheduler routine to make the process computable. If the priority of any of these processes allows it to preempt a current process, a rescheduling interrupt is requested.

SCH$UNLOCK or SCH$UNLOCK_QUAD then releases the SCHED spinlock, restoring the IPL at entry, and returns to its invoker.

9.7.5 Accessing a Mutex from System Context

Although mutexes were originally designed for use from process context, it is possible for a system thread of execution to acquire a mutex. This enables a system thread to synchronize its access with those of full processes to a database protected by a mutex. In general, this capability is limited to nonpageable databases, since the executive bugchecks in response to page faults occurring above IPL 2. Currently, the capability is only used by fork processes to acquire the I/O database mutex.

The I/O database mutex basically synchronizes the lists of I/O data structures, for example, the linked list of UCBs associated with a particular device. A device driver that clones new device units from template devices must insert new units into the UCB list and remove units being deleted. Although these insertions and deletions are usually done from process context, in some cases they must be done from fork process context. For example, when the disk class driver fork process receives a message from an MSCP server that a new disk unit has come on line, it must clone a UCB and add it to the list.

The following routines in module MUTEX serve this need:

► SCH$LOCKWEXEC and SCH$LOCKWEXEC_QUAD—Acquire write ownership of a mutex from a system thread
► SCH$LOCKREXEC and SCH$LOCKREXEC_QUAD—Acquire read ownership of a mutex from a system thread
► SCH$UNLOCKEXEC and SCH$UNLOCKEXEC_QUAD—Release a mutex from a system thread

The main difference between these routines and their process context counterparts is that they return a failure status if the mutex is unavailable. There is no mechanism that transparently stalls a fork process and awakens it when the mutex becomes available. If a fork process receives a failure status, it must wait itself by using the fork and wait mechanism described in Chapter 5.

These routines acquire the SCHED spinlock, which is held at IPL$_ SCHED. This mechanism is therefore restricted to threads of execution that run at IPL 8 or below and that hold no higher ranking spinlock.

9.8   **RELEVANT SOURCE MODULES**

Source modules described in this chapter include

    [LIB]CPUDEF.SDL
    [LIB]IPLDEF.SDL
    [LIB]MTXDEF.SDL
    [LIB]MUTEXDEF.SDL
    [LIB]SPLCODDEF.SDL
    [LIB]SPLDEF.SDL
    [LIB]SYSMAR.MAR
    [SYS]FORKCNTRL.MAR
    [SYS]LDAT.MAR
    [SYS]MUTEX.MAR
    [SYS]SPINLOCKS.MAR

10   Event Flags

I claim not to have controlled events, but confess plainly that
events have controlled me.

Abraham Lincoln, Letter to A. G. Hodges, April 4, 1864

Event flags are status bits maintained by the OpenVMS AXP operating system for general programming use. Each event flag can be either set or clear,
and its status can be tested.

System services read, set, and clear event flags. A process can specify that
an event flag be set at the completion of an operation such as an I/O request.
When the process can proceed no further until the request is complete, the
process can request a system service to wait for the event flag to be set.

This chapter describes the implementation of event flags and the services
that support them.

10.1   EVENT FLAGS

An event flag can be used within a single process for synchronization with
the completion of certain system services, such as I/O, lock, information,
and timer requests. Each of these services includes an argument identifying
the event flag associated with the request. When a process requests such a
system service, that event flag is cleared. It is subsequently set when the
request has been completed as a signal to the process that the operation is
complete. Event flags can also be used as application-specific synchronization tools.

Event flags can be local to one process or shared among processes in the
same user identification code (UIC) group. Shared event flags are called common event flags. Processes sharing common event flags must be running on
a single VMScluster member; that is, common event flags are not visible
clusterwide.

Each process has available to it 64 local (process-specific) event flags, in
two clusters of 32 flags each, and can access 64 common event flags at once,
in two clusters of 32 flags each. Before a process can refer to the flags in a
particular common event flag cluster, it must explicitly associate with the
cluster (see Section 10.1.2), specifying which numbers it will use to refer to
the flags.

The operating system assigns no inherent meaning to any particular event
flag, although it does reserve certain flags for its own use (see Section 10.1.1).
A process defines the meaning of a flag by the way it uses the flag. For example, when a process requests the Queue I/O Request ($QIO) system service,
specifying event flag 10 as the EFN argument, the process can subsequently

284

wait for completion of that I/O request by waiting for event flag 10 to be set. After the process's wait is satisfied, the meaning of event flag 10 is undefined.

If the process concurrently uses event flag 10 in two different ways, the meaning of its being set is ambiguous. Under some circumstances, concurrent uses of the same flag within a process can lead to a spurious signal of completion; under others, concurrent uses can lead to an indefinite wait. Use of the Run-Time Library procedures LIB$GET_EF and LIB$FREE_EF (see the *OpenVMS RTL Library (LIB$) Manual*) can help prevent inadvertent concurrent use of the same flags.

The services for which an event flag argument can be specified include

- Breakthrough [and Wait] ($BRKTHRU[W])
- Enqueue Lock Request [and Wait] ($ENQ[W])
- Get Device/Volume Information [and Wait] ($GETDVI[W])
- Get Job/Process Information [and Wait] ($GETJPI[W])
- Get Lock Information [and Wait] ($GETLKI[W])
- Get Queue Information [and Wait] ($GETQUI[W])
- Get Systemwide Information [and Wait] ($GETSYI[W])
- Queue I/O Request [and Wait] ($QIO[W])
- Send to Job Controller [and Wait] ($SNDJBC[W])
- Set Timer ($SETIMR)
- Synchronize ($SYNCH)
- Update Section File on Disk [and Wait] ($UPDSEC[W])

10.1.1 Local Event Flags

The 64 local event flags are contained in each process's process header (PHD), at offset PHD$Q_LEFC. The quadword is divided into two longwords whose names are PHD$L_LEFC_0 and PHD$L_LEFC_1. All local event flags are initialized to zero during process creation.

Local event flags 0 to 31 make up cluster 0. Bit 0 in PHD$L_LEFC_0 corresponds to event flag 0, bit 1 to event flag 1, and so on. Local event flags 32 to 63 make up cluster 1. Bit 0 in PHD$L_LEFC_1 corresponds to event flag 32, bit 1 to event flag 33, and so on.

OpenVMS VAX local event flags are in a process's process control block (PCB). Their relocation in OpenVMS AXP to the PHD makes it possible for the wait-for services to test them in an outer mode, as described in Section 10.6.

Event flag 0 is the default event flag. Whenever a process requests a system service with an event flag number argument, but does not specify a particular flag, event flag 0 is used. Consequently, it is more likely than others to be used incorrectly for multiple concurrent requests.

Event flag numbers 24 through 31 are reserved for system use; this means they can be set and cleared at any time by executive software and should not be used by application software.

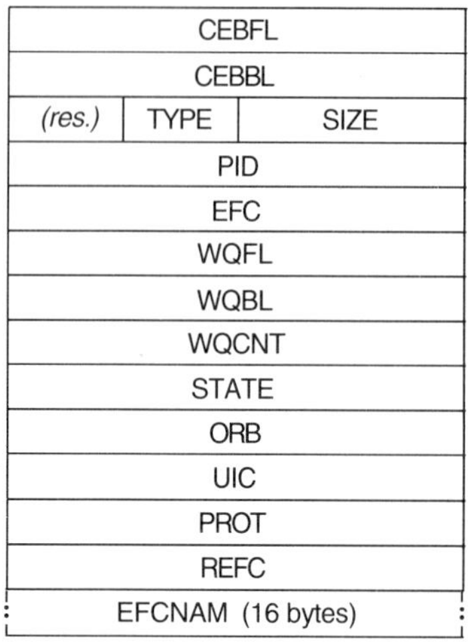

CEBFL		
CEBBL		
(res.)	TYPE	SIZE
PID		
EFC		
WQFL		
WQBL		
WQCNT		
STATE		
ORB		
UIC		
PROT		
REFC		
EFCNAM (16 bytes)		

Figure 10.1
Layout of Common Event Block (CEB)

10.1.2   Common Event Flags

A process creates a common event flag cluster dynamically, by requesting the Associate Common Event Flag Cluster ($ASCEFC) system service (see Section 10.3). Each common event flag cluster is described by a nonpaged pool data structure called a common event block (CEB), whose layout is shown in Figure 10.1.

The process specifies whether it will access the flags in that cluster using event flag numbers 64 through 95 (cluster 2) or 96 through 127 (cluster 3). If the flags are associated as cluster 2, the field PCB$L_EFC2P contains the address of their CEB. Otherwise, PCB$L_EFC3P contains its address.

CEB$L_CEBFL and CEB$L_CEBBL link each CEB into a systemwide list whose listhead is SCH$GQ_CEBHD (see Figure 10.2). The system global SCH$GW_CEBCNT contains the number of CEBs in the list. The mutex EXE$GL_CEBMTX synchronizes access to the CEB list. Chapter 9 describes the use of mutexes.

A particular common event flag cluster is identified by its name, CEB$T_ EFCNAM, and UIC group, CEB$W_GRP. (CEB$W_GRP is the high-order word of CEB$L_UIC.) There cannot be more than one cluster with the same name and group.

Two bits are defined in CEB$L_STS:

▶ CEB$V_PERM, when set, indicates that the cluster is a permanent one rather than a temporary one.
▶ CEB$V_NOQUOTA, when set, indicates that no quota was charged for the creation of the cluster.

Creation of a temporary cluster is charged against a job's timer queue entry

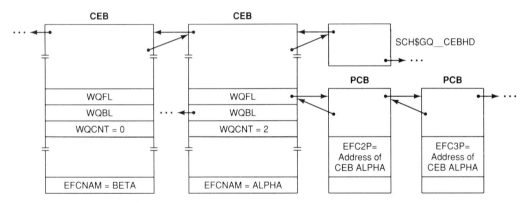

Figure 10.2
Common Event Flag Wait Queues

(TQE) quota. Creation of a permanent cluster uses no quota but requires the privilege PRMCEB. A temporary cluster exists only as long as a process is associated to it, whereas a permanent cluster must be explicitly deleted.

CEB$L_PID contains the internal process ID (IPID) of the master process in the job tree of the process that created the cluster.

The field CEB$L_EFC contains the 32 event flags. These are all initialized to zero when the cluster is created.

The fields CEBL_WQFL, CEBL_WQBL, CEB$L_WQCNT, and CEB$L_STATE form a wait queue (see Chapter 13) for processes waiting for flags in that cluster.

CEB$L_UIC contains the UIC of the creating process.

Only processes within the same UIC group can share common event flags. CEB$L_PROT contains the value 0 if other processes in the same UIC group are permitted access; otherwise, it contains the value 1.

CEB$L_REFC contains the number of processes that are currently associated to the cluster.

10.2   PCB FIELDS RELATED TO EVENT FLAGS

Figure 10.3 shows the PCB fields related to the use of event flags. Section 10.1.2 describes the meaning of the fields PCB$L_EFC2P and PCB$L_EFC3P.

The other fields are significant for a process in an event flag wait. PCB$L_WEFC contains the number of the cluster containing the flags for which a process waits. PCB$L_EFWM contains a mask that is the 1's complement of the flags in the cluster for which the process is waiting. The PCB$L_STS bit PCB$V_WALL, when set, indicates that the process is waiting for all those flags to be set.

These fields are loaded only when a process initiates an event flag wait. Consequently, for a process in a state other than event flag wait, they may be

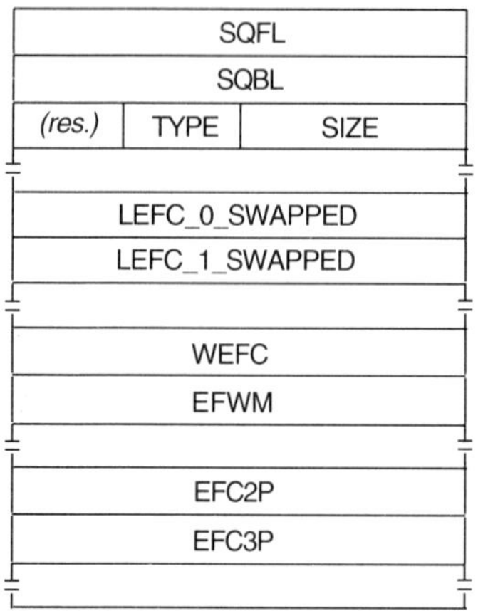

SQFL		
SQBL		
(res.)	TYPE	SIZE

LEFC_0_SWAPPED
LEFC_1_SWAPPED

WEFC
EFWM

EFC2P
EFC3P

Figure 10.3
Process Control Block (PCB) Fields That Support Event
Flags

stale. Furthermore, the field PCB$L_EFWM has an additional use: it identi-
fies the resource waited for by a process in a miscellaneous wait state.

When a process is outswapped, its PHD may be outswapped as well, leaving the local event flags in its PHD inaccessible to a routine trying to set any
of them. When outswapping a process, the swapper therefore copies the local
event flags from the PHD to PCB$Q_LEFC_SWAPPED. The quadword is di-
vided into two longwords whose names are PCB$L_LEFC_0_SWAPPED and
PCB$L_LEFC_1_SWAPPED. When inswapping a process, the swapper copies
the flags from the PCB to the PHD.

10.3 ASSOCIATING TO A COMMON EVENT FLAG CLUSTER

A process requests the $ASCEFC system service to create a named common
event flag cluster if it does not already exist and to access its flags. The
process specifies the name of the cluster and implicitly, through its PCB$L_
UIC field, the UIC group of the cluster.

The $ASCEFC system service procedure, EXE$ASCEFC in module SYS-
ASCEFC, runs in kernel mode. It takes the following steps:

1. EXE$ASCEFC confirms that the event flag number is within cluster 2
   or 3, returning the error status SS$_ILLEFC if it is not.
2. It locks the CEB mutex for write access.
3. It searches the CEB list for a cluster with the same name and group.
4. If one exists, EXE$ASCEFC checks whether the process can access it. If
   the process's UIC matches that of the CEB owner or if the CEB protection code allows group access, the process is allowed to associate to the
   cluster.

If the process is allowed access, EXE$ASCEFC continues with step 7. Otherwise, it unlocks the mutex and returns the error status SS$_NO-PRIV.

5. If the common event flag cluster does not already exist, the process is requesting its creation.

   - If the process requests a permanent cluster, it must have the privilege PRMCEB. If it does not have the privilege, EXE$ASCEFC unlocks the mutex and returns the error status SS$_NOPRIV.
   - If the process is not requesting a permanent cluster, EXE$ASCEFC charges it against the job's TQE quota. If the process has insufficient quota, EXE$ASCEFC unlocks the mutex and returns the error status SS$_EXQUOTA.

6. EXE$ASCEFC allocates a CEB from nonpaged pool and initializes it. It sets CEB$V_PERM in CEB$L_STS if the cluster is a permanent one. It increments SCH$GW_CEBCNT, the number of CEBs, and links the new CEB into the list.

7. Whether or not the cluster existed previously, the routine associates the process and the cluster by incrementing the cluster's reference count and by storing the address of the CEB in either PCB$L_EFC2P or PCB$L_EFC3P.

   First, however, it saves the old contents of PCB$L_EFC2P or PCB$L_EFC3P. If they are not zero, the process has been using those event flag numbers to associate with another cluster. EXE$ASCEFC severs the connection between the process and the other cluster by taking the steps described in Section 10.4.

8. It unlocks the mutex and returns.

10.4   DISSOCIATING FROM A COMMON EVENT FLAG CLUSTER

A process dissociates itself from a common event flag cluster explicitly by requesting the Disassociate Common Event Flag Cluster ($DACEFC) system service with an event flag number within that cluster. Implicitly, the service is requested on behalf of the process when it associates a new event flag cluster with a cluster number already in use.

The $DACEFC system service procedure, EXE$DACEFC in module SYS-ASCEFC, runs in kernel mode. It takes the following steps:

1. EXE$DACEFC confirms that the event flag number is within cluster 2 or 3, returning the error status SS$_ILLEFC if it is not.

2. It locks the CEB mutex for write.

3. It locates the CEB using the PCB pointer to the cluster and clears the pointer.

4. If the pointer was zero, the process did not have an associated cluster. The routine simply unlocks the mutex and returns.

5. Otherwise, it decrements the cluster's reference count. If there are other processes associated to the cluster or if the cluster is a permanent one, it unlocks the mutex and returns.

6. Otherwise (the cluster is temporary and has no processes still associated with it), EXE$DACEFC deletes it by taking the following steps:

   a. If CEB$V_NOQUOTA in CEB$L_STS is clear, EXE$DACEFC returns quota to the job against which it was originally charged.

   b. EXE$DACEFC removes the CEB from the CEB list, deallocates it to nonpaged pool, and decrements SCH$GW_CEBCNT.

   c. EXE$DACEFC unlocks the mutex and returns.

During image rundown, a process is automatically dissociated from any common event flag clusters to which it had associated.

10.5   **DELETING AN EVENT FLAG CLUSTER**

To delete a permanent event flag cluster, a process requests the Delete Common Event Flag Cluster ($DLCEFC) system service with the name of the cluster to be deleted.

A cluster cannot be deleted if processes are still associated with it. In such a case, the $DLCEFC service transforms the permanent cluster to a temporary one so that it will be deleted when the last process associated with the cluster requests the $DACEFC service.

The $DLCEFC system service procedure, EXE$DLCEFC in module SYSASCEFC, runs in kernel mode. It takes the following steps:

1. EXE$DLCEFC locks the CEB mutex for write.

2. It scans the CEB list for a cluster of the specified name and a group code matching that of the process. If it fails to find one, it unlocks the mutex and simply returns.

3. If it finds one, it tests whether the process is allowed to access the CEB. If the process's UIC is not that of the CEB and if the CEB protection does not allow a group member to delete it, EXE$DLCEFC unlocks the mutex and returns the error status SS$_NOPRIV.

   If the process does not have the privilege PRMCEB, EXE$DLCEFC also returns the error status SS$_NOPRIV.

4. Unless the process is deleting a temporary CEB, EXE$DLCEFC clears CEB$V_PERM and sets CEB$V_NOQUOTA in CEB$L_STS. This effectively changes the cluster to a temporary one for which no quota need be returned. The cluster's deletion is always deferred until all processes have dissociated from it.

5. EXE$DLCEFC increments the cluster's reference count and transfers to code within EXE$DACEFC, described in step 5 in Section 10.4. (The increment balances a decrement in EXE$DACEFC.)

10.6   WAITING FOR AN EVENT FLAG

A process can be placed into an event flag wait state to wait for the setting of one or more flags. When a process waits for more than one flag, all the flags must be in the same cluster. A process waits for event flags by performing any of the following actions:

- Requesting one of the three event flag wait system services directly:
  - Wait for Single Event Flag ($WAITFR)
  - Wait for Logical OR of Event Flags ($WFLOR)
  - Wait for Logical AND of Event Flags ($WFLAND)
- Requesting the $SYNCH system service, which combines $WAITFR and a status block test to wait for service completion (thus minimizing spurious completions caused by multiple concurrent uses of the same flag)
- Requesting the synchronous version of the services listed in Section 10.1, each of which incorporates $SYNCH
- Requesting Record Management Services (RMS) as a synchronous operation, which results in requesting $WAITFR

The distinction between $WFLOR and $WFLAND lies in how many of the flags must be set for the wait condition to be satisfied. If any of the flags in the mask is set when $WFLOR is requested, the process is not placed into a wait state. Instead, the service immediately returns to its caller.

Each of the flags specified in the $WFLAND system service argument must have been set for the wait to be satisfied. Although the flags need not be set simultaneously, clearing one of the flags in the mask can result in an indefinite wait, as described later in this section.

However the wait-for system service is requested, it examines the current state of the event flag or flags. If the event flag wait condition is satisfied, it returns control to the process. Otherwise, it places the process into a wait state until the flag or flags are set. The wait-for system services are described in the following paragraphs. The $SYNCH system service and synchronous RMS completions are described in Chapter 7.

The wait-for system service procedures, EXE$WAITFR, EXE$WFLOR, and EXE$WFLAND, which are in module SYSWAIT, are mode of caller services. The three mode of caller service procedures have the same form. Each checks whether the flag or flags are local or common and whether the wait-for condition is already met:

- If the flags are local, each service tests the flags in the PHD to see if the wait-for condition is already met and, if so, executes an MB instruction and returns the status SS$_WASSET.

  An event flag is process state that can be set asynchronously by a thread of execution running on another processor as a signal that other process state can now be accessed, for example, an I/O buffer. The explicit MB

291

instruction orders sensing the state of the flag with access to any other process state. (Spinlock acquisitions in the kernel mode services described in the next paragraphs result in implicit memory barriers.) Under these circumstances, the services can complete without the overhead of changing mode to kernel.

▶ If the flags are local, but the wait-for condition is not met, each service requests a corresponding system service whose name has the form $*wait_* INT, for example, $WAITFR_INT.

▶ If the flags are common, each service requests a corresponding system service whose name has the form $*wait*_COMMON, for example, $WFLOR_ COMMON.

The corresponding system service procedures are in module SYSWAIT and all execute in kernel mode. Each EXE$*wait*_COMMON and EXE$*wait*_ INT procedure copies the wait mask argument and transfers control to EXE$WAIT, in module SYSWAIT.

EXE$WAIT is entered with a mask identifying the flags to be waited for, the number of a flag in that cluster, and a wait-all flag that is set if the entry is from $WFLAND.

EXE$WAIT takes the following steps:

1. It checks that the event flag number is legal, returning the error status SS$_ILLEFC if the number is out of range.
2. EXE$WAIT raises interrupt priority level (IPL) to 2 to block delivery of a kernel mode asynchronous system trap (AST) procedure that might request another wait-for service.
3. It determines which cluster contains that event flag and records the cluster number in PCB$L_WEFC.
4. If the cluster number is 2 or 3, indicating a common event flag cluster, EXE$WAIT first checks that there is an associated cluster and returns the error status SS$_UNASEFC if there is none.

   If there is an associated cluster, it gets the CEB address from either PCB$L_EFC2P or PCB$L_EFC3P, depending on the cluster number.
5. It tests whether proactive memory reclamation from processes that wake periodically has been enabled and whether this process is potentially subject to working set reduction. If so, it invokes EXE$CHK_WT_BHVR, in module RSE, to reduce the working set if appropriate. Chapter 13 describes the routine and this form of memory reclamation in more detail.
6. EXE$WAIT acquires the SCHED spinlock, raising IPL to IPL$_SCHED, to block concurrent access to the event flags by SCH$POSTEF (see Section 10.7) and to synchronize access to the scheduler database.
7. It tests whether the event flag wait condition is satisfied by the current state of the flags.
8. If the wait condition is satisfied, EXE$WAIT releases the spinlock and returns to the mode of caller service procedure, which had requested ei-

ther $wait_INT or $wait_COMMON. The mode of caller service returns to its requestor.

9. If the event flag wait condition is unsatisfied, the routine checks whether the wait is wait-all. If so, it sets the PCB$V_WALL bit in PCB$L_STS.

10. EXE$WAIT stores a mask representing the flags to be waited for in PCB$L_EFWM:

   • If the process requested $WFLOR, the PCB$L_EFWM mask contains the 1's complement of the input mask passed to the system service.

   • If the process requested $WAITFR, the PCB$L_EFWM mask contains a 1 in every bit except the bit number corresponding to the specified flag. (The $WAITFR mask is thus a special case of a wait for any one of a group of flags to be set.)

   • If the process requested $WFLAND, EXE$WAIT clears any bits in the input mask corresponding to currently set flags, complements it, and then stores it in PCB$L_EFWM.

11. EXE$WAIT calls SCH$WAIT_PROC, in module SCHED_ROUTINES, to change the process's scheduling state to either a local or common event flag wait state, depending on the cluster number. It returns the status SS$_WAIT_CALLERS_MODE to the change mode dispatcher. In response to that status the change mode dispatcher initiates a context swap. Chapter 13 describes this sequence in greater detail.

   There are two systemwide local event flag wait states (LEF and LEFO) and two corresponding wait queue listheads (SCH$GQ_LEFWQ and SCH$GQ_LEFOWQ). Only one common event flag wait state exists for both resident and outswapped processes. However, there is a separate common event flag wait queue listhead (see Figure 10.1) in each common event flag cluster. Each has the same overall structure as any other wait queue listhead (see Figure 10.2). Both resident and outswapped processes waiting for flags in a common event flag cluster are queued to the same CEB wait queue. Having one queue in each CEB makes it easier to locate processes whose wait is satisfied by the setting of a flag in that cluster.

The value of the program counter (PC) saved for the waiting process depends upon whether event flag wait is for local or common flags. In either case, the process waits at the access mode at which it requested the mode of caller wait-for service. In either case, whenever the process is placed into execution, it will repeat the test for whether the event flag wait is satisfied. If the process became computable because the flags were set, it exits from the system service, as long as the flags are still set. If the process became computable as the result of AST enqueuing, at the completion of the AST it reexecutes the service and is placed back into a wait. Chapter 13 gives additional information.

While this technique permits ASTs to be delivered to a process waiting for event flags to be set, it constrains the ways in which event flags can be used: flags for which a process is waiting should not be cleared by other threads of execution. The result of clearing an event flag might be that a process becomes computable as the result of the flag's having been set but reenters the event flag wait state indefinitely when it reexecutes the event flag wait service and finds the flag no longer set. This could happen, for example, if process A waited for a common event flag set and then cleared by process B.

An indefinite wait is also possible when a local flag is used concurrently to signal multiple events. The sequence that follows is one example:

1. The mainline code requests a synchronous service and waits for local flag *N* to be set.
2. An AST is queued to the process, making it computable.
3. The AST procedure begins to execute.
4. The event associated with the mainline code's service occurs, and the local flag is set.
5. The AST procedure requests an asynchronous service, specifying the same flag.
6. The service procedure, in preparation for a possible wait request, clears the flag; initiates the requested task; and returns to the AST procedure, which also returns.
7. The mainline code repeats its event flag wait test. Because the flag has been cleared, the mainline code reenters its wait state.

This constraint applies to all wait-for services but has additional significance for the $WFLAND system service. The $WFLAND system service generates a wait mask based on the input mask flags that are not already set at the time the service is requested. However, each time the process is placed back into execution as a result of AST delivery, the process reexecutes the $WFLAND service and, each time, the event flag wait mask is built anew. No record is kept that some of the flags have been set and should not be waited for again if the service is reexecuted.

10.7 SETTING AN EVENT FLAG

A process sets an event flag directly by requesting the system service Set Event Flag ($SETEF). A process can use this service at AST level to communicate with its mainline code. It can also use this service to set common event flags to communicate with other processes.

The executive sets event flags in response to I/O completion, timer expiration, the granting of a lock request, and completion of any of the system services listed in Section 10.1.

The $SETEF system service and any other executive code that sets an event flag invokes SCH$POSTEF, in module POSTEF. SCH$POSTEF performs the actual event flag setting and checks whether a process's event flag wait is satisfied. Its arguments are the number of the flag to be set, the IPID of the process in whose context that flag number is defined, and a priority increment class number (see Chapter 13).

SCH$POSTEF runs in kernel mode. It takes the following steps:

1. It first acquires the SCHED spinlock, raising IPL to IPL$_SCHED, to block concurrent access to the flags from a wait-for service and to synchronize access to the scheduler database. (Note that the spinlock acquisition causes execution of an MB instruction, which orders any prior writes with the setting of the event flag.)

2. It then confirms that the specified process still exists. If not, it releases the spinlock and returns the error status SS$_NONEXPR.

3. It checks that the event flag number is legal, returning the error status SS$_ILLEFC if the number is out of range.

4. It then determines what kind of event flag is being set. For a common event flag, it continues with step 8.

5. If a local event flag is being set, SCH$POSTEF sets it using the load-locked/store-conditional mechanism to synchronize against concurrent writes to the flags. (For example, a process context thread of execution might be clearing one flag while I/O postprocessing code sets another.)

   It checks whether this flag satisfies a wait request for this process. In the case of a $WFLOR wait, this flag merely has to match one of the flags being waited for. For a $WFLAND wait, all the flags in the mask must be set to satisfy the process's wait request.

6. If the process's wait is satisfied, SCH$POSTEF reports an event-flag-setting event for the process by invoking SCH$REPORT_EVENT, in module RSE. Note that SCH$POSTEF examines PCB event-flag-related fields to decide if a wait is satisfied but ignores the process's scheduling state. Thus, SCH$POSTEF's event report may be based on stale values in these fields. SCH$REPORT_EVENT confirms that the process is in an event flag wait state prior to acting on the event report.

7. Whether or not a wait was satisfied, SCH$POSTEF releases the SCHED spinlock and returns the success status SS$_WASSET or SS$_WASCLR, depending on the initial state of the flag. This completes its processing for a local event flag.

8. If a common event flag is being set, SCH$POSTEF first checks that there is an associated common event flag cluster, returning the error status SS$_UNASEFC if there is none.

9. It gets the CEB address, using the contents of either PCB$L_EFC2P or PCB$L_EFC3P, depending on the flag number. It sets the flag using the load-locked/store-conditional mechanism to synchronize against concurrent writes to the flags. SCH$POSTEF must also scan the list of

PCBs in the CEB wait queue to determine which, if any, of the processes waiting for flags in this cluster has its wait request satisfied. SCH$POSTEF reports an event-flag-setting event for each such process.
10. It releases the SCHED spinlock, restoring the previous IPL, and returns.

SCH$REPORT_EVENT ignores an event-flag-setting event reported for a process not in an event flag wait state and simply returns. When an event-flag-setting event is reported for a process in an event flag wait state, SCH$REPORT_EVENT changes its state to computable resident (COM) or computable outswap (COMO) and, if appropriate, applies a priority boost, based upon the priority increment class number passed from SCH$POSTEF. SCH_REPORT_EVENT may request a rescheduling interrupt on behalf of the process or awaken the swapper process. Chapter 13 gives more details.

10.8 READING AND CLEARING EVENT FLAGS

The Read Event Flag ($READEF) system service is informational. It has no effect on the computability of any process. The $READEF system service procedure, EXE$READEF in module SYSEVTSRV, runs in kernel mode. It determines which cluster to read from its EFN argument. It copies the flags from either the PHD or the CEB that contains them to the location specified by its caller. It executes an MB instruction to order sensing the state of the flag with any subsequent actions the process might make based on its state. It returns the success status SS$_WASSET if any flag was set; otherwise, it returns SS$_WASCLR, which is equal to SS$_NORMAL.

The Clear Event Flag ($CLREF) system service simply clears the event flag specified by its EFN argument. The $CLREF system service procedure, EXE$CLREF in module SYSEVTSRV, runs in kernel mode. It locates the cluster that contains the specified flag and clears the flag using the load-locked/store-conditional mechanism. It executes an MB instruction to order sensing the state of the flag with any subsequent actions the process might make based on its state. It returns the success status SS$_WASCLR or SS$_WASSET, depending on the initial state of the flag. It has no immediate effect on the scheduling state of any process.

10.9 INTERPROCESS SYNCHRONIZATION THROUGH COMMON EVENT FLAGS

The use of common event flags is one method of interprocess synchronization. One process can reach a critical point in its execution and wait for a common event flag. Another process can enable this process to continue its execution by setting the flag.

A common event flag can also be used as a semaphore to gain access to a resource shared among processes. One such application is outlined here. It first requires creation of a common event flag cluster with all its flags set.

Each flag can be used as an individual lock. Each cooperating process must associate to the common event flag cluster.

Before any process uses the resource represented by a particular event flag, it must execute a sequence such as the following, which uses event flag number 65 as an example:

```
5$:    $CLREF_S    EFN=#65          ;Clear the event flag
       CMPL        R0,#SS$_WASSET   ;Was its previous state = 1?
       BEQL        10$              ;Branch if yes
       $WAITFR_S   EFN=#65          ;Else wait for flag
       BRB         5$
10$:                                ;Proceed to access resource
       .
       .
       .
       $SETEF_S    EFN=#65          ;Set the event flag
```

Clearing an event flag is an interlocked operation implemented by the executive. Only one process at a time can clear the flag and cause the transition in its state from set to clear. That process then "owns" the flag and its associated resource. Any other process that clears the flag receives a was-clear status and must wait for the flag to be set.

The process that owns the flag can then access the resource without synchronization problems. When the process's accesses to the resource are complete, the process sets the flag, relinquishing ownership of the flag and resource. The processes that were waiting for the flag are made computable and repeat their attempts to cause the event flag transition from set to clear.

10.10   RELEVANT SOURCE MODULES

Source modules described in this chapter include

[LIB]CEBDEF.SDL
[LIB]PCBDEF.SDL
[SYS]POSTEF.MAR
[SYS]SYSASCEFC.MAR
[SYS]SYSEVTSRV.MAR
[SYS]SYSWAIT.MAR

11   Lock Management

'Tis in my memory lock'd,
And you yourself shall keep the key of it.

Shakespeare, *Hamlet*, 1, iii

This chapter provides a brief overview of locks and related terminology. It describes lock management data structures, lock management system services, and deadlock detection.

The treatment in this chapter assumes that the reader is familiar with the description of the OpenVMS AXP lock management system services found in the *OpenVMS System Services Reference Manual*. Although VMScluster distributed lock management is briefly discussed here, its details are beyond the scope of this book.

11.1   OVERVIEW

Lock management system services enable cooperating processes to synchronize their accesses to global sections, files, and other entities. Through these services, a process assigns a name to an entity and requests a lock on the name. The services do not maintain a permanent link between the named resource and an actual entity. Processes requiring synchronized access to an entity must explicitly cooperate by locking the resource name representing the entity.

A lock is characterized by the extent to which it allows shared access with other locks on the same resource, that is, resource name. Locks that permit mutual shared access are termed compatible. Processes holding compatible locks on a resource have concurrent access to it and, if they behave consistently, to the entity it represents. A process requesting an incompatible lock is denied access. Optionally, such a process can be placed into a wait state until blocking locks are released and the resource becomes available.

The following system services, described in Section 11.3, allow a process to enqueue and dequeue lock requests and to get information about locks:

- Enqueue Lock Request [and Wait] ($ENQ[W])
- Dequeue Lock Request ($DEQ)
- Get Lock Information [and Wait] ($GETLKI[W])

In response to the first request to lock a given resource name, the executive creates a data structure called a resource block, described in Section 11.2.1, to represent the resource and grants the requestor access to the resource. When a subsequent request is made to lock the same name, the executive checks the resource block to determine whether the requested lock mode is compatible with the granted lock mode. If so, the executive grants the second requestor access also.

A data structure called a lock block, described in Section 11.2.3, represents a lock request. When a lock request is granted, its lock block is placed on the resource's granted queue. A lock granted in one mode can later be converted to another mode; a lock block representing a conversion request is placed on a resource's conversion queue. A lock block representing a request for incompatible access to a resource for which another process holds a lock is placed on the resource's wait queue.

When two processes compete for incompatible access to a resource, only one gets access; the other process's request is not granted until the competing process releases the lock or converts the lock to a mode compatible with the other's request. If an application is poorly designed, two or more competing processes can potentially wait for each other to release a lock. Such waits can never be satisfied. This condition is called a deadlock. The executive does not prevent applications from creating deadlock conditions. It does, however, detect and break deadlocks, as described in Section 11.4.

Lock management is central to VMScluster operation. Lock management system services provide clusterwide synchronization to OpenVMS AXP facilities and user applications. Appendix H describes the manner in which some of the facilities define resources and use locks.

Resource names are clusterwide in scope. Resource blocks and lock blocks, as well as other lock management data structures, are distributed among the nodes of a VMScluster system. A system application called the distributed lock manager assists the lock management system services in maintaining the clusterwide lock database. Participating cluster nodes share lock management overhead while keeping internode traffic at a minimum level. A detailed description of the distributed lock manager is outside the scope of this book. Its basic operation is presented in Section 11.2.6.

11.2   LOCK MANAGEMENT DATA STRUCTURES

The lock database consists of the following kinds of structures:

- ▶ Resource blocks (RSBs), which represent the entities for which locks have been requested
- ▶ One resource hash table, which locates the RSBs
- ▶ Lock blocks (LKBs), which describe locks requested by processes
- ▶ One lock ID table, which locates the LKBs

11.2.1   Resource Blocks

An RSB is allocated from nonpaged pool whenever a process requests the $ENQ system service specifying a resource not already defined.

A resource is uniquely identified by the following combination:

▸ Resource name string of 1 to 31 characters
▸ User identification code (UIC) group number (or zero if the resource is systemwide)
▸ Access mode
▸ Address of parent RSB, if any

Two resources with identical resource name strings are different unless their UIC groups, access modes, and parents match.

Resources can be hierarchical. For example, a resource can be defined to represent a particular file, with subresources for particular records in the file. The file resource is a parent resource to the resources representing records in the file. A record subresource may be a parent resource to additional subresources that represent fields in the record. The combination of a resource and all its subresources is called a resource tree. The top-level resource in the tree, the one with no parent, is called the root resource.

The first lock request for a resource can specify the parent of the resource, thereby defining its relationship in a tree. If no parent is specified, the resource becomes a root resource. To synchronize access to a subresource, a process must first lock the root resource and each subresource in the branches of the resource tree leading down to the target subresource, including the target subresource. For example, before locking a field in a record, a process must lock the associated file and record.

The root resource list, whose listhead is the global symbol LCK$GL_ RRSFL, links the root resources known by the local system. Subresources are linked to these root RSBs. The maximum depth of a resource tree is 127.

Figure 11.1 shows the layout of an RSB. RSB$T_RESNAM and RSB$B_ RSNLEN contain the resource name string and its length. Together with RSBW_GROUP, RSBB_RMOD, and RSB$L_PARENT, these fields uniquely identify a particular resource.

RSB$B_DEPTH indicates the position of the resource in a resource tree; a root resource has a depth of 0. The depth of a subresource is set to 1 more than its parent's RSB$B_DEPTH. Root resources are linked to form a queue through their RSB$L_RRSFL and RSB$L_RRSBL fields. All subresources of the root resource are linked to form a queue through the fields RSB$L_SRSFL and RSB$L_SRSBL. Each subresource contains the address of its root RSB in RSB$L_RTRSB; a root resource contains its own address. Figure 11.2 shows this linkage of root and subresources. RSB$W_ACTIVITY tracks the local node's use of the resource; a root resource with a low value is more likely to be remastered (see Section 11.2.6).

If the resource has a parent resource, its access mode is taken from the parent. Otherwise, the access mode is specified by the $ENQ system service argument ACMODE. The argument is maximized with the mode from which the service was requested, which is the default if the argument is omitted.

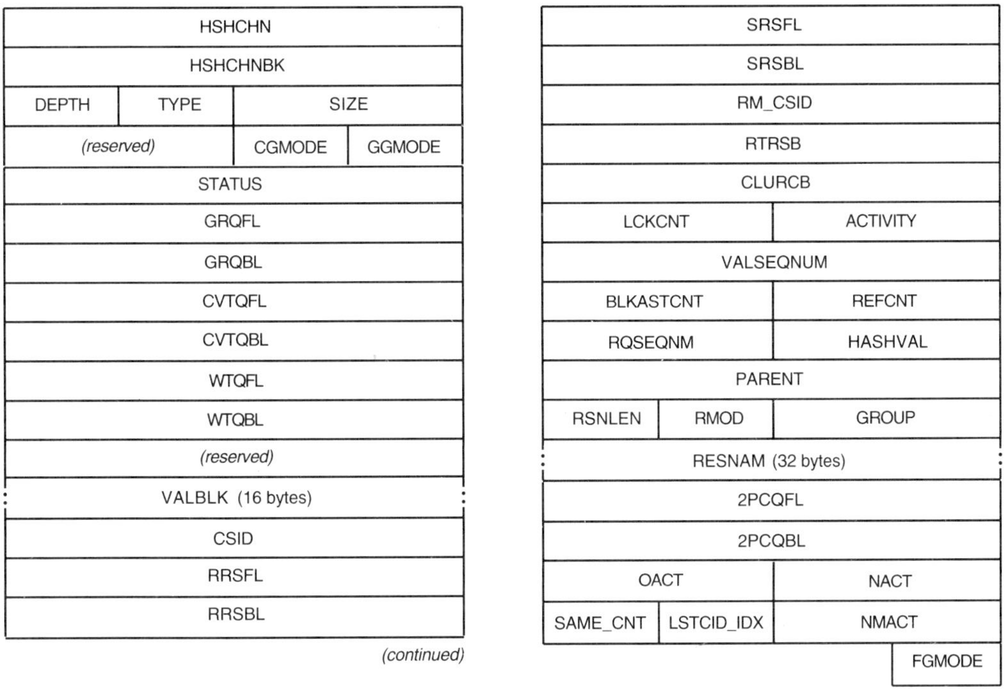

HSHCHN			
HSHCHNBK			
DEPTH	TYPE	SIZE	
(reserved)		CGMODE	GGMODE
STATUS			
GRQFL			
GRQBL			
CVTQFL			
CVTQBL			
WTQFL			
WTQBL			
(reserved)			
VALBLK (16 bytes)			
CSID			
RRSFL			
RRSBL			

(continued)

SRSFL		
SRSBL		
RM_CSID		
RTRSB		
CLURCB		
LCKCNT		ACTIVITY
VALSEQNUM		
BLKASTCNT		REFCNT
RQSEQNM		HASHVAL
PARENT		
RSNLEN	RMOD	GROUP
RESNAM (32 bytes)		
2PCQFL		
2PCQBL		
OACT		NACT
SAME_CNT	LSTCID_IDX	NMACT
		FGMODE

Figure 11.1
Layout of a Resource Block (RSB)

The resource's access mode defines the name space in which the resource exists. It specifies the least privileged mode from which locks can be queued to the resource and from which information about the locks can be obtained. In a parent RSB, RSB$W_REFCNT counts the number of its immediate subresources.

An RSB contains listheads for the granted, conversion, and wait queues of LKBs associated with the resource. The listhead for the granted LKB queue consists of the fields RSB$L_GRQFL and RSB$L_GRQBL. The listhead for the conversion queue is the fields RSB$L_CVTQFL and RSB$L_CVTQBL. The listhead for the wait queue is the fields RSB$L_WTQFL and RSB$L_WTQBL. Section 11.2.3 describes the significance of these queues.

An RSB also contains 16 bytes that form the value block for the resource at the field RSB$Q_VALBLK. RSB$L_VALSEQNUM contains the sequence number associated with the contents of the value block.

Other RSB fields are described in later sections of this chapter.

For enhanced performance, preallocated RSBs are cached. The routine that allocates RSBs first attempts to remove one from an RSB lookaside list at global location LCK$GL_RSB_HEAD. If the lookaside list is empty, the routine allocates an RSB from nonpaged pool. When an RSB is no longer needed, it is put into the lookaside list. To ensure that the list does not grow out of

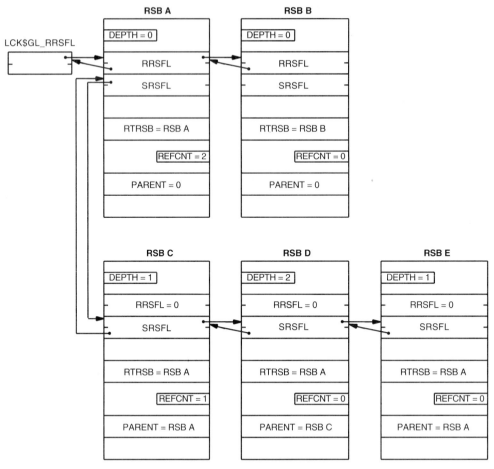

Figure 11.2
Root Resources and Subresources

proportion, a routine periodically trims the list by deallocating excess RSBs back to nonpaged pool.

11.2.2 Resource Hash Table

The resource hash table locates all the RSBs in use. The combination of the resource name string and its length, resource access mode, UIC group number, and parent RSB hash value is hashed, and the result is stored in RSB$W_HASHVAL. The hashing algorithm is similar to the algorithm used for hashing logical names, described in Chapter 38. The contents of RSB$W_HASHVAL index a particular entry in the resource hash table. More than one resource name can hash to the same value. Each longword entry in the hash table is either zero or a pointer to a list of RSBs with that hash value. If a longword entry in the resource hash table contains a zero, there is no RSB with that hash value.

Because the RSBs are maintained in a list that is doubly linked but not circular (the resource hash table itself contains no backward pointers), the list of RSBs is termed a chain. The first two longwords in each RSB contain the forward and backward pointers for the resource hash chain. The last block in each chain has a zero forward pointer.

Figure 11.3 shows the structure of the resource hash table and its relation to hash chains.

The resource hash table is allocated from nonpaged pool. The global location LCK$GL_HASHTBL contains its address. The number of longword entries in the resource hash table is determined by the SYSGEN parameter RESHASHTBL. Note that the parameter does not limit the number of RSBs that can be created. However, the combination of a small hash table and many RSBs can result in longer hash chains than might be desirable.

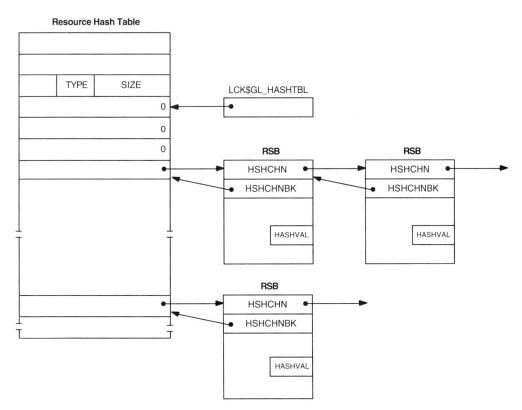

Figure 11.3
Resource Hash Table and Hash Chains

11.2.3 Lock Blocks

The $ENQ system service allocates an LKB from nonpaged pool in response to a process's first lock request on a resource. The LKB is assigned a unique lock ID used to identify the lock in subsequent lock conversion or dequeue requests. The LKB is owned only by the creator process. When a process dequeues a lock, the LKB is deallocated. When a process is deleted, all its locks are dequeued. Figure 11.4 shows the layout of a lock block.

Table 11.1 lists the lock modes, their meanings, and the other granted lock modes with which each lock is compatible.

A lock granted at one mode can later be converted to another mode. LKB$B_RQMODE specifies the requested lock mode of the lock, and LKB$B_GRMODE, the granted lock mode.

A lock can be granted, converting, or waiting, depending on the lock modes of other locks on the resource. A new lock is granted and its LKB placed on the RSB granted queue if its lock mode is compatible with those of locks already granted on the resource and if the conversion and wait queues are empty. Otherwise, it is placed at the end of the wait queue. A subsequent attempt to convert a granted lock to a more restrictive lock mode can result in the insertion of its LKB at the end of the conversion queue. Conversion

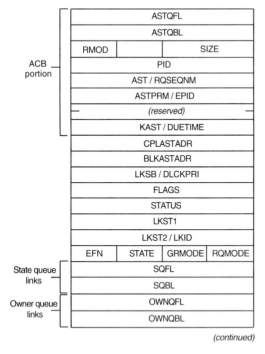

(continued)

Figure 11.4
Layout of a Lock Block (LKB)

Table 11.1   Meaning and Compatibility of Lock Modes

Mode of Requested Lock	*Meaning*	*Compatible with*
NL	Null—grants no access; used as an indicator of interest or a placeholder for future lock conversion	NL, CR, CW, PR, PW, EX
CR	Concurrent read—grants read access and allows resource sharing with other readers and writers	NL, CR, CW, PR, PW
CW	Concurrent write—grants write access and allows resource sharing with other writers	NL, CR, CW
PR	Protected read—grants read access and allows resource sharing with other readers, but not writers	NL, CR, PR
PW	Protected write—grants write access and allows resource sharing with CR-mode readers, but not writers	NL, CR
EX	Exclusive—grants write access and prevents resource sharing with any other readers or writers	NL

requests have precedence over all waiting requests and all new lock requests. Waiting requests have precedence over all new lock requests.

LKB$B_STATE specifies the current lock condition, for example, granted, waiting, or in a conversion queue. LKB$L_SQFL and LKB$L_SQBL link the LKB into the appropriate state queue in its RSB. Typically, a lock in the conversion or wait queue is also queued to the lock timeout queue through the fields LKB$L_ASTQFL and LKB$L_ASTQBL. If the lock request is not granted within a certain amount of time, a deadlock search is triggered (see Section 11.4.1).

A lock with a parent lock and resource is termed a sublock. An LKB describing a sublock contains the address of the parent LKB in field LKB$L_PARENT; the parent LKB has no corresponding pointer to the sublock. The RSB associated with the sublock points to the parent resource through the field RSB$L_PARENT; the parent resource has no corresponding pointer to the subresource. These relations are shown in Figure 11.5. LKB$W_REFCNT specifies how many sublocks have that LKB as their parent.

The first part of an LKB is an asynchronous system trap (AST) control block (ACB). When a lock request is granted, the LKB/ACB can be queued to

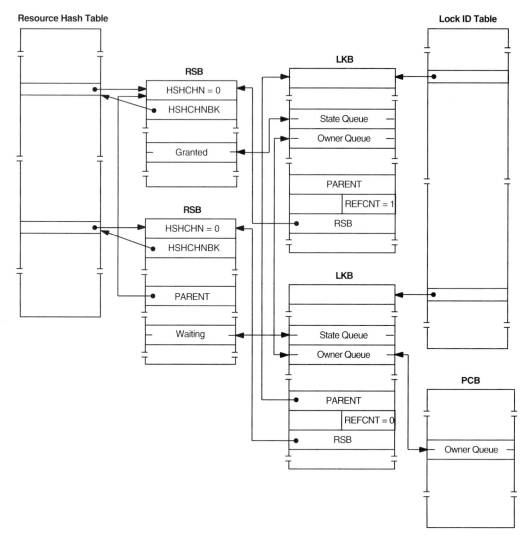

Figure 11.5
Relations Between Locks and Sublocks

the process's PCB through the fields LKB$L_ASTQFL and LKB$L_ASTQBL. Queued as an ACB, it describes a special kernel mode AST, a blocking AST, or a completion AST (see Section 11.3.4). LKB$L_PID contains the internal process ID of the process that requested the lock.

LKB$B_RMOD specifies the access mode at which completion and blocking ASTs for this lock are delivered. The access mode from which the $ENQ system service is requested, rather than an $ENQ service argument, determines the value of LKB$B_RMOD. This field also specifies the least privileged access mode from which the lock can be converted or dequeued. If a lock has a parent, the lock's access mode must not be more privileged than that of its parent.

LKB$L_EPID contains the extended process ID (see Chapter 27). LKB$L_CPLASTADR and LKB$L_BLKASTADR contain the procedure values of the completion and blocking AST procedures requested by the process. LKB$L_LKSB contains the address of the request's lock status block (LKSB). LKB$L_LKST1 contains the condition value to be copied to the lock status block. The second longword of lock status, LKB$L_LKID, contains the lock ID itself.

Other LKB fields are described in later sections of this chapter.

For enhanced performance, preallocated LKBs are cached. The routine that allocates LKBs first attempts to remove one from an LKB lookaside list at global location LCK$GL_LKB_HEAD. If the lookaside list is empty, the routine allocates an LKB from nonpaged pool. When an LKB is no longer needed, it is put into the lookaside list. To ensure that the list does not grow out of proportion, a routine periodically trims the list by deallocating excess LKBs back to nonpaged pool.

11.2.4 Lock ID Table

The lock ID table, shown in Figure 11.6, locates all LKBs. A lock ID consists of an index into the lock ID table and a sequence number identifying this particular use of that index. When a lock index is in use, its entry in the lock ID table contains the address of the associated LKB.

The entry for an unused index has two pieces of information. The high-order byte contains the updated sequence number for that index. The low-order three bytes contain the index of the next unused entry in the lock ID table. The unused entries in the lock ID table are thus linked together, with the listhead at global location LCK$GL_NXTID. When a new lock is requested, its index is taken from LCK$GL_NXTID, which is updated to point to the next unused entry. Global location LCK$GL_LSTFREE contains the index of the last free lock ID.

A lock to be dequeued is identified by its lock ID. The lock ID locates the corresponding lock ID table entry. The table entry has the address of the LKB to be deallocated. When the LKB is deallocated to nonpaged pool, the corresponding lock ID's sequence number byte is incremented, the last free lock ID's index is initialized with the index of the lock ID being deallocated, and the deallocated lock ID's index is stored in LCK$GL_LSTFREE. Note that while an LKB is on the lookaside list, its lock ID is, in effect, cached as well.

Because it is possible that an erroneous value can be passed as a lock ID to a lock management system service, the system services validate the lock ID. They compare the requestor's process identification (PID) and access mode with the PID and access mode stored in the LKB. The PIDs must match

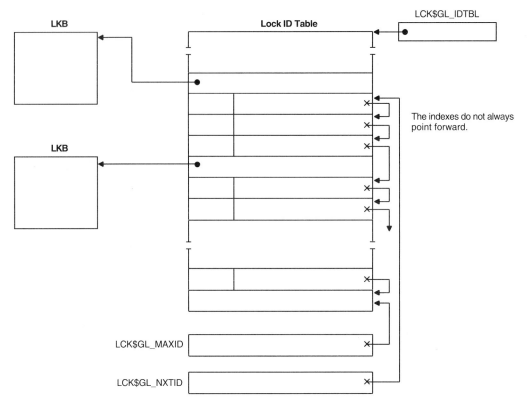

Figure 11.6
Structure of the Lock ID Table

and the requestor's access mode must be at least as privileged as that of the lock. If the comparison fails, the service exits with the error status SS$_IVLOCKID.

The global symbol LCK$GL_IDTBL points to the lock ID table. The SYS-GEN parameters LOCKIDTBL and LOCKIDTBL_MAX control the size of the lock ID table. LOCKIDTBL_MAX specifies the maximum size of the lock ID table and thus the maximum number of locks. LOCKIDTBL specifies the initial size of the lock ID table.

During system initialization enough system page table entries (SPTEs) are allocated to map LOCKIDTBL_MAX + 256 longwords for lock IDs. Physical pages are allocated for LOCKIDTBL + 256 longwords and mapped through the first SPTEs. All remaining SPTEs map a zeroed physical page. Global location LCK$GL_LKIDFREE keeps a running count of free lock IDs, and LCK$GL_LKIDCNT, the total number of lock IDs. LCK$GL_NXTID is initialized to contain the index of the first entry in the table. Each lock ID is initialized to contain the index to its successor, starting with the first one. LCK$GL_MAXID contains the index to the last entry in the lock ID table.

When a new lock is requested and no lock ID is free (LCK$GL_LKIDFREE is zero), the lock ID table must be expanded unless it already contains LOCK-IDTBL_MAX entries. To expand the table, the executive allocates a physical page and maps it with the first free SPTE. Each longword in that page represents a new lock ID. Starting with the first one, the executive initializes each new lock ID to contain the index to its successor. The executive adjusts the last entry in the lock ID table to contain the index of the first entry in the new page, and updates LCKGL_MAXID, LCKGL_LKIDFREE, and LCK$GL_LKIDCNT.

Although the lock ID sequence number field is only a byte field, a lock ID will be reused only after at least 65,535 others are used. By adding 256 to LOCKIDTBL and LOCKIDTBL_MAX and not including the additional count in LCK$GL_LKIDFREE and LCK$GL_LKIDCNT, the executive guarantees that there will always be at least 256 lock IDs in the chain of free lock IDs. When LCK$GL_LKIDFREE goes down to zero, there are still 256 free lock IDs in the chain, although they cannot be used until the lock ID table is expanded. If the lock ID table can no longer be expanded, the executive generates the fatal bugcheck LOCKMGRERR, even though, at this point, there would still be 256 free lock IDs.

Earlier, both the lock ID sequence number and the lock ID index were word fields. This limited the maximum number of lock IDs on a system to 65,536. Expanding the lock ID index field to three bytes allows for a theoretical maximum of 16,777,216 locks, although the supported maximum is 4,194,304 locks.

11.2.5   Relations in the Lock Database

There are three ways in which the lock database can be accessed:

► As described in Section 11.2.2, the RSB for a given resource name can be located through the resource hash table. All locks associated with the resource can be located through the RSB state queue heads.
► As described in Section 11.2.4, the LKB for a given lock ID can be located through the lock ID table. The resource address field in the LKB points to the resource associated with the lock.
► All locks owned by a specific process can be located through the process lock queue.

Each process has a lock queue, a doubly linked list of all the locks it has requested. The listhead is in the PCB at the fields PCB$L_LOCKQFL and PCB$L_LOCKQBL. An LKB is linked into this list through the fields LKB$L_OWNQFL and LKB$L_OWNQBL. That is, PCB$L_LOCKQFL points not to the beginning of the first LKB in the queue but to field LKB$L_OWNQFL in that LKB. All granted locks are first, followed by converting and waiting locks. The locks are ordered this way to facilitate deadlock detection (see Section 11.4.2.2).

11.2.6 **VMScluster Lock Database**

Lock management data structures, RSBs and LKBs, are distributed among the nodes of a VMScluster system. This section provides an overview of how the lock management database is organized. In the following paragraphs, wherever a node is said to perform an operation, the agent responsible for that operation is actually the distributed lock manager system application.

Each resource has a node responsible for granting locks on the resource, called the master node. The first node to define a root resource becomes the master node for that resource tree. The master node maintains a list of granted locks and a queue of waiting requests for the resource. Since the master node is responsible for granting a lock, a node must communicate a lock request to the master node as a first step in servicing the request.

Each node holding a lock on a resource mastered by another node has its own copy of the resource and lock blocks. The RSB on a node not mastering the resource contains the cluster system ID (CSID) of the mastering node in the field RSB$L_CSID. The RSB on the mastering node contains zero in that field to indicate that it is the master RSB. The CSID field is also zero on a system that is not a VMScluster node.

In a VMScluster system, a process's lock request can be represented by two LKBs on two different nodes. Depending on whether a resource is mastered on the same node as a process requesting a lock on the resource, an LKB can be a local copy, a process copy, or a master copy:

- ▸ A local copy is an LKB for a lock request on one node whose resource is mastered on that same node. This LKB is the only one representing the process's lock. This is similar to the nonclustered case.
- ▸ A process copy is an LKB for a lock request on one node whose resource is mastered on another node. The process copy describes the process's interest in the resource. The other node has the master copy of the lock. The field LKB$L_REMLKID in the process copy identifies the lock ID of the master copy. (Lock IDs are specific to a single node.) RSB$L_CSID identifies the master node.
- ▸ A master copy is an LKB that exists on a node mastering a resource but that represents the lock of a process on a different node. The field LKB$L_REMLKID in the master copy identifies the lock ID of the process copy. The field LKB$L_CSID in the master copy identifies the node of the process copy.

The three types of LKB can be distinguished based on the setting of the bit LKB$V_MSTCPY in LKB$L_FLAGS and the contents of RSB$L_CSID in the associated resource's RSB.

- Local copy—LKB$V_MSTCPY is zero and RSB$L_CSID is zero.
- Process copy—LKB$V_MSTCPY is zero and RSB$L_CSID is nonzero.
- Master copy—LKB$V_MSTCPY is nonzero and RSB$L_CSID is zero.

Each resource has a directory node responsible for mapping a resource's name to its master node. Given a resource name, the resource's directory node can be determined through a simple algorithm using the name string and the number of directory nodes. A node can serve as the directory node for a subset of all root resources in a VMScluster.

When a lock is requested for a resource not locally defined, the local node first determines the directory node for the resource and sends a lock request message to it using system communication services (SCS). The directory node responds in one of the following ways:

- If the directory node finds the resource undefined, it sends a message to the requesting node to master the resource itself.
- If the directory node is the same as the master node, it performs the lock request and sends a confirmation message to the requesting node.
- If the directory node is not the same as the master node, it sends the identity of the master node to the requesting node.

The directory node for a particular resource maintains its directory entry RSB. A directory entry RSB has the RSB$V_DIRENTRY bit set in the RSB$L_STATUS field and the CSID of the resource's master node in the RSB$L_CSID field. If the directory node is also the resource's master node, the RSB$L_CSID field contains a zero, and one RSB serves both functions; if not, there are RSBs on both the directory and master nodes. Thus, there can potentially be an RSB on the directory node, an RSB on the master node, and an RSB on each node with a lock on the resource.

A node's relative participation in resource mastership is based on the value of its SYSGEN parameter LOCKDIRWT. The higher the value of LOCK-DIRWT, the more a node participates in directory activity. In general, a LOCKDIRWT value of 0 is used for satellite nodes and a value of 1 for the central nodes.

If a node that has mastered a resource tree is not the node on which most locking activity for that resource occurs, there is a potential performance loss because messages have to be exchanged between the master node and the nodes on which locking activity occurs. (This performance loss could be offset if the processing power of the master node is significantly higher than the nodes on which the locking activity occurs.) Mastership of a resource tree can move from one node to another during normal operation through dynamic remastering.

When the node mastering a resource tree receives a lock request from another node, it performs a quick test to determine whether the requesting node would be a more efficient master node.

▶ If the requesting node's LOCKDIRWT value is lower, then mastership does not need to change.

▶ If the requesting node's LOCKDIRWT value is higher, then that node should become the master.

▶ If the requesting node's LOCKDIRWT value is the same, then if the requesting node has a higher activity value for the resource, the requesting node should become the master.

If the resource should be remastered, the executive flags this and services the current request. At some later point, another code thread actually performs dynamic remastering.

11.3   LOCK MANAGEMENT SYSTEM SERVICES

The $ENQ system service attempts to grant a new lock request or lock conversion immediately. If the new lock request or conversion cannot be granted, the service places the LKB on the RSB's wait or conversion queue. The $DEQ system service dequeues or cancels a lock from a resource and then searches the resource's state queues for locks to grant that are compatible with the currently granted locks. The $GETLKI system service returns information about a specified lock or locks.

The following sections describe the operations of these system services on a single node. VMScluster operation is mentioned, but the details are beyond the scope of this book.

The asynchronous forms of the $ENQ and $GETLKI system services validate the request and arguments, build appropriate data structures to represent the request, and return a status to the requestor that indicates whether the request was valid. The requestor can continue processing or wait for the service to complete. When either service completes, it returns information in the LKSB associated with the request. Optionally, each system service can also deliver a completion AST. The synchronous forms of these services, $ENQW and $GETLKIW, return control to the requestor only after the service is complete. Chapter 7 provides more information concerning synchronous and asynchronous system services.

11.3.1   The $ENQ[W] System Service

The $ENQ system service procedure, EXE$ENQ in module SYSENQDEQ, runs in kernel mode. EXE$ENQ first validates the event flag and lock mode arguments and tests accessibility of the lock status block. If any of these tests fails, EXE$ENQ returns to its requestor with an error status. If the tests succeed, EXE$ENQ tests whether LCK$V_CONVERT is set in the FLAGS argument to determine whether this is a new lock request or conversion of an existing lock. Section 11.3.2 describes lock conversions.

EXE$ENQ raises IPL to IPL$_SCS and acquires the SCS spinlock to synchronize access to the lock database. All exit and error paths release the SCS spinlock and lower IPL to IPL 2 before exiting.

When a new lock is requested, EXE$ENQ allocates an LKB and RSB from the lookaside lists or from nonpaged pool. EXE$ENQ allocates the RSB on the assumption that the resource is being defined for the first time.

If the requestor specified the PARID argument, EXE$ENQ verifies that the parent lock ID is valid, that the access mode of the $ENQ requestor is not more privileged than that of the parent lock, and that the parent lock's PID matches that of the current process. If any of these tests fails, EXE$ENQ returns the error status SS$_IVLOCKID to its requestor. If the tests complete successfully but the parent lock request has not been granted, EXE$ENQ returns the error status SS$_PARNOTGRANT. If the parent lock request has been granted, EXE$ENQ increments the reference count in the parent's lock and stores the parent lock's address in the new lock's LKB$L_PARENT field.

If the requestor requested a UIC-specific resource, EXE$ENQ stores the process's UIC group in the RSB. Otherwise, if the requestor requested a systemwide resource name by specifying the FLAGS argument bit LCKV_SYSTEM, EXEENQ checks that the process either has the SYSLCK privilege or requested the $ENQ system service from kernel or executive mode. If neither condition is true, EXE$ENQ returns the error status SS$_NOSYSLCK to its requestor.

EXE$ENQ charges the lock against the job quota JIB$L_ENQCNT unless the request specified the FLAGS argument bit LCK$V_NOQUOTA, which requires that the request was made from executive or kernel mode. (Use of this flag is reserved to Digital.) If this request would exceed the job's ENQLM quota, EXE$ENQ returns the error status SS$_EXENQLM. Otherwise, EXE$ENQ allocates a lock ID, expanding the lock ID table if necessary, and stores the address of the LKB in the table entry for that lock ID.

EXE$ENQ then determines whether the resource already exists on this node. It computes the resource hash value, indexes into the resource hash table, and searches the resource hash chain for the named RSB. The resource specified by the lock request must match an RSB with the same values in the following fields: parent RSB address, UIC group number, access mode, and resource name.

If it does not find the RSB for the named resource, EXE$ENQ links the new RSB to the end of the hash chain. EXE$ENQ initializes the remaining RSB fields, including the three lock queue headers, the value block and sequence number, and the reference count.

If the resource has no parent, EXE$ENQ places it at the tail of the systemwide list of root resources whose listhead is LCK$GL_RRSFL. The RSB's own address is stored in its root resource field, RSB$L_RTRSB.

If the resource has a parent, the new resource inherits its CSID from the parent resource. The parent RSB's reference count is incremented. Resource depth is initialized to 1 more than the parent resource depth. If maximum lock depth is exceeded, EXE$ENQ puts the RSB and LKB into the looka-side lists and returns the error status SS$_EXDEPTH. The new resource also inherits the parent's root resource, RSB$L_RTRSB. It is inserted into the sub-resource queue of its parent.

If the resource is new and mastered locally, no further checks are neces-sary; the new lock is granted immediately (see Section 11.3.4).

If an RSB for the named resource is found, the new RSB is superfluous and is put into the RSB lookaside list. If the resource is mastered locally, the new lock is granted immediately when the conversion and wait queues are empty and the request mode in the LKB is compatible with the currently granted locks (see Section 11.3.4). EXE$ENQ returns the success code SS$_SYNCH to its requestor if the FLAGS argument bit LCK$V_SYNCSTS is set. The event flag and completion AST are omitted in this case. Otherwise, EXE$ENQ returns the status SS$_NORMAL and proceeds to set the event flag and deliver the completion AST, if requested.

If an RSB is found but not mastered locally, the local node sends a lock request to the master node and waits the process requesting the lock for resource RSN$_SCS while cluster communication occurs on its behalf.

If the lock cannot be granted immediately, the FLAGS argument bit LCK$V_NOQUEUE determines EXE$ENQ's action:

▶ If LCK$V_NOQUEUE is set, EXE$ENQ puts the LKB into the LKB looka-side list and returns the failure status SS$_NOTQUEUED to its requestor.

▶ If LCK$V_NOQUEUE is clear, EXE$ENQ sets the lock state to LKB$K_WAITING and places the LKB at the end of the wait queue in the RSB. The wait queue is maintained in first-in/first-out (FIFO) order. If the waiting LKB is not a master copy LKB, it is also queued onto PCB$L_LOCKQFL in the PCB of the requesting (current) process. If the LKB is not a process copy and has not disabled deadlock wait (LCK$V_NODLCKWT is clear), and if deadlock wait is enabled on the system (LCK$GL_WAITTIME is nonzero), then a due time is computed and the LKB is inserted into the timeout queue. Section 11.4.1 describes deadlock searches initiated by timeouts.

A null mode lock request on a resource that is currently granted in exclu-sive mode is a valid and compatible request. Such a request would normally be placed at the end of the resource's wait queue if another request is cur-rently on the wait queue or conversion queue. If the LCK$V_EXPEDITE flag was specified in the $ENQ system service request, however, the request is granted immediately.

The asynchronous form of the system service ($ENQ) returns to its re-questor. The synchronous form of the system service ($ENQW) waits both for the event flag associated with the request to be set and for status to be returned in the LKSB.

To speed checks for compatibility with the currently granted locks, each RSB contains a single field indicating the highest granted lock mode of all locks in both the granted and conversion queues for that resource. This field is termed the group grant mode. Note that locks on the conversion queue retain their original grant mode while waiting for their conversion requests to complete. It is the original grant mode of these locks that is used in calculating the group grant mode, not their request mode.

The value of the group grant mode is stored in the RSB at the field RSB$B_GGMODE. Because this value is calculated when a lock is granted and maintained in the RSB, compatibility checking involves only one compare operation. Note that in a VMScluster system the group grant mode is maintained only in the master RSB.

11.3.2   Lock Conversions

When a process requests the $ENQ system service, the value of the LCK$V_CONVERT bit in the FLAGS argument differentiates between a new lock request and a lock conversion. When LCK$V_CONVERT is set, EXE$ENQ performs a lock conversion. EXE$ENQ obtains the lock ID of the lock to be converted from the LKSB argument and uses the LKMODE argument as the request mode.

Four lock modes affect EXE$ENQ's actions:

▶ The current mode of the converting lock, called its grant mode and stored in LKB$B_GRMODE.
▶ The converting lock's desired new value, called its request mode and stored in LKB$B_RQMODE when the lock is on the conversion or wait queue.
▶ The most restrictive grant mode found in a lock on the resource's conversion or granted queues, called the group grant mode and stored in RSB$B_GGMODE.
▶ The blocking condition to compare against when locks are removed from the granted queue, called the conversion grant mode and stored in RSB$B_CGMODE.

The conversion grant mode prevents a lock from blocking its own conversion and determines when an attempt to grant queued lock conversions is worthwhile. Most of the time, the conversion grant mode contains the same value as the group grant mode. The conversion grant mode differs from the group grant mode when both of the following are true:

▶ The grant mode of the lock at the head of the conversion queue is the most restrictive lock mode for the resource.
▶ No other locks are granted at that same lock mode.

In this case, the resource's conversion grant mode summarizes only the grant modes of locks on the granted queue. It contains a less restrictive lock mode than the group grant mode does, because group grant mode includes the grant modes of locks on the conversion queue.

EXE$ENQ begins by removing the lock specified by the lock ID from the granted queue. If no locks remain on the granted or conversion queue, the converting lock is granted immediately and EXE$ENQ attempts to grant any waiting locks after clearing the group and conversion grant modes. Section 11.3.4 describes the grant procedure.

When additional locks exist on the conversion or grant queue, the conversion grant mode and the lock's grant mode are compared:

▶ If they are not equal, the compatibility of the converting lock's request mode and the resource's group grant mode determines whether the lock is granted or placed at the tail of the conversion queue. Because the converting lock was not the most restrictive lock on the granted queue, its conversion has no effect on locks in the conversion or wait queue. EXE$ENQ will not attempt to grant any locks except the converting lock.

▶ If the lock's grant mode matches the resource's conversion grant mode, the converting lock was granted in the most restrictive lock mode present on the granted queue. The resource's group and conversion grant modes must be recalculated without including the grant mode of the converting lock, to prevent it from blocking its own conversion.

If the recalculated grant value proves compatible with the lock's request mode, the value is stored in the group grant and conversion grant fields and the lock conversion is granted. Since the change in this lock's status may be significant for other locks on the conversion or wait queue, EXE$ENQ attempts to grant locks first from the conversion queue, then from the wait queue, until it reaches a lock that it cannot grant.

In either case, if the lock's request mode is incompatible, EXE$ENQ tests the LCK$V_NOQUEUE bit:

▶ If LCK$V_NOQUEUE is set, EXE$ENQ inserts the lock back into the granted queue and returns the status SS$_NOTQUEUED to the requestor.

▶ If LCK$V_NOQUEUE is clear, EXE$ENQ clears the lock state and places the LKB at the tail of the FIFO conversion queue. EXE$ENQ does not alter the group grant mode but sets the conversion grant field to the recalculated value if the lock is first in the conversion queue. EXE$ENQ also moves the LKB to the end of the PCB queue. The PCB queue has granted locks first, followed by waiting and converting locks. If the LKB is not a process copy, if the conversion request did not disable deadlock wait, and if deadlock wait is enabled on the system (LCK$GL_WAITTIME is nonzero), then EXE$ENQ computes a due time and inserts the LKB into the timeout queue. Section 11.4.1 gives more information on deadlock searches initiated by timeouts.

Locks on the conversion or wait queue are granted later, by EXE$DEQ when blocking locks are removed from the granted or conversion queue, and by EXE$ENQ when blocking locks are converted to less restrictive lock modes.

Lock conversions, like lock grants, take place on the VMScluster node mastering the resource. If the resource is mastered on another node, the local node sends a lock conversion request to the master node and waits the process requesting the lock for resource RSN$_SCS while cluster communication occurs on its behalf.

11.3.3   **The $DEQ System Service**

A process requests the $DEQ system service to dequeue locks or sublocks that are granted or to cancel ungranted lock requests. The $DEQ system service procedure, EXE$DEQ in module SYSENQDEQ, runs in kernel mode. EXE$DEQ examines the LKID argument and the FLAGS argument bit LCK$V_DEQALL to determine whether a specific lock or a number of locks are to be dequeued.

▶ If the FLAGS argument has the LCK$V_DEQALL bit set, then the process is requesting the dequeuing of multiple locks. The locks to be dequeued are determined by the $DEQ access mode argument ACMODE and by the LKID argument. The ACMODE argument is maximized with the access mode from which the $DEQ system service was requested. If omitted, it defaults to the access mode from which the system service was requested.

  • If the LKID argument is specified, EXE$DEQ dequeues all sublocks of that lock whose access modes are not more privileged than the dequeue access mode. Note that if LKID is specified with LCK$V_DEQALL, sublocks of that lock are dequeued, but the lock itself is not dequeued.
  • Otherwise, if the LKID argument is zero, EXE$DEQ checks every lock held by the process and dequeues each one whose lock access mode is not more privileged than the dequeue access mode.

▶ If the FLAGS argument has the LCK$V_DEQALL bit clear, then the process is requesting that one lock be dequeued or canceled. In this case, EXE$DEQ uses the LKID argument to locate the LKB and the FLAGS argument bit LCK$V_CANCEL to determine the operation.

To dequeue each individual lock, EXE$DEQ acquires the SCS spinlock and raises IPL to IPL$_SCS. It verifies that the access mode of the $DEQ requestor is not less privileged than that of the lock (LKB$B_RMOD) and that the lock PID matches that of the current process. If either of these tests fails, EXE$DEQ returns the error status SS$_IVLOCKID to its requestor. Once the lock is verified, EXE$DEQ checks whether the lock has sublocks. Before a lock is deleted, its sublocks must be dequeued. Unless the LCK$V_DEQALL flag is set, EXE$DEQ returns the error status SS$_SUBLOCKS.

All exit and error paths release the SCS spinlock and lower IPL to 2 before exiting. When dequeuing multiple locks, EXE$DEQ releases and reacquires the spinlock between individual lock requests.

EXE$DEQ removes the LKB from whichever resource queue it is found on.

▶ If the lock is dequeued from the granted queue, EXE$DEQ checks whether the LKB is the only lock on the resource. If so, EXE$DEQ removes the RSB from its resource hash chain and deallocates it. If other locks remain, EXE$DEQ recomputes the resource's group grant mode and conversion grant mode and attempts to grant locks on the conversion and wait queues.

▶ If the lock is dequeued from the conversion queue, it might have blocked other lock requests. If it was at the head of the queue, or if its grant mode is equal to the resource's conversion grant mode, EXE$DEQ recomputes the resource's group grant mode and conversion grant mode. EXE$DEQ attempts to grant locks beginning with the new first lock in the conversion queue. It repeats this with the conversion and wait queues until it reaches a lock whose lock mode is incompatible with the resource group grant mode.

▶ If the lock is dequeued from the head of the wait queue and the conversion queue is empty, EXE$DEQ tries to grant the first lock in the wait queue. If it succeeds, EXE$DEQ continues with the next lock in the wait queue. It repeats this until it reaches a lock whose lock mode is incompatible with the resource group grant mode.

If the lock being dequeued was a sublock, EXE$DEQ decrements its parent lock's reference count. It releases the lock ID and removes the LKB from the process's PCB lock queue.

If the lock was waiting or in the conversion queue, EXE$DEQ sets the event flag associated with the lock request and queues the LKB as an ACB to the process to return final lock status. The LKB is deallocated when the AST is delivered.

If the lock was granted, its LKB may still be queued as an ACB. If the ACB was merely to deliver a blocking AST, EXE$DEQ removes the LKB/ACB from the ACB queue and deallocates the LKB. Otherwise, the LKB/ACB will be deallocated when the AST is delivered. Whenever the LKB is deallocated, the lock quota is returned to the process.

11.3.4 Granting a Lock

The routine LCK$GRANT_LOCK, in module SYSENQDEQ, is invoked to grant a lock request. LCK$GRANT_LOCK is invoked under three different sets of circumstances:

▶ EXE$ENQ receives a request for a lock on a new resource or a resource with locks whose modes are compatible. The lock request can be granted immediately, synchronously with the original system service call.

▶ EXE$ENQ converts a lock on a resource to a less restrictive lock mode. Another lock that was blocked can now be granted, asynchronously to its original lock request.

▶ EXE$DEQ dequeues or cancels a lock on a resource. Another lock that was blocked can now be granted, asynchronously to its original lock request.

LCK$GRANT_LOCK takes the following steps in granting a lock:

1. If the mode of the lock being granted is more restrictive than the existing group grant mode, LCK$GRANT_LOCK copies the mode of the lock being granted to the group grant mode field and the conversion grant mode field.

2. It places the LKB on the granted queue, changing its state to granted. LCK$GRANT_LOCK writes the requested lock mode in LKB$B_GR-MODE.

3. If the lock is a master copy completing asynchronously, it invokes LCK$SND_GRANTED to send a granted message to the VMScluster node waiting for this lock.

4. If the lock is being granted asynchronously, it might be on the timeout queue. If so, LCK$GRANT_LOCK removes it.

5. After processing the AST delivery requirements described subsequently, the routine invokes SCH$POSTEF to set the event flag associated with the lock request (LKB$B_EFN). If the process was waiting for this event flag to be set, its scheduling priority and state may be altered. Chapter 10 discusses event flags, and Chapter 13 gives information about process scheduling.

LCK$GRANT_LOCK makes a series of tests to determine whether an AST should be queued to the process whose lock request it granted. Three ASTs can be requested:

▶ A special kernel mode AST
▶ A user-requested blocking AST
▶ A user-requested completion AST

These three ASTs are independent of each other. Consequently, it is possible that no AST will be requested or that as many as three ASTs will be required to serve all needs.

LCK$GRANT_LOCK must queue a blocking AST to the process if it requested one and if the newly granted lock is blocking another lock. No blocking AST is necessary if none was requested or if the lock is not blocking another lock.

If the process requested a completion AST, LCK$GRANT_LOCK queues one unless the lock request was granted synchronously and the FLAGS argument bit LCK$V_SYNCSTS was set.

The special kernel mode AST must be queued if the lock request completed asynchronously. The special kernel mode AST routine writes the status to the process's LKSB and possibly a value to the lock value block. Even if the lock request completed synchronously, the special kernel mode AST routine is necessary to perform cleanup if a completion or blocking AST is to be queued.

An ACB can describe one normal AST procedure or one special kernel mode AST routine. An ACB can also describe a special kernel mode AST routine piggybacked on a normal AST procedure. Chapter 8 gives a detailed description of ASTs. If an AST is required, LCK$GRANT_LOCK invokes SCH$QAST to queue an ACB to the process. The LKB is used as the ACB.

LCK$GRANT_LOCK chooses one of the following:

▸ It does not queue an ACB if the lock request is synchronous and neither a blocking nor a completion AST is required.

▸ It queues an ACB specifying a special kernel mode AST if the lock request is asynchronous and neither a blocking nor a completion AST is required.

▸ It queues an ACB specifying a piggyback special kernel mode AST if either or both a blocking and a completion AST are required.

Because the ACB can contain the procedure value of only one AST procedure, special treatment is required when both completion and blocking ASTs must be delivered. When the lock is granted, LCK$GRANT_LOCK writes the procedure value of the completion AST procedure (stored at the field LKB$L_CPLASTADR) in the field LKB$L_AST. It then queues the LKB as an ACB.

Just before entering the completion AST procedure, the AST delivery service routine dispatches to the piggyback special kernel mode AST routine. This routine writes the procedure value of the blocking AST (stored at the field LKB$L_BLKASTADR) in LKB$L_AST. It then requeues the LKB as an ACB. When the piggyback special kernel mode AST routine exits, the completion AST procedure executes. When the completion AST procedure exits, the blocking AST is delivered.

11.3.5   System-Owned Locks

Some locks, called system-owned locks, are not associated with any process. A system-owned lock, its resource, and thus its value block remain in existence when no process has any interest in the resource. A system-owned lock has zero in its LKB$L_PID field and is not queued to any PCB lock queue. The scope of its resource name may be systemwide or qualified by UIC group. Note the distinction between a system-owned lock and a resource that is defined systemwide.

A system-owned lock may only be requested from kernel or executive mode. The special $ENQ system service FLAGS argument LCK$V_CVTSYS indicates that the lock should be granted as a system-owned lock or converted from a process-owned lock to a system-owned lock.

Although the service request must be made from kernel or executive mode, the access mode of the resource is determined by the $ENQ system service argument ACMODE, as it would be for any resource. One additional restriction applies—if a lock is system-owned, its parent lock (if any) must also be system-owned. A process-owned lock may have a system-owned lock as its parent, but a system-owned lock must not be a sublock of a process-owned lock.

The only possible state of a system-owned lock is granted. That is, a lock in a wait or conversion queue cannot be system-owned. This restriction exists partly because delivery of a completion AST or special kernel mode AST requires a process context. Furthermore, locks in the wait and conversion queues are examined during deadlock detection on the assumption that each lock is owned by a process.

When the FLAGS argument bit LCK$V_CVTSYS is set in a new lock request, EXE$ENQ sets the LCK$V_SYNCSTS and LCK$V_NOQUEUE flags as well. When LCK$V_NOQUEUE is set, EXE$ENQ returns the error status SS$_NOTQUEUED if it cannot grant the lock immediately. If it can grant the lock immediately and LCK$V_SYNCSTS is set, it does not queue a completion AST or set an event flag.

By specifying the FLAGS argument bit LCK$V_CVTSYS with LCK$V_CONVERT, a process can request the conversion of a process-owned lock to a system-owned lock or a system-owned lock to a less restrictive lock mode.

A process can request conversion of a system-owned lock to a more restrictive mode, but the request can succeed only if the conversion can complete immediately. Otherwise, the system-owned lock is converted to a process-owned lock, the lock remains granted at its original lock mode, and EXE$ENQ returns the error status SS$_BADPARAM.

A mechanism is defined for delivery of a blocking AST for a system-owned lock. The field LKB$L_BLKASTADR in a system-owned lock contains the procedure value of a blocking AST routine in system space. Instead of queuing a blocking AST to a process, the lock management services dispatch to that routine at IPL$_SCS holding the SCS spinlock.

Certain OpenVMS AXP components, such as the Files-11 Extended QIO Processor (XQP), use system-owned locks. The XQP synchronizes access to the individual entries in its I/O buffer cache through system-owned locks. The XQP, running in the context of each process in the system, maintains a systemwide cache of blocks read from the on-disk file structure. A process's XQP requests a lock on a buffer cache entry only while it is reading or writing that entry in the cache. The cache entry exists, however, even when no process is accessing it. The lock management data structures representing the cache entry must also continue to exist.

The use of system-owned locks is reserved to Digital. Any other use is strongly discouraged by Digital and completely unsupported.

11.3.6   Fork Process-Owned Locks

Lock management system services can be requested only from process context at IPL 0. Certain system components that execute in system context, such as the virtual I/O cache implementation, require access to locks also. The executive provides an internal interface to lock management functionality for fork processes. The use of this interface is strictly reserved to Digital; any other use is completely unsupported.

Locks created through this interface are called fork process-owned locks. The LKB$L_LCKCTX field of a fork process-owned lock points to an auxiliary structure called the lock context block (LCKCTX); for other types of lock, this field contains a zero. The LKB$L_PID field of a fork process-owned lock contains zero just as that of a system-owned lock does. Deadlock detection is not possible for fork process-owned locks, just as it is not possible for system-owned locks. Unlike a system-owned lock, however, a fork process-owned lock can be waited or converted.

11.3.7   The $GETLKI[W] System Service

The $GETLKI[W] system service enables a process to obtain information about one or more locks that it is allowed to interrogate. The process may only obtain information about locks on resources on the same node in a VMScluster system with access modes equal to or less privileged than the access mode at which the $GETLKI request is issued. For example, a process running in user mode cannot obtain information about locks on executive mode resources. The field RSB$B_RMOD defines the resource access mode.

The process can be further limited to a subset of the resource name space by its lack of privilege. Without any privilege, a process can interrogate only locks on resources with the same UIC group number as its own. With WORLD privilege, a process can interrogate locks on resources of any UIC group. Obtaining information about the locks of systemwide resources requires either that the process have SYSLCK privilege or that it make the $GETLKI request from kernel or executive mode.

The $GETLKI system service procedure, EXE$GETLKI in module SYS-GETLKI, runs in kernel mode. The system service is called with a LKSB argument that either identifies a particular lock or specifies a wildcard operation. First, EXE$GETLKI locates the LKB associated with the specified lock ID and verifies that the process can interrogate it. If the process specified a wildcard operation, EXE$GETLKI locates the first LKB that the process can interrogate. EXE$GETLKI begins with lock index 0 and scans the lock ID table. On each successive call, it returns information about one lock, maintaining the lock index context for the next call.

EXE$GETLKI is called with the address of an item list that includes, for each specified item, which kind of lock information is to be returned, the size and address of the buffer to receive the information, and a location to receive the size of the information returned. EXE$GETLKI checks each item in the item list for correctness: its item code must be valid; its buffer descriptor and buffer must be writable in the access mode of $GETLKI's requestor. In general, it then copies the requested information, either from the LKB or its RSB, to the buffer and records the size of the returned information in the specified location.

Certain types of information are not obtainable through simply copying data structure fields, for example, a list of all locks blocking the specified lock. EXE$GETLKI contains special routines for getting such information.

When EXE$GETLKI has either processed all items in the item list or found one that is incorrect or that has an inaccessible buffer, it is done. It sets the event flag associated with the request and queues a completion AST if one was requested and if the system service completed without error. EXE$GETLKI then returns to its requestor with completion status in R0.

11.4   HANDLING DEADLOCKS

A deadlock occurs when several locks are waiting for each other in a circular fashion. The executive resolves deadlocks by choosing a participant in the deadlock cycle and refusing that participant's lock request. The participant chosen to break the deadlock is termed the victim. The victim's lock or conversion request fails and the error status SS$_DEADLOCK is returned in the victim's lock status block.

None of the victim's already granted locks are affected, even when they are part of the deadlock. Resolution of the deadlock is the responsibility of the victim.

There are three phases of deadlock handling:

1. A deadlock is suspected.
2. A deadlock search proves that a deadlock actually exists.
3. A victim is chosen.

These three phases are described in subsequent sections. The descriptions are limited to handling of deadlocks within one system that is not a VMScluster node. VMScluster deadlock handling is beyond the scope of this book.

11.4.1   Initiating a Deadlock Search

Because deadlock detection is time-consuming, it is not desirable to search for deadlocks every time a lock or conversion request is blocked. Instead, the executive searches for a deadlock only when a lock request has been waiting for a resource for a specified amount of time. The SYSGEN parameter DEAD-LOCK_WAIT specifies how many seconds a blocked lock request must have been waiting before a deadlock search is initiated.

A way of restricting a particular lock's participation in deadlock searches is provided through the special $ENQ FLAGS arguments LCK$V_NODLCKWT and LCK$V_NODLCKBLK. The LCK$V_NODLCKWT flag in a lock or conversion request inhibits the deadlock search mechanism on a per-lock basis. Locks requested in this manner cannot initiate conversion deadlock searches because they never time out. They are disregarded in multiple resource deadlock searches initiated for other locks. Incorrect use of this flag may cause genuine deadlocks to be ignored, however. For more information, see the *OpenVMS System Services Reference Manual*.

When a lock request specifies a blocking AST procedure that dequeues the blocking lock or converts it to a less restrictive mode, that lock request may also specify the LCK$V_NODLCKBLK flag. This exempts the LKB from multiple resource deadlock searches on the assumption that the potential deadlock condition will be resolved by the blocking AST procedure. Again, incorrect use of this flag may cause genuine deadlocks to be ignored. For more information, see the *OpenVMS System Services Reference Manual*.

When an LKB requested without the flag LCK$V_NODLCKWT is placed into a conversion or wait queue, EXE$ENQ also places the LKB into the lock timeout queue. The lock timeout queue listhead is at global location LCK$GL_TIMOUTQ. The AST queue fields in the LKB link it into the lock timeout queue. Figure 11.7 shows LKBs on the timeout queue.

When an LKB is placed into the timeout queue, the time at which the lock request will time out is computed and stored in LKB$L_DUETIME. (LKB$L_DUETIME is actually a double use of the special kernel mode AST procedure value field, LKB$L_KAST.) The due time is the sum of DEADLOCK_WAIT, stored in LCK$GL_WAITTIME, and the current system uptime in seconds, EXE$GL_ABSTIM.

Once every second, the routine EXE$TIMEOUT, in module TIMESCHDL, executes. EXE$TIMEOUT has various functions (see Chapter 12). One of them is to check whether the first entry in the lock timeout queue has timed out by comparing its LKB$L_DUETIME to the contents of EXE$GL_ABSTIM. Because the queue is time-ordered, checking the due time of the first entry is sufficient to determine whether a deadlock search is necessary.

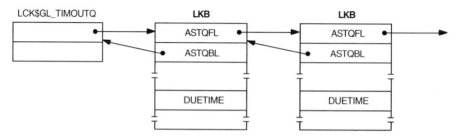

Figure 11.7
Lock Timeout Queue Ordered by LKB$L_DUETIME

If the first entry has not timed out, no other entry could have. If the first entry has timed out, EXE$TIMEOUT initiates a deadlock search by invoking the routine LCK$SEARCHDLCK, in module DEADLOCK.

11.4.2 **Deadlock Detection**

There are two forms of deadlock, each requiring a different detection method. A conversion deadlock is easily detected because it is restricted to locks for a single resource. A multiple resource deadlock is harder to detect, requiring a more complex search.

11.4.2.1 **Conversion Deadlocks.** A conversion deadlock can occur when there are at least two LKBs in an RSB's conversion queue for a resource. If the request mode of one lock in the queue is incompatible with the grant mode of another lock in the queue, a deadlock exists.

For example, assume there are two protected read (PR) mode locks on a resource. The process with one PR mode lock requests a conversion to EX mode. Because PR mode is incompatible with EX mode, the conversion request must wait. While the first conversion request is waiting, the process with the second PR mode lock also requests a conversion to EX mode. The first lock cannot be granted because its request mode, EX, is incompatible with the second lock's grant mode, PR. The second conversion request cannot be granted because it is waiting behind the first.

The search for a conversion deadlock begins with the first LKB on the lock timeout queue. The LKB's state queue backward link points to the previous LKB in the conversion queue. The grant mode of the previous lock is compared with the request mode of the lock that timed out. If the modes are compatible, the next previous lock in the conversion queue is examined. The test is repeated until an incompatible lock is found or the beginning of the queue is reached. The flags LCK$V_NODLCKWT and LCK$V_NODLCKBLK are ignored.

If a lock with an incompatible grant mode is found, a deadlock exists. A victim LKB is selected (see Section 11.4.3). If the beginning of the queue is reached, a conversion deadlock does not exist, and a search for a multiple resource deadlock is initiated.

11.4.2.2 **Multiple Resource Deadlocks.** A multiple resource deadlock occurs when a circular list of processes are each waiting for one another on two or more resources.

For example, assume process A locks resource 1 and process B locks resource 2. Process A then requests a lock on resource 2 that is incompatible with B's lock on resource 2, and thus process A must wait. Note that at this point, a circular list does not exist. When process B then requests a lock on resource 1 that is incompatible with A's lock on resource 1, it must wait. A multiple resource deadlock now exists. Processes A and B are both waiting

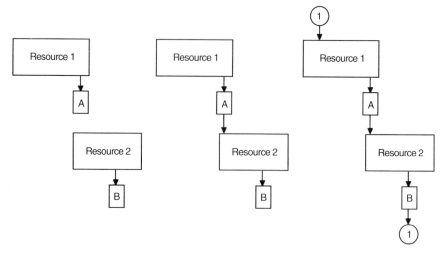

Figure 11.8
Example of a Deadlock

for each other to release different resources. These steps are shown in Figure 11.8. In the figure, locks that are blocking a resource (incompatible with waiting locks) are shown beneath the resource; locks that are waiting for a resource are shown above the resource.

This type of deadlock normally involves two or more resources, unless one process locks the same resource twice. (Usually a process does not lock the same resource twice. However, if the process is multithreaded, double locking can occur. Double locking can result in a multiple resource deadlock.)

To verify that a multiple resource deadlock exists, LCK$SEARCHDLCK uses a recursive algorithm. Its approach is based upon the following:

▶ A waiting lock is blocked by locks owned by other processes.
▶ Any of the other processes might themselves have waiting locks.
▶ Those waiting locks are blocked by locks that are owned by other blocking processes.

LCK$SEARCHDLCK starts with the lock that timed out on the lock timeout queue. It saves the extended process ID (EPID) of the owner process of the lock that timed out and invokes the multiple resource deadlock routine (LCK$SRCH_RESDLCK). If it finds a lock with the same owner EPID blocking a resource, a deadlock exists.

Each time LCK$SRCH_RESDLCK is invoked, a stack frame is pushed onto the stack. Each stack frame contains information on the current position in the search. Figure 11.9 shows the contents of the stack frame.

The search algorithm is recursive. The SYSGEN parameters KSTACK-PAGES and DLCKEXTRASTK limit the number of kernel stack bytes that can be used for deadlock searches, and hence the amount of recursion.

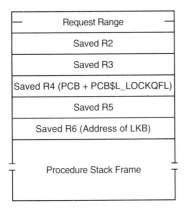

— Request Range —
Saved R2
Saved R3
Saved R4 (PCB + PCB$L_LOCKQFL)
Saved R5
Saved R6 (Address of LKB)
Procedure Stack Frame

Figure 11.9
Stack Frame Built for LCK$SRCH_RESDLCK

KSTACKPAGES is the size of the kernel stack, and DLCKEXTRASTK is the number of kernel stack bytes that cannot be used for deadlock searches. The difference between the available kernel stack and DLCKEXTRASTK is the amount of stack space available for LCK$SRCH_RESDLCK's stack frames. The reserved stack space allows interrupt service routines, which execute on the current process's kernel stack, to have sufficient stack space for execution.

Each invocation of LCK$SRCH_RESDLCK specifies the address of a waiting LKB. The resource associated with the LKB is located, and the resource state queues are searched for LKBs whose granted or requested lock mode is incompatible with that of the waiting LKB. If an incompatible LKB is found, that lock is considered to be blocking the waiting LKB unless it has the LCK$V_NODLCKBLK bit set in the LKB$L_FLAGS field.

When a blocking lock is found, its EPID is compared to that of the lock that initiated the deadlock search:

▶ If they are the same, the list is proved to be circular and a deadlock exists. A victim lock is chosen (see Section 11.4.3), and deadlock detection returns control to EXE$TIMEOUT.

▶ If the EPID of the blocking lock is not the same as the saved EPID and the search bitmap does not indicate that this process has been visited already, the PCB lock queue of the process owning the blocking lock is searched. If an LKB is found in a convert or wait state with the LCK$V_NODLCKWT bit clear, another invocation of LCK$SRCH_RESDLCK is made, specifying that LKB's address.

Each time LCK$SRCH_RESDLCK is invoked, it searches the state queues associated with the specified LKB to see if it is waiting for a resource.

When all the state queues for a given resource have been searched and no blocking lock has been found for that LKB, the routine removes the stack frame and returns control to its invoker. If the invoker itself was LCK$SRCH_RESDLCK, the previous search for blocked locks on the resource can now be resumed.

A process bitmap is maintained to reduce the number of repeated searches for blocking locks on a particular process. Each time a new blocking PCB is located, a bit corresponding to that process is set. If the bit for the PCB is set already, the search for locks blocking that process is terminated because its locks have been searched already.

11.4.2.3   **Unsuspected Deadlocks.** Note that the use of the process bitmap speeds the location of the suspected deadlock but prevents the accidental detection of unsuspected deadlocks. An unsuspected deadlock is one that exists within the lock management database but that has not been detected so far because none of its locks has timed out on the lock timeout queue. This behavior is accepted for the following reasons:

> ▸ Applications are assumed to be designed so that deadlocks are rare.
> ▸ Finding a process a second time in a deadlock search does not necessarily indicate that an unsuspected deadlock exists.
> ▸ The occurrence of unsuspected deadlocks should be rarer still.
> ▸ Any deadlock search that does not find a deadlock wastes processor time.
> ▸ The unsuspected deadlock will become a suspected deadlock when one of its own locks times out on the lock timeout queue and a deadlock search is initiated on its behalf.

Figure 11.10 shows two deadlocks. In the figure, locks that are blocking a resource (incompatible with waiting locks) are shown beneath the RSB; locks that are waiting for a resource are shown above the RSB. One deadlock is suspected and a search is in progress for it. The heavy arrows in the figure show the path of that deadlock cycle. The other is unsuspected. This figure is an extension of the deadlock cycle shown in Figure 11.8.

In this case, the deadlock search was initiated as a search for the locks blocking process A. Because process C's lock is the first one found granted for resource 2, it is the first lock that is investigated for participation in the deadlock cycle. Process C is waiting for resource 3. The bit corresponding to process C is set in the process bitmap. The context of the search is saved on the stack, and LCK$SRCH_RESDLCK is invoked to search for processes blocking process C's lock.

Process D has a blocking lock on resource 3. Process D is also waiting for resource 2. The bit corresponding to process D is set in the process bitmap. The context of the search is saved on the stack and LCK$SRCH_RESDLCK is invoked to search for processes blocking process D's lock. Process C has a blocking lock on resource 2. This situation is a deadlock. However, because the bit corresponding to process C was set in the process bitmap, the deadlock search for process C is abandoned. One by one, the stack frames are

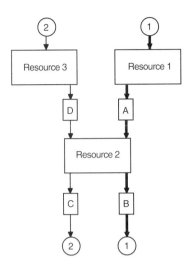

Figure 11.10
Suspected and Unsuspected Deadlocks

removed and the search whose context was saved continues. Eventually the deadlock search continues with locks blocking resource 2, and the deadlock cycle of processes A and B is discovered.

Eventually one of the locks requested by processes C and D will time out, and a deadlock search will be initiated.

11.4.2.4   Example of a Search for a Multiple Resource Deadlock. Figure 11.11 shows a series of locks that result in a deadlock. In the figure, locks that are blocking a resource (incompatible with waiting locks) are shown beneath the RSB; locks that are waiting for a resource are shown above the RSB. The heavy arrows in the figure show the path of the deadlock cycle.

Assume that the lock owned by process A timed out. Process A is waiting for a lock on resource 1. The deadlock search routine saves process A's EPID and invokes LCK$SRCH_RESDLCK, passing the address of process A's LKB.

The first incompatible lock on resource 1 is owned by process C. Process C has no other waiting locks, so LCK$SRCH_RESDLCK moves on to the next incompatible lock. This lock is owned by process D. When LCK$SRCH_RESDLCK follows the PCB queue for process D, it finds that this process is waiting for a lock on resource 3.

LCK$SRCH_RESDLCK invokes itself, passing the address of the LKB owned by process D. The new invocation of LCK$SRCH_RESDLCK pushes a stack frame showing the position of the search on resource 1. LCK$SRCH_RESDLCK starts to search for locks on resource 3 that are incompatible with process D's lock. Resource 3 has two incompatible locks, owned by processes E and F. Neither of these processes is waiting for a lock, so the search on resource 3 terminates. The contents of the stack frame are restored

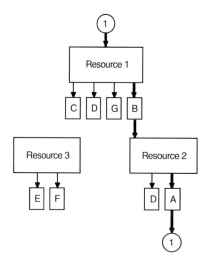

Figure 11.11
Example of a Multiple Resource Deadlock

and LCK$SRCH_RESDLCK returns to its previous invocation. The search for processes blocking process A resumes.

The next incompatible lock found on resource 1 is owned by process G. Process G has no waiting locks, so the search continues with process B. The PCB queue for process B shows that it is waiting for a lock on resource 2.

Again, LCK$SRCH_RESDLCK invokes itself, passing the address of the LKB owned by process B. The new invocation of LCK$SRCH_RESDLCK pushes a new stack frame onto the stack, and LCK$SRCH_RESDLCK finds that process D owns a lock that is incompatible with the lock owned by process B. However, because locks owned by process D have been searched already (the bit for process D is set in the process bitmap), the search moves on to the next process.

The next incompatible lock is owned by process A. Because the EPID of process A matches the EPID that was saved initially, the list is proved to be circular and a deadlock exists. Now a victim must be chosen.

11.4.3   Victim Selection

Because conversion deadlocks involve only two processes, the victim selection routine simply chooses the process with the lower deadlock priority, stored in the PCB at the field PCB$L_DLCKPRI.

For a multiple resource deadlock, the victim selection routine is only slightly more complicated. The frames that were pushed onto the stack in each recursion into the deadlock location routine are searched for the lowest deadlock priority. Each time a lower deadlock priority value is found, the priority and the owner process are noted. If a deadlock priority of zero is found, that process is immediately chosen as the victim. When all frames have been searched or a deadlock priority of zero is found, the stack pointer is restored and the process with the lowest deadlock priority is chosen as the victim.

Note that the current OpenVMS AXP implementation initializes the deadlock priority of all new processes to zero. Thus, it is not possible to determine which process will be chosen as the victim. With the current implementation, victim selection depends primarily on timing.

11.5   RELEVANT SOURCE MODULES

Source modules described in this chapter include

> [LIB]LKBDEF.SDL
> [LIB]RSBDEF.SDL
> [SYS]DEADLOCK.MAR
> [SYS]DSTRLOCK.MAR
> [SYS]INIT.MAR
> [SYS]LCKMGR_MACROS.MAR
> [SYS]SYSENQDEQ.MAR
> [SYS]SYSGETLKI.MAR
> [SYS]TIMESCHDL.MAR

PART IV / Scheduling and Time Support

12 Time Support

Love, all alike, no season knows, nor clime,
Nor hours, days, months, which are the rags of time.

John Donne, *The Sun Rising*

Support for any activity that requires either the date and time or the measurement of an interval of time is implemented in both the AXP hardware and the OpenVMS AXP operating system.

12.1 OVERVIEW

To support time-related activities, the Alpha AXP architecture requires that each AXP system provide a battery-backed watch chip, an interval timer interrupt that repeats at a system-specific interval, and a process cycle counter. Console software and the privileged architecture library code (PALcode) cooperate to provide a system cycle counter based on the process cycle counter.

Using these hardware features, the operating system keeps time and services time-dependent requests from processes and system threads of execution. The executive uses the battery-backed watch chip to initialize and maintain the system time across system bootstraps, power failures, and shutdowns. It uses interval timer interrupts to maintain the current date and time (the system time) as well as the time elapsed since the system was bootstrapped (the system uptime). The executive uses the system cycle counter for timing very short intervals, typically with a granularity of a few tens of nanoseconds or less.

In addition to maintaining the system time, the interval timer interrupt service routine is also responsible for checking whether the current process has reached quantum end and whether time-dependent requests must be serviced. If the current process's quantum has ended, the routine requests an interrupt priority level (IPL) 7 software timer interrupt to initiate quantum-end processing. If the most imminent time-dependent request has become due, the routine queues an IPL 8 fork process to execute the software timer fork routine, which services time-dependent requests.

The system manager can adjust the system date and time using the SETTIME Digital command language (DCL) command or the Set Time ($SETIME) system service. The Get Time ($GETTIM) system service enables users to read the current date and time. Several other services, described briefly in Chapter 39, convert the date and time between ASCII and binary formats. Application software can also call a number of Run-Time Library procedures, described in the *OpenVMS RTL Library (LIB$) Manual*, to convert or format the date and time.

To support users' time-dependent requests, the executive provides two system services, Set Timer ($SETIMR) and Schedule Wakeup ($SCHDWK).

12.2 ARCHITECTURAL TIMERS

This section describes the architecturally defined timers available to the OpenVMS AXP operating system.

12.2.1 Interval Timer

All AXP systems provide an interval timer that generates an IPL 22 interrupt at the minimum rate of 1,000 times per second, with a minimum accuracy of 0.0005 percent. An interval timer interrupt is sometimes called a tick. The interrupt rate is implementation-dependent and is passed to the operating system by console software through the hardware restart parameter block (HWRPB) at offset HWRPB$IQ_CLOCK_INT_FREQ. On a symmetric multiprocessing (SMP) system, all processors are interrupted by interval timer interrupts; however, only the primary processor keeps the time.

All currently available AXP systems generate interval timer interrupts at the rate of 1,024 per second.

12.2.2 Battery-Backed Watch Chip

A battery-backed watch chip maintains the date and time across system reboots and power failures. At system initialization the operating system reads the battery-backed watch chip to determine the date and time (see Section 12.3.1).

The internal time representation of the battery-backed watch chip is implementation-dependent. All currently available AXP systems use a watch chip that maintains the time in an internal 24-hour binary format.

The battery-backed watch chip is initialized during bootstrap if the executive determines that its contents are invalid or whenever an operator changes the system time. The executive accesses the battery-backed watch chip through system-specific routines, as outlined in Section 12.3.5.

On an SMP system, only the primary processor is allowed to write the battery-backed watch chip. The Alpha AXP architecture guarantees that the primary processor can access the battery-backed watch chip but makes no such guarantees for other processors. Having only one processor access the chip provides a simple synchronization method.

12.2.3 Process and System Cycle Counters

An AXP processor maintains two cycle counters:

► The process cycle counter (PCC)
► The system cycle counter (SCC)

On an SMP system, each processor has its own PCC and SCC. Both cycle counters count at the same frequency and are suitable for timing very short intervals, typically with a granularity of a few tens of nanoseconds. Software can calculate the duration of an interval by reading a cycle counter at the start and end of the interval and dividing the number of elapsed cycles by the cycle counter frequency. The frequency can be derived from the cycles-per-second value passed to the executive by console software through the HWRPB at offset HWRPB$IQ_CYCLE_COUNT_FREQ.

The PCC is a process-specific 32-bit counter that increments once per n CPU cycles, where n is a fixed implementation-specific integer between 1 and 16. At overflow, it wraps to 0.

In actual implementation, the PCC is maintained as two longword quantities. The first longword, called the PCC counter, constantly increments and wraps at overflow even across process context switches. Adding the second longword, called the PCC offset, to the PCC counter yields the current process-specific PCC value.

PALcode records the PCC value in a hardware privileged context block (HWPCB) longword when it saves a process's context. When it loads a process's context, PALcode computes the new PCC offset based on the recorded PCC value and the current PCC counter. The nonprivileged RPCC instruction returns a quadword value whose high-order longword is the offset and low-order longword is the counter. An application must compute the PCC value by adding the two longwords; the *Alpha AXP Architecture Reference Manual* contains an instruction sequence that can be used for this purpose.

Because unsigned arithmetic is used, the PCC value can be correctly computed even if it has wrapped once between the start and end of a timing operation. If the PCC value has wrapped more than once during a timing operation, however, it is useless. For this reason, a process can only use the PCC value for accurately measuring process time intervals of very short duration—typically starting at tens of nanoseconds (possibly even less) but not exceeding 2^{32} times the PCC interval (roughly 20 to 30 seconds for current AXP processors).

No executive component uses the PCC. Hardware increments a process's PCC counter regardless of whether system interrupts are being serviced on the process's kernel stack. For this reason, despite its name, the PCC is of limited use in process performance measurement.

The SCC is an always-increasing per-CPU 64-bit counter that tracks the number of CPU cycles (or a multiple thereof) elapsed since the processor was initialized. Console software initializes the SCC to zero during processor initialization. When the SCC is viewed as two longwords, its low-order longword is the same as the PCC counter and its high-order longword tracks the number of times the low-order longword has wrapped. The SCC is unaffected by process context switching. PALcode maintains the SCC based on the PCC counter. The nonprivileged CALL_PAL RSCC instruction returns the SCC value in R0.

Because each CPU has its own SCC, a process using the SCC for timing purposes on an SMP system should ensure that it does not migrate to another processor before the timing operation has been completed. Because the RPCC instruction consumes no PALcode overhead, a process may be able to measure very short process-specific intervals more accurately using the PCC than using the SCC if it can block interrupts or if the inclusion of interrupts is acceptable.

The executive provides procedures and macros that use the SCC to implement timeouts and delays of very short duration. Drivers and other privileged software can call these procedures, outlined in Section 12.9.

12.3 SYSTEM TIMEKEEPING

During system initialization the executive determines the date and time from the battery-backed watch chip, from a value previously recorded on the system disk, from a value entered by the operator, or in a VMScluster system, from a node that has already joined the cluster (see Section 12.3.1). The executive maintains the system time in the global location EXE$GQ_SYSTIME. The interval timer interrupt service routine updates this and other global locations that represent time (see Section 12.6).

The executive maintains the system uptime in two different formats. EXE$GL_ABSTIM contains the number of seconds elapsed since system bootstrap, and EXE$GL_ABSTIM_TICS contains the number of soft ticks elapsed during the same period. The term *soft tick* refers to a 10-millisecond event that simulates a VAX-style interval timer interrupt, as explained in Section 12.3.4.

Table 12.1 summarizes some global locations used for timekeeping.

Table 12.1   Time-Related Cells

Name	*Description*
EXE$GQ_SYSTIME	System date and time in 100-nanosecond intervals from midnight, November 17, 1858
EXE$GL_ABSTIM	System uptime in seconds
EXE$GL_ABSTIM_TICS	System uptime in elapsed soft ticks (10-millisecond units)
EXE$GQ_SAVED_HWCLOCK	Time of last adjustment of EXE$GQ_SYSTIME in system time format
EXE$GQ_1ST_TIME	Expiration time in system time format of the most imminent time-dependent request
EXE$GQ_BOOTTIME	Time of last bootstrap in system time format

12.3.1   Date and Time Initialization

Whenever the system operator or a system management component adjusts the system time cell, the executive copies its value to EXE$GQ_SAVED_ HWCLOCK. The executive updates the contents of EXE$GQ_SAVED_HW-CLOCK both in memory and on disk in the base image file, SYS$BASE_IMAGE.EXE. The record on disk is nonvolatile and survives across system bootstraps. When a system must boot unattended and its battery-backed watch chip cannot be read, the value in EXE$GQ_SAVED_HWCLOCK is used to initialize the system time cell.

During system initialization the SYSINIT process (see Chapter 34) invokes the routine EXE$INIT_HWCLOCK, in module [SYSLOA]TIMROUT, to initialize EXE$GQ_SYSTIME from the battery-backed watch chip, from EXE$GQ_SAVED_HWCLOCK, or from a date and time entered by the operator. For a node joining a VMScluster system, SYSINIT obtains the date and time from a node that has already joined and calls EXE$SETIME_INT, described in Section 12.3.3, to set the date and time. When a new VMScluster system is being formed, the time from one system is sent to all other nodes, each of which invokes EXE$SETIME_INT.

Later, after the system disk is mounted, SYSINIT requests the $SETIME system service to record the new value of EXE$GQ_SAVED_HWCLOCK in the SYS$BASE_IMAGE.EXE base image on disk.

EXE$INIT_HWCLOCK performs the following steps:

1. If the SYSGEN parameter SETTIME is 0, EXE$INIT_HWCLOCK reads the battery-backed watch chip by calling a system-specific procedure described in Section 12.3.5.

2. If SETTIME is 1, or if the battery-backed watch chip cannot be read for some reason, EXE$INIT_HWCLOCK examines the SYSGEN parameter TIMEPROMPTWAIT to determine how to initialize the system time:

    a. A TIMEPROMPTWAIT value of zero means that the routine is to reset the time without human intervention. EXE$INIT_HWCLOCK computes the new system time as the contents of EXE$GQ_SAVED_ HWCLOCK incremented by 1.

    b. A nonzero TIMEPROMPTWAIT value causes the routine to prompt for the date and time on the console terminal and wait until the operator enters valid data. If TIMEPROMPTWAIT is negative, the system will not proceed unless the operator enters the date and time. If TIME-PROMPTWAIT is positive, its value represents an upper limit, in microfortnights, on the amount of time EXE$INIT_HWCLOCK waits for the operator to enter a new date and time. (A microfortnight is treated as equivalent to a second.) If that time elapses without the input of valid data, EXE$INIT_HWCLOCK proceeds as if TIMEPROMPT-WAIT had been zero.

3. EXE$INIT_HWCLOCK calls EXE$SETIME_INT, an internal entry point for the $SETIME system service (see Section 12.3.3), to initialize the system time and update EXE$GQ_SAVED_HWCLOCK in memory. The SYS$BASE_IMAGE.EXE base image on disk cannot be modified until the system disk is mounted.

12.3.2 Date and Time Maintenance

EXE$GQ_SYSTIME, the system time cell, contains the number of 100-nanosecond intervals that have elapsed since 00:00 hours, November 17, 1858, the base time for the Smithsonian Institution astronomical calendar. It is initialized during system initialization (see Section 12.3.1) and updated by the interval timer interrupt service routine (see Section 12.6). EXE$GQ_SYSTIME is the reference for nearly all user-requested time-dependent software activities in the system. For example, the $GETTIM system service simply writes this quadword value into a user-defined buffer.

EXE$GL_ABSTIM, the system uptime cell, contains the number of seconds that have elapsed since the system was bootstrapped. It is zero at system initialization and incremented by the interval timer interrupt service routine every second (see Section 12.6). EXE$GL_ABSTIM is the reference time for a number of operations. In particular, it is used to check periodically for I/O device, I/O controller, mount verification, and lock request timeouts.

EXE$GL_ABSTIM_TICS contains the number of 10-millisecond intervals that have elapsed since the system was bootstrapped. It is zero at system initialization and incremented by the interval timer interrupt service routine (see Section 12.6). EXE$GL_ABSTIM_TICS is the reference time for the scheduling subsystem. Its contents are recorded in the field PCB$L_WAITIME whenever a process is placed into a wait state and in the field PCB$L_ONQTIME when a process incurs quantum end. A comparison between PCB$L_WAITIME and EXE$GL_ABSTIM_TICS enables outswap scheduling code to determine if the process can be considered to be in a long wait, and a comparison between PCB$L_ONQTIME and EXE$GL_ABSTIM_TICS, to determine if the process is dormant (see Chapter 20).

EXE$GQ_SYSTIME is adjusted at powerfail recovery by routine EXE$RESTART, in module POWERFAIL (see Chapter 36), and through the $SETIME system service. EXE$GL_ABSTIM and EXE$GL_ABSTIM_TICS are never adjusted.

12.3.3 $SETIME System Service

The $SETIME system service allows a system manager or operator to adjust the system time while the operating system is running. This may be necessary because of a power failure longer than the battery backup time of the battery-backed watch chip or changes between standard and daylight saving time, for example. The new system time is passed as the optional single argument of the system service.

The system service procedure EXE$SETIME, in module SYSSETIME, runs in kernel mode. Running on a uniprocessor or on the primary processor in an SMP system, it performs the following steps:

1. It first validates the request. If the requesting process does not have the OPER and LOG_IO privileges, EXE$SETIME returns the error SS$_NO-PRIV. If the input quadword cannot be read, the procedure returns the error SS$_ACCVIO.

2. If no time argument, or an argument of zero, is passed to the system service, EXE$SETIME invokes EXE$READ_HWCLOCK to read the battery-backed watch chip and return the current time in system time format. Otherwise, the time argument contains the target system time in system time format.

3. EXE$SETIME acquires the TIMER and HWCLK spinlocks. It writes the new system time into the cells EXE$GQ_SYSTIME and EXE$GQ_SAVED_HWCLOCK. It also updates the battery-backed watch chip. It then releases the HWCLK spinlock.

4. EXE$SETIME adjusts the expiration time of each time-dependent request that specifies a relative (or delta) time by the difference between the previous system time and the new system time. This modification preserves the correct relative time across the modification to the system time. EXE$SETIME does not adjust a request made for an absolute time; this ensures that the requested action will occur at the time specified by the user. EXE$SETIME then releases the TIMER spinlock.

   Section 12.4 describes time-dependent requests and the timer queue entries that represent them.

5. EXE$SETIME records the contents of EXE$GQ_SAVED_HWCLOCK in its corresponding disk block in the base image file SYS$BASE_IM-AGE.EXE. The boot control block field BOO$L_TIMELBN contains the logical block number of that block on the system disk.

The $SETIME system service can also be entered directly at a special entry point, EXE$SETIME_INT. This entry point is used during system initialization to compute the system time from the contents of the battery-backed watch chip and system variables. The difference between EXE$SETIME and EXE$SETIME_INT is that the latter is called at a point in SYSINIT before the system disk is mounted and hence must disable recording the value of EXE$GQ_SAVED_HWCLOCK on disk (see Section 12.3.1).

12.3.4   Simulated 10-Millisecond Clock

To facilitate the porting of VAX VMS, the OpenVMS AXP interval timer interrupt service routine simulates a VAX-style 10-millisecond clock. As a result, a number of time-related VAX VMS modules and interfaces are largely unchanged despite significant changes in the underlying hardware mechanisms. For example, parts of the OpenVMS AXP interval timer interrupt service routine and time-related scheduling functions, such as quantum-end processing, work much the same as their VAX counterparts.

The 10-millisecond event is sometimes called a soft tick to differentiate it from the interval timer interrupt. Depending on the interval timer interrupt frequency, soft ticks may not occur precisely at 10-millisecond intervals. If the duration between interval timer interrupts were an integral factor of 10 milliseconds, a soft tick could be generated precisely every 10 milliseconds. On current implementations, however, the soft tick is not precise. Instead, the interval timer interrupt service routine uses an algorithm that ensures that over a large number of interrupts, the average interval between soft ticks is 10 milliseconds. This imprecision does not affect the accuracy of any other clocks, such as system time, that depend on hardware mechanisms.

Any VAX VMS software being ported to OpenVMS AXP that relies on an exact 10-millisecond duration for the 10-millisecond clock must be changed.

12.3.5 Battery-Backed Watch Chip Access Routines

The system-specific routines for accessing the battery-backed watch chip are part of the system-specific SYS$CPU_ROUTINES_*xxyy* image, where *xx* is the system type designator and *yy* is the processor type designator. (Appendix G lists system and processor designations.) These routines are all in module [SYSLOA]TIMROUT:

- ▶ EXE$INIT_HWCLOCK, which uses the battery-backed watch chip to initialize the system time
- ▶ EXE$READ_HWCLOCK, which reads the battery-backed watch chip
- ▶ EXE$WRITE_HWCLOCK and EXE$WRITE_LOCAL_HWCLOCK, which write the battery-backed watch chip

EXE$READ_HWCLOCK and EXE$WRITE_HWCLOCK are the routines generally used to access the battery-backed watch chip. When either routine is invoked from a secondary processor, it initiates an interprocessor dialogue (see Chapter 37) to request code running on the primary processor to perform the actual access to the watch chip.

EXE$READ_HWCLOCK and EXE$WRITE_HWCLOCK call EXE$READ_BBW, EXE$WRITE_BBW, and EXE$WRITE_LOCAL_HWCLOCK, procedures that can be executed on the primary processor only. EXE$READ_BBW and EXE$WRITE_BBW are in module [SYSLOA]BBW_COMMON. These procedures in turn call READ_SYSTEM_BBW or WRITE_SYSTEM_BBW, in module [CPU*xxyy*]BBW_ROUTINES_*xxyy*, to perform the actual register access of the battery-backed watch chip.

12.4 TIME-RELATED DATA STRUCTURES

The executive describes each time-dependent request with a data structure called a timer queue entry (TQE). It maintains an absolute queue of TQEs,

ordered by their expiration times, at the system global location EXE$GL_
TQFL. The TIMER spinlock synchronizes access to the timer queue.

Time-dependent requests, also known as timer requests, may be characterized in the following ways:

▶ What action the executive takes at expiration time, for example, setting an
  event flag or waking up a process
▶ Whether the request is a recurring one, to be repeated at specified intervals
▶ How the expiration time is determined

A user can specify that the executive take action at a particular absolute
time, at a time relative to the time of the request, or when the process
has accumulated a certain amount of CPU time. Accumulated CPU time
is maintained in the process control block (PCB) cell PCB$L_CPUTIM; it is
the number of soft ticks of CPU time the process has accumulated since its
creation.

TQEs are generally allocated from nonpaged pool and inserted into the
timer queue as a result of $SETIMR and $SCHDWK system service requests
(see Section 12.5). The allocation of TQEs is governed by the pooled job quota
JIB$L_TQCNT.

The layout of a TQE is shown in Figure 12.1. The link fields TQE$L_TQFL
and TQE$L_TQBL, the TQE$W_SIZE field, and the TQE$B_TYPE field are
characteristic of system data structures allocated from pool.

The TQE$B_RQTYPE field describes the timer request. Its two low-order
bits define the type of timer request: process timer request, system routine
request, or process wake request. Bit TQE$V_REPEAT is set if the request is
a repeating request rather than a one-time request. Bit TQE$V_ABSOLUTE is

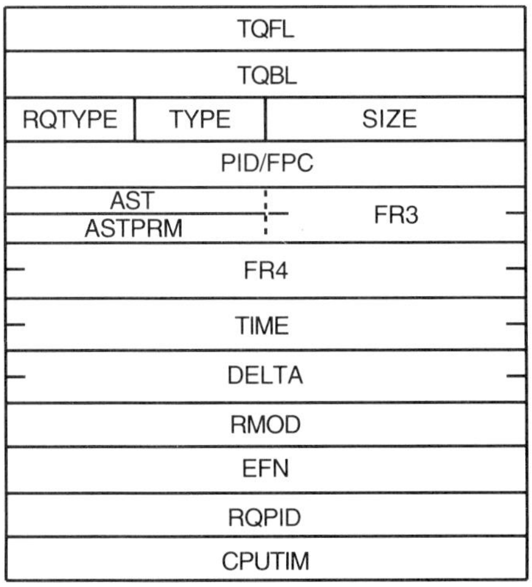

| TQFL |
| TQBL |
| RQTYPE | TYPE | SIZE |
| PID/FPC |
| AST / ASTPRM | FR3 |
| FR4 |
| TIME |
| DELTA |
| RMOD |
| EFN |
| RQPID |
| CPUTIM |

RQTYPE Bits

Bit	Value	Meaning
0 – 1	0	Process timer request
	1	System routine request
	2	Scheduled wake request
2	0	One–time request
	1	Repeating request (not allowed for process timer requests)
3	0	Relative time request
	1	Absolute time request
4	1	Timer is based on CPU time accumulated
5		*(reserved)*
6	1	AST is associated with timer event (same as AST quota bit)
7		*(reserved)*

Figure 12.1
Layout of a Timer Queue Entry (TQE)

343

set if the executive is to take action at a particular absolute time rather than at a relative interval from when the request was made. Bit TQE$V_CHK_CPUTIM is set if the executive is to take action when the target process has accumulated a certain amount of CPU time. Figure 12.1 summarizes the bits in TQE$B_RQTYPE.

The interpretation of the next several fields depends upon the type of timer request. For a system routine request, TQE$L_FPC contains the procedure value of the system routine; TQE$Q_FR3, the value to be restored to R3; and TQE$Q_FR4, the value to be restored to R4. For a process request, TQE$L_PID contains the process ID (PID) of the target process; TQE$L_AST, the procedure value of an asynchronous system trap (AST) procedure to execute; and TQE$L_ASTPRM, an optional parameter to be passed to the AST procedure.

For both process and system routine requests, the field TQE$Q_TIME is the quadword system time at which the executive is to take action. The field TQE$Q_DELTA is the absolute value of the repeat interval time for repeating requests.

Several fields are meaningful only for process requests. The access mode from which the service was requested is stored in TQE$L_RMOD. Bit ACB$V_QUOTA of TQE$L_RMOD is set if an AST is to be delivered at expiration time. The number of the event flag to be set at expiration time is stored in TQE$L_EFN. TQE$L_RQPID contains the PID of the process that made the initial timer request, since the requesting process is not necessarily the same as the target process whose ID is stored in TQE$L_PID.

For a request based on accumulated CPU time, TQE$L_CPUTIM contains the amount of CPU time, in soft ticks, that the process should accumulate for the timer request to expire.

A special fork block called the software timer fork block is used to request the execution of the software timer fork routine, described in Section 12.8. The TIMER spinlock is the fork lock associated with this fork block. The fork block has a busy bit, which, when set, means that execution of the software timer fork routine has been requested.

12.5 TIMER SYSTEM SERVICES

Application software can use two system services, $SETIMR and $SCHDWK, to request time-dependent services. Two complementary services, Cancel Wakeup ($CANWAK) and Cancel Timer Request ($CANTIM), both in module SYSCANEVT, cancel time-dependent requests.

12.5.1 $SETIMR System Service

The $SETIMR system service creates TQEs for nonrecurring process timer requests. Five arguments control the actions taken by this service:

▶ The EFN argument specifies an event flag number.

▶ The DAYTIM argument is the address of a timer expiration time.

▶ The ASTADR argument is the procedure value of an AST procedure.

▶ The REQIDT argument is a request identification parameter.

▶ The FLAGS argument specifies some flags.

Running in kernel mode, its system service procedure, EXE$SETIMR in module SYSSCHEVT, performs the following steps:

1. The event flag specified by the EFN argument is cleared in preparation for a subsequent setting at expiration time.

2. If the FLAGS argument is nonzero, this timer request is based on the CPU time accumulated by this process; EXE$SETIMR sets the TQE$V_CHK_CPUTIM bit in the TQE that it builds for this request.

3. EXE$SETIMR checks the request to ascertain that

   • The location specified by the DAYTIM argument is accessible to the requesting process

   • The requesting process does not exceed its PCB$L_ASTCNT quota if an AST is to be associated with this timer request

4. EXE$SETIMR decrements JIB$L_TQCNT to charge the allocation of the TQE. If the job runs out of the pooled resource JIB$L_TQCNT, then EXE$SETIMR puts the process into a miscellaneous wait state with its PCB$L_EFWM field containing the address of the job information block (JIB), and bit JIB$V_TQCNT_WAITERS set in JIB$L_FLAGS. When JIB$L_TQCNT is restored, this process will resume execution at the next step.

5. EXE$SETIMR allocates a TQE from nonpaged pool and initializes it from the system service arguments of time, request type, and PID.

6. If the DAYTIM argument is negative, indicating that it is a relative time, EXE$SETIMR calculates the absolute expiration time of the request by adding the absolute value of this argument to the current system time, EXE$GQ_SYSTIME. Bit TQE$V_ABSOLUTE is cleared for this element if this was a relative time request; otherwise, the bit is set.

7. EXE$SETIMR stores the access mode from which the system service was requested in the TQE$L_RMOD field. If AST notification was requested, EXE$SETIMR decrements the process PCB$L_ASTCNT to indicate the future AST delivery and sets bit ACB$V_QUOTA of TQE$L_RMOD to indicate the AST accounting.

8. EXE$SETIMR copies the REQIDT argument, which is used as the AST parameter, and the event flag number to the TQE.

9. If bit TQE$V_CHK_CPUTIM is set in the TQE, the DAYTIM argument represents the amount of CPU time the process must accumulate for the timer request to come due. EXE$SETIMR estimates the earliest absolute time at which this could happen and stores it in the TQE$Q_TIME field.

   It also calculates the total number of soft ticks the process must accumulate for this and stores it in TQE$L_CPUTIM. Later, when the TQE

expires, this value is compared with either PHD$L_CPUTIM or PCB$L_
CPUTIM, depending on whether the process is resident, to determine if
the timer request is indeed due. If it is not, the TQE is requeued with a
new expiration time (see Section 12.8.1).

10. EXE$SETIMR invokes EXE$INSTIMQ, in module EXSUBROUT, which
inserts the TQE into the right place in the timer queue while holding the
TIMER spinlock and returns.

11. EXE$SETIMR returns to its requestor.

12.5.2 $CANTIM System Service

The $CANTIM system service removes one or more TQEs before expira-
tion. Two arguments, the request identification parameter and the access
mode, control the actions taken by this service. The system service procedure, EXE$CANTIM in module SYSCANEVT, invokes EXE$RMVTIMQ,
in module EXSUBROUT, to remove and deallocate each TQE on the timer
queue that meets all the following criteria:

▶ The current process's ID is the same as TQE$L_PID.

▶ The access mode from which the service was requested is at least as privileged as the access mode stored in the TQE. This ensures that no request can be deleted for an access mode more privileged than that of the
requestor.

▶ The request identification parameter argument is the same as that stored
in the TQE. If the argument value is zero, then all TQEs meeting the first
two criteria are removed.

EXE$RMVTIMQ removes TQEs from the timer queue while holding the
TIMER spinlock.

12.5.3 $SCHDWK System Service

The logic for managing process scheduled wakeup requests is similar to that
of $SETIMR requests. Two differences are the ability to specify repeating
scheduled wakeup requests and the ability to schedule wakeup requests for
another process. The $SCHDWK system service procedure, EXE$SCHDWK
in module SYSSCHEVT, runs in kernel mode. It performs the following
actions:

1. EXE$SCHDWK invokes EXE$NAM_TO_PCB, in module SYSPCNTRL,
to locate the PCB of the process to be awakened.

    EXE$NAM_TO_PCB determines whether the input arguments spec-
ify a target process on this VMScluster node or on another node. In the
former case, EXE$NAM_TO_PCB confirms the existence of the target
process and the ability of the current process to delete it. (Chapter 14
describes the possible relations between the two processes and the privileges required in each case.) If the process is identified as one on another

VMScluster node, EXE$NAM_TO_PCB cannot make those checks; it can only confirm that the VMScluster node identification is valid.

If further action is possible, EXE$NAM_TO_PCB returns at IPL$_SCHED with the SCHED spinlock held; otherwise, it returns at IPL 0. In either case, it returns an appropriate status.

2. If EXE$NAM_TO_PCB returns the status SS$_REMOTE_PROC, indicating that the process may exist on another VMScluster node, EXE$SCHDWK validates the time arguments and transfers control to a clusterwide process service (CWPS) routine in module SYSPCNTRL. The routine transmits the wakeup request to the appropriate VMScluster node and places the requesting process into a wait state, waiting for resource RSN$_SCS. A cooperating CWPS routine on the other node performs the request and transmits status back to this node. Through mechanisms described in Chapter 14, control returns to a CWPS routine running in the context of the $SCHDWK requestor. This routine exits from the $SCHDWK system service, returning the status transmitted from the other node.

3. If EXE$NAM_TO_PCB returns any other error status, EXE$SCHDWK returns the error status to its requestor.

4. If EXE$NAM_TO_PCB returns a status indicating that the target process exists on this node and that the requesting process may affect the target process, EXE$SCHDWK continues.

5. It tests the repeat time argument to determine whether the request is a one-time or repeating scheduled wakeup.

6. If it is a repeating request, EXE$SCHDWK converts the requested repeat time into system time format. If the repeat time is less than the duration between two interval timer interrupts, it is increased to that value. If the expiration time plus the repeat time is less than the current time, EXE$SCHDWK returns the error status SS$_IVTIME. Note that Open-VMS AXP allows a finer granularity of repeating request than OpenVMS VAX, because the interval between interval timer interrupts is 1 millisecond or less on an AXP system.

7. EXE$SCHDWK allocates a TQE from nonpaged pool and initializes its repeat time, request time, and requesting and target process ID fields.

8. If the initial scheduled wakeup time was expressed as a relative time, then EXE$SCHDWK clears bit TQE$V_ABSOLUTE and calculates the expiration time as the sum of the absolute value of the initial delta time and the current system time. If the initial scheduled wakeup time was expressed as an absolute time, it sets bit TQE$V_ABSOLUTE.

9. It decrements the PCB$L_ASTCNT quota of the requesting process to account for the allocation of the TQE.

10. EXE$SCHDWK decrements JIB$L_TQCNT to charge the allocation of the TQE. If the job runs out of the pooled resource JIBL_TQCNT, EXESCHDWK puts the process into a miscellaneous wait state with

its PCB$L_EFWM field containing the address of the JIB, and bit JIB$V_TQCNT_WAITERS set in JIB$L_FLAGS. When JIB$L_TQCNT is restored, this process will resume execution at the next step.

11. It invokes EXE$INSTIMQ, which inserts the TQE into the right place in the timer queue while holding the TIMER spinlock and returns.

12. EXE$SCHDWK returns to its requestor.

When the expiration time is reached, the target process is awakened (see Section 12.8.3). Deallocation of the TQE occurs after delivery of a one-time scheduled wakeup request or as a result of a $CANWAK system service request.

12.5.4 $CANWAK System Service

The $CANWAK system service cancels all one-time and repeating scheduled wakeup requests for a target process. The system service procedure, EXE$CANWAK in module SYSCANEVT, first tests that the requesting process has the ability to affect the target process. It then deallocates each canceled TQE to nonpaged pool and, if the requesting process still exists, returns its PCB$L_ASTCNT quota to indicate the deallocation.

12.6 INTERVAL TIMER INTERRUPT SERVICE ROUTINE

The interval timer interrupt service routine, EXE$HWCLKINT in module TIMESCHDL, performs the following major functions:

- ► It updates the system time.
- ► It performs process and CPU accounting.
- ► It implements the sanity timer mechanism in an SMP system.
- ► It checks whether the current process has reached quantum end.
- ► It checks whether the most imminent TQE is due.

In an SMP system, the interval timer interrupt is taken by all processors, and all of them execute EXE$HWCLKINT. However, only the primary CPU is responsible for updating the system time and system uptime and checking the timer queue.

Unless otherwise stated, EXE$HWCLKINT performs the following actions on a uniprocessor or on each member of an SMP system:

1. Running on a uniprocessor or on the primary processor of an SMP system, EXE$HWCLKINT performs the following steps:

   a. It acquires the HWCLK spinlock.

   b. It updates the system time quadword, EXE$GQ_SYSTIME, by adding to it the value in EXE$GL_TICKLENGTH. In addition, whenever a certain number of ticks have passed, EXE$HWCLKINT adds to EXE$GQ_SYSTIME a value called the accuracy bonus, described later in this section.

EXE$GL_TICKLENGTH is used to maintain the system time relative to an external time standard. Normally, EXE$GL_TICKLENGTH is initialized to the value in EXE$GL_SYSTICK, the OpenVMS AXP representation of the duration between two interval timer interrupts. A privileged OpenVMS application, however, can adjust EXE$GL_TICKLENGTH, thus speeding up or slowing down the OpenVMS clock until it is synchronized with the reference time. Varying the tick length guarantees a monotonically increasing system time and avoids the pitfalls of other means of changing the system time. Use of the cells EXE$GL_SYSTICK and EXE$GL_TICKLENGTH is reserved to Digital and otherwise completely unsupported.

c. EXE$HWCLKINT compares the updated system time with the quadword EXE$GQ_1ST_TIME, the expiration time of the most imminent TQE. If this TQE is due, EXE$HWCLKINT checks whether the special fork block for the software timer fork routine has already been inserted into the primary processor's IPL 8 fork queue. If not, it inserts the fork block into the queue, and, if the queue was empty, requests an IPL$_TIMER software interrupt.

d. It releases the HWCLK spinlock.

2. EXE$HWCLKINT updates time statistics fields maintained as an array in the per-CPU database (see Chapter 37) at CPU$Q_KERNEL. The meaning of each counter in this array of seven quadwords is explained in Table 12.2.

   EXE$HWCLKINT determines that it is executing in system context if bit 2, the interrupt-in-progress bit, is set in the processor status saved in the interrupt stack frame.

   Chapter 1 describes system context, and Chapter 3, the interrupt stack frame.

3. EXE$HWCLKINT decrements CPU$L_SOFT_TICK by 1 and, if that brings CPU$L_SOFT_TICK to 0, proceeds to step 4. Otherwise, it dismisses the interval timer interrupt.

Table 12.2   Per-CPU Statistics Counters

Index	Meaning
0	Kernel mode in process context; no spinlock busy wait is active
1	Executive mode
2	Supervisor mode
3	User mode
4	Kernel mode in system context; no spinlock busy wait is active
5	Kernel mode in process or system context; spinlock busy wait is active
6	In scheduler idle loop

CPU$L_SOFT_TICK contains a running count of the number of interval timer interrupts left until the next soft tick. During system initialization INI$TIMER_QUEUE, in module TIMESCHDL, computes the initial value of CPU$L_SOFT_TICK based on the interval timer interrupt frequency.

When every soft tick occurs, EXE$HWCLKINT recomputes the value of CPU$L_SOFT_TICK such that the next soft tick will occur within a specified maximum deviation from the actual next 10-millisecond point. Section 12.3.4 outlines the reason that soft ticks may not occur precisely at 10-millisecond intervals.

4. In an SMP system, EXE$HWCLKINT performs the operations necessary to implement this processor's part of the sanity timer mechanism, as described in Chapter 37.

5. Running on a uniprocessor or on the primary processor of an SMP system, EXE$HWCLKINT increments EXE$GL_ABSTIM_TICS, and, every hundredth time through, EXE$GL_ABSTIM. In effect, EXE$HWCLKINT increments EXE$GL_ABSTIM every second.

6. EXE$HWCLKINT determines whether this soft tick should be charged to the current process. If the processor was running in system context at the time of the interrupt, the tick is not charged, and EXE$HWCLKINT continues with step 8.

Otherwise, EXE$HWCLKINT increments the appropriate element of the current process's per-mode soft tick counter, a four-longword array at PCB$L_KERNEL_COUNTER. The layered Portable Operating System Interface (POSIX) subsystem uses the contents of this array for per-mode CPU time accouting.

EXE$HWCLKINT increments the process's accumulated CPU time, PHD$L_CPUTIM, and its quantum, PHD$L_QUANT. If the quantum, initialized to a negative value, reaches zero, EXE$HWCLKINT requests an IPL 7 software interrupt to initiate quantum-end processing for this process.

7. EXE$HWCLKINT checks the interrupt program counter (PC) saved in the interrupt stack frame. If the saved PC is a system space address, EXE$HWCLKINT increments the PHD$L_CPUTIM field in the system header.

8. It dismisses the interval timer interrupt.

The interval timer interrupt service routine increments EXE$GQ_SYSTIME by an integral number. This could introduce a rounding error depending on the value of the interval timer frequency. For example, the value 9,765.625 represents the number of 100-nanosecond intervals in 1/1024th of a second, where 1,024 is the interval timer interrupt frequency. There is a rounding error of 0.625 (in hundreds of nanoseconds) for each interrupt.

EXE$HWCLKINT makes up for this rounding error by adding a value called an accuracy bonus once every *n* ticks. The value of *n* for current implementations is 20,000. The accuracy bonus is simply the product of the rounding error and 20,000, which amounts to 12,500 100-nanosecond intervals, or 0.00125 seconds. This value is added every 20,000 * 0.9765, or 19.53125, seconds.

12.7   SOFTWARE TIMER INTERRUPT SERVICE ROUTINE

The software timer interrupt service routine, EXE$SWTIMINT in module TIMESCHDL, is entered through the IPL 7 software interrupt. The software timer interrupt is requested by the interval timer interrupt service routine when the current process has reached quantum end.

Prior to VAX VMS Version 5.5, the IPL 7 software timer interrupt service routine serviced the timer queue. In later versions of VAX VMS and in OpenVMS AXP, an IPL 8 fork process running the software timer fork routine, described in Section 12.8, services the timer queue.

EXE$SWTIMINT gets the current process's PCB from CPU$L_CURPCB in the processor's per-CPU database and locates the process's header. It tests PHD$L_QUANT to determine whether the current process on this processor has reached quantum end. This field is initialized to the negative value of the SYSGEN parameter QUANTUM and incremented by the interval timer interrupt service routine. A zero or positive quantum value indicates quantum expiration. If the process has reached quantum end, EXE$SWTIMINT invokes routine SCH$QEND, in module RSE, to perform quantum-end processing (see Chapter 13).

12.8   SOFTWARE TIMER FORK ROUTINE

The software timer fork routine, EXE$SWTIMER_FORK in module TIMESCHDL, has been added to the executive to service the timer queue through an IPL 8 interrupt. This redesign reduces the latency to run EXE$TIMEOUT. EXE$TIMEOUT, a periodic system routine, runs every second as a result of the expiration of a permanent TQE. This routine performs device and controller timeout detection (see Section 12.8.2), a crucial part of device driver processing. In early versions of the VAX VMS operating system, when the IPL 7 software timer interrupt service routine serviced the timer queue, EXE$TIMEOUT could be stalled for unacceptable periods of time when there was heavy IPL 8 activity.

EXE$SWTIMER_FORK is entered by the fork dispatcher as a fork process at IPL 8, with the TIMER spinlock held. EXE$SWTIMER_FORK clears the busy bit in the software timer fork block. Holding the HWCLK spinlock to synchronize with the interval timer interrupt service routine, it checks whether the system time, EXE$GQ_SYSTIME, is greater than or equal to the expiration time of the first entry in the timer queue. If it is, then the timer request is due. EXE$SWTIMER_FORK removes the TQE from the timer queue, releases the HWCLK and TIMER spinlocks, lowering IPL to IPL$_TIMER, and performs one of three sequences of code depending upon the type of timer request. The following sections describe these sequences.

12.8.1 Process Timer Requests

If the TQE is a process timer request, created by a $SETIMR system service request, then EXE$SWTIMER_FORK performs the following operations:

1. If bit TQE$V_CHK_CPUTIM is set to indicate that the timer request is in terms of CPU time accumulated by the process, then it takes the following steps:

   a. If the requesting process is not in the system any more, it simply deallocates the TQE.

   b. Otherwise, it obtains the CPU time from PHD$L_CPUTIM if the requesting process is resident and from PCB$L_CPUTIM if it is not. (The swapper copies PHD$L_CPUTIM to PCB$L_CPUTIM when it outswaps a process.) EXE$SWTIMER_FORK compares the process's CPU time to TQE$L_CPUTIM to see whether the timer request has expired.

   If the timer has expired, the routine proceeds with step 2 as if this were a normal TQE expiration. Otherwise, it converts the difference between PCB$L_CPUTIM and TQE$L_CPUTIM, that is, the remaining number of soft ticks, to system time format. It adds that value to the expiration time, making a new estimate of when the process might have accumulated enough CPU time. It then reinserts the TQE into the queue and continues with step 6.

2. Holding the SCHED spinlock, it sets the event flag associated with this timer request by invoking SCH$POSTEF with the contents of the TQE$L_PID and TQE$L_EFN fields. A software priority boost of 3 may be applied to the process (see Chapter 13).

3. If the target process is no longer in the system, or if the event flag number is illegal, EXE$SWTIMER_FORK simply deallocates the TQE.

4. It increments the process's JIB$L_TQCNT quota to indicate the pending deallocation of the TQE. It tests JIB$L_FLAGS to determine if any processes in the same job are waiting for TQE quota. For each such process, it invokes EXE$WAIT_QUEUE_RELEASE, in module MUTEX, to make the process computable.

5. If ACB$V_QUOTA in TQE$L_RMOD is set, the user requested AST notification. EXE$SWTIMER_FORK copies the TQE$L_RMOD field to TQE$B_RQTYPE to reformat the TQE into an AST control block (ACB). EXE$SWTIMER_FORK invokes SCH$QAST to queue the ACB to the process (see Chapter 8).

6. When the processing of this TQE has been completed, EXE$SWTIMER_ FORK checks whether the next TQE is due.

Note that process timer requests are strictly one-time requests. Any repetition of timer requests must be implemented by the requesting process. A process can request $SETIMR events only on its own behalf.

12.8.2   Periodic System Routine Requests

The second type of TQE, a system routine request, is a system-initiated time-dependent request to execute a specified system routine. EXE$SWTIMER_ FORK handles this type of TQE by performing the following actions:

1. It loads R3 and R4 from the TQE$Q_FR3 and TQE$Q_FR4 fields. R5 has the address of the TQE.
2. It invokes the system routine whose procedure value the TQE$L_FPC field contains.
3. EXE$SWTIMER_FORK assumes that on return from the system routine, R5 has a valid TQE address. It tests the TQE$V_REPEAT bit for this TQE. If the bit is set, EXE$SWTIMER_FORK reinserts the TQE into the timer queue, having computed a new expiration time from TQE$Q_ DELTA.

    Note that even if the TQE is not reinserted into the queue, EXE$SW-TIMER_FORK does not deallocate the TQE. As a result, this type of TQE can be defined in a static nonpaged portion of system space or within a device driver data structure.
4. EXE$SWTIMER_FORK then checks whether the next TQE is due.

One example of this type of request is the once-per-second execution of the routine EXE$TIMEOUT, in module TIMESCHDL. The TQE for EXE$TIME-OUT is permanently defined in the same module, and the timer queue is initialized with this TQE as the first entry in the queue. EXE$TIMEOUT performs the following steps:

1. Holding the SCHED spinlock, it invokes the routine SCH$SWPWAKE to awaken the swapper process, if appropriate (see Chapter 20).
2. It invokes the routine ERL$WAKE, in module ERRORLOG, to awaken the ERRFMT process, if appropriate (see Chapter 35).
3. EXE$TIMEOUT scans the I/O database for devices that have exceeded their timeout intervals. Holding the appropriate fork lock and device lock, it invokes the driver for each such device at its timeout entry point (see Chapter 24).

    This scan also invokes the driver's timeout routine for terminal timed reads that have expired.
4. It scans the list of controller request blocks (CRBs) on the list IOC$GL_ CRBTMOUT for any that have timed out. The CRB timeout mechanism

enables a driver to be entered periodically for controller-related functions. The driver stores the procedure value of a timeout routine in the field CRB$L_TOUTROUT and an expiration time in CRB$L_DUETIME and invokes IOC$THREADCRB, in module IOSUBNPAG, to thread its CRB into the list. EXE$TIMEOUT compares the expiration time with EXE$GL_ABSTIM and, if the CRB due time has arrived, invokes the timeout routine holding the appropriate fork lock.

The Digital Storage Architecture (DSA) class and port drivers employ this mechanism. The DSA disk class driver, for example, must send its server periodic messages to inform the server that the host system is running. The DSA disk class driver timeout routine also checks that the server has made progress on the oldest outstanding request.

5. If a process is running the Monitor utility to display disk and disk queue length information, EXE$TIMEOUT scans the I/O database to collect information about disk queue lengths.

6. Next, it scans the fork and wait queue. Chapter 5 describes this queue and its use by fork processes.

7. It checks the first entry on the lock manager timeout queue to see if it has expired. If it has, it initiates a deadlock search by invoking LCK$SEARCHDLCK, in module DEADLOCK (see Chapter 11).

8. EXE$TIMEOUT invokes SCH$ONE_SEC, in module RSE, whose primary task is to invoke SCH$PIX_SCAN, also in module RSE. SCH$PIX_SCAN gives selected computable resident (COM) and computable outswapped (COMO) processes a priority boost, as described in Chapter 13.

9. Invoking SCH$RAVAIL, EXE$TIMEOUT declares several system resources available: RSN$_NPDYNMEM, RSN$_PGDYNMEM, RSN$_MAILBOX, and RSN$_ASTWAIT. This is necessary because, in certain rare cases, these resources are not declared available when they should be.

10. EXE$TIMEOUT returns to its invoker.

Another example of a repeating system timer routine is one the terminal driver uses to implement its modem polling. The controller initialization routine in the terminal driver loads the expiration time field in a TQE in the terminal driver with the current system time, sets the repeat bit, and loads the repeat interval with the SYSGEN parameter TTY_SCANDELTA. When the timer routine expires, it polls each modem looking for state changes.

12.8.3 Scheduled Wakeup Requests

The third type of TQE is a request for a scheduled wakeup ($SCHDWK) of a hibernating process. This type of request may be either one-time or repeating and may be requested by a process other than the target process.

EXE$SWTIMER_FORK performs the following operations for a scheduled wakeup TQE.

1. It invokes SCH$WAKE, in module RSE, to awaken the target process, which is identified by TQE$L_PID.

   If the target process is no longer in the system, or if the request is a one-time request, indicated by a zero TQE$V_REPEAT bit in the TQE$B_RQTYPE field, then EXE$SWTIMER_FORK performs the following steps:

   a. If the requesting process (TQE$L_RQPID) still exists, it increments the process's PCB$L_ASTCNT quota.

   b. It increments the requesting process's JIB$L_TQCNT quota to indicate the pending deallocation of the TQE.

      It tests JIB$L_FLAGS to determine if any processes in the same job are waiting for TQE quota. For each such process, it invokes EXE$WAIT_QUEUE_RELEASE, in module MUTEX, to make the process computable.

   c. It deallocates the TQE to nonpaged pool.

2. If the request is a repeating type, then it adds the repeat interval, TQE$Q_DELTA, to the request's expiration time, TQE$Q_TIME, computing its new expiration time. Based on this value, it reinserts the TQE at the appropriate position in the timer queue by invoking EXE$INSTIMQ, in module EXSUBROUT.

3. EXE$SWTIMER_FORK then checks whether the next TQE is due.

12.9   HIGH-RESOLUTION DELAYS AND TIMED WAITS

The OpenVMS AXP executive provides a number of procedures that drivers and other kernel mode code can call to implement very short delays and timed waits. Although the time argument to these procedures is typically a number of nanoseconds, the minimum delay that these procedures can provide is system-specific, in effect, equal to a small multiple of the SCC's granularity.

The procedure EXE$DELAY, in module [SYSLOA]TIMEDWAIT, can be used to wait unconditionally for a specified number of nanoseconds. The procedure converts its input argument to an end SCC value and loops at its caller's IPL until the end SCC value is reached before returning to its caller.

Two complementary executive procedures, EXE$TIMEDWAIT_SETUP and EXE$TIMEDWAIT_COMPLETE, both in module [SYSLOA]TIMED-WAIT, can be used to implement timed waits. A timed wait is a wait for a condition to occur within a specified time period. The following pseudocode fragment illustrates how these procedures can be used:

```
status = EXE$TIMEDWAIT_SETUP(
        delta,              !delta = number of
                            ! nanoseconds to wait
        end_time_token      !end_time_token = target SCC,
    );                      ! return value
```

355

```
do
!
!Insert code to test for event completion here.
!
while (EXE$TIMEDWAIT_COMPLETE(end_time_token) = SS$_CONTINUE);

!
!If here, the event either completed or timed out.
```

EXE$TIMEDWAIT_SETUP computes the value of the SCC after *delta* nanoseconds have elapsed and returns this value in *end_time_token*. The procedure EXE$TIMEDWAIT_COMPLETE compares this value to the current SCC value to determine whether the timeout condition has occurred. If so, it returns the status value SS$_TIMEOUT; otherwise, it returns SS$_CONTINUE.

The MACRO-32 macros BUSYWAIT, TIMEDWAIT, and TIMEDELAY use these executive procedures to implement delays and timed waits of the SCC's granularity. The BUSYWAIT macro is used by spinlock support routines. The TIMEDWAIT and TIMEDELAY macros are used by a number of device drivers.

Example 12.1 shows a sample invocation of the TIMEDWAIT macro, in module [DRIVER]PKCDRIVER, and its expansion.

Example 12.1
TIMEDWAIT Macro Expansion

```
; Macro invocation
;
TIMEDWAIT TIME=#<30*1000>,-              ;No. of 10-μs intervals to wait
          INS1=<PUSHL R0>,-
          INS2=<READ_CSR REG=STATUS,DEST=R3>,-
          INS3=<POPL R0>,-
          INS4=<BBS #PMAZ$V_STATUS_INT,-
                R3,-
                MSO_BUS_SERV>,-
          DONELBL=MSO_BUS_SERV
BLBS      R0,100$                        ;Branch if no timeout
;
; Macro expansion
;
; First, quadword align stack, handling arbitrary stack alignment.

    SUBL2    #^X18,SP                    ;Make space for two
                                         ; quad-aligned items
    ADDL3    #7,SP,R1                    ;Round up SP, place into R1
    BICL2    #7,R1                       ;Compute quad-aligned base
    PUSHAB   8(R1)                       ;Spare copy of END_VALUE address
    MOVL     #30000,R0                   ;Load 10-μs count into R0
    EVAX_MULQ #10000,R0,R0               ;Compute nanosecs
                                         ; (10*1000 per 10 μs)
```

(continued)

Example 12.1 *(continued)*
TIMEDWAIT Macro Expansion

```
    EVAX_STQ  R0,(R1)                  ;Save delta time
    PUSHAQ    8(R1)                    ;Place argument #2 (END_VALUE addr)
    PUSHAQ    (R1)                     ;Place argument #1 (DELTA addr)
    CALLS     #2,G^EXE$TIMEDWAIT_SETUP ;Set up end value
    BLBC      R0,L1                    ;Just exit on error
;
; Embedded label and user-specified instructions
;
; First, set up INS<N> instructions for existing invocations.
; Then add USERINS instruction list.

IMBEDLBL:
    PUSHL     R0                       ;INS1
    READ_CSR  REG=STATUS,DEST=R3       ;INS2
    POPL      R0                       ;INS3
    BBS       #PMAZ$V_STATUS_INT,-     ;INS4
              R3,-
              MSO_BUS_SERV

; End of loop test - check for completion (timeout).

    PUSHL     (SP)                     ;Copy END_VALUE pointer
    CALLS     #1,G^EXE$TIMEDWAIT_COMPLETE ;Check for completion
    BLBS      R0,IMBEDLBL              ;Loop if not yet done

; Exit point - clean up stack.

MSO_BUS_SERV:
L1:
    ADDL2     #<^X18+4>,SP             ;Restore SP
```

12.10   RELEVANT SOURCE MODULES

Source modules described in this chapter include

> [LIB]IOMAR.MAR
> [LIB]TQEDEF.SDL
> [SYS]SYSCANEVT.MAR
> [SYS]SYSSCHEVT.MAR
> [SYS]SYSSETIME.MAR
> [SYS]TIMESCHDL.MAR
> [SYSLOA]BBW_COMMON.M64
> [SYSLOA]TIMEDWAIT.MAR
> [SYSLOA]TIMROUT.MAR

13   Scheduling

It is equally bad when one speeds on the guest unwilling to go,
and when he holds back one who is hastening. Rather one should
befriend the guest who is there, but speed him when he wishes.

Homer, *The Odyssey*

Only one process can run on a processor at once. Scheduling is the mechanism that selects a process to run.

The characteristics most significant to the scheduling of a process are

▶ Process priority, which determines the precedence of various processes for execution

▶ Scheduling state, which defines the readiness of a process to be scheduled for execution, its computability or lack thereof

▶ Processor capability or affinity requirements, which constrain the set of processors of a symmetric multiprocessing (SMP) system on which a process can execute

Running on a particular processor, the scheduler identifies and selects for execution the highest priority process that can execute on that processor and places it into execution. A process currently executing enters a wait state when it makes a direct or indirect request for a system operation that cannot complete immediately. A waiting process becomes computable as the result of system events, such as the setting of an event flag or the queuing of an asynchronous system trap (AST), and may preempt a current process.

This chapter first describes the data structures related to scheduling and the significance of process priority, scheduling state, capabilities, and affinity. It then describes the dynamics of their interactions—how changes in one characteristic can affect the others and the mechanisms by which the characteristics change. Finally, it describes the rescheduling interrupt service routine in detail.

13.1   SCHEDULING DATA STRUCTURES

This section describes most of the system data structures that are relevant to scheduling.

The fundamental data structure is the process control block (PCB). It specifies the scheduling state, process priority, and capability and affinity requirements of a process and records many other process characteristics. Section 13.1.1 describes fields in the PCB relevant to scheduling.

One PCB, the null PCB, is defined statically as a placeholder. In early versions of the VAX/VMS operating system, the null PCB described a process called the null process. This process no longer exists, but there is still a need for a placeholder PCB so that each system pointer to a PCB can point to a valid PCB, even when there is no associated process.

Section 13.1.2 describes the process scheduling state queues, the queues in which PCBs of processes in the same scheduling states are linked.

The PCB contains the address of the process header (PHD). The PHD includes several fields related to scheduling and contains a hardware privileged context block (HWPCB), a structure in which privileged context is loaded and stored through the CALL_PAL SWPCTX instruction. Section 13.2.1 describes the HWPCB, and Section 13.1.3, the other fields.

The data structure called the per-CPU database supports SMP. The per-CPU database records processor-specific information. Each CPU has its own per-CPU database. Section 13.1.4 describes the fields in this structure relevant to scheduling.

Each CPU is identified by an ID, a number from 0 to 31. The system mask SCH$GL_IDLE_CPUS has a bit corresponding to each CPU. When set, the bit indicates that the CPU is idle and has no current process. The bit is cleared as a signal to indicate that the CPU should repeat its attempt to select a process to execute.

Several other systemwide data structures related to process priority are described in Section 13.3.

The set of PCBs, process scheduling state queues, and related data structures is known as the scheduler database. The SCHED spinlock synchronizes access to the set of data structures, although not necessarily to all fields within each structure. Chapter 9 describes the implementation and use of spinlocks.

13.1.1 PCB Fields Related to Scheduling

When a process is created, a PCB is allocated for it from nonpaged pool. A process continues to use the same PCB until the process is deleted and its PCB deallocated.

Figure 13.1 illustrates the fields of the PCB that are particularly important to scheduling. Others are shown in other chapters, in particular, in Chapters 8, 9, and 10.

PCB$W_SIZE and PCB$B_TYPE are the standard dynamic data structure fields.

The scheduling state of a process is specified by its PCB$L_STATE field. All processes in the system are in the current (CUR) state, a wait state, computable resident (COM) state, or computable outswapped (COMO) state. Section 13.4 summarizes the scheduling states and the transitions among them.

The PCBs of processes in most scheduling states are queued together with those of other processes in the same state so that they can be located

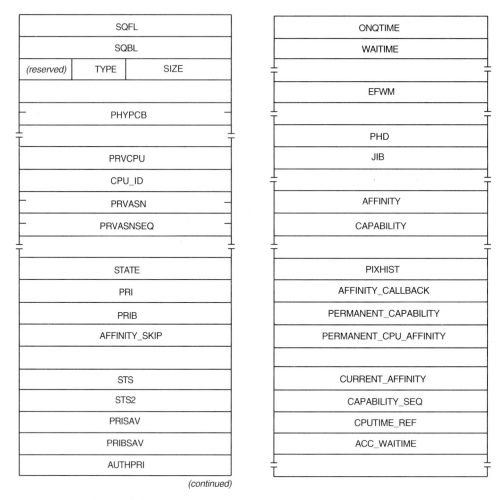

Figure 13.1
Process Control Block (PCB) Fields Used in Scheduling

more easily by scheduling routines. The scheduling state queue link fields, PCB$L_SQFL and PCB$L_SQBL, link a PCB into a process scheduling state queue (hereafter referred to as a process state queue). The various process state queues are described in Section 13.1.2.

The physical address of a process's HWPCB is stored in its PCB field PCB$Q_PHYPCB.

PCB$L_STS and PCB$L_STS2, the process status longwords, contain various flags describing the status of the process. The bit PCB$V_RES in PCB$L_STS is of particular significance to scheduling. When set, it indicates that the process is in memory rather than outswapped. Table 27.2 describes the flags in the process status longwords.

Several PCB fields are related to process priority. Section 13.3 describes these fields.

When a process is in an event flag wait (see Section 13.4.3.1) or a miscellaneous wait state (see Section 13.4.3.3), PCB$L_EFWM identifies the flags or resource for which the process waits.

PCB$L_PHD contains the address of the PHD (see Section 13.1.3).

PCB$L_JIB contains the address of the job information block (JIB). The PCBs of all processes in a job tree share the JIB, which contains information common to all processes in the job, notably pooled quotas.

PCB$L_CPU_ID contains the processor ID of the CPU on which the process is currently executing or has last executed.

PCB$L_PRVCPU contains the ID of the last CPU on which this process's hardware context was saved. PCB$Q_PRVASN contains the address space number (ASN) assigned to the process during its execution on that CPU, and PCB$Q_PRVASNSEQ the sequence number associated with the ASN. Section 13.1.4 describes the meaning of these fields.

PCB$L_WAITIME contains the system absolute time in units of 10-millisecond intervals, or soft ticks, at which a process was most recently placed into a wait state.

PCB$L_ONQTIME records the system absolute time in soft ticks at which a process most recently reached quantum end.

PCB$L_CPUTIME_REF records the amount of CPU time the process had accumulated the last time its ratio of wait time to compute time was calculated. This ratio is calculated to determine whether memory should be reclaimed from a process's working set. PCB$L_ACC_WAITIME records the amount of wait time the process has accumulated since then. Section 13.6.1.6 describes the use of these fields in more detail.

PCB$L_PIXHIST is described in Section 13.6.7.

The other PCB fields shown in Figure 13.1 are discussed in Section 13.5.

13.1.2 Process State Queues

PCBs of processes in most scheduling states are linked with those of other processes in the same states. There are queues for computable processes and for processes in different wait states. The listheads for all these queues are defined in the module SYSTEM_DATA_CELLS. There is no queue of current processes; instead, the per-CPU database of each CPU has a pointer to the PCB of its current process.

There are 64 queues for COM processes, one for each possible process priority. The quadword listheads of these queues are defined as an array whose starting address is global location SCH$AQ_COMH. A process is inserted into the queue corresponding to the internal value of its current process priority (see Section 13.3). There is a similar array of 64 quadword listheads for the COMO state at global location SCH$AQ_COMOH.

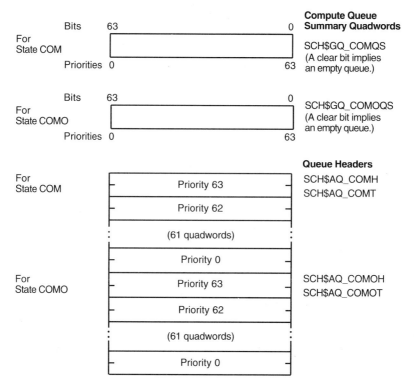

Figure 13.2
Computable (Executable) State Queues

The condition (empty or not) of each computable queue is summarized by a bit. If the queue contains one or more PCBs, the bit is set; if the queue is empty, the bit is clear. The 64 bits describing the COM queues are in the quadword at global location SCH$GQ_COMQS; the COMO queues are summarized in the quadword SCH$GQ_COMOQS. Bit 0 in each quadword corresponds to the queue for process priority 63, bit 1 for priority 62, and so forth. (Section 13.3 explains the inverted order.) These summary quadwords facilitate selection of the next process to execute and selection of the next process to be inswapped. Figure 13.2 shows the computable queues and their summary quadwords.

Figure 13.3 shows the array of scheduler wait queue headers. Each header is a listhead for processes in one of the wait states. The first two longwords are the links to the PCBs in this queue. The field WQH$L_WQSTATE contains the numerical value corresponding to the scheduling state of this queue (see Table 13.1 in Section 13.4). All PCBs in a process state queue have PCB$L_STATE values identical to the state value of the wait queue header. The field WQH$L_WQCNT contains the number of PCBs currently in this state and queue.

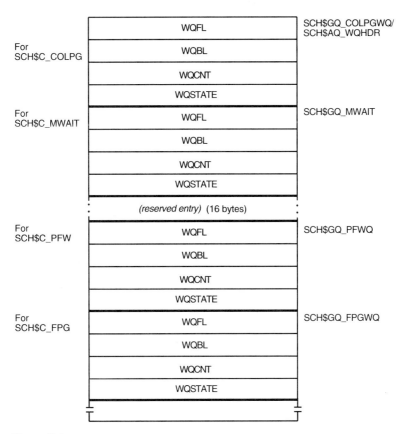

Figure 13.3
Array of Wait Queue Headers

The wait queue headers for all wait states except common event flag (CEF) wait are defined within this array ordered by increasing state number, with the collided page wait state first. Each wait queue header except CEF has its own global pointer. A scheduling routine can access a particular wait queue by specifying its global name or using its state number as an index into the wait queue header array. The global location SCH$AQ_WQHDR is the address of the beginning of the array and corresponds to index number 1. (There is no state whose numeric value is 0.) Note that there is no actual header with an index value of 3, or CEF, although space is reserved.

A process waiting for one or more common event flags is queued to a wait queue in the common event block (CEB) defining the common event flag cluster with which the process is associated. A CEB includes four longwords corresponding to a wait queue header. The format of the CEB is shown in Chapter 10. Having a wait queue in each CEB makes it easier to determine which CEF processes are computable when a common event flag is set. The wait queue in the CEB contains resident and outswapped processes.

13.1.3   PHD Fields Related to Scheduling

Figure 13.4 illustrates some PHD fields that are particularly important to scheduling (the layout of the HWPCB is shown in Figure 13.6). Others are shown in other chapters, in particular, Chapter 16 and Appendix E.

PHD$L_CPULIM contains zero if the process is allowed unlimited CPU time, or the number of soft ticks it is allowed. PHD$L_CPUTIM contains the number of soft ticks the process has accumulated. PHD$L_QUANT contains the amount of quantum, measured in soft ticks, remaining to the process (see Section 13.6.2).

If the image running in the process performs floating-point arithmetic, when the process is taken out of execution the contents of its floating-point registers are saved in its PHD, beginning at PHD$Q_F0. The contents of the floating-point control processor register are saved in PHD$Q_FPCR. When the process is placed back into execution, the contents of these registers are restored from the PHD.

PHD$L_FLAGS2 contains two flags related to scheduling:

▸ PHD$V_SW_FEN mirrors the state of the process's floating-point enable register. When set, it indicates that the process is performing floating-point arithmetic. Examining the PHD copy of a current process's floating-point enable register takes less time than examining the register through the CALL_PAL MFPR instruction.

▸ PHD$V_AST_PENDING, when set, means that a deliverable AST is pend-

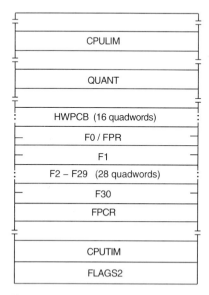

Figure 13.4
Process Header (PHD) Fields Used in Scheduling

ing for the process. Its use in optimizing AST delivery to a process being placed back into execution is described in Section 13.7.1.

13.1.4   Per-CPU Database Fields Related to Scheduling

The per-CPU database records processor-specific information such as the address of the PCB of the process current on that processor, the address of the processor's system context stack, and the processor's fork queues. Chapter 37 contains further information, including a detailed description of the per-CPU database. Figure 13.5 illustrates the fields of the per-CPU database that are related to scheduling.

CPU$L_CURPCB contains the PCB address of the process currently executing on this processor. CPU$L_CUR_PRI contains the process's current priority. If the processor is idle, CPU$L_CURPCB contains the address of the null PCB, and CPU$L_CUR_PRI contains –1.

CPU$L_PHY_CPUID contains the ID of the processor, a number from 0 to 31. CPU$L_CPUID_MASK is a mask of all zeros with one bit set corresponding to the CPU ID.

Several fields are used by the idle loop, which executes when there is no computable resident process to run. The idle loop zeros free pages of

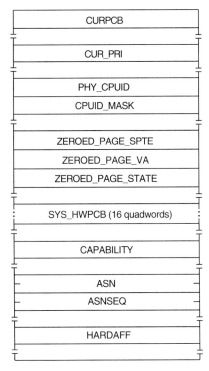

Figure 13.5
Per-CPU Database Fields Used in Scheduling

physical memory to provide a supply for allocation of demand zero pages and level 1 page tables (L1PTs). During system initialization a system page table entry (SPTE) is reserved for each processor to use in zeroing pages. The address of the SPTE is recorded in CPU$L_ZEROED_PAGE_SPTE, and the starting system virtual address mapped by that SPTE, in CPU$L_ZEROED_PAGE_VA. While zeroing a page, the idle loop records its current position in CPU$L_ZEROED_PAGE_STATE. Section 13.7.3 describes the idle loop.

Beginning at CPU$Q_SYS_HWPCB is a HWPCB for use by the processor when there is no current process to run. The Alpha AXP architecture requires that there always be a current HWPCB to define a context for CPU execution. During system initialization a HWPCB and kernel stack are allocated for each processor as part of the per-CPU data area. When there is no computable resident process to place into execution, the rescheduling interrupt service routine swaps to this context. Chapter 37 contains further details.

CPU$L_CAPABILITY is a bit mask with bits set to represent the capabilities of this processor. The low bit, when set, means that this CPU is the primary processor. The macro $CPBDEF defines symbolic values for the bits in this field. CPU$L_HARDAFF is the number of processes that have affinity for this CPU. Section 13.5 describes the meaning and use of these two fields.

CPU$Q_ASN contains the ASN most recently assigned to a process on this CPU. On a CPU that supports ASNs, the current process's ASN is an implicit input for translation buffer (TB) lookups and invalidation of single TB entries. As a result, when process context is swapped, process-private TB entries need not be flushed from the TB. Instead, the executive is responsible for initiating invalidation of process-private entries when necessary.

CPU$Q_ASN is initialized to the maximum ASN possible on the CPU and decremented as each ASN is assigned. (The maximum number possible is CPU-specific; on a DEC 7000 Model 610, for example, the maximum number is $3F_{16}$.) When CPU$Q_ASN is decremented to zero and ASN 0 is assigned, all possible ASNs have been assigned on this CPU. CPU$Q_ASN is reset to its maximum possible value, and the next ASN to be assigned is one that has already been assigned.

If multiple processes used the same ASN concurrently, one process's virtual address could be translated using another's page table entry (PTE) contents, resulting in corruption of both virtual address spaces. To prevent this possibility, the executive associates a sequence number with an ASN assignment. When a process is assigned an ASN, the current sequence number, the contents of CPU$Q_ASNSEQ, are copied to its PHD.

Whenever the executive resets CPU$Q_ASN to its maximum, it increments the sequence number as a signal that all ASNs previously assigned on this CPU are invalid and cannot be reused. It invalidates all process-private TB entries.

When a process is taken out of execution, the ID of the CPU it ran on is stored in PCB$L_PRVCPU, and its ASN and ASNSEQ are stored in PCB$Q_

PRVASN and PCB$Q_PRVASNSEQ. Whenever a process is about to be placed into execution, the executive examines PCB$L_PRVCPU to see if the process is running on the same CPU as the last time it executed. If it is and if the saved sequence number matches the current contents of CPU$Q_ASNSEQ, the process continues to use the same ASN. If it is not running on the same CPU, the process is assigned a new ASN. If the process is running on the same CPU, but its saved sequence number does not match the current contents of CPU$Q_ASNSEQ, the process is assigned a new ASN.

13.2   HARDWARE CONTEXT

The definition of a process from the viewpoint of the hardware is known as hardware context. It includes the following registers:

- Integer registers: R0 through R29, and stack pointer (SP)
- If the process is using floating-point, the floating-point registers: F0–F30 (F31 is always read as zero), floating-point control (FPCR) processor register, and floating-point enable (FEN) processor register
- Per-process stack pointers for kernel, executive, supervisor, and user mode stacks
- Program counter (PC) and processor status (PS)
- Page table base (PTBR) processor register (see Chapter 15)
- ASN processor register
- AST enable (ASTEN) processor register (see Chapter 8)
- AST summary (ASTSR) processor register (see Chapter 8)
- Data alignment trap fixup (DATFX) processor register, which controls whether data alignment traps, which are fixed up by privileged architecture library (PALcode) routines, generate exceptions (see Chapter 39)
- Process cycle counter (see Chapter 12)
- Process unique value, a value used in support of multithread software such as DECthreads
- Performance monitoring enable (PME) processor register

While a process is current, its hardware context is updated continuously. When a process is taken out of execution, its hardware context must be copied from registers to memory, where it is saved until the process executes again. OpenVMS AXP scheduling routines ensure that the integer registers, PC, and PS are saved on the process's kernel stack and, if necessary, that the floating-point registers are saved in the PHD (see Section 13.2.2). The PAL-code routine that implements the swap process context instruction, CALL_PAL SWPCTX, saves a subset of the hardware context in the HWPCB.

13.2.1   Hardware Privileged Context Block

Figure 13.6 shows the layout of the HWPCB. Symbolic offsets for its fields begin with the string PHD$.

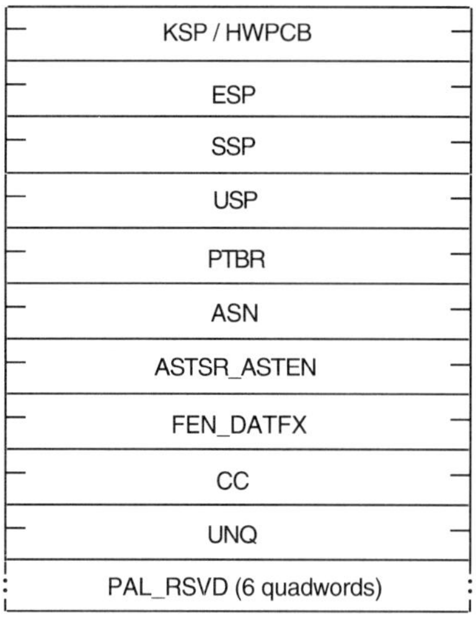

KSP / HWPCB
ESP
SSP
USP
PTBR
ASN
ASTSR_ASTEN
FEN_DATFX
CC
UNQ
PAL_RSVD (6 quadwords)

Figure 13.6
Layout of the Hardware Privileged Context Block
(HWPCB)

The executive creates a HWPCB for each process in the fixed part of its
PHD beginning at a naturally aligned 128-byte boundary. The process's PCB
field PCB$Q_PHYPCB contains the physical address of its HWPCB. The
swapper initializes this field when it swaps a process into memory. While
a process is current, the HWPCB base (PCBB) processor register contains the
physical address of its HWPCB, and the processor is said to own the HW-
PCB. If software (other than PALcode routines) attempts read or write access
to any of the HWPCB fields other than PHD$Q_ASTSR_ASTEN while the
processor owns it, the results are unpredictable. (The rescheduling interrupt
service routine, described in Section 13.7.1, examines this field as a faster
way to read the contents of the process's ASTSR and ASTEN registers.)

Figure 13.7 illustrates access to the HWPCB.

When the executive selects a new process to place into execution, it copies
the process's PCB$Q_PHYPCB field to R16 before executing the instruction
CALL_PAL SWPCTX. The PALcode SWPCTX routine gets the address of the current process's HWPCB from the PCBB processor register, saves its privileged
context, reloads the PCBB processor register with the address of the new
process's HWPCB, and loads its privileged context. The CALL_PAL SWPCTX instruction returns ownership of the former current process's HWPCB to the
executive. Section 13.7.2 provides further details.

13.2.2 Canonical Kernel Stack

The term *canonical kernel stack* refers to the unprivileged hardware context
saved on a process's kernel stack. Figure 13.8 shows the arrangement of the
canonical kernel stack.

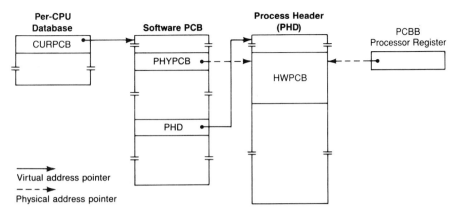

Figure 13.7
Access to the Hardware Privileged Context Block

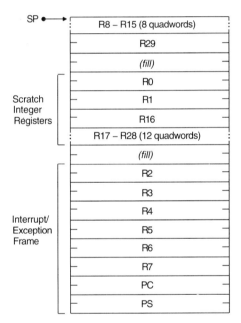

Figure 13.8
Arrangement of the Canonical Kernel Stack

The context is ordered based partly on the sequence that saves it in the rescheduling interrupt service routine. The oldest context (at the highest addresses) on the stack is an interrupt/exception stack frame. The stack frame is followed by the scratch integer registers, saved to enable the rescheduling code to call other procedures prior to context swap without overwriting the register contents. In this chapter, the term *scratch integer registers* refers to integer registers that may be modified by a called procedure without being restored.

369

The quadword of fill between the interrupt/exception stack frame and scratch integer registers is present to align the stack on an octaword boundary. This alignment enables the rescheduling interrupt service routine to call other procedures after the scratch integer registers have been saved. The scratch integer registers are followed by another quadword of fill and the non-scratch integer registers other than R2 through R7. The stack alignment enables the rescheduling interrupt service routine to call other procedures after completing the canonical kernel stack and prior to swapping this process's context.

When the process is placed back into execution by a CALL_PAL SWPCTX instruction, the rescheduling routine restores from the stack the integer registers other than R2 through R7 and executes a CALL_PAL REI instruction to restore registers R2 through R7 and resume execution in the process (see Section 13.7.1).

For a process to be placed back into execution by the same code sequence, regardless of its state prior to the context switch, every noncurrent process must have the same arrangement of saved hardware context. Moreover, a canonical kernel stack is created for each new process as the process is created; when the rescheduling routine swaps to the process's context and executes a CALL_PAL REI instruction, it transfers control to EXE$PROCSTRT (see Chapter 27).

13.3   PROCESS PRIORITY

Two different mechanisms whose names contain the term *priority* are associated with each process. Interrupt priority level (IPL) applies to process-based and system-based code alike. IPL governs the hardware precedence of interrupts, as described in Chapter 3.

Process priority determines the precedence of a process for execution and memory residence. Throughout this book, the term *priority* used without qualification refers to process priority.

Process priorities have two different representations, an external representation for presentation to the user and an internal one for use by most scheduling code. External process priorities take on values from 0 to 63; 0 is the lowest priority, and 63 is the highest. This representation matches the tendency of most users to associate higher values with higher priorities.

The range of 64 priorities is divided into two parts. The priorities from 16 to 63 are assigned to real-time processes, and the priorities from 0 to 15 are assigned to normal processes. The scheduling of a process is significantly affected by its type (either normal or real-time) and by its assigned priority level.

Traditionally, OpenVMS priorities are in the range 0 to 31, which is divided into a real-time half and a normal half. The OpenVMS AXP priority range includes additional real-time priorities in preparation for future real-time Portable Operating System Interface (POSIX) support.

Internal process priorities are stored in an inverted order. For example, 0, the lowest external priority, is stored internally as 63; external priority 63 is stored internally as 0. Subtracting one priority form from 63 converts it to the other form.

In the original operating system design, the values were inverted in this way to facilitate selection of the next process to execute and the next process to be inswapped; on OpenVMS VAX systems, these functions use the find first set (FFS) instruction, which begins its search for a set bit at bit position 0. The OpenVMS AXP executive uses the same representation for compatibility and ease of porting. (In other data structures, external priority is used instead, for convenience of the code referencing them.) As a result of this inversion, priority promotions or boosts are implemented through subtract or decrement instructions.

System utilities, such as the System Dump Analyzer (SDA), MONITOR, and the code that implements the Digital command language (DCL) command SHOW SYSTEM, convert internal priorities to external ones for display. The Get Job Process Information ($GETJPI) system service returns an external priority when a process priority is requested.

All discussions in this book use external priority representation unless otherwise noted. This convention should be taken into account when relating descriptions in this book to the actual routines in the listings, where internal priorities predominate.

Several fields of the PCB describe process priority. The values in these fields are in internal priority representation. The field PCB$L_PRI defines the current process priority, which is used to make scheduling decisions. PCB$L_PRIB defines the base priority of the process, from which the current priority is calculated. For normal or time-sharing processes, these priority values are sometimes different, while real-time processes always have identical current and base priority values.

When a process is first created, its base priority is initialized from an argument to the Create Process ($CREPRC) system service. Subsequently, if the process executes the LOGINOUT.EXE image, it may reset the base priority using the value from the user's record in the system authorization file.

A process with the ALTPRI privilege can raise and lower its current and base priorities without constraint, using the Set Priority ($SETPRI) system service or the DCL command SET PROCESS/PRIORITY. Chapter 14 describes the operation of the $SETPRI system service. The field PCB$L_AUTHPRI contains the base priority authorized at the time the process was created. A process without the ALTPRI privilege may raise and lower its priorities only between 0 and the contents of PCB$L_AUTHPRI.

System mechanisms that adjust priority dynamically are described in Section 13.3.3.

The fields PCB$L_PRIBSAV and PCB$L_PRISAV record the base and current priority values at the time a process first locks a mutex, before it receives a temporary elevation into the real-time range. When the process unlocks the mutex, its priority values are restored from these fields.

SCH$AQ_PREEMPT_MASK is a 64-quadword array of constants, with one quadword for each priority. The array is indexed by internal priority; the quadword at SCH$AQ_PREEMPT_MASK corresponds to internal priority 0. The quadword for a priority represents the priorities that it can preempt. Each bit in the quadword represents a priority, with bit 0 representing *external* priority 0. The bits are organized that way because they are masked against the data in SCH$GQ_ACTIVE_PRIORITY, described later in this section.

During system initialization the preemption masks that represent the rules for normal priority processes are altered in accordance with the SYSGEN parameter PRIORITY_OFFSET, whose default value is 0.

When a resident process becomes computable, scheduling code must decide whether the process should preempt one currently executing. Scheduling code indexes the preemption array using the priority of the newly computable process. The selected mask indicates which priorities the process can preempt. The values in the masks implement two preemption rules and thus simplify the decision code:

▶ A real-time process can preempt any process of lower priority.
▶ A normal process at external priority n can preempt a process at priority $n - (\text{PRIORITY\_OFFSET} + 1)$.

Altering this parameter enables the system manager to reduce the number of times a current process is preempted by a newly computable process. Preventing preemption by a newly computable process only one or two priority levels higher than a current process improves overall system performance. It minimizes unnecessary rescheduling and helps to minimize movement of a process from one processor to another on an SMP system. If no other scheduling events intervene, such a newly computable process will be favored at quantum end of the current process.

A system in which one class of users is to have significantly better responsiveness than another class requires that the base priorities for the two classes must differ by the value of the SYSGEN parameter PRIORITY_OFFSET + 1.

The per-CPU database field CPU$L_CUR_PRI contains the internal form of the current priority of the process current on that CPU. If the CPU is idle and has no current process, the field contains –1.

The priorities of the processes current on each member of an SMP system are described by two system data structures, defined in SYSTEM_DATA_CELLS.

▶ SCH$AL_CPU_PRIORITY is a 64-longword array with one longword for each priority. The array is indexed by internal priority; the longword at SCH$AL_CPU_PRIORITY corresponds to internal priority 0. Each bit in a longword represents one SMP member, with bit 0, for example, corresponding to CPU ID 0. Bit m set in longword n means that the process current on CPU ID m is at internal priority n.

▶ SCH$GQ_ACTIVE_PRIORITY, summarizing SCH$AL_CPU_PRIORITY, has a bit for each priority. When set, a particular bit indicates that one or more SMP members have a current process at that priority. Bit 0, for example, corresponds to external priority 0. Originally, the quadword was designed to be indexed by external priority so that VAX scheduling code could execute a FFS instruction to locate the lowest priority current process.

Figure 13.9 shows how these data structures might look for an SMP system of two members with CPU IDs 0 and 2. CPU 0 is executing a process at external priority 5, and CPU 2, a process at external priority 8. For simplicity, most of the bits are omitted.

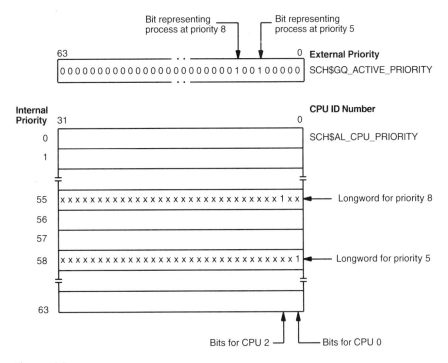

Figure 13.9
SMP Priority Summary Data Structures

13.3.1   Real-Time Priority Range

Processes with priority levels 16 through 63 are considered real-time processes. Two scheduling characteristics distinguish real-time processes from normal processes:

- ▶ The current priority of a real-time process does not change over time unless there is a direct program or operator request to change it. No dynamic priority adjustment (see Section 13.3.3) is applied by the executive.
- ▶ A real-time process executes until it is preempted by a higher priority process or it enters a wait state (see Section 13.4.3). A real-time process is not susceptible to quantum end (see Section 13.6.2); that is, it is not removed from execution because some interval of execution time has expired.

Taken in isolation, the real-time range of priorities provides a scheduling environment like traditional real-time systems: preemptive, priority-driven scheduling without a time slice or quantum.

13.3.2   Normal Priority Range

Most user processes are normal processes. All system processes except the swapper and the Files-11 Extended QIO Processor (XQP) cache server process are normal processes.

The current priority of a normal process varies over time, while its base priority remains constant unless there is a direct program or operator request to change it. This behavior is the result of dynamic priority adjustment applied by the executive to favor I/O-bound processes and processes performing terminal I/O over those performing other types of I/O and compute-bound processes. The mechanism of priority adjustment is discussed in Section 13.3.3.

Normal processes run in a time-sharing environment that allocates time slices (or quanta) to processes in turn. A normal process executes until one of the following events occurs:

- ▶ It is preempted by a higher priority computable process. For one normal process to preempt another, the priority of the preempting process must be at least PRIORITY_OFFSET + 1 more than that of the preempted process.
- ▶ It enters a resource or event wait state.
- ▶ It has used its current quantum, and there is another computable process at the same or higher priority.

Processes with identical current priorities are scheduled on a round-robin basis. That is, apart from the affinity and capability constraints described in Section 13.5, each process at a given priority level executes in turn before any other process at that level executes again.

Most normal processes experience round-robin scheduling because, by default, the user authorization file defines the base priority for users as the value of SYSGEN parameter DEFPRI. Its usual value is 4.

13.3.3   Dynamic Priority Adjustment

Normal processes do not generally execute at a single priority level. Rather, the priority of a normal process changes over time in a range of zero to six priority levels above the base process priority. Two mechanisms provide this priority adjustment:

▶ When a condition for which the process has been waiting is satisfied or a needed resource becomes available, its current priority may be increased to improve the scheduling response for the process. The size of the possible increase varies (see Section 13.6.6).

▶ Each time the process executes without further system events (see Section 13.6.5), the current priority is lowered by one priority level until its base priority is reached (see Section 13.7.1).

Over time, compute-bound process priorities tend to remain at their base priority levels, whereas I/O-bound processes tend to have average current priorities somewhat higher than their base priorities.

An example of priority adjustment that occurs over time for several processes is described in Section 13.6.6 and illustrated in Figure 13.14.

A normal process occasionally has its priority boosted by the pixscan mechanism, described in Section 13.6.7.

Temporary priority adjustment can also occur as a result of locking a mutex and through action by the $GETJPI system service, which is described in Chapter 14.

13.4   SCHEDULING STATES

This section describes the various scheduling states and some of the transitions among them. Figure 13.10 shows the common transitions but omits a few of the less frequent ones.

The symbolic name for a scheduling state is represented by SCH$C_*mnemonic*, for example, SCH$C_COM. These symbolic names are defined by the macro $STATEDEF. Table 13.1 lists the scheduling states and the corresponding PCB$L_STATE values.

Certain wait conditions are represented by two different scheduling states: one resident and one outswapped. A process waiting for a local event flag is in the LEF or the LEFO state, depending on its residence. Other scheduling states, such as CEF, include both resident and outswapped processes. The PCB$V_RES bit in PCB$L_STS always specifies whether the process is resident or outswapped, regardless of its scheduling state.

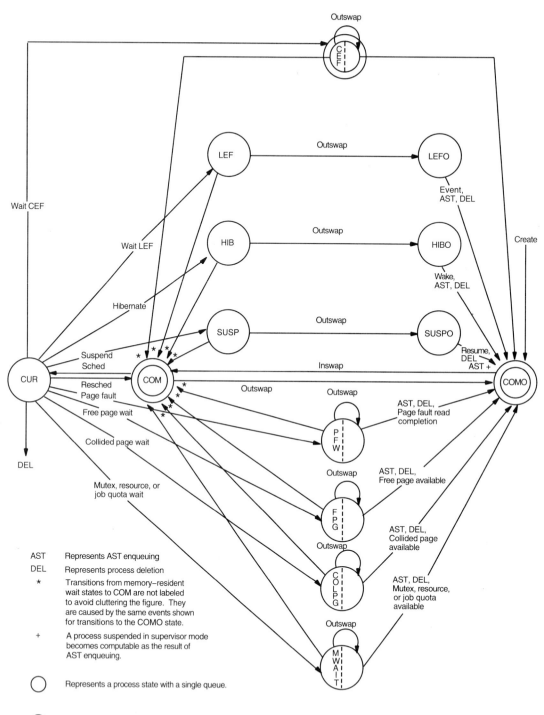

Figure 13.10
State Transitions

Table 13.1 Scheduling States

State Name	Mnemonic	Value
Collided page wait	COLPG	1
Miscellaneous wait	MWAIT	2
Mutex wait		
Resource wait		
Job quota wait		
Common event flag wait	CEF	3
Page fault wait	PFW	4
Local event flag wait (resident)	LEF	5
Local event flag wait (outswapped)	LEFO	6
Hibernate wait (resident)	HIB	7
Hibernate wait (outswapped)	HIBO	8
Suspend wait (resident)	SUSP	9
Suspend wait (outswapped)	SUSPO	10
Free page wait	FPG	11
Computable (resident)	COM	12
Computable (outswapped)	COMO	13
Currently executing process	CUR	14

13.4.1   Current State

A process in the CUR state is currently being executed. Its PCB address is recorded in its processor's per-CPU database at CPU$L_CURPCB.

A CUR process makes a transition to the COM state when it is preempted by a higher priority process. A CUR process of normal priority also makes this transition when it reaches quantum end and there is another computable process of higher or equal priority. A CUR process can make a transition to any of the resident wait states by directly or indirectly requesting a system operation that cannot complete immediately.

Direct requests for system services like Hibernate ($HIBER) and Suspend Process ($SUSPND) place the process into the voluntary wait states HIB and SUSP. Direct requests for system services like Queue I/O Request and Wait ($QIOW), Synchronize ($SYNCH), and Wait for Single Event Flag ($WAITFR) place the process into the voluntary wait states LEF or CEF.

Indirect wait requests occur as a result of paging or contention for system resources. A process does not request PFW, FPG, COLPG, or MWAIT transitions. Rather, the transitions to these wait states occur because direct service requests to the system cannot be completed or satisfied at the moment.

Deletion of a process can only occur while it is CUR. The process's address space and PHD are accessible only while it is current. Furthermore, process deletion in the context of the process being deleted enables the use of system services, such as Deassign I/O Channel ($DASSGN) and Delete Virtual Address Space ($DELTVA). Chapter 31 describes process deletion in detail.

13.4.2   Computable States

A process in the COM state is not waiting for events or resources, other than acquiring control of the CPU for execution. A COM process enters the CUR state after having been selected as the next process to run (see Section 13.7.1).

A COM process enters the COMO state when it is outswapped.

A process in the COMO state is waiting for the swapper process to bring it into memory. As a COM process, it can then be scheduled for execution. Processes are created in the COMO state.

A COM process selected for execution can enter the RWCAP miscellaneous wait state if its capability and affinity requirements have no match on any active member of an SMP system. (This transition is not shown in Figure 13.10.) Section 13.5 describes capability and affinity requirements.

13.4.3   Wait States

A process that is not current or computable is waiting for the availability of a system resource or the occurrence of an event. The process is in one of several distinct wait states. The wait state reflects the particular condition that must be satisfied for the process to become computable again.

A process in a wait state makes the transition to COM or COMO through a system event such as the availability of a requested resource or the satisfaction of a wait condition. For most process wait states, the queuing of an AST makes a process computable even if the wait condition is not satisfied.

13.4.3.1   Voluntary Wait States.

Several scheduling states are associated with event flag waits: LEF, LEFO, and CEF. A process enters the LEF or CEF state as a result of requesting the $WAITFR, $SYNCH, Wait for Logical OR of Event Flags ($WFLOR), and Wait for Logical AND of Event Flags ($WFLAND) system services directly or indirectly, for example, with a $QIOW or $ENQW system service call, issued either by the process or on its behalf by some system component such as Record Management Services (RMS). A process enters the LEF state when it waits for local event flags or the CEF state when it waits for flags in a common event flag cluster.

An LEF process enters the LEFO state when it is outswapped. The transition from the LEF, LEFO, or CEF states to the computable (COM or COMO) states can occur as a result of an event flag's being set that satisfies the wait condition, AST queuing, or process deletion (a special case of AST queuing). Chapter 10 describes event flag waits in more detail.

There are separate resident and outswapped states and queues for hibernating and suspended processes. The $HIBER and $SUSPND system services cause processes to enter the HIB and SUSP wait states. Outswapping a HIB or SUSP process causes it to enter the HIBO or SUSPO state.

A process makes the transition from the HIB or HIBO state to COM or

COMO as a result of execution of the Wake ($WAKE) or Schedule Wakeup ($SCHDWK) system service, AST queuing, or process deletion.

The SUSP and SUSPO states are categorized by the access mode of the suspension as either supervisor mode or kernel mode. A process in supervisor mode suspension, the default, is made computable by the queuing of an AST. (The nature of its wait, however, enables only executive and kernel mode ASTs to be delivered.) A process in kernel mode suspension is not made computable by the enqueuing of an AST. A process in either type of suspension is made computable when another process requests the Resume Process ($RESUME) system service for the suspended process. Chapter 8 contains further information on ASTs, and Chapter 14, on the implementation of the $SUSPND and $HIBER system services.

Process deletion, implemented with a kernel mode AST, makes any process that is being deleted computable, even one in the SUSP or SUSPO state, because the target process is resumed before the AST is queued.

13.4.3.2 **Memory Management Wait States.** Three process wait states are associated with memory management. For each there is a single queue that includes resident and outswapped processes. In addition, several resource waits, described in Section 13.4.3.3.1, are associated with memory management. Memory management wait states are discussed in more detail in Chapter 18.

A process enters the page fault (PFW) wait state when code running in its context refers to a page that is not in physical memory. While the page read is in progress, the process is placed into the PFW state. Completion of the page read, AST queuing, or process deletion can cause a PFW process to become COM or COMO, depending upon its PCB$V_RES bit value when the satisfying condition occurs. If AST queuing makes the process computable before the page read completes, when the process reexecutes the instruction that caused the page fault, it is placed back into a page fault wait.

Usually a process enters the free page (FPG) wait state when it requests a physical page to be added to its working set but there are no free pages to be allocated from the free page list. In addition, a process requesting a lock through the Enqueue Lock Request ($ENQ) system service can be placed into this wait state when the lock ID table is full and a page of physical memory to extend it cannot be allocated. This state is essentially a resource wait that ends when the supply of free pages is replenished through modified page writing, working set trimming, process outswapping, or virtual address space deletion. When a physical page becomes available, all FPG processes are made COM or COMO. The first process to execute allocates the page. If the free page list is empty as a result, when the other processes execute, they are placed back into a FPG wait.

A process enters the collided page (COLPG) wait state when more than one process causes page faults on the same shared page at the same time. The initial faulting process enters the PFW state, while the second and succeeding processes enter the COLPG state. All COLPG processes are made COM or COMO when the read operation completes.

13.4.3.3   **Miscellaneous Wait State.** A process in the miscellaneous wait (MWAIT) state waits for the availability of a depleted system resource or job quota or a locked mutex. The contents of the field PCB$L_EFWM identify the entity for which the process waits:

- ▶ A small positive integer identifies a system resource.
- ▶ The system virtual address of the process's JIB specifies that the process is waiting for a job quota.
- ▶ The system virtual address of a mutex specifies that the process is waiting for that mutex.

There is a single MWAIT queue for resident and outswapped processes.

13.4.3.3.1   *System Resource Miscellaneous Waits.* A process may enter a resource wait if a resource it needs is not available. Common examples are the depletion of nonpaged pool or an already full mailbox. The process becomes computable when an executive routine declares the resource available. AST enqueuing makes the process computable, temporarily at least (see Section 13.6.1.5).

Table 13.2 lists the resources associated with the MWAIT state. Their symbolic values are defined by the $RSNDEF macro. System utilities such as SDA, MONITOR, and the DCL command SHOW SYSTEM display the state of a process in a resource wait using one of the mnemonic names in this table.

The system global SCH$GL_RESMASK summarizes the system resources for which processes in the MWAIT state are currently waiting. For example, bit 3 corresponds to RSN$_NPDYNMEM. When set, it indicates that one or more PCBs are in the MWAIT queue waiting for nonpaged pool to become available.

When an executive routine releases a resource for which processes might be waiting, it invokes SCH$RAVAIL, in module MUTEX, to declare the resource available for any waiting processes. SCH$RAVAIL tests and clears the bit in SCH$GL_RESMASK corresponding to the resource. If the bit was set, the routine scans the MWAIT queue for processes whose PCB$L_EFWM matches the available resource. For any such process it finds, it makes the process COM or COMO, as appropriate.

RWAST is a general-purpose resource wait used primarily when the wait is expected to be satisfied by the queuing or delivery of an AST to the process. There is no concrete resource corresponding to the name RSN$_ASTWAIT. The $QIO system service can place a process into this resource wait when the process is not allowed to issue another buffered or direct I/O request until one completes. Another use of RSN$_ASTWAIT is to wait for all the I/O requests on a channel to complete after the process has requested the

Table 13.2   Types of Resource MWAIT State

Resource Wait Name	Mnemonic	Symbolic Name	Number
AST wait (wait for system or special kernel mode AST)	RWAST	RSN$_ASTWAIT	1
Mailbox full	RWMBX	RSN$_MAILBOX	2
Nonpaged dynamic memory	RWNPG	RSN$_NPDYNMEM	3
Page file full	RWPFF	RSN$_PGFILE	4
Paged dynamic memory	RWPAG	RSN$_PGDYNMEM	5
Breakthrough [1]	RWBRK	RSN$_BRKTHRU	6
Image activation lock [1]	RWIMG	RSN$_IACLOCK	7
Job pooled quota [1]	RWQUO	RSN$_JQUOTA	8
Lock identifier [1]	RWLCK	RSN$_LOCKID	9
Swap file space [1]	RWSWP	RSN$_SWPFILE	10
Modified page list empty	RWMPE	RSN$_MPLEMPTY	11
Modified page writer busy	RWMPB	RSN$_MPWBUSY	12
Distributed lock manager wait	RWSCS	RSN$_SCS	13
VMScluster transition	RWCLU	RSN$_CLUSTRAN	14
CPU capability	RWCAP	RSN$_CPUCAP	15
VMScluster server process	RWCSV	RSN$_CLUSRV	16
Reserved [1]	RWSNP	RSN$_SNAPSHOT	17
POSIX fork creation	PSXFR	RSN$_PSXFRK	18

[1] This resource wait is not currently used.

$DASSGN system service. A process about to be suspended or deleted waits for the RSN$_ASTWAIT resource until all its Files-11 XQP activity completes (see Chapter 8).

A process is placed into RWMBX wait when it has resource wait mode enabled and tries to write to a mailbox that is full or has insufficient buffer space.

A process is placed into RWNPG wait when it is unsuccessful in allocating nonpaged pool. With the expandability of nonpaged pool, this wait is relatively rare.

A process is placed into RWPAG wait when it is unsuccessful in allocating paged pool.

A process in RWMPE wait is waiting for the modified page writer to signal that it has flushed the modified page list. The only process placed into this wait is one running the OPCCRASH image, which forces a flush of the modified page list prior to stopping the system.

A process is placed into RWPFF wait when it faults a modified page with page file backing store out of its working set and the associated page file has not yet been initialized.

A process that faults a modified page out of its working set can be placed into RWMPB wait when either of the following is true:

- ► The modified page list contains more pages than the SYSGEN parameter MPW_WAITLIMIT.
- ► The modified page list contains more pages than the SYSGEN parameter MPW_LOWAITLIMIT and the modified page writer is active, writing modified pages.

Generally, this resource wait occurs on a system whose modified page list has grown faster than it could be written. A process in such a wait becomes computable when enough modified pages have been written so that there are MPW_LOWAITLIMIT or fewer pages left on the list.

Chapter 18 contains further details on RWPFF and RWMPB waits.

The lock manager uses RWSCS to stall the execution of a process on a VMScluster node when the lock manager must wait for a response from a remote system that has information about a particular lock resource.

A process that issues any lock requests on any node of a VMScluster in transition (that is, while a node is being added or removed) is placed into RWCLU wait until the VMScluster membership stabilizes.

A computable process that requires one or more CPU capabilities that cannot all be satisfied by a single active member of the SMP system is placed into RWCAP wait (see Section 13.5).

There is a maximum number of outstanding transfer requests from one VMScluster node to a remote node's cluster server process. When this limit has been reached and a process requests a service that would initiate another such transfer, the process is placed into RWCSV wait until transfer requests complete.

The resource wait PSXFR is implemented to support the layered POSIX subsystem. It provides synchronization between a parent and child process during a POSIX fork operation.

The Set Resource Wait Mode ($SETRWM) system service can cause a subsequent system service to return an error status rather than placing the process into the MWAIT state. The $SETRWM system service sets the PCB$V_SSRWAIT bit in PCB$L_STS. Disabling resource wait affects many directly requested operations (such as I/O requests or timer requests) but has no effect on allocation requests by the system on behalf of the user. Although a process can respond to a depleted resource error from a system service call or an RMS request, it has no means of reacting to a similar error in case of an unexpected event such as a page fault. For example, when the page fault service routine is unable to allocate an I/O request packet for a page read, it

places the process into an MWAIT wait regardless of the value of PCB$V_
SSRWAIT.

13.4.3.3.2   *Mutex Miscellaneous Waits.* A system routine that accesses data structures protected by a mutex places a process into the MWAIT state if the requested mutex ownership cannot be granted. Thus, the mutex wait state indicates a locked resource and not necessarily a depleted one. When the mutex is unlocked, each process waiting to lock that mutex is made COM or COMO to repeat its attempt to lock the mutex. AST queuing makes a mutex-waiting process computable only temporarily; the IPL at which the process is waited is 2, blocking the AST delivery interrupt. The process repeats its attempt to lock the mutex, and if it is locked, the process is placed back into a wait.

Chapter 9 lists the names of mutexes whose addresses can be stored in PCB$L_EFWM and describes the mutex lock and unlock routines. System utilities such as SDA, MONITOR, and the DCL command SHOW SYSTEM display the state of a process waiting for a mutex as MUTEX.

13.4.3.3.3   *Job Quota Miscellaneous Waits.* Another type of miscellaneous wait is a wait for a depleted job quota. Currently, there are two job quotas for which a process may have to wait:

> ► Buffered I/O byte count quota—used in a large number of ways, including I/O requests buffered in nonpaged pool, temporary mailboxes, and window control blocks
> ► Timer queue entry (TQE) quota—used for timer requests and common event flag cluster creation

When a job has one or more processes in such a wait, the field JIB$L_FLAGS has a bit set to indicate each job quota for which processes in that job are waiting. Bit 0, when set, means that one or more processes are waiting for JIB$L_BYTCNT. Bit 1, when set, means that one or more processes are waiting for TQE quota.

When another process in the job returns one of these quotas, the corresponding bit is checked to see if there is any waiting process. If there is, the waiting process is made computable to repeat its attempt to charge against the job quota.

A process in a job quota wait has the address of its JIB in PCB$L_EFWM. System utilities such as SDA, MONITOR, and the DCL command SHOW SYSTEM display the state of a process waiting for a jobwide resource as MUTEX.

13.5   **CAPABILITIES AND AFFINITY**

A capability represents a CPU attribute that a given process requires in order to execute. Generally a capability is a hardware feature. In an SMP system, a process's requirement for a particular capability may limit its execution to a subset of the available processors. For example, a process might require the capability CPB$V_PRIMARY and thus only be able to execute on the primary processor.

Affinity is the requirement that a process execute on a specific processor of an SMP system. OpenVMS provides for both explicit and implicit affinity. A process must explicitly request explicit affinity and must explicitly dismiss it. Explicit affinity might allow processes to be segregated by CPU. In contrast, a process acquires implicit affinity for a processor when there are advantages to its continuing execution on that processor. For example, a process that executed on a CPU with a large physical memory cache might have data still cached if it were placed back into execution on that CPU. Or a process placed back into execution on the same CPU on which it last executed might have process-private TB entries still cached.

Each processor's per-CPU database field CPU$L_CAPABILITY describes its set of capabilities. When a new CPU joins the SMP system, its capability mask is copied from the system default one, SCH$GL_DEFAULT_CPU_CAP. The default CPU capabilities are as follows:

▶ CPB$V_RUN, when set, means the CPU can schedule processes. The run capability is removed from a processor by the image that implements the DCL command STOP/CPU.
▶ CPB$V_QUORUM, when set, means that the CPU (or the entire SMP system) is an active member of a VMScluster that has quorum. The VMScluster connection manager removes the quorum capability from every cluster member when quorum has been lost and restores it when quorum is regained. Because most processes are created requiring this capability, removing this capability from a CPU blocks the execution of most processes. Certain processes that take part in the cluster transition do not require this capability and continue to run.

The 32-longword array SCH$AL_CPU_CAP, indexed by CPU ID, collects that information for all CPUs, simplifying a search for a CPU with a set of particular capabilities. Each set bit in a CPU's longword represents a capability of that CPU. The capability of being primary is set at system initialization in the primary processor's capability field and entered in the SCH$AL_CPU_CAP array.

The routines SCH$ADD_CPU_CAP and SCH$REMOVE_CPU_CAP, both in module CAPABILITY, provide for dynamic changes to CPU capabilities. The contents of SCH$GL_CAPABILITY_SEQUENCE indicate to which generation the data in SCH$AL_CPU_CAP belongs; whenever the data changes by the addition or removal of a CPU capability, SCH$GL_CAPABILITY_SEQUENCE is incremented. Keeping track of the generation enables processes with capability constraints to detect changes in the set of processors available to meet those constraints.

Fields in each process's PCB describe its current and permanent capability requirements and affinity.

PCB$L_CAPABILITY and PCB$L_PERMANENT_CAPABILITY are the current and permanent capability requirements. When a process is created, the permanent capability mask is copied from the system default one, SCH$GL_DEFAULT_PROCESS_CAP, currently defined so as to require that the process execute on a CPU with quorum and the run capability. The routines SCH$REQUIRE_CAPABILITY and SCH$RELEASE_CAPABILITY, both in module CAPABILITY, provide for dynamic changes to process requirements. These routines initialize the target process's PCB$L_CURRENT_AFFINITY as a mask with bits set to represent the CPUs that satisfy the capability requirements. These are the CPUs on which the process can execute. The routines also copy the current value of SCH$GL_CAPABILITY_SEQUENCE to PCB$L_CAPABILITY_SEQ for future use as a validity check on the current affinity mask.

Two process capability mask bits represent affinity:

► CPB$V_IMPLICIT_AFFINITY, when set, means that the process has acquired implicit affinity for a particular CPU.

► CPB$V_EXPLICIT_AFFINITY, when set, means that the process has acquired explicit affinity for a particular CPU.

SCH$REQUIRE_CAPABILITY can be called to request that a particular process acquire current or permanent explicit affinity for a particular CPU. The procedure stores a new value with only one bit set in the affected process's PCB$L_CURRENT_AFFINITY and stores the CPU ID of the processor in PCB$L_AFFINITY. If the request was for permanent affinity, it also stores the CPU ID in PCB$L_PERMANENT_CPU_AFFINITY and sets the capability bit in PCB$L_PERMANENT_CAPABILITY. The processor's CPU$L_HARDAFF is incremented as a count of processes that have explicit affinity for it.

Following are examples of executive routines that employ capabilities and explicit affinity:

► The Get Environment Variable ($GETENV) system service must run on the primary processor when it calls a console subsystem procedure to get the current value of a particular environment variable (see Chapters 33 and 39).

► The undocumented Diagnose ($DIAGNOSE) system service enables a process with DIAGNOSE privilege to acquire or remove explicit affinity to a specified CPU or to whichever CPU is primary. Use of this service is reserved to Digital; any other use is unsupported.

- The Set Time ($SETIME) system service must run on the primary processor when it reads and writes the battery-backed watch.
- The routine IOC$LAST_CHAN, in module IOSUBNPAG, entered when a process deassigns its last channel to a device, tests whether the device's registers can only be accessed from a limited set of processors. If so, the routine acquires explicit affinity for the primary processor, which is always presumed to be a member of every device's affinity set. Chapter 37 describes the concept of device affinity set in more detail.
- The interval timer interrupt service routine runs on each SMP member but performs system timekeeping functions only on the primary processor. It tests the low bit of the current processor's per-CPU database field CPU$L_CAPABILITY to determine whether it is running on the primary.

The procedure SCH$ACQUIRE_AFFINITY can be called to request that a target process acquire implicit affinity for a particular CPU. The routine stores a new value for PCB$L_CURRENT_AFFINITY with only one bit set and the CPU ID in PCB$L_AFFINITY. It sets CPB$V_IMPLICIT_AFFINITY in the target process's PCB$L_CAPABILITY. When a process with implicit affinity is selected for execution, if its affinity is not for the current CPU, the scheduler returns the process to the compute queue and attempts to select a process to run whose priority is high enough so that it could not be preempted by the process with implicit affinity.

Potentially, the process can be skipped for execution in this manner repeatedly up to the number in PCB$L_AFFINITY_SKIP, which is decremented at each failed attempt. PCB$L_AFFINITY_SKIP is initialized from the SYSGEN parameter AFFINITY_SKIP, whose default value is 2. When PCB$L_AFFINITY_SKIP reaches 0 or whenever the scheduler cannot find an alternative process that can execute on this CPU, it breaks implicit affinity. That is, a process's having implicit affinity for one CPU is not a compelling reason to leave another CPU idle. If PCB$L_AFFINITY_CALLBACK is nonzero, the scheduler calls the specified procedure to perform any processor-specific cleanup associated with breaking affinity. The procedure is called with the SCHED spinlock held, at IPL$_SCHED, and with two arguments, the address of the PCB and the ID of the CPU.

Currently, no use is made of implicit affinity.

At image rundown, a process's capability mask is restored from its permanent capability mask and affinity from the permanent affinity. Explicit affinity counts in the per-CPU database are adjusted. If there is any change in required capabilities or affinity, the image rundown routine requests an IPL 3 interrupt for the scheduler to determine where the process should run.

At deletion of a process with explicit affinity, the CPU$L_HARDAFF field of its associated processor is decremented.

13.6	**SCHEDULING DYNAMICS**

In general, on an OpenVMS system in equilibrium, the available processors execute the highest priority COM processes. A number of events can alter this equilibrium and require that the scheduler reschedule: that is, select another process to run and swap its context with that of the current process, taking the current process out of execution and placing the new one into execution.

The following are the principal events that require rescheduling:

► A current process goes into a wait state.
► A current process reaches the end of its quantum, and there is another COM process of equal or higher priority.
► A current process requests explicit rescheduling through the Initiate Rescheduling Interrupt ($RESCHED) system service.
► A current process changes its priority, and there is a higher priority COM process.
► There is no longer a match between the capabilities required by a current process and the processor on which it is executing.
► A system event alters the scheduling state of a noncurrent process to COM, and its priority permits it to preempt a current process.

Figures 13.12, 13.13, and 13.15 show the relations among the routines involved in these events. The sections that follow describe the events and the routines that handle them. Section 13.7 describes the rescheduling interrupt.

13.6.1	**Placing a Current Process into a Wait State**

When a process directly or indirectly requests a system operation for which it must wait, the process is placed into a wait state. Placing a process into a wait state consists of making the associated scheduler database changes and saving the process's hardware context. Saving the process's hardware context requires saving integer registers on its kernel stack to complete the canonical kernel stack (see Section 13.2.2) and possibly saving floating-point registers before swapping process context. Although this precise stack arrangement requires MACRO-64 routines, MACRO-32 routines can update the scheduler database.

Several routines update the scheduler database so as to place a process into a particular wait state; several form the canonical kernel stack and transfer control to the scheduling code that performs the actual context switch; and several perform all three functions. Which of these is used depends upon

► The mode in which the process is to wait
► The wait state into which the process is to be placed

To illustrate the necessary steps, this section describes one particular sequence, which waits a process in an outer mode.

When a process requests a system service that must place the process into a wait for some event or resource before it can complete the request, the service procedure typically waits the process in the mode from which the service was requested. As a result, the process will be able to receive ASTs for that mode and more privileged ones. In order to wait the process in the outer mode, the service procedure must return the status SS$_WAIT_CALLERS_MODE to its caller, the change mode dispatcher, requesting that it clean up the stack and wait the process. (Each system service that can return this status must have been described as such when it was loaded. The description further specifies whether the service is to be reexecuted when it is placed back into execution.)

Figure 13.11 shows some of the main steps in the sequence leading to this type of process wait. The numbers in the figure correspond to those in the following list:

① The process requests the system service by calling its system service transfer routine.

② The transfer routine executes a CALL_PAL CHMK instruction, generating an exception. The exception service routine for CHMK exceptions is the change mode dispatcher, EXE$CMODKRNL in module SYSTEM_SERVICE_DISPATCHER. The exception frame created by this exception forms the first part of a potential canonical kernel stack.

③ Determining that the service may return SS$_WAIT_CALLERS_MODE, the change mode dispatcher saves the service arguments on the kernel stack before calling the service procedure.

④ When the service procedure determines that the process must wait, it first acquires the SCHED spinlock and then typically calls SCH$WAIT_PROC, in module SCHED_ROUTINES, to update the scheduler database.

⑤ SCH$WAIT_PROC is entered in process context and with the SCHED spinlock held. Its arguments specify the address of the PCB of the current process and the address of the wait queue into which the PCB is to be inserted. It takes the following steps:

   a. It changes the process scheduling state to that in the WQH$L_WQSTATE field of the specified wait queue header, inserts the PCB into the wait queue, and increments WQH$L_WQCNT to show the addition of a process to the queue.

   b. It charges the SYSGEN parameter IOTA against the process quantum, as described in Section 13.6.2. It also adjusts PHD$L_TIMREF by the value of IOTA. PHD$L_TIMREF and the process quantum must be adjusted together for automatic working set limit adjustment to be responsive (see Chapter 19).

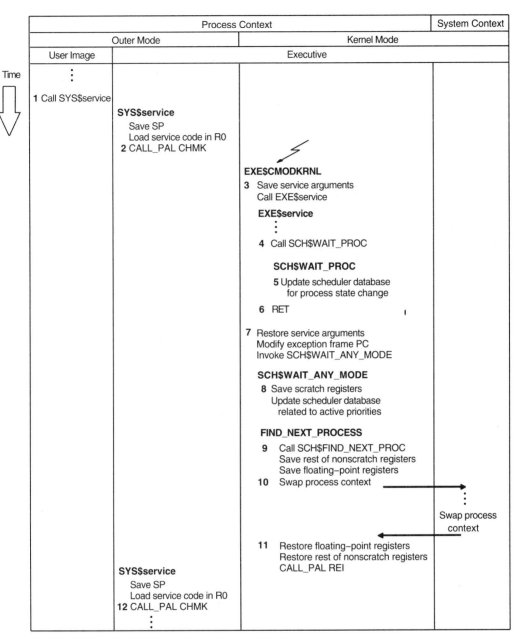

Figure 13.11
Process Wait Sequence

c. SCH$WAIT_PROC copies the contents of the system global EXE$GL_ ABSTIM_TICS, the system time in soft ticks, to PCB$L_WAITIME, to record the time at which the process began its wait. If the process remains in a wait state for long, it will become a candidate for working set shrinkage and possibly outswapping (see Chapter 20).

d. It returns to the service procedure.

At this point, although the scheduler database shows the process as being in a wait state, the service procedure and the code described in the following steps continue to run in the process's hardware context until a CALL_ PAL SWPCTX instruction is executed.

⑥ Still holding the SCHED spinlock, the service procedure returns the status SS$_WAIT_CALLERS_MODE to the change mode dispatcher.

⑦ In response to that status, the change mode dispatcher tests whether this is a service procedure that is to be reexecuted after the wait condition is satisfied. (Most service procedures that return this status must be reexecuted.) If so, it restores the argument registers (which may have been overwritten during service execution) from the kernel stack and subtracts 12 from the PC in the exception frame so that it contains the address of the beginning of the system service transfer routine.

In either case, the change mode dispatcher then invokes SCH$WAIT_ ANY_MODE, in module SCHEDULER. Chapter 7 describes the change mode dispatcher in more detail.

⑧ SCH$WAIT_ANY_MODE is entered with the SCHED spinlock still held and nothing on the kernel stack except the CHMK exception stack frame. It takes the following steps:

a. It reserves space on the stack for all the scratch integer registers but saves only the system service argument registers. The contents of the others are irrelevant because the system service was entered through a procedure call, across which scratch integer register contents are never preserved.

b. It tests at what IPL the process is to be waited and, if it is less than 2, reads the process's ASTSR and ASTEN registers to determine whether a deliverable AST has been queued to the process but not yet delivered. This test prevents an AST event that should take the process out of its wait from being ignored. If a deliverable AST has been queued, SCH$WAIT_ANY_MODE reports an AST queuing event to SCH$REPORT_EVENT (see Section 13.6.5), which changes the process's scheduling state to COM.

c. It gets the address of the current process's PCB and its current priority from the per-CPU database.

d. It clears the bit representing the CPU's ID in the longword corresponding to the priority in the array at SCH$AL_CPU_PRIORITY.

e. If there are no other processes at this priority current on any CPU,

it clears the bit corresponding to that priority in SCH$GQ_ACTIVE_
PRIORITY.

    f. At this point, SCH$WAIT_ANY_MODE and the rescheduling inter-
    rupt service routine converge, at label FIND_NEXT_PROCESS.

⑨ The rescheduling interrupt service routine selects the next process to
execute and saves the rest of the nonprivileged hardware context of the
process being waited. The canonical kernel stack is now complete.

⑩ It executes the instruction CALL_PAL SWPCTX. Section 13.7.1 describes the
selection of a new process and the context swap.

⑪ Later, when the process's wait is ended, it is placed back into execution in the outer mode at the beginning of the system service transfer
routine.

⑫ The process reexecutes the transfer routine and then reenters the service
procedure.

Procedures that update the scheduler database to reflect a state change for
a process being placed into a wait include

▶ SCH$WAIT_PROC, in module SCHED_ROUTINES, intended for a process
to be placed into a specified wait in an outer mode

▶ SCH$RESOURCE_WAIT_SETUP, in module MUTEX, intended for a pro-
cess to be placed into an MWAIT for a specified system resource to be
available

▶ MMG$RESRCWAIT, in module PAGEFAULT, intended for a page faulting
process to be placed into an MWAIT for a specified system resource to be
available

▶ MMG$PGFLTWAIT, in module PAGEFAULT, intended for a page faulting
process to be placed into a specified wait

The actions to complete a canonical kernel stack and initiate context swap
are centralized in several routines in module SCHEDULER:

▶ SCH$WAIT_ANY_MODE—Wait a process in the access mode specified by
the PS in its interrupt/exception stack frame.

▶ SCH$WAIT_KERNEL_MODE—Wait a process in kernel mode using the
current PS and caller's return address as the PC.

▶ SCH$WAIT_KERNEL_MODE_PS—Wait a process in kernel mode using a
specified PS and caller's return address as the PC.

As shown in Figure 13.12, those routines are invoked by procedures such
as the following:

▶ EXE$WAIT, in module SYSWAIT, to place a process requesting the $WAIT-
FR, $WFLOR, or $WFLAND system service into an LEF or CEF wait (see
Chapter 10)

▶ EXE$HIBER, in module SYSPCNTRL, to place a process into a HIB wait
(see Chapter 14)

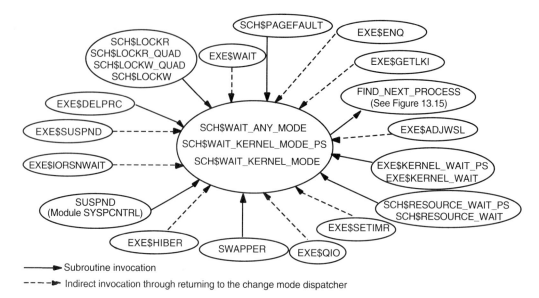

Figure 13.12
Paths Leading to a Process Wait

- ▶ EXE$SUSPND and SUSPND, in module SYSPCNTRL, to place a process into a SUSP wait (see Chapter 14)
- ▶ Various other system service procedures that return the status SS$_WAIT_CALLERS_MODE to the change mode dispatcher
- ▶ Swapper process main loop, in module SWAPPER, to place the swapper into a HIB wait state when it has no work to do
- ▶ SCH$PAGEFAULT, in module SCHEDULER, to place a process into PFW and other memory management related waits
- ▶ EXE$KERNEL_WAIT_PS, in module MUTEX, to place a process into an MWAIT for JIB byte count quota
- ▶ The various mutex lock routines, in module MUTEX, to place a process into an MWAIT for a mutex (see Chapter 9)
- ▶ SCH$RESOURCE_WAIT and SCH$RESOURCE_WAIT_PS, in module MUTEX, to place a process into an MWAIT for a system resource

One of the responsibilities of all the procedures that place a process into a wait is to ensure that the process can reenter the appropriate wait state, if necessary, after the process is placed back into execution as the result of AST delivery. (Recall that AST enqueuing makes a process in most wait states computable.) These routines therefore determine values for the PC and PS at which the process is to wait. These values are stored in the interrupt/exception stack frame, at the bottom of the canonical kernel stack, that is used when the process executes a CALL_PAL REI instruction after being placed back into execution.

The PC and PS control which thread of execution will run, and its access mode and IPL. Its access mode affects AST delivery: only ASTs equally or more privileged can be delivered. If the access mode is kernel, then the wait IPL is also significant: an IPL of 2 blocks AST delivery interrupts. Several different techniques for placing a process into a wait are used, depending on the particular wait state being entered.

13.6.1.1 **Context for HIB Wait States.** When a process enters a HIB wait state, the change mode dispatcher uses the system service transfer routine CHMK exception PS as the wait PS. Consequently, the process waits in the access mode in which the system service was issued.

For the wait PC, the change mode dispatcher subtracts 12 from the CHMK exception PC in the exception stack frame so that it contains the address of the beginning of the system service transfer routine. Chapter 7 contains more information about system service transfer routines and change mode exceptions.

If an AST is delivered to a process in such a wait state, when the AST exits, the AST delivery interrupt service routine's CALL_PAL REI returns control to the system service transfer routine.

13.6.1.2 **Context for LEF or CEF Wait State.** The OpenVMS AXP event flag wait system services are mode of caller services. These services can check whether a local event flag is set without the overhead of changing to kernel mode. If the flag is clear, each service must request a kernel mode form of the service to recheck the state of the flag and wait the process if necessary.

When a process enters an LEF wait state, the change mode dispatcher does not modify the exception stack frame. Consequently, the process is waited in such a way that it will be placed back into execution within the mode of caller service at the outer mode, just after the request for the kernel mode form of the service.

Checking the state of common event flags requires kernel mode. When these services are requested to wait for common flags, they must each request a kernel mode form of the service to locate the flags, check them, and wait the process if necessary.

When a process enters a CEF wait state, the change mode dispatcher subtracts 12 from the PC in the exception stack frame so that when the process is placed back into execution, it will rerequest the kernel mode form of the service. Chapter 10 describes these services in more detail.

13.6.1.3 **Context for Memory Management Wait States.** SCH$PAGEFAULT, in module SCHEDULER, the page fault exception service routine (see Chapter 18) places processes into the three wait states associated with memory management. This routine uses the PC and PS in the page fault exception stack frame as the wait PC and PS. Because the PS reflects the access mode in which the page fault occurred, ASTs can be delivered for that and all inner access modes.

After an AST executes in such a process, the process executes the faulting instruction again. If the reason for the fault has been removed (a free page became available or the page read completed) while the AST was being delivered or was executing, the process simply continues with its execution. If the situation that caused the process to page fault still exists, the process reincurs the page fault and will be placed back into a memory management wait state. Note that a process that was initially in a PFW state for a shared page could be placed into a COLPG state by such a sequence of events.

13.6.1.4 **Context for a SUSP Wait.** A process is suspended as the result of executing an AST. The access mode of the AST can be supervisor or kernel mode, depending on which form of suspend is requested. The default is supervisor mode. While a process is suspended in kernel mode, the wait PC is an address in the kernel AST that caused the process to enter the suspend state. The saved PS indicates kernel mode and IPL 0. ASTs can be queued, but not delivered, to a process suspended in kernel mode. That is, when an AST is queued to a kernel mode suspended process, the AST event is ignored.

While a process is suspended in supervisor mode, the saved PC is an address in the $SUSPND system service transfer routine, requested from within the supervisor mode AST, which remains active. AST enqueuing makes the process computable. When the process is placed into execution, a kernel or executive mode AST can be executed, but a user or supervisor mode AST cannot: the new AST control block remains queued, and the interrupt is dismissed. In either case, a CALL_PAL REI instruction is executed, which causes control to return to the wait PC. It repeats the system service request and repeats the test that suspended the process. If the process has not been resumed, it is suspended again.

13.6.1.5 **Context for an MWAIT Wait.** When a process is placed into a wait for a mutex, its saved PC is one of the lock routines in module MUTEX. Its saved PS indicates kernel mode and IPL 2, making it impossible for a process in an MWAIT state waiting for a mutex to receive ASTs.

A process can also be placed into an MWAIT state while waiting for an arbitrary system resource. In this case, the caller of SCH$RESOURCE_WAIT or SCH$RESOURCE_WAIT_PS determines the wait PC and PS.

A process with resource wait mode enabled can be placed into an MWAIT state while waiting for a job quota, either byte count or TQE quota.

In the case of byte count, the routine EXE$DEBIT_BYTCNT, in module EXSUBROUT, checks whether the job has sufficient byte count quota for a particular request. If it does not, EXE$DEBIT_BYTCNT calls EXE$KERNEL_WAIT_PS to place the process into a wait with kernel access mode and IPL equal to that at entry to EXE$DEBIT_BYTCNT. Typically, this routine and its subentry points are invoked from device driver preprocessing routines at IPL 2, and thus the process is waited at IPL 2. The wait PC is an address within EXE$DEBIT_BYTCNT that repeats the test.

In the case of TQE quota, the process is placed into a wait similar to that for HIB and CEF—its wait PC is the address of the CHMK instruction in the system service transfer routine and its PS is the change mode exception PS, so that the process waits in the access mode from which it requested the service.

13.6.1.6 **Proactive Memory Reclamation from Periodically Waking Processes.** The routines EXE$HIBER and EXE$WAIT are responsible for implementing the policy of proactive memory reclamation from periodically waking processes. The policy is enabled when the low bit of SYSGEN parameter MMG_CTLFLAGS is set, as it is by default. If enabled, the proactive memory reclamation mechanism becomes active only when memory is low. Each of the services checks whether the mechanism is active, whether the process has a normal priority, and whether it has accumulated 30 seconds of wait time (PCB$L_ACC_WAITIME) since the last time its execution history was checked. If all the conditions are met, each procedure invokes EXE$CHK_WAIT_BHVR, in module RSE.

EXE$CHK_WAIT_BHVR takes the following steps:

1. It checks whether the process has any outstanding direct I/O and, if so, returns immediately.
2. It checks whether the process has a high ratio of wait time to execution time since this routine was last called to check this process. If the process's accumulated CPU time is at least 1 percent of its wait time, the routine continues with step 5.
3. It tests whether the process has disabled automatic working set adjustment (PCB$V_DISAWS in PCB$L_STS is set) or whether the executive has temporarily blocked changes to its working set (PHD$V_NO_WS_CHNG in PHD$L_FLAGS is set). If either is true, EXE$CHK_WAIT_BHVR continues with step 5.
4. Holding the MMG spinlock, it tries to reduce the process's working set size by 25 percent. It does not alter the working set limit.
5. It copies the accumulated CPU time from PHD$L_CPUTIME to PCB$L_CPUTIME_REF for use the next time the routine is executed. It clears PCB$L_ACC_WAITIME and returns.

13.6.2 **Quantum Expiration**

The SYSGEN parameter QUANTUM defines the size of the time slice for the round-robin scheduling of normal processes. The quantum also determines, for most process states, the minimum amount of time a process remains in memory after an inswap operation, but it is not an absolute guarantee of memory residence. The swapper's use of the initial quantum flag in selecting an outswap candidate is described in Chapter 20. The value of QUANTUM is the number of 10-millisecond intervals (soft ticks) in the quantum. The default QUANTUM value of 20, therefore, produces a scheduling interval of 200 milliseconds.

A process's quantum is expressed as a negative number of soft ticks. After each 10-millisecond interval, the interval timer interrupt service routine increments the PHD$L_QUANT field in the current process's PHD. When this value becomes zero or positive, the interrupt service routine requests a software timer interrupt. The software timer interrupt service routine signals a quantum-end event by invoking the subroutine SCH$QEND, in module RSE.

An additional deduction from quantum is governed by the special SYSGEN parameter IOTA. Its default value is 2, representing two soft ticks. This value is charged against PHD$L_QUANT each time a process enters a wait state. This mechanism ensures that all processes experience quantum-end events with some regularity. Processes that are compute-bound experience quantum end as a result of using a certain amount of CPU time. Processes that are I/O-bound experience quantum end as a result of performing a reasonable number of I/O requests.

The routine SCH$QEND is executed whenever a current process reaches quantum end. It runs on the same CPU as the process, as part of the software timer interrupt service routine.

Its first action is to enable or disable alignment fault reporting for the current process (see Chapter 39). After acquiring the SCHED spinlock, its subsequent minimum actions are to reset the field PHD$L_QUANT to the full quantum value; clear the initial quantum flag, PCB$V_INQUAN in the field PCB$L_STS; and record EXE$GL_ABSTIM_TICS in PCB$L_ONQTIME. It performs those actions for both real-time and normal processes.

For a normal process, SCH$QEND takes the following additional steps:

1. SCH$QEND updates PCB$L_PIXHIST, the pixscan history summary longword (see Section 13.6.7), by shifting it left one bit.

2. SCH$QEND tests whether a CPU time limit has been imposed and, if so, compares the process's limit field, PHD$L_CPULIM, against its accumulated CPU time, PHD$L_CPUTIM, to determine whether that limit has been reached. If the CPU limit has been reached, each access mode has an interval of time to clean up or run down before the image exits and the process is deleted. The size of the warning interval for each access mode is defined by the SYSGEN parameter EXTRACPU, which has a default value of 10 seconds.

3. SCH$QEND checks whether automatic working set limit adjustment is enabled and appropriate for this process. If both are true, the limit of

the process working set list may be expanded or contracted. Chapter 19 describes automatic working set limit adjustment.

4. If there is an inswap candidate (if SCH$GQ_COMOQS is nonzero, indicating at least one nonempty COMO state queue), SCH$QEND sets the current priority of the process to its base priority. It changes, as appropriate, CPUL_CUR_PRI, SCHAL_CPU_PRIORITY, and SCH$GQ_ACTIVE_PRIORITY.

   Furthermore, it invokes SCH$SWPWAKE, in module RSE, to awaken the swapper. As a computable, resident, real-time process of software priority 16, the swapper is likely to be the next process scheduled.

5. SCH$QEND checks whether there is a COM process of equal or higher priority. If not, this process will continue to execute. If its current priority is not equal to its base priority, SCH$QEND decrements its current priority, making the appropriate changes to CPUL_CUR_PRI, SCHAL_CPU_PRIORITY, and SCH$GQ_ACTIVE_PRIORITY. This decrement is equivalent to the one made every time a process is placed into execution. SCH$QEND then releases the SCHED spinlock and returns to the software timer interrupt service routine.

   This behavior saves unnecessary context switches when this process continues to be the best candidate to execute.

6. If there is a COM process of equal or higher priority, SCH$QEND requests an IPL 3 rescheduling interrupt and returns. When the interrupt is granted, the current process will be taken out of execution and another selected to execute.

In Figure 13.15, SCH$QEND is shown as a requestor of a rescheduling interrupt.

13.6.3 Changing the Priority of a Current Process

Several routines change the priority of a current process:

▶ SCH$QEND, when a normal process reaches quantum end and there is a COMO process

▶ SCH$QEND, when a normal process that is not yet at its base priority will continue to execute (see Section 13.6.2 for a description of quantum-end processing)

▶ EXE$SETPRI, in module SYSSETPRI, when a process requests the $SET-PRI system service (see Chapter 14)

▶ The mutex lock routines in module MUTEX, when a normal process locks a mutex and gets a temporary boost to priority 16

▶ SCH$UNLOCK and SCH$UNLOCK_QUAD, in module MUTEX, when a normal process unlocks a mutex and has its priority restored (see Chapter 9 for information on locking and unlocking mutexes)

▶ EXE$GETJPI, in module SYSGETJPI, when the target process's original priority is restored after a boost (see Chapter 39)

▶ EXE$RESCHED, in module SYSPARPRC, when a process requests the $RESCHED system service to lower its priority to its base and request a rescheduling interrupt (see Chapter 14)

The actions to change the priority of a current process are centralized in the routine SCH$CHANGE_CUR_PRIORITY, in module RSE. All the routines in the previous list except the first invoke SCH$CHANGE_CUR_PRIORITY. Figure 13.15 shows its invokers.

SCH$CHANGE_CUR_PRIORITY is entered at IPL$_SCHED and with the SCHED spinlock held. It can run in system context, invoked from SCH$QEND; in the context of the process whose priority is changing; or in the context of a process requesting the $SETPRI service on behalf of another process. Its arguments specify the address of the PCB of the target process, the one whose priority is to be changed; the address of the per-CPU database of its CPU; and the new priority.

SCH$CHANGE_CUR_PRIORITY takes the following steps:

1. It clears the bit corresponding to the CPU's ID in the longword corresponding to the priority in the array at SCH$AL_CPU_PRIORITY.

2. If there are no other processes at this priority current on any CPU, it clears the bit corresponding to that priority in SCH$GQ_ACTIVE_PRIORITY.

3. It copies the new priority to PCB$L_PRI and CPU$L_CUR_PRI.

4. It sets the bit corresponding to the CPU's ID in the longword corresponding to the priority in the array at SCH$AL_CPU_PRIORITY.

5. It sets the bit corresponding to the process's new priority in SCH$GQ_ACTIVE_PRIORITY.

6. It locates the least significant set bit in the quadword SCH$GQ_COM-QS. The located bit position indicates the highest priority nonempty computable resident state queue.

7. It compares the changed priority of the target process with that of the highest priority COM process. If the changed priority is higher or equal, SCH$CHANGE_CUR_PRIORITY returns.

8. Otherwise, it requests a rescheduling interrupt on the CPU on which the target process is current.

   • If SCH$CHANGE_CUR_PRIORITY and the target process are executing on the same CPU, this is simply an IPL 3 software interrupt request.

   • If the CPUs are different, SCH$CHANGE_CUR_PRIORITY requests an interprocessor interrupt on the other CPU so that the IPL 3 interrupt can be requested there. Chapter 37 describes interprocessor interrupts.

Clearly, this priority comparison can result in rescheduling when the priority of a current process is lowered. Moreover, under some circumstances, it could also result in rescheduling even when the priority of a current process is raised a small amount. Because preemption of a current process by a newly computable process requires a priority difference of PRIORITY_OFFSET + 1, a normal computable process might continue to execute despite the existence of a slightly higher priority process that had just become computable. Under these circumstances, if the current process were to raise its priority to a value less than that of the newly computable process, the current process would be rescheduled.

13.6.4 Capability Mismatch

This section describes how a mismatch in capability requirements can occur between a current process and the processor on which it is executing and how the mismatch is handled.

There are several routines that can affect process capability and affinity requirements and CPU capabilities so as to produce a mismatch.

SCH$ACQUIRE_AFFINITY, in module CAPABILITY, can be called to request that a current process acquire implicit affinity for a processor other than the one on which it is executing. If the process already has implicit affinity or has explicit affinity for a different CPU, the routine returns an error status. Otherwise, it performs the following steps:

1. It initializes PCB$L_AFFINITY_SKIP and sets the bit CPB$V_IMPLICIT_AFFINITY in PCB$L_CAPABILITY. It stores the procedure value of the routine to be called if implicit affinity is broken.
2. It stores the intended CPU ID in PCB$L_AFFINITY and tests whether the process is current.
3. If so, it compares PCB$L_AFFINITY to PCB$L_CPU_ID. If the two are different, SCH$ACQUIRE_AFFINITY requests a rescheduling interrupt. If the process is current on a different CPU than the one on which SCH$ACQUIRE_AFFINITY is executing, the routine requests an interprocessor interrupt so that the rescheduling interrupt is requested on the right CPU.

SCH$REMOVE_CPU_CAP, in module CAPABILITY, is called to remove a capability from one or all CPUs. It takes the following steps, looping through them if all CPUs are to be affected:

1. It clears the bit corresponding to the capability in the target CPU's per-CPU database field CPU$L_CAPABILITY and its longword in the SCH$AL_CPU_CAP array.
2. It increments SCH$GL_CAPABILITY_SEQUENCE to indicate a change in the capabilities of the active members of the SMP system.
3. It gets the address of the process current on that CPU from CPU$L_CURPCB and examines its capability mask.

4. If this capability is not required by the process current on the target CPU, the routine returns.

5. Otherwise, it requests a rescheduling interrupt, through an interprocessor interrupt if necessary.

SCH$REQUIRE_CAPABILITY, in module CAPABILITY, is called for a particular process to acquire a new capability requirement. It takes the following steps:

1. It acquires the SCHED spinlock, raising IPL to IPL$_SCHED.

2. It sets the capability requirement in the target process's PCB$L_CAPABILITY.

3. If a different explicit affinity is being requested than was previously set, the routine decrements CPU$L_HARDAFF of the current CPU and increments it for the new CPU. It stores the new CPU ID in PCB$L_AFFINITY and, if this is a request to make a permanent change, in PCB$L_PERMANENT_CPU_AFFINITY as well.

4. It stores the new capability mask in PCB$L_CAPABILITY and, if this is a request to alter permanent capabilities, in PCB$L_PERMANENT_CAPABILITY as well.

5. It invokes SCH$CALCULATE_AFFINITY to get the new current affinity mask.

6. It then checks whether the process is current.

7. If so, it tests whether the bit represented by PCB$L_CPU_ID is set in PCB$L_CURRENT_AFFINITY. If not, the routine requests a rescheduling interrupt, through an interprocessor interrupt if necessary.

8. It releases the SCHED spinlock.

EXE$RUNDWN, in module SYSRUNDWN, implements the Image Rundown ($RUNDWN) system service. It takes the following steps to reset the process's current capability requirements:

1. It acquires the SCHED spinlock, raising IPL to IPL$_SCHED.

2. It compares the process's current capability and affinity requirements with its permanent ones. If neither has changed, this part of rundown is complete. EXE$RUNDWN releases the SCHED spinlock and continues with other processing.

3. If there is an affinity change, then the routine decrements CPU$L_HARDAFF for the CPU to which the process currently has explicit affinity, if any, and increments it for the CPU to which the process has permanent affinity, if any.

4. It resets PCB$L_CAPABILITY and PCB$L_AFFINITY and clears PCB$L_CURRENT_AFFINITY and PCB$L_CAPABILITY_SEQ. It then requests a rescheduling interrupt so that the rescheduling interrupt service routine will determine where the process should continue execution.

5. EXE$RUNDWN releases the SCHED spinlock, restoring the previous IPL and permitting the rescheduling interrupt to be granted.

13.6.5   **Event Reporting**

This section describes how a process makes a transition to a COM state and how it preempts a current process.

A system event potentially changes the scheduling state of a process, making it computable, memory-resident, or outswapped. Examples of system events include the setting of an event flag for which a process is waiting, AST queuing, and page fault I/O completion. An executive routine aware of a system event that may take a process out of a wait state reports it on behalf of the affected process.

Holding the SCHED spinlock and running at IPL$_SCHED, such a routine invokes the RPTEVT macro, which generates the following code:

```
MOVL    #EVT$_event_name,R0
JSB     SCH$REPORT_EVENT
```

The event value identifies the event being reported.

SCH$REPORT_EVENT is responsible for making many of the process state transitions shown in Figure 13.10. Figure 13.13 shows the invokers of SCH$REPORT_EVENT and its entry points SCH$CHSE and SCH$CHSEP.

SCH$REPORT_EVENT is also passed the address of the PCB of the affected process and a priority increment class. If the event makes the process computable, the process may receive a priority boost, depending on the priority class, its current priority, and its base priority.

SCH$REPORT_EVENT and routines it invokes, all in module RSE, perform the following operations:

1. SCH$REPORT_EVENT indexes an internal table with the event value to determine whether the event is significant for the process, based on its current state.

   Each event has a bit mask defining which states this event can affect. The current state of the process is obtained from the PCB$L_STATE field.

   • For example, a wake event is only significant for processes that are hibernating (HIB or HIBO states).
   • An outswap event is only significant for the four states (COM, HIB, LEF, and SUSP) where a wait queue change is required.
   • The queuing of an AST is significant to all process states except kernel mode SUSP and SUSPO, COM, COMO, and CUR, and results in a transition to COM or COMO.

2. If the event is not significant for the current process state, the routine ignores the event and simply returns.

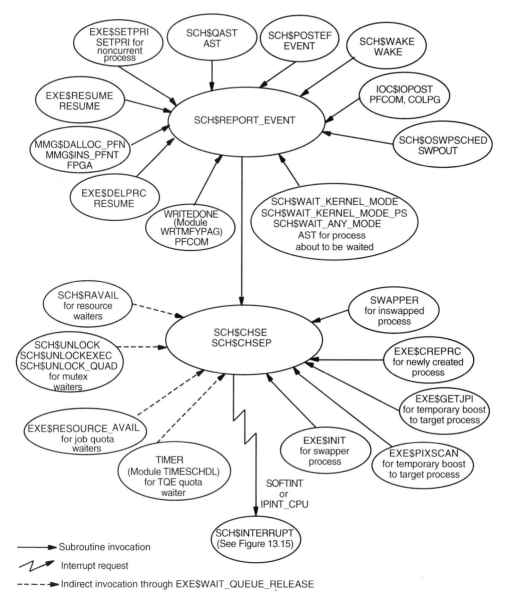

Figure 13.13
Paths to Event Reporting

3. For an outswap event producing an LEF to LEFO, HIB to HIBO, or SUSP to SUSPO transition, SCH$REPORT_EVENT removes the PCB of the process from the resident wait queue and inserts it into the corresponding outswapped wait queue. It adjusts the corresponding wait queue header count fields and PCB$L_STATE and returns.

4. For an outswap event producing a COM to COMO transition, SCH$RE-PORT_EVENT removes the PCB from the COM priority queue corresponding to PCB$L_PRI and inserts it into the corresponding COMO priority queue. It changes PCB$L_STATE. It clears the SCH$GQ_COMQS summary bit corresponding to PCB$L_PRI if that COM queue is now empty and unconditionally sets the corresponding SCH$GQ_COMOQS bit. It then returns.

5. For any transition that makes a process computable, SCH$REPORT_EVENT removes the process from its wait queue and decrements the wait queue header count.

6. It subtracts PCB$L_WAITIME from the current time in soft ticks and adds the result to the process's accumulated wait time, PCB$L_ACC_WAITIME.

7. SCH$REPORT_EVENT performs whatever priority adjustment is appropriate (see Section 13.6.6) and removes the process from whatever wait queue it is in.

8. If the now computable process is outswapped, SCH$REPORT_EVENT changes its state to COMO and inserts the process into the COMO queue corresponding to its priority, and unconditionally sets the summary bit in SCH$GQ_COMOQS corresponding to the selected priority queue. It awakens the swapper and returns. Later, after the process is inswapped, it will become eligible for execution.

9. If the now computable process is resident, SCH$REPORT_EVENT alters its state to COM and inserts the process into the COM queue corresponding to its priority, and unconditionally sets the summary bit in SCH$GL_COMQS corresponding to the selected priority queue.

   It compares the process's current affinity mask with the mask of idle CPUs. If there are potential CPUs on which the process can execute, SCH$REPORT_EVENT clears their bits in SCH$GL_IDLE_CPUS as a signal to each of them to try to reschedule (see Section 13.7.1). If it appears that there are no potential CPUs, SCH$REPORT_EVENT checks that the process's PCB$L_CAPABILITY_SEQ is current, recalculating current affinity if it is not. If there are still no idle candidate CPUs and the process's priority is not high enough for it to preempt any active process, SCH$REPORT_EVENT simply returns.

   If the process's priority permits it to preempt some active processes, SCH$REPORT_EVENT searches for a candidate to preempt on a CPU whose capabilities fit. If it finds one, it requests either an interprocessor interrupt or an IPL 3 interrupt, depending on where the process to be preempted is executing. When the interprocessor interrupt is granted, its service routine will request an IPL 3 interrupt to cause rescheduling.

   On a uniprocessor system, the issue is simpler: if there is a current process, can it be preempted by the newly computable process? The preemption test is based upon the SCH$AQ_PREEMPT_MASK array, described in Section 13.3. If there is no current process or if it can be preempted by the newly computable one, SCH$REPORT_EVENT requests an IPL 3 software interrupt. The routine then returns.

13.6.6   **System Events and Associated Priority Boosts**

System routines that report events to SCH$REPORT_EVENT not only describe the event and the process to which it applies but also specify one of five classes of priority increments or boosts that may be applied to the base priority of the process. Table 13.3 lists the events, priority class, and potential amount of priority increment applied to the process. The table does not show AST queuing, because system routines queuing ASTs to a process can select any of the priority increment classes to be associated with the queuing of an AST.

The actual software priority of the process is determined by the following steps:

1. The priority boost for the event class (see Table 13.3) is added to the base priority of the process (PCB$L_PRIB).
2. If the process has a current priority higher than the result of step 1, the current priority is retained (as occurs in Figure 13.14, event 13).
3. If the higher priority of steps 1 and 2 is more than 15, then the base priority of the process is used. Note that this test accomplishes two checks at the same time. First, all real-time processes fit this criterion, with the result that real-time processes do not have their priorities adjusted in response to system events. Second, priority boosts cannot move a normal process into the real-time priority range.

A side effect of step 3 is that real-time processes always execute at their base priorities. Further, note that normal processes with base priorities from 10 to 15 do not always receive priority increments as events occur. As the base priority of a normal process is moved closer to 15, the process spends a greater amount of time at its base priority. Priority 14 and 15 processes experience no priority boosts. This strategy benefits those processes that most need it, that is, I/O-bound and interactive processes with base priorities of 4 through 9. Processes with elevated base priorities do not need this help because they are always at these levels.

An example of priority adjustment that occurs over time for several processes is given in Figure 13.14. In this example, the value of the SYSGEN parameter PRIORITY_OFFSET is assumed to be 2. The following notes relate to the event numbers along the time axis of the figure:

1. Process C becomes computable. Process A is preempted.
2. C hibernates. A executes again, one priority level lower.

Table 13.3   System Events and Associated Priority Boosts

Event	Priority Class [1]	Priority Boost
Page fault read complete	0 (PRI$_NULL)	0
Inswap	0	0
Outswap	0	0
Collided page available	0	0
Quantum end	0	0 [2]
$GETxxI completion [3]	0	0
$SNDJBC completion [3]	0	0
Direct I/O completion [3]	1 (PRI$_IOCOM)	2
Nonterminal buffered I/O completion [3]	1	2
Update section write completion [3]	1	2
Set priority	1	2
Event flag set through $SETEF	1	2
Modified write of deleted page complete	1	2
Resource available	2 (PRI$_RESAVL)	3
Mutex available	2	3
Job quota returned	2	3
Free page available	2	3
Resource lock granted [3]	2	3
Wake a process	2	3
Resume a process	2	3
Resume a process for deletion	2	3
Timer request expiration [3]	2 (PRI$_TIMER)	3
Terminal output completion [3]	3 (PRI$_TOCOM)	4
Terminal input completion [3]	4 (PRI$_TICOM)	6
Process creation	4	6

[1] Routines that report system events pass an increment class to the scheduler. The scheduler uses this class as a longword index into a table of values (local symbol B_PINC in module RSE) to compute the actual boost.

[2] When a normal process reaches quantum end, its priority is lowered to its base if there is a COMO process. Otherwise, the process's priority is decremented.

[3] This priority boost is part of reporting that the event flag associated with the request has been set. An AST may be queued to the process as well, with the same boost specified. The process priority is affected only if the process is in a wait.

3. A experiences quantum end. Because there is a computable outswapped process (B), A's priority is lowered to its base. It continues to run.

4. The swapper process now executes to complete its inswap of B, previously initiated, and B is scheduled for execution.

5. B is preempted by C.

6. B executes again, one priority level lower.

7. B requests an I/O operation to a device other than a terminal. A executes at its base priority.

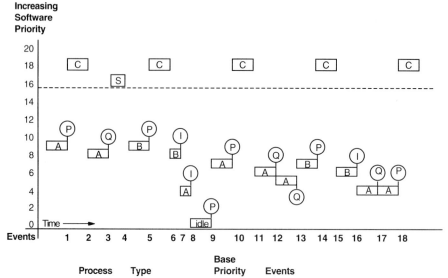

Figure 13.14
Priorities and Priority Adjustments

8. A requests a terminal output operation and waits for its completion. There is no process that can be scheduled. The idle loop (see Section 13.7.3) executes.

9. A executes following I/O completion at its base priority + 3. (The applied boost was 4, and A's priority was subsequently decremented when it was rescheduled.)

10. A is preempted by C.

11. A executes again, one priority level lower.

12. A experiences quantum end, and its priority is lowered by 1. It continues to execute. A's priority is not lowered to its base because there is no computable outswapped process.

13. B's output completes. A priority boost of 2 is not applied to B's base priority because the result would be less than B's current priority. Although B's priority is higher than that of A, it is not high enough to preempt A, which continues to execute until quantum end. B then executes.

14. B is preempted by C.

15. B executes again, one priority level lower.

16. B requests an I/O operation. A executes again, one priority level lower. (A has reached its base priority.)

17. A experiences quantum end, and because there are no other computable

processes of equal or higher priority, A continues to execute at the same priority (its base priority).

18. A is preempted by C.

13.6.7   PIXSCAN Priority Boosts

The pixscan mechanism gives occasional priority boosts to normal priority COM and COMO processes. The SYSGEN parameter PIXSCAN specifies the maximum number of processes that can receive this boost each second. The priority boost prevents a high-priority, compute-intensive job from continuously blocking lower priority processes and causing potential deadlocks. A deadlock might occur, for example, if a low-priority process acquired a volume lock on a critical disk but could not receive enough CPU time to complete its use of the lock and release it.

The mechanism is implemented in the routine SCH$PIXSCAN, in module RSE, invoked once a second from EXE$TIMEOUT (see Chapter 12).

SCH$PIXSCAN takes the following steps:

1. It first tests whether SGN$GW_PIXSCAN, the SYSGEN parameter, is 0. A zero value disables this mechanism, and SCH$PIXSCAN simply returns to its invoker. Its default value is 1.

2. A nonzero value in SGN$GW_PIXSCAN is the maximum number of processes that may be boosted. SCH$PIXSCAN acquires the SCHED spinlock. No IPL change is necessary because it is already executing at IPL 8.

3. SCH$PIXSCAN determines whether any processes are eligible for boost, that is, COM and COMO processes with external priorities 0 through 15. If there are none, it releases the SCHED spinlock and returns.

4. If there are eligible processes, it determines the priority of the highest priority normal process that is CUR, COM, or COMO. This is the value to which selected processes will be boosted.

5. SCH$PIXSCAN uses the low bit of EXE$GL_ABSTIM as a "coin" to determine whether to begin scanning each priority level's compute queues with the COM or COMO queue. In an outer loop, it scans the COM and COMO queues, starting with the (external) priority 0. SCH$PIXSCAN stops when one of the following occurs:

   • It reaches the queues with the same priority as the boost value computed in step 4.
   • It has boosted the maximum number of processes.
   • It reaches a process that has reached quantum end within a time interval less than the SYSGEN parameter DORMANTWAIT.

   Examining the processes in a particular nonempty compute queue, SCH$PIXSCAN performs the following steps for each process.

a. It compares PCB$L_ONQTIME plus the SYSGEN parameter DORMANTWAIT, expressed in 10-millisecond units, to the current absolute time, EXE$GL_ABSTIM_TICS. If the latter is less, the process is not dormant and has not been waiting for the CPU long enough to get a boost. By implication, no other process in that or any higher priority queue is likely to be dormant. The default value of DORMANTWAIT is 2 seconds.

b. If the process is dormant, SCH$PIXSCAN sets the low-order bit in its pixscan history longword, PCB$L_PIXHIST. This longword is shifted left at each quantum end to record whether the process had a pixscan boost during its past executions. The pixscan history of a process is significant for quantum-end automatic working set limit reductions, as described in Chapter 19. It invokes SCH$CHSEP, in module RSE, to boost the process's priority.

6. SCH$PIXSCAN releases the SCHED spinlock and returns.

13.7 RESCHEDULING INTERRUPT

The IPL 3 interrupt service routine schedules processes for execution. The function of this interrupt service routine is to remove the currently executing process by saving the current process's hardware registers and replacing it with that of the highest priority computable resident process. This operation, known as context switching, is accompanied by modifications to the process state, current priority, and state queue of the affected processes.

In some cases, a rescheduling interrupt is requested because a resident process has become computable whose priority is high enough to preempt the current process. In other cases, the current process enters a wait state, and the executive transfers into the rescheduling interrupt service routine to select another process to run. If there is no computable resident process, the interrupt service routine swaps to the hardware context called the system HWPCB (see Section 13.1.4).

The Alpha AXP architecture was designed so that it could be extended to assist the software in performing critical, commonly performed operations, such as context switching; it provides the instruction CALL_PAL SWPCTX to swap two processes' privileged hardware contexts.

13.7.1 Rescheduling Interrupt Service Routine

The IPL 3 interrupt service routine consists of a central MACRO-64 interrupt service routine, SCH$INTERRUPT in module SCHEDULER, and several MACRO-32 routines.

As shown in Figure 13.15, SCH$INTERRUPT is requested as an IPL 3 software interrupt by several different routines:

▶ SCH$REPORT_EVENT and SCH$CHSE/SCH$CHSEP, when a resident

process becomes computable whose priority allows it to preempt the current process

- ▸ SCH$QEND, when a current process reaches quantum end, it is a normal process, and there is a COM process of equal or higher priority
- ▸ SCH$CHANGE_CUR_PRIORITY, when a current process changes its priority and there is a COM process whose priority is higher
- ▸ SCH$ACQUIRE_AFFINITY, when a current process acquires implicit affinity for a processor other than the one on which it is executing
- ▸ SCH$REMOVE_CPU_CAP, when a current process is executing on a CPU that just lost a capability required by the process
- ▸ SCH$REQUIRE_CAPABILITY, when a current process requires a capability not present on the CPU on which it is executing
- ▸ EXE$RUNDWN, when a process's just-restored permanent capability requirements do not match the capabilities of the CPU on which it is executing
- ▸ EXE$RESCHED, when it responds to a process's explicit request for rescheduling

Note that sometimes an IPL 3 interrupt can be directly requested on the appropriate CPU. Other times, an interprocessor interrupt must be requested first so that the IPL 3 interrupt can be requested on the appropriate CPU by the interprocessor interrupt service routine.

Under some circumstances, there may not be a current process to be saved by SCH$INTERRUPT. In these cases, executive routines transfer control directly into the middle of SCH$INTERRUPT for process selection.

The routines that transfer into the middle of SCH$INTERRUPT include the following:

- ▸ SCH$WAIT_ANY_MODE, SCH$WAIT_KERNEL_MODE, SCH$WAIT_KERNEL_MODE_PS, when a current process has been placed into a wait state
- ▸ DELETE, in module SYSDELPRC, when a current process has been deleted, through MACRO-64 routine SCH$DELETE_CALLBACK, in module SCHEDULER
- ▸ EXE$INIT, in module INIT, leaving system context during system initialization, to schedule the first process on the primary processor (or only processor), through MACRO-64 routine SCH$INIT, in module SCHEDULER
- ▸ SMP$START_SECONDARY, the routine that performs secondary processor initialization, leaving system context on a secondary processor, to schedule its first process, also through SCH$INIT
- ▸ SCH$PAGEFAULT, when a current process has been placed in a wait state as a result of a page fault

SCH$INTERRUPT runs in kernel mode, initially on the kernel stack of

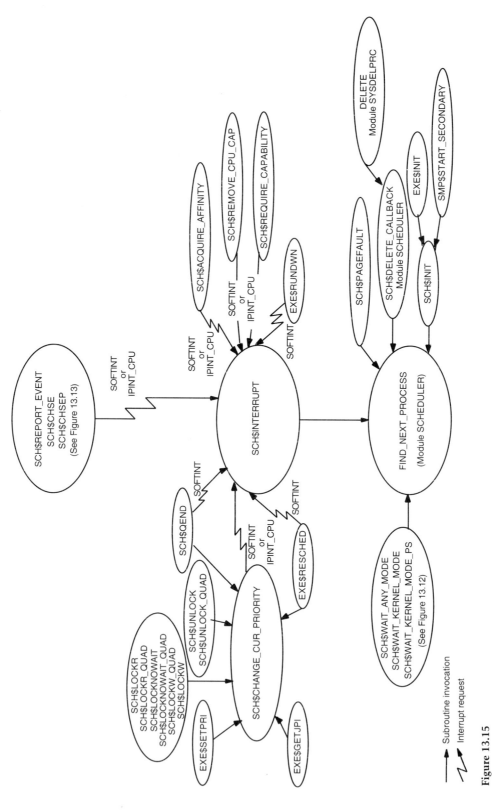

Figure 13.15
Paths to Rescheduling

the process being taken out of execution. The first part of the canonical kernel stack, the interrupt/exception stack frame, is already present. It performs the following steps:

1. SCH$INTERRUPT first saves all the scratch registers (R0, R1, R16–R28) on the kernel stack so that it can call other procedures.

2. It calls SCH$STATE_TO_COM, in module SCHED_ROUTINES, to update the scheduler database for the current process.
   SCH$STATE_TO_COM proceeds as follows:

   a. It acquires the SCHED spinlock, raising IPL to IPL$_SCHED to block concurrent access to and modification of the scheduler database.

   b. It gets the address of the current process's PCB and its current priority from the per-CPU database.

   c. It clears the bit representing the CPU's ID in the longword corresponding to the priority in the array at SCH$AL_CPU_PRIORITY.

   d. If there are no other processes at this priority current on any CPU, it clears the bit corresponding to that priority in SCH$GQ_ACTIVE_PRIORITY.

   e. SCH$STATE_TO_COM sets the bit corresponding to the process's priority in the compute queue summary quadword, SCH$GQ_COMQS.

   f. It changes the state of the process from CUR to COM by updating the PCB$L_STATE field.

   g. It inserts the PCB at the tail of the COM queue corresponding to the process's current priority.

   h. It clears SCH$GL_IDLE_CPUS to signal any idle CPU that it should attempt to reschedule. The scheduler idle loop is described in Section 13.7.3.

   i. SCH$STATE_TO_COM returns to SCH$INTERRUPT. At this point, although the scheduler database shows the process as COM, SCH$INTERRUPT is still running in its hardware context.

3. Still holding the SCHED spinlock, SCH$INTERRUPT calls SCH$FIND_NEXT_PROC, in module SCHED_ROUTINES, to select the next process to execute on this CPU. SCH$FIND_NEXT_PROC takes the following steps:

   a. It scans SCH$GQ_COMQS to find the least significant bit set. The located bit position indicates the highest priority nonempty computable resident state queue. As an optimization, it first tests whether there are any computable resident processes and, if not, returns immediately. If there are, it uses a mask to test whether there are any at priorities 0 through 46. Typically, there are none, and the scan begins at bit 47 of SCH$GQ_COMQS, saving 47 fruitless scan iterations. Bit 47 corresponds to external priority 16, the priority of the swapper process, which is often the highest priority computable process.

b. It uses the bit number as an index into the COM listheads to get the address of the listhead of the selected computable resident queue.

c. It removes the first PCB in the selected queue.

d. If the removed PCB was the only one in the queue, SCH$FIND_NEXT_PROC clears the corresponding SCH$GQ_COMQS bit to indicate that the queue is empty.

e. It confirms that the structure removed from the queue is actually a PCB, generating the fatal bugcheck INCON_SCHED if not.

f. SCH$FIND_NEXT_PROC tests whether the process's capability requirements, including explicit affinity, match the capabilities of the CPU. If they do not match, it tests further to see if the requirements can be met by any active SMP member. If they cannot, it places the process into a RWCAP resource wait state and selects another process to run. If the process has implicit affinity for a different CPU, SCH$FIND_NEXT_PROC tries to honor it but may not (see Section 13.5).

g. If the capabilities match, it stores the address of the new current process PCB in the per-CPU database.

h. It changes the state of the process to current by storing the value SCH$C_CUR in the PCB$L_STATE field.

i. It stores the CPU's ID in PCB$L_CPU_ID.

j. It examines the current process priority and potentially modifies it. If the process is a real-time process or a normal process already at its base priority, then the process is scheduled at its current or base priority (they are the same). If the current process is a normal process above its base priority, then a decrease of one software priority level is performed before scheduling. Thus, priority demotions always occur before execution, and a process executes at the priority of the queue to which it will be returned (not at the priority of the queue from which it was removed).

k. SCH$FIND_NEXT_PROC copies the process's current priority to the per-CPU database.

l. It clears the bit corresponding to this CPU in SCH$GL_IDLE_CPUS to indicate that the CPU is not idle.

m. It sets the bit corresponding to the CPU's ID in the longword corresponding to the priority in the array at SCH$AL_CPU_PRIORITY.

n. SCH$FIND_NEXT_PROC sets the bit corresponding to the process's current priority in SCH$GQ_ACTIVE_PRIORITY.

o. Still holding the SCHED spinlock, it returns to SCH$INTERRUPT with the address of the PCB or, if it found no computable process that could run on this CPU, the value 0.

4. If there is no computable resident process, SCH$INTERRUPT executes the idle loop code, described in Section 13.7.3.

5. Before it saves the remainder of the current process's hardware context, SCH$INTERRUPT checks whether the current process is the same as the newly selected process. If so, it releases the SCHED spinlock and continues with step 16.

6. If they differ, it saves on the kernel stack the nonscratch registers whose contents have not already been saved (R8–R15, R29). This completes the canonical kernel stack.

7. SCH$INTERRUPT saves the current process's ASN and the associated sequence number in PCB$Q_PRVASN and PCB$Q_PRVASNSEQ and the CPU ID in PCB$L_PRVCPU. (This information will be used to determine whether process-private TB entries must be invalidated when the process is next placed into execution.)

8. If the process is using floating-point arithmetic, SCH$INTERRUPT saves the contents of the floating-point registers (F0–F30) and the FPCR in the PHD.

9. It then tests whether the newly selected process needs a new ASN. If the process last executed on this same processor and if CPU$Q_ASNSEQ has not changed since the process was taken out of execution, the process uses the same ASN, and SCH$INTERRUPT continues with step 10.

    If either of those tests fails, SCH$INTERRUPT decrements the current contents of CPU$Q_ASN as the new ASN. When decrementing the number past zero, SCH$INTERRUPT takes the following additional steps:

    a. SCH$INTERRUPT resets CPU$Q_ASN to the maximum possible number on this type of processor and increments CPU$Q_ASNSEQ, the sequence number to be associated with the next uses of the address space numbers.

    b. It stores the new sequence number in PHD$Q_ASNSEQ.

    It stores the ASN in the target process's PHD$Q_ASN, which is part of its HWPCB, and in CPU$Q_ASN.

10. It copies the physical address of the HWPCB for the scheduled process from PCB$L_PHYPCB to R16.

11. It executes a CALL_PAL SWPCTX instruction (see Section 13.7.2) to swap the privileged part of the two hardware contexts. SCH$INTERRUPT is now running in the context of the newly scheduled process and on its kernel stack.

12. If SCH$INTERRUPT incremented CPU$Q_ASNSEQ in step 9a, any process-private TB entries based on the old uses of the ASNs are stale and must be flushed. SCH$INTERRUPT executes the instruction CALL_PAL MTPR_TBIAP to flush all TB entries whose address space match bits are clear.

13. If the newly scheduled process is performing floating-point arithmetic, SCH$INTERRUPT restores the contents of its floating-point registers (F0–F30) and the FPCR from the PHD.

14. SCH$INTERRUPT restores the process's nonscratch registers from its canonical kernel stack, leaving the scratch registers and interrupt/exception stack frame.

15. SCH$INTERRUPT tests and clears the PHD$V_AST_PENDING flag in PHD$L_FLAGS2. It releases the SCHED spinlock. If the flag was clear, it continues with step 18.

16. If the flag was set, indicating that a deliverable AST has been queued to the process, SCH$INTERRUPT examines the PS in the interrupt/exception stack frame to determine at what mode and IPL the process will resume execution. If IPL is 2 or higher, no AST delivery is possible, and SCH$INTERRUPT continues with step 18.

    If IPL is less than 2, it examines PHD$Q_ASTEN_ASTSR to get the contents of the process's AST summary and enable registers. It determines the mode of the most privileged pending AST. It checks whether the process is to resume execution at that or a less privileged mode and whether delivery to that mode is enabled. If either condition is false, it continues with step 18.

17. SCH$INTERRUPT has determined that the pending AST is deliverable. If the routine were to execute a CALL_PAL REI instruction now, an AST delivery interrupt would be requested and granted. To save some of the overhead associated with those steps, SCH$INTERRUPT instead clears the appropriate ASTSR bit and simulates the interrupt:

    a. It restores the scratch integer registers from the canonical kernel stack.

    b. It builds an interrupt stack frame whose PC is the address of the appropriate AST delivery interrupt service routine, whose PS specifies a current mode of kernel and IPL 2, and whose R3 is the linkage pointer for the service routine.

    c. It executes a CALL_PAL REI instruction, transferring control to the AST delivery interrupt service routine. After the AST procedure exits, the process will resume execution at the place at which it was taken out of execution.

    Chapter 8 contains further information about AST delivery.

18. SCH$INTERRUPT restores the scratch integer registers from the canonical kernel stack.

19. It executes a CALL_PAL REI instruction to pass control to the scheduled process through the interrupt/exception stack frame that formed the first part of the canonical kernel stack. Execution of the CALL_PAL REI instruction has the following additional effects:

    • The IPL is dropped from IPL$_SCHED.

• The access mode is typically changed from kernel to a less privileged one.

13.7.2   **SWPCTX PALcode Routine**

The swap process context routine, which executes in response to the CALL_ PAL SWPCTX instruction, performs several operations. It expects to be entered with the following conditions:

▶ The PCBB processor register contains the physical address of the HWPCB for the current process.

▶ R16 contains the physical address of the HWPCB for the process that is to become current.

The PALcode routine performs the following operations:

1. It checks that current access mode is kernel, generating a privileged instruction exception if not.
2. It checks that the address in R16 is on a 128-byte boundary.
3. It stores SP in the HWPCB for the current process as the value of the kernel stack pointer. It stores the per-process stack pointers for the other three access mode stacks in the HWPCB unless this is a processor type that implements only the HWPCB forms of them.
4. It stores the ASTEN and ASTSR registers in the HWPCB unless this is a processor type that implements only the HWPCB forms of them.
5. It uses the process cycle counter to determine the current CPU cycles accumulated by the process and stores the longword value in the HWPCB.
6. It copies the process unique value from its internal storage unless this is a processor type that implements only the HWPCB copy.
7. At this point, all the privileged context of the current process has been saved, and the PALcode routine begins loading the new process's context.
   First, it copies the contents of R16 to the PCBB processor register.
8. If this is a CPU type that does not support ASNs, it invalidates process-private TB entries. A TB caches virtual page numbers and the numbers of the physical pages to which they are mapped, thus speeding up address translation. Without ASNs, all the process-private TB entries belong to the previous process. The invalidation prevents mistranslation of virtual addresses and protects the data of both processes.
9. It loads the set of processor registers whose contents it saved in the old process's HWPCB from the new process's HWPCB.
   In addition, it loads the page table base (PTBR) processor register, FEN register, DATFX processor register, and process unique value.
10. It calculates and loads the current value of this process's cycle counter.

The CALL_PAL SWPCTX instruction is found in just a few locations in the executive.

▶ The rescheduling interrupt service routine executes this instruction to swap the context of the current process with that of the next process to be run. The current process might be still computable or being placed in a wait state.

▶ At the end of process deletion, the context of the process being deleted is swapped for the context of the system HWPCB with a CALL_PAL SWPCTX instruction.

▶ SMP$START_SECONDARY, executing on a secondary processor, swaps context from the termination HWPCB to the system HWPCB (see Chapter 33).

13.7.3   The Idle Loop

If SCH$INTERRUPT finds no computable process to execute, it swaps to the system HWPCB and executes code known as the idle loop. The idle loop's responsibilities are as follows:

▶ To shut down the CPU or enter the benign state if the CPU no longer has the run capability

▶ To execute a computable resident process as soon as there is one available

▶ To maintain a supply of zeroed free pages, up to the maximum specified by SYSGEN parameter ZERO_LIST_HI, whose default value is 16

▶ To increment PMS$GQ_IDLE_LOOP as a count of iterations through the idle loop

The idle loop, routine SCH$IDLE in module SCHED_ROUTINES, performs the following operations:

1. It sets the bit corresponding to the CPU in SCH$GL_IDLE_CPUS to indicate that the CPU is idle.

2. It stores the address of the null PCB and a priority value of –1 in the CPU's per-CPU database.

3. Having made those changes, it can release the SCHED spinlock, lowering IPL to IPL$_RESCHED (3), the IPL of the rescheduling interrupt. This IPL permits software interrupts on this processor that can alter the scheduler database.

4. It tests whether the CPU still has run capability and, if not, invokes SMP$SHUTDOWN_CPU, described in Chapter 37.

5. It tests whether its bit in SCH$GL_IDLE_CPUS is clear. If the bit is still set, it continues with the next step.

   The bit is cleared as a signal that a resident computable process is available. The time during which the routine loops is counted as null time, which the Monitor utility displays as "Idle Time."

   When this CPU's idle bit is cleared, SCH$IDLE sets bit CPU$V_ SCHED in its per-CPU database to indicate that it is still idle and trying to acquire the SCHED spinlock. If an interval timer interrupt occurs while this bit is set, the interval timer interrupt service routine accounts for the CPU time as null time rather than as busy wait (MPSYNCH) time. SCH$IDLE tries to acquire the SCHED spinlock. Once successful, it clears CPU$V_SCHED and branches back to SCH$INTERRUPT to repeat the attempt to select a process to execute.

If another idle processor has already scheduled the computable process, this CPU may reexecute the idle loop.

6. It increments PMS$GQ_IDLE_LOOP.

7. If the supply of free pages needs replenishing, it allocates a free page of physical memory whose virtual contents are of no more interest and initializes the SPTE whose address is in CPU$L_ZEROED_PAGE_SPTE to map the allocated page. It zeros the page 32 bytes at a time, checking whether its idle bit has been cleared in between chunks.

After clearing an entire page, SCH$IDLE reinitializes its page frame number database record, inserts it on the zeroed page list, increments the count of zeroed pages at MMG$GQ_ZEROED_LIST_COUNT, and continues with step 4.

13.8   RELEVANT SOURCE MODULES

Source modules described in this chapter include

[LIB]CPUDEF.SDL
[LIB]PCBDEF.SDL
[LIB]PHDDEF.SDL
[LIB]RSNDEF.SDL
[LIB]STATEDEF.SDL
[LIB]WQHDEF.SDL
[SYS]MUTEX.MAR
[SYS]RSE.MAR
[SYS]SCHEDULER.M64
[SYS]SCHED_ROUTINES.MAR
[SYS]SYSWAIT.MAR

14 Process Control and Communication

I was alone and unable to communicate with anyone. I did not
know the names of anything. I did not even know things had
names. Then one day, after she had tried a number of approaches,
my teacher held my hand under the water pump on our farm.
As the cool water ran over my hand and arm, she spelled the
word water in my other hand. She spelled it over and over, and
suddenly I knew there was a name for things and that I would
never be completely alone again.

Helen Keller, *The Story of My Life*

The executive provides a number of services that allow one process to control the execution of another. It also provides a variety of mechanisms by
which processes can obtain information about each other and communicate
with one another.

Process control system services enable a process to affect its own scheduling state or that of another process, either on the local system or on a remote VMScluster node. These services also enable a process to alter some of
its own characteristics (such as name or priority). The process information
system services allow a process to obtain detailed information about other
processes, both on the local system and on other VMScluster nodes. This
chapter describes the implementation of the process control and process information system services.

Communication mechanisms available to processes include event flags,
mailboxes, lock management system services, global shared data sections,
and shared files. Other chapters describe the implementation of these mechanisms. This chapter briefly discusses the manner in which a process might
use these mechanisms to communicate with another process.

Table 14.1 summarizes the system services related to process control and
process information.

14.1 REQUIREMENTS FOR AFFECTING ANOTHER PROCESS

Before a process can obtain information on another process or alter it in
any way, it must have a means of uniquely identifying the process within
a VMScluster system. In addition, it must have appropriate privileges or user
identification code (UIC) based access to the process.

Process identification and privilege checking are centralized in the routine
EXE$NAM_TO_PCB, in module SYSPCNTRL. Process control and process

Table 14.1   Summary of Process System Services

Service Name	Scope of Processes Affected	Privileges Checked
Hibernate ($HIBER)	Issuing process [1]	None
Wake Process from Hibernation ($WAKE)	Same VMScluster	GROUP or WORLD
Schedule Wakeup ($SCHDWK)	Same VMScluster	GROUP or WORLD
Cancel Wakeup ($CANWAK)	Same VMScluster	GROUP or WORLD
Suspend Process ($SUSPND)	Same VMScluster	GROUP or WORLD
Resume Process ($RESUME)	Same VMScluster	GROUP or WORLD
Exit ($EXIT)	Issuing process	None
Force Exit ($FORCEX)	Same VMScluster	GROUP or WORLD
Create Process ($CREPRC)	Same node	DETACH for different user identification codes
Delete Process ($DELPRC)	Same VMScluster	GROUP or WORLD
Set AST Enable ($SETAST)	Issuing process	Access mode check
Set Power Recovery AST ($SETPRA)	Issuing process	Access mode check
Set Priority ($SETPRI)	Same VMScluster	ALTPRI and either GROUP or WORLD
Set Process Name ($SETPRN)	Issuing process	None
Set Resource Wait Mode ($SETRWM)	Issuing process [2]	None
Set System Service Failure Exception Mode ($SETSFM)	Issuing process [2]	Access mode check
Set Process Swap Mode ($SETSWM)	Issuing process [2]	PSWAPM
Reschedule Process ($RESCHED)	Issuing process	None
Get Job/Process Information ($GETJPI)	Same VMScluster	GROUP or WORLD
Process Scan ($PROCESS_ SCAN)	Same VMScluster	GROUP or WORLD

[1] As part of the $CREPRC system service, a process can specify that the process being created hibernate before a specified image executes.

[2] Through the $CREPRC system service, a process can be created with this characteristic.

information system services that can affect processes other than their requestor all invoke EXE$NAM_TO_PCB; thus they all identify processes and check privileges in the same manner.

Earlier, the scope of the process control and process information system services was restricted to the local node; the scope became VMScluster-wide with the addition of clusterwide process service (CWPS) routines. These routines provide a transparent mechanism by which a process can affect a target process on another VMScluster node. Section 14.1.3 contains more information on CWPS routines.

14.1.1 Identifying the Target Process

Process control and process information system services have arguments that specify the target process by process name and process ID (PID). If the process requesting the system service does not specify the target process using one or the other of these arguments, the target process is assumed to be the requesting process.

Process name is always implicitly qualified by UIC group. That is, a process can identify by name only processes within the same UIC group as itself. The PRCNAM argument can identify a process on another VMScluster node. It can include up to six characters for the node name, followed by a double colon.

Two forms of PID identify a process: an internal PID, called an IPID, and an extended PID, called an EPID. The IPID, stored in PCB$L_PID, uniquely identifies a process on a single node. The low word of the IPID is the index of the process control block (PCB) in the local PCB vector. The EPID uniquely identifies a process in a VMScluster system by including a VMScluster node identifier. It is stored in PCB$L_EPID. Chapter 27 describes the layout and creation of the IPID and EPID.

Because the IPID is only relevant to kernel mode code on the local node, most system utilities, such as SHOW SYSTEM and the Monitor utility, display EPIDs. An EPID is passed as a system service argument to identify a process by its PID.

A legitimate EPID never has its high-order bit set; the Get Job/Process Information ($GETJPI) and Process Scan ($PROCESS_SCAN) system services can thus use a negative value in an EPID field as a wildcard indicator.

14.1.2 Locating the Process and Checking Privileges

Regardless of how the target of a process control or process information service is specified, the executive must determine whether the process exists within the VMScluster system and whether the requesting process has the ability to affect the target. These two checks are centralized in EXE$NAM_TO_PCB.

EXE$NAM_TO_PCB's argument list includes the EPID of the target process and the process name from the process control system service's PRCNAM argument. When neither argument is specified, the most common case, the requesting process is also the target process. EXE$NAM_TO_PCB is optimized for this case. When both arguments are present, EXE$NAM_TO_PCB uses the EPID to identify the target.

EXE$NAM_TO_PCB performs the following:

1. If the requesting process is also the target process, privilege checks are unnecessary; EXE$NAM_TO_PCB returns successfully to the system service with the IPID, the PCB address, and optionally the EPID, holding the SCHED spinlock.

2. If the requesting process is not the target process, EXE$NAM_TO_PCB attempts to locate the target process using the EPID or, if the EPID is not specified, the process name.

   If the EPID or process name indicates that the process is a valid local one, EXE$NAM_TO_PCB acquires the SCHED spinlock, raising interrupt priority level (IPL) to IPL$_SCHED, and proceeds to step 3.

   If the target process is not valid locally, the EPID or the process name must designate a legitimate remote VMScluster node. Only the remote node can determine if the target process is valid.

   - If the EPID or process name indicates that the target process is on a valid VMScluster node, EXE$NAM_TO_PCB returns the error status SS$_REMOTE_PROC. Section 14.1.3 describes the steps taken to locate a target process on a remote node.
   - If the EPID specifies an unknown VMScluster node, EXE$NAM_TO_PCB returns the error status SS$_NONEXPR, which becomes the system service's return status.
   - If the process name specifies a VMScluster node that is unknown, EXE$NAM_TO_PCB returns the error status SS$_NOSUCHNODE.
   - If the process name uses an incorrect format for the node name, EXE$NAM_TO_PCB returns the error status SS$_IVLOGNAM.

3. For a local target process, EXE$NAM_TO_PCB invokes EXE$CHECK_PCB_PRIVS, in module SYSPCNTRL, to determine whether the requesting process has the ability to examine or modify its target.

   EXE$CHECK_PCB_PRIVS returns a success status if any of the following is true:

   - The requesting and target processes are in the same job tree, that is, they share a job information block (JIB).
   - The requesting and target processes have the same UIC.
   - The requesting process has WORLD privilege.
   - The requesting and target processes are members of the same UIC group and the requesting process has GROUP privilege.

4. If EXE$CHECK_PCB_PRIVS returns a success status, EXE$NAM_TO_PCB returns successfully to the system service, still holding the SCHED spinlock.

421

Otherwise, EXE$NAM_TO_PCB releases the SCHED spinlock and returns the error status SS$_NOPRIV, which becomes the system service's return status.

14.1.3   Servicing a Request for a Remote Process

An EPID identifies the VMScluster node on which a process might exist and the PCB vector slot on that node that contains the process's PCB. EPID validation occurs in two steps. The node identifier part is validated first, followed by the PCB vector slot on the identified VMScluster node.

A process control or process information system service invokes the routine EXE$NAM_TO_PCB to locate its target process. If EXE$NAM_TO_PCB does not locate the target process on the local node, it invokes a CWPS routine to verify that the node identified by the EPID or PRCNAM argument exists within the VMScluster system. Executive code running on the identified node must subsequently confirm the existence of the target process.

If the CWPS routine successfully identifies the remote VMScluster node, it returns the error status SS$_REMOTE_PROC. In response to this status, the system service procedure routes the request to CWPS. CWPS allocates and initializes a structure to describe the service request and the requesting process, and transmits it to the remote node using system communication services (SCS). If the system service is a synchronous one, such as $SUSPND, the process enters the RSN$_CLUSRV resource wait state until a response is received from the remote node. For a system service such as $GETJPI[W], the status SS$_NORMAL is returned to the requestor for the asynchronous form or to a synchronization routine for the synchronous form.

On the remote node, a CWPS dispatch routine executing in system context receives the service request. It allocates a composite structure to describe the request locally. It then queues a kernel mode asynchronous system trap (AST) to the CLUSTER_SERVER process, determining the procedure value of the AST routine from the function to be performed; for example, a process control function causes the CLUSTER_SERVER process to execute CWPS$SRCV_PCNTRL_AST, in module [SYSLOA]CWPS_SERVICE_RECV.

For a typical process control function, the CLUSTER_SERVER process initializes a structure that mimics the PCB of the requesting process and invokes EXE$NAM_TO_PCB. Thus, EXE$NAM_TO_PCB performs privilege and access checks, which require a PCB, regardless of whether a request is remote or local. If EXE$NAM_TO_PCB detects an error, the CWPS routine returns the error status to the requesting process on the original node. Otherwise, it requests the system service on behalf of the requesting process. The system service returns status and information to the CWPS routine, which transmits that information to a CWPS receiver on the initiating node. This routine returns the status and data to the original requestor of the system service. (In the case of an asynchronous service like $GETJPI, the standard kernel mode AST is delivered at service completion.)

Figure 14.1 shows this sequence of events, slightly simplified, for an asynchronous process control system service such as $GETJPI.

14.2 PROCESS INFORMATION SYSTEM SERVICES

The process information system services, $GETJPI and $PROCESS_SCAN, return selected information about a process or group of processes within a VMScluster system.

The $PROCESS_SCAN system service functions as an adjunct to the $GETJPI system service. It creates and maintains a search context that filters the information returned by $GETJPI. In the traditional form of $GETJPI wildcard processing, an image requests the $GETJPI service from a loop, obtaining information about the next sequential process with each request. The image tests the returned information to decide whether the process really is of interest; for example, an image looking for all processes belonging to a particular user name obtains the user name field through the $GETJPI service and compares each returned user name with its desired user name.

The $PROCESS_SCAN service simplifies this path; an image requests the service to record its search criteria in a context block and passes the context block address on subsequent $GETJPI requests. When the $GETJPI system service procedure is passed a context block address, it invokes process scan subroutines for the actual processing. Its requestor only receives information on processes matching the search criteria and is not required to filter the data itself.

14.2.1 Data Structures Related to the $PROCESS_SCAN System Service

The $PROCESS_SCAN system service uses fields in the process header (PHD), context blocks, $GETJPI buffer areas, and CWPS structures to service requests.

An image can request the $PROCESS_SCAN service multiple times with different search criteria to create multiple context blocks. For example, to search a VMScluster system, the image could either create one context block matching all cluster nodes, or create a separate context block for each node and conduct the remote scans in parallel. The PHD contains a listhead for a process's context blocks at offset PHD$Q_PSCANCTX_QUEUE. At PHD$L_PSCANCTX_SEQNUM, the PHD contains a sequence number that matches the value in the PSCANCTX$W_SEQNUM field of valid context blocks.

The context block, pictured in Figure 14.2, is the primary data structure created and maintained by the $PROCESS_SCAN service. The $PSCAN-CTXDEF macro defines its header; the size of the structure varies. The item

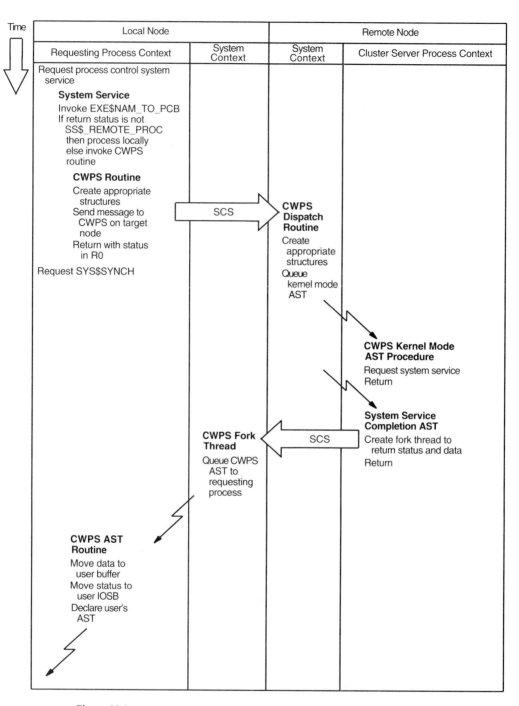

Figure 14.1
CWPS Remote Request Processing

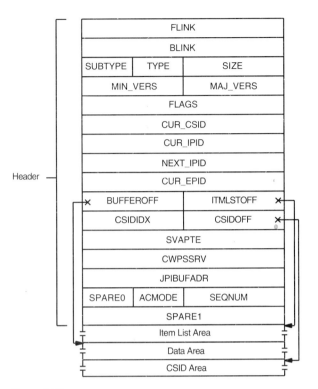

Figure 14.2
$PROCESS_SCAN Context Block (PSCANCTX)

list and data areas follow the header. They contain copies of the $PROCESS_
SCAN items comprising the process filter and the associated comparison data. PSCANCTX$W_ITMLSTOFF and PSCANCTX$W_BUFFEROFF
contain the offsets from the PSCANCTX structure to these areas. The
$PROCESS_SCAN service allocates this structure from the process alloca-
tion region.

If a search involves VMScluster nodes other than the local node, the context block includes a cluster system ID (CSID) area. This area contains the
CSID of each node where the search is to be conducted. PSCANCTX$W_
CSIDOFF contains the offset to this area. PSCANCTX$L_CUR_CSID stores
the CSID of the node currently being scanned, with zero indicating the local
node. The context block fields PSCANCTX$L_CUR_IPID, PSCANCTX$L_
CUR_EPID, and PSCANCTX$L_NEXT_IPID track local PCB vector scans
(see Section 14.2.3).

Only one $GETJPI request at a time can use a particular context block to
reference other VMScluster nodes. PSCANCTX$V_BUSY in PSCANCTX$L_
FLAGS locks the context block; Section 14.2.3 describes its use.

When a remote node is scanned, the offset PSCANCTX$L_CWPSSRV
contains the address of a structure whose symbolic offsets are defined by

425

the $CWPSSRV macro. Allocated from nonpaged pool, this variable-sized structure contains information to be passed to the remote node by CWPS. CWPSSRV$L_EXT_OFFSET contains the index to a CWPSSRV extension created for a $GETJPI request, defined by the $CWPSJPI macro. Figure 14.3 shows this linkage.

To execute more efficiently on a wildcard request in a VMScluster system, an image can request that the $PROCESS_SCAN and $GETJPI services bundle information about several target processes rather than return the information one process at a time. If the image requests this $GETJPI buffering, the $PROCESS_SCAN service allocates a buffer from the process allocation region and stores its address in PSCANCTX$L_JPIBUFADR. This variable-sized structure, whose header offsets are defined by the $PSCANBUFDEF macro, contains a copy of the requested $GETJPI item codes followed by the area where returned data is stored.

14.2.2 $PROCESS_SCAN System Service

The $PROCESS_SCAN system service procedure, EXE$PROCESS_SCAN in module PROCESS_SCAN, executes in kernel mode. The service includes additional routines in modules PROCESS_SCAN_ITMLST and PROCESS_SCAN_CHECK.

The service has two arguments: PIDCTX and ITMLST.

▶ PIDCTX is a longword in which the service returns the address of the context block. The system service requestor must pass the returned PIDCTX argument as the PID input argument to the $GETJPI system service.

▶ ITMLST is the address of an item list composed of one or more entries. Each entry contains the coded value of a selection criterion for $PROCESS_SCAN, either the value or the address of the item, and flags controlling

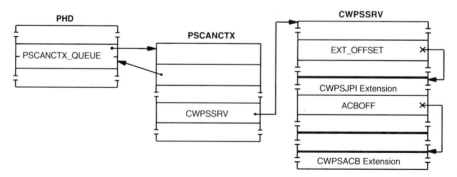

Figure 14.3
Structure Linkage

the manner in which the $PROCESS_SCAN and $GETJPI services use the item.

EXE$PROCESS_SCAN takes the following steps:

1. It verifies that the PIDCTX argument was supplied and that it specifies a location writable from the access mode of the requestor. If not, it returns the error status SS$_INVSRQ or SS$_ACCVIO, as appropriate.

2. If EXE$PROCESS_SCAN discovers that the PIDCTX argument contains the address of a previous context block, it removes the context block from the process's queue of active context blocks and deallocates the block and any data structures linked to it. (Otherwise, context blocks are deallocated at image exit.)

3. If no ITMLST argument is specified, EXE$PROCESS_SCAN merely returns a success status to its caller, accomplishing no useful work. Otherwise, EXE$PROCESS_SCAN checks each item in the item list for the following conditions:
   - The requested item code is recognized.
   - The length of the buffer is appropriate for the item code.
   - The buffer descriptor and the buffer contents are readable.
   - The flags specified for a particular item code are appropriate.

   In addition, the item list must be well-formed; for example, the last item cannot specify the flag PSCAN$V_OR.

4. Some item codes apply to processes; others, like PSCAN$_NODE_CSID and PSCAN$_HW_NAME, apply to VMScluster nodes. If the node is part of a VMScluster system and a specified item code indicates a node context, EXE$PROCESS_SCAN invokes a CWPS routine to create a list of the current VMScluster nodes and their characteristics. From this, it eliminates nodes that do not meet the search criteria and constructs a table of the remaining CSIDs. Only processes on these nodes are scanned.

5. EXE$PROCESS_SCAN allocates memory from the process allocation region for the context block. The structure size is the sum of the sizes of the fixed header, the item list entries that apply to processes, their associated data for comparison, and the CSID area (see Figure 14.2). If a $GETJPI buffer was requested, its size is included in the allocation as well.

6. It increments the process scan sequence number in the PHD, copies that value to the context block, and inserts the new context block into the PHD queue.

7. EXE$PROCESS_SCAN initializes the context block, including the offset to the item list (PSCANCTX$W_ITMLSTOFF), the offset to the data area (PSCANCTX$W_BUFFEROFF), the CSID table and the offset to the table

(PSCANCTX$W_CSIDIDX), the item list and data areas, the address of the $GETJPI buffer (PSCANCTX$L_JPIBUFADR), and the flags.

8. Finally, it negates the address of the context block. This indicates a wild-card context yet also locates the context block and differentiates the context from the traditional $GETJPI wildcard indicator, –1 in the high word of the PID. EXE$PROCESS_SCAN returns this value to its requestor in the PIDCTX location.

The $GETJPI service can now be requested to use the context created by $PROCESS_SCAN.

14.2.3 $GETJPI System Service

The $GETJPI[W] system service provides selected information about a specified process: the process requesting the $GETJPI service (the default), a process explicitly identified by EPID, or the next process located in a wild-card scan. The service can obtain information from the PCB, JIB, PHD, and control region.

$GETJPI arguments include the following:

▶ EFN contains the number of an event flag to be set when the request is complete. If none is specified, event flag 0 is used.

▶ PID contains the EPID of one process from which to collect information, a traditional $GETJPI wildcard indicator, or a context block from $PROCESS_SCAN.

▶ PRCNAM contains the node and process name of the target process, used if the process ID is not specified.

▶ ITMLST contains the address of an item list. The item list can contain multiple entries, each of which includes a code indicating the information to be returned, the size and address of a buffer to hold the information, and a location to contain the actual size of the returned information. The item list terminates with a longword of zero.

▶ IOSB contains the address of an I/O status block where $GETJPI records final status information.

▶ ASTADR and ASTPRM contain the procedure value and parameter of an AST procedure to be called when the request completes.

The $GETJPI system service procedure, EXE$GETJPI in module SYS-GETJPI, executes in kernel mode. It performs the following operations:

1. EXE$GETJPI allocates a storage area on the stack for local context items, such as the PCB address and a set of control flags.

2. EXE$GETJPI tests the first item list entry. Like all item list entries, it must be readable from the access mode of the requestor. The first item list entry is the only legal location for the item code JPI$_GETJPI_CONTROL_FLAGS. This item code allows the requestor to limit EXE$GET-

JPI's behavior with outswapped processes, to restrict AST delivery, and to obtain information on processes that are suspended or marked for deletion. EXE$GETJPI copies the control flags, if specified, to its local context area.

3. It checks the PID argument; a value of zero indicates the current process, a positive value indicates an EPID, and a negative value indicates a wild-card specification.

- For zero or a possible EPID, EXE$GETJPI continues at step 6.
- For a negative value, EXE$GETJPI invokes the process scan routine EXE$PSCAN_LOCKCTX, in module PROCESS_SCAN, which negates the argument and compares it to the context blocks in PHD$Q_PSCANCTX_QUEUE.

  If no matching context block is found, EXE$GETJPI attempts to process the argument as a traditional $GETJPI wildcard. It obtains the next EPID (see Section 14.2.6) and continues at step 6.

  If a matching context block exists, EXE$PSCAN_LOCKCTX sets PSCANCTX$V_BUSY in it to lock the context. Only one $GETJPI request at a time can use a context block to reference other VMScluster nodes. PSCANCTX$V_BUSY in PSCANCTX$L_FLAGS locks the context block; if the bit is set when the process attempts to acquire the context block, it is waited for resource RSN$_ASTWAIT until the context block is available. When the request referencing the context block completes, the process is reentered with an AST routine that clears PSCANCTX$V_BUSY. On return from the AST routine, the process reexecutes the test of the busy bit, acquires the context block, and continues from this point.

4. EXE$GETJPI invokes the process scan routine EXE$PSCAN_NEXT_PID to obtain the next EPID and update the context block.

5. EXE$PSCAN_NEXT_PID, in module PROCESS_SCAN, tries to find a local process that matches the search criteria in the context block and that the $GETJPI requestor can access. To scan the local node, it steps through the PCB vector one process at a time. It updates the process index with each iteration, and the next request using the same context begins where the previous scan left off. The context block fields PSCANCTX$L_CUR_IPID, PSCANCTX$L_CUR_EPID, and PSCAN-CTX$L_NEXT_IPID track this local scan.

   When EXE$PSCAN_NEXT_PID discovers a process matching the search criteria, it returns the EPID of the matching process to EXE$GET-JPI, and EXE$GETJPI continues at step 6.

   If it does not find a local process, EXE$PSCAN_NEXT_PID returns the CSID of the next node to search and the error status SS$_REMOTE_PROC. EXE$GETJPI passes control to CWPS$GETJPI_PSCAN, which continues the $GETJPI processing (see Section 14.2.4).

If it does not find a local process and the context block contains no more CSIDs to search, EXE$PSCAN_NEXT_PID returns the error status SS$_NOMOREPROC, which becomes the $GETJPI status return.

6. EXE$GETJPI invokes EXE$NAM_TO_PCB to obtain the target PCB address and check privileges. As described in Section 14.1.2, EXE$NAM_TO_PCB determines whether the current process has the ability to obtain information about the target.

   If the target is not on the local node, EXE$NAM_TO_PCB returns the error SS$_REMOTE_PROC. EXE$GETJPI passes control to CWPS$GETJPI, which continues the $GETJPI processing (see Section 14.2.4).

   If the target process is on the local node, EXE$GETJPI continues with the steps that follow. These steps apply only to a target process on the local node.

7. EXE$GETJPI checks for write access to the I/O status block (IOSB) and clears the IOSB, if one was specified.

8. It clears the specified event flag or event flag 0.

9. If AST notification was requested, EXE$GETJPI checks that the process has sufficient AST quota. If so, it charges for the AST; otherwise it returns the error status SS$_EXASTLM.

10. EXE$GETJPI examines each item in the item list to check for the following conditions:

    • The buffer descriptor must be readable and the buffer writable.
    • The requested item must be a recognized one.

11. If these conditions are met, then the requested item can be retrieved. All data about the current process and PCB and JIB data about another process can be obtained directly without entering the context of the target process. (The PCB and JIB are nonpaged pool data structures allocated for the life of the process and job.) In addition, data from the PHD of another process can be obtained directly if the PHD is resident (if the PCB$V_PHDRES bit in PCB$L_STS is set). EXE$GETJPI moves all such information to the user-defined buffers for each corresponding item.

12. If no information remains to be gathered, then EXE$GETJPI returns to the requestor after performing the following actions:

    • Setting the specified event flag
    • Queuing AST notification, if it was requested
    • Writing status to an IOSB, if one was supplied

13. Information in the target process's control region can be retrieved only by executing in the context of the target process. Information stored in the target process's process header may not be available if the process is outswapped. To collect information from the control region or from an outswapped process header, EXE$GETJPI queues a special kernel mode AST to the target process, enabling EXE$GETJPI code to execute in the target context.

The $GETJPI requestor can control this behavior through two $GETJPI control flags, JPI$V_NO_TARGET_INSWAP and JPI$V_NO_TARGET_AST.

- If the requestor specifies JPI$V_NO_TARGET_INSWAP, EXE$GETJPI does not queue an AST to the target unless it is resident. Thus, EXE$GETJPI is unable to obtain any information about an outswapped process, but it can obtain information from the PHD and from the control region of a resident process.
- If the requestor specifies JPI$V_NO_TARGET_AST, EXE$GETJPI never queues an AST to the target process. Thus, it returns data from a resident PHD but never from the control region.

Depending on the control flags, EXE$GETJPI allocates nonpaged pool for an extended AST control block (ACB) and an information buffer. It charges the pool against the process's JIB$L_BYTCNT quota. EXE$GETJPI initializes the normal ACB fields, then stores descriptors of all the information that must be retrieved while executing in the context of the other process into the extension. It creates a buffer to receive the retrieved information for transmission to the requesting process.

14. EXE$GETJPI checks the status and state of the target process. If the target process is in any of the following states, information from it cannot be obtained:

- It no longer exists.
- Deletion or suspension is pending.
- The state is suspended (SUSP), suspended outswapped (SUSPO), or miscellaneous wait (MWAIT) (see Chapter 13).

If the process is in any of these states, EXE$GETJPI deallocates the nonpaged pool and restores the quota charged. If the process no longer exists, EXE$GETJPI returns the error status SS$_NONEXPR to its requestor. For the other conditions, EXE$GETJPI's behavior is based on the $GETJPI control flag JPI$V_IGNORE_TARGET_STATUS. If the flag is specified, EXE$GETJPI returns the status SS$_NORMAL to its requestor; otherwise it returns the error status SS$_SUSPENDED. Even in this case, at step 11 EXE$GETJPI has already moved data from the PCB, JIB, and possibly the PHD into user-defined buffers.

Note that the completion mechanisms are all triggered if any error condition occurs. That is, the event flag is set, an AST (if requested) is queued, and an IOSB (if specified) is written with the failure status.

15. EXE$GETJPI queues the ACB to the target process with a priority increment class of PRI$_TICOM. If, however, the target process is computable (COM) or computable outswapped (COMO), queuing the AST does not result in a priority boost. (Chapter 13 discusses event reporting.) In that case, EXE$GETJPI boosts the target process's priority enough to make it equal to the priority of the requesting process (unless the

requesting process is a real-time process or its priority is lower than that of the target process). The target priority boost ensures that even a low-priority target process will eventually return an answer to the requestor.

16. The asynchronous form of the system service returns to the requestor. The requestor can either wait for the information to be returned or continue processing. The synchronous form of the system service waits for the event flag associated with the request to be set and status to be returned. Chapter 7 gives details on synchronous and asynchronous system services.

14.2.4   Remote $GETJPI Support

The CWPS routines CWPS$GETJPI and CWPS$GETJPI_PSCAN, in module CWPS_GETJPI, dispatch $GETJPI requests to other VMScluster nodes and return status and item list information to the original requestor. EXE$GETJPI passes control to CWPS$GETJPI when no context block is associated with the request, merely an EPID or process name identifying a remote VMScluster node. It passes control to the alternative entry point CWPS$GETJPI_PSCAN when a context block exists.

CWPS$GETJPI performs the same argument list validation as EXE$GETJPI does, that is, checking the IOSB for write access and clearing it, clearing the specified event flag, checking and charging AST quota, and validating the item list.

If these checks succeed, CWPS$GETJPI allocates sufficient nonpaged pool to describe the $GETJPI request. It creates a variable-sized data structure with space for the context block, item list, return buffer, and an ACB. The $CWPSSRV macro defines the symbolic offsets for the fields in the structure header. The $CWPSJPI macro defines symbolic offsets for the fields in an extension for $GETJPI requests.

CWPS$GETJPI initializes this structure and stores its address in the context block at offset PSCANCTX$L_CWPSSRV. It invokes a CWPS subroutine to transmit the request to the appropriate remote node using SCS.

On the remote node, a CWPS dispatch routine executing in system context receives the service request. It allocates a structure to describe the request, including the context block. It then queues a kernel mode AST to the CLUSTER_SERVER process, determining the procedure value of the AST procedure from the function to be performed; in this case, CWPS$SRCV_GETJPI_AST in module [SYSLOA]CWPS_SERVICE_RECV.

CWPS$SRCV_GETJPI_AST, executing in the context of the CLUSTER_SERVER process, builds a structure that mimics the PCB of the requesting process. If it did not receive a context block, it merely requests the $GETJPI system service on behalf of the original requestor. Otherwise, it inserts the context block into the PHD queue in the CLUSTER_SERVER process and invokes the process scan routines EXE$PSCAN_LOCKCTX and EXE$PSCAN_NEXT_PID as EXE$GETJPI does. These locate the EPID of the next process matching the search context. CWPS$SRCV_GETJPI_AST then requests the $GETJPI service with the explicit EPID of a local process, specifying a completion AST procedure. EXE$GETJPI follows the steps described in Section 14.2.3 for a local process.

When the $GETJPI request completes, the completion AST procedure passes control to another CWPS routine to return status and data to the originating node using SCS.

When the response arrives from the remote node, a cleanup routine tests the status returned from the remote node. On a successful return, it copies the returned data to the $GETJPI requestor's buffer area after suitable accessibility checks, updates the context block, and clears the busy flag. It sets the event flag, queues an AST (if requested), and returns the status in the IOSB, if one is specified.

14.2.5 $GETJPI Special Kernel Mode ASTs

To obtain information about a target process on the local node, EXE$GETJPI must sometimes queue a special kernel mode AST to the target. From either the context of the requesting process (if the requestor is local) or the context of the CLUSTER_SERVER process, EXE$GETJPI queues this AST when the required information resides in an outswapped PHD or in the control region of the target process.

The special kernel mode AST routine executes in the context of the target process to access the information. Once the AST has obtained the information, it queues another special kernel mode AST to the requesting process or the CLUSTER_SERVER process, to pass the information back to the service requestor.

A summary of the operations performed by these two special kernel mode AST routines follows:

1. The first special kernel mode AST routine runs when the target process is placed into execution. It examines the extended ACB to determine the requested information and stores it in the associated system buffer. It reformats the extended ACB to deliver a second special kernel mode AST, this time to the requesting process or the CLUSTER_SERVER process. It queues the extended ACB to the requesting process if it still exists and is not marked for deletion. (The CLUSTER_SERVER process cannot be deleted or suspended.) Otherwise, it deallocates the ACB and returns.

2. The second kernel mode AST routine executes in the context of the requesting process or CLUSTER_SERVER process. If the PHD image counter has changed since the service was requested, then the requesting image has been run down. In this case, the AST routine deallocates

the block of nonpaged pool, restores the JIB$L_BYTCNT quota, and returns.

3. If the image counter in the PHD agrees with the image counter in the extended ACB, the special kernel mode AST routine copies the retrieved data from the system buffer into the user-defined buffers.

Note that the asynchronous nature of this aspect of the system service requires that the IOSB and all data buffers be probed again for write accessibility. This check ensures that the original requestor of $GETJPI has not altered the IOSB and data buffer protection in the interval between the $GETJPI request and the delivery of the return special kernel mode AST.

4. The event flag is set and the IOSB is written if it was specified.

5. If a completion AST was requested, the extended ACB is reused to queue an AST to the requesting process in the requestor's access mode. Otherwise, the ACB is deallocated to nonpaged pool.

The CLUSTER_SERVER process always specifies CWPS$SRCV_GET-JPI_SRV_AST as its completion AST procedure when requesting the $GETJPI system service. Therefore, for a remote request, the ACB is always reused.

14.2.6   Traditional Wildcard Support in $GETJPI

In addition to the wildcard search available through the $PROCESS_SCAN system service, the executive preserves the traditional $GETJPI wildcard behavior. The $GETJPI system service provides the ability to obtain information about all processes on the local node. An image requests this feature by passing −1 as the PID argument to the $GETJPI system service. An internal routine in EXE$GETJPI searches the PCB vector for the first slot containing a valid PCB and passes information back to the requestor about the associated process.

EXE$GETJPI alters the process index field of the requestor's PID argument to contain the process index of the target process. When the $GETJPI service is requested again, the negative sequence number (in the high-order word of the process ID) indicates that a wildcard operation is in progress, and the positive process index indicates the offset in the PCB vector where the search should continue.

Chapter 27 provides more information on the PCB vector. Note that the user image will not work correctly if it alters the value of the PID argument between $GETJPI requests.

The image continues to request the $GETJPI service until the status SS$_NOMOREPROC is returned, indicating that the PCB vector search routine has reached the end of the PCB vector. The *OpenVMS System Services Reference Manual* contains a sample program using $GETJPI wildcards.

14.3   **SYSTEM SERVICES AFFECTING PROCESS COMPUTABILITY**

The controlling process in a multiprocess application typically creates other processes to perform designated work. When these processes have completed their work, the controlling process may delete them or place them into some wait state in anticipation of additional work. Chapter 27 describes the detailed operation of process creation. Process deletion is described in Chapter 31.

Hibernation and suspension are the two different ways in which a process can temporarily stall execution. The system services Hibernate ($HIBER) and Suspend Process ($SUSPND) implement hibernation and suspension. The associated services Wake Process ($WAKE), Schedule Wakeup ($SCHDWK), and Resume Process ($RESUME) cause execution to recommence.

14.3.1   **Hibernate/Wake**

A process requests the $HIBER service to place itself into hibernation; it cannot put another process into the HIB state. The $HIBER system service procedure is EXE$HIBER, in module SYSPCNTRL, which performs the following steps:

1. It tests whether proactive memory reclamation from processes that wake periodically has been enabled and is currently active, and whether this process is potentially subject to working set reduction. If so, it invokes EXE$CHK_WAIT_BHVR, in module RSE, to reduce the working set if appropriate. Chapter 13 describes the routine and this form of memory reclamation in more detail.

2. EXE$HIBER acquires the SCHED spinlock, raising IPL to IPL$_SCHED.

3. It tests and clears the state of the wake pending flag, PCB$V_WAKEPEN in PCB$L_STS.

4. If the flag was set, a wake request preceded the hibernate request. EXE$HIBER merely releases the spinlock and returns to its requestor at IPL 0.

5. Otherwise, if the flag was clear, EXE$HIBER calls SCH$WAIT_PROC, in module SCHED_ROUTINES, to place the process's PCB into the hibernate wait queue. It then returns the status SS$_WAIT_CALLERS_MODE to the system service dispatcher, causing the process to be taken out of execution.

   The system service dispatcher alters the saved program counter (PC) to contain the address of the beginning of the system service transfer routine. Thus, if the process receives an AST while hibernating, it reexecutes EXE$HIBER upon completion of the AST routine. Since EXE$HIBER tests the wake pending flag, a hibernating process is easily awakened if an AST procedure requests the $WAKE service. Chapter 7 describes the actions of the system service dispatcher.

$HIBER's complementary services are $WAKE and $SCHDWK, which remove a process from hibernation. To awaken itself, a process can request $WAKE from an AST procedure or schedule a wake through $SCHDWK. Alternatively, another process with the ability to affect the hibernating process can request $WAKE or $SCHDWK on the process's behalf.

The $WAKE system service procedure, EXE$WAKE in module SYSP-CNTRL, runs in kernel mode. It invokes EXE$NAM_TO_PCB, described in Section 14.1.2. For a local process, EXE$WAKE invokes SCH$WAKE in module RSE. SCH$WAKE sets the wake pending flag, PCB$V_WAKEPEN, and reports the awakening event to the scheduler routine SCH$REPORT_EVENT, specifying the priority boost class PRI$_RESAVL for the awakening process. SCH$REPORT_EVENT removes the process from the HIB or HIBO queue and places it into the COM or COMO queue corresponding to its updated priority.

The next time the process is scheduled at non-AST level, EXE$HIBER re-executes because of the altered PC. Since SCH$WAKE set the wake pending flag, EXE$HIBER clears the flag and returns immediately. Note that if a process is awakened from any state other than HIB or HIBO, the net result is to leave the wake pending flag set with no other change in the process scheduling state.

If the process is remote, EXE$WAKE branches to CWPS$P_CNTRL, in module SYSPCNTRL. Section 14.1.3 summarizes the result.

Chapter 13 provides further details on SCH$REPORT_EVENT, priority boosts, and process state queues, and Chapter 12 describes the $SCHDWK system service.

14.3.2   Suspend/Resume

Because one process can suspend other processes within the VMScluster system, the implementation of process suspension is more complicated than that of hibernation. The executive's scheduling philosophy illustrated in Figure 13.10 assumes that processes enter various wait states from the state of being the current process and in no other way. This assumption requires that the process being suspended (the target) become the current process on some CPU, possibly replacing the requestor of the $SUSPND system service.

To accommodate this scheduling constraint, a process is suspended as the result of executing a kernel or supervisor mode AST. AST execution ensures that the process is first made current before being placed into the SUSP scheduling state.

A process can be suspended either in kernel mode or in supervisor mode through the $SUSPND system service. Kernel mode suspension is called hard suspension; supervisor mode suspension is called soft suspension. No ASTs can be delivered to a hard-suspended process, whereas executive and kernel mode ASTs can be delivered to a soft-suspended process. The $RE-SUME system service makes a suspended process computable.

14.3.2.1   **Process Suspension.** Process suspension occurs in two phases. In the first phase, the $SUSPND system service procedure, EXE$SUSPND, queues a supervisor mode (default) or kernel mode (depending on the request) AST procedure to the process that is to be suspended. In the second phase, the AST procedure executes in the target process's context.

14.3.2.1.1   *EXE$SUSPND.* This system service procedure executes the following steps in kernel mode:

1. EXE$SUSPND checks for the presence of its FLAGS argument. If the low bit of the FLAGS argument is clear or the argument is not specified, the request is for supervisor mode suspension. Bit 1 of the FLAGS argument has a special meaning: when set, it indicates that the $SUSPND service was requested from the supervisor mode AST procedure (see Section 14.3.2.1.3). Use of this bit is reserved to Digital; any other use is unsupported.

2. If the request is for kernel mode suspension, EXE$SUSPND checks whether it was requested from either kernel or executive mode; if not, it returns the error status SS$_NOPRIV.

3. EXE$SUSPND invokes EXE$NAM_TO_PCB to identify the target process and perform access checking.

4. If the target process is not local, EXE$NAM_TO_PCB returns the error status SS$_REMOTE_PROC. EXE$SUSPND passes the request to a CWPS routine for transmission to a remote VMScluster node. If the local process has appropriate access to the remote target process, a CWPS routine on the remote node eventually executes the $SUSPND request from the context of the CLUSTER_SERVER process. It transmits status to a CWPS receiver on the requesting node, which reenters the context of the requesting process via an AST to return the status to the user image.

5. Otherwise, if the target process is local, EXE$NAM_TO_PCB returns holding the SCHED spinlock. EXE$SUSPND continues with the steps that follow. (Exit paths from EXE$SUSPND must release this spinlock and lower IPL to 0.)

6. It checks the delete pending bit PCB$V_DELPEN, in PCB$L_STS, in the PCB of the target process. If the process is marked for deletion, it returns the error status SS$_NONEXPR.

7. It checks the bit PCB$V_NOSUSPEND in PCB$L_STS. If EXE$SUSPND cannot safely suspend the process, it returns the error status SS$_NOSUSPEND.

8. It tests and sets PCB$V_SUSPEN, the suspend pending bit in PCB$L_

STS. If suspension is pending, EXE$SUSPND tests the bit PCB$V_SOFT-SUSP. If the pending suspension is supervisor mode, PCB$V_SOFTSUSP is set; otherwise, a kernel mode suspension is pending.

If a kernel mode suspension is pending, EXE$SUSPND returns the status SS$_NORMAL.

Otherwise, if a supervisor mode suspension is pending or no suspension is pending, EXE$SUSPND's actions depend on the mode of the new suspension request:

- If the new suspension request is for kernel mode, EXE$SUSPND queues the kernel mode AST (the second part of suspension) to the target process (possibly the same as the requesting process).

- If the new suspension request is for supervisor mode, EXE$SUSPND determines whether it is executing within the context of its supervisor mode AST procedure. If not, it marks the process for soft suspension by setting PCB$V_SOFTSUSP. It then queues a supervisor mode AST to the target process. Otherwise, if EXE$SUSPND is executing within its supervisor mode AST context, as indicated by bit 1 of the FLAGS argument being set, it performs the steps described in Section 14.3.2.1.3.

Through the normal scheduling selection process, the target process eventually executes the kernel or supervisor mode AST procedure.

14.3.2.1.2   *Kernel Mode AST Procedure.* The kernel mode AST procedure SUSPND, in module SYSPCNTRL, executes in the context of the target process. SUSPND obtains the current PCB address and acquires the SCHED spinlock. It then tests the bit PCB$V_SOFTSUSP in PCB$L_STS. A set bit indicates supervisor mode suspension. Since kernel mode suspension preempts supervisor mode suspension, SUSPND clears PCB$V_SOFTSUSP and sets PCB$V_PRE-EMPTED.

SUSPND checks and clears the resume pending flag PCB$V_RESPEN, in PCB$L_STS. This check prevents the deadlock that might otherwise occur if the associated $RESUME system service request preceded the execution of the AST procedure. If the resume pending flag is set, the AST procedure simply clears the suspend pending bit, releases the SCHED spinlock, lowers IPL to 0, and returns. The process continues execution.

If the resume pending flag is clear, the kernel mode AST procedure checks whether there is a Files-11 Extended QIO Processor (XQP) operation in progress. Chapter 8 discusses this check and the action taken if an operation is in progress.

If no Files-11 operation is in progress, the kernel mode AST procedure places the process into the SUSP wait state. Its saved PC is an address in the AST procedure and the saved processor status (PS) indicates kernel mode and IPL 0. ASTs can be queued to a process suspended in kernel mode but they cannot be delivered. When an AST is queued to a process suspended in kernel mode, SCH$REPORT_EVENT ignores the AST event. Only the $RESUME system service can cause a process suspended in kernel mode to continue with execution. At that time, the process reexecutes the check of the resume pending flag, which would be set, causing the process to return successfully from the AST.

14.3.2.1.3 *Supervisor Mode AST Procedure.* The supervisor mode AST procedure, SUS-PEND_SOFT in module SYSPCNTRL, executes in the context of the target process. Its only action is to request the $SUSPND system service with bit 1 of the FLAGS argument set, thus reentering EXE$SUSPND.

When EXE$SUSPND is reentered, it determines that it is executing within the context of its supervisor mode AST procedure. It tests the bit PCB$V_PREEMPTED in PCB$L_STS. If it is set, the supervisor mode suspension was preempted by a kernel mode suspension. If PCB$V_PREEMPTED is set and PCB$V_SOFTSUSP is clear, EXE$SUSPND clears PCB$V_SUSPEN and PCB$V_PREEMPTED and returns successfully to the requestor.

If the supervisor mode suspension was not preempted by a kernel mode suspension, PCB$V_PREEMPTED is clear. If PCB$V_RESPEN is also clear, indicating that the process has not been resumed, EXE$SUSPND calls SCH$WAIT_PROC to place the process's PCB in the suspension queue. It then returns the status SS$_WAIT_CALLERS_MODE to the system service dispatcher, causing the process to be taken out of execution. Chapter 7 describes the actions of the system service dispatcher.

While a process is suspended in supervisor mode, its saved PC contains the address of the beginning of the SYS$SUSPND system service transfer routine. Its saved PS indicates supervisor mode. The process's supervisor mode AST active bit is set, blocking delivery of another supervisor mode AST. The enqueuing of an AST makes the process computable. When the process is placed into execution, a kernel or executive mode AST can be executed, but a user or supervisor mode AST cannot; the AST control block is queued and the interrupt is dismissed.

In either case, the CALL_PAL REI instruction is executed, which causes the $SUSPND system service to be reexecuted. EXE$SUSPND repeats the test that suspended the process. If PCB$V_RESPEN is not set, the process is once more suspended.

14.3.2.2   **Operation of the $RESUME System Service.** The $RESUME system service is very simple. It invokes EXE$NAM_TO_PCB and, for an accessible process on the local system, sets the resume pending flag PCB$V_RESPEN in the target process PCB. It then reports a resume event, invoking SCH$REPORT_EVENT. As with all other system events, this report may result in a rescheduling interrupt request, a request to wake the swapper process, or nothing at all.

If the target process is not local, the $RESUME request is passed to a CWPS routine for transmission to a remote VMScluster node. If the local process has appropriate access to the remote target process, a CWPS routine on the remote node eventually executes the $RESUME request from the context of the CLUSTER_SERVER process. It transmits status to a CWPS receiver on the requesting node, which reenters the context of the requesting process via an AST to return the status to the user image.

14.3.3 Exit and Forced Exit

The Exit ($EXIT) system service terminates the currently executing image. If the process is executing a single image without a command language interpreter, image exit usually results in process deletion. A detailed discussion of the $EXIT system service is given in Chapter 28.

The Force Exit ($FORCEX) system service enables one process to force a target process to request the $EXIT system service. The system service procedure EXE$FORCEX, in module SYSFORCEX, locates the process through EXE$NAM_TO_PCB.

If the target process is not local, EXE$NAM_TO_PCB returns the error status SS$_REMOTE_PROC. EXE$FORCEX passes the request to a CWPS routine for transmission to a remote VMScluster node. If the local process has appropriate access to the remote target process, a CWPS routine on the remote node eventually executes the $FORCEX request in the context of the CLUSTER_SERVER process, performing the steps described in the following paragraphs. The remote CWPS routine transmits status to a CWPS receiver on the requesting node, which reenters the context of the requesting process via an AST to return the status to the user image.

For a local process, EXE$FORCEX simply sets the force exit pending flag, PCB$V_FORCPEN in PCB$L_STS, and queues a user mode AST to the target process. This AST procedure, executing in user mode, requests the $EXIT system service after clearing the AST active flag by requesting the Clear AST ($CLRAST) system service. Note that the AST procedure cannot execute if the target process has disabled AST delivery.

Chapter 8 provides more information on this instruction. The $EXIT request executes in the context of the target process. Execution proceeds as if the target process had requested the system service itself.

14.4 MISCELLANEOUS PROCESS ATTRIBUTE CHANGES

Several system services allow a process to alter its characteristics, such as its response to resource allocation failures, its priority, and its process name. Some of these changes (such as priority elevation or swap disabling) require privilege. The Set Priority ($SETPRI) system service is the only service described in this section that a process can issue for a target other than itself.

14.4.1   **Set Priority**

The $SETPRI system service allows a process to alter its own priority or the priority of other processes within the VMScluster system, limited by the privilege checks in EXE$NAM_TO_PCB (see Section 14.1.2). A process with the ALTPRI privilege can change priority to any value between 0 and 64. A process without this privilege is restricted to the range between zero and the authorized base priority of its target process (PCB$L_AUTHPRI) or the current base priority of its target process (PCB$L_PRIB), whichever is higher.

The system service procedure, EXE$SETPRI in module SYSSETPRI, runs in kernel mode. It locates the target process via EXE$NAM_TO_PCB.

If the target process is not local, EXE$NAM_TO_PCB returns the error status SS$_REMOTE_PROC. EXE$SETPRI passes the request to a CWPS routine for transmission to a remote VMScluster node. If the local process has appropriate access to the remote target process, a CWPS routine on the remote node eventually executes the $SETPRI request in the context of the CLUSTER_SERVER process, performing the steps described in the following paragraphs. The remote CWPS routine transmits status to a CWPS receiver on the requesting node, which reenters the context of the requesting process via an AST to return the status to the user image.

For a local process, EXE$SETPRI changes the base priority in the PCB at offsets PCB$L_PRIBSAV and PCB$L_PRIB and the saved base priority at offset PCB$L_PRISAV. (For a target process at elevated priority with a mutex locked, EXE$SETPRI only alters PCB$L_PRIBSAV and PCB$L_PRISAV.) Chapter 13 provides further information on these PCB fields.

If the target process is currently executing, EXE$SETPRI invokes the routine SCH$CHANGE_CUR_PRIORITY, in module RSE, to alter its current priority, stored in offset PCB$L_PRI, and other priority-related systemwide data structures. Chapter 13 describes SCH$CHANGE_CUR_PRIORITY.

EXE$SETPRI reports a set-priority system event for the target process by invoking SCH$REPORT_EVENT with a priority boost class of PRI$_IOCOM. SCH$REPORT_EVENT takes the following steps:

1. If the target process is in the COM or COMO state, it removes the process's PCB from its current COM or COMO queue. It places the PCB into the queue corresponding to the new current priority.
2. It clears and sets, as appropriate, the bits in SCH$GQ_COMQS or SCH$GQ_COMOQS.
3. It requests a rescheduling interrupt if the target process is resident and can preempt a current process.
4. If the target process is outswapped, SCH$REPORT_EVENT attempts to awaken the swapper process.

Chapter 13 further details SCH$REPORT_EVENT's actions.

14.4.2   **Reschedule Current Process**

The Initiate Rescheduling Interrupt ($RESCHED) system service provides run-time support for the parallel processing features of DEC FORTRAN and DEC C. It enables the currently executing process to request rescheduling, allowing other processes at the same base priority to run.

The $RESCHED system service procedure, EXE$RESCHED in module SYSPARPRC, runs in kernel mode. It takes the following steps:

1. It acquires the SCHED spinlock, raising IPL to IPL$_SCHED.
2. It copies the contents of EXE$GL_ABSTIM_TICS, the number of 10-millisecond intervals elapsed since bootstrap, into PCB$L_ONQTIME.
3. It invokes SCH$CHANGE_CUR_PRIORITY, described in Chapter 13, to lower the process's priority to its base.
4. It requests a rescheduling interrupt.
5. It releases the SCHED spinlock, restoring the previous IPL (thus enabling the rescheduling interrupt to be granted).
6. It returns a success status to its requestor.

14.4.3   **Set Process Name**

The Set Process Name ($SETPRN) system service allows a process to change or eliminate its own process name. The new name cannot contain more than 15 characters. If no other process in the same group has the same name, EXE$SETPRN, in module SYSPCNTRL, places the new name into the PCB at offset PCB$T_LNAME. Note that this service allows more flexibility in establishing a process name than is available from the usual channels, such as the user name, $JOB card, or Digital command language (DCL) command SET PROCESS /NAME, because there are no restrictions imposed by the service on characters that can make up the process name.

14.4.4   **Process Mode Services**

The PCB field PCB$L_STS records the current software status of the process. Table 14.2 lists each of the flags in the longword and the direct or indirect ways to set or clear these flags. Each of these flags has a symbolic name of the form PCB$V_*name*, where *name* is one of those listed in the table.

The module SYSSETMOD contains three miscellaneous system services whose only action is to set or clear a bit in PCB$L_STS. These are the Set Resource Wait Mode ($SETRWM), Set System Service Failure Exception Mode ($SETSFM), and Set Swap Mode ($SETSWM) system services. To disable swapping, a process must possess the PSWAPM privilege. The other two services require no privilege.

Several system services (such as $DELPRC, $FORCEX, $RESUME, and $SUSPND) set or clear bits in PCB$L_STS as an indication that the service's primary operation has been initiated.

442

14.5   INTERPROCESS COMMUNICATION

In applications with more than one process, the processes commonly share data or transfer information from one to the other. The executive provides mechanisms to accomplish this exchange. These mechanisms vary in the amount of information that can be transmitted, transparency of the transmission, and amount of synchronization provided by the operating system.

This section discusses event flags, mailboxes, logical names, global sections, and lock management system services. Processes running on different nodes of a VMScluster system cannot communicate using the first four methods. The executive also provides file sharing, described in *Guide to OpenVMS File Applications*, and DECnet task-to-task communication, described in *DECnet for OpenVMS Networking Manual*.

14.5.1   Event Flags

Common event flags can be treated as a method for several processes to share single bits of information. A common event flag is typically used, however, as a synchronization tool for other, more complicated, communication techniques.

Common event flags can be shared by processes in the same UIC group executing on processors accessing common memory, that is, processors participating in a symmetric multiprocessing system. They cannot be shared by processes on different VMScluster nodes. Chapter 10 contains more information on the implementation of common event flags.

14.5.2   Lock Management System Services

The lock management system services (also known as the lock manager) enable a process to name an arbitrary resource and share it VMScluster-wide. A process can request locks on the named resource in a variety of lock modes to control the manner in which the process shares the resource with other processes. In each lock request, the process can declare a blocking AST procedure, which is invoked by the lock manager if the process's granted lock blocks another request for the resource. The process can also specify the lock manager behavior when access to a resource cannot be granted immediately: either that it wait until the resource is available, or return immediately with notification of the failure.

Each resource includes a 16-byte area available to store process data. The lock manager synchronizes access to this area, allowing cooperating processes to read and write the area using lock value blocks.

Chapter 11 describes the implementation of the lock management system services. Appendix H provides examples of operating system modules that use lock management system services to coordinate access to system resources.

Table 14.2   Meanings of Flags in PCB$L_STS

Flag Name	Meaning if Set	Set by	Cleared by
RES	Process is resident	Swapper	Swapper
DELPEN	Process deletion is pending	$DELPRC	
FORCPEN	Forced exit is pending	$FORCEX	Image rundown, Process rundown
INQUAN	Process is in initial quantum after inswap	Swapper	SCH$QEND
PSWAPM	Process swapping is disabled	$SETSWM, $CREPRC	$SETSWM
RESPEN	Resume is pending (skip suspend)	$RESUME	Suspend AST
SSFEXC	Enable system service exceptions for kernel mode	$SETSFM	$SETSFM, Process rundown
SSFEXCE	Enable system service exceptions for executive mode	$SETSFM	$SETSFM, Process rundown
SSFEXCS	Enable system service exceptions for supervisor mode	$SETSFM	$SETSFM, Process rundown
SSFEXCU	Enable system service exceptions for user mode	$SETSFM, $CREPRC	$SETSFM, Image rundown
SSRWAIT	Disable resource wait mode	$SETRWM, $CREPRC	$SETRWM
SUSPEN	Suspend is pending	$SUSPND	Suspend AST
WAKEPEN	Wake is pending (skip hibernate)	$WAKE, $SCHDWK	$HIBER
WALL	Wait for all event flags in mask	$WFLAND	Next $WFLOR or $WAITFR
BATCH	Process is a batch job	$CREPRC	
NOACNT	No accounting records for this process	$CREPRC	
NOSUSPEND	Do not suspend this process	CWPS, Audit Server	Audit Server
ASTPEN	AST is pending (not used)		
PHDRES	Process header is resident	Swapper	Swapper
HIBER	Hibernate after initial image activation	$CREPRC	
LOGIN	Log in without reading the authorization file	$CREPRC	
NETWRK	Process is a network job	$CREPRC	
PWRAST	Process has declared a power recovery AST	$SETPRA	Queuing of recovery AST, Image rundown, Process rundown
NODELET	Do not delete this process	CWPS, NETACP	NETACP
DISAWS	Disable automatic working set adjustment on this process	SET WORK /NOADJUST, $CREPRC	SET WORK /ADJUST
INTER	Process is interactive job	$CREPRC	

Table 14.2   Meanings of Flags in PCB$L_STS *(continued)*

Flag Name	Meaning if Set	Set by	Cleared by
RECOVER	(Reserved)		
SECAUDIT	Perform mandatory process auditing	LOGINOUT, $CREPRC	LOGINOUT
HARDAFF	(Reserved)		
ERDACT	Exec mode rundown active	Process rundown	Process rundown
SOFTSUSP	Process is soft suspended	$SUSPND	$SUSPND
PREEMPTED	Hard suspend has preempted soft	$SUSPND	$SUSPND

14.5.3   Mailboxes

Mailboxes are software-implemented I/O devices that are read and written through Record Management Services (RMS) requests or the Queue I/O Request ($QIO) system service on a local node. Though process-specific or systemwide parameters may control the amount of data that can be written to a mailbox in one operation, there is no limit on the total amount of information that can be passed through a mailbox with a series of reads and writes.

Typically, one process reads messages written to a mailbox by one or more other processes. In the simple method of synchronizing mailbox I/O, the receiving process initiates its read of the mailbox and waits until the read completes. The read completes when another process writes to the mailbox. Since the receiving process cannot do anything else while waiting for data, this technique is restrictive. Processes running on different nodes of a VMScluster system cannot share a mailbox.

In most applications, the receiving process performs other tasks in addition to servicing the mailbox. Putting such a process into a wait state for the mailbox prevents it from servicing any of its other tasks. In such an application, the receiving process could read the mailbox asynchronously with AST notification. Alternatively, the receiving process could queue a read attention AST request to the mailbox driver. These techniques allow a process to continue its mainline processing and to handle mailbox requests from other processes only when such work is needed.

Chapter 25 discusses the implementation of mailboxes, and Chapter 8 describes attention ASTs.

14.5.4   Logical Names

The executive makes extensive use of logical names to provide device independence in the I/O subsystem. Logical names can be used for many other purposes also. For example, one process can pass information to another process by creating a logical name in a shared logical name table and storing information in the equivalence string. The receiving process simply translates the name to retrieve the data.

Processes using logical name translation for interprocess communication should use proper synchronization rather than relying on an error status such as SS$_NOTRAN from the Translate Logical Name ($TRNLNM) system service for synchronization. For example, the cooperating processes can use a common event flag. An exception to this rule is when a process creates a subprocess or detached process and passes data to the new process in the equivalence strings for SYS$INPUT, SYS$OUTPUT, or SYS$ERROR. Processes running on different nodes of a VMScluster system cannot share a logical name. Chapter 38 describes the implementation of logical names.

14.5.5 Global Sections

Global sections provide the fastest method for one process to pass information to another process on the same system. Because the processes map the data area into their address space, no movement of data takes place; the data is shared. The sharing, however, is not transparent. Each process must map the global section, and the participating processes must agree upon a synchronization technique to coordinate the reading and writing of the global section and provide notification of new data. It can be implemented with event flags, lock management system services, or some similar mechanism.

A global section implemented on a multiprocessor system can be simultaneously accessed by multiple processes. Synchronization in such an environment requires use of MACRO-32 interlocked statements or their equivalents in other languages, or a protocol based on event flags or locks. Processes running on different nodes of a VMScluster system cannot share a global section. Chapter 9 briefly describes synchronization of shared memory.

Chapter 17 describes the implementation of global sections.

14.6 RELEVANT SOURCE MODULES

Source modules described in this chapter include

```
[LIB]CWPSDEF.SDL
[LIB]PSCANCTXDEF.SDL
[STARLET]PSCANDEF.SDL
[SYS]CWPS_GETJPI.MAR
[SYS]PROCESS_SCAN.MAR
[SYS]PROCESS_SCAN_CHECK.MAR
[SYS]PROCESS_SCAN_ITMLST.MAR
[SYS]SYSFORCEX.MAR
[SYS]SYSGETJPI.MAR
[SYS]SYSPARPRC.MAR
[SYS]SYSPCNTRL.MAR
[SYS]SYSSETMOD.MAR
[SYS]SYSSETPRI.MAR
[SYSLOA]CWPS_SERVICE_RECV.MAR
```

PART V / Memory Management

15 Memory Management Overview

> One must have a good memory to be able to keep the promises
> one makes.
>
> Friedrich Wilhelm Nietzsche, *Human, All Too Human*

Virtual memory support for the OpenVMS AXP operating system is based upon Alpha AXP architectural features and is designed to provide maximum compatibility with OpenVMS VAX memory management.

This chapter describes the Alpha AXP memory management architecture and provides an overview of OpenVMS AXP memory management.

15.1 OVERVIEW

Physical memory is the real memory supplied by the hardware. A virtual memory environment supports software that has memory requirements greater than the available physical memory. An individual process can require more memory than is available, or the total requirements of multiple processes can exceed available memory. A virtual memory system simulates real memory by transparently moving the contents of memory to and from block-addressable mass storage, usually disks.

An AXP processor and the executive cooperate to support virtual memory. (As used here, the term *processor* includes both the CPU and its privileged architecture library (PALcode) address translation routine. Section 15.3.3 differentiates their roles.) In normal operation, the processor interprets all instruction and operand addresses as virtual addresses (addresses in virtual memory) and translates virtual addresses to physical addresses (addresses in physical memory) as it executes instructions.

This execution time translation capability enables the executive to execute an image in whatever physical memory is available. It also enables the executive and an AXP processor in combination to restrict access to selected areas of memory, a capability known as memory protection.

The term *memory management* describes not only virtual memory support but also the ways in which the executive exploits this capability. Memory management is fundamentally concerned with the following issues:

▸ Movement of code and data between mass storage and physical memory as required to simulate a virtual memory larger than the physical one
▸ Support of memory areas in which individual processes can run without interference from others, areas in which system code can be shared but not modified by its users, and common memory for shared code and data
▸ Arbitration among competing uses of physical memory to optimize system operation and allocate memory equitably

449

15.2   **VIRTUAL MEMORY CONCEPTS**

Support for virtual memory enables a process to execute an image that only partly resides in physical memory at any given time. Only the portion of virtual address space actually in use need occupy physical memory. This enables the execution of images larger than the available physical memory. It also makes it possible for parts of different processes' images and address spaces to be resident simultaneously. Address references in an image built for a virtual memory system are independent of the physical memory in which the image actually executes.

Virtual memory is implemented in such a way that each process has its own address space. The executive is mapped into the same address range in each process's address space and is shared among all processes. That address range is called system space. Only the process itself can access the nonshared part of its address space, which is called process-private space, or simply process space. Each process is thereby protected against references from other processes.

Physical memory consists of storage locations, each with its own address. Physical address space is the set of all physical addresses that identify unique memory storage locations and I/O space locations. A physical address can be transmitted by the processor over the processor-memory interconnect, typically to a memory controller.

During normal operations, an instruction accesses memory using the virtual address of a byte. A virtual address is an unsigned integer. The processor translates the virtual address to a physical address using information provided by the operating system. The set of all possible virtual addresses is called virtual memory, or virtual address space. In the Alpha AXP architecture, a virtual address is represented as a 64-bit unsigned integer.

Virtual address space and physical memory are divided into units called pages. Each page is a group of contiguous bytes that starts on an address boundary that is a multiple of the page size in bytes. The virtual page is the unit of address translation and the unit of memory protection. Each virtual page has protection bits specifying which access modes can read and write it.

The processor treats all instruction-generated addresses as virtual and translates them to physical addresses using first a CPU component called a translation buffer and, if that fails, a set of software data structures. The data structures, known as page tables, provide a complete association of virtual to physical pages. A page table consists of page table entries (PTEs), each of which associates one page of virtual address space with its physical location, either in memory or on a mass storage medium. (This description is slightly simplified; Section 15.3.1 and Chapter 16 contain more details.)

A translation buffer is a small cache of recently used PTEs. A translation buffer can be accessed and searched faster than a page table.

A PTE contains a bit called the valid bit, which, when set, means that the virtual page is currently in some page of physical memory. A PTE whose valid bit is set contains the number of the physical page occupied by the virtual page. The physical page number, called a page frame number (PFN), consists of all the bits of the physical page's address except for those that specify the byte within the page. When a reference is made to a virtual address whose PTE valid bit is set, the processor uses the PFN to transform the virtual address into a physical address. This transformation is called virtual address translation. Sections 15.3.1 and 15.3.3 contain more information on the Alpha AXP address translation algorithm, and Section 15.3.2 describes the contents of a PTE in more detail.

When a reference is made to a virtual address whose PTE valid bit is clear, the processor cannot perform address translation and instead generates a translation-not-valid exception, more commonly known as a page fault. The page fault exception service routine, called the page fault handler, examines the PTE to determine the physical location of the invalid page. If the invalid page is in physical memory, the page fault handler simply updates the PTE. Otherwise, it obtains an available page of physical memory and initiates I/O to read the virtual page into it from mass storage. When this occurs, the process is said to be faulting the page in.

When the I/O completes successfully, the page fault handler sets the PTE valid bit and dismisses the exception. With the virtual page now valid, control returns to the instruction whose previous execution triggered the page fault, and it is reexecuted. Reading a virtual page into memory in response to an attempted access is called demand paging.

The set of a process's valid virtual pages is called its working set. The executive limits the number of pages of physical memory a process can use at the same time by setting a maximum size for its working set. When this limit has been reached and the process incurs a page fault, the page fault handler selects one of the process's virtual pages to remove from physical memory. When this occurs, the process is said to be faulting the page out. Removing one virtual page from a process's working set to make room for another is called replacement paging.

The mass storage location from which a virtual page is read is called its backing store. A common example of backing store is a set of blocks in an image file. If the virtual page is guaranteed not to change (that is, it contains code or read-only data), the page fault handler need not write the page to mass storage when it is faulted out (thus saving the I/O) and can reread it from the image file as often as required. Thus, the backing store file remains the image file. If, however, the virtual page contains writable data of which each process gets its own copy, the page is faulted in once from the image and later faulted out to page file backing store, from which any subsequent faults will be satisfied.

Chapter 18 describes in detail how the page fault handler deals with various types of page fault.

15.3   ALPHA AXP MEMORY MANAGEMENT ARCHITECTURE

Virtual and physical memory are divided into pages. The Alpha AXP architecture supports a page size of 8 KB, 16 KB, 32 KB, or 64 KB. Each of the systems supported by this release of OpenVMS AXP, however, has a page size of 8 KB (8,192 bytes). For simplicity, therefore, this volume usually describes virtual addresses and address translation in terms of a page size of 8 KB. In contrast, all VAX processors have the same page size, 512 bytes. To distinguish the two architectures' pages, the term *pagelet* identifies a VAX page, or a 512-byte unit of memory.

Each page is a group of 8 K contiguous bytes starting on an 8 KB address boundary. The first page starts at address 0, the second at address 2000_{16} (or 8192_{10}), the third at address 4000_{16} (or 16384_{10}), and so on.

Each physical page has an identifying number called a PFN. A PFN is simply the portion of the physical address that specifies the physical page, namely, all but the low-order bits that specify the byte offset within the page. Generally, physical memory page numbers start at 0 and increase toward higher numbers.

The maximum amount of memory addressable on any processor is limited by the layout of the PTE, which has space for a 32-bit PFN. Thus, the maximum architecturally defined physical address space is 2^{32} pages. The maximum number of bytes of physical address space varies with page size.

Each process has its own address space and its own set of page tables. One process at a time executes on a processor. (On a symmetric multiprocessing system, one process at a time executes on each processor.) As a process is placed into execution, its page tables become the working page tables for that processor.

When an attempted virtual access cannot be completed, a memory management exception occurs, and the operating system is notified. Section 15.3.3 summarizes memory management exceptions.

The Alpha AXP architecture includes support for a feature called a granularity hint region. A granularity hint region is made up of a number of physically and virtually contiguous pages that are treated as a unit during address translation (see Section 15.3.5).

Memory management is always enabled on an AXP processor. The processor treats all instruction-generated addresses as virtual. It is possible, however, for kernel mode code to access a physical address directly by executing the instruction `CALL_PAL STQP` or `CALL_PAL LDQP`.

15.3.1   Virtual Addresses and Page Table Hierarchy

Although instruction execution generates 64-bit virtual addresses, a particular processor implements a smaller virtual address whose size is a function of the processor's page size. For example, a processor with an 8 KB page supports a 43-bit virtual address. On a processor that supports a 43-bit virtual address,

63	43 42	33 32	23 22	13 12	0
Sign extension bits	Level 1	Level 2	Level 3	Byte within page	

Figure 15.1
Parts of an Alpha AXP Virtual Address

a correct 64-bit virtual address must have identical values in bits $\langle 63:43 \rangle$, and the value of these sign extension bits must be the same as the value of bit 42, the high bit of the level fields (see Figure 15.1). The significant bits in a virtual address are those in the three level fields and in the byte within page field; the sign extension bits have no significance in a correct virtual address. That is, correct virtual addresses are in the range 0 to 000003FF FFFFFFFF$_{16}$ or the range FFFFFC00 00000000$_{16}$ to FFFFFFFF FFFFFFFF$_{16}$.

An Alpha AXP virtual address is divided into five parts whose sizes and starting bit positions vary with page size. Figure 15.1 shows the parts of a virtual address on a system with a page size of 8 KB. Table 15.1 shows the sizes of the virtual address parts for all other supported page sizes.

The processor translates a virtual address to a physical address using a three-level hierarchy of page tables. Each level diagramed in Figure 15.1 indexes a different level of page table, and each is used in translating the virtual address. An Alpha AXP page table of any level is one page long, and each PTE in it is eight bytes long. The value in a level field is thus multiplied by 8 to select a PTE.

A page table on a system with a page size of 8 KB contains 1,024 PTEs $(8{,}192/8 = 1{,}024)$. On such a system, a level field must identify one of 1,024 PTEs and thus must be ten bits wide $(1{,}024 = 2^{10})$. Byte within page must be 13 bits wide $(8{,}192 = 2^{13})$. Thus, a virtual address on a system with an 8 KB page has 43 bits of significance; the high 21 bits are simply sign extension bits.

A level 3 page table (L3PT) contains 1,024 L3PTEs, each of which can map a code or data page. A level 2 page table (L2PT) contains 1,024 L2PTEs, each of which can map an L3PT. A level 1 page table (L1PT) contains 1,024

Table 15.1   Effects of Page Size on Alpha AXP Virtual Addresses

Page Size	Byte Offset Bits	Level Bits	Maximum Bytes	Virtual Address Bits	Physical Address Bits
8 KB	13	10	8 TB	43	45
16 KB	14	11	128 TB	47	46
32 KB	15	12	2,048 TB	51	47
64 KB	16	13	32,768 TB	55	48

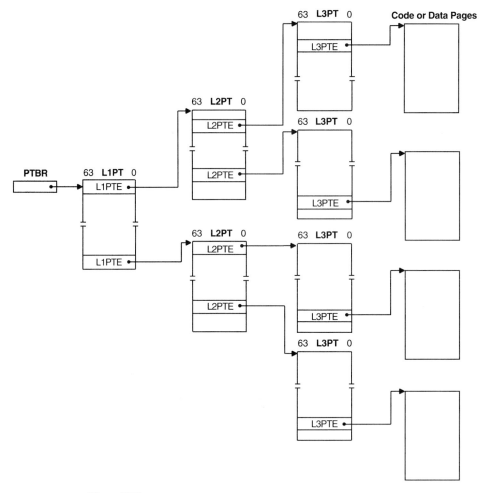

Figure 15.2
Page Table Hierarchy

L1PTEs, each of which can map an L2PT. Figure 15.2 shows the relations among the three levels of page table.

Each process has its own L1, L2, and L3 page tables. The page table base (PTBR) processor register contains the PFN of the L1PT. The PTBR is part of the hardware privileged context and is swapped with process context.

Figure 15.3 illustrates the fundamental steps of address translation for an example virtual address whose three level fields contain the values L1, L2, and L3. These basic steps are as follows:

1. The PTBR points to the L1PT.
2. The contents of the level 1 field in the virtual address index the L1PT to select an L1PTE, which contains the PFN of an L2PT.

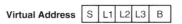

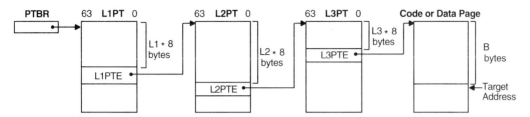

Figure 15.3
Example of Address Translation

3. The contents of the level 2 field in the virtual address index the L2PT to select an L2PTE, which contains the PFN of an L3PT.

4. The contents of the level 3 field in the virtual address index the L3PT to select an L3PTE, which contains the PFN of the page containing the code or data at that virtual address.

5. The contents of the byte within page field are concatenated with the PFN to form the target physical address.

The Alpha AXP architecture supports a sparse virtual address space. Whether a particular virtual page is defined is independent of the state of its neighboring pages. Unlike the VAX architecture, the Alpha AXP architecture has no page table length registers and does not require multiple physically contiguous page tables. Moreover, holes in the virtual address space need not be represented by page tables. The architecture requires only that the L1PT be resident; it permits L2PTs and L3PTs to be pageable. Section 15.5.2 describes OpenVMS AXP treatment of L2PTs and L3PTs.

15.3.2   PTE Contents

Figure 15.4 shows the architectural definition of a valid PTE.

Bit $\langle 0 \rangle$ in the PTE is set to indicate that the virtual page is valid and that the processor can interpret bits $\langle 63:32 \rangle$ as a PFN. Bits $\langle 3:1 \rangle$, the fault-on bits, are briefly explained in Section 15.3.3. Bit $\langle 4 \rangle$, the address space match bit, is set in a PTE that maps a page shared at the same address range in all processes' address spaces. A nonzero value in bits $\langle 6:5 \rangle$, the granularity hint bits, identifies the page as one of a group of physically and virtually contiguous pages, called a granularity hint region. The address space match and granularity hint bits affect translation buffer operation and are described further in Section 15.3.5. Bit $\langle 7 \rangle$ is architecturally reserved.

Bits $\langle 15:8 \rangle$ of the PTE are the protection bits for the virtual page. There are two bits for each access mode, one a read enable (mRE) and one a write enable (mWE). The first, when set, enables read references to the page from

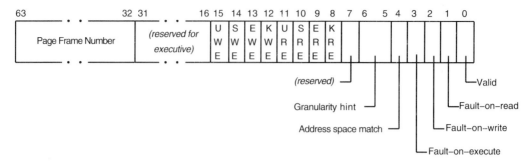

Figure 15.4
Valid Page Table Entry

that mode. The other enables write references. If a write enable bit is set but the corresponding read enable is not, the operation of the processor is undefined.

The architecture reserves bits ⟨31 : 16⟩ for use by the executive, which maintains a modify bit in one of them. (Unlike a VAX PTE, the architecturally defined Alpha AXP PTE has no modify bit. It is the responsibility of the operating system to record whether a page has been modified.) OpenVMS AXP use of the reserved bits is explained further in Chapters 16 and 18.

15.3.3   Virtual Address Translation

Alpha AXP address translation involves both the CPU and a PALcode routine. As a performance optimization, an AXP CPU includes a cache called a translation buffer (TB), which records virtual address translations. Section 15.3.5 describes the TB in more detail; this section summarizes its role in address translation, as defined by the Alpha AXP architecture.

Each entry cached in the TB associates a virtual address with information from its L3PTE, in particular, the PFN, protection, and fault-on bits. Only information from valid L3PTEs is cached. (An attempted translation that results in a page fault is not cached; however, after the page is read in from backing store, the faulting instruction will be reexecuted and the then valid PTE will be cached.) The only address translations directly performed by an AXP CPU itself are through TB lookups.

If a virtual address to be translated is present in the TB (a hit), the CPU examines the cached L3PTE information to test whether the reference should be allowed:

1. The CPU tests the access mode and intended type of reference against the protection bits to determine whether the reference is legal. For this purpose, an instruction fetch is considered a read.

   If the protection on the page prohibits the access, the CPU generates an exception called an access violation.

2. If the protection bits allow the access, the CPU checks the intended reference against the fault-on bits. For this purpose, an instruction fetch is considered an attempted execution. If the corresponding fault-on bit is set, the CPU invalidates the TB entry and generates a fault-on-read, fault-on-write, or fault-on-execute exception, as appropriate. (The TB entry is invalidated on the presumption that the exception service routine will alter the PTE to clear the fault-on bit so that the instruction can reexecute without faulting. Having altered a valid PTE, the exception service routine would otherwise have to request the invalidation explicitly.)

3. If the access is allowed and no fault-on exception need be generated, the CPU forms the physical address by concatenating the PFN in the TB entry with the low-order bits of the virtual address, the byte offset within page.

If a virtual address to be translated is not present in the TB (a miss), the CPU dispatches to the PALcode TB miss routine to fetch the L3PTE for that virtual address and store it in the TB. The PALcode routine takes the following steps:

1. It checks that the bit values in the sign extension field of the virtual address are the same as the value of bit 42 (the high bit of the significant virtual address fields), indicating a correct virtual address. If they are not the same, the routine generates an access violation.

2. It calculates the physical address of the L1PTE corresponding to the target virtual address by concatenating the contents of the PTBR with the level 1 field in the virtual address multiplied by 8, the number of bytes in a PTE.

3. It fetches the L1PTE and tests its valid bit.

   • If the L1PTE valid bit is clear, the routine also tests that the L1PTE permits kernel read access. If it does not, the routine generates an access violation. If it does, the routine generates a page fault exception.

   • If the L1PTE valid bit is set, the PFN in it identifies the page containing the L2PT. The routine calculates the physical address of the L2PTE corresponding to the target virtual address by concatenating the PFN in the L1PTE with the contents of the level 2 field in the virtual address multiplied by 8.

4. It fetches the L2PTE and makes the tests just described to determine whether the L2PTE is valid or whether a page fault or access violation exception should be generated.

5. If the L2PTE is valid, the PFN in it identifies the page containing the L3PT. The routine calculates the physical address of the L3PTE corresponding to the target virtual address by concatenating the PFN

in the L2PTE with the contents of the level 3 field in the virtual address multiplied by 8.

6. The routine fetches the L3PTE and tests the intended reference to the target virtual address and the mode from which it is being made against the protection bits in the L3PTE. If the page is protected against the intended reference, the routine generates an access violation. Because this test is made whether or not the page is valid, the legality of an intended reference to an invalid page can be checked without having to fault the page into memory.

7. The routine tests the valid bit in the L3PTE and, if it is clear, generates a page fault exception.

8. If the valid bit is set, the routine loads a TB entry with information from the L3PTE and exits.

When the PALcode TB miss routine exits, the CPU retries its translation of the address that incurred the TB miss. This time the L3PTE information is cached in the TB. The CPU checks the intended reference against the fault-on bits and calculates the target physical address.

The basis for the PALcode routine's fetch of the L3PTE is indeed the page table hierarchy, as just described. The architecture, however, defines an alternative preferred method of accessing the L3PTE that sometimes eliminates the need for fetches from the L1PT and L2PT. Section 15.3.4 describes this method.

Before dispatching to any memory management exception service routine (access violation, translation-not-valid, or fault-on), PALcode loads the following exception parameter information into registers:

▶ R4—The exact virtual address whose attempted reference caused the exception

▶ R5—The memory management flag quadword, whose possible values are
  - $00000000\ 00000000_{16}$ for a faulting data read
  - $00000000\ 00000001_{16}$ for a faulting instruction fetch
  - $80000000\ 00000000_{16}$ for a faulting data write

The saved program counter (PC) field in the exception stack frame (see Chapter 3) contains the address of the instruction whose fetch failed, or of the load, store, or CALL_PAL instruction that incurred the fault.

The *Alpha AXP Architecture Reference Manual* contains further details of the architecturally defined address translation mechanism.

15.3.4 Page Table Virtual Address Region

As previously mentioned, the Alpha AXP architecture defines an alternative method for locating and accessing an L3PTE that is often faster than locating it through the page table hierarchy.

The alternative method requires that every L3PT have a virtual address in a new virtual address region, one used only by the PALcode TB miss routine. This virtual address region, known as the page table virtual address region, is laid out as a linear array of all possible L3PTEs in a given process address space. On a system with an 8 KB page size this array is $2\,00000000_{16}$ bytes, or 8 GB, long.

In this array, any L3PTE can be located by using the concatenated level 1, level 2, and level 3 parts of a virtual address as a single linear index. The linear layout and single index eliminate the necessity for the L1PTE and L2PTE accesses.

The page table virtual address region is constructed from the same page table pages as the normal page tables, but it is unique in not only consisting of page tables but also being mapped by them.

To construct this separate virtual address region, two elements are required. First, an otherwise unused L1PTE must point to the L1PT containing it. This self-mapped L1PT creates a page table hierarchy that is shifted one level up from its use in a normal page table. The self-mapped L1PT becomes an L2PT as well; each normal L2PT becomes, in the shifted hierarchy, an L3PT; and the normal L3PTs become the data pages, the ultimate target of virtual address translation.

Second, a processor register must identify the starting address of the page table virtual address region. The virtual page table base (VPTB) processor register contains the virtual (not physical) address of the base of the linear array of L3PTEs.

The page table virtual address region can map 1 L1PT, 1,023 L2PTs, and $1,023 * 1,024$ L3PTs. Because the L1PT also serves as an L2PT and as an L3PT, one might also say that the region maps 1 L1PT, 1,024 L2PTs, and $1,024 * 1,024$ L3PTs.

The existence of the page table virtual address region alters the address translation flow described in Section 15.3.3. After a TB miss, the CPU dispatches to the PALcode TB miss routine, which proceeds as follows:

1. It checks that the bits in the sign extension field of the virtual address are the same as bit 42 of the address. If not, the routine generates an access violation.

2. It effectively extracts the concatenated level 1, level 2, and level 3 fields of the address to form a virtual page number. It multiplies the virtual page number by 8, the size of a PTE, to form an offset into the array of L3PTEs in the page table virtual address region.

3. It adds the offset to the contents of the VPTB to form the page table region virtual address of the L3PTE for the virtual address to be translated. It tries to fetch the contents of that virtual address.

4. If the fetch completes without causing another TB miss, the PALcode routine has the L3PTE and continues with step 6 of the flow in Section 15.3.3.

5. If the fetch causes a TB miss, the PALcode routine is reentered. The routine's subsequent steps are implementation-dependent. It must use the three-level page table fetch described in Section 15.3.3 to fetch the L3PTE, but it can start with either the original virtual address to be translated or the virtual address of the L3PTE. In either case, in the course of translating the original virtual address, the routine fills two TB entries, one for the original virtual address and one for the address of the L3PTE.

The operating system creates the page table virtual address region by identifying its virtual address range and initializing the corresponding L1PTE to map the L1PT itself. During system initialization the operating system selects a virtual address range for this region that meets the following constraints:

▸ It must be a virtual address range not otherwise in use.
▸ It must be as large as the number of bytes that are mapped by one L1PTE.
▸ It must begin on a boundary that is a multiple of its size in bytes.

The operating system initializes the L1PTE corresponding to the base of this virtual address range with the PFN of the L1PT, valid bit set, kernel mode read and write enabled, and all other bits zero.

The operating system then loads the base of this virtual address range into the VPTB processor register. Whenever a new process is created, the operating system must initialize the corresponding L1PTE in the process's L1PT to map the L1PT and thereby the page table virtual address region. Section 15.4.5 explains the mapping of this address region and shows its layout.

15.3.5   Translation Buffer

As described in Section 15.3.3, a TB is a CPU component that caches the result of recent successful virtual address translations of valid pages. Each TB entry caches one translation: a virtual page number and, minimally, its corresponding PFN, address space match, and protection bits.

Like a physical memory cache, a TB is a relatively small amount of relatively fast memory that the CPU can access more quickly than physical memory. Because there are considerably fewer TB entries than virtual pages, a one-to-one mapping between virtual pages and TB entries is impossible. Each TB entry has an associated valid bit; when the bit is set, the entry represents a valid translation that the CPU can use. Each valid TB entry identifies the specific virtual address whose L3PTE information it contains. When all the TB entries are in use and another translation must be cached, one of the entries must be replaced with the new translation.

The size and organization of a TB are CPU-specific. Some CPUs have both an instruction stream TB (ITB) and a data stream TB (DTB). The ITB caches translations performed as the result of instruction fetches. The DTB caches translations performed as the result of loading or storing memory operands. The information in each type of TB entry can be different. For example, on CPUs supported by OpenVMS AXP Version 1.5, the ITB does not include the fault-on bits. Therefore no TB entry is made for a page whose fault-on-execute bit is set. Instead, it is always the PALcode's responsibility to generate this fault.

The architecture defines a processor register related to TB use called TB check (TBCHK). The operating system can execute the instruction CALL_ PAL MFPR, specifying the TBCHK register and a virtual address to determine whether the translation for a particular virtual page is cached in the TB. The presence of a TB entry for a page indicates the page has been referenced recently and may therefore not be a good candidate to remove from a process working set.

The contents of a TB entry that represents a valid translation can remain valid until they are superseded by a later translation of a different virtual address that maps to the same TB entry. The operating system is responsible, therefore, for flushing stale, no longer correct entries from the TB; for example, it must invalidate a TB entry corresponding to a no longer valid PTE that maps a page being deleted or removed from a process's working set.

Because all processes have the same virtual address range, all TB entries are process-specific. In theory, the entire TB would have to be invalidated when process context is swapped. However, in practice, a TB entry that represents a physical page shared at the same virtual address in all processes need not be invalidated. The L3PTE mapping such a page has the address space match bit set to indicate it maps a virtual address whose translation is the same in any process context. When process context is swapped, the swap privileged context (SWPCTX) PALcode routine invalidates only entries whose address space match bits are clear.

On a multiprocessor system, each CPU has its own TB. Although each CPU executes a different process, a shared page accessed from different processes can be represented in multiple processors' TBs. When the operating system changes the L3PTE of a valid page whose address space match bit is set, it is responsible for invalidating the page in all processors' TBs.

The architecture includes support for a feature called address space number (ASN), whereby a TB entry is tagged with a number identifying the process whose address translation the TB entry represents. (TB entries for pages whose address space match bits are set are not tagged in this way.) The processor register ASN is part of hardware privileged context on a CPU that supports this feature. The current process's ASN is an implicit input for all TB lookups, invalidation of single TB entries, and examination of the TBCHK register.

On a CPU that supports this feature, the SWPCTX PALcode routine does not invalidate TB entries. Instead, the operating system is responsible for ensuring that unique ASNs are assigned to different processes and for invalidating all TB entries if an ASN in current use must be reassigned. On a multiprocessor system that supports this feature, the operating system is also responsible for ensuring either that a process always runs on the same CPU or that it is assigned a new ASN if it executes on a different CPU than the one on which it last ran.

The operating system can invalidate one or more TB entries by executing the CALL_PAL MTPR instruction with one of the following possible processor registers specified:

- ▸ TBIA—TB invalidate all
- ▸ TBISD—TB invalidate a single DTB entry
- ▸ TBISI—TB invalidate a single ITB entry
- ▸ TBIS—TB invalidate a single TB entry from both the ITB and DTB
- ▸ TBIAP—TB invalidate all process entries (those whose address space match bits are clear)

A CPU implementation is allowed to flush more entries than the register specifies.

An Alpha AXP TB optionally supports a feature called a granularity hint, by means of which one TB entry can represent a group of physically and virtually contiguous pages with identical PTE characteristics (protection, validity, and fault-on bits), known as a granularity hint region. Use of granularity hints improves performance by increasing the number of apparent TB entries and thus reducing TB misses.

The number of pages in a group specified by one TB entry can be 8, 64, or 512 pages and is specified in the PTE of each page in the group. If the TB holds an entry for any virtual page in the group, the CPU uses that entry to translate any virtual address in the entire group. The details of a particular TB, such as how many entries support granularity hints and group size, vary with CPU type.

A granularity hint region must be on a naturally aligned boundary. For example, a granularity hint region of 64 pages must be on a physical and virtual 64-page boundary. For the operating system to make use of granularity hints, it must reserve blocks of physical memory and virtual address space early in system initialization to ensure that the address constraints can be met. Section 15.4.4 summarizes OpenVMS AXP use of granularity hint regions, and Chapters 16 and 32 provide more information.

15.4 THE EXECUTIVE'S USE OF MEMORY MANAGEMENT FEATURES

This section summarizes how the executive uses the features and mechanisms defined by the Alpha AXP memory management architecture.

15.4.1   Page Size

Although all the CPUs supported in this release have a page size of 8 KB, the page size may increase in future CPU implementations. The console subsystem passes the page size to the executive during system initialization, and the executive defines various global cells accordingly. The following is a partial list of these cells and their contents for a page size of 8 KB:

- MMG$GL_PAGE_SIZE—Size of page in bytes (00002000_{16})
- MMG$GL_VA_TO_VPN—Number of bits to shift right to derive the virtual page number from a virtual address ($FFFFFFF3_{16}$)
- MMG$GL_VPN_TO_VA—Number of bits to shift left to derive the virtual address from a virtual page number ($0000000D_{16}$)
- MMG$GL_BWP_MASK—Mask of set bits corresponding to the byte offset field bits in a virtual address ($00001FFF_{16}$)

Executive routines use these and similar cells as parameters for page size dependent code. An application program can determine the page size by requesting the Get System Information ($GETSYI) system service to return information about item SYI$_PAGESIZE.

15.4.2   Virtual Address Space Regions Supported by the Executive

OpenVMS AXP virtual address space is largely based upon VAX VMS virtual address space, which is defined by the VAX architecture. The VAX architecture defines a 32-bit virtual address space.

The low half of the VAX virtual address space (addresses between 0 and $7FFFFFFF_{16}$) is called process-private space. This space is further divided into two equal pieces called P0 space and P1 space. Each is 1 GB long. The P0 space range is from 0 to $3FFFFFFF_{16}$. P0 space starts at location 0 and expands toward increasing addresses. The P1 space range is from 40000000_{16} to $7FFFFFFF_{16}$. P1 space starts at location $7FFFFFFF_{16}$ and expands toward decreasing addresses.

The upper half of the VAX virtual address space is called system space. The lower half of system space (the addresses between 80000000_{16} and $BFFFFFFF_{16}$) is called S0 space. S0 space begins at 80000000_{16} and expands toward increasing addresses. Although the original VAX architecture specified that the upper half of system space was undefined and reserved to Digital, the architecture has since been modified to permit S0 space to expand to $FFFFFFFF_{16}$. The expanded address range results in 2 GB of system space.

The VAX architecture associates a page table with each region of virtual address space. The processor translates system space addresses using the system page table. Each process has its own P0 and P1 page tables. A VAX page table does not map the full virtual address space possible; instead, it maps only the part of its region that has been created.

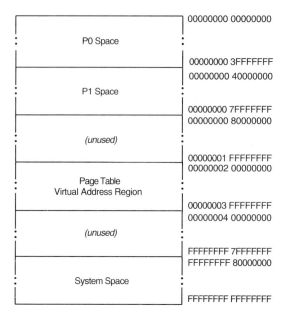

Figure 15.5
Alpha AXP Virtual Address Regions

A key goal of OpenVMS AXP memory management is to maximize compatibility with OpenVMS VAX. For normal use, therefore, OpenVMS AXP currently supports only the three VAX virtual address space ranges and the page table virtual address region, which is described in Sections 15.3.4 and 15.4.5. Figure 15.5 shows these four regions.

The P0 and P1 virtual address space ranges are identical to their VAX counterparts. OpenVMS AXP defines them from 0 to 00000000 7FFFFFFF$_{16}$. It defines the system space range as FFFFFFFF 80000000$_{16}$ to FFFFFFFF FFFFFFFF$_{16}$. Thus, the Alpha AXP 64-bit addresses are sign-extended versions of the VAX 32-bit ones. Because the AXP LDL instruction sign-extends in loading a longword from memory into a quadword register, addresses can be stored as longwords in memory. (Remember that an AXP instruction requires its address operands to be in registers.) Defining system space at that range also avoids using an address range that would be a natural extension to process-private address space at a later stage of OpenVMS AXP.

15.4.3 Page Table Hierarchy

When a process is created, the executive allocates a physical page for its L1PT. It zeros most of the L1PTEs and initializes three valid L1PTEs:

▶ An L1PTE at offset 0 to map a process-private L2PT for P0 and P1 space
▶ An L1PTE to map the page table virtual address region

▸ An L1PTE, byte offset $1FF8_{16}$ in an 8 KB page, to map a shared L2PT for system space

At system initialization the console subsystem allocates and initializes an L1PT initially for use by bootstrap code and later for use by system threads of execution, such as the code that runs in the context of the system hardware privileged context block (HWPCB). The only valid L1PTEs in it are those that map the page table virtual address region and the shared L2PT for system space.

Figure 15.6 shows the relations among the levels of page table that map P0, P1, and system space. For simplicity, it omits the page table virtual address region and other self-mappings of page tables.

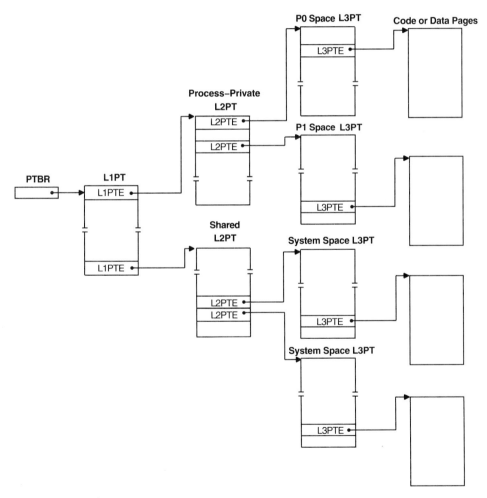

Figure 15.6
Page Table Hierarchy Mapping P0, P1, and System Space

Defining system space at the high end of virtual address space rather than at 00000000 80000000$_{16}$ has another advantage: the L3PTEs that map system space are not mapped by the process-private L2PT, which would otherwise map them. If they were, they would need to be copied to the L2PT created at each process's creation.

15.4.4 Use of PTE Contents

The system space address region is mapped at the same place in all processes' address spaces and is shared. The executive therefore sets the address space match bit in the L2PTEs and L3PTEs that map system space. As a result, TB entries mapping system space have the address space match bit set and are thus more likely to remain in the TB.

By default, one or more granularity hint regions in system space are allocated for each of the following purposes:

▸ Base and executive images' nonpaged code and resident images' code
▸ Base and executive images' nonpaged data
▸ Nonpaged system data that is not part of an executive image, such as the PFN database, which describes the state of physical memory

The appropriate granularity hint bits as well as the address space match bit are set in each of the L3PTEs that map these regions.

The fault-on-read bit is also set in each L3PTE that maps pages in the first granularity hint region, the one containing executive nonpaged code and resident image code sections. It sets all mRE bits for these pages, which can contain mode of caller system service procedures and Run-Time Library procedures. That the protection bits enable read access means that any mode can fetch and execute instructions from these pages. The set fault-on-read bit, however, causes data fetches to fault. This mechanism blocks undesirable read accesses to these pages.

After all installations are complete, any unused physical pages that were part of the code granularity hint region are released to the free page list and the system space L3PTEs that mapped them are zeroed. Even though the L3PTE that mapped such a page is zeroed, the granularity hint feature permits virtual addresses to be translated to physical addresses within the released page. If the TB holds an entry for any valid virtual page in the granularity hint region, the CPU uses that entry to translate any virtual address in the entire region, which still includes the released pages.

Once on the free page list, a released page can be reallocated for another use and mapped by some other L3PTE. Such a page can have two mappings: one, for example, in process-private space, and the other through the system space address range for the granularity hint region. If one process tries to read from a page reallocated to another process by using its former system virtual address, the CPU generates a fault-on-read exception. The exception service routine currently advances the PC in the exception stack frame past the instruction that incurred the exception and dismisses the exception. Chapter 17 describes a method by which the contents of these pages can be accessed as data.

The fault-on-write bit is set in the L3PTE of a writable page when it is faulted with read intent. After the page becomes valid, if any attempt is made to write it, the processor generates a fault-on-write exception. The exception service routine clears the fault-on-write bit and sets the modify bit in the L3PTE. (In contrast, when a writable page is faulted with write intent, the modify bit in its L3PTE is set when the page fault I/O completes.) Chapter 18 describes in more detail how the modify bit is maintained.

The fault-on-execute bit is set in a page faulted as the result of anything but an instruction fetch. Use of the bit minimizes TB invalidates on a system with both an ITB and a DTB. Any later attempt to execute an instruction from the page results in a fault-on-execute exception. The exception service routine clears the fault-on-execute bit and returns. If no instruction is executed from the page, the fault-on-execute bit remains set. If, when the page is removed from the working set, the fault-on-execute bit is still set, there cannot be a TB entry for the page in the ITB, and the executive needs to invalidate only the DTB. If, however, the fault-on-execute bit is clear when the page is removed from the working set, the executive must invalidate both the DTB and ITB.

The executive also uses fault-on-execute to restrict access to translated image pages that the Translated Image Environment (TIE) facility identifies as no-execute. These are image pages that contain VAX instructions. Any attempt to execute instructions from such a page results in a fault-on-execute exception. The exception service routine signals an access violation to the TIE's condition handler. Chapter 29 describes the use of this mechanism in more detail.

In bits ⟨15 : 8⟩, the executive defines a subset of the possible combinations of protections. For compatibility with VAX VMS applications, the executive uses only those combinations that implement protections consistent with the VAX architecture. These combinations obey the following rules:

▶ If a given access mode has write access to a specific page, then that access mode also has read access to that page.

▶ If a given access mode can read a specific page, then all more privileged access modes can read the same page.

▶ If a given access mode can write a specific page, then all more privileged access modes can write the same page.

15.4.5   Mapping of Page Table Virtual Address Region

The executive identifies the L1PTE that maps the L1PT as the one whose byte offset is MMG$C_PTSPACE_OFFSET. In this release, the symbol has a

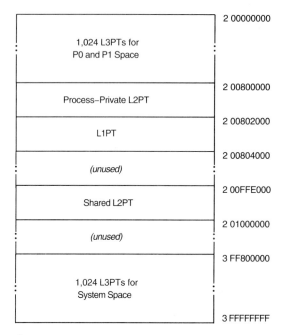

1,024 L3PTs for P0 and P1 Space	2 00000000
Process–Private L2PT	2 00800000
L1PT	2 00802000
(unused)	2 00804000
Shared L2PT	2 00FFE000
(unused)	2 01000000
1,024 L3PTs for System Space	3 FF800000
	3 FFFFFFFF

Figure 15.7
Page Table Virtual Address Region

value of 8. On a system with an 8 KB page size, that L1PTE maps the virtual address region 2 00000000$_{16}$ to 3 FFFFFFFF$_{16}$.

Figure 15.7 shows the resulting organization of the page table virtual address region on a system with an 8 KB page size.

Figure 15.8 shows the transformation of the page table hierarchy of Figure 15.6 into the page table virtual address region. Each page table in Figure 15.8 has two labels: one identifying its use in mapping the page table virtual address region (PTVAR), and the other, in parentheses, identifying its normal use in mapping any other virtual address.

The page table containing the L1PTE is not only the L1PT but is now also an L2PT (and an L3PT and a data page). The page table virtual address region L3PTs it maps are normally used as L2PTs. The page table virtual address region data pages are normally used as L3PTs.

15.5 VIRTUAL MEMORY

This section summarizes OpenVMS AXP use of each of the virtual address space regions and the data structures associated with those uses.

15.5.1 Use of Virtual Address Space Regions

The three regions of address space are used differently:

▶ System space contains the executive, systemwide data structures, and any images installed permanently resident by the system manager.

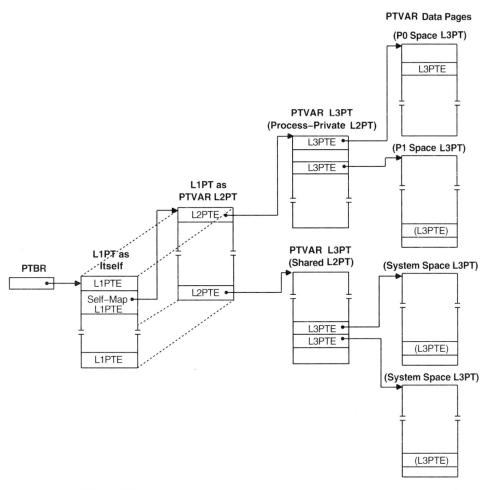

Figure 15.8
Transforming the Page Table Hierarchy into the Page
Table Virtual Address Region

▶ P1 space contains the process stacks and permanent process control
   information maintained by the executive. It also contains address space
   used on the process's behalf by inner access mode components such as
   Record Management Services, the file system, and a command language
   interpreter.
▶ P0 space maps whatever images the user activates.

Appendix F describes the layout of system and P1 virtual address space in
more detail.

Different areas of virtual address space have different protections. The protection codes on most system space data pages prohibit access from all but
kernel and executive modes. System space pages occupied by executive code
allow any access mode to execute code in them. Certain parts of P1 space

are protected against access from outer access modes. The protection on P0 space pages usually allows read access from user mode and sometimes write access as well.

Virtual address space is created (and recreated) at different times during system operation. System space is formed once and mapped in each process's address space. Process-private address space is created for each process and mapped only when that process is current.

SYSBOOT and other initialization routines load executive images into system space, form the dynamic memory pools, and initialize the other regions of system space. Chapters 33 and 34 describe the formation and initialization of system space in detail. Even after initialization is done, the size of system space is not fixed. The architecture does not require that the system page table be physically contiguous, and it permits a sparse mapping. Thus, system space can be expanded during normal operation, as described in Chapter 32. Individual system page table entries can be altered to create, delete, or modify particular pages of system space.

When a process is created, its P1 space is created in several stages, as described in Chapters 27 and 30. The global cell CTL$GL_CTLBASVA contains the address that is the boundary between the permanent and temporary portions of P1 space. The regions of P1 space below this address, namely, the user stack and a possible replacement image I/O section, are recreated by the image activator when it activates an executable image. P1 space can expand toward lower addresses during image execution as a result of system services requested explicitly by the image or implicitly on its behalf.

P0 space and the nonpermanent part of P1 space are deleted at image rundown and recreated with each new image run. The image activator creates address space for the image and every shareable image that it references. During image execution it creates additional P0 address space as necessary to activate images requested through the Run-Time Library procedure LIB$FIND_ IMAGE_SYMBOL. P0 and P1 space can also change during image execution as a result of system services requested explicitly by an image or implicitly on its behalf.

As the image activator processes images, it creates process sections for the image sections it encounters. (A process section can also be created dynamically in response to a system service request.) A process section is a group of contiguous virtual pages with the same characteristics, such as writability and shareability.

The VAX architecture limits P0 and P1 space to 1 GB each. In supporting VAX-like address regions, the OpenVMS AXP executive enforces this limit. Their combined sizes may be further constrained by the SYSGEN parameter VIRTUALPAGECNT, the page file quota available to the process, and some additional factors, as described in Chapter 17.

Chapter 28 describes the image activator and the memory management system services it requests to map the sections of an image. Chapter 17 describes those system services.

15.5.2   Virtual Address Space Data Structures

The major data structures that describe virtual address space are

- ▶ System page table (SPT), consisting of a number of L3PTs
- ▶ System section table (also known as the global section table)
- ▶ Process-private page tables (P0PT and P1PT), consisting of a number of L3PTs
- ▶ Process section table (PST)
- ▶ L2PTs to map the L3PTs
- ▶ L1PT to map the L2PTs

During system initialization SYSBOOT allocates physical memory for the shared L2PT that maps system space and as many L3PTs as necessary to map initial system space requirements. These L3PTs make up the SPT and are in contiguous virtual pages. The SPT is expanded as needed. A maximum of 256 L3PTs would be needed to map a 2 GB system space.

When the executive creates a process, it allocates a page of physical memory for the process's L1PT and stores the physical address of the L1PT in the process's HWPCB. When the process context is made current, that physical address is loaded into the PTBR processor register.

The executive uses the PTBR to calculate addresses within the L1PT that it accesses physically through `CALL_PAL LDQP` and `CALL_PAL STQP` instructions. The executive does not access a process's L1PT accessed through virtual addresses.

The executive also builds a data structure called a process header (PHD) to record memory management data about the process. The process-private L2PT is allocated as part of a process's header and is permanently locked in its working set. Its L2PTEs map the L3PTs that make up the P0 and P1 page tables. These L3PTs are also part of the process's header, but they are pageable.

Chapter 16 describes page tables in further detail.

The PHD also contains the PST, which typically has one process section table entry (PSTE) to describe each process section created in that process's address space. A PSTE contains information necessary to resolve a page fault for a page in the section. The PTE for an invalid page that is part of a process section contains a pointer to the section's PSTE.

Chapter 16 contains more information on the PST. It also discusses systemwide structures analogous to the process-specific PHD and PST: the system header and its section table, which contain descriptions of system space sections and global sections.

15.6   **PHYSICAL MEMORY**

The OpenVMS AXP system allocates some pages of physical memory permanently, for example, the pages that contain the SPT or the system base images. More typically, the system allocates a physical page of memory for a particular need, such as a virtual page in a process's address space, and deallocates the page when it is no longer needed.

This section summarizes the management of physical memory and its associated data structures.

15.6.1   **Physical Memory Data Structures**

A database called the PFN database, described in Chapter 16, records significant information about each physical page, such as whether it is currently in use and for what purpose.

The pages of physical memory allocated to a process are called its working set. A structure within the PHD called the working set list represents just those pages in a compact form. (In contrast, L3PTEs describing valid pages are scattered among those describing invalid pages in process-private L3PTs.) The working set list is briefly described in Chapter 16 and in more detail in Chapter 19. A working set list within the system header describes pageable system pages that are valid.

Physical pages available for allocation are linked together into a list called the free page list. A page is allocated from the front of the list and generally deallocated to the back of the list. At allocation a physical page is associated with a virtual page: the PFN of the physical page is placed in the PTE corresponding to the virtual page, and the contents of the virtual page are read into the physical page from mass storage. The physical page retains its virtual contents until it is allocated for a new use. Even when the physical page is removed from a process's working set and the valid bit in the virtual page's PTE is cleared, the PTE still contains the physical page's PFN. Until the physical page is reused, it is possible to resolve a fault for the virtual page by removing the physical page from the free page list and setting the PTE valid bit again. A page fault resolved in this manner without the need for mass storage I/O is sometimes called a soft page fault.

When a physical page that has been modified is removed from a process's working set, the page is inserted at the back of another list, called the modified page list. The modified page list differs from the free page list in that a physical page on the modified page list cannot be reused until its contents are written to backing store, for example, a page file or the section file to which the virtual page belongs. Once the swapper has written the contents of the modified page to backing store, the swapper moves the page to the back of the free page list. (Acting in this capacity, the swapper is referred to as the modified page writer.)

While a physical page is on either the modified or free page list, a page fault for its virtual page can be resolved without I/O. Thus these lists act as systemwide caches of recently used virtual pages.

When the system has no current process to run, the executive removes a page from the free page list that has no more ties to a virtual page, for example, a page whose contents have been deleted, and zeros it. Afterward, it inserts the page into a list of similar pages called the zeroed page list, from which demand zero pages are allocated. Zeroing an 8 KB or larger page when the system would otherwise be idle reduces the overhead incurred to allocate a page of all zeros. (Chapter 13 provides further details.)

15.6.2   Sharing Physical Memory

The page is the unit of sharing. Because system space addresses are mapped into each process's address space, the physical memory occupied by system pages is shared by all processes. In addition, multiple processes' PTEs can map the same physical pages to enable the processes to share physical memory. For example, multiple processes using the same command language interpreter can share the read-only pages of the image. (However, each process needs a private copy of its writable data pages.) Sharing physical pages makes more efficient use of memory and reduces the number of page faults that require mass storage I/O.

Multiple processes share physical memory through a mechanism called a global section. All the pages of a global section have the same attributes. A global section resembles a process section and is dealt with similarly by the page fault handler.

Several data structures are associated with global sections:

► Global section table
► Global section descriptors
► Global page table

The global section table (GST) is analogous to a process section table and contains a global section table entry (GSTE) for each global section. Like a PSTE, a GSTE has information necessary to resolve a page fault for a page in the section.

A global section descriptor (GSD) identifies a particular global section by name and associates the name with a GSTE. A GSD contains information used to determine whether a particular process is allowed to access the global section.

The global page table (GPT) contains global PTEs that serve as templates for the process PTEs that map global pages. Unlike other PTEs, GPTEs are not accessed in the course of translating virtual addresses; they are only accessed by memory management routines.

When multiple processes are mapped to a global section, all processes can potentially benefit from each other's page faults. When process A incurs a page fault for a global page not in its working set, if the page is not valid, it is read in from its backing store. After the page fault completes, the GPTE is modified to show that the global page is valid. If process B then incurs a page fault for that page, the page fault handler copies the information from the GPTE to B's PTE and resolves the fault without the need for I/O.

Chapter 16 contains more details on all these structures, and Chapter 18 discusses global page faults.

15.6.3 Managing Physical Memory

Physical memory is used in the following ways:

- Permanently, by pages occupied by the resident executive (system base images and the nonpageable sections of executive images) and its systemwide nonpageable data structures (for example, system context stacks, the PFN database, and nonpaged pool)
- Permanently, by images other than executive images that have been installed resident in system space, for example LIBOTS.EXE and LIBRTL.EXE
- Dynamically, by pages on the free, modified, and zeroed page lists
- Dynamically, by pages in processes' working sets
- Dynamically, by pages in the system working set (pageable sections of executive images and pageable system data)

The executive apportions physical memory among these uses based on

- SYSGEN parameters that specify various minimum and maximum limits, such as the sizes of the free and modified page lists and the systemwide maximum process working set size
- Process quotas and limits that specify process-specific minimum and maximum working set sizes
- Statistics and measurements that describe the current environment, such as the size of the free page list and the rate at which a particular process has been page faulting recently

15.7 SOFTWARE MEMORY MANAGEMENT MECHANISMS

This section provides an overview of the mechanisms by which physical and virtual memory are managed. OpenVMS AXP memory management is based upon VAX VMS memory management.

VAX VMS memory management mechanisms are best introduced from a historical perspective. Historically, the system has had two basic mechanisms to control its allocation of physical memory to processes: paging and swapping. Several auxiliary mechanisms, such as automatic working set limit adjustment and swapper trimming, supplement these fundamental ones.

15.7.1   **Original Design**

An important goal of the initial release of the VAX/VMS operating system was to provide an environment for a variety of applications, including real-time, batch, and time-sharing, on a family of VAX processors with a wide range of performance and capacity. The memory management subsystem was designed to adjust to the changing demands of time-sharing loads and to meet the more predictable performance required by real-time processes.

The major problems common to virtual memory systems that concerned the original designers were the following:

▸ The negative effect that one heavily paging process has on other processes' performance

▸ The high cost of starting a process that is required to fault all its pages into memory

▸ The high I/O load imposed by paging

VAX/VMS support of virtual memory was designed to address these problems. With some modifications, the original design remains intact in the OpenVMS AXP operating system.

The original VAX/VMS designers chose to implement process-local page replacement instead of global replacement. A process pages against itself, for the most part, rather than against other processes. This minimizes the risk of page fault thrashing among processes and also makes possible more predictable performance for a real-time process.

A process is created with a working set quota that limits its maximum use of physical memory. The default and maximum sizes of each process's working set are specified at process creation. As a process executes and faults pages, they are read into memory from backing store and added to the process's working set. When the process's working set grows to its maximum size, a subsequent page fault must be a replacement page fault, requiring that a page first be removed from the working set. In this manner, the process pages against itself. (Note, however, that a heavily paging process that causes the contents of the free and modified page lists to turn over rapidly can indirectly affect other processes.)

Unlike some virtual memory architectures, neither the VAX nor the Alpha AXP architecture includes a reference bit in each PTE by means of which less recently referenced pages can be identified. Instead, the executive uses the order of working set list entries to determine length of residence. The working set list, which describes the pages in the process's working set, is a ring buffer with a pointer to the entry most recently added to the working set. In general, the page most likely to be removed from the working set is the one following the most recently added, that is, the oldest.

Although this working set replacement algorithm is simple to implement and has low CPU overhead, its selection of a page to be removed is not optimal and may cause more page faults. For those reasons, the original algorithm has been enhanced. Chapter 19 describes the current algorithm.

To minimize the performance impact of this algorithm, the executive caches pages removed from a working set so that they can be faulted back into it without the need for mass storage I/O; the executive inserts a page removed from a working set at the tail of the free page list or the modified page list, depending on whether the page had been modified. When a process needs a physical page of memory, for example, to fault a nonresident page, the executive allocates the physical page at the head of the free page list. Thus an unmodified page is cached for a length of time proportional to the size of the free page list and the frequency with which pages are allocated from it. When the modified page list grows beyond a certain size or the free page list shrinks below a certain size, the executive writes modified pages to their backing store, typically a page file, and then inserts them at the tail of the free page list. A modified page is thus cached while it is on both the modified and free page lists.

As previously noted, the working set replacement algorithm typically removes the oldest page in the working set rather than the least recently used. The page list caches, however, make it possible to fault the page back in as the newest page in the working set with little overhead. Because the working set list thereby tends to become somewhat ordered by use, the page list caches considerably improve the performance of the working set list replacement algorithm, bringing it close to that possible with a least-recently-used algorithm but with less overhead. (Note that a heavily paging process can affect others indirectly by causing the page lists to turn over more rapidly, thus reducing their effectiveness as caches for the other processes.)

The executive provides services by which a process can exercise some control over its working set list: it can lock and unlock selected pages into its working set and purge its working set of pages in a specified address range. At image exit, the executive deletes P0 space and the nonpermanent part of P1 space, thereby removing these pages from the working set. Before a process executes a new image, the executive purges the working set of no longer needed pages, such as command language interpreter code and data.

The VAX/VMS system was designed to manage memory by both paging and swapping. Paging occurs in response to process page fault exceptions and results in moving virtual pages into and out of physical memory. Swapping, which occurs in response to events detected by the executive, results in moving whole working sets into and out of physical memory. Swapping all of a process's working set minimizes the time to reactivate the process and the number of I/O operations required to remove its pages from memory and to read them back in. Swapping makes it possible for more processes to coexist even when their working sets cannot all fit into memory at once.

Processes in certain long-lasting wait states are more likely to be outswapped than computable processes. When an outswapped process becomes computable, it is eventually inswapped. Chapter 20 describes the relation between process scheduling states and the swapper's selection of inswap and outswap candidates. A privileged process can prevent itself from being swapped.

To reduce the I/O overhead of paging, the executive reads and writes multiple pages at a time in units called clusters. A page fault cluster size is defined for each pageable entity, for example, an image section or a process page table. When a page is faulted, the executive tries to read a cluster's worth of pages. It writes modified pages in clusters also, to reduce I/O overhead. A SYSGEN parameter specifies the number of modified pages written to a page file at once. Within this larger cluster, the modified page writer groups related virtual pages so that they can be faulted back in as a cluster. Chapter 18 describes both types of clustering.

Simply deferring the writing of modified pages reduces I/O overhead to some extent: some pages are deleted before they are written; some pages are faulted in from the modified page list and modified again before they are written.

In VAX/VMS Version 1, the following characteristics of the memory management subsystem could be controlled by SYSGEN parameters and process authorization limits:

▶ The minimum sizes of the free and modified page lists
▶ The maximum size the modified page list could grow before the system began to write its pages to a page file
▶ The maximum number of concurrently resident processes
▶ For each process, a default and maximum working set size

As processes were created, used free pages, and faulted pages, the free page list would shrink and the modified page list would grow. If the free page list shrunk too low, the swapper would write modified pages and, if necessary, outswap a process. If the modified page list grew too large, the swapper would write modified pages. Occasionally, the swapper would have to write the entire modified page list, or flush it, in order to force specific pages out of memory. A process could alter its working set size from its default to its maximum through a system service to use that many more pages. Its working set size would be reset to its default at image exit.

15.7.2   Auxiliary Mechanisms

VAX/VMS Version 2 added a mechanism called automatic working set limit adjustment, by which a process's working set size was altered in response to its page fault rate. The working set of a heavily faulting process grew so as to reduce its page fault rate. The working set of a process that incurred very few page faults was shrunk. With expansion considered the more significant part of the mechanism, it was triggered at quantum end, based on the idea that a process that could not execute even for a quantum did not need its working set limit adjusted. Chapter 19 describes automatic working set limit adjustment.

VAX/VMS Version 2 also employed an enhancement to the VAX architecture that made it possible to test whether a page had been referenced recently enough so that its PTE was in the TB cache. (The Alpha AXP architecture also supports this capability through the TBCHK processor register.)

In VAX/VMS Version 3, automatic working set limit adjustment was enhanced to permit a heavily faulting process to grow beyond its normal maximum working set if the free page list was sufficiently large. An alternative mechanism for reclaiming physical pages was added, called swapper trimming. The basic idea was that when the swapper process detected that the free page list had shrunk too low, it could reclaim memory from the working sets of processes expanded in times of plenty. If more memory was needed, it could either outswap a process or shrink a process working set as low as the SYSGEN parameter SWPOUTPGCNT. This added considerable flexibility to the original design; by altering this and several other parameters, a system manager could tune the system to favor swapping over paging, or vice versa.

VAX/VMS Version 4 refined swapper trimming, correcting a failure to reclaim memory from a low-priority compute-bound process whose working set had expanded when the system was lightly loaded. As a result of the pixscan mechanism, described in Chapter 13, the refinement was not always effective.

In VAX VMS Version 5 there were several changes to the modified page writer, the most significant being that it no longer flushed the modified page list to force specific pages out of memory. Instead, it could be requested to search the list for selected pages and write them, leaving the rest of the pages as cache. Swapper trimming was further refined to reclaim memory more quickly from certain kinds of processes, in some cases by outswapping rather than trimming them.

Based on VAX VMS Version 5, the OpenVMS AXP operating system uses these same mechanisms.

15.7.3 Comparison of Paging and Swapping

The executive uses both paging and swapping to make efficient use of available physical memory. The page fault handler executes in the context of the process that incurs a page fault. It supports programs with virtual address spaces larger than physical memory. The swapper enables a system to support more active processes than can fit into physical memory at one time. The swapper's responsibilities are more global and systemwide than those of the page fault handler. Table 15.2 compares the page fault handler and the swapper in its role as working set swapper.

Table 15.2   Comparison of Paging and Swapping

DIFFERENCES

Paging	*Swapping*
The page fault handler moves pages in and out of process working sets.	The swapper moves entire processes in and out of physical memory.
The page fault handler is an exception service routine that executes in the context of the process incurring the page fault.	The swapper is a separate process that is awakened from its hibernating state by components that detect a need for swapper activity.
The unit of paging is the page, although the page fault handler attempts to read more than one page with a single disk read.	The unit of swapping is the process or, actually, the pages of the process currently in its working set.
Page read requests for process pages are queued to the driver according to the base priority of the process incurring the page fault. [1]	Swapper I/O requests are queued according to the value of the SYSGEN parameter SWP_PRIO. Modified page write requests are queued according to the SYSGEN parameter MPW_PRIO. [1]
Paging supports images with very large address spaces.	Swapping supports a large number of concurrently active processes.

SIMILARITIES

The page fault handler and swapper work from a common database. The most important structures used for both paging and swapping are the process page tables, the working set list, and the PFN database.

The page fault handler and swapper do conventional I/O. The details of pager and swapper I/O are not very different from the normal Queue I/O Request ($QIO) system service mechanism.

Both components attempt to maximize the number of blocks read or written with a given I/O request. The page fault handler accomplishes this with read clustering. The swapper attempts to inswap or outswap the entire working set in one or a small number of I/O requests. The modified page writer writes clusters of pages.

[1] This consideration has meaning for few mass storage device drivers. The priority at which an I/O request is queued to many drivers is largely irrelevant because they handle most requests immediately by queuing them to the device, which is likely to reorder them based on considerations such as disk head position.

15.8   FURTHER INFORMATION

▶ Chapter 16, for a description of the data structures used by the memory management subsystem

▶ Chapter 17, for a description of the system services that an image requests to alter a process's virtual address space

▶ Chapter 18, for a discussion of the translation-not-valid fault (page fault)

handler, the exception service routine that responds to page faults and brings virtual pages into memory

- ▸ Chapter 19, for a description of the working set list and the mechanisms that alter, shrink, and expand it
- ▸ Chapter 20, for an examination of the swapper process, a system process that manages physical memory by writing modified pages, shrinking process working sets, and swapping processes
- ▸ Chapter 21, for a description of the various pools from which virtual memory is allocated for transient needs, such as creation of dynamic data structures
- ▸ *Alpha AXP Architecture Reference Manual*, Part II, Chapter 3, for information on OpenVMS AXP memory management support

16 Memory Management Data Structures

> ... but there's one great advantage in it, that one's memory
> works both ways.
>
> Lewis Carroll, *Through the Looking Glass*

This chapter describes data structures used by the memory management subsystem. These include the following:

- Structures that describe process memory, including process-private page tables
- Structures that describe the state of physical memory
- System page table
- Structures that enable processes to share memory through global sections
- Structures that describe the state of page and swap files

The other memory management chapters discuss how the routines that compose the memory management subsystem use these structures.

16.1 PROCESS DATA STRUCTURES

Most memory management information about a process is maintained in its process header (PHD). The PHD includes a list of valid virtual process pages, a description of the sections that make up the process-private address space, and the process-private page tables that map the process-private address space.

The process control block (PCB) is the key data structure that represents a process. The executive can transform a process's ID into the address of its PCB. The PCB contains some information related to memory management, in particular, the address of the PHD.

The PHD and PCB are both allocated in system space. When a process is created, a PCB for it is allocated from nonpaged pool. A region of system space called the balance set slots contains space for the PHDs of the maximum number of resident processes. When a process is created, a slot is reserved for its PHD. If the process is outswapped, its PHD may be outswapped as well. The PCB and PHD are described in the sections that follow.

16.1.1 Process Control Block

A PCB is allocated for the life of the process and remains in nonpaged pool whether the process is resident or outswapped. When a process is

481

outswapped, the PCB remains as the representation of the existence of that process and must contain all information that the swapper requires to inswap the process. Figure 16.1 shows the PCB fields related to memory management.

As described in Chapter 15, the Alpha AXP architecture supports a feature called address space number as part of process hardware privileged context. On a CPU that supports this feature, each translation buffer (TB) entry is tagged with a number identifying the process whose address translation the entry represents. Thus the TB does not need to be flushed of process-private translations when process context is swapped. The executive is responsible for assigning unique address space numbers to processes. It records information about the assigned address space number in the PCB. PCB$Q_PRVASN contains the address space number the process was using when its context was last saved, and PCB$Q_PRVASNSEQ, the sequence number associated with that address space number. Chapter 13 provides more information.

PCB$L_STS contains several status bits relevant to memory management:

▶ PCB$V_RES, when set, means that the process (that is, its PHD and its working set) is resident in memory.

▶ PCB$V_PSWAPM, when set, means that the process has disabled outswapping of itself.

▶ PCB$V_PHDRES, when set, means that the process's PHD is resident. (When a process is outswapped, its header may remain in memory.)

▶ PCB$V_DISAWS, when set, means that the process has disabled automatic working set limit adjustment.

PCB$L_STS2 contains one status bit related to memory management: PCB$V_PHDLOCK. When set, this bit means that the process has one or more pages locked in memory through the Lock Pages in Memory ($LCKPAG) system service. The PHD of such a process may not be outswapped.

PCB$L_APTCNT only has meaning for an outswapped process; the swapper records in it the number of pages of PHD outswapped in the process's swap slot.

PCB$L_GPGCNT contains the number of global pages in the process's working set, and PCB$L_PPGCNT, the number of process-private pages. The sum of these two fields is the number of physically resident pages, the size of the process's working set.

When a process is newly created, PCB$L_WSSWP is cleared to signal the swapper that the process's initial pages come from the shell (see Chapter 27). The field has a different use later in the life of the process: when a process is outswapped, PCB$L_WSSWP contains its mass storage location. If the process has been outswapped in one extent, PCB$L_WSSWP contains a systemwide page file index (see Section 16.8.2) identifying the swap file and the

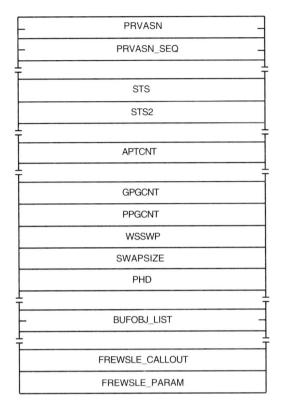

Figure 16.1
PCB Fields Related to Memory Management

starting virtual block number. The high bit of PCB$L_SWAPSIZE is set to indicate such a process; the low 31 bits of PCB$L_SWAPSIZE contain its outswapped size in pages. If the process is outswapped in more than one extent, PCB$L_WSSWP contains the address of a page/swap file mapping window block (PFLMAP), a data structure that lists the locations and sizes of the extents. Chapter 20 describes the PFLMAP and process swapping.

PCB$L_PHD contains the address of the PHD, if PCB$V_PHDRES in PCB$L_STS is set.

PCB$Q_BUFOBJ_LIST is the list head for buffer object descriptors. Each buffer object descriptor describes a buffer object, a piece of address space used for a particular kind of I/O. Section 16.5 contains further information on buffer objects and their descriptors.

PCB$A_FREWSLE_CALLOUT, if nonzero, is the procedure value of a procedure to be called when a page is selected for removal from the process's working set. The procedure is called with arguments identifying the process and the page and with the contents of PCB$L_FREWSLE_PARAM. Chapter 19 gives further information.

16.1.2   Process Header

The most important process-specific memory management information about a process is contained in its PHD. A PHD consists of a fixed part and several variable-length substructures:

- ► The working set list describes the subset of process-private page table entries (PTEs) that are currently valid.
- ► The process section table (PST) contains entries that associate the process sections created in the process's address space with the corresponding sections in the files where the pages originate.
- ► Several arrays contain information about the pages of the PHD itself. The swapper uses this information when it outswaps the PHD.
- ► The process-private page tables are the largest contributors to the size of the PHD and contain the complete description of the process-private virtual address space in use by the process, including both valid and invalid pages. These page tables are the level 3 page tables (L3PTs) that make up the P0 and P1 page tables and the process-private level 2 page table (L2PT) that maps them.

The maximum sizes of these substructures are fixed by SYSGEN parameters, but their actual sizes vary in response to process needs. Pointers or indexes in the fixed portion of the PHD locate each substructure. Although the substructures vary in size, the balance set slots in which PHDs reside are of fixed size to enable memory management routines to associate easily the address of a process PTE with the process, as described in Section 16.7.3.

The P0 and P1 page tables are at a fixed place (for a given set of SYSGEN parameters) at the high-address portion of the PHD. The P0 page table grows toward increasing addresses and the P1 page table toward decreasing addresses. The system virtual addresses of the page tables must remain stable while the process is resident or has I/O in progress. The page frame number (PFN) database record for each physical page occupied by a virtual page contains a pointer to the PTE that maps the virtual page. Any outstanding direct I/O request refers to its buffer using the system virtual address of the buffer's PTEs.

The dynamic growth area of the PHD must accommodate the growth of both the PST and the working set list. Expansion in either of these can result in moving the PST to higher addresses in the PHD. Section 16.1.2.3 describes PST/working set list expansion.

Figure 16.2 shows the parts of the PHD. The smaller figure to the right shows the relative sizes of the portions of the PHD on a typical system. Figure E.8 shows the detailed layout of the PHD. Specific fields in the PHD are described, where appropriate, in this and the other memory management chapters.

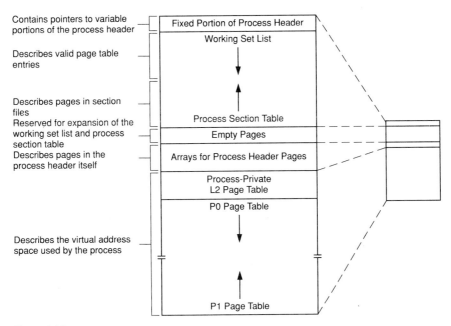

Figure 16.2
Discrete Portions of the Process Header

The PHD has several unusual characteristics that distinguish it from other data structures:

► The PHD is swappable. When a process is outswapped, its PHD can be outswapped as well. When later inswapped, the PHD is likely to be placed in a different balance set slot at a different system space address. (Section 16.7.1 describes balance set slots.)

► The PHD is referenced using addresses in several different address regions. It is located in system space so that the swapper and other memory management code can access it. The PHD, excluding the process-private page tables, is also mapped in P1 space and accessed through global pointer CTL$GL_PHD. This P1 window to the PHD is at a fixed virtual address range and remains the same across outswaps and inswaps. The exact location of the window varies with system version; its size varies with several SYSGEN parameters. Chapter 20 contains more information on the double mapping of the PHD.

As described in Chapter 15, a process's page table hierarchy is also mapped in the page table virtual address region so that it can be accessed by the TB miss privileged architecture library (PALcode) routine.

► The PHD has both pageable and nonpageable parts. The L3PTs that make up the P0 and P1 page tables are pageable; the rest of the PHD, including the process-private L2PT, is not pageable.

485

The memory-resident portion of the PHD is described by the process's working set list, and its nonpageable portion is locked into the working set. PHD pages are the only pages with system virtual addresses that are part of a process working set.

An attempt by one process to fault a page in another process's PHD is viewed as an error. The page fault handler simulates an access violation for any such attempted fault.

The swappability and pageability of the PHD result in several different methods for synchronizing access to fields within it. Because a PHD can be inswapped to a different balance set slot than it last occupied, accesses to a PHD that use its system space address must be synchronized against swapper interference. Accesses from a current process can be made with the SCHED spinlock held to block any rescheduling and possible swapping of the process. Holding the MMG spinlock is another way to block swapping.

Setting bit PHD$V_NO_WS_CHNG in PHD$L_FLAGS (see Chapter 19) blocks not only swapping of the process but also certain changes to its working set list.

Alternatively, executive code that runs in process context can access the doubly mapped part of the PHD through the P1 window and thus avoid the need for blocking possible movement of the PHD to a different balance set slot.

None of these alternatives provides a way to read, write, or update process-private PTEs in the L3PTs in the PHD. The L3PTs are not doubly mapped and are accessible only through the system space address of the PHD.

OpenVMS VAX memory management code is able to calculate the address of a process-private PTE and access it in a single instruction. The instruction references the PTE with register deferred indexed addressing mode, using the P1 window to get the contents of the process's P0 or P1 base register.

In order to perform the analogous operation, OpenVMS AXP code requires multiple instructions, during which the process could be interrupted and subsequently outswapped and inswapped to a different balance set slot. Performing this sequence with the MMG or SCHED spinlock held is not a solution because the L3PTs are pageable, and a page fault at elevated IPL would result in a system crash. To solve this problem, the PHD$V_LOCK_HEADER flag has been added to PHD$L_FLAGS as an interlock. When set, the PHD$V_LOCK_HEADER flag indicates that a memory management routine is accessing process-private L3PTs and that the process may not be swapped.

The sections that follow describe the fixed part of the PHD and its memory management substructures.

16.1.2.1   **Fixed Part of the PHD.** In addition to the pointers and indexes that locate variable-length parts of the PHD, the fixed area contains cells for process accounting information and several process quotas and limits. The hardware privileged context block (HWPCB), the area in which the privileged register context of the process is saved, is also in the fixed part of the PHD.

This part of the PHD also contains space to save the contents of floating-point registers when the process is not current.

16.1.2.2   **Working Set List.** Another memory management data structure located in the PHD is the working set list. The working set list describes the subset of a process's pages that are currently valid. Pages described in a process's working set list are P0, P1, or PHD pages. Its capacity to describe pages is the upper limit on the number of physical pages the process can occupy.

The page fault handler and swapper use the working set list to determine which virtual page to discard (to mark invalid) when it is necessary to remove a physical page from the process. The swapper also uses the working set list to determine which virtual pages need to be written to the swap file when the process is outswapped.

Chapter 19 describes the organization and use of the working set list and the layout of a working set list entry (WSLE).

16.1.2.3   **Process Section Table.** The process section table is also located in the PHD. It contains process section table entries (PSTEs). A PSTE describes the association between a contiguous portion of virtual address space and a contiguous portion of a file. Both these portions are known as sections and consist of pages with identical characteristics, for example, protection, owner access mode, writability, and file location. Virtual address space is largely managed in units of sections.

When an image is activated (see Chapter 28), the file containing the image is opened and a process section is created for each process-private image section. Although each image section is mapped separately, the image file is opened only once, and the image's sections page using the same assigned channel and window control block.

A process section is also created when

▸ A process opens a file and requests the Create and Map Section ($CRMPSC) system service to map the file or some part of it into its address space
▸ A shareable image is activated that is not shared (that is, one that has not been installed with the /SHARED qualifier through the Install utility)
▸ A shared image is activated that has a copy-on-reference section

PSTEs enable the memory management subsystem to keep track of process pages in different sections, potentially in different files on different mass storage devices.

Figure 16.3 shows the location of the PST within the PHD. PHD$L_PST-BASOFF contains the byte offset from the beginning of the PHD to the high-address end of the PST.

Each PSTE within the table is 40 bytes long and is located through a negative longword index from the base of the PST. The first PSTE has an index of $-A_{16}$, the second -14_{16}. Successive PSTEs are at lower addresses. Since all references to a PSTE are relative to PHD$L_PSTBASOFF, the PST can be moved within the PHD without requiring changes in process PTEs that contain process section table indexes. Allocating or deleting a PSTE is synchronized at IPL 2, to block other threads in the process.

The following operations compute the address of a particular PSTE:

1. Add the contents of PHD$L_PSTBASOFF to the address of the PHD. The result is the address of the base of the PST.
2. Multiply the negative process section table longword index by 4.
3. Add the (negative) result to the address of the PST.

A PST is organized into a variable number of linked lists of PSTEs. Figure 16.3 shows a typical PST with free and allocated PSTEs; the allocated PSTEs are shaded. The negative index in PHD$L_PSTLAST is the largest index of any entry ever allocated and is thus a "high-water mark."

All the process sections that page from the same section file using the same assigned channel are linked together. The entries are linked together through the backward and forward link index fields of each entry.

When a section is deleted, the PSTE that mapped the section is placed on the list of free entries so that it can be reused. The negative index PHD$L_PSTFREE points to the most recent addition to the free list. If no entry has been deleted, PHD$L_PSTFREE contains zero. The first longword in a PSTE on the free list contains the negative index to the previous element on the free list. When a section is created, the PSTE allocation routine first checks the free list. If there is no free PSTE, a new one is created from the expansion region between the working set list and the PST, and PHD$L_PSTLAST is modified.

The executive attempts to keep the working set list and PST virtually adjacent, partly to simplify and shorten manipulation of the PHD during outswap and inswap and partly to minimize the chances of wasting physical memory for partial pages of both. When the executive must expand the working set list into the area already occupied by the PST or expand the PST into the area already occupied by the working set list, it allocates space from the existing empty page area (see Figure 16.3). Then, it moves the entire PST into the allocated space at higher addresses and stores the new base address in PHD$L_PSTBASOFF.

The longword at PHD$L_PSTBASMAX/PHD$L_BAK specifies the maximum size of the PST. This longword points to the high-address end of the

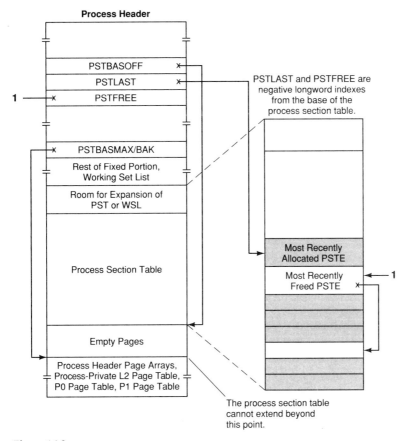

Figure 16.3
Process Section Table

empty page area. It contains a longword index from the beginning of the PHD.

Room is reserved in the PHD for the maximum PST and working set list, specified by the SYSGEN parameters PROCSECTCNT and WSMAX. It is possible for the PST to grow larger than PROCSECTCNT specifies, at the expense of the working set list.

Figure 16.4 shows the layout of a process/global section table entry. (Section 16.6.2 describes global section table entries.) Field names within a section table entry are defined by the STARLET.MLB macro $SECDEF and begin with SEC$.

The first longword in the PSTE has two names: in a PSTE, SEC$L_CCB contains the address of the channel control block (CCB) on which the section file has been opened; in a GSTE, SEC$L_GSD contains the address of the global section descriptor (GSD) for that section.

CCB/GSD
SEXFL
SEXBL
PFC
WINDOW
VBN
FLAGS
REFCNT
UNIT_CNT
VPX

PSTE Flags

Bit	Meaning
0	Global
1	Copy on reference
2	Demand zero
3	Writable
4–5	*(reserved)*
6–7	Access mode for writing
8–9	Owner access mode
10–13	*(reserved)*
14	Permanent
15	0 = Group global
	1 = System global

Figure 16.4
Layout of Process/Global Section Table Entry
(PSTE/GSTE)

SEC$L_SEXFL and SEC$L_SEXBL contain negative indexes from the base of the section table to the previous and next section table entry. These link an entry in use into a list of others that page using the same CCB. They also link all free entries together.

SEC$L_PFC is the number of section pages that the page fault handler attempts to read in together when a page fault occurs.

SEC$L_WINDOW is the address of the window control block (WCB) that describes the locations of the section file on a mass storage volume. The WCB points to the unit control block (UCB) for the volume.

SEC$L_VBN specifies the starting virtual, or file-relative, block number (VBN) of the section file at which the pages in this section begin.

SEC$L_FLAGS contains flag bits that describe the section.

SEC$L_REFCNT contains the number of PTEs that refer to the section.

SEC$L_UNIT_CNT contains the number of units in the section. A PFN-mapped section is measured in units of physical pages. Any other type of section is measured in 512-byte pagelets. A pagelet is the size of a mass storage block. Note that a section file can occupy an arbitrary number of blocks or pagelets but a section must be created as a number of pages. If the number of blocks in a section file is not an integral multiple of blocks per page, the last page in the section is said to be partial.

For a process-private section, SEC$L_UNIT_CNT is initially related to SEC$L_REFCNT. If the section has no partial pages, then SEC$L_UNIT_CNT is initialized as an integral multiple of SEC$L_REFCNT. On a system with an 8 KB page size, SEC$L_UNIT_CNT would be SEC$L_REFCNT multiplied by 16. If the section ends with a page not completely backed up by section file blocks, SEC$L_UNIT_CNT is less than an integral multiple of SEC$L_REFCNT. For a global section, SEC$L_REFCNT is the number of PTEs that refer to the section's units from all the processes that have mapped it. For either type of section, SEC$L_REFCNT is decreased when a process deletes pages in its address space that map the section.

SEC$L_VPX contains the starting virtual page number at which the section's pages are mapped in the address space.

Most fields in a PSTE are initialized when the section is created and not modified subsequently. SEC$L_REFCNT is modified as the process deletes section pages from its address space. It is modified with the MMG spinlock held, since it can be accessed from process context and also by I/O postprocessing code. SEC$L_FLAGS is modified using the load-locked/store-conditional mechanism.

The following steps locate a virtual page in a section file through information in the PSTE:

1. Subtract the section's starting virtual page number from the virtual page number of the faulting page to obtain the page offset into the section.
2. Multiply the page offset by the number of pagelets per page.
3. Add the contents of SEC$L_VBN to the block offset computed in step 2 to get the VBN of the virtual page within the file.

   (In page faulting from a section file or writing a modified page back to a section file, the executive checks whether the section file has a page's worth of blocks beginning at that VBN. It compares the contents of SEC$L_UNIT_CNT, the number of pagelets (and therefore blocks) in the section file, to the sum of that VBN and the number of blocks in a page. If the section does not have enough blocks, the executive transfers only as many blocks as exist in the section file for that virtual page and zeros the rest of the page.)
4. Use the mapping information in the WCB to transform the VBN to a logical block number on a mass storage volume.

16.1.2.4 **Process Header Page Arrays.** When a PHD is outswapped, some information about each PHD page is stored in the PHD page array portion of the outswapped PHD. Figure 16.5 shows this area. Two of the arrays, the BAK and WSLX arrays, save information about each PHD page in the working set, copied either from the PFN database (see Section 16.2) or from the system page table entry (SPTE) that maps that PHD page.

While a PHD is resident, the backing store location of each of its valid or transition pages is stored in the PFN database; the backing store location of a PHD page in a page file is stored in the SPTE that maps the PHD page. For a valid page in a resident PHD, the PFN database stores information about the

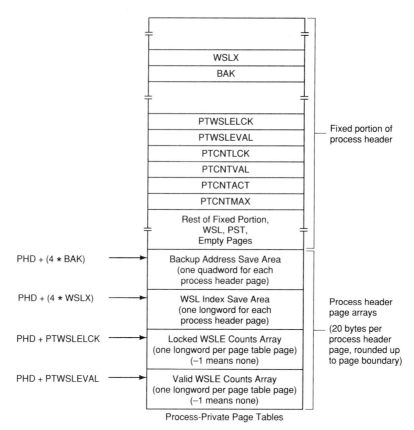

Figure 16.5
Process Header Page Arrays

location of the page's entry in the process's working set list. When the PHD is outswapped, both the physical pages and the balance set slot it occupied are released for other uses. The PHD BAK array records the backing store information for each PHD page, which would otherwise be lost.

The PHD WSLX array records the location in the working set list of each PHD page. Without this information, locating the page table pages in the working set list at inswap, in order to lock them into the working set list as the pages that they map are reconnected, would require an inefficient search of the working set list.

The other two arrays, locked WSLE count and valid WSLE count, contain a reference count for each L3PT page. They are described in greater detail in Chapter 18.

16.1.3   Process Page Tables

As shown in Figure 15.6, each process has its own page table hierarchy. When a process is created, the executive allocates and initializes a page of physical memory for use as the process's level 1 page table (L1PT). After being initialized, a process's L1PT is not accessed virtually (except through the page table virtual address region by the TB miss PALcode routine), and it has no permanent system space mapping. The executive accesses only three L1PTEs in an L1PT: those that map the process-private L2PT, the shared L2PT, and the L1PT itself. The L1PT is not outswapped with the process; instead, the page is released at outswap and a new L1PT is initialized at process inswap.

The executive also creates a process-private L2PT for the process. The L2PT is part of the PHD, and PHD$L_L2PT_VA contains the system virtual address of the L2PT. The L2PT is nonpageable and permanently locked into the process's working set list. The process-private L2PT maps the L3PTs that make up the process's P0 and P1 space. On a system with an 8 KB page size, the first 256 L2PTEs are sufficient to map the full process-private address space supported in this release: 1 GB of P0 space and 1 GB of P1 space.

Figure 16.6 shows the process-private page tables in the PHD and the fields in the fixed portion of the PHD that locate the process-private L2PT, P0, and P1 page tables.

A P0 or P1 page table can grow as required to reflect expansion of the address space it maps. The executive merely maps additional page table pages into the virtual addresses contiguous to the end of the page table. Because the dynamic growth of a process page table can accommodate the dynamic expansion of a process's virtual address space, the size of a process's page tables can be adjusted to suit its needs. The executive does not need to allocate maximum-size process page tables for all processes. Furthermore, P0 and P1 page tables can themselves be paged.

The P0 page table consists of L3PTs that contain PTEs for all pages currently defined in P0 space. The L3PTEs that make up the P0 page table are called P0PTEs. The starting system space virtual address of the P0 page table is stored in offset PHD$L_L3PT_VA. The current size of the P0 page table in bytes is stored in offset PHD$L_P0LENGTH. The number of PTEs in it is its length in bytes divided by 8.

PHD$L_FREP0VA contains the virtual address corresponding to the first unmapped page in P0 space. The P0 page table maps process addresses from 0 to the contents of PHD$L_FREP0VA less 1. In other words, the contents of PHD$L_FREP0VA are the product of the page size in bytes and the number of P0PTEs.

In a similar manner, the P1 page table contains P1PTEs for the pages in P1 space. Its base address and length are stored in fields PHD$L_L3PT_VA_ P1 and PHD$L_P1LENGTH. Like P1 space itself, the P1 page table grows toward smaller addresses. The base address of the P1 page table is the virtual address of the P1PTE that would map virtual address 40000000_{16}, that is, virtual page 0 in P1 space. This allows a P1 virtual page number to be used as an index into the P1 page table. PHD$L_P1LENGTH contains the size

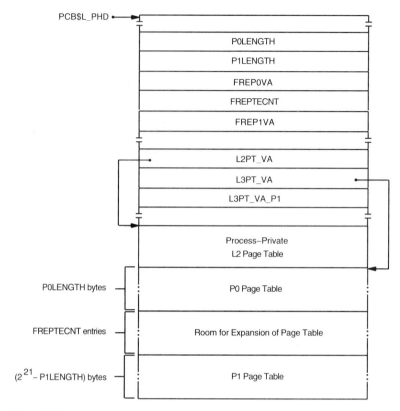

Figure 16.6
Process Page Tables

in bytes of the P1PTEs between virtual page 0 and the first defined (that is, lowest) page of P1 space.

The virtual address corresponding to the first unmapped page in P1 space is stored at offset PHD$L_FREP1VA. The P1 page table maps addresses from the contents of PHD$L_FREP1VA plus the size of a page in bytes to $7FFFFFFF_{16}$.

The SYSGEN parameter VIRTUALPAGECNT is the upper limit on the maximum combined number of L3PTEs in the P0 and P1 page tables. Chapter 17 describes additional limits to the growth of virtual address space. The number of L3PTEs available for the expansion of either P0 space or P1 space is stored in offset PHD$L_FREPTECNT. This number is the SYSGEN parameter VIRTUALPAGECNT minus the current sizes of the P0 and P1 page tables.

Because the P0 page table, P1 page table, and L2PT are part of the PHD, they are all mapped by SPTEs. Figure 16.7 shows this double mapping. In this figure, each pointer represents a PFN. When a P0 or P1 page table page

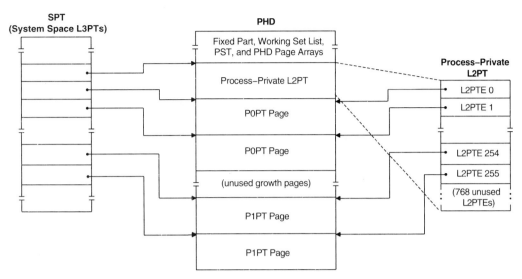

Figure 16.7
P0 and P1 Page Tables Mapped by L2PT and SPT

is valid, both the SPTE and the L2PTE that map it contain the same value. When a P0 or P1 page table page is removed from a process's working set, both possible TB entries must be invalidated. (In addition, because process page tables are also mapped in the page table virtual address region, a possible TB entry representing that address must also be invalidated.) Backing store information about the page is stored in the SPTE, and the L2PTE is cleared except for the bit enabling kernel read.

Figure 16.8 shows the various forms of valid and invalid PTE that can appear in an L3PT. The shaded bits in each PTE are either reserved or bits whose contents are irrelevant for that form of PTE.

Chapter 15 describes the architecturally defined bits in a valid PTE: bits $\langle 15:0 \rangle$ and bits $\langle 63:32 \rangle$.

Bits $\langle 31:16 \rangle$ are reserved for software. The executive defines a number of them:

▶ Bit 16 in a valid PTE is the window bit. When set, it means that the virtual page is a double mapping of a physical page. When the virtual page is deleted, the PFN database for the physical page should not be altered.

▶ Bit 20 in a valid PTE is the modify bit. When set, it means that the virtual page has been modified and not yet been written to backing store.

▶ Bits $\langle 29:28 \rangle$ specify how the page should be copied when a process's address space is cloned during a Portable Operating System Interface (POSIX) fork operation.

495

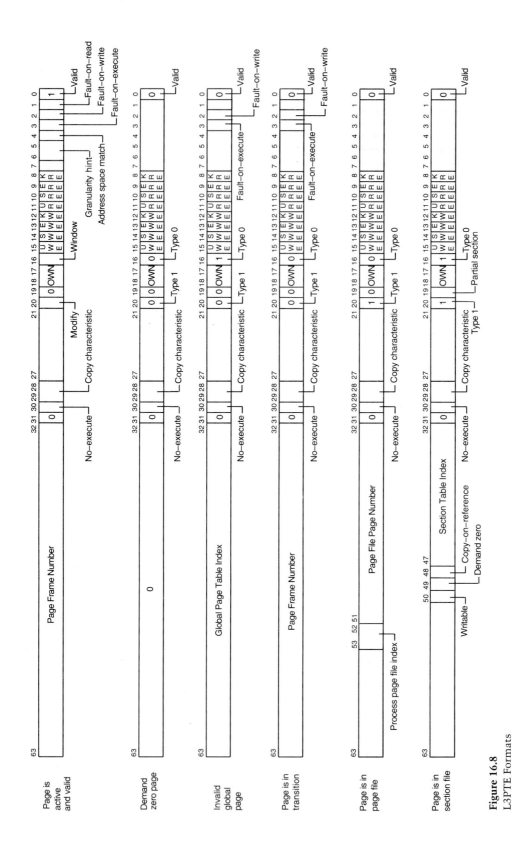

Figure 16.8
L3PTE Formats

▶ Bit 30, when set, specifies that no execution access to the page is permitted. The Translated Image Environment (TIE) facility identifies a VAX image page containing untranslated code as no-execute. The executive sets the fault-on-execute bit as well so that an attempted instruction fetch from such a page triggers an exception.

▶ Bit 31 always contains zero to distinguish a PTE from the system virtual address of a PTE, whose bit 31 is set.

Notice that the valid bit, protection bits, owner access mode bits, copy characteristic bits, and bit 31 have the same meaning in all forms of PTE.

The owner access mode bits record the access mode that owns that page. The executive allows a process to modify the characteristics of a virtual page or delete it from an access mode equal to or more privileged than the page's owner access mode.

A PTE for an invalid page contains either the location of the page or a pointer to further information about the page. The page fault handler uses the type bits, bits ⟨16⟩ and ⟨20⟩, in the invalid PTE to distinguish the different forms of invalid PTE. These are described in the sections that follow. Chapter 18 describes the processing of page faults for various types of invalid PTE.

One form of invalid PTE not pictured in Figure 16.8 is a null page, a quadword of zero. A PTE with a zero protection code disallows any access to the page by any mode. This form of PTE describes an unmapped page of address space.

16.1.3.1 **PTE Containing a Process Section Table Index.** The PTE of each page in a process section contains the index of the PSTE describing that section. The PSTE has information about the location of the file mapped into the process address space and about the mapping between virtual file blocks and section pages.

The PSTE also contains control bits that are copied to the PTE of each page in the section:

▶ Bit PTE$V_CRF (bit 48) is set to indicate the page is copy-on-reference.
▶ Bit PTE$V_DZRO (bit 49) is set to indicate the page is demand zero.
▶ Bit PTE$V_WRT (bit 50) is set to indicate the page is writable.

In addition, bit PTE$V_PARTIAL_SECTION (bit 19) is set in a PTE that maps a page not entirely backed by a section file. With page size not equal to disk block size, any section file whose block count is not an integral multiple of pages has a last page with this attribute.

Section 16.1.2.3 describes the PST organization and layout of the PSTE.

16.1.3.2 **PTE Containing a Page File Page Number.** A process can page in up to four different page files. Each process has a four-byte array in its PHD, beginning at offset PHD$B_PRCPGFL, that identifies the page files it can use. Each byte can contain a different systemwide page file index, an index into the page-and-swap-file vector. Section 16.8.2 contains more information on the page-and-swap-file vector, and Chapter 18 discusses the assignment of a process to a page file.

When a virtual page has been faulted out to a page file, its PTE contains the number of the page within the page file and a two-bit number starting at bit PTE$V_PRCPGFLX (bits ⟨53 : 52⟩) indicating the page file in which the page is located. The two-bit number, referred to as a process-local page file index, indexes the PHD array at PHD$B_PRCPGFL. (VAX VMS Version 5 introduced this extra level of indirection because there were insufficient spare bits in the PTE to specify an eight-bit page file index. The OpenVMS AXP executive retained this form for ease of porting.)

A process has a current page file in which pages have been reserved for its use as backing store. PHD$L_PRCPAGFIL contains the process-local index of the process's current page file. PHD$B_PAGFIL contains the corresponding systemwide index into the page-and-swap-file vector.

The quadword PHD$Q_PAGFIL, of which PHD$B_PAGFIL is the high-order byte, is a template for a virtual page that requires a page file backing store address. When such a page is first faulted, the template is copied to the PFN$Q_BAK field in the PFN database record (see Section 16.2.2) for the physical page. Bits ⟨53 : 52⟩ of the template contain the same value as PHD$L_PRCPAGFIL. Bits ⟨41 : 32⟩ contain zero. A PFN$Q_BAK field containing such a template backing store address indicates that blocks in the specified page file have been reserved for the virtual page but not yet allocated.

16.1.3.3   **PTE Containing a Global Page Table Index.** The PTE of an invalid process page mapped to a global page contains an index into the global page table, where an associated global PTE contains the information used to locate the page. Section 16.6.4 describes the contents of global PTEs.

16.1.3.4   **PTE of a Page in Transition.** When a physical page is removed from a process working set, it is not discarded but put on the free or modified page list. The invalid virtual page, still associated with the physical page, is called a transition page. Its PTE contains a PFN, but the valid bit is clear. The two type bits are also clear. Retaining the connection to a physical page enables the executive to fault the virtual page back into the working set with minimal overhead until the physical page is reallocated for another use.

Another type of transition page is a virtual page in transit between mass storage and physical memory. When a process faults a page not in memory, the page fault handler allocates a physical page and requests an I/O operation to read the virtual page from its backing store. While the I/O request is in progress, the virtual page has a transition PTE.

A transition page is described further by its physical page's record in the

PFN database (see Section 16.2). In particular, the PFN$L_PAGE_STATE field in the PFN database record (see Section 16.2.3) identifies the state of the page and distinguishes among the different types of transition page.

16.1.3.5   **PTE of a Demand Zero Page.** One form of transition PTE has a zero in the PFN field. This zero indicates a special form of page called a demand-allocate, zero-fill page, or demand zero page for short. A demand zero page is a writable page of address space, created on demand instead of being read in from backing store, and zeroed. When a page fault occurs for such a page, the page fault handler first tries to allocate a physical page from the zeroed page list. If the zeroed page list is empty, the page fault handler must allocate a physical page from the free page list and fill the page with zeros. In either case, it then inserts the PFN into the PTE, sets the valid and modify bits, and dismisses the exception.

16.2   **PFN DATABASE**

The memory management data structures contain information about each page of physical memory, including those reserved for use by the console subsystem. The fact that this information must be accessible while the page is in use means that it cannot be stored in the page itself. In addition, the caching strategy for the free and modified page lists requires physical page information to be accessible even when pages are not currently active and valid. The PFN database records this information.

The OpenVMS AXP PFN database consists of one 32-byte record, or structure, for each page of physical memory (see Figure 16.9). Its starting address is stored in cell PFN$PL_DATABASE, and access to it is synchronized by the MMG spinlock. Each record is aligned on a 32-byte virtual and physical address boundary.

Each field in the record contains a specific item of information about that physical page of memory. Table 16.1 summarizes the information in each

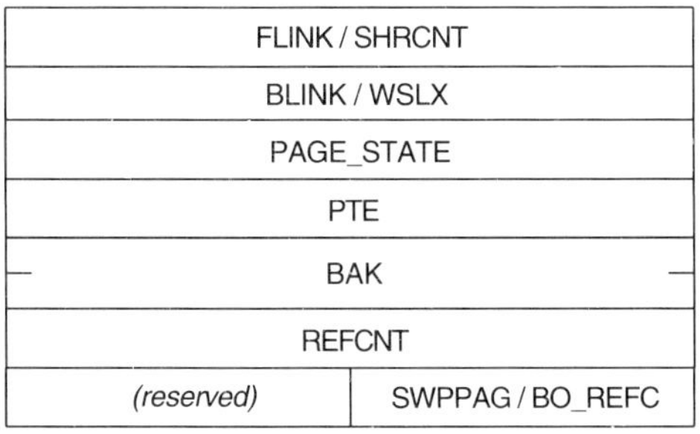

FLINK / SHRCNT	
BLINK / WSLX	
PAGE_STATE	
PTE	
BAK	
REFCNT	
(reserved)	SWPPAG / BO_REFC

Figure 16.9
Layout of PFN Database Record

Table 16.1   PFN Database Record Fields

Contents	Name	Size	Comments
Global share count	SHRCNT	Longword	Overlays FLINK
Forward link	FLINK	Longword	Figure 16.12; Overlays SHRCNT
Working set list index	WSLX	Longword	Overlays BLINK
Backward link	BLINK	Longword	Figure 16.12; Overlays WSLX
Physical page state and type	PAGE_STATE	Longword	Figure 16.11
System virtual address of PTE	PTE	Longword	
Backing store address	BAK	Quadword	Figure 16.10
Reference count	REFCNT	Longword	
Swap file page number	SWPPAG	Word	Overlays BO_REFC
Buffer object reference count	BO_REFC	Word	Overlays SWPPAG

PFN database record. In listing the names of the fields in each record, the table omits the prefix PFN$*x*_, where *x* identifies the data type.

Although the OpenVMS VAX PFN database contains the same basic information, its organization is quite different: it consists of multiple arrays, each containing a different type of information with an element for each page.

Typically, executive code accesses more than one kind of information about a particular page when it accesses the PFN database. Thus, to make cache hits more likely and to improve performance, the OpenVMS AXP PFN database is organized as a set of records, each one holding different types of information about the same page.

During system initialization SYSBOOT determines how many pages of physical memory are present on the system and how big the PFN database must be to describe them all. It allocates enough system space from the granularity hint region for systemwide writable data (see Section 16.4) and zeros the entire database. It then initializes each page's type to PFN$C_UN-KNOWN.

Most of the information in a PFN record for a page relates to the current virtual use of that physical page. For a physical page that has no connection to a virtual page, the only meaningful information is found in the PFNL_FLINK, PFNL_BLINK, and PFN$L_PAGE_STATE fields.

The page frame number of a physical page is the index of its record in the PFN database; that is, information about a particular page is located by indexing the PFN database with the PFN of that page. To transform a PFN into the address of its PFN database record, the OpenVMS AXP system provides a macro called PFN_TO_ENTRY for use by MACRO-32 code. An example of its use follows:

```
PFN_TO_ENTRY -                      ;Get PFN database record address
PFN = R0,-                          ;PFN of interest (input)
ENTRY = R15                         ;Address of its record (output)
EVAX_LDQ R2,PFN$Q_BAK(R15)          ;Get backing store information
MOVL     PFN$L_PTE(R15),R3          ;Get address of PTE mapping page
```

This transformation currently consists of multiplying the size of each record by the page's PFN and adding that offset to the base address of the PFN database.

The global location MMG$GL_MINPFN contains the lowest valid PFN in the PFN database. It is currently initialized to zero. The global location MMG$GL_MAXPFN contains the highest PFN described in the PFN database, that is, not necessarily the highest PFN on the system but rather the PFN of the highest physical page that the operating system or the console subsystem can use. The two maxima can differ if the SYSGEN parameter PHYSICAL_MEMORY has been defined to be less than the amount of memory present on the system.

The sections that follow describe the fields that make up each PFN record.

16.2.1   PFN$L_PTE Field

The PFN$L_PTE field contains the system virtual address of the PTE that maps that physical page. If no virtual page is mapped to a physical page, its PFN$L_PTE field contains zero. The PFN$L_PTE field for a global page contains the virtual address of the global PTE.

Since a buffer object (see Section 16.5) page is locked into memory, its PFN$L_PTE field can be initialized so that incorrect use of it triggers a system crash; it contains an illegal system space address whose low-order word contains the process index of the buffer object creator.

When assigning a physical page to a new use, the executive examines its PFN$L_PTE field to determine whether the page is a transition page and still pointed to by a PTE associated with its previous use. If the field contents are not zero, the executive must take steps to sever the connection between the physical page and its previous use.

16.2.2   PFN$Q_BAK Field

The PFN$Q_BAK field contains the backing store location for the virtual page occupying a physical page. When a physical page is assigned to another use, the PTE, if any, that currently maps the page must be updated. The executive replaces information about the location of the virtual page in memory (the PFN of the physical page that contains it) with information about its location in mass storage copied from the PFN$Q_BAK field.

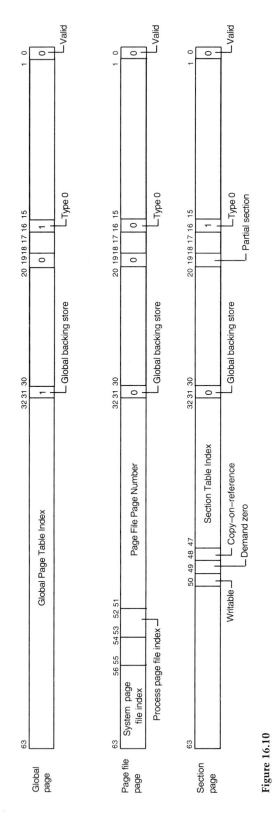

Figure 16.10
Possible Contents of PFN$Q_BAK Field

502

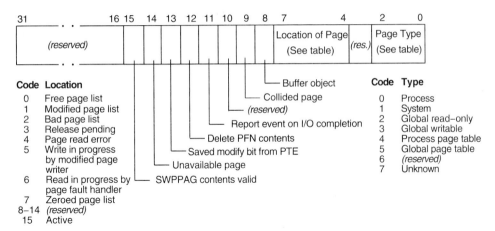

Figure 16.11
Contents of PFN$L_PAGE_STATE Field

Figure 16.10 shows the possible contents of a PFN$Q_BAK field. The shaded bits in each form are either reserved or bits whose contents are irrelevant for that form of backing store information.

16.2.3   PFN$L_PAGE_STATE Field

The PFN$L_PAGE_STATE field, shown in Figure 16.11, indicates the state, type, and location of a physical page.

As shown in the figure, bits $\langle 2:0 \rangle$ of this field identify the type of virtual page that occupies the corresponding physical page, for example, whether it is a process or system page or page table page. The page fault handler, swapper, and other parts of the executive take actions dependent on page type.

Bits $\langle 7:4 \rangle$ contain the page location code, indicating, for example, whether the page is on the free page list or valid in a working set.

Several page location codes require further explanation:

▶ Release pending means that the virtual page has been removed from a working set but still has a nonzero reference count. When the reference count is decremented to zero at I/O completion, the physical page will be placed on the free or modified page list.

▶ Page read error means that a nonrecoverable I/O error occurred during an attempt to read the virtual page from its backing store into the physical page. During postprocessing of the I/O request, when the error is noted, this code is stored in the PFN$L_PAGE_STATE field. Consequently, when the page is later refaulted, the page fault handler will signal a page read error exception.

▶ Write in progress means that the modified page writer has initiated I/O to write the page to its backing store.

▶ Read in progress means that the page fault handler has initiated I/O to read the page from its backing store.

▶ A page on the zeroed page list is a free page that was completely zeroed when the system would otherwise have been idle. Such a page can be allocated as a demand zero page, as a page most of whose contents are zero, or as a section page only partly represented on disk.

The PFN$L_PAGE_STATE field also has a number of status bits.

The buffer object bit (PFN$V_BUFOBJ), when set, means the page is part of a buffer object or is a page table page that maps a buffer object (see Section 16.5).

The collided page bit (PFN$V_COLLISION) is set when a page fault occurs for a virtual page that is already being read in from its backing store (one whose location bits show it as read in progress). This can happen, for example, if multiple processes fault a shared page. It can also happen if a process in a page fault wait is interrupted for asynchronous system trap (AST) delivery and then reexecutes the instruction that triggered the page fault. When I/O completes for a page with this bit set, I/O postprocessing code clears the bit and reports the system event collided page available for all processes in the collided page wait state. Chapter 13 describes system events. Collided pages are discussed briefly in Chapter 18.

The report event bit (PFN$V_RPTEVT) is set when an attempt is made to delete a virtual page that cannot be deleted immediately, for example, because the modified page writer is writing the page to its backing store. The executive places the process into a page fault wait. When the modified page writer's I/O completes, it reports a page fault completion system event. When the process is placed back into execution, the page deletion proceeds.

The delete contents bit (PFN$V_DELCON) is set to indicate that the connection between a physical page and its virtual contents should be severed. When the reference count of a physical page whose delete contents bit is set becomes zero, the PFN$L_PTE field in its PFN database record is cleared. The physical page is then put at the front of the free page list, where it will be reused before pages that are still associated with virtual pages.

The modify bit (PFN$V_MODIFY) is set to indicate a modified page that has not yet been written to its backing store. It determines whether a physical page is put on the free page list or the modified page list when the page's reference count reaches zero. The modify bit is set under a number of circumstances, including the following:

▶ On the first attempt to write to a writable virtual page, the executive sets the modify bit in its PTE. When a virtual page is removed from a working set, the modify bit in its PTE is logically ORed into the saved modify bit in the PFN$L_PAGE_STATE field for the physical page. The modify bit must be recorded in the PFN$L_PAGE_STATE field because that bit in an invalid PTE has another use as the TYP1 bit.

▸ When a page is used as a direct I/O read buffer, the executive routine that locks down pages, MMG$IOLOCK, in module IOLOCK, sets the modify bit in its PTE. When the page is removed from the process's working set, the OR operation described in the previous item sets the modify bit in PFN$L_PAGE_STATE.

▸ When a copy-on-reference page is faulted into a working set, the executive sets the modify bit in the PFN$L_PAGE_STATE field of the physical page. Thus, even if the virtual page is not modified while it is valid, when the page is removed from the working set, the physical page is inserted into the modified list. This ensures that it will be written to page file backing store, from where it will be read on a subsequent page fault.

▸ When a demand zero page is faulted into a process's working set, the modify bit in PFN$L_PAGE_STATE is set.

▸ When a buffer object is created, the modify bit is set in PFN$L_PAGE_STATE for each of its pages.

The swap page valid bit (PFN$V_SWPPAG_VALID) bit is set by the swapper to indicate that the contents of PFN$W_SWPPAG represent a swap file page number.

The unavailable page bit (PFN$V_UNAVAILABLE), when set, means the page is not available for the operating system to use. Typically, it means that the page is in a memory region reserved for the console subsystem's use.

16.2.4 PFN$L_FLINK and PFN$L_BLINK Fields

A physical page not occupied by a valid virtual page is in one of four lists: the free, modified, bad, or zeroed page list. The heads of the first three lists are in an array of longwords that begins at global location PFN$AL_HEAD. Their list tails are in the array PFN$AL_TAIL. Each array has three elements, the first for the free page list, the second for the modified page list, and the third for the bad page list.

These three page lists must all be doubly linked lists because a page is often arbitrarily removed from the middle of the list. The links cannot exist in the pages themselves because the contents of each page must be preserved. The forward link (FLINK) and backward link (BLINK) fields in a PFN database record implement the links for each page. The PFN$L_FLINK field contains the PFN of the successor page, and the PFN$L_BLINK field that of the predecessor page.

A zero in one of the link fields indicates the end of the list, rather than being a pointer to physical page 0. This is one reason why physical page 0 cannot be used in any dynamic function. Another reason is that the representation of invalid demand zero PTEs assumes that a PFN of zero can never appear in an invalid PTE (see Figure 16.8). However, it can be used by a system virtual page that is always resident. Physical page 0 is usually in an area of memory reserved for the console subsystem.

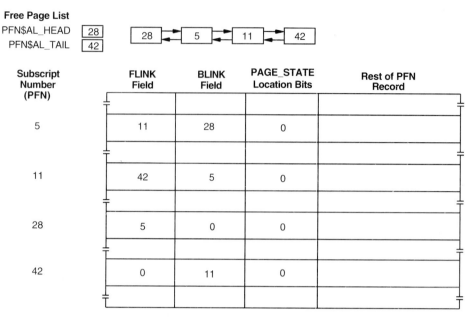

Figure 16.12
Example of Free Page List Showing Linkage Method

Figure 16.12 shows an example of pages on the free page list, along with their corresponding PFN$L_FLINK and PFN$L_BLINK fields. The PFN$L_PAGE_STATE location bit for each page contains zero, indicating that the physical page is on the free page list.

The zeroed page list head is at MMG$GQ_ZEROED_LIST. The list is singly linked so that pages can be inserted at and removed from the head of the list with the load-locked/store-conditional mechanism. The number of pages on the list is in cell MMG$GQ_ZEROED_LIST_COUNT. The SYS-GEN parameter ZERO_LIST_HI specifies the maximum number of pages on this list. The list serves as a source of demand zero pages that have already been zeroed. When there is no computable process to execute, the scheduler idle loop removes a page from the free page list that has no connection to any virtual page and clears the page. After clearing the entire page, the idle loop inserts the page on the zeroed page list.

16.2.5   PFN$L_REFCNT Field

The PFN$L_REFCNT field counts the number of reasons a physical page should not be placed on the free or modified page list. For instance, the count is incremented if a page is in a process working set; is part of a direct I/O buffer with I/O in progress; or is part of a buffer object or a page table page mapping a buffer object.

I/O completion and working set replacement use the same mechanism to decrement the reference count. When the reference count goes to zero, the physical page is released to the free or modified page list, depending on the saved modify bit in its PFN$L_PAGE_STATE field. Manipulations of the reference count are illustrated and described in greater detail in Chapter 18.

16.2.6   PFN$L_SHRCNT Field

A second form of reference count is kept for global pages. PFN$L_SHRCNT, the share count field in a PFN database record, counts the number of process PTEs that are mapped to a particular global page. When the share count for a particular page goes from 0 to 1, the PFN$L_REFCNT field is incremented. Further additions to the share count do not affect the reference count.

As the global page is removed from the working set of each process mapped to the page, the share count is decremented. When the share count finally reaches zero, the PFN$L_REFCNT field for the page is also decremented.

Because a physical page with a nonzero share count cannot be on one of the page lists, the forward and backward link fields are not needed for such a page. The PFN$L_SHRCNT field overlays the PFN$L_FLINK field.

Process and global page table pages also use the PFN$L_SHRCNT field. When this count goes from zero to nonzero, the page table page is dynamically locked into a working set: a process page table page into a process working set, and a global page table page into the system working set. Chapter 18 describes the share count in further detail.

16.2.7   PFN$L_WSLX Field

The working set list index field, PFN$L_WSLX, for a valid page contains a longword index from the beginning of the process (or system) header to the WSLE for that page. The PFN$L_WSLX field is used, for example, during the deallocation of a page of memory. If the virtual page is valid, the WSLE that describes it must be altered. Without the contents of the PFN$L_WSLX field, it would be necessary to search the working set list to locate the WSLE.

Because a physical page in a working set is not on one of the page lists, the PFN$L_FLINK and PFN$L_BLINK fields are not needed for such a page. The PFN$L_WSLX field overlays the PFN$L_BLINK field.

The PFN$L_WSLX field for a global page counts the number of times the page has been locked into memory.

16.2.8   PFN$W_SWPPAG Field

The swap file page number field, PFN$W_SWPPAG, supports the outswap of a process with read I/O in progress. When such an outswap occurs, the swapper sets bit PFN$V_SWPPAG_VALID in PFN$L_PAGE_STATE and records in PFN$W_SWPPAG the page offset in the process body part of the swap slot into which the locked down page should be written.

When the swapper I/O is completed, the locked page is marked release pending. When the original I/O is completed, the I/O postprocessing routine sees that the page is in the release pending state and has the saved modify bit set, and inserts the page on the modified page list. The modified page writer checks the PFN$V_SWPPAG_VALID bit and, if it is nonzero, diverts a modified page from its normal backing store address to the designated location in the swap file.

Because a physical page in a buffer object or a page table page that maps a buffer object cannot be outswapped, this field is not needed to describe such a page. The PFN$W_BO_REFC field overlays the PFN$W_SWPPAG field.

16.2.9   PFN$W_BO_REFC Field

Another form of reference count is kept for buffer object pages (see Section 16.5). The buffer object reference count field, PFN$W_BO_REFC, counts the number of processes in whose address space a buffer object page has been mapped. When the reference count for a particular buffer object page goes from 0 to 1, its PFN$L_REFCNT field is incremented. Further additions to the buffer object reference count do not affect the PFN reference count. For a page table page that maps one or more buffer objects, PFN$W_BO_REFC contains the number of buffer object pages mapped by the page table page.

Because a physical page in a buffer object or a page table page that maps a buffer object cannot be outswapped, the PFN$W_SWPPAG field is not needed to describe such a page. The PFN$W_BO_REFC field overlays the PFN$W_SWPPAG field.

16.3   SYSTEM DATA STRUCTURES

There are several systemwide memory management data structures analogous to process data structures.

16.3.1   System Header and System PCB

The executive maintains two data structures for itself that parallel process structures: the system PCB and system header. Using these, the page fault handler can treat page faults of system pages almost identically to page faults for process pages.

The system PCB, whose address is in MMG$AR_SYSPCB, contains a base priority used for I/O requests for page faults of system space pages and global pages. It also has a pointer to the system header, parallel to the PHD pointer in any process PCB.

The system header, whose address is in MMG$GL_SYSPHD, occupies part of the granularity hint region for systemwide writable data. As shown in Figure 16.13, the system header contains a working set list and a section table. Its working set list governs page replacement for pageable system pages (other than those within the balance set slots). Pageable system pages come

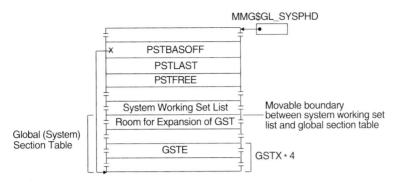

Figure 16.13
System Header Containing the System Working Set List
and the Global Section Table

from pageable sections in executive images, paged pool, and the global page table. These are all paged in the system working set list. Its size in pagelets is determined by the SYSGEN parameter SYSMWCNT. Unlike other working set lists, the system working set list does not expand or contract in response to system page fault rate. Once the system working set fills, replacement paging is required. Changes to the system working set list are synchronized by the MMG spinlock.

The backing store for pageable writable executive data and page file global sections is within page files. Like a PHD, the system header contains a four-byte array at PHD$B_PRCPGFL with systemwide indexes of the page files that have been assigned. PHD$L_PRCPAGFIL contains the process-local index of the current page file, and PHD$B_PAGFIL, the systemwide index of the current page file.

The section table in the system header contains entries for sections in files that contain pageable system pages and for global sections. The SYSGEN parameter GBLSECTIONS specifies the number of entries in the section table.

16.3.2   System Page Table

During system initialization SYSBOOT allocates one physical page for the shared L2PT that maps system space and initializes it. SYSBOOT stores its PFN in the cell MMG$GL_SHARED_L2PT_PFN and its system virtual address in the system header field PHD$L_L2PT_VA. The shared L2PT is not itself part of the system header.

While SYSBOOT is executing, it creates system space beginning at location FFFFFFFF 80000000$_{16}$. It creates as much as needed for executive images and data structures, such as the balance set slots. It allocates physical pages of memory for the L3PTs that make up the SPT and stores their PFNs in the appropriate L2PTEs. SYSBOOT allocates only enough L3PTs to map the amount of system space it created. Because the Alpha AXP architecture supports a sparse address space and does not require page tables that map virtually contiguous address regions to be physically contiguous, additional L3PTs can be allocated after system initialization.

The SPT, therefore, does not need to map the entire 2 GB of possible system space. If, during system operation, there are insufficient SPTEs, the SPT can be extended beyond its current size by allocating a physical page for another L3PT, initializing the next available L2PTE to map that page, and initializing the new L3PTEs. (In contrast, the VAX architecture requires a physically contiguous SPT. OpenVMS VAX SYSBOOT must calculate the maximum size of system space and allocate the entire SPT. It uses SYSGEN parameters such as SPTREQ to estimate the maximum size.)

On a system with an 8 KB page size, the last 256 L2PTEs are sufficient to map a full 2 GB of system space. The other 768 L2PTEs are unused. The 769th L2PTE (counting from 1) maps the first L3PT that makes up the SPT. The last L2PTE contains its own PFN (it maps itself). Thus, the L2PT also has a role as an L3PT.

As a result of this self-mapping, the L2PT and the L3PTs it maps can be accessed through system space virtual addresses by memory management routines altering SPTEs, for example, in response to system space page faults. This self-mapping should not be confused with the self-mapping by which an L1PTE maps the L1PT as an L2PT to create the page table virtual address region beginning at $2\ 00000000_{16}$. As described in Chapter 15, the page table virtual address region is used solely by the TB miss PALcode routine.

Figure 16.14 illustrates the page table hierarchy that results from the self-mapping.

Because of the self-mapping, the L3PTs that make up the SPT map the shared L2PT and a possible 1,024 L3PTs, most of which are not used. Figure 16.15 shows this self-mapping. The left-hand part of the figure shows the entire address space mapped by the last L1PTE (not to scale). Three-fourths of it is unused in this OpenVMS AXP release. The high fourth of it, from $FFFFFFFF\ 80000000_{16}$ to $FFFFFFFF\ FFFFFFFF_{16}$, is available for system space.

The middle part of the figure shows the part of this address space that would map 1,024 L3PTs if all shared L2PTEs were used. The first 768 L3PTs are unused and correspond to the unused 6 GB in the left-hand part of the figure. The first L3PT of those that make up the SPT begins at $FFFFFFFF\ FFE00000_{16}$. The last L3PT in this region is also the L2PT.

The right-hand part of the figure shows the L2PT. Its first 768 entries are unused. The next entry is the one that maps the first page of SPT. The last entry is the one that maps the L2PT itself.

The global cell MMG$GL_SPTBASE contains the system virtual address of the system page table. For the most part, SPTEs can take on the same formats as valid and invalid process PTEs (see Figure 16.8). The one exception is that an invalid SPTE cannot have the global page table index format.

Additionally, invalid SPTEs that are unused and available for allocation are

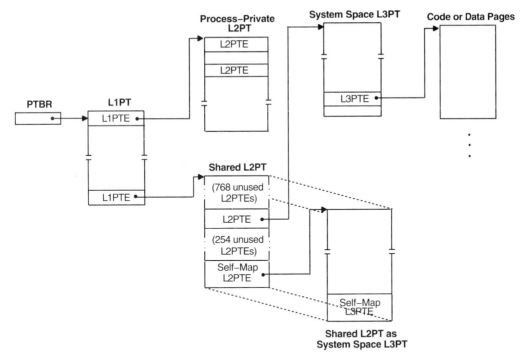

Figure 16.14
System Space Page Table Hierarchy

linked together in a list. The SPTEs themselves contain information such as a pointer to the next group of free SPTEs and the number of free SPTEs in this group. Chapter 32 shows the contents of SPTEs used in this way.

The MMG spinlock synchronizes changes to SPTEs and allocation from the list of available SPTEs.

16.4   **GRANULARITY HINT REGIONS AND HUGE PAGES**

An Alpha AXP TB supports granularity hints, by which a single TB entry can represent a group of pages that are virtually and physically contiguous. Chapter 15 describes the role of this feature in address translation. During system initialization physical memory and system address space for granularity hint regions are reserved. By default, one or more granularity hint regions are allocated for each of the following purposes:

▸ Nonpaged dynamically allocated system data, such as the PFN database
▸ Base and executive images' nonpaged code and resident images' code
▸ Base and executive images' nonpaged data

The granularity hint region or regions associated with each of these uses are commonly referred to as a huge page. A huge page consists of more than one region if it requires more physical pages than can be mapped by one TB entry.

511

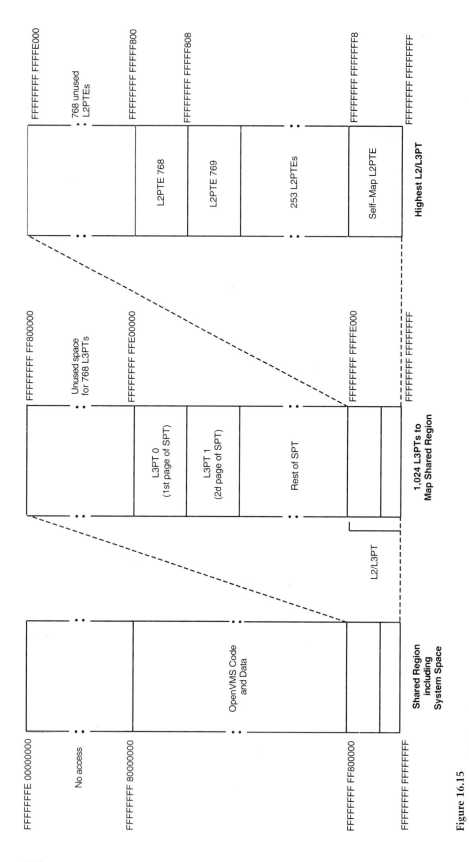

Figure 16.15
System Space Self-Mapping

512

One region is always created for nonpaged dynamically allocated system data. The SYSGEN parameter ITB_ENTRIES and the flags in the SYSGEN parameter LOAD_SYS_IMAGES control whether other regions are created and what use is made of them. Bit 1 of LOAD_SYS_IMAGES, SGN$V_EXEC_SLICING, when set, specifies that executive images should be loaded with their nonpaged code sections in the code huge page and their data in a data huge page. The macro $SYSPARDEF defines symbolic values for these flags.

The SYSGEN parameter ITB_ENTRIES specifies the maximum number of instruction stream TB (ITB) entries to map granularity regions containing code. Its default value is 1, as a result of which a 512-page huge code page is created. The nonpaged code sections of executive images are mapped into this region, as are all code sections of images installed resident, such as LIBOTS and LIBRTL. Chapter 32 describes how executive images are loaded sliced into huge pages, and Chapter 28 describes the use and installation of resident images.

By default, at the end of system initialization, some or all unused pages in the huge page code region are released to the free page list. The contents of SYSGEN parameter GH_RSRVPGCNT specify how many pages are to be left available for mapping images installed resident after system initialization is complete. By default its value is zero.

If executive image slicing is enabled, a data huge page is allocated as two granularity hint regions, each 64 pages long. At the end of system initialization, if space is left unused in the data huge page, the data huge page is shrunk to a multiple of eight-page regions.

Each huge page is described by a nonpaged pool data structure called a loader huge page descriptor (LDRHP) and a bitmap that reflects allocations within the huge page. Three LDRHPs are allocated together, followed by three bitmaps. Each bitmap begins on a quadword boundary. The starting address of these structures is recorded in LDR$GQ_HPDESC. Once SYSINIT begins to execute, access to these structures and bitmaps is synchronized with the base image mutex, EXE$GQ_BASIMGMTX. Figure 16.16 shows the layout of these structures.

LDRHP$Q_TYPE identifies the type of huge page: read-only image sections, writable image sections, or systemwide writable data. LDRHP$Q_SIZE contains the size of the huge page in bytes; LDRHP$Q_PA, its starting physical address; and LDRHP$Q_VA, its starting virtual address.

LDRHP$Q_SLICE_SIZE contains the granularity of allocation, or slice, from this huge page. On current Alpha AXP implementations, the granularity of allocation is 8 KB for the image code page and systemwide data page and 512 bytes for the image data page. LDRHP$Q_FREE_SLICES contains the number of available slices left in the huge page. LDRHP$Q_USED_SLICES contains the number of slices in the page that are in use. LDRHP$Q_STARTUP_PAGES contains the number of pages in use in the huge page at

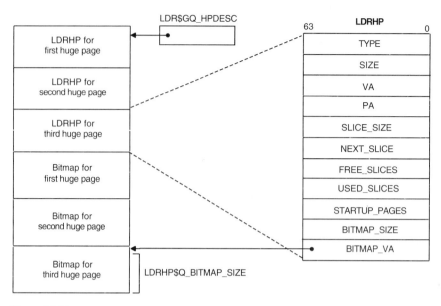

Figure 16.16
Layout of Huge Page Data Structures

the end of system initialization. The AUTOGEN utility uses the contents of this field in the code huge page to determine the appropriateness of the GH_RSRVPGCNT parameter value.

The bitmap, whose starting virtual address is in LDRHP$Q_BITMAP_VA, has one bit per slice. If the value of the bit is 1, the slice is available; if its value is 0, it has been allocated. The size in bytes of the bitmap is in LDRHP$Q_BITMAP_SIZE. LDRHP$Q_NEXT_SLICE contains the number of the first free slice.

16.5   BUFFER OBJECTS

A buffer object is a special kind of I/O buffer. The pages that make up a buffer object are locked into physical memory and are doubly mapped in system space and process-private space. I/O can be initiated to or from the buffer with minimal overhead; in particular, there is no need to probe the buffer or lock its pages into memory. The body and process header of a process with I/O in progress to a buffer object can both be swapped. Although a process page table page that maps a buffer object is locked in memory, it is not locked into the process's working set, and its use in mapping a buffer object does not prevent the process's header from being outswapped. Buffer objects are reserved for use by Digital; any other use is unsupported.

A buffer object is created when a process requests the undocumented Create Buffer Object ($CREATE_BUFOBJ) system service (see Chapter 17), specifying an existing process-private address range to be mapped as a buffer object.

Each buffer object is described by a nonpaged pool data structure called a buffer object descriptor (BOD), shown in Figure 16.17. All the BODs for buffer objects created by a particular process are linked together in a list whose head is in the process's PCB$Q_BUFOBJ_LIST field.

BODs enable the memory management subsystem to keep track of the buffer objects the process created and their associated system virtual addresses. When an image exits, the executive examines the process's BOD list and deletes buffer objects that still exist.

BOD$L_FLINK and BOD$L_BLINK link a BOD into the PCB list of others by the same process.

BOD$W_SIZE and BOD$B_TYPE are the standard dynamic data structure header fields. A BOD has a type of DYN$C_BOD.

BOD$L_ACMODE contains the owner access mode of the buffer object.

BOD$L_SEQNUM contains a sequence number that identifies the buffer object.

BOD$L_REFCNT contains the number of references to the buffer object and the number of reasons the buffer should not be deleted. Creating a buffer object establishes the reference count as 1. In addition, a device driver can increment the reference count when it processes an I/O request that uses the buffer and decrement the reference count when the I/O completes.

BOD$L_FLAGS contains flag bits that describe the section. BOD$V_DELPEN, when set, means that a request to delete the buffer object has been made and that its deletion is pending. BOD$V_NOQUOTA, when set, means

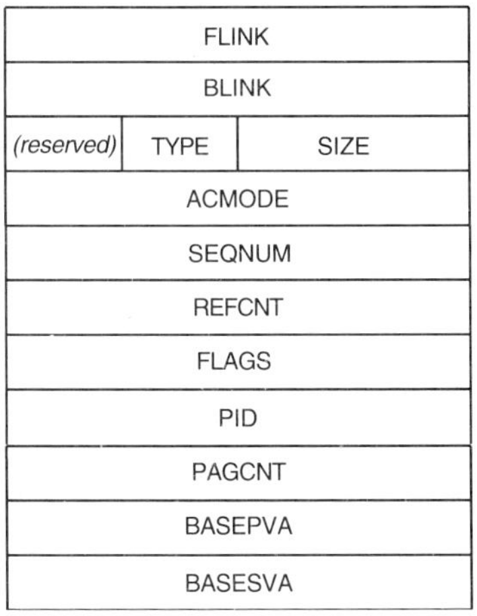

FLINK		
BLINK		
(reserved)	TYPE	SIZE
ACMODE		
SEQNUM		
REFCNT		
FLAGS		
PID		
PAGCNT		
BASEPVA		
BASESVA		

Figure 16.17
Layout of Buffer Object Descriptor (BOD)

that the buffer object pages were not charged against the process's buffered I/O byte count quota when the buffer object was created.

BOD$L_PID contains the internal ID of the process that created the buffer object.

BOD$L_PAGCNT contains the number of pages in the buffer object.

BOD$L_BASEPVA contains the process virtual address at which the buffer object is mapped, and BOD$L_BASESVA, the system virtual address.

16.6 DATA STRUCTURES FOR GLOBAL PAGES

The treatment of global pages is somewhat different from that of process-private pages; the executive must keep additional systemwide data to describe global pages and sections. The sections that follow describe these data structures.

16.6.1 Global Section Descriptor

All global sections are created by the Create and Map Section ($CRMPSC) system service, requested directly from a user image or indirectly through the Install utility. When the service creates a global section, it allocates a GSD, a paged pool data structure, to describe the section. Figure 16.18 shows the layout of a GSD. A GSD associates the global section name to its GSTE. The information in the GSD is only used when some process attempts to

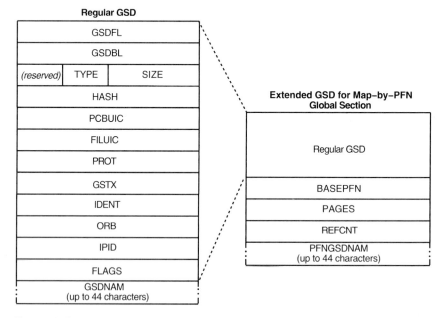

Figure 16.18
Layout of Global Section Descriptor (GSD)

map to or delete the section. The page fault handler does not use this data structure.

GSD$L_GSDFL and GSD$L_GSDBL link the GSD into one of several GSD lists maintained by the system. All system global sections are linked into one list, whose listhead is formed by global cells EXE$GL_GSDSYSFL and EXE$GL_GSDSYSBL. Group global sections (independent of group number) are linked into the other list, at EXE$GL_GSDGRPFL and EXE$GL_GSD-GRPBL. When a request is made to delete a global section to which processes are still mapped, its GSD is removed from its current list and inserted into a list of delete-pending GSDs, the listhead of which is at EXE$GL_GSDDELFL and EXE$GL_GSDDELBL. The mutex EXE$GL_GSDMTX (see Chapter 9) serializes access to all three lists.

GSD$W_SIZE and GSD$B_TYPE are the standard dynamic data structure fields.

GSD$L_HASH contains a hashed representation of the global section name. Comparing hash values rather than section names speeds up a search for a global section with a particular name.

GSD$L_PCBUIC is the user identification code (UIC) from the software PCB of the creating process. GSD$L_FILUIC is the UIC of the owner of the section file.

GSD$L_PROT contains the protection that is specified by the global section creator.

GSD$L_GSTX contains the global section table index for the section's GSTE.

GSD$L_IDENT contains the version identification of the global section. The value is specified by the $CRMPSC system service requestor. The Install utility copies it from the image header of the image being installed.

GSD$L_ORB contains the address of the associated object rights block (ORB). In the case of a section that maps a file, the global section shares the ORB associated with the open file.

When a process requests that a global section be deleted, its internal process ID is copied to GSD$L_IPID. If the global section is writable, when all its modified pages have been written, the modified page writer queues an AST to that process to perform the cleanup and deletion of the global section.

GSD$L_FLAGS contains flags that describe the section.

GSD$T_GSDNAM contains a counted ASCII string that is the section's name.

A global section created with the PFN map option of the $CRMPSC system service has no associated GSTE; its pages are not paged. Such a section has an extended GSD, as shown in Figure 16.18. In the extended GSD, GSD$L_BASEPFN contains the starting PFN of the section. GSD$L_PAGES specifies its size in pages. GSD$L_REFCNT specifies how many PTEs map to this section. GSD$T_PFNGSDNAM, rather than GSD$T_GSDNAM, contains the section name.

16.6.2   Global Section Table Entries

The section table in the system header serves a second purpose. When a global section is created, a section table entry that describes the global section file is allocated from the section table in the system header. Because of this use, the system header's section table is usually called the global section table (GST).

The layout of a GSTE is nearly identical to the layout of a PSTE. Figure 16.4 illustrates both kinds of section table entry.

A GSTE is accessed in a similar way to a PSTE, with a negative longword index from the bottom of the GST (see Section 16.1.2.3). The global section table index (GSTX) in the GSD is such an index, associating a GSD with a GSTE.

The allocation and deletion of GSTEs are synchronized by the MMG spinlock.

16.6.3   Global Page Table

Like other L3PTs, the global page table (GPT) describes the state of the pages it maps. Unlike the others, the GPT is not accessed by the TB miss PALcode routine to load an entry into the TB. It is only accessed by OpenVMS AXP memory management routines. The MMG spinlock synchronizes access to the GPT.

The executive locates a specific GPTE in the GPT using a global page table index (GPTX) as a quadword context index from the contents of MMG$GL_GPTBASE, the cell that contains the starting address of the GPT.

When a process maps a portion of its address space to a global section, its process PTEs that map the section are initialized to the GPTX form of PTE (see Figure 16.8). A global section is mapped by a set of contiguous GPTEs, one for each global page plus two additional GPTEs, one at the beginning of the set and one at the end. The two additional GPTEs are cleared and serve as stoppers to limit modified page write clustering (see Chapter 18). The process PTE that maps the first global section page contains the GPTX of the GPTE that maps the first page in the global section. Each successive process PTE contains the next higher GPTX, so that each PTE effectively points to the GPTE that maps that particular page in the global section.

The relation between process PTEs and GPTEs is shown in Figure 16.19. In the figure, the first M GPTEs are in use for other sections, and the global section shown is mapped by $N + 2$ GPTEs beginning with GPTE $M + 1$. GPTE M is a stopper.

When a process first accesses an invalid global section page, it incurs a page fault. Determining that the invalid page is a global page, the page fault handler indexes the GPT with the GPTX to locate the GPTE that describes the global page.

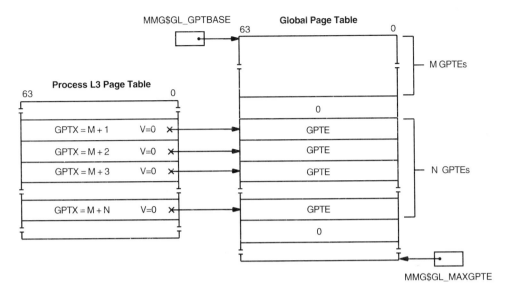

Figure 16.19
Relation Between Process PTEs and GPTEs

16.6.4   Global Page Table Entries

Each page in a global section is described by a GPTE. GPTEs are restricted to the following forms of PTE (see Figure 16.20). The shaded bits in each GPTE are either reserved or are irrelevant for that form of GPTE.

► The GPTE can be valid, indicating that the global page is in at least one process working set.
► The GPTE can indicate a page in some transition state. The corresponding PFN$L_PAGE_STATE field identifies the transition state.
► For a global page in a global section file, the GPTE contains a global section table index.
► The GPTE can indicate a demand zero page in a global page-file section.
► The GPTE can indicate a global page-file section page that has been created and is in use.

When a global page is faulted in, the bits shown in Figure 16.20 labeled Global and Global Write are incorporated into the PFN$L_PAGE_STATE field for the physical page and the entry corresponding to the page in the working set lists of processes that have mapped to it.

Additionally, invalid GPTEs that are unused and available for allocation are linked together in a list. The first two GPTEs in each group of adjacent free GPTEs themselves contain information, such as a pointer to the next group of free GPTEs and the number of free GPTEs in this group. The organization of the list is the same as that of the variable-length paged pool list,

519

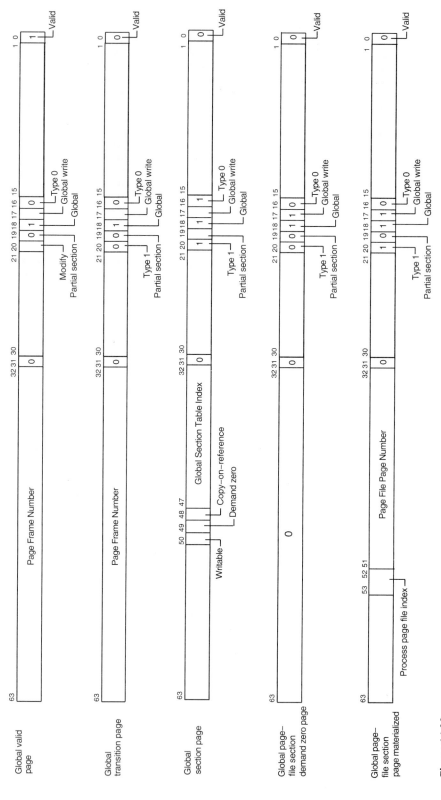

Figure 16.20
GPTE Formats

520

and the routines that allocate and deallocate GPTEs are the routines used for paged pool allocation. Chapter 21 shows the form of such a list and describes the allocation and deallocation routines.

16.6.5   **Relations among Global Section Data Structures**

Figure 16.21 shows the relations among the GSD, GSTE, and GPTEs for a given section on a system with a page size of 8 KB:

▸ The central shaded structure is the GSTE (see Figure 16.4 for its layout) within the GST. The first longword in the GSTE points to the GSD.

▸ The virtual page number field (which contains J in Figure 16.21) contains the GPTX of the first GPTE that maps this section.

▸ The global section consists of K pages and, in this example, none of them is partial. That is, the number of mass storage blocks in the section is an integral multiple of the number of blocks per page. Given a system with a page size of 8 KB, the SEC$L_UNIT_CNT field in the GSTE therefore contains the number of pages in the section multiplied by 16, the number of mass storage blocks per page.

▸ The GSD contains a GSTX that locates the GSTE.

▸ The original form of each GPTE contains the same GSTX found in the GSD. When any given GPTE is either valid or in transition, the GSTX is stored in the corresponding PFN database record PFN$Q_BAK field. Note that a GPTE for a global page-file section contains a page file backing store address.

The allocation and initialization of global section data structures are described along with the $CRMPSC and Map Global Section ($MGBLSC) system services in Chapter 17.

16.7   **DATA STRUCTURES USED FOR SWAPPING**

The following three data structures are used primarily by the swapper but also indirectly by the page fault handler.

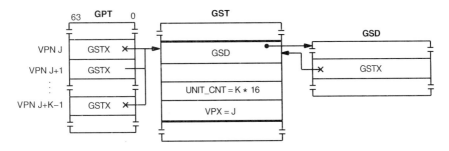

Figure 16.21
Relations among Global Section Data Structures

- Balance set slots
- PHD reference count array
- Process index array

The SYSGEN parameter BALSETCNT, whose global name is SGN$GL_BALSETCT, specifies the number of elements in each array.

16.7.1 Balance Set Slots

A balance set slot is a piece of system virtual address space reserved for a PHD. The number of balance set slots defines the maximum number of concurrently resident processes.

When the system is initialized, an amount of system virtual address space equal to the size of a PHD times BALSETCNT is allocated. The location of the beginning of the balance set slots is stored in global cell SWP$GL_BALBASE. The size of a PHD in pages is stored in global location SWP$GL_BSLOTSZ.

Figure 16.22 shows this area. Appendix F describes the calculations performed by SYSGEN to determine the size of the PHD.

16.7.2 Balance Set Slot Arrays

As shown in Figure 16.23, the system maintains two word arrays describing each process with a PHD stored in a balance set slot. Both of the word arrays are indexed by the balance set slot number occupied by the resident process. The balance set slot number is stored in the fixed portion of the PHD at offset PHD$L_PHVINDEX. Entries in the first array contain the number of

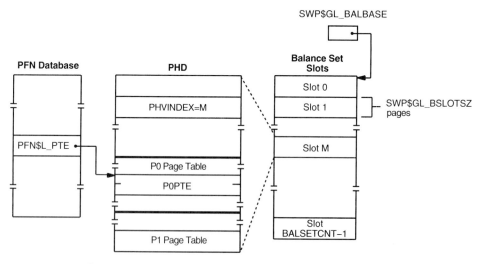

Figure 16.22
Balance Set Slots Containing Process Headers

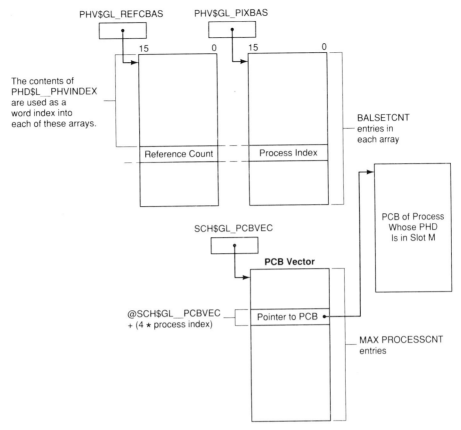

Figure 16.23
Process Header Vector Arrays

references to each PHD. Entries in the second array contain an index into a longword array that points to the PCB for each PHD.

Global cell PHV$GL_REFCBAS contains the starting address of the reference count array. Each of its elements counts the number of reasons why the corresponding PHD cannot be removed from memory. Chapter 18 lists the circumstances under which an element is incremented and decremented. A value of –1 in a reference count array element means that the corresponding balance set slot is not in use.

Global cell PHV$GL_PIXBAS contains the starting address of the process index array. Each of its elements contains an index into the longword array, based at the global pointer SCH$GL_PCBVEC. An element in the longword PCB vector contains the address of the PCB of the process with that process index. Figure 16.23 illustrates how the address of a PHD is transformed into the address of the PCB for that process, using the entry in the process index array.

A value of 0 in the process index array entry means that the corresponding balance set slot is not in use. A value of –1 in a process index array entry means that the process whose PHD used that balance set slot has been deleted and its PHD can be deleted to reclaim physical memory as well as the balance set slot.

If the PHD address is known, the balance set slot index can be calculated, as described in the next section. By using this as a word index into the process index array, the longword index into the PCB vector is found. The array element in the PCB vector is the address of the PCB, whose PCB$L_PHD entry points back to the balance set slot. Chapter 27 contains a more detailed description of the PCB vector and its use by the Create Process ($CREPRC) system service.

16.7.3 Comment on Equal-Size Balance Set Slots

The choice of equal-size balance set slots, at first sight seemingly inefficient, has some subtle benefits for portions of the memory management subsystem. There are several instances, most notably within the modified page writer, when it is necessary to obtain a PHD address from a physical page's PFN. With fixed-size balance set slots, this operation is straightforward.

As shown in Figure 16.22, a PFN database record's PFN$L_PTE field points to a PTE somewhere in the balance set slot area. Subtracting the contents of SWP$GL_BALBASE from the PFN$L_PTE contents and dividing the result by the size of a balance set slot (the size of a PHD) in bytes produces the balance set slot index. If this index is multiplied by the size of the PHD in bytes and added to the contents of SWP$GL_BALBASE, the final result is the address of the PHD containing the PTE that maps the physical page in question.

Furthermore, as described in the previous section, the balance set slot index can locate the process index and its PCB address.

16.8 DATA STRUCTURES THAT DESCRIBE THE PAGE AND SWAP FILES

Page and swap files are used by the memory management subsystem to save physical page contents or process working sets. Page files are used to save the contents of modified pages that are not in physical memory. Both the swap and page files are used to save the working sets of processes that are not in the balance set.

16.8.1 Page File Control Blocks

Each page and swap file in use is described by a data structure called a page file control block (PFL). A page or swap file can be placed in use either automatically during system initialization or manually through SYSGEN commands. In either case, code in module [SYSINI]INITPGFIL allocates a PFL from nonpaged pool and initializes it.

Initializing the PFL includes the following operations:

1. The file is opened and a special window control block is built to describe all the file's extents. The special WCB, called a cathedral window, ensures that the memory management subsystem does not have to take a window turn (see Chapter 23), which could lead to a system deadlock.
2. The address of the WCB is stored in the PFL.
3. A bitmap is allocated from nonpaged pool and initialized to all 1's. Each bit in the map represents one page's worth of mass storage blocks. A set bit indicates the availability of the blocks corresponding to that page.

Figure 16.24 shows the layout of a PFL. PFL$L_BITMAP is the address of the start of the bitmap that describes the state of the blocks in the file. PFL$L_BITMAPSIZ is the length of the bitmap in bytes. PFL$L_STARTBYTE is the address of the bitmap byte at which the next scan for free blocks should begin.

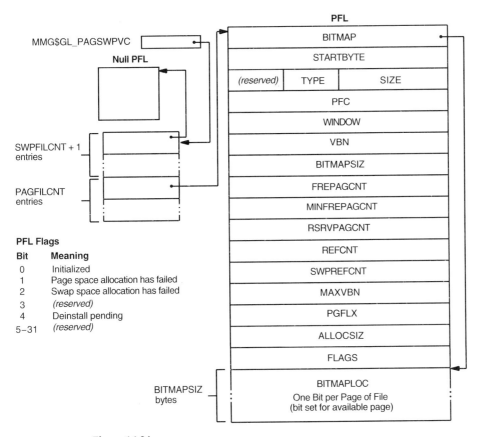

Figure 16.24
Page and Swap File Database

PFL$W_SIZE and PFL$B_TYPE are the standard dynamic data structure fields.

PFL$L_PFC is the number of pages to cluster together on a page read.

PFL$L_WINDOW is the address of the WCB that describes the mapping extents of the file so that file-relative, or virtual, block numbers can be converted to volume-relative, or logical, block numbers.

Generally, PFL$L_VBN contains zero; in the case of a primary page file in use as a crash dump file, it contains a number that reserves enough pages in the page file for the dump. If the dump has already been analyzed, one page's worth of blocks are reserved. If there is a valid unanalyzed dump in the file, PFL$L_VBN contains the size of the dump in blocks rounded up to the next multiple of a page's worth of mass storage blocks. Chapter 35 discusses use of the primary page file as a dump file.

PFL$L_VBN has an additional use for a page file larger than $FFFFF_{16}$ pages. When installing such a file, SYSGEN divides it into segments of $FFFFF_{16}$ blocks. It initializes a PFL for each segment, plus one for the last partial segment. PFL$L_VBN indicates the starting virtual block number of each segment. A page in a segment is represented by the combination of page file index and a page number relative to the start of the segment. The page number is thus small enough to fit into the page file page number portion of a page file backing store PTE. To calculate the actual backing store address, the page file page number is multiplied by the blocks per page and then added to the contents of the associated PFL$L_VBN.

When installing a swap file larger than $FFFFFF_{16}$ pages, SYSGEN similarly divides it into segments of $FFFFFF_{16}$ pages.

Note that the PFL contains a WCB field, virtual block number field, and page fault cluster factor field at the same relative offsets as they are in a section table entry. Because all fields are present and at the same offsets, page file and section file I/O requests can be processed by common code, independent of the data structure that describes the file being read or written.

PFL$L_FREPAGCNT is the number of pages, less 1, that can be allocated.

PFL$L_MINFREPAGCNT is the "low-water mark" for the file and represents the smallest number of pages free during the use of the file.

PFL$L_RSRVPAGCNT is the number of pages that can be reserved without overcommitting the page file.

PFL$L_REFCNT contains the number of processes using the file for paging or swapping. PFL$L_SWPREFCNT contains the number using it only for swapping.

PFL$L_MAXVBN is the mask applied to a PTE with a page file backing store address. For a swap file, it contains the value $FFFFFF_{16}$; for a page file, the value $FFFFF_{16}$.

PFL$L_PGFLX is the systemwide index number of the page-and-swap-file vector entry that contains the address of the PFL.

PFL$L_ALLOCSIZ is the current allocation request size in the file, the number of contiguous pages the modified page writer or the swapper tries to allocate. It is initialized to the value of the SYSGEN parameter MPW_WRTCLUSTER and adjusted dynamically with available space in the file.

PFL$L_FLAGS contains bits describing the state of the file.

At offset PFL$L_BITMAPLOC the bitmap begins. It has one bit for each page in the file. A value of 0 means the page is in use; a value of 1 means the page is free.

Chapter 18 describes the use of page files, and Chapter 20, of swap files.

16.8.2   Page-and-Swap-File Vector

Pointers to the PFLs are stored in a nonpaged pool array called the page-and-swap-file vector. The number of longwords in this array is the maximum number of page and swap files that can be in use on the system (the sum of SYSGEN parameters SWPFILCNT and PAGFILCNT) plus 1. A page or swap file is identified by an index number indicating the position of its PFL address in this array. This is called a systemwide index to distinguish it from a two-bit process-local page file index (see Section 16.1.3.2). The page-and-swap-file vector can contain up to 128 pointers.

During system initialization the routine EXE$INIT, in module INIT (see Chapter 34), allocates and initializes the page-and-swap-file vector, which is a standard dynamic data structure.

The first two longwords of its header are unused. The third longword of its header contains the size of the data structure, a type value of DYN$C_PTR, and a subtype value of DYN$C_PFL. The fourth longword contains the number of pointers in the array. The data begins at the fifth longword. EXE$INIT stores the address of the beginning of the actual data in global location MMG$GL_PAGSWPVC. Figure 16.24 shows the use of the page-and-swap-file vector data area to point to PFLs.

EXE$INIT initializes each pointer with the address of the null page file control block, the contents of MMG$AR_NULLPFL. For the most part, this address serves as a zero value, indicating that no page or swap file with this index is in use.

The SYSINIT process (see Chapter 34) places in use the primary page file, SYS$SPECIFIC:[SYSEXE]PAGEFILE.SYS, if it exists. (Any page file installed at a later stage of system initialization or operation is not considered a primary page file, even if it is the first page file installed.) SYSINIT builds a PFL and places its address in the page-and-swap-file vector. The primary page file has a systemwide index value equal to 1 more than the SYSGEN parameter SWPFILCNT.

SYSINIT also installs SYS$SPECIFIC:[SYSEXE]SWAPFILE.SYS, if it exists, as the primary swap file. (A swap file installed at a later stage is not a primary

527

swap file, even if it is the first one.) The first swap file installed has index 1. If there is no swap file, index 1 points to the null PFL. If the value of the SYSGEN parameter SWPFILCNT is zero, index 1 points to the primary page file.

If there are no swap files, all swap operations are performed to page files. Although the system can run this way, it is desirable that there be at least one swap file. For example, after several large processes are outswapped into a page file, the page file may be sufficiently full that modified page write clustering is hindered.

Any additional page and swap files are placed in use by SYSGEN in response to the commands INSTALL/PAGEFILE and INSTALL/SWAPFILE. Installing page files other than the primary one on different disks allows for balancing the paging load. A system with alternative swap files can support a greater number of processes or processes with larger working sets.

An inactive page or swap file can be removed from use. After a privileged user enters the SYSGEN command DEINSTALL to initiate the removal of a page or swap file, no new allocations are made from it. However, the actual removal from use is deferred until the file is inactive and PFL$L_REFCNT has gone to zero.

16.9 SWAPPER AND MODIFIED PAGE WRITER PAGE TABLE ARRAYS

The I/O subsystem enables an image to make a direct I/O request (direct memory access transfer) to a virtually contiguous buffer. There is no requirement that pages in a buffer be physically contiguous, only virtually contiguous. This capability is called scatter-read/gather-write or, more simply, scatter/gather.

16.9.1 Direct I/O and Scatter/Gather

A combination of hardware and I/O subsystem software supports I/O to and from physically noncontiguous pages. The manner in which this is supported varies with processor type and I/O adapter type.

Regardless of the manner of the support, a direct I/O request typically involves locking the pages of a virtually contiguous buffer into memory. The I/O locking mechanism brings each page into the working set of the requesting process, makes it valid, and increments that page's reference count in its PFN database record to reflect the pending read or write. The buffer is generally described in the I/O request packet (IRP) through three fields:

▶ IRP$L_SVAPTE contains the system virtual address of the first PTE that maps the buffer.

▶ IRP$L_BOFF and IRP$L_BCNT are used to calculate how many PTEs are required to map the buffer.

A driver processes this I/O request in a manner suitable to the processor and I/O adapter.

16.9.2   Swapper I/O

The swapper is presented with a more difficult problem. It must write a collection of process pages to disk that are not virtually contiguous. It solves this problem elegantly.

When the system is initialized, a private L2PT is allocated for the swapper and as many L3PTs as required to map the largest possible working set. The L3PTs make up the swapper's P0 page table. The starting address of the first L3PT is stored in the field PHD$L_L3PT_VA in the swapper's PHD. To facilitate porting, the address is also stored in global cell SWP$GL_MAP.

When the swapper scans the working set list of the process that is being outswapped, it copies the PFNs in every valid PTE to successive entries in its P0 page table. The swapper stores the address of the base of its P0 page table in the field IRP$L_SVAPTE before the IRP is passed to the driver. (The swapper can exercise this control because it builds a portion of its own IRP.) The P0 page table looks just like any other page table to the hardware/software combination that implements scatter/gather I/O.

What the swapper has succeeded in doing is making pages that were not virtually contiguous into pages that are virtually contiguous in its own P0 space, the process that is actually requesting the I/O. At the same time that each PTE is processed, any special actions based on the type of page are also taken care of. The whole operation of outswap and the complementary steps taken when the process is swapped back into memory are discussed in Chapter 20.

The swapper P0 page table supports only one use at a time. When an inswap or outswap operation is in progress, the swap-in-progress flag (SCH$V_SIP), in location SCH$GL_SIP, is set to indicate its use.

16.9.3   Modified Page Writer PTE Arrays

The modified page writer, in its attempt to write many pages to backing store with a single write request (so-called modified page write clustering), is faced with a problem similar to that of the swapper. The modified page writer must build a table of PTEs just as the swapper does.

Unlike the swapper, which can perform only one swap operation at a time, the modified page writer can perform concurrent multiple modified page writes. The SYSGEN parameter MPW_IOLIMIT specifies its maximum number of concurrent I/O operations.

When the modified page writer is building an I/O request, it can encounter three different types of page.

▶ Pages bound for a swap file (PFN$V_SWPPAG_VALID set) are written individually.

▶ Pages bound for a section file are not necessarily virtually contiguous; these pages will be written as a group only if they are virtually contiguous.

▶ Pages on the modified page list that are to be written to a particular page file may not only be noncontiguous within one process address space but may also belong to several processes. It is these pages that the modified page writer must cluster so they appear virtually contiguous.

During system initialization the modified page writer's initialization routine, MPW$INIT in module WRTMFYPAG, allocates nonpaged pool to build I/O maps. It allocates MPW_IOLIMIT number of structures and links them into a lookaside list. Each structure is large enough for an IRP and two arrays, each of MPW_WRTCLUSTER elements. One is a quadword array, and the other a word array.

When modified pages are written, the quadword array is filled with PTEs containing PFNs in a manner analogous to the way in which the swapper map is used. The word array contains an index into the PHD vector for each page in the map. In this way, each page that is put into the map and written to its backing store location is related to the PHD containing the PTE that maps this page. The operation of the modified page writer, including its clustered writes to a page file, is discussed in detail in Chapter 18.

16.10 RELEVANT SOURCE MODULES

Source modules described in this chapter include

[LIB]BODDEF.SDL
[LIB]GSDDEF.SDL
[LIB]LDRHPDEF.SDL
[LIB]PCBDEF.SDL
[LIB]PFLDEF.SDL
[LIB]PFNDEF.SDL
[LIB]PHDDEF.SDL
[LIB]PTEDEF.SDL
[STARLET]SECDEF.SDL

17 Memory Management System Services

A place for everything and everything in its place.

Isabella Mary Beeton, *The Book of Household Management*

This chapter describes those system services that affect a process's virtual address space and several others:

▶ Create Virtual Address Space ($CRETVA), by which a process creates demand zero pages in P0 or P1 space

▶ Expand Region ($EXPREG), by which a process creates demand zero pages at the high end of P0 space or the low end of P1 space

▶ Create and Map Section ($CRMPSC), by which a process creates a process-private or global section that maps the blocks of a file to a portion of process address space

▶ Map Global Section ($MGBLSC), by which a process maps to an existing global section

▶ Delete Virtual Address Space ($DELTVA), by which a process deletes P0 or P1 pages

▶ Contract Region ($CNTREG), by which the upper end of P0 space or the lower end of P1 space is deleted

▶ Delete Global Section ($DGBLSC), by which a global section is marked for deletion when no more processes are mapped to it

▶ Create Buffer Object ($CREATE_BUFOBJ), by which a buffer object is created

▶ Delete Buffer Object ($DELETE_BUFOBJ), by which a buffer object is deleted

▶ Set Process Swap Mode ($SETSWM), by which process swapping can be enabled or disabled

▶ Set Protection on Pages ($SETPRT), by which the protection on a page of virtual address space can be changed

▶ Set Fault Characteristic ($SETFLT), by which the fault-on-execute bit for a page can be set

▶ Copy Fault on Read Page ($COPY_FOR_PAGE), by which data is read from a page with fault-on-read set

Chapter 19 describes the system services that control a process's working set list. Chapter 18 describes the Update Section File on Disk ($UPDSEC) system service, by which the contents of all modified pages in a section are written to their backing store.

17.1   COMMON CHARACTERISTICS

A process's ability to use the services described in this chapter may be limited by access mode, process quotas, limits, privileges, and SYSGEN parameters.

The page table entry (PTE) associated with each page of virtual address space contains an owner field (see Figure 16.8) that specifies which access mode owns the page. The memory management system service checks the owner field to determine whether the requestor of the service is at least as privileged as the owner of the page and thus able to manipulate the page in the desired fashion.

In general, a process is only permitted to affect process-private address space with these services.

Almost all the memory management system services accept a desired virtual address range as an input argument. Many of the services can partly succeed, that is, affect only a portion of the specified address range. A system service indicates partial success by returning an error status and the address range for which the operation completed in the optional RETADR argument.

Many of the memory management system services have a common sequence. First, each creates scratch space on the stack to record information about the service request. The macro $MMGDEF defines symbolic offsets into this scratch space, which is pointed to by the frame pointer (FP) register while the system service procedure is executing. Figure 17.1 shows the layout of stack scratch space. Some fields are used by only a few system services; others are common to all.

MMG$L_ACCESS_MODE contains the access mode associated with the

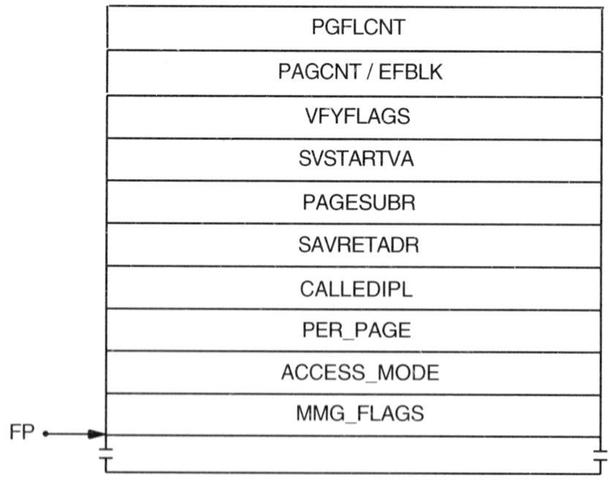

PGFLCNT
PAGCNT / EFBLK
VFYFLAGS
SVSTARTVA
PAGESUBR
SAVRETADR
CALLEDIPL
PER_PAGE
ACCESS_MODE
MMG_FLAGS

FP →

Figure 17.1
Layout of Stack Scratch Space

operation, the less privileged of the mode from which the service was requested and the mode specified in the ACMODE argument.

MMG$L_MMG_FLAGS contains flag bits associated with the operation:

▸ Bit MMG$V_CHGPAGFIL in this longword, when set, means page file quota should be charged for the operation.

▸ Bit MMG$V_NOWAIT_IPL0, when set, means that a memory management routine should return with an error status rather than waiting at interrupt priority level (IPL) 0 for I/O completion.

▸ Bit MMG$V_NO_OVERMAP, when set, means that the address space to be created may not overlap existing address space.

▸ Bit MMG$V_PARTIAL_FIRST, when set, means that the first page to be mapped is only partially backed by section file.

▸ Bit MMG$V_PARTIAL_LAST, when set, means that the last page to be mapped is only partially backed by section file.

▸ Bit MMG$V_NO_IRP_DELETE, when set, means that an I/O request packet created by the $UPDSEC system service is currently in use and should not be deallocated to nonpaged pool.

▸ Bit MMG$V_DELPAG_NOP, when set, means that not all pages in the specified region could be deleted.

MMG$L_PER_PAGE is the per-page processing context area. It contains one defined flag, MMG$V_DELGBLDON. When set, the bit means that global pages in the range have already been purged.

MMG$L_CALLEDIPL records the IPL from which the service was requested, typically 0.

MMG$L_SAVRETADR contains the value of the optional service RETADR argument, the address of a two-longword array to receive the starting and ending virtual addresses affected by the service.

MMG$L_PAGESUBR contains the procedure value of the executive routine that performs the requested service on a single page.

MMG$L_SVSTARTVA saves the starting virtual address specified by the user.

MMG$L_VFYFLAGS contains the section flags passed as an argument to a service such as $CRMPSC and verified by the service.

MMG$L_PAGCNT and MMG$L_EFBLK are two names for the same field. MMG$L_PAGCNT, used by services related to buffer objects, contains the number of pages in a buffer object being created or deleted. MMG$L_EFBLK contains the number of the end-of-file block for a section file.

MMG$L_PGFLCNT contains the number of pages of page file quota that have been reserved against the job's quota for this request.

After creating and initializing the stack scratch space, such a memory management system service takes the following steps.

1. It raises IPL to 2 to block the delivery of an asynchronous system trap (AST). In addition to blocking process deletion, this prevents the execution of AST code that could cause unexpected changes to the page tables, working set list, and data structures.

2. If appropriate, it checks page ownership to ensure that a less privileged access mode is not attempting to alter the properties of pages owned by a more privileged access mode.

3. It invokes the routine MMG$CREDEL, in module SYSCREDEL, passing it the procedure value of a per-page service-specific routine to accomplish the desired action of the system service. MMG$CREDEL performs general page processing and invokes the per-page routine for each page in the desired range.

4. It returns the address range actually affected by MMG$CREDEL's actions in the optional RETADR argument.

5. It restores the entry IPL and returns to its invoker.

In some cases, step 3 in that sequence is replaced by the invocation of a routine that affects all pages in the desired range.

MMG$CREDEL takes the following steps:

1. It tests the starting and ending addresses of the range and, if either is in system space, returns the error status SS$_NOPRIV.

2. It initializes MMG$L_PAGESUBR and MMG$L_SVSTARTVA in the scratch space and stores in integer registers information such as process control block (PCB) address, process header (PHD) address, page count, starting virtual address, and ending virtual address.

3. MMG$CREDEL invokes the per-page routine. Unless the routine returns an error status, MMG$CREDEL continues to invoke it, once per page.

4. When an error occurs or there are no more pages, MMG$CREDEL returns to its invoker with a status code and the address of the last affected page in registers.

17.2 PROCESS-PRIVATE VIRTUAL ADDRESS SPACE CREATION

Among the most basic memory management services are those that create process-private virtual address space: $CRETVA, $EXPREG, $CRMPSC, and $MGBLSC. The image activator requests these services during image activation, as described in Chapter 28. An image can request these services directly to alter the process address space.

P0 and P1 space are each described by a single process-private level 2 page table (L2PT) and by level 3 page tables (L3PTs), with a level 3 page table entry (L3PTE) for each page of address space. The L3PTs that map addresses 0 to $3FFFFFFF_{16}$ make up the P0 page table (P0PT). The L3PTs that map addresses 40000000_{16} to $7FFFFFFF_{16}$ make up the P1 page table (P1PT).

These process-private page tables are in the PHD. Figure 16.6 shows the process-private page tables and the fields that describe them.

Creating address space typically requires expanding the appropriate page table and modifying the PHD fields that delimit it. It always requires initializing L3PTEs to map the new address space. If the L3PTEs to be initialized occupy one or more as yet unused pages of the L3PT, then one or more L2PTEs must also be initialized. In the case of address space associated with a process-private section file, creating address space also involves allocating and initializing a process section table entry.

There are several limits on the amount of process-private virtual address space that can be created:

▶ The SYSGEN parameter VIRTUALPAGECNT controls the total number of L3PTEs (P0PTEs plus P1PTEs) that any process can have. The division of these pages between P0 space and P1 space is arbitrary and process-specific; VIRTUALPAGECNT limits only their sum.

▶ The size of a process working set can also constrain the size of that process's address space. When a process tries to expand its address space, the executive checks whether there is enough room in the dynamic working set list for the fluid working set (PHD$L_WSFLUID, initialized from the SYSGEN parameter MINWSCNT), plus the worst-case number of page table pages required to map it, to allow the process to perform useful work. If this check succeeds, the virtual address space creation can proceed. Otherwise, if the process's working set list is smaller than its quota, the working set list is expanded. If the working set list is full and cannot be expanded (see Chapter 19), the virtual address space creation fails with the error status SS$_INSFWSL.

▶ Another constraint on the total size of the process address space is page file quota. Each demand zero page and copy-on-reference section page is charged against the job's page file quota, JIB$L_PGFLCNT. (Although the page file quota is externally represented as pagelets, the quota is internally maintained in pages.)

▶ Creation of address space with page file backing store may be limited by the number of page files to which the process has been assigned. The form of invalid PTE that describes a page in a page file has a two-bit process-local page file index and a 20-bit page number. Thus, for each page file to which the process has been assigned, it can create a theoretical maximum of 2^{20} pages of pageable address space that requires page file backing store (for example, demand zero or copy-on-reference sections). The current theoretical maximum is stored in PHD$L_PPGFLVA and decremented by each page of such address space the process creates. Each time a process is assigned or deassigned to a page file, the cell is increased or decreased by 2^{20}. The cell is decremented for each demand zero or copy-on-reference page the process creates and incremented when each such page is deleted.

17.3   **DEMAND ZERO VIRTUAL ADDRESS SPACE CREATION**

The simplest form of address space creation is the creation of a series of demand zero pages through the $CRETVA and $EXPREG system services. The services initialize PTEs, that is, create address space, to map the demand zero pages. A demand zero page is not itself created until the first time the process accesses it.

For the $EXPREG system service, PTEs to map demand zero pages are initialized at the end of the designated process-private address region. For the $CRETVA system service, PTEs are initialized to map the specified address range. If any pages already exist in the requested range, they must be deleted first. On the other hand, if the requested range begins beyond the end of the region, the address space between them must also be created.

These two system services can partly succeed. That is, a number of pages smaller than the number originally requested may be mapped. After several pages have already been successfully mapped, the service can run into one of the limits to address space creation.

17.3.1   **$CRETVA System Service**

The $CRETVA system service procedure, EXE$CRETVA in module SYSCRE-DEL, runs in kernel mode. Its alternative entry point MMG$CRETVA_K is called from code already in kernel mode, such as image activator routines and EXE$PROCSTRT in module PROCSTRT. The alternative entry point has additional arguments that enable the caller to specify the protection of the new address space, whether the new space may overlap existing space, and the contents of the copy characteristic and no-execute bits in each L3PTE.

EXE$CRETVA takes the following steps:

1. It creates and initializes the stack scratch space.
2. It constructs template L3PTE contents for the new pages.
   The template L3PTE indicates a demand zero page, with owner access mode the less privileged of the requesting access mode and the ACMODE argument. In the case of a normal system service request, the L3PTE has protection bits enabling read and write access to the owner mode. In the case of entry through MMG$CRETVA_K, the protection is specified by the caller.
3. EXE$CRETVA raises IPL to 2 to block AST delivery.
4. It tests the starting and ending addresses and, if either is a system space address, returns the error status SS$_NOPRIV.
5. It rounds the starting and ending addresses down to an AXP page boundary and calculates the desired page count based on the difference between them. It checks whether the specified address range overlaps any existing space. If there is overlap, EXE$CRETVA continues with step 8.
6. Typically, there is no overlap; the process is requesting the creation of

536

address space just beyond the end of what has already been defined. As an optimization for this common case, EXE$CRETVA invokes MMG$TRY_ALL, in module SYSCREDEL, to test further whether the entire space can be created.

MMG$TRY_ALL tests whether there are enough free L3PTEs, enough room in the dynamic working set list, enough page file quota, and enough PHD$L_PPGFLVA capacity. If all tests pass, it adjusts PHD$L_PxLENGTH, PHD$L_FREPTECNT, and PHD$L_FREPxVA; and charges against page file quota and PHD$L_PPGFLVA. If necessary, it initializes L2PTEs to map new L3PT pages. It returns a status indicating its findings.

If the entire address space cannot be created, EXE$CRETVA proceeds with step 8.

7. If none of the limits to growth of the process's virtual address space has been reached, EXE$CRETVA invokes MMG$FAST_CREATE, in module SYSCREDEL.

   MMG$FAST_CREATE determines in which region space is being created and with which starting L3PTE. It loops, initializing four L3PTEs in each iteration. (During this loop, while MMG$FAST_CREATE modifies L3PTEs at IPL 2, bit PHD$V_LOCK_HEADER in PHD$L_FLAGS is set to prevent possible outswap and subsequent inswap of the PHD into a different balance set slot.) Creating the address space in this manner is significantly faster than creating it one page at a time.

   EXE$CRETVA continues with step 9.

8. If any of the limits to virtual address space growth described in the previous section prevents creation of the entire space, EXE$CRETVA creates it one page at a time, stopping when the limit is reached. Page-by-page creation is also necessary if the specified address space overlaps already existing space, since the existing pages must first be deleted. In either of these cases, EXE$CRETVA invokes MMG$CREDEL, specifying MMG$CREPAG, in module SYSCREDEL, as the per-page service-specific routine.

9. EXE$CRETVA returns any unused page file quota, records peak page file usage and virtual size statistics, and stores return information in the optional RETADR argument.

10. It restores the IPL at entry and returns to its requestor.

MMG$CREPAG is the per-page service-specific routine for the $CRETVA and $EXPREG system services. It is invoked with an argument specifying the L3PTE contents for the new page. It takes the following steps:

1. It tests whether the page is to be mapped beyond the limit of its defined address space and, if not, continues with step 3.

2. If the page is outside its address space, MMG$CREPAG tests whether there are enough free L3PTEs and enough room in the dynamic working

set list to expand the region to add all the desired pages. If so, it adjusts PHD$L_PxLENGTH, PHD$L_FREPxVA, and PHD$L_FREPTECNT.

MMG$CREPAG must deal with the possibility that the requested page may not be adjacent to the current end of the region and that the intervening address space must also be created.

- If there are insufficient L3PTEs to allow expansion up to the requested starting virtual address, MMG$CREPAG returns the error status SS$_VASFULL to its invoker.
- If there are insufficient L3PTEs to allow the full expansion, but the region can be expanded at least to the first requested page, the routine adjusts the items previously listed to show expansion of as many pages as there are L3PTEs left.
- If there is insufficient room in the dynamic working set list for expansion up to the first requested page, the routine returns the error status SS$_INSFWSL.
- If there is insufficient room in the dynamic working set list for the full expansion but enough for at least the first requested page, the routine adjusts the listed items to show expansion through the first requested page.
- If there are both sufficient L3PTEs and sufficient room in the dynamic working set list, MMG$CREPAG adjusts the listed items to include the total expansion.

This step is taken only for the first page of address space; it is not repeated in subsequent invocations of MMG$CREPAG.

3. MMG$CREPAG tests whether the page to be created already exists. If it does and no address overmap was specified, MMG$CREPAG returns the status SS$_VA_IN_USE to its invoker, which returns it as the system service status. (The image activator specifies the NO_OVERMAP flag when it requests the $CRETVA system service.)

4. If the page already exists but overmap is allowed, MMG$CREPAG invokes MMG$DELPAG, described in Section 17.5.2, to delete the virtual page.

5. If page file quota does not need to be charged, MMG$CREPAG continues with step 6. Otherwise, it must charge the pages against MMG$L_PGFLCNT and PHD$L_PPGFLVA.

   If no more reserved quota is left, MMG$CREPAG tries to reserve more quota from the process's job page file quota, JIB$L_PGFLCNT.

   If PHD$L_PPGFLVA would be exceeded, MMG$CREPAG tries to assign the process to another page file.

   If either charge cannot be made, MMG$CREPAG adjusts PHD$L_PxLENGTH, PHD$L_FREPxVA, and PHD$L_FREPTECNT to show expansion up to but not including the page that could not be mapped. It returns the error status SS$_EXQUOTA.

6. It stores the requested value into the L3PTE.

7. It returns to its invoker.

17.3.2 $EXPREG System Service

The $EXPREG system service is very similar to the $CRETVA system service. Its system service procedure, EXE$EXPREG in module SYSCREDEL, runs in kernel mode. Depending on the region that is to be expanded, EXE$EXPREG uses either PHD$L_FREP0VA or PHD$L_FREP1VA as one end of the address range.

It converts its PAGCNT argument, the number of pagelets by which the region is to be expanded, to a number of physical pages, rounding up if necessary. It adds the number of bytes corresponding to that many physical pages to the end of the address range to form the new end of the address region.

It forms template L3PTE contents for the new page, as EXE$CRETVA does.

As an optimization, EXE$EXPREG first checks whether the entire address space can be created. If so, EXE$EXPREG creates it all at once rather than page by page, invoking the routine MMG$FAST_CREATE. Otherwise, it invokes the routine MMG$CREDEL, specifying MMG$CREPAG as the per-page service-specific routine. Section 17.3.1 describes these routines.

17.3.3   Automatic User Stack Expansion

A special form of P1 space expansion occurs when a request for user stack space exceeds the remaining size of the user stack. The processor can detect such a request made implicitly through an access violation.

Several executive software routines can also detect the need to expand the user stack:

▶ The AST delivery interrupt service routine (see Chapter 8), when it is unable to copy AST-related information from the kernel stack to the user stack

▶ The Adjust Outer Mode Stack Pointer ($ADJSTK) system service

▶ The exception dispatching routine, EXE$EXCEPTION in module EXCEPTION, when it is unable to copy the exception context area onto the user stack (see Chapter 6)

These routines invoke EXE$EXPANDSTK, in module SYSADJSTK, to try to expand the user stack. EXE$EXPANDSTK is also invoked by the access violation exception service routine, EXE$ACVIOLAT in module EXCEPTION, for an access violation that occurred in user mode. EXE$EXPANDSTK checks that

▶ A length violation or an attempt to access an empty page occurred rather than a protection violation

▶ The inaccessible address is in P1 space and less than the high end of the user stack

If these conditions are true, EXE$EXPANDSTK requests the $CRETVA system service to expand P1 space from its current low-address end to the specified inaccessible address. For the usual case, one in which a program requires more user stack space than requested at link time, the expansion typically occurs one page at a time.

Because this automatic expansion cannot be disabled on a process-specific or systemwide basis, a runaway program that uses stack space without returning it is not aborted immediately. Instead, the program runs until it reaches one of the limits to growth of virtual address space described in Section 17.2.

Another side effect of automatic expansion occurs when a program makes a possibly incorrect reference to an arbitrary P1 address lower than the top of the user stack. Rather than exiting with some error status, the program will probably continue to execute (after the creation of many demand zero pages).

If the stack expansion fails for any reason, the process is notified in a way that depends on the invoker of EXE$EXPANDSTK:

▶ The $ADJSTK system service can fail with several of the error codes returned by the $CRETVA system service.

▶ An attempt to deliver an AST to a process with insufficient user stack space results in an AST delivery stack fault condition reported to the process.

▶ If the user stack cannot be expanded in response to a P1 space length violation, then an access violation fault is reported to the process.

▶ If there is not enough user stack to report an exception, EXE$EXCEPTION first tries to reset the user stack pointer to the high-address end of the stack. If that fails, EXE$EXCEPTION requests the $CRETVA system service in an attempt to recreate the address space. If that fails, EXE$EXCEPTION bypasses the normal condition handler search and reports the exception directly to the last chance handler. Typically, this handler aborts the currently executing image. Chapter 6 contains more details.

17.4   PROCESS AND GLOBAL SECTIONS

The $CRMPSC system service is an alternative method of creating address space, one that enables a process to associate a portion of its address space with a specified portion of a file. The section may be specific to a process (called a process-private section or sometimes simply a process section) or it may be a global section, shared among several processes.

The $CRMPSC system service also provides special options. For example, a process with PFNMAP privilege can map virtual address space to specific physical addresses. Typically, a process uses this capability to access a physical page in I/O space in order to communicate with a particular I/O device. The $CRMPSC service also enables the creation of global page-file sections, demand zero global sections whose pages are backed by a page file.

The $MGBLSC system service is another way to create address space, one that enables a process to map a portion of its address space to an already existing global section.

The image activator (see Chapter 28) requests both these services to map portions of process address space to sections in image files and to previously installed global sections.

Table 17.1 summarizes the different types of section that can be created through these services, and the source of and backing for their pages.

17.4.1 $CRMPSC System Service

The $CRMPSC system service creates a process-private or global section and maps it into process address space. The particular actions it takes are determined by the options or flags with which the service is requested. The *OpenVMS System Services Reference Manual* describes the system service arguments and shows which flags can be used together.

The sections that follow describe creation of a process-private section backed by section file, a PFN-mapped process-private section, and global sections of each type.

Table 17.1   Section Types and Backing Store

Section Type	Source of Contents	Backing Store
DEMAND ZERO PAGES CREATED BY $CRETVA OR $EXPREG SYSTEM SERVICE		
	Demand zero page	Page file
PROCESS-PRIVATE SECTIONS		
Demand zero	Demand zero page	Section file
Copy-on-reference	Section file	Page file
Read-only	Section file	Section file
Writable (and not copy-on-reference)	Section file	Section file
PFN-mapped	Physical page or I/O space locations	None
GLOBAL SECTIONS		
Demand zero	Demand zero page	Section file
Page-file	Demand zero page	Page file
Copy-on-reference	Section file	Page file
Read-only	Section file	Section file
Writable (and not copy-on-reference)	Section file	Section file
PFN-mapped	Physical page or I/O space locations	None

17.4.1.1   **Process-Private Section Creation.** The $CRMPSC system service proce-
dure, EXE$CRMPSC in module SYSCRMPSC, runs in kernel mode. When
EXE$CRMPSC is requested to map a process-private section, it takes the
following steps:

1. EXE$CRMPSC checks the INADR argument:

    a. It checks whether the starting or ending address is in system space
    and, if so, returns the error status SS$_NOPRIV.

    b. Unless the expand-region flag was specified in the FLAGS argument, it
    confirms that the starting address is on an AXP page boundary and
    that the ending address is one byte less than a page boundary. (It takes
    into account the possibility that the addresses have been specified
    in reverse order.) If the addresses are not correct, it returns the error
    status SS$_INVARG.

2. It creates and initializes the stack scratch space.

3. It invokes MMG$VFY_SECFLG, in module SYSDGBLSC, to test the
compatibility of the FLAGS arguments with each other and with the
process's privileges, and then confirms that the CHAN argument was supplied. (The requestor must have already opened the section file on the
specified channel.) If the flags are incompatible or the argument is absent, it returns the error status SS$_IVSECFLG.

4. It confirms that the specified channel has been assigned; that its associated device is directory-structured, files-oriented, and random access;
and that a file is open on the channel. In case of error, it returns the error
status SS$_NOTFILEDEV or SS$_IVCHNLSEC.

5. It checks whether the associated window control block (WCB) maps the
entire file. When the image activator opens a file, it does so specifying
that all extents of the file should be mapped. However, an image may
open a file itself and then request the $CRMPSC system service; in that
case, the WCB might not contain a complete description of the file.

    The memory management subsystem cannot take a window turn (see
    Chapter 23) on pages within a section. It therefore requires that the
    WCB describe all the extents of the mapped file. If the WCB does not,
    EXE$CRMPSC queues an I/O request to remap the file with a cathedral
    WCB, one that does describe all the file extents. Once the file is mapped
    completely, EXE$CRMPSC copies the end-of-file virtual block number
    from the file control block to MMG$L_EFBLK.

    Because the WCB occupies nonpaged pool, its extension is charged
    against the job's buffered I/O byte count quota (JIB$L_BYTCNT). Because
    the quota charge persists until the section is deleted, this charge is also
    made against the job's JIB$L_BYTLM, which limits the maximum charge
    against JIB$L_BYTCNT. When a job has insufficient JIB$L_BYTCNT for
    a request, the executive checks that the request is not larger than JIB$L_

BYTLM before placing the process in resource wait. Charging the WCB extension against JIB$L_BYTLM prevents placing the process into what might otherwise be a never-ending resource wait.

6. If the section to be mapped is a copy-on-reference section, EXE$CRMPSC sets bit MMG$V_CHGPAGFIL in MMG$L_MMG_FLAGS as a signal that the section must be charged against the job's page file quota and PHD$L_PPGFLVA.

7. It checks that the PAGCNT argument is positive and, if not, returns the error SS$_ILLPAGCNT.

8. It raises IPL to 2 to block AST delivery.

9. Prior to allocating a process section table entry (PSTE), it invokes MMG$DALCSTXSCN, in module PHDUTL, to check whether any PSTEs can be deallocated. A section table entry cannot always be deallocated synchronously on request. For example, if direct I/O is in progress to pages in the section, those pages cannot be deleted and hence the section cannot be. After the I/O completes, a subsequent invocation of MMG$DALCSTXSCN will result in deallocation of the section table entry (see Section 17.4.3).

10. Unless the section is copy-on-reference and demand zero, EXE$CRMPSC allocates a PSTE (whose layout is shown in Figure 16.4) and initializes it. (A copy-on-reference demand zero section does not need a PSTE; its page faults require no I/O from a section file.)

    When the process section is being created as a part of image activation (see Chapter 28), the original source for much of the data stored in the PSTE is an image section descriptor in the image file.

    a. EXE$CRMPSC copies the section flags to SEC$L_FLAGS.

    b. EXE$CRMPSC stores in SEC$L_WINDOW the address of the WCB from the channel control block (CCB) or from the PSTE to which the CCB points. Recall that if multiple sections are mapped from the same file, there is one PSTE for each section but only one CCB and one WCB.

    c. It checks that the file has been opened in a manner consistent with the section flags: if the section is writable but not copy-on-reference, the file must have been opened for write access. If the file was opened for write access, then EXE$CRMPSC sets the writable flag in SEC$L_FLAGS.

    d. It copies the VBN argument to SEC$L_VBN. If the VBN argument is 0, its default, EXE$CRMPSC replaces it with 1.

    e. It copies the PAGCNT argument, if present, to SEC$L_UNIT_CNT after checking that the file contains at least that many blocks between SEC$L_VBN and its end of file. If the argument is absent, EXE$CRMPSC initializes SEC$L_UNIT_CNT to the difference between the end-of-file block and SEC$L_VBN.

f. If this is the first section mapped on this file, EXE$CRMPSC stores the section index in CCB$L_WIND and in the PSTE forward and backward links. If this is not the first section, EXE$CRMPSC inserts the PSTE into the chain of other PSTEs paging on that channel.

g. It initializes SEC$L_REFCNT to 1 and sets the section table entry flag SEC$V_INPROG to ensure that the section is not inadvertently deleted before its PTEs are initialized. If the system service cannot complete, it may place the process into a wait state at IPL 0. If the process were deleted at that point, the Delete Process ($DELPRC) system service would be able to detect such a section by the set SEC$V_INPROG flag and decrement the biased reference count.

h. EXE$CRMPSC converts the section pagelet fault cluster argument, PFC, to a page fault cluster value and stores the minimum of that and 127 in SEC$L_PFC.

i. It clears SEC$L_VPX, the virtual page index.

11. EXE$CRMPSC forms a template L3PTE for the section's pages (see Figure 16.8). The L3PTE has both type bits set; the section table index in bits ⟨47 : 32⟩ (or zero for a copy-on-reference demand zero section); and the WRT, CRF, and DZRO bits copied from the section flags. EXE$CRMPSC calculates the page owner mode and protection bits based on MMG$L_ACCESS_MODE, the writable flag in SEC$L_FLAGS, and the input section flags specifying the mode allowed to write the section pages.

12. If the expand-region flag was specified in the FLAGS system service argument, EXE$CRMPSC calculates the starting and ending addresses to map based on the pagelet count multiplied by 512 and the contents of PHD$L_FREPxVA. The INADR argument identifies in which process-private region the section is to be created.

If the expand-region flag was not specified, EXE$CRMPSC calculates the actual and useful address ranges to be mapped, based on the INADR and PAGCNT arguments and, depending on the section type, number of blocks in the section file.

In either case, an integral number of AXP pages will be mapped. If the pagelet count does not represent an integral number of pages, the page at the high-address end of the section will be only partly occupied by the section. Its L3PTE will have the PTE$V_PARTIAL_SECTION bit set. Either MMG$V_PARTIAL_FIRST or MMG$V_PARTIAL_LAST in MMG$L_MMG_FLAGS is set, indicating that the first or last page to be mapped is partial. Which is partial depends on the order of mapping, which depends on how the address range was specified in the INADR argument.

13. EXE$CRMPSC determines whether the new address space overmaps existing space.

- If the space does not already exist and can all be created, EXE$CRMPSC sets PHD$V_LOCK_HEADER in PHD$L_FLAGS, to disable swapping of this process temporarily, and initializes the section's L3PTEs. If the section is not an integral number of physical pages, EXE$CRMPSC sets PTE$V_PARTIAL_SECTION in the L3PTE that maps the page with the highest address. It clears PHD$V_LOCK_HEADER. It then increases the section's reference count by the number of pages just mapped.
- If the space to be created overmaps existing space or cannot all be created, EXE$CRMPSC invokes MMG$CREDEL, described in Section 17.1, specifying MAPSECPAG as the per-page routine.

14. EXE$CRMPSC calculates the starting virtual page number of the section and stores it in SEC$L_VPX.
15. It decrements SEC$L_REFCNT to remove the extra reference, unnecessary now that the reference count reflects the mapped L3PTEs, and clears the SEC$V_INPROG flag.
16. EXE$CRMPSC returns any unused page file quota, records peak page file use and virtual size statistics, and stores return information in the optional RETADR argument.
17. It restores the IPL at entry and returns to its requestor.

MAPSECPAG, in module SYSCRMPSC, is the per-page service-specific routine for $CRMPSC. It is invoked with a number of arguments, including the L3PTE contents for the new page, number of pages in the section, number of pages to be mapped, and address of the section table entry.

For a process section, it takes the following steps:

1. Within initialization code, executed only once, MAPSECPAG sets the NO_OVERMAP flag in MMG$L_MMG_FLAGS if it is set in MMG$L_VFYFLAGS. It minimizes the requested number of pages to be mapped with the number of pages in the section.

   For a section file section being mapped in reverse order (from high address to low) whose highest address page is partial, it maps the first page with PTE$V_PARTIAL_SECTION set. It increments the section's reference count.

   It replaces its own address in MMG$L_PAGESUBR so as to bypass the initialization code the next time it is entered.

2. MAPSECPAG invokes MMG$CREPAG, described in Section 17.3.1, which stores the template L3PTE contents into the next L3PTE and charges against job page file quota and PHD$L_PPGFLVA.
3. MAPSECPAG increments the section table entry's reference count to reflect that one more L3PTE maps a page in that section.
4. It returns to its invoker, MMG$CREDEL, which continues to invoke it until there are no more pages to be mapped or until one of the limits to growth is reached.

   For a section file section being mapped in forward order (from low

545

address to high) whose highest address page is partial, MAPSECPAG maps the last page with PTE$V_PARTIAL_SECTION set.

17.4.1.2   **PFN-Mapped Process Section Creation.** The $CRMPSC system service enables a process with PFNMAP privilege to map a portion of its virtual address space to a specific range of physical addresses. Although the primary purpose of this feature is to map process address space to I/O addresses, it is also used to map specific physical memory pages. When such a section is larger than one page, it maps physically contiguous pages.

When a process section mapped by a page frame number (PFN) is created, the effect is to add a series of valid L3PTEs to the process page table. The PFN fields in these L3PTEs contain the requested physical page numbers. The window bit is set in each L3PTE to indicate that the virtual page is PFN-mapped. These pages do not count against the process working set. They cannot be paged, swapped, or locked in the process working set. Moreover, no record is maintained in the PFN database that such pages are PFN-mapped.

Requested to create a PFN-mapped section, EXE$CRMPSC takes the following steps:

1. EXE$CRMPSC checks the INADR argument:
   a. It checks whether the starting or ending address is in system space and, if so, returns the error status SS$_NOPRIV.
   b. Unless the expand-region flag was specified in the FLAGS argument, it confirms that the starting address is on an AXP page boundary and that the ending address is one byte less than a page boundary. (It takes into account the possibility that the addresses have been specified in reverse order.) If the addresses are not correct, it returns the error status SS$_INVARG.
2. It creates and initializes the stack scratch space.
3. It invokes MMG$VFY_SECFLG to test the compatibility of the section flags.
4. It raises IPL to 2 to block AST delivery.
5. It confirms that the process has PFNMAP privilege, returning the error status SS$_NOPRIV if not.
6. It invokes MMG$DALCSTXSCN, described in Section 17.4.3, to deallocate any process section whose reference count has gone to zero.
7. EXE$CRMPSC forms a template L3PTE for pages in the section. The L3PTE has the valid and window bits set. EXE$CRMPSC calculates its page owner mode and protection bits based on MMG$L_ACCESS_MODE, the writable flag in SEC$L_FLAGS, and the flags in the FLAGS argument specifying the mode allowed to write the section pages. The PFN in the first L3PTE is specified by the VBN argument (named for its more typical use).
8. If the expand-region flag was specified in the FLAGS system service ar-

gument, EXE$CRMPSC calculates the starting and ending section addresses based on the page count and contents of PHD$L_FREPxVA. (Note that for a PFN-mapped section, the PAGCNT argument specifies a number of pages, not pagelets.) The INADR argument identifies in which process-private region the section is to be created.

If the flag is absent, the starting and ending addresses are determined by the INADR argument.

9. If the address space to be created does not overmap existing address space and it can all be created, EXE$CRMPSC checks whether the PFN-mapped section meets the requirements for a granularity hint region:

- The page count must be 8, 64, or 512.
- The starting virtual and physical addresses must be aligned multiples of the page count.

If the section meets the requirements, EXE$CRMPSC inserts the granularity hint value corresponding to the page count into the template L3PTE. It sets PHD$V_LOCK_HEADER in PHD$L_FLAGS, to disable swapping of this process temporarily and initializes the P0 or P1 L3PTEs, incrementing the PFN for each L3PTE. It clears PHD$V_LOCK_HEADER and proceeds with step 11.

This feature is primarily used by DECwindows for sections containing video frame buffers. Chapter 15 describes how granularity hint regions improve translation buffer (TB) performance.

10. EXE$CRMPSC invokes MMG$CREDEL, described in Section 17.1, specifying MAPSECPAG as the per-page routine.
11. EXE$CRMPSC records peak virtual size statistics and stores return information in the optional RETADR argument.
12. It restores the IPL at entry and returns to its requestor.

Invoked to create a PFN-mapped section page, MAPSECPAG takes the following steps:

1. Within initialization code, executed only once, MAPSECPAG sets the NO_OVERMAP flag in MMG$L_MMG_FLAGS if it is set in MMG$L_VFYFLAGS. It minimizes the number of pages requested in the PAGCNT argument with the number of pages in the address range specified by the INADR argument. It replaces its own address in MMG$L_PAGESUBR so as to bypass the initialization code the next time it is entered.
2. MAPSECPAG invokes MMG$CREPAG, described in Section 17.3.1, which stores the template L3PTE contents into the next L3PTE. It sets PHD$V_NO_WS_CHNG in PHD$L_FLAGS and touches the page table page containing the newly created page, faulting it if necessary. It acquires the MMG spinlock, clears PHD$V_NO_WS_CHNG, locks the page table page into the process's working set list, releases the spinlock, and returns.

3. MAPSECPAG calculates the contents of the next L3PTE by increment-ing or decrementing the PFN value from the current PTE, depending on the order of mapping.

4. It returns to its invoker, MMG$CREDEL, which continues to invoke it until there are no more pages to be mapped or until one of the limits to growth is reached.

17.4.1.3   **Global Section Creation.** The $CRMPSC system service enables a process to create a global section or, if the section already exists, to map to it. The Install utility requests the $CRMPSC system service to create one or more global sections when an image is installed with the /SHARED qualifier.

A global section can be a group global section to be shared by processes in the same user identification code (UIC) group, or a systemwide global sec-tion. Creation of the latter requires the SYSGBL privilege. The global section can be a temporary one that is deleted as soon as no process is mapped to it or a permanent one that must be explicitly deleted through the $DGBLSC system service. Creation of the latter requires the PRMGBL privilege.

The creation of a global section is similar to the creation of a process sec-tion except that additional data structures are involved. Chapter 16 shows the layouts of these data structures and describes them and their interrela-tions in more detail.

► A global section descriptor (GSD; see Figure 16.18), which enables subse-quent $MGBLSC system service requests to determine whether the named section exists and to locate its global section table entry (GSTE).

► A GSTE (see Figure 16.4), analogous to the PSTE but part of the system header rather than of a PHD.

► Global page table entries (GPTEs), each of which describes the state of one global page in the section. GPTEs are used by the page fault handler when a process incurs a page fault for a global page. They are not used in address translation.

When a process maps to a global section, its L3PTEs that describe the specified address range are initialized with global page table indexes (GPTXs; see Figure 16.19).

Like a process-private section, a global section can consist of specific pages of memory or I/O address space. Creation of a global PFN-mapped section re-quires the PFNMAP privilege. The only data structure necessary to describe a global PFN-mapped section is a special form of GSD (see Figure 16.18). There are no GPTEs nor is there a GSTE. When a process maps to such a section, its L3PTEs are initialized with the valid and window bits set and PFNs based on GSD$L_BASEPFN.

Another type of global section is a demand zero section whose pages are backed in a page file. This type of section is called a global page-file section. Record Management Services (RMS) uses this type of section to implement global buffers on a file. The SYSGEN parameter GBLPAGFIL specifies the maximum number of page file pages that can be put to this use.

Requested to create or map a global section, EXE$CRMPSC takes the following steps:

1. As described in Section 17.4.1.1, it initializes stack scratch space, determines the actual and useful ranges to be mapped, and tests the compatibility of the FLAGS argument. It examines the specified flags to determine what type of global section is to be created and what further checks are required.

   - If a global section is to be mapped and the requestor specified a value for the RELPAG argument, the RETADR must also have been specified.
   - If a PFN-mapped section or global page-file section is to be created, the CHAN argument should not be present.
   - If a section file section is to be created, the CHAN argument must be present, the file must have been opened, and the WCB must map the entire file. If the section already exists, the CHAN argument need not be present.
   - If the section is to be copy-on-reference, EXE$CRMPSC sets MMG$V_CHGPAGFIL in MMG$L_MMG_FLAGS.

2. It locks the GSD mutex for write access, raising IPL to 2 as a side effect. The GSD mutex synchronizes access to both the systemwide and group GSD lists.

3. It invokes MMG$DALCSTXSCN1, in module PHDUTL, described in Section 17.4.3, to check the global (system) section table for any sections to be deleted.

4. It invokes MMG$GSDSCAN, in module SYSDGBLSC, to find the GSD, if any, that corresponds to the GSDNAM argument. MMG$GSDSCAN attempts logical name translation of the GSDNAM argument (see the *Open-VMS Programming Concepts* manual). If the translation fails, it uses the string specified by the service requestor as the global section name.

   MMG$GSDSCAN scans the group or systemwide GSD list, depending on the kind of section. In scanning the group list, it first compares the process's UIC group code with the high word of GSD$L_PCBUIC. If they are equal, it then compares the global section names. Because a character string comparison is relatively lengthy, the routine first confirms that one is necessary by requiring that the hash values and the character string lengths be the same for the target section name and the one in the candidate GSD. If they are not the same, the global section names cannot be.

   If the names match, MMG$GSDSCAN checks the match control information specified in the IDENT argument against GSD$L_IDENT. If there is a version incompatibility, MMG$GSDSCAN continues to scan the list until it reaches the end or finds a match. Multiple versions of

549

a global section with different version identifications and match control information can be installed. If a newer one were installed last and had match control specifying upward compatibility (match less or equal), it could be used with executables linked against it or earlier versions. If it had match control specifying no upward compatibility (match equal), an executable linked against an earlier version would not match; EXE$CRMPSC would continue to scan the list and find the earlier one.

5. If MMG$GSDSCAN located a matching GSD, EXE$CRMPSC is being requested to map to an existing section, and it transfers control to EXE$MGBLSC, at step 7 in the description in Section 17.4.2.

6. If no match is found, EXE$CRMPSC is being requested to create a new section. It first checks whether the process has the required privileges for the requested section type. If not, EXE$CRMPSC unlocks the GSD mutex and returns the error status SS$_NOPRIV.

7. It allocates paged pool for a GSD. The size of the GSD depends on whether the global section is PFN-mapped. If pool is unavailable, it unlocks the GSD mutex and returns the error status SS$_GSDFULL.

8. EXE$CRMPSC begins to initialize the GSD, copying the section name to GSD$T_GSDNAM, storing the hash value in GSD$L_HASH, and clearing GSD$L_IPID.

9. If the section is PFN-mapped, EXE$CRMPSC clears GSD fields irrelevant to this type of section and copies the vbn argument to GSD$L_BASEPFN, the section name to GSD$T_PFNGSDNAM, the contents of the pagcnt argument to GSD$L_PAGES, and the prot argument to GSD$L_PROT. (Note that for a PFN-mapped section, the pagcnt argument specifies a number of pages, not pagelets.)

10. If the section is to map a file, EXE$CRMPSC stores the address of the object rights block (ORB) associated with the open file in GSD$L_ORB.

    If the section is a PFN-mapped or global page-file section, it allocates an ORB from paged pool and initializes it, copying PCB$L_UIC to ORB$L_OWNER and the prot argument to ORB$W_PROT. If pool for the ORB is unavailable, it deallocates the GSD, unlocks the GSD mutex and returns the error status SS$_GSDFULL.

11. EXE$CRMPSC copies PCB$L_UIC to GSD$L_PCBUIC and initializes GSD$L_FLAGS from the section flags and access mode. It initializes GSD$L_IDENT from the ident argument.

12. If the section is PFN-mapped, EXE$CRMPSC continues with step 22.

13. Otherwise, it allocates a GSTE from the system header. If none is available, it deallocates the ORB and GSD, unlocks the mutex, and returns the error status SS$_SECTBLFUL.

14. EXE$CRMPSC takes most of the same steps to initialize a GSTE as for a PSTE for a process section (see steps 10a through 10i in Section 17.4.1.1). One additional step required for a global section is making the WCB a

"shared" one if it is not already. This chiefly involves returning the byte count quota charged for it to the appropriate job, setting the bit WCB$V_ SHRWCB in WCB$B_ACCESS, and incrementing WCB$W_REFCNT to indicate one more reason the file should not be closed.

15. It stores the GSTE index in GSD$L_GSTX and the PROT argument in GSD$L_PROT.

16. If the section is a section file section rather than a global page-file section, EXE$CRMPSC copies the file owner to GSD$L_FILUIC.

17. If the section is a global page-file section, EXE$CRMPSC subtracts its page count from MMG$GL_GBLPAGFIL, the number of pages of page file that can be used for this purpose, which is initialized from the SYS-GEN parameter GBLPAGFIL. It must also charge the section's pages against PHD$L_PPGFLVA in the system header.

   If mapping this section would exceed the allowed global page file count or if it would exceed PHD$L_PPGFLVA and another page file cannot be assigned, EXE$CRMPSC deallocates the GSD, ORB, and GSTE, unlocks the mutex, and returns the error status SS$_EXGBLPAGFIL.

18. It converts the number of pagelets in the section to pages and allocates a set of contiguous GPTEs, one for each global page plus two additional GPTEs, one at the beginning of the set and one at the end. The two additional GPTEs are cleared and serve as "stoppers," limits to modified page write clustering (see Chapter 18).

   If there are insufficient GPTEs, EXE$CRMPSC deallocates the data structures it built, restores the page file charges, unlocks the mutex, and returns the error status SS$_GPTFULL.

19. It calculates the virtual page number of the second GPTE (skipping the stopper GPTE) and stores that in SEC$L_VPX.

20. It forms template PTE contents for the GPTEs. Figure 16.20 shows the format of the section table index form of GPTE.

21. EXE$CRMPSC then loops, initializing GPTEs:

    a. It faults the page of global page table that contains the GPTE, if it is not valid.

    b. It acquires the MMG spinlock, raising IPL to IPL$_MMG.

    c. It confirms that the page table page is still valid. If not, it releases the MMG spinlock and returns to step a.

    d. It increments the PFN$L_SHRCNT field in the PFN database record for the physical page in which the global page table page resides.

    e. If the share count makes the transition from 0 to 1 (this is the first GPTE in the page to be initialized), EXE$CRMPSC locks it into the system working set list; increments the system header field PHD$L_ PTCNTACT, the number of active page table pages; and increments the reference count for the system header.

    f. If necessary, it sets PTE$V_PARTIAL_SECTION in the highest GPTE to indicate that the page will be only partly occupied by global section data.

    g. It releases the MMG spinlock, restoring an IPL of 2.

22. It inserts the GSD at the front of the group or systemwide list.

23. The global section has been created. EXE$CRMPSC transfers control to EXE$MGBLSC to map it into the process's virtual address space as an existing section. It transfers control to EXE$MGBLSC at step 10 in the description in Section 17.4.2.

17.4.2   **$MGBLSC System Service**

The $MGBLSC system service can be considered a special case of the $CRMPSC system service, one in which the global section already exists. This service maps a range of process addresses to the named global section. It usually has no effect on the global database other than to include the latest mapping in various reference counts.

When a process maps to a global section backed by a file rather than a PFN-mapped section, each of its process L3PTEs in the designated range is initialized with a GPTX (see Figures 16.8 and 16.19). A GPTX is a pointer to the GPTE that records the current state of the global page.

The $MGBLSC system service procedure, EXE$MGBLSC in module SYS-CRMPSC, runs in kernel mode. It takes the following steps:

1. It creates and initializes stack scratch space.
2. EXE$MGBLSC checks the INADR argument:
   a. It checks whether the starting or ending address is in system space and, if so, returns the error status SS$_NOPRIV.
   b. Unless the expand-region flag was specified in the FLAGS argument, it confirms that the starting address is on an AXP page boundary and that the ending address is one byte less than a page boundary. (It takes into account the possibility that the addresses have been specified in reverse order.) If the addresses are not correct, it returns the error status SS$_INVARG.
3. It invokes MMG$VFY_SECFLG, in module SYSDGBLSC, to test the compatibility of the section flags with each other. If the flags are incompatible, it returns the error status SS$_IVSECFLG.
4. It locks the GSD mutex for write access to synchronize access to the GSD lists, raising IPL to 2.
5. It invokes MMG$DALCSTXSCN1, described in Section 17.4.3, to check the global (system) section table for any sections to be deleted.
6. It invokes MMG$GSDSCAN to scan the GSD list for the specified global section. Section 17.4.1.3 describes MMG$GSDSCAN's actions.

    If the section is not found, EXE$MGBLSC unlocks the GSD mutex and returns MMG$GSDSCAN's error status to the system service requestor.

7. If the global section is mapped to a file, EXE$MGBLSC calculates the address of its GSTE from GSD$L_GSTX and the contents of PHD$L_PSTBASOFF in the system header.

8. If the section is copy-on-reference, it sets MMG$V_CHGPAGFIL in MMG$L_MMG_FLAGS so that the section pages will be charged against the process's page file quota and PHD$L_PPGFLVA.

9. It compares the section access mode with the mode bits in MMG$L_ACCESS_MODE to determine if the system service requestor is allowed to map the section. If not, EXE$MGBLSC unlocks the GSD mutex and returns the error status SS$_NOPRIV.

10. If the section is not PFN-mapped, it increments SEC$L_REFCNT so that the section cannot inadvertently be deleted before its pages are mapped into the process's address space.

    If the section is PFN-mapped, EXE$MGBLSC increments GSD$L_REFCNT to prevent section deletion. (Recall that a PFN-mapped global section has no associated GSTE.)

11. With the section's deletion blocked, EXE$MGBLSC can safely unlock the GSD mutex.

12. If the expand-region flag was specified in the FLAGS system service argument, EXE$MGBLSC calculates the starting and ending section addresses based on the RELPAG argument, the section page count (GSD$L_PAGES for a PFN-mapped section or SEC$L_UNIT_CNT multiplied by pagelets per page for all others), and contents of PHD$L_FREPxVA. The INADR argument simply identifies in which process-private region the section is to be created.

    If the expand-region flag was not specified, EXE$MGBLSC calculates the virtual address range to be mapped based on the RELPAG argument (in units of pages or pagelets, depending on section type), the section page count (GSD$L_PAGES for a PFN-mapped section or SEC$L_UNIT_CNT multiplied by pagelets per page for all others), and the INADR argument.

    In either case, an integral number of AXP pages will be mapped. If the pagelet count does not represent an integral number of pages, the highest address page of the section will be only partly occupied by section. Its L3PTE will have the PTE$V_PARTIAL_SECTION bit set.

13. EXE$MGBLSC forms a template L3PTE for pages in the section.

    • If the section is PFN-mapped, the L3PTE has the valid and window bits set, and its PFN is based upon the contents of GSD$L_BASEPFN. (The L3PTE that maps the lowest address page of the section will have that PFN.)

    • If the section is backed by a section file, the L3PTE has the type 0 bit set and the type 1 bit clear to indicate a global page, and its GPTX is based upon the contents of SEC$L_VPX. (The L3PTE that maps the lowest address page of the section will have that GPTX.)

EXE$MGBLSC calculates the L3PTE protection bits based on MMG$L_ACCESS_MODE, the writable flag in SEC$L_FLAGS, and the input section flags specifying the mode allowed to write the section pages.

14. It tests whether the process has the necessary access (read, write, or execute) to the section based on the process's access rights list and the ORB associated with the section.

    If the process does not have the desired access, EXE$MGBLSC decrements the appropriate reference count, based on the section type; invokes security auditing code, which may record the unsuccessful access; and returns an error status.

    If the process is allowed access, EXE$MGBLSC also invokes security auditing code, which checks whether a successful access should be audited, and if so, builds a message to be logged before the service exits.

15. EXE$MGBLSC determines whether the address space into which the section will be mapped overmaps existing space and whether the section is a PFN-mapped section.

    - If the space does not exist, the number of pages in the section is equal to the number of pages to be mapped, the section is not a PFN-mapped section, and all pages can be created, EXE$MGBLSC sets PHD$V_LOCK_HEADER in PHD$L_FLAGS to block outswapping and process page table movement. It increases the section's reference count by the number of pages to be mapped. It initializes each of the process's L3PTEs by inserting the appropriate GPTX along with the template L3PTE. It clears PHD$V_LOCK_HEADER.
    - If the space to be created overmaps existing space or cannot all be created, or if the section is a PFN-mapped section, EXE$MGBLSC invokes MMG$CREDEL, specifying MAPSECPAG, described in Section 17.4.1.1, as the per-page routine.

16. EXE$MGBLSC returns any unused page file quota, records peak page file use and virtual size statistics, and stores return information in the optional RETADR argument.

17. It decrements the section reference count to remove the extra reference, unnecessary now that the reference count reflects the mapped PTEs.

18. It invokes MMG$DELGBLWCB to close open files associated with temporary global sections whose reference counts have gone to zero and to delete their WCBs. Section 17.4.3 describes this routine in more detail.

19. It invokes a security audit routine, which may log successful access to the section.

20. It restores the IPL at entry and returns to its requestor.

17.4.3 $DGBLSC System Service

Deleting a global section is more complex than creating one because the section must be reduced from one of many states to nonexistence. In addition, global writable pages must be written to their backing store before a global section can be fully deleted. To avoid stalling the process requesting the service until all associated I/O completes, the final steps in the deletion of a global section are often deferred to a time after the system service request and return.

The actual section deletion cannot occur until the reference count in the GSTE, the count of process PTEs mapped to the section, goes to zero. Although the reference count can be zero when the $DGBLSC service is requested, more commonly global section deletion occurs as a side effect of virtual address deletion, which itself might occur as a result of image exit or process deletion.

The $DGBLSC system service procedure, EXE$DGBLSC in module SYS-DGBLSC, runs in kernel mode. It takes the following steps:

1. It creates and initializes stack scratch space.
2. It confirms that the process has PRMGBL privilege and, if the section to be deleted is a system global section, SYSGBL privilege. If the process lacks a necessary privilege, EXE$DGBLSC returns the error status SS$_NOPRIV.
3. It invokes MMG$VFY_SECFLG to test the compatibility of the specified section flags.
4. It locks the GSD mutex for write access, raising IPL to 2.
5. It invokes MMG$GSDSCAN, described in Section 17.4.1.3, to locate the GSD for the specified global section. If the section does not exist, it unlocks the mutex and returns the error status SS$_NOSUCHSEC.
6. If the global section is a PFN-mapped section, EXE$DGBLSC confirms that the process has PFNMAP privilege, unlocking the mutex and returning the error status SS$_NOPRIV if not. A PFN-mapped section is described solely by a GSD; there are no GSTE, no GPTEs, and no section reference count. The section can be deleted immediately. EXE$DGBLSC deallocates the ORB and GSD to paged pool. It continues with step 8.
7. If the global section is mapped to a file, EXE$DGBLSC removes the GSD from its current list and inserts it on the delete pending list, at global location EXE$GL_GSDDELFL. It clears the global section's permanent flag, SEC$V_PERM in GSD$L_FLAGS and, if there is an associated GSTE, in SEC$L_FLAGS as well. This step changes the section to a temporary global section that can be deleted when its reference count becomes zero.

   If the reference count in the GSTE is zero, the section can be deleted now; EXE$DGBLSC sets PHD$V_DALCSTX in PHD$L_FLAGS in the system header as a signal for MMG$DALCSTXSCN.
8. It invokes MMG$DALCSTXSCN, described later in this section, in case this section or any other can be deleted now.
9. It unlocks the GSD mutex.

10. It invokes MMG$DELGBLWCB, described later in this section.

11. It restores the IPL at entry and returns to its requestor.

MMG$DALCSTXSCN, in module PHDUTL, is invoked to locate and deal with deletable section table entries, in both the global section and process section tables. Section deletion cannot occur until the section reference count goes to zero, generally as the result of virtual address space deletion or modified page writing. A scan for deletable GSTEs is initiated from the $MGBLSC and $DGBLSC system services, and from the $CRMPSC system service when it is creating a global section.

MMG$DALCSTXSCN is entered at IPL 2 in kernel mode, with the address of a PHD whose section table should be scanned. In the case of deleted global sections, it is entered with the address of the system header and with the GSD mutex locked. At alternative entry point MMG$DALCSTXSCN1, the routine first gets the address of the system header and then merges with MMG$DALCSTXSCN.

MMG$DALCSTXSCN takes the following steps:

1. It tests and clears PHD$V_DALCSTX, returning immediately if the bit was already clear.

2. It scans the list of section table entries, returning when it reaches the end of the list. It examines each entry's reference count, skipping to the next one if the count is nonzero.

3. If the reference count is zero, MMG$DALCSTXSCN tests whether the section is permanent and, if so, continues with step 2.

4. Otherwise, it tests whether the section is a global section. If it is, it invokes MMG$DELGBLSEC to delete it and then continues with step 2.

5. For a process-private section, MMG$DALCSTXSCN checks whether this section is the only one still mapped from its section file.

   - If so, it restores the address of the WCB to CCB$L_WIND and inserts the section table entry into the free page list.
   - If there are other sections still mapped, it removes this one from the chain, inserts it into the free page list, and, if necessary, adjusts CCB$L_WIND to point to a section table entry other than the one being deleted.

   In either case, it continues with step 2.

MMG$DELGBLSEC, in module SYSDGBLSC, is invoked to delete a temporary global section whose reference count has gone to zero, that is, one with no pages mapped by any process.

1. It removes the GSD from its current list, which could be the group or systemwide list or the delete pending list, and inserts it into the delete pending list so that no more processes can map to it.

556

2. Starting with SEC$L_UNIT_CNT, the number of pagelets in the section, it calculates the number of pages in the section.

3. It gets the starting GPTX from the GSTE.

4. It acquires the MMG spinlock, raising IPL to IPL$_MMG.

5. It scans the section's GPTEs to determine the state of the global pages. If it reaches the last GPTE rather than one of the end conditions in the following list, it continues with step 8.

   - If it finds a transition page on the free page list, it invokes MMG$DEL_PFNLST, in module ALLOCPFN, to delete the page's virtual contents. The PFN is moved from its current position on the free page list to the head of the list, so that it can be reallocated before pages whose contents might still be useful. Its PFN record fields are reinitialized. The reference count for the global page table page that contains the GPTE is decremented. When an entire page of GPTEs is freed, the global page table page can be unlocked from the system working set. MMG$DELGBLSEC continues its scan of the section's GPTEs.

   - If it finds a global page-file section page on the modified page list, it clears the saved modify bit in the physical page's PFN$L_PAGE_STATE field and invokes MMG$DEL_PFNLST as described. It continues its scan of the section's GPTEs.

   - If it finds a transition page on the modified page list that is not part of a global page-file section, the page must be written to its backing store before the section is deleted, and MMG$DELGBLSEC goes to step 6.

   - If it finds a transition page that is not on the free or modified page list, the page is being read in from its backing store. That I/O must complete before the section is deleted, and MMG$DELGBLSEC goes to step 7.

6. It requests the modified page writer to perform a selective purge of the modified page list to write this section's global pages to their backing store and release them (see Chapter 18).

7. It releases the MMG spinlock, restoring IPL to 2, stores the process ID of the current process in GSD$L_IPID as the target of an eventual cleanup AST, sets PHD$V_DALCSTX in the system header, and returns.

8. If MMG$DELGBLSEC has scanned all the GPTEs for the section and found none for whose I/O it must wait, it scans the GPTEs again, this time to decrement the global page table page reference count and to release page file backing store.

   - If it finds a global page in a page file, it deallocates that page, decrements the global page table page reference count, and clears the GPTE.

   - If it finds a demand zero global page, it simply decrements the global page table reference count and clears the GPTE.

9. It releases the MMG spinlock, setting IPL to 2.

10. It deallocates the GPTEs.

11. If there is a file open on the section, it decrements the reference count in the WCB. If the count is now zero, it inserts the WCB into a queue of delete pending WCBs.

12. If this was a global page-file section, MMG$DELGBLSEC adds its page count back to MMG$GL_GBLPAGFIL and to PHD$L_PPGFLVA in the system header.

13. It removes the GSD from the delete pending list and deallocates it to paged pool, with the ORB, unless the ORB is still in use for an open section file.

14. It inserts the GSTE into the free page list.

15. It allocates nonpaged pool, forms it into an AST control block, queues a normal kernel mode AST to the current process, and returns to its invoker. The specified AST procedure is GSD_CLEAN_AST.

GSD_CLEAN_AST executes as a normal kernel mode AST procedure in the context of the process that requested the system service that triggered MMG$DELGBLSEC, possibly but not necessarily the process that requested deletion of the global section. Its enqueuing can be requested from MMG$DELGBLSEC or the modified page writer, and also by the routines that decrease section reference count, MMG$SUBSECREF and MMG$DECSECREF in module PHDUTL, when a temporary global section's reference count goes to zero. It takes the following steps:

1. GSD_CLEAN_AST tests whether the process is being deleted or already has this procedure active. If either is true, it returns.

2. It requests the Clear AST ($CLRAST) system service so that a subsequent kernel mode AST can be delivered.

3. If PHD$V_DALCSTX in the system header is set, it locks the GSD mutex; invokes MMG$DALCSTXSCN; and unlocks the mutex.

4. It invokes MMG$DELGBLWCB, described later in this section, to close the section file.

5. It returns.

MMG$DELGBLWCB, in module SYSDGBLSC, is invoked to close an open file associated with a temporary global section whose reference count has gone to zero and to delete the WCB. It takes the following steps:

1. It makes several consistency checks, returning immediately if it is executing within a process that owns any mutexes, has kernel mode AST delivery disabled, has an active kernel mode AST, or if the file system impure area in this process is not yet initialized. Its subsequent processing requires delivery of a kernel mode AST, IPL 0 execution, and file system processing.

2. It removes a WCB from the delete pending list, returning if there is none.

3. It finds an available channel control block and stores in it the address of the unit control block on which the file represented by the WCB is

open; the address of the WCB; and an indication that the channel has been assigned in kernel mode.

4. It lowers IPL to 0 and requests the Deassign Channel ($DASSGN) system service, the actions of which result in closing the file.

5. It raises IPL back to 2 and continues with step 2.

17.5 VIRTUAL ADDRESS SPACE DELETION

Page deletion is generally more complicated than page creation. Creation involves taking the process from one known state (the address space does not yet exist) to another known state (for example, the process PTEs contain demand zero L3PTEs). Page deletion must deal with initial conditions that include all possible states of a virtual page.

Page creation may first require that the specified pages be deleted to put the process page tables into their known state. Thus, page deletion is often an integral part of page creation.

A process deletes part of its address space by requesting the $DELTVA system service.

17.5.1 Page Deletion and Process Waits

A page that has I/O in progress cannot be deleted until the I/O completes. A process trying to delete such a private page is placed into a page fault wait state (with a request that a system event be reported when I/O completes) until the page read or write completes. Deleting a page in the write-in-progress transition state has the same effect. A page in the read-in-progress transition state is faulted, with the immediate result that the process is placed into the collided page wait state.

Special action must be taken for a global page with I/O in progress because there is no way to determine if the process deleting the page is also responsible for the I/O. Hence, if the process has any direct I/O in progress, the process is placed into a resource wait for the resource RSN$_ASTWAIT until its direct I/O completes.

17.5.2 $DELTVA System Service

The $DELTVA system service procedure, EXE$DELTVA in module SYSCRE-DEL, runs in kernel mode. EXE$DELTVA takes the following steps:

1. It creates and initializes the stack scratch space and raises IPL to 2.
2. It invokes MMG$CREDEL (see Section 17.1), specifying MMG$DELPAG as the per-page service-specific routine.
3. It invokes MMG$DALCSTXSCN (see Section 17.4.3) to see if any process sections can be deleted.
4. EXE$DELTVA sets PHD$V_LOCK_HEADER in PHD$L_FLAGS to prevent outswapping and page table movement.

5. It checks whether as the result of the deletion there are now null pages at the end of that P0 or P1 region, enabling the region to be contracted. If there are null pages, it adjusts the following PHD fields (see Chapter 16):
   - PHD$L_FREPTECNT—Number of free L3PTEs
   - PHD$L_FREPxVA—First free address in the region
   - PHD$L_PxLENGTH—Page table length
6. It checks whether the contraction resulted in freeing an entire L3PT and, if so, clears the corresponding L2PTE.
7. It clears PHD$V_LOCK_HEADER.
8. It restores the IPL at entry.
9. EXE$DELTVA records peak page file use and virtual size statistics, and stores return information in the optional RETADR argument.
10. It executes an instruction memory barrier to flush any instructions that might have been prefetched from the deleted address space.
11. It returns to its requestor.

When a virtual page is deleted, MMG$DELPAG (and routines it invokes) must return all process and system resources associated with the page. These can include the following:

▸ A physical page of memory for a valid or transition page
▸ A page file page for a page whose backing store address indicates already allocated blocks
▸ A working set list entry for a page in a process working set list
▸ Page file quota for a page with a page file backing store address and the charge against PHD$L_PPGFLVA, even if the page has not yet been allocated a block in a page file

Deleting a process-private section page results in decrementing the reference count in the PSTE (see Figure 16.4). If the reference count goes to zero, the PSTE itself can be released. Deleting a global section page results in decrementing the reference count in the GSTE. If the reference count goes to zero, the GSTE itself can be released.

In addition, a valid or modified page with a section file backing store address rather than a page file backing store address must have its latest contents written back to the section file. (The contents of a page with a page file backing store address are unimportant after the virtual page is deleted and do not have to be saved before the physical page is reused.)

Deleting the contents of a physical page means that the PFN$L_PTE field in its PFN database record is cleared, destroying all ties between the physical page and any process virtual address. In addition, the page is placed at the head of the free page list, so that it can be reallocated before other pages whose contents might still be useful.

MMG$DELPAG is the per-page service-specific routine for the $DELTVA and $CNTREG system services. It is invoked with an argument specifying the address to be deleted. It takes the following steps:

1. It clears MMG$L_PER_PAGE in the stack scratch area.
2. With bit PHD$V_NO_WS_CHNG in PHD$L_FLAGS set to block out-swap and working set shrinking or trimming, it gets the address of the L3PTE that maps the specified virtual address and faults the page table page into the process's working set list. It acquires the MMG spinlock and clears PHD$V_NO_WS_CHNG.
3. It examines the L3PTE that maps the page to be deleted.
4. If the L3PTE contains zero, the page is a null page and has already been deleted. MMG$DELPAG returns to its invoker after releasing the MMG spinlock and restoring the previous IPL.
5. It compares the requestor access mode with that of the page owner. If the access mode is insufficiently privileged, it releases the MMG spinlock and returns the error status SS$_PAGOWNVIO.
6. Otherwise, it determines the type of the virtual page, based on the valid and type bits in the L3PTE that maps it.
7. If the page is in a page file, MMG$DELPAG deallocates the occupied page of page file, restores job page file quota and PHD$L_PPGFLVA, clears the L3PTE, releases the MMG spinlock, and returns.
8. If the page is from a demand zero process section, MMG$DELPAG releases the MMG spinlock, lowers IPL, touches the page to fault it into the working set, and continues with step 2. Faulting it into the working set first ensures that an untouched demand zero page backed by a section file will be written back to it as all zeros. Handling it in this way minimizes the need for complex code to handle a relatively rare case.
9. If the page is an invalid page from any other type of process section, MMG$DELPAG decrements the section reference count. If the page is copy-on-reference, MMG$DELPAG increments the job page file quota and PHD$L_PPGFLVA. It clears the L3PTE, releases the MMG spinlock, and returns.
10. If the page is a demand zero page (created by the $CRETVA or $EXPREG system service), MMG$DELPAG restores job page file quota and PHD$L_PPGFLVA, clears the L3PTE, releases the MMG spinlock, and returns.
11. If the page is any other type of transition page, MMG$DELPAG examines the page's PFN$L_PAGE_STATE record to see where the page is.

   • If the page is on the free page list, it invokes MMG$DEL_PFNLST, in module ALLOCPFN, to delete the page's virtual contents and modify the L3PTE. The PFN is moved from its current position on the free page list to the head of the list. Its PFN record is reinitialized. PFN$V_

DELCON is set in the page's PFN$L_PAGE_STATE field. The PFN$L_SHRCNT field for the page table page that maps it is decremented. If the count goes to zero, the page table page is released from the working set list. It releases the MMG spinlock and returns.

- If the page is on the modified page list and has page file backing store, MMG$DELPAG clears the saved modify bit in the page's PFN$L_PAGE_STATE field so that the page, when deleted, will be inserted into the free page list, and invokes MMG$DEL_PFNLST, as just described. It releases the MMG spinlock and returns.

  If the page is on the modified page list but it is a section file page, MMG$DELPAG releases the MMG spinlock, lowers IPL, touches the page to fault it into the working set, and continues with step 2. Handling the page this way simplifies MMG$DELPAG's subsequent steps to write the page to its section file.

- If the page state is read in progress or release pending, MMG$DELPAG releases the MMG spinlock, lowers IPL, touches the page to fault it into the working set, and continues with step 2.

- If the page state is active, or if there was an I/O error reading the page in from mass storage, MMG$DELPAG continues with the next step.

12. If the page is valid (or a transition page that is active or that incurred a page read I/O error), MMG$DELPAG examines its PFN$L_PAGE_STATE field to determine its type.

- If the page is a PFN-mapped section page, it tests whether the process has direct I/O in progress. If not, it clears the valid, fault-on-read, and fault-on-write bits in the L3PTE. It decrements the appropriate PHD$L_PTWSLELCK array longword for the page table page that maps the section page to indicate one less reason for that page table page to be locked into the working set list. It invalidates any cached translation in the TB and clears the entire L3PTE. (Note that if the page being deleted is part of a PFN-mapped granularity hint region, the granularity hint bits are cleared in all other L3PTEs that map pages in the granularity hint region.)

  If the process has direct I/O in progress, its I/O must complete before this page can be deleted. When direct I/O is in progress to a typical process page, its PFN$L_REFCNT field is incremented. Thus a value larger than 1 indicates I/O in progress. A PFN-mapped page may have other processes mapped to it, some of which could be doing I/O to it, so its REFCNT value is not precise enough to determine whether the page is in use as an I/O buffer for this process. Furthermore, a page mapped by PFN may be one without any PFN database to examine.

  If bit MMG$V_NOWAIT_IPL0 in MMG$L_MMG_FLAGS is set, as

it would be if the page were being deleted as a side effect of creating a process section that overmapped the page, the process cannot wait at IPL 0 for the I/O to complete, and MMG$DELPAG releases the MMG spinlock and returns the error status SS$_ABORT to its invoker. Otherwise, it releases the MMG spinlock and places the process into a resource wait for resource RSN$_ASTWAIT (effectively, wait for an I/O completion) at IPL 0. When the process is placed back into execution, MMG$DELPAG raises IPL to 2 and resumes at step 2.

- If the page is permanently locked into the working set, MMG$DELPAG simply releases the MMG spinlock and returns a success code. Such a page cannot be deleted until the process is deleted or outswapped.
- If the process has locked the page into its working set, MMG$DELPAG releases the MMG spinlock; invokes MMG$LCKULKPAG, in module SYSLKWSET (described in Chapter 19) to unlock the page; and then resumes at step 2.
- If the PFN$L_REFCNT field for this (process-private) page contains a value larger than 1, the page is in use as an I/O buffer. MMG$DELPAG tests whether the page is part of a buffer object (see Section 17.6) and, if so, releases the MMG spinlock and returns the error status SS$_VA_IN_USE to its invoker. If the page is not part of a buffer object, MMGDELPAG tests against MMG$V_NOWAIT_IPL0 as previously described and either returns an error status or places the process into a wait until the I/O completes.
- If the page has been modified but has page file backing store, or if the page has not been modified, MMG$DELPAG sets the PFN$V_DELCON bit and clears the saved modify bit in the PFN$L_PAGE_STATE field so the page's contents will be deleted when it is inserted into the free page list. It clears the valid, modify, fault-on-execute, and fault-on-write bits in the L3PTE; invalidates any possible TB entry; removes the page from the working set list; and decrements its PFN$L_REFCNT field.

  If PFN$L_REFCNT is still greater than zero, the page is being written, and MMG$DELPAG must wait for I/O completion as previously described.

  If PFN$L_REFCNT contains zero, MMG$DELPAG deallocates the associated physical page, as a result of which the L3PTE once again contains a backing store format, and then resumes with step 2, deleting the page as an invalid unmodified page-file section page.
- If the page has been modified and is backed by a section file rather than a page file, it has to be written to its backing store before it can be deleted. MMG$DELPAG invokes a routine that is part of the $UPDSEC system service to write the page to its backing store. When the I/O is being initiated, MMG$DELPAG changes the PFN$L_PAGE_

STATE location to write in progress and takes the actions previously described for a modified page with page file backing store.

13. If the process page is an invalid global page, MMG$DELPAG examines its GPTE to determine the page type and validity of the master page.

- If the master page is a demand zero page or a page in a global page-file section, MMG$DELPAG decrements the global section reference count and clears the process L3PTE. It releases the MMG spinlock and returns to its invoker.
- If the global page is in transition being faulted from its backing store, MMG$DELPAG tests and sets MMG$V_DELGBLDON in MMG$L_PER_PAGE. If the bit was already set, it continues with the next step. Otherwise, MMG$DELPAG must free the process's working set list entry associated with the global page. It invokes a routine within the Purge Working Set ($PURGWS) system service to remove that page and any other global pages in the address range being deleted from the working set list and to change the PFN database accordingly. It resumes with step 2.
- If the global page is valid or in transition, has I/O in progress, and the process has outstanding direct I/O, the direct I/O may be to the global page that the process is trying to delete. MMG$DELPAG therefore places the process into a resource wait, as previously described, until the I/O completes. It resumes with step 2.

  If the process has no outstanding direct I/O, MMG$DELPAG continues with the next step.
- If the global page is valid with no I/O in progress, invalid and in a section file, or a transition page with no I/O in progress, MMG$DELPAG examines its PFN$Q_BAK field to determine the type of section. If the section is demand zero, it continues with the next step. If the section is copy-on-reference, it first increments the job page file quota and PHD$L_PPGFLVA. For any type of section that is not demand zero, MMG$DELPAG decrements the global section reference count, clears the process PTE, releases the MMG spinlock, and returns.
- If the global page is invalid and a page from a demand zero writable section, MMG$DELPAG allocates a physical page and maps it temporarily to zero it. MMG$DELPAG initializes the page's PFN database record, storing the address of the global table entry in PFN$L_PTE and setting PFN$L_PAGE_STATE global writable and active. It decrements the global section's reference count and invokes MMG$INCPTREF, in module PAGEFAULT, to lock the global page table page. MMG$DEL-PAG then inserts the page onto the modified page list, clears the process L3PTE, releases the MMG spinlock, and returns. These steps ensure that an untouched demand zero page backed by a global section file will be written back to it as all zeros. This requirement is similar

to that for a demand zero page in a writable process section. However, MMG$DELPAG takes these steps rather than fault the page in first as it does a process-private page, for better performance in a more common case.

17.5.3 $CNTREG System Service

The $CNTREG system service procedure, EXE$CNTREG in module SYS-CREDEL, runs in kernel mode. The $CNTREG system service is a special case of the $DELTVA system service. EXE$CNTREG simply converts the requested number of pagelets into a P0 or P1 page range and merges with EXE$DELTVA at step 2 in the description in Section 17.5.2.

17.6 BUFFER OBJECT CREATION AND DELETION

A buffer object is a special kind of I/O buffer doubly mapped in both process-private space and system space. Multiple I/O requests can be initiated to or from an existing buffer object with less overhead than with the standard I/O mechanisms, direct and buffered I/O.

The pages of a standard direct I/O buffer are probed and locked into memory when the I/O request is initiated. The PFN$L_REFCNT in the PFN database record of each page is incremented to lock the page. The page table pages that map the buffer pages are locked into the process's working set and into memory, and the process's header cannot be outswapped. When the I/O request completes, for each page of the buffer, PFN$L_REFCNT is decremented, and page table pages are unlocked.

Buffered I/O is initiated to or from a buffer allocated in nonpaged pool. On output, data is copied from the user's buffer to the pool buffer. On input, data is copied from the pool buffer to the user's buffer.

In contrast, the pages of a buffer object are probed only once and the pages are locked only once, at buffer creation. Because the pages always have a system space virtual mapping, there is no need to lock the process-private page table pages into the working set. Because the pages have a process-private mapping, there is no need to copy data between a process buffer and a system buffer. Tests for buffer object pages in the swapper make it possible to outswap a process body and header even though I/O may be in progress to its buffer object.

The pseudo terminal driver, [PTD]SYS$FTDRIVER, uses the buffer object mechanism. A process interacts with this driver through system services (in the privileged shareable image [PTD]PTD$SERVICES_SHR.EXE) that create and manage the process's buffer objects. The DECwindows terminal class driver, [DECW$XTERMINAL]DECW$XTDRIVER.EXE, also uses the buffer object mechanism. Use of buffer objects and these services is reserved to Digital. Any other use is unsupported.

An image creates a buffer object by requesting the $CREATE_BUFOBJ system service. (Actually, a user's image requests a pseudo terminal system service that requests the $CREATE_BUFOBJ system service.) The system service creates a data structure called a buffer object descriptor (BOD, described in detail in Chapter 16) that contains the process-private and system space addresses of the buffer.

An image deletes a buffer object by requesting the $DELETE_BUFOBJ system service. At image exit, any buffer objects created by that image that still exist are deleted by image rundown code.

Chapter 18 provides additional information on the transitions of buffer object pages and their page tables.

17.6.1 $CREATE_BUFOBJ System Service

The $CREATE_BUFOBJ system service procedure, EXE$CREATE_BUFOBJ in module SYSLKWSET, runs in kernel mode. The service is requested with the following arguments:

- ▶ INADR, RETADR, and ACMODE—The standard memory management service arguments
- ▶ FLAGS—Flags to specify that quota should not be charged for the buffer object and that the RETADR argument addresses should be the system space addresses
- ▶ CREBUF_HANDLE—The address of a two-longword array to receive the buffer handle of the created buffer object

A buffer handle identifies the buffer object in later $DELETE_BUFOBJ and I/O requests. The first longword of a buffer handle contains the address of the BOD. The second longword contains a sequence number, copied from BOD$L_SEQNUM, which is used to validate the buffer handle itself.

EXE$CREATE_BUFOBJ takes the following steps:

1. It creates and initializes stack scratch space.
2. It raises IPL to 2 to block AST delivery.
3. It allocates nonpaged pool for a BOD, charging the pool against the process's byte count quota and limit.
4. It initializes the BOD, copying the process ID to BOD$L_PID and the access mode to BOD$L_ACMODE, and links it to the tail of the PCB list at PCB$Q_BUFOBJ_LIST.
5. EXE$CREATE_BUFOBJ determines the number of pages the buffer object is to contain. If the no-quota flag was specified on a request made from kernel mode, EXE$CREATE_BUFOBJ sets BOD$V_NOQUOTA in BOD$L_FLAGS. Otherwise, it charges the number of bytes in the buffer object against the process's byte count quota and limit.
6. It allocates system page table entries (SPTEs) to map the buffer into sys-

tem space and stores the corresponding starting system virtual address in BOD$L_BASESVA.

7. It increments the master buffer object sequence number and stores that number in BOD$L_SEQNUM.

8. EXE$CREATE_BUFOBJ invokes MMG$CREDEL (see Section 17.1), specifying LCKBUFOBJPAG as the per-page service-specific routine.

9. When MMG$CREDEL returns, EXE$CREATE_BUFOBJ checks whether the buffer object contains all requested pages. If not, it restores unused byte count quota and limit to the process and deallocates unused SPTEs.

10. It restores the IPL at entry.

11. It records peak page file use and virtual size statistics, and stores return information in the optional RETADR argument.

12. It returns to its requestor.

LCKBUFOBJPAG, in module SYSLKWSET, is the per-page service-specific routine for $CREATE_BUFOBJ. It takes the following steps:

1. It tests that the process-private page is writable from the requesting access mode and, if not, returns the error status SS$_ACCVIO, which is returned to the service requestor.

2. It acquires the MMG spinlock, raising IPL to IPL$_MMG, and gets the address of the L3PTE that maps the page.

3. It tests whether the page is valid. If not, it releases the spinlock, touches the page to fault it, and resumes with step 2.

4. LCKBUFOBJPAG makes several consistency tests on the page, checking that its owner mode is not more privileged than the mode in MMG$L_ACCESS_MODE, the page is a process page, and the page is not a PFN-mapped page. If any test fails, LCKBUFOBJPAG returns an appropriate error status, which is passed back to the service requestor.

5. If the tests succeed, LCKBUFOBJPAG increments the physical page's PFN$W_BO_REFC. It increments the page's PFN$L_REFCNT, sets PFN$V_BUFOBJ in PFN$L_PAGE_STATE, and stores an illegal address containing the process index in the page's PFN$L_PTE as a troubleshooting aid. (Correct treatment of a buffer object page should never result in access of this field.)

6. It modifies the PFN database record for the page table page that maps this buffer object page. It increments PFN$W_BO_REFC. If this is the first buffer object page mapped by this page table page, it also sets the modify and PFN$V_BUFOBJ bits in PFN$L_PAGE_STATE and increments PFN$L_REFCNT.

7. It sets the modify bit in the buffer object page's PFN$L_PAGE_STATE and initializes the SPTE that doubly maps the buffer object page with the PFN, kernel mode read and write enabled, kernel mode owner, valid address space match, modify, no-execute, fault-on-execute, and window bits set.

8. It increments BOD$L_PAGCNT to show that another page has been added to the buffer object.
9. It releases the MMG spinlock and returns.

17.6.2   **$DELETE_BUFOBJ System Service**

The $DELETE_BUFOBJ system service procedure, EXE$DELETE_BUFOBJ in module SYSLKWSET, runs in kernel mode. The service is requested with the address of a buffer handle describing the buffer object to be deleted.

EXE$DELETE_BUFOBJ takes the following steps:

1. It probes accessibility of the buffer handle and in case of error returns the error status SS$_BADPARAM to its requestor.
2. It acquires the MMG spinlock, raising IPL to IPL$_MMG.
3. It checks the following:
   - The BOD is actually linked into the process's BOD list at PCB$Q_BUFOBJ_LIST.
   - The buffer handle is valid.
   - The requesting process's ID is the same as BOD$L_PID.
   - The access mode from which the service was requested is at least as privileged as the creator of the buffer object.

   If any consistency check fails, EXE$DELETE_BUFOBJ releases the MMG spinlock and returns either SS$_BADPARAM or SS$_NOPRIV.
4. It tests and sets BOD$V_DELPEN in BOD$L_FLAGS. If the bit was already set, EXE$DELETE_BUFOBJ releases the spinlock and returns the error status SS$_BADPARAM. Once BOD$V_DELPEN is set, no further I/O can be initiated to this buffer object.
5. It decrements BOD$L_REFCNT and, if the count is still positive, indicating outstanding I/O requests in progress, simply returns.
6. If the reference count is zero, EXE$DELETE_BUFOBJ removes the system mapping of the buffer object pages, one page at a time:
   a. It clears the SPTE and flushes any cached translation from the TB.
   b. It decrements the physical page's PFN$W_BO_REFC and clears bit PFN$V_BUFOBJ in its PFN$L_PAGE_STATE field.
   c. It restores the virtual address of the process's PTE that maps this buffer object to the page's PFN$L_PTE.
   d. It tests whether the page table page that maps the buffer object is valid and, if not, frees a working set list entry for it and makes it valid. It decrements the page table page's PFN$W_BO_REFC. If the reference count is now zero, EXE$DELETE_BUFOBJ clears PFN$V_BUFOBJ in PFN$L_PAGE_STATE for the page and decrements its PFN$L_REFCNT.
   e. If the buffer object page is in a release pending state, EXE$DELETE_BUFOBJ invokes MMG$INCPTREF, in module PAGEFAULT, to increment the PFN$L_SHRCNT of the process page table page that mapped

it. (To allow the page table page to be removed from the working set, its PFN$L_SHRCNT was decremented even though it continued to map a buffer object page in transition.)

    f. EXE$DELETE_BUFOBJ decrements the buffer object page's PFN$L_REFCNT. If the count is now zero, the page is released to the modified page list.

It deallocates the SPTEs that doubly mapped the buffer object.

7. It clears BOD$L_SEQNUM to ensure invalidity of any subsequent reference to the deleted buffer object through its handle, removes the BOD from the PCB queue, and deallocates the BOD to nonpaged pool.

8. It restores the byte count quota and limit charged against the process for the BOD and buffer object pages.

9. It returns to its requestor.

17.7 $SETSWM SYSTEM SERVICE

A process with PSWAPM privilege can lock and unlock itself into the balance set by requesting the $SETSWM system service. A process locked into the balance set cannot be outswapped.

The $SETSWM system service procedure, EXE$SETSWM in module SYSSETMOD, runs in kernel mode. EXE$SETSWM checks that the process has privilege and simply sets (or clears) the PCB$V_PSWAPM bit in PCB$L_STS, the status longword in the software PCB. While setting or clearing the bit, EXE$SETSWM holds the SCHED spinlock.

When the swapper is searching for suitable outswap candidates, a process whose PCB$V_PSWAPM bit is set is passed over.

17.8 $SETPRT SYSTEM SERVICE

A process can alter the protection of a set of pages in its address space by requesting the $SETPRT system service.

The $SETPRT system service procedure, EXE$SETPRT in module SYSSETPRT, runs in kernel mode. It takes the following steps:

1. It transforms the contents of the PROT argument from a VAX protection encoding to the analogous Alpha AXP protection bits.

2. It creates and initializes stack scratch space.

3. It raises IPL to 2 to block AST delivery.

4. EXE$SETPRT invokes MMG$CREDEL, specifying SETPRTPAG as the per-page service-specific routine.

5. It restores the IPL at entry and returns to its requestor.

SETPRTPAG, in module SYSSETPRT, takes the following steps:

1. With PHD$V_NO_WS_CHNG in PHD$L_FLAGS set to block outswap and working set shrinking or trimming, it gets the address of the L3PTE

569

that maps the specified virtual address and faults the page table page into the process's working set list. It acquires the MMG spinlock and clears PHD$V_NO_WS_CHNG.

2. It tests whether the L3PTE is zero, indicating a null page, and, if so, releases the MMG spinlock and returns the error status SS$_ACCVIO, which is passed back to the $SETPRT requestor.

3. It compares the requestor access mode in MMG$L_ACCESS_MODE with that of the page owner. If the access mode is insufficiently privileged, it releases the MMG spinlock and returns the error status SS$_ PAGOWNVIO.

4. Otherwise, it determines the type of the virtual page, based on the valid and type bits in the L3PTE that maps it.

- If the page is a transition or demand zero page that is to become read-only, SETPRTPAG releases the MMG spinlock, lowers IPL, touches the page to make it valid, and continues at step 1.
- If the page is a demand zero page and will remain writable or is a page file page, SETPRTPAG continues with step 5.
- If the page is a process-private section page and the protection change would make a writable page read-only, SETPRTPAG continues with step 5.

  If the page is already writable from some mode or is a copy-on-reference page, SETPRTPAG continues with step 5.

  If the protection change would make a read-only page writable, SETPRTPAG must change the page to be a copy-on-reference page: it charges the page against the process's job page file quota and PHD$L_ PPGFLVA, and changes the page's backing store to a page file. It continues with step 5, also setting the copy-on-reference bit in the L3PTE. An inability to charge the page against quota or PHD$L_PPGFLVA results in an error return.

- If the page is valid, SETPRTPAG checks that it is not a PFN-mapped page and that it is a process page. If either is false, it returns the error status SS$_NOPRIV.

  If the page is a valid process page and the protection change would make a writable page read-only, SETPRTPAG continues with step 5, also clearing the fault-on-write bit if it was set.

  If the page is a valid process page and the protection change does not make a read-only page writable or if the page already has page file backing store, SETPRTPAG continues with step 5.

  Otherwise, it changes the PFN$Q_BAK field for the physical page to a page file backing store form and decrements the section's reference count. It completes changing the page to a copy-on-reference page, taking the same steps as for a process-private section page.

- If the page is a global section page, SETPRTPAG determines the page type from the global PTE. If it contains anything but a global section index for a copy-on-reference page, SETPRTPAG returns the error status SS$_NOPRIV. Otherwise, it continues.

5. It modifies the L3PTE to change the page's protection and invalidates any cached TB entry for the page.
6. It releases the MMG spinlock, restoring the previous IPL of 2, and returns to its invoker.

In general, the operation of this service is straightforward. However, its actions have one interesting side effect. If a section page for a read-only section has its protection set to writable, the copy-on-reference bit is set. This set bit forces the page to have its backing store address changed to the page file when the page is faulted, preventing a later attempt to write the modified section pages back to a file to which the process may be denied write access.

17.9 $SETFLT SYSTEM SERVICE

A process can set the no-execute characteristic for each of a group of pages in its address space by requesting the undocumented $SETFLT system service. Use of this service is reserved to Digital. Any other use is unsupported.

The $SETFLT system service procedure, EXE$SETFLT in module SYSSETPRT, runs in kernel mode. It takes the following steps:

1. It creates and initializes stack scratch space.
2. It performs several consistency checks on the arguments, returning the error status SS$_BADPARAM if the FLAGS argument specifies anything other than no-execute or the error status SS$_ACCVIO if other arguments are inaccessible.
3. It raises IPL to 2 to block AST delivery.
4. EXE$SETFLT invokes MMG$CREDEL (see Section 17.1), specifying SETFLTPAG as the per-page service-specific routine.
5. If MMG$CREDEL returns successfully, EXE$SETFLT executes an instruction memory barrier to flush any instructions that might have been prefetched from the pages whose fault-on-execute bit has just been set.
6. It restores the previous IPL and returns to its requestor.

SETFLTPAG, in module SYSSETPRT, takes the following steps:

1. With PHD$V_NO_WS_CHNG in PHD$L_FLAGS set to block outswap and working set shrinking or trimming, it gets the address of the L3PTE that maps the specified virtual address and faults the page table page into the process's working set list. It acquires the MMG spinlock and clears PHD$V_NO_WS_CHNG.
2. It compares the requestor access mode with that of the page owner. If the access mode is insufficiently privileged, it releases the MMG spinlock

and returns the error status SS$_PAGOWNVIO, which is passed back to the $SETFLT requestor.

3. Otherwise, it determines the type of the virtual page, based on the valid and type bits in the L3PTE that maps it.

- If the page is a transition or demand zero page, SETFLTPAG releases the MMG spinlock, lowers IPL, touches the page to make it valid, and continues at step 1.

- If the page is valid, SETFLTPAG checks that it is a process page and not a PFN-mapped page, returning the error status SS$_NOPRIV if either is false. If both are true, it sets the no-execute and fault-on-execute bits in the L3PTE.

- If the page is a global page, a page file page, or a section page, SETFLT-PAG sets the no-execute bit in the L3PTE.

4. It invalidates any possible TB entry for the page; releases the MMG spinlock, lowering IPL; and returns.

17.10 $COPY_FOR_PAGE SYSTEM SERVICE

A process can read data from a page whose fault-on-read bit is set by requesting the undocumented $COPY_FOR_PAGE system service. The service is requested with three arguments specifying the number of bytes to be copied, the source virtual address, and the destination virtual address. As described in Chapter 15, the executive sets the fault-on-read bit in the SPTEs mapping the granularity hint region that contains executive and other installed resident images' code sections. The protection on these pages permits user access so that instructions in mode of caller system services and images installed resident can be executed by any access mode. Data fetches, in contrast, are blocked by the fault-on-read bit.

The System Dump Analyzer (SDA) utility and debuggers use this service when they are requested to display instructions in system space. This service provides the ability to fetch data from system pages set fault-on-read for the few instances in which it is required. Use of this service is reserved to Digital. Any other use is unsupported.

The $COPY_FOR_PAGE system service procedure, EXE$COPY_FOR_PAGE in module COPY_FOR_PAGE, runs in kernel mode. It takes the following steps:

1. It confirms that the data to be read is in system space, returning the error status SS$_BADPARAM if not.

2. It probes the protection on the system page to confirm that the access mode from which the service was requested is allowed to read the page and, if not, returns the error status SS$_ACCVIO.

3. It probes the output buffer page to confirm that the requesting access mode has write access and, if not, returns the error status SS$_ACCVIO.

4. It acquires the MMG spinlock, raising IPL to IPL$_MMG.

5. EXE$COPY_FOR_PAGE examines the SPTE containing the start of the data.

   • If the page is invalid but the fault-on-read bit is set, the SPTE is inconsistent and EXE$COPY_FOR_PAGE generates the fatal bugcheck INCONMMGST.

   • If the page is valid and the fault-on-read bit is not set, EXE$COPY_FOR_PAGE releases the MMG spinlock and simply copies the data to the requestor's output buffer.

   • If the page is valid and the fault-on-read bit is set, EXE$COPY_FOR_PAGE temporarily double-maps the physical page or pages containing the data. The temporary mapping permits kernel read access and has the fault-on-read bit clear. The alternative to the double mapping is temporarily clearing the fault-on-read bit in the original SPTE. That alternative would not only make it possible for other threads of execution to fetch data from the page but would also require clearing and then resetting the bit in each SPTE that maps any page within the granularity hint region.

     EXE$COPY_FOR_PAGE releases the spinlock, lowering IPL. Using the temporary mapping of the physical page, it copies the data to the requestor's output buffer. It reacquires the spinlock to unmap the page or pages and releases the spinlock.

6. It returns to its requestor.

17.11   RELEVANT SOURCE MODULES

Source modules described in this chapter include

[LIB]MMGDEF.SDL
[SYS]COPY_FOR_PAGE.B32
[SYS]PHDUTL.MAR
[SYS]SYSADJSTK.MAR
[SYS]SYSCREDEL.MAR
[SYS]SYSCRMPSC.MAR
[SYS]SYSDGBLSC.MAR
[SYS]SYSLKWSET.MAR
[SYS]SYSSETMOD.MAR
[SYS]SYSSETPRT.MAR

18 Paging Dynamics

> I consider that a man's brain originally is like a little empty attic,
> and you have to stock it with such furniture as you choose. . . .
> Now, the skillful workman is very careful indeed as to what he
> takes into his brain-attic. He will have nothing but the tools
> which may help him in doing his work, but of these he has a
> large assortment, and all in the most perfect order. It is a mistake
> to think that that little room has elastic walls and can distend to
> any extent. Depend upon it, there comes a time when for every
> addition of knowledge you forget something that you knew
> before. It is of highest importance, therefore, not to have useless
> facts elbowing out the useful ones.
>
> Sir Arthur Conan Doyle, *A Study in Scarlet*

This chapter's subject is paging dynamics, the movement of pages of code
and data between memory and mass storage. Specifically, it describes the
transitions a page makes as it is faulted into and out of a working set list,
and as it moves between its backing store and memory.

The chapter also discusses modified page writing, the allocation and use of
page files, and the operation of the Update Section File on Disk ($UPDSEC)
system service.

18.1 OVERVIEW

A typical virtual page begins life as a demand zero page or as a number of
blocks in a section file on a mass storage medium. As discussed in Chapter 15, the size of a virtual or physical page on an AXP processor varies with
processor type. On all processors supported by this version of the operating
system, page size is 8 KB, or 16 512-byte blocks.

Commonly, a virtual page comes from an image. A process initiates execution of the image by requesting the Image Activate ($IMGACT) system
service, better known as the image activator. The image activator, described
in detail in Chapter 28, maps the entire image into the process's address
space, using the memory management system services described in Chapter 17. The image activator initializes data structures such as process section
table entries (PSTEs) and page table entries (PTEs) to associate blocks of the
image file with the process pages they are to occupy. Chapter 16 discusses
the various memory management data structures.

When an image begins to execute, few of its pages have been read into
memory from the image file, and most of the level 3 page table entries
(L3PTEs) that map the image have a clear valid bit. (The image activator did
access some pages to relocate and fix up address references within the image.)

When an image page whose valid bit is clear is referenced, a translation-not-valid exception results. The processor changes access mode to kernel and switches to the kernel stack. It dispatches to the translation-not-valid exception service routine, more commonly known as the page fault handler.

The page fault handler examines the memory management data structures to determine what kind of virtual page this is and takes appropriate actions:

▶ For example, in the case of a demand zero page, it finds an available entry in the process's working set list, allocates a page of zeroed memory, and stores its page frame number (PFN) in the L3PTE with a set valid bit. It dismisses the exception. The process reexecutes the instruction whose attempted execution caused the page fault. This time, with the L3PTE valid bit set, the processor translates the virtual address to a physical address and execution continues.

▶ In the case of a virtual page in a mass storage file, the page fault handler determines which blocks contain the virtual page that triggered the fault, finds an available entry in the process's working set list, allocates a physical page of memory from the free page list, stores its PFN in the L3PTE with a clear valid bit, and requests an I/O operation to read those blocks into the allocated page. It places the process into a page fault wait state.

When the I/O completes, I/O postprocessing code sets the valid bit in the L3PTE and makes the process computable. When the process is placed back into execution, it reexecutes the instruction whose attempted execution caused the page fault. This time, with the L3PTE valid bit set, the processor translates the virtual address to a physical address and execution continues.

Although many steps in page fault handling are common to most types of page, some depend on page type and state. Section 18.2 describes the common steps in page fault handling and serves as a framework for details of type- and state-specific processing described in subsequent sections.

Faulted in, a page remains valid and in the working set until removed. Reasons for removal include the following:

▶ Room is required for another page (see Chapter 19).
▶ The Purge Working Set ($PURGWS) system service removes it (see Chapter 19).
▶ Swapper trimming removes it (see Chapter 20).
▶ Proactive memory reclamation removes it (see Chapters 13 and 20).
▶ Working set limit adjustment removes it (see Chapter 19).

Removed from the working set list, the page is inserted into the modified page list, if it has been modified; otherwise, it is inserted into the free page list. Sometime later, the swapper, in response to insufficient free pages or an excess of modified pages, writes modified pages to their backing store, typically a page file. It then inserts them into the free page list. Acting in this capacity, the swapper is called the modified page writer.

While the page is on the free or modified page list, it is essentially cached; the page fault handler can resolve a fault for it by simply updating the memory management data structures and placing the page back into the process's working set list.

This chapter shows how the page fault handler manipulates the various memory management data structures in response to faults for different types of virtual page. It presents page fault handler action largely in terms of modifications to data structures and state transitions. It also describes the transitions that a virtual page makes when it is removed from a working set list.

Section 18.3 discusses the transitions of different kinds of process page. Section 18.4 covers the transitions of global pages. Section 18.5 describes the transitions of system space pages, process page table pages, and global page table pages.

18.2 PAGE FAULT HANDLING

The page fault handler is entered in response to a translation-not-valid fault, described in detail in Chapter 15. When it is entered, the stack contains the standard exception stack frame, pictured in Figure 3.4. The page fault is described by the contents of the following registers:

▶ R4—The fault virtual address
▶ R5—One of the following values:

$80000000\ 00000000_{16}$ for a write data fault
$00000000\ 00000000_{16}$ for a read data fault
$00000000\ 00000001_{16}$ for a read instruction fault

The page fault handler is implemented in a combination of MACRO-64 assembly language and MACRO-32:

▶ SCH$PAGEFAULT, in MACRO-64 assembly language module SCHEDULER
▶ MMG$PAGEFAULT, in MACRO-32 module PAGEFAULT

Assembly language is required to save all the scratch registers so they can be restored when the exception is dismissed. Forming the canonical kernel stack (see Chapter 13) in case the process must be placed into a wait state also requires assembly language.

18.2.1 Common Steps in Page Fault Handling

Figure 18.1 summarizes the main steps in handling a typical fault for a page on a mass storage medium. The numbers in the figure are keyed to the explanations that follow.

① Entered first, SCH$PAGEFAULT saves the scratch registers on the stack and calls MMG$PAGEFAULT.

② MMG$PAGEFAULT checks the interrupt priority level (IPL) at which the page fault occurred. If the IPL is higher than 2, it generates the fatal PGFIPLHI bugcheck. Page faults above IPL 2 are not allowed for the following reasons:

- Code executes at an elevated IPL to perform a series of synchronized instructions. If a page fault occurs, the faulting process might be removed from execution, allowing another process to execute the same routine or access the same protected data structure. The alternative, looping in process context at elevated IPL until the page fault I/O completes, would reduce system performance and responsiveness. Moreover, any loop at IPL 4 or above would block the I/O postprocessing necessary for page fault resolution. On a uniprocessor system, a loop above IPL 2 blocks swapper execution and would result in a deadlock if the free page list were empty and the page fault required allocation of a page of memory.

- When the system is executing at an IPL higher than 2, it may be running in system context. MMG$PAGEFAULT and related routines perform operations that require process context.

③ MMG$PAGEFAULT acquires the MMG spinlock, raising IPL to IPL$_MMG. It locates the L3PTE that maps the page containing the fault virtual address in the following manner:

- It determines which set of level 3 page tables (L3PTs) contain the L3PTE by examining bits ⟨31 : 30⟩ of the virtual address. If bit 31 of the virtual address is set, the L3PTs that make up the system page table contain the L3PTE. If bit 31 is clear, the value of bit 30 specifies whether the address is a P0 or P1 space address and which process-private set of L3PTs contain the L3PTE.

- On a processor with an 8 KB page size, MMG$PAGEFAULT extracts bits ⟨31 : 13⟩ of a system virtual address or bits ⟨30 : 13⟩ of a process-private virtual address to get the virtual page number of the faulting page. Multiplying the virtual page number by 8, the size of a PTE, it indexes the P0, P1, or system space set of L3PTs.

Before examining the L3PTE, it determines whether the system PTE (SPTE) that maps the page table page containing the L3PTE is itself valid. (Recall that all page table pages are mapped in system space.) This check avoids the necessity of making the page fault handler recursive.

If the SPTE is invalid, MMG$PAGEFAULT transforms the page fault into one for the page table page. After the page table page has been faulted in, its SPTE made valid, and the exception dismissed, the instruction that caused the original fault will reexecute and refault, and the page fault handler will fault in the process page.

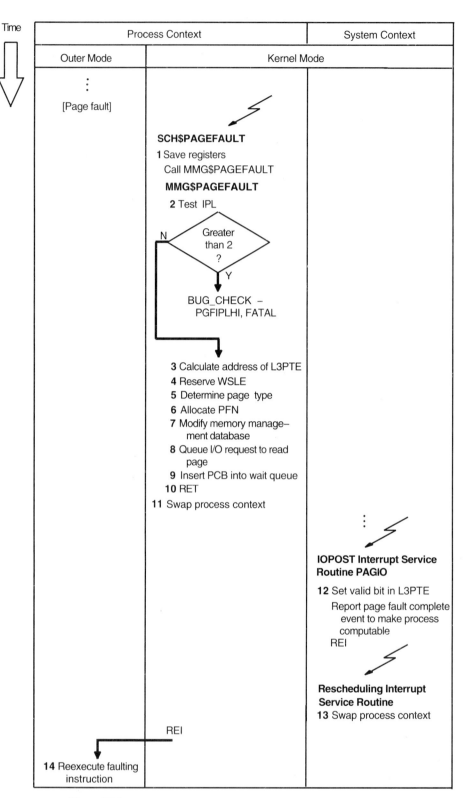

Figure 18.1
Main Steps in Faulting a Page from a Mass Storage
Medium

④ It invokes MMG$FREWSLE, in module PAGEFAULT, to find room in the working set list for a new page, possibly by removing a page from it (see step 4 in Section 18.3.1).

If MMG$FREWSLE returns an error status indicating that a free working set list entry (WSLE) is not currently available, MMG$PAGEFAULT releases the MMG spinlock, acquires the SCHED spinlock, inserts the process's process control block (PCB) into the resource wait queue, loads the status SS$_WAIT_CALLERS_MODE into R0, and continues with step 10.

If a free WSLE is available, MMG$PAGEFAULT retests the validity of the SPTE mapping the page table page (one of whose L3PTEs maps the virtual address). This is done in case MMG$FREWSLE has removed the L3PT from the working set. If the SPTE is no longer valid, MMG$PAGEFAULT transforms the fault into one for the L3PT. After the page table page has been faulted in, its SPTE made valid, and the exception dismissed, the instruction that caused the original fault will reexecute and refault, and the page fault handler will fault in the process page.

⑤ It determines the type of page. Its subsequent actions depend on the nature of the invalid page. Figure 16.8 shows the different forms of invalid L3PTE, and Chapter 17 describes how most of them are initialized in response to various system service requests.

⑥ If necessary, MMG$PAGEFAULT allocates a physical page of memory. (If the virtual page is already in memory, for example, occupying a physical page on the free page list, this step is unnecessary.)

If a page of memory is not currently available, MMG$PAGEFAULT releases the MMG spinlock, acquires the SCHED spinlock, inserts the PCB into the free page wait queue, loads the status SS$_WAIT_CALLERS_MODE into R0, and continues with step 10.

⑦ MMG$PAGEFAULT updates the memory management data structures.

⑧ If the page does not need to be read, perhaps because it is a demand zero page or a page faulted from the free page list, MMG$PAGEFAULT releases the MMG spinlock, loads the status SS$_NORMAL into R0, and continues with step 10.

If the page must be read in from a mass storage device, MMG$PAGE-FAULT builds an I/O request packet (see Section 18.12) that describes the read to be done, releases the MMG spinlock, and queues the request to the driver.

⑨ MMG$PAGEFAULT acquires the SCHED spinlock. Before placing the process into a page fault wait state, it tests whether the faulted page is still invalid. On a symmetric multiprocessing (SMP) system, where MMG$PAGEFAULT is running on one processor, concurrent processing of the I/O request on another may have already made the page valid. If the page is valid, MMG$PAGEFAULT releases the SCHED spinlock, loads the status SS$_NORMAL into R0, and continues with step 10.

If the page is still invalid, it inserts the PCB into the page fault wait queue and loads the status SS$_WAIT_CALLERS_MODE into R0.

⑩ MMG$PAGEFAULT returns to SCH$PAGEFAULT.

⑪ SCH$PAGEFAULT's actions depend on the status from MMG$PAGE-FAULT.

If MMG$PAGEFAULT returned the status SS$_NORMAL, indicating that page fault handling is complete, SCH$PAGEFAULT restores the saved scratch registers and executes a CALL_PAL REI instruction to dismiss the page fault.

If MMG$PAGEFAULT returned the status SS$_WAIT_CALLERS_MODE, indicating that the process must wait, SCH$PAGEFAULT takes the following actions:

a. It updates several systemwide data cells to reflect that this process is no longer current.

b. It selects a computable resident process with whose hardware context that of the waiting process can be swapped. If none is available, it will swap to the system hardware context.

c. It saves the nonscratch integer registers on the stack and, if the process is using floating-point arithmetic, the floating-point registers in the process header (PHD).

d. It swaps process context.

e. Running in the new process's context, it releases the SCHED spinlock, restores the new process's nonprivileged hardware context, and reenters it by executing the instruction CALL_PAL REI.

⑫ Page read completion occurs as part of I/O postprocessing (see Chapter 23) and runs in system context. The I/O postprocessing routine PAGIO, in module IOCIOPOST, sets the valid bit in the L3PTE and reports the scheduling event page fault completion for the process to make it computable. PAGIO's actions are described in Section 18.7.

When the event is reported, if the process is resident and its priority is sufficiently high that it should preempt, a rescheduling interrupt is requested. For simplicity, the figure shows this step as occurring in system context, although it is more likely to occur in the context of whatever process is current. Section 18.13 describes the various wait states associated with page faults.

⑬ The rescheduling interrupt service routine selects the page faulting process for execution, swaps to its context, and then executes a CALL_PAL REI instruction.

⑭ The process reexecutes the instruction that caused the page fault, this time with the page valid.

18.2.2   **Error Returns to SCH$PAGEFAULT**

MMG$PAGEFAULT can return these error statuses to SCH$PAGEFAULT:

▸ SS$_ACCVIO
▸ SS$_PAGRDERR
▸ SS$_PAGRDERRXM

If the process has tried to access another process's header, MMG$PAGE-
FAULT returns the error status SS$_ACCVIO; in response SCH$PAGE-
FAULT restores the scratch registers and transfers to EXE$ACVIOLAT, in
module EXCEPTION. EXE$ACVIOLAT, described in Chapter 6, simulates
an access violation exception to be reported to the access mode that incurred
the page fault. If the fault occurred in an inner mode, the system may crash.

If the system incurred a hardware error on a previous attempt to read the
faulted page, MMG$PAGEFAULT determines the access mode in which this
page fault occurred and the mode of the page owner. It returns the error
status SS$_PAGRDERR when either of the following is true:

▸ The page fault occurred in user or supervisor mode.
▸ The page fault occurred in executive or kernel mode and the page is owned
  by executive or kernel mode.

If the page fault occurred in executive or kernel mode but the page is
owned by user or supervisor mode, MMG$PAGEFAULT returns the error
status SS$_PAGRDERRXM. This set of circumstances is called a cross-mode
page read error.

In response to either status, SCH$PAGEFAULT restores the scratch
registers and then transfers to EXE$PAGRDERR, in module EXCEPTION.
EXE$PAGRDERR, described in Chapter 6, generates the special condition
SS$_PAGRDERR or SS$_PAGRDERRXM and reports it to the access mode
that incurred the page fault.

If no other condition handler handles either condition, the condition is
passed to the last chance condition handler for that mode. For executive
mode, the last chance condition handler is EXE$EXCPTNE, in module EX-
CEPTION_ROUTINES; for kernel mode, the handler is EXE$EXCPTN, in
the same module.

Each of these handlers checks whether the condition is SS$_PAGRD-
ERRXM and, if so, requests the Exit ($EXIT) system service, specifying SS$_
PAGRDERRXM as the reason for exit. Exiting the image from either executive or kernel mode will cause its process to be deleted. In the case of a
cross-mode page read error, the process cannot continue execution, but the
system is not affected.

For any other type of condition, in particular, SS$_PAGRDERR, the exec-
utive mode last chance condition handler generates the nonfatal bugcheck
SSRVEXCEPT and requests the $EXIT system service, causing the process to

be deleted. When such conditions occur in kernel mode, the kernel mode last chance condition handler generates the fatal bugcheck SSRVEXCEPT. In the case of a read error for a page owned by kernel mode, system operation may be affected and the executive crashes the system rather than risk system and file integrity.

18.3   PAGE TRANSITIONS FOR PROCESS PAGES

This section describes the transitions that different types of process page undergo. Many of the transitions depend upon the initial location of the virtual page and the location of its backing store.

Initially, a process page is faulted in from a section file on a mass storage medium or created on demand as a page of all zeros, a demand zero page. (One other possibility is a page in a PFN-mapped section. Such a page remains valid throughout its life and is thus outside the scope of this chapter.) A page from a section file is further characterized by whether it is read-only or writable. All demand zero pages are writable.

When a read-only page is removed from the working set, there is no need to record its current contents; the page can be refaulted from its original location. When a writable modified page is removed from the working set, its current contents must be recorded to retain the modifications. The term *backing store* refers to the mass storage location of the modified page.

A writable section page can be characterized by whether it is copy-on-reference. The backing store for a copy-on-reference page is the page file. The backing store for one that is not copy-on-reference is the section file. When a copy-on-reference page is first faulted in, it is assigned a backing store location. Removed from the working set, the page is eventually recorded in its backing store location. Subsequently faulted, it is read from the backing store. (This approach simplifies the management of the page at the cost of having to write the page to its backing store even when it has not been modified.)

Most demand zero pages are created through the Create Virtual Address Space ($CRETVA) or the Expand Region ($EXPREG) system service. The backing store for such pages is the page file. It is also possible, however, for a process to create a section of demand zero pages backed by a section file.

Chapter 17 describes the system services that create various kinds of virtual address space.

The sections that follow describe the transitions for several kinds of process page. Typically, the first transition occurs when the page is faulted in from a mass storage device. In subsequent transitions the page is removed from the working set. It may be placed into the free page list, or it may be placed into the modified page list and written to its backing store. During any of these transitions, the page may be faulted again.

Section 18.2.1 describes the page fault handling steps common to many types of page fault but omits the details of concomitant memory management data structure changes. The sections that follow describe the data structure changes.

Section 18.3.1 describes the initial fault and subsequent transitions of a process section page that is not copy-on-reference; and Section 18.3.2, of a process section page that is copy-on-reference. Section 18.3.3 describes the initial fault of a demand zero page. Its subsequent transitions depend on whether it is a demand zero section page backed in a section file or a simple demand zero page backed in the page file. Section 18.3.4 summarizes some additional kinds of page fault common to the page types already described. Section 18.3.5 discusses the transitions of a process page that is part of a buffer object page.

18.3.1 Process Section Page That Is Not Copy-on-Reference

The L3PTE for a page that is not copy-on-reference initially contains a process section table index (PSTX) with the copy-on-reference bit (PTE⟨48⟩) clear. The transitions that such a page can make are illustrated in Figure 18.2. The numbers in the figure are keyed to the explanations that follow. For simplicity, clustered reads and writes are ignored here. Sections 18.6 and 18.8.4 discuss the clustering aspects of paging I/O.

① The first transition is faulting the page in from the file that contains it. As described in Section 18.2.1, MMG$PAGEFAULT locates the L3PTE that maps the faulting page and ensures the validity of the page table page containing it. MMG$PAGEFAULT uses three other routines in module PAGEFAULT to perform some of the related updates to memory management data structures:

- MMG$ININEW_PFN allocates a physical page from the head of the free page list into which the virtual page will be read. It stores the address of the L3PTE in the PFN$L_PTE field of that page's PFN database record and a type code of process page in PFN$L_PAGE_STATE.
- MMG$INCPTREF updates some of the data structures describing the page table page that maps the faulted page (see Section 18.5.1).
- MMG$MAKE_WSLE updates data structures related to the working set list. It initializes the WSLE with the virtual address and page type of the page being faulted and sets its valid bit. It initializes several data structures related to the page table page (see Section 18.5.1). It increments the field PCB$L_PPGCNT to indicate one more process page in the working set. It stores the index of the WSLE in the PFN$L_WSLX field of the PFN database record for the physical page and increments its PFN$L_REFCNT field to indicate that the page is in a working set list.

MMG$PAGEFAULT itself also increments the PFN$L_REFCNT field for the allocated physical page, bringing the count to 2, to indicate the I/O

583

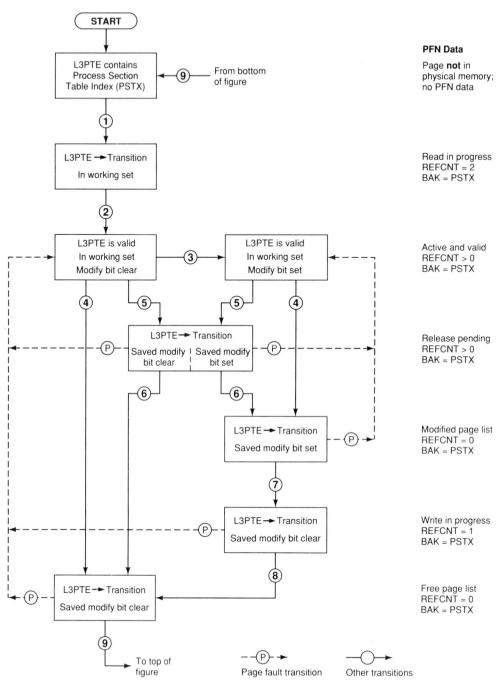

Figure 18.2
Page Transitions for a Process Section Page That Is Not
Copy-on-Reference

request about to be queued for this page. It initializes the page's PFN$Q_
BAK field from the L3PTE's type and partial section bits and bits (63 : 32).

It inserts the PFN of the allocated page into the L3PTE, leaving the
protection, owner, and copy characteristics bits as they were. It initializes
the type bits to indicate a transition page. If the page is writable but was
faulted with read intent, it sets the fault-on-write bit. It sets fault-on-
execute either if the no-execute bit was set or if the page was faulted
with read or write data intent rather than with execute intent. Chapter 15
discusses the significance of the fault-on bits and the executive's use of
them.

MMG$PAGEFAULT initializes the location bits in the page's PFN$L_
PAGE_STATE field to read in progress.

It builds an I/O request packet (see Section 18.12) that describes the
read to be done. From the PSTX in the original L3PTE contents, it locates
the corresponding PSTE in the PHD. From information in the PSTE, it
can calculate which virtual blocks in the file contain the virtual page.

If the last page in the section has the partial section bit set and is in the
cluster to be read, MMG$PAGEFAULT must take extra steps. A partial
section is one whose size in blocks is not an exact multiple of the number
of blocks in a page. Thus, its last page is not entirely backed by section
file. For this kind of page fault, MMG$PAGEFAULT calculates the I/O
request byte count such that the last page's contribution to the count
includes only those pagelets that have backing store. It temporarily maps
the PFN with a reserved SPTE and clears the part of the partially backed
page that has no backing store.

It queues the request to the driver for the device containing the page.

(2) Because most of the work was done in response to the initial fault, there
is little left to do when the page read completes. Holding the MMG spinlock, routine PAGIO decrements PFN$L_REFCNT. In the usual case, the
reference count remains greater than zero. In that case, PAGIO changes
the PFN$L_PAGE_STATE location bits to active and sets the valid bit in
the process L3PTE. If the page is writable, PAGIO tests the fault-on-write
bit. If it is clear, indicating that the page was faulted with write intent,
PAGIO sets the modify bit in the L3PTE.

It is, however, possible for PAGIO to decrement the reference count to
zero. This can happen if the page was removed from the working set list,
for example, through swapper trimming or automatic working set limit
adjustment, before the page read completes. The page would have been
put in the release pending state with a reference count of 1. If PAGIO
decrements the reference count to zero, then instead of setting the valid
bit, it inserts the page into the free page list.

(3) One transition that a valid page can undergo and still remain valid occurs
when the page is modified as a result of instruction execution. When an
attempt is made to write to a page that was originally faulted with read

intent and one whose fault-on-write bit is set, the processor generates a fault-on-write exception. The exception service routine clears the fault-on-write bit in the L3PTE and sets the modify bit. The change is not noted at this time in the PFN database.

④ A valid page becomes invalid when it is removed from the working set list as a result of any of the conditions described in Section 18.1. Most of those result in the invocation of MMG$FREWSLE or its alternative entry point, MMG$FREWSLX. Of most relevance here are the changes to memory management data structures when a non-copy-on-reference page is removed from the process working set list:

   a. The modify bit in the L3PTE is saved. The valid, modify, fault-on-write, and fault-on-execute bits are cleared. Its PFN field is unchanged.

   b. The translation buffer (TB) is invalidated to remove the cached but now obsolete contents of the L3PTE.

   c. The saved modify bit from the L3PTE is inserted into the PFN$L_PAGE_STATE field, saving its value.

   d. The page's PFN$L_REFCNT is decremented. If the reference count goes to zero, the page is put into the free or modified page list, according to the setting of the saved modify bit in PFN$L_PAGE_STATE. Since the PFN$L_BLINK field overlays the PFN$L_WSLX field, inserting the page into the free or modified page list supplants the PFN$L_WSLX field contents. The page's new location (free or modified page list) is inserted into the PFN$L_PAGE_STATE field.

   e. The WSLE is zeroed. The PHD$L_PTWSLEVAL array element for the page table page mapping this page is decremented. If the count makes the transition to –1, PHD$L_PTCNTVAL is also decremented (see Section 18.5.1). PCB$L_PPGCNT is decremented to indicate one less process page.

⑤ If the reference count (decremented in step 4d) does not go to zero, there is outstanding direct I/O for this page. MMG$FREWSLX changes the page's PFN$L_PAGE_STATE location bits from active to release pending.

⑥ When direct I/O for the page completes, the I/O postprocessing routine invokes MMG$UNLOCK, in module IOLOCK. It invokes MMG$DECPTREF, in module PAGEFAULT, once for each L3PT that maps I/O buffer pages. MMG$DECPTREF decrements the PFN$L_SHRCNT field in the PFN database record for the L3PT (incremented when the I/O was initiated) to indicate one less reason for it to remain in existence (see Section 18.5.1).

For each page in the I/O buffer, MMG$UNLOCK decrements the page's PFN$L_REFCNT. If it goes to zero, MMG$UNLOCK puts the page into either the free or the modified page list, based on the setting of the saved modify bit, and changes PFN$L_PAGE_STATE accordingly. It releases the MMG spinlock and returns.

If the page was placed into the free page list, the next stages in its processing are as described in step 9.

⑦ If the page was placed into the modified page list, the modified page writer eventually removes the page and initiates a write of it to the backing store address in its PFN$Q_BAK field. A writable page that is not copy-on-reference is written back to the file where it originated.

The modified page writer sets the PFN$L_PAGE_STATE location bits for the page to write in progress and clears the saved modify bit. The reference count of 1 reflects the outstanding I/O operation.

Note that a section containing writable process pages that are not copy-on-reference cannot be produced by the linker. Such a section must be created with the Create and Map Section ($CRMPSC) system service.

⑧ When the modified page write completes, the page's reference count is decremented to zero. Because the saved modify bit is clear, the page is put into the free page list.

⑨ A page placed on the free page list normally remains attached to the process for some time; that is, the L3PTE contains its PFN, and the PFN$L_PTE field in the PFN database record for that page contains the address of the process L3PTE.

When the physical page is allocated for another purpose, several steps must be taken to break the ties between the process virtual page and the physical page that is about to be reused. The routine MMG$DELCON_PFN, in module ALLOCPFN, performs those steps:

a. It locates the L3PTE from the contents of the PFN$L_PTE field.

b. The L3PTE must be altered to reflect the backing store address of the page. For a non-copy-on-reference page, it restores some of the L3PTE's contents before the initial page fault, namely, the PSTX from the page's PFN$Q_BAK. It leaves the protection, owner, copy characteristics, and no-execute bits as they were.

c. It invokes MMG$DECPTREF, which decrements the PFN$L_SHR-CNT field in the PFN database record for the L3PT to indicate one less reason for it to remain valid (see Section 18.5.1).

d. MMG$DELCON_PFN reinitializes the PFN database record for the physical page before reallocating it. In particular, it clears PFN$L_PTE, the connection from the PFN database to the process page table.

A subsequent fault requires rereading the page from the section file.

18.3.2   Process Section Page That Is Copy-on-Reference

The more common type of writable process page is a copy-on-reference page. The initial value in the L3PTE (START 1 in Figure 18.3) is a PSTX; the copy-on-reference bit (PTE⟨48⟩) is set. The writable bit (PTE⟨50⟩) is usually set. Figure 18.3 illustrates the transitions that such a page makes from its initial

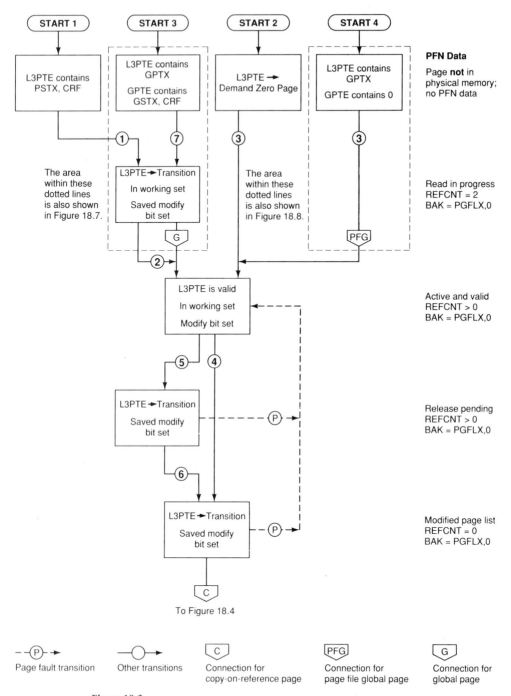

Figure 18.3
Page Transitions for Process and Global Copy-on-
Reference Pages and for Demand Zero Pages

page fault until it is written to page file backing store. The numbers in the figure are keyed to the explanations that follow.

Many of the transitions that occur here resemble the case just described. This section notes each transition but elaborates only those areas that are different.

① When a page fault occurs, MMG$PAGEFAULT performs the actions described in step 1 of Section 18.3.1. It also takes several additional steps:

  a. First, it updates the PFN$L_PAGE_STATE field location bits to the value read in progress, with the saved modify bit set. The page's backing store will be a page file, not a section file; the copy of the page in the section file must not be modified, yet each of the potentially many copies of the page may be modified. Setting the saved modify bit guarantees that an initial copy of the page will be written to the page file when it is first paged out, whether or not it has been modified.

  b. Second, it assigns the page a backing store (namely, the process's current page file) and copies PHD$Q_PAGFIL to the PFN$Q_BAK field. (Section 18.11 provides further details on page file assignment, reservation, and allocation.) At this time, all ties to the original section file have been broken. When the modified page writer first writes this page to its backing store (as it eventually will because the saved modify bit was just set), it will allocate actual blocks in the page file.

  c. If the last page in the section has the partial section bit set in its L3PTE and is in the cluster to be read, MMG$PAGEFAULT calculates the I/O request byte count accordingly and clears the part of the page without backing store, as described in step 1 of Section 18.3.1. In addition, it clears the partial section flag in PFN$Q_BAK, because once the page is faulted in, it is no longer partially backed; its backing store is a whole page in the page file.

② After the read completes, PAGIO decrements the reference count of each page in the page fault cluster. If the reference count is greater than zero, it updates the PFN$L_PAGE_STATE location bits to active and sets the L3PTE valid bit. If the reference count is decremented to zero because the page has been removed from the working set list, it places the page into the modified page list and changes its PFN$L_PAGE_STATE location bits accordingly.

  PAGIO also subtracts the number of pages read from the PSTE's reference count to show that many fewer L3PTEs mapping pages from that section file.

③ This transition is described in Section 18.3.3.

④ When the copy-on-reference page is removed from the working set and its reference count goes to zero, the page is placed into the modified page list.

If the page has been modified and its assigned page file backing store, if any, contains an obsolete copy, that storage is deallocated and the page number in the PFN$Q_BAK field is cleared. The process-local page file index remains intact.

⑤ If the reference count did not go to zero when the page was removed from the process working set, the physical page is placed into the release pending state until the I/O completes.

⑥ At that time, the page is put into the modified page list.

⑦ This transition is described as transition 3 in Section 18.4.3.

When the modified page writer writes the page to its backing store in a page file, the page makes a transition from the modified page list. Figure 18.4, the diagram for faults from the page file, shows this transition. The connection between Figure 18.3 and Figure 18.4 is indicated by path C in the two figures. A subsequent fault for the page is resolved from the page file.

The transitions for a page faulted from the page file (see Figure 18.4) resemble those described for a page that is not copy-on-reference (see Figure 18.2). The only difference in the PFN data between the two figures is that the PFN$Q_BAK field value in Figure 18.4 indicates that the page belongs in a page file, whereas the PFN$Q_BAK field value in Figure 18.2 contains a PSTX.

The other difference between the two figures is the entry point into the transition diagram. A page can start out in a section file (the L3PTE contains a PSTX) but a page can never start out in a page file. The entry into Figure 18.4 is from path C in Figure 18.3, from one of several initial states that eventually result in the physical page contents' being written to the page file.

18.3.3 Demand Zero Page

An L3PTE to map a typical demand zero page is initialized by the $CRETVA or the $EXPREG system service. These services can be requested explicitly by an image or implicitly by the system on behalf of the process, for example, as part of image activation. Also, a process can request the $CRMPSC system service to create a demand zero section backed by a section file. An L3PTE to map such a section has a PSTX with the copy-on-reference bit clear and the demand zero bit set. Either type of demand zero page is created the first time it is faulted.

Figure 18.3 (START 2) and Figure 18.4 illustrate the transitions of a typical demand zero page, one backed in a page file.

The transitions of a demand zero section page resemble those in Figure 18.2 except for the steps to get to the active and valid state.

The following description corresponds to step 3 in Figure 18.3 for a simple demand zero page and to the entry into Figure 18.2 for a demand zero section page.

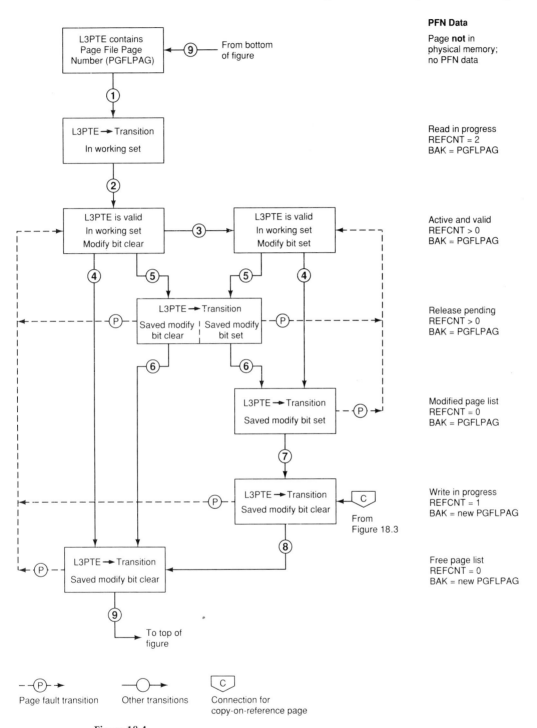

Figure 18.4
Page Transitions for a Page Located in a Page File

③ When MMG$PAGEFAULT detects a page fault for a demand zero page, it invokes MMG$ININEW_PFN_DZRO, in module PAGEFAULT, an alternative entry point to MMG$ININEW_PFN, to allocate a free page from the zeroed page list. If the zeroed page list is empty, a page is allocated from the free page list. MMG$INCPTREF and MMG$MAKE_WSLE update related memory management data structures. Step 1 of Section 18.3.1 and step 1 of Section 18.5.1 describe these routines.

MMG$PAGEFAULT makes additional updates to memory management data structures:

a. It changes the PFN$L_PAGE_STATE location bits to active.
b. It assigns the page a backing store:

If the page is a simple demand zero page, it copies PHD$Q_PAGFIL to the PFN$Q_BAK field of the page's PFN database record to assign backing store in the process's current page file. Allocation of actual blocks in the page file is done later by the modified page writer.

If the page is a demand zero section page, its backing store is the section file.

c. If the page was allocated from the free page list rather than from the zeroed page list, it must be zeroed. MMG$PAGEFAULT temporarily maps the PFN using a reserved SPTE and zeros the page.
d. It inserts the PFN into the L3PTE associated with the fault, setting the valid and modify bits, and leaving the protection, owner, copy characteristics, and no-execute bits as they were. If the no-execute bit is set, MMG$PAGEFAULT also sets fault-on-execute.

Subsequent transitions for a demand zero page are shown in Figure 18.3 and described throughout Sections 18.3.1, 18.3.2, and 18.3.4.

18.3.4 Page Faults out of Transition States

Figures 18.2, 18.3, and 18.4 show some of the transitions that can occur when a virtual page is faulted while the associated physical page is in the transition state. While these changes back to the active state are straightforward, certain details about each fault should be mentioned. Most of the following transitions are represented in the figures by a P within a circle.

▶ MMG$PAGEFAULT resolves a page fault from the free page list by first removing the page from the list. It invokes MMG$MAKE_WSLE (see step 1 of Section 18.3.1) to update the memory management data structures to reflect the fact that the page is in the working set list. These updates include the page's PFN database record PFN$L_WSLX and PFN$L_REFCNT fields and PCB$L_PPGCNT.

MMG$PAGEFAULT changes the PFN$L_PAGE_STATE location bits for the page to active. It sets the fault-on-execute bit in the L3PTE either if the no-execute bit was set or if the page was faulted with read or write intent. If the page is writable but has not been modified, MMG$PAGEFAULT sets the fault-on-write bit in the L3PTE. It sets the valid bit in the L3PTE. (Recall that a transition PTE retains the PFN of the physical page in which the virtual page resides.)

▸ A page fault from the modified page list is resolved in exactly the same way. Figures 18.2 to 18.4 show that the page was previously modified but never written to its backing store by returning the page to its modified state. That is, the saved modify bit in its PFN$L_PAGE_STATE field remains set, causing the page to be put into the modified page list when it is removed from the working set again.

▸ A page fault from the release pending state is similar to the previous two except that the page does not have to be removed from a page list.

Artistic license is taken in the figures to differentiate physical pages that were modified from pages that were not.

▸ A transition deserving special comment is a page fault that occurs while the modified page writer is writing the page to its backing store. The saved modify bit is cleared before the write begins so that the page will be placed into the free page list when the write completes. Although the page has not yet been completely backed up, it is assumed that the write will complete successfully. A page fault for the page can thus put it into the active but unmodified state. The only difficulty occurs in the event of a write error. The modified page writer's I/O completion routine, WRITEDONE in module WRTMFYPAG, detects this and resets the saved modify bit.

▸ A page fault for a process page being read in response to a previous page fault results in placing the process into a page fault wait state. In early versions of the VAX/VMS operating system, the process would have been placed into a collided page fault wait instead. This change minimizes spurious wakeups for processes in collided page fault wait.

18.3.5   Buffer Object Page

A buffer object is a special kind of I/O buffer. The pages that make up a buffer object are locked into physical memory and double-mapped in system space and process space. Because the pages are already locked into memory, there is no need for a device driver to lock them when initiating an I/O request and no need for the I/O postprocessing routine to unlock them. The implementation of buffer objects enables the body and process header of a process with I/O in progress to a buffer object to be swapped.

Chapter 17 details the system services that create and delete buffer objects, and Chapter 16 discusses the buffer object descriptor data structure associated with each buffer object.

A buffer object page begins life as a process page, perhaps a demand zero page. Its initial transitions therefore are no different from those of that page type. The transitions particular to a buffer object page are illustrated in Figure 18.5. The numbers in the figure are keyed to the explanations that follow.

Figure 18.5 begins with the page already valid, in the process's working set. The Create Buffer Object ($CREATE_BUFOBJ) system service faults it into the working set if it is not already valid.

① The $CREATE_BUFOBJ system service locks this page (and any other in the buffer object) into memory by incrementing the page's reference count, PFN$L_REFCNT; sets the buffer object and saved modify bits in PFN$L_PAGE_STATE; and increments the page's PFN$W_BO_REFC to 1.

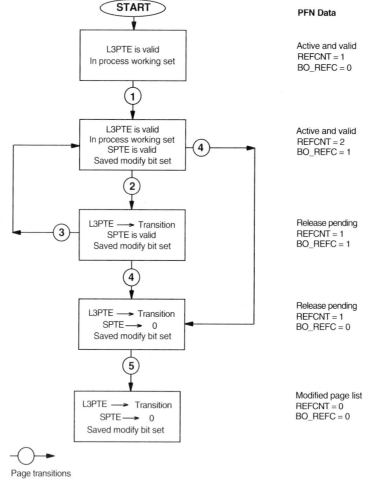

Page transitions

Figure 18.5
Page Transitions for a Buffer Object Page

It makes similar modifications to the PFN database record for the process-private page table page that maps the buffer object.

The system service initializes an SPTE to double-map the buffer object page.

② When the buffer object page is removed from the working set, for example, as a result of replacement paging, the valid and modify bits in the process-private L3PTE that map it are cleared. The page's reference count is decremented to 1, and the location bits in PFN$L_PAGE_STATE are set to release pending. The share count for the process-private page table page that maps it is decremented.

③ When the buffer object page is faulted back into the working set, its state is changed to active and its reference count is incremented. The share count for the process-private page table page that maps it is incremented.

④ When the buffer object is deleted, the Delete Buffer Object ($DELETE_BUFOBJ) system service clears the SPTE that double-maps the page and invalidates any cached entry from the TB. It decrements the page's PFN$W_BO_REFC to zero and clears the buffer object bit in its PFN$L_PAGE_STATE field.

It decrements PFN$W_BO_REFC for the process-private page table page that maps the buffer object and, if that goes to zero, clears the buffer object bit in its PFN$L_PAGE_STATE field and decrements the page's reference count. Since the former buffer object page is in a release pending state, the service increments the page table page's share count.

⑤ It decrements the former buffer object page's reference count. If the reference count is now zero, the page is released to the modified page list.

18.4   PAGE TRANSITIONS FOR GLOBAL PAGES

The transitions of a global page resemble those of process pages. A major difference, however, is the presence of both a global page table entry (GPTE) and potentially multiple process L3PTEs that refer to the same page.

18.4.1   Global Read-Only Page

This section assumes much of the detail shown earlier in Figure 18.2 and focuses on an example in which two processes map the same global page. Figure 18.6 illustrates the transitions that occur for a global read-only page in an already created section that is mapped by two processes. The numbers in the figure are keyed to the explanations that follow.

When the global section is initially created, as described in Chapter 17, the data structures described in Chapter 16 are initialized. The GPTE for the page represented in Figure 18.6 contains a global section table index (GSTX), which locates the global section table entry (GSTE) containing information about the global section file.

1. When process A maps the section, each L3PTE representing a page in the section is initialized with a global page table index (GPTX), effectively a pointer to the associated GPTE.

2. When process B maps the section, its L3PTEs contain exactly the same GPTXs as those in process A's L3PTEs.

3. Process B happens to fault the global page first. After reserving an entry in process B's working set list, MMG$PAGEFAULT takes the following steps, many of which are the same as those taken for a process section page (see step 1 in Section 18.3.1):

   a. Because process B's L3PTE contains a GPTX, MMG$PAGEFAULT indexes the global page table with it to get the GPTE. The GPTE contains a GSTX, indicating that the global page resides on mass storage.

   b. MMG$ININEW_PFN allocates a physical page. It stores in PFN$L_PTE the address of the GPTE rather than of a process L3PTE, and a type code of global page in PFN$L_PAGE_STATE.

   c. MMG$INCPTREF updates the data structures describing the global page table page that maps the faulted page. It increments the global page table page's share count to indicate one more transition or valid GPTE.

   d. MMG$MAKE_WSLE updates the data structures related to process B's working set list, initializing the WSLE. WSLX information is not kept for a global page. Instead, MMG$MAKE_WSLE increments the share count for the page and, because the count makes the transition from 0 to 1, its reference count as well.

      It invokes MMG$INCPTREF, which updates some of the data structures describing B's process page table that maps the global page. MMG$MAKE_WSLE updates others and increments PCB$L_GPGCNT to indicate that process B has one more global page in its working set.

   e. MMG$PAGEFAULT inserts the PFN of the allocated page into the L3PTE, leaving the protection, owner, and copy characteristics bits as they were. It initializes the type bits to indicate a transition page.

   f. It sets the PFN$L_PAGE_STATE location bits to read in progress.

   g. It stores the GSTX in the PFN$Q_BAK field.

   h. It sets fault-on-execute in B's L3PTE either if the no-execute bit was set or if the page was faulted with read data intent.

   MMG$PAGEFAULT initiates a read of the faulted page from its section file. While the read is in progress, the GPTE contains a transition PTE but process B's L3PTE still contains the GPTX. The reference count for the page indicates two references: one for the read in progress and one because the page is in process B's working set (the share count field is nonzero).

4. After the read completes, the I/O postprocessing routine PAGIO takes the following steps for each page in the page fault cluster.

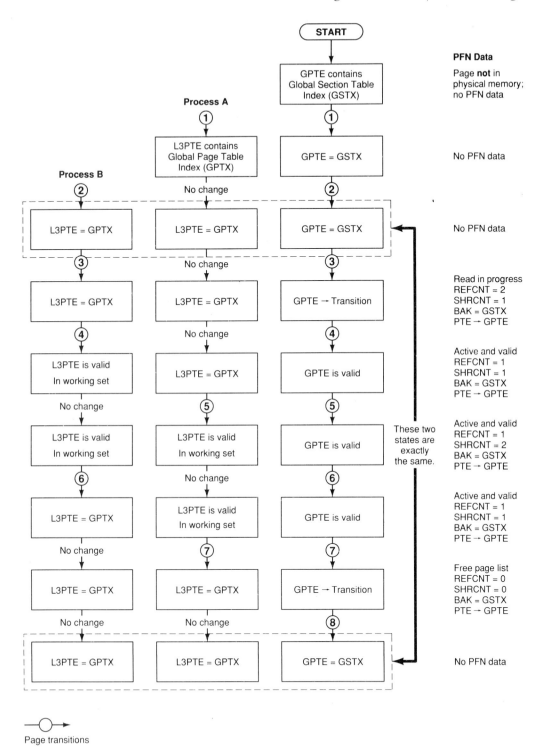

Figure 18.6
Page Transitions for a Global Read-Only Page Mapped by
Two Processes

a. It decrements the page's reference count. (The reference and share counts are both 1 at this point.)

b. It changes the PFN$L_PAGE_STATE location bits to active.

c. It sets the valid bit in the GPTE to record the fact that this page is physically resident and in a process working set.

d. It locates the process L3PTE through an address stored in the I/O request packet. It inserts the PFN from the GPTE into the L3PTE, leaving the protection, owner, copy characteristics, and no-execute bits as they were and setting the valid bit.

PAGIO reports the scheduling event page fault completion for process B so that it becomes computable.

⑤ When process A faults the same global page, MMG$PAGEFAULT's initial action is the same as it was in step 3, because the L3PTE contains a GPTX. Now, however, MMG$PAGEFAULT finds a valid GPTE. Resolution of this page fault is simple.

Through MMG$MAKE_WSLE and MMG$INCPTREF, whose actions are described in more detail in step 3d and Section 18.5.1, MMG$PAGEFAULT initializes the WSLE for process A, increments its PCB$L_GPGCNT, and increments the share count for the global page to 2.

MMG$PAGEFAULT inserts the PFN from the GPTE into process A's L3PTE, leaving the protection, owner, copy characteristics, and no-execute bits as they were and setting the valid bit.

⑥ When MMG$FREWSLE removes the global page from process B's working set, it invalidates any cached TB entry for that virtual page and restores process B's L3PTE to its previous state (rather than some transition form). Because the page's PFN$L_PTE field contains the address of the GPTE, MMG$FREWSLE must recalculate the GPTX.

The calculation is straightforward. MMG$FREWSLE subtracts the contents of MMG$GL_GPTBASE from the contents of PFN$L_PTE, divides the result by 8, and inserts the quotient in process B's L3PTE as a GPTX.

It invokes MMG$DECPTREF, which decrements the share count for the L3PT to indicate that it maps one less page.

MMG$FREWSLE decrements the share count for the page itself. The share count is still positive, and thus the GPTE remains valid. It updates the data structures related to process B's working set list, for example, clearing the WSLE (see Section 18.5.1). It decrements process B's PCB$L_GPGCNT.

⑦ When MMG$FREWSLE removes the global page from process A's working set, it restores the process L3PTE as described in step 6.

It decrements the share count, this time to zero. It therefore clears the valid, fault-on-read, fault-on-write, and modify bits in the GPTE to turn it into a transition PTE and decrements the page's reference count. A global read-only page with a reference count of zero, such as this one, is placed into the free page list and its PFN$L_PAGE_STATE location bits are updated accordingly. The other PFN database record fields are unchanged.

(8) When the physical page is reused, the ties must be broken between the physical page and, in this case, the GPTE. (None of the processes mapped to this page are affected in any way by this step.)

The contents of the PFN$Q_BAK field, a GSTX, are inserted into the GPTE located by the contents of PFN$L_PTE. MMG$DECPTREF, described in Section 18.5.1, is invoked to update the data structures describing the global page table page that contains the GPTE. The PFN$L_PTE field is then cleared, breaking the connection between the physical page and the global page table.

These steps return the process and global page tables to the state following step 2 (although it is pictured here as a different state to simplify the figure).

18.4.2   Global Writable Page

The transitions that occur for a global writable page are the same as those for a process page that is not copy-on-reference. The only difference between such transitions and those illustrated in Figure 18.2 is that the GPTE, not the process L3PTE, is affected by the transitions of the physical page.

The process L3PTE for a global page contains a GPTX up to the time that the page is made valid. Only then is a PFN inserted into the process L3PTE. As soon as the page is removed from the process working set, the GPTX is restored to the process L3PTE. All ties to the PFN database are made through the GPTE, which retains the PFN while the physical page is in the various transition states.

18.4.3   Global Copy-on-Reference Page

A global copy-on-reference page is shared only in its initial state. As soon as the fault occurs, the page is treated exactly like a process page.

Figure 18.7 illustrates the transitions that occur for a global copy-on-reference page. The numbers in the figure are keyed to the explanations that follow.

(1) The initial conditions are identical to those in Figure 18.6. After the section is created, each of its GPTEs contains a GSTX. In this case, the copy-on-reference bit is set in each GPTE.

(2) Process A maps the page; the GPTX is stored in its L3PTE.
   Process B maps the page; the same GPTX is stored in its L3PTE. Up to this point, nothing is different from Figure 18.6.

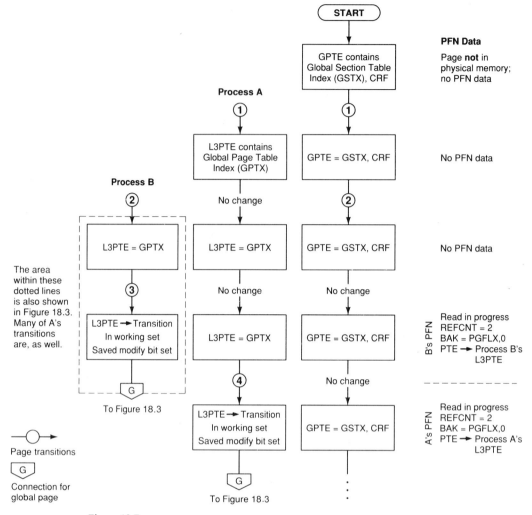

Figure 18.7
Page Transitions for a Global Copy-on-Reference Page

③ When process B faults the page, MMG$PAGEFAULT locates the GPTE from the GPTX and notes that the page is located in a global section file and is copy-on-reference. MMG$PAGEFAULT, in concert with the routines described in step 1 of Section 18.3.1, allocates a page from the free page list and updates the pertinent memory management data structures as follows:

a. The GPTE is not altered and retains its GSTX contents.
b. The PFN$L_PTE field gets the address of process B's L3PTE.
c. The share count for the page table page containing process B's L3PTE

is incremented. Section 18.5.1 details other changes to data structures related to the page table page.

d. The PFN$L_PAGE_STATE type bits for the physical page are set to process page.

e. An entry in process B's working set list is initialized to describe the faulted page.

f. The PFN$L_WSLX field is set to the index of the WSLE.

g. PCB$L_PPGCNT is incremented.

h. The reference count is incremented twice, once for the page's membership in the working set and once for the I/O in progress.

i. Process B's L3PTE is changed to a transition PTE with the PFN of the allocated page. The protection, owner, and copy characteristics bits are left as they were. If the page is writable but was faulted with read intent, MMG$PAGEFAULT sets the fault-on-write bit. It sets fault-on-execute either if the no-execute bit was set or if the page was faulted with read or write data intent.

j. A backing store is assigned to the page, typically a reserved page from the process's current page file.

k. The page's PFN$Q_BAK field is initialized from the GPTE's type and partial section bits, $\langle 63 : 32 \rangle$, and the assigned backing store.

l. The PFN$L_PAGE_STATE location bits are set to read in progress with the saved modify bit set.

Note that all ties between process B and the global section are broken. The page is now treated like a process copy-on-reference page. The two boxes for process B within the dotted lines in Figure 18.7 are also pictured within dotted lines in Figure 18.3.

MMG$PAGEFAULT initiates a read of the faulted page.

④ When process A faults the same page, the same steps are taken, this time with a different physical page.

Thus, both process A and process B get the same initial copy of the global page from the global section file but, from that point on, each process has its own private copy of the page to modify.

18.4.4   Global Page-File Section Page

A global page-file section provides a way for processes to share global pages without a backing store file. A global page-file section page is initially faulted as a demand zero page and from then on is indistinguishable from other global writable pages except that its backing store is in a page file.

Figure 18.8 illustrates the transitions of a global page-file section page. The numbers in the figure are keyed to the explanations that follow.

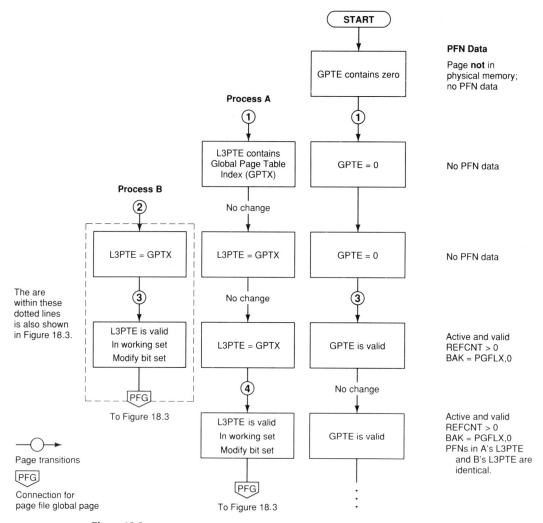

Figure 18.8
Page Transitions for a Global Page-File Section Page

① The initial conditions are identical to those in Figure 18.6. The section is created; each of its GPTEs contains a zero in the PFN field.

② Process A maps the page; the GPTX is stored in its L3PTE.
    Process B maps the page; the same GPTX is stored in its L3PTE.

③ When process B faults this page, MMG$PAGEFAULT locates the GPTE from the GPTX and notes that the page is demand zero. It invokes MMG$ININEW_PFN_DZRO to allocate a free page from the zeroed page list. If the list is empty, a page is allocated from the free page list. MMG$PAGEFAULT, in concert with MMG$ININEW_PFN and the other routines described in step 1 of Section 18.3.1, makes the following modifications to the pertinent memory management data structures.

a. The share count for the global page table page containing the GPTE is incremented.

b. The PFN$L_PTE field for the allocated page points to the GPTE.

c. The PFN$L_PAGE_STATE type bits for the allocated global page are set to global writable.

d. An entry in process B's working set list is initialized to describe the faulted page.

e. The share count for the page table page containing process B's L3PTE is incremented. Section 18.5.1 details other changes to data structures related to the page table page.

f. PCB$L_GPGCNT is incremented.

g. The share and reference counts for the allocated page are incremented.

h. Its PFN$L_PAGE_STATE location bits are set to active.

i. MMG$PAGEFAULT assigns the page a backing store (namely, the current page file in use for system working set list paging) and copies PHD$Q_PAGFIL to the PFN$Q_BAK field of the page's PFN database record. Allocation of actual blocks in the page file is done later by the modified page writer.

j. If the page was allocated from the free page list rather than from the zeroed page list, it must be zeroed. MMG$PAGEFAULT temporarily maps the PFN using a reserved SPTE and zeros the page.

k. It inserts the PFN into the process-private L3PTE, setting the valid and modify bits, and leaving the protection, owner, copy characteristics, and no-execute bits as they were. If the no-execute bit is set, MMG$PAGEFAULT also sets fault-on-execute.

l. It inserts the PFN into the GPTE, setting the valid and modify bits and leaving the protection, owner, copy characteristics, and no-execute bits as they were.

(4) When process A faults the same page, MMG$PAGEFAULT locates the GPTE from the GPTX and finds that the GPTE is valid. It inserts the PFN, valid, and modify bits from the valid GPTE into process A's L3PTE, leaving the protection, owner, copy characteristics, and no-execute bits as they were. If the no-execute bit is set, MMG$PAGEFAULT also sets fault-on-execute.

Transitions for a global page-file section page resemble those of a page located in a page file (see Figure 18.4). However, for a global page-file section page, the GPTE, not the process L3PTE, is affected by the transitions of the physical page. Once the global page is removed from a process's working set, the process L3PTE reverts to the GPTX form.

18.5   PAGE TRANSITIONS FOR SYSTEM SPACE PAGES

This section describes page faults for pages in system space. The following are the kinds of pageable system space pages.

- ► Process page table pages
- ► System pages, which include
  - • Read-only pages from pageable image sections in executive images
  - • Writable pages from pageable image sections in executive images
  - • Paged pool pages
- ► Global page table pages

A process's valid page table pages are described in its own working set list. When valid, the other types of pages are described in the working set list in the system header.

The only pageable sections in system space are from executive images. In theory, the base images, SYS$BASE_IMAGE.EXE and SYS$PUBLIC_VEC-TORS.EXE, can contain pageable code and data. In OpenVMS AXP Version 1.5, however, they have no pageable sections. By default, when an executive image is mapped, a section table entry in the system section table (which also serves as the global section table) is initialized to describe each pageable section in the image. Each SPTE that maps a page in a pageable section has both type bits set to indicate the process section index form of invalid L3PTE and contains the index of the section's entry in the system section table. Note that it is possible to disable paging of executive images by setting the SYSGEN parameter S0_PAGING to a nonzero value.

If the section is writable, each of its SPTEs also has the copy-on-reference and writable bits set. Chapter 32 describes the mapping of executive images in detail.

The SPTEs that map both paged pool and the global page table initially have the demand zero page form of invalid PTE.

18.5.1 Process Page Table Pages

When MMG$PAGEFAULT determines that a page fault for a system space page is within the balance set slots, it makes an additional sanity check. It checks whether one process is trying to fault a page table page in another process's PHD. Unlike other system pages, PHD pages belong to the associated process; pageable PHD pages are part of its working set. A process is therefore not allowed to fault a page in another process's PHD. When MMG$PAGEFAULT detects this type of fault, it transforms the page fault into an access violation.

It is possible, however, for a process to fault a page in its own PHD and immediately be context-switched. If the process is outswapped and inswapped before its next execution, the swapper may have moved its PHD to a different balance set slot. At inswap, the swapper sets the bit PHD$V_NOACCVIO in PHD$L_FLAGS to signal this possibility.

If the PHD does occupy a different balance set slot when the process resumes execution in MMG$PAGEFAULT, the faulting virtual address in R4 is now an address in the balance set slots but not in the process's own PHD. For this reason, MMG$PAGEFAULT checks further before deciding the access is in error: it tests and clears PHD$V_NOACCVIO in PHD$L_FLAGS.

If the bit was set, MMG$PAGEFAULT dismisses the page fault, and the faulting instruction reexecutes with the PHD$V_NOACCVIO bit clear. If the instruction again faults a page in another process's balance set slot, MMG$PAGEFAULT releases the MMG spinlock and returns to SCH$PAGE-FAULT, indicating that it should simulate an access violation, employing the page fault exception parameters as access violation parameters (see Section 18.2.1).

As described in Chapter 16, the L3PTs that make up a process's P0 and P1 page tables are part of its PHD and are mapped by both SPTEs and L2PTEs. The executive accesses the L3PTs through system space addresses. Only the TB miss PALcode routine uses the L2PTEs.

The L3PTs that map permanent P1 space are created with the process. All others are represented by demand zero SPTEs. When the process requests a system service to create address space, the system service must initialize the L3PTEs that map that space. Accessing an L3PTE in a page mapped by a demand zero SPTE causes a page fault.

Many of the transitions of a process page table page resemble those of other demand zero pages, described in Section 18.3.3. Some aspects of page table page transitions are unique, however. Some of the transitions that such a page can make are illustrated in Figure 18.9. The numbers in the figure are keyed to the following explanations. For simplicity, some of the transitions shown in Figures 18.3 and 18.4 are omitted here.

(1) When MMG$PAGEFAULT detects a page fault for a process page table page that has not yet been created, it takes the following steps:

   a. MMG$PAGEFAULT uses other routines in module PAGEFAULT to perform some of the related updates to memory management data structures:

      MMG$ININEW_PFN_DZRO allocates a free page from the zeroed page list. It stores the address of the SPTE in the PFN$L_PTE field of that page's PFN database record and initializes the page's PFN$L_PAGE_STATE type bits to process page table.

      MMG$MAKE_WSLE initializes the process's WSLE with the system virtual address of the L3PT and page type of process page table and sets the WSLE's valid bit. It increments PCB$L_PPGCNT. It stores the index of the WSLE in the PFN$L_WSLX field of the PFN database record for the page table page and also increments its reference count to indicate that the page is in a working set list.

   b. MMG$PAGEFAULT updates the PFN$L_PAGE_STATE location bits to active.

   c. It assigns the page a backing store (namely, the process's current page file) by copying PHD$Q_PAGFIL to the PFN$Q_BAK field of the page's

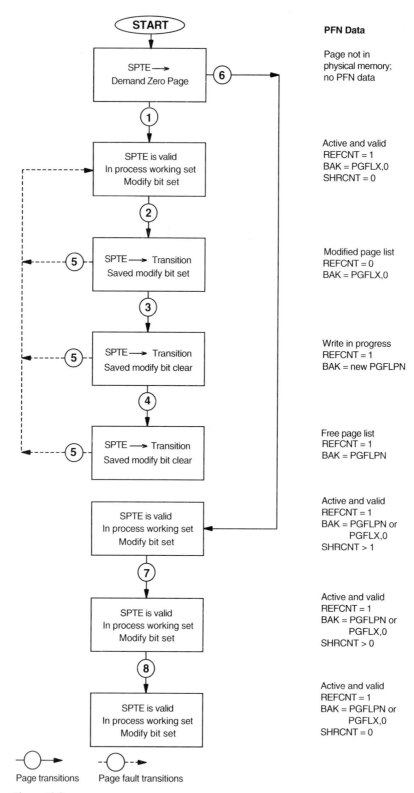

Figure 18.9
Page Transitions for Process Page Table Pages

606

PFN database record. Allocation of actual blocks in the page file is done later by the modified page writer.

d. It inserts the PFN into the SPTE associated with the fault, setting the valid, modify, fault-on-execute, and address space match bits, and leaving the protection, owner, copy characteristics, and no-execute bits as they were.

e. It copies the contents of the SPTE, except for the address space match bit, to the process's L2PTE that maps this page of L3PT.

f. Finally, MMG$PAGEFAULT returns the status SS$_NORMAL to SCH$PAGEFAULT.

Control returns to the system service, which initializes L3PTEs, for example, to map a section. When done, the system service returns.

② If none of the pages is made valid, the process page table page can be removed from the working set as a result of replacement paging. MMG$FREWSLE increments the PHD's entry in the array at PHV$GL_REFCBAS, the number of reasons the PHD should remain in memory, to account for the page table page as a transition page. Decrementing the page's reference count to zero, it inserts the page into the modified page list. It also decrements PCB$L_PPGCNT and clears the WSLE that was associated with the page.

③ The modified page writer eventually removes the page from the modified page list and writes it to the page file identified by its PFN$Q_BAK field.

④ When the write completes, the page is placed into the free page list.

⑤ When the process later tries to access a page mapped by this L3PT, it incurs a page fault. MMG$PAGEFAULT calculates the system virtual address of the L3PTE mapping the target address and discovers that the L3PT is not valid. It transforms the fault for the target address into one for the L3PT.

In Figure 18.9, the fault is shown as happening before the physical page containing the L3PT is reallocated for another use. MMG$PAGEFAULT faults the page from the free page list, updates the data structures that describe the page, and returns the status SS$_NORMAL to SCH$PAGEFAULT. When SCH$PAGEFAULT dismisses the exception, the instruction that attempted access to a page mapped by this L3PT is reexecuted.

⑥ When MMG$PAGEFAULT processes the first page fault for a page mapped by this L3PT, it and its associated routines take the actions described in step 1 of Section 18.3.1 and the following actions, which are not detailed in that section:

a. MMG$INCPTREF updates structures related to the L3PT. It increments the share count for the page table page to indicate that it maps one more valid page. If this is the first valid page mapped by the page table page (that is, if the share count makes the transition from 0 to 1), MMG$INCPTREF locks the WSLE for the page table page into the process's working set list by setting the WSL$V_WSLOCK bit and also increments PHD$L_PTCNTACT, the number of active page table pages for the process, and the PHD's entry in the array at PHV$GL_REFCBAS.

b. When updating the data structures related to the working set list, such as the WSLE for the faulted page, MMG$MAKE_WSLE also increments the PHD$L_PTWSLEVAL array element corresponding to the page table page to indicate one more valid entry in the process's working set list mapped by that page table page. If the count makes the transition from –1 to 0, MMG$MAKE_WSLE also increments PHD$L_PTCNTVAL, the number of page table pages that map valid WSLEs.

Whenever the process faults another page mapped by this L3PT, the L3PT's share count and PHD$L_PTWSLEVAL array element are incremented.

⑦ Whenever one of the pages mapped by this L3PT is removed from the working set, MMG$FREWSLE decrements the PHD$L_PTWSLEVAL array element to indicate the L3PT maps one less valid page. When the count makes the transition to –1, the page table page is dead, and MMG$FREWSLE also decrements PHD$L_PTCNTVAL.

Once the page table page is dead, its WSLE is a candidate for reuse by a page being newly faulted into the working set. While the page table page describes transition pages, however, it cannot be reused. To free the WSLE, MMG$FREWSLE severs all ties between the transition pages on the free page list and the page table page, moves those pages to the head of the free page list, and requests a selective purge of the modified page list (see Section 18.8). Chapter 19 contains further information on how a dead page table page is removed from the working set.

⑧ As the contents of each page are deleted, MMG$DECPTREF is invoked to update the data structures describing the L3PT. It decrements the share count for the L3PT to indicate one less reason for it to remain valid.

When the share count makes the transition from 1 to 0, MMG$DECPTREF takes the following additional steps:

a. It decrements the PHD's entry in the array at PHV$GL_REFCBAS, the number of reasons the PHD should remain in memory. If that count goes to 0, MMG$DECPTREF wakes the swapper process to outswap the PHD.

b. It locates the WSLE for the page table and clears its WSL$V_WSLOCK bit to unlock it from the process's working set list.

c. It decrements PHD$L_PTCNTACT, the number of active page table pages for the process.

18.5.2   **System Page That Is Not Copy-on-Reference**

The transitions for a read-only system section page resemble those described in Section 18.3.1. This section mainly notes the details that differ from those for a process section page that is not copy-on-reference. The numbers that follow correspond to those in Figure 18.2.

(1) MMG$PAGEFAULT locates an entry in the system working set list for the faulted page. It allocates a page from the free page list. There is no need to update data structures describing the page table page that contains the SPTE. The SPT does not page; its page table pages are always valid. The page type stored in the PFN$L_PAGE_STATE type bits is system page. The system header does not have a PHD$L_PTWSLEVAL array, nor is there any need to record the number of page table pages with valid WSLEs; the system working set list is not outswapped.

MMG$PAGEFAULT initializes the page's PFN$Q_BAK field from the SPTE's type and partial section bits and bits ⟨63 : 32⟩. It locates the system section table entry just as it would a PSTX and calculates which virtual blocks contain the faulted page.

(2) After the I/O completes, PAGIO, the I/O postprocessing routine, reports a page fault completion event for the process that faulted the page. PAGIO sets the address space match bit in the L3PTE when setting the valid bit.

(4) The system working set is not subject to purging, swapper trimming, or working set limit adjustment. A page is removed from the system working set list only when space is required for another page. Also, unloading an executive image may result in deletion of pages.

On an SMP system, when a page is removed from the system working set list, the cached SPTE contents must be flushed from the TBs of all members of the system. Chapter 37 describes how the processors cooperate to perform the invalidation.

18.5.3   **System Page That Is Copy-on-Reference**

The transitions for a copy-on-reference system section page resemble those described in Section 18.3.2 and shown in Figure 18.3.

Field PHD$Q_PAGFIL in the system header is a template backing store value for writable system pages.

The page type stored in the PFN$L_PAGE_STATE type bits is system page.

18.5.4   **Demand Zero System Page**

The transitions for a demand zero system page resemble those described in Section 18.3.3 and shown in the path labeled START 2 in Figure 18.3.

One difference worth noting is that the page type stored in the PFN$L_PAGE_STATE type bits is either global page table page or, for paged pool, system page.

Another difference is that a nonresident page of global page table is faulted into the system working set when one of its GPTEs is allocated for a global section being created. The share count for the global page table page is incremented for each GPTE that maps a global section page. When the share count transitions from 0 to 1, that is, when the first GPTE is allocated, the global page table page is locked into the system working set. The share count for a global page table page is also incremented when a physical page is allocated for a page it maps.

18.6 PAGE READ CLUSTERING

To make reading and writing as efficient as possible, MMG$PAGEFAULT implements a feature called clustering. It checks whether pages adjacent to the virtual page being faulted are located in the same file in adjacent virtual blocks. If so, it requests a multiple-page read so that a cluster of pages will be brought into the working set at one time. One *N*-page request has less CPU and I/O overhead than *N* one-page requests. This section discusses clustering in page read I/O.

The modified page writer and the $UPDSEC system service also cluster their write operations, both to make their writes as efficient as possible and to allow subsequent clustered reads for the pages that are being written. Section 18.8.4 summarizes clustering by the modified page writer, and Section 18.9, by the $UPDSEC system service.

Table 18.1 indicates the limit to which the object of each type of memory management I/O request is clustered.

When MMG$PAGEFAULT determines that a read is required to satisfy a page fault, it attempts to identify a cluster of pages to be read at once. The manner in which this cluster is formed depends on the initial state of the faulting PTE, as described in the next sections.

18.6.1 Terminating Conditions for Clustered Reads

Beginning with the PTE of the faulting page, MMG$PAGEFAULT scans adjacent PTEs in the direction of higher virtual addresses, checking for adjacent virtual pages that have the same backing store location. It continues until it reaches the desired cluster size or until it reaches one of the following other terminating conditions:

▸ It encounters a type of PTE different from that of the original faulting PTE (see Section 18.6.2).
▸ The page table page containing the next PTE is itself not valid.
▸ Another WSLE is not available. (Each page in the cluster must be added to the working set.)
▸ No physical page is available.

610

Table 18.1   Cluster Factor in I/O Requests Issued
by Memory Management

Type of I/O Request	*Cluster Factor*
PROCESS PAGE READ	
Page in section file	pfc/PFCDEFAULT [1]
Page in page file	PFCDEFAULT [2]
Page table page	PAGTBLPFC [2]
SYSTEM PAGE READ	
System section page [3]	SYSPFC [2]
Paged pool page	PFCDEFAULT [2]
Global page table page	1
GLOBAL PAGE READ	
Global page	pfc/PFCDEFAULT [1]
Global copy-on-reference page	pfc/PFCDEFAULT [1]
MODIFIED PAGE WRITE	
To page file	MPW_WRTCLUSTER [2]
To private section file	MPW_WRTCLUSTER [2]
To global section file	MPW_WRTCLUSTER [2]
To swap file (set bit PFN$V_ SWPPAG)	1
$UPDSEC WRITE	
Private section	MPW_WRTCLUSTER [2]
Global section	MPW_WRTCLUSTER [2]
SWAPPER I/O	
Swapper I/O	n/a

[1] The cluster factor for a private or global section can be specified at link time or when the cluster is mapped by explicitly declaring a cluster factor (pfc). If unspecified, the SYSGEN parameter PFCDEFAULT is used.

[2] This is a SYSGEN parameter.

[3] Pageable executive routines originate in executive image sections, described by section table entries in the system header.

If, after scanning the adjacent PTEs toward higher virtual addresses, it has not formed a cluster of at least two pages, MMG$PAGEFAULT scans toward lower virtual addresses with the same terminating conditions. The scan is made initially toward higher virtual addresses because programs typically execute sequentially toward higher virtual addresses and these pages are more likely to be needed soon. If that scan does not form a cluster of at least two pages, MMG$PAGEFAULT scans for pages at lower virtual addresses on the assumption that pages at lower virtual addresses but near the faulting page are likely to be needed soon.

18.6.2   Matching Conditions During the Page Table Scan

The match criterion for adjacent PTEs depends on the form of the initial PTE:

▶ If the original PTE contains a PSTX, successive PTEs must contain exactly the same PSTX.

▶ If the original PTE contains a page file page number, successive PTEs must contain PTEs with the same page file index and successively increasing (or decreasing) page numbers.

▶ If the original PTE contains a GPTX, successive PTEs must contain successively increasing (or decreasing) indexes. In addition, the GPTEs must all contain exactly the same GSTX.

18.6.3   Maximum Cluster Size for Page Read

The maximum number of pages that can make up a cluster is a function of the type of page being read:

▶ Global page table pages are not clustered because they are only faulted during global section creation and remain valid while they map any global pages.

▶ The cluster factor for process page table pages is taken from PHD$L_ PGTBPFC. The default value of this field is the special SYSGEN parameter PAGTBLPFC, whose default value is two pagelets, resulting in a cluster factor of one page. Increasing this value is likely to have a negligible effect on most systems.

▶ The cluster factor for pages read from a page file is taken from the PFL$L_ PFC field of the page file control block (see Figure 16.24). This field usually contains zero, in which case the default page fault cluster is used. (Just as for clustered reads from the page file, this default is taken from PHD$L_ DFPFC.)

There are two methods by which the cluster factor of a process or global section can be controlled. At link time, the page fault cluster factor in an image section descriptor can be set to nonzero through the linker cluster option and its PFC argument:

CLUSTER = *cluster-name*, [*base-address*] ,*pfc*,*file-spec*[, . . .]

Second, the page fault cluster factor for a section mapped through the $CRMPSC system service can be specified through the optional PFC argument.

18.7   PAGE READ COMPLETION

The I/O postprocessing routine IOC$IOPOST, in module IOCIOPOST, detects page read completion when the flags IRP$V_PAGIO and IRP$V_FUNC in IRP$L_STS are both set.

Page read completion is not reported to the faulting process in the normal fashion with a special kernel mode asynchronous system trap (AST) because none of the postprocessing has to be performed in the context of the faulting process. Holding the MMG spinlock, the I/O postprocessing routine PAGIO performs the postprocessing needed. It performs the following steps for each page in the page fault cluster that was successfully read:

1. It decrements the reference count in the page's PFN database record, indicating that the read in progress has completed.
2. If the reference count is now zero, it puts the page into the free or modified page list, depending on the value of the saved modify bit, and continues with the next page.
3. If the reference count is nonzero, it sets the location bits in PFN$L_PAGE_STATE to active.
4. It sets the valid bit in the L3PTE. For a system space page, it also sets the address space match bit. For a writable page that was faulted with write intent, it also sets the modify bit.
5. If the page is a global page that is not copy-on-reference, the valid bit set in step 4 was actually in the GPTE. In this case, the process (slave) L3PTE must also be altered: PAGIO inserts the PFN, partial section, type 0, global, global write, and valid bits from the GPTE into the slave L3PTE. If appropriate, it sets the modify bit in the slave L3PTE.
6. If the page is a process page table, PAGIO calculates the address of the process-private L2PTE that maps it. PAGIO copies the contents of the SPTE that maps the process page table page to the L2PTE but clears the address space match bit in the L2PTE.

After processing the pages that were read successfully, PAGIO tests for an I/O error. If one occurred, it takes the following steps for the page that incurred the error:

1. It decrements the reference count in the page's PFN database record, indicating that the read in progress has completed.
2. It changes the page's PFN$L_PAGE_STATE location bits to read error, setting the delete-contents bit and clearing the saved modify bit.
3. If the virtual page is a copy-on-reference page, PAGIO restores its backing store location to the physical page's PFN$Q_BAK field. If the error occurred on the last page of the transfer and that page was partially backed, it sets the partial section flag in PFN$Q_BAK.
4. If the page's reference count is now zero and the process is memory-resident, PAGIO releases the page to the free page list. (If the process is outswapped, PAGIO inserts the page into the bad page list instead. When the process is inswapped, the page will be removed from the bad page list.)

After tending to the individual pages, PAGIO determines whether the pages are from a copy-on-reference section. If so, it subtracts the number of pages read from the section's reference count.

PAGIO reports the scheduling event page fault completion for the page faulting process so that it is made computable. The priority increment value is zero; that is, there is no boost to the process's scheduling priority. If any of the pages just read were collided pages, it also makes all processes in the collided page wait state computable. Collided pages are discussed in Section 18.13.3.

If an error occurred and more of the transfer remains to be done, PAGIO updates the IRP to describe the rest of the transfer (excluding any pages already done and the page that incurred the error) and requeues the IRP to the device driver.

18.8   MODIFIED PAGE WRITING

Once a second, the executive checks whether any of the swapper's tasks need to be performed and wakes it if necessary; one such task is writing pages from the modified page list to mass storage. The modified page writer, MMG$WRTMFYPAG, in module WRTMFYPAG, is a subroutine of the swapper process. Within its main loop, the swapper invokes MMG$WRTMFYPAG to form a cluster of modified pages that have the same backing store and request a write I/O operation.

At completion of the write I/O operation, the modified page writer's special kernel mode AST routine is entered to place the pages into the free page list and, if appropriate, to initiate the writing of more modified pages.

18.8.1   Requesting the Modified Page Writer

During system operation other executive routines request the writing of modified pages by invoking the routine MMG$PURGEMPL, in module WRTMFYPAG, with arguments identifying the requested operation and its scope. The possible operations are writing pages to shrink the modified list to a target size (called a MAINTAIN request), writing pages within a virtual address range (an SVAPTE request), and writing all pages backed by section files (an OPCCRASH request).

Modified page writing is requested in a number of circumstances:

▶ When the modified page list has exceeded its high limit, defined by the SYSGEN parameter MPW_HILIMIT (MAINTAIN)
▶ When the free page list is below its low limit and can be replenished by writing modified pages (MAINTAIN)
▶ When particular modified pages must be written to their backing store (SVAPTE)
▶ When the OPCCRASH image, running during system shutdown, must write all pages in the list that are backed by section files to their backing store (OPCCRASH)

Originally, the modified page list was sometimes emptied, or flushed, during normal operations. In VAX VMS Version 5, the flushing was replaced by selective purging, that is, writing all modified pages whose PTEs fall within a specified system virtual address range (the SVAPTE request). For selective purging of process-private space modified pages, the PTEs of interest are L2PTEs or L3PTEs. For selective purging of writable global pages, the PTEs of interest are GPTEs.

Selective purging is requested under the following circumstances:

▶ When a process body has been outswapped but its PHD, whose slot is needed, cannot be outswapped because some of its L2 or L3PTEs map transition pages on the modified page list (see Chapter 20)
▶ When a writable global section with transition pages still on the modified page list is deleted (see Chapter 17)
▶ When a process needs to reuse a WSLE that describes a page table page that is now inactive but still maps transition pages on the modified page list (a dead page table page, described in Chapter 19)

The modified page writer may be requested multiple times before it is actually invoked by the swapper. MMG$PURGEMPL therefore records information about the request. It stores the requested command with the highest rank in MPW$GL_STATE; from low to high rank, the ordering is MAINTAIN, SVAPTE, and OPCCRASH.

For a MAINTAIN request, the modified page writer typically compares the target modified page list size with the value of the SYSGEN parameter MPW_LOLIMIT and uses the larger as a target size. (If a previous MAINTAIN request has been made, MMG$PURGEMPL uses the lesser of its target size and the current target size.) It records the target size in SCH$GL_MFYLOLIM and SCH$GL_MFYLIM.

For an SVAPTE request, it also records the highest addressed PTE of interest in MPW$GL_SVAPTEHIGH and the lowest in MPW$GL_SVAPTELOW. If there are multiple outstanding SVAPTE requests, the count of such requests is stored in MPW$GL_REQCNT, and the low and high SVAPTE addresses of each request are stored in elements of a 32-quadword array beginning at MPW$GQ_SVAPTE.

MPW$GL_SVAPTEHIGH and MPW$GL_SVAPTELOW record the highest and lowest addresses of any PTE in any of the requests. When the modified page writer scans the list for a page that meets any of the SVAPTE requests, it can easily reject one whose PTE address is outside that range without having to compare its PTE address to all the ranges. These cells facilitate the scan of the modified page list.

For an OPCCRASH request, MMG$PURGEMPL stores 80000000_{16} in MPW$GL_SVAPTELOW and $FFFFFFFF_{16}$ in MPW$GL_SVAPTEHIGH so that all pages on the modified page list will match the PTE address range.

Once modified page writing to shrink the list (MAINTAIN) is initiated, the modified page writer continues writing modified pages until the size of the list is at or below the contents of SCH$GL_MFYLOLIM. Chapter 20 describes the calculation of the target modified page list size for the different circumstances in which the swapper initiates modified page writing.

When an SVAPTE or OPCCRASH request initiates modified page writing to purge or flush the list, both the lower and upper limits for the modified page list are set to zero. For an SVAPTE request, the modified page writer scans the entire list and writes all pages whose PTE addresses fall within the specified range. For an OPCCRASH request, the modified page writer scans the entire list and writes all pages not backed by a page file.

Before the modified page writer exits, it restores its two limits to the values contained in the SYSGEN parameters MPW_HILIMIT and MPW_LOLIMIT.

18.8.2 Operation of the Modified Page Writer

Invoked by the swapper, the modified page writer initiates the writing of modified pages. The modified page writer forms a cluster and queues an I/O request. When the I/O request completes, the modified page writer's special kernel mode AST routine is entered. After performing necessary processing on the pages that have been written, it checks whether more modified pages must be written and, if so, forms another cluster. At the completion of that request, the special kernel mode AST routine may queue yet another request.

The modified page writer can initiate up to SYSGEN parameter MPW_IOLIMIT concurrent I/O requests. The default value of MPW_IOLIMIT is 4. As described in Chapter 16, during system initialization MPW_IOLIMIT nonpaged pool data structures are allocated. Each contains an IRP and two arrays that describe the pages in the cluster. These structures are queued to a listhead at MPW$GL_IRPFL and MPW$GL_IRPBL. Figure 18.10 shows the layout of this data structure, known as a modified page writer I/O request packet (MPW IRP).

Associated with each MPW IRP is a preallocated kernel process block (KPB). Preallocating the KPB minimizes the overhead in the driver to process the IRP and helps prevent deadlocks. Chapter 24 discusses the implementation of a device driver that runs as a kernel process.

MMG$WRTMFYPAG proceeds in the following fashion:

1. It compares the number of pages on the modified page list to SCH$GL_MFYLIM. If there are fewer pages on the list, it simply exits.
2. It tests whether any page files have been installed and, if not, exits. (Although the system requires the use of page files during normal operations, it can run without any during system startup.)
3. It acquires the MMG spinlock, raising IPL to IPL$_MMG.
4. It sets bit SCH$V_MPW in SCH$GL_SIP to indicate that modified page

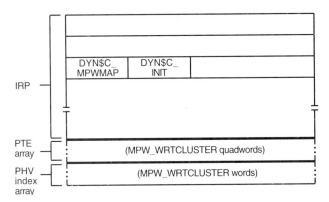

Figure 18.10
Layout of Modified Page Writer IRP (MPW IRP)

writing is active. If the bit was already set, MMG$WRTMFYPAG re-
leases the MMG spinlock and exits.

5. Otherwise, it tests whether this is a SVAPTE request and, if so, whether
   1 second has elapsed since the previous one. If not, it clears SCH$V_
   MPW in SCH$GL_SIP, releases the MMG spinlock, and exits. This test
   helps limit the time the modified page writer spends scanning the modified page list.

6. MMG$WRTMFYPAG invokes MMG$PURGEMPL, specifying the default command of MAINTAIN to shrink the list to MPW_LOWAIT-
   LIMIT pages.

   • If a previous SVAPTE request has been made and not yet satisfied,
     MMG$PURGEMPL returns immediately.
   • If no previous SVAPTE or other MAINTAIN requests have been made,
     it changes MPW$GL_STATE to MAINTAIN and stores the larger of
     MPW_LOWAITLIMIT and SCH$GL_MFYLOSV in SCH$GL_MFYLIM
     and SCH$GL_MFYLOLIM.
   • If a previous MAINTAIN request has been made, it stores the lesser
     of the previous and current requested limits in SCH$GL_MFYLIM and
     SCH$GL_MFYLOLIM.

7. MMG$WRTMFYPAG removes an MPW IRP from the list. If none is
   available, it continues with step 20.

8. It scans the modified page list to find a page with which to begin a
   cluster. Entered the first time, it begins with the first page on the
   list. Subsequently, it typically resumes with the page at which the
   last scan stopped. If that page is no longer on the modified page list,
   MMG$WRTMFYPAG tries the pages that preceded and followed it on
   the list. If neither of them is still on the list, it selects the first page on
   the list.

617

Its processing of that page depends on the type of request it is performing (the value of MPW$GL_STATE):

- If performing a MAINTAIN request, it accepts the page.
- If performing an SVAPTE request, it tests whether the address of the page's PTE falls within any of the requested ranges. If not, it goes on to the next page in the list.
- If performing an OPCCRASH request, it tests whether the page's backing store is something other than a page file. If not, it goes on to the next page in the list.

9. MMG$WRTMFYPAG determines the type of the first page in the cluster from its PFN database record PFN$L_PAGE_STATE type bits.

10. Based on the page type, it gets the address of the relevant PHD, either that of a process or of the system.

11. It examines the PFN$Q_BAK field to determine the type of backing store: page file, section file, or swap file page (see Section 18.8.5).

12. If the backing store is in a page file, MMG$WRTMFYPAG tests whether its last attempt to allocate space in that page file failed. If so, it rejects this page as a starting point and goes on to the next page in the modified page list, continuing with step 8. The allocation failure information is cleared each time MMG$WRTMFYPAG is invoked. If the last attempt to allocate space in the page file was successful, MMG$WRTMFYPAG allocates a cluster of pages in that page file (see Section 18.8.6).

13. Unless the backing store is a swap file page, MMG$WRTMFYPAG tries to form a cluster of pages, as described in Section 18.8.5. It scans adjacent PTEs (first toward lower virtual addresses and then toward higher virtual addresses), looking for transition PTEs that map pages on the modified page list, until either the desired cluster size is reached or one of the other terminating conditions described in Section 18.8.4 is reached.

    This scan begins first toward smaller virtual addresses for the same reason that the page read cluster routine begins toward larger addresses. Given that the program is more likely to reference higher addresses, it would be inefficient to initiate a write operation only to have the page immediately faulted and likely modified again. The modified page writer writes first those pages with a smaller likelihood of being referenced in the near future.

14. When it can no longer cluster, it records the PTEs and their associated PHD vector indexes in the MPW IRP.

15. If the cluster is one of page file pages, MMG$WRTMFYPAG updates the PFN$Q_BAK field for each page to show the actual page file page allocated.

16. MMG$WRTMFYPAG removes each page from the modified page list, decrementing SCH$GL_MFYCNT to show one less modified page.

17. It changes the PFN$L_PAGE_STATE location bits for each page to write in progress and also clears the saved modify bit. It increments the reference count for each page to reflect the I/O in progress. If the page is a page table page, MMG$WRTMFYPAG also increments the PHV$GL_REFCBAS array element corresponding to the PHD.

18. It releases the MMG spinlock, fills in the MPW IRP, and queues it to the backing store driver.

19. MMG$WRTMFYPAG reacquires the MMG spinlock and goes to step 7 to try to form another cluster of pages to write.

20. In local routine MMG$MPW_END, the modified page writer performs end processing. Depending on the operation performed, the modified page writer may declare as available the resource RSN$_MPWBUSY or the resource RSN$_MPLEMPTY. If no modified page write I/O requests are outstanding, it clears SCH$V_MPW in SCH$GL_SIP.

21. The modified page writer releases the MMG spinlock and processes any global section descriptors (GSDs) on the delete pending list, possibly queuing a kernel mode AST to the creator of each global section. Chapter 17 describes this processing in detail.

Whenever a modified page write request completes, MMG$WRTMFY-PAG's special kernel mode AST routine is entered. Section 18.8.3 describes this routine.

18.8.3   Modified Page Write Completion

The modified page writer's special kernel mode AST routine, WRITEDONE in module WRTMFYPAG, takes the following steps:

1. It acquires the MMG spinlock, raising IPL to IPL$_MMG.

2. It deallocates the MPW IRP to its own lookaside list.

3. It examines the characteristics of each page in the cluster:

   a. If the page is a page table page, it decrements the PHV$GL_REFCBAS array element corresponding to that PHD.

   b. If the page's backing store was a swap file page, WRITEDONE clears PFN$V_SWPPAG_VALID in the PFN$L_PAGE_STATE field to indicate that the contents of PFN$W_SWPPAG are no longer valid.

   c. It decrements the reference count for the page. If the count goes to zero, it places the page into the free page list.

   d. If the RPTEVT bit in the PFN$L_PAGE_STATE field is set, WRITE-DONE reports a page fault completion scheduling event for the process that owns the page. This bit is set when deletion of the page has been stalled while it is being written to its backing store.

4. WRITEDONE attempts to form another MPW cluster, rejoining the flow described in Section 18.8.2 at step 7.

18.8.4 **Modified Page Write Clustering**

The modified page writer scans the page table, attempting to form a cluster. The terminating conditions for its scan include the following:

▶ The page table page is not valid, implying that there are no transition pages in this page table page. The special check avoids an unnecessary page fault.

▶ The PTE does not indicate a transition page.

▶ The PTE indicates a page in transition, but the physical page is not on the modified page list.

▶ Bit PFN$V_SWPPAG_VALID in the page's PFN$L_PAGE_STATE field is set. Such a page is treated in a special way by the modified page writer.

▶ The contents of the PFN$Q_BAK field for the first page in the cluster and the page in question indicate that their backing store location is a process or global section file, but the section indexes are not the same.

▶ The PFN$Q_BAK field for the first page in the cluster and the page in question indicate that the pages are to be written to a page file, but they have different page file indexes.

The maximum size of the cluster depends on its type (see Section 18.8.5).

18.8.5 **Backing Store for Modified Pages**

The modified page writer attempts to cluster when writing modified pages to their backing store addresses. It encounters three different clustering situations for the three possible backing store locations.

The set bit PFN$V_SWPPAG_VALID in PFN$L_PAGE_STATE indicates that the process has been outswapped and this page remained behind, probably as the result of an outstanding read request. The modified page writer writes a single page to the swap file page whose number is in PFN$W_SWP-PAG. It does not attempt to cluster because virtually contiguous pages in an I/O buffer are unlikely to be adjacent in the outswapped process body. The process body is outswapped with pages ordered as they appear in the working set list, not in virtual address order. A description of how the PFN$W_SWPPAG field is loaded is found in Chapter 20, where the entire outswap operation is discussed.

If the backing store address is in a section file, the modified page writer creates a cluster up to the value of the SYSGEN parameter MPW_WRTCLUSTER. Any of the terminating conditions listed in the previous section can limit the size of the cluster. If the last page in the section is in the cluster and the partial section bit is set in its L3PTE, the modified page writer calculates the I/O request byte count such that the last page's contribution to the count includes only those pagelets that have backing store.

If the backing store address is in a page file, adjacent pages bound for the same page file are written at the same time. The modified page writer attempts to allocate a number of pages in the page file equal to MPW_WRT-

CLUSTER. The desired cluster factor is reduced to the number of pages actually allocated. Section 18.8.6 describes allocation of space within the page file.

The cluster created for a write to a page file consists of several smaller clusters, each representing a series of virtually contiguous pages (see Figure 18.11):

1. The modified page writer creates a cluster of virtually contiguous pages, all bound for the same page file.

2. If the desired cluster size has not yet been reached, the modified page list is searched until another physical page bound for the same page file is found.

3. Pages virtually contiguous to this page form the second minicluster that is added to the eventual cluster to be written to the page file.

4. The modified page writer continues in this manner until either the cluster size is reached or no more pages on the modified page list have the designated page file as their backing store address. The modified page writer is building a large cluster that consists of a series of smaller clusters. The large cluster terminates only when the desired size is reached or when the modified page list contains no more pages bound to the page file in question. Each smaller cluster can terminate on any of the conditions listed in the previous section, or on the two terminating conditions for the large cluster.

18.8.6 Page File Space Allocation

Before the modified page writer searches for more pages to form a cluster bound for a page file, it must determine the maximum size of the write cluster. To do this, it determines the number of contiguous pages that can be allocated in the page file associated with the current page.

The modified page writer invokes MPW$ALLOCPAGFIL1, in module PAGEFILE, to allocate a cluster of pages in that page file. The number of pages it tries to allocate is stored in the page file control block at the offset PFL$L_ALLOCSIZ and is usually equal to MPW_WRTCLUSTER. If that many pages are not available, MMG$WRTMFYPAG reduces the PFL$L_ALLOCSIZ size by 16 pages, if it can, and invokes MPW$ALLOCPAGFIL1 again to search for contiguous blocks starting back at the beginning of the page file.

The allocation size is raised sometime later when space frees up in the page file. When the page file deallocation routine determines that it has freed a large enough cluster, it increases the allocation size by 8, to a maximum of MPW_WRTCLUSTER.

When the allocation size for the page file is less than or equal to 16, the modified page writer invokes MPW$ALLOCPAGFIL2, in module PAGEFILE, a special-case allocation routine. This routine searches for and allocates the first available cluster, starting from the beginning of the page file. The routine can allocate between 1 and 16 contiguous pages. If the first available cluster is not in the first quarter of the page file, MPW$ALLOCPAGFIL2 issues the following message on the console terminal:

```
%SYSTEM-W-PAGEFRAG, page file filling up; please create more space
```

If the first available cluster is in the last quarter, MPW$ALLOCPAGFIL2 issues the following message on the console terminal:

```
%SYSTEM-W-PAGECRIT, page file nearly full; system trying to continue
```

Each of these messages is issued only once during a boot of the system, even if more than one page file becomes full. The first message is issued when one page file becomes fragmented or full; the second, when the same or a different page file becomes fragmented or full. These messages on the console terminal may be a good indication that the system requires an(other) alternative page file. However, because of the nature of the checks, it is possible for the system to run out of page file space without any message having been displayed.

If the modified page writer is unable to allocate any pages in a particular page file, it skips any pages with backing store in that page file.

18.8.7 **Example of Modified Page Write to a Page File**

Figure 18.11 illustrates a sample cluster for writing to a page file. The modified page list, pictured in the upper right-hand corner of the figure, is shown as a sequential array to simplify the figure.

1. The first page on the modified page list is PFN A. By scanning backward through the process's page table, the modified page writer locates first PFN F and then PFN H. The L3PTE preceding the one that contains PFN H is also a transition PTE, but the page is on the free page list. This page terminates the backward search.
2. The modified page writer's map begins with PFN H, PFN F, and PFN A. The search now goes in the forward direction, with each page bound for the same page file added to the map up to and including PFN E. Because the next L3PTE is valid, the first minicluster is terminated.
3. The next page on the modified page list, PFN B, leads to the addition of a second cluster to the map. This cluster begins with PFN G and ends with PFN J. The backward search was terminated with an L3PTE containing a section table index. The forward search terminated with a demand zero PTE.

   Note that this second cluster consists of pages belonging to a different process than that of the first cluster. The difference is reflected in the process header vector index array, which contains a word element for each L3PTE in the map (see Figure 18.10).

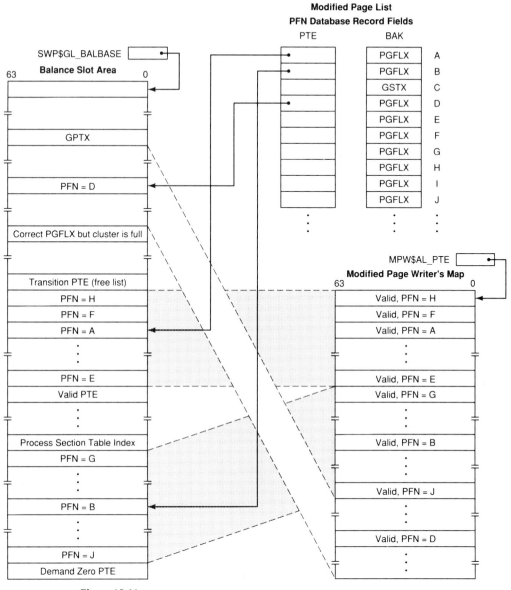

Figure 18.11
Clustered Write to a Page File

4. The next page on the modified page list is PFN C. This page belongs in a global section file and is skipped during the current scan.

5. PFN D leads to a third cluster that was terminated in the backward direction by an L3PTE that contains a GPTX. The search in the forward direction terminates when the desired cluster size is reached, even though the next PTE was bound to the same page file. The cluster size is either

MPW_WRTCLUSTER or the number of adjacent pages available in the page file, whichever is smaller. In any case, this cluster will be written with a single write request.

6. Note that reaching the desired cluster size resulted in leaving some pages on the modified page list bound for the same page file, such as PFN I.

18.9 $UPDSEC SYSTEM SERVICE

The $UPDSEC[W] system service enables a process to write a specified range of pages in a process or global section to their backing store in a controlled fashion, without waiting for the modified page writer to do the backup. This system service is especially useful for frequently accessed pages that may never be written by the modified page writer because they are always being faulted from the modified page list back into the working set before they are backed up.

This system service is a cross between modified page writing and a normal write request. As for any I/O request, the requestor can request completion notification with an event flag and I/O status block or an AST. The number of pages written is specified by the address range that is passed as an input parameter to the service. The cluster factor is the minimum of MPW_ WRTCLUSTER and the number of pages in the input range. The direction of search for modified pages is determined by the order in which the address range is specified to the service.

The system service procedure EXE$UPDSEC, in module SYSUPDSEC, runs in kernel mode. It checks the validity of the input address range, clears the event flag associated with the I/O request, charges the process direct I/O quota, and allocates nonpaged pool to serve as an extended I/O packet. The pool is used to queue one or more modified page write I/O requests and to keep track of how much of the section the service has processed.

EXE$UPDSEC then invokes MMG$CREDEL, in module SYSCREDEL, specifying UPDSECPAG, in module SYSUPDSEC, as the per-page service-specific routine. (Chapter 17 describes the actions of MMG$CREDEL and its use of per-page service-specific routines.) Routines UPDSECQWT, PTEPFN-MFY, MMG$WRT_PGS_BAK, and MMG$UPDSECAST, all in module SYS-UPDSEC, are also part of this system service.

UPDSECPAG invokes UPDSECQWT to form the first cluster and to initialize and queue the IRP to the driver for the backing store device.

UPDSECQWT takes the following steps:

1. It touches the next page table page that maps pages in the specified range to fault it into the working set list.
2. It acquires the MMG spinlock, raising IPL to IPL$_MMG.
3. It scans in the specified direction of the range for the first candidate page: one whose owner access mode is not more privileged than that of the

service requestor; that is a valid or transition page (or a valid or transition global page); that is writable but not copy-on-reference; and that has been modified.

4. Having found one candidate page, it invokes MMG$WRT_PGS_BAK.

5. MMG$WRT_PGS_BAK scans in the specified direction for adjacent pages that have similar characteristics; in particular, the backing store for the pages must be the same. The adjacent pages do not necessarily have to have been modified but they do all have to be valid or transition, that is, resident.

   In the case of process pages, it forms a cluster from the first modified page through the last modified page in the MPW_WRTCLUSTER adjacent pages.

   In the case of global pages, determining which pages have been modified is not feasible. The system service runs in the context of one process and can scan its PTEs for set modify bits. However, to determine whether a particular page has been modified requires looking at the PFN database and the PTEs of all processes mapped to this global page. (The state of the saved modify bit in the GPTE does not necessarily reflect the state of the page.) Because there are no back pointers for valid global pages, this information is unavailable. Therefore, all pages in a global section are written to their backing store location, regardless of whether the pages have been modified.

   By setting the low bit of the FLAGS parameter, the requestor can indicate that it is the only process whose modifed pages should be written. In that case, the process's L3PTEs and the PFN database are used to select candidate pages for backing up. Only pages modified by this process can be the beginning and end pages of a cluster.

6. Having formed a cluster, MMG$WRT_PGS_BAK modifies the PFN database records for the pages in it. It increments the PFN$L_REFCNT field for each page. If the page is on the free or modified page list, it removes it from the list and changes its PFN$L_PAGE_STATE location bits to write in progress and clears the saved modify bit. If the page was valid, it also clears the modify bit in the PTE.

7. If the last page in the section is in the cluster and has the PTE$V_PARTIAL_SECTION bit set, MMG$WRT_PGS_BAK calculates the I/O request byte count such that the last page's contribution to the count includes only those pagelets that have backing store.

8. It initializes an IRP, releases the MMG spinlock, and queues the I/O request to the backing store driver.

When the write completes, the process that requested the $UPDSEC system service receives a special kernel mode AST. AST routine MMG$UPDSECAST first checks whether all the pages that were requested by the system service call have been written or whether another write is required.

To perform the check, it invokes UPDSECQWT, which forms another cluster and queues another write request if necessary. If all requested pages have been written, MMG$UPDSECAST enters the normal I/O completion path, which involves event flags, I/O status blocks, and user-requested ASTs, thus notifying the process.

18.10 REFERENCE COUNTS

Much of the memory management subsystem's activity is asynchronous, initiated in response to process actions but completed in other contexts. The memory management database keeps track of the current state of various structures and resources through reference counts. Certain count transitions trigger additional memory management subsystem activity. This section summarizes those reference counts and the activities triggered by their transitions. These counts are mentioned throughout this and the other memory management chapters.

Table 18.2 lists these reference counts with a brief description of each. The sections that follow describe each count in more detail.

Table 18.2   Memory Management Reference Counts

Reference Count Location	*Meaning*
PFN$L_REFCNT	Number of reasons the current contents of physical page should stay in memory
PFN$L_SHRCNT for process page table page	Number of valid and transition pages it maps
PFN$L_SHRCNT for global page table page	Number of GPTEs that map global section pages
PFN$L_SHRCNT for global page	Number of L3PTEs that are mapped to it
PHD$L_PTWSLELCK array element	Number of locked WSLEs and window PTEs mapped by this process page table page
PHD$L_PTWSLEVAL array element	Number of valid WSLEs mapped by this process page table page
PHD$L_PTCNTACT	Number of active page table pages with nonzero PTEs
PHD$L_PTCNTLCK	Number of page table pages with non-negative PHD$L_PTWSLELCK counts
PHD$L_PTCNTVAL	Number of page table pages with non-negative PHD$L_PTWSLEVAL counts
PHV$GL_REFCBAS array element	Number of reasons the PHD should remain resident

18.10.1   PFN$L_REFCNT

PFN$L_REFCNT counts the number of reasons a physical page should retain its current contents. A value of zero means the associated page is on the free, modified, zeroed, or bad page list. The count is incremented for the following reasons:

▸ The associated virtual page is being faulted in.
▸ A page is locked as part of a direct I/O buffer with I/O in progress.
▸ The associated virtual page is added to a working set list.
▸ The associated virtual page is part of a buffer object.
▸ The associated virtual page is a process page table page whose PFN$W_BO_REFC is greater than zero.
▸ A section page is being written to its backing store.
▸ A page is being outswapped as part of a process header or body.
▸ A page has just been inswapped as part of a process header or body.

PFN$L_REFCNT is decremented for the following events:

▸ Page fault I/O completes.
▸ Modified page write I/O completes.
▸ Any other type of direct I/O completes when the buffer pages are unlocked.
▸ Outswap completes.
▸ A buffer object is deleted.
▸ PFN$W_BO_REFC transitions to zero, indicating that a process page table page no longer maps any buffer objects.

When a page's reference count transitions from 1 to 0, the page is inserted into the free or modified page list, depending on the state of its saved modify bit.

18.10.2   PFN$L_SHRCNT and PHD$L_PTCNTACT

As shown in Table 18.2, the meaning of PFN$L_SHRCNT depends on the type of virtual page occupying the physical page.

For a process page table page, PFN$L_SHRCNT is the number of valid and transition pages it maps. A count of zero means the page table page maps no valid and no transition pages. The count is incremented for the following events:

▸ A physical page is allocated for a virtual page being faulted.
▸ A transition page mapped by that page table page is made valid and locked as part of a direct I/O buffer.
▸ At inswap, a valid process body page is remapped by that page table page.
▸ At inswap, the process is remapped by that page table page to a buffer object page.
▸ A buffer object page mapped by that page table page is being deleted (but the virtual address space that it occupied still exists).

The count is decremented for the following events:

▶ A page mapped by that page table page is removed from the process working set list.
▶ Contents of a virtual page mapped by that page table page are deleted and the associated physical page is deallocated.
▶ A page mapped by that page table page is part of a direct I/O buffer being unlocked at I/O completion.
▶ At outswap, a buffer object page mapped by that page table page is being disconnected from the process working set list.

When the share count for a page table page transitions from 0 to 1, the executive increments PHD$L_PTCNTACT to indicate one more process page table page mapping valid or transition pages and also increments the appropriate PHV$GL_REFCBAS array element. When the count transitions from 1 to 0, the executive decrements PHD$L_PTCNTACT and also decrements the appropriate PHV$GL_REFCBAS array element.

For a global page table page, PFN$L_SHRCNT is the number of GPTEs in it that map global section pages. The count is incremented for the following events:

▶ A global section page is created and mapped by that global page table page.
▶ At inswap, a valid global section page with no other sharers is remapped.

The count is decremented for the following events:

▶ A global section page mapped by that global page table page is deleted.
▶ The contents of a virtual page mapped by that global page table page are deleted and the associated physical page is deallocated.
▶ At outswap, a global writable page is dropped from a process working set list.
▶ At outswap, a global page with no other sharers is outswapped with a process working set list.

For a global page, PFN$L_SHRCNT is the number of L3PTEs that map to the global page. The count is incremented for the following events:

▶ At inswap, a process is reconnected to a valid global page.
▶ An unmodified global demand zero page is materialized rather than faulted in to expedite deletion of the page.

The count is decremented for the following events:

▶ A global page is removed from a process's working set.
▶ After outswap, a process is disconnected from a valid global page.
▶ Prior to outswap, a process is disconnected from a valid writable global page.

When the share count for a global page transitions from 0 to 1, the executive increments PFN$L_REFCNT to indicate one more reason for the page to remain resident. When the count transitions from 1 to 0, the executive decrements PFN$L_REFCNT.

One other use is made of PFN$L_SHRCNT for system pages. The count records the number of times a particular page has been locked into the system working set through the routine MMG$LOCK_SYSTEM_PAGES, in module LOCK_SYSTEM_PAGES. Such a page is unlocked through routine MMG$UNLOCK_SYSTEM_PAGES, in the same module. When the share count transitions from 1 to 0, the routine actually unlocks it from the system working set. Chapter 19 describes these routines.

18.10.3   PHD$L_PTWSLEVAL Array Element and PHD$L_PTCNTVAL

PHD$L_PTWSLEVAL contains the offset to an array in the PHD. The array has one element for each of the maximum number of L3PTs the PHD can accommodate. An element corresponding to a process page table page contains the number of valid pages mapped by that page table page. A value of –1 for an element means the PHD page maps no such pages (or is not currently in use as an L3PT).

The count is incremented for the following events:

▶ A page mapped by that page table page is faulted into the working set list.
▶ A transition page mapped by that page table page is added to the working set list so that it can be locked as part of a direct I/O buffer.

The count is decremented for the following events:

▶ A page mapped by that page table page is removed from the working set list.
▶ A valid, unmodified process page mapped by that page table page is being deleted.
▶ At outswap, a transition process page mapped by that page table page is removed from the working set list because its page fault I/O has not completed.
▶ At outswap, either a global page in transition or a valid global writable page mapped by that page table page is removed from the working set list.

When the count transitions from –1 to 0, the executive increments PHD$L_PTCNTVAL to indicate one more process page table page mapping valid pages. When the count transitions from 0 to –1, the page table page is considered dead; the executive decrements PHD$L_PTCNTVAL.

18.10.4   PHD$L_PTWSLELCK Array Element and PHD$L_PTCNTLCK

PHD$L_PTWSLELCK contains the offset to an array in the PHD. The array has one element for each of the maximum number of L3PTs the PHD can accommodate. An element corresponding to a process page table page contains the number of locked pages and window pages mapped by that page table page. A window page is a virtual page that is a double mapping of a physical page. For example, a virtual page in a section mapped by PFN is a window page. A value of –1 for a PHD$L_PTWSLELCK array element means the page table page maps no such pages (or is not currently in use as an L3PT).

The count is incremented for the following events:

▶ A virtual page is created that maps a window page and that is mapped by that page table page.

▶ A page mapped by that page table page is locked into the working set list or into memory.

The count is decremented for the following events:

▶ A window page or PFN-mapped process page mapped by that page table page is deleted.

▶ A page mapped by that page table page is unlocked from the working set list or from memory.

When the count transitions from –1 to 0, the executive increments PHD$L_PTCNTLCK to indicate one more process page table page mapping locked or window pages. When the count transitions from 0 to –1, the executive decrements PHD$L_PTCNTLCK.

18.10.5 PHV$GL_REFCBAS Array Element

PHV$GL_REFCBAS contains the address of an array with one element for each balance set slot (see Chapter 16). Each element counts the number of reasons the current PHD must continue to occupy that balance set slot, that is, the number of process page table pages tightly connected to that PHD slot. A value of –1 for an element means the corresponding balance set slot does not contain any PHD. A value of 0 means that the slot has been assigned to a process.

A PHV$GL_REFCBAS element is incremented for the following reasons:

▶ A process page table page is being faulted in from a page file.

▶ A process page table page (that does not map a buffer object) has been removed from the working set list and is on the free or modified page list.

▶ A process page table page maps valid or transition pages.

Typically, either MMG$DECPHDREF or MMG$DECPHDREF1, both in module PAGEFAULT, is invoked to decrement a PHV$GL_REFCBAS element. A PHV$GL_REFCBAS element is decremented for the following events:

▶ A process page table page is deleted (inserted into the free page list with the delete contents bit set in its PFN$L_PAGE_STATE field).

▶ Page fault I/O for a process page table page completes.

▶ Modified page write I/O for a process page table page completes.

▶ A process page table page (that does not map a buffer object) is faulted from the free or modified page list.

▶ A process page table page's PFN$L_SHRCNT transitions to zero, indicating the page table maps no valid or transition pages.

When the count transitions to 0, the swapper is awakened to clean up the slot so that it is available for another process.

<table>
<tr><td>18.11</td><td>**USE OF PAGE FILES**</td></tr>
</table>

During system initialization and operation one or more page files are placed into use. When a process is created, it is assigned to a page file, and space in that page file is reserved for it. When a process faults a copy-on-reference or demand zero page, the page is charged against the reserved space. Allocation of particular blocks in the page file is deferred until the modified page writer actually prepares to write the page. A process can be assigned concurrently to as many as four page files during its lifetime.

This section describes the data structures and mechanisms related to page file use.

<table>
<tr><td>18.11.1</td><td>**Related Data Structures**</td></tr>
</table>

A nonpaged pool data structure called a page file control block (PFL) describes each page file in use. Space in a page file is managed in page-sized units. Chapter 16 shows the PFL (see Figure 16.24) and describes its fields. Those with particular importance to this discussion are PFL$L_FREPAGCNT, the number of pages that can be allocated, and PFL$L_RSRVPAGCNT, the number of pages that can be reserved without overcommitting the file. Both fields are initialized to the number of available pages.

PFL$L_FREPAGCNT is the actual number of pages that can be accommodated by the free blocks in the page file. This field is not decremented until the modified page writer actually assigns space to a particular virtual page. It is incremented whenever a page file page is released, either because its virtual page is being deleted or its contents are known to be obsolete. (That is, when a page previously assigned space in a page file is placed into the modified page list, its backing store copy can no longer be regarded as good.)

In contrast, PFL$L_RSRVPAGCNT is charged when page file space is reserved for a process's use. Reserved space is only a logical claim on the page file; actual allocation is not made until the modified page writer is about to write a cluster of pages to the file. The executive computes the ratio of reservable space to total size for each page file to select the most lightly loaded one, when reserving space for a newly created process or one that has used its current reservation. PFL$L_RSRVPAGCNT can, in fact, become negative if the number of pages assigned backing store in the file

631

exceeds the physical size of the file. On most systems, however, only a small percentage of reserved space is written; thus, an overcommitment is viewed as benign. (The display for the Digital command language SHOW MEMORY/FILES command shows the overcommitment as a negative number.)

A number of PHD fields describe the process's connection to page files.

Beginning at PHD$B_PRCPGFL, a four-byte array represents the page files to which the process has been assigned. The array is indexed by a two-bit process-local page file number. The elements of this array are initialized to zero to indicate no assignment. When a process is assigned to a page file, that file's index (see Figure 16.24) is stored in the next available element of PHD$B_PRCPGFL.

The low four bits of PHD$L_PGFLCNT contain the number of page files to which the process has been assigned, that is, the number of valid elements in the four-byte array. Each of the high four bits, when set, means that the corresponding page file has a pending deassign.

PHD$B_PAGFIL contains the systemwide index of the page file in which the process has reserved blocks. It is the high-order byte of the field PHD$Q_PAGFIL, which contains the corresponding process-local page file index in bits $\langle 53:52 \rangle$ and zero elsewhere. This field serves as template backing store for the construction of a PTE with a page file backing store address. PHD$L_PRCPAGFIL contains the process-local index associated with that page file.

PHD$L_PRCPGFLOPAGES contains the total reserved pages in the current page file, including space already allocated by the modified page writer. PHD$L_PRCPGFLPAGES contains the reserved pages not yet allocated in the current page file.

Beginning at PHD$L_PRCPGFLREFS is a four-longword array indexed by the two-bit process-local page file index. Each of its elements represents the number of process PTEs currently associated with that page file. The elements count downward from 100000_{16}, 1 larger than the maximum page file page number that can be accommodated in a PTE, $FFFFF_{16}$. (Counting downward simplifies the test for whether the number has reached its maximum.) The difference between 100000_{16} and an array element's contents represents the total number of pages in the page file referenced by that process's PTEs. The array element for the current page file is updated only when the currently reserved pages have been used. Thus, for the current page file, the difference between PHD$L_PRCPGFLOPAGES and PHD$L_PRCPGFLPAGES represents additional referenced pages.

18.11.2 Assignment and Deassignment to a Page File

When a process is created, MMG$ASNPRCPGFLP, in module PAGEFILE, is invoked to assign to it the page file estimated to have the most available space, the one with the largest ratio of reservable pages to total pages. The routine stores the systemwide index of that page file in PHD$B_PAGFIL and in the byte at PHD$B_PRCPGFL and a process-local index of zero in PHD$L_PRCPAGFIL.

MMG$RSRVPRCPGFL2, in module PAGEFILE, is invoked to reserve a number of pages in the page file for the process's use. The number is stored in PHD$L_PRCPGFLOPAGES and PHD$L_PRCPGFLPAGES and subtracted from PFL$L_RSRVPAGCNT in the page file block.

Whenever the process faults a page that requires page file backing store, MMG$PAGEFAULT decrements PHD$L_PRCPGFLPAGES and copies PHD$Q_PAGFIL to the PFN$Q_BAK field for the page. When no more reserved pages remain (when PHD$L_PRCPGFLPAGES becomes zero), then MMG$PAGEFAULT invokes MMG$SWITCH_PRCPGFL, in module PAGE-FAULT, to reserve more page file space for the process.

MMG$SWITCH_PRCPGFL subtracts PHD$L_PRCPGFLOPAGES from the PHD$L_PRCPGFLREFS element corresponding to the current page file, generating the fatal bugcheck BADPRCPGFLC if the result is negative.

MMG$SWITCH_PRCPGFL invokes MMG$ASNPRCPGFL to select the best page file for a new reservation. Unless the process has already been assigned to four page files, the best page file is the one estimated to have the most available space; it may be the same one the process was just using. If the process has been assigned to four page files, the new reservation must come from one of them. If the process has not been assigned space in the chosen page file, MMG$ASNPRCPGFL stores its systemwide page file index in the next available slot in the array at PHD$B_PRCPGFL and increments PHD$L_PGFLCNT to point to the next slot. It initializes PHD$Q_PAGFIL and PHD$L_PRCPAGFIL.

MMG$SWITCH_PRCPGFL invokes MMG$RSRVPRCPGFL2 to reserve the SYSGEN parameter RSRVPAGCNT number of pages in that page file. The default value of this parameter is 128. MMG$RSRVPRCPGFL2 subtracts that many pages from PFL$L_RSRVPAGCNT of the chosen page file and adds it to PHD$L_PRCPGFLPAGES and PHD$L_PRCPGFLOPAGES.

Section 18.8.6 describes the allocation of actual pages in the page file.

When a process page backed by a page file is deleted, MMG$DALCPRC-PGFL, in module PAGEFILE, is invoked to deallocate the page file page, if any, and return the reservation. It increments the appropriate PHD$L_PRCPGFLREFS longword; if, as a result, there are no more references to that page file, the routine deassigns the process from the page file.

After a process is deleted, when the swapper deletes its header, the swapper deassigns the process from any remaining page file assignments.

18.12   INPUT AND OUTPUT THAT SUPPORT PAGING

There is little special-purpose code in the I/O subsystem to support page and swap I/O. MMG$PAGEFAULT and the swapper each build their own IRPs but queue these packets to a device driver in the normal fashion. These are the only differences.

► Special Queue I/O Request ($QIO) entry points for page and swap I/O (in module SYSQIOREQ) bypass many of the usual $QIO checks to minimize overhead.

► An IRP describing a page or swap request is distinguished from other IRPs by a flag in IRP$L_STS. These flags are detected by the I/O postprocessing routine, which dispatches to special completion paths for page read and other types of memory management I/O.

Tables 18.3 to 18.5 summarize the I/O requests issued by memory management components. The first table lists the type of paging or swapping I/O, the priority of each such request, the relevant process identification, and information about the priority boost the process receives at I/O completion. For more information on priority classes and boosts, see Chapter 13.

Tables 18.4 and 18.5 list more information about each type of I/O request, summarizing the unusual uses to which the memory management components put several fields in the IRP. These fields are not required for their more typical uses and can thus be used for storing other information needed by these components.

The columns SVAPTE, PARAM_0, and PARAM_1 in Table 18.4 describe the contents of IRP fields IRPL_SVAPTE, IRPQ_PARAM_0, and IRP$Q_PARAM_1 for each type of read operation requested by the memory management subsystem. For write requests, listed in Table 18.5, the fields IRPL_SVAPTE, IRPL_AST, and IRP$L_ASTPRM are used. The SVAPTE column identifies the type of PTE whose address is in that field. In most cases it is an L3PTE in a process's P0 or P1 page table.

Table 18.3   Summary of I/O Requests Issued by Memory Management—Part I

Type of I/O Request	Priority IRP$B_PRI	Process ID IRP$L_PID	Priority Boost
Process page read, Global page read, Process page table	Base priority of faulting process	PID of faulting process	0
System page read, Global page table	Base priority from system PCB—16	PID of faulting process	0
Modified page write	MPW_PRIO [1]	PID of swapper [2]	None [3]
$UPDSEC write	Base priority of caller	PID of caller	2
Swapper I/O	SWP_PRIO [1]	PID of swapper	None [3]

[1] This is a SYSGEN parameter.
[2] The modified page writer is a subroutine of the swapper process.
[3] The swapper is a real-time process and is therefore not subject to priority boosts.

Table 18.4   Summary of I/O Requests Issued by Memory Management—Part II (Read Requests)

Type of I/O Read Request	SVAPTE	PARAM_0	PARAM_1	WCB Source
PROCESS PAGE READ				
Page in section file	L3PTE	0	0/PSTX [1]	PSTE
Page in page file	L3PTE	0	0	PFL
Page table page	SPTE	0	0	PFL [2]
SYSTEM PAGE READ				
System section page [3]	SPTE	0	0	SSTE
Paged pool page	SPTE	0	0	PFL
GLOBAL PAGE READ				
Global page	GPTE	Slave L3PTE address	0	GSTE
Global copy-on-reference page	L3PTE	GPTE contents	GPTX	GSTE
Global page table page	SPTE	0	0	PFL [2]

[1] If the page is copy-on-reference, IRP$Q_PARAM_1 contains the PSTX.

[2] Process page tables and global page tables originate as demand zero pages whose backing store is a page file.

[3] Pageable executive routines originate in executive images, described by section table entries in the system header.

For write requests, the ASTPRM field contains the address of a special kernel mode AST (KAST) routine. The column WCB Source specifies from which memory management data structure the address of the window control block (WCB) is obtained. This address is stored in the field IRP$L_WIND.

18.13   PAGING AND SCHEDULING

Page fault handling can influence the scheduling state of processes in several ways. If a read is required to satisfy a page fault, the faulting process is placed into a page fault wait state. If a resource such as physical memory is not available, the process is placed into an appropriate wait state. There are several other wait states that a process may be placed into as a result of a page fault. The process waits with its program counter (PC), processor status (PS), and other registers reflecting its state at the time it executed the instruction that generated the page fault.

Table 18.5   Summary of I/O Requests Issued by Memory Management—Part III
(Write Requests)

Type of I/O Write Request	SVAPTE	AST	ASTPRM	WCB Source
MODIFIED PAGE WRITE				
To page file	MPW map	0	MPW KAST, WRITEDONE	PFL
To private section file	MPW map	0	MPW KAST, WRITEDONE	PSTE
To global section file	MPW map	0	MPW KAST, WRITEDONE	GSTE
To swap file (nonzero SWPPAG)	MPW map	0	MPW KAST, WRITEDONE	PFL
$UPDSEC WRITE				
Private section	L3PTE	AST address	AST argument	PSTE
Global section	GPTE	AST address	AST argument	GSTE
SWAPPER I/O				
Swapper I/O	Swapper map	0	Swapper KAST, IODONE	PFL

Chapter 13 describes process scheduling, wait states, priority increment classes, resource waits, and the reporting of scheduler events.

18.13.1   Page Fault Wait State

A process is placed into page fault wait when a read is required to resolve a page fault. The I/O postprocessing routine PAGIO detects that a page read has completed and reports the scheduling event page fault completion for the process. As a result, the process is removed from the page fault wait state and made computable. No priority boost is associated with page fault read completion.

18.13.2   Free Page Wait State

If not enough physical memory is available to satisfy a page fault, the faulting process is placed into a free page wait state. Whenever a page is deallocated and the free page list was formerly empty, routine MMG$DALLOC_PFN, in module ALLOCPFN, checks for processes in this state. It reports the scheduling event free page available so that each process in the free page wait state is made computable.

MMG$DALLOC_PFN makes no scheduling decision about which process will get the page. There is no first-in/first-out approach to the free page wait state; rather, all processes waiting for the page are made computable. The next process to execute will be the highest priority resident computable process.

18.13.3   Collided Page Wait State

It is possible for a page fault to occur for a page that is already being read from its backing store. If the page is anything but a process page, it is referred to as a collided page. The collided bit is set in the PFN$L_PAGE_STATE field, and the process placed into the collided page (COLPG) wait state.

When the page fault I/O is complete, the page read completion code in PAGIO checks if the collided bit was set for any page in the cluster just read. If so, it reports the scheduling event collided page available for each process in that wait state. It does not check whether a process is waiting for the collided page that was faulted in.

This lack of checking has two advantages:

- ▶ No special code determines which process executes first. All processes are made computable, and the normal scheduling algorithm selects the process that executes next.
- ▶ The probability of a collided page is small. The probability of two different collided pages is even smaller. If a process waiting for another collided page is selected for execution, that process will incur a page fault and be placed back into the collided page wait state. Nothing unusual occurs, and the operating system avoids a lot of special-case code to handle a situation that rarely, if ever, occurs.

18.13.4   Resource Wait States

Several types of resource wait are associated with memory management. A process waiting for one of these resources is placed into the miscellaneous wait state (see Chapter 13) until the resource is available.

Early versions of the VAX/VMS operating system also could place a process into a wait for resource RSN$_SWPFILE (RWSWP). When a process was unable to increase its swap file allocation to accommodate a larger working set, it was placed into this resource wait until space became available in the swap file. The timing and form of VAX VMS swap file allocation changed, and this resource wait is not used by the OpenVMS AXP executive.

18.13.4.1   Resource Wait for RSN$_ASTWAIT (RWAST). A process that faults a page is placed into this wait when the process has no direct I/O quota left against which the page fault I/O request can be charged.

18.13.4.2   **Resource Wait for RSN$_NPDYNMEM (RWNPP).** A process that faults a page is placed into the RWNPP resource wait when MMG$PAGEFAULT is not able to allocate nonpaged pool for an I/O request packet for the page fault I/O.

18.13.4.3   **Resource Wait for RSN$_PGFILE (RWPFF).** A process that faults a modified page with page file backing store out of its working set may be placed into this resource wait when the page file identified by the page file index has not yet been initialized.

The process is not placed into this wait unless all the following conditions are true:

- ▸ The process holds no mutexes.
- ▸ The process is not the swapper process.
- ▸ Bit MMG$V_NOWAIT in MMG$GB_FREWFLGS is clear.
- ▸ One or more page files have been installed.

If any of them is not true, waiting the process could lead to a process or system hang, and MMG$PAGEFAULT simply continues processing the page fault.

18.13.4.4   **Resource Wait for RSN$_MPWBUSY (RWMPB).** A process that faults a modified page out of its working set may be placed into this resource wait when either of the following is true:

- ▸ The modified page list contains more pages than the SYSGEN parameter MPW_WAITLIMIT.
- ▸ The modified page list contains more pages than the SYSGEN parameter MPW_LOWAITLIMIT and the modified page writer is active, writing modified pages.

In addition, the conditions listed in the previous section must also all be true.

The modified page writer declares the availability of the resource RSN$_MPWBUSY in processing a MAINTAIN request when it has written enough modified pages so that the list is left with MPW_LOWAITLIMIT or fewer pages.

18.13.4.5   **Resource Wait for RSN$_MPLEMPTY (RWMPE).** A process in RWMPE is waiting for the modified page writer to signal that it has flushed the modified page list. The only process currently placed into this wait is one running the OPCCRASH image, which forces a flush of the modified page list prior to stopping the system.

18.14   RELEVANT SOURCE MODULES

Source modules described in this chapter include

    [SYS]ALLOCPFN.MAR
    [SYS]EXCEPTION.M64
    [SYS]EXCEPTION_ROUTINES.MAR
    [SYS]IOCIOPOST.MAR
    [SYS]IOLOCK.MAR
    [SYS]PAGEFAULT.MAR
    [SYS]PAGEFILE.MAR
    [SYS]SCHEDULER.M64
    [SYS]SYSLKWSET.MAR
    [SYS]SYSUPDSEC.MAR
    [SYS]WRTMFYPAG.MAR

19 Working Set List Dynamics

> "Then you keep moving round, I suppose?" said Alice.
>
> "Exactly so," said the Hatter, "as the things get used up."
>
> "But what happens when you come to the beginning again?"
> Alice ventured to ask.
>
> "Suppose we change the subject," the March Hare
> interrupted, yawning. "I'm getting tired of this. I vote the young
> lady tell us a story."
>
> Lewis Carroll, *Alice's Adventures in Wonderland*

The pages of physical memory in use by a process are called its working set. A data structure within the process header (PHD) called the working set list describes just those pages in a compact form.

This chapter describes the composition of the working set list, the ways in which it shrinks and expands to describe a varying number of pages, and the system services by which a process affects its working set and working set list.

19.1 OVERVIEW

The term *working set* refers to the virtual pages of a process that are currently valid and in physical memory. A valid page is one whose page table entry (PTE) valid bit is set.

As a process executes an image, it faults code, data, and page table pages into its working set. Chapter 18 describes the page fault mechanism in detail. Execution of asynchronous system trap (AST) procedures, condition handlers, and system services that touch pageable process space can cause additional faults into the working set. The working set continues to grow as the process faults pages until the process occupies as much physical memory as it requires or is allowed. Each subsequent page fault requires that a page be removed from the working set to make room for the new page.

The executive maintains a list of working set pages for each process, called the working set list. The list facilitates

- Selecting a page to remove from the working set when a process needs to fault in a page but already occupies all the physical memory it is currently allowed, or when the process's working set is being shrunk
- Determining which pages to write when a process is outswapped
- Determining which pages to read when a process is inswapped

Section 19.2 describes the structure and makeup of the working set list. Section 19.3 gives a detailed description of replacement paging, that is, removing one virtual page from the working set to make room for another.

The size of the working set list and the number of its entries constrain a process's use of physical memory. The working set list size varies over the process's lifetime. It can be affected by the authorization file entry for an interactive user, SYSGEN parameters, availability of physical memory, and the recent paging history of the process. Section 19.4 describes these effects, and Section 19.2.3 discusses the capacity of the working set list.

By requesting the following system services, a process can affect its own working set and working set list:

- Adjust Working Set Limit ($ADJWSL)
- Lock Pages in Working Set ($LKWSET)
- Lock Pages in Memory ($LCKPAG)
- Unlock Pages from Working Set ($ULWSET)
- Unlock Pages from Memory ($ULKPAG)
- Purge Working Set ($PURGWS)

These services are described in later sections of this chapter.

Section 19.9 explains the means by which a process can prevent the removal of a particular page from its working set.

Chapter 16 describes the system working set list. This chapter is primarily concerned with the process working set list, although much of it is equally applicable to the system working set list.

19.2 THE WORKING SET LIST

A process working set includes the process's P0 and P1 space pages and the system space pages that contain its PHD. The working set also includes global pages in use by the process. Each of these pages is described by a working set list entry (WSLE). Because the data structure containing the WSLEs, the working set list, is part of the PHD, the working set list is self-describing, containing WSLEs that describe the working set list itself as well as the other PHD pages.

Pages that are part of a section mapped by page frame number (PFN) are valid for the entire time the process maps such pages, and they do not appear in the working set list. The page containing a process's level 1 page table (L1PT) is dedicated to that use while the process is resident, but it has no virtual mapping and is not represented in the working set list.

19.2.1 The WSLE

The format of a valid WSLE is shown in Figure 19.1. Note that the upper bits are the same as the upper bits of a virtual address. (As described in Chapter 15, the format of a virtual address varies with processor page size. On a processor with an 8 KB page size, the upper 19 bits specify the address.) This allows the WSLE to be passed as a virtual address to several utility routines that ignore the byte offset bits (WSLE control bits). Table 19.1 shows

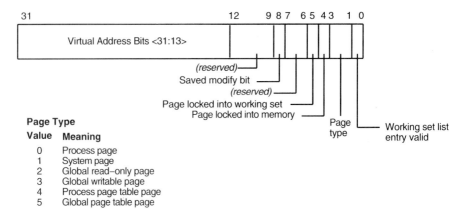

Figure 19.1
Format of a WSLE

the meanings of the WSLE control bits. The MACRO-32 macro $WSLDEF defines their symbolic values, which begin with the string WSL$V_.

19.2.2   Regions of the Working Set List

The working set list is divided into three regions: one containing entries for pages that are permanently locked; one containing entries for pages locked after process creation, chiefly by user request; and one containing dynamic entries. These regions are described in more detail later in this section.

Figure 19.2 shows the fields in the fixed portion of the PHD that describe the working set list. Many of them locate the different regions of the working set list through a longword index to a particular WSLE. For example, the following steps compute the address of the beginning of the working set list from the longword index in PHD$L_WSLIST:

1. Multiply the contents of PHD$L_WSLIST by 4.
2. Add the result to the address of the beginning of the PHD.

Three of the fields shown, PHD$L_DFWSCNT, PHD$L_WSQUOTA, and PHD$L_WSEXTENT, do not locate region boundaries but instead represent a number of WSLEs. These fields nonetheless contain longword indexes, providing easier comparison with fields that do locate boundaries. The following steps convert such a field into the number of WSLEs it represents:

1. Subtract the contents of PHD$L_WSLIST from it.
2. Add 1 to the result.

This chapter refers to the converted contents of a longword index field using its field name without the PHD$L_ prefix, for example, WSQUOTA. Note that names used in this way represent a number of WSLEs, or pages.

Table 19.1   WSLE Control Bits

Field Name	Meaning
VALID	When set, this bit indicates that the WSLE is in use.
PAGTYP	This field (a duplicate of the contents of the PFN$L_PAGE_STATE type bits) identifies the page type and specifies the action required when the page is removed from the working set.
PFNLOCK	When set, this bit indicates that the page has been locked into physical memory with the $LCKPAG system service.
WSLOCK	When set, this bit indicates one of the following types of page locked into the working set:

    ▸ Permanently locked page
    ▸ Page locked with the $LKWSET system service
    ▸ Process-private page table page that maps one or
      more valid or transition pages

MODIFY	This bit, used when the process is outswapped, records the logical OR of the modify bit in the PTE and the saved modify bit in the page's PFN$L_PAGE_STATE field.

Two of the fields shown, PHD$L_WSSIZE and PHD$L_EXTDYNWS, each contain an actual number of WSLEs. This chapter refers to their contents as WSSIZE and EXTDYNWS.

The permanently locked region of the working set list describes pages that are forever a part of the process working set. Pages whose WSLEs are in this region cannot be unlocked and are not candidates for working set replacement. They include the following:

▸ Kernel stack page or pages
▸ Page containing the P1 pointer area
▸ PHD pages that are not page table pages—the fixed portion, the PHD page arrays, the maximum process section table, and enough pages for a working set list of as many entries as the SYSGEN parameter PQL_DWSDEFAULT, converted from pagelets to pages
▸ The P1 level 3 page table (L3PT) that maps the kernel stack, the page containing the P1 pointer area, and the P1 window to the PHD (see Chapter 16)
▸ The process-private level 2 page table (L2PT) that maps P0 and P1 L3PTs

The value in PHD$L_WSLIST is a longword index to the first WSLE in this region. Its value, calculated during process creation, is the same for all processes running on a particular version of the operating system. Because

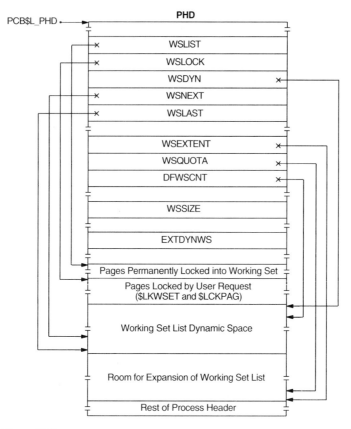

Figure 19.2
Working Set List

WSLIST represents a pointer to the beginning of the working set list, its value is simply a function of the size of the fixed PHD that precedes it.

The second region contains WSLEs for pages that are locked by user request, specifically through the $LKWSET and $LCKPAG system services. Pages whose WSLEs are in this region are not candidates for working set replacement. Any process-private page table page that maps a PFN-mapped section is also locked into this region of the working set list, as are PHD expansion pages resulting from working set list growth.

PHD$L_WSLOCK contains the longword index to the first WSLE in the locked region. PHD$L_WSDYN points to the WSLE immediately following the last WSLE in this region. To lock a page into the working set list, the executive swaps its WSLE with that pointed to by PHD$L_WSDYN and increments PHD$L_WSDYN. Consequently, the user-locked region is increased by one WSLE and the dynamic region is decreased by one.

The two locked regions of the working set list are completely filled with valid WSLEs. Rather than keep a count of locked pages, the executive can simply calculate the difference between the contents of PHD$L_WSDYN and PHD$L_WSLIST.

The dynamic region of the working set list describes process-private and global pages that have not been locked into the working set list and process-private page table pages. Process-private and global pages are candidates for working set replacement.

A process-private page table page that maps valid or transition pages is locked into this region of the working set list through the WSLOCK bit in the WSLE and is not a candidate for working set replacement while still locked. Page table pages locked in this manner remain in the dynamic region, although locked, for a number of reasons. They are considered dynamic because they are unlocked when all the valid and transition pages they map are removed from the working set. Leaving them in the dynamic region results in less CPU overhead than switching them into and out of the locked region. Note that a page table page that maps no valid or transition pages other than buffer object pages is not locked into the working set list. Chapter 17 provides further information.

The dynamic region begins at the entry identified by the contents of PHD$L_WSDYN. PHD$L_WSLAST contains the longword index for the last WSLE; its contents identify the end of the dynamic region. The dynamic region is treated as a ring buffer for page replacement. The entry most recently inserted into the working set list is pointed to by PHD$L_WSNEXT. The entry following it is the point in the ring buffer at which page replacement typically occurs. The page replacement algorithm, explained in Section 19.3, is a modified first-in/first-out (FIFO) scheme.

The dynamic region of the working set list is not necessarily dense; there may be empty entries between those specified by PHD$L_WSDYN and PHD$L_WSLAST.

19.2.3   Size of the Working Set List

Three critical parameters govern the dynamics of the working set list: size, limit, and capacity (see Figure 19.3).

The process's working set size is the number of WSLEs currently in use. No single field contains this value; instead, it is the sum of two separately maintained counts, PCB$L_PPGCNT and PCB$L_GPGCNT.

The maximum number of WSLEs the process is allowed to use is known as its working set limit. It is maintained in a field that is somewhat confusingly called PHD$L_WSSIZE. Despite its name, it contains the working set limit, not the size (which is the sum of the two fields listed in the previous paragraph).

The amount of memory allocated in the PHD for the working set list varies during the life of a process. The amount of memory currently allocated in the PHD for the working set list (PHD$L_WSLAST minus PHD$L_WSLIST,

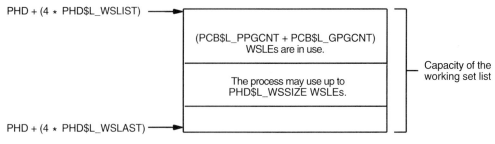

PHD + (4 * PHD$L_WSLIST)

(PCB$L_PPGCNT + PCB$L_GPGCNT)
WSLEs are in use.

The process may use up to
PHD$L_WSSIZE WSLEs.

Capacity of the
working set list

PHD + (4 * PHD$L_WSLAST)

Figure 19.3
Working Set List Parameters

plus 1) is referred to in this chapter as the working set list capacity. When the capacity increases, the working set list data structure itself may grow and consume more physical memory.

When the working set limit is reduced, the working set list capacity is not necessarily altered. The working set list simply becomes more sparsely populated with valid WSLEs and more heavily populated with invalid WSLEs.

Table 19.2 shows process-specific and systemwide working set list parameters, quotas, and limits. Note that for compatibility with OpenVMS VAX, user authorization file quotas and SYSGEN parameters related to the working set list are typically specified externally in units of pagelets and converted to pages for internal use by the executive.

During system initialization enough virtual address space is reserved in each PHD for the maximum-size working set list, one with as many entries as the number of pages represented by the SYSGEN parameter WSMAX.

Each process is created with its initial working set limit and working set list capacity set to the same value, the process's default working set limit, DFWSCNT (assuming that DFWSCNT is less than or equal to WSMAX converted to pages). For a typical interactive process, DFWSCNT is specified by the user authorization file (UAF) entry. The executive thus initially allocates physical memory for only a relatively small working set list.

When a process runs an image, it begins faulting pages; the working set size increases, growing toward the working set limit. Once it reaches the limit, subsequent page faults require the removal of pages from the working set. With the working set limit, the executive governs the amount of physical memory a process may use.

The process can increase its default working set limit through the Digital command language (DCL) command SET WORKING_SET. A running image can increase the process's current working set limit by requesting the $ADJWSL system service. The executive can increase a process's working set limit through automatic working set limit adjustment. These mechanisms are discussed in Section 19.4.

Table 19.2   Working Set Lists: Limits and Quotas

Description	*Location or Name*	*Comments*
Working set limit	PHD$L_WSSIZE	Set by LOGINOUT; Altered by $ADJWSL; Altered by automatic working set limit adjustment, image exit, swapper trimming
Working set size in pages	PCB$L_PPGCNT + PCB$L_GPGCNT	Updated each time a page is added to or removed from the working set; Reduced by proactive memory reclamation
Index of last WSLE (determines capacity of list)	PHD$L_WSLAST	May be altered by $ADJWSL, page fault handler, image exit, or automatic working set limit adjustment
Index of first WSLE	PHD$L_WSLIST	The same for all processes on all systems of the same version
Index of first locked WSLE	PHD$L_WSLOCK	The same for all processes in a given system
Index of first dynamic WSLE	PHD$L_WSDYN	Altered by $LKWSET, $LCKPAG, $ULWSET, and $ULKPAG
Index of most recently inserted WSLE	PHD$L_WSNEXT	Updated each time an entry is added to or released from working set
Default working set limit	PHD$L_DFWSCNT	Set by LOGINOUT; Altered by DCL command SET WORKING_ SET/LIMIT
Normal maximum working set limit (index)	PHD$L_WSQUOTA	Set by LOGINOUT; Altered by DCL command SET WORKING_ SET/QUOTA
Extended maximum working set limit (index)	PHD$L_WSEXTENT	Set by LOGINOUT; Altered by DCL command SET WORKING_ SET/EXTENT
Upper limit to normal maximum working set limit (index)	PHD$L_WSAUTH	Set by LOGINOUT; Cannot be altered

(continued)

Table 19.2   Working Set Lists: Limits and Quotas *(continued)*

Description	Location or Name	Comments
Upper limit to extended maximum working set limit (index)	PHD$L_WSAUTHEXT	Set by LOGINOUT; Cannot be altered
Sufficient number of dynamic WSLEs for a process to execute without continuous faults	PHD$L_WSFLUID	Set by SHELL to the value of MINWSCNT
Number of dynamic WSLEs not counting PHD$L_WSFLUID process pages and a reasonable number of page table pages	PHD$L_EXTDYNWS	Updated each time size of dynamic working set region is changed
Authorized default working set limit in pagelets	UAF$L_DFWSCNT	Converted to pages and copied to PHD$L_DFWSCNT
Authorized normal maximum working set limit in pagelets	UAF$L_WSQUOTA	Converted to pages and copied to PHD$L_WSAUTH and PHD$L_WSQUOTA
Authorized extended maximum working set limit in pagelets	UAF$L_WSEXTENT	Converted to pages and copied to PHD$L_WSEXTENT and PHD$L_WSAUTHEXT
Systemwide minimum number of fluid working set pages	MINWSCNT	SYSGEN parameter
Systemwide maximum working set limit in pagelets	WSMAX	SYSGEN parameter
System working set limit in pagelets	SYSMWCNT	SYSGEN parameter
Default value for working set limit default in pagelets (used by $CREPRC)	PQL_DWSDEFAULT	SYSGEN parameter
Minimum value for working set limit default in pagelets (used by $CREPRC)	PQL_MWSDEFAULT	SYSGEN parameter
Default value for normal maximum working set limit in pagelets (used by $CREPRC)	PQL_DWSQUOTA	SYSGEN parameter

Table 19.2   Working Set Lists: Limits and Quotas *(continued)*

Description	Location or Name	Comments
Minimum value for normal maximum working set limit in pagelets (used by $CREPRC)	PQL_MWSQUOTA	SYSGEN parameter
Default value for extended maximum working set limit in pagelets (used by $CREPRC)	PQL_DWSEXTENT	SYSGEN parameter
Minimum value for extended maximum working set limit in pagelets (used by $CREPRC)	PQL_MWSEXTENT	SYSGEN parameter

Whenever the working set limit would exceed the working set list capacity, the capacity must grow as well to accommodate the new limit. As described in Chapter 16, the working set list capacity is dynamic; it grows toward the process section table (PST). When the working set list must expand into the area already occupied by the PST, the PST is moved to higher addresses. However, there is not always room in the PHD for the expanded working set list. The total space available for both the working set list and the PST is determined by the two SYSGEN parameters WSMAX and PROCSECTCNT. Because a process is allowed to create more than PROC-SECTCNT sections, the PST can grow into space that would have been available for the working set list. In that case, the working set list capacity can grow no further, and the process must make do with its current capacity.

Furthermore, because the working set list contains WSLEs for all the PHD pages in physical memory, its size and the size of the PHD are interrelated. As the working set grows, the working set list in the PHD grows, and more WSLEs are required to describe the PHD pages in memory. The size of the PHD (excluding the page table pages) is constrained to be no larger in pages than half of the process's working set quota. This constraint preserves a reasonable number of WSLEs for non-PHD pages. A process with a large value for working set extent and a relatively small value for working set quota may have the expansion of its working set limited by this constraint.

The process's working set size decreases as the result of its deleting virtual address space (explicitly or, for example, at image exit) and requesting the

$PURGWS system service. The executive may reduce the working set size of a long-waiting process or a periodically waking process to reclaim memory for an insufficiently large free page list. This mechanism, called proactive memory reclamation, and the conditions that trigger it are described in Chapters 13 and 20. A process's working set size can also decrease as an effect of having its working set limit decreased below its working set size.

A programmer with a good understanding of an image's paging behavior can voluntarily reduce the process's working set limit by requesting the $ADJWSL system service. There are several other less direct mechanisms by which the working set limit is decreased:

▶ Automatic working set limit adjustment can reduce the limit (see Section 19.4.3).

▶ The swapper process can initiate a reduction of the working set limit with a mechanism known as swapper trimming or working set shrinking. In an effort to acquire needed physical memory, the swapper reduces the working sets and working set limits of processes in the balance set before actually removing processes from the balance set. Process selection is performed by a table-driven, prioritized scheme. Chapter 20 describes the conditions that trigger this mechanism and the criteria by which processes are selected. (Swapper trimming differs from proactive memory reclamation in that the latter reduces the working set size but not the limit.)

▶ The process working set limit is also reset at image exit to its default value, DFWSCNT (see Chapter 28).

At image exit, in addition to reducing the process's working set limit, the executive may reduce the working set list capacity; if possible, the executive resets PHD$L_WSLAST by moving it toward lower addresses past any invalid WSLEs. It continues until it reaches a valid WSLE or until the working set list capacity is just equal to the working set limit. Additionally, when the executive is scanning the working set list to find an entry for a page being faulted, it may move PHD$L_WSLAST in the same way, compressing invalid entries at the high-address end of the working set list. The executive must strike a balance between spending too much overhead compressing empty entries so that PHD$L_WSLAST is precise and spending too much overhead searching for a valid replacement WSLE when the working set list is sparse (see Section 19.3.1).

The executive guarantees a minimum size for the dynamic region of the working set list. Although most Alpha AXP instructions generate few memory references, the executive must ensure that an instruction that references memory can execute. All the pages referenced in an instruction must be valid for the instruction to complete execution. If the dynamic region of the working set is too small, an infinite page fault loop could occur during the attempted execution of one instruction. An instruction could begin to execute, incur a page fault, restart, incur a different page fault, replace the first faulted page in the working set list, restart, reincur the first page fault, and so on, unable to complete execution. More realistically, the dynamic region of the working set should be large enough to allow a typical image to make reasonable progress without continual page faults.

During system initialization the SYSGEN parameters that affect minimum working set sizes are adjusted to allow for at least this minimum. That is, SYSBOOT ensures that the values of PQL_MWSDEFAULT and PQL_DWSDEFAULT represent a number of pages large enough to accommodate the sum of the following:

▸ The SYSGEN parameter MINWSCNT, the minimum number of fluid pages in the working set
▸ The worst-case number of page table pages to map MINWSCNT pages, namely, MINWSCNT
▸ The maximum process header, not counting page table pages
▸ The kernel stack page or pages
▸ The page containing the P1 pointer area
▸ The minimum number of page tables to map the P1 space defined by the SHELL*xx* module

Subsequently, the executive checks that the dynamic working set list has enough space whenever it adjusts the working set limit or locks pages into the working set list. For a typical process and address space, the executive checks that the number of dynamic WSLEs is at least twice MINWSCNT. In this check, it ignores any working set list extension above WSQUOTA, since any extension above quota is subject to swapper trimming. To facilitate the check, the executive maintains the field PHD$L_EXTDYNWS, which effectively contains the number of WSLEs in the dynamic region of the working set list beyond the minimum number required. The calculation of PHD$L_EXTDYNWS is based upon a working set no bigger than WSQUOTA.

For example, when a process tries to lock a page into its working set list, the executive checks that PHD$L_EXTDYNWS has a value of at least 2, one entry for the page and another for its page table page.

The manner in which a process is created determines how values for WSQUOTA and WSEXTENT are defined. They are defined and potentially redefined several times during different steps of process creation. In the case of the typical interactive process, the values come from its authorization file record and are minimized with WSMAX. Chapters 27 and 30 supply further information.

19.3   WORKING SET REPLACEMENT

When a process references an invalid virtual page, the page fault handler must take steps to make the page valid. It must also create a WSLE for the page. If there is no room in the working set list for another entry, one must be removed. The page fault handler uses the dynamic region of the working set list to determine which virtual page to discard.

The dynamic region of the working set list can contain unused WSLEs. When the working set limit is reduced, the working set list capacity is usually left intact, resulting in a sparse working set list. This makes adding a page to the working set slightly more complex. That a WSLE is empty does not necessarily mean the process can make use of it; the size of the working set must be less than the working set limit. If the process is already at its limit, a nonempty WSLE must be found whose virtual page can be removed from the working set to make room for the new page.

The executive uses a modified FIFO scheme for its working set list replacement algorithm. The entry most likely to have been in the working set list for the longest time, the one following that pointed to by PHD$L_WSNEXT, is the one first considered for replacement.

19.3.1 Scan of the Working Set List

When the page fault handler needs an empty WSLE, it invokes routine MMG$FREWSLE, in module PAGEFAULT. The following steps summarize its flow. Subsequent sections describe more details of particular aspects of its flow.

MMG$FREWSLE scans the working set list. It begins by checking whether the WSLE whose index is in PHD$L_WSNEXT is empty. If not, it starts with the next WSLE.

1. If the WSLE is empty (contents are zero), MMG$FREWSLE checks whether the entry can be used (see Section 19.3.2). If it can be used, it is selected.

2. If the WSLE is not empty (contents are nonzero) but is an active page table page (one that maps valid pages), the WSLE cannot be used.

3. If the WSLE is not empty but is a process-private page table page that maps no valid pages, it may be usable. MMG$FREWSLE takes the steps described in Section 19.3.3 to determine whether the page table page can be released and its WSLE reused.

4. If the WSLE is not empty and is not a process-private page table page, MMG$FREWSLE makes additional checks to see whether the WSLE is suitable for reuse. If not, the WSLE is skipped (see Section 19.3.4).

5. If the WSLE is selected for reuse and is not empty, MMG$FREWSLE takes the actions described in Section 19.3.5.

6. If the WSLE is not selected, the index is incremented, and the steps in this list are repeated until a usable WSLE is found. If the index exceeds the end of the list, it is reset to the beginning of the dynamic working set list.

Once a WSLE is selected for reuse, PHD$L_WSNEXT is updated to contain its longword index.

19.3.2   **Using an Empty Entry in the Working Set List**

When an empty WSLE is found, MMG$FREWSLE checks whether a page can be added to the working set. If there are fewer pages in the working set than WSQUOTA, a new physical page may be added to the working set. It may also be possible to add physical pages to the working set above WSQUOTA (up to WSEXTENT), depending on the size of the free page list.

The following checks are required for an empty WSLE to be usable:

1. If the working set size (PCB$L_PPGCNT plus PCB$L_GPGCNT) equals the working set limit, the empty WSLE may not be used, and a page in the working set must be replaced.
2. If the working set size has not reached its limit, the size is compared to WSQUOTA. If the size is less than WSQUOTA, a new page is allowed into the working set. The empty WSLE is used.
3. If the working set has WSQUOTA or more pages, the number of pages on the free page list is compared to the SYSGEN parameter GROWLIM. If there are more than GROWLIM pages on the free page list, a new page is allowed into the working set. The empty WSLE is used.

   Note that to extend the working set size above WSQUOTA, the working set limit must have been extended above WSQUOTA. For the working set limit to be extended above WSQUOTA, the free page list must contain more than the SYSGEN parameter BORROWLIM pages. For more information on working set limits, BORROWLIM, and automatic working set limit adjustment, see Section 19.4.

If an empty but unusable WSLE is found at the end of a working set list that has reached its limit, the working set list capacity is reduced; PHD$L_WSLAST is reset to point to the last unavailable (nonzero) WSLE in the working set list.

19.3.3   **Releasing a Dead Page Table Page**

MMG$FREWSLE invokes SCANDEADPT, in module PAGEFAULT, to determine whether a WSLE describing a page table page can be reused to describe a page being faulted into the working set list. There are several possible outcomes:

▶ The WSLE describes a page table page that maps valid pages and is therefore not reusable.
▶ The WSLE describes a page table page that maps transition pages and can be released from its current use for reuse after the ties between the transition pages and the page table page are severed, that is, after no virtual pages mapped by the page table page are cached in the free or modified page list.
▶ The WSLE describes such a reusable page table page, but the working set list contains enough dynamic entries that this one need not be released now. An attempt is made to leave a page table page in the working set list

to keep its virtual pages cached on page lists, in case the process refaults them.

SCANDEADPT first determines whether the process has any dead page table pages. A dead page table page is one that maps no valid pages. It may, however, map pages on the free or modified page list. SCANDEADPT checks this by comparing PHD$L_PTCNTVAL, the number of page table pages with valid WSLEs, to PHD$L_PTCNTACT, the number of active page table pages. If PHD$L_PTCNTACT is larger than PHD$L_PTCNTVAL, the difference between them is the number of dead page table pages. If there are none, SCANDEADPT returns immediately. MMG$FREWSLE skips this WSLE and continues its scan of the working set list.

If there are any dead page table pages, SCANDEADPT checks how full the working set list is. It checks whether the dynamic region of the working set list has at least twice MINWSCNT entries, not counting those that describe dead page table pages or page table pages that map pages locked into memory or into the working set list. If so, it has sufficient dynamic entries; the dead page table page scan is postponed, and SCANDEADPT returns. MMG$FREWSLE skips this WSLE and continues its scan of the working set list.

If there are not sufficient dynamic WSLEs to leave a potentially dead page table page in the working set list, SCANDEADPT checks whether this page is a dead page table page. If the page's element in the PHD$L_PTWSLEVAL array is non-negative, the page table page maps pages in the working set list and cannot be released. SCANDEADPT returns, and MMG$FREWSLE goes on to the next WSLE.

Having determined that the WSLE describes a dead page table page, SCAN-DEADPT must scan each PTE within the page table page to determine whether it is a transition PTE. If the page table page contains transition PTEs for pages on the free page list, SCANDEADPT must modify the PFN database for those pages before the WSLE can be reused. It moves each such page to the front of the free page list and sets the delete contents bit in the page's PFN$L_PAGE_STATE field.

If the page table page contains transition PTEs for pages on the modified page list, those pages must be written to their backing store before the page table page can be released from the working set list. SCANDEADPT sets the delete contents bit in each page's PFN$L_PAGE_STATE field and requests a selective purge of the modified page list so that those pages will be written. SCANDEADPT returns to MMG$FREWSLE with a status indicating it should return to its invoker to wait. The process is placed into a resource wait for RSN$_PGFILE if any of the modified pages are backed by a page file that has not yet been initialized. The process is placed into a resource wait for RSN$_MPWBUSY until the modified page list is selectively purged. Chapter 18 describes the selective purge mechanism and the resource waits.

19.3.4 Skipping WSLEs

The operating system uses both frequency-of-use information maintained by the hardware and process-specific criteria to modify its strict FIFO page replacement algorithm. The working set replacement routine can skip a limited number of WSLEs with particular characteristics. The number is specified by the special SYSGEN parameter TBSKIPWSL.

The architecture defines a processor register related to translation buffer (TB) use called TB check (TBCHK). Kernel mode code can execute the instruction CALL_PAL MFPR, specifying the TBCHK register and a virtual address to determine whether the translation for a particular virtual page is cached. The presence of a TB entry for a page indicates the page has been referenced recently and may therefore be a poor candidate to remove from the working set.

Additionally, a process can declare a procedure to be notified of every pending removal from its working set list. The procedure can return a status indicating that this page is a poor choice. This mechanism is limited to kernel mode applications and is currently intended for support of a graphics subsystem. Accessing its own copy of the process page table, the graphics hardware determines how to treat a particular page based on its valid bit. The device driver for the graphics hardware requests notification of working set list removals so it can maintain the copy of the page table. If a page selected for removal is currently in use by the graphics hardware, the driver indicates that the page is a poor choice. Use of this mechanism is reserved to Digital; any other use is unsupported.

Kernel mode software running in process context, like the device driver just described, calls the routine MMG$DECLARE_WSL_PAGER, in module SYSLKWSET, with two arguments. One is the procedure value of a routine to be called when a page is about to be removed from that process's working set. The other is a parameter to be passed to that procedure. Because the working set list removal procedure may be called from outside the context of that process, the procedure must be within code loaded into system space. MMG$DECLARE_WSL_PAGER stores the procedure value in PCB$A_FREWSLE_CALLOUT and the parameter in PCB$L_FREWSLE_PARAM.

The modified working set list replacement algorithm works in the following manner. Before a valid WSLE is reused, a check is first made to see if a translation for the virtual page described by that WSLE is in the TB. If the translation for that page is cached in the TB, and fewer than TBSKIPWSL entries have been skipped during this scan of the working set list, MMG$FREWSLE skips that WSLE and resumes the search for an available WSLE with the next one.

If the translation is not cached in the TB, and if PCB$A_FREWSLE_CALLOUT is nonzero, MMG$FREWSLE calls the working set removal procedure with the specified parameter, the virtual address, a flag, and the addresses of the PCB and PHD. Initially the value of the flag is zero. If the procedure returns the status SS$_RETRY, MMG$FREWSLE skips that WSLE and resumes the search for an available WSLE with the next one.

After TBSKIPWSL WSLEs have been skipped in this manner, both checks are abandoned and the next valid WSLE is simply reused. First, however, if there is a working set removal procedure, MMG$FREWSLE calls it with a flag value indicating that the selected page will definitely be removed from the working set.

If the value of TBSKIPWSL is set to zero, the skipping of WSLEs is disabled; although the working set removal procedure is still called, it is called with the flag value indicating that the selected page will definitely be removed from the working set. The default value of TBSKIPWSL is 8.

19.3.5   Reusing WSLEs

The virtual page that the WSLE represents must be removed before the WSLE can be reused. Typically, the virtual page is valid and must be made invalid. This section confines itself to a description of valid WSLEs.

For such a page, MMG$FREWSLE takes the following steps:

1. If the page has been modified, MMG$FREWSLE tests whether its backing store is an uninitialized page file and how full the modified page list is.

   a. If the backing store is an uninitialized page file, MMG$FREWSLE proceeds with step c.

   b. If the modified page list has fewer pages than the SYSGEN parameter MPW_WAITLIMIT, or if modified page writing is in progress and the list has fewer pages than the SYSGEN parameter MPW_LOWAIT-LIMIT, MMG$FREWSLE proceeds with step 2.

   c. Otherwise, to avoid deadlocks, MMG$FREWSLE checks that the process does not hold any mutexes, that the process is not the swapper, that bit MMG$V_NOWAIT in MMG$GB_FREWFLGS is clear, and that at least one page file has been installed. If any condition is false, MMG$FREWSLE proceeds with step 2.

      If all are true, it returns a status to the page fault handler indicating that the process should be placed into a resource wait. The process is placed into the resource wait RSN$_PGFILE until a page file is installed or into the resource wait RSN$_MPWBUSY until the modified page list has dropped below MPW_LOWAITLIMIT pages.

2. At alternative entry point MMG$FREWSLX, the routine saves the modify bit from the associated PTE in the page's PFN$L_PAGE_STATE field. It clears the valid, modify, fault-on-execute, fault-on-write, and address space match bits in the PTE. If the fault-on-execute bit was set, it invalidates any cached copy of the PTE from the data stream translation

buffer (DTB). If the bit was clear, it invalidates any cached copy from either the instruction stream translation buffer (ITB) or the DTB (see Section 19.3.6).

3. If the page being removed is an L3PT, MMG$FREWSLX reinitializes the L2PTE that mapped it and removes any cached copy of the L2PTE from the DTB.

   If the page being removed is an L3PT that no longer maps any P0 or P1 address space, MMG$FREWSLX decrements its reference count, restores the system page table entry (SPTE) that mapped it to a demand zero PTE, deallocates the L3PT's backing store, and inserts the physical page on the zeroed page list.

   It proceeds with step 6.

4. If the page is a global page, MMG$FREWSLX changes the PTE to the global page table index form. It invokes MMG$DECPTREF, in module PAGEFAULT, to update the data structures describing the process page table page that maps the page.

   MMG$DECPTREF decrements the share count for the process page table page to indicate that it maps one less valid or transition page. If this was the last valid or transition page mapped by the page table page (that is, if the share count makes the transition from 1 to 0), MMG$DECPTREF locates the WSLE for the page table page and clears its WSL$V_WSLOCK bit. It also decrements PHD$L_PTCNTACT, the number of active page table pages for the process, and the PHD's entry in the array at PHV$GL_REFCBAS, the number of reasons the PHD should remain in memory.

   MMG$FREWSLX decrements the share count for the global page to indicate one less process is mapping it. If the count is still nonzero, MMG$FREWSLX proceeds with step 6. If the count goes to zero, it clears the valid, modify, fault-on-write, fault-on-execute, and address space match bits in the global page table entry (GPTE).

5. For a page that is a process page or a global page with a zero share count, MMG$FREWSLX decrements the reference count for the page to indicate one less reference to it.

   If the reference count goes to zero, it invokes MMG$REL_PFN, in module ALLOCPFN, to insert the page at the end of the free or modified page list, depending on the state of its saved modify bit. If the page has been modified and has an assigned page file backing store, MMG$REL_PFN releases its backing store, which has a now-obsolete copy of the page. The PFN$Q_BAK field is reset to a process-local page file index and a page number of zero.

   If the reference count is nonzero, indicating possible direct or paging I/O in progress, MMG$FREWSLX examines the PFN$L_PAGE_STATE field and, if the page is not active, changes its state to release pending.

6. MMG$FREWSLX invokes MMG$DELWSLEX, in module PAGEFAULT.

MMG$DELWSLEX decrements the appropriate element in the PHD$L_PTWSLEVAL array to indicate the page table page that mapped this page maps one less valid page. If that count goes to –1, it also decrements PHD$L_PTCNTVAL to indicate one less page table page mapping valid pages. It decrements either PCB$L_PPGCNT or PCB$L_GPGCNT, depending on page type. It clears the WSLE and returns.

7. MMG$FREWSLX returns to its invoker.

19.3.6   TB Invalidation

As described in Chapter 15, a TB is a CPU component that caches the results of recent successful virtual address translations of valid pages. Each TB entry caches one translation: a virtual page number and, minimally, its corresponding PFN, address space match, and protection bits. The size and organization of a TB are CPU-specific. Some CPUs have both an ITB and a DTB.

The operating system is responsible for flushing stale, no longer correct, entries from the TB. For example, it must invalidate a TB entry corresponding to a no longer valid PTE that maps a page being deleted or removed from a process's working set. It must also invalidate the TB entry for a valid page whose protection is changing.

Each process has its own virtual address space, and all TB entries are process-specific. System virtual space, however, is shared and mapped by all processes. A PTE and a TB entry that represent such a page are identified by a set address space match bit. Because a process runs on only one processor at a time, its process-private TB entries, those with a clear address space match bit, need be flushed only from the TB of the processor on which the process is running.

Some CPU types support a feature called address space number (ASN), whereby a TB entry is tagged with a number identifying the process whose address space translation the TB entry represents. ASN is a CPU-specific designation; although each member of a symmetric multiprocessing (SMP) system uses the same range of ASNs, a specific ASN on one CPU does not necessarily represent the same virtual address space as that ASN on another CPU. On a CPU that supports ASNs, the current process's ASN is an implicit input for all TB lookups and invalidation of single TB entries.

On a CPU that does not support ASNs, process-private entries are flushed from the TB whenever process context is switched. On a CPU that does support ASNs, process-private entries are not flushed at context swap. Instead, the executive must flush them explicitly by writing to the TB invalidate all process entries (TBIAP) processor register. Chapter 13 describes how the executive assigns ASNs and determines when to flush process-private entries.

Executive modules typically invalidate TB entries through one of several MACRO-32 macros.

▸ TBI_ALL—Invalidate all TB entries.

▸ TBI_SINGLE and TBI_SINGLE_64—Invalidate a single entry from both the ITB and the DTB.

▸ TBI_DATA_64—Invalidate a single DTB entry for a page whose fault-on-execute bit is still set.

Each of the macros that invalidate single entries includes an argument to specify the virtual address to be invalidated. All the listed macros have an ENVIRON argument whose default value is MP. If one of the macros is invoked with the ENVIRON argument specified as LOCAL, the macro merely generates a CALL_PAL MTPR instruction whose processor register depends on the macro. (Chapter 15 lists the processor registers associated with TB invalidation.) These macros are invoked this way when the virtual address is known to be process-private, one whose address space match bit is clear.

As described in Chapter 15, the executive sets the fault-on-execute bit in the PTE of each page faulted as the result of a data fetch. If an attempt is made to execute an instruction from the page, a fault-on-execute exception occurs. The exception service routine clears the fault-on-execute bit. When the fault-on-execute bit is still set for a page whose TB entries must be invalidated, the executive invokes the TBI_DATA_64 macro because there can be no ITB entry for the page.

On an SMP system, each CPU has its own TB. Although each CPU executes a different process, a shared page accessed from different processes at the same virtual address can be represented in multiple processors' TBs. When the executive changes the L3PTE of a valid page whose address space match bit is set, it is responsible for invalidating the page in all processors' TBs. In practice, only system space pages have the address space match bit set.

To invalidate a TB entry for a page whose address space match bit is set, the executive invokes the appropriate TB invalidate macro and explicitly specifies the ENVIRON argument as MP or implicitly specifies it that way by omitting the argument. When the macro ENVIRON argument has a value of MP, code is generated that transfers control to one of several subroutines in module PAGEFAULT:

▸ MMG$TBI_ALL

▸ MMG$TBI_SINGLE and MMG$TBI_SINGLE_64

▸ MMG$TBI_DATA_64

Each of these subroutines tests whether SMP is enabled and, if not, merely executes a CALL_PAL MTPR instruction specifying the appropriate processor register. If SMP is enabled, each subroutine calls either MP_INVALIDATE or MP_INVALIDATE_DATA, in module PAGEFAULT. Chapter 37 describes these routines and the means by which one processor notifies the other members to flush one or all TB entries.

19.4 WORKING SET LIMIT ADJUSTMENT

A process's working set limit (see Table 19.2) varies over its lifetime as a result of events such as image execution and exit, dynamic working set limit adjustment, and swapper trimming.

The working set limit can be altered with the $ADJWSL system service. Requested explicitly by the process, the system service can alter the working set limit up to WSEXTENT.

The service can also be requested automatically on behalf of the process, for example, as part of the quantum-end routine when it performs automatic working set limit adjustment. Through this means, the maximum size to which the working set limit can grow is WSQUOTA, unless there are sufficient pages on the free page list (more than the SYSGEN parameter BORROWLIM). In that case, automatic working set limit adjustment can enlarge the limit up to WSEXTENT.

Once the working set limit is increased, if there are more than the SYSGEN parameter GROWLIM pages on the free page list, the executive allows the process to use the extended limit by adding more pages to its working set without removing already valid entries. Adding pages to a process's working set decreases the probability that the process will incur a page fault.

Section 19.4.3 describes the automatic working set limit adjustment mechanism.

19.4.1 $ADJWSL System Service

The $ADJWSL system service is requested to alter the process's working set limit by a number of pagelets. Its procedure, EXE$ADJWSL in module SYSADJWSL, runs in kernel mode, at interrupt priority level (IPL) 2 and above. EXE$ADJWSL first converts its input argument from pagelets to pages, rounding up if necessary. It then determines whether the request is to increase or reduce the limit.

To increase the limit, EXE$ADJWSL first checks and possibly reduces the size of the increase. The new limit must be less than or equal to the value of the SYSGEN parameter WSMAX, converted from units of pagelets to pages; less than or equal to the process's extended maximum working set limit; and within the system's physical memory capacity.

If the new working set limit is within the current capacity of the working set list, EXE$ADJWSL computes a new value for PHD$L_EXTDYNWS and returns. Otherwise, EXE$ADJWSL first invokes MMG$ALCPHD, in module PHDUTL, to increase the working set list capacity.

MMG$ALCPHD tests whether there is a gap between the high-address end of the working set list and the low-address end of the PST that is large enough for the working set list expansion. If not, it tries to compress enough unused entries from the low-address end of the PST to accommodate the expansion. If that also fails, MMG$ALCPHD tries to shift the PST to higher addresses by moving it to as yet unused pages of the PHD. As previously described, the PHD cannot be expanded in this manner if the number of pages in the nonpageable part of the current PHD is half the size of the process's WSQUOTA.

If expanded working set list pages are created, they must be locked into the working set list. It is possible that locking all the expansion pages at once would leave insufficient extra dynamic entries in the existing working set list. However, if the working set list were partially expanded, the number of dynamic entries would increase, allowing more expansion pages to be locked. Thus, expanding the working set limit may require multiple iterations.

MMG$ALCPHD returns the number of entries by which it increased the capacity of the working set list. If no increase was possible, it returns zero.

If MMG$ALCPHD added any new entries, EXE$ADJWSL changes PHD$L_WSNEXT to point to the first of the newly added WSLEs and clears the WSLEs to initialize them. It adds the number of new WSLEs to both PHD$L_WSLAST and PHD$L_WSSIZE. It recalculates PHD$L_EXTDYNWS and returns to its requestor.

To decrease the limit, EXE$ADJWSL first acquires the MMG spinlock, raising IPL to IPL$_MMG, to block swapper trimming and possible quantum-end and working set limit adjustment. It invokes MMG$SHRINKWS, in module SYSADJWSL.

MMG$SHRINKWS checks and possibly reduces the size of the decrease. The new limit must allow for at least the SYSGEN parameter MINWSCNT WSLEs in the dynamic portion of the working set list. In addition, PHD$L_EXTDYNWS cannot be reduced below zero.

MMG$SHRINKWS modifies the working set limit. If the process's working set size is already less than or equal to the new limit, it simply returns to EXE$ADJWSL. Otherwise, MMG$SHRINKWS repeatedly invokes MMG$FREWSLE (see Section 19.3.1), in module PAGEFAULT, for each page to be removed from the process's working set. The reduced list can be sparse, that is, can contain unused and unusable WSLEs; the working set capacity is not necessarily decreased with the working set limit. Control returns to EXE$ADJWSL.

EXE$ADJWSL releases the spinlock, recalculates PHD$L_EXTDYNWS, and returns.

19.4.2 SET WORKING_SET Command

The DCL command SET WORKING_SET enables the user to alter the default working set limit (DFWSCNT), the normal maximum working set limit (WSQUOTA), or the extended maximum working set limit (WSEXTENT). None of these can be set to a value larger than the authorized extended maximum working set limit (WSAUTHEXT). For OpenVMS VAX compatibility, the command's qualifiers are expressed in units of pagelets.

Altering the default limit affects the working set list reset operation per-formed by the routine MMG$IMGRESET, in module PHDUTL, which is in-voked at image exit. Altering the normal maximum working set limit affects the maximum working set limit when physical memory is not plentiful. It changes the upper limit for future $ADJWSL system service requests.

With the /[NO]ADJUST qualifier to this command, a user can also disable or reenable automatic working set limit adjustment. Use of that qualifier sets or clears the process control block (PCB) status longword bit PCB$V_DISAWS.

19.4.3   Automatic Working Set Limit Adjustment

In addition to adjusting working set limit through an explicit $ADJWSL re-quest or as a side effect of image exit, the executive also provides automatic working set limit adjustment to keep a process's page fault rate within lim-its set by one of several SYSGEN parameters. Note that no such adjustment takes place for real-time processes or for a process that has disabled auto-matic working set limit adjustment through the DCL command SET WORK-ING_SET/NOADJUST. The executive can also use automatic working set limit adjustment to reclaim an extension to the working set of a low-priority process.

Table 19.3 shows the parameters that control automatic working set limit adjustment. All the SYSGEN parameters listed in this table are dynamic and can be altered without rebooting the system.

The automatic working set limit adjustment takes place as part of the quantum-end routine (see Chapter 13).

The quantum-end routine, SCH$QEND in module RSE, adjusts the work-ing set limit in several steps:

1. It makes the following checks, and if any of these conditions is true, SCH$QEND performs no adjustment.

    • If the process's priority is in the real-time range, adjustment of this process is disabled.
    • If the user has entered the DCL command SET WORKING_SET/NO-ADJUST, PCB$V_DISAWS is set and automatic working set limit ad-justment for the process has been disabled.
    • If PHD$V_NO_WS_CHNG is set, the executive has temporarily blocked changes to the working set list of this process.
    • If the WSINC parameter is set to zero, the adjustment is disabled on a systemwide basis.

2. If the process has not been executing long enough since the last ad-justment (if the difference between accumulated CPU time, PHD$L_CPUTIM, and the time of the last adjustment attempt, PHD$L_TIMREF,

Table 19.3 Process and System Parameters Used by Automatic Working Set Limit Adjustment

Description	Location or Name	Comments
Total amount of CPU time charged to this process	PHD$L_CPUTIM	Updated by interval timer interrupt service routine
Amount of CPU time at last adjustment check	PHD$L_TIMREF	Updated by quantum-end routine when adjustment check is made; Altered when process is placed into a wait
Total number of page faults for this process	PHD$L_PAGEFLTS	Updated each time this process incurs a page fault
Number of page faults at last adjustment check	PHD$L_PFLREF	Updated by quantum-end routine when adjustment check is made
Most recent page fault rate for this process	PHD$L_PFLTRATE	Recorded at each adjustment check; Compared to PFRATH and PFRATL
Process automatic working set limit adjustment flag	PCB$V_DISAWS in PCB$L_STS	When set, disables adjustment for process
Amount of CPU time process must accumulate before page fault rate check is made	AWSTIME [1]	
Lower limit page fault rate	PFRATL [1]	When 0, disables adjustment based on page fault rate for entire system
Number of pagelets by which to decrease working set limit	WSDEC [1]	Also, amount to reclaim from low-priority process with extended working set
Lower bound in pagelets for decreasing working set list size	AWSMIN [1]	Do not adjust if PCB$L_PPGCNT is less than or equal to this
Upper limit page fault rate	PFRATH [1]	
Number of pagelets by which to increase working set limit	WSINC [1]	When 0, disables adjustment for entire system

(continued)

Table 19.3 Process and System Parameters Used by Automatic Working Set Limit Adjustment *(continued)*

Description	Location or Name	Comments
Free page list size that allows growth of working set	GROWLIM [1]	Add new page to working set only if free page list has more pages than this value
Free page list size that allows extension of working set limit	BORROWLIM [1]	Extend working set limit beyond WSQUOTA only if free page list has more pages than this value; When −1, disables working set limit extension for entire system

[1] This value is a SYSGEN parameter.

is less than the SYSGEN parameter AWSTIME), no adjustment based on page fault rate is made. SCH$QEND proceeds with step 5.

If the process has accumulated enough CPU time, the reference time is updated (PHD$L_CPUTIM is copied to PHD$L_TIMREF), and the rate checks are made.

Between adjustment checks, PHD$L_TIMREF is also altered when the process is placed in a wait. As described in Chapter 13, when a process goes into a wait, the SYSGEN parameter IOTA is charged against its quantum. To balance the quantum charge, IOTA is subtracted from PHD$L_TIMREF, so that the last check for adjustment appears to have taken place longer ago than it really did and AWSTIME is more quickly reached. This subtraction helps ensure the expansion of the working set limit of a process that is faulting heavily. Without it, a process that undergoes many page fault waits could reach quantum end without having accumulated AWSTIME worth of CPU time and thus not be considered for automatic working set limit adjustment.

3. SCH$QEND calculates the current page fault rate. The philosophy for automatic working set limit adjustment is based on two premises. If the page fault rate is low enough, the system can reclaim physical memory from the process, by reducing its working set limit, without harming the process by causing it to fault heavily. If the page fault rate is too high, the process can benefit from a larger working set limit because it will incur fewer faults without degrading the system.

4. If the page fault rate is too high (greater than or equal to PFRATH), SCH$QEND checks if the working set limit should be increased.

- If the working set size is less than 75 percent of the current working set limit, the working set limit is not expanded.
- If the current working set limit is below WSQUOTA, it is expanded by WSINC, converted to pages.
- If the working set limit is greater than or equal to WSQUOTA, the number of pages on the free page list is compared to the SYSGEN parameter BORROWLIM.

    If there are BORROWLIM or more pages on the free page list, the working set limit is increased by WSINC, converted to pages. It can be increased to a maximum limit of WSEXTENT.

    If there are fewer than BORROWLIM pages on the free page list, the working set limit is not increased.

    Setting BORROWLIM to −1 disables working set limit expansion above WSQUOTA for the entire system.

    Once the working set limit has been expanded, newly faulted pages may be added to the working set. The page fault handler adds pages to the working set above WSQUOTA only when there are more than the SYSGEN parameter GROWLIM pages on the free page list.
    SCH$QEND proceeds with step 6.

5. If WSDEC is zero, shrinking the working set by automatic working set limit adjustment is disabled and no adjustment occurs. If WSDEC is nonzero, two types of decrease to the working set limit are possible.

    First, if the current page fault rate is low enough (less than PFRATL), the working set limit is shrunk by WSDEC, converted to pages. However, if the contents of PCB$L_PPGCNT are less than or equal to AWSMIN, no adjustment takes place. This decision is based on the assumption that many of the pages in the working set are global pages and therefore the system will not benefit (and the process may suffer) if the working set limit is decreased.

    Note that PFRATL is zero by default. This default value effectively disables this method of working set limit reduction in favor of swapper working set trimming. The rationale for this change is explained at the end of this list.

    Second, even if a meaningful interval has not elapsed for computing a page fault rate, the process's working set limit will be shrunk, whatever its page fault rate and whatever the value of PFRATL, if all the following are true:

    - The process has had a pixscan priority boost in its last 32 execution quantums (PCB$L_PIXHIST is nonzero). Chapter 13 describes the pixscan mechanism.
    - The free page list contains fewer than GROWLIM pages.
    - The process's working set limit is larger than WSQUOTA.

    Its working set limit will be decreased by the smaller of WSDEC, converted to pages, and the amount by which its working set limit exceeds WSQUOTA. This mechanism reclaims working set growth beyond WSQUOTA, which is regarded as temporary growth to be permitted only when sufficient memory is available.

6. The actual working set limit adjustment is accomplished by a kernel mode AST that requests the $ADJWSL system service. The AST parameter passed to this AST is the amount of previously determined increase or decrease. This step is required because the system service must be called from process context (at IPL 0) and SCH$QEND is executing in system context in response to the IPL$_TIMERFORK software timer interrupt.

Two problems are inherent in the quantum-end scheme of automatic working set limit adjustment: processes that are compute-intensive will reach quantum end many times, and images that have been written to be efficient with respect to page faults (and incur a low page fault rate) will qualify for working set limit reduction, because their page fault rate is lower than PFRATL. In both these cases, working set limit reduction is not desirable. In contrast, swapper trimming (summarized in Section 19.2.3 and detailed in Chapter 20) selects processes starting with those that are less likely to need large working sets.

Working set limit reduction based on page fault rate at quantum end is disabled by setting the default value of PFRATL to zero. Swapper trimming and the image exit reset are the primary methods used to reduce working set limit. In contrast to automatic working set limit reduction, swapper trimming shrinks the working set limit (and size) only when free pages are needed. The executive also uses automatic working set limit adjustment at quantum end to reclaim extensions from the working sets of low-priority processes.

19.5 $LKWSET SYSTEM SERVICE

A process requests the $LKWSET system service to lock a virtual page into its process working set and thus prevent page faults from occurring on references to the page. Locking a page into the working set guarantees that when the process is current, the locked page is always valid. This service has obvious benefit for time-critical applications and other situations in which a program must access code or data without incurring a page fault.

The $LKWSET system service is also requested by process-based kernel mode routines that execute at IPLs above 2, to ensure the validity of code and data pages. Page faults at IPLs above 2 are prohibited; if one occurs, the page fault handler generates the fatal bugcheck PGFIPLHI.

Pages locked into a process working set do not necessarily remain resident in physical memory when the process is not current; the entire working set might be outswapped. To guarantee residency of the pages, a process must request either the $LCKPAG system service or both the $LKWSET and the Set Swap Mode ($SETSWM) system services.

The $LKWSET system service procedure, EXE$LKWSET in module SYS-LKWSET, executes in kernel mode. It takes the following steps:

1. It creates and initializes scratch space on the stack and raises IPL to 2.
2. It sets the bit PHD$V_NO_WS_CHNG in PHD$L_FLAGS to block swapper trimming of the working set and automatic working set limit adjustment (see Section 19.9).
3. If necessary and possible, EXE$LKWSET increases the working set limit to have sufficient extra dynamic entries to accommodate the pages to be locked and a page table page for each such page.

   If the process has disabled working set limit adjustment, or if its working set limit is already larger than its quota, no increase is possible. As a result, MMG$LCKULKPAG may be able to lock only a limited number of pages.
4. EXE$LKWSET invokes MMG$CREDEL, in module SYSCREDEL, specifying MMG$LCKULKPAG, in module SYSLKWSET, as the per-page service-specific routine. Chapter 17 describes the memory management stack scratch space, the actions of MMG$CREDEL, and its invocation of the specified service-specific routine.
5. When MMG$CREDEL returns, EXE$LKWSET clears PHD$V_NO_WS_CHNG.
6. It restores the previous IPL and returns to its requestor with the status from MMG$CREDEL.

To lock a page into the working set, MMG$LCKULKPAG takes the following steps:

1. It tests whether the page is readable from the system service requestor's access mode. If the page is inaccessible, it returns the error status SS$_ACCVIO, which becomes the status returned by the system service.
2. It acquires the MMG spinlock, raising IPL to IPL$_MMG.
3. It examines the L3PTE that maps the page. If the page is not valid, MMG$LCKULKPAG releases the MMG spinlock, faults the page, and continues with step 2.
4. It compares the page owner access mode with the mode of the system service requestor. If the page is owned by a more privileged mode, the requestor is not allowed to alter its state, and MMG$LCKULKPAG releases the MMG spinlock and returns the error status SS$_PAGOWNVIO.
5. It tests whether the window bit is set in the L3PTE and, if so, immediately returns the success status SS$_WASSET. A virtual page whose

L3PTE's window bit is set is always valid and is not described by a WSLE, so no further action is appropriate.

6. MMG$LCKULKPAG examines the PFN$L_PAGE_STATE field in the page's PFN database record to determine if the page type is process or read-only global. If neither, it releases the MMG spinlock and returns the error status SS$_NOPRIV; a process is not permitted to lock any other type of page into its working set. In particular, it may not lock global writable pages because when a process is outswapped, the swapper must be able to remove global writable pages from the working set. The removal avoids any ambiguity at inswap concerning the location of the most recent copy of a global writable page.

7. MMG$LCKULKPAG gets the working set list index (WSLX) for a process page from its PFN$L_WSLX field. WSLX information is not kept for a global page; instead, MMG$LCKULKPAG must scan the process's working set list to locate the entry for the page.

8. MMG$LCKULKPAG examines the WSLE. If the page is already locked into the working set, the routine releases the MMG spinlock and returns the success status SS$_WASSET.

9. Otherwise, it checks that PHD$L_EXTDYNWS is at least 2 (to allow for the page table page as well as the page being locked). This ensures that the process will have enough dynamic WSLEs after the page is locked into its working set. If not, it releases the MMG spinlock and returns the error status SS$_LKWSETFUL.

10. It sets the WSL$V_WSLOCK bit in the WSLE of the newly locked page.

11. It must reorganize the working set list, pictured in Figure 19.2, so that the locked page is in the user-locked region of the working set list, following the PHD$L_WSLOCK pointer. MMG$LCKULKPAG accomplishes this reorganization by exchanging the newly locked WSLE with the entry pointed to by PHD$L_WSDYN and incrementing PHD$L_WSDYN to point to the next entry in the list. If PHD$L_WSDYN pointed to a valid WSLE, it exchanges the contents of the PFN$L_WSLX fields for the two valid pages; otherwise, it updates the PFN$L_WSLX field for the newly locked page.

12. MMG$LCKULKPAG increments the PHD$L_PTWSLELCK array element corresponding to the page table page mapping the locked page. If the count goes to zero, it also increments PHD$L_PTCNTLCK, the number of page table pages mapping locked WSLEs.

13. It checks that PHD$L_WSNEXT is still pointing into the dynamic part of the working set list (and not at the former PHD$L_WSDYN, which is now in the user-locked region), moving it if necessary to point to the same WSLE as PHD$L_WSLAST.

14. It recalculates PHD$L_EXTDYNWS.

15. It releases the MMG spinlock and returns to MMG$CREDEL.

19.6   **$LCKPAG SYSTEM SERVICE**

The $LCKPAG system service procedure, EXE$LCKPAG in module SYS-LKWSET, is similar to that of the $LKWSET system service. However, the $LCKPAG service guarantees permanent residency for the specified virtual address range in addition to performing an implicit working set lock of those pages. The pages remain resident until the process specifies them in an $ULKPAG system service request. Because this operation permanently allocates a system resource, physical memory, it requires the privilege PSWAPM.

Executing in kernel mode, EXE$LCKPAG tests whether the process has the privilege PSWAPM and, if not, returns the error status SS$_NOPRIV. It raises IPL to 2, sets the PHD$V_NO_WS_CHNG flag, and increases the working set limit as necessary and possible.

It invokes MMG$CREDEL, specifying MMG$LCKULKPAG as the per-page service-specific routine. MMG$LCKULKPAG is invoked with a flag that specifies the page is to be locked into memory rather than into the working set.

Although the results of invoking the two lock services are similar, the following differences exist:

▶ The WSLE of a page locked into memory has the WSL$V_PFNLOCK bit set rather than the WSL$V_WSLOCK bit.
▶ A PHD that maps a page locked into memory must be locked into memory itself to ensure the residency of the page table page mapping the locked page. A global writable page can be locked into memory, although it cannot be explicitly locked into the working set.

19.7   **$ULWSET AND $ULKPAG SYSTEM SERVICES**

These system services unlock pages from either the working set or physical memory. The two system service procedures are EXE$ULWSET and EXE$ULKPAG, both in SYSLKWSET. Both, executing in kernel mode, invoke MMG$CREDEL with MMG$LCKULKPAG as the per-page service-specific routine. Both execute at IPL 0; working set trimming and adjustment do not interfere with unlocking pages.

MMG$LCKULKPAG is invoked with one flag that specifies the operation is an unlock and a second flag that specifies whether the page is to be unlocked from the working set or from memory. It takes the following steps to unlock each page:

1. Its first steps are identical to steps 1 through 7 described for MMG$LCK-ULKPAG in Section 19.5.
2. MMG$LCKULKPAG examines the WSLE. If the page is not locked into the working set, the routine releases the MMG spinlock and returns the success status SS$_WASCLR.
3. Otherwise, depending on the operation requested, it clears the appropriate WSLE bit (WSL$V_WSLOCK or WSL$V_PFNLOCK).

669

4. If one of the lock bits is still set, it goes on to step 6. Otherwise, it decrements PHD$L_WSDYN and swaps the WSLE of the page being unlocked with the one pointed to by PHD$L_WSDYN, thus making the unlocked WSLE the first one in the dynamic region. If PHD$L_WSDYN pointed to a valid WSLE, it exchanges the contents of the PFN$L_WSLX fields for the two valid pages; otherwise, it updates the PFN$L_WSLX field for the newly unlocked page.

   MMG$LCKULKPAG decrements the PHD$L_PTWSLELCK array element corresponding to the page table page mapping the locked page. If the count goes to –1, it also decrements PHD$L_PTCNTLCK, the number of page table pages mapping locked WSLEs.
5. It recalculates PHD$L_EXTDYNWS.
6. It releases the MMG spinlock and returns to MMG$CREDEL.

19.8 $PURGWS SYSTEM SERVICE

A process requests the $PURGWS system service to remove all virtual pages in a specified address range from its working set. A process might request this service if a certain set of routines or data were no longer required. By voluntarily removing entries from the working set, a process can exercise some control over the working set list replacement algorithm, increasing the chances for frequently used pages to remain in the working set.

The executive uses this service as part of the image startup sequence (see Chapter 28) to ensure that a program starts its execution without unnecessary pages such as command language interpreter command processing routines in its working set.

The $PURGWS system service procedure, EXE$PURGWS in module SYSPURGWS, runs in kernel mode. It takes the following steps:

1. It creates and initializes the stack scratch space and raises IPL to 2.
2. It invokes MMG$CREDEL, specifying PURGWSPAG, in module SYSPURGWS, as the per-page service-specific routine.
3. EXE$PURGWS returns the status from MMG$CREDEL to its requestor.

PURGWSPAG immediately invokes MMG$PURGWSSCN, in module SYSPURGWS, which takes the following steps:

1. It acquires the MMG spinlock, raising IPL to IPL$_MMG.
2. It scans the dynamic region of the working set list, examining each WSLE.

   • If the WSLE is not valid, is locked into the working set, or is that of a page table page, or if the address of the associated virtual page does not fall within the boundaries specified by the system service requestor, MMG$PURGWSSCN goes on to the next entry.
   • Otherwise, MMG$PURGWSSCN invokes MMG$FREWSLX, described

in Section 19.3.5, to take steps to release the WSLE and change the state of the page.

3. When MMG$PURGWSSCN reaches the end of the dynamic region, it releases the MMG spinlock, restoring the entry IPL, and returns.

19.9   KEEPING A PAGE IN THE WORKING SET LIST

Occasionally it is desirable or necessary to fault a page into the working set and have it remain valid, perhaps for improved or more predictable performance. Code executing in kernel mode at elevated IPL, however, has a different concern. Because a page fault at IPL 3 or above results in a PGFIPLHI fatal bugcheck, a code thread executing at elevated IPL must ensure the residency of all code, data, and linkage section pages it accesses.

The issues related to the residency of particular pages in process and system working set lists include

▸ Specifying the pages of interest
▸ For elevated IPL execution, ensuring that all relevant pages are resident
▸ Keeping the pages in the working set

This section summarizes the first issue briefly; its focus is on the others.

Specifying the particular pages generally requires identifying the starting and ending addresses symbolically or identifying the starting address symbolically and specifying the length of the area of interest. How simple these steps are depends on whether the area of interest contains simply data, code and its associated linkage section, or all three. It also depends on whether the language in which the source modules are written supports such capabilities.

In general, data pages are easier to specify and can be identified through data cell names at the beginning and end of the data. The organization of code written in any language cannot be taken for granted: a compiler may reorder code, convert routine invocations to in-line code, and so on. This makes it difficult to identify the boundaries of code to be made resident.

A number of events can lead to replacement paging or the removal of pages from a process's working set list:

▸ Execution in the process's context of a code thread of any access mode that incurs page faults, whether mainline code, procedure in a shareable image, inner access mode service (Record Management Services, system, or command language interpreter callback), AST thread, or condition handler
▸ Execution of a code thread that directly locks an invalid page into memory or the working set list or indirectly locks buffer pages by requesting direct I/O operations
▸ Quantum-end automatic working set limit adjustment of a current process
▸ Swapper trimming of a noncurrent process
▸ Proactive memory reclamation from the working set of a long-waiting process or a periodically waking process about to go into a wait

For a process to fault a page into its working set list and have it remain there, it must either ensure that the page is not a candidate for replacement paging or prevent all the events previously listed that lead to replacement paging.

The most straightforward measure, available in any access mode, is to lock the page with the $LKWSET system service. As a result, the page's WSLE is placed in the user-locked region of the working set list and is not a candidate for replacement paging. The page remains in the working set list regardless of the process's scheduling state and throughout any outswap and inswap. The only page type for which this mechanism fails is a global writable page. The executive prohibits locking global writable pages into the working set list to avoid ambiguity at inswap concerning the location of the most recent version of the page. To ensure the residency of a global writable page, a process must lock the page into memory. Note that locking a global page into memory does not prevent process page faults for it.

For kernel mode code, typically the issue is one of preventing any page fault during elevated IPL execution. The OpenVMS VAX technique of "poor man's lockdown" does not work on an OpenVMS AXP system. That technique involves executing a single instruction that both faults one or more pages into the working set and raises IPL, for example:

```
        ASSUME NEWIPL - .LE 511   ;Check that instruction and target
                                  ; IPL are on the same or
                                  ; adjacent pages
        MTPR    NEWIPL,#PR$_IPL   ;Raise IPL to level in NEWIPL
            .                     ;Code to be faulted into
            .                     ; the working set
NEWIPL: .LONG 8
```

For that instruction to execute on a VAX processor, the page or pages containing the instruction and NEWIPL must both be resident. The processor generates page faults if the instruction and pages it references are not resident, and the executive must page them in before the instruction can successfully execute. At the completion of the instruction, IPL is raised, after which no further page faulting is possible. Running at IPL 3 or above blocks the delivery of an AST that might cause unexpected instruction execution and potential page faults. It also blocks the delivery of the automatic working set limit adjustment AST and the rescheduling interrupt, thus also preventing swapper trimming.

That technique would fail on an AXP system for several reasons:

▶ The sequence requires the execution of multiple instructions, making it impossible to reference the IPL and raise IPL atomically.

▶ Except for programs written in MACRO-64 for OpenVMS AXP, the compiler may move code around, making it difficult to delimit sections to be locked.

▶ The sequence does not lock linkage section pages.

▶ By default Alpha AXP compiler technology puts code and data, for example, the longword containing the IPL, in different program sections. It is possible to link an image so as to cluster code, data, and linkage section pages together, but such an image must not be installed resident in a granularity hint region.

Kernel mode code, whether running as part of an image or as part of the executive, may be able to request the $LKWSET system service to lock pages into a process working set list. The $LKWSET system service, however, cannot be used to lock pages into the system working set list.

Code that runs at elevated IPL must also make its associated linkage section and any other data resident. Another issue for elevated IPL code is that the compiler may generate calls to Run-Time Library or other language support routines. These routines must also be made resident and furthermore must be appropriate for execution in kernel mode at elevated IPL.

OpenVMS AXP provides two sets of MACRO-32 macros to facilitate locking code and linkage section pages into the working set list. One set is for use with image code intended to be locked for the duration of the image's execution. The other set is for use with code to be locked and unlocked. The two sets of macros should not be mixed in one image.

The first set of macros is $LOCKED_PAGE_START and $LOCKED_PAGE_END, which delimit the area to be locked by creating special program sections (PSECTs) for the code and its associated linkage section, and the macro $LOCKED_PAGE_INIT, which should be invoked from within initialization code in the image to generate the appropriate $LKWSET requests.

The other set of macros comprises $LOCK_PAGE and $UNLOCK_PAGE, which delimit the code to be locked. These macros can be invoked multiple times within an image. All delimited code is placed into a separate PSECT, and the linkage section associated with that code is also placed into a separate PSECT. Code generated by the $LOCK_PAGE macro makes $LKWSET requests for both the code and linkage section areas, and code generated by the $UNLOCK_PAGE macro makes the corresponding $ULWSET requests.

These macros are described in more detail in *Migrating to an OpenVMS AXP System: Porting VAX MACRO Code*. Both sets of macros are primarily intended for elevated IPL execution. Care must be taken to ensure that the delimited code does not call Run-Time Library or other procedures. The MACRO-32 compiler for OpenVMS AXP generates calls to routines to emulate certain VAX instructions. An image that uses these macros must link against the system base image (using the /SYSEXE qualifier) to resolve references to emulation routine symbols with the routines supplied in a nonpageable executive image.

These macros may not be suitable for all applications. One alternative option for kernel mode code involves the PHD$V_NO_WS_CHNG bit. The general sequence is to raise IPL to 2, set the bit, and fault the page or pages into the working set list. Setting this bit blocks swapper trimming, automatic working set limit adjustment, and proactive memory reclamation. The code must execute a constrained instruction sequence to ensure the continued residency of the page, since the working set list is still subject to replacement paging. The memory management subsystem and other parts of the executive employ this option, setting the bit for relatively brief periods of time. Use of this bit is reserved to Digital; any other use is unsupported.

Neither of these alternatives is suitable for locking pages into the system working set list, pages such as paged pool or pageable data in executive images. The $LKWSET system service rejects an attempt to lock pages into the system working set. The system working set is still subject to replacement paging when the PHD$V_NO_WS_CHNG bit is set in the system header, and on an SMP system, system working set list replacement paging could be triggered by code executing on any of the other processors.

For kernel mode code that needs to fault pages into the system working set list and have them remain there, two routines are provided. The routine MMG$LOCK_SYSTEM_PAGES, in module LOCK_SYSTEM_PAGES, can lock pages into the system working set. For each page to be locked, the routine takes the following steps:

1. It faults the page.
2. It acquires the MMG spinlock.
3. It tests whether the page is still valid and, if not, releases the spinlock and returns to step 1.
4. It increments PFN$L_SHRCNT in the PFN database record for the physical page occupied by the virtual page, gets the WSLX from the PFN$L_WSLX field, and sets the WSL$V_WSLOCK bit in the WSLE in the system working set list.
5. It releases the MMG spinlock.

The routine returns to its caller.

When the caller no longer requires the pages to be resident, it calls MMG$UNLOCK_SYSTEM_PAGES, in module LOCK_SYSTEM_PAGES, which clears the WSL$V_WSLOCK bit and decrements the PFN$L_SHRCNT field for each page.

Locking many pages into a working set list is not always possible or desirable. In cases where elevated IPL execution is not an issue, a process can do the following to minimize page faults once the desired pages are in the working set:

▸ Prevent swapper trimming with the DCL command SET WORKING_SET/QUOTA=*authquota* and /EXTENT=*authquota*, where *authquota* is the authorized normal maximum working set limit. This prevents first-level swapper trimming by ensuring that the working set limit is not above the authorized maximum limit.

► Disable automatic working set limit adjustment and second-level swapper trimming with the DCL command SET WORKING_SET/NOADJUST. This also blocks proactive memory reclamation from a process classified as a periodically waking process.

► Lock itself into the balance set in case, as a result of its execution characteristics, it is classified as a long-waiting process and becomes subject to proactive memory reclamation.

► Execute a constrained sequence of already resident code that touches already resident data and linkage section pages. In general, such code must block AST delivery, cause no exceptions, signal no conditions, and call no procedures outside the address space already resident.

19.10   RELEVANT SOURCE MODULES

Source modules described in this chapter include

[CLIUTL]SETMISC.B32
[LIB]UAFDEF.SDL
[LIB]WSLDEF.SDL
[LOGIN]INITUSER.B32
[SYS]LOCK_SYSTEM_PAGES.MAR
[SYS]PAGEFAULT.MAR
[SYS]PHDUTL.MAR
[SYS]RSE.MAR
[SYS]SYSADJWSL.MAR
[SYS]SYSLKWSET.MAR
[SYS]SYSPURGWS.MAR

20 The Swapper

A time to cast away stones and a time to gather stones
together . . .

Ecclesiastes 3:5

The amount of physical memory present on the system is not a hard limit
to the number of processes in the system. The OpenVMS AXP operating
system effectively extends physical memory by keeping a subset of active
processes resident at once. It maximizes the number of such processes by
limiting the number of pages that each process has in memory at any given
time. Processes not resident in memory reside on mass storage in swap files;
that is, they are outswapped.

The swapper process is the systemwide physical memory manager. Its responsibilities include maintaining an adequate supply of physical memory
and ensuring that the highest priority computable processes are resident in
memory.

This chapter summarizes the top-level flow through the swapper process
and concentrates on its inswap and outswap operations. Chapter 18 describes
how the swapper writes modified pages to their backing store; and Chapter 19, how it limits processes' use of physical memory.

20.1 OVERVIEW

This section reviews some basic swapper concepts.

20.1.1 Swapper Responsibilities

The swapper has several main responsibilities:

- Ensuring that the balance set contains the most important processes
- Maintaining a minimum free page list size
- Maintaining a maximum modified page list size

Its first responsibility is to ensure that the currently resident processes are
the highest priority computable processes in the system. When a nonresident
process becomes computable, the swapper must bring it back into memory if
its priority and the available memory allow.

The swapper maintains the number of free pages (the sum of pages on the
free and zeroed page lists) above the threshold established by the SYSGEN
parameter FREELIM. Free physical pages are needed for resolving page faults
and inswapping computable processes. The swapper keeps the number of free
pages above FREELIM by means of four operations, described in more detail
in subsequent sections.

1. The swapper deletes process headers (PHDs) of already deleted processes. It outswaps any PHDs that are associated with previously outswapped process bodies and that are eligible for outswap.
2. It invokes the modified page writer routine to write modified pages.
3. It shrinks the working sets of one or more resident processes.
4. If necessary, the swapper selects an eligible process for outswap and removes that process from memory. The table that determines outswap selection also determines the order in which processes are selected for working set reduction.

The swapper stops reclaiming pages when the number of free pages exceeds the SYSGEN parameter FREEGOAL.

The swapper ensures that there are fewer pages on the modified page list than the threshold established by the SYSGEN parameter MPW_HILIMIT. When the modified page list grows above this limit, the swapper invokes the modified page writer routine to write the contents of some modified pages to their backing store and to move the physical pages to the free page list.

20.1.2   System Events That Trigger Swapper Activity

The swapper spends its idle time hibernating. Executive components that detect a need for swapper activity wake the swapper by invoking routine SCH$SWPWAKE, in module RSE. In addition, SCH$SWPWAKE is invoked once a second from system timer code. SCH$SWPWAKE performs a series of checks to determine whether there is a real need for the swapper to run. If so, it awakens the swapper. If not, it simply returns. Performing these checks in SCH$SWPWAKE rather than in the swapper process itself avoids the overhead of two needless context switches.

Table 20.1 lists the system events that trigger a possible need for swapper activity, the module containing the routine that detects each need, and the action the swapper takes in response.

The swapper can be awakened in another, more indirect way: clearing the cell that contains the modified page list high limit so that a subsequent test for whether the list size exceeds its high limit will fail. The routine MMG$PURGEMPL, in module WRTMFYPAG, uses this method. This routine, invoked to request the writing of modified pages, is described in Chapter 18.

20.1.3   Swapper Implementation

The swapper is implemented as a separate process with a priority of 16, the lowest real-time priority. It is selected for execution like any other process in the system.

The swapper executes entirely in kernel mode. All swapper code resides in system space. Except for some initialization code, all swapper code is in module SWAPPER. The swapper uses its P0 space only to swap processes. It

Table 20.1   Events That May Cause the Swapper to Be Awakened

System Event	Routine Name (Module)	Swapper Action
Process that is outswapped be-comes computable	SCH$CHSE (RSE)	The swapper attempts to make this process resident.
Quantum end	SCH$QEND (RSE)	The swapper may be able to perform an outswap previously blocked by initial quantum flag setting or process priority.
Modified page list exceeds upper limit	MMG$DALLOCPFN, MMG$INS_PFNH/T (ALLOCPFN)	The swapper writes modified pages.
Free page list drops below low limit	MMG$REM_PFN (ALLOCPFN)	The swapper increases the free page count, taking the steps summarized in Section 20.1.1.
Balance set slot of deleted process becomes available	DELETE_IN_SYS_CONTEXT (SYSDELPRC)	The swapper can delete the PHD and may be able to perform a previously blocked inswap.
PHD reference count goes to zero	MMG$DECPHDREF (PAGEFAULT)	The swapper can outswap a PHD to join the previously outswapped process body.
Powerfail recovery	EXE$RESTART_CONT (POWERFAIL)	The swapper queues a power recovery AST to any process that requested one.
System timer subroutine executes once a second	EXE$TIMEOUT (TIMESCHDL)	The swapper is awakened if there is any work for it.

has a small amount of P1 space to eliminate the need for a number of special-case checks for swapper process context.

The swapper serves as a convenient process context for several system functions. In particular, during system initialization it performs those initialization tasks that require process context and must be performed prior to the creation of any other process, for example, initializing paged pool and creating the SYSINIT process. Chapter 34 describes these functions of the swapper.

In addition, the file system uses the swapper as a process context for the execution of certain asynchronous system trap (AST) procedures. Cluster-wide file system cache coherency and volume locking are implemented through system-owned file system locks (see Chapter 11 and Appendix H). When one VMScluster node's lock blocks a second node's progress, the second requests execution of a blocking routine on the first. Running in system context on the first node, the blocking routine queues an AST to the swapper process. Running in process context on the first node, the AST procedure can request standard system services to convert the associated lock to a less restrictive mode or dequeue it.

20.2 **SWAPPER USE OF MEMORY MANAGEMENT DATA STRUCTURES**

Chapter 16 describes the memory management data structures used by both the page fault handler and the swapper. The discussion here reviews those structures and adds descriptions of the structures used exclusively by the swapper.

20.2.1 **Process Header**

Most of the information used by the swapper in managing the details of inswapping or outswapping is contained in the PHD of the process to be swapped:

▶ Working set list
▶ Process-private page tables
▶ Process header page arrays

The working set list describes the portion of a process's virtual address space that must be written to the swap file or otherwise dealt with when the process is outswapped. The working set list is trimmed to a maximum of WSQUOTA pages before outswap. When the process is inswapped, the working set list in its PHD describes the process pages in the swap file. The swapper's scan of the working set list at outswap is discussed in Section 20.5.

The working set list does not supply the swapper with all the information necessary to outswap a process. Other information about a virtual page is contained in its level 3 page table entry (L3PTE) or in the page frame number (PFN) database record for that physical page. Each working set list entry (WSLE) effectively points to an L3PTE that contains a PFN. When outswapping, the swapper copies the L3PTE contents to its own P0 page table (see Section 20.2.2). It then inserts the contents of the PFN$Q_BAK field for this physical page into the L3PTE, dissociating it from the physical memory that its virtual page occupied.

PHD pages are also part of a process's working set. These pages reside in system space; system page table entries (SPTEs) map the balance set slot in which the PHD resides. As part of outswapping, the swapper dissociates the PHD pages from their SPTEs so that it can reuse the balance set slot. Thus, unlike those of process pages, PHD pages' L3PTEs are not available to hold these pages' backing store addresses while they are outswapped.

Instead, when a process is outswapped, the contents of the PFN$Q_BAK field for each PHD page currently in the working set are stored in the corresponding array element in the PHD page BAK array (see Figure 16.5).

When the process is inswapped, the PHD page arrays can be scanned and the BAK contents copied from the array back into the PFN$Q_BAK fields of the PFN database records for the physical pages that contain the PHD.

The swapper also records where each PHD page fits into the working set list. It stores the PFN$L_WSLX field in the corresponding PHD page working set list index (WSLX) array element. The use of this array while the PHD is being rebuilt following inswap prevents a prohibitively long search of the working set list for each PHD page.

20.2.2 Swapping I/O Data Structures

Like the page fault handler, the swapper makes standard I/O requests. During system initialization it allocates an I/O request packet (IRP) to be used for swap I/O. Because most disk drivers execute as kernel processes (see Chapter 5), the swapper also allocates a kernel process block and physical memory for a kernel process stack. The preallocation prevents any possible deadlock when an outswap is requested to free memory because there are not enough free pages.

To perform an inswap or outswap, the swapper initializes some of the fields that will be interpreted in a special manner by the I/O postprocessing routine. After these fields have been filled in, it invokes one of the swapper I/O entry points in module SYSQIOREQ (EXE$BLDPKTSWPR or EXE$BLDPKTSWPW) that fills in an appropriate function code and queues the packet to the appropriate disk driver.

Tables 18.3 to 18.5 show how the IRP is used by the swapper for its I/O activities.

The swapper uses its own P0 page table to read or write a process working set, a collection of virtually noncontiguous pages, in one or more I/O requests. The swapper P0 page table is an array of quadwords whose address is stored in the global cell SWP$GL_MAP. The number of quadwords in the array is the number of pages equivalent to the value of the SYSGEN parameter WSMAX, which is in units of pagelets. It can describe one outswap or one inswap operation at a time.

Certain swapper operations complete asynchronously. The swapper maintains two bits in the cell SCH$GL_SIP as signals of ongoing operation: when set, SCH$V_SIP means that an inswap or outswap is in progress and is described by the swapper P0 page table; when set, SCH$V_MPW means that modified page writes are in progress.

At outswap, the PFN of each page to be written to a swap file is stored in a page table entry (PTE) in the swapper's P0 page table. The address of the beginning of the page table is passed to the I/O system as the system virtual address of the L3PTE that maps the first page of the I/O buffer. At inswap, the swapper allocates physical pages of memory for the working set being inswapped and records their PFNs in its P0 page table. The swap image is read into these pages. As the swapper rebuilds the working set list and page tables, it copies the PFN from each P0 page table entry (P0PTE) to the appropriate system or process L3PTE.

20.2.3   Swap File Data Structures

The system maintains a page file control block for each page and swap file in the system. Figure 16.24 shows the layout of this data structure and describes its fields. Both page and swap files can be used for swapping.

During system initialization the SYSINIT process opens the primary swap file SYS$SPECIFIC:[SYSEXE]SWAPFILE.SYS, if it exists, and initializes its page file control block. When any additional swap file is installed (with the SYSGEN command INSTALL), SYSGEN initializes its page file control block.

In early versions of VAX/VMS, the executive required that there be a swap slot large enough to outswap the process at its current size, up to the maximum of its authorized quota. When a process was created, space for its working set was assigned in the first swap file with enough free space. When the process working set grew too large for the swap space, a replacement swap slot was allocated. When the working set limit was adjusted at image reset, a smaller swap slot was allocated. Each swap slot consisted of virtually contiguous blocks within a single swap file.

In VAX VMS Version 5, swap space allocation changed considerably, reflecting the fact that processes are outswapped relatively infrequently and that they are typically outswapped with shrunken working sets. Swap space is not assigned until a process is selected for outswap, subsequent to any swapper trimming. The executive attempts to allocate virtually contiguous space in a single swap or page file. If that fails, however, it allocates multiple file extents in a number of swap and page files. (A file extent is a group of consecutively numbered logical blocks.) This approach requires less dedicated swap file space than did early VAX/VMS versions and results in less fragmentation of swap and page files. The overhead of allocating and deallocating seldom-used swap space has been eliminated.

Based on VAX VMS Version 5, the OpenVMS AXP executive allocates swap space in a similar manner; the one difference is that swap space is allocated in units of pages rather than disk blocks.

Two fields in the process control block (PCB) of an outswapped process contain information about its swap space: PCB$L_WSSWP, its location, and PCB$L_SWAPSIZE, its size in pages.

The value in PCB$L_WSSWP has several interpretations:

▶ When a process is first created, its PCB$L_WSSWP is zeroed to indicate to the swapper that this process requires an inswap from the shell.

▶ A positive value indicates that the swap space consists of a single extent. The upper byte is a longword index into the page-and-swap-file vector (see Figure 16.24). The indexed element of the array contains the address of the page file control block that describes the process's swap file. The other three bytes specify the starting page number of the swap space.

▶ A negative value is the system virtual address of a nonpaged pool data structure called a page file map (PFLMAP). Whenever the swap space consists of more than one extent, the swapper allocates a PFLMAP with one pointer for each extent.

Figure 20.1 shows the layout of a PFLMAP. PFLMAP$L_PAGECNT is the total number of pages described in all the PFLMAP's pointers. PFLMAP$W_SIZE and PFLMAP$B_TYPE are the standard dynamic data structure fields. The size of a PFLMAP depends on the number of pointers it contains. Its maximum size is 512 bytes. PFLMAP$B_ACTPTRS is the number of pointers in the structure. The pointers begin at offset PFLMAP$Q_PTR.

Each pointer is a quadword. Its first longword contains a swap file index and starting page number, just like the contents of PCB$L_WSSWP for a single-extent swap space. The second longword contains the number of pages in the extent. Bit 31 is set in the second longword of the last pointer to flag it as the end.

In the case of a single-extent swap space, PCB$L_SWAPSIZE contains the size of the slot, with bit 31 set to indicate it is the only pointer. Thus, the executive can treat the quadword beginning at PCB$L_WSSWP as a pointer with the same form as one in a PFLMAP.

Figure 20.2 shows the relations among the data structures involved in swap file use and also the structure of a single-extent swap space. The upper byte

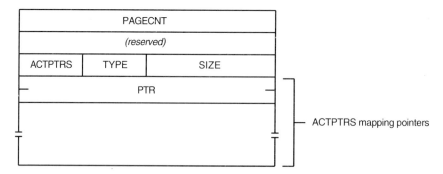

Figure 20.1
Layout of a Page File Map (PFLMAP)

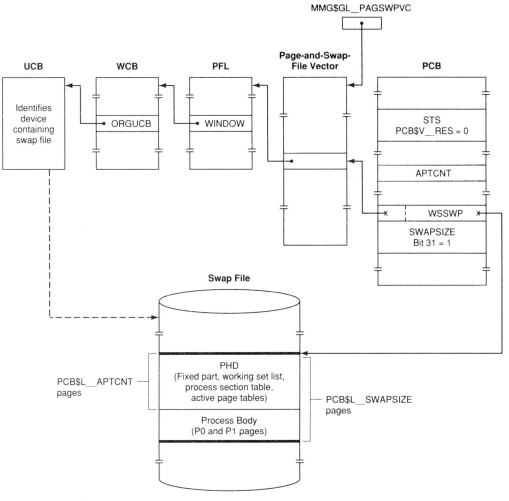

Figure 20.2
Swap File Database

of PCB$L_WSSWP indexes the page-and-swap-file vector array element that contains the address of the page file control block for that swap file. The page file control block field PFL$L_WINDOW contains the address of the window control block (WCB) describing the location of the swap file on a mass storage medium. The field WCB$L_ORGUCB contains the address of the unit control block for that device.

Within the swap file, the process's slot begins at the page whose number is in the low three bytes of PCB$L_WSSWP. It must contain room for the PHD and the process body (the P0 and P1 pages belonging to the process). The total size of the swap space is contained in PCB$L_SWAPSIZE. It is the smallest multiple of SYSGEN parameter SWPALLOCINC large enough to accommodate the process's working set size, which is the sum of PCB$L_PPGCNT and PCB$L_GPGCNT.

The field PCB$L_APTCNT contains the size of the first part of the space, which is reserved for the PHD. This field has no meaning for a resident process; the swapper calculates its value by scanning the working set list of a process about to be outswapped.

20.3   **SWAPPER MAIN LOOP**

The swapper does not determine why it was awakened. Every time it is awakened, it tends to all the tasks for which it is responsible. The main loop of the swapper consists of the following steps:

1. It invokes local routine BALANCE, which tests the number of free pages.
   - If there are sufficient free pages, BALANCE invokes local routine OUTSWAP to clean up deleted PHDs and possibly outswap a suitable process.
   - If there are insufficient free pages and the size of the modified page list is large enough, BALANCE requests the writing of modified pages to make up the deficit; otherwise, it invokes OUTSWAP, which may trigger the shrinking of process working sets in addition to cleaning up deleted PHDs and possibly outswapping a process.

   Section 20.3.1 describes BALANCE in more detail.

2. The swapper invokes the modified page writer routine, MMG$WRT-MFYPAG in module WRTMFYPAG, which initiates modified page writing in response to any pending requests. For example, if the size of the modified page list exceeds its current upper limit, modified pages are written until the size of the list falls below the SYSGEN parameter MPW_LOWAITLIMIT. Chapter 18 describes the modified page writer.

3. The swapper invokes local routine SWAPSCHED to identify the highest priority computable outswapped process. If there is none, SWAPSCHED returns. Otherwise, it calculates the size of that process's working set and tests whether there are enough free pages to accommodate it without reducing the number of free pages below its minimum, SYSGEN parameter FREELIM.
   - If there are enough pages, SWAPSCHED invokes local routine INSWAP to initiate the inswap.
   - If there are not enough pages, SWAPSCHED invokes the OUTSWAP routine to make up the free page deficit.

   Section 20.3.2 discusses SWAPSCHED in more detail.

4. Because the swapper is a system process that executes fairly frequently, it is a convenient vehicle for testing whether a powerfail recovery has occurred and, if so, notifying all processes that have requested power recov-

ery AST notification through the Set Power Recovery AST ($SETPRA) system service. This delivery mechanism is described in Chapter 36.

5. Finally, the swapper puts itself into the hibernate state, after checking its wake pending flag. If any thread of execution, including the swapper itself in one of its routines, has requested swapper activity since the swapper began execution, the hibernate is skipped and the swapper goes back to step 1.

20.3.1   The BALANCE Routine

Figure 20.3 shows the basic decisions and flow of the BALANCE routine. In the figure, FREECNT refers to the contents of SCH$GL_FREECNT, the sum of the number of pages on the free and zeroed page lists, and MFY-CNT refers to the contents of SCH$GL_MFYCNT, the number of pages on the modified page list. The numbers in the figure correspond to those in the following list.

BALANCE takes the following steps:

① BALANCE acquires the MMG and SCHED spinlocks, raising interrupt priority level (IPL) to IPL$_MMG.

② It compares the number of free pages (the contents of SCH$GL_FREE-CNT) to its low limit, the SYSGEN parameter FREELIM. If the number of free pages is larger than FREELIM, BALANCE goes on to step 6.

③ If the number of free pages is smaller than FREELIM, BALANCE tests whether modified page writing is already in progress. If it is, BALANCE checks whether enough modified pages are being written to make up the difference between the number of free pages and SYSGEN parameter FREEGOAL. (The number of free pages will be replenished to a target size of FREEGOAL pages.) If so, it subtracts FREEGOAL from FREECNT and stores the difference in R3 as its working copy of the free page deficit. It continues with step 6.

④ If modified page writing is not in progress, BALANCE tests whether the modified page list contains as many pages as the SYSGEN parameter MPW_THRESH. If the threshold has been reached, BALANCE further tests that the difference between the list's current size and its low limit (the SYSGEN parameter MPW_LOLIMIT) is large enough to satisfy the deficit. That is, the modified page list must contain enough pages to pass both tests before the swapper can replenish the free page list from it. If the modified page list is not large enough, BALANCE goes to step 8.

⑤ If the modified page list is large enough, BALANCE invokes the routine MMG$PURGEMPL, in module WRTMFYPAG, to request that enough pages be written from the modified page list to make up the free page deficit. (Chapter 18 describes MMG$PURGEMPL and the modified page writer.) BALANCE releases the spinlocks and returns.

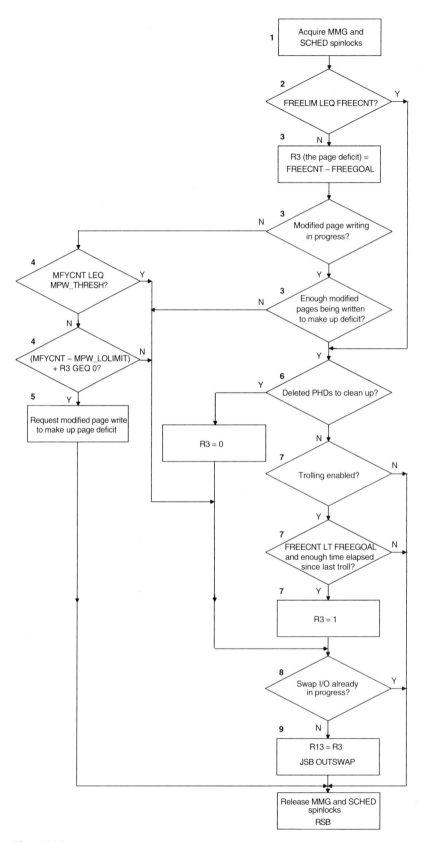

Figure 20.3
BALANCE Operations

⑥ BALANCE tests whether there are any PHDs belonging to deleted processes from which to reclaim memory and, if so, clears R3 and continues with step 8.

⑦ If there are no deleted PHDs, BALANCE tests bit 1 in SYSGEN parameter MMG_CTLFLAGS to see if the mechanism known as trolling is enabled. If trolling is enabled, BALANCE tests whether there are fewer free pages than FREEGOAL and whether enough time has elapsed since the last troll attempt. If both are true, it initializes R3 to 1 to indicate that OUTSWAP should look for a suitable process to outswap proactively.

⑧ BALANCE tests and sets SCH$V_SIP in SCH$GL_SIP. If the swapper already has an inswap or outswap in progress, BALANCE releases the spinlocks and returns.

⑨ If no swap I/O is in progress, BALANCE transfers to routine OUTSWAP, with R13 a copy of R3 and SWP$GB_ISWPRI set to zero. Section 20.3.3 discusses OUTSWAP and the meaning of its arguments.

20.3.2   The SWAPSCHED Routine and Selection of Inswap Process

SWAPSCHED takes the following steps:

1. It acquires the MMG spinlock.
2. It tests and sets bit SCH$V_SIP in SCH$GL_SIP. If the bit was already set, indicating that the swapper P0 page table is in use, SWAPSCHED releases the spinlock and returns.

   Otherwise, it acquires the SCHED spinlock to synchronize access to the scheduler database.
3. It selects the highest priority nonempty computable outswap (COMO) queue. It removes a process from that queue, if one exists, to inswap.

   The scheduling subsystem maintains 64 quadwords as listheads for COMO processes, one for each software priority (see Figure 13.2). These queues are identical to the 64 queues of the computable resident (COM) processes. The steps taken by the swapper to decide which process to inswap parallel the steps taken by the rescheduling interrupt service routine (see Chapter 13) to select the next process for execution.
4. If there is no COMO process, SWAPSCHED clears SCH$V_SIP, releases the spinlocks, and returns.
5. If a COMO process exists and there are enough pages for its working set, SWAPSCHED invokes INSWAP to read the process into memory.
6. If a COMO process exists but there are insufficient pages for its working set, SWAPSCHED attempts an optimization aimed at minimizing swapping on systems with more compute-bound processes than can fit into available memory. It makes two checks. One is whether the process's priority is no higher than the SYSGEN parameter DEFPRI, the default process priority. The other is whether less time than the SYSGEN parameter SWPRATE (a time interval with a default value of 5 seconds) has

elapsed since the last inswap of a process with a priority as low as DEF-PRI. If both are true, SWAPSCHED abandons the inswap.

Otherwise, it sets SWP$GB_ISWPRI to the priority of the inswap process and R13 to the complement of the free page deficit and invokes OUTSWAP to reclaim enough memory for the inswap.

Whenever enough pages become available, the swapper executes the IN-SWAP routine, which initiates reading the selected process into memory. Later, when the inswap I/O request completes, the swapper rebuilds the working set list and process page tables. The swapper invokes routine SCH$CHSEP, in module RSE, to change the state of the newly inswapped process to computable from computable outswapped. Section 20.6 describes these steps in more detail. The newly inswapped process will be scheduled when the processor (or a member of a symmetric multiprocessing system) is available and the process is the highest priority computable resident process.

20.3.3 The OUTSWAP Routine

The swapper executes the OUTSWAP routine to perform one or more tasks related to memory reclamation. OUTSWAP is entered with the MMG and SCHED spinlocks held. It has one explicit argument, the contents of R13, the desired function:

▶ A value of 0 signifies OUTSWAP is to free deleted PHDs and, if possible, outswap a PHD to join its outswapped process body.
▶ A value of 1 signifies that OUTSWAP is to outswap a suitable process proactively.
▶ A value of 80000000_{16} signifies OUTSWAP is to free a balance set slot, either by outswapping a PHD or, less immediately, by outswapping a process body.
▶ Any other negative value is the complement of the free page deficit that OUTSWAP is to make up any way possible.

OUTSWAP has one implicit argument, SWP$GB_ISWPRI, which contains zero or the priority of the inswap candidate. SCH$OSWPSCHED, invoked by OUTSWAP, compares this priority to that of certain processes to determine if they are suitable candidates for shrinking or outswapping. Because an internal priority of zero represents the highest priority, when SWP$GB_ISWPRI is zero all those processes are considered suitable. Section 20.4 provides details on the selection of shrink and outswap candidates.

OUTSWAP takes the following steps:

1. If R13 contains the value 1, OUTSWAP continues with step 7.
2. Otherwise, it first attempts to reclaim memory by releasing the PHD of a previously deleted process or by outswapping the PHD of a previously

outswapped process. It scans the PHD reference count array for a suitable header.

3. If OUTSWAP finds a PHD with a zero reference count, it tests the corresponding PHV$GL_PIXBAS array element.

- If it contains –1, the process has been deleted and the swapper can release its PHD slot and its level 1 page table (L1PT). In routine DELPHD, the swapper zeros the three level 1 page table entries (L1PTEs) that are used (see Chapter 15) and inserts the L1PT into the zeroed page list. It dissociates the process from all assigned page files. DELPHD scans the SPTEs that map the slot, releases any valid pages to the free page list, and deallocates any page file backing store associated with any invalid pages. When done, it invokes MMG$DINS_PRCPGFLS, in module PAGEFILE, in case a pending page file deinstallation can be carried out now that all page file backing store associated with the process has been released.

  DELPHD invalidates all translation buffer (TB) entries to remove stale translations representing the deleted PHD slot. It clears the PHV$GL_PIXBAS array element and changes the PHD reference count to –1. It returns to OUTSWAP, which returns to its invoker.

- If the corresponding PHV$GL_PIXBAS array element contains a positive value, the process has been outswapped and its PHD can be outswapped as well, as described in Section 20.5.3.2. After the I/O is initiated, control returns to OUTSWAP's invoker.

4. If the PHD has a nonzero reference count and belongs to an outswapped process, OUTSWAP determines whether the PHD maps any pages locked in memory by testing bit PCB$V_PHDLOCK in PCB$L_STS2. If so, the PHD cannot be outswapped, and OUTSWAP returns to step 2 to scan for another PHD.

   If the PHD maps no locked pages, OUTSWAP usually records the slot number of the process and returns to step 2 to continue the scan, in case there is a deleted PHD to clean up. To avoid always picking the same slot to outswap, one time in eight OUTSWAP does not record the slot number of the first candidate.

5. After scanning all the slots without finding one that contains the PHD of a deleted process, OUTSWAP checks whether it has found a PHD belonging to an outswapped process. If so, it takes the steps described in Section 20.5.3.1 to attempt to sever all the connections between the PHD and memory so it can be outswapped. If the reference count goes to zero, outswap of the PHD is initiated and control returns to OUTSWAP's invoker.

   If the reference count does not go to zero, the header probably maps modified pages, which must be written first. Thus, OUTSWAP invokes MMG$PURGEMPL, in module WRTMFYPAG, to request that any modified pages mapped by that header's page tables be written when modified page writing is initiated.

OUTSWAP returns to step 2, to scan for another PHD.

6. If OUTSWAP scans all the balance set slots without finding a PHD to release or outswap, it tests R13.

   - If the argument is zero, OUTSWAP returns to its invoker.
   - If the argument is negative, OUTSWAP continues with the next step.

7. OUTSWAP invokes SCH$OSWPSCHED, in module OSWPSCHED. Depending upon the contents of R13, SCH$OSWPSCHED may shrink working sets or select a process to outswap. Section 20.4 describes its operations.

   Whenever SCH$OSWPSCHED shrinks a working set, it checks if the free page deficit has been made up. If the deficit has not yet been made up, it makes checks similar to those previously described to determine whether writing the modified page list is appropriate and whether it would satisfy the deficit. If it would, SCH$OSWPSCHED invokes MMG$PURGEMPL to request that enough modified pages be written to make up the free page deficit.

   If SCH$OSWPSCHED selects a process to outswap, it allocates swap space for the process's working set and reports a SWPOUT scheduling event to change the process's scheduling state from a resident one to an outswapped one.

8. If SCH$OSWPSCHED returns with an identified outswap candidate, OUTSWAP takes the steps described in Section 20.5 to outswap that process. After initiating the I/O to outswap the process body, OUTSWAP returns to its invoker. Later, after the process body outswap I/O completes, the process header may be outswapped as well.

   If SCH$OSWPSCHED returns without an identified outswap candidate, OUTSWAP simply returns to its invoker.

20.4 SELECTION OF SHRINK AND OUTSWAP PROCESSES

When the swapper needs physical memory or a balance set slot, it invokes the routine SCH$OSWPSCHED. It specifies that it needs a certain number of pages of memory, that a suitable process should be swapped proactively, or that it needs a balance set slot. SCH$OSWPSCHED can shrink the working sets of selected processes, select a process to be outswapped, or perform both operations.

When bit 1 of SYSGEN parameter MMG_CTLFLAGS is set, the mechanism known as trolling is enabled and, as its first action, SCH$OSWPSCHED searches for a suitable process to outswap. The search is driven by the TROLL table, described in Section 20.4.1. Section 20.4.3 describes how this table is used.

If bit 1 of MMG_CTLFLAGS is clear, or if the trolling routine found no suitable process to outswap, SCH$OSWPSCHED searches more extensively for processes to shrink or swap. Its search is also table-driven. Section 20.4.1 describes the OSWPSCHED table, and Section 20.4.2, how the table is used.

If SCH$OSWPSCHED selects a process to be outswapped, it returns the process's PCB address to routine OUTSWAP, which is responsible for the actual outswap.

20.4.1 The OSWPSCHED and TROLL Tables

This section describes both the traditional OSWPSCHED table and the table used by the trolling routine. Because the table that drives the trolling routine is a subset of the OSWPSCHED table, the latter is described first.

The OSWPSCHED table is divided into sections, each specifying one or more resident process scheduling states and a set of conditions associated with each state. Table 20.2 lists the individual entries and sections in the OSWPSCHED table. States in the same section are considered equivalent. Selection of shrink and outswap candidates depends on the factors named in the column heads of Table 20.2.

SCH$OSWPSCHED scans the scheduling queues in the order shown in the State column. It checks whether any process in that state queue satisfies the conditions in the second through sixth columns. If a process satisfies those conditions, it is a candidate for shrinking and possibly for swapping.

SCH$OSWPSCHED can perform two levels of shrinking: in first-level trimming, it shrinks an extended working set back to the normal maximum working set limit (WSQUOTA); in second-level trimming, it attempts to shrink a working set to the number of pages represented by the SYSGEN parameter SWPOUTPGCNT. Before performing any second-level trimming, it shrinks all working sets that have been extended. SCH$OSWPSCHED stops trimming after reclaiming the requested number of pages.

When SCH$OSWPSCHED finds a candidate process, its subsequent action depends on the flags described in the last column.

The conditions in the table entries discriminate among processes, based on their likelihood of becoming computable in a short while and the effects of shrinking or swapping them. When the system needs to reclaim physical memory, process working sets extended in times of plentiful memory are shrunk first. In general, the intent is to prevent the outswap of a process that is about to become computable when the only reason for the swap is to bring a computable process of equal priority into memory. Overall system performance may be improved by shrinking processes rather than swapping them. However, a process in some states may be affected less by being swapped than by having its working set reduced.

Table 20.2   OSWPSCHED Table

State	I/O	Priority	Initial Quantum	Long Wait	Dormant	Flags
SUSP	No buffered	n/a	n/a	n/a	n/a	Swap (SWAPASAP)
SUSP	Buffered	n/a	n/a	n/a	n/a	Second (SWPOGOAL)
COM	n/a	n/a	n/a	n/a	Yes	First only (LVL1_TRIM)
HIB	n/a	n/a	n/a	Yes	n/a	Second
LEF	No direct	n/a	n/a	Yes	n/a	Second
CEF	No direct	n/a	n/a	n/a	n/a	Second
HIB	n/a	n/a	n/a	No	n/a	Second
LEF	No direct	n/a	n/a	No	n/a	Second
FPG	n/a	Yes	n/a	n/a	n/a	n/a
COLPG	n/a	Yes	n/a	n/a	n/a	n/a
MWAIT	n/a	n/a	n/a	n/a	n/a	n/a
CEF	Direct	Yes	Yes	n/a	n/a	n/a
LEF	Direct	Yes	Yes	n/a	n/a	n/a
PFW	n/a	Yes	Yes	n/a	n/a	n/a
COM	n/a	Yes [1]	Yes	n/a	No	n/a

[1] This constraint is not present in the OSWPSCHED table; however, it is present in the algorithm and thus shown here.

Descriptions of the various conditions and flags follow:

▶ I/O. A table entry in this column can specify No direct, Direct, No buffered, Buffered, and n/a.

When a process that is in a local event flag (LEF) or common event flag (CEF) scheduling state has an outstanding direct I/O request, there is a high probability that the process is waiting for the direct I/O to complete. If so, the process will soon become computable and thus be a less desirable shrink or outswap candidate. SCH$OSWPSCHED therefore distinguishes between processes with and without outstanding I/O requests.

A suspended process, by default, can receive kernel and executive ASTs. To prevent such a process from being outswapped and then becoming computable again as the result of buffered I/O completion, the table distinguishes between suspended processes with and without outstanding buffered I/O requests.

In this column, n/a means that the existence of either type of outstanding I/O request is irrelevant. No test is made for either.

▸ Priority. A table entry in this column can specify Yes or n/a.

Yes in this column means that SCH$OSWPSCHED compares the priority of the inswap process with that of any process that may be shrunk or outswapped. A process that is computable or likely to be computable soon is not considered a candidate, unless its priority is less than or equal to that of the potential inswap process, stored in global location SWP$GB_ISWPRI. (The swapper zeros SWP$GB_ISWPRI before invoking SCH$OSWPSCHED to make up a free page list deficit.)

In this column, n/a means no test is made.

▸ Initial Quantum. A table entry in this column can specify Yes or n/a.

Yes in this column means that SCH$OSWPSCHED rejects a process that is in its initial memory residency quantum. A process likely to become computable soon is not considered a candidate for second-level trimming or outswapping if it is within its initial memory residency quantum. If SWP$GB_ISWPRI is less than or equal to 47, indicating the inswap candidate is a real-time process, the constraint is ignored. The intent is to leave the process in memory long enough to do useful work, after the system has expended the overhead of inswapping it. This reduces the possibility of swap thrashing, a condition in which the system spends more time swapping in and out than in process execution.

In this column, n/a means that SCH$OSWPSCHED does not test if the process is in its initial quantum.

▸ Long Wait. A table entry in this column can specify Yes, No, or n/a.

Either Yes or No in this column means that SCH$OSWPSCHED determines whether a process has been waiting in an LEF or hibernate (HIB) state longer than the SYSGEN parameter LONGWAIT. Yes means that for a process to be a candidate, it must be in a long wait. A process that has been waiting a long time is likely to wait longer still; one that has been waiting a short time is more likely to become computable soon. For example, a process waiting for terminal input longer than a LONGWAIT interval is likely to remain in LEF longer still.

No in this column means that the process must not have been waiting a long time; n/a means that SCH$OSWPSCHED does not test for this condition.

▸ Dormant. A table entry in this column can specify Yes, No, or n/a.

Either Yes or No in this column means that SCH$OSWPSCHED determines whether a computable process is dormant, that is, one whose priority is less than or equal to the SYSGEN parameter DEFPRI and that has been on a COM or COMO queue for longer than the SYSGEN parameter DORMANTWAIT. Yes in this column means that the process must be dormant to be a candidate. A dormant process is considered a very good candidate to be shrunk. An example of such a process is a compute-bound process with a priority too low to get CPU time. This condition was added to expedite the shrinking and outswap of a process such as a low-priority batch job. While the process runs at night on a lightly loaded system, its working set is expanded and it can acquire extensive physical memory, but once interactive users log in, the process cannot get CPU time.

No in this column means the process must not be dormant to be a candidate; n/a means that SCH$OSWPSCHED does not test for this condition.

This older mechanism for dealing with dormant processes persists in case the system manager has disabled the newer, preferred mechanism, the combination of PIXSCAN priority boost and quantum-end working set trimming. Chapter 19 contains information on quantum-end trimming, and Chapter 13 describes the PIXSCAN mechanism.

▶ Flags. Three flags direct SCH$OSWPSCHED to take specific action on a particular pass through the table. In this column, n/a means no specific action is indicated.

The LVL1_TRIM flag, shown in the table as First Only, means that the working set of a process selected by this entry should be trimmed only to WSQUOTA. Such a process is ignored in the second pass of the table.

The SWAPASAP flag, shown in the table as Swap, means that SCH$O-SWPSCHED should outswap a process selected by this entry after reducing its working set to WSQUOTA. When the outswapped process becomes computable again, it will not have to waste compute time rebuilding its working set.

The SWPOGOAL flag, shown in the table as Second, indicates that SCH$OSWPSCHED must try to shrink the working set size of a process selected by that table entry to the number of pages represented by SWP-OUTPGCNT. Shrinking the working set of such a process may reclaim enough memory that the process need not be outswapped.

In addition to conditions imposed by the table entries, there are several implicit constraints on the suitability of a particular process to be shrunk or outswapped:

▶ A process cannot be outswapped if it has locked itself into the balance set.

▶ The working set of a process that has disabled automatic working set adjustment cannot be shrunk.

▶ A real-time process's working set cannot be shrunk below WSQUOTA.

▶ If the executive has temporarily blocked changes to the working set list and PTEs of a process (by setting the bit PHD$V_NO_WS_CHNG in PHD$W_FLAGS), the working set cannot be shrunk or outswapped.

▶ If the executive has temporarily blocked movement of the PHD (by setting bit PHD$V_LOCK_HEADER in PHD$L_FLAGS), the process cannot be swapped.

▶ A process that is already outswapped cannot be shrunk or outswapped.

The TROLL table consists of three entries within one section. Its first entry specifies the SUSP scheduling state. Its other two entries are HIB and LEF, with the LONGWAIT flag set for each. The actual order of these two entries varies, depending on which queue had the longest waiting process the last time the trolling routine executed.

20.4.2   Passes Through the OSWPSCHED Table

SCH$OSWPSCHED scans the scheduler database looking for processes to be shrunk or outswapped. Whenever it gains free pages from shrinking a working set, it checks whether there are enough pages on the free and modified page lists to satisfy the swapper's need. If enough pages are available, SCH$OSWPSCHED returns. It also returns if it finds a process to be outswapped. The search for a candidate process is table-driven.

SCH$OSWPSCHED makes two passes through the table. On its first pass, it potentially traverses all sections of the table, performing first-level trimming of any candidate processes. If it has been entered with a request to outswap a process to free a balance set slot, the first candidate process that is shrunk and that has not locked itself into the balance set is also selected as an outswap candidate.

If SCH$OSWPSCHED has been entered to satisfy a free page deficit, it continues reclaiming memory from working sets that had been extended until it reaches the end of the table, reclaims enough free pages to satisfy the deficit, or finds a process to be outswapped. A suitable outswap candidate is one that meets the scheduling state and conditions of a table entry that includes the SWAPASAP flag and that has not locked itself into the balance set.

If SCH$OSWPSCHED reaches the end of the table without satisfying the deficit or locating an outswap candidate, it makes a second pass through the table, starting its scan at the beginning of the table. If it has been entered to satisfy a free page deficit, it performs second-level trimming. If it has been entered to free a balance set slot, it selects for outswap with no trimming the first candidate process that has not locked itself into the balance set.

In second-level swapper trimming, SCH$OSWPSCHED can scan each section of the table twice. First, if the entry contains the SWPOGOAL flag, SCH$OSWPSCHED shrinks the working set of a process selected by this entry (unless the process has disabled automatic working set adjustment). The working set is reduced, if possible, to the number of pages represented by the SYSGEN parameter SWPOUTPGCNT. If the deficit is not satisfied, SCH$OSWPSCHED continues scanning through processes selected by the table section. When it gets to the end of the section, it restarts at the beginning of the section, looking for a process to outswap. When SCH$OSWPSCHED gets to the end of the section for the second time, it goes to the next section. The pass ends when the deficit is satisfied or a process is found to outswap. If outswapping a process does not satisfy the deficit, eventually the swapper will reexecute the OUTSWAP and SCH$OSWPSCHED routines.

The swapper maintains a swap failure counter that records the number of times it has failed to locate a candidate to shrink or swap. This count is maintained across invocations of SCH$OSWPSCHED. It is intended to loosen the constraints in situations where the normal conditions have failed to produce candidates. When this count reaches a value equal to SWPFAIL, the swapper ignores certain constraints when selecting a process to shrink or outswap: it ignores the initial quantum condition for all processes and the priority constraint for all processes except COM ones. The counter is reset each time an outswap candidate is successfully located.

When the swapper scans a series of processes in a particular scheduling queue, the scan begins with the least recently queued entry (at the tail of the queue). This starting point ensures that the longer a process has been in a wait queue, the more chance it has of being shrunk or swapped. (A process is inserted into a wait queue at the front of the list, unlike most queues.)

20.4.3 Trolling

The trolling routine, TROLLER, in module OSWPSCHED, first tests whether the free page list has fewer pages than FREELIM. If so, the test for whether a process has been waiting a long enough time will be based on half the value of the LONGWAIT parameter. TROLLER then takes the following steps:

1. Scanning the SUSP wait queue, it tests each process to check that the process has not locked itself into the balance set and that the executive has set neither PHD$V_LOCK_HEADER nor PHD$V_NO_WS_CHNG in PHD$L_FLAGS. If all these constraints are met, TROLLER has found a candidate to outswap and continues with step 4.

2. If TROLLER failed to find a suspended process to outswap, it scans the HIB and LEF wait queues. Which one it scans first depends on which had the longest waiting process the last time TROLLER executed. A suitable process in either scheduling state must have been waiting long enough and must meet the constraints just listed.

3. If it processes the entire TROLL table and finds no candidate, it returns a failure status to SCH$OSWPSCHED.

4. When it finds a candidate to outswap, TROLLER tests if SCH$OSWP-SCHED was entered to free up a balance set slot or make up a free page deficit. In the first case, TROLLER reduces the process's working set to its WSQUOTA; in the second case, to SWPOUTPGCNT. In either case, it removes pages from the working set list without reducing the working set limit.

5. It allocates swap space for the outswap candidate.

6. TROLLER scans both the HIB and LEF wait queues to determine the longest waiting swappable process in either state and calculates how soon that process could meet the LONGWAIT constraint TROLLER established at its entry.

7. It recalculates the next time at which the trolling routine should be entered as the later of 5 seconds from the current time and the time at which the oldest swappable HIB or LEF process will have waited long enough to meet the LONGWAIT constraint. Because the trolling routine is automatically entered every time SCH$OSWPSCHED is, the result of this calculation represents a maximum interval between trolls.

8. If necessary, it switches the second and third entries in the TROLL table so that the queue that currently has the oldest process will be scanned first on TROLLER's next execution.

9. It returns to SCH$OSWPSCHED with the address of the PCB of the outswap candidate.

SCH$OSWPSCHED clears PCB$V_RES in PCB$L_STS for that process, reports a SWPOUT event for the process to change its scheduling state, resets the swap failure count, and returns the process's PCB address to OUTSWAP.

20.5   OUTSWAP OPERATION

Outswap is described before inswap because it is easier to explain inswap in terms of what the swapper puts into the swap file. The swapper does not remove processes from the balance set indiscriminately. In general, unless trolling is enabled, the swapper tries to satisfy the free page deficit first by shrinking working sets, deleting or outswapping PHDs, and writing modified pages. The swapper outswaps a process if one of the following conditions is true:

▶ Trolling is enabled, and an existing process meets the trolling constraints.
▶ The steps just described fail to free enough pages.
▶ SCH$OSWPSCHED encounters a process that meets the constraints of a table entry with the SWAPASAP flag.
▶ The system needs a balance set slot (PHD slot).

20.5.1   Selection of an Outswap Candidate

As described in Section 20.4, the outswap selection is driven by an ordered table of scheduling states and associated conditions. The swapper selects a process less likely to benefit from remaining in memory. Once a candidate is selected, the swapper prepares the working set of that process for outswap.

20.5.2   Outswap of the Process Body

The swapper outswaps the process body (P0 and P1 pages) separately from the PHD for the following reasons:

▶ Fields in the PHD (most notably WSLEs and process L3PTEs) are modified as the working set list is processed.

▶ The PHD may not be swappable at the same time as the body because of outstanding I/O, pages on the modified page list, or some other reason.

Even though the PHD is outswapped separately, space in the swap file is reserved for it at the beginning of the swap slot.

20.5.2.1   **Scanning the Working Set List.** To prepare the process body for outswap, the swapper scans the working set list. It must examine each page in the working set list to determine if any special action is required. The swapper looks at a combination of the page type (found in the WSLE as well as the PFN$L_PAGE_STATE field in the PFN database record) and the valid bit.

A page in the working set can be in one of the following three states:

▶ The page is valid.
▶ The page is currently being read into memory. The swapper treats page reads like any other I/O in progress when swapping a process.
▶ The process L3PTE contains a global page table index (GPTX), and the indexed global page table entry (GPTE) indicates a transition state. The swapper handles global pages in a special manner when outswapping a process.

Table 20.3 lists all combinations of page type and valid bit setting that the swapper encounters and the action it takes for each. Several combinations are discussed further in the following sections. (One type of page not discussed further is a page locked into memory, one whose WSLE PFNLOCK bit is set. Apart from setting PCB$V_PHDLOCK in the process's PCB$L_STS2 as an indication that its PHD cannot be outswapped, the swapper ignores such pages; they remain in memory, and no other action is required.)

The basic step the swapper takes as it scans the working set list is to add a description of each swappable page to its P0 page table. As a result, the virtually noncontiguous pages in the process's working set appear virtually contiguous in the swapper's P0 address space to the I/O system (see Figures 20.5 and 20.8).

For each page, the swapper performs the following steps:

1. It locates the L3PTE from the virtual page number in the WSLE.
2. It determines any special action, based on page validity and page type.
3. It copies the PFN from the L3PTE to the swapper P0 page table.
4. It records the modify bit (logical OR of L3PTE modify bit and PFN$L_PAGE_STATE field saved modify bit) in the WSLE.
5. For a valid process page, it sets the delete contents bit in the PFN$L_PAGE_STATE field. This bit causes the page to be placed at the head of the free page list when its reference count goes to zero (normally, when the swap write completes).

Note that the swapper does not explicitly restore each L3PTE to the contents of its physical page's PFN$Q_BAK field. The contents will be replaced

Table 20.3   Scan of Working Set List of Outswap Process

Page Type WSLE ⟨3 : 1⟩	Page Validity L3PTE	Action of Swapper for This Page
Process page	Transition	(Page state = Read in Progress) Treat as page with I/O in progress. Special action may be taken at inswap or by the modified page writer. (Page state = Read Error) Drop from working set. No other transition states are possible for a page in the working set.
Process page	Valid	Outswap page. If there is outstanding I/O and the page is modified, store in its PFN record the number of the swap file page where the updated page contents should be written when the I/O completes. If the page is part of a buffer object, decrement its page table's share count.
System page	n/a	It is impossible for a system page to be in a process working set. The swapper generates the fatal IVWSETLIST bugcheck.
Global read-only	Transition	If the process L3PTE still contains a PFN, this page is an active transition page. Outswap the page. If the process L3PTE contains a GPTX, then the global page table must contain a transition L3PTE. The page is dropped from the process working set.
Global read-only	Valid	If share count = 1, outswap. If share count > 1, drop from working set. It is highly likely that a process can fault such a page later without I/O. This check avoids multiple copies of the same page in the swap file.
Global writable	n/a	Drop from working set. At inswap, it would be difficult to determine whether the page in memory is more up-to-date than the swap file copy.
Page table page	n/a	Not part of the process body. However, while the swapper is scanning the process body, the virtual address field in the working set list is modified to reflect the offset from the beginning of the PHD because page table pages will probably be located at different virtual addresses following inswap.

when the page is released (after the swap write completes and all other references to the page are eliminated).

20.5.2.2   **Pages Within Buffer Objects.** If the swapper encounters a page whose reference count is greater than 1, it checks whether bit PFN$V_BUFOBJ is set in PFN$L_PAGE_STATE. If so, the page is part of a buffer object. The swapper decrements the share count of the page table page that maps it so that the PHD can be released. For simplicity, the virtual page will be outswapped along with the rest of the process body, but its contents will be superseded at inswap by the current contents of that physical page.

20.5.2.3   **Pages with Direct I/O in Progress.** If, in the swapper's scan of the working set list, it encounters a modified page with outstanding I/O, it stores in the page's PFN$W_SWPPAG field the location in the swap file where that page belongs and sets PFN$V_SWPPAG_VALID in PFN$L_PAGE_STATE. The page will be swapped along with the rest of the process body to reserve a place for it in the swap file.

If the I/O operation is a write (from memory to mass storage) and the page was not otherwise modified, the contents currently being written to the swap file are good. The page will be inserted into the free page list when the I/O operation completes.

If the I/O operation is a read (or if it is a write and some other action has caused the page to be modified), the physical page will be placed into the modified page list when the I/O completes. The modified page writer takes special action for a modified page whose PFN$V_SWPPAG_VALID bit is set. That is, it writes the page to the swap file page whose number is in PFN$W_SWPPAG rather than to its normal backing store address.

20.5.2.4   **Global Pages.** Global pages are also given special treatment at outswap. A writable global page is dropped from the working set before the process is outswapped. The task of determining whether the contents that are swapped are up-to-date when the process is brought back into memory is more complicated than simply refaulting the page (often without I/O) when the process is swapped back into memory.

A global read-only page is swapped only if its global share count is 1. In all other cases, the page is dropped from the working set and must be refaulted (most likely without I/O) after the process is inswapped. (Global pages that are locked into the working set are not dropped from it.) Global transition pages are also dropped from the working set.

20.5.2.5   **Example of a Process Body Outswap.** Figures 20.4 through 20.6 show some of the special cases the swapper encounters while it is scanning the process's working set list. The key information about each page is a combination of the L3PTE validity and the page type. The order of the scan is defined by the order of the working set list. Figure 20.4 shows the working set, the process page tables, and the associated PFN database records before the swapper begins its working set scan. Figure 20.5 shows the modified working set and

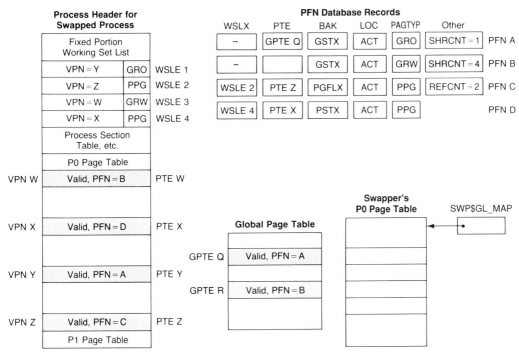

Figure 20.4
Example Working Set List before Outswap Scan

the swapper P0 page table after the working set list scan but before the I/O request is initiated. Figure 20.6 shows the state of the L3PTEs after the swap write has completed and the physical pages have been released.

1. WSLE 1 is a global read-only page. The VPN field of the WSLE locates the L3PTE. The PFN field of the L3PTE locates the PFN database record associated with this physical page. In particular, the PFN$L_SHRCNT field for this page contains 1. (This process is the only process that currently has this page in its working set.) The swapper writes this page out as part of the swap image for this process. Thus, PFN A is the first page in the swapper's P0 page table (see Figure 20.5).

   When the outswap I/O completes, the swapper will delete the page. That is, it will clear the PFN$L_PTE field and place the page at the head of the free page list (see Figure 20.6).

2. WSLE 2 is a process page that also has I/O in progress (a reference count of 2.) This page will be swapped; its PFN is shown in the swapper's P0 page table.

   If the page was previously modified (if either the L3PTE modify bit or saved modify bit in PFN$L_PAGE_STATE is set), the address in the

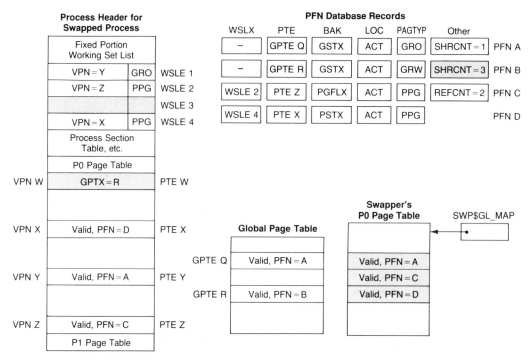

Figure 20.5
Example Working Set List after Outswap Scan

swap file where the page belongs is stored in the PFN$W_SWPPAG field and bit PFN$V_SWPPAG_VALID is set in PFN$L_PAGE_STATE. A set PFN$V_SWPPAG_VALID bit causes the page to be placed into the modified page list when it is released. If the process is still outswapped when the modified page writer writes this page, the page will be written to the page reserved for it in the swap file.

The page is marked for deletion. That is, when the PFN$L_REFCNT for the page reaches zero (because of completion of both the outstanding I/O and the swapper's write), the page is placed at the head of the free page list and its PFN$L_PTE field cleared.

3. WSLE 3 is a global writable page. The page is dropped from the process working set (see Figure 20.5); the process L3PTE contents are replaced with the GPTX of GPTE R, and the PFN$L_SHRCNT for PFN B is decremented. Notice that PFN B is not included in the swapper's P0 page table, which contains a list of the physical pages that will be written to the swap file.

4. WSLE 4, the last WSLE in this example, is an ordinary process page. The page is added to the swapper's P0 page table (PFN D) and it is marked for deletion. The deletion will actually occur after the swapper's write operation completes.

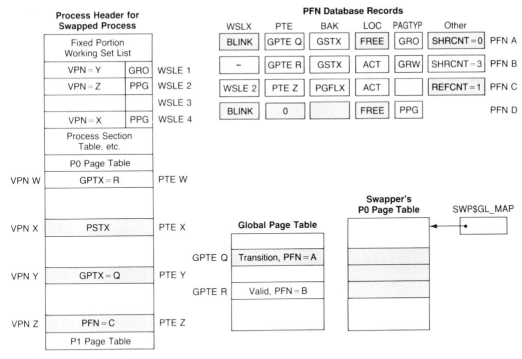

Figure 20.6
Changes after Swapper's Write Completes

20.5.3   Outswap of the Process Header

The PHD is not outswapped until after the process body has been success-fully written to the swap file. Before the PHD can be outswapped, ties be-tween physical pages and the process page tables must be severed, including pages that were in the working set and written to the swap file and also pages that are in some transition state, notably pages on the free and modified page lists.

20.5.3.1   Partial Outswap.
After the process body has been outswapped, the PHD be-comes eligible for outswap. In fact, the header of an outswapped process is one of the first things that the swapper looks for in an attempt to add pages to the free page list.

The indication that a PHD cannot be outswapped yet is a nonzero PHD reference count. An element in the PHD vector reference array (see Fig-ure 16.23) represents the number of reasons (transition pages, active page table pages, and so on) the PHD cannot be outswapped.

Because the outswap of the header need not immediately follow the body outswap (a situation referred to as a partial outswap), it is possible that a PHD will not be swapped in the time between the outswap and subsequent inswap of its process body. In the corresponding partial inswap, the swapper need not allocate a balance set slot and bring the PHD into memory because it is already resident.

If, in routine OUTSWAP, the swapper locates a PHD with a nonzero reference count belonging to an outswapped process, it takes whatever actions are required to remove the ties that bind the PHD to physical memory. First, it eliminates any transition L3PTEs whose physical pages are on the free page list.

It locates a transition L3PTE by scanning the free page list for a page whose PFN$L_PTE field contents lie within the P0 or P1 page tables of the PHD being examined. It starts its scan at the back of the list with the most recently queued entries, on the assumption that the transition pages are more frequently in the back half of the list. Whenever it finds such a page, it invokes MMG$DELCON_PFN, in module ALLOCPFN, which restores the backing store information in the physical page's PFN$Q_BAK field to the process L3PTE, reinitializes the PFN database record to indicate the page is not attached to any virtual page, moves the page from its current location to the head of the free page list, and decrements the corresponding page table page share count.

Because the free page list is only one of several transition states, the scan of the free page list may not free the PHD for removal. Pages may be in some other transition state. A page in a transition state that represents some form of I/O in progress (release pending, read in progress, write in progress) is left alone because there is nothing that the swapper can do until the I/O completes. After the free page list is scanned, if the process still has transition pages, the swapper invokes MMG$PURGEMPL to request that all modified pages be written that are mapped by page tables in the PHD or that are in the PHD itself. A modified page written to its backing store is released to the free page list. Later, after the pages have been selectively purged from modified page list, the swapper will scan the free page list again.

If the swapper succeeds in releasing a PHD with the previously described free page list scan, it can take the steps described in the next section to outswap the PHD.

20.5.3.2 **Preparing the Process Header for Outswap.** Once the reference count for the PHD reaches zero, it can be outswapped and the balance set slot freed. The outswap of the PHD is similar to the outswap of a process body, in that the PFNs corresponding to most of the PHD pages are inserted into the swapper's P0 page table to form a virtually contiguous transfer for the I/O subsystem. The process-private level 2 page table (L2PT) page and any level 3 page table (L3PT) pages that map buffer objects are omitted.

There are several differences, however, between the outswap of a PHD and a process body. When a process body is outswapped, the header that maps that body is still resident. When the swapper's write completes and each physical page is being deleted, the contents of the PFN$Q_BAK field in the PFN database record for each page are restored to the process L3PTE.

PHD pages are mapped by SPTEs for that balance set slot. The SPTEs are not available to hold the PFN$Q_BAK field contents because they will be used by the next occupant of this balance set slot. Instead, the PHD page BAK array (see Section 20.2.1) serves this purpose. As the PHD is processed for outswap, the contents of the PFN$Q_BAK field for each active header page are stored in the corresponding PHD page BAK array element.

At the same time, the location of each header page within the working set list is stored in the WSLX array. This array prevents a prohibitively long search to rebuild the PHD when the process is swapped back into memory.

A page table page that maps a buffer object receives special treatment. For a page table page that maps no working set pages, the swapper resets the associated PFN$L_PTE to an illegal address whose low-order word is the process index, clears its entry in the PHD WSLX array, sets its BAK array entry to the contents of the SPTE, and clears the SPTE. For a page table page that is active and maps a buffer object, the swapper fills in the WSLX and BAK array entries, also setting the TYPE 0 bit in the BAK array entry to distinguish this page type. It leaves the SPTE and the PFN$L_PTE field intact.

Routine RELPHD, in the SWAPPER module, prepares the PHD to be outswapped. In addition to the actions previously described, it takes the following steps:

1. It copies the local event flags from the PHD to the PCB (see Chapter 10).
2. It stores the index of the PHD slot in PCB$L_PHD and clears PCB$V_PHDRES in PCB$L_STS as indications that the process no longer has a resident PHD.
3. It subtracts the address of the PHD from PHDL_L2PT_VA, PHDL_L3PT_VA, and PHD$L_L3PT_VA_P1 to transform their contents from system virtual addresses to offsets into the PHD.
4. The L1PT is not outswapped, since it has only three quadwords of information. Instead it is released to the free page list and its PFN database record updated accordingly.

   The L2PT is not outswapped, since it is faster to reconstruct it at inswap. RELPHD clears the valid, fault-on-execute, fault-on-write, modify, and address space match bits in the SPTE that maps it and releases the page to the free page list.

Once the header is successfully outswapped, routine RELEASE_PROCESS_HEADER, in module SWAPPER, runs. It releases each outswapped header page to the front of the free page list, reinitializing the SPTE that mapped it and its PFN database record. It initializes the PHD reference count, clears the PHV$GL_PIXBAS element corresponding to the slot, and clears the process's PCB$L_PHD. The balance set slot is now available for further use.

20.6   INSWAP OPERATION

The inswap is exactly the opposite of the outswap operation. The swapper brings the PHD, including active page tables and the process body, back into physical memory. It then uses the contents of the working set list to rebuild the process page tables, an operation that primarily involves updating each valid PTE to reflect the new PFN used by that PTE. As each page is processed, the swapper can resolve any special case that existed when the process was outswapped.

20.6.1   Selection of an Inswap Candidate

As described in Section 20.3.2, the swapper selects a process for inswap, much as the scheduler selects a candidate for execution. The following processes are candidates for inswap:

▶ Newly created processes
▶ Processes that are in some outswapped wait state and that were just made computable
▶ Processes that were outswapped while in the computable state

The highest priority COMO process is the one selected for inswap.

20.6.2   Preparation for Inswap

Before inswapping a process, the swapper must locate a free balance set slot for the process's PHD, unless it is still resident, and allocate pages of physical memory for its working set.

In routine SWAPSCHED, the swapper calculates the number of pages required as the sum of PCBL_PPGCNT, PCBL_GPGCNT, and one additional page for the L1PT. If the PHD is still resident, SWAPSCHED subtracts the number of header pages (PCB$L_APTCNT) from the number of pages to be allocated. SWAPSCHED tests whether the number of free pages is large enough for the required number of pages to be allocated. If not, it invokes OUTSWAP, specifying the number of free pages to be reclaimed. Sometime later, after the outswap is completed, the swapper will try to inswap again, selecting a candidate from the highest priority COMO queue.

If the number of free pages is large enough, SWAPSCHED invokes INSWAP to inswap the process header and body. If the PHD has been outswapped, INSWAP scans the PHD reference count array for a balance set slot with a negative reference count. If it fails to find one, it invokes OUTSWAP, specifying that a process should be outswapped to free a balance set slot. (Section 20.3.3 summarizes OUTSWAP's actions.) Sometime later, after the outswap is completed, the swapper will try to inswap again, selecting a candidate from the highest priority COMO queue.

If INSWAP finds a free balance set slot, it zeros the PHD reference count for that slot, stores the low word of the process's ID in the corresponding

PHV$GL_PIXBAS array element, and stores in PCB$L_PHD the byte offset of the slot from the beginning of the balance set slot area.

It then allocates as many free physical pages as required to accommodate the process's working set. It updates the PFN database record for each page by incrementing the page's reference count and setting its state to active. For each page, it initializes a swapper P0PTE with the PFN of the allocated page and a protection of ERKW and sets the valid, fault-on-execute, and no-execute bits. INSWAP flushes the translation buffer to remove any stale entries for its P0 space.

INSWAP records the PCB of the inswap process in SWP$GL_INPCB and resets the swap failure count. It initiates the inswap I/O.

20.6.3   Inswap of the Process Header

After the inswap I/O completes, the routine SETUP, in module SWAPPER, executes.

If the PHD was outswapped, SETUP must reestablish it in memory before the process body can be reconstructed. SETUP must adjust those process parameters that are tied to a specific balance set slot (that is, specific system virtual or physical addresses) to reflect the PHD's new location.

SETUP takes the following steps:

1. It adds the address of the beginning of the balance set slots to the contents of PCB$L_PHD, which were the byte offset of the slot, and sets PCB$V_PHDRES in PCB$L_STS as indications that the PHD is resident.
2. It copies the local event flags from the PCB to the PHD (see Chapter 10).
3. It stores the index of the slot in PHD$GL_PHVINDEX.
4. It adds the address of the PHD to PHDL_L2PT_VA, PHDL_L3PT_VA, and PHD$L_L3PT_VA_P1 to transform their contents from offsets into the PHD to system virtual addresses.
5. Each SPTE that maps the balance set slot must be initialized. The SPTE for each page of the PHD read from the swap image is initialized with the PFN from the swapper's P0 page table, a protection of ERKW, and set valid, fault-on-execute, no-execute, and address space match bits. The PFN database record for that page of memory is updated.

   The swapper does this work in a simple loop in local routine FILLPHD, invoked from SETUP. The loop is executed once for each header page. The simplicity of the loop results from the use of the two PHD page arrays in the PHD. These arrays enable the PFN$Q_BAK and PFN$L_WSLX fields to be loaded from the information copied to the two header arrays when the process was outswapped. To access these arrays, the swapper examines the PHD through the swapper's P0 space addresses.

   Page table pages that map buffer objects receive special treatment. For a page table page that mapped no working set pages at outswap, FILLPHD inserts the BAK array element contents into the SPTE and stores the address of the new SPTE in PFN$L_PTE. For a page table page that was active and valid when the process was outswapped, the swapper inserts a protection of ERKW and the BAK array element contents into the appropriate SPTE, clearing the TYPE 0 bit and setting the valid, fault-on-execute, no-execute, and address space match bits. It stores the address of the new SPTE in PFN$L_PTE.

6. SETUP invokes SWP$FILL_L1L2_PT, in module SWAPPER, to initialize the L1PT and L2PT. Neither was swapped, but physical pages for both were allocated along with memory for the working set inswap. SWP$FILL_L1L2_PT takes the following steps:

   a. The L2PT is mapped in the swapper's P0 address space. Using that mapping, the routine zeros the L2PT.

   b. It copies the contents of SPTEs that map process P0 and P1 page tables into the corresponding L2PTEs, clearing the address space match bit in each such L2PTE. In each invalid L2PTE that maps addresses within the defined boundaries of P0 or P1 space, it stores the protection KR.

   c. SWP$FILL_L1L2_PT updates the PFN database for the page that is to contain the process's L1PT.

   d. It temporarily maps the page, using an SPTE reserved for swapper use, and zeros it.

   e. It initializes the three L1PTEs that are used.

7. SETUP sets PHD$V_NOACCVIO in PHD$L_FLAGS as an indication that the header has just been inswapped, possibly to a different balance set slot, and that the first reference the process makes to another balance set slot could be the result of a swap at an inopportune time. Chapter 18 describes how the page fault handler tests and clears this bit.

8. The physical address of the hardware privileged context block (HWPCB) is calculated and stored in the field PCB$L_PHYPCB.

9. It initializes PCB$L_PRVCPU to −1 to ensure that when the process is next executed, it is assigned a new address space number. This step eliminates the need to flush stale process-private translation buffer entries.

10. SETUP initializes the P1 PTEs that double-map the PHD pages that are not page table pages.

    This P1 mapping provides invariant addresses for the nonpageable part of the PHD. The system space mapping is subject to change with outswap and inswap: if the header is outswapped, it is likely to be inswapped into a different balance set slot. Chapter 16 describes the conventions for accessing the PHD.

    The P1 window to the PHD has the following implications:

    • The physical pages that are doubly mapped are not kept track of through reference counts. However, these header pages are a permanent part of the process working set.

  • The P1 page table page that maps these pages must also be a permanent member of the process working set.

20.6.4   Rebuilding the Process Body

After the PHD is in a known state, the process body can be restored to the state it was in before the process was outswapped.

20.6.4.1   Rebuilding the Working Set List and Process Page Tables. Rebuilding the process body involves scanning both the swapper's P0 page table and the process working set list. Recall that at outswap the processing of each page was determined by a combination of page type and validity. On inswap, the key to the processing of each page is the contents of the PTE located by the virtual address field in the WSLE. An approximation of swapper activity for each page is as follows:

1. The L3PTE is located from the virtual address in the WSLE.
2. In the usual case, the original contents of the L3PTE are stored in the PFN$Q_BAK field, and the PFN from the swapper P0PTE is inserted into the now valid L3PTE.
3. If, for some reason, a copy of the page already exists in memory (for example, if the page was locked into memory with the $LCKPAG system service), that copy is put into the process working set. The duplicate page from the swapper's P0 page table is released to the front of the free page list.

If the virtual address field represents a system space address, the WSLE describes a page in the PHD. The swapper must calculate the new system virtual address corresponding to that page and modify the WSLE.

Table 20.4 details the different cases the swapper can encounter when rebuilding the process page tables. At inswap time, the swapper uses the contents of the L3PTE to determine what action to take for each particular page.

20.6.4.2   Pages with I/O in Progress when Outswap Occurred. Pages that had I/O in progress when the process was outswapped were written to the swap file anyway to reserve space. If the page was previously unmodified, it would have been put into the free page list when both the swap write and the outstanding write operation completed. If the page was previously modified, it would have been put into the modified page list when both the swap write and the outstanding write operation completed (because bit PFN$V_ SWPPAG_VALID was set).

In either case, it is possible for the process to be inswapped before one of these physical pages is reused. The swapper uses the physical page that is already contained in the process L3PTE (as a transition page) and releases the

Table 20.4 Rebuilding the Working Set List and the Process Page Tables

Type of Page Table Entry	*Action of Swapper for This Page*
L3PTE is valid.	Page was not released at outswap. ▸ If the page was locked into memory, no action is required. ▸ If the page is part of a buffer object, the stale copy of the page that was outswapped must be released.
L3PTE indicates a transition page (probably because of outstanding I/O when process was outswapped).	Fault transition page into process working set. Release duplicate page that was just inswapped.
L3PTE contains a GPTX. (Page must be global read-only because global read/write pages were dropped from the working set at outswap time.)	Swapper action is based on the contents of the GPTE: ▸ If the GPTE is valid, copy the PFN in the GPTE to the process L3PTE and release the duplicate page. ▸ If the GPTE indicates a transition page, make the GPTE valid, add that physical page to the process working set, and release the duplicate page. ▸ If the GPTE indicates a GSTX, then keep the page just inswapped and make that the master page in the GPTE as well as the slave page in the process L3PTE.
L3PTE contains a page file index or a process section table index.	These are the usual contents for a page that did not have outstanding I/O or other page references when the process was outswapped. The PFN in the swapper's P0 page table is inserted into the process page table. Its PFN database record is initialized.

duplicate physical page from the swapper's P0 page table to the front of the free page list.

In the case of a page on the free page list, this decision is simply one of convenience. In the case of a page on the modified page list, the contents of the page in the swap image are out-of-date, and the swapper must use the physical page that is already in memory.

20.6.4.3 Resolution of Global Read-Only Pages. The only type of global page that can be in the swap file is a global read-only page that had a share count of 1 when the process was outswapped (or a page that was explicitly locked). All other global pages were dropped from the process working set before the process was outswapped.

There are two cases that the swapper can find when rebuilding the process page tables. At inswap, the process L3PTE for a global read-only page always contains a GPTX. The swapper's treatment of the page is determined by the contents of the GPTE indexed by the GPTX:

▸ If no other process has mapped the global page, the GPTE contains a GSTX. The swapper stores the PFN from the swapper's P0 page table in both the process L3PTE and the GPTE.

▸ If some other process referenced the global page while this process was outswapped, the GPTE can indicate a valid or a transition page. In either case, the swapper releases the duplicate page to the free page list and stores the PFN from the GPTE in the process PTE. If the page is in transition, the swapper makes it valid.

20.6.4.4   **Example of an Inswap Operation.** Figures 20.7 through 20.9 show an inswap operation that illustrates some of the special cases the swapper encounters when inswapping a process body. Note that this example is not related to the outswap example shown in Figures 20.4 to 20.6.

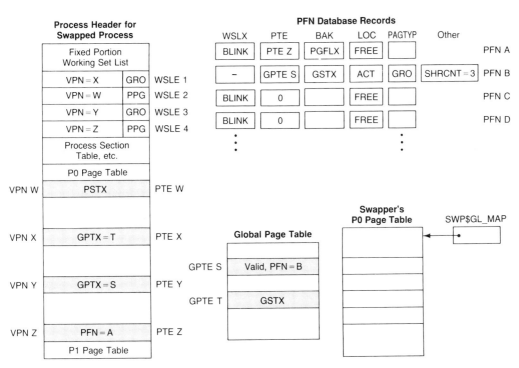

Figure 20.7
Working Set List and Swapper P0 Page Table before
Physical Page Allocation

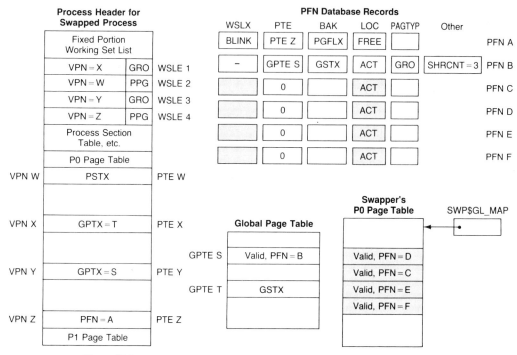

Figure 20.8
Working Set List and Swapper P0 Page Table after Physical
Page Allocation

Figure 20.7 shows the state of the PHD after the process has been selected
to be inswapped. Figure 20.8 shows that four physical pages have been allocated to contain the four working set papers that the example describes. Figure 20.9 shows the rebuilt process page tables and the PFN database changes
that result from rebuilding the working set and process page tables.

1. WSLE 1 locates virtual page number X. This L3PTE contains a GPTX.
   The referenced GPTE (GPTE T) contains a GSTX, indicating that the
   GPTE is not valid.

   PFN D is inserted into the L3PTE. The swapper also inserts PFN D in
   the GPTE, sets the GPTE valid bit (see Figure 20.9), and updates the PFN
   database record for physical page D to reflect its new state.

2. WSLE 2 is a process page mapped by L3PTE W (see Figure 20.8). This
   L3PTE contains a process section table index. The L3PTE is updated to
   contain PFN C, and the PSTX is stored in the PFN$Q_BAK field for that
   page (see Figure 20.8). Other PFN record fields are updated accordingly.

3. WSLE 3, which locates L3PTE Y, is exactly like the first, as far as the
   process data is concerned. However, the GPTE (GPTE S) is valid, indicating that another copy of this page already exists. (This could occur only if
   another process had faulted the page while this process was outswapped.)

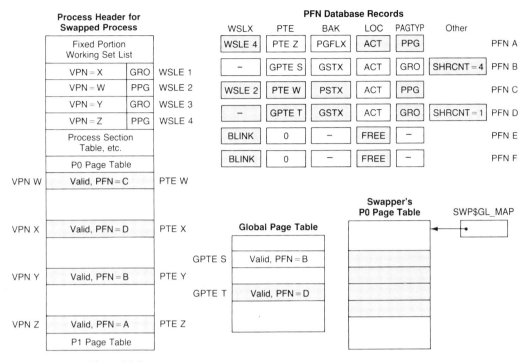

Figure 20.9
Working Set List and Rebuilt Page Tables

The duplicate page (PFN E) is released to the front of the free page list. The process L3PTE is altered to contain the physical page that already exists (PFN B), and the share count for that page is incremented (from 3 to 4).

4. WSLE 4 resembles WSLE 2. However, the process L3PTE indicates a transition page. (This implies that the header in this example was never outswapped.)

The action taken here is similar to step 3, where a duplicate global page was discovered. The page just read (PFN F) is released to the head of the free page list. The transition page (PFN A) is faulted back into the process working set by removing the page from the free page list, changing its state to active, and setting the valid bit in the L3PTE.

20.6.4.5   Final Processing of the Inswap Operation. After the working set list has been scanned and the process page tables rebuilt, several other steps must be taken before the process is executable.

Local routine SETAST_CONTEXT takes these steps:

1. It calculates contents for the AST summary register (ASTSR) and stores them in the HWPCB. (ASTs may have been queued to the process while

it was outswapped. The HWPCB, which contains a copy of the ASTSR, was not available while the header was not resident.)

2. The resident bit, PCB$V_RES, and the initial quantum bit, PCB$V_INQUAN, are set in PCB$L_STS.

3. It clears bit PCB$V_PHDLOCK in PCB$L_STS2 (see Section 20.5.2.1).

4. The process's swap space is deallocated.

5. A new quantum interval is stored in the PHD.

6. SETAST_CONTEXT invokes SCH$CHSEP to change the process's scheduling state to COM from COMO.

7. It clears SCH$V_SIP in SCH$GL_SIP.

20.7   RELEVANT SOURCE MODULES

Source modules described in this chapter include

[LIB]PFLMAPDEF.SDL
[SYS]OSWPSCHED.MAR
[SYS]SWAPPER.MAR

21 Pool Management

In this bright little package, now isn't it odd?
You've a dime's worth of something known only to God!

Edgar Albert Guest, *The Package of Seeds*

The OpenVMS AXP operating system creates and uses many data structures in the course of its work. It creates some of them at system initialization; it creates others when they are needed and destroys them when their useful life is finished. It maintains distinct areas of virtual address memory, called pools, in which it allocates and deallocates data structures. Each such area has different characteristics. This chapter describes these memory areas, their uses, and their allocation and deallocation algorithms.

21.1 SUMMARY OF POOL AREAS

Almost all executive data structures created after system initialization are volatile; they are allocated on demand and deallocated when no longer needed. These data structures have a common header format (see Section 21.4). Their memory requirements vary in a number of ways:

- Pageability—Data structures accessed by code running at interrupt priority level (IPL) 2 or below can be pageable; data structures accessed at higher IPLs cannot.
- Virtual location—Some data structures are local to one process, mapped in process-private address space; others must be mapped in system space, accessible to multiple processes and to system context code.
- Protection—Many dynamic data structures are created and modified only by kernel mode code, but some data structures are accessed by outer modes.

The executive provides different storage areas to meet the memory requirements of dynamic data structures, based on two different allocation schemes: variable-length allocation and fixed-length allocation.

There are three pools of storage for variable-length allocation:

- A nonpageable system space pool, known as nonpaged pool
- A pageable system space pool, known as paged pool
- A pageable process space pool, known as the process allocation region

The executive also provides the following lookaside lists of fixed-length packets:

- 80 lookaside lists out of nonpaged pool, with element sizes starting from 64 bytes and going up to 5,120 bytes in 64-byte increments

- ▸ A kernel process block (KPB) lookaside list out of nonpaged pool
- ▸ A process quota block (PQB) lookaside list out of paged pool
- ▸ A process-private kernel request packet (KRP) lookaside list out of P1 space for each process

A lookaside list is a linked list of equal-sized packets, each of which is ready for allocation through a quick unlinking operation. Lookaside lists enable faster allocation and deallocation of the most frequently used sizes and types of storage.

Throughout this chapter, *packet* refers to a preformed, fixed-length allocation, and *block* refers to a variable-length allocation. The pool areas are summarized in Table 21.1.

Table 21.1   Comparison of Different Pool Areas

SYSTEM SPACE

NONPAGED POOL VARIABLE-LENGTH REGION

Protection	ERKW
Synchronization technique	Spinlock
Type of list	Variable-length blocks; singly linked absolute list
Allocation	Multiple of 64 bytes; mask is EXE$M_NPAGGRNMSK [1]
Minimum request size	1 byte
Characteristics	Nonpageable; expandable

NONPAGED POOL LOOKASIDE LISTS

Protection	ERKW
Synchronization technique	Load-locked/store-conditional mechanism
Type of list	Fixed-length packets; singly linked absolute list
Allocation	Multiple of 64 bytes; mask is EXE$M_NPAGGRNMSK [1]
Minimum request size	1 byte
Characteristics	Nonpageable; packets are initially allocated out of the nonpaged pool variable-length region and deallocated to these lists

NONPAGED POOL KPB LOOKASIDE LIST

Protection	ERKW
Synchronization technique	Load-locked/store-conditional mechanism
Type of list	Fixed-length packets; singly linked absolute list
Allocation	KPB$C_LENGTH
Minimum request size	KPB$C_LENGTH
Characteristics	Nonpageable; packets are initially allocated out of the nonpaged pool variable-length region and deallocated to this list

PAGED POOL

Protection	ERKW
Synchronization technique	Mutex

Table 21.1   Comparison of Different Pool Areas *(continued)*

SYSTEM SPACE

PAGED POOL

Type of list	Variable-length blocks; singly linked absolute list
Allocation	Multiple of 16 bytes; mask is EXE$M_PAGGRNMSK [1]
Minimum request size	1 byte
Characteristics	Pageable

PAGED POOL PQB LOOKASIDE LIST

Protection	ERKW
Synchronization technique	Self-relative queue operations
Type of list	Fixed-length packets; doubly linked self-relative queue
Allocation	PQB$C_LENGTH
Minimum request size	PQB$C_LENGTH
Characteristics	Pageable; PQBs are initially allocated out of paged pool and deallocated to this list

PROCESS-PRIVATE SPACE

PROCESS ALLOCATION REGION

Protection	UREW
Synchronization technique	Access mode and IPL
Type of list	Variable-length blocks; singly linked absolute list
Allocation	Multiple of 16 bytes; mask is EXE$M_P1GRNMSK [1]
Minimum request size	1 byte
Characteristics	Pageable; expandable into P0 space

P1 SPACE KRP LOOKASIDE LIST

Protection	URKW
Synchronization technique	Access mode and absolute queue operations
Type of list	Fixed-length packets; doubly linked absolute queue
Allocation	CTL$C_KRP_SIZE
Minimum request size	CTL$C_KRP_SIZE
Characteristics	Pageable

[1] See Section 21.2 for a description of allocation masks.

21.2   **VARIABLE-LENGTH ALLOCATION**

Pools that permit allocation of variable-length blocks have a common structure. Each system space pool has a global location containing the virtual address of the beginning of the pool and a listhead containing the virtual address of the first unused block in the pool. The first two longwords of each unused block describe the block. As illustrated in Figure 21.1, the first

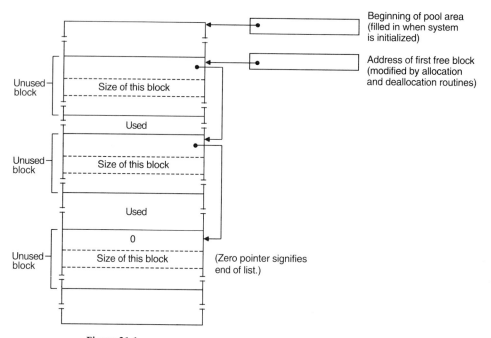

Figure 21.1
Layout of Unused Areas in Variable-Length Pools

longword in a block contains the address of the next unused block in the list. The second longword contains the size in bytes of the unused block inclusive of the first two longwords. Each successive unused block is found at a higher address. Thus, the unused blocks in each pool area form a singly linked, memory-ordered list. The shaded areas in the figure represent unused blocks.

All pool areas are initially page-aligned. The allocation routines for the variable-length pools round the requested size up to the next multiple of 16 or 64 bytes to impose a granularity on both the allocated and unused areas. The granularity of nonpaged pool allocation is 64 bytes; the granularity of the other pools is 16 bytes. The symbol EXE\$M_*xxx*GRNMSK is a mask that indicates allocation granularity, where *xxx* is NPAG for nonpaged pool, PAG for paged pool, and P1 for the process allocation region. For increased maintainability, any code that needs these values should use the symbol rather than a hard-coded value.

Table 21.2 summarizes variable-length allocation listheads and routines. In the table, the @ symbol precedes the address of each location containing a specified value, and all routines are in module MEMORYALC unless marked otherwise.

Each variable-length pool has its own set of allocation and deallocation routines. The various routines invoke the lower level routines EXE\$ALLO-CATE and EXE\$DEALLOCATE, in module MEMORYALC, which support

Table 21.2   Variable-Length Allocation Listheads and Routines

SYSTEM SPACE

NONPAGED POOL VARIABLE-LENGTH REGION

Beginning address	@MMG$GL_NPAGEDYN [1]
First free block's address	@(EXE$GL_NONPAGED+4) [2]
Expansion area's address	@MMG$GL_NPAGNEXT [2]
Allocation routines	EXE$ALONPAGVAR, [3]
	EXE$ALONONPAGED, [3]
	EXE$ALONONPAGED_ALN [3]
Deallocation routines	EXE$DEANONPAGED, [3]
	EXE$DEANONPGDSIZ [3]

PAGED POOL

Beginning address	@MMG$GL_PAGEDYN [1]
First free block's address	@EXE$GL_PAGED [2]
Allocation routine	EXE$ALOPAGED
Deallocation routine	EXE$DEAPAGED

PROCESS-PRIVATE SPACE

PROCESS ALLOCATION REGION

First free block's address	@CTL$GQ_ALLOCREG, [2]
	@CTL$GQ_P0ALLOC [2]
Allocation routines	EXE$ALOP1IMAG,
	EXE$ALOP1PROC,
	EXE$ALOP0IMAG
Deallocation routine	EXE$DEAP1

[1] The static contents of this location are recorded during system initialization.
[2] The contents of this location are dynamic.
[3] This routine is in module MEMORYALC_DYN.

the structure common to the variable-length lists. Each routine has two arguments: the address of the pool listhead and the size of the data structure to be allocated or deallocated. These general-purpose routines are also used for several other pools, including symbol table space of the Digital command language (DCL) interpreter, the process space pool of the network ancillary control process (NETACP), and the global page table.

21.2.1   Variable-Length Block Allocation

When the low-level allocation routine EXE$ALLOCATE is invoked, it searches from the beginning of the list until it encounters an unused block large enough to satisfy the request. If the fit is exact, the allocation routine simply adjusts the previous pointer to point to the next free block. If the fit is not exact, it subtracts the allocated size from the original size of the block, puts the new size into the remainder of the block, and adjusts the previous pointer to point to the remainder of the block. That is, if the fit is not exact, the low-address end of the block is allocated, and the high-address end is placed back in the list. The two possible allocation situations (exact and inexact fit) are illustrated in Figure 21.2. The shaded areas in the figure represent unused blocks.

21.2.2 Variable-Length Block Allocation Examples

The first part of Figure 21.2 (Initial Condition) shows a section of paged pool; MMG$GL_PAGEDYN, which points to the beginning of paged pool; and EXE$GL_PAGED, which points to the first available block of paged pool. In this example, allocated blocks of memory are identified only by the total

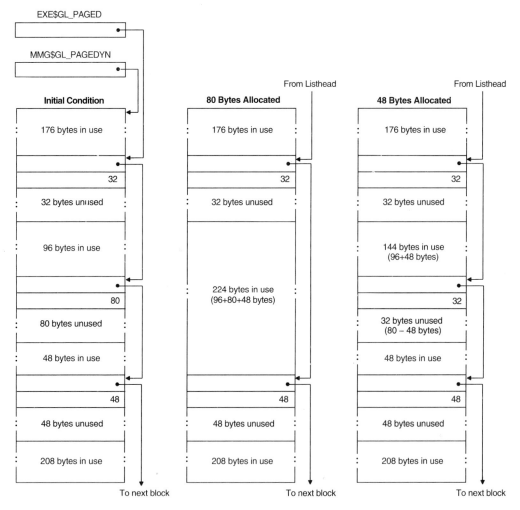

Figure 21.2
Examples of Variable-Length Block Allocation

number of bytes in use, with no indication of the number and size of the individual data structures within each block.

The second part of Figure 21.2 (80 Bytes Allocated) shows the structure of paged pool after the allocation of an 80-byte block. Note that the discrete portions of 96 bytes and 48 bytes in use and the 80 bytes that were allocated are now combined to show a 224-byte block of paged pool in use.

The third part of Figure 21.2 (48 Bytes Allocated) shows an alternative scenario, the structure of paged pool after the allocation of a 48-byte block. The 48 bytes were taken from the first unused block large enough to contain it. Because this allocation was not an exact fit, an unused 32-byte block remains.

21.2.3   Variable-Length Block Deallocation

When a block is deallocated, it must be inserted into the list according to its address. EXE$DEALLOCATE follows the unused area pointers until it encounters a block whose address is higher than the address of the block to be deallocated. If the deallocated block is adjacent to another unused block, the two blocks are merged into a single unused area.

This merging, or agglomeration, can occur at the end of the preceding unused block or at the beginning of the following block (or both). Because merging occurs automatically as a part of deallocation, there is no need for any externally triggered routine to consolidate pool fragmentation.

21.2.4   Variable-Length Block Deallocation Examples

Figure 21.3 shows three sample deallocations, two of which illustrate merging. The first part of the figure (Initial Condition) shows an area of paged pool containing logical name blocks for three logical names: ADAM, GREGORY, and ROSAMUND. These three logical name blocks are bracketed by two unused portions of paged pool, one 64 bytes long, the other 176 bytes long.

The second part of Figure 21.3 (ADAM Deleted) shows the result of deleting the logical name ADAM. Because the logical name block was adjacent to the high-address end of an unused block, the blocks are merged. The size of the deallocated block is simply added to the size of the unused block. No pointers need to be adjusted.

The structure shown in the third part of Figure 21.3 (GREGORY Deleted) shows an alternative scenario, which is the result of deleting the logical name GREGORY. The pointer in the unused block of 64 bytes is altered to point to the deallocated block; a new pointer and size longword are created within the deallocated block.

The fourth part of Figure 21.3 (ROSAMUND Deleted) shows the result of deleting the logical name ROSAMUND. In this case, the deallocated

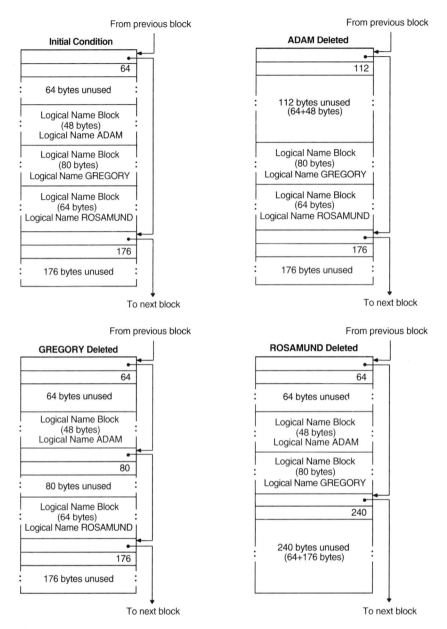

Figure 21.3
Examples of Variable-Length Block Deallocation

block is adjacent to the low-address end of an unused block, so the blocks are merged. The pointer to the next unused block that was previously in the adjacent block is moved to the beginning of the newly deallocated block. The following longword is loaded with the size of the merged block (240 bytes).

21.3   FIXED-LENGTH ALLOCATION

Fixed-length lists, also known as lookaside lists, consist of fixed-length packets available for allocation. Fixed-length lists expedite the allocation and deallocation of the most commonly used sizes and types of storage. In contrast to variable-length allocation, fixed-length allocation is very simple. There is minimal overhead searching for a sufficiently large block of free memory to accommodate a specific request.

In VAX VMS Version 5 each fixed-length list is a doubly linked list, either an absolute queue or a self-relative queue. Each element of an absolute queue contains the addresses of the previous and next elements in the list. Each element of a self-relative queue contains the displacements to the previous and next elements in the list.

The OpenVMS AXP operating system uses absolute and self-relative queues for some fixed-length packet lists, and a new type of singly linked list for others. The Alpha AXP architecture implements queue insertions and removals through privileged architecture library (PALcode) routines. The new type of singly linked lookaside list provides an efficient way to insert and remove packets atomically without using PALcode routines.

Insertion and removal of an element from the head or tail of a queue is atomic with no other synchronization necessary:

▶ For an absolute queue, each such modification is atomic with respect to any other threads of execution on the same processor.

▶ For a self-relative queue, each such modification is atomic with respect to all other threads of execution on all members of a symmetric multiprocessing (SMP) system.

Chapter 9 contains further information on queues and synchronizing access to them.

Figure 21.4 (Initial Condition) shows the general form of a fixed-length list that is either a self-relative queue or an absolute queue.

A packet is allocated by removing the first element from the front of the list (see Figure 21.4, Packet Removed from Head). A packet is deallocated by inserting it at the back of the list (see Figure 21.4, Packet Inserted at Tail).

Shown in Figure 21.5, the new type of lookaside list is singly linked and absolute. Its listhead is a naturally aligned quadword. The first longword of the list contains the address of the first packet, or zero if the list is empty. The second longword is a sequence number used in synchronizing access to the list. Packets are always allocated from and deallocated to the front of this kind of list. The first longword of each packet contains the address of the next packet in the list; the first longword of the last packet contains zero.

Routines EXE$LAL_REMOVE_FIRST and EXE$LAL_INSERT_FIRST, in module LOOK_ASIDE_LIST, allocate and deallocate packets from this list.

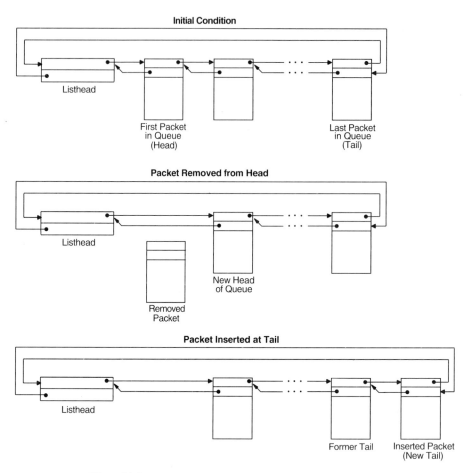

Figure 21.4
Fixed-Length Packet Allocation and Deallocation from a
Queue

The insertions and removals are atomic with respect to all threads of execution on all SMP system members.

To deallocate a packet, EXE$LAL_INSERT_FIRST does the following:

1. It copies the address of the first packet in the list from the listhead to the forward link of the packet being deallocated.
2. It executes a memory barrier (MB) instruction to ensure that the first write is visible before the next write.
3. It executes a load-locked instruction (LDL_L) to refetch the address of the first packet from the listhead.
4. If that address has changed, it restarts the insertion at step 1. Otherwise, it conditionally stores (STL_C) the address of the packet being deallocated in the listhead.

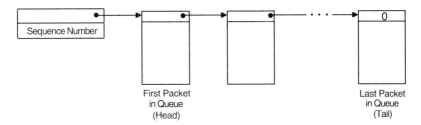

Figure 21.5
Singly Linked Lookaside List

If the store operation fails, another thread of execution has interrupted this one (or accessed the list concurrently on another SMP system member); in that case, EXE$LAL_INSERT_FIRST restarts the insertion at step 1.

5. If the store operation succeeds, EXE$LAL_INSERT_FIRST returns to its invoker.

Because the store-conditional instruction will fail should a memory reference occur between the load and the store, allocating a packet is somewhat more complex than deallocating one. To allocate a packet, EXE$LAL_REMOVE_FIRST takes the following steps:

1. It loads both the sequence number and address of the first packet in the list. If the list is empty, it returns a failure status to its invoker.
2. It loads the address of the second packet in the list from the forward link of the first.
3. It executes a load-locked (LDQ_L) instruction to refetch the sequence number and address of the first packet. If either has changed, it restarts the removal at step 1.
4. It forms the new contents of the listhead as the incremented sequence number and address of the second packet.
5. It conditionally stores (STQ_C) these contents. If the store operation fails, it restarts the removal at step 1.
6. If the store operation succeeds, EXE$LAL_REMOVE_FIRST confirms that the forward pointer of the packet just allocated is the same as the address it loaded in step 2. If the addresses are the same, it returns to its invoker with the address of the allocated packet.

   If the addresses are not the same, it generates the fatal bugcheck BADQHDR. This sanity check has a high probability of detecting the unlikely event that between steps 1 and 3, 2^{31} other accesses occurred to the list (so that the sequence number wrapped around to itself) and the first packet in the list at step 1 was again the first packet in the list at step 3.

EXE$LAL_REMOVE_FIRST could also generate the fatal bugcheck BADQHDR in the unlikely event that the store operation had to be repeated at step 1 more than 917,504 times during one invocation.

Table 21.3 summarizes fixed-length allocation listheads and routines. In the table, the @ symbol precedes the address of a location containing the specified value, and each routine is in module MEMORYALC unless marked otherwise.

Table 21.3   Fixed-Length Allocation Listheads and Routines

SYSTEM SPACE

NONPAGED POOL LOOKASIDE LISTS

Type of list	Singly linked absolute list
Listhead address	IOC$GQ_LISTHEADS + *listhead_offset* [1,2]
Allocation routines	EXE$ALONONPAGED, [3] EXE$ALLOCBUF, EXE$ALLOC*xyz* [3,4]
Deallocation routines	EXE$DEANONPAGED, [3] EXE$DEANONPGDSIZ [3]

KPB LOOKASIDE LIST

Type of list	Singly linked absolute list
Listhead address	IOC$GQ_KPBLAL [2]
Allocation routine	EXE$KP_ALLOCATE_KPB [5]
Deallocation routine	EXE$KP_DEALLOCATE_KPB [5]

PQB LOOKASIDE LIST

Type of list	Self-relative queue
Listhead address	EXE$GQ_PQBIQ [2]

PROCESS-PRIVATE SPACE

KRP LOOKASIDE LIST

Type of list	Absolute queue
Beginning address	@CTL$A_KRP
First free block's address	@CTL$GL_KRPFL [2]
Last free block's address	@CTL$GL_KRPBL [2]

[1] The address of the nonpaged pool lookaside listhead for a specific size is static. Given the packet size, this address can be computed using the formula *listhead_offset* = *(packet_size*/40_{16}*)* *8. The contents of the listhead, namely, the address of the first packet in the list, are dynamic.

[2] The contents of this location are dynamic.

[3] This routine is in module MEMORYALC_DYN.

[4] *xyz* is the name of a data structure, such as PCB (process control block) or JIB (job information block).

[5] This routine is in module KERNEL_PROCESS.

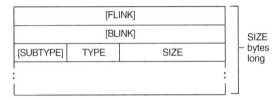

Figure 21.6
Format of Dynamic Data Structures

21.4   DYNAMIC DATA STRUCTURES

Almost all dynamic data structures have a common header format, shown in Figure 21.6:

▸ The first two longwords are available to link the data structure into a list or queue

▸ The third longword contains the size, type, and (optional) subtype fields at byte offsets 8, 10, and 11

The type field enables system components to distinguish different data structures and to confirm that a piece of dynamic storage contains the expected data structure type. Data structures with a type code value equal to or larger than 96 also have a one-byte subtype code at offset 11. The macro $DYNDEF defines the possible values for the type and subtype fields.

The high-order bit of the type field is zero, that is, the possible values for type are in the range 0 to 127. Note that values in the range 128 to 255 are reserved for future use by Digital.

When a dynamic data structure is deallocated to the variable-length list, the size field specifies how much storage is being returned. For fixed-length packet deallocations, the size field selects the lookaside list into which the packet will be placed.

The System Dump Analyzer (SDA) utility uses the type, subtype, and size fields to produce a formatted display of a dynamic data structure and to determine the portions of variable-length pool that are in use.

21.5   NONPAGED POOL

Nonpaged dynamic memory contains data structures used by components that run in system context, such as unit control blocks and I/O request packets. For these parts of the operating system, only system space is accessible. Furthermore, they execute at IPLs above 2, where page faults are not permitted.

Nonpaged dynamic memory, commonly known as nonpaged pool, also contains data structures that are shared by multiple processes and that may be accessed above IPL 2. Nonpaged pool is the most heavily used of the pool areas.

The protection on nonpaged pool is ERKW, allowing it to be read from executive and kernel modes but written only from kernel mode.

Nonpaged pool consists of a variable-length list and a number of fixed-length lookaside lists. The lookaside lists provide for the most frequently allocated nonpaged pool data structures. Section 21.5.2 discusses allocation in detail.

Early versions of the VAX/VMS executive had only one lookaside list, whose primary use was for I/O request packets; it was called the I/O request packet lookaside list. Later versions of the VAX/VMS executive have three lookaside lists: for large request packets (LRPs), intermediate (and I/O) request packets (IRPs), and small request packets (SRPs). A separate nonpaged region is reserved for each of these lookaside lists, which are created and populated at system initialization. SYSGEN parameters govern the sizes of each of the regions. VAX VMS Version 5 implements these lists as self-relative queues.

The OpenVMS AXP executive provides 80 lookaside lists for packets ranging in size from 64 to 5,120 bytes in increments of 64 bytes. These lookaside lists are of the new singly linked absolute type. An array of listheads for these lists begins at global location IOC$GQ_LISTHEADS, in the executive image SYSTEM_PRIMITIVES. Figure 21.7 shows the array and an example lookaside list.

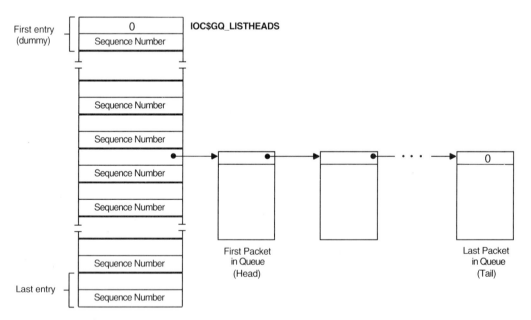

Figure 21.7
Nonpaged Pool Lookaside Lists

A nonpaged pool allocation routine attempting to service a request first rounds up the requested size to the next multiple of 64 and checks the list-head corresponding to the requested size. If there is no packet on that list, the allocation routine allocates pool from the variable-length list. Thus, all packets on OpenVMS AXP nonpaged pool lookaside lists originate in the nonpaged pool variable-length region.

A nonpaged pool deallocation routine does not return pool directly to the variable-length list. Rather, the deallocation routine inserts it into the lookaside list corresponding to the packet's size.

Packets do not remain on the lookaside lists forever. They are either consumed by later allocation requests or returned to the variable-length list through a process called pool reclamation. When there is no packet on a request size's corresponding list and there is insufficient memory in the non-paged pool variable-length region, the executive initiates pool reclamation. The executive also initiates pool reclamation periodically to ensure sufficient memory on the nonpaged pool variable-length list. Section 21.5.4 describes nonpaged pool reclamation.

Called adaptive nonpaged pool management, this new mechanism simplifies system management by automatically adapting to varying workloads, thereby eliminating a number of SYSGEN parameters used with the earlier style of pool management.

When a nonpaged pool request cannot be satisfied even after pool reclamation, the executive attempts to expand nonpaged pool. Section 21.5.5 describes nonpaged pool expansion.

In addition to the standard lookaside lists, the OpenVMS AXP executive provides a lookaside list of KPBs, used primarily by device driver fork processes. KPBs, initially allocated from nonpaged pool, are deallocated to the KPB lookaside list. The KPB allocation routine attempts to allocate a KPB from this list as a faster alternative to general nonpaged pool allocation. Each KPB points to an associated kernel process stack. Allocation and initialization of a kernel process stack is a time-consuming process. Maintaining the KPBs on a separate lookaside list allows the executive to reuse KPBs and their associated stacks. Chapter 5 describes kernel processes and KPBs.

21.5.1 Nonpaged Pool Initialization

SYSGEN parameters NPAGEDYN and NPAGEVIR specify the size of nonpaged pool. NPAGEDYN is the initial size of nonpaged pool in bytes, and NPAGEVIR is the maximum size, in bytes, to which it can expand. Both are rounded down to a number representing an integral number of pages. During system initialization SYSBOOT allocates a slice of the nonpaged system data huge page for the initial size of nonpaged pool. Chapter 15 describes huge pages and slices. SYSBOOT also reserves enough virtual address space contiguous to this region for nonpaged pool to expand to its maximum size.

SYSBOOT initializes the nonpaged pool variable-length list and the global locations EXE$GL_NONPAGED, MMG$GL_NPAGEDYN, and MMG$GL_NPAGNEXT.

The array of nonpaged pool lookaside listheads is created as a completely zeroed array of longwords during compilation of module MEMORYALC_DYN.

21.5.2   Nonpaged Pool Allocation

A number of routines in module MEMORYALC allocate nonpaged pool. Some of these routines, such as EXE$ALLOCPCB or EXE$ALLOCTQE, allocate pool for a particular type of data structure, filling in its size and type. Some routines, intended for use only within process context, conditionally place the process into a resource wait (see Chapter 13) for resource RSN$_NPDYNMEM if pool is unavailable. All these routines invoke EXE$ALONONPAGED, the general nonpaged pool allocation routine.

A consumer of nonpaged pool must use an appropriate executive procedure, such as EXE$ALLOCTQE or EXE$ALONONPAGED, for allocation and deallocation. Direct allocation from or deallocation to a nonpaged pool lookaside list is not allowed. That is, directly manipulating the lookaside list through the EXELAL_REMOVE_FIRST/EXELAL_INSERT_FIRST routines or through the load-locked/store-conditional mechanism is not allowed.

Because allocation from and deallocation to a lookaside list are so much faster than the equivalent operations involving the variable-length list, EXE$ALONONPAGED checks to determine whether a requested block can be allocated from one of the lookaside lists. It allocates requests from the variable-length list only if the requested size is larger than 5,120 bytes or if the lookaside list corresponding to the requested size is empty.

EXE$ALONONPAGED and EXE$ALONPAGVAR are entry points to the same procedure, EXE$ALONONPAGED_INT in module MEMORYALC_DYN, which allocates nonpaged pool by performing the following steps:

1. It rounds up the requested size to the nearest multiple of 64.
2. If the rounded value of the requested size is larger than 5,120 bytes, it proceeds with step 4.
3. It invokes EXE$LAL_REMOVE_FIRST (described in Section 21.3) to allocate the first packet from the lookaside list corresponding to the requested size. If a packet was successfully allocated, EXE$ALONONPAGED_INT returns to its invoker with a success status. Otherwise, it continues.
4. If the current IPL is greater than IPL$_POOL, EXE$ALONONPAGED_INT tests the BOOSTATE$V_SWAPPER flag in EXE$GL_STATE. If that is set, indicating that system initialization has completed, EXE$ALONONPAGED_INT returns to its invoker with the error status SS$_INSFMEM. Otherwise, it continues.

5. It invokes EXE$ALONPAGVAR_INT, in module MEMORYALC_DYN, to allocate a nonpaged pool block of the requested size and returns the status from EXE$ALONPAGVAR_INT to its invoker.

EXE$ALONPAGVAR_INT allocates pool only from the variable-length list. It performs the following steps:

1. It rounds the request size up to a multiple of 64.
2. It increments PMS$GL_NPAGDYNREQ, which tracks the number of allocation requests for variable-length pool (see Table 21.4 in Section 21.10).
3. It acquires the POOL spinlock, raising IPL to IPL$_POOL.
4. It invokes the lower level routine EXE$ALLOCATE, described in Section 21.2.
5. It releases the POOL spinlock, restoring the previous IPL. If EXE$ALLOCATE succeeded, EXE$ALONPAGVAR_INT returns the size and address of the allocated block.
6. If the allocation failed, EXE$ALONPAGVAR_INT checks whether pool reclamation was already performed for this request. If not, it invokes EXE$RECLAIMLISTS, in module MEMORYALC_DYN, to attempt to reclaim nonpaged pool (see Section 21.5.4). Upon return from EXE$RECLAIMLISTS, regardless of whether pool was reclaimed, EXE$ALONPAGVAR_INT retries pool allocation beginning with step 3.
7. If pool reclamation was already attempted for this request, EXE$ALONPAGVAR_INT instead invokes EXE$EXTENDPOOL, in module MEMORYALC, to attempt pool expansion (see Section 21.5.5).

   If the expansion succeeds, EXE$ALONPAGVAR_INT repeats the allocation attempt. If the expansion fails, EXE$ALONPAGVAR_INT invokes EXE$FLUSHLISTS, in module MEMORYALC_DYN. This routine performs much the same operations as EXE$RECLAIMLISTS, described in Section 21.5.4, with the following differences:

   • It removes all packets from each lookaside list. (EXE$RECLAIMLISTS only takes one packet from each lookaside list.)
   • It stops processing as soon as the current allocation request can be satisfied.

   If, despite the expansion and flushing effort, the nonpaged pool request cannot be satisfied, EXE$ALONPAGVAR_INT increments PMS$GL_NPAGDYNREQF and updates PMS$GL_NPAGDYNFPAGES (listed in Table 21.4) and returns the error status SS$_INSFMEM to its invoker.

Since nonpaged pool allocation granularity is 64 bytes and nonpaged pool begins at a page boundary, all nonpaged pool packets and blocks are guaranteed to be at least 64-byte aligned. A consumer requiring greater than 64-byte alignment can invoke the routine EXE$ALONONPAGED_ALN, in module

MEMORYALC_DYN, which attempts nonpaged pool allocation to the specified alignment constraint.

21.5.3   Nonpaged Pool Deallocation

In order to deallocate nonpaged pool, a consumer of nonpaged pool invokes EXE$DEANONPAGED or EXE$DEANONPGDSIZ. EXE$DEANONPAGED determines the size of the block being returned and invokes EXE$DEANONPGDSIZ.

EXE$DEANONPGDSIZ returns the deallocated block either to one of the lookaside lists or to the variable-length region, performing the following steps:

1. It rounds up the deallocation request size to a multiple of 64.
2. If the rounded deallocation size is less than or equal to 5,120 bytes, it determines the appropriate listhead in the array at IOC$GQ_LISTHEADS and invokes EXE$LAL_INSERT_FIRST to return the deallocated packet to the front of that list. It then returns to its invoker.
3. If the rounded deallocation size is larger than 5,120 bytes, EXE$DEANONPGDSIZ acquires the POOL spinlock, raising IPL to IPL$_POOL; invokes EXE$DEALLOCATE, the lower level routine described in Section 21.2; and then releases the POOL spinlock, restoring the previous IPL.

21.5.4   Nonpaged Pool Reclamation

As previously described, nonpaged pool deallocation routines insert a packet on a lookaside list rather than returning it to the variable-length list. Returning a packet to a lookaside list enables faster allocation of packets of that size. On a running system, however, the demanded allocation sizes are somewhat unpredictable. As more packets are put on lookaside lists, remaining space on the variable-length list gets smaller. Without a process for reclaiming space from unused lookaside list packets, nonpaged pool exhaustion or excessive fragmentation can occur, slowing down or preventing further allocation.

Through a process called nonpaged pool reclamation, packets from nonpaged pool lookaside lists are moved to the nonpaged pool variable-length list.

Reclamation can be gentle or aggressive. The executive performs gentle reclamation periodically. When performing gentle reclamation, the executive reclaims pool from the first packet of each lookaside list that has two or more packets. The executive performs aggressive reclamation when an allocation request cannot be satisfied from either the appropriate lookaside list or the variable-length list. When performing aggressive reclamation, the executive reclaims pool from one packet on each nonempty lookaside list starting with the list for the minimum allocation size.

Reclamation is not possible if there are no packets on any of the lookaside lists.

Nonpaged pool reclamation is initiated by invoking EXE$RECLAIMLISTS with an argument specifying whether the reclamation is to be gentle or aggressive. If the argument is zero, the routine performs gentle reclamation. Otherwise, it performs aggressive reclamation.

EXE$RECLAIMLISTS is invoked by one of two routines:

▶ INI$ESTAB_RECLAIM_TQE, in module MEMORYALC_DYN, which runs every 30 seconds as a repeating system timer routine (see Chapter 12)
▶ EXE$ALONPAGVAR_INT, when it determines that there is insufficient space in the nonpaged pool variable-length list to satisfy a request

INI$ESTAB_RECLAIM_TQE requests gentle reclamation; EXE$ALONPAG-VAR_INT requests aggressive reclamation.

EXE$RECLAIMLISTS performs the following steps:

1. It acquires the POOL spinlock, raising IPL to IPL$_POOL, to synchronize access to the variable-length list. This also synchronizes access to an array into which EXE$RECLAIMLISTS collects the addresses of reclaimed packets.
2. Starting with the list for the smallest allocation size and progressing to the list for the largest allocation size, it performs the following operation for each nonempty nonpaged pool lookaside list:
   • In gentle reclamation, EXE$RECLAIMLISTS removes the first packet from the list only if the list has at least two elements.
   • In aggressive reclamation, it removes the first packet on the list, if there is one.

   In either case, it records the addresses of removed packets in an array that is processed at step 3.
3. EXE$RECLAIMLISTS invokes EXE$DEALLOCATE for each removed packet, returning pool to the variable-length list. Recall that EXE$DEAL-LOCATE maintains the variable-length list as an ordered list, agglomerating adjacent blocks as necessary to reduce fragmentation.
4. It releases the POOL spinlock, dropping IPL to the level at entry to EXE$RECLAIMLISTS.
5. It invokes EXE$KP_RECLAIM_KPB, in module KERNEL_PROCESS, passing it the same argument that was passed to EXE$RECLAIMLISTS.

   The algorithm for KPB reclamation is similar to that for general nonpaged pool reclamation and can be gentle or aggressive. Chapter 5 describes KPBs and KPB reclamation.

21.5.5   Nonpaged Pool Expansion

Dynamic nonpaged pool expansion creates additional nonpaged pool as it is needed. At system initialization SYSBOOT allocates space in the nonpaged system data huge page for the size of nonpaged pool specified by NPAGE-DYN and reserves enough contiguous virtual address space for nonpaged pool to expand up to NPAGEVIR pages. When an attempt to allocate nonpaged pool fails, the pool can be expanded by allocating more physical memory for it and altering the system page table (SPT) accordingly. Note that expanded pool is not within the nonpaged system data huge page, although it is virtually contiguous to it. EXE$EXTENDPOOL is the routine that attempts to expand pool. When pool reclamation does not yield sufficient space to satisfy an allocation request, EXE$ALONPAGVAR_INT invokes EXE$EXTENDPOOL.

EXE$EXTENDPOOL synchronizes nonpaged pool expansion by first acquiring the MMG spinlock if it can, unless the current CPU already holds the MMG spinlock, in which case EXE$EXTENDPOOL skips this step. The MMG spinlock also synchronizes access to the page frame number (PFN) database. If EXE$EXTENDPOOL was entered from an interrupt service routine running above IPL$_SYNCH or is running on a CPU that owns the SCHED spinlock but not the MMG spinlock, EXE$EXTENDPOOL creates an IPL$_QUEUEAST fork process to expand nonpaged pool at some later time and returns an allocation failure status to its caller. (IPL$_SYNCH is the MMG spinlock's IPL, and the SCHED spinlock is ranked higher than the MMG spinlock.)

EXE$EXTENDPOOL then attempts to allocate 32 KB of physical memory. First, it checks whether the physical pages can be allocated without reducing the number of physical pages available to the system below the minimum required. Pool expansion must leave sufficient fluid pages to accommodate the sum of the maximum swap image (the lesser of the number of pages represented by WSMAX and SWP$GL_SWAP_IMAGE_SIZE_MAX pages), the modified list low limit, and the free page list low limit. This check may result in fewer pages being allocated for the expansion.

If the memory sufficiency check fails, the routine attempts to broadcast a message to the operator's console and logs an expansion failure event (see Section 21.9).

For each allocated page, EXE$EXTENDPOOL places its PFN in the next invalid system page table entry (SPTE) and sets the valid bit. EXE$EXTEND-POOL acquires the POOL spinlock, invokes EXE$DEALLOCATE to add the new virtual pages to nonpaged pool, and releases the POOL spinlock. If EXE$EXTENDPOOL acquired the MMG spinlock, it releases that spinlock also.

If EXE$EXTENDPOOL is able to expand nonpaged pool, it reports that the resource RSN$_NPDYNMEM is available for any waiting processes.

Nonpaged pool expansion provides a degree of automatic system tuning. The penalty for undersizing NPAGEDYN is the increased overhead in allocating requests that cause expansion. An additional penalty is the performance loss associated with not having the expanded pages within a huge page (and thus its granularity hint region). Chapter 15 explains how huge pages improve system performance.

The penalties for oversizing NPAGEVIR are one quadword (the SPTE) for each unused page and one associated unusable page of system virtual address space.

If NPAGEVIR is too small, processes may be placed into a resource wait state, waiting for nonpaged pool to become available.

The AUTOGEN facility can also adjust SYSGEN parameters that govern the initial size of nonpaged pool according to a given system's workload, as outlined in Section 21.9.

Nonpaged pool expands, but it does not contract. No mechanism returns PFNs from nonpaged pool to the free page list. The nonpaged pool region returns to its original size only at the next bootstrap, if NPAGEDYN has not changed.

21.5.6   Nonpaged Pool Synchronization

The POOL spinlock serializes access to the nonpaged pool variable-length list. Acquiring the POOL spinlock raises IPL to IPL$_POOL. The allocation, deallocation, reclamation, and expansion routines for nonpaged pool acquire and release the POOL spinlock.

Device drivers running at fork level frequently allocate dynamic storage. The POOL spinlock ranks higher than all fork locks and the MAILBOX spinlock. This allows a CPU executing a driver fork process to acquire the POOL spinlock while owning the MAILBOX or any of the IOLOCKx fork locks. However, a CPU executing at device IPL may not acquire the POOL spinlock because device IPL is higher than IPL$_POOL.

Each nonpaged pool allocation routine that runs in process context, such as EXE$ALLOCCEB or EXE$ALLOCIRP, invokes EXE$ALONONPAGED without acquiring the SCHED spinlock. If this attempt to allocate pool is successful, the routine has avoided the overhead of SCHED spinlock acquisition and release.

If EXE$ALONONPAGED fails to allocate the pool, the routine acquires the SCHED spinlock, raising IPL to IPL$_SCHED and synchronizing access to the scheduler database, and invokes EXE$ALONONPAGED again. If the second allocation attempt fails, the routine tests PCB$V_SSRWAIT in PCB$L_STS. If it is clear, EXE$ALONONPAGED returns a failure status to its invoker; otherwise, EXE$ALONONPAGED invokes a scheduling routine to place the process into a resource wait state, waiting for RSN$_NPDYNMEM.

A process in such a wait state will be made computable whenever RSN$_NPDYNMEM is declared available. In earlier versions of VAX/VMS, the resource was declared available each time nonpaged pool was deallocated. Because resource waits occur less frequently than deallocations, OpenVMS AXP reduces overhead by avoiding this declaration at deallocation. Instead, the resource is declared available once a second by EXE$TIMEOUT, in module TIMESCHDL (see Chapter 12). It is also declared available by EXE$EXTENDPOOL whenever nonpaged pool is expanded.

Code executing as the result of an interrupt at IPL$_SCHED or above deallocates nonpaged pool through routine COM$DRVDEALMEM, in module MEMORYALC. COM$DRVDEALMEM deallocates any packet up to 5,120 bytes in size by simply invoking EXE$DEANONPGDSIZ. Such a packet is returned to the lookaside list. Access to the lookaside list is synchronized using special instructions, as described in Section 21.3. For a larger packet, if IPL is below IPL$_POOL, COM$DRVDEALMEM simply invokes EXE$DEANONPGDSIZ. If COM$DRVDEALMEM is invoked from IPL$_POOL or above, however, it transforms the block that is to be deallocated into a fork block (see Figure 5.1) and requests an IPL$_QUEUEAST software interrupt.

The code that executes as the IPL$_QUEUEAST fork process (the saved procedure value in the fork block) simply invokes EXE$DEANONPAGED to deallocate the block. Because EXE$DEANONPAGED is entered at IPL$_QUEUEAST, the synchronized access to the scheduler's database is preserved.

By convention, process context code that allocates a nonpaged pool data structure executes at IPL 2 or above as long as the data structure's existence is recorded solely in a temporary process location, such as in a register or on the stack. Running at IPL 2 blocks AST delivery and prevents the possible loss of the pool if the process were to be deleted.

21.5.7   Uses of Nonpaged Pool

This section summarizes typical uses of nonpaged pool, which serves many purposes.

Nonpaged pool is allocated during early stages of system initialization. The use of nonpaged pool by system initialization code is described in Chapter 34.

The following executive data structures are allocated from nonpaged pool:

- Buffered I/O buffers
- I/O data structures, such as I/O request packets, unit control blocks, controller request blocks, adapter control blocks, window control blocks, file control blocks, class driver data blocks, and class driver request packets
- Lock management data structures, such as lock blocks and resource blocks
- Synchronization data structures, such as common event blocks and dynamic spinlocks

- ▶ Process data structures, such as process control blocks and job information blocks
- ▶ Kernel process blocks
- ▶ Other miscellaneous systemwide data structures, such as timer queue entries

21.6   PAGED POOL

Paged dynamic memory, commonly known as paged pool, contains data structures that are used by multiple processes but that are not required to be permanently memory-resident. Its protection is ERKW, allowing it to be read from executive and kernel modes but written only from kernel mode.

During system initialization SYSBOOT reserves system space for paged pool, placing its starting address in MMG$GL_PAGEDYN. The SYSGEN parameter PAGEDYN specifies the size of this area in bytes. Paged pool is created as a set of demand zero pages. BOO$INIT_POOL, in module [SYS-BOOT]SYSBOOT, places the address of the beginning of the paged pool area in EXE$GL_PAGED. System initialization code running in the context of the swapper process initializes the pool as one data structure encompassing the entire pool. That initialization incurs a page fault and thus requires process context.

Process context kernel mode code invokes the routine EXE$ALOPAGED to allocate paged pool and the routine EXE$DEAPAGED to deallocate paged pool. These routines, both in module MEMORYALC, invoke the lower level variable-length allocation and deallocation routines described in Section 21.2.

If an allocation request cannot be satisfied, EXE$ALOPAGED returns to its invoker with a failure status. The invoker may return an error, for example, SS$_INSFMEM, to the user program, or the invoker may place the process into a resource wait state, waiting for resource RSN$_PGDYNMEM.

Whenever paged pool is deallocated, EXE$DEAPAGED invokes SCH$RA-VAIL, in module MUTEX, to declare the availability of paged pool for any waiting process. Chapter 13 describes process resource waits.

Unused paged pool requires little system overhead: one SPTE per page of pool and one corresponding reserved page of system virtual address space. Because paged pool is created as demand zero SPTEs (see Chapter 16), it expands on demand through page faults.

Because this area is pageable, code that accesses it must run at IPL 2 or below while accessing it. Elevated IPL, therefore, cannot be used for synchronizing access to the paged pool list or to any data structures allocated from it. The EXE$GL_PGDYNMTX mutex serializes access to the paged pool list. Both EXE$ALOPAGED and EXE$DEAPAGED lock this mutex for write access.

By convention, process context code that allocates a paged pool data structure executes at IPL 2 as long as the data structure's existence is recorded solely in a temporary process location, such as in a register or on the stack. Running at IPL 2 blocks AST delivery and prevents the possible loss of the pool if the process were to be deleted.

The following data structures are located in the paged pool area:

▸ The shareable logical name tables and logical name blocks

▸ The Files-11 Extended QIO Processor (XQP) I/O buffer cache, which is used for data such as file headers, index file bitmap blocks, directory file data blocks, and quota file data blocks

▸ Global section descriptors, which are used when a global section is mapped or unmapped

▸ Mounted volume list entries, which associate a mounted volume name with its corresponding logical name and unit control block address

▸ Access control list elements, which specify what access to an object is allowed for different classes of users

▸ Object rights blocks that are accessed at IPL 2 and below

▸ Data structures required by the Install utility to describe known images

   Any image that is installed has a known file entry created to describe it. Some frequently accessed known images also have their image headers permanently resident in paged pool. These data structures are described in more detail in Chapter 28.

▸ PQBs, which are temporarily used during process creation to store the quotas and limits of the new process

   PQBs, initially allocated from paged pool, are not deallocated back to the paged pool list. Instead, they are queued to a lookaside list, the self-relative queue at global label EXE$GQ_PQBIQ. Process creation code attempts to allocate a PQB by removing an element from this queue as a faster alternative to general paged pool allocation.

21.7   PROCESS ALLOCATION REGION

The process allocation region contains variable-length data structures that are used only by a single process and are not required to be permanently memory-resident. (Process allocation region pages are pageable.) Its protection is set to UREW, allowing executive and kernel modes to write it and any access mode to read it.

The process allocation region consists of a P1 space variable-length pool and may include a P0 space variable-length pool as well. The P0 space allocation pool is useful only for image-specific data structures that do not need to survive image exit. The P1 space pool can be used for both image-specific data structures and data structures that must survive the rundown of an image, such as logical name tables.

During process startup EXE$PROCSTRT reserves P1 address space for

the process allocation region. The SYSGEN parameter CTLPAGES specifies the number of pagelets in the P1 pool. Free space in the P1 process
allocation region is maintained in a singly linked, memory-ordered list, as described in Section 21.2. EXE$PROCSTRT initializes the pool and its listhead,
CTL$GQ_ALLOCREG. There is no global pointer that locates the beginning
of the process allocation region.

Executive mode code or kernel mode code running in process context
invokes EXE$ALOP1PROC, EXE$ALOP1IMAG, or EXE$ALOP0IMAG to
allocate space from the process allocation region, and EXE$DEAP1 to de-
allocate a data structure to the region. These routines are in module
MEMORYALC. When the data structure must be allocated from the P1
pool, EXE$ALOP1PROC is used. When the data structure is image-specific,
EXE$ALOP1IMAG or EXE$ALOP0IMAG is used.

EXE$ALOP1IMAG and EXE$ALOP0IMAG differ in which region they first
attempt the allocation. EXE$ALOP1IMAG tries the P1 region first, while
EXE$ALOP0IMAG tries the P0 region first. If EXE$ALOP1IMAG finds that
there is insufficient space, or EXE$ALOP0IMAG finds that allocation in the
P0 region is disallowed, each attempts to allocate from the other region.
Neither routine can allocate from P1 space if the P1 process allocation region
reaches a threshold of use specified by the SYSGEN parameter CTLIMGLIM.
If the current image is one that was linked with the NOP0BUFS option,
allocation from P0 space is prevented. If the allocation fails, these routines
return the SS$_INSFMEM error status.

The CTLIMGLIM limit does not apply to EXE$ALOP1PROC. The lat-
ter may allocate space until the P1 allocation region is exhausted. The
arithmetic difference between CTLPAGES and CTLIMGLIM guarantees a
minimum number of pagelets exclusively for EXE$ALOP1PROC. EXE$ALO-
P1PROC only allocates space from the P1 region. If an allocation fails, it returns the error status SS$_INSFMEM.

Free space in the P0 process allocation region is maintained in a singly
linked, memory-ordered list, as described in Section 21.2. During compilation of the SHELL*xx*K module, where *xx* is the system page size of 8, 16, 32,
or 64 KB, the P0 process allocation region listhead, CTL$GQ_P0ALLOC, is
initialized to zero. The image rundown routine deletes P0 space and zeros
the listhead.

If not prevented by the presence of the NOP0BUFS linker option, EXE$AL-
OP1IMAG and EXE$ALOP0IMAG create and expand the P0 process alloca-
tion region by invoking the routine MMG$EXPREG, in module SYSCRE-
DEL. This routine functions much like the Expand Program/Control Region
($EXPREG) system service. EXE$ALOP1IMAG and EXE$ALOP0IMAG ex-
pand the P0 region as needed to satisfy allocation requests, but always by at
least one virtual page. Each time one of these routines expands the P0 region,
it invokes EXE$DEALLOCATE to link the new space into the free list.

The current image and other executive routines may also expand the P0 virtual address space for their own purposes. Depending on the sequence of these expansions, multiple P0 allocation region expansions can result in a noncontiguous P0 allocation region. Note that this contrasts with the paged, nonpaged, and P1 allocation pools, which are always contiguous.

EXE$ALOP1PROC, EXE$ALOP1IMAG, and EXE$ALOP0IMAG each stores the address of the appropriate listhead in a register and invokes EXE$ALLOCATE to perform the variable-length allocation described in Section 21.2.1. EXE$DEAP1 determines whether the block being deallocated is from the P0 or P1 space pool and invokes EXE$DEALLOCATE with the address of the appropriate listhead.

No special synchronization mechanism is currently used for either the process allocation region or for the process logical names found there. However, the allocation routines change to kernel mode and execute at IPL 2, effectively blocking any other mainline or AST code from executing and perhaps attempting a simultaneous allocation from the process allocation region.

The data structures in the following list are located in the process allocation region:

▸ The process-private logical name tables and logical name blocks
▸ Image control blocks, built by the image activator to describe what images have been activated in the process
▸ Rights database identifier blocks, which contain Record Management Services context (internal file and stream identifiers) for the rights database file
▸ A context block in which the Breakthrough ($BRKTHRU) system service maintains status information as the service asynchronously broadcasts messages to the terminals specified by the user
▸ Process scan context blocks, used by the Process Scan ($PROCESS_SCAN) system service, described in Chapter 14

There is enough room in the process allocation region for privileged application software to allocate process-specific data structures of reasonable size.

21.8   KRP LOOKASIDE LIST

The KRP lookaside list is a P1 space list for process-private kernel mode data structures that are not required to be permanently memory-resident. The list is a doubly linked absolute queue, whose listhead contains the addresses of the first and last blocks in the list. The protection on this storage area is URKW, allowing it to be read from any mode but modified only from kernel mode.

Address space for this list is defined at compilation time of the SHELL*xx*K module, which defines the fixed part of P1 space. Two global symbols,

CTL$C_KRP_COUNT and CTL$C_KRP_SIZE, control the number of KRP packets created and the size of each packet. Routine EXE$PROCSTRT, in module PROCSTRT, initializes the list, forming packets and inserting them into the list at CTL$GL_KRPFL and CTL$GL_KRPBL.

A KRP is used as pageable storage, local to a kernel mode subroutine. KRPs should be used only for temporary storage that is deallocated before the subroutine returns. The most common use of KRPs is to store an equivalence name returned from a logical name translation.

Allocation and deallocation to this list is through CALL_PAL INSQUEL and CALL_PAL REMQUEL PALcode instructions. Both allocation and deallocation are always done from the front of the list. There is no need for synchronization other than that provided by the PALcode operations. Because KRPs are used only for storage local to the execution of a procedure, a failure to allocate a KRP is very unexpected and indicates a serious error rather than a temporary resource shortage. Kernel mode code that is unsuccessful at allocating from this list thus generates the fatal bugcheck KRPEMPTY.

21.9   COLLECTING POOL ALLOCATION STATISTICS

The executive requires adequate pool space to operate properly. Inadequate pool space can contribute to poor system performance and, in extreme cases, can cause the system to become totally unresponsive. The AUTOGEN facility has a feedback mechanism which, based on data gathered by various operating system components, can adjust SYSGEN parameter values to a given system's workload.

The pool allocation and expansion routines described in this chapter store pool allocation and failure statistics in data cells. (An allocation request that results in a pool expansion is not classified as a failure; pool expansion is assumed to be a routine event.) From these statistics, AUTOGEN's feedback mechanism can calculate new values for the SYSGEN parameters that control the system paged and nonpaged pool sizes.

A variable-length list (paged or nonpaged) allocation fails when no sufficiently large free block is found and, in the case of nonpaged pool, the list cannot be expanded.

An epoch is the 10-second period starting at a variable-length pool allocation failure. The routine that detects the allocation failure keeps a total of the number of bytes that fail to be allocated during an epoch. At the end of an epoch, the routine converts that to a whole number of pages and adds it to the appropriate data cell. It collects four categories of statistics for paged pool and variable-length nonpaged pool:

▸ Total number of allocation attempts
▸ Number of allocation failures
▸ Number of epochs during which allocation attempts failed
▸ Total number of pages that could not be allocated

Table 21.4   Pool Allocation Statistics

Statistic	Location	Maintained By
	NONPAGED POOL	
Total number of expansion failures	PMS$GL_NPAGDYNEXPF	EXTENDPAGE
Number of allocation attempts	PMS$GL_NPAGDYNREQ	EXE$ALONPAGVAR
Number of allocation failures	PMS$GL_NPAGDYNREQF	EXTEND_FAIL
Number of allocation failure epochs	PMS$GL_NPAGDYNF	EXTEND_FAIL
Total number of pages that failed to be allocated	PMS$GL_NPAGDYNFPAGES	EXTEND_FAIL
	PAGED POOL	
Number of allocation attempts	PMS$GL_PAGDYNREQ	EXE$ALOPAGED
Number of allocation failures	PMS$GL_PAGDYNREQF	EXE$ALOPAGED
Number of allocation failure epochs	PMS$GL_PAGDYNF	EXE$ALOPAGED
Total number of pages that failed to be allocated	PMS$GL_PAGDYNFPAGES	EXE$ALOPAGED

Table 21.4 lists the data collected and the routines responsible for updating the data cells. The program AGEN$FEEDBACK.EXE (part of the MANAGE facility) reads these data cells during the SAVPARAMS phase of AUTOGEN.COM. The *OpenVMS System Manager's Manual* provides a description of AUTOGEN's operational phases and the instructions for running it.

21.10   DETECTING POOL CORRUPTION

Certain pool misuses can lead to obscure problems if left unchecked. The operating system implements two mechanisms to help troubleshoot pool corruption problems: pool poisoning and pool history. Both are optional and enabled through the SYSGEN parameter POOLCHECK. Pool poisoning occurs dynamically, as packets or blocks are allocated and deallocated, and can result in timely detection of fatal errors. Pool history facilitates troubleshooting of problems after a crash has occurred.

21.10.1   **Pool Poisoning**

The pool poisoning mechanism can detect pool misuses such as

- ▶ Continued use of a block of pool after it is deallocated
- ▶ Use of uninitialized fields in a block of allocated pool
- ▶ Use of a block of pool that was not allocated

The mechanism applies to the variable-length pools (paged pool, nonpaged pool, and process allocation region) and to the nonpaged pool lookaside lists. It involves

- ▶ Filling deallocated pool with a unique pattern, called the FREE or "poison" pattern
- ▶ Checking that the poison pattern is intact in pool being allocated and generating the fatal bugcheck POOLCHECK if the pattern is not intact
- ▶ Filling allocated pool with a second pattern, called the ALLO pattern

This section describes the POOLCHECK SYSGEN parameter, which controls the mechanism. It explains the mechanism's workings and lists some limits to its ability to detect corruption.

21.10.1.1   **POOLCHECK Parameter.** The dynamic SYSGEN parameter POOLCHECK consists of four eight-bit fields, one of which must be zero (see Table 21.5 and Figure 21.8). The bits in the FLAGS byte enable and disable pool filling and checking and specify which pools are affected. The rest of this section describes the individual bits. The FREE and ALLO bytes specify the patterns written into pool when the space is deallocated and allocated. The default value of POOLCHECK is zero. Note that its value should be changed only for a specific purpose, such as debugging a device driver; there is a severe performance penalty when this parameter is nonzero.

Bits in the FLAGS byte put the mechanism into one of three states:

- ▶ Do not fill or check blocks
- ▶ Fill blocks only upon deallocation
- ▶ Fill blocks upon deallocation; check and fill blocks upon allocation

Bits 0 and 7 enable the filling of blocks during deallocation. Bit 0 enables the filling, with the FREE pattern, of blocks deallocated to the variable-length paged and nonpaged pools and to the nonpaged pool lookaside lists. Bits 0 and 7 together enable the filling of blocks deallocated to the process allocation region.

Table 21.5   POOLCHECK Parameter FLAGS Bits

Bit	Meaning if Set
0	Fill with FREE pattern on deallocation
1	On allocation, check for FREE pattern and fill with ALLO pattern; enable pool checking
2–6	Unused
7	Perform pool-checking operations for process allocation region also

ALLO	FREE	Must be zero	FLAGS

Figure 21.8
POOLCHECK Parameter

When set in combination with the other bits, bit 1 enables the checking and filling of blocks during allocation. If set with bit 0, it enables the checking and filling, with the ALLO pattern, of blocks allocated from the variable-length paged and nonpaged pools and from the nonpaged pool lookaside lists. If set with bit 7, it enables the checking and filling of blocks allocated from the process allocation region.

21.10.1.2   **Pool-Poisoning Routine.** The routine POISON_PACKET, in module MEMO-RYALC, is invoked to fill pool space with a predictable pattern under several circumstances:

▶ Space is deallocated by EXE$DEANONPAGED, EXE$DEANONPGDSIZ, or EXE$DEALLOCATE.
▶ A deallocated variable-length block is agglomerated with free blocks.
▶ Space is returned to variable-length pool by EXE$ALLOCATE as a result of an inexact fit.
▶ Space is added to variable-length nonpaged pool as a result of pool expansion.

The macro $PFREEDEF defines offsets to a free block or packet of pool. Figure 21.9 shows the effects of pool poisoning on a free piece of pool. The first nine longwords form a header, of which the first eight remain unchanged by pool poisoning:

▶ The first three longwords contain the forward pointer to the next free block; the size of the block, if it is a variable-length block; and the original size, type, and subtype fields.
▶ When POISON_PACKET is invoked by EXE$DEANONPAGED and EXE$DEANONPGDSIZ, the fourth longword of the header contains the

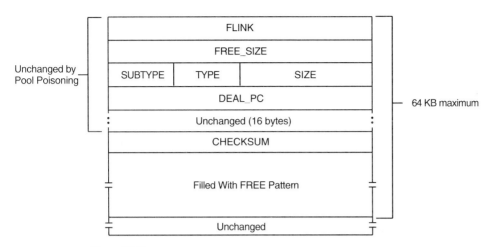

Figure 21.9
Format of Poisoned Pool Space

return address of the deallocation routine's invoker. When POISON_
PACKET is invoked by EXE$DEALLOCATE, that is, for a variable-length
block, this longword contains stale data that is still potentially useful in
crash dump analysis.

▶ The next two quadwords contain data that POISON_PACKET does not
use.

If enabled by the previously described bits, POISON_PACKET poisons
deallocated pool as follows:

1. It calculates a checksum by adding (ignoring any carry) the following:
    - FREE pattern byte
    - The deallocated block's address
    - Contents of the longword at PFREE$W_SIZE
    - Contents of the longword at PFREE$L_DEAL_PC
    - Contents of the longword beginning at EXE$GQ_BOOTTIME + 1

    It stores the checksum in the longword at offset PFREE$L_CHECKSUM
    of the block.

      Under certain circumstances, it is possible for the contents of memory
    to be preserved from one bootstrap of the operating system to the next.
    The last longword used in calculating the checksum enables the check-
    ing routine to differentiate between stale poisoned pool and pool space
    poisoned during this bootstrap of the operating system.

2. It initializes the remainder of the space, up to a maximum of 64 KB, with
    the FREE pattern.

21.10.1.3   Pool-Checking Routine. The routine CHECK_PACKET, in module MEMO-
RYALC, checks pool space. It is invoked by the following routines.

▶ EXE$ALLOCATE, when allocating variable-length pool space from paged pool, nonpaged pool, or the process allocation region

▶ EXE$ALONONPAGED, when allocating a lookaside packet

CHECK_PACKET calculates the expected checksum using the algorithm described in Section 21.10.1.2. If the expected checksum does not match that found in the PFREE$L_CHECKSUM longword, CHECK_PACKET assumes the block is unpoisoned and makes no further checks. (Since POOLCHECK is a dynamic SYSGEN parameter, it is possible that pool poisoning was disabled for a time, resulting in unpoisoned blocks on the free list. Alternatively, the block may have been poisoned during a previous bootstrap.)

If the checksum matches, CHECK_PACKET examines the remainder of the block for the FREE pattern. If the FREE pattern is not intact, it generates the fatal bugcheck POOLCHECK after pushing a reason code onto the stack. Table 21.6 summarizes these reason codes.

If the FREE pattern is intact, CHECK_PACKET fills the entire block (including the first nine longwords) with the ALLO pattern.

21.10.1.4 **Constraints on the Pool-Checking Mechanism.** Some circumstances can circumvent the pool-checking mechanism:

▶ Any corruption of pool space that corrupts the third, fourth, or ninth (checksum) longword effectively disables checking for that block.

▶ Checking occurs only at allocation time. Corruption that occurs after a block is allocated is not detected.

▶ When a block being deallocated to variable-length pool is merged with a free block above or below it, the entire resulting free block is filled. This masks any corruption that may have previously occurred in an adjacent free block.

▶ The mechanism fills and checks a maximum of 65,500 bytes (64 KB less the nine-longword header).

Disabling and reenabling pool poisoning with the same FREE pattern can lead to false POOLCHECK bugchecks. If EXE$DEALLOCATE concatenates a variable-length block to the bottom of a poisoned free block while pool

---

Table 21.6   POOLCHECK Bugcheck Reason Codes

Value	Meaning
0	Packet is corrupted
1, 2	Unused
3	Paged block extends outside of paged pool
4	Nonpaged block extends outside of nonpaged pool
5	P1 space allocation attempted at too high an IPL
6	Block could not be agglomerated

poisoning is disabled, only the top part of the resulting free block contains the FREE pattern. If pool checking is subsequently enabled with the same FREE pattern and this free block is allocated, CHECK_PACKET interprets it as being corrupt.

21.10.2   Pool History

The pool history mechanism records information about pool allocations and deallocations in a nonpaged pool ring buffer. If the system crashes as a result of pool corruption, information about the most recent allocations and deallocations can be displayed using the SDA utility.

The pool history mechanism is enabled by bootstrapping the system with a nonzero POOLCHECK SYSGEN parameter. In that case, SYSBOOT, the secondary bootstrap program, loads the SYSTEM_PRIMITIVES.EXE executive image rather than SYSTEM_PRIMITIVES_MIN.EXE. SYSTEM_PRIMI-TIVES.EXE contains the code described in this section.

During system initialization the executive image's initialization routine, INI$ESTAB_RECLAIM_TQE, in module MEMORYALC_DYN, allocates a block of nonpaged pool for a nonpaged pool history buffer ring. This block can hold 256 nonpaged pool history buffers. It stores the address of this block in IOC$AR_RINGBUF and IOC$AR_NEXTNPH.

The routines EXE$ALONONPAGED_INT, EXE$ALONONPAGED_ALN_LIST, EXE$DEANONPAGED_INT, and EXE$DEANONPGDSIZ_INT, all in module MEMORYALC_DYN, call procedure UPDATE_RINGBUF, also in module MEMORYALC_DYN, as part of their operation. UPDATE_RING-BUF maintains the nonpaged pool history buffer ring.

Each time it is called, UPDATE_RINGBUF updates IOC$AR_NEXTNPH to point to the next available history buffer. If all history buffers have been used, it initializes IOC$AR_NEXTNPH with the contents of IOC$AR_RINGBUF, the beginning of the history buffer area. UPDATE_RINGBUF records the following information in the history buffer:

- ▶ The return address of the caller of the allocation or deallocation routine
- ▶ The address of the nonpaged pool packet or block being allocated or deallocated
- ▶ Size, type, and subtype of data structure being allocated or deallocated
- ▶ A value indicating whether the data structure was allocated from or deallocated to a lookaside list or the variable-length region

The layout of a pool history buffer is shown in Figure 21.10. The macro $NPHDEF defines the offsets to the fields in this structure.

The SDA command SHOW POOL/RING_BUFFER displays information stored in the history buffers. Note that this command cannot display useful information on a running system because of the dynamic nature of pool; it is used mainly in crash dump analysis.

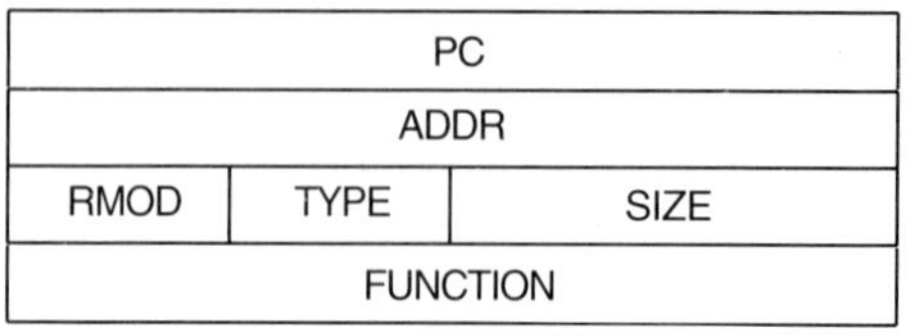

PC		
ADDR		
RMOD	TYPE	SIZE
FUNCTION		

Function Value	Meaning
0	Lookaside list allocation
1	Variable region allocation
2	Lookaside list deallocation
3	Variable region deallocation

Figure 21.10
Layout of Nonpaged Pool History Buffer

21.11   RELEVANT SOURCE MODULES

Source modules described in this chapter include

[LIB]NPOOL_DATA.SDL
[LIB]PFREEDEF.SDL
[SYS]LOOK_ASIDE_LIST.M64
[SYS]MEMORYALC.MAR
[SYS]MEMORYALC_DYN.B32

PART VI / Input/Output

22 Overview of the I/O Subsystem

Out of intense complexities intense simplicities emerge.
Winston Churchill

This chapter provides an overview of the OpenVMS AXP I/O subsystem. The major I/O subsystem components are device drivers and their data structures, ancillary control processes, I/O support routines, and I/O system services.

The following chapters describe different aspects of the I/O subsystem in more detail:

▶ Chapter 2 provides an overview of the Alpha AXP I/O hardware architecture and the terms that describe its components.
▶ Chapter 23 describes I/O system services and their use.
▶ Chapter 24 describes driver I/O processing.
▶ Chapter 25 describes software I/O mailboxes.
▶ Chapter 26 describes the terminal driver, pseudo devices, disk bad block processing, and other I/O-related topics.

The manual *OpenVMS AXP Device Support: Creating a Step 1 Driver from an OpenVMS VAX Device Driver* describes device drivers from the point of view of adding a device driver to the system.

22.1 OVERVIEW

User images initiate most I/O operations. The executive initiates I/O operations for swapping, paging, file system, and other miscellaneous functions.

All I/O operation requests are eventually handled by a system software component called a device driver, or simply, a driver. The driver is primarily responsible for communicating system and user I/O requests to the I/O hardware and ensuring that they are carried out correctly within a reasonable time. Each type of device has a separate driver. Section 22.3 provides an overview of drivers.

Figure 22.1 shows various software components involved in user-initiated I/O operations. User images and most components request an I/O operation through the Queue I/O Request ($QIO) system service. User images can indirectly request the $QIO system service using Record Management Services (RMS) or a higher level language interface such as a FORTRAN WRITE statement or the C language `printf()` function.

The $QIO system service provides a device-independent user interface to drivers. If the device-independent parameters of a user's I/O request are valid,

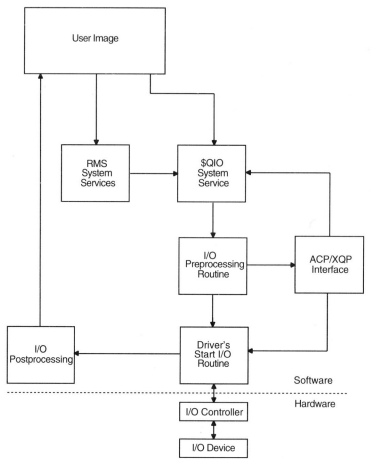

Figure 22.1
Overview of OpenVMS AXP I/O Processing

the service allocates and builds an I/O request packet (IRP). The IRP describes the I/O request and its context until the request completes successfully. The $QIO system service passes the IRP to the driver's I/O preprocessing routine for device- and function-specific validation. This I/O preprocessing routine may, for example, check the accessibility of the $QIO requestor's buffer in preparation for a direct memory access (DMA) transfer. $QIO and related system services are described in Chapter 23.

The driver's I/O preprocessing routine, also known as a function decision table (FDT) routine, delivers the IRP to the driver's start I/O routine if all the following conditions are met:

▶ The I/O request is valid.
▶ No ancillary control process (ACP) assistance is required.

▶ The function that was requested cannot be completed by the I/O preprocessing routine.

▶ No further I/O preprocessing is required.

Chapter 23 elaborates on the steps taken by the driver's I/O preprocessing routine.

The start I/O routine interacts with the controller to perform the requested I/O operation. It and other driver routines are summarized in Section 22.3.2.

If the I/O preprocessing routine requires ACP assistance, it delivers the IRP to the ACP. An ACP assists a device driver with its complex functions. For example, the network ACP (NETACP) assists the network device driver (NETDRIVER) with creating links to other systems, performing routing and switching functions, and so on. The ACP can issue $QIO requests of its own to process a user's I/O request, or it can deliver the IRP to the driver's start I/O routine.

The executive provides I/O support routines that assist drivers at many levels. Section 22.5 summarizes these routines.

22.2   I/O DATABASE

The I/O database serves the following main functions:

▶ It describes individual I/O hardware components, such as devices, controllers, adapters, and widgets, as well as device drivers.

▶ It describes system topology, that is, the configuration of and interrelations among I/O hardware components.

▶ It maintains the context of I/O operations.

This section gives a brief overview of the I/O database and the structures within it. *OpenVMS AXP Device Support: Creating a Step 1 Driver from an OpenVMS VAX Device Driver* provides a detailed treatment of the data structures that make up the I/O database. Figure 22.2 shows the relations among the principal data structures in the I/O database.

22.2.1   I/O Hardware Components and Their Data Structures

Each I/O hardware component has one or more data structures associated with it.

22.2.1.1   Data Structures for I/O Devices.
The I/O database is unit-oriented. The item of interest to a process that requests the I/O operation is the target device unit. In most cases, the I/O controller, I/O adapter, and so on, are significant to the requesting process only because they communicate between the CPU and the device unit.

The executive creates a unit control block (UCB) for each I/O device attached to the system. A typical UCB, shown in Figure 22.3, defines the characteristics and current state of an individual device and is the focal point for

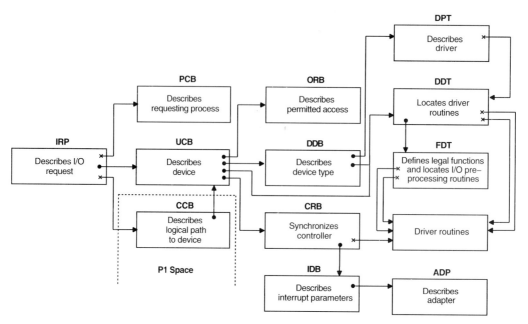

Figure 22.2
The I/O Database

controlling access to it. It contains a fork block (FKB) substructure (described in Chapter 5). When a driver is stalled or interrupted, the driver's context is stored in the FKB. The UCB also contains pointers to various related data structures, and a queue header for the device's pending I/O requests. A UCB can have one or more device-specific extension areas.

The executive creates an object rights block (ORB) for each device when it creates the associated UCB. An ORB, pictured in Figure E.6, describes the rights a process must have to access the object associated with the ORB. A UCB is not the only entity that has an associated ORB; although ORBs are a part of the I/O database, they are not unique to it.

A device data block (DDB) contains information common to all devices of the same type connected to a particular controller. A DDB is not used directly for controlling access either to the device controller or to associated devices. Shown in Figure 22.4, a DDB records the generic device name (TT, for example) concatenated with the controller designator (A or B, for example). When combined with the unit number for the device, the generic device name forms the OpenVMS name for the device (TTA10:, for example).

The device's allocation class is combined with this name to form a unique device name in a VMScluster. A DDB also points to the driver prologue and driver dispatch tables.

IOC$GL_DEVLIST is the listhead for the list of all DDBs on a system. Offset DDB$PS_LINK in each DDB points to the next DDB in the list. The

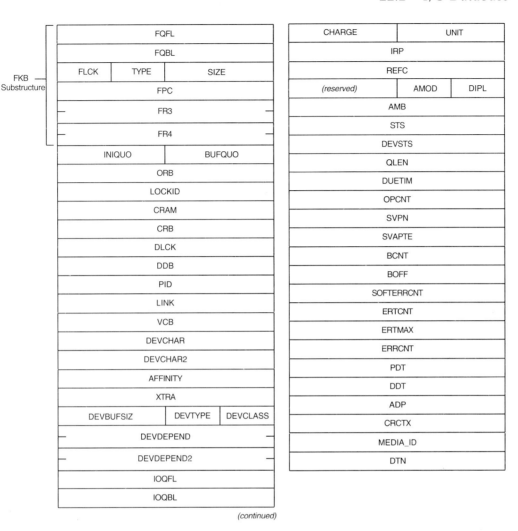

CHARGE	UNIT	
IRP		
REFC		
(reserved)	AMOD	DIPL
AMB		
STS		
DEVSTS		
QLEN		
DUETIM		
OPCNT		
SVPN		
SVAPTE		
BCNT		
BOFF		
SOFTERRCNT		
ERTCNT		
ERTMAX		
ERRCNT		
PDT		
DDT		
ADP		
CRCTX		
MEDIA_ID		
DTN		

FQFL		
FQBL		
FLCK	TYPE	SIZE
FPC		
FR3		
FR4		
INIQUO	BUFQUO	
ORB		
LOCKID		
CRAM		
CRB		
DLCK		
DDB		
PID		
LINK		
VCB		
DEVCHAR		
DEVCHAR2		
AFFINITY		
XTRA		
DEVBUFSIZ	DEVTYPE	DEVCLASS
DEVDEPEND		
DEVDEPEND2		
IOQFL		
IOQBL		

FKB Substructure

(continued)

Figure 22.3
Unit Control Block (UCB)

last DDB in the list has zero in its DDB$PS_LINK field. Figure 22.5 shows the DDB list. IOC$GL_DEVLIST is actually an alternative name for the field SB$PS_DDB in the statically allocated system block (SB) that describes the system. (On a system that is a VMScluster node, there is an SB for each node in the cluster. The SB for each node has a list of DDBs for devices on that node that are mounted clusterwide.)

Offset DDB$PS_UCB in each DDB points to the first in a list of UCBs for units of the same type attached to the controller associated with the DDB. The next UCB in this list is located through the UCB offset UCB$PS_LINK, as shown in Figure 22.5. The last UCB in the list has zero in its UCB$PS_LINK field.

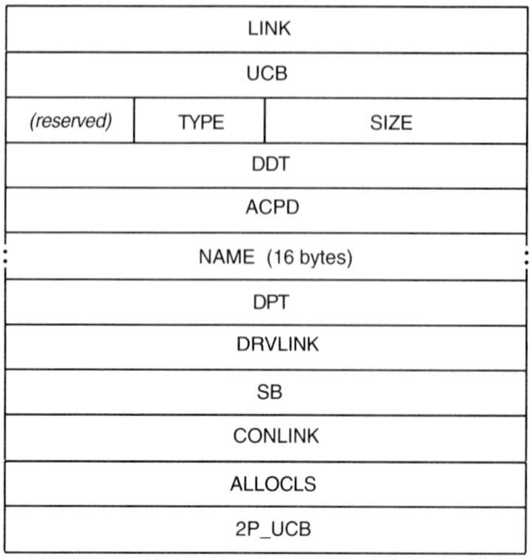

LINK		
UCB		
(reserved)	TYPE	SIZE
DDT		
ACPD		
NAME (16 bytes)		
DPT		
DRVLINK		
SB		
CONLINK		
ALLOCLS		
2P_UCB		

Figure 22.4
Device Data Block (DDB)

The Assign Channel ($ASSIGN) system service, for example, searches the DDB list to locate the DDB corresponding to a user-specified generic device name. It then searches the DDB's UCB list to locate the UCB corresponding to the user-specified unit number.

All DDBs associated with a driver are linked together in a list that begins at offset DPT$PS_DDB_LIST in the driver prologue table (DPT). Offset DDB$PS_DRVLINK in each DDB points to the next DDB in this list, as shown in Figure 22.6. This list can be used to find all devices associated with a given driver. Section 22.3.1.1 describes the driver prologue table.

The class driver data block (CDDB) field CDDB$PS_DDB for a controller is the listhead of all DDBs associated with that controller. Offset DDB$PS_CONLINK in each DDB points to the next DDB in this list.

22.2.1.2 **Data Structures for I/O Controllers.** The executive creates a controller request block (CRB) to represent and control access to an I/O controller. Shown in Figure 22.7, a CRB defines the current state of the controller. It contains an FKB substructure and a listhead of fork processes waiting for controller access. It also contains one interrupt transfer vector (VEC) substructure, shown in Figure 22.8, for each of the controller's interrupt vectors.

A VEC substructure provides information about a device's interrupt: the location of its service routine and the address of the interrupt dispatch block (IDB) to be used by the service routine. The purpose and use of the VEC substructure are described in Chapter 24.

The executive creates an IDB for every CRB it creates. An IDB, shown in Figure 22.9, stores parameters for the device's interrupt service routine that

756

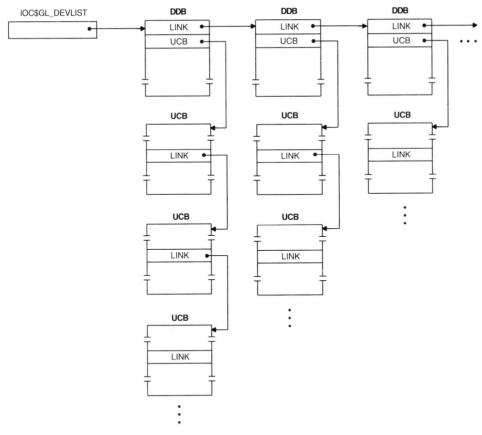

Figure 22.5
DDB List

enable it to determine which of the controller's units should be serviced. An IDB holds the address of the I/O controller's base control/status register (CSR), a list of controller register access mailboxes (CRAMs), and for some controllers, a list of UCBs associated with the controller.

An IDB also contains the system control block (SCB) vector offset for the controller's interrupts. If more than one interrupt vector is associated with the controller, its IDB points to an auxiliary structure called the vector list extension (VLE), shown in Figure 22.10. A VLE has an array of SCB vector offsets for the controller's interrupts. Chapters 4 and 24 give more information on interrupts and interrupt dispatching.

A CRAM can be associated with an I/O controller or an I/O device. Shown in Figure 22.11, a CRAM contains a hardware mailbox, a pointer to the local I/O adapter's mailbox pointer register (MBPR), and various parameters that govern the hardware mailbox access operation. Chapter 26 describes hardware mailbox access support.

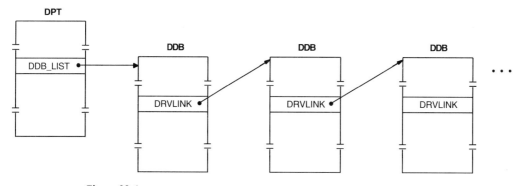

Figure 22.6
Driver's DDB List

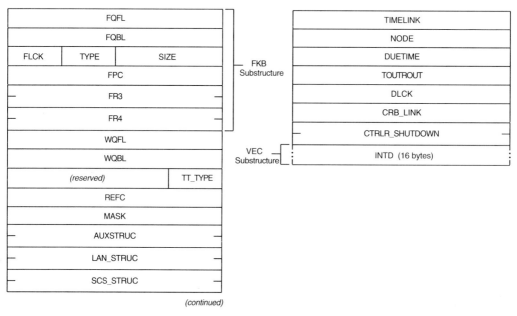

(continued)

Figure 22.7
Controller Request Block (CRB)

22.2.1.3 **Data Structures for Interconnects, I/O Adapters, and I/O Widgets.** An Open-VMS VAX adapter control block (ADP) simply represents a hardware block that connects one interconnect to another. In OpenVMS AXP, the ADP's function has been extended to include information about the interconnect and the system configuration.

Despite its name, therefore, an ADP, shown in Figure 22.12, can now represent one of the following: the processor-memory interconnect (PMI), a tightly coupled I/O interconnect, or a multichannel I/O widget.

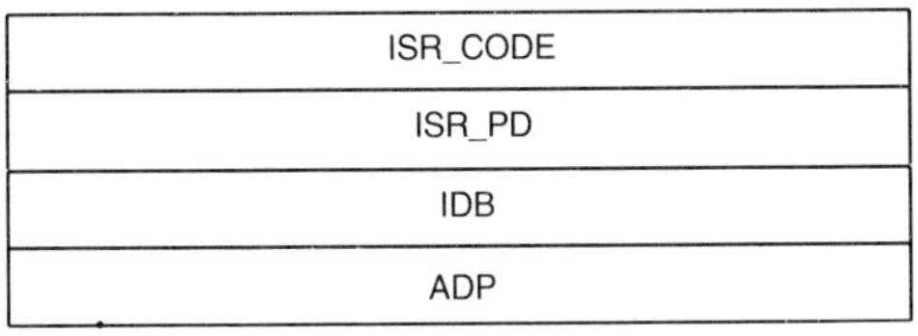

ISR_CODE
ISR_PD
IDB
ADP

Figure 22.8
Interrupt Transfer Vector (VEC)

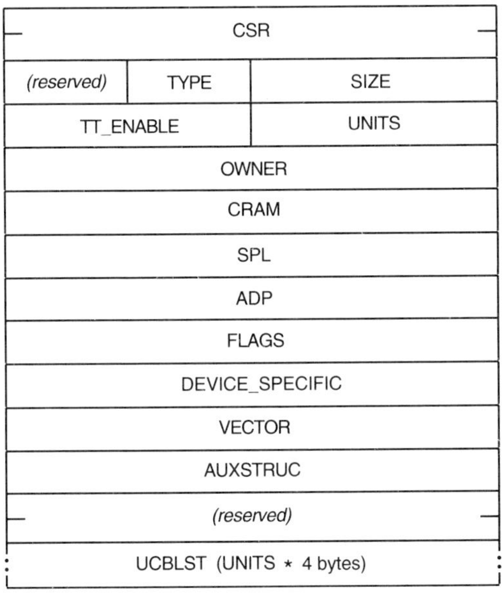

CSR		
(reserved)	TYPE	SIZE
TT_ENABLE		UNITS
OWNER		
CRAM		
SPL		
ADP		
FLAGS		
DEVICE_SPECIFIC		
VECTOR		
AUXSTRUC		
(reserved)		
UCBLST (UNITS ∗ 4 bytes)		

Figure 22.9
Interrupt Dispatch Block (IDB)

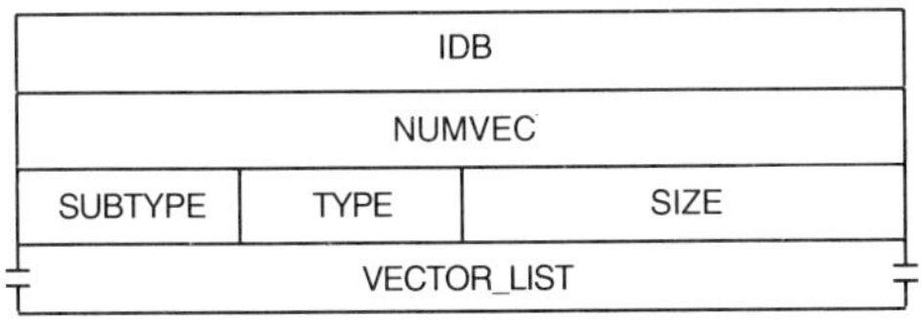

IDB		
NUMVEC		
SUBTYPE	TYPE	SIZE
VECTOR_LIST		

Figure 22.10
Vector List Extension (VLE)

The system ADP represents the PMI. It has an auxiliary bus array structure that describes all PMI nodes. An ADP other than the system ADP represents either a tightly coupled I/O interconnect or a multichannel I/O widget.

An ADP for a tightly coupled I/O interconnect contains information related to hardware mailbox support, system topology, adapter interrupts, and

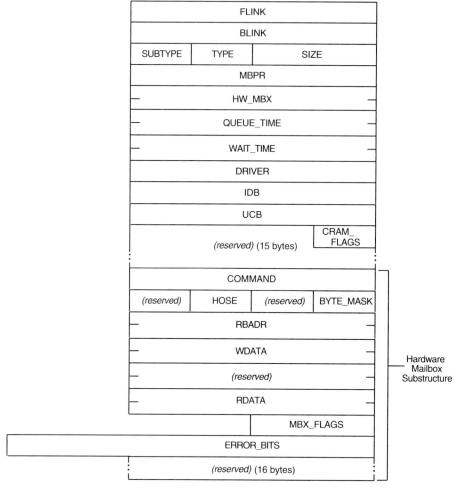

Figure 22.11
Controller Register Access Mailbox (CRAM)

related items. It also contains information about the I/O adapter that connects the interconnect to the PMI or to a parent tightly coupled I/O interconnect. The adjective *parent* in this context describes the tightly coupled I/O interconnect that is closer to the PMI.

Information relating to an I/O widget is normally maintained only in a widget-specific data structure defined and used by the widget's driver. Information that is common to all loosely coupled I/O interconnects connected to a multichannel I/O widget is, however, maintained in an ADP.

An ADP can have up to four auxiliary data structures: adapter bus array (BUSARRAY), pointed to by ADP$PS_BUS_ARRAY; adapter command table (CMDTABLE), pointed to by ADP$PS_COMMAND_TBL; counted resource

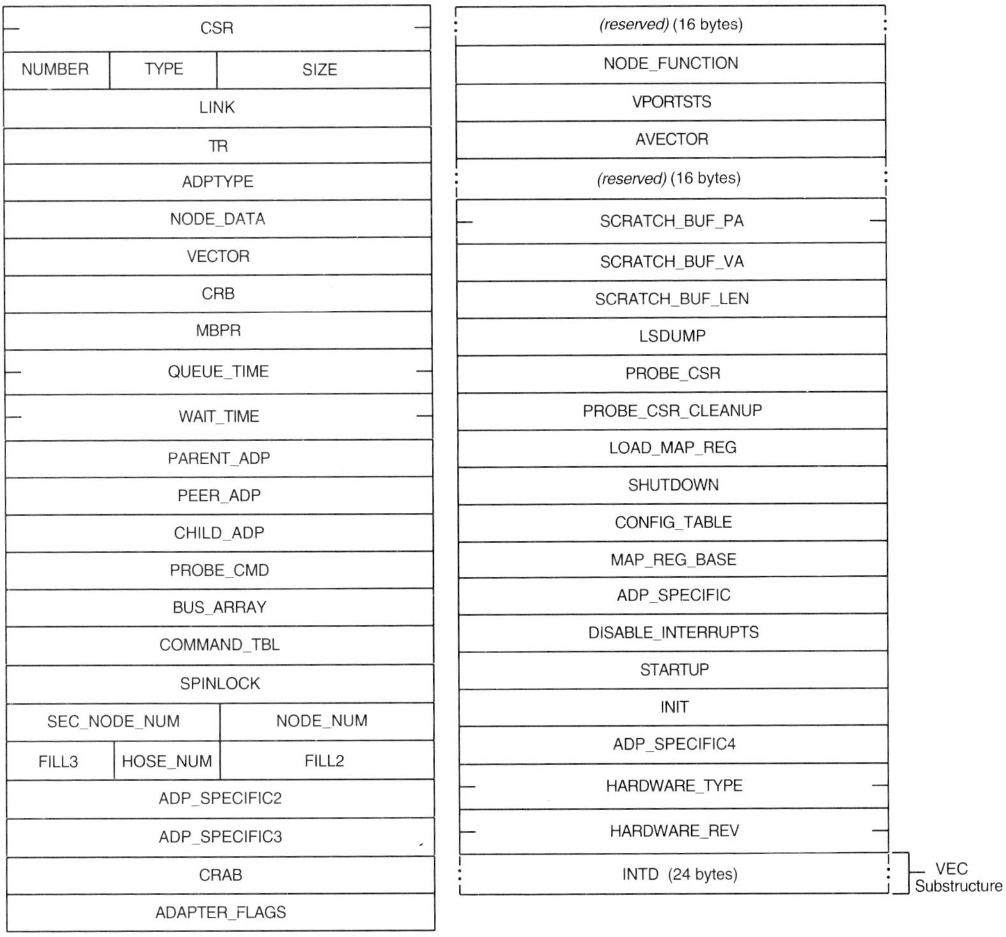

CSR		
NUMBER	TYPE	SIZE
LINK		
TR		
ADPTYPE		
NODE_DATA		
VECTOR		
CRB		
MBPR		
QUEUE_TIME		
WAIT_TIME		
PARENT_ADP		
PEER_ADP		
CHILD_ADP		
PROBE_CMD		
BUS_ARRAY		
COMMAND_TBL		
SPINLOCK		
SEC_NODE_NUM	NODE_NUM	
FILL3	HOSE_NUM	FILL2
ADP_SPECIFIC2		
ADP_SPECIFIC3		
CRAB		
ADAPTER_FLAGS		

(reserved) (16 bytes)
NODE_FUNCTION
VPORTSTS
AVECTOR
(reserved) (16 bytes)
SCRATCH_BUF_PA
SCRATCH_BUF_VA
SCRATCH_BUF_LEN
LSDUMP
PROBE_CSR
PROBE_CSR_CLEANUP
LOAD_MAP_REG
SHUTDOWN
CONFIG_TABLE
MAP_REG_BASE
ADP_SPECIFIC
DISABLE_INTERRUPTS
STARTUP
INIT
ADP_SPECIFIC4
HARDWARE_TYPE
HARDWARE_REV
INTD (24 bytes) — VEC Substructure

(continued)

Figure 22.12
Adapter Control Block (ADP)

allocation block (CRAB), pointed to by ADP$PS_CRAB; and interrupt vector table, pointed to by ADP$PS_VECTOR. The BUSARRAY structure is described later in this section.

IOC$GL_ADPLIST is the listhead for the list of all ADPs, shown in Figure 22.13. The first ADP on this list is always the system ADP. Offset ADP$PS_LINK in each ADP points to the next ADP in the list. The last ADP in the list has zero in its ADP$PS_LINK field. In response to the command IO SHOW BUS, the SYSMAN utility traverses and displays this list.

The hierarchy of tightly coupled I/O interconnects on a system is represented by the interconnections between ADPs in the ADP list. In conjunction with the auxiliary BUSARRAY structure (shown in Figure 22.14) for

761

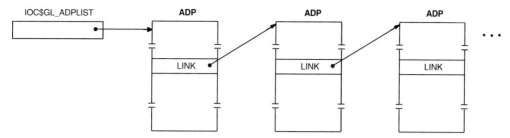

Figure 22.13
ADP List

each ADP, this information represents a system's configuration. For example, Figure 22.15 shows how ADPs and their auxiliary BUSARRAY structures represent the DEC 7000 Model 600 system configuration.

At the root of the hierarchical ADP list is the system ADP. Offset ADP$PS_CHILD_ADP in the system ADP points to an ADP for a tightly coupled I/O interconnect at the next level in the hierarchy—one that connects to the PMI directly, that is, without other intervening tightly coupled I/O interconnects. In Figure 22.15, the system ADP's ADP$PS_CHILD_ADP points to the first Extended Memory Interconnect (XMI) ADP.

Offset ADP$PS_PEER_ADP in the system ADP always contains the value zero because the PMI has no peers. On a DEC 7000 Model 600 system, for example, up to four XMIs can be connected to the PMI through an I/O module. Offset ADP$PS_PEER_ADP in each XMI ADP points to the next XMI ADP if one exists. Offset ADP$PS_PEER_ADP in the last XMI ADP in the chain contains zero.

The BUSARRAY structure contains information about nodes on a tightly coupled I/O interconnect. It consists of a fixed portion and an array of entries. The fixed portion contains the tightly coupled I/O interconnect type, the number of nodes, and a pointer to the ADP. There is one array entry for each tightly coupled I/O interconnect node. Each entry records the node number, hardware identification of the node, an ADP pointer, and a CRB pointer. If the node is either an I/O adapter or a multichannel I/O widget, device autoconfiguration code initializes the ADP pointer to an ADP address and the CRB pointer to zero. If the node is an I/O widget instead, device autoconfiguration code initializes the CRB pointer to a CRB address and the ADP pointer to zero. For a node connected manually through the SYSMAN IO CONNECT command, both pointers contain zero.

22.2.2 Context of I/O Operations

The executive maintains the context of user I/O requests in the channel control block (CCB) and the IRP, the latter pictured in Figure 22.16. Before an image can perform I/O operations to a device, it must assign an I/O chan-

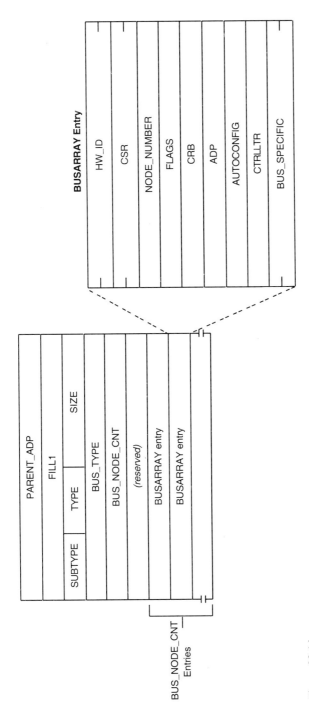

Figure 22.14
Adapter Bus Array (BUSARRAY)

763

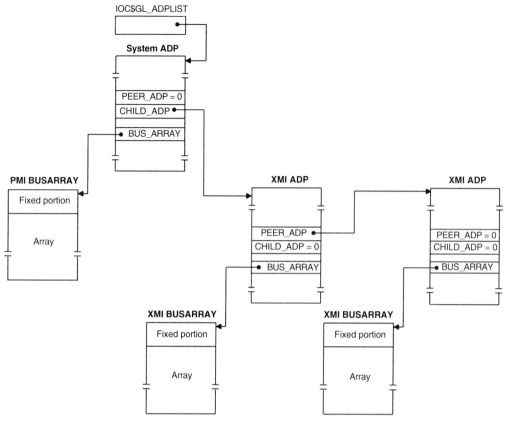

Figure 22.15
ADP Hierarchy and System Configuration

nel to the device. It does this by requesting the $ASSIGN system service, which allocates a CCB to describe the channel. Unlike other I/O data structures described here, CCBs are located in the P1 space of each process. An I/O channel, described by the CCB, is the software mechanism that links a process to the target device of an I/O operation. The I/O channel and CCB are described in Chapter 23.

When an image requests the $QIO system service for an I/O operation, the $QIO system service procedure, in cooperation with the driver's preprocessing routine, constructs an IRP to describe the I/O request in a standard format. The device-independent arguments of the I/O request are recorded in the IRP. Additionally, if the operation involves data transfer, the user buffer's address and size are recorded in the IRP. The IRP has an asynchronous system trap (AST) control block (ACB) substructure, a pointer to the UCB for the target device, addresses of other related data structures, and a class driver request packet (CDRP) substructure. Class drivers are described in Section 22.3.

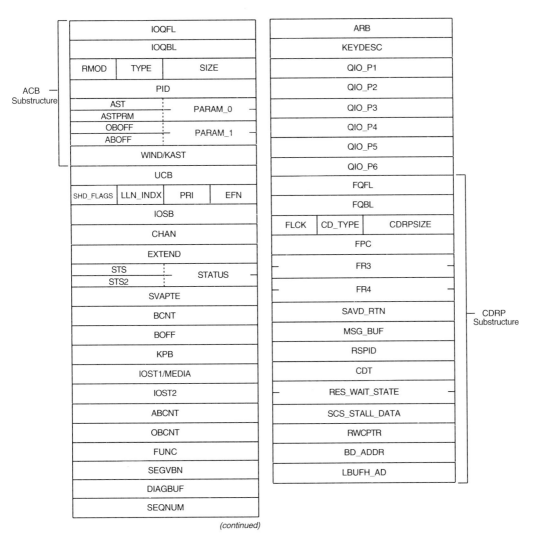

Figure 22.16
I/O Request Packet (IRP)

The CDRP substructure describes a request to be handled by a system communication services (SCS) port driver. Such requests are generated, for example, by the Mass Storage Control Protocol (MSCP) disk and tape class drivers. To save time in these drivers, each IRP includes enough space for a CDRP, although the space is not always used for that purpose.

When the I/O subsystem initiates an I/O operation, it creates a fork process thread of execution in which driver code executes. The fork process's context is maintained in a fork block, which is usually a substructure of a larger structure, for example, a UCB or a CDRP. A driver fork process that requires more context to be maintained can execute as a kernel process, a thread of execution with a private stack. A kernel process block (KPB) describes each kernel process. Chapter 5 contains further details on fork and kernel processes, FKBs, and KPBs.

22.2.3 Synchronizing Access to the I/O Database

The following methods are used to synchronize access to the I/O database: mutexes, interrupt priority level (IPL), spinlocks, and lock management system services.

The I/O database mutex, IOC$GL_MUTEX, synchronizes access to the I/O database. This mutex does not synchronize access to any of the hardware components of the I/O subsystem. Its major purpose is to synchronize the addition or deletion of data structures with searches of the I/O database.

The spinlocks of most interest to the I/O subsystem are fork locks and device locks. Fork locks synchronize fork processing. A device lock synchronizes access to the device controller data structures and therefore to the controller.

IPL synchronization of the I/O database normally occurs as part of spinlock acquisition and release. Less frequently, IPL is used to synchronize access in a context where coordination with other processors in a symmetric multiprocessing system is irrelevant. For example, a driver fork process raises IPL to IPL$_POWER (31) to block powerfail interrupts on the local processor just before initiating device activity.

Chapter 9 discusses the use of IPL, spinlocks, and mutexes for synchronization. *OpenVMS AXP Device Support: Creating a Step 1 Driver from an OpenVMS VAX Device Driver* describes the use of IPL and spinlocks for synchronization from the perspective of device drivers. Chapter 11 describes lock management system services.

If the system is a VMScluster node, lock management system services synchronize access to the UCBs for devices that are cluster-available (DEV$V_CLU set in UCB$L_DEVCHAR2). Each such device is described by a resource name that is the string SYS$ concatenated with the allocation class device name. Appendix H gives more information on specific locks.

22.3 DEVICE DRIVERS

A device driver is a collection of routines and tables that assist the executive in performing I/O operations on a device. The key functions of a device driver are as follows:

▶ Defining an I/O device for the rest of the operating system
▶ Preparing an I/O device and its controller for operation during system initialization, during connection of the device by the driver-loading procedure, and during recovery from a power failure
▶ Validating device-dependent parameters of a user's I/O request

► Translating user I/O requests into device-specific commands
► Activating the I/O device by accessing one or more interface registers
► Responding to device interrupts
► Responding to device timeout conditions
► Responding to I/O request cancellations
► Logging errors
► Returning device status to the I/O requestor

There are two OpenVMS AXP driver models—the traditional model, in which the entire driver is contained in one image, and the class/port model, in which the driver consists of more than one image.

In the class/port model, the class driver performs functions common to a class of device, such as an MSCP disk or a Small Computer System Interface (SCSI) tape, for example. The port driver contains controller-specific subroutines for the class driver. For any given device, a class driver is bound to a port driver through the UCB or a port-specific data structure. The functional division into class and port drivers simplifies maintenance and integration of software when new devices and controllers are introduced.

The following are different categories of class/port driver, distinguished on the basis of the interaction between class and port driver:

► MSCP drivers
► SCSI drivers
► Terminal drivers
► Communications drivers

Class/port drivers are discussed in more detail in Chapter 26. The term *driver* when used by itself usually refers to a traditional driver.

22.3.1   Driver Tables

The following tables—driver prologue table, driver dispatch table, and function decision table—are included in most drivers.

22.3.1.1   Driver Prologue Table.

A driver prologue table, shown in Figure 22.17, is a statically defined data structure within the driver image. It contains information that helps the driver-loading procedure load the driver into memory and create the driver's I/O database. (SYS$LOAD_DRIVER, in module [IOGEN]INIT_LOAD_DRIVER, is the driver-loading procedure.) For example, a DPT defines the size of the device's UCB, the number of per-unit and per-controller CRAMs, and the driver's name. It also points to the driver dispatch table and to procedure descriptors for various driver routines that assist the driver-loading procedure in preparing the device's I/O database.

After loading the driver, the driver-loading procedure chains the DPT to the systemwide list of DPTs starting at global location IOC$GL_DPTLIST.

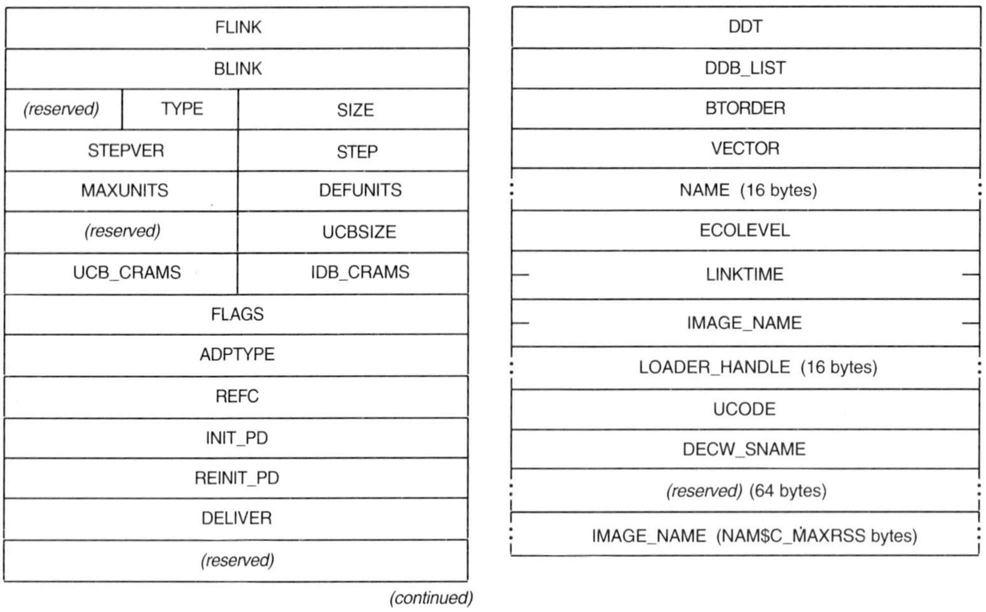

FLINK		
BLINK		
(reserved)	TYPE	SIZE
STEPVER		STEP
MAXUNITS		DEFUNITS
(reserved)		UCBSIZE
UCB_CRAMS		IDB_CRAMS
FLAGS		
ADPTYPE		
REFC		
INIT_PD		
REINIT_PD		
DELIVER		
(reserved)		

DDT
DDB_LIST
BTORDER
VECTOR
NAME (16 bytes)
ECOLEVEL
LINKTIME
IMAGE_NAME
LOADER_HANDLE (16 bytes)
UCODE
DECW_SNAME
(reserved) (64 bytes)
IMAGE_NAME (NAM$C_MAXRSS bytes)

(continued)

Figure 22.17
Driver Prologue Table (DPT)

22.3.1.2 **Driver Dispatch Table.** Each device driver has a set of standard routines, described in Section 22.3.2, that the executive can invoke to perform device-related operations. The executive locates these routines through the driver dispatch table (DDT), shown in Figure 22.18.

A DDT is a statically defined data structure within the driver image. In addition to containing procedure values for a driver's start I/O routine, controller initialization routine, unit initialization routine, and other routines, a DDT also points to the driver's function decision table and defines the sizes of a driver's diagnostic and error log buffers.

22.3.1.3 **Function Decision Table.** A function decision table, shown in Figure 22.19, lists all valid I/O function codes for the device and associates valid codes with the addresses of I/O preprocessing routines, also referred to as FDT routines.

Statically defined within the driver image, an FDT consists of a fixed portion followed by an array of FDT entries. The fixed portion consists of two 64-bit masks: the legal function mask, and the buffered function mask.

I/O function codes have values ranging from 0 to 63. Each bit in a mask corresponds to an I/O function code. For example, bit 33 in a mask corresponds to I/O function code 33. Bits set in the legal function mask indicate which function codes are supported for the associated devices. Bits set in the

(reserved)	
START	
(reserved)	SIZE
ERRORBUF	DIAGBUF
(reserved)	FDTSIZE
CTRLINIT	
UNITINIT	
CLONEDUCB	
FDT	
CANCEL	
REGDUMP	
ALTSTART	

MNTVER
MNTV_SSSC
MNTV_FOR
MNTV_SQD
AUX_STORAGE
AUX_ROUTINE
CHANNEL_ASSIGN
CANCEL_SELECTIVE
STACK_BCNT
REG_MASK
KP_STARTIO

(continued)

Figure 22.18
Driver Dispatch Table (DDT)

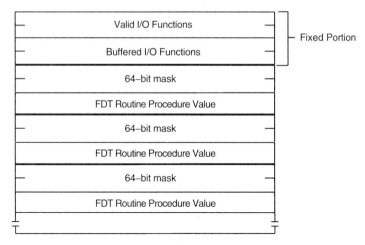

Figure 22.19
Function Decision Table (FDT)

buffered function mask indicate which function codes represent buffered I/O operations.

Each FDT entry consists of a 64-bit mask and the procedure value of an FDT routine. The $QIO system service invokes the FDT routine if the bit corresponding to a requested function is set in the associated mask. An FDT

769

routine validates the device- and function-dependent parameters of an I/O request and prepares the IRP for the driver's start I/O routine.

22.3.2 Driver Routines

Table 22.1 provides a summary of OpenVMS AXP driver routines. It classifies driver routines loosely into the following categories based on their major functions:

▶ Routines that prepare the I/O database. With the exception of the cloned UCB routine, these routines are invoked by the driver-loading procedure to set up and maintain the driver's I/O database.

After loading a driver, the driver-loading procedure creates the following data structures for the device and its associated components, based on information in the DPT: DDB, UCB, ORB, CRB, IDB, VLE, and possibly CRAMs. If the CRB and IDB were already created during system initialization, they are not recreated.

The driver-loading procedure initializes device-independent fields in the device's I/O database, that is, the device's associated I/O data structures. It then calls the driver's I/O database initialization routine, which initializes various device-specific fields in the I/O database. The driver-loading procedure also calls the driver's I/O database reinitialization routine, which initializes fields in the I/O database that could change if the driver were reloaded.

Traditionally, OpenVMS VAX initialization of a device's I/O database has been divided into fields initialized only once when the device driver is first loaded and those initialized again whenever the driver is reloaded. Although OpenVMS AXP does not currently support driver reloading, it reflects OpenVMS VAX in providing both kinds of initialization.

If a driver provides a unit delivery routine, the OpenVMS AXP auto-configuration procedure calls it to determine whether to configure a given device unit.

EXE$ASSIGN, the $ASSIGN system service procedure, invokes a device's cloned UCB routine when an image assigns an I/O channel to a software template device such as the NET: device (see Chapter 23). The cloned UCB routine performs device-specific initialization of the software device's cloned UCB.

▶ Routines that prepare controllers and devices. A controller initialization routine prepares a controller for I/O operations by initializing its interface registers, permanently allocating controller-specific resources, and performing other necessary steps. It is invoked by the driver-loading procedure.

A unit initialization routine prepares an individual device unit for operation; it is invoked by the driver-loading procedure for each unit

Table 22.1   Summary of Driver Routines

Routine	Function	Located Through	Called/Invoked by
ROUTINES THAT PREPARE THE I/O DATABASE			
I/O database initialization	Prepares the driver's I/O database when a driver is loaded	DPT$PS_INIT_ PD	SYS$LOAD_DRIVER
I/O database reinitialization	Initializes the part of a driver's I/O database that would be reinitialized if the driver were reloaded	DPT$PS_REINIT_PD	SYS$LOAD_DRIVER
Unit delivery	For a multiunit controller, determines which units exist	DPT$PS_DELIVER	SYS$LOAD_DRIVER
Cloned UCB	Performs device-specific initialization of a pseudo device's cloned UCB	DDT$PS_CLONEDUCB	EXE$ASSIGN
ROUTINES THAT PREPARE CONTROLLERS AND DEVICES			
Controller initialization	Prepares a controller for operation	DDT$PS_CTRLINIT	IOC$CTRLINIT
Unit initialization	Prepares a device for operation; for a single unit controller, prepares the controller as well	DDT$PS_UNITINIT	IOC$UNITINIT
ROUTINES THAT PREPARE USER I/O REQUESTS			
I/O preprocessing (FDT)	Performs function- and device-specific I/O request preprocessing	FDT entries	EXE$QIO
ROUTINES THAT PROCESS I/O REQUESTS			
Start I/O	Initiates and processes an I/O operation on a device	DDT$PS_START	IOC$INITIATE, IOC$REQCOM
Alternate start I/O	Initiates and processes an I/O request on a device whose driver supports multiple concurrent I/O operations	DDT$PS_ALTSTART	EXE$ALTQUEPKT
Interrupt service	Services device interrupts	VEC substructure in CRB or ADP	IO_INTERRUPT
Cancel I/O	Cancels an in-progress I/O request	DDT$PS_CANCEL	EXE$CANCEL, EXE$DALLOC, EXE$DASSGN
Register dumping	Copies interface registers to a diagnostic or error log buffer	DDT$PS_REGDUMP	ERL$DEVICERR, ERL$DEVICTMO, ERL$DEVICEATTN, IOC$DIAGBUFILL

771

of a multiunit controller. It also initializes device-specific fields of the UCB and sets the UCB$V_ONLINE bit to make the device usable by software.

▶ Routines that prepare user I/O requests. An image requests the $QIO system service for each I/O operation. EXE$QIO, the $QIO system service procedure, validates the request using the legal and buffered function masks in the FDT (see Section 22.3.1.3). Subsequently, it allocates and builds the device-independent portion of the IRP. The function-specific parameters of the I/O request can only be processed and entered into the IRP with the help of FDT routines, function-specific routines in the driver.

▶ Routines that process I/O requests. A start I/O routine is the starting point for the system thread of execution that carries an I/O request through to completion. It is entered by the executive after an I/O request has been validated. It translates a function request to a device-specific command and initiates device action, typically by writing to one or more device interface registers, sending command messages, or other means. Subsequently, it waits for the device to signal completion of device action through an interrupt, an end message, or other means. The device's interrupt service routine responds to a device interrupt by reactivating the thread of execution that was responsible for the device interrupt. When device processing completes successfully, or when an error or timeout condition occurs, a start I/O routine initiates I/O request postprocessing to post the status of the I/O request to the requestor. Chapter 24 details the actions of a driver's start I/O routine.

An alternate start I/O routine performs actions similar to a start I/O routine except that it supports the processing of multiple concurrent I/O requests.

A cancel I/O routine provides driver-specific processing to cancel an I/O request in progress, that is, one currently being processed by the start I/O routine. The Cancel I/O ($CANCEL) system service can cancel pending (that is, not yet in progress) I/O requests because no driver-specific processing is required; it simply deallocates IRPs from the pending I/O queue of the device UCB.

Drivers log errors to the system error log file typically through one of three routines: ERL$DEVICERR, ERL$DEVICTMO, or ERL$DEVICE-ATTN, all in module ERRORLOG (see Chapter 35). These routines, as well as IOC$DIAGBUFILL, in module IOSUBNPAG, invoke a driver's register-dumping routine. IOC$DIAGBUFILL provides support to drivers that perform diagnostic I/O. The register-dumping routine copies device interface registers and other important information to the error log or diagnostic buffer that its invoker allocates.

22.4   ANCILLARY CONTROL PROCESSES

A driver executes mostly at elevated IPL with minimal context; it cannot request system services. This makes it difficult to implement complex functions in drivers. An ACP is a separate thread of execution running in process context that implements complex driver functions.

As shown in Figure 22.1, a driver's FDT routine passes an I/O request either to an ACP or to a driver's start I/O routine, depending on the I/O function requested. A complex function request such as opening a disk file or establishing a network logical link, for example, is typically handled by an ACP.

An ACP image usually hibernates, waiting to be awakened to service I/O requests. An I/O request is passed to the ACP by queuing the IRP to the ACP queue block (AQB), shown in Figure 22.20, and waking up the ACP if necessary.

The OpenVMS AXP operating system provides the following ACPs:

- ▸ MTAAACP—Magnetic tape ACP
- ▸ NETACP—DECnet ACP
- ▸ REMACP—Remote terminal ACP
- ▸ F11BXQP—Files-11 On-Disk Structure Level 2 extended QIO processor
- ▸ F11CACP—Files-11 ACP for compact disk read-only memory (CD-ROM) in International Standards Organization (ISO) 9660 on-disk format
- ▸ F11DACP—Files-11 ACP for CD-ROM in High Sierra on-disk format

In VAX/VMS Version 4, the Files-11 On-Disk Structure Level 2 ACP, F11B-ACP, was converted to F11BXQP, also simply called the XQP. The XQP implements the Files-11 On-Disk Structure Level 2 on mass storage devices, and assists their drivers with file system function requests. Unlike other ACPs, the XQP runs in the context of the process that issued the I/O re-

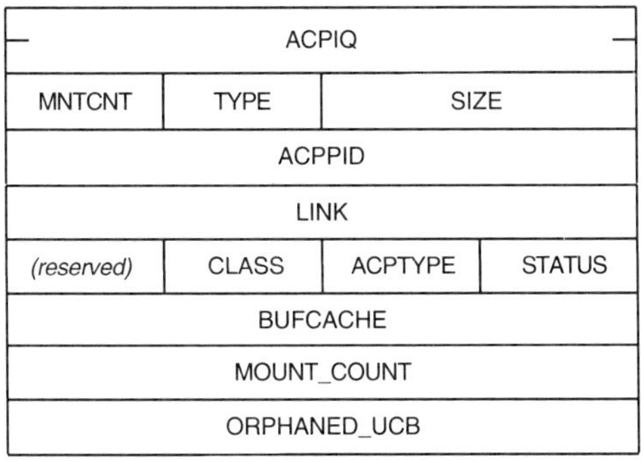

ACPIQ			
MNTCNT	TYPE	SIZE	
ACPPID			
LINK			
(reserved)	CLASS	ACPTYPE	STATUS
BUFCACHE			
MOUNT_COUNT			
ORPHANED_UCB			

Figure 22.20
ACP Queue Block (AQB)

quest. The mechanism of IRP delivery to the XQP is also different, as briefly described in Chapter 24.

For the purposes of this chapter, the XQP is simply another form of ACP; unless explicitly mentioned, the term *ACP* also refers to the XQP.

Two data structures are common to most ACPs—an AQB, which holds information specific to the ACP, and a volume control block (VCB), which describes a volume that is serviced by an ACP.

An AQB has a queue header for IRPs waiting to be processed, the process ID of the ACP, the ACP's class and type, and a mount count, which typically indicates the number of volumes the ACP is servicing. All AQBs on a system are linked together. The global location IOC$GL_AQBLIST is the listhead for this list. Offset AQB$L_LINK points to the next AQB in the list, as shown in Figure 22.21.

The term *volume* refers to a set of one or more devices that is treated as a single entity by an ACP; an ACP is responsible for maintaining the structure of data on a volume. The following are examples of a volume:

► A disk unit, serviced by the XQP
► A set of disk units (also called a volume set), serviced by the XQP
► The DECnet network, serviced by NETACP
► A tape unit, serviced by MTAAACP

A VCB describes a volume. A device's UCB points to the VCB for the volume to which the device belongs. A VCB may be known by a different name within the ACP. For example, the DECnet ACP's VCB is known as a routing control block (RCB). Typically, a VCB contains information about the organizational structure of a device.

A VCB has a fixed portion, shown in Figure 22.22, followed by an ACP-specific extension. One example of an ACP-specific extension is the VCB disk extension, shown in Figure 22.23, which is used by the XQP. Another example, shown in Figure 22.24, is the VCB magnetic tape extension, used by MTAAACP. Figure 22.25 shows how a device's VCB and AQB can be located.

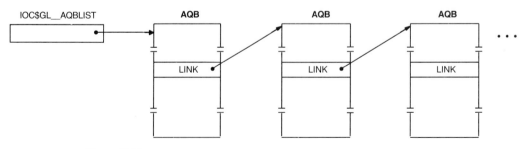

Figure 22.21
AQB List

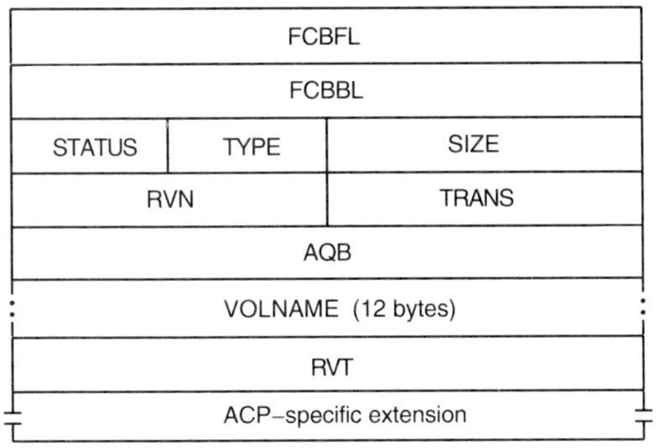

FCBFL

FCBBL

STATUS	TYPE	SIZE

RVN	TRANS

AQB

VOLNAME (12 bytes)

RVT

ACP–specific extension

Figure 22.22
Volume Control Block (VCB)

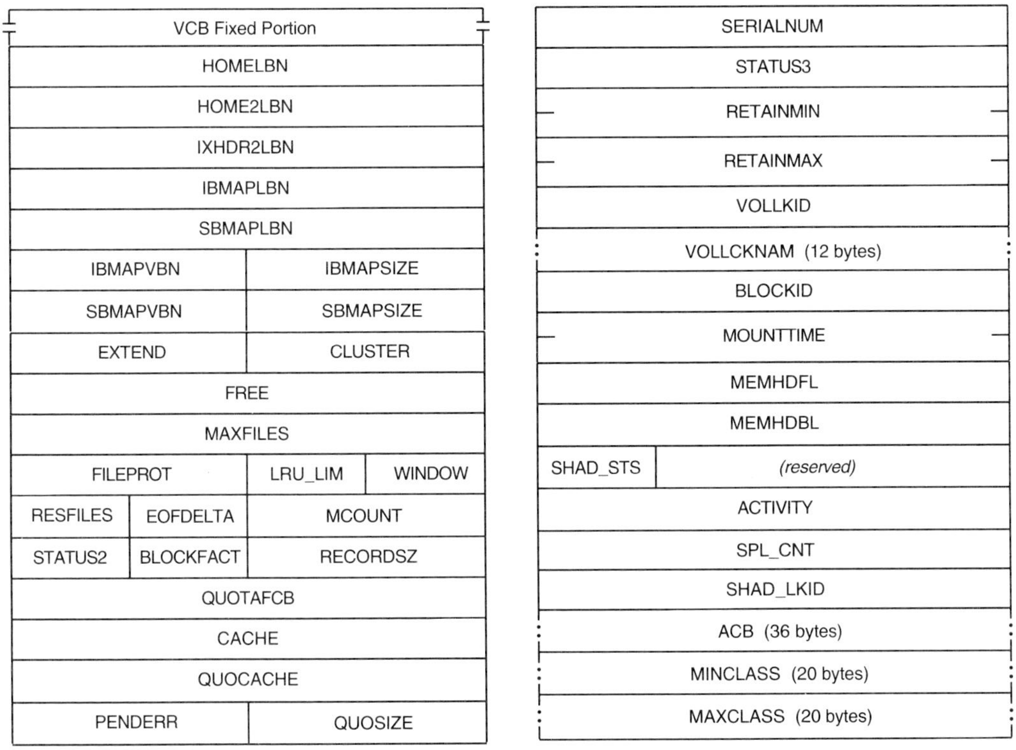

VCB Fixed Portion			
HOMELBN			
HOME2LBN			
IXHDR2LBN			
IBMAPLBN			
SBMAPLBN			
IBMAPVBN		IBMAPSIZE	
SBMAPVBN		SBMAPSIZE	
EXTEND		CLUSTER	
FREE			
MAXFILES			
FILEPROT		LRU_LIM	WINDOW
RESFILES	EOFDELTA	MCOUNT	
STATUS2	BLOCKFACT	RECORDSZ	
QUOTAFCB			
CACHE			
QUOCACHE			
PENDERR		QUOSIZE	

SERIALNUM	
STATUS3	
RETAINMIN	
RETAINMAX	
VOLLKID	
VOLLCKNAM (12 bytes)	
BLOCKID	
MOUNTTIME	
MEMHDFL	
MEMHDBL	
SHAD_STS	(reserved)
ACTIVITY	
SPL_CNT	
SHAD_LKID	
ACB (36 bytes)	
MINCLASS (20 bytes)	
MAXCLASS (20 bytes)	

(continued)

Figure 22.23
VCB Disk Extension

775

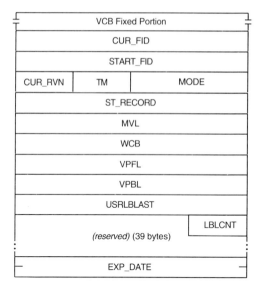

Figure 22.24
VCB Magnetic Tape Extension

22.5   I/O SUPPORT ROUTINES

The executive provides a number of I/O support routines that enable common driver functions to be performed in a consistent fashion. These routines, which are documented in the manual *OpenVMS AXP Device Support: Creating a Step 1 Driver from an OpenVMS VAX Device Driver*, perform a variety of functions needed by drivers. They are categorized as follows:

▸ I/O preprocessing support routines. These FDT routines perform preprocessing for common functions such as validating a user-specified buffer, locking a user buffer into memory, translating a logical or virtual function request to the corresponding physical function request, and copying function-specific parameters to the IRP.

▸ Fork and kernel process support routines. A driver's start I/O routine invokes these routines for fork or kernel process support. As described in Chapters 5 and 24, the executive creates a fork process for every I/O operation it initiates. The fork process can execute as a kernel process if it requires additional context.

▸ I/O request completion support routines. These routines complete driver I/O operations. Some are invoked by a driver's FDT routine; others by a driver's start I/O routine.

▸ Hardware mailbox support routines. These routines manage the allocation and use of hardware mailboxes. Architectural aspects of hardware mailbox access are outlined in Chapter 2.

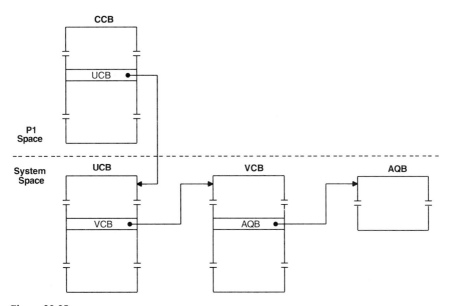

Figure 22.25
Locating a Device's VCB and AQB

- Spinlock support routines. Drivers acquire and release static and dynamic spinlocks using these routines, which are described in Chapter 9.
- Diagnostic and error logging support routines. These routines assist in debugging drivers and in reporting and recording device-specific errors. Chapter 35 describes error logging.
- Timer queue and timed wait support routines. These routines assist drivers in allocating, inserting, and removing timer queue entries, and implementing timers and interconnect-specific delay intervals. Chapter 12 describes these routines.
- Buffer allocation support routines. These routines assist drivers in allocating nonpaged pool, and in enforcing user process quotas. Chapter 21 summarizes routines that allocate nonpaged pool.

A number of miscellaneous routines assist drivers with various other tasks as well.

22.6   RELEVANT SOURCE MODULES

Source modules described in this chapter include

[LIB]ADPDEF.SDL
[LIB]AQBDEF.SDL
[LIB]BUSARRAYDEF.SDL
[LIB]CRAMDEF.SDL

[LIB]CRBDEF.SDL
[LIB]DDBDEF.SDL
[LIB]DDTDEF.SDL
[LIB]DPTDEF.SDL
[LIB]IDBDEF.SDL
[LIB]IRPDEF.SDL
[LIB]UCBDEF.SDL
[LIB]VCBDEF.SDL
[LIB]VECDEF.SDL
[LIB]VLEDEF.SDL

23   I/O System Services

Delay not Caesar! Read it instantly!
Shakespeare, *Julius Caesar*, 3, i

Here is a letter, read it at your leisure.
Shakespeare, *Merchant of Venice*, 5, i

An image performs I/O operations on a device by requesting I/O system services. System components such as Record Management Services (RMS), ancillary control processes (ACPs), and the Files-11 Extended QIO Processor (XQP) also request I/O system services on behalf of a process. This chapter describes the basic I/O system services and the device-independent portions of the flow of an I/O request. Chapter 24 describes the device-dependent portion of that flow.

23.1   OVERVIEW

The basic I/O system services are

- ► Allocate Device ($ALLOC), by which an image reserves a particular device for exclusive use
- ► Deallocate Device ($DALLOC), by which an image relinquishes such a device
- ► Assign I/O Channel ($ASSIGN), by which an image creates a logical link to a device
- ► Deassign I/O Channel ($DASSGN), by which an image deletes the logical link
- ► Queue I/O Request [and Wait] ($QIO[W]), by which an image requests an I/O operation on a particular logical link to a device
- ► Cancel I/O on Channel ($CANCEL), by which an image cancels outstanding I/O requests on a particular logical link to a device

The OpenVMS AXP operating system provides other I/O system services in addition to those discussed in this chapter (see the *OpenVMS Programming Concepts* manual).

All the system service procedures discussed in this chapter that have a device name argument also accept a logical name instead of a device name. Each procedure uses the same criteria to process the device name argument. *OpenVMS Programming Concepts* describes these criteria. Logical names and logical name translation are discussed in Chapter 38.

A typical service sequence for an image is shown in Figure 23.1. The numbers in the figure correspond to those in the following list.

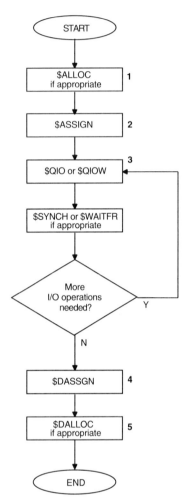

Figure 23.1
Typical Use of I/O System Services

① If appropriate (see Section 23.4), the image requests the $ALLOC system service.

② It requests the $ASSIGN system service.

③ The image requests either the $QIO system service followed by an event flag wait system service (for example, Wait for Single Event Flag, $WAITFR, or Synchronize, $SYNCH) or the $QIOW system service. This step is repeated for each I/O operation.

④ When the image has completed its I/O operations, it requests the $DAS-SGN system service. This service can be requested explicitly, or implicitly as part of image rundown or process deletion.

⑤ If necessary, the image explicitly requests the $DALLOC system service.

This service can also be requested implicitly as part of image rundown or process deletion.

An I/O request is processed in a number of steps and threads of execution. A typical sequence is shown, with some simplifications, in Figure 23.2. The numbers in the figure correspond to those in the following list:

1. The image requests the $QIO[W] system service.

2. EXE$QIO, the $QIO system service procedure, runs in process context. It validates its device-independent arguments and builds a data structure, called an I/O request packet (IRP), that describes the I/O request. Although it is entered at interrupt priority level (IPL) 0, it raises IPL to 2 before it allocates the IRP.

3. It invokes one or more function decision table (FDT) action routines specific to the device and I/O function. The FDT action routines, also running in process context, complete argument validation and any necessary I/O request preprocessing. An FDT routine can allocate a nonpaged pool buffer for use by the driver, or it can lock user buffer pages into memory so that they can be accessed by a direct memory access (DMA) device.

4. In general, the last FDT action routine invokes an executive routine to pass the IRP to the device driver and to return control to the user. An FDT action routine can also abort or complete the I/O request and return control to the user.

5. The device driver's start I/O routine initiates the device activity corresponding to the I/O request and then waits for the device interrupt that signals completion of the activity. The start I/O routine can be entered in either process context or system context. Although this example describes a situation in which the routine would be entered in process context, for simplicity, Figure 23.2 shows the start I/O routine in the System Context column.

6. The device interrupt service routine (ISR), which executes at device IPL, copies device status and then forks to dismiss the interrupt and resume the start I/O routine at a lower IPL.

7. Reentered as a fork process, the start I/O routine verifies that the request has been satisfied, copies status to the IRP, and queues the IRP for postprocessing.

8. The I/O postprocessing interrupt service routine, running in system context, performs some postprocessing functions, for example, it unlocks buffer pages, restores charged quota, and sets the event flag associated with the I/O request. It queues a special kernel mode asynchronous system trap (AST) to the process whose I/O completed.

9. Running in the context of the process that requested the I/O, the special kernel mode AST routine can copy I/O status to the image's I/O status block (IOSB) and copy input data from a nonpaged pool buffer to a user

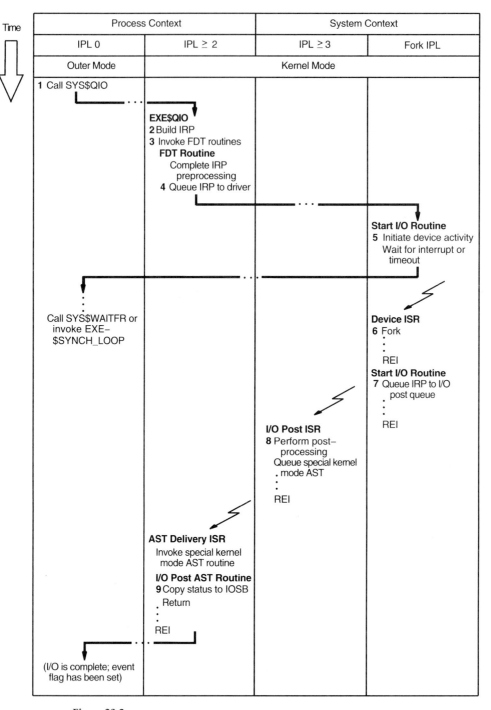

Figure 23.2
Flow of an I/O Request

buffer. If the user requested AST notification of the I/O completion, the special kernel mode AST routine queues a normal AST.

23.2 DEVICE DRIVERS AND SPINLOCKS

Device drivers synchronize access to I/O devices and controllers with fork locks and device locks, both of which are types of spinlocks.

The effect of the FORKLOCK macro on a uniprocessing system is simply to raise IPL to the fork IPL for the device. The fork IPL is determined from the device's fork lock index in UCB$B_FLCK. Similarly, the effect of the DEVICELOCK macro on a uniprocessing system is to raise IPL to the device IPL, which is stored in UCB$B_DIPL by the device driver during its initialization. Chapter 9 gives more details on fork locks and device locks.

23.3 DEVICE ATTRIBUTES

The term *device* is defined in Chapter 2.

The executive assigns every device one or more attributes that describe the device to the I/O system services and the rest of the system. Table 23.1 shows a selected list of device attribute flags as defined by the STARLET $DEVDEF macro. These flags, which represent the characteristics of a device, are in the unit control block (UCB) fields UCB$L_DEVCHAR and UCB$L_DEVCHAR2.

A device may or may not have a physical embodiment. A device without a physical embodiment is called a pseudo device; it is a software emulation.

The bit UCB$V_TEMPLATE in UCB$L_STS, when set, indicates a template device. A template device, discussed in Section 23.5.2.2.2, is a pseudo device whose UCB is cloned whenever an image assigns a channel to it.

23.4 ALLOCATING AND DEALLOCATING DEVICES

An I/O device can be declared shareable or nonshareable by its driver. A disk, for example, is typically declared shareable so as to allow concurrent access to multiple users, whereas a line printer is always declared nonshareable because access to it must be serialized. A device is typically declared nonshareable if its I/O is inherently sequential; such a device is designed to service I/O requests from one user at a time. The executive allows multiple processes to access a shareable device concurrently; under very constrained conditions, it is also possible for multiple processes to access a nonshareable device concurrently.

Before a process can issue I/O requests to a nonshareable device, it must allocate the device for its exclusive use. A process can also allocate a device that is declared shareable, thus temporarily acquiring exclusive access to it.

A device allocated to a process can nonetheless be used by another process under the following conditions.

Table 23.1   Selected Device Attribute Flags

Flag	Meaning if Set
DEV$V_REC	Device is record-oriented
DEV$V_CCL	Device supports carriage control
DEV$V_TRM	Device is a terminal
DEV$V_DIR	Device is directory-structured
DEV$V_SQD	Device is sequential and block-oriented
DEV$V_SPL	Device is being spooled
DEV$V_NET	Device is a network device
DEV$V_FOD	Device is file-oriented
DEV$V_DUA	Device is dual-ported
DEV$V_SHR	Device is shareable
DEV$V_AVL	Device is available for use
DEV$V_MNT	Device is mounted
DEV$V_MBX	Device is a mailbox
DEV$V_DMT	Device is marked for dismount
DEV$V_ELG	Device has error logging enabled
DEV$V_ALL	Device is allocated
DEV$V_FOR	Device is mounted foreign
DEV$V_IDV	Device can provide input
DEV$V_ODV	Device can provide output
DEV$V_CLU	Device is available clusterwide
DEV$V_DET	Device is a detached terminal
DEV$V_RED	Device is a redirected terminal

▸ The other process is a subprocess of the first. This condition provides, for example, flexible access to an interactive terminal among a user's process and its spawned subprocesses.

▸ The other process is a part of the same Portable Operating System Interface (POSIX) session.

▸ The other process has the SHARE privilege. For example, the print symbiont uses the SHARE privilege to access a disk mounted privately when the owner queues files on the disk for printing.

Under any circumstances, the processes sharing the device are responsible for arbitrating their accesses to it.

There are two forms of device allocation: explicit, requested by the process through the $ALLOC system service, and implicit, performed as necessary on behalf of the process by the $ASSIGN system service. In either form, the process ID (PID) of the process that allocated the device is stored in the UCB device owner field, UCB$L_PID.

Explicit allocation differs from implicit allocation in several ways:

▸ An implicitly allocated device is transparently deallocated when its last channel is deassigned; an explicitly allocated device must be explicitly deallocated.

▶ A process can request explicit allocation of a generic device type or a specific device unit.

▶ In the case of explicit allocation, the device-allocated bit, DEV$V_ALL in UCB$L_DEVCHAR, is set and the device reference count, UCB$L_REFC, is incremented twice, once by $ALLOC and once by $ASSIGN. In the case of implicit device allocation, the device-allocated bit is clear and the device reference count is incremented only once, by $ASSIGN.

A process requests the $ALLOC system service to allocate a device explicitly. The device can be released only through the $DALLOC system service, requested by the process directly or by code running on its behalf at image rundown or process deletion.

For a nonshareable device that a process has not explicitly allocated, the $ASSIGN system service (see Section 23.5.2) performs implicit allocation.

23.4.1 $ALLOC System Service

The $ALLOC system service has five arguments, of which only the DEVNAM argument is required:

▶ The DEVNAM argument identifies the device to be allocated.

▶ The PHYBUF argument specifies where the $ALLOC system service should return the name of the device.

▶ The PHYLEN argument specifies where it should return the length of the device name.

▶ The ACMODE argument identifies the access mode to be associated with the device. It is maximized with the mode of the requestor. Once allocated, the device can only be deallocated from the same or a more privileged mode.

▶ The FLAGS argument contains only one flag, the low bit. When set, the low bit indicates that any device of a particular type can be allocated, not just a specific device.

The $ALLOC system service procedure, EXE$ALLOC in module SYS-DEVALC, will not allocate the device if any one of the following conditions is true:

▶ The device is already allocated by another process (UCB$L_PID is nonzero and does not match PCB$L_PID).

▶ The device reference count is nonzero.

▶ A volume is mounted on the device.

▶ The device is spooled (DEV$V_SPL in UCB$L_DEVCHAR is set), and the process does not have the ALLSPOOL privilege.

▶ The requesting process does not have access rights to allocate the device, based on the device owner's user identification code (UIC) and protection and its access control list.

▶ The device is not available (DEV$V_AVL in UCB$L_DEVCHAR is clear) or not online (UCB$V_ONLINE in UCB$L_STS is clear).

▶ The device is a template device.

▶ The device is cluster-available and a conflicting resource lock exists.

EXE$ALLOC runs in kernel mode. It takes the following steps to allocate a device:

1. It invokes SCH$IOLOCKW, in module MUTEX, to lock the I/O database mutex for write access.
2. It verifies that the DEVNAM argument's string descriptor is read-accessible.
3. If the FLAGS argument is specified, EXE$ALLOC verifies that it is read-accessible and does not have undefined bits set.
4. It invokes IOC$SEARCH, in module IOSUBPAGD, to locate a suitable device.

   • If the FLAGS argument is not specified or is 0, EXE$ALLOC requests a search for the exact device specified by the DEVNAM argument.

   • If the FLAGS argument is 1, EXE$ALLOC requests a search for the first available device matching the type specified by the DEVNAM argument.

   IOC$SEARCH invokes IOC$TRANDEVNAM, in module IOSUB-PAGD, to translate the DEVNAM argument. It then searches the I/O database for either the specific device or one of the particular type. IOC$SEARCH and routines it invokes verify the suitability of the device and its accessibility to this process.

   If the device is cluster-available, it invokes IOC$LOCK_DEV, in module IOSUBPAGD. IOC$LOCK_DEV requests the Enqueue Lock Request ($ENQ) system service to queue an exclusive mode resource lock on the device. IOC$LOCK_DEV stores the lock ID in UCB$L_LOCKID.

5. EXE$ALLOC returns the translated device name if the PHYBUF argument is specified, the descriptor is readable, and the buffer is writable. If the PHYLEN argument is also specified and is write-accessible, EXE$ALLOC also returns the length of the device name.
6. It allocates the device:

   a. It sets the device-allocated bit, DEV$V_ALL in UCB$L_DEVCHAR.

   b. It maximizes the ACMODE argument with the access mode of its requestor and stores the result in UCB$B_AMOD.

   c. It increments the device reference count, UCB$L_REFCNT.

   d. It copies the PID, PCB$L_PID, to the UCB device owner field, UCB$L_PID.

7. It invokes SCH$IOUNLOCK, in module MUTEX, to unlock the I/O database mutex, lowers IPL to 0, and returns to the requestor with the success status SS$_NORMAL.

23.4.2 $DALLOC System Service

An image can deallocate a single device or all devices allocated to the process by requesting the $DALLOC system service. The $DALLOC system service is also requested during image rundown to deallocate all devices allocated in user-mode and during process deletion to deallocate all devices still allocated to the process. Image rundown is discussed in Chapter 28, and process deletion, in Chapter 31.

The $DALLOC system service has two optional arguments:

▶ The DEVNAM argument specifies the device to be deallocated. If the DEVNAM argument is specified, it must translate to a physical device name. If the DEVNAM argument is not specified, all devices allocated by the process from access modes equal to or less privileged than that specified by the ACMODE argument are deallocated.

▶ The ACMODE argument specifies the access mode on behalf of which the deallocation is to be performed. It is maximized with the mode of the requestor.

The $DALLOC system service procedure, EXE$DALLOC in module SYSDEVALC, runs in kernel mode. It performs the following steps:

1. EXE$DALLOC maximizes the ACMODE argument with the access mode of its requestor.

2. It locks the I/O database mutex for write access.

3. It determines if the DEVNAM argument is present.

   • If the argument is present, it invokes IOC$SEARCHDEV, in module IOSUBPAGD, to locate the specified device.

   • If the argument is absent, it invokes IOC$SCAN_IODB, in module IOSUBNPAG, to find the first UCB in the I/O database.

4. In either case, EXE$DALLOC makes the following checks before deallocating the device.

   • The UCB$L_PID field must match the PCB$L_PID field of the process requesting the $DALLOC system service.

   • The access mode in UCB$B_AMOD must be greater than or equal to the access mode computed in step 1.

   • The device must have been explicitly allocated.

   • The device must not be mounted (DEV$V_MNT in UCB$L_DEVCHAR must be clear) unless the device is a terminal (DEV$V_TRM in UCB$L_DEVCHAR is set). A DECnet remote terminal is marked as mounted but need not be interlocked against deallocation because only the owner process has access to it.

5. It deallocates the device by invoking IOC$DALLOC_DEV, in module IOSUBPAGD, which takes the following steps:

   a. It clears the device-allocated bit.

   b. If the device is shareable, it clears the device owner field.

   c. It decrements the device reference count.

   d. If the reference count is now zero, IOC$DALLOC_DEV clears the owner field in the UCB and invokes IOC$LAST_CHAN, which performs last channel processing (see Section 23.5.4).

e. If the device is cluster-available, IOC$DALLOC_DEV invokes the routine IOC$UNLOCK_DEV, in module IOSUBPAGD, to deal with the resource lock on the device. IOC$UNLOCK_DEV tests UCB$L_LOCKID to determine whether there is a resource lock. It also tests the device reference count to determine whether there are still channels assigned to the device (see Section 23.5).

If there is no resource lock, or if the device is still allocated, the routine returns.

If there is a resource lock and channels are still assigned to the device, the routine requests the $ENQ system service to convert the resource lock to concurrent read mode.

If there is a resource lock and no channel is still assigned, the routine requests the Dequeue Lock Request ($DEQ) system service to dequeue the resource lock.

6. If the DEVNAM argument was present, EXE$DALLOC is done. It unlocks the I/O database mutex and returns to its requestor with the success status SS$_NORMAL.

Otherwise, EXE$DALLOC goes to step 3 to get the next UCB in the I/O database. When no more UCBs are found, EXE$DALLOC is done and exits as described.

23.5 ASSIGNING AND DEASSIGNING CHANNELS

The software mechanism that links a process to a device is called a channel. To perform I/O on a device, an image first creates a channel to it by requesting the $ASSIGN system service. The image then identifies the device to the $QIO system service through its channel identifier. When the image is done with the device, it requests the $DASSGN system service to break the link between the process and the device.

23.5.1 Channel Control Block

A channel is described by a process-specific data structure called a channel control block (CCB), shown in Figure 23.3. A process's CCBs are contained in a table located in its P1 space (see Figure 1.7 and Table F.5). The global location CTL$GA_CCB_TABLE contains the address of the table. The number of CCBs in the table is determined by the SYSGEN parameter CHANNELCNT.

IOC$CREATE_CCB_TABLE, in module IOCHANUTILS, creates the CCB table during process creation. A value called the channel identifier identifies a particular CCB in the table. IOC$ALLOCATE_CCB, in module IOCHANUTILS, allocates a CCB from the CCB table and returns the chan-

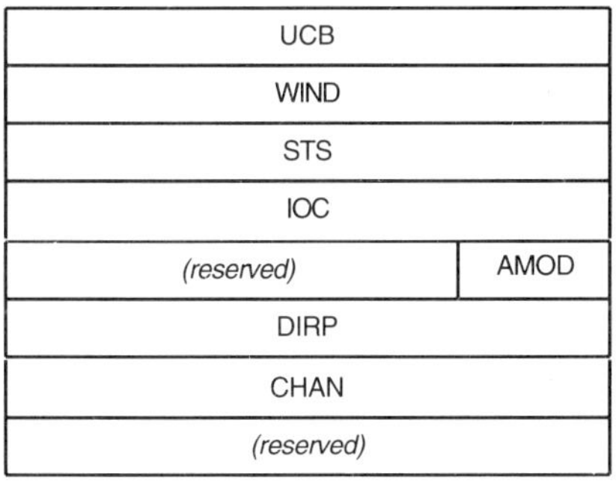

UCB	
WIND	
STS	
IOC	
(reserved)	AMOD
DIRP	
CHAN	
(reserved)	

Figure 23.3
Layout of a Channel Control Block (CCB)

nel identifier. IOC$CHAN_TO_CCB, in module IOCHANUTILS, returns the CCB that corresponds to a given channel identifier.

Note that in OpenVMS VAX and in OpenVMS AXP Version 1.0, the layouts of the CCB, the CCB table, and the channel identifier are different from the layouts described here. For OpenVMS AXP Version 1.5, code that makes any assumption about the layout of the CCB table or the channel identifier must be changed to call the appropriate procedure, for example, IOC$CHAN_TO_CCB or IOC$ALLOCATE_CCB. The field CCB$L_CHAN contains the channel identifier.

The field CCB$B_AMOD contains 0 if the channel is unassigned. Otherwise, it contains the access mode from which the channel was assigned, biased by 1. For example, the value 1 indicates that the channel was assigned from kernel mode. A $QIO system service request on a particular channel must be made from an access mode at least as privileged as the mode from which the channel was assigned.

CCB$L_UCB contains the address of the UCB of the device to which the channel is assigned.

Any comparison of CCB$B_AMOD with an access mode value must be a signed comparison. The Files-11 XQP prevents deassignment of its channel when the channel is inactive by storing –1 in CCB$B_AMOD. (The XQP reserves this channel for itself during process initialization.) Prior to using the channel, the XQP transforms the CCB into a normal kernel mode channel to the device of the XQP's choice.

If a file has been opened on the channel, CCB$L_WIND contains the address of its window control block (WCB). If the file is associated with a process section, CCB$L_WIND contains the process section index. CCB$L_WIND contains an unnamed flag in the low bit that is set to indicate either an access (open) request in progress or a deaccess (close) request waiting for all other outstanding I/O requests to be completed.

▶ If an access request is pending, CCB$L_WIND contains a 1.

▶ If a deaccess request is pending, CCB$L_WIND contains the result of a logical OR operation of the WCB address or process section index with 1. CCB$L_DIRP contains the address of the IRP that describes the deaccess request. Since WCB addresses and process section indexes are always even, system routines can recover these values by masking out the low bit of CCB$L_WIND.

CCB$L_STS contains several status bits. CCB$L_IOC counts the number of outstanding I/O requests on the channel.

23.5.2 $ASSIGN System Service

The $ASSIGN system service has five arguments; the first two are required, the next two are optional, and the last one is a placeholder:

▶ The DEVNAM argument is the name of the device to which to assign the channel.

▶ The CHAN argument is the address of the word in which to return the assigned channel identifier.

▶ The ACMODE argument, indicating the access mode to be associated with the channel, is maximized with the mode of the requestor.

▶ The MBXNAM argument is the name of the mailbox to be associated with the channel. An image associates a mailbox with a nonshareable device to receive status information, such as the arrival of unsolicited input from a terminal. The device driver for the device either uses or ignores this associated mailbox.

▶ The NULLARG argument is a placeholder.

The $ASSIGN system service procedure, EXE$ASSIGN in module SYSAS-SIGN, performs special processing for DECnet remote devices. A DECnet remote device is one whose device name specification includes the string :: . A device that is not a DECnet remote device is, for the purposes of the $AS-SIGN system service, called a local device. Note that even a local device can be external to the system; the device's driver can hide the details of device implementation from the $ASSIGN system service. A local area transport (LAT) device, for example, is a local device by this definition, even though the physical terminal associated with such a device can be connected to the system through a network.

EXE$ASSIGN runs in the requestor's mode. It performs the following steps:

1. It requests the $ASSIGN_LOCAL system service, passing it the same arguments as listed for $ASSIGN. EXE$ASSIGN_LOCAL, in module SYSASSIGN, is the $ASSIGN_LOCAL system service procedure. It assigns a channel to a local device and returns the status SS$_NON-LOCAL for a device whose name has the string :: embedded in it.

The actions of EXE$ASSIGN_LOCAL are described in the next several sections.

2. If EXE$ASSIGN_LOCAL returns the success status SS$_NONLOCAL, EXE$ASSIGN calls NETWORK_ASSIGN, also in module SYSASSIGN, to assign a channel to a DECnet remote device. The advantage of splitting local and network processing in this manner is that the requesting process can be waited in the requestor's mode, rather than kernel mode, during a network device assignment.

3. EXE$ASSIGN returns to its requestor.

Figure 23.4 shows the steps in the control flow of EXE$ASSIGN_LOCAL that are described in the following sections.

23.5.2.1   **Common Initial Steps for Local and Remote Device Assignment.** Running in kernel mode, EXE$ASSIGN_LOCAL performs the following steps for both local and DECnet remote device assignment:

1. It verifies that the CHAN argument is write-accessible.
2. If the MBXNAM argument was specified, EXE$ASSIGN_LOCAL verifies that it is read-accessible.
3. It verifies that the DEVNAM argument is read-accessible.
4. EXE$ASSIGN_LOCAL maximizes the ACMODE argument with the access mode of its requestor.
5. If this is a reassign request made by a POSIX component, EXE$ASSIGN_LOCAL calls IOC$REALLOCATE_CCB, in module IOCHANUTILS, to reallocate the specified CCB. Otherwise, EXE$ASSIGN_LOCAL calls IOC$ALLOCATE_CCB, in module IOCHANUTILS, to allocate a CCB. (When the controlling process of a POSIX session terminates unexpectedly, or the POSIX terminal driver detects a hangup, each channel assigned by every POSIX process in that session is reassigned to the POSIX hangup device. Use of reassign requests is reserved to Digital.)

    IOC$ALLOCATE_CCB begins its search for a free CCB at the low-address end of the CCB table. It examines offset CCB$B_AMOD to determine whether the CCB is free. If the CCB is in use, IOC$ALLOCATE_CCB examines the next CCB, repeating its test. This sequence continues until IOC$ALLOCATE_CCB locates a free CCB or reaches the end of the table.

    If IOC$ALLOCATE_CCB locates a CCB, it returns the address of the free CCB and a channel identifier. The channel identifier will be returned in the CHAN argument of the system service request.

    If no free CCB is located, IOC$ALLOCATE_CCB returns the error status SS$_NOIOCHAN to EXE$ASSIGN_LOCAL.

6. EXE$ASSIGN_LOCAL locks the I/O database mutex for write access.
7. If the MBXNAM argument was specified, EXE$ASSIGN_LOCAL invokes IOC$SEARCHDEV to get the address of the specified mailbox UCB. The

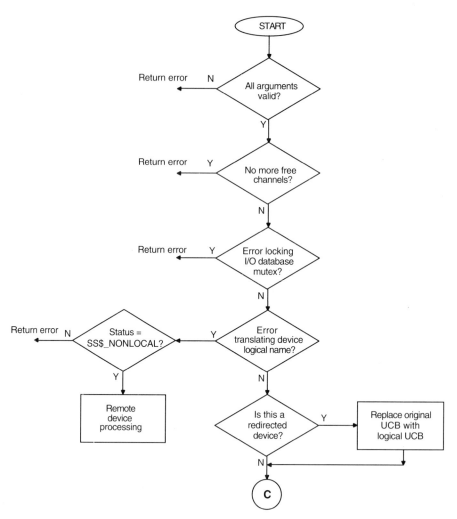

Figure 23.4
Major Steps in EXE$ASSIGN_LOCAL

device must be a mailbox device (DEV$V_MBX in UCB$L_DEVCHAR is set) but not a network device.

8. It invokes IOC$SEARCH to locate the device specified in the DEVNAM argument. If the device name is a logical name, IOC$SEARCH invokes IOC$TRANDEVNAM to perform logical name translation.

If IOC$TRANDEVNAM returns a success status, IOC$SEARCH then scans the I/O database for a device with the resulting equivalence name.

- If IOC$SEARCH locates the device, it returns the address of the device's UCB. EXE$ASSIGN_LOCAL then takes the steps discussed in Section 23.5.2.2.

- If IOC$SEARCH does not locate the device, EXE$ASSIGN_LOCAL un-

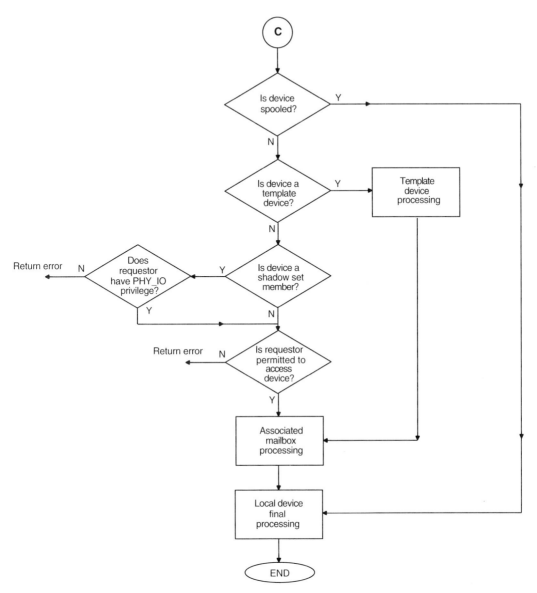

Figure 23.4 *(continued)*
Major Steps in EXE$ASSIGN_LOCAL

    locks the I/O database mutex and returns to the requestor with the error status from IOC$SEARCH.

9. If the device name contains a node delimiter (::), IOC$TRANDEVNAM returns the error status SS$_NONLOCAL, and EXE$ASSIGN_LOCAL takes the steps described in Section 23.5.2.3 for DECnet remote device assignment.

10. If IOC$TRANDEVNAM returns any other error status, EXE$ASSIGN_

LOCAL unlocks the I/O database mutex by invoking SCH$IOUNLOCK and returns to the requestor with that error status.

23.5.2.2 **Local Device Assignment.** EXE$ASSIGN_LOCAL first checks for several special kinds of device:

1. If the UCB is a redirected UCB (DEV$V_RED in UCB$L_DEVCHAR2 is set), EXE$ASSIGN_LOCAL replaces the original UCB address with the address of the logical UCB by using the value in field UCB$L_TT_LOGUCB of the original UCB. This mechanism associates the assigned channel with the virtual rather than the physical terminal. (The physical terminal can be a pseudo device such as a LAT terminal.) Only terminal UCBs can be redirected (see Chapter 26).

2. If the device is set spooled, EXE$ASSIGN_LOCAL goes directly to local device final processing, described in Section 23.5.2.2.4.

EXE$ASSIGN_LOCAL then determines whether the device is a template device. If it is, EXE$ASSIGN_LOCAL clones the UCB to create a new device, as described in Section 23.5.2.2.2.

23.5.2.2.1 *Nontemplate Device Processing.* Before assigning a channel to a local nontemplate device, EXE$ASSIGN_LOCAL confirms the following:

▸ If the device is a shadow set member (DEV$V_SSM or DEV$V_SHD in UCB$L_DEVCHAR2 is set), the requesting process must have the PHY_IO privilege.

▸ If the device is allocated (UCB$L_PID is nonzero) and nonshareable, one of the following conditions must be true:

• The requesting process must be the owner of the device or a descendant of the owner process.
• The requesting process must be a part of the same POSIX session.
• The requesting process must have the SHARE privilege, and the volume protection and owner UIC must allow access.

▸ If the device is not allocated, the volume protection and owner UIC must allow access.

If the requestor is allowed to assign a channel to the device, EXE$ASSIGN_LOCAL handles the associated mailbox, if any, and performs final processing (see Section 23.5.2.2.4).

If the requestor is not allowed to assign the channel, EXE$ASSIGN_LOCAL unlocks the I/O database mutex by invoking SCH$IOUNLOCK and returns to the requestor with an error status.

23.5.2.2.2 *Template Device Processing.* If the device is a template device, EXE$ASSIGN_LOCAL creates a new UCB, called the cloned UCB, by copying the template UCB, and assigns the channel to the cloned UCB as follows.

1. If the template device is a network device, it verifies that the process has NETMBX privilege.

2. EXE$ASSIGN_LOCAL invokes IOC$CHKUCBQUOTA, in module UCBCREDEL, to verify that the process has as much BYTLM quota as the sum of the size of the template UCB plus 256 additional bytes to satisfy process deletion needs.

   IOC$CHKUCBQUOTA invokes EXE$DEBIT_BYTCNT_BYTLIM_NW, in module EXSUBROUT, to check and charge the quota. Both the byte count quota (JIB$L_BYTCNT) and limit (JIB$L_BYTLIM) are charged. Since the amount charged by IOC$CHKUCBQUOTA will not be restored until the UCB is deleted, the process has effectively had its byte limit reduced by the amount of the charge. EXE$DEBIT_BYTCNT_BYTLIM_NW decrements the byte limit as well to reflect this fact.

3. EXE$ASSIGN_LOCAL invokes IOC$CLONE_UCB, in module UCB-CREDEL, to create the cloned UCB and an object rights block (ORB).

   IOC$CLONE_UCB copies the template UCB and then makes several modifications to the cloned UCB, of which the following are of particular interest:
   - It sets the reference count to 1.
   - It marks the unit online.
   - It clears the template bit.
   - It stores the size of the UCB in UCB$W_CHARGE.
   - It gives the UCB a unique unit number between 1 and 9999.
   - It links the UCB into the UCB chain of the related device data block (DDB).

4. EXE$ASSIGN_LOCAL stores the current process's UIC in the ORB owner field (ORB$L_OWNER). At this point, the owner field of the cloned UCB is still clear.

5. It sets UCB$V_DELETEUCB in UCB$L_STS to mark the cloned UCB for deletion when its reference count goes to 0.

6. If the template UCB is a mailbox, it sets the mailbox delete bit (UCB$V_DELMBX in UCB$L_DEVSTS). This is done because special steps are required to delete a mailbox UCB.

7. It clears the device reference count, which was set to 1 by IOC$CLONE_UCB. Later, when channel assignment is complete, the reference count is incremented.

8. EXE$ASSIGN_LOCAL invokes IOC$DEBIT_UCB, in module UCBCRE-DEL, to record the master PID charged for the UCB (JIB$L_MPID) into the charge PID field (UCB$L_CPID).

9. EXE$ASSIGN_LOCAL invokes the driver at the entry point specified by DDT$L_CLONEUCB, passing it the addresses of the template and cloned UCBs. The driver can perform any additional checks necessary. If the driver returns any error status, the process of cloning the UCB is undone and $ASSIGN completes with failure.

The driver's cloned UCB routine runs in the context of the process that requested the $ASSIGN system service. It executes at IPL 2 because the I/O database mutex is owned by the process.

10. If the device is not shareable, EXE$ASSIGN_LOCAL copies the process's PID to UCB$L_PID, implicitly allocating it.

11. It takes the steps described in Section 23.5.2.2.3.

23.5.2.2.3 *Associated Mailbox Processing.* If an associated mailbox was requested, EXE$ASSIGN_LOCAL stores the address of the associated mailbox UCB in the UCB$L_AMB field of the UCB to which the channel is being assigned. It increments the reference count in the associated mailbox UCB and sets CCB$V_AMB for later storage in CCB$L_STS to indicate that there is an associated mailbox.

No association is made if either of the following is true:

▸ The device is a file-oriented device (DEV$V_FOD in UCB$L_DEVCHAR is set) or the device is shareable. In either case, the request for an associated mailbox is simply ignored.

▸ The device already has an associated mailbox (UCB$L_AMB is nonzero), and the MBXNAM argument specifies a different mailbox. In this case, EXE$ASSIGN_LOCAL unlocks the I/O database mutex and returns the failure status SS$_DEVACTIVE.

Upon completing any steps required for the associated mailbox, EXE$AS-SIGN_LOCAL proceeds to final processing.

23.5.2.2.4 *Local Device Final Processing.* At this point, EXE$ASSIGN_LOCAL has found a free channel, verified the existence of the device (creating the UCB in the case of a template device), and verified that the process has access to the device. It completes the assignment of an I/O channel to a local device in the following steps:

1. If appropriate, it invokes IOC$LOCK_DEV, described in Section 23.4.1, to queue a concurrent read mode resource lock on the device. The following conditions must all be met for EXE$ASSIGN_LOCAL to take this action:
   - The device reference count is 0.
   - The system is an active node of a VMScluster system.
   - The device is cluster-available.

2. If the device is not shareable and not currently owned, EXE$ASSIGN_LOCAL implicitly allocates the device to the current process by storing the current process's PID (PCB$L_PID) in UCB$L_PID.

3. It copies the device's UCB address to CCB$L_UCB.

4. It increments the device reference count.

5. It stores the access mode biased by 1 in CCB$B_AMOD.

6. It sets CCB$L_STS appropriately. The only bit that can be set as a result of this step is CCB$V_AMB.

7. EXE$ASSIGN_LOCAL writes the channel identifier to the word specified by the CHAN argument.

8. It unlocks the I/O database mutex by invoking SCH$IOUNLOCK and returns the success status SS$_NORMAL to its requestor.

23.5.2.3   **Assigning a Channel to a DECnet Remote Device.** This section assumes familiarity with transparent and nontransparent network communication, described in the *DECnet for OpenVMS Networking Manual*. If the device is a DECnet remote device, EXE$ASSIGN performs the first step in transparent network communication, converting the transparent network communication into the related nontransparent network communication.

If IOC$TRANDEVNAM returns the failure status SS$_NONLOCAL (see Section 23.5.2.1), EXE$ASSIGN_LOCAL converts it to a success status. EXE$ASSIGN_LOCAL then invokes SCH$IOUNLOCK to unlock the I/O database mutex and to return the now-modified SS$_NONLOCAL status to EXE$ASSIGN. In response to this, EXE$ASSIGN calls NETWORK_ASSIGN, in module SYSASSIGN.

NETWORK_ASSIGN, running in the access mode from which the $ASSIGN system service was requested, initiates nontransparent network communication by taking the following steps:

1. It establishes a condition handler in case system service failure exception mode has been enabled. This condition handler will resignal any conditions other than SS$_NOLOGNAM, which occurs normally in logical name translation and should not be passed back to the requestor of the $ASSIGN system service.

2. It allocates a buffer on the stack for use as the data area for logical name translation and initializes this area to request the equivalence name and its attributes.

3. It requests the Translate Logical Name ($TRNLNM) system service to translate the DEVNAM argument. This repetition of the logical name translation done at the beginning of EXE$ASSIGN_LOCAL is necessary because the result of the earlier translation was not saved.

   The result of this step should be a network connect block suitable for use in an outbound connection request operation. NETWORK_ASSIGN makes no attempt to ensure that the result of this step is in the proper format. If it is not, an error will be returned when the connection is attempted in the next step.

4. NETWORK_ASSIGN requests the $ASSIGN system service with the following items in the argument list:

   • The DEVNAM argument is the network device name, _NET.

- The CHAN argument is a stack location that temporarily holds the assigned channel identifier.
- The ACMODE argument is the ACMODE argument of the original $AS-SIGN request, maximized with the access mode of the requestor.
- The MBXNAM argument is the same argument passed in the original $ASSIGN system service request.

Since NET0 is a template device, the unit to which the channel is assigned is a new unit, created as described in Section 23.5.2.2.2.

5. It requests the $QIOW system service to establish a connection to the DECnet remote device:

- The FUNC argument is IO$_ACCESS ORed with IO$M_ACCESS.
- The event flag is EXE$C_SYSEFN.
- The CHAN argument is the one to which the device was assigned in the previous step.
- The network connect block is the one obtained in step 3.

6. If $QIOW completes successfully, NETWORK_ASSIGN records the channel identifier from step 4 in the word specified by the CHAN argument of the original $ASSIGN system service request. It then returns the success status SS$_REMOTE to its requestor.

7. If $QIOW fails, NETWORK_ASSIGN requests the $DASSGN system service to deassign the channel. It then returns the failure status from the $QIOW system service to its requestor.

23.5.3 $DASSGN System Service

The $DASSGN system service deassigns a previously assigned I/O channel and clears the linkage and control information in the corresponding CCB, freeing the CCB for reuse. Any outstanding I/O request on the device is terminated in the process. $DASSGN has only one argument, the CHAN argument, which specifies the identifier of the channel to be deassigned.

The $DASSGN system service procedure, EXE$DASSGN in module SYS-DASSGN, runs in kernel mode. It takes the following steps:

1. It invokes IOC$VERIFYCHAN, in module IOSUBPAGD, which in turn calls IOC$VERIFY_CHAN, in module IOCHANUTILS, which does the following:

   a. It verifies that the channel is legal.

   b. It verifies that the channel was assigned from an access mode no more privileged than the access mode from which it is to be deassigned. CCB$B_AMOD must be greater than the previous mode field in the processor status (PS).

   c. It returns the address and the identifier of the CCB for the channel.

2. EXE$DASSGN calls EXE$CANCELN with a reason code of CAN$C_DASSGN (channel is being deassigned) to cancel all outstanding I/O on

the channel. EXE$CANCELN is an entry point in the $CANCEL system service, discussed in Section 23.9.

3. It invokes IOC$VERIFYCHAN again in case the cancel I/O operation triggered a kernel mode AST routine that requested the $DASSGN system service again. This second call to $DASSGN could have completely deassigned the channel.

4. If a file is open on the channel (CCB$L_WIND is nonzero), EXE$DAS-SGN requests the $QIOW system service to close the file. It specifies a function code of IO$_DEACCESS and event flag number 30. Event flag 30 is used to avoid conflict with the use of event flag 31 (EXE$C_SYSEFN) by $CANCEL.

   If a network logical link rather than a file was open on the channel, the deaccess operation dissolves the link.

5. EXE$DASSGN raises IPL to 2 and examines CCB$L_IOC to determine if any I/O is outstanding on the channel. If there is, EXE$DASSGN must wait for its completion AST before proceeding further. EXE$DASSGN acquires the SCHED spinlock and tests whether the process has a pending kernel mode AST whose delivery has been blocked by EXE$DAS-SGN's execution at IPL 2 and above.

   • If there is a pending kernel mode AST, EXE$DASSGN releases the spinlock, lowers IPL to 0, and transfers control to step 3. Lowering IPL to 0 triggers the interrupt that delivers the pending kernel mode AST.

   • If there is not, EXE$DASSGN calls SCH$RESOURCE_WAIT_PS, in module MUTEX, to place the process into a resource wait. SCH$RE-SOURCE_WAIT_PS releases the SCHED spinlock and waits the process at IPL 0 and at a PC corresponding to step 3.

   Chapter 8 discusses ASTs in more detail, and Chapter 13, wait states.

6. It locks the I/O database mutex for write access.

7. It clears CCB$B_AMOD.

8. If there is an associated mailbox (CCB$V_AMB in CCB$L_STS is set), EXE$DASSGN dissociates the mailbox by taking the following steps:

   a. It clears UCB$L_AMB in the device UCB.

   b. It decrements the reference count in the mailbox UCB.

   c. If the mailbox reference count is now 0, it invokes IOC$LAST_CHAN_AMBX, in module IOSUBNPAG, to perform last channel processing for an associated mailbox (see Section 23.5.4).

9. It decrements the reference count in the device UCB.

10. If the device reference count is now 0, indicating that the device was not explicitly allocated, EXE$DASSGN takes the following steps:

    a. It clears the device owner field, deallocating the device.

    b. If the device is cluster-available, it invokes IOC$UNLOCK_DEV to remove the resource lock on the device (see Section 23.4.2).

    c. It invokes IOC$LAST_CHAN to perform last channel processing.

11. If the device reference count is 1 and the device has been explicitly allocated, EXE$DASSGN invokes IOC$LAST_CHAN to perform last channel processing.
12. It calls IOC$DEALLOCATE_CCB, in module IOCHANUTILS, to deallocate the CCB.
13. It invokes SCH$IOUNLOCK to unlock the I/O database mutex, lowers IPL to 0, and returns the success status SS$_NORMAL to its requestor.

23.5.4   Last Channel Processing

Last channel processing is performed when the last channel to a device is deassigned:

- When the device reference count goes to 0, and the device was not explicitly allocated
- When the device reference count goes to 1, and the device was explicitly allocated

There are two entry points to last channel processing: IOC$LAST_CHAN and IOC$LAST_CHAN_AMBX. The latter routine is invoked when the device is an associated mailbox, the former routine in all other cases. They differ only in their initial steps:

- IOC$LAST_CHAN is invoked with the channel identifier and the address of the UCB of the device assigned to the channel. It saves the reason code CAN$C_DASSGN for later use.
- IOC$LAST_CHAN_AMBX is invoked with the address of the mailbox UCB, not the UCB of the device assigned to the channel. (The channel is not assigned to the mailbox and is not needed by the mailbox driver. The current IRP is also not needed by the mailbox driver.) It saves the reason code CAN$C_AMBXDGN for later use.

At this point, IOC$LAST_CHAN and IOC$LAST_CHAN_AMBX converge in the following steps:

1. If the UCB specifies primary affinity and the process does not already require primary affinity, the routine calls SCH$REQUIRE_CAPABILITY, in module CAPABILITY, to acquire affinity for the primary CPU. This is done to handle those cases where the device registers should be accessed only from the primary processor in a symmetric multiprocessing (SMP) system. Chapter 13 discusses processor affinity.
2. The routine acquires the device fork lock, raising IPL to the associated fork IPL. This step synchronizes access to the UCB.
3. It invokes the device driver's cancel I/O routine, passing the reason code saved previously.
4. The routine releases the fork lock without changing IPL.
5. It lowers IPL to 2, leaving it there to prevent process deletion.

6. If primary affinity was acquired, the routine releases it.

7. If the device is explicitly allocated, the routine returns to its invoker.

8. If the device is a terminal or mailbox, the routine clears DEV$V_OPR in UCB$L_DEVCHAR, disabling the device as an operator terminal.

9. If UCB$V_DELETEUCB in UCB$L_STS is set, the routine takes the following two steps:

   a. It invokes IOC$CREDIT_UCB, in module UCBCREDEL, to return the quota charged against the byte count and byte limit.

   b. It invokes IOC$DELETE_UCB, in module UCBCREDEL, to delete the UCB and the associated ORB.

10. The routine returns to its invoker.

23.6 $QIO SYSTEM SERVICE

The $QIO system service performs device-independent preprocessing and, via FDT routines, device-dependent preprocessing. It then queues an I/O request to the driver for the device associated with a channel. Any additional work to be done is performed by the device driver's start I/O routine.

The $QIO system service has the following arguments:

▶ The EFN argument is the number of the event flag to be associated with the I/O request. Since this argument is passed by value, omitting it is the same as specifying event flag 0.

▶ The CHAN argument is the identifier of the I/O channel. This is the same as the CHAN argument returned by the $ASSIGN system service.

▶ The FUNC argument identifies what operation is to be performed by the device driver. It is divided into two portions, the function code proper and function modifiers. Throughout the chapter, the term *function code* means just the function code proper; the term FUNC means the entire argument.

▶ The IOSB argument is the address of the IOSB, a quadword to receive final status of the I/O operation. The *OpenVMS System Services Reference Manual* and the *OpenVMS I/O User's Reference Manual* provide a detailed description of the format of the IOSB.

▶ The ASTADR argument is the address of an AST procedure to be executed in the mode of the requestor when the I/O operation completes.

▶ The ASTPRM argument is the parameter to be passed to the AST procedure.

▶ There are six optional device- and function-specific parameters, P1 through P6.

The CHAN and FUNC arguments must be specified. All others are optional and, if not specified, default to a value of zero.

23.6.1   Device-Independent Preprocessing

The $QIO system service procedure, EXE$QIO in module SYSQIOREQ, executes in kernel mode.

To perform device-independent preprocessing, EXE$QIO validates and processes all its arguments except for P1 through P6. It takes the following steps:

1. It clears the specified event flag so that the process will be placed into a wait state until the I/O operation completes, should the caller request either the $SYNCH system service or one of the event flag wait system services to wait for the I/O operation to complete.

2. It verifies that the channel identifier is valid and has been assigned from an access mode no more privileged than the mode of the $QIO requestor by performing the following checks:

   • The channel identifier is greater than zero and less than or equal to the contents of CTL$GW_CHINDX. CTL$GW_CHINDX contains the identifier of the highest assigned channel. Note that not all the channels whose identifiers are less than the contents of CTL$GW_CHINDX are necessarily currently assigned. They could have been deassigned since the channel whose identifier is stored in CTL$GW_CHINDX was last assigned. (For performance considerations, EXE$QIO verifies the channel identifier as mentioned. The supported way to verify a channel identifier is to call IOC$VERIFY_CHAN, in module IOCHANUTILS rather than to assume the format of the channel identifier.)

   • The access mode of the requestor (specified by the previous mode field, PSL$V_PRVMOD, of the current PS) is less than the access mode specified by the CCB access mode field. This ensures that the channel is used only from access modes at least as privileged as the access mode from which the channel was assigned.

3. If an access or deaccess request is pending on the channel (low bit in CCB$L_WIND is set), the process is placed into an AST wait state, to wait for the access or deaccess to complete. When the AST wait is satisfied, EXE$QIO will restart at the beginning.

4. It extracts the function code from the FUNC argument.

5. If the device is spooled and the function code specifies a virtual I/O function, EXE$QIO substitutes the intermediate device UCB for the UCB specified in the CCB. The intermediate device UCB address is stored in UCB$L_AMB of the UCB specified by the CCB. Virtual I/O to a spooled device is assumed to be I/O that should be spooled. I/O done by the software implementing spooling, for example, the print symbiont, would be logical or physical I/O.

6. Under some circumstances, EXE$QIO must verify the process's access to the device. If the device is file-oriented, then a file processor (ACP or Files-11 XQP) has been or will be involved in checking the process's access to the device when it opens a file. If the device is neither file-oriented nor shareable, the process's access has already been checked as part of implicit or explicit device allocation.

   However, when a process requests a read or write operation from a shareable, non-file-oriented device (for example, a device mounted foreign), EXE$QIO checks whether the access is allowed. It invokes either EXE$CHKRDACCES or EXE$CHKWRTACCES, in module EX-SUBROUT. If the process has the needed access, the routine sets the appropriate bit (CCB$V_RDCHKDON or CCB$V_WRTCHKDON) in CCB$L_STS.

Note that EXE$QIO contains two lists of functions, one for reads and one for writes. While the interpretation of function codes is almost entirely up to the device driver, EXE$QIO does know that the "correct" interpretation of certain codes is a read or a write operation and performs access checking based on this interpretation.

In step 16, EXE$QIO performs additional access checks based on whether the I/O function is physical, logical, or virtual.

7. EXE$QIO verifies that the function code is a legal function by checking the legal function mask in the FDT (see Chapter 22).

8. If the device is offline, EXE$QIO checks that the function code is either IO$_DEACCESS or IO$_ACPCONTROL. If it is not, EXE$QIO returns the error status SS$_DEVOFFLINE.

9. If the IOSB argument is nonzero, EXE$QIO verifies that the IOSB can be written by the requesting mode and then clears it.

10. EXE$QIO uses the buffered I/O function mask in the FDT to determine whether the function code specifies a direct or buffered operation.

11. It raises IPL to 2 to prevent process deletion. This step is necessary for two reasons:

   • EXE$QIO will allocate an IRP. The fact that this IRP is allocated to this process will not be reflected in any data structure until much later. If the process were to be deleted before this allocation were recorded, the IRP would be lost.

   • In steps 12 and 14, EXE$QIO indicates that this process has outstanding I/O. If process deletion were begun after these steps, but before the request was actually queued, the process would become deadlocked, trying to run down nonexistent I/O. Chapter 31 gives more information on process deletion.

12. EXE$QIO determines whether the process has sufficient I/O quota (direct or buffered, depending upon the previous determination) and, if so, charges against it.

   If the process does not have sufficient quota, EXE$QIO lowers IPL to 0 and invokes EXE$SNGLQUOTA_LONG, in module EXSUBROUT, to place the process into an AST wait if the process has resource wait mode enabled. When the I/O quota is returned to the process, the process resumes execution at the next step at IPL 2.

13. It allocates an IRP from nonpaged pool (see Chapter 21).

14. It increments the outstanding I/O count in the CCB.

15. It initializes the IRP. Most of this initialization is straightforward, for example, storing the EFN argument in IRP$B_EFN and copying each of the six function-dependent $QIO arguments to IRP$L_QIO_P*n*, where *n* corresponds to the function-dependent argument number. There are some steps that deserve special comment:

- If the ASTADR argument is nonzero, EXE$QIO charges the process AST quota for an AST control block (ACB). It also sets ACB$V_QUOTA in IRP$B_RMOD to indicate that the process has been charged for the ACB.
- If the function code specifies a buffered I/O operation, EXE$QIO sets IRP$V_BUFIO in IRP$L_STS. Otherwise, it clears the bit.
- EXE$QIO clears the fields that describe the buffer, IRPL_SVAPTE, IRPL_BOFF, and IRP$L_BCNT, the transfer parameters.
- If CCB$L_WIND is nonzero, the channel is associated with either a file or a process section. If the channel is associated with a file, CCB$L_WIND contains the system space address of a WCB, a negative number. EXE$QIO stores the address of this WCB in IRP$L_WIND.

  If the channel is associated with a process section, CCB$L_WIND contains the process section index, a positive number. EXE$QIO uses this value to index the process section table (PST) and obtain the address of the WCB associated with the process section. EXE$QIO stores the address of this WCB in IRP$L_WIND. Chapter 16 gives details on the PST.
- If the function code is a virtual read or write to a non-file-oriented device, EXE$QIO converts the function code into the corresponding logical function code. It stores the converted function code in IRP$L_FUNC and uses the converted function code for all further checking it performs. EXE$QIO stores the function modifiers specified in the FUNC argument in IRP$L_FUNC without change.

16. If the device is not spooled, shareable, or file-oriented, EXE$QIO does not perform any additional privilege checks. Otherwise, it verifies that the process has the necessary privilege to access the device based on whether the I/O function is physical, logical, or virtual.

17. If the request specifies a diagnostic buffer, EXE$QIO allocates the buffer and stores its address in IRP$L_DIAGBUF.

The device-independent preprocessing is complete. EXE$QIO invokes FDT routines to perform device-dependent preprocessing.

23.6.2   Device-Dependent Preprocessing (FDT Routines)

The primary purpose of FDT routines is to validate and process the device-dependent $QIO parameters, P1 to P6. A device driver can include custom FDT routines or use some of the general-purpose routines that are part of the executive. Regardless of the location of FDT routines, they are logically device-dependent extensions of the $QIO system service.

EXE$QIO searches the FDT entries looking for a mask that specifies the function code. When such a mask is found, EXE$QIO invokes the associated FDT routine. If the FDT routine returns control to EXEQIO, EXEQIO continues its search. Successive FDT routines are invoked until an FDT routine invokes one of the routines that terminates FDT processing. These routines are described in the next section.

Note that no FDT entry marks the end of the FDT. It is possible for the search of the FDT to continue past the end of the FDT. Such an occurrence would be an error and would cause unpredictable results.

FDT routines execute in the context of the process that requested the $QIO system service. Therefore, they have access to data in the process's P0 and P1 address space. FDT routines communicate information about the I/O request to the driver through IRP fields. FDT routines can also modify I/O database structures associated with the device assigned to the channel.

FDT routines for direct I/O (I/O done directly between a user buffer and the device) ensure that each buffer page is locked into memory by incrementing its reference count in the page frame number (PFN) database (see Chapter 16).

In the case of direct I/O, these routines initialize the transfer parameters to describe the buffer as follows:

▶ IRP$L_SVAPTE contains the system virtual address of the first page table entry that maps the buffer.
▶ IRP$L_BOFF contains the buffer's offset in bytes from the beginning of that page.
▶ IRP$L_BCNT is the number of bytes to be transferred.

FDT routines for buffered I/O operations must allocate a buffer from nonpaged pool that will be used by the driver for the actual transfer. If the operation is a buffered write, the FDT routine copies data that is being written to this buffer.

The use of system space buffers permits the device driver to access the data in the buffer when the process is no longer current.

In the case of buffered I/O, these routines initialize the transfer parameters to describe the buffer as follows:

▶ IRP$L_SVAPTE is the address of the nonpaged pool buffer, which begins with a 12-byte header, shown in Figure 23.5 (see Section 23.7.3.1).
▶ IRP$L_BOFF is the amount charged against the process's job byte count quota.
▶ IRP$L_BCNT is the number of bytes to be transferred.

Transfers that can take a long time to complete (such as a terminal read or write) are often implemented as buffered I/O operations, whereas transfers that should complete quickly (such as a disk read or write) are implemented as direct I/O operations. Direct I/O requires locking process pages and page tables into memory, tying up the process header, and thus the balance set slot, for the duration of the I/O request. Chapter 20 contains more information on the complexity of swapping a process with direct I/O in progress.

23.6.3 I/O Completion

It is important to distinguish between completion of the $QIO system service request, which signals either that the I/O is underway or that the service was requested incorrectly, and the completion of the I/O request itself.

Passing a status in R0, EXE$QIO returns through the change mode dispatcher to the access mode from which it was requested. If the status is not a success, control returns to the image at a point following its service request. If the status is a success and the image requested the asynchronous form ($QIO) of the service, control returns to the image, which later will request the $SYNCH system service or an event flag wait service to await I/O completion. If the status is a success and the image requested the synchronous form ($QIOW), the executive places the process into an event flag wait until the I/O completes (see Section 23.6.4). Chapter 7 provides more information on how a synchronous system service waits a process.

An I/O request can complete when EXE$QIO returns to its requestor, or it can be passed on to the device driver for device action or some other processing. An FDT routine typically determines how an I/O request completes:

1. If an I/O request is ill formed, the FDT routine invokes EXE$ABORTIO, in module SYSQIOREQ, to abort the request.
2. If no device action or further processing is necessary, or a device-specific error occurs in the FDT routine, it invokes either EXE$FINISHIO or EXE$FINISHIOC, both in module SYSQIOREQ, to complete the I/O request.
3. If an ACP function was requested, or if ACP intervention is required before the I/O request can be delivered to the driver, the FDT routine invokes EXE$QIOACPPKT, in module SYSQIOREQ.
4. If device action or some further driver processing is needed, the FDT routine invokes either EXE$QIODRVPKT or EXE$ALTQUEPKT, both in module SYSQIOREQ.

The next section explains how EXE$QIO itself completes an I/O request. Subsequent sections describe each of the routines that an FDT routine can invoke to complete the request in other ways.

23.6.3.1 $QIO Completion by EXE$QIO.
EXE$QIO itself completes an I/O request only if an error occurs.

As discussed previously, EXE$QIO makes certain checks before it allocates an IRP; for example, the CHAN argument must specify a usable channel. If

EXE$QIO detects an error before allocating an IRP, it takes the following steps:

1. It invokes SCH$POSTEF, in module POSTEF, to set the event flag specified by the EFN argument.
2. It returns an error status in R0 to the requestor.

If EXE$QIO detects an error after it has allocated an IRP, it aborts the I/O, as described in Section 23.6.3.2.

23.6.3.2 **Aborting an I/O Request—EXE$ABORTIO.** If EXE$QIO (after it has allocated an IRP) or an FDT routine detects a device-independent error (for example, insufficient privilege), it loads the final status of the system service in R0 and invokes EXE$ABORTIO, in module SYSQIOREQ, to abort the I/O. EXE$ABORTIO takes the following steps:

1. EXE$ABORTIO copies the error status from R0 to IRP$L_IOST1, clears IRP$L_IOST2, and sets the IRP$V_ABORTIO bit in the IRP$L_STS2 field.
2. It then acquires the device fork lock, raising IPL to fork IPL.
3. It clears IRP$L_IOSB, the address of the IOSB, so that no status is written to it.
4. It clears ACB$V_QUOTA in IRP$B_RMOD and increments the process's AST quota if the bit was set. This prevents a user-specified AST procedure from being called.
5. It inserts the IRP into the current CPU's per-CPU I/O postprocessing queue and requests an IPL$_IOPOST interrupt (see Section 23.7). During postprocessing, any quotas charged will be restored and buffers deallocated or unlocked, if necessary.
   Use of the per-CPU I/O postprocessing queue ensures that I/O postprocessing occurs before the system service completes. If, instead, the systemwide I/O postprocessing queue were used and the process were not current on the primary processor, it is possible that the process would run before the I/O postprocessing occurred. Chapter 37 contains details on the two types of I/O postprocessing queues.
6. EXE$ABORTIO releases the device fork lock.
7. It lowers IPL to 0 and returns to the system service requestor.

The effect of these steps is to complete the system service request without performing any I/O operation. EXE$ABORTIO subjects the IRP to I/O postprocessing because EXE$ABORTIO could have been invoked at any stage of I/O preprocessing: I/O postprocessing guarantees that the I/O request will be aborted cleanly, that is, any allocated buffers will be returned, any locked pages will be released, and so on.

23.6.3.3 **Completing the I/O Request in the FDT Routine—EXE$FINISHIO(C).** Some I/O requests can be completed by an FDT routine without the need for driver processing and device operation. There are two circumstances under which this can occur:

- ▸ If the FDT routine detects a device-specific error, for example, a buffer not properly aligned
- ▸ If the FDT routine can perform all requested operations, for example, an IO$_SENSEMODE operation that returns only fields in the UCB

The FDT routine takes essentially the same action in both cases; the difference is in the status it returns.

The FDT routine invokes either EXE$FINISHIO or EXE$FINISHIOC, both in module SYSQIOREQ. These are alternative entry points to the same routine.

1. EXE$FINISHIOC clears R1. It then continues as if entry had been at EXE$FINISHIO.
2. EXE$FINISHIO increments the operation count in the UCB.
3. It stores R0 and R1 in IRP$L_IOST1 and IRP$L_IOST2. R0 on entry to both routines contains the first longword to be stored in the IOSB. R1 on entry to EXE$FINISHIO contains the second longword to be stored in the IOSB.
4. EXE$FINISHIO acquires the device fork lock, raising IPL to fork IPL.
5. It loads the success status SS$_NORMAL in R0 as the final status of the $QIO system service. Note that the final status of the I/O operation, now in the low-order word of IRP$L_IOST1, can be a failure status.
6. It inserts the IRP into the current CPU's per-CPU I/O postprocessing queue and requests an IPL$_IOPOST interrupt.
7. EXE$FINISHIO releases the device fork lock.
8. It lowers IPL to 0 and returns to the system service requestor.

23.6.3.4 **Entering the Driver's Start I/O Routine—EXE$QIODRVPKT.** To initiate I/O on a device, an FDT routine typically invokes EXE$QIODRVPKT. If the device is idle, EXE$QIODRVPKT invokes the driver's start I/O routine; otherwise, EXE$QIODRVPKT inserts the IRP into the wait queue in the device's UCB.

EXE$QIODRVPKT invokes EXE$INSIOQ, in module SYSQIOREQ, which performs the following actions:

1. It acquires the device fork lock, raising IPL to fork IPL.
2. If UCB$V_BSY in UCB$L_STS is set, indicating that the device is busy, EXE$INSIOQ invokes EXE$INSERT_IRP, in module SYSQIOREQ, to insert the IRP into the device's queue of pending I/O requests. The queue, whose listhead is at UCB$L_IOQFL, is ordered according to the base

Table 23.2   Flags in UCB$L_STS

Flag	*Meaning if Set*
UCB$V_BSY	Device start I/O routine is currently processing an I/O request
UCB$V_INT	An interrupt is expected from this device
UCB$V_TIM	This device has an I/O operation being timed
UCB$V_TIMOUT	This device has timed out
UCB$V_CANCEL	Current I/O on the device has been canceled
UCB$V_POWER	The system recovered from a power failure

priority of the process that requested the I/O. When EXE$INSERT_IRP returns, control is transferred to step 5.

3. If the device is idle, EXE$INSIOQ marks it busy by setting UCB$V_BSY in UCB$L_STS and invokes IOC$INITIATE, in module IOSUBNPAG, to initiate device I/O.

   IOC$INITIATE determines whether the device on which the I/O was requested has affinity for the current CPU by examining the device's affinity mask, UCB$L_AFFINITY. If the device does not have affinity for this CPU, then IOC$INITIATE decrements UCB$L_QLEN, clears the UCB$V_BSY bit in UCB$L_STS, and calls SMP$CPU_SWITCH, in module SMPROUT. SMP$CPU_SWITCH creates a fork process on the CPU with the lowest physical CPU identification for which this device has affinity; this fork process invokes EXE$INSIOQC, in module SYSQIOREQ. EXE$INSIOQC obtains the fork lock, increments UCB$L_QLEN, sets the UCB$V_BSY bit in UCB$L_STS, and reinvokes IOC$INITIATE.

   Running on a CPU for which the device has affinity, IOC$INITIATE performs the following steps:

   a. It saves the IRP address in UCB$L_IRP.

   b. It copies IRPL_SVAPTE, IRPL_BCNT, and IRP$L_BOFF to UCB$L_SVAPTE, UCB$L_BCNT, and UCB$L_BOFF. This step is an optimization for direct I/O operations and is unnecessary for most buffered I/O operations.

   c. It clears UCB$V_TIMOUT and UCB$V_CANCEL in UCB$L_STS. Table 23.2 explains the significance of these and other flags in UCB$L_STS.

   d. If a diagnostic buffer is associated with the current I/O request, IOC$INITIATE obtains its address and records the current system time in it as the operation start time.

      A process requests diagnostic I/O to a driver that supports it by making a physical I/O request and specifying the address of a diagnostic buffer as a function-specific parameter. If the requesting process has the DIAGNOSE privilege, EXE$QIO allocates a system diagnostic buffer from nonpaged pool and records its address in IRP$L_DIAGBUF. EXE$QIO also sets IRP$V_DIAGBUF in IRP$L_STS. Various components of the executive support diagnostic I/O by filling in different parts of the diagnostic buffer if IRP$V_DIAGBUF is set. The system diagnostic buffer is copied to the requesting process's diagnostic buffer by the I/O completion AST routine, as described in Section 23.7.3.2.

  e. IOC$INITIATE gets the address of the driver dispatch table (DDT) from the UCB, locates the driver's start I/O routine through DDT$L_START, and invokes it.

4. The driver's start I/O routine eventually returns to IOC$INITIATE, and IOC$INITIATE returns to EXE$INSIOQ, as discussed in Chapter 24.

5. EXE$INSIOQ releases the device fork lock, restoring the IPL at entry, and returns control to EXE$QIODRVPKT.

6. EXE$QIODRVPKT restores IPL to 0 and returns to the image that requested the I/O. The status returned in R0 indicates that the I/O request was queued to the driver successfully. The $QIO requestor cannot determine the status of the I/O operation until the I/O postprocessing routine writes the I/O status block for this I/O request.

23.6.3.5 Entering the Driver's Alternate Start I/O Routine—EXE$ALTQUEPKT.

An FDT routine invokes EXE$ALTQUEPKT to enter a driver's alternate start I/O routine. The terminal driver's write FDT routine, for example, enters the alternate start I/O routine when a write to a full duplex terminal is requested.

A driver can queue an I/O request to another driver by using that driver's alternate start I/O routine in conjunction with an I/O postprocessing system completion routine (see Section 23.7.1). NETDRIVER, for example, uses this mechanism to interact with its communications drivers.

A driver with an alternate start I/O routine must be able to deal with multiple concurrent I/O requests.

EXE$ALTQUEPKT invokes the driver's alternate start I/O routine regardless of the setting of the UCB$V_BSY bit, as follows:

1. It acquires the device fork lock, raising IPL to fork IPL.

2. It tests UCB$V_ALTBSY in UCB$L_STS. When set, this flag indicates that another thread of execution is in the process of being restarted on a processor for which the device has affinity. If UCB$V_ALTBSY is set, EXE$ALTQUEPKT inserts the IRP into the device's alternate I/O request wait queue at UCB$L_ALTIOWQ, releases the fork lock, and returns.

   Synchronizing with the UCB$V_ALTBSY bit ensures that alternate start I/O requests are processed in the same order in which they are issued, regardless of the CPU on which an alternate start I/O request is made.

3. If UCB$V_ALTBSY is clear, EXE$ALTQUEPKT gets the current CPU's

physical CPU ID from the per-CPU database field CPU$L_PHY_CPUID and checks the device affinity mask in UCB$L_AFFINITY to determine if the device has affinity for this CPU. If not, EXE$ALTQUEPKT sets UCB$V_ALTBSY and calls SMP$CPU_SWITCH, in module SMPROUT, to create a fork process on the CPU with the lowest physical CPU ID for which the device has affinity. The fork process resumes processing at step 5.

4. If the device does have affinity for this CPU, EXE$ALTQUEPKT gets the address of the driver's DDT from the UCB, locates its alternate start I/O routine through offset DDT$L_ALTSTART, and invokes it.

When the driver's alternate start I/O routine returns, EXE$ALTQUE-PKT releases the device fork lock, restoring the IPL at entry, and returns to its invoker, the FDT routine.

5. Running on a CPU for which the device has affinity, EXE$ALTQUEPKT obtains the fork lock and invokes the device's alternate start I/O routine. When the driver's alternate start I/O routine returns, EXE$ALTQUEPKT processes the remaining IRPs, if any, on the device's alternate I/O wait queue, invoking the driver's alternate start I/O routine for each IRP from a CPU for which the device has affinity.

When all IRPs on the alternate I/O wait queue have been processed, EXE$ALTQUEPKT clears the UCB$V_ALTBSY bit, releases the fork lock, and dismisses the fork process.

23.6.3.6   **Initiating ACP I/O—EXE$QIOACPPKT.** Some I/O requests must be processed by a device's ACP. For example, when a file system function such as IO$_ACCESS is requested, or when a window turn is required to map a requested virtual block number (VBN) to a logical block number (LBN), a disk driver requires assistance from the XQP, which is a form of ACP (see Chapter 22). A window turn updates file retrieval information in the WCB (see Section 23.8.2).

An ACP transforms an I/O request into one more suitable for the driver and queues the request to the driver. Alternatively, it requests one or more I/O operations itself to perform the requested function. After it has performed the function, the ACP initiates I/O postprocessing.

EXE$QIOACPPKT is invoked by file system FDT routines in module SYSACPFDT when an I/O request requires action by the XQP. It is also invoked by other FDT routines for I/O requests that require ACP assistance. EXE$QIOACPPKT performs the following actions:

1. It locates the volume control block (VCB) of the device from the UCB. From the VCB, it locates the ACP queue block (AQB) and tests AQB$L_ACPPID. Chapter 22 discusses ACPs, the VCB, and the AQB.

EXE$QIOACPPKT makes a distinction between the XQP and other ACPs. The XQP runs in the I/O requestor's process context, whereas other ACPs run as separate processes. In the XQP's AQB, AQB$L_ACP-PID is zero. For other ACPs, the field contains the PID of the ACP.

2. If AQB$L_ACPPID is nonzero, EXE$QIOACPPKT places the IRP at the tail of the interlocked I/O request queue at AQB$L_ACPIQ.

   a. If the queue was not empty, EXE$QIOACPPKT returns a successful status to its requestor, indicating that the I/O request is queued.

   b. If this IRP is the first to be inserted into the queue, EXE$QIOACPPKT gets the ACP's PID from AQB$L_ACPPID and invokes SCH$WAKE, in module RSE, to wake up the ACP. If SCH$WAKE returns a success status, EXE$QIOACPPKT returns a success status for the $QIO request.

      Later, when the ACP is placed into execution, the ACP removes the request from its queue, performs the requested function, and initiates I/O postprocessing by queuing the IRP to the systemwide postprocessing queue. Section 23.7 and Chapter 24 discuss I/O postprocessing.

3. If AQB$L_ACPPID is zero, EXE$QIOACPPKT enters EXE$QXQPPKT, in module SYSQIOREQ. EXE$QXQPPKT generates a file system request in the context of the current process:

   a. Using the portion of the IRP that begins at offset IRP$L_IOQFL as an ACB, it stores the procedure value of the XQP procedure F11X$RCV_PKT, in module [F11X]DISPAT, in ACB$L_AST.

   b. EXE$QXQPPKT stores the address of the IRP itself in ACB$L_AST-PRM.

   c. It then invokes SCH$QAST, in module ASTDEL, to queue the IRP as a kernel mode AST to the current process.

   d. When SCH$QAST returns, EXE$QXQPPKT lowers IPL to 0 and returns control to the $QIO system service requestor.

Before control returns to the $QIO requestor, the kernel mode AST is delivered and F11X$RCV_PKT is called. F11X$RCV_PKT queues the IRP to the per-process XQP queue in the XQP's data area. If the XQP is not busy servicing another IRP, F11X$RCV_PKT resumes the XQP's thread of execution; otherwise F11X$RCV_PKT simply returns, dismissing the kernel mode AST. When the XQP has finished processing its current I/O request, it removes the next IRP from its per-process queue and begins processing it.

When the XQP has serviced the request, it performs I/O postprocessing by invoking special entry points in IOC$IOPOST, in module IOCIOPOST.

23.6.4 $QIOW System Service

The $QIOW system service is the synchronous form of the $QIO system service. It takes the same arguments as the latter. EXE$QIOW, the $QIOW system service procedure, executes in its requestor's access mode. It simply copies the arguments to the current stack and requests the $QIO system service.

If the $QIO system service returns an error, the $QIOW system service returns the error status to its requestor. Otherwise, EXE$QIOW invokes EXE$SYNCH_LOOP, in module SYSSYNCH. EXE$SYNCH_LOOP places the process into a wait state until the event flag associated with the I/O request is set. When the process resumes as a result of the setting of the event flag, EXE$SYNCH_LOOP verifies that the IOSB was updated through the completion of the I/O operation. If the IOSB was not updated, EXE$SYNCH_ LOOP clears the event flag and places the process into a wait state for the same event flag. The $QIOW request does not complete until the IOSB is updated.

If the IOSB argument was omitted in the $QIOW request, EXE$SYNCH_ LOOP returns to the $QIOW requestor once the event flag is set. Note, however, that unless a unique event flag was associated with the $QIOW operation, there is no guarantee that the I/O operation completed; the completion of another operation that was associated with the event flag may have set the event flag.

23.7 I/O POSTPROCESSING

The executive performs I/O postprocessing after an associated driver completes an I/O operation. The I/O postprocessing routine IOC$IOPOST, in module IOCIOPOST, is the interrupt service routine for the IPL$_IOPOST software interrupt. It implements the device-independent steps necessary to complete an I/O request.

Some I/O postprocessing operations, for example, unlocking buffer pages and deallocating buffers, are performed by IOC$IOPOST. Other operations, such as writing the IOSB, are performed by a special kernel mode AST routine, discussed in Section 23.7.3.

There is one systemwide I/O postprocessing queue and one per-CPU I/O postprocessing queue for each CPU. IOC$IOPOST always removes entries from the per-CPU queue for the current CPU. It removes entries from the systemwide queue only when it is running on the primary processor. When running on the primary, it checks the systemwide queue and then, when the systemwide queue is empty, the per-CPU queue. For simplicity, the following discussion treats these queues as if they were one. Chapter 37 describes the need for both types of queue.

IOC$IOPOST removes the first IRP in the I/O postprocessing queue. It takes one of two paths, depending upon the value in IRP$L_PID. If the value in IRP$L_PID is negative, IOC$IOPOST performs system I/O completion. If the value in IRP$L_PID is positive, IOC$IOPOST performs normal I/O completion. These two paths are described in the following sections.

In either path, if the virtual I/O cache is enabled, IOC$IOPOST invokes CACHE$IOPOST, in module VCC_CACHE, to perform virtual I/O cache-related postprocessing on I/O requests to nonsequential devices. Chapter 26 briefly describes the virtual I/O cache, but the details of its implementation are outside the scope of this book.

23.7.1   System I/O Completion

A negative value in IRP$L_PID is the procedure value of the system I/O completion (end action) routine. IOC$IOPOST invokes this routine. When it returns, IOC$IOPOST removes the next IRP from the queue and processes it.

Various components use system I/O completion routines to perform specialized I/O postprocessing. For example, the VMScluster connection manager uses them for the I/O to the quorum disk. The connection manager, which runs as a fork process, creates the IRP and inserts it into the driver's request queue. Although the driver does not do anything unusual to process the request, IOC$IOPOST cannot perform its usual process-related I/O completion tasks. Instead, the specified system completion routine returns data and status to the connection manager and deallocates the IRP.

23.7.2   Normal I/O Completion

A positive value in IRP$L_PID is the PID of the I/O requestor. IOC$IOPOST determines the type of I/O operation by testing IRP$V_BUFIO in IRP$L_STS. If the bit is set, the I/O operation is buffered; otherwise, it is direct. IOC$IOPOST performs actions appropriate to the type of I/O operation and then queues a special kernel mode AST to the requestor. The AST routine will perform the completion that must be done in the context of the requestor.

23.7.2.1   Buffered I/O Completion. Buffered I/O involves a transfer to or from a system space buffer in nonpaged pool. IOC$IOPOST takes the following initial steps in the case of buffered I/O:

1. It increments PCB$L_BIOCNT, the number of concurrent buffered I/O requests allowed.
2. If IRP$V_FILACP in IRP$L_STS is set, IOC$IOPOST also increments PCB$L_DIOCNT, the number of concurrent direct I/O requests allowed. Routine BUILDACPBUF, in module SYSACPFDT, sets this bit for most ACP I/O requests. FDT routines for most common ACP function requests invoke BUILDACPBUF.
3. IOC$IOPOST invokes the routine EXE$CREDIT_BYTCNT, in module EXSUB-ROUT, to restore the byte count quota that was charged for the system buffer. Note that IRP$L_BOFF does not contain a buffer offset in this case; it contains a byte count. The FDT routine that allocated the system buffer stored the size of the buffer in IRP$L_BOFF and charged the job information block (JIB) for the buffer.

4. IOC$IOPOST stores the procedure value of the special kernel mode AST routine in the IRP at offset ACB$L_KAST. The IRP will also be used as an ACB. ACB$L_KAST and IRP$L_WIND are the same offset. At this point, the WCB address is no longer needed and that location can be safely reused.

The special kernel mode AST routine, in module IOCIOPOST, has two entry points: BUFPOST, for buffered read completion, and DIRPOST, for all others. The first case differs from the others in that data must be copied from the system buffer to the process buffer before the process is informed that I/O is complete. In the case of a buffered write, however, there is no need to copy data between the process buffer and the system buffer. It was copied earlier from the process buffer to the system buffer by an FDT routine. In the case of direct I/O, there is no system buffer.

It is possible that there was no need for a system buffer; an I/O request with no transfer of data is usually performed as a buffered I/O request. If a buffer was needed, its address is in IRP$L_SVAPTE.

- If IRP$L_SVAPTE is nonzero and IRP$V_FUNC in IRP$L_STS is set, the I/O function is a read requiring a buffer. In this case, IOC$IOPOST stores the procedure value of BUFPOST in ACB$L_KAST.

- Otherwise, IOC$IOPOST stores the procedure value of DIRPOST in ACB$L_KAST. If IRP$L_SVAPTE is nonzero, IOC$IOPOST deallocates the buffer.

5. It performs the steps described in Section 23.7.2.3.

23.7.2.2   **Direct I/O Completion.** Direct I/O requests involve the transfer of data directly to or from the process buffer, which can be paged. Since paging must not occur during the processing of the I/O request, the pages are locked in memory by one of the FDT routines invoked by EXE$QIO.

For direct I/O operations other than swapping and paging I/O, which are discussed in Chapters 18 and 20, IOC$IOPOST takes the following initial steps:

1. It performs the steps necessary to handle segmented transfers, if needed, as described in Section 23.8.

2. It determines the number of pages the direct I/O buffer occupies from IRP$L_BOFF and IRP$L_BCNT. IRP$L_SVAPTE contains the address of the first page table entry that maps the buffer. It unlocks the pages by invoking MMG$UNLOCK, in module IOLOCK, which decrements the pages' associated reference counts in the PFN database (see Chapter 16). This step can result in the pages being placed on the free or modified page list.

3. An IRP by itself can describe only one direct I/O buffer. If a direct I/O request has more than one buffer, an FDT routine allocates one or more IRP extensions (IRPEs) to describe them. Each IRPE can describe two

buffers. An IRP with an IRPE has bit IRP$V_EXTEND set in IRP$L_STS and the address of the IRPE in IRP$L_EXTEND. Similarly, each IRPE can point to another IRPE.

IOC$IOPOST tests whether IRPEs are present; if so, it unlocks the additional buffers they describe.

No drivers that are part of the OpenVMS AXP operating system use IRPEs.

4. It increments PCB$L_DIOCNT, the number of allowed concurrent direct I/O requests.
5. It stores the procedure value of DIRPOST in ACB$L_KAST.
6. It performs the steps described in Section 23.7.2.3.

23.7.2.3   **Final Steps in IOC$IOPOST.** IOC$IOPOST performs the same final steps for each buffered and direct I/O request:

1. If appropriate, it invokes SCH$POSTEF, in module POSTEF, to set the specified event flag for the process whose I/O just completed.
2. It queues a postprocessing special kernel mode AST to the process.

Whether IOC$IOPOST or its AST routine sets the event flag is determined by the type of flag: if the flag is local, IOC$IOPOST sets it; otherwise, the AST routine sets it.

A potential synchronization problem could occur if a process whose event flag wait is satisfied executes before the postprocessing AST routine copies possible buffered input to a process buffer and records status in the IOSB. This race condition could occur under two sets of circumstances:

▸ Multiple processes were waiting for a common event flag associated with an I/O request and one of them executed before the process that requested the I/O could execute the postprocessing AST routine. IOC$IOPOST avoids this race condition by not setting a common event flag itself; instead, its AST routine does.

▸ IOC$IOPOST and the newly computable process execute on different processors and the process begins to execute before the AST routine is queued. IOC$IOPOST avoids this race condition by acquiring the SCHED spinlock before setting the flag and not releasing it until the AST is queued.

SCH$POSTEF invokes SCH$REPORT_EVENT, in module RSE, if setting the event flag satisfies the wait. SCH$REPORT_EVENT changes the process's state to computable or computable outswapped. Chapter 10 gives more information on event flag waits, and Chapter 13, on SCH$REPORT_ EVENT.

If the process is current (possibly on another member of an SMP system), IOC$IOPOST invokes SCH$QAST before it invokes SCH$POSTEF. This ensures that the special kernel mode AST routine runs before the process can detect that the event flag is set.

IOC$IOPOST sets ACB$V_KAST in IRP$B_RMOD to indicate that this is a special kernel mode AST and invokes SCH$QAST, in module ASTDEL, to queue the AST to the process identified by the IRP$L_PID field. The IRP is used as the ACB for SCH$QAST, as described in Chapter 8. Except for ACB$L_KAST and ACB$V_KAST, IOC$IOPOST does not change any fields in the IRP/ACB.

IOC$IOPOST attempts to remove another IRP from the I/O postprocessing queue. If it is successful, it processes that IRP. Otherwise, it executes a CALL_ PAL REI instruction to exit the interrupt service routine.

23.7.3   I/O Completion Special Kernel Mode AST Routine

The I/O completion special kernel mode AST routine has two entry points: BUFPOST and DIRPOST. BUFPOST performs certain steps unique to buffered read completion and then falls into DIRPOST.

23.7.3.1   Buffered Read Completion.
BUFPOST copies data from system buffers allocated by an FDT routine to user buffers in process-private address space. BUFPOST processes three types of system buffer, identified by IRP$L_STS bits:

▶ Simple buffer—IRP$V_COMPLEX clear. Simple buffers are used for most buffered and diagnostic I/O operations.
▶ Complex buffer—IRP$V_COMPLEX set and IRP$V_CHAINED clear. Most ACP FDT routines in module SYSACPFDT use complex buffers to process ACP I/O requests.
▶ Chained complex buffer—IRP$V_COMPLEX and IRP$V_CHAINED set. Chained complex buffers are used by network device drivers.

When a simple buffer is associated with an I/O request, IRP$L_SVAPTE contains its address and IRP$L_BCNT contains the number of bytes of data in the buffer. Figure 23.5 shows the layout of a simple buffer.

The first longword of the buffer points to the data, beyond the header. The second longword contains the address of the user buffer. The next word contains the size of the simple I/O buffer. The next byte contains the type,

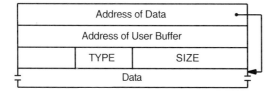

Figure 23.5
Layout of a Simple Buffer

typically DYN$C_BUFIO. The next byte is spare. The rest of the buffer contains the data.

BUFPOST invokes routine MOVBUF, in module IOCIOPOST, to move the data. MOVBUF takes the following steps:

1. It verifies that the user buffer is still write-accessible to the access mode in IRP$B_RMOD.

    If it is not write-accessible, MOVBUF modifies the final status in IRP$L_IOST1 to be SS$_ACCVIO.

2. Otherwise, MOVBUF copies the data from the system buffer to the user buffer.

3. It deallocates the system buffer to nonpaged pool.

4. It returns to its invoker.

If the I/O request is a mailbox read (IRP$V_MBXIO in IRP$L_STS is set), BUFPOST invokes SCH$RAVAIL, in module MUTEX, to declare the mailbox resource available in case a process is waiting for this resource. Resources are discussed in Chapter 13.

When a complex buffer is associated with an I/O request, IRP$L_SVAPTE contains its address and IRP$L_BCNT contains the number of descriptors in the packet.

The layout of a complex buffer is shown in Figure 23.6. The first longword points to the first descriptor. The second longword is ignored by BUFPOST. The third longword contains the size and type. There can be space between the third longword and the first descriptor. The rest of the buffer consists of descriptors and the associated data buffers.

Each descriptor has the same format. The offset field contains the offset from the start of the descriptor to the data buffer in the packet. The size field contains the number of bytes in the data buffer; the size can be zero. The user

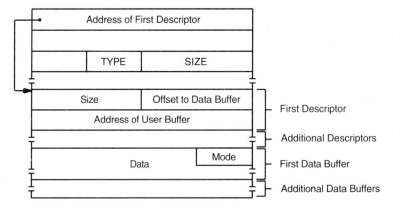

Figure 23.6
Layout of a Complex Buffer

buffer address is the address of the process-private space user buffer. The first byte in the data buffer is the access mode associated with the user buffer.

One common instance of the complex buffer is the ACP I/O buffer (AIB) used by the XQP. In the AIB, the third longword is followed by an access rights block (ARB) copied from the requestor's PCB. The descriptors apply to input data as well as output data. In the case of input data, the size field in the descriptor is set to zero before the IRP is completed by the file system. The file system can also reduce the count of descriptors in IRP$L_BCNT; this is done when the last descriptors are for input data. Since the size contained in the third longword of the buffer reflects the entire buffer, no space is lost when the buffer is deallocated to nonpaged pool.

BUFPOST processes the buffer in the following steps:

1. It gets the address of the first descriptor.
2. If the size field is zero, BUFPOST goes to step 5.
3. If the user buffer is write-accessible, BUFPOST transfers the data from the data buffer to the user buffer.
4. If the user buffer is not write-accessible, BUFPOST modifies the final status in IRP$L_IOST1 to be SS$_ACCVIO and goes to step 6.
5. If there are more descriptors, BUFPOST gets the address of the next descriptor and then goes to step 2.
6. It deallocates the buffer to nonpaged pool.

When a chained complex buffer is associated with an I/O request, IRP$L_SVAPTE contains the address of the first chained complex buffer and IRP$L_BCNT contains the size of the user buffer.

Chained complex buffers are used by some of the communications drivers. They provide a mechanism for one logical buffer to be split into several segments that are not combined until they are transferred to the user buffer.

The layout of a chained complex buffer is shown in Figure 23.7. The first longword contains the address of the data area. The second longword contains the address of the user buffer; this field is valid only in the first descriptor in the chain. CXB$W_SIZE contains the size of the chained complex buffer. CXB$B_TYPE contains the type, DYN$C_CXB. CXB$W_LENGTH contains the size of the data area. CXB$L_LINK contains the address of the next chained complex buffer in the chain; zero indicates the end of the chain.

BUFPOST processes the chained complex buffers in the following manner:

1. It verifies that the user buffer is write-accessible to the access mode in IRP$B_RMOD.
2. If the user buffer is not write-accessible, BUFPOST modifies the final status in IRP$L_IOST1 to be SS$_ACCVIO. It then goes to step 6.
3. If the user buffer is write-accessible, BUFPOST sets CXB$W_LENGTH to be the smaller of the amount of space left in the user buffer and the original contents of CXB$W_LENGTH.

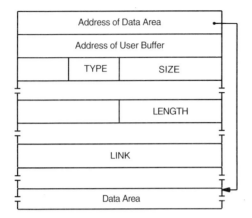

Figure 23.7
Layout of a Chained Complex Buffer

4. It moves that amount of data from the data area to the user buffer and reduces the amount of space left in the user buffer by the amount occupied by the transferred data.

5. If there is space left in the user buffer, BUFPOST moves to the next buffer. If there is a next buffer, BUFPOST goes to step 3.

6. BUFPOST deallocates all the buffers to nonpaged pool.

23.7.3.2   **Common Completion for Buffered and Direct I/O.** DIRPOST performs the completion common to buffered and direct I/O requests:

1. It increments either PHD$L_DIOCNT or PHD$L_BIOCNT, the process's cumulative totals of completed direct I/O and buffered I/O requests.

2. If a user's diagnostic buffer was associated with the I/O request, DIRPOST invokes routine MOVBUF to copy the diagnostic information from the system diagnostic buffer to the user's diagnostic buffer. DIRPOST then deallocates the system diagnostic buffer. The system diagnostic buffer has the same format as a simple buffered I/O buffer.

3. It decrements the CCB count of I/O requests in progress on this channel.

4. If this was the last I/O for the channel and there is a deaccess request for the channel pending, DIRPOST queues that deaccess request to the ACP by invoking IOC$WAKACP, in module IOCIOPOST.

5. If the I/O request specified an IOSB, DIRPOST copies the quadword at IRP$L_IOST1 to the IOSB.

6. If a common event flag is associated with the I/O request, DIRPOST invokes SCH$POSTEF to set the flag.

7. If any IRPEs were used, it deallocates them.

8. If ACB$V_QUOTA is set in IRP$B_RMOD, then the user requested AST notification of I/O completion. The AST procedure value and the op-

tional AST argument were originally stored in the IRP (now used as an ACB). DIRPOST invokes SCH$QAST to queue the IRP as an ACB, this time for a normal AST in the access mode at which the I/O request was made.

9. Otherwise, if ACB$V_QUOTA is clear, DIRPOST deallocates the IRP/ACB to nonpaged pool.

10. It returns to its invoker, SCH$ASTDEL in module ASTDEL.

23.8   SEGMENTED VIRTUAL AND LOGICAL I/O

Under certain circumstances, the I/O subsystem must break I/O transfer requests involving a block-addressable mass storage device into segments and pass the request to the device driver segment by segment. This section describes the means by which such requests are segmented and successive segments are passed on to a device driver.

A file is stored on such a device in a series of blocks. There are three ways of referring to the blocks: file-relative (virtual), volume-relative (logical), and absolute (physical). An image performing I/O to a file describes its request in terms of the starting VBN and the number of bytes to be transferred. The I/O subsystem must convert the VBN into its corresponding LBN for the device driver. For some devices, the LBN must be converted into the corresponding physical block number.

A logically contiguous series of blocks in a file is called an extent. An extent is described by its starting LBN and the number of blocks in it. Most files are made up of multiple extents; a logically contiguous file has only one extent. Each file has an on-disk data structure called a file header that lists the extents that make up the file. When a file is opened, information about its extents is copied from the file header into the WCB. If the image's I/O request crosses a file extent boundary, the I/O subsystem must break the request into segments, each of which fits within one extent.

Figure 23.8 shows the layout of a WCB with two map entries. Offsets for the first two map entries of each WCB are defined by the $WCBDEF macro.

Certain mass storage devices and their associated drivers cannot handle transfers greater than 64 KB at one time. In this case the I/O subsystem must break the transfers into segments no greater than 64 KB. Note that the request can already have been segmented to fit within file extents, which may be greater than 64 KB.

23.8.1   Segmentation by FDT Routines

Usually, a mass storage device driver specifies the following FDT routines: ACP$READBLK for reads and ACP$WRITEBLK for writes, both in module SYSACPFDT. These routines store the total byte count of the request in the original byte count field of the IRP, IRP$L_OBCNT, and clear the accumulated byte count field of the IRP, IRP$L_ABCNT.

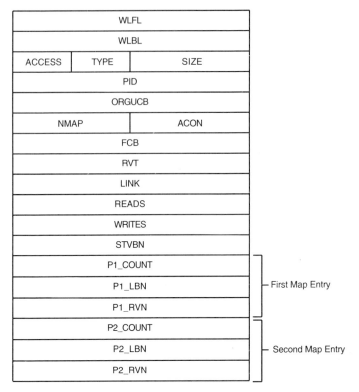

WLFL			
WLBL			
ACCESS	TYPE	SIZE	
PID			
ORGUCB			
NMAP		ACON	
FCB			
RVT			
LINK			
READS			
WRITES			
STVBN			
P1_COUNT			
P1_LBN			
P1_RVN			
P2_COUNT			
P2_LBN			
P2_RVN			

First Map Entry (P1_COUNT, P1_LBN, P1_RVN)

Second Map Entry (P2_COUNT, P2_LBN, P2_RVN)

Figure 23.8
Layout of a Window Control Block (WCB)

23.8.1.1 **Segmenting Virtual I/O.** If the transfer is a virtual I/O transfer, these routines then invoke IOC$MAPVBLK, in module IOSUBRAMS, to perform the actual conversion from VBNs to LBNs. IOC$MAPVBLK (see Section 23.8.2) returns the number of bytes not mapped.

If the number of bytes mapped is nonzero, each FDT routine takes the following steps:

1. It computes the number of bytes mapped by subtracting the number of bytes not mapped from IRP$L_OBCNT and stores this number in IRP$L_BCNT.
2. It stores the starting LBN in IRP$L_IOST1.
3. It stores the starting VBN in IRP$L_SEGVBN.
4. It converts the I/O function to the equivalent physical I/O function.
5. It takes the steps discussed in Section 23.8.1.2.

If the number of bytes mapped by IOC$MAPVBLK is zero, the FDT routines store the starting VBN in IRP$L_SEGVBN and the number of bytes not mapped (in this case, the total number of bytes requested) in IRP$L_BCNT

822

and then invoke EXE$QIOACPPKT, in module SYSQIOREQ, to send the IRP to the ACP.

When the file system processes this IRP, it detects that the WCB does not map the requested virtual range and performs a window turn. It reads the file header to obtain the mapping information necessary for the transfer in question and stores the information in the WCB, replacing other mapping information already contained there. The file system performs the equivalent steps that IOC$MAPVBLK performs and then queues the IRP to the driver. Note that the number of bytes mapped at this point is nonzero.

23.8.1.2 **Segmenting Logical and Physical I/O.** If the function is not a physical I/O function, the FDT routines convert it to the equivalent physical I/O function. The FDT routines then take the steps necessary to handle transfers greater than 64 KB, as discussed in Section 23.8.3. Note that these steps are not required for all disk devices.

The routines then queue the IRP to the driver. The driver performs the transfer without regard for whether the entire range is to be transferred. IOC$IOPOST will check whether the entire range has been transferred when the driver completes the I/O request and will take the necessary action, as described in Section 23.8.4.

23.8.2 **IOC$MAPVBLK**

IOC$MAPVBLK uses the information passed (via registers and the IRP) to convert the VBNs to LBNs. The goal is to convert the starting VBN to the related LBN. The gating factor is the information stored in the WCB (the address of the WCB is obtained from CCB$L_WIND) that was created by the file system when the file was opened.

If the WCB contains enough mapping information to convert the entire virtual range of the transfer into corresponding LBNs on the volume, then the virtual I/O transfer will be handled directly by the driver and IOC$IOPOST, even if the transfer consists of several logically noncontiguous pieces. If the WCB does not contain enough information to completely map the virtual range of the transfer, the intervention of the file system will be required at some time to complete the transfer. This intervention is known as a window turn.

Because a deadlock situation could occur if a file mapped by the memory management subsystem required a window turn, the memory management subsystem must avoid window turns. To do this, each file mapped by the memory management subsystem must have all its mapping information in the WCB. A special, large variation of the WCB is used, called a cathedral window.

IOC$MAPVBLK can encounter one of the following situations.

▶ The virtual range is logically contiguous and the WCB contains the needed mapping information. In this case, all that IOC$MAPVBLK needs to do is convert the starting VBN into the related LBN. The driver can transfer the data without further conversion of VBNs into LBNs.

▶ The WCB contains mapping information for the beginning of the virtual range but not for the entire virtual range. In this case, IOC$MAPVBLK converts the starting VBN into the related LBN. The driver can transfer the start of the virtual range but will need further conversion of VBNs into LBNs to transfer the rest of the range.

In this case, the virtual range may be logically contiguous, but not enough mapping information is contained in the WCB to verify this. A window turn will be needed later.

▶ The virtual range is not logically contiguous, but the WCB does contain mapping information for the beginning of the virtual range. IOC$MAP-VBLK handles this case in the same way it handles the previous case.

The driver can transfer the start of the virtual range but will need further conversion of VBNs into LBNs to transfer the rest of the range. The WCB may or may not contain the needed information. If it does not, a window turn will be needed. Whether a window turn will be needed later is irrelevant at this point.

▶ The mapping information that maps the first virtual block in the range to its logical counterpart is not in the WCB. A window turn is needed before any data can be transferred.

In all cases, IOC$MAPVBLK returns the number of bytes not mapped. If the number of bytes mapped is nonzero, IOC$MAPVBLK also returns the starting LBN.

23.8.3   Segmenting Transfers Greater Than 64 KB

The OpenVMS AXP operating system supports I/O transfers greater than 64 KB for mass storage devices, even though a device and its driver may only support transfers up to 64 KB. This is done by breaking the transfer into segments no larger than the maximum transfer size supported by the driver. The UCB$L_MAXBCNT field contains the largest transfer size supported by the driver. If it is zero, it is assumed to be 65,024 (64 KB minus 512).

If the IRP$L_BCNT field is greater than the maximum transfer size specified by UCB$L_MAXBCNT, the FDT routines set IRP$L_BCNT to the maximum transfer size accepted by the driver. Otherwise, they do not modify IRP$L_BCNT. Remember that the FDT routines store the requested size in IRP$L_OBCNT, as noted in Section 23.8.1.

As a result, the first transfer will be the size specified by UCB$L_MAX-BCNT. The remainder will be transferred as a result of the steps taken by IOC$IOPOST, as described in Section 23.8.4.

824

23.8.4   **IOC$IOPOST Processing of Segmented Transfers**

Whenever IOC$IOPOST encounters an IRP for a direct I/O data transfer request, it determines if another segment must be transferred by comparing the original byte count to the number of bytes transferred thus far. If the difference is not zero, another segment must be transferred. If the two numbers agree, the request is completed exactly like other direct I/O requests.

If the two numbers do not agree, IOC$IOPOST prepares the IRP for the transfer of the next segment by taking the following steps:

1. If the transfer is a virtual I/O transfer, IOC$IOPOST invokes IOC$MAP-VBLK.

    The same cases exist here as when IOC$MAPVBLK is invoked by the FDT routines. IOC$IOPOST takes the equivalent steps in each case for the transfer that starts at the VBN in IRP$L_SEGVBN. If there is a total mapping failure of the remaining transfer, IOC$IOPOST invokes IOC$QTOACP to pass the IRP to the ACP. Otherwise, IOC$IOPOST continues.

2. It places the lesser of the remaining byte count and the maximum transfer size accepted by the driver in IRP$L_BCNT.

3. It updates the starting VBN in IRP$L_SEGVBN by the number of blocks transferred in the last transfer.

4. It invokes EXE$INSIOQC, in module SYSQIOREQ, to queue the IRP to the driver.

Thus, in a fashion transparent to the requestor, the original request is segmented to satisfy the limitations of the WCB or the maximum transfer size permitted by the device.

23.9   **$CANCEL SYSTEM SERVICE**

The $CANCEL system service cancels pending I/O requests on a specified channel. These include queued I/O requests as well as the request in progress. The $CANCEL system service can be requested by an image. It is also requested by the $DASSGN system service, which is requested during image and process rundown. The $CANCEL system service has only the CHAN argument, which specifies the I/O channel on which I/O is to be canceled.

The $CANCEL system service procedure, EXE$CANCEL in module SYS-CANCEL, executes in kernel mode. Kernel mode code can request a second form of the $CANCEL system service by calling the system service procedure directly at an alternative entry point, EXE$CANCELN. This form of the system service has two arguments:

► The CHAN argument
► The optional CODE argument, the reason for the cancellation

EXE$CANCELN determines if the CODE argument is present. If it is present, the procedure saves it for later use. Otherwise, the procedure saves a reason code of CAN$C_CANCEL. EXE$CANCEL, on the other hand, always saves a reason code of CAN$C_CANCEL. Once the reason code has been saved, EXE$CANCEL and EXE$CANCELN converge.

1. EXE$CANCEL invokes IOC$VERIFYCHAN, as discussed in Section 23.5.3, to verify the channel.
2. If the driver specifies primary processor affinity and the process has not already acquired primary affinity, EXE$CANCEL calls SCH$REQUIRE_CAPABILITY to acquire primary affinity. Chapter 13 gives details on processor affinity.
3. EXE$CANCEL raises IPL to 2 to block process deletion.
4. It page faults the CCB in such a way as to lock it into the working set and then acquires the device fork lock, raising IPL to fork IPL.
5. It searches the IRPs queued to the UCB (starting at UCB$L_IOQFL), looking for those that meet the following criteria:

   - The requesting PID (PCB$L_PID) matches the PID in IRP$L_PID.
   - The channel identifier in IRP$L_CHAN is the same as the requested channel.
   - The request is not a virtual request (IRP$V_VIRTUAL in IRP$L_STS is clear). In general, I/O cannot be canceled on disk or tape devices. Drivers for these devices ensure that IRP$V_VIRTUAL is set on all requests that cannot be canceled.

   For each IRP that satisfies these criteria, EXE$CANCEL takes the following steps and then resumes the search:

   a. It removes the IRP from the queue.
   b. It clears the buffered read bit (IRP$V_FUNC in IRP$L_STS) for buffered I/O functions. Since this I/O operation has not been started, there is no data to be transferred to the user's buffers.
   c. It places the error status SS$_CANCEL in the low-order word of IRP$L_IOST1 and clears the high-order word. This is the final status of the I/O operation.
   d. It inserts the IRP at the tail of the systemwide I/O postprocessing queue and requests an IPL$_IOPOST interrupt (see Section 23.7).

6. After scanning the IRP queue, EXE$CANCEL invokes the driver's cancel I/O routine, whose procedure value is stored in the driver dispatch table. The driver is passed the cancel reason saved at the start of EXE$CANCEL or EXE$CANCELN. The driver should perform any actions appropriate to canceling I/O.
7. EXE$CANCEL tests the device type to determine whether canceling its active request is appropriate. If the device is a disk, it is likely that the request will complete quickly enough that canceling it is unnecessary. If

canceling the active request is not appropriate, EXE$CANCEL exits, as described in step 8. Otherwise, EXE$CANCEL continues with step 9.

8. If primary processor affinity was acquired, EXE$CANCEL relinquishes it. EXE$CANCEL releases the device fork lock, lowers IPL to 0, and returns the success status SS$_NORMAL to its requestor.

9. If there is no outstanding I/O (CCB$L_IOC is zero) and there is no file activity (CCB$L_WIND is zero), EXE$CANCEL exits, as described in step 8. (If there is file activity, then CCB$L_WIND contains the address of the WCB associated with the channel or a process section index. At this point, the distinction is not significant.)

10. If the device is not mounted or is mounted foreign, EXE$CANCEL exits, as described in step 8.

11. If there is a process section associated with the channel, EXE$CANCEL exits, as described in step 8.

12. At this point, EXE$CANCEL has determined that there is a file open on this channel. If WCB$V_NOTFCP in WCB$B_ACCESS is set, it exits, as described in step 8.

    The WCB$V_NOTFCP bit identifies a WCB created by special routines that run only during system startup. These routines open files before the Files-11 XQP is available. When these files are opened again after the XQP is available, new WCBs are created. The original WCBs are not destroyed and are not used by the XQP.

13. At this point, EXE$CANCEL has determined that there is a user file open on the channel. It attempts to allocate an IRP to request an IO$_ACPCONTROL function. If it cannot allocate an IRP, it does one of two things:

    • If the process does not have resource wait mode enabled, EXE$CANCEL exits, as described in step 8, with a status indicating the reason that EXE$CANCEL could not allocate an IRP.
    • Otherwise, EXE$CANCEL calls SCH$RESOURCE_WAIT_PS to place the process into an RSN$_NPDYNMEM wait, after relinquishing the device fork lock. If primary affinity was acquired, it is relinquished prior to invoking SCH$RESOURCE_WAIT_PS. When the wait completes, EXE$CANCEL returns to step 3.

14. It initializes the IRP as follows:

    a. The PID of the requestor is set to the value in PCB$L_PID.
    b. The AST procedure value and parameter are cleared (no user AST).
    c. The WCB address is set to the value in CCB$L_WIND.
    d. The UCB address is stored in IRP$L_UCB.
    e. The function code is set to IO$_ACPCONTROL.
    f. The event flag is set to EXE$C_SYSEFN.
    g. The priority is set to the process's base priority.
    h. The IOSB address is set to zero.

    i. The channel identifier is stored in IRP$L_CHAN.

    j. The I/O is marked as buffered I/O with no buffer.

    k. The access rights block address is set to the value in PCB$L_ARB.

The I/O function code IO$_ACPCONTROL is special because it has no associated I/O buffer. It is ignored by disk ACPs and the XQP. It is recognized by the magnetic tape ACP as a special I/O abort function (equivalent to invoking the driver's cancel I/O routine) that causes the ACP to abort the mounting of a multivolume tape file.

15. EXE$CANCEL charges the user's buffered I/O quota, PCB$L_BIOCNT, for an I/O request.

16. The device fork lock is released.

17. If primary affinity was acquired, it is relinquished.

18. EXE$CANCEL invokes EXE$QIOACPPKT to queue the packet to the file system. EXE$QIOACPPKT returns control to the requestor of the system service.

23.10   RELEVANT SOURCE MODULES

Source modules described in this chapter include

    [F11X]DISPAT.B32
    [F11X]WITURN.B32
    [LIB]CCBDEF.SDL
    [LIB]CXBDEF.SDL
    [LIB]WCBDEF.SDL
    [SYS]ASTDEL.MAR
    [SYS]EXSUBROUT.MAR
    [SYS]IOCHANUTILS.B64
    [SYS]IOCIOPOST.MAR
    [SYS]IOSUBNPAG.MAR
    [SYS]IOSUBPAGD.MAR
    [SYS]IOSUBRAMS.MAR
    [SYS]MUTEX.MAR
    [SYS]POSTEF.MAR
    [SYS]RSE.MAR
    [SYS]SMPROUT.MAR
    [SYS]SYSACPFDT.MAR
    [SYS]SYSASSIGN.MAR
    [SYS]SYSCANCEL.MAR
    [SYS]SYSDASSGN.MAR
    [SYS]SYSDEVALC.MAR
    [SYS]SYSQIOREQ.MAR
    [SYS]SYSSYNCH.MAR
    [SYS]UCBCREDEL.MAR

24   I/O Processing

"Open the pod-bay doors, HAL."
Arthur C. Clarke, *2001: A Space Odyssey*

Once a user's I/O request is preprocessed and validated by the Queue I/O Request ($QIO) system service and a device driver's function decision table (FDT) action routine, the OpenVMS AXP executive invokes the driver's start I/O routine to perform the requested function. Chapter 23 describes the preprocessing and validation of the I/O request. This chapter describes how a driver's start I/O routine interacts with the executive to perform a user-requested function and how the executive dispatches I/O device interrupts.

24.1   DEVICE DRIVER MODELS

There are two basic device driver models: the traditional model, in which the entire driver is contained in one image, and the class/port model, in which the driver is implemented by more than one image.

The class/port driver model evolved from the traditional model and retains the same user interface. In the class/port driver model, the class driver performs functions common to a class of device, such as a Small Computer Systems Interface (SCSI) disk or tape, for example. The port driver contains controller-specific subroutines for the class driver. Chapter 26 gives more information on class/port drivers.

OpenVMS VAX support routines and MACRO-32 macros for traditional drivers have been ported to OpenVMS AXP to allow Digital to port existing OpenVMS VAX drivers with minimal change to the OpenVMS AXP operating system. Use of these driver-porting mechanisms is unsupported; moreover, they will change in a future release.

This chapter describes I/O processing in terms of the ported OpenVMS VAX mechanisms for traditional drivers.

24.2   THE START I/O ROUTINE

The heart of a driver, regardless of driver model, is its start I/O routine. The start I/O routine services I/O requests by interacting with the device controller.

A start I/O routine usually performs at least the following steps:

1. It allocates controller- and device-specific resources.
2. It initiates device activity.
3. It awaits device activity completion.

4. It deallocates controller- and device-specific resources, if allocated in step 1.

5. It initiates I/O request completion processing.

A simple traditional driver's start I/O routine is shown in Example 24.1. How it interacts with the executive to perform some of the preceding steps is the subject of discussion in this chapter. Chapter 26 describes allocation and deallocation of controller- and device-specific resources.

Example 24.1 shows how the macros WFIKPCH, IOFORK, and REQCOM create the framework for a simple start I/O routine. These and other related macros are documented in the manual *OpenVMS AXP Device Support: Creating a Step 1 Driver from an OpenVMS VAX Device Driver*. The macros, provided as a convenience to the driver writer, invoke executive routines described in this chapter.

24.2.1 Driver-Controller Interface

The design of the driver-controller interface determines the actions of a driver's start I/O routine. Chapter 2 describes two categories of driver-controller interface: a simple interface, in which a driver communicates with a controller exclusively through interface registers, and a more sophisticated interface, in which a driver uses command and response buffers in memory in addition to controller interface registers.

The driver used as an example in this section implements a simple driver-controller interface.

24.2.2 Device Activity Initiation

A start I/O routine that implements a simple driver-controller interface initializes one or more interface registers to inform the device controller of required action and to initiate device activity.

Example 24.1
Simple Start I/O Routine

```
STARTIO:  .JSB_ENTRY <R2,R3,R4,R5>
            :
            :

; Initiate device activity by informing controller
; of required action

            :
            :
          WFIKPCH    DEVTMO,#6      ;Wait for interrupt or timeout
            :
            :                       ;Execution resumes here upon interrupt
          IOFORK                    ;Request to defer further
                                    ; processing to a lower IPL
            :
            :
          REQCOM                    ;Initiate I/O request completion
                                    ; processing
```

A start I/O routine that implements a more complex driver-controller interface might create one or more command messages in memory and access a controller interface register to notify the controller of awaiting command messages.

The executive invokes a traditional driver's start I/O routine when a user requests an I/O operation and the device is idle. Figure 24.1 shows the flow of control from a user image to the start I/O routine and back. Note that in Figures 24.1, 24.2, and 24.3 portions of the start I/O routine that are not relevant to the control flow, but aid in understanding it, are shaded.

The numbers in Figure 24.1 correspond to the numbered steps that follow:

① The user image requests the $QIO system service.

② The $QIO system service procedure, EXE$QIO in module SYSQIOREQ, validates the function-independent parameters of the request, allocates and builds an IRP, and invokes the driver's FDT routine for the requested function.

③ The FDT routine validates function-dependent parameters of the I/O request, sets up any necessary I/O buffers, and invokes EXE$QIODRVPKT, in module SYSQIOREQ. Chapter 23 provides details on FDT routine processing and the control flow into the driver's start I/O routine.

④ EXE$QIODRVPKT invokes EXE$INSIOQ, also in module SYSQIOREQ. Chapter 23 describes EXE$INSIOQ.

⑤ EXE$INSIOQ acquires the fork lock for the UCB and tests UCB$V_BSY. If the device is not busy, it invokes IOC$INITIATE, in module IOSUBNPAG.

⑥ IOC$INITIATE locates the driver's start I/O routine and invokes it.

⑦ The start I/O routine acquires the device lock to synchronize its activity with device interrupts. It then initializes one or more device interface registers with information such as function requested and address of I/O buffer.

⑧ Typically, a simple driver-controller interface includes a bit, sometimes called the GO bit, that indicates to the device that the driver has provided the device with all necessary information for a transfer. The setting of this bit is a cue that the device can start the transfer. After the start I/O routine sets this bit, it must stall until the device signals completion through an interrupt. It does this by invoking the WFIKPCH macro.

The WFIKPCH macro has two required arguments:

▸ The address of the timeout routine
▸ The number of seconds within which the interrupt must occur

If the interrupt occurs within the specified time, the executive resumes the start I/O routine at the MACRO-32 statement following the WFIKPCH macro; otherwise, the executive resumes the start I/O routine at the timeout routine specified. The WFIKPCH macro invocation in Example 24.1 expands to the code shown in Example 24.2.

Example 24.2
Expansion of the WFIKPCH Macro

```
; Expansion of WFIKPCH DEVTMO,#6

        MOVL    #6,R1                       ;Timeout time = 6 seconds
        MOVL    (SP)+,R2                    ;IPL to restore
        MOVAB   L1,UCB$L_FPC(R5)            ;Processing will resume at
                                            ; L1 after interrupt
        JSB     IOC$PRIMITIVE_WFIKPCH       ;
        RSB                                 ;Return to start I/O
                                            ; routine's invoker
                                            ;
L1:     .JSB_ENTRY INPUT=<R3,R4,R5>,SCRATCH=<R0,R1,R2>
                                            ;
        BITL    #UCB$M_TIMOUT, -            ;Did interrupt arrive
                UCB$L_STS(R5)               ; on time?
        BNEQ    DEVTMO                      ;If not zero, device
                                            ; timed out
```

Note that when IOC$PRIMITIVE_WFIKPCH is invoked, UCB$L_FPC contains the procedure value of entry point L1, which the WFIKPCH macro generated.

24.2.3 Waiting for Device Activity Completion

A controller that implements a simple driver-controller interface signals completion of each I/O request by generating an I/O interrupt. A controller that implements a more sophisticated interface can signal the completion of multiple I/O requests by creating multiple response messages in memory and generating a single interrupt; each response message holds the completion status of a command message.

This section describes how IOC$PRIMITIVE_WFIKPCH, in module IO-SUBNPAG, stalls the simple driver's start I/O routine of Example 24.1 until the target device interrupts.

The following steps correspond to those pictured in Figure 24.1.

⑨ IOC$PRIMITIVE_WFIKPCH performs the following steps:

a. It saves register R3 in UCB$Q_FR3 and R4 in UCB$Q_FR4.

b. It sets UCB$V_INT in UCB$L_STS to indicate that an interrupt is expected from this device and UCB$V_TIM to indicate the device interrupt is being timed.

c. It adds the timeout value in R1 to the system uptime, EXE$GL_ABSTIM, and stores the result in UCB$L_DUETIM. This value is the system uptime at which this request will expire.

d. IOC$PRIMITIVE_WFIKPCH clears UCB$V_TIMOUT in UCB$L_STS. If the interrupt does not occur within the stipulated time, EXE$TIMEOUT, in module TIMESCHDL, will set the bit. Chapter 12 describes EXE$TIMEOUT.

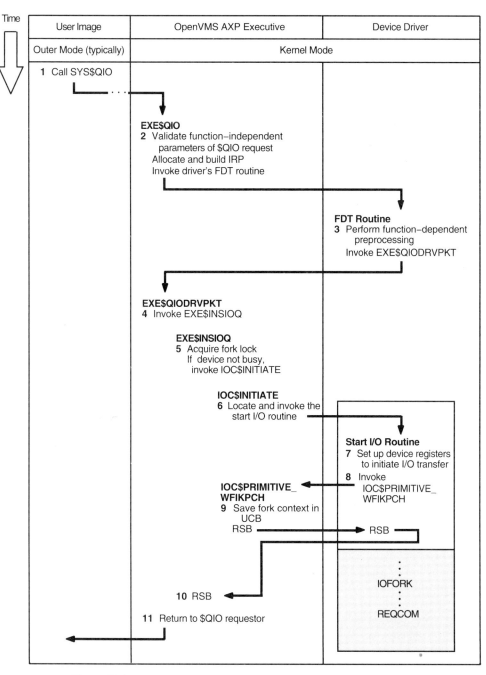

Figure 24.1
Entering the Start I/O Routine

833

e. IOC$PRIMITIVE_WFIKPCH releases the device lock and returns to the driver start I/O routine, which immediately returns to its invoker, EXE$INSIOQ.

Effectively, the WFIKPCH macro invocation saves the context of the driver's start I/O routine in the UCB fork block. The start I/O routine will be resumed after the device interrupt.

⑩ EXE$INSIOQ returns to EXE$QIODRVPKT.

⑪ EXE$QIODRVPKT returns control to the I/O requestor, as described in Chapter 23.

24.2.4 Servicing the Device Interrupt

When a device has performed a requested function, it interrupts the processor. On a symmetric multiprocessing (SMP) system, the processor that is interrupted is the primary processor. Interrupt dispatching, the mechanism by which the executive invokes a device's interrupt service routine (ISR), is described in Section 24.3.

Figure 24.2 shows how the ISR resumes the start I/O routine. The numbers in the figure correspond to the numbered steps that follow.

① The common I/O interrupt dispatcher, IO_INTERRUPT, in module IOCINTDISP, saves integer registers R0, R1, and R16 through R29 on the stack. It then calls the device's ISR, passing it the address of the interrupt dispatch block (IDB) as an argument.

② Example 24.3 shows a simple ISR for a simple driver.

Typically, an ISR must perform the following steps:

a. Obtain the UCB address for the device that interrupted.

b. Acquire the device lock.

The UCB contains the address of the device lock. The device lock normally synchronizes access to controller and device registers and certain UCB fields. Every code thread that accesses these registers or UCB fields must acquire the device lock first. A driver writer determines which registers and fields the device lock synchronizes based on the nature of the device and the interaction among driver routines like initialization, timeout, start I/O, and interrupt service routines.

c. Test whether the interrupt is expected.

If UCB$V_INT is not set, the interrupt is not expected; the ISR simply releases the device lock and returns to IO_INTERRUPT. Note that for a device such as a terminal, unexpected interrupts are quite normal and would be serviced within its driver.

d. If the interrupt is expected, the ISR restores fork R3 from the UCB fork block and resumes the start I/O routine at the entry point whose procedure value is in UCB$L_FPC. The processor remains at device IPL. Note that fork R4 is never restored; instead, the second instruction in

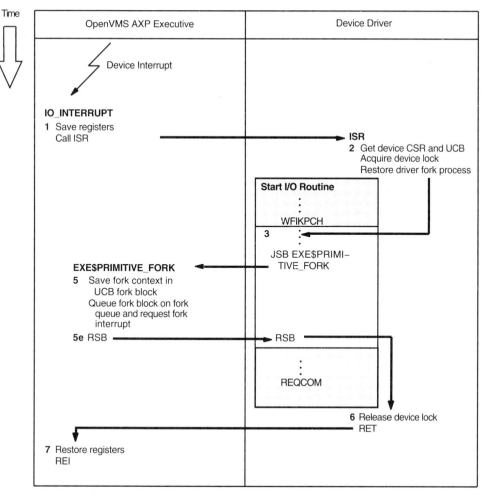

Figure 24.2
ISR Resumes the Start I/O Routine

the ISR stores the address of the device's control/status register (CSR) in R4.

③ The procedure value in UCB$L_FPC identifies the entry point L1 in Example 24.2. If the interrupt arrives within the specified time interval, L1 proceeds to step 4; otherwise, it enters DEVTMO.

④ The start I/O routine performs any device-specific processing that requires execution at device IPL with the device lock held. All other processing is deferred to the fork process.

Since this part of the start I/O routine has been resumed from the ISR at device IPL, it may not directly lower the IPL. The Alpha AXP architecture

Example 24.3
Simple Interrupt Service Routine

```
ISR:   .CALL_ENTRY

       MOVL    4(AP), R4                 ;Get IDB in R4
       MOVL    IDB$PS_OWNER(R4), R5      ;Get owner UCB in R5
       DEVICELOCK -
               LOCKADDR=UCB$L_DLCK(R5)   ;Acquire device lock
       BBCC    #UCB$V_INT, -             ;Is interrupt expected?
               UCB$L_STS(R5), 10$        ;If not, go to 10$
       MOVQ    UCB$Q_FR3(R5), R3         ;Otherwise, restore fork R3
       JSB     @UCB$L_FPC(R5)            ;Resume start I/O routine
10$:   DEVICEUNLOCK -                    ;Release device lock
               LOCKADDR=UCB$L_DLCK(R5)

       RET                               ;Return to common interrupt
                                         ; dispatcher
```

prohibits an interrupt thread of execution from lowering IPL below the level at which it was initiated.

The executive provides the IOFORK macro so that a driver can request the resumption of a thread of execution at a lower IPL. If it is used without any of its optional arguments (that is, in a form compatible with its use in OpenVMS VAX), the macro expands to the following MACRO-32 code sequence:

```
        BICL    #UCB$M_TIM, UCB$L_STS(R5)
; What follows is the expansion of the FORK macro,
; which the IOFORK macro invokes
        MOVAB   L1,FKB$L_FPC(R5)
        JSB     EXE$PRIMITIVE_FORK
        RSB
L1:     .JSB_ENTRY INPUT=<R3,R4,R5>,SCRATCH=<R0,R1,R2>
```

Clearing UCB$V_TIM in UCB$L_STS indicates that the device no longer has an I/O operation being timed for the delivery of an interrupt.

(5) EXE$PRIMITIVE_FORK, in module FORKCNTRL, requests the resumption of the fork process at its fork IPL as follows:

a. It stores registers R3 and R4 in UCB$Q_FR3 and UCB$Q_FR4. (The beginning of the UCB acts as the fork block.)

b. It gets the fork IPL of the fork thread from the array SMP$AL_IPLVEC indexed by the fork lock index in UCB$B_FLCK.

c. EXE$PRIMITIVE_FORK locates the head of the fork queue for this fork IPL in the per-CPU database for the processor on which it is running and inserts the fork block into this queue. Chapter 5 describes fork queues.

d. If the fork block is the first to be inserted on the fork queue, it requests a software interrupt at fork IPL.

e. It then returns to the start I/O routine, which returns to the ISR.

⑥ The ISR releases the device lock and returns to IO_INTERRUPT.

⑦ IO_INTERRUPT restores registers R0, R1, and R16 through R29. It then dismisses the interrupt with a CALL_PAL REI instruction.

Subsequently reentered at fork IPL, the start I/O routine will resume execution at the MACRO-32 statement following the IOFORK macro.

24.2.5   **I/O Request Completion Processing**

Figure 24.3 shows the control flow when the fork dispatcher resumes the driver's start I/O routine. The numbers in the figure correspond to the numbered steps in the description that follows.

When processor IPL falls below the fork IPL of the device, the processor grants the requested software interrupt at that IPL. The software ISR is one of the EXE$FRKIPLxDSP routines in module FORKCNTRL, where x is 6, 8, 9, 10, or 11, one of the fork IPL values. All these routines converge in EXE$FORKDSPTH, also in module FORKCNTRL.

① EXE$FORKDSPTH removes one fork block at a time from the appropriate fork queue and performs the following steps:

a. It acquires the fork lock whose index is in FKB$B_FLCK.

b. It restores R3 and R4 from FKB$Q_FR3 and FKB$Q_FR4 of the fork block. For a UCB, these are the same as offsets UCB$Q_FR3 and UCB$Q_FR4.

c. It invokes the routine whose procedure value is stored in FKB$L_FPC, thus resuming the fork process.

d. When the fork process returns, EXE$FORKDSPTH releases the fork lock.

In Example 24.1, EXE$FORKDSPTH resumes the start I/O routine at the MACRO-32 statement following the invocation of the IOFORK macro.

② The start I/O routine performs device-dependent I/O postprocessing, which includes checking for a device error condition. It then constructs in the low-order longwords of registers R0 and R1 the final status of the I/O operation; this is the status to be returned in the I/O requestor's I/O status block.

Upon completion of device-dependent I/O postprocessing, the start I/O routine invokes the REQCOM macro to initiate device-independent I/O postprocessing performed by the executive. The REQCOM macro expands to the following MACRO-32 statements:

```
JSB IOC$REQCOM
RSB
```

③ IOC$REQCOM, in module IOSUBNPAG, queues the IRP to the systemwide postprocessing queue and requests the IPL$_IOPOST software

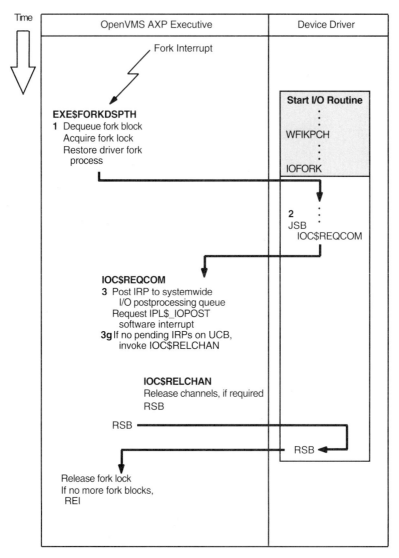

Figure 24.3
Fork Dispatcher Resumes the Start I/O Routine

interrupt. It performs the following steps (details of processing related to mount verification have been omitted):

a. If there is an associated error log buffer (UCB$V_ERLOGIP in UCB$L_STS is set), IOC$REQCOM transfers the necessary information to the error log buffer and invokes ERL$RELEASEMB, in module ERROR-LOG, to complete the error log activity for this I/O operation.

b. It increments the I/O operation count in the UCB.

c. It stores the final I/O status in IRP$L_IOST1 and IRP$L_IOST2.

d. It saves the current IPL.

e. IOC$REQCOM inserts the IRP in the interlocked systemwide I/O postprocessing queue, IOC$GQ_POSTIQ.

   If it is running on a uniprocessing system, or on the primary processor of a multiprocessing system, IOC$REQCOM simply requests an IPL$_IOPOST interrupt. If it is running on a secondary processor of an SMP system, IOC$REQCOM requests the IPL$_IOPOST software interrupt on the primary processor using the IPINT_CPU macro. Chapter 5 describes software interrupts, and Chapter 37, interprocessor interrupts.

f. IOC$REQCOM restores the saved IPL.

g. It attempts to remove a pending IRP from the head of the device's queue of pending I/O requests at UCB$L_IOQFL.

   If there is one, IOC$REQCOM invokes IOC$INITIATE to initiate the I/O. IOC$INITIATE invokes the driver's start I/O routine. When that instance of the start I/O routine returns, perhaps after stalling through WFIKPCH to wait for device activity, IOC$INITIATE returns to IOC$REQCOM.

   If there are no pending I/O requests for the device, IOC$REQCOM clears UCB$V_BSY in UCB$L_STS and invokes IOC$RELCHAN to release any device controllers to which the start I/O routine had acquired exclusive access.

h. IOC$REQCOM returns to its invoker, the start I/O routine.

④ The start I/O routine returns to its invoker, which, in this example, is EXE$FORKDSPTH.

24.3   I/O INTERRUPT DISPATCHING

The Alpha AXP architecture reserves system control block (SCB) vector offsets 800_{16} through $7FF0_{16}$ for I/O interrupts. How these vectors are allocated to devices and actually used is implementation-dependent.

In response to an I/O device interrupt, the processor enters the initiate exception, interrupt, or machine check (IEI) privileged architecture library (PALcode) routine. The IEI PALcode routine determines the device interrupt vector in a system-specific manner and uses it as the SCB vector offset to locate the interrupt's corresponding SCB entry. Chapter 3 describes the IEI PALcode routine.

An SCB entry consists of two quadwords. The first quadword of each SCB entry for an I/O interrupt contains the same value: the code address of the common I/O interrupt dispatcher, IO_INTERRUPT. The second quadword contains the address of the interrupt transfer vector (VEC) for the interrupting device. The VEC is usually a substructure of a controller request block (CRB) or an adapter control block (ADP), as described in Section 24.3.2.

PALcode loads R3 with the contents of the second quadword, the VEC address, before entering IO_INTERRUPT, which locates the interrupt's service routine from information in the VEC.

24.3.1 Common I/O Interrupt Dispatcher

Example 24.4 shows a code fragment from IO_INTERRUPT, in module IOCINTDISP, which is written in MACRO-64 assembly language.

Running in kernel mode on the interrupted process's kernel stack, IO_INTERRUPT performs the following steps:

1. It saves registers R0, R1, and R16 through R29 on the current stack.
2. IO_INTERRUPT records the contents of VEC$L_IDB(R3) in R16 as the single argument for the ISR to be called. VEC$L_IDB(R3) points to an IDB or an ADP, depending on whether the interrupt is directly or indirectly vectored, as described in Section 24.3.2.
3. It uses VEC$PS_ISR_CODE and VEC$PS_ISR_PD to call the ISR.
4. When the ISR returns control, IO_INTERRUPT restores the saved registers and then executes a CALL_PAL REI instruction to dismiss the interrupt.

24.3.2 Directly and Indirectly Vectored Interrupts

Device interrupt requests are conveyed to an Alpha AXP processor from two sources: local I/O widgets and local I/O adapters (see Chapter 2). Interrupt

Example 24.4
Common I/O Interrupt Dispatcher

```
IO_INTERRUPT::
        .
        .
        .
        MB                              ;Issue memory barrier
        LDA     SP,-SAVE_LENGTH(SP)     ;Allocate stack space
        STQ     R0,SAVR0(SP)            ;Save registers R0, R1,
                                        ; R16-R29
        .
        .
        .
        STQ     R29,SAVR29(SP)          ;
        LDL     R16,VEC$L_IDB(R3)       ;Set up parameter to driver
        LDA     R25,1(R31)              ;One argument
        LDL     R26,VEC$PS_ISR_CODE(R3) ;Get code address of ISR
        LDL     R27,VEC$PS_ISR_PD(R3)   ;Get ISR's procedure
                                        ; value
        JSR     R26,(R26)               ;Call the ISR
        LDQ     R0,SAVR0(SP)            ;Restore registers R0, R1,
                                        ; R16-R29
        .
        .
        .
        LDQ     R29,SAVR29(SP)          ;
        LDA     SP,SAVE_LENGTH(SP)      ;Restore stack pointer
        REI                             ;Now dismiss the interrupt
```

requests generated by devices attached to remote I/O widgets are conveyed to the processor through one or more intervening I/O adapters.

If the executive can directly dispatch a device interrupt to the interrupting device's ISR, the interrupt is said to be directly vectored; otherwise, it is indirectly vectored.

Whether the executive can directly vector a device interrupt depends primarily on system and PALcode implementation. If PALcode cannot directly determine an interrupting device's vector, the device's interrupts cannot be directly vectored. Such a device's interrupts are vectored through an intermediate interrupt service routine, typically that of the local I/O adapter or multichannel I/O widget that conveys the device's interrupt requests to the processor.

When PALcode can directly determine an interrupting device's vector, the executive can implement either method of vectoring, depending on other system-specific factors.

Whether a device interrupt is directly vectored is transparent to IO_INTERRUPT, which uses the area pointed to by R3 as a VEC substructure.

For a device with directly vectored interrupts, the VEC is a CRB substructure, and VEC$L_ISR_CODE and VEC$L_ISR_PD describe the interrupting device's ISR. The control flow from IO_INTERRUPT to the device's ISR is shown in Figure 24.4.

For a device with indirectly vectored interrupts, the VEC is a substructure of the ADP for the local I/O adapter or multichannel I/O widget that conveys the device's interrupt request to the processor; VEC$L_ISR_PD and VEC$L_ISR_CODE describe the ISR for the local I/O adapter or multichannel I/O widget.

The control flow from IO_INTERRUPT to the device's ISR for an indirectly vectored interrupt is shown in Figure 24.5. IO_INTERRUPT calls the adapter's ISR with the ADP address as an argument (see Section 24.3.1). The adapter ISR determines the interrupting device's vector in a device- and interconnect-specific manner. It then uses the interrupt vector as an index into the adapter's interrupt vector table. The interrupt vector table, pointed to by ADP$L_VECTOR, is an array of pointers to VEC substructures. Indexed by device interrupt vector, an entry in the array points to the CRB VEC substructure for a controller whose interrupts are indirectly vectored through the adapter's ISR. The adapter's ISR calls the interrupting device's ISR using information in the appropriate CRB VEC substructure.

24.4 DRIVER KERNEL PROCESSES

As explained in Section 24.2, for every I/O that the executive initiates, it creates a fork process thread of execution in which driver code executes. A fork process's context is maintained in the fork block, which is usually part of a larger data structure such as the UCB or the IRP. A driver fork

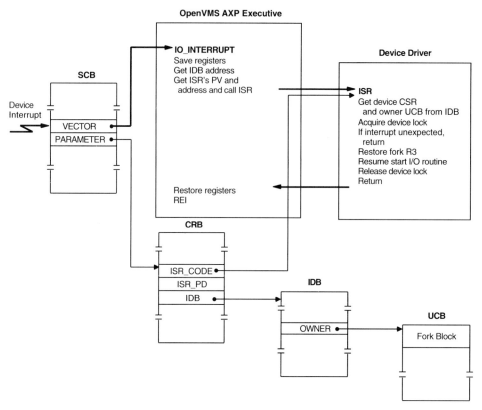

Figure 24.4
Control Flow for a Directly Vectored Interrupt

process that requires more context can execute as a kernel process. A kernel process has a private stack on which it can maintain context across stalls and restarts. Chapter 5 describes fork processes and kernel processes in detail.

A MACRO-32 driver being ported from OpenVMS VAX to OpenVMS AXP can be converted to use the kernel process mechanism through macros provided by the OpenVMS AXP executive. In general, these macros are named KP_STALL_*xxx* or KP_*xxx*, where *xxx* is the name of the equivalent Open-VMS VAX macro, if one exists. The manual *OpenVMS AXP Device Support: Creating a Step 1 Driver from an OpenVMS VAX Device Driver* provides more information on these macros.

Example 24.5 shows the simple driver's start I/O routine of Example 24.1, modified to use the kernel process mechanism. To use the kernel process mechanism, a MACRO-32 device driver must follow certain conventions. The numbers in the following list correspond to those in Example 24.5.

① The DDTAB macro invocation must identify EXE$KP_STARTIO, in module KERNEL_PROCESS, as the START argument and the start I/O routine within the driver as the KP_STARTIO argument.

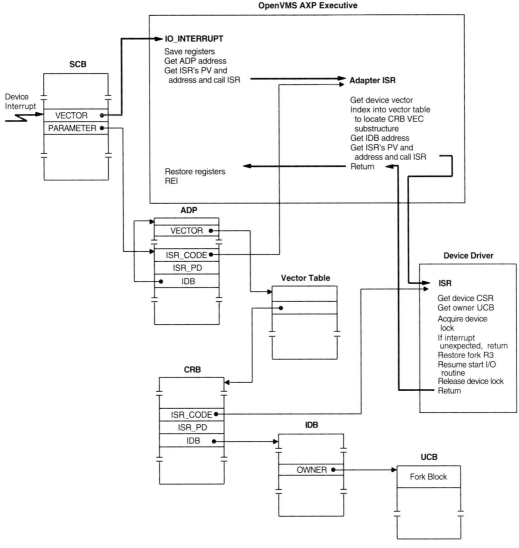

Figure 24.5
Control Flow for an Indirectly Vectored Interrupt

② The start I/O routine within the driver must be a standard-conforming procedure.

③ The start I/O procedure must retrieve the addresses of the IRP and UCB from the kernel process block (KPB) associated with the kernel process.

④ The start I/O procedure must use the KP_STALL_*xxx* or KP_*xxx* macros instead of equivalent OpenVMS VAX macros.

What follows is a brief description of the control flow of an I/O operation through the start I/O procedure of Example 24.5. Although the details of

843

Example 24.5
Simple Start I/O Routine That Uses the Kernel Process
Mechanism

```
                  .
                  .
                  .
         DDTAB -
                  .
                  .
             START=EXE$KP_STARTIO,-  ①
             KP_STARTIO=STARTIO,-            ;Miscellaneous other
                                             ; required changes ignored
                  .
                  .
                  .
STARTIO:     .CALL_ENTRY <R2,R3,R4,R5>   ②
             MOVL   4(AP),R0                 ;Get KPB address
             MOVL   KPB$PS_UCB(R0),R5   ③   ;Get UCB address
             MOVL   KPB$PS_IRP(R0),R3        ;Get IRP address
                  .
                  .
             KP_STALL_WFIKPCH DEVTMO,#6 ④   ;Wait for interrupt
                                             ; or timeout
                  .
                  .
             KP_STALL_IOFORK                 ;Wait until IPL drops
                                             ; to fork IPL
                  .
                  .
             KP_REQCOM                       ;Complete request
```

the interaction between the start I/O procedure and the executive are quite different from the interaction described in Section 24.2, the overall structure of a driver that uses the kernel process mechanism is much the same as that of a driver using the fork process mechanism.

The vertical bars in the rightmost column of Figures 24.6, 24.7, and 24.8 represent stack execution: the right-hand bar, execution on the kernel process's stack, and the left-hand bars, execution on another kernel stack.

24.4.1 Driver Kernel Process Startup

Control flow from EXE$QIO to IOC$INITIATE is identical for drivers using the kernel process mechanism and drivers using the fork process mechanism. IOC$INITIATE locates the driver's start I/O routine and invokes it; in this example, it invokes EXE$KP_STARTIO, in module KERNEL_PROCESS, the routine identified by the DDTAB macro START argument.

EXE$KP_STARTIO performs the following steps to create a kernel process thread of execution running procedure STARTIO. The numbers in Figure 24.6 correspond to those in the following list:

① EXE$KP_STARTIO checks whether the IRP is one that is being used by the modified page writer; if so, it goes to step 4, skipping the KPB allocation because the modified page writer uses preallocated KPBs.

② It computes the kernel process's required stack size as the larger of

844

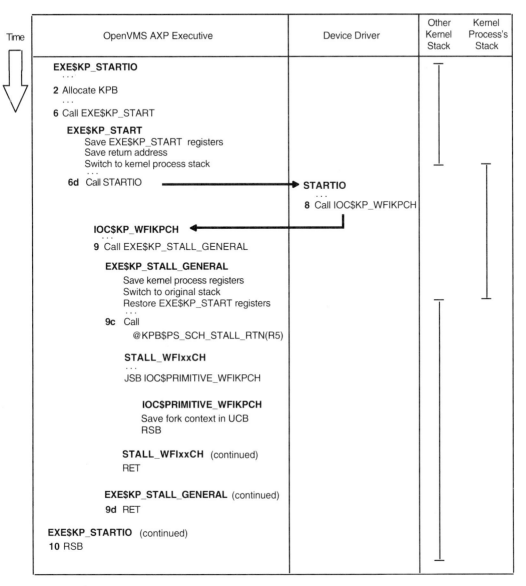

Figure 24.6
Driver Kernel Process Startup

KPB$K_MIN_IO_STACK and DDT$IS_STACK_BCNT and then calls EXE$KP_ALLOCATE_KPB to allocate a KPB and that much stack.

③ If EXE$KP_ALLOCATE_KPB returns a success status, EXE$KP_STARTIO proceeds to the next step.

If EXE$KP_ALLOCATE_KPB returns the failure status SS$_INSFRPGS (insufficient free pages), SS$_INSFSPTS (insufficient system page table entries), or SS$_INSFMEM (insufficient memory), EXE$KP_STARTIO

Example 24.6
Expansion of the KP_STALL_WFIKPCH Macro

```
; Expansion of KP_STALL_WFIKPCH DEVTMO,#6

                            ;Top of stack has IPL to
                            ; restore after setting up wait
        PUSHL   #6          ;Timeout value
        PUSHL   KPB         ;KPB address
        CALLS   #3,IOC$KP_
                WFIKPCH     ;
        BLBC    R0,DEVTMO   ;If operation timed out,
                            ; enter timeout routine
```

calls EXE$KP_ALLOCATE_KPB once a second until the operation is successful or the I/O request is canceled. If the I/O request is canceled, EXE$KP_STARTIO completes the request by setting the completion status to SS$_ABORT and invoking the REQCOM macro. Upon successful return from EXE$KP_ALLOCATE_KPB, EXE$KP_STARTIO proceeds to the next step.

If EXE$KP_ALLOCATE_KPB returns any other error status, EXE$KP_STARTIO generates the fatal bugcheck INCONSTATE.

④ EXE$KP_STARTIO initializes KPB$PS_IRP and KPB$PS_UCB with the IRP and UCB addresses.

⑤ It copies STARTIO's register save mask from DDT$IS_REG_MASK into R0. It then performs some logical operations on R0 to create a register save mask that includes all registers that kernel process support routines need saved but none that need not be saved (R0, R1, R16–R25, R27, R28, R30, R31).

⑥ EXE$KP_STARTIO calls EXE$KP_START, in module KERNEL_PROCESS_MAGIC. EXE$KP_START starts a driver kernel process thread of execution by taking the steps summarized in the following list (see Chapter 5 for further details):

a. EXE$KP_START saves the registers specified in R0's register save mask on the current stack.

b. It saves the current stack pointer in KPB$PS_SAVED_SP.

c. It switches to the kernel process's stack by loading the stack pointer (SP) from KPB$PS_STACK_BASE.

d. It calls STARTIO, the procedure whose procedure value is in DDT$PS_KP_STARTIO, with the KPB address as the single argument.

⑦ STARTIO loads R3 and R5 from the IRP and UCB addresses in the KPB. It then acquires the device lock and initiates device activity.

⑧ After initiating device activity, STARTIO invokes the macro KP_STALL_WFIKPCH, which, for the given example, expands as shown in Example 24.6.

⑨ IOC$KP_WFIKPCH, in module KERNEL_PROCESS, validates its arguments and copies them to the KPB. It records the procedure value of STALL_WFIxxCH, also in module KERNEL_PROCESS, in KPB$PS_SCH_STALL_RTN and calls EXE$KP_STALL_GENERAL, in module KERNEL_PROCESS_MAGIC, to stall the kernel process.

The actions of EXE$KP_STALL_GENERAL are detailed in Chapter 5. Steps that are relevant to this control flow are summarized in the following list:

a. EXE$KP_STALL_GENERAL saves the kernel process's context on the kernel process's stack.

b. It restores the stack and register contexts that were current when the kernel process was entered.

c. It calls STALL_WFIxxCH (the routine whose procedure value is in KPB$PS_SCH_STALL_RTN).

   STALL_WFIxxCH invokes the WFIKPCH macro, specifying the macro statement RET as the return mechanism. The WFIKPCH macro invocation generates an entry point in STALL_WFIxxCH and stores its procedure value in UCB$L_FPC. It then invokes IOC$PRIMITIVE_WFIKPCH, which records the fork context of the driver kernel process, releases the device lock, and returns to STALL_WFIxxCH. STALL_WFIxxCH returns to EXE$KP_STALL_GENERAL.

d. EXE$KP_STALL_GENERAL loads the success status SS$_NORMAL into R0 and returns to the routine whose return address was saved on the kernel stack, which, for this example, is EXE$KP_STARTIO.

⑩ When control returns from EXE$KP_STALL_GENERAL, EXE$KP_STARTIO tests the status in R0. If R0 contains a success status, EXE$KP_STARTIO returns to its invoker, which, in this example, is IOC$INITIATE. If R0 contains an error, EXE$KP_START was unable to start the kernel process for some reason and EXE$KP_STARTIO generates the fatal bugcheck INCONSTATE.

The control flow from IOC$INITIATE back to the $QIO requestor is the same as that for a driver using fork processes.

24.4.2 Device Interrupt Resumes Driver Kernel Process

Figure 24.7 shows the control flow when the device activity completion interrupt resumes the driver kernel process. The numbers in the following list correspond to those in Figure 24.7. Most of the details are left out of the steps here because they are given elsewhere in this chapter or in Chapter 5.

① When the device interrupts, the IEI PALcode routine invokes IO_INTERRUPT, in module IOCINTDISP, as discussed in Section 24.3.2.

② IO_INTERRUPT calls the device's ISR.

③ At step 9c in Section 24.4.1, STALL_WFIxxCH invoked the WFIKPCH macro. The WFIKPCH macro invocation generated an entry point in

STALL_WFIxxCH, and stored its procedure value in UCB$L_FPC. The device's ISR obtains the device lock and resumes STALL_WFIxxCH at this entry point.

④ STALL_WFIxxCH calls EXE$KP_RESTART.

⑤ EXE$KP_RESTART saves the register context of its caller, switches to the kernel process's stack, and restores the kernel process's registers. The most recent call frame on the kernel process's stack was left there when the driver kernel process earlier called IOC$KP_WFIKPCH. EXE$KP_RESTART returns to the STARTIO procedure from its call to IOC$KP_WFIKPCH.

⑥ The STARTIO procedure performs device-specific status checks of the I/O operation that just completed. It performs only the steps that must be performed at device IPL, before invoking the KP_STALL_IOFORK macro to resume the kernel process at the lower fork IPL. The KP_STALL_IO-FORK macro expands as follows:

```
MOVL    IRP$PS_KPB(R3),R0       ;Get pointer to KPB
MOVL    KPB$PS_UCB(R0),R1       ;Point to UCB
BICL    #UCB$M_TIM,UCB$L_STS(R1) ;Clear TIM bit
PUSHL   R1                      ;Point to FKB (in UCB)
PUSHL   R0                      ;Point to KPB
CALLS   #2,EXE$KP_FORK          ;Stall the kernel process
```

Clearing UCB$V_TIM in UCB$L_STS indicates that the device no longer has an I/O operation being timed for the delivery of an interrupt.

⑦ EXE$KP_FORK saves the kernel process's fork context in the UCB fork block. It places the procedure value of STALL_FORK, also in module KERNEL_PROCESS, into KPB$PS_SCH_STALL_RTN and calls EXE$KP_STALL_GENERAL.

⑧ EXE$KP_STALL_GENERAL saves the kernel process's register context in the KPB, switches to the original kernel stack, and restores the registers that were saved in step 5, when the kernel process was resumed. It then calls STALL_FORK, the procedure whose procedure value is in KPB$PS_SCH_STALL_RTN.

⑨ STALL_FORK stores the procedure value of COMMON_FORK_RTN, in module KERNEL_PROCESS, in KPB$PS_FPC, and invokes EXE$PRIMITIVE_FORK.

⑩ EXE$PRIMITIVE_FORK saves the fork registers R3 and R4 in the UCB fork block, inserts the UCB fork block into the appropriate fork queue, requests a fork IPL interrupt if appropriate, and returns to STALL_FORK.

⑪ STALL_FORK returns to its caller, EXE$KP_STALL_GENERAL.

⑫ At this point, the most recent call frame on the original kernel stack is the one left there by STALL_WFIxxCH when it called EXE$KP_RESTART. EXE$KP_STALL_GENERAL returns to STALL_WFIxxCH.

⑬ STALL_WFIxxCH returns to the ISR.

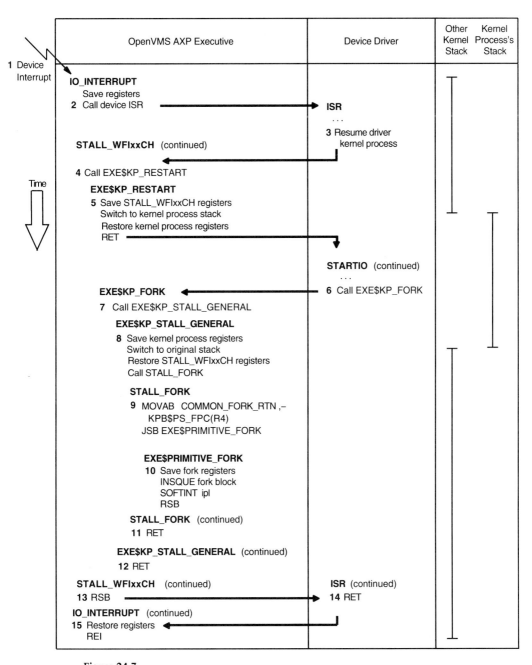

Figure 24.7
Device Interrupt Resumes Driver Kernel Process

849

⑭ The ISR releases the device lock and returns to IO_INTERRUPT.

⑮ IO_INTERRUPT restores the registers it saved and dismisses the interrupt with a `CALL_PAL REI` instruction.

24.4.3   Fork Interrupt Resumes Driver Kernel Process

Figure 24.8 shows the control flow when the fork IPL software interrupt resumes the driver kernel process. The numbers in the following list correspond to those in Figure 24.8. Most of the details are left out of the steps here because they are given elsewhere in this chapter or in Chapter 5.

① When processor IPL drops below the fork IPL, the fork IPL software interrupt is granted. The fork dispatcher ISR, EXE$FRKIPL*x*DSP, where *x* is 6, 8, 9, 10, or 11, one of the fork IPLs, is entered. This example assumes a fork IPL of 8.

② EXE$FRKIPL8DSP obtains the offset to the IPL 8 fork queue listhead (see Chapter 5) and enters EXE$FORKDSPTH.

③ EXE$FORKDSPTH is a common entry point used by all fork IPL ISRs. It resumes pending fork processes by performing the following steps:

   a. It removes a fork block from the fork queue. If no fork block was removed, it dismisses the fork IPL interrupt using the `CALL_PAL REI` instruction.

   b. It acquires the fork lock whose index is in FKB$B_FLCK.

   c. It resumes the fork process.

④ The fork process invokes COMMON_FORK_RTN.

⑤ COMMON_FORK_RTN calls EXE$KP_RESTART.

⑥ EXE$KP_RESTART saves the fork process's register context on the current stack. R4 contains the KPB address of the kernel process that must be resumed. EXE$KP_RESTART switches to the kernel process's stack, restores the kernel process's registers, and resumes the kernel process by executing the MACRO-32 statement RET.

   The most recent call frame on the kernel process's stack is the one left by EXE$KP_FORK when it earlier called EXE$KP_STALL_GENERAL. Thus the RET statement resumes EXE$KP_FORK.

⑦ EXE$KP_FORK returns to its caller, the STARTIO procedure.

⑧ The STARTIO procedure completes device-specific I/O postprocessing and invokes the KP_REQCOM macro. The KP_REQCOM macro expands to the following MACRO-32 statements:

```
JSB IOC$REQCOM
RET
```

⑨ After IOC$REQCOM performs the actions detailed in Section 24.2.5, it returns to the STARTIO procedure.

⑩ At this point, the most recent call frame on the kernel process's stack is the one left there by EXE$KP_START when it earlier started up the

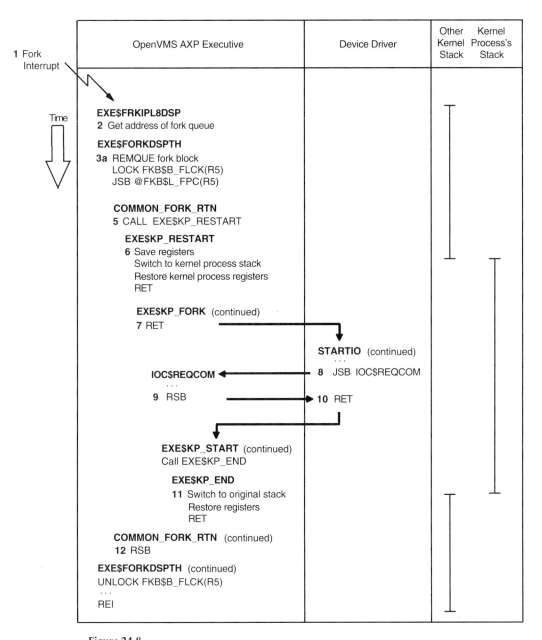

Figure 24.8
Fork Interrupt Resumes Driver Kernel Process

driver kernel process and called the STARTIO procedure (see step 6d, Section 24.4.1). STARTIO returns to EXE$KP_START. EXE$KP_START calls EXE$KP_END to end the kernel process.

⑪ At this point, the most recent call frame on the original kernel stack

851

is the one left there by COMMON_FORK_RTN when it earlier called EXE$KP_RESTART. EXE$KP_END switches to the original kernel stack, restores registers that were saved by EXE$KP_RESTART, and returns to COMMON_FORK_RTN.

⑫ COMMON_FORK_RTN returns to EXE$FORKDSPTH, which releases the fork lock and proceeds to step 3a.

24.5   RELEVANT SOURCE MODULES

Source modules described in this chapter include

[LIB]IOMAR.MAR
[LIB]KPMAR.MAR
[SYS]FORKCNTRL.MAR
[SYS]IOCINTDISP.M64
[SYS]IOSUBNPAG.MAR
[SYS]KERNEL_PROCESS.MAR
[SYS]KERNEL_PROCESS_MAGIC.M64

25 Mailboxes

Knowing how to answer one who speaks,
To reply to one who sends a message.

Amenemope, *The Instruction of Amenemope*

An OpenVMS mailbox is a virtual I/O device for interprocess communication. One process writes a message to a mailbox for another process to read. A process reads or writes mailbox messages using standard I/O mechanisms.

This chapter discusses mailboxes: the data structures that define them, the system services that create and delete them, and the driver that implements mailbox I/O. It briefly describes some examples of their use by the executive and system components.

25.1 OVERVIEW

The Alpha AXP architecture defines an entity called a hardware mailbox that should not be confused with the type of mailbox described in this chapter. Chapter 2 describes hardware mailboxes.

A mailbox is a virtual I/O device implemented in software. A mailbox device is described by the same basic data structures as any other device. Mailbox data structures are created dynamically in response to a process's Create Mailbox and Assign Channel ($CREMBX) system service request.

Mailbox messages are read and written through the standard I/O mechanisms. The mailbox driver, MBDRIVER, services Queue I/O ($QIO) system service requests to mailbox devices. The driver stores messages written to a mailbox device in nonpaged pool until they are read.

Two or more processes running on the same system can share a mailbox. The executive allows driver fork processes to write to mailboxes, although it does not allow driver fork processes to read from mailboxes. Processes sharing a mailbox generally identify it by an agreed-upon logical name, which translates to the mailbox device name. Processes running on different VMScluster system nodes cannot share a mailbox.

Typically, a mailbox is used as a one-way communication path between two or more processes; one process reads messages written to the mailbox by one or more other processes. By default the mailbox driver associates each write request with a single read request. Mailbox messages are read in the order in which they are written. A message written to a mailbox cannot be broadcast; it is read by only one process. There are no restrictions on the order in which read and write requests can be issued, although the order influences the order of request completion.

A mailbox is created with a specified maximum byte count to buffer messages written to it that have not yet been read. Thus, a process can write a message to a mailbox whether or not there is a pending read request. If there is a pending read request, the message is read immediately; otherwise, the message is buffered. By default a write request does not complete until another process reads the entire message, although a process can specify that its write request complete immediately.

When a process issues a read request to a mailbox, a buffered message may or may not be present. By default a read request does not complete until another process writes a message to the mailbox, although a process can specify that its read request complete immediately.

The executive provides two forms of mailbox I/O: the traditional record I/O and a new form called stream I/O.

With record I/O, the mailbox driver matches a read request with at most one write request, even if the size of the read data buffer and the amount of data provided by the buffered write message are not the same.

▶ If the read data buffer is longer, the driver ignores the space at the end of it.
▶ If the write message is longer, the driver copies the first part of it to the read data buffer and discards the rest.

With stream I/O, a process can specify exactly how much data is to be read. The driver matches as many reads to as many writes as necessary:

▶ If the read data buffer is longer, the driver copies the write message to the first part of the data buffer and completes the write request. The driver does not complete the read request until it has copied the requested number of bytes to the read buffer or until the mailbox is emptied.
▶ If the write message is longer, the driver copies the first part of it to the read data buffer and completes the read request. It retains the rest of the write message for a subsequent read request.

The mailbox driver can handle any sequence of stream and record I/O operations to a mailbox predictably; an application performing the I/O operations must ensure that the sequence is meaningful. A mailbox read operation can be forced to complete immediately, using a function request modifier, if no channel with write capability is assigned to the mailbox. Similarly, a mailbox write operation can be forced to complete immediately if no channel with read capability is assigned.

There are two kinds of mailboxes: temporary and permanent. A temporary mailbox is deleted automatically when no more processes have channels assigned to it. A permanent mailbox must be explicitly marked for deletion using the Delete Mailbox ($DELMBX) system service. Once marked for deletion, a permanent mailbox is deleted when no more processes have channels assigned to it.

The *OpenVMS I/O User's Reference Manual* provides more information on using mailboxes.

25.2   **LOGICAL NAMES OF MAILBOXES**

Like any other I/O device, a mailbox has a device name specification in the form *ddcu*. The mailbox device type, *dd*, is MB. Its controller designation, *c*, is A. The unit number, *u*, is an integer from 1 to 9999.

Unlike those for other I/O devices, a particular unit number is not usually associated with a particular mailbox. The only mailboxes created with specific unit numbers are those permanently defined in the executive (see Section 25.3). When a mailbox is created, it is assigned the next available unit number. Its unit number cannot be determined before the mailbox is created.

Therefore, a process creating a mailbox usually also requests the creation of a logical name that translates to the mailbox device name. Other processes identify the mailbox by its logical name when they assign a channel to it. Although a user-specified logical name is not required, accessing a mailbox without one is difficult.

Every logical name is associated with a logical name table. The $CREMBX system service creates a logical name for a mailbox in one of the following tables:

▸ The table LNM$TEMPORARY_MAILBOX for a temporary mailbox
▸ The table LNM$PERMANENT_MAILBOX for a permanent mailbox

LNM$TEMPORARY_MAILBOX is itself a logical name, whose default translation is LNM$JOB, the jobwide logical name table. The default translation of LNM$PERMANENT_MAILBOX is LNM$SYSTEM, the systemwide logical name table. Thus, temporary mailboxes, by default, can only be shared by processes in the same job tree. Processes not in the same job tree may share a temporary mailbox by redefining LNM$TEMPORARY_MAILBOX to some shared logical name table. The manual *OpenVMS Programming Concepts* contains more information on the subject of mailbox logical names.

In addition to automatic logical name creation for a mailbox being created, the executive provides automatic logical name deletion for a mailbox being deleted.

Directed by the $CREMBX system service, the Create Logical Name ($CRELNM) system service stores the address of the logical name data structure in the mailbox unit control block field UCB$L_LOGADR and the address of the mailbox unit control block in the logical name data structure. If, however, the mailbox logical name is a process-private name, $CRELNM clears UCB$L_LOGADR to prevent possible race conditions at process deletion, when all process-private logical names are deleted.

25.3   MAILBOX DATA STRUCTURES

A mailbox device uses many of the same basic data structures that other I/O devices use (see Chapter 22). These include

- Device data block (DDB)
- Controller request block (CRB)
- Unit control block (UCB) for each unit
- Object rights block (ORB) for each unit

Since a mailbox is not a physical device and does not service interrupts, it does not require an interrupt dispatch block (IDB) or an adapter control block (ADP).

Unlike those of most devices, the mailbox DDB and CRB are not created dynamically. Instead, they and four permanent mailbox UCBs and ORBs are built into the module PERMANENT_DEVICE_DATABASE. Permanent unit MBA0 is the template from which $CREMBX clones other mailboxes (see Chapter 23 for a description of template device processing). Section 25.6 describes the use of the special permanent mailbox units MBA1, MBA2, and MBA3.

For every write request, the mailbox driver allocates a nonpaged pool data structure called a message block. The layout of this structure is shown in Figure 25.1. A message block representing a pending write request is queued to the UCB's write request queue; it contains a pointer to its associated I/O request packet (IRP).

For a stream read request of nonzero length, the mailbox driver allocates a nonpaged pool data structure called a read system buffer. The layout of this structure is shown in Figure 25.2. An IRP representing a pending stream read

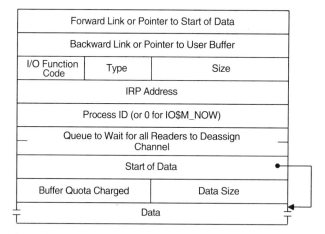

Figure 25.1
Layout of Mailbox Message Block

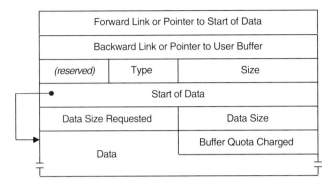

Figure 25.2
Layout of Read System Buffer

request is queued to the UCB's read request queue; its IRP$L_SVAPTE field points to the associated read system buffer. When processing a record read request, the mailbox driver directly copies data to the I/O requestor's buffer; no buffering, and hence no read system buffer, is involved.

A mailbox UCB (see Figure 25.3) contains a number of device-specific fields. The $UCBDEF macro defines offsets into this structure.

UCB$L_MB_MSGQFL and UCB$L_MB_MSGQBL form a listhead for an absolute queue of message blocks.

A process can request notification through an attention asynchronous system trap (AST) when any of the following events occurs:

▸ A read request is issued to the mailbox, and no corresponding write message has been queued.

▸ A write request is issued to the mailbox, and no corresponding read request has been queued.

▸ Room has potentially become available for write requests.

The driver builds an AST control block (ACB) to represent each request for an attention AST. It maintains a singly linked list of ACBs for each type of attention AST. Their listheads are in the mailbox UCB:

▸ UCB$L_MB_R_AST, for read attention ASTs
▸ UCB$L_MB_W_AST, for write attention ASTs
▸ UCB$L_MB_ROOM_NOTIFY, for room attention ASTs

Section 25.5.4.1 describes the mailbox driver's use of attention ASTs.

UCB$W_MSGCNT contains the number of write requests queued to the mailbox. The mailbox driver maintains a copy of this value in UCB$L_DEVDEPEND for use by the Get Device/Volume Information ($GETDVI) system service.

UCB$W_INIQUO contains the number of bytes of nonpaged pool that can be used to buffer messages written to the mailbox. UCB$W_INIQUO is set

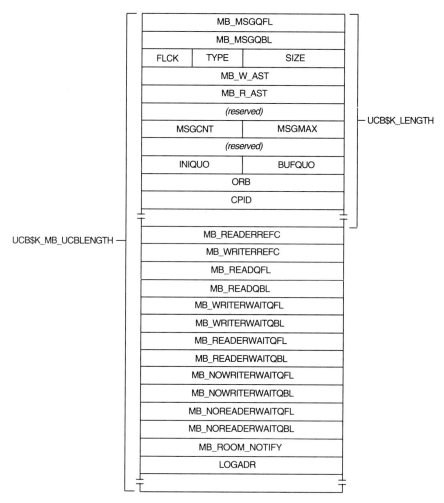

Figure 25.3
Layout of Mailbox UCB

to the $CREMBX argument BUFQUO if the argument is specified. Otherwise, the SYSGEN parameter DEFMBXBUFQUO is used.

UCB$W_BUFQUO contains the space currently available for new messages. Initially, UCB$W_BUFQUO contains the value stored in UCB$W_INIQUO. When a message is written to the mailbox, UCB$W_BUFQUO is reduced by the size of the message. When the message is read, UCB$W_BUFQUO is increased by the size of the message. For the special mailboxes MBA1, MBA2, and MBA3, buffer quota is set to the maximum permissible value, 65535.

Despite its name, UCB$W_MSGMAX is not used by the mailbox driver. Instead, for a mailbox UCB, the standard UCB field UCB$W_DEVBUFSIZ contains the maximum byte size of a message that can be queued to the mailbox.

UCB$L_MB_READERREFC contains the reader reference count, that is, the number of read only or read/write channels assigned to the mailbox. When a channel with read capability is assigned, the count is incremented, and when the channel is deassigned, the count is decremented. UCB$L_MB_WRITERREFC contains the writer reference count, that is, the number of write only or read/write channels assigned to the mailbox. When a channel with write capability is assigned, the count is incremented, and when the channel is deassigned, the count is decremented. The capability to assign a read only or a write only mailbox channel was newly introduced along with stream I/O.

UCB$L_MB_READQFL and UCB$L_MB_READQBL form the listhead for an absolute queue of read IRPs waiting for messages to be written to the mailbox. This queue is called the read request queue.

Through a set mode function request to the mailbox driver, a process can request to wait until a channel with read or write capability is assigned to a specified mailbox. UCB$L_MB_WRITERWAITQFL and UCB$L_MB_WRITERWAITQBL form the listhead for an absolute queue of set mode IRPs waiting for a write channel to be assigned to the mailbox. UCB$L_MB_READERWAITQFL and UCB$L_MB_READERWAITQBL form the listhead for an absolute queue of set mode IRPs waiting for a read channel to be assigned to the mailbox.

UCB$L_MB_NOWRITERWAITQFL and UCB$L_MB_NOWRITERWAIT-QBL form the listhead for an absolute queue of read IRPs waiting for all write channels on the mailbox to be deassigned. UCB$L_MB_NOREADER-WAITQFL and UCB$L_MB_NOREADERWAITQBL form the listhead for an absolute queue of message blocks waiting for all read channels on the mailbox to be deassigned.

UCB$L_LOGADR contains the address of the mailbox device's logical name block.

25.4   MAILBOX CREATION AND DELETION

Two system services are related specifically to mailbox use: $CREMBX and $DELMBX.

25.4.1 $CREMBX System Service

The $CREMBX system service procedure, EXE$CREMBX in module SYS-MAILBX, runs in kernel mode. It creates a virtual mailbox device named MBA*n* and assigns an I/O channel to it or, if the mailbox already exists, merely assigns an I/O channel. $CREMBX has eight arguments:

▶ PRMFLG, a flag specifying whether the mailbox is to be a permanent or a temporary one

859

▶ CHAN, the address of a word in which the channel identifier assigned to the mailbox by EXE$CREMBX is written

▶ MAXMSG, the maximum size of a message that can be written to the mailbox

▶ BUFQUO, the number of bytes of nonpaged pool that can be used to buffer messages written to the mailbox

▶ PROMSK, the protection mask to be associated with the created mailbox

▶ ACMODE, the access mode to be associated with the channel to which the mailbox is assigned

▶ LOGNAM, the logical name to be assigned to a new mailbox or translated to locate an existing mailbox

▶ FLAGS, a value specifying whether the mailbox is read/write, read only, or write only

The CHAN argument is required; all others are optional.

EXE$CREMBX takes the following initial steps:

1. It verifies that the FLAGS argument has a legal value.
2. It verifies that the CHAN argument is write-accessible.
3. EXE$CREMBX raises the interrupt priority level (IPL) to 2 to prevent process deletion and invokes IOC$FFCHAN to find a free channel control block (CCB). IOC$FFCHAN is discussed in Chapter 23.
4. It checks that the process has the necessary privilege to create the type of mailbox specified in the PRMFLG argument: PRMMBX for a permanent mailbox or TMPMBX for a temporary mailbox.
5. It locks the I/O database mutex for write access.
6. If the LOGNAM argument was omitted, EXE$CREMBX presumes that the mailbox does not exist and must be created. It creates the mailbox by taking the steps described later in this section. It then clears UCB$L_LOGADR to indicate that the mailbox has no associated logical name and continues with step 10.
7. If the LOGNAM argument was specified, EXE$CREMBX requests the Translate Logical Name ($TRNLNM) system service to obtain the address of the mailbox UCB, if one exists. It passes the following arguments to $TRNLNM:

   • The name of the mailbox logical name table
   • The logical name specified by the LOGNAM argument
   • The maximized access mode, that is, the less privileged of the access mode specified by the ACMODE argument and the access mode of the requestor
   • An item list element requesting the back pointer, that is, the address of the mailbox UCB associated with the logical name

8. If the specified logical name does not exist, EXE$CREMBX presumes that the mailbox does not exist and creates the mailbox by taking the steps described later in this section. It continues with step 10.

9. If the logical name exists, EXE$CREMBX uses its back pointer contents as the UCB address and proceeds to step 11.

10. EXE$CREMBX requests the $CRELNM system service to create the logical name specified by the LOGNAM argument. It passes the following arguments to the $CRELNM system service:
    - The name of the mailbox logical name table
    - The logical name specified by the LOGNAM argument
    - The maximized access mode
    - An item list element directing the $CRELNM system service to store the address of the logical name block in UCB$L_LOGADR

11. EXE$CREMBX increments the reference count for that mailbox and assigns a channel to the mailbox by taking the following steps:
    a. It stores the mailbox UCB address in CCB$L_UCB.
    b. It stores in CCB$B_AMOD the access mode at which the channel was assigned (plus 1). The access mode is biased by 1 because a 0 in CCB$B_AMOD indicates an unassigned channel. As usual, the access mode at which the channel is assigned is the less privileged of the access mode specified by the ACMODE argument and the access mode of the requestor.
    c. The FLAGS argument specifies the type of access permitted on the channel: read/write, read only, or write only. Based on this value, EXE$CREMBX sets the CCB$V_NOWRITEACC bit or the CCB$V_NOREADACC bit in CCB$L_STS as appropriate. If the FLAGS argument is zero, or is unspecified, the channel is assigned for both read and write access.
    d. EXE$CREMBX invokes MB$CHANUNWAIT, in module MBDRIVER, passing it the CCB address. Among other things, MB$CHANUNWAIT, described in Section 25.5.4.2, increments the reader reference count if read access is permitted, and the writer reference count if write access is permitted.

12. EXE$CREMBX stores the channel identifier in the address specified by the CHAN argument. It unlocks the I/O database mutex, lowers IPL to 0, and finally returns the success status SS$_NORMAL to its requestor.

If the mailbox does not exist, EXE$CREMBX creates it. It can create a temporary or a permanent mailbox depending on the value of the PRMFLG argument. To create a temporary mailbox, a process must have sufficient byte count quota for the mailbox messages and UCB. The quota is charged at mailbox creation and returned at mailbox deletion. Because a permanent mailbox may survive the deletion of its creating process, quota is not charged for its creation. Instead, PRMMBX, a privilege less lightly granted than TMPMBX, is required for a process to create a permanent mailbox.

To create a mailbox, EXE$CREMBX takes the following steps:

1. For a temporary mailbox, it invokes IOC$CHKMBXQUOTA, in module UCBCREDEL, to determine if the process buffered I/O byte count quota (JIB$L_BYTCNT) can accommodate both of the following with a margin of 256 bytes left:

   - The size of a mailbox UCB
   - The space to buffer mailbox messages, specified either by the optional BUFQUO argument or by the SYSGEN parameter DEFMBXBUFQUO if the BUFQUO argument is absent.

   IOC$CHKMBXQUOTA invokes EXE$DEBIT_BYTCNT_BYTLM_NW to charge the process buffered I/O byte count quota and byte limit (JIB$L_BYTLM) for the size of the mailbox UCB and the mailbox message block. If the quota is insufficient, IOC$CHKMBXQUOTA returns an error status to EXE$CREMBX, which returns the error to its caller.

2. EXE$CREMBX invokes IOC$CLONE_UCB, in module UCBCREDEL, to clone a new UCB and ORB from the template mailbox unit MBA0.

   IOC$CLONE_UCB allocates nonpaged pool into which it copies the template UCB and ORB. It increments the contents of UCB$W_UNIT_SEED and checks whether a mailbox with that unit number exists. If so, it tries the next value. It continues until it finds an available unit number. If it increments the unit number past 9999, it continues at unit number 1.

   IOC$CLONE_UCB initializes the new UCB: it links the new UCB into the UCB list, sets the reference count to 1, marks the device online, and stores the new ORB address into UCB$L_ORB.

3. EXE$CREMBX further initializes the cloned UCB:

   a. It initializes the queue headers outlined in Section 25.3, such as the read request queue and UCB$L_MB_WRITERWAITQFL, as empty.

   b. It stores the buffer quota in the buffer quota and initial buffer quota fields, UCB$W_BUFQUO and UCB$W_INIQUO.

   c. It clears the owner field, UCB$L_PID.

   d. It modifies the ORB associated with the UCB to specify the system, owner, group, and world format protection mask, and stores the PROMSK argument in ORB$W_PROT.

   e. It stores the current process's user identification code (UIC) in the ORB owner UIC field.

   f. It initializes the UCB device buffer size field with either the MAXMSG argument or the SYSGEN parameter DEFMBXMXMSG.

   g. It initializes UCB$L_DEVDEPEND to zero. The mailbox driver keeps a copy of the current message count in this field.

   h. It stores the sum of the UCB size and the buffer quota in UCB$W_CHARGE.

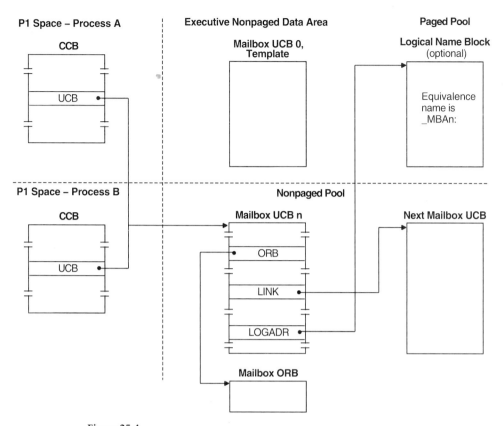

Figure 25.4
Data Structures Associated with Mailbox Creation

    i. If the mailbox is permanent, EXE$CREMBX sets bit UCB$V_PRM-MBX in UCB$L_DEVSTS.

    j. If the mailbox is temporary, EXE$CREMBX sets bit UCB$V_DELMBX in UCB$L_DEVSTS to mark the mailbox for deletion when the last channel to it is deassigned. It invokes IOC$DEBIT_UCB, in module UCBCREDEL, to copy the master process ID charged for the UCB (JIB$L_MPID) into the charge PID field (UCB$L_CPID).

Figure 25.4 shows the data structures associated with mailbox creation.

25.4.2 $DELMBX System Service

The $DELMBX system service marks a mailbox UCB for deletion; it does not actually delete the UCB. UCB deletion occurs during last channel processing. Requesting $DELMBX to mark a temporary mailbox for deletion is superfluous; it can be deleted simply by deassigning all its channels. The $DELMBX system service has only one argument: CHAN, the identifier of the channel assigned to the mailbox to be deleted.

863

The $DELMBX system service procedure, EXE$DELMBX in module SYS-MAILBX, runs in kernel mode. It invokes IOC$VERIFYCHAN to verify the channel identifier and get the address of the CCB. EXE$DELMBX gets the UCB address from CCB$L_UCB and verifies the following:

▸ The UCB is a mailbox (DEV$V_MBX in UCB$L_DEVCHAR is set).
▸ If the mailbox is permanent, the process has PRMMBX privilege.

If these conditions are met, EXE$DELMBX marks a permanent mailbox for deletion by setting bit UCB$V_DELMBX in UCB$L_DEVSTS. The $CREMBX system service set bit UCB$V_DELMBX for a temporary mailbox when the mailbox UCB was created.

The mailbox is actually deleted by IOC$DELETE_UCB, in module UCB-CREDEL, when the reference count goes to zero, that is, when the last channel assigned to it is deassigned. Last channel processing is performed by IOC$LAST_CHAN, in module IOSUBNPAG. IOC$LAST_CHAN invokes the driver's cancel I/O routine with an appropriate cancellation reason code. The mailbox driver's cancel I/O routine deletes the logical name, if any, as part of last channel processing. Chapter 23 discusses last channel processing.

25.5 MAILBOX DRIVER

The following sections describe the functions of the mailbox driver. Earlier versions of the mailbox driver were written completely in MACRO-32. In current versions of OpenVMS VAX and in OpenVMS AXP, most of the mailbox driver is written in BLISS, in module MBDRIVER. Module MB-DRIVER_HEADER, written in MACRO-32, contains the driver table declarations. Unlike most other drivers, which are separate executive images, the mailbox driver is implemented as a part of the SYSDEVICE.EXE executive image.

MBDRIVER uses IPL$_MAILBOX, the highest fork IPL, as its IPL. It does this to prevent possible synchronization problems with other driver fork processes that reference mailboxes, for example, to send a "device is offline" message to the operator's mailbox.

MBDRIVER differs from a traditional OpenVMS device driver in that it has no separate start I/O routine. The steps typically performed by a start I/O routine are performed by MBDRIVER's function decision table (FDT) routines:

▸ MB$FDT_READ—Used for IO$_READxBLK function requests, where x is P for physical, V for virtual, and L for logical (MBDRIVER makes no distinction between these three forms)
▸ MB$FDT_WRITE—Used for IO$_WRITExBLK and IO$_WRITEOF function requests

▶ MB$FDT_SETMODE—Used for IO$_SETMODE function requests

▶ MB$FDT_SENSEMODE—Used for IO$_SENSEMODE function requests

25.5.1 Mailbox Write Request Processing

One or more of the following modifiers can be specified with an IO$_WRITExBLK or an IO$_WRITEOF request:

▶ IO$M_READERCHECK—Abort operation if no read channels are assigned to the mailbox.

▶ IO$M_NOW—Complete operation immediately; do not wait for readers.

▶ IO$M_NORSWAIT—Abort operation if the mailbox is full, rather than placing the requestor in a wait state.

An image can request the IO$_WRITExBLK function to write a message to a specific mailbox, or it can request the IO$_WRITEOF function to write an end-of-file message. The FDT routine MB$FDT_WRITE services either type of request by taking the following steps:

1. If the CCB$V_NOWRITEACC flag in the CCB is set, indicating that this is a read-only channel, it aborts the I/O request with the SS$_ILLIOFUNC error status.

2. If the CCB$V_WRTCHKDON flag in the CCB is clear, MB$FDT_WRITE invokes EXE$CHKWRTACCES, in module EXSUBROUT, to check whether the process has write access to this mailbox. If EXE$CHKWRTACCES returns an error status, the routine aborts the I/O request with that error status. Otherwise, it sets the CCB$V_WRTCHKDON flag to avoid making this check for future write requests on the same channel.

3. If the IO$_WRITEOF function was requested, it initializes IRP$L_BOFF and IRP$L_BCNT to zero and IRP$L_MEDIA to its own address and proceeds to step 5.

4. MB$FDT_WRITE verifies the following:

   • The message size must be less than or equal to the maximum message size (UCB$W_DEVBUFSIZ) for the mailbox. If the message size exceeds the maximum, the request is aborted with the error status SS$_MBTOOSML.

   • The process must have read access to the buffer from which the mailbox message will be copied, as determined by EXE$WRITECHK, in module SYSQIOFDT.

   It saves the address of the I/O requestor's buffer in IRP$L_MEDIA.

5. It invokes EXE$ALONONPAGED, in module MEMORYALC_DYN, to allocate a message block from nonpaged pool.

   If allocation was unsuccessful and the IO$M_NORSWAIT modifier was present, MB$FDT_WRITE aborts the I/O request with the error status SS$_INSFMEM. If allocation was unsuccessful and the modifier was not present, the routine invokes EXE$IORSNWAIT, in module SYSQIOFDT, to place the process into a wait for resource RSN$_NP-DYNMEM (RWNPP).

6. It initializes the message block (see Figure 25.1).

7. It acquires the MAILBOX spinlock, raising IPL to IPL$_MAILBOX.

8. If the IO$M_READERCHECK modifier is present, and no channels with read capability are assigned to the mailbox, MB$FDT_WRITE releases the MAILBOX spinlock, restoring IPL, deallocates the message block to nonpaged pool, and completes the I/O request with the error status SS$_NOREADER.

9. MB$FDT_WRITE determines if enough buffer quota remains for the message. If not, it checks whether the message size is less than the total space allowed for messages and whether any read requests are queued to the mailbox. Outstanding read requests consume buffer quota, and completing the write request will free buffer quota by completing the read requests. The routine proceeds to step 10.

   If there are no outstanding read requests and no remaining buffer quota, MB$FDT_WRITE releases the spinlock, restores the saved IPL, and deallocates the message block to nonpaged pool. It then performs one of the following actions:

   - If the message size is less than the total space allowed for messages and the IO$M_NORSWAIT modifier was not present, MB$FDT_WRITE invokes EXE$IORSNWAIT to place the process into a wait for resource RSN$_MAILBOX (RWMBX).
   - If the message size is less than the total space allowed and the modifier was present, it aborts the I/O request with the error status SS$_MBFULL.
   - If the message size is larger than the total space allowed, it aborts the I/O request with the error status SS$_MBTOOSML.

10. If there is enough room for the message, or if this write request will free up buffer quota for the mailbox, MB$FDT_WRITE puts the message on the mailbox queue as follows:

    a. It increments the message count, UCB$W_MSGCNT, and copies this value to UCB$L_DEVDEPEND.

    b. If there is enough room for the message, it charges buffer quota by decrementing the message size from UCB$W_BUFQUO. If the message size is zero, or if this is an end-of-file message, MB$FDT_WRITE charges one byte.

    c. It queues the message to the write request queue.

    d. If the read request queue is not empty, it invokes MB$FINISHREAD, in module MBDRIVER, to complete the read request. Section 25.5.3

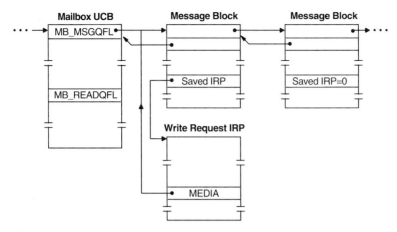

Figure 25.5
Queued Mailbox Messages

describes MB$FINISHREAD's actions. When MB$FINISHREAD returns, MB$FDT_WRITE proceeds to step 11.

e. If the read request queue is empty, MB$FDT_WRITE queues the message block to wait for a read request, unless the IO$M_NOW modifier is present, or the IO$M_READERCHECK modifier is present and no read channel is assigned to the mailbox.

f. MB$FDT_WRITE invokes COM$DELATTNAST, in module COMDRVSUB, to deliver any write attention ASTs to the appropriate processes.

11. It releases the MAILBOX spinlock, restoring the saved IPL.

12. If the IO$M_NOW modifier was present, MB$FDT_WRITE invokes EXE$FINISHIOC, in module SYSQIOREQ, to record the I/O status block (IOSB) information in the IRP and complete the I/O request with a status of SS$_NORMAL.

If the IO$M_NOW modifier was not present, MB$FDT_WRITE invokes EXE$QIORETURN, in module SYSQIOREQ, to return to the I/O requestor. I/O completion of the write request is stalled until a read request is issued.

Figure 25.5 shows the data structures involved in mailbox write request completion.

25.5.2 Mailbox Read Request Processing

One or more of the following modifiers can be specified with an IO$_READxBLK request:

▸ IO$M_WRITERCHECK—Abort operation if no write channels are assigned to the mailbox.

▸ IO$M_NOW—Complete operation immediately; do not wait for writers.

▸ IO$M_STREAM—Perform a stream read.

When an image requests the IO$_READxBLK function to read a message from a specific mailbox, the FDT routine MB$FDT_READ takes the following steps:

1. If the CCB$V_NOREADACC flag in the CCB is set, indicating that read access is not allowed on this channel, MB$FDT_READ aborts the I/O request with the error status SS$_ILLIOFUNC.

2. If the message size is larger than the maximum message size permitted for this mailbox, MB$FDT_READ aborts the I/O request with the error status SS$_MBTOOSML.

3. Unless this read request is a zero-byte one, MB$FDT_READ invokes EXE$READCHK, in module SYSQIOFDT, to verify that the process has write access to the buffer into which the mailbox message is to be copied.

4. For a zero-byte stream read request, MB$FDT_READ completes the I/O request by invoking EXE$FINISHIOC with the status SS$_NORMAL.

5. MB$FDT_READ sets the IRP$V_MBXIO bit in IRP$L_STS to indicate that it is a mailbox I/O request. The I/O postprocessing special kernel mode AST routine declares the availability of the mailbox resource when it processes an I/O request with this bit set.

6. MB$FDT_READ saves the current IPL and acquires the MAILBOX spinlock, raising IPL to IPL$_MAILBOX.

7. If the IO$M_STREAM modifier is present, MB$FDT_READ takes the following steps:

   a. It checks whether the mailbox's write request queue has any messages, and if so, whether the first outstanding message's data size is the same as this read request's. If so, it proceeds to step 8.

   b. Otherwise, MB$FDT_READ must allocate a read system buffer to save information about this read request, because this single read request may require multiple writes to the mailbox. MB$FDT_READ allocates a nonpaged pool buffer and initializes it (see Figure 25.2). It saves the address of the read system buffer in IRP$L_SVAPTE.

   c. It determines if enough buffer quota remains for the read system buffer. If not, it checks whether the read system buffer size is less than the total space allowed for messages and whether any write requests are queued to the mailbox. Outstanding write requests consume buffer quota, and completing the read request will free buffer quota by completing the write requests. MB$FDT_READ proceeds to step 8.

   If the message size exceeds the total space allowed, or if there are no outstanding read requests, MB$FDT_READ releases the MAILBOX spinlock, deallocates the read system buffer, and aborts the I/O request with the error status SS$_EXQUOTA.

8. If the IO$M_WRITERCHECK modifier is present, if no write channel is assigned to the mailbox, and if there are no outstanding messages, MB$FDT_READ releases the MAILBOX spinlock, returns any buffer quota charged, deallocates the read system buffer, and completes the I/O request with the error status SS$_NOWRITER.

9. If the IO$M_NOW modifier is present and there are no outstanding messages, MB$FDT_READ releases the MAILBOX spinlock, returns any buffer quota charged, deallocates the read system buffer, and completes the I/O request with the error status SS$_ENDOFFILE.

10. If the IO$M_WRITERCHECK modifier is present and a write channel is assigned to the mailbox, MB$FDT_READ checks whether the current channel has write access and whether any outstanding messages are in the mailbox. If both conditions are true, MB$FDT_READ queues the IRP (at offset IRP$L_NOPARTNERQFL) to the UCB$L_MB_NOWRITERWAITQFL queue. Otherwise, MB$FDT_READ initializes IRP$L_NOPARTNERQFL to zero.

11. MB$FDT_READ queues the IRP to the UCB's read request queue.

12. If the UCB's write request queue is not empty, it invokes MB$FINISH-READ to complete the read operation. Otherwise, it invokes COM$DEL-ATTNAST to deliver any read attention ASTs that were requested.

13. It releases the MAILBOX spinlock and returns to the $QIO requestor.

Figure 25.6 shows the other data structures that are involved in read request completion.

25.5.3   Mailbox Read and Write Request Completion

MB$FINISHREAD is the read and write request completion routine. It is invoked by the read or write FDT routine when a matching write or read request is found to be queued to the mailbox. MB$FINISHREAD matches a read request to a write request in the following manner:

▶ For a record read, it completes both the read and write requests (case 1).
▶ For a stream read, it does one of the following:

  • If the read request size exactly matches the write request size, it completes both requests (case 1).
  • If the read request size is less than the write request size, it completes the read request, updates the write message block, and looks for more read requests (case 2).
  • If the read request size is greater than the write request size, it completes the write request, updates the read system buffer and the read IRP, and looks for more write requests (case 3).

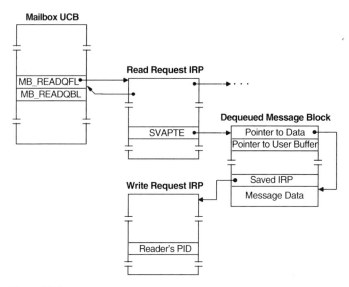

Figure 25.6
Read Request Completion

MB$FINISHREAD performs the following steps:

1. It gets the addresses of the first message block and the first IRP queued to the mailbox.
2. It determines which of the three cases is true and proceeds as described in the sections that follow.
3. If it needs to check for more read or write requests, it goes to step 1.
4. If, during processing, it freed up buffer quota for the mailbox, it invokes COM$DELATTNAST to deliver any pending room availability attention ASTs.
5. It returns to its invoker.

25.5.3.1   **Case 1: Record Read or Matching Request Sizes.** For a record read, or a stream read request whose size exactly matches the write request size, MB$FINISHREAD performs the following steps:

1. It dequeues the first message block from the write request queue and the first pending read IRP from the read request queue.
2. For a stream read, it initializes IRP$L_SVAPTE with the address of the read system buffer. For a record read, it initializes IRP$L_SVAPTE with the address of the message block.
3. If the IRP is on the UCB$L_MB_NOWRITERWAITQFL queue, MB$FINISHREAD removes the IRP from that queue. If the message block is on the UCB$L_MB_NOREADERWAITQFL queue, it dequeues the message block from that queue.
4. For a stream read, MB$FINISHREAD copies data from the message block into the read system buffer. During I/O completion processing of the

stream read IRP, data from the read system buffer will be copied to the I/O requestor's data buffer.

For a record read, MB$FINISHREAD initializes the message block in the format of a buffered I/O buffer, with the first longword pointing to the data area and the second longword pointing to the I/O requestor's data buffer. During I/O completion processing of a record read IRP, data from the message block will be copied to the I/O requestor's data buffer. Chapter 23 describes the format of a buffered I/O buffer and I/O completion processing.

5. If one or more processes are waiting for resource RSN$_MAILBOX, MB$FINISHREAD creates a fork process to declare the mailbox resource available.

6. It prepares the read IRP's IRP$L_IOST1 and IRP$L_IOST2 fields for I/O postprocessing:

   - If the read data size is less than the write data size, MB$FINISHREAD sets the read completion status in the low-order word of IRP$L_IOST1 as SS$_BUFFEROVF. If the write is a write end-of-file request, it sets the read completion status as SS$_ENDOFFILE. Otherwise, it sets the status as SS$_NORMAL.
   - It initializes the high-order word of IRP$L_IOST1 with the number of bytes read.
   - It initializes IRP$L_IOST2 with the PID of the process that wrote the message.

   It invokes COM$POST to initiate I/O postprocessing for the read IRP. I/O postprocessing code eventually copies these fields into the I/O requestor's IOSB. For mailbox reads and writes, the layout of the IOSB is shown in Figure 25.7.

7. MB$FINISHREAD increments the UCB message count and copies the value to UCB$L_DEVDEPEND.

8. If the write IRP still exists, MB$FINISHREAD completes the write request as follows:

   a. It sets the completion status as SS$_NORMAL and the byte count as the number of bytes copied.
   b. It initializes IRP$L_IOST2 with the PID of the process that read the message.
   c. It invokes COM$POST to initiate I/O postprocessing.

   If the message block does not contain the address of an associated IRP,

Byte Count	Status
Reader or Writer Process ID	

Figure 25.7
Layout of Read and Write IOSB

the write request was already completed; MB$FINISHREAD deallocates the message block.

25.5.3.2 Case 2: Read Request Size Less Than Write Request Size.

If the size of the stream read request is smaller than that of the write request, MB$FINISH-READ performs the following steps:

1. It dequeues the read IRP from the read request queue, leaving the corresponding message block on the write request queue. It gets the address of the read system buffer from IRP$L_SVAPTE.
2. If the IRP is on the UCB$L_MB_NOWRITERWAITQFL queue, it dequeues the IRP from that queue.
3. If one or more processes are waiting for resource RSN$_MAILBOX, MB$FINISHREAD creates a fork process to declare the mailbox resource available.
4. It copies IRP$L_BCNT bytes of data from the message block to the read system buffer.
5. It subtracts the number of bytes copied from the message block's data size cell. It adds the same number to the data area pointer of the message block.
6. It initializes IRP$L_IOST1 and IRP$L_IOST2 of the read IRP (see Section 25.5.3.1) and invokes COM$POST to complete the read request.
7. If the read request queue is empty, or if the next read request is a zero-byte one, MB$FINISHREAD completes the write request corresponding to the message block. Otherwise, it goes to step 1 of Section 25.5.3.

25.5.3.3 Case 3: Read Request Size Greater Than Write Request Size.

If the size of the stream read request is larger than that of the write request, MB$FINISH-READ performs the following steps:

1. It dequeues the message block from the mailbox's write request queue, leaving the corresponding read IRP on the read request queue.
2. If the message block is in the UCB$L_MB_READERWAITQFL queue, it dequeues the message block from that queue.
3. It initializes the first two longwords of the message block as a buffered I/O buffer (see Section 25.5.3.1).
4. If one or more processes are waiting for resource RSN$_MAILBOX, MB$FINISHREAD creates a fork process to declare the mailbox resource available.
5. It copies all the data from the message block to the data area of the read system buffer. It decrements the read IRP's IRP$L_BCNT by the size of the data transferred to reflect the remaining number of bytes to be read.
6. It updates the read system buffer's data size and data area pointer cells by adding the number of bytes copied to them.

7. It decrements the UCB's message count and copies the value to UCB$L_
   DEVDEPEND.

8. If a write IRP exists, MB$FINISHREAD initializes the write IRP's IRP$L_
   IOST1 and IRP$L_IOST2 fields (see Section 25.5.3.1) and invokes
   COM$POST to complete the write request.

   If the message block does not contain the address of the associated
   IRP, the write request was already completed; MB$FINISHREAD simply
   deallocates the message block.

9. If the write request queue is empty, or if the next write request is a
   write end-of-file request, MB$FINISHREAD completes the read request,
   as outlined in step 10. Otherwise, it goes to step 1 of Section 25.5.3.

10. MB$FINISHREAD performs the following steps:
    a. It copies the read system buffer's data size cell to IRP$L_BCNT.
    b. It dequeues the read IRP from the read request queue.
    c. If the IRP is in the UCB$L_MB_NOWRITERWAITQFL queue, the rou-
       tine removes it.
    d. It initializes IRP$L_IOST1 and IRP$L_IOST2 (see Section 25.5.3.1) and
       invokes COM$POST to complete the read request.

25.5.4   Processing Set Mode Requests

A process can use the IO$_SETMODE function to request MBDRIVER to
perform various operations. The function modifier determines the specific
operation. One, and only one, of the following modifiers may be specified:

▶ IO$M_READATTN—Deliver an AST when a read request is issued to the
  mailbox and no write request is pending.

▶ IO$M_WRTATTN—Deliver an AST when a write request is issued to the
  mailbox and no read request is pending.

▶ IO$M_MB_ROOM_NOTIFY—Deliver an AST when room becomes avail-
  able in the mailbox buffer.

▶ IO$M_READERWAIT—Wait until a read channel is assigned to the mail-
  box.

▶ IO$M_WRITERWAIT—Wait until a write channel is assigned to the
  mailbox.

▶ IO$M_SETPROT—Set protection on the mailbox.

If more than one modifier is present, the FDT routine aborts the request with
the error status SS$_ILLIOFUNC.

25.5.4.1   AST Notification of Read or Write Requests. When an image requests a
set mode function to establish either a read or a write attention AST, MB-
DRIVER's set mode FDT routine, MB$FDT_SETMODE, takes the following
steps:

1. It verifies that the channel is read- or write-accessible, as appropriate.

2. It invokes COM$SETATTNAST, in module COMDRVSUB, to allocate, initialize, and queue an ACB to the appropriate listhead in the mailbox UCB. MB$FDT_SETMODE passes the address of the listhead, either UCB$L_MB_R_AST for a read attention AST request, or UCB$L_MB_W_AST for a write attention AST request. Chapter 8 provides more information on attention ASTs.

3. It acquires the MAILBOX spinlock, raising IPL to IPL$_MAILBOX, to synchronize access to the mailbox UCB.

4. It determines whether the notification condition is met:

   • If the request is for a read attention AST, there must be at least one IRP queued in the mailbox's read request queue.

   • If the request is for a write attention AST, there must be at least one message queued to the mailbox, that is, UCB$W_MSGCNT must be nonzero.

   If the appropriate condition is met, MB$FDT_SETMODE invokes COM$DELATTNAST, in module COMDRVSUB, to queue the attention AST to the current process.

   Otherwise, MBDRIVER will queue the attention AST to the process later, when the notification condition is met.

5. MB$FDT_SETMODE releases the MAILBOX spinlock and then invokes EXE$FINISHIOC, in module SYSQIOREQ, to complete the I/O request (see Chapter 23).

25.5.4.2 **Waiting for a Reader or Writer.** When an image requests that the current thread of execution be put in a wait state until a read channel or a write channel is assigned to a specific mailbox, MB$FDT_SETMODE takes the following steps:

1. It checks the appropriate reference count:

   • For an IO$M_READERWAIT request, the reader reference count
   • For an IO$M_WRITERWAIT request, the writer reference count

   If the reference count is nonzero, indicating that a read or a write channel is already assigned to the mailbox, it invokes EXE$FINISHIOC to complete the I/O request immediately.

2. Otherwise, it inserts the IRP into the mailbox's reader wait queue or writer wait queue and invokes EXE$QIORETURN to return to the I/O requestor. If the synchronous form of the $QIO system service had been requested, the requesting process waits in the requestor's mode until the wait condition is met. If the asynchronous form of the service had been requested, control returns to the requestor; the requestor synchronizes with the I/O completion using an event flag or an AST, as described in Chapter 23.

Later, when a read or a write channel is assigned to the mailbox, EXE$CRE-

MBX invokes MB$CHANUNWAIT, in module MBDRIVER, to perform the following steps:

1. MB$CHANUNWAIT makes a copy of the CCB on the stack, allowing the CCB's contents to be read at high IPL. (CCBs are in a pageable part of P1 space.)
2. MB$CHANUNWAIT acquires the MAILBOX spinlock, raising IPL to IPL$_MAILBOX, to synchronize access to the mailbox UCB.
3. If read access is permitted on this channel, the routine increments the reader reference count.
4. If write access is permitted on this channel, it increments the writer reference count.
5. Depending on whether the channel provides read access, write access, or both, MB$CHANUNWAIT removes all IRPs from the following queues:
   - The reader wait queue, if read operations are permitted on the channel
   - The writer wait queue, if write operations are permitted on the channel

   For each IRP removed, MB$CHANUNWAIT initializes the IRP$L_IO-ST1 and IRP$L_IOST2 fields and invokes COM$POST to complete the I/O request. I/O postprocessing code eventually copies IRP$L_IOST1 and IRP$L_IOST2 to the I/O requestor's IOSB (see Chapter 23).
6. It releases the MAILBOX spinlock, restoring the previous IPL, and returns to EXE$CREMBX.

25.5.4.3   **AST Notification of Room Availability in a Mailbox.** When an image requests that an attention AST be delivered when room is available in a specific mailbox, MB$FDT_SETMODE takes the following steps:

1. It verifies that the channel is read-accessible. If not, it aborts the I/O request.
2. It invokes COM$SETATTNAST to allocate, initialize, and queue an ACB to the listhead at UCB$L_MB_ROOM_NOTIFY.
3. It invokes EXE$FINISHIOC to complete the I/O request.

Later, when a completing read or write request returns buffer quota to the mailbox UCB, MBDRIVER invokes COM$DELATTNAST to queue the attention AST to the requesting process. The AST delivery is only an indication that room has potentially become available; the process must retry its write operation or use a sense mode request to determine how much room is left. For example, a room attention AST can be delivered when a zero-byte read completes, although very little room (one byte) has become available.

25.5.4.4   **Specifying Access Protection of a Mailbox.** When an image requests a set mode function to set the protection on a mailbox, MB$FDT_SETMODE takes the following steps:

1. It verifies that the requesting process either has BYPASS privilege or that

it has allocated the device by invoking EXE$CHKPRO_INT, in module EXESUBROUT.

2. It acquires the MAILBOX spinlock, raising IPL to IPL$_MAILBOX, to synchronize access to the UCB.

3. It sets the flag specifying that the standard system, owner, group, world protection mask is valid and moves the P2 argument of the $QIO request to the ORB's protection mask field, ORB$W_PROT.

4. It releases the MAILBOX spinlock and invokes EXE$FINISHIOC to complete the I/O request.

25.5.5 Mailbox Sense Mode Request Processing

A process can use the IO$_SENSEMODE function to request the driver to check whether at least one read or write channel is assigned to the mailbox. One, and only one, of the following modifiers may be specified:

▶ IO$M_READERCHECK—Check whether at least one read channel is assigned to the mailbox.

▶ IO$M_WRITERCHECK—Check whether at least one write channel is assigned to the mailbox.

When an image requests a sense mode function, MB$FDT_SENSEMODE, MBDRIVER's sense mode FDT routine, takes the following steps:

1. If this is a reader check request and the reader reference count is zero, the routine sets the return status as SS$_NOREADER. If this is a writer check request and the writer reference count is zero, it sets the return status as SS$_NOWRITER.

2. It acquires the MAILBOX spinlock, raising IPL to IPL$_MAILBOX, to synchronize access to the mailbox UCB's write request queue.

3. It loops through each message block on the queue to determine the total size in bytes of all the messages queued to the mailbox.

4. It releases the MAILBOX spinlock, restoring the previous IPL.

5. It invokes EXE$FINISHIOC to complete the I/O request with an IOSB, illustrated in Figure 25.8.

25.5.6 Mailbox Cancel I/O Routine

The mailbox driver's cancel I/O routine, MB$CANCEL, is invoked when an outstanding I/O request to a mailbox is canceled or when a process deassigns

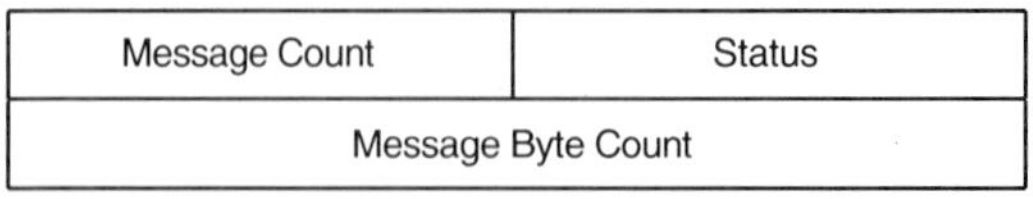

Message Count	Status
Message Byte Count	

Figure 25.8
Layout of Sense Mode IOSB

a channel to a mailbox. The routine performs three functions depending on the cancellation reason code: CANC_CANCEL, CANC_AMBXDGN, or CAN$C_DASSGN.

▶ For a reason code of CANC_CANCEL, MBCANCEL cancels the oldest outstanding I/O request and aborts all other outstanding I/O requests for a particular process and channel on a mailbox unit. It then flushes the mailbox's attention AST queues (see Chapter 8) and declares the resource RSN$_MAILBOX available if necessary.

▶ For a reason code of CAN$C_AMBXDGN, MB$CANCEL tests the bit UCB$V_DELMBX in UCB$L_DEVSTS. If it is set, MB$CANCEL synchronizes its access to the logical name table and deletes the mailbox logical name if one exists. It then deallocates all queued message blocks to nonpaged pool and sets the UCB$V_DELETEUCB bit in UCB$L_STS so that the UCB will be deleted when its reference count falls to zero.

▶ For a reason code of CANC_DASSGN, MBCANCEL performs all the functions associated with the CAN$C_CANCEL reason code. Additionally, MB$CANCEL checks whether the mailbox's reference count has fallen to zero. If so, it performs all the functions associated with the CAN$C_AMBXDGN reason code.

MBDRIVER also provides a selective cancel I/O routine, MB$SELECT_CANCEL, which cancels I/O requests corresponding to a specified list of IOSBs.

25.5.7   Mailbox Messages from Drivers

EXE$SNDEVMSG, in module MBDRIVER, builds a device-specific mailbox message and inserts it into a message queue. A device driver cannot assume process context and therefore cannot use the $QIO system service to write a message, for example, to the operator communication (OPCOM) process's mailbox. It invokes EXE$SNDEVMSG instead.

EXE$SNDEVMSG must be invoked at or below IPL$_MAILBOX. The driver provides its device UCB address, the address of a mailbox UCB to which to queue a message, and the type of message to create.

EXE$SNDEVMSG performs the following steps:

1. It verifies that the specified mailbox device is really a mailbox. If it is not, the routine returns the error status SS$_DEVNOTMBX.
2. It verifies that it was invoked at or below IPL$_MAILBOX. If not, it generates the fatal bugcheck SPLIPLHIGH.
3. It acquires the MAILBOX spinlock, raising IPL to IPL$_MAILBOX.
4. It determines the device name in the form *node$controller* by invoking IOC$CVT_DEVNAM, in module IOSUBNPAG. If IOC$CVT_DEVNAM returns an error status, EXE$SNDEVMSG generates the fatal bugcheck INCONSTATE.

5. In a temporary storage area, it constructs a device message block containing the message code, the target device unit number, and the target device name.

6. It invokes EXE$WRTMAILBOX, described in Section 25.5.8, to queue the message to the appropriate mailbox unit.

7. EXE$SNDEVMSG releases the MAILBOX spinlock and returns.

25.5.8   **Alternative Mailbox Write Request Processing**

EXE$WRTMAILBOX performs message block allocation and message queuing just as MB$FDT_WRITE does. However, it executes within the limitations of system context. In addition, it does not reference any IRP fields, so it is available to driver code that bypasses the $QIO system service and that has no IRP to describe its mailbox I/O request. System routines such as EXE$SNDEVMSG and EXE$SNDOPR invoke EXE$WRTMAILBOX to complete mailbox message processing.

EXE$WRTMAILBOX performs the following steps:

1. It verifies that it was invoked at or below IPL$_MAILBOX. If not, it generates the fatal bugcheck SPLIPLHIGH. If IPL is not at least IPL 2, it raises IPL to IPL 2.

2. It invokes EXE$ALONONPAGED to allocate nonpaged pool for the message block. If EXE$ALONONPAGED returns a failure status, EXE$WRTMAILBOX restores the previous IPL and returns the error status SS$_INSFMEM.

   If the message block was successfully allocated, EXE$WRTMAILBOX initializes it (see Figure 25.1) and copies the invoker's data buffer to it. It clears the message block's IRP address field because no IRP is associated with the request.

3. It acquires the MAILBOX spinlock, raising IPL to IPL$_MAILBOX.

4. It tests the UCB$V_DELETEUCB bit in UCB$L_STS to determine whether the mailbox has been marked for deletion. If it has, EXE$WRTMAILBOX releases the MAILBOX spinlock, invokes COM$DRVDEALMEM to deallocate the message block, and returns the error status SS$_NOSUCHDEV.

5. EXE$WRTMAILBOX determines how much buffer quota is left. If there is sufficient, it continues with step 6.

   If there is insufficient buffer quota for this message and there are no pending read requests, EXE$WRTMAILBOX releases the MAILBOX spinlock, invokes COM$DRVDEALMEM to deallocate the message block, and returns the error status SS$_MBFULL. If there are pending stream read requests, EXE$WRTMAILBOX processes the write request. Doing so will complete any pending stream read requests and release buffer quota.

6. If the message size exceeds the maximum permitted message size,

EXE$WRTMAILBOX releases the MAILBOX spinlock, invokes the routine COM$DRVDEALMEM to deallocate the message block, and returns the error status SS$_MBTOOSML.

7. It determines the current process's PID and stores it in the message block. Since EXE$WRTMAILBOX might be executing in system context, this PID is not necessarily relevant.

8. It increments the mailbox's message count and copies the value to UCB$L_DEVDEPEND.

9. Unless it had determined in step 5 that there is insufficient buffer quota, it decrements UCB$W_BUFQUO by the message size. If the message size is zero, it decrements UCB$W_BUFQUO by 1.

10. It inserts the message onto the mailbox's write request queue.

11. If the mailbox's read request queue is not empty, it invokes MB$FINISH-READ to complete one or more pending read requests. Otherwise, it invokes COM$DELATTNAST to deliver any queued write attention ASTs.

12. EXE$WRTMAILBOX releases the MAILBOX spinlock, restoring the previous IPL, and returns.

25.6   MAILBOX USE BY THE EXECUTIVE AND SYSTEM COMPONENTS

The executive uses mailboxes in a number of ways:

▶ A process establishes a termination mailbox to receive status information about a subprocess it creates. Chapters 27 and 31 give more information on termination mailboxes.

▶ A process can monitor error logging activity as it happens through the use of an error log mailbox. Chapter 35 describes the error log mailbox mechanism.

▶ When a process assigns a channel to a nonshareable device, it can request an associated mailbox to receive device status information such as the arrival of unsolicited input. The description of the Assign I/O Channel ($ASSIGN) system service in Chapter 23 provides more information.

When a process spawns a subprocess through the Digital command language (DCL) interpreter, DCL establishes a termination mailbox for the spawned subprocess. It also creates a mailbox to write logical names and symbol definitions to the subprocess and another mailbox to receive attach requests from the subprocess. Chapter 30 describes the use of these mailboxes in more detail.

The sections that follow describe the use of mailboxes to communicate with the job controller, OPCOM, the audit server, and the file system.

25.6.1   Job Controller Mailbox Use

The executive communicates with the job controller through the job controller's input mailbox, MBA1. Various modules in the executive pass information and requests to the job controller through this mailbox. System services that request information from the job controller, such as Send Job Controller ($SNDJBC) and Get Queue Information ($GETQUI), package some of their requests as mailbox messages. Unsolicited terminal input, connection manager notification that a node has left the VMScluster, and notification of process termination are all events communicated to the job controller though messages to MBA1.

INI$DEVICE_DATABASE, in module PERMANENT_DEVICE_DATABASE, stores the UCB address of MBA1 into the field SYS$AR_JOBCTLMB during system initialization. The mailbox is defined with a reference count of 1, which protects it from allocation and deletion.

The job controller's initialization routine uses the symbol SYS$C_JOBCTLMB, which has the value MBA1, to assign a channel to the input mailbox.

25.6.2 Operator Communication Process Mailbox Use

A device or process communicates with OPCOM, the operator communication process, through OPCOM's input mailbox, MBA2. INI$DEVICE_DATABASE stores the address of the OPCOM mailbox's UCB in SYS$AR_OPRMBX during system initialization. This mailbox is defined with a reference count of 1 and cannot be allocated or deleted.

OPCOM's initialization routine assigns a channel to its mailbox and sets the mailbox protection. It posts an initial mailbox read request, specifying the AST procedure READ_MAILBOX, in module [OPCOM]OPCOMMAIN.

The AST is triggered by a write to OPCOM's mailbox. The AST procedure allocates a work queue element, reads the OPCOM mailbox, and copies the data from the mailbox into the work queue element. It inserts the element into OPCOM's work queue, wakes the main loop, and reissues the mailbox read request.

The main loop services the work queue, reading messages from it and servicing each based on its function code. Most messages come through the Send Message to Operator ($SNDOPR) system service, although device online/offline messages, for example, are sent through EXE$SNDEVMSG.

25.6.3 Audit Server Mailbox Use

Communication with AUDIT_SERVER, the audit server process, occurs through the audit server mailbox, MBA3. During system initialization INI$DEVICE_DATABASE stores the UCB address of MBA3 into the field SYS$AR_AUDSRVMBX. The audit server's initialization routine assigns a channel to this mailbox and then posts an initial mailbox read request, specifying the AST procedure AUDSRV$QUEUE_MESSAGE, in module [AUDSRV]AUDSERVER.

[CLIUTL]SETAUDIT, which implements the DCL SET AUDIT command, passes information and requests to the audit server through this mailbox. It triggers the AST by writing to the mailbox. The AST procedure allocates a message queue element, reads the AUDIT_SERVER mailbox, and copies the data from the mailbox into the message queue element. It inserts the element on AUDIT_SERVER's work queue, wakes the main loop, and reissues the mailbox read request.

OPCOM's initialization routine also assigns a channel to the audit server mailbox. While security auditing is enabled, OPCOM inserts a message into the audit server mailbox whenever a security alarm is generated. The $NSADEF macro defines the format of both the security alarm messages and the SET AUDIT messages.

25.6.4 File System Bad Block Mailbox

File system initialization creates a permanent mailbox named ACP$BAD-BLOCK_MBX. This mailbox provides a path for communication with bad block recovery processes.

When a driver notifies the file system (through I/O postprocessing) of a suspected bad block, the file system flags the file header. When the file containing the detected bad block is deleted, another file system routine performs further processing. It assigns a channel to the bad block mailbox, writes a message to the mailbox indicating the device UCB and file ID number, and creates a process running the image BADBLOCK. The bad block process assigns a channel to the mailbox and reads the message for instructions. Chapter 26 gives more information on bad block processing.

25.7 RELEVANT SOURCE MODULES

Source modules described in this chapter include

> [AUDSRV]AUDSERVER.B32
> [F11X]INIFCP.B32
> [F11X]SNDBAD.B32
> [LIB]UCBDEF.SDL
> [OPCOM]OPCOMMAIN.B32
> [SYS]COMDRVSUB.MAR
> [SYS]MBDRIVER_HEADER.MAR
> [SYS]MBDRIVER.B32
> [SYS]PERMANENT_DEVICE_DATABASE.MAR
> [SYS]SYSMAILBX.MAR
> [SYS]SYSQIOFDT.MAR
> [SYS]UCBCREDEL.MAR

26 Miscellaneous I/O Topics

Lull'd in the countless chambers of the brain,
Our thoughts are link'd by many a hidden chain;
Awake but one, and lo, what myriads arise!
Each stamps its image as the other flies.

Alexander Pope

This chapter presents a number of I/O-related topics. The first few sections give a description of techniques used by selected device drivers that can help in understanding the OpenVMS AXP I/O subsystem. No attempt is made to discuss each device driver, nor is every feature of a particular driver described. The *OpenVMS I/O User's Reference Manual* provides detailed descriptions of the features and capabilities provided by each supported device driver.

This chapter also discusses other topics, such as counted resource management, controller register access mailbox (CRAM) support procedures, the virtual I/O cache, disk bad block processing, the Breakthrough ($BRKTHRU) system service, and other informational system services.

26.1 CLASS AND PORT DRIVERS

The operating system uses a layered approach for certain device drivers. The functional layer, called the class driver, handles operations on a certain class of device, such as disk, tape, or terminal. The communications layer, called the port driver, handles operations that depend on the protocol and hardware used to communicate with the actual device and controller.

OpenVMS AXP class and port device drivers include the following (names listed are image file names without the .EXE file type):

- The terminal class driver, SYS$TTDRIVER
- Terminal port drivers, such as SYS$LTDRIVER, SYS$OPDRIVER, and SYS$YRDRIVER
- The Mass Storage Control Protocol (MSCP) disk class driver, SYS$DUDRIVER
- The Small Computer System Interconnect (SCSI) disk class driver, SYS$DKDRIVER
- The tape MSCP (TMSCP) class driver, SYS$TUDRIVER
- The SCSI tape class driver, SYS$MKDRIVER
- System communication services (SCS) port drivers, such as SYS$PNDRIVER and SYS$PEDRIVER
- Digital Storage Systems Interconnect (DSSI) port drivers, such as SYS$PIDRIVER

▶ SCSI port drivers, such as SYS$PKCDRIVER, SYS$PKJDRIVER, and SYS$PKZDRIVER

In each case, the class driver is bound to a specific port driver through a system data structure. Through this binding, the class driver is able to invoke port driver routines in a generic fashion, and vice versa.

For example, using the following MACRO-32 statement, the MSCP disk class driver invokes a port-specific routine to send a message over the port:

```
JSB @PDTVEC$L_SENDMSG(R4)
```

In this example, the binding data structure is the port descriptor table (PDT), which contains pointers to port-specific subroutines. Usually, there is a port-specific subroutine for each well-defined function, such as sending a message over the port or receiving one. A port driver is really a set of port-specific subroutines for one or more class drivers.

Both the MSCP disk class driver and the TMSCP tape class driver support devices that communicate using a Digital protocol known as systems communication architecture (SCA). Figure 26.1 shows a conceptual diagram of SCA, and Section 26.1.1 briefly describes it.

SCSI disk and tape class drivers implement many of the same features as their MSCP counterparts; however, they use a different protocol to communicate with the controllers. SCSI drivers are not discussed in this book.

The terminal class and port drivers differ substantially from the other drivers and are discussed in Section 26.2.

26.1.1   OpenVMS AXP Implementation of SCA

SCA defines a communications layer and the external interface to that layer. The OpenVMS AXP implementation of SCA is known as SCS. The executive image SYS$SCS.EXE implements the port-independent part of SCS. An SCA port driver implements the port-dependent part of SCS on a specific port device. OpenVMS AXP SCA port drivers include the following:

▶ SYS$PNDRIVER, for computer interconnect (CI) adapters such as CIXCD

▶ SYS$PUDRIVER, for an adapter such as the KDM70, which supports Digital's proprietary storage system port (SSP) architecture

▶ SYS$PEDRIVER, which implements SCA over the network interconnect (NI), either Ethernet or Fiber Distributed Data Interconnect (FDDI)

▶ SYS$PIDRIVER for DSSI controllers, which are integrated with disks such as the RF30 and RF71

An SCA class driver uses SCS as a communications medium for some higher level functions or protocols. A class driver implements the functional layer and performs operations on a user-visible device without regard for the SCA communications transport used.

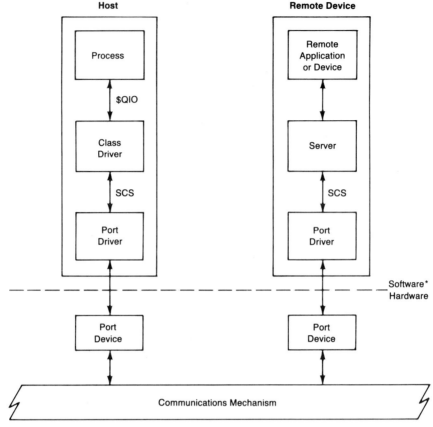

Host

Process

$QIO

Class
Driver

SCS

Port
Driver

Remote Device

Remote
Application
or Device

Server

SCS

Port
Driver

Software*
Hardware

Port
Device

Port
Device

Communications Mechanism

*It is possible for the remote device to implement the port driver and server in hardware.

Figure 26.1
Conceptual Diagram of Systems Communication
Architecture

Currently there are two protocols in the function layer that call SCS to
communicate information:

▶ MSCP, a general protocol designed to describe all types of disk operation. It
is implemented by controllers for Digital Storage Architecture (DSA) disks,
such as the KDM70 and the HSC70, and by the software MSCP server
supplied with the OpenVMS AXP operating system. The MSCP disk class
driver is SYS$DUDRIVER.

▶ TMSCP, a general tape protocol designed to describe all types of tape operations. It is implemented by controllers for DSA tape drives, such as the
TA78, TA81, and TA90. The TMSCP class driver is SYS$TUDRIVER.

The disk class driver can communicate to an MSCP server through any
SCA port driver. Similarly, the tape class driver can use any SCA port driver
to communicate to a TMSCP device.

26.1.2   **I/O Processing**

To perform I/O through a class and port driver, a user application must first assign a channel to the class driver. The application can then request I/O operations on that channel.

The following sequence shows how a process on a host system communicates information to a remote device through an SCA class and port driver.

1. The process on the host system requests an I/O operation of a class driver. The Queue I/O Request ($QIO) system service validates the I/O request, describes it in an I/O request packet (IRP), and passes the IRP to the class driver.

2. The class driver translates portions of the IRP to an MSCP request. Parameters of the MSCP request include the following:

   • Unit number of the device
   • Function code, for example read or write, of the operation requested
   • Starting logical block number
   • Number of bytes to transfer

   The class driver then initializes fields in a class driver request packet (CDRP). A CDAP contains information necessary for SCS operations. Figure 26.2 shows the layout of a CDRP. As a convenience to the $QIO/class driver interface, a CDRP is designed to be an extension of an IRP.

3. The class driver then invokes SCS to transmit the MSCP request to the MSCP server.

4. The SCS operations are interpreted by the port driver, which then communicates the I/O request to a remote port driver.

5. The remote port driver passes the request to the MSCP server.

6. The server acts on the MSCP request and passes the I/O request to the remote application or device.

26.2   **TERMINAL DRIVER**

The terminal driver is made up of one class driver and a number of device-specific port drivers. The terminal class driver consists of device-independent routines for terminal I/O processing. A terminal port driver contains routines that are specific to the actual transmission and reception of characters on a particular type of hardware. This section presents a brief overview of terminal I/O processing.

Note that the terminal class and port drivers do not communicate using the SCS protocol, nor do the terminal port devices conform to the SCA standards. The terminal class driver, SYS$TTDRIVER, contains function decision table (FDT) routines and other device-independent routines. The port drivers contain interrupt service routines and other controller-specific subroutines. The logical components of the terminal I/O subsystem are illustrated in Figure 26.3.

885

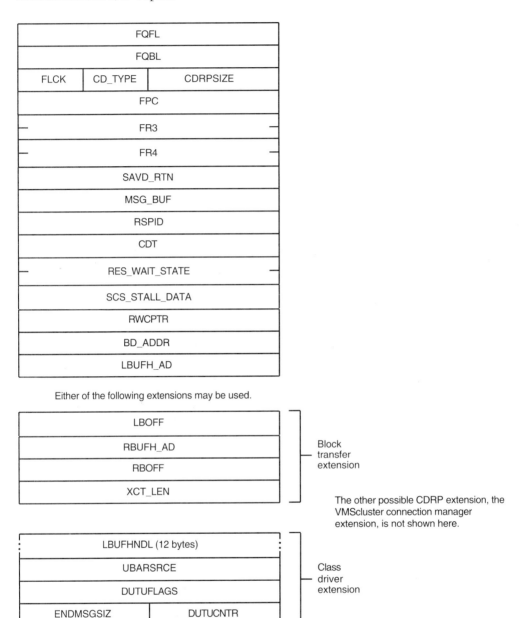

Figure 26.2
Layout of a Class Driver Request Packet (CDRP)

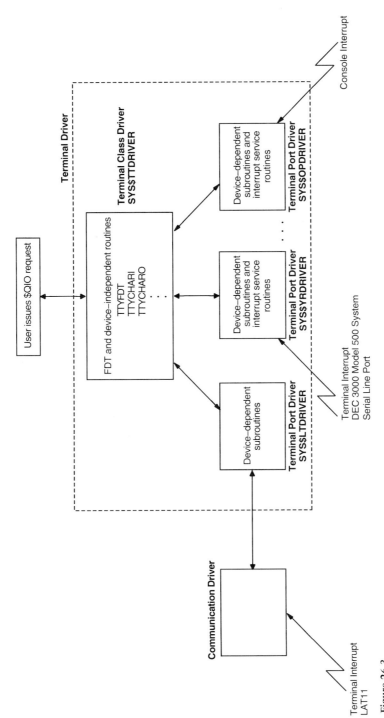

Figure 26.3
Terminal I/O System

The class and port driver images are separate images. Support for a new terminal controller can be added in a new port driver. The following port drivers are currently supplied:

► SYS$YRDRIVER for certain serial line controllers
► SYS$OPDRIVER, the console port driver
► SYS$LTDRIVER, the local area terminal port driver (see Section 26.2.4)

When the system is bootstrapped, the secondary bootstrap program, SYS-BOOT, loads SYS$OPDRIVER, the console port driver image. Later, the executive initialization routine EXE$INIT, in module INIT, loads the terminal class driver, SYS$TTDRIVER, and creates the necessary linkages between the terminal class driver and the console port driver. The device-specific extension of a terminal unit control block (UCB) contains pointers to the class and port vector dispatch tables. EXE$INIT locates the address of the dispatch tables for the two drivers and stores them in the console UCB.

Later in system initialization, autoconfiguration code identifies the terminal controllers present and loads the appropriate port drivers. The controller and unit initialization routines of these port drivers initialize the UCB extensions.

The relations among the terminal class driver, console port driver, and the console UCB are shown in Figure 26.4, as an example of how the terminal class driver and its various port drivers are bound together.

The SYSGEN parameter TTY_CLASSNAME is initialized with the prefix SYS$ followed by the next two ASCII characters of the terminal class driver name to be loaded by SYSBOOT. This facilitates the debugging of new terminal class driver images. If a new terminal class driver image contains errors that prevent the system from completing its initialization sequence, TTY_CLASSNAME can be set conversationally to the first two ASCII characters of an alternative terminal class driver image during a system reboot. Digital does not support user-written alternative terminal class drivers.

26.2.1 Full-Duplex Operation

The terminal driver implements partial full-duplex operation by default. Full-duplex operation is based upon an alternate start I/O routine entry point to the terminal class driver. Whenever a write request is issued to a full-duplex terminal, the write FDT routine TTY$FDTWRITE, in module [TTDRVR]TTYFDT, allocates and initializes a write buffer packet to describe the write request. It then invokes EXE$ALTQUEPKT, in module SYSQIOREQ, to enter the driver's alternate start I/O routine.

Normally, an FDT routine invokes EXE$QIODRVPKT, in module SYS-QIOREQ, to enter the driver's start I/O routine. EXE$QIODRVPKT tests whether the driver is already active for that unit. If the unit is already busy,

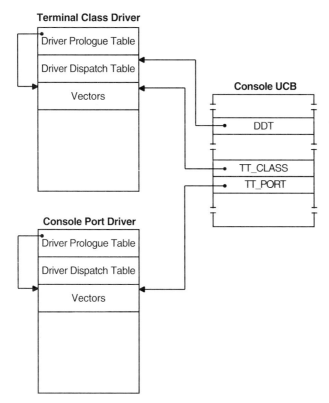

Figure 26.4
Terminal Driver Initialization

EXE$QIODRVPKT queues the IRP to the UCB rather than entering the start I/O routine.

EXE$ALTQUEPKT differs from EXE$QIODRVPKT as follows:

▶ It does not test the UCB busy flag. The flag may be set as the result of a read request in progress. Full-duplex operation means that a read request can be interrupted by a write request.

▶ It does not clear the UCB$V_CANCEL and UCB$V_TIMOUT bits in UCB$L_STS because they may be in use by the current IRP for a read request.

▶ It does not copy the SVAPTE, BCNT, and BOFF fields from the IRP to the UCB because this would affect the current I/O operation if the UCB were busy.

▶ It enters the alternate start I/O routine in the driver rather than the regular start I/O routine.

Chapter 24 gives more information on EXE$QIODRVPKT and EXE$ALT-QUEPKT.

TTY$WRTSTARTIO, in module [TTDRVR]TTYSTRSTP, is the alternate start I/O routine entry point. It obtains the device spinlock to synchronize with the interrupt service routine, raising interrupt priority level (IPL) to device IPL, and processes the packet as follows:

1. If a write is currently in progress, it queues the write buffer packet.
2. If a read operation or a read with prompt operation is in progress but the I/O function modifier specifies write breakthrough (IRP$V_BREAK-THRU), it starts the write operation.
3. If a read is occurring but no read data has echoed yet, it starts the write operation.
4. Otherwise, it queues the write buffer packet to the UCB.

To complete a write I/O request for full-duplex operation, the driver's start I/O routine exits by invoking routine COM$POST, in module COM-DRVSUB. COM$POST places the IRP on the systemwide I/O postprocessing queue, requests an IPL$_IOPOST software interrupt (on the primary CPU, if this is a symmetric multiprocessing system), and returns. A traditional driver issues the REQCOM macro to complete an I/O request. REQCOM invokes IOC$REQCOM, in module IOSUBNPAG.

IOC$REQCOM is avoided for full-duplex write requests because it would attempt to initiate processing of the next IRP queued to the UCB while there is still an active IRP. However, all read requests and half-duplex writes are terminated through IOC$REQCOM (see Chapter 24), so that the next request of this type can be processed in the normal fashion.

In full-duplex operation, the device can expect more than one interrupt at a time, one for a read request and one for a write request. Therefore, two fork program counters (PCs) must be stored. A traditional driver expects only one interrupt at a time and stores the fork PC in UCB$L_FPC. The terminal driver stores more than one fork PC by altering the value of R5, which normally points to the UCB, to point to the write buffer packet or the IRP before invoking the FORK macro.

A fork block is thereby formed in the write buffer packet or in the IRP. The fork block in the UCB is not used for read or write requests, although it is used at other times, for example, when a type-ahead buffer is allocated or when unsolicited input is being handled.

Any number of outstanding I/O requests could be handled by a driver entered at the alternate start I/O routine entry point. The driver, however, must be able to distinguish which interrupt is associated with which fork block and synchronize I/O operations. Such a driver might maintain queues for outstanding I/O requests and operate almost exclusively at device IPL, as the terminal port drivers do, blocking out device interrupts to achieve synchronization with multiple I/O request processing.

26.2.2   **Type-Ahead Buffer**

SYS$TTDRIVER allocates a type-ahead buffer from nonpaged pool for each terminal device. Every character typed on the terminal is placed into this buffer whether a read request is active or not, unless the terminal is set /PASTHRU and a read request is active. This ensures that characters typed at a terminal are not lost even if there is no application at the moment to read them.

The size of the type-ahead buffer is usually specified by the SYSGEN parameter TTY_TYPAHDSZ. This is the systemwide default and applies to all terminals that do not have the TT2$V_ALTYPEAHD characteristic. If the terminal has the characteristic TT2$V_ALTYPEAHD, then the SYSGEN parameter TTY_ALTYPAHD specifies the type-ahead buffer size.

If the terminal has been set /HOSTSYNC (using the Digital command language (DCL) command SET TERM/HOSTSYNC), then when the buffer is within eight characters of being full, the driver sends an XOFF character to the terminal to tell it to stop sending data. If the terminal has the alternative size type-ahead buffer, the SYSGEN parameter TTY_ALTALARM is the threshold for determining when to send an XOFF. When the buffer is emptied, the driver sends an XON character to the terminal to tell it to start sending data. This technique prevents loss of characters during block I/O transmission from high-speed terminals.

26.2.3   **Virtual Terminal Support**

A process that is associated with a virtual terminal device rather than a physical terminal can freely break and reestablish its connection to the virtual terminal. A virtual terminal device is associated with a physical terminal by the terminal driver upon process login. The connection between a physical terminal and the virtual terminal may be broken by a line disconnect caused by modem signals or broken local area transport (LAT) terminal server communication, or by the DCL DISCONNECT command. This section explains how the terminal driver implements virtual terminal support.

When a terminal device that is not associated with any process receives unsolicited input, SYS$TTDRIVER forks to invoke the routine UNSOL, in module [TTDRVR]TTYSUB. UNSOL notifies the job controller of such an occurrence by sending a message to the job controller's permanent mailbox. The message contains the unsolicited data and the name of the terminal device. The name of the device can be that of the physical device or that of a virtual terminal, which is created by UNSOL.

If the terminal that received unsolicited data has the TT2$V_DISCON-NECT characteristic and if the device VTA0 exists on the system, UNSOL invokes CLONE_UCB, in module [TTDRVR]TTYSUB, to create a virtual device corresponding to the physical terminal.

CLONE_UCB clones the UCB for the virtual device from the UCB for VTA0. The virtual device is called VTA*n*, where *n* is the unit number. The virtual device UCB has a pointer, UCB$L_TL_PHYUCB, to the physical device's UCB. Similarly, the physical device's UCB has a pointer, UCB$L_TT_LOGUCB, to the virtual device's UCB.

UNSOL then passes the terminal device UCB to the job controller along with the unsolicited data notification.

When the job controller receives notification of unsolicited data on an unowned terminal, it creates a detached process running LOGINOUT.EXE, which begins a login session at the specified terminal. Chapter 27 provides more information on process creation by the job controller.

SYS$TTDRIVER FDT routines operate on the terminal UCB regardless of whether it is a physical or a virtual terminal. For a virtual terminal in a disconnected state, SYS$TTDRIVER queues any I/O requests to the UCB.

SYS$TTDRIVER's start I/O routine gets the physical device's UCB from offset UCB$L_TL_PHYUCB in the device UCB on which it operates. For a physical terminal, UCB$L_TL_PHYUCB points to itself (that is, the physical terminal's UCB). SYS$TTDRIVER's alternate start I/O routine operates in the same manner.

26.2.4 Local Area Transport Terminal Server Support

Support for a LAT terminal server such as the LAT11 is implemented in the framework of the same terminal port/class driver model. The terminal driver treats a LAT terminal device as a physical terminal device. A LAT terminal device has a name of the form LTA*n*, where *n* is the unit number. SYS$LTDRIVER, the driver for LAT terminal ports, interacts with SYS$TTDRIVER through the terminal driver port/class interface.

26.2.5 Remote Terminals

DECnet allows users to log in on a remote OpenVMS system and perform operations on that remote system just as they would at the local system. The communication from the remote system to the controlling terminal is performed through a pseudo device on the remote system called a remote terminal. The driver for remote terminals is SYS$CTDRIVER.

Although the focus here is on DECnet communication between two OpenVMS AXP systems, the discussion is equally applicable to DECnet communication between an OpenVMS AXP system and a VAX system running VAX/VMS Version 4 or later. If the remote VAX system is running a version of VAX/VMS earlier than Version 4, a different protocol and a remote terminal driver named SYS$RTTDRIVER are used on the AXP system.

In addition to DECnet, three images are required to support remote terminals: the local system uses the image RTPAD.EXE; the remote system uses the images REMACP.EXE and SYS$CTDRIVER.EXE. REMACP.EXE is created from modules in facility [REM]. SYS$CTDRIVER.EXE and RTPAD.EXE are created from modules in facility [RTPAD].

A user on a local system logs in on a remote system as follows:

1. When a user on a local system issues the DCL command SET HOST, DCL runs the image RTPAD.EXE.
2. RTPAD uses DECnet to request a connection to a network object on the specified node. On a remote OpenVMS system, the object is REMACP.
3. The image REMACP.EXE, running on the remote system in the REMACP process, creates a UCB for the remote terminal device whose name is of the form RTAn, where n is the unit number.
4. REMACP returns information about the remote system to RTPAD.

    Using the information returned from REMACP, RTPAD determines which operating system is communicating with the local system. RTPAD has routines for communicating with a number of different Digital operating systems, including RSTS/E, RSX-11M, TOPS-20, OpenVMS AXP, and OpenVMS VAX.
5. REMACP links the UCB into the driver tables by invoking SYS$CTDRIVER's unsolicited input service routine.
6. SYS$CTDRIVER sends a message to the job controller's mailbox, located through the global location SYS$AR_JOBCTLMB, indicating that an unsolicited interrupt was received from the remote terminal.
7. The job controller creates a detached process running LOGINOUT on terminal RTAn. The user can now log in to the remote system.

RTPAD converts all I/O requests on the user's local terminal to messages it sends over the DECnet link. SYS$CTDRIVER does the same for all I/O requests on the remote terminal. The protocol for the exchange of messages between RTPAD and SYS$CTDRIVER is proprietary to Digital.

When the user logs off from the remote system, REMACP deletes the remote terminal UCB.

26.3   PSEUDO DEVICES

The OpenVMS AXP operating system supports a number of virtual devices, also called pseudo devices, including

- Null device, NL:
- Network devices, NETn:
- Virtual terminal devices, VTAn:
- Remote terminal devices, RTAn:
- Mailboxes, MBAn:

where n is the unit number.

A user assigns a channel to a pseudo device and issues I/O requests as though it were a real device. Chapter 25 discusses mailboxes. Section 26.2

discusses remote terminals and virtual terminals. The following sections highlight some features of the device drivers for other pseudo devices.

26.3.1 Null Device Driver

The null device driver, NLDRIVER, is assembled and linked with the executive image SYSDEVICE.EXE. It is a simple driver, consisting of two FDT routines, one to complete read requests and one to complete write requests. The read FDT routine responds to read requests by returning the status SS$_ENDOFFILE. The write FDT routine responds to write requests by returning the status SS$_NORMAL. No data is transferred, nor are any privilege or quota checks made.

26.3.2 Network Device Driver

The network device, NET:, is a mechanism for DECnet users to access network functions. An image requests the Assign I/O Channel ($ASSIGN) system service to assign a channel to the NET: device. The system service procedure clones a network UCB from the NET0: template device, giving it a new unit number to produce a unique device name, such as NET100:. The assigned channel points to the newly created UCB. This channel can then be used to perform access, control, and other I/O operations on the network. When the image deassigns the last channel to the network UCB, the UCB is deleted. Chapter 23 describes this system service in more detail.

The following images are used for network communication:

- The network device driver, NETDRIVER
- NETACP.EXE, running in the network ancillary control process, NETACP
- Network communication device drivers

NETDRIVER creates links to other systems, performs switching and routing functions, breaks user messages into manageable pieces for transmission, and reassembles the messages on reception. An appropriate communication device driver performs the actual I/O operations. For example, SYS$FCDRIVER performs network communications for TURBOchannel FDDI adapters.

NETACP performs the following tasks:

- Creates processes to accept inbound connects
- Parses network control blocks and supplies defaults when a user issues an IO$_ACCESS function code to create a logical link
- Transmits and receives routing messages to maintain a picture of the network
- Maintains the volatile network database

NETDRIVER and other communication drivers support two I/O request interfaces:

▸ The $QIO interface is standard and works as it would for any driver.

▸ Internal IRPs are built by kernel mode modules, such as other device drivers, and passed to the driver's alternate start I/O interface. This interface bypasses the $QIO system service, which performs a number of validation checks considered unnecessary at this level.

For example, SYS$CTDRIVER, the remote terminal driver, uses NET-DRIVER's internal IRP interface in network communication. NETDRIVER passes I/O requests to a lower level device driver such as SYS$FCDRIVER through the internal IRP interface.

Figure 26.5 illustrates some network I/O functions. The *DECnet for Open-VMS Networking Manual* and the *DECnet for OpenVMS Network Management Utilities* manual provide more information on DECnet.

<table>
<tr><td>26.4</td><td>

CONTROLLER REGISTER ACCESS MAILBOX SUPPORT ROUTINES

</td></tr>
</table>

Chapter 2 describes the two models of device interface register access on Alpha AXP systems: direct access and hardware mailbox access. It also describes the structure and use of a hardware mailbox. This section describes the use of hardware mailboxes, CRAMs, and the CRAM support mechanism.

Invented initially to facilitate hardware mailbox access for device drivers, the CRAM support mechanism can now also be used by drivers to access device interface registers without regard to the underlying access model. The present description assumes that the underlying model is hardware mailbox access, although, for the most part, it is valid for direct access also.

Each hardware mailbox structure is part of a CRAM data structure (see Figure 22.11). A CRAM also contains pointers to a few associated data structures and some fields that allow the efficient management of CRAMs. The macro $CRAMDEF defines offsets within the CRAM structure.

To access a device interface register through a hardware mailbox, a device driver fills in the hardware mailbox with a CRAM command and other appropriate information. Then the driver writes the physical address of the hardware mailbox into the mailbox pointer register (MBPR). Writing to the MBPR triggers an associated I/O adapter to perform the desired access.

A CRAM command is an interconnect-specific command to read or write to an I/O space location (see Chapter 2). Each interconnect has an associated table of CRAM command definitions that is initialized by interconnect-specific initialization code. CRAM command indices offer a uniform way of describing device interface register access for most interconnects. The adapter control block (ADP) associated with an interconnect contains a pointer to the CRAM command table for the interconnect.

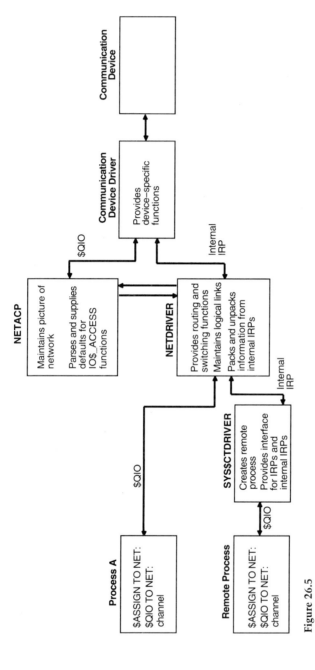

Figure 26.5
Processing Network I/O Requests

896

The executive provides support procedures for device interface register access:

- ▶ IOC$ALLOCATE_CRAM—To allocate and initialize a CRAM
- ▶ IOC$DEALLOCATE_CRAM—To deallocate a CRAM
- ▶ IOC$CRAM_CMD—To initialize target interconnect-specific fields of the CRAM
- ▶ IOC$CRAM_QUEUE—To queue a CRAM for a mailbox operation and return
- ▶ IOC$CRAM_WAIT—To wait for the completion of a queued mailbox operation or timeout
- ▶ IOC$CRAM_IO—To queue a CRAM for a mailbox operation and wait for its completion

IOC$ALLOCATE_CRAM and IOC$DEALLOCATE_CRAM are in module CRAM-ALLOC, and the remaining procedures are in module [SYSLOA] CRAM-IO. MACRO-32 macros such as CRAM_IO and CRAM_QUEUE generate calls to these procedures. On a system that supports direct access, such as a DEC 3000 system, a different set of procedures, typically in module [CPU*xxyy*]IO_SUPPORT_*xxyy*, is called to perform interface register access. Appendix G contains more information on the system designator *xx* and the CPU designator *yy*.

A device driver can follow one of the following models of CRAM use:

- ▶ It can preallocate a CRAM for each device register. A MACRO-32 driver can specify two new parameters, UCB_CRAMS and IDB_CRAMS, in the driver prologue table macro (DPTAB) invocation. UCB_CRAMS specifies the number of CRAMs to be preallocated to a unit when a new unit's UCB is created. Similarly, IDB_CRAMS specifies the number of CRAMs to be preallocated to a controller when an IDB is created. A preallocated CRAM is linked to the UCB or the IDB, as appropriate.
- ▶ If there are a large number of device registers, a driver can preallocate a CRAM for each type of access, for example, one CRAM for every read access and another for every write access.
- ▶ A driver can dynamically allocate a CRAM for each device register access. An error register that is rarely accessed, for example, can be accessed in this manner. This method is not used for performance-sensitive accesses, however.

26.5 DEVICE DRIVER COUNTED RESOURCE MANAGEMENT

A driver fork process can allocate and deallocate device resources such as map registers through a set of generic OpenVMS AXP counted resource management procedures. Device drivers supplied with the system normally use these procedures only for managing map registers; however, the procedures can manage any other resource with similar allocation characteristics.

897

The counted resource management procedures operate on two data structures: the counted resource allocation block (CRAB) and the counted resource context block (CRCTX), described in detail in *OpenVMS AXP Device Support: Creating a Step 1 Driver from an OpenVMS VAX Device Driver.*

A CRAB describes a counted resource, such as a set of map registers available on an I/O adapter, that needs to be shared among cooperating driver fork or kernel processes. The initialization routine for an I/O adapter that has such a resource allocates the CRAB from nonpaged pool and initializes it. Among other things, a CRAB contains

- The number of resource items
- An array of descriptors that record the location and length of a set of available contiguous resource items
- The allocation granularity
- The head of a wait queue of CRCTXs that describe unsatisfied resource requests

A CRCTX describes a specific request for a counted resource. A driver calls an executive procedure to create a CRCTX before it makes an allocation request. Among other things, a CRCTX contains

- The number of items of the resource requested
- A fork block in which to store the context of a requesting fork process, should the request be stalled
- The procedure value of a callback routine to be invoked when a stalled request is granted

A driver fork process typically calls counted resource management procedures to perform direct memory access (DMA) in the following manner:

1. It calls IOC$ALLOC_CRCTX, in module ALLOC_CNT_RES, to allocate a CRCTX from nonpaged pool and initialize it.
2. It calls IOC$ALLOC_CNT_RES, in module ALLOC_CNT_RES, to allocate map registers, passing it as arguments the CRAB and the CRCTX. IOC$ALLOC_CNT_RES performs the following steps:

   a. It acquires the dynamic spinlock associated with the CRAB.
   b. If this is a high-priority request, or no other thread is waiting for map registers associated with the CRAB, it attempts to allocate the requested map registers immediately.

      If allocation fails for a high-priority request, IOC$ALLOC_CNT_ RES proceeds with step d.
   c. For a normal-priority request, if allocation fails because of an insufficient number of map registers being available, IOC$ALLOC_CNT_ RES does the following.

If the requestor specified a callback routine, IOC$ALLOC_CNT_
RES saves the thread's fork process context in the CRCTX, inserts
the CRCTX at the tail of the CRAB's wait queue, and proceeds with
step d. Later, another driver fork process will release map registers
associated with the CRAB by calling IOC$DEALLOC_CNT_RES.
IOC$DEALLOC_CNT_RES will resume the driver thread that was
suspended by IOC$ALLOC_CNT_RES.

If the requestor did not specify a callback routine, IOC$ALLOC_
CNT_RES simply proceeds to the next step.

    d. IOC$ALLOC_CNT_RES releases the dynamic spinlock associated
with the CRAB and returns the allocation status to its caller.

3. The driver fork process calls IOC$LOAD_MAP, in module [SYSLOA]
MISC_SUPPORT, to load the allocated map registers.

4. It sets up appropriate device interface registers to initiate device activity.

5. It calls IOC$DEALLOC_CNT_RES, in module ALLOC_CNT_RES, to
deallocate the map registers.

6. It calls IOC$DEALLOC_CRCTX, in module ALLOC_CNT_RES, to de-
allocate the CRCTX.

The preceding description assumes that a driver allocates and deallocates
map registers dynamically as required. Depending on the availability of map
registers and the performance requirements, a driver might allocate map
registers permanently rather than on a per-request basis.

A driver kernel process can call the counted resource management support
procedures also, provided that the process itself ensures that its context is
saved and restored appropriately.

26.6   THE VIRTUAL I/O CACHE

Since VAX/VMS Version 4, the Files-11 extended $QIO processor (XQP) has
maintained a cache of logical blocks, known as the buffer cache, containing
file system information, such as file headers and directory files. The XQP's
buffer cache trades off virtual memory for increased speed in accessing file
system information.

The virtual I/O cache, or data cache, introduced in OpenVMS VAX Version 6 and OpenVMS AXP Version 1.5, trades off physical memory for increased speed in reading data from disk files. It provides transparent caching
of data for any application that performs virtual I/O to read and write data
files from a disk, subject to the restriction that the cache will be invalidated
whenever logical I/O is performed to the same disk. (The disk can also be a
Files-11 On-Disk Structure Level 2 format compact disk read-only memory.)
Virtual I/O caching is disabled for page files, swap files, and any executable
image file that is writable. Since the virtual I/O cache caches virtual disk
blocks, it is sometimes called the virtual block number (VBN) cache.

The virtual I/O cache is write-through: a virtual block that is modified is immediately written back to the disk. This provides for reliable operation but also implies that the virtual I/O cache improves performance only for read operations.

The executive image SYS$VCC.EXE implements support for the virtual I/O cache. Its routines are invoked by various parts of the executive:

▶ The XQP routines that perform file operations such as access (open), deaccess (close), mount, and dismount operations invoke CACHE$ACCESS, CACHE$DEACCESS, CACHE$MOUNT, and CACHE$DISMOUNT, in module VCC_FILE.

▶ The file system FDT routines that support virtual block I/O, namely ACP$READBLK and ACP$WRITEBLK, in module SYSACPFDT, invoke CACHE$QIO, in module VCC_CACHE.

▶ I/O postprocessing code invokes CACHE$IOPOST, in module VCC_CACHE, if virtual I/O caching is enabled. CACHE$IOPOST invalidates the virtual I/O cache for a disk on which a logical write operation has been performed.

The file control block (FCB) of a file whose data is being cached contains a pointer to the cache file control block (CFCB), the primary virtual I/O cache substructure. The CFCB points to other virtual I/O cache-related data structures. The MMG spinlock synchronizes access to the virtual I/O cache data structures; used in this way, it is also called the CACHE spinlock.

The SYSGEN parameter VCC_FLAGS controls whether virtual I/O caching is enabled. Its default value of 1 enables caching. The SYSGEN parameter VCC_MAXSIZE specifies the number of disk blocks that can be simultaneously cached. Its default value is 6,400 disk blocks, which is equivalent to 3.2 MB of memory. The initialization routine for the SYS$VCC.EXE executive image allocates physical memory for the cache based on VCC_MAXSIZE, up to a maximum of half the size of physical memory.

On an OpenVMS VAX system, the virtual I/O cache is a clusterwide cache. On an OpenVMS AXP Version 1.5 system, the virtual I/O cache is disabled when the system joins or forms a VMScluster.

The DCL command SHOW MEMORY/CACHE/FULL displays virtual I/O cache statistics.

26.7 BAD BLOCK PROCESSING ON DISKS

26.7.1 Static Bad Block Handling

A non-DSA disk is typically tested to detect bad blocks before the disk is put into use. Each cluster containing a bad block is allocated to a special file called [000000]BADBLK.SYS, so that the bad blocks cannot be allocated to user files. (The smallest unit of file system allocation is the disk cluster.) This is known as static bad block handling. As the disk is used, additional blocks may become bad. Dynamic bad block handling deals with those blocks.

26.7.2 Dynamic Bad Block Handling

Dynamic bad block handling is a cooperative effort among driver FDT routines, I/O postprocessing, and the XQP. FDT routines for IO$_READVBLK and IO$_WRITEVBLK construct an IRP and set the IRP$V_VIRTUAL bit in IRP$L_STS. When the I/O postprocessing routine discovers a transfer error on a virtual I/O function, it routes the IRP to the XQP.

The XQP, using information in the IRP, calculates the bad block address and stores that information in the file [000000]BADLOG.SYS. This file contains a list identifying suspected bad blocks on the volume that are not currently contained in the volume's bad block file. In addition, the XQP sets a bit in the FCB to indicate the presence of a bad block and returns an error status to the requesting process. When the file is closed, an equivalent bit is set in the file's header on disk.

When such a file is deleted, the XQP creates a process running the image BADBLOCK.EXE to diagnose the file. It writes worst-case test patterns over the blocks of the file and reads them back, comparing the data to the original pattern. If a bad block is found, the image uses privileged file system functions to allocate the disk cluster containing the block to the bad block file [000000]BADBLK.SYS;1. In addition, the entry in the [000000]BADLOG.SYS file that describes this bad block is removed.

Note that a dynamic bad block is not discovered until it is already part of a file and is not allocated to the bad block file until that file is deleted.

Dynamic bad block handling is restricted to virtual I/O functions (that is, file I/O). Processes performing logical or physical I/O functions must provide their own bad block handling. Dynamic bad block handling is performed only for non-DSA disks.

26.7.3 Bad Block Replacement on DSA Disks

A DSA disk maintains a given set of logical block numbers (LBNs) regardless of bad blocks. It maintains a number of spare blocks that are used as replacement blocks for LBNs that are detected to be bad. If the disk controller detects that a given LBN has a nonrecoverable error, it initiates a procedure known as bad block replacement (BBR). BBR remaps the bad LBN to a good replacement block.

None of the disk controllers supported on OpenVMS AXP systems requires host assistance for BBR, unlike some of the older controllers, such as the KDM50, supported on OpenVMS VAX systems.

A forced error flag is associated with each block on a DSA disk. When a read operation to a DSA disk block results in a nonrecoverable error, the block is reassigned to a replacement block on the disk and the forced error flag for this block is set. The forced error flag is a signal that the data in the block is questionable. When a block with this flag set is read, the driver returns the error status SS$_FORCEDERROR to the requestor of the I/O operation. A subsequent successful write to the block clears the forced error flag.

Note that it is possible to have blocks assigned to [000000]BADBLK.SYS;1 on a DSA disk. This happens, for example, when the disk size in blocks is odd, and the disk cluster size is even. (The cluster size of a disk is the minimum unit of allocation on a disk in blocks and is specified by the DCL command INITIALIZE/CLUSTER_SIZE.) In that case, one or more of the last blocks on the disk become unusable.

26.7.4 Bad Block Replacement on SCSI Disks

The SCSI disk class driver (SYS$DKDRIVER) performs bad block replacement for SCSI disks. However, there is no forced error flag associated with SCSI disk blocks.

When a read operation to a SCSI disk results in a nonrecoverable error, the SCSI disk class driver returns the status SS$_PARITY to the requestor of the I/O operation. BBR does not occur for this block. This is because BBR at this point would result in undetected user data corruption, since there is no forced error flag associated with SCSI disk blocks.

The file system then performs the same bad block processing discussed in Section 26.7.2.

26.8 $BRKTHRU SYSTEM SERVICE

The $BRKTHRU system service sends a specified message to one or more terminals. All its eleven arguments except the MSGBUF argument are optional:

- ▶ The number of the event flag to be set when the message has been written to the specified terminals, the EFN argument
- ▶ The message buffer containing the text that is to be written, the MSGBUF argument
- ▶ The name of the terminal or user name to which to send the text, the SENDTO argument
- ▶ The type of terminal to which to send the message, the SNDTYP argument
- ▶ The address of an I/O status block (IOSB) that will receive the I/O completion status of the $BRKTHRU system service, the IOSB argument
- ▶ The carriage control to be used with the message, the CARCON argument
- ▶ Options for the $BRKTHRU system service, the FLAGS argument
- ▶ The class requestor identification, which identifies the application or image that is requesting the $BRKTHRU system service, the REQID argument
- ▶ The number of seconds that must elapse before an attempted write by the $BRKTHRU system service is considered to have failed, the TIMOUT argument

▶ The address of the AST procedure to be executed after the message has been sent to the specified terminals, the ASTADR argument

▶ The AST parameter to be passed to the AST procedure specified by the ASTADR argument, the ASTPRM argument

The $BRKTHRU system service procedure, EXE$BRKTHRU in module SYSBRKTHR, runs in kernel mode. Its processing consists of three major steps:

1. It allocates a breakthrough message descriptor block (BRK) from the P1 space process allocation region, initializes it, and stores the formatted message in it, as discussed in Section 26.8.1. The $BRKTDEF macro defines the layout of the BRK (see Figure 26.6).

2. It initiates a write to a given terminal, as discussed in Section 26.8.2.

3. It responds to the completion of a given write, as discussed in Section 26.8.3.

EXE$BRKTHRU sends two types of messages: the unformatted, user-specified message and the screen message. The screen message is a formatted version of the user-specified message that is sent to video terminals. It consists of the following fields, which are mainly escape sequences that envelop the message:

▶ Escape sequences to save the cursor's position and attributes, position it in column 1 of the correct line, and erase to the end of the line.

▶ One escape sequence for every line to be erased. The number of lines to be erased is specified by the low byte of the FLAGS argument.

▶ The text specified by the MSGBUF argument.

▶ An escape sequence to restore the cursor position and attributes.

26.8.1 Initial Processing

EXE$BRKTHRU begins by clearing the event flag specified by the EFN argument. Since the EFN argument is passed by value, it defaults to zero. If an IOSB is specified, EXE$BRKTHRU verifies that the caller has write access to it and clears it.

It verifies the accessibility of the message buffer specified by the MSGBUF argument.

It computes the size of the BRK needed for the request as the sum of the following items, rounded up to an integral number of longwords:

▶ The basic size (BRK$C_LENGTH) of the BRK

▶ Space for the name of the terminal to which to send the mailbox message (16 bytes)

▶ The size of the unformatted message

▶ Space for the screen message (208 bytes plus the size of the unformatted message)

▶ Space for four $QIO context areas

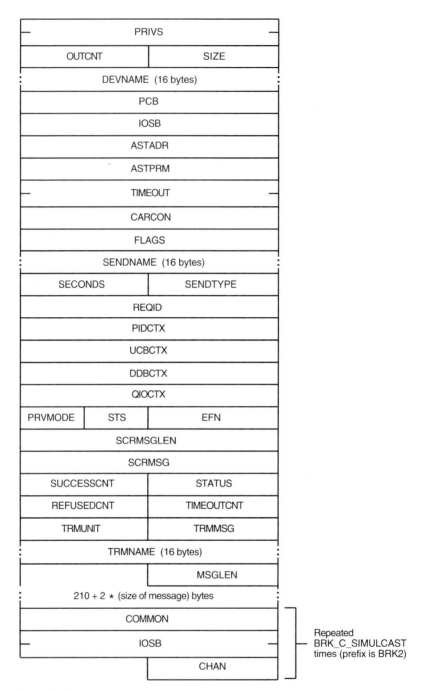

Figure 26.6
Layout of a Breakthrough Message Descriptor Block (BRK)

Table 26.1   Meanings of the SNDTYP and SENDTO Arguments

SNDTYP	SENDTO	Comments
BRK$C_USERNAME	User name	Send message to a single user
BRK$C_DEVICE	Device name	Send message to a specific device
BRK$C_ALLUSERS	—	Send message to all users
BRK$C_ALLTERMS	—	Send message to all devices

It allocates space from the process allocation region in P1 space for the BRK and initializes it as follows:

1. It clears the BRK from BRK$Q_PRIVS up to BRK$T_MSGBUF.
2. EXE$BRKTHRU stores the size of the BRK in BRK$W_SIZE.
3. It locks the entire BRK structure in the process's working set through the Lock Pages in Working Set ($LKWSET) system service.
4. It stores the address of the $QIO context area in BRK$L_QIOCTX.
5. It stores the length of the screen message in BRK$L_SCRMSGLEN.
6. It stores the address of the requestor's PCB in BRK$L_PCB.
7. EXE$BRKTHRU stores the address of the IOSB in BRK$L_IOSB.
8. It stores the length of the unformatted message in BRK$W_MSGLEN and then copies the unformatted message text to the buffer starting at BRK$T_MSGBUF.
9. It stores the address of the first byte after the message in BRK$L_SCRMSG. It will store the screen message at this address.
10. It validates the SNDTYP argument.
11. EXE$BRKTHRU sets up the BRK to reflect the SNDTYP and SENDTO arguments. Table 26.1 explains the meanings of these arguments.

    - If the SNDTYP argument is BRK$C_USERNAME or BRK$C_DEVICE, EXE$BRKTHRU invokes EXE$PROBER_DSC, in module [SYS]EXSUBROUT, to verify the accessibility of the user name or device specified by the SENDTO argument.
    - If the SNDTYP argument is BRK$C_USERNAME, it copies the SENDTO argument to BRK$T_SENDNAME and compares it with the current user name. If the two names are equal, it has completed this step. If they are not equal, it verifies that the process has OPER privilege.
    - If the SNDTYP argument is BRKC_DEVICE, EXEBRKTHRU requests the Get Device/Volume Information ($GETDVI) system service to get the physical name of the device. EXE$BRKTHRU copies the name returned to BRK$T_DEVNAM and sets BRK$V_CHKPRV in BRK$B_STS to indicate that it should check the process's privilege to send to the specified device at a later step.
    - If the SNDTYP argument is either BRK$C_ALLUSERS or BRK$C_ALLTERMS, EXE$BRKTHRU verifies that the process has OPER privilege.

12. If the TIMOUT argument was specified, EXE$BRKTHRU ensures that it is at least BRK_C_MINTIME (4 seconds). It converts the argument to clock ticks and stores the resulting quadword in BRK$Q_TIMEOUT.

13. It stores the default VMScluster timeout value BRK_C_CLUTIMEOUT (15 seconds) in BRK$W_SECONDS.

14. EXE$BRKTHRU determines whether the sender has the privileges to access the target terminal. If the sender has the BYPASS and SHARE privileges, the sender can access the terminal. If not, then if the sender has either of the OPER or WORLD privileges, the sender can access the terminal; in this case, EXE$BRKTHRU will later temporarily enable the BYPASS and SHARE privileges for the sender (see Section 26.8.2.4). Note that the privileges are required even when the sender and the target terminal's owner are the same.

    In this step, EXE$BRKTHRU stores a privilege mask in BRK$Q_PRIVS. The mask has at most two set bits, those corresponding to the BYPASS and SHARE privileges. The mask specifies which privilege or privileges the process does not have.

15. It copies the remaining $BRKTHRU arguments to the BRK.

16. It verifies that the REQID argument is less than or equal to 63.

17. It stores the success status SS$_NORMAL in BRK$W_STATUS.

18. It stores the mailbox prefix code MSG$_TRMBRDCST in BRK$W_TRMMSG. Note that the BRK contains a mailbox message in fields BRK$W_TRMMSG through the end of the unformatted message stored at BRK$T_MSGBUF.

19. It stores the access mode from which the $BRKTHRU service was requested in BRK$B_PRVMODE.

20. It stores –1 in BRK$L_PIDCTX as the wildcard PID that will be an argument to the Get Job/Process Information ($GETJPI) system service later.

21. It requests the Formatted ASCII Output ($FAO) system service to format the message. $FAO stores the length of the screen message in BRK$L_SCRMSGLEN and the screen message at the address in BRK$L_SCRMSG. At this point, the BRK contains the unformatted message starting at BRK$T_MSGBUF and the screen message immediately following it. BRK$L_SCRMSGLEN and BRK$L_SCRMSG constitute a descriptor for the screen message.

EXE$BRKTHRU is now ready to send messages. It does so as follows:

1. It requests the Set AST Enable ($SETAST) system service to disable delivery of kernel mode ASTs. This is necessary to prevent image exit before the CCB$V_IMGTMP bit is set in the channel control block (CCB) of the channel through which EXE$BRKTHRU will write to a terminal. This is discussed in further detail in Section 26.8.2.4.

2. It attempts to initiate BRK_C_SIMULCAST (four) message writes, as discussed in Section 26.8.2.

3. If the system is a VMScluster node and the BRK$V_CLUSTER flag was specified in the $BRKTHRU request, EXE$BRKTHRU invokes EXE$CSP_BRKTHRU, in module [SYSLOA]CSPCLIENT, to send a clusterwide process service (CWPS) message to all other nodes in the VMScluster system. The CLUSTER_SERVER process on each of the other nodes responds to such a message by invoking CSP$BRKTHRU, in module [SYSLOA]CSPBRKTHR. CSP$BRKTHRU requests the $BRKTHRU system service to broadcast the message on that system. Chapter 14 provides more information on the CWPS mechanism.

4. If all writes have been completed, EXE$BRKTHRU deallocates the BRK, as described in Section 26.8.3.3.

5. It requests the $SETAST system service to reenable kernel mode AST delivery.

The asynchronous form of the system service, $BRKTHRU, returns to its requestor. Its requestor can either wait for I/O completion or continue processing. The synchronous form of the system service, $BRKTHRUW, waits for the event flag associated with the request to be set and status to be returned. Chapter 7 contains more information on synchronous and asynchronous system services.

26.8.2   Writing the Breakthrough Message

EXE$BRKTHRU takes two major steps when it attempts to initiate writing a message: selecting the next terminal to which to write, and starting the actual I/O operation. If it does not find a terminal to which to write, it skips the second of these. Each time it finds an acceptable terminal UCB, it initiates a write.

The steps EXE$BRKTHRU takes to find the next terminal depend upon the SNDTYP argument.

26.8.2.1   Finding a Specific Terminal.
If the SNDTYP argument was BRKC_DEVICE, EXEBRKTHRU has already found the terminal when it requested the $GETDVI system service to initialize the BRK. All that it does now is set BRK$V_DONE in BRK$B_STS.

26.8.2.2   Finding All Terminals for a Specific User.
If the SNDTYP argument was BRK$C_USERNAME, EXE$BRKTHRU must find all terminals on which the given user is logged in. It accomplishes this by finding all processes belonging to that user and the terminal, if any, associated with each of those processes.

EXE$BRKTHRU requests the $GETJPI system service to perform a wildcard operation. On each $GETJPI request, EXE$BRKTHRU requests the user name and the name of the process's login terminal. Each time $GETJPI returns, EXE$BRKTHRU verifies that the process is an interactive process and belongs to the correct user. If the process does not meet these criteria, EXE$BRKTHRU requests $GETJPI to get information about the next process.

Once EXE$BRKTHRU finds an interactive process belonging to the correct user, it invokes IOC$SEARCHDEV, in module IOSUBPAGD, to locate the UCB and the device data block (DDB) for the terminal. EXE$BRKTHRU then verifies that the UCB and the device it describes meet the following criteria:

- It is a terminal UCB.
- It is available.
- It is not a network device, a spooled device, or a detached terminal.
- It does not have the broadcast class specified by the REQID argument disabled.
- It does not have broadcasts disabled or pass-all enabled unless there is a broadcast mailbox associated with the UCB.

If the UCB does not meet these criteria, EXE$BRKTHRU requests the $GETJPI service to get information about the next process.

If the UCB meets these criteria, EXE$BRKTHRU verifies that the requestor has the privilege to access the device. If BRK$V_CHKPRIV in BRK$B_STS is clear, no further check is necessary. Otherwise, EXE$BRKTHRU verifies that at least one of the following conditions is met:

- The sender process's PID matches the owner PID, UCB$L_PID, of the terminal.
- The process is a descendant of the owner of the UCB. EXE$BRKTHRU follows the process control block (PCB) process owner chain until it finds a process whose PID matches the device owner. If the end of the process owner chain is reached without a match, then the next condition must be met.
- The process has OPER privilege.

If the process has the necessary privilege to access the device, EXE$BRK-THRU invokes IOC$CVT_DEVNAM, in module IOSUBNPAG, to convert the device name to the form *ddcn* and store the name starting at BRK$T_DEVNAM + 1. EXE$BRKTHRU stores the length of the name in BRK$T_DEVNAM, the unit number in BRK$W_TRMUNIT, and the contents of DDB$T_NAME in BRK$T_TRMNAME.

26.8.2.3 **Finding All Terminals and All Users.** If the SNDTYP argument was BRK$C_ALLTERMS or BRK$C_ALLUSERS, EXE$BRKTHRU must find all terminals on the system. It does this by invoking IOC$SCAN_IODB, in module IO-SUBNPAG, to find each UCB in the system.

Any invoker of IOC$SCAN_IODB must pass a DDB and UCB address to it at each invocation. From this context IOC$SCAN_IODB determines where to start its search of the I/O database. If the addresses are zero, it starts at the beginning of the I/O database.

EXE$BRKTHRU passes IOC$SCAN_IODB the addresses in BRK$L_UCB-CTX and BRK$L_DDBCTX. These fields were cleared when the BRK was initialized. EXE$BRKTHRU stores the results from invoking IOC$SCAN_IODB in these fields. Each time IOC$SCAN_IODB finds a UCB, it returns a success status. When IOC$SCAN_IODB reaches the end of the I/O database, it returns a failure status.

After each successful call to IOC$SCAN_IODB, EXE$BRKTHRU makes sure that the UCB is acceptable:

▶ It must be a terminal UCB.
▶ It must be online.
▶ If the terminal is not allocated, the terminal must not be set autobaud.

If the UCB is not acceptable, EXE$BRKTHRU invokes IOC$SCAN_IODB again to get another UCB. If IOC$SCAN_IODB finds another UCB, EXE$BRKTHRU checks that UCB. EXE$BRKTHRU continues this loop until it gets an acceptable UCB or all UCBs have been found. When all UCBs have been found, EXE$BRKTHRU sets BRK$V_DONE in BRK$B_STS.

26.8.2.4   **Performing the Breakthrough I/O.** EXE$BRKTHRU now has in the BRK the information necessary to send the message to a specific terminal. It takes the following steps to send the message:

1. If TT2$V_BRDCSTMBX in UCB$L_DEVDEPND2 is set and UCB$L_AMB is nonzero, EXE$BRKTHRU invokes EXE$WRTMAILBOX, in module MBDRIVER, to write the message to the associated mailbox. Note that the BRK contains the message already formatted for the mailbox write starting at BRK$W_TRMMSG.

2. It verifies that broadcasts to the terminal are not disabled and that the terminal is not in pass-all mode. There are two reasons for checking these bits now. If they were checked earlier, they could have changed since the earlier check was performed. If the terminal has an associated mailbox, EXE$BRKTHRU did not check these bits earlier.

3. If BRK$Q_PRIVS is nonzero, EXE$BRKTHRU requests the Set Privilege ($SETPRIV) system service to enable the privileges specified by BRK$Q_PRIVS. The process temporarily acquires BYPASS and SHARE privileges if it does not already have them.

4. It requests the $ASSIGN system service to assign a channel to the terminal UCB, with the CHAN argument specifying BRK2$W_CHAN. If BRK$Q_PRIVS is nonzero, after the $ASSIGN system service completes EXE$BRKTHRU requests $SETPRIV to disable the privileges specified by BRK$Q_PRIVS.

5. It sets CCB$V_IMGTMP in the CCB of the channel just assigned to ensure that the channel will be deassigned if the image exits before EXE$BRKTHRU completes (see Chapter 28). As a result, SYS$RUN-

DWN will deassign this channel on image exit if the channel has not been deassigned previously.

6. It requests the $QIO system service to write the message to the terminal. Note that each concurrent write uses a different $QIO context area. Since there are four such areas, only four writes can be outstanding at any one time. The following arguments are specified:

- If BRK$V_SCREEN was specified in the FLAGS argument and TT2$V_DECCRT in UCB$L_DEVDEPND2 is set, the screen message is written. The message length is the value in BRK$L_SCRMSGLEN; the message is the one at the address stored in BRK$L_SCRMSG; the carriage control is a zero.

  Otherwise, the unformatted message is written. The message length is the value in BRK$W_MSGLEN; the message is the one stored at BRK$T_MSGBUF; the carriage control is the value in BRK$L_CARCON.

- The channel is the one specified by BRK2$W_CHAN.
- The IOSB is the one at BRK2$Q_IOSB.
- The AST procedure address is QIO_DONE, in module SYSBRKTHR. This procedure is discussed in Section 26.8.3.2.
- The AST parameter is the address of the $QIO context area, BRK2$L_COMMON.
- The function code is write virtual block, with the refresh, cancel CTRL/O, and breakthrough modifiers.
- The event flag is BRK_C_QIOEFN (31).

7. EXE$BRKTHRU increments BRK$W_OUTCNT to reflect another outstanding write request.

8. If the TIMOUT argument was specified, EXE$BRKTHRU requests the Set Timer ($SETIMR) system service, specifying QIO_TIMEOUT, in module SYSBRKTHR, as the AST procedure to be called when the timer expires and the value in BRK$Q_TIMEOUT as the time. QIO_TIMEOUT is discussed in Section 26.8.3.1.

EXE$BRKTHRU has now initiated writing the breakthrough message to a given terminal.

26.8.3   Completion Actions

EXE$BRKTHRU performs the following actions related to completion:

▸ It responds to the expiration of a timer.
▸ It responds to the completion of a write to a terminal.
▸ It checks for completion of the $BRKTHRU system service.

It performs the first two within AST procedures. It performs the last in a subroutine.

26.8.3.1   **Timer Expiration.** If the timer expires before the I/O completion AST is executed, the executive calls the AST procedure QIO_TIMEOUT with an argument that is the address of the $QIO context area. QIO_TIMEOUT requests the $CANCEL system service to cancel the write request. This will result in QIO_DONE being invoked as part of completing the I/O request; any further processing required will be performed by QIO_DONE.

26.8.3.2   **I/O Completion AST.** The I/O completion AST procedure, QIO_DONE, is called when the I/O operation requested via the $QIO system service completes. Its one argument is the address of the $QIO context area for the completed write. QIO_DONE takes the following steps:

1. If BRK$Q_TIMEOUT is nonzero, it requests the Cancel Timer ($CANTIM) system service to cancel the timer requested via the $SETIMR system service. Note that the timer may have expired already.
2. It requests the $DASSGN system service to deassign the channel.
3. It decrements BRK$W_OUTCNT to reflect the completion of the write request.
4. It attempts to initiate another write operation by taking the steps described in Section 26.8.2.
5. It then checks for completion of the $BRKTHRU request by taking the steps described in Section 26.8.3.3.

26.8.3.3   **Completion Checks.** CHECK_COMPLETE is invoked to check for completion of the $BRKTHRU request:

1. It checks BRK$W_OUTCNT. If it is nonzero, there is at least one write request outstanding, and CHECK_COMPLETE exits.
2. It stores the final status in the IOSB if the requestor specified an IOSB.
3. If the $BRKTHRU request specified a completion AST, CHECK_COMPLETE requests the Declare AST ($DCLAST) system service, specifying the AST procedure and parameter recorded in the BRK.
4. It requests the Set Event Flag ($SETEF) system service to set the specified event flag.
5. It requests the Unlock Pages from Working Set ($ULWSET) system service to unlock the BRK from the working set.
6. Finally, it deallocates the BRK to the P1 allocation region.

26.9   **DEVICE INFORMATION SYSTEM SERVICES**

Images frequently require information about particular devices on the system. Device information can be characterized as device-dependent or device-independent.

Device-independent information is present for each device on the system. Its interpretation is the same for all devices. It is obtained by reading fields in the UCB that are present for all devices on the system. Examples include the device unit number, UCB$W_UNIT; device characteristics, UCB$L_DEVCHAR; and the device type, UCB$B_DEVTYPE.

The interpretation of device-dependent information varies from device to device. Examples include the information contained in the fields UCB$L_DEVDEPEND and UCB$L_DEVDEPND2. It can also be information that is present only for certain devices, such as the logical UCB address in a physical terminal UCB, UCB$L_TT_LOGUCB.

Each device has primary and secondary device characteristics. These two sets of characteristics are identical unless one of the following conditions holds:

▶ If the device has an associated mailbox, the primary characteristics are those of the assigned device and the secondary characteristics are those of the associated mailbox.

▶ If the device is spooled, the primary characteristics are those of the intermediate device and the secondary characteristics are those of the spooled device.

▶ If the device represents a logical link on the network, the secondary characteristics contain information about the link.

The OpenVMS AXP operating system provides several system services to obtain specific information about a particular device. This section describes the $DEVICE_SCAN system service, which returns the names of all devices that match a set of search criteria, and the $GETDVI system service, which can return most information contained in UCB fields that are common to all devices, including certain device-dependent information, such as that in UCB$L_DEVDEPEND.

The $QIO system service can obtain device-dependent information that is not available through the $GETDVI system service. Two function codes, IO$_SENSEMODE and IO$_SENSECHAR, can request a device driver to return device-dependent information to the caller. The specific information returned depends on the device. The *OpenVMS I/O User's Reference Manual* contains details about what information is returned by specific OpenVMS AXP device drivers.

26.9.1 $DEVICE_SCAN System Service

The $DEVICE_SCAN system service searches for devices that match user-specified search criteria. The search criteria, specified in an item list, include the device type, the device class, and the wildcarded device name.

In response to an initial request, the $DEVICE_SCAN system service searches for the first occurrence of a device that matches the search criteria. It maintains context information so that on subsequent $DEVICE_SCAN requests, it can return other matching device names, until no more matching devices exist. At that time, the service returns the error status SS$_NOMOREDEV.

$DEVICE_SCAN arguments include the following:

► The address of a buffer in which $DEVICE_SCAN returns the name of a matching device

► A location to contain the length of the returned device name

► The name of a device for which to search, which can include the standard wildcard characters

► The address of an item list, in which each entry includes an item code, an input buffer address and length, and a reserved field

► The address of a context quadword, initially zeroed, where $DEVICE_SCAN maintains search context information across service requests

The $DEVICE_SCAN system service procedure, EXE$DEVICE_SCAN in module SYSGETDVI, executes in kernel mode. It performs the following operations:

1. It checks each item in the item list for correctness: its item code must be valid; its buffer descriptor and buffer must be readable. The $DVS-DEF macro defines two legal item codes, one indicating that the buffer contains a device class (defined by the $DCDEF macro) and one indicating that the buffer contains a device type (also defined by $DCDEF) for which to search.

2. It restores the search context information, either zeros on the first service request or the unit number and the DDB of the matching device located in the previous search.

3. It invokes SCH$IOLOCKR, in module MUTEX, which raises IPL to 2 to prevent process deletion and locks the I/O database mutex for read access. Thus, the structure of the I/O database cannot change until $DEVICE_SCAN unlocks the mutex. Chapter 22 describes the I/O database.

4. EXE$DEVICE_SCAN invokes IOC$SCAN_IODB_USRCTX, in module IOSUBNPAG, which sequentially scans the I/O database. EXE$DEVICE_SCAN tests each returned device and reinvokes IOC$SCAN_IODB_USRCTX if the device type and class do not match the search criteria.

5. Otherwise, it invokes IOC$CVT_DEVNAM, in module IOSUBNPAG, to convert the matching device's name and unit number to a physical device name string. If the device allocation class is nonzero and the device is file-oriented, it returns a string of the form $*DeviceAllocation-Class*$ddC*n*, where *dd* is the device name, *C* is the controller designation, and *n* is the unit number. Otherwise, it returns a string of the form *VMSclusterNodeName*$ddC*n*.

6. If the user specified a device name in the search criteria, EXE$DEVICE_SCAN invokes EXE$MATCH_NAME, also in module IOSUBNPAG, to perform the wildcard comparison.

7. When it locates a device that matches all criteria, EXE$DEVICE_SCAN returns its device name and length to the requestor after storing the unit number and DDB address in the context block and unlocking the I/O database mutex, lowering IPL to 0.

26.9.2 $GETDVI System Service

The $GETDVI system service can obtain device-independent information about a device. It can also return a device's primary and secondary characteristics. It is requested with the following arguments:

- The event flag number to set when the request completes
- The identifier of an I/O channel assigned to the device
- The device name (possibly obtained via the $DEVICE_SCAN system service), used if no channel identifier is specified
- The address of an item list, each entry of which includes an item code, the size and address of a buffer to receive information, and a location to store the size of the information returned
- An IOSB to receive final status information
- The procedure value and parameter for an AST procedure to call when the request completes
- A place-holding null argument

The $GETDVI system service procedure, EXE$GETDVI in module SYS-GETDVI, executes in kernel mode. It performs the following operations:

1. EXE$GETDVI clears the specified event flag.
2. It checks the IOSB, if specified, for write access and clears the IOSB.
3. It checks and charges the process's AST quota if AST notification is requested. If the AST quota is insufficient, it returns the error status SS$_EXASTLM.
4. If a channel identifier is specified, EXE$GETDVI verifies the channel and obtains the UCB of the device accessed on the channel. It invokes SCH$IOLOCKR to lock the I/O database mutex for read access.
5. Otherwise, if a device name is specified, EXE$GETDVI invokes SCH$IO-LOCKR to lock the I/O database mutex for read access and invokes IOC$SEARCHDEV, in module IOSUBPAGD, to search the I/O database for the specified device and return the addresses of the device UCB and DDB.

   If the request is for secondary device characteristics, EXE$GETDVI locates the appropriate structures at this point.
6. For each item, EXE$GETDVI performs the following:

   a. It checks each item in the item list for correctness: its item code must be valid; its buffer size, buffer, and return length must be readable or writable as appropriate.

    b. It processes the item code, locating the appropriate structure and off-set and copying the desired information into the user buffer.

7. EXE$GETDVI unlocks the I/O database mutex.

8. It sets the specified event flag by invoking routine SCH$POSTEF, in module POSTEF.

9. It stores a status value in the IOSB, if specified.

10. If the user requested AST notification, EXE$GETDVI requests the $DCLAST system service to queue the ACB as a completion AST and returns.

11. If the user did not request AST notification, EXE$GETDVI returns.

26.10   RELEVANT SOURCE MODULES

Source modules described in this chapter include

    [LIB]BRKTDEF.SDL
    [SYS]ALLOC_CNT_RES.BLI
    [SYS]CRAM-ALLOC.MAR
    [SYS]SYSBRKTHR.MAR
    [SYS]SYSGETDVI.MAR
    [SYSLOA]CRAM-IO.MAR
    [TTDRVR]TTYFDT.MAR
    [TTDRVR]TTYSTRSTP.MAR
    [TTDRVR]TTYSUB.MAR

PART VII / Life of a Process

27   Process Creation

All things in the world come from being.
And being comes from non-being.

Lao-tzu, *Tao Tê Ching*

This chapter describes the phases in which a new process is created: creation in the context of an existing process, new process inswap, and finally, initialization in the context of the new process.

27.1   OVERVIEW

The creation of a new process takes place in several phases:

1. Creation begins in the context of an existing process that requests the Create Process ($CREPRC) system service. The $CREPRC system service performs the following steps:

   a. It makes privilege and quota checks.

   b. It allocates and initializes the process control block (PCB); the job information block (JIB), unless it is creating a subprocess; and the process quota block (PQB). Explicit $CREPRC arguments and implicit parameters are taken from the context of the creator.

   c. It places the data structures describing the new process into the scheduler database.

2. The initial scheduling state of the new process is computable outswapped (COMO). Thus, execution of the new process is suppressed until the swapper process moves the new process into the balance set. The following steps are performed in the context of the swapper process:

   a. The swapper moves the template for the new process context into the balance set from the executive image SHELLxK (the shell), where x is 8, 16, 32, or 64, the system's page size in kilobytes.

   b. It builds the process header (PHD) according to the values of SYSGEN parameters for this configuration.

   c. It requests that the new process be scheduled for execution.

3. The final steps of process initialization take place in the context of the new process in the routine EXE$PROCSTRT. EXE$PROCSTRT performs the following steps:

   a. It copies the arguments from the PQB to the PHD and various locations in P1 space, converting pagelets to units of pages as necessary.

   b. It requests the image activator to activate the image that was specified in the $CREPRC request.

   c. It calls the image at its entry point.

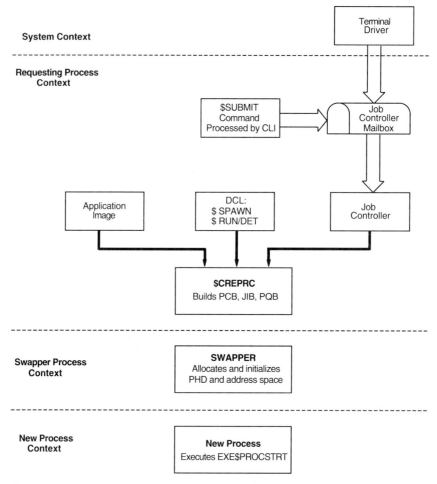

Figure 27.1
Process Creation

Figure 27.1 shows these phases of process creation and the context within which each phase occurs.

The Portable Operating System Interface (POSIX) creates a minimal process in response to the fork() POSIX system call. Support for this is implemented by EXE$CRE_MIN_PROCESS, in module SYSCREPRC, and by EXE$PSX_FORK_PROCSTRT, in module POSIX_ROUTINES, in addition to some procedures described in this chapter. A description of the minimal process or its implementation is outside the scope of this book.

27.2 $CREPRC SYSTEM SERVICE

The $CREPRC system service establishes the parameters of the new process. Some of these parameters are passed to the system service by the requestor.

The system service copies others from the context of the requestor: the requestor's PCB, PHD, JIB, and P1 space (see Figure 27.2).

The $CREPRC system service can copy information to the PCB or the JIB of the new process but cannot access its PHD or P1 space because neither exists at this stage of process creation. It stores the parameters to be copied to the PHD or P1 space in the PQB, a temporary data structure, until the new process comes into existence and has a virtual address space and a PHD. Table 27.1 lists the contents of the PQB.

27.2.1 **Control Flow of the $CREPRC System Service**

The $CREPRC system service procedure, EXE$CREPRC in module SYSCRE-PRC, runs in kernel mode. It performs the following steps:

1. It verifies that the address specified in the PIDADR argument is accessible to the mode from which EXE$CREPRC was requested. If not, it returns the error status SS$_ACCVIO.

2. It creates either a top-level process, detached from its creator, or a sub-process, attached to its creator's job tree. EXE$CREPRC's actions depend on the UIC argument and the PRC$V_DETACH bit in the STSFLG argument.

   • If the requestor specified a nonzero UIC argument, EXE$CREPRC creates a top-level process. The process is further classified as interactive, network, batch, or detached based on EXE$CREPRC's STSFLG argument.

   • If the UIC argument is zero, the default, and the requestor did not set the PRC$V_DETACH bit in the STSFLG argument, EXE$CREPRC creates a subprocess.

   • If the UIC argument is zero, the default, but the requestor set the PRC$V_DETACH bit in the STSFLG argument, EXE$CREPRC creates a top-level, detached process with the same user identification code (UIC) as that of the requestor.

   EXE$CREPRC tests whether the specified UIC is zero or the same as that of the requestor. If it is, no privilege is necessary to create a top-level process. Otherwise, the requestor needs either the DETACH or CMKRNL privilege. If the requestor requested creation of a top-level process without the necessary privilege, EXE$CREPRC returns the error status SS$_NOPRIV.

3. EXE$CREPRC raises interrupt priority level (IPL) to 2 and allocates a PCB from nonpaged pool. Next, it allocates a PQB from either the PQB lookaside list or paged pool, and completely zeros it except for its header. Chapter 21 describes nonpaged pool, paged pool, and the PQB lookaside list.

   EXE$CREPRC remains at IPL 2 or above from this point to prevent process deletion and the loss of allocated but unrecorded memory. If

921

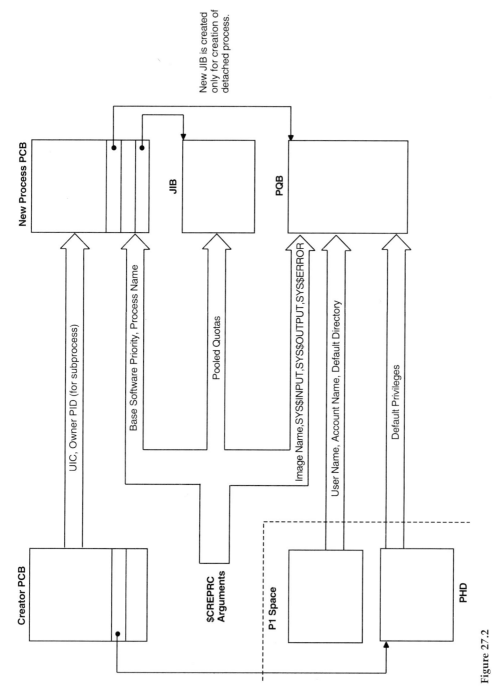

Figure 27.2
Sample Movement of Parameters in Process Creation

922

Table 27.1 Contents of the Process Quota Block

Item	Size (bytes)	Units
Privilege mask	8	–
Size of PQB	2	Bytes
Type code	1	–
Status	1	–
AST limit	4	ASTs
Buffered I/O limit	4	Requests
Reserved	4	–
CPU time limit	4	10-ms intervals (soft ticks)
Direct I/O limit	4	Requests
Reserved	16	–
Working set quota	4	Pagelets
Working set default	4	Pagelets
Lock limit	4	Locks
Working set extent	4	Pagelets
Logical name table quota	4	Bytes
Flags	2	–
Default message flags	1	–
Reserved	1	–
Authorization file flags	4	–
Process creation flags	4	–
Minimum authorized security class	20	–
Maximum authorized security class	20	–
SYS$INPUT attributes	4	–
SYS$OUTPUT attributes	4	–
SYS$ERROR attributes	4	–
SYS$DISK attributes	4	–
CLI image name	32	–
CLI command table name	256	–
Spawn CLI image name	32	–
Spawn CLI command table name	256	–
Equivalence name for SYS$INPUT	256	–
Equivalence name for SYS$OUTPUT	256	–
Equivalence name for SYS$ERROR	256	–
Equivalence name for SYS$DISK	256	–
Default directory string	256	–
Image name	256	–
Account name	8	–

an error occurs, EXE$CREPRC deallocates the PCB, PQB, and JIB (if necessary) before returning the error status to the requestor.

4. JIB initialization differs for top-level processes and subprocesses:

   • If EXE$CREPRC is creating a top-level process, it allocates a JIB from nonpaged pool. It initializes the JIB's jobwide list of mounted volumes as an empty list, then copies the account and user name fields from the creating process's JIB and zeros the JIB to its end.

- If EXE$CREPRC is creating a subprocess, no JIB allocation is necessary; the subprocess shares its creator's JIB. EXE$CREPRC increments JIB$L_PRCCNT, the count of subprocesses in the job tree.

Before accessing JIB$L_PGFLCNT, the process page file quota, EXE$CREPRC acquires the MMG spinlock, raising IPL to IPL$_MMG. It charges JIB$L_PGFLCNT for the number of process page file pages contributed by the shell and releases the MMG spinlock, lowering IPL to 2.

If the job has insufficient page file quota, EXE$CREPRC deallocates the newly acquired data structures and returns the error status SS$_EXQUOTA to its requestor. Otherwise, it increments JIB$L_PRCCNT and compares it to JIB$L_PRCLIM, the maximum number of processes in the job tree. If JIB$L_PRCCNT exceeds JIB$L_PRCLIM, the job tree is at its maximum size. EXE$CREPRC decrements JIB$L_PRCCNT, deallocates the PCB and PQB, and returns the error status SS$_EXQUOTA to its requestor. Figure 27.3 shows the relation between the JIB and the PCBs of several processes in the same job.

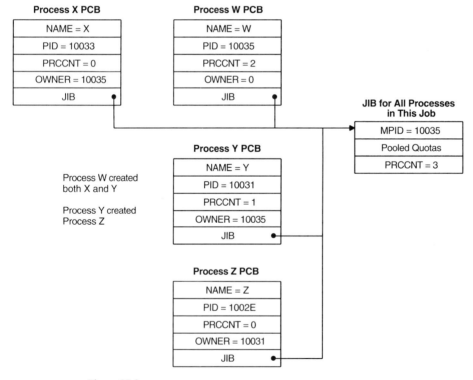

Figure 27.3
Relation Between the JIB and the PCBs of Several Processes in the Same Job

Note that the process count field within a PCB (PCB$L_PRCCNT) tracks the number of subprocesses created by one process. JIB$L_PRC-CNT counts the total number of subprocesses in the entire job.

5. For both top-level processes and subprocesses, EXE$CREPRC stores the address of the JIB in PCB$L_JIB.
6. EXE$CREPRC copies the creator's account name from CTL$T_AC-COUNT to the PQB.
7. It initializes several fields in the PCB to nonzero values:

   a. It sets up five asynchronous system trap (AST) queues, one for each of the four access modes and one for special kernel ASTs, as empty listheads.
   b. It sets up the PCB's lock queue as an empty listhead.
   c. It sets up the PCB's buffer object queue (see Chapter 16) as an empty listhead.
   d. It initializes the PCB's current and permanent CPU capability requirement fields to the system default value found in SCH$GL_DEFAULT_PROCESS_CAP.
   e. It copies the default affinity skip value from SCH$GL_AFFINITY_SKIP to the PCB.
   f. If the system default capability mask enables implicit affinity, it copies the CPU ID of the processor for which the current process has affinity to the new process's PCB$L_AFFINITY field. Chapter 13 describes process affinity.
   g. It copies the default file protection from SYS$GW_FILEPROT, the system default file protection, unless the process is a subprocess, in which case it uses the default file protection from the creating process's PCB.
   h. It copies the access rights block (ARB) from the creating process's ARB. If the creator has an extended rights list, EXE$CREPRC allocates a nonpaged pool buffer into which it copies the extended rights list.

      The ARB is currently located within the PCB. However, executive routines that check a process's access rights use the ARB pointer, PCB$L_ARB, to locate the process rights and UIC. All programs should follow this convention, since the ARB may become an independent structure in the future. Any programs that do not use the ARB pointer will require modification when this occurs.
   i. EXE$CREPRC copies the unit number of the termination mailbox from the MBXUNIT argument. The termination mailbox number is not used until the process is eventually deleted. At that time, the process deletion routine writes a termination message to the specified mailbox if the unit number is nonzero.
   j. It initializes the process-private page count, PCB$L_PPGCNT, to the number of pages required for the new process header and the shell pages.

k. EXE$CREPRC copies the process name, if one exists, into the PCB.

8. It determines the process privileges of the new process and stores them in the PQB:

   - If no privilege argument is present, EXE$CREPRC uses the current working privileges of the creator.
   - If a privilege argument is present and the creator has SETPRV privilege, EXE$CREPRC uses the privilege argument with no modification.
   - If a privilege argument is present and the creator does not have SET-PRV privilege, EXE$CREPRC stores the logical AND of the working privileges of the creator and the privileges specified in the argument. In short, a process cannot receive privileges that its creator does not have.

   Table 28.2 summarizes the various privilege masks associated with a process.

9. EXE$CREPRC determines the software priority of the new process and stores it in the PCB base priority and current priority fields. The system service macro $CREPRC_S, used from MACRO-32, specifies a default value of 2 for the BASPRI argument. The default value for other languages is determined by the treatment of missing arguments by the language processor.

   If the creator has ALTPRI privilege, EXE$CREPRC uses the priority specified in the argument list. If the creator does not have ALTPRI privilege, EXE$CREPRC uses the smaller of the creator's base priority and the priority in the argument list.

10. EXE$CREPRC determines the UIC of the new process and stores it in the PCB. The UIC argument is used if the requestor specified that argument. Otherwise, EXE$CREPRC uses the UIC of the creator. Therefore, a subprocess always has the same UIC as its creator—if the UIC argument had been specified, EXE$CREPRC would have created a top-level process.

11. If the new process is a subprocess, EXE$CREPRC copies the internal process ID (IPID) of the creator to the PCB$L_OWNER field of the new PCB and the extended process ID (EPID) of the creator to the field PCB$L_EOWNER. Section 27.2.3 describes internal and extended process IDs.

    If the new process is a top-level process, the PCB$L_OWNER and PCB$L_EOWNER fields remain zero.

12. EXE$CREPRC tests that the process name is unique within the UIC group. It examines the process name fields of all PCBs in the system with the same group number. If the process name is not unique, EXE$CREPRC returns the error status SS$_DUPLNAM to its requestor. Process name is always qualified by UIC group number.

13. EXE$CREPRC copies several text strings to the PQB, taking the image name and the equivalence names for SYS$INPUT, SYS$OUTPUT, and SYS$ERROR from the $CREPRC argument list. For most processes, the image is LOGINOUT.EXE.

14. It translates the logical name SYS$DISK in the table LNM$FILE_DEV and stores its equivalence name in the PQB. For compatibility with previous releases of VAX VMS, SYS$DISK is translated only once. Thus, its equivalence name must be either a shareable logical name or a physical device name.

15. EXE$CREPRC copies the minimum and maximum authorized security clearance records from the creator's PHD to the new process's PQB.

16. It copies the following information from the P1 space of the creator process:

    - Default directory string
    - Command language interpreter (CLI) name
    - Command table name
    - CLI name for use by spawned subprocesses
    - Command table name for use by spawned subprocesses

17. It copies the default message flags and flags specified in the creator's authorization file record from the P1 space of the creator to the PQB.

18. It extracts the status flags for the new process from the $CREPRC argument list and sets the corresponding flags in the PCB and PQB. Table 27.2 describes the status flags. All PCB flags listed in the table are found in the field PCB$L_STS. The IMGDMP flag is eventually stored in the field PHD$L_FLAGS, but since the PHD does not exist yet, the PQB temporarily maintains the flag. EXE$CREPRC always propagates the flag PCB$V_SECAUDIT from the creator process.

    It checks the creator process's privilege mask for any flags requiring privilege.

19. If the process being created is not a subprocess, and it is not a batch, network, or interactive process, then it must be a true detached process. In that case, EXE$CREPRC copies JIB$W_MAXJOBS and JIB$W_MAX-DETACH from the creator's JIB to that of the new process. If either count is nonzero, indicating a limit, EXE$CREPRC must check whether creation of this process would exceed one of those limits.

    It acquires the SCHED spinlock, raising IPL to IPL$_SCHED. Holding the spinlock, it scans all existing processes except for the swapper process. It looks for a process that is not a network process or a subprocess and that has the same user name as the process being created. If it finds one, it increments the total count of jobs with that user name. If the process is neither interactive nor batch, it also increments the total count of detached processes with that user name.

    After scanning all the processes, EXE$CREPRC releases the SCHED spinlock and restores IPL to 2. If either job limit has been exceeded, EXE$CREPRC returns the error status SS$_EXPRCLM to its requestor.

20. It determines the quotas for the new process and stores them in the PQB. Section 27.2.2 describes the steps taken to determine the quota list for the new process.

Table 27.2   Status Flags Specified at Process Creation

Flag Argument	Meaning if Set	Destination
PRC$V_SSRWAIT	Disable system service resource wait mode	PCB$V_SSRWAIT
PRC$V_SSFEXCU	Enable system service exceptions for user mode	PCB$V_SSFEXCU
PRC$V_PSWAPM [1]	Inhibit process swapping	PCB$V_PSWAPM
PRC$V_NOACNT [2]	Suppress accounting	PCB$V_NOACNT
PRC$V_BATCH [3]	Batch (noninteractive) process	PCB$V_BATCH
PRC$V_HIBER	Hibernate process before calling image	PCB$V_HIBER
PRC$V_NOUAF	Log in without reading the authorization file	PCB$V_LOGIN
PRC$V_NETWRK	Process is a network connect object	PCB$V_NETWRK
PRC$V_DISAWS	Disable system-initiated working set list adjustment	PCB$V_DISAWS
PRC$V_DETACH [4]	Process is detached	PCB$V_DETACH
PRC$V_INTER	Process is interactive	PCB$V_INTER
PRC$V_IMGDMP	Enable image dump	PHD$V_IMGDMP
PRC$V_NOPASSWORD	Disable prompt for user name and password	PCB$V_NOPASSWORD

[1] Requires PSWAPM privilege.
[2] Requires NOACNT privilege.
[3] Requires DETACH privilege.
[4] Flag ignored unless same UIC.

21. EXE$CREPRC processes the ITMLST argument, if one was supplied. This argument is reserved for use by the executive to pass logical name attributes for SYS$INPUT, SYS$OUTPUT, and SYS$ERROR to EXE$CREPRC, which in turn copies the attributes into the PQB.

22. EXE$CREPRC stores the address of the PQB in the field PCB$L_PQB. PCB$L_PQB is the same longword as the event flag wait mask field, PCB$L_EFWM. The field PCB$L_PQB is available until the process executes in its own context and is placed into a resource or event flag wait state. At that time, its contents are overwritten by an event flag wait mask. Therefore, the initial instructions of EXE$PROCSTRT, the first code to run in the new process's context, are nonpageable and immediately copy the PQB address elsewhere. Section 27.4 describes EXE$PROCSTRT.

23. EXE$CREPRC acquires the MMG and SCHED spinlocks, raising IPL to IPL$_MMG. It searches the PCB vector for an empty slot (see Section 27.2.3.1). If none is available, it returns the error status SS$_NOSLOT to its requestor after releasing the SCHED and MMG spinlocks. The PCB vector is pictured in Figure 27.4.

Otherwise, having found an available PCB vector slot, EXE$CREPRC tests the maximum process count. If the maximum process count has been exceeded (SCH$GW_PROCCNT's contents are larger than those of SCH$GW_PROCLIM), EXE$CREPRC returns the error status SS$_NOSLOT to its requestor after releasing the SCHED and MMG spinlocks.

EXE$CREPRC increments SCH$GW_PROCCNT regardless of process type.

If the new process is interactive, EXE$CREPRC increments SYS$GL_IJOBCNT, the current interactive job count for the system. Since all interactive jobs begin by executing the LOGINOUT image, the comparison of SYS$GL_IJOBCNT to the SYSGEN parameter IJOBLIM is handled by LOGINOUT.

If the new process is a batch job, EXE$CREPRC increments SYS$GL_BJOBCNT, the current batch job count for the system.

24. EXE$CREPRC stores the new PCB address in the available PCB vector slot.
25. It fabricates internal and extended process IDs (see Section 27.2.3.1) and stores them in the PCB of the new process.
26. If the new process is not a subprocess, EXE$CREPRC stores its IPID in the master process ID field of the JIB (JIB$L_MPID).
27. EXE$CREPRC invokes the routine SCH$CHSE, in module RSE, to insert the process into the COMO scheduling queue. It specifies the priority increment class PRI$_TICOM to boost the base priority by 6.
28. If it is creating a subprocess, EXE$CREPRC increments the count of subprocesses owned by the creator (PCB$L_PRCCNT in the creator's PCB). In addition, if a CPU time limit is in effect for the creator, EXE$CREPRC deducts the amount of CPU time passed to the new process from the creator.
29. Finally, it releases the SCHED and MMG spinlocks, lowers IPL to 0, and returns the EPID of the new process (if requested) to the requestor.

27.2.2   Establishing Quotas for the New Process

The $CREPRC system service uses two tables in the executive to set up quotas for the new process: a minimum quota table and a default quota table. Each quota or limit in the system has an entry in both tables. The contents of the minimum table are determined by the SYSGEN parameters whose names are of the form PQL_M*quota-name*; the contents of the default table are of the form PQL_D*quota-name*. Following is a list of the steps EXE$CREPRC takes to determine the value for each quota or limit that is passed to the new process:

1. It places the default value for each quota into the PQB as initial value.
2. It replaces the default values in the PQB by any quotas specified in the argument list to the $CREPRC system service.
3. It forces each quota to at least its minimum value.

4. It checks to ensure that the creator possesses sufficient quota to cover the quota that it is giving to the new process:

   a. If the creator has either the DETACH or the CMKRNL privilege and is creating a top-level process, quotas are unrestricted and no check is performed.

   b. If the creator has neither privilege and is creating a top-level process with the same UIC, then the new process quotas must be less than or equal to those of the creator.

   c. If a subprocess is being created and the quota is neither pooled nor deductible (the only deductible quota currently implemented is CPU time limit), then the subprocess quota must be less than or equal to the creator's quota.

   d. Pooled quotas require no special action when a subprocess is being created because they already reside in the JIB, a structure that is shared by all processes in the job (see Figure 27.3).

   e. If a subprocess is being created and the quota in question is the CPU time limit quota, EXE$CREPRC's actions depend on how much quota the creator process possesses. If the creator has an infinite CPU time limit, then no check is performed. If the creator has a finite CPU time limit and specifies an infinite CPU time limit for the subprocess, half of the creator's CPU time limit is passed to the subprocess. If the creator has a finite CPU time limit and specifies a finite CPU time limit for the subprocess, the amount passed to the subprocess must be less than the creator's original quota, or the creation is aborted.

5. EXE$CREPRC places pooled quotas directly into the JIB, if newly allocated. It places other quotas into the PCB or stores them temporarily in the PQB.

Table 27.3 lists the quotas that are passed to a new process when it is created, whether each quota is deductible or pooled, and where the limit is stored in the context of the new process. Further discussion of quotas can be found in the *OpenVMS System Manager's Manual* and in the *OpenVMS System Services Reference Manual*.

With the exception of CPU time limit and subprocess count, all active counts start at their process limit values and decrement to zero. An active count of zero indicates no quota remaining. An active count equal to the corresponding process limit indicates no outstanding requests.

27.2.3 Process Identification

The executive provides two forms of process identifier (PID) for each process. The internal, traditional form—the IPID—identifies a process within the context of a single system. The EPID is a compressed version of the IPID that additionally identifies the VMScluster node of a process. In this book, the unqualified term *process ID* or *PID* refers to the internal, traditional form.

Table 27.3 Storage Areas for Process Quotas

Quota/Limit Name	Location of Active Count	Location of Process Limit	Count/Limit Stored by [1]
NONDEDUCTIBLE QUOTAS			
AST limit	PCB$L_ASTCNT	PHD$L_ASTLM	C/P
Buffered I/O limit	PCB$L_BIOCNT	PCB$L_BIOLM	C/C
Direct I/O limit	PCB$L_DIOCNT	PCB$L_DIOLM	C/C
Working set quota	n/a [2]	PHD$L_WSQUOTA	/P
Working set default	n/a [2]	PHD$L_DFWSCNT	/P
Working set extent	n/a [2]	PHD$L_WSEXTENT	/P
DEDUCTIBLE QUOTA			
CPU time limit	PHD$L_CPUTIM	PHD$L_CPULIM	P/P [3]
POOLED QUOTAS (SHARED BY ALL PROCESSES IN THE SAME JOB)			
Buffered I/O byte limit	JIB$L_BYTCNT	JIB$L_BYTLM	C/C [4]
Open file limit	JIB$L_FILCNT	JIB$L_FILLM	C/C [4]
Page file page limit	JIB$L_PGFLCNT	JIB$L_PGFLQUOTA	C/C [4]
Subprocess limit	JIB$L_PRCCNT	JIB$L_PRCLIM	C/C [4]
Timer queue entry limit	JIB$L_TQCNT	JIB$L_TQLM	C/C [4]
Enqueue limit	JIB$L_ENQCNT	JIB$L_ENQLM	C/C [4]

[1] The slash (/) separates the count from the limit: C/ indicates that the count value is stored by EXE$CREPRC; /C indicates that the limit value is stored by EXE$CREPRC; P/ indicates that the count value is stored by EXE$PROCSTRT; /P indicates that the limit value is stored by EXE$PROCSTRT.

[2] Working set list quotas are handled differently from other quotas (see Chapter 19).

[3] CPUTIM starts at zero and increments for each 10-ms interval (soft tick) that the process is current. If limit checking is in effect (CPULIM nonzero), then CPUTIM may not exceed CPULIM.

[4] The contents of the JIB are loaded by EXE$CREPRC when a detached process is created. Subprocess creation uses an existing JIB.

Executive routines use the IPID or EPID to locate a process's PCB. All process PCB addresses are stored in the PCB vector. The IPID or EPID provides an index into the PCB vector and a parallel array called the sequence vector. The number of entries in each array (and therefore the maximum number of processes allowed at any given time on a system) is determined by the SYSGEN parameter MAXPROCESSCNT.

The executive generally identifies a process internally by its IPID, although code such as the lock management system services and the cluster-wide process services may use both forms of PID. System services accept and return EPIDs, and system utilities display EPIDs, but the format of the EPID is subject to change in future versions of the operating system. No program should attempt to partition the EPID fields. Instead, the executive provides the following routines (in the module SYSPCNTRL) for transformation or manipulation of an EPID by kernel mode code.

- EXE$CVT_EPID_TO_PCB—Convert an EPID to address of corresponding PCB
- EXE$CVT_EPID_TO_IPID—Convert an EPID to IPID
- EXE$CVT_IPID_TO_EPID—Convert an IPID to EPID
- EXE$CVT_IPID_TO_PCB—Convert an IPID to address of corresponding PCB

27.2.3.1 **Fabricating PIDs.** EXE$CREPRC fabricates a process's IPID and EPID after obtaining a free PCB vector slot (and implicitly the associated sequence vector slot).

The PCB vector is allocated from nonpaged pool during system initialization, and its address is stored in SCH$GL_PCBVEC. It contains a longword slot for each possible process in the system. The first entry in the vector contains the address of the null PCB. The second entry contains the address of the swapper process PCB. All other entries in the vector initially contain the address of the null PCB.

When EXE$CREPRC creates a process, it searches the PCB vector for an empty slot into which to insert the address of the new PCB it has built. It considers an entry that contains the address of the null PCB to be an empty slot. EXE$CREPRC excludes the first two PCBs (the null PCB and the swapper process) from its scan of the PCB vector. It begins the scan with the slot most recently allocated and wraps to the slot after the swapper process if it exceeds the maximum entry. The index of the maximum entry is stored in SCH$GL_MAXPIX.

Figure 27.4 provides an example of the contents of the PCB vector.

As processes are created and deleted on the system over time, the slots in the PCB vector are reused. The sequence vector tracks the reuse of these PCB vector slots.

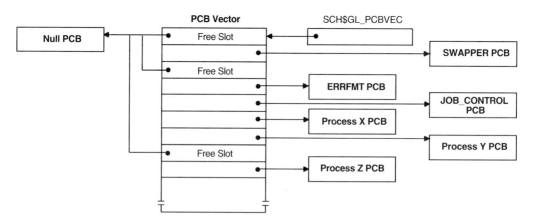

Figure 27.4
Sample PCB Vector

All entries in the sequence vector are cleared during system initialization. Each time EXE$CREPRC uses a PCB vector slot, it increments the value in the corresponding sequence vector slot. This sequence number becomes the high-order word of the IPID. Thus, executive routines use the sequence number as a consistency check to determine that a number alleged to be an IPID corresponds to a real process in the system.

When a process is deleted, the executive stores the address of the null PCB in its PCB vector slot to indicate that the slot is available. The sequence number, however, is not incremented until the slot is reassigned by EXE$CREPRC.

The sequence number increments to 32,767, then cycles back to 0. Therefore, when IPIDs are interpreted as signed integers, they are never negative. This allows the I/O subsystem to treat a negative value in the IRP$L_PID field of an I/O request packet (IRP) in a special manner. The I/O postprocessing interrupt service routine interprets a negative IRP$L_PID value as the (system virtual) address of an internal I/O completion routine.

A PCB contains four fields related to process identification. EXE$CREPRC loads them all, because it has access to the PCB of the creator process and it fabricates the IPID and EPID of the new process.

▶ PCB$L_PID—Internal process ID
▶ PCB$L_EPID—Extended process ID
▶ PCB$L_OWNER—Internal process ID of process's creator
▶ PCB$L_EOWNER—Extended process ID of process's creator

27.2.3.2   **Internal PID.** The IPID is a longword value. Its low-order word contains an index into the PCB vector and the sequence vector, unique across the local system but not across the nodes of a VMScluster system. Its high-order word is the sequence number from the sequence vector.

The executive uses the sequence number to check the validity of an IPID. The high-order word of the IPID must match the sequence number in the sequence vector offset indexed by the low-order word of the IPID. Additionally, the PCB vector slot must contain the address of a PCB other than the null PCB.

To optimize the IPID validity check, the executive routines EXE$CVT_IPID_TO_PCB and EXE$NAM_TO_PCB, in module SYSPCNTRL, rely on two PCB characteristics. First, a PCB contains its own IPID at offset PCB$L_PID. Second, the null PCB contains a zero in its PCB$L_PID field, and it is the only PCB whose IPID is zero. To verify that an IPID is valid, these routines index into the PCB vector using the low-order word of the IPID. They obtain the PCB address and compare its PCB$L_PID to the IPID being checked. The test fails under two conditions:

▶ If the process specified has been deleted and the slot has been reused, the

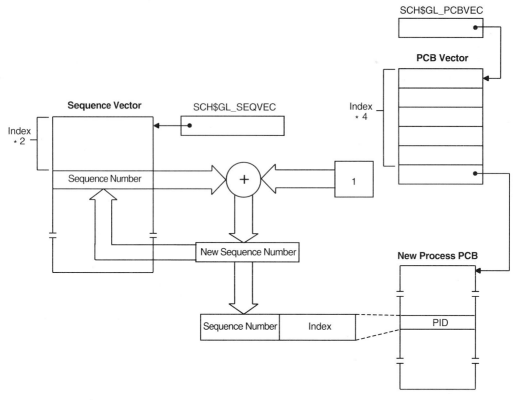

Figure 27.5
Fabrication of an Internal Process ID (IPID)

new PCB's IPID contains an incremented sequence number and does not match.

▶ If the process specified has been deleted but the slot has not been reused, the PCB vector contains the address of the null PCB. The null PCB contains zero in its PCB$L_PID field and can never match the IPID being checked.

Figure 27.5 shows how an IPID is constructed.

27.2.3.3   **Extended PID.** The EPID serves as a VMScluster-wide process identification and is currently constructed from the IPID. Figure 27.6 shows its layout. Its low-order 21 bits contain the IPID in two fields. The widths of these two fields vary, depending on the value of the SYSGEN parameter MAX-PROCESSCNT. The first field, beginning at bit 0, contains the process index. The size of the field is computed at system initialization and stored in global location SCH$GL_PIXWIDTH. The second field contains the sequence number. Its size is 21 minus the size of the first field.

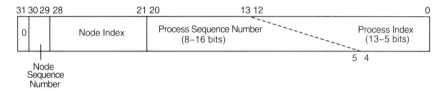

Figure 27.6
Layout of an Extended Process ID (EPID)

Bit 31 of the EPID is zero, preserving the rule that an EPID or IPID is never negative. The other ten high-order bits identify the VMScluster node. The node identification is similar to process identification in that it consists of an index into a node table and a sequence number that counts how many times the index has been reused. On a system that is not a VMScluster node, these bits are all zero.

After a system becomes a VMScluster node, the EPIDs of any existing processes must be updated with the node information, which comes from the node's cluster system identification (CSID). The low-order ten bits from the global location SCH$GW_LOCALNODE are inserted into the field PCB$L_EPID of each process and, if appropriate, into the field PCB$L_EOWNER.

27.3   SWAPPER'S ROLE IN PROCESS CREATION

Minimally, two data structures are required to represent a process: the software PCB and the PHD. In addition, a process must have some P1 pages, in particular, a kernel stack. Creating a process requires creating and initializing these structures and connecting them to each other and to other system data structures.

As described in Section 27.2, EXE$CREPRC creates a new process's PCB. The swapper creates a new process's PHD and its required P1 pages.

The PHD is a complex data structure with a fixed part and a variable part. The swapper copies the fixed part of the PHD from the executive image SHELLxK, also simply called the shell. It creates the variable part of the PHD based on page table pages from the shell and various SYSGEN parameters. Because the PHD is mapped in both system space and the process's P1 space, the swapper must initialize both system page table entries (SPTEs) and P1 page table entries (P1PTEs) to map it.

The swapper creates a new process's kernel stack by copying a prefabricated one from the shell. The initial contents of the prefabricated kernel stack, shown in Figure 27.7, are equivalent to the interrupt stack frame and saved integer registers found on the kernel stack of any noncurrent process (see Chapter 13). The initial program counter (PC) and processor status (PS)

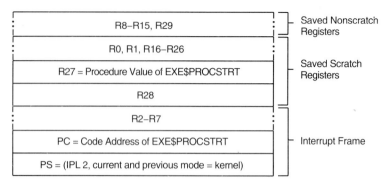

Figure 27.7
Initial Kernel Stack

on this kernel stack are defined to cause the execution of the final routine involved in process creation (see Section 27.4).

A PHD includes a hardware privileged context block (HWPCB) that defines the process's initial privileged context. The combination of the HWPCB and the information on the prefabricated kernel stack specifies the new process's hardware context.

The swapper copies other required P1 pages from the shell and locks some of them permanently into the process's working set.

The sections that follow describe these steps in more detail. Chapter 16 contains information on page tables and the address translation algorithm, and Appendix F discusses the layout of P1 space.

27.3.1 Shell Layout

The shell contains a template for a process's initial P1 pages and for the fixed part of its PHD. Table 27.4 lists the contents of the first six shell pages. In addition to these pages, the shell also contains SWP$SHELL_INIT, a routine that the swapper calls to initialize a newly created process.

27.3.2 Moving the Shell into Process Context

The swapper takes the following steps in preparation for the inswap of any process:

1. It allocates physical memory for the process, the number of pages specified by PCB$L_PPGCNT plus PCB$L_GPGCNT.
2. It records the page frame numbers (PFNs) of these pages in its P0 page table (P0PT).
3. It allocates a balance set slot, an entry in the system space array that contains the PHDs of resident processes.

Table 27.4   Shell Pages Used by the Swapper

Item	Size (Pages)	Locked	Page Number
Template for fixed part of PHD	1 [1]	Yes	1
P1 level 3 page table page	1	Yes	2
Process-private level 2 page table page	1	Yes	3
P1 pointer area	1	Yes	4
RMS data area	1	No	5
Kernel stack	1	Yes	6

[1] The ultimate size of the PHD depends on the values of several SYSGEN parameters. Appendix F describes how the size of the PHD is calculated by SYSBOOT, the secondary bootstrap program.

As described in Chapter 16, the PHD is also mapped in the process's P1 space.

In the case of a newly created process, EXE$CREPRC has cleared PCB$L_GPGCNT and initialized PCB$L_PPGCNT to the value in SWP$GL_SHELLSIZ. Computed during system initialization as a function of SYSGEN parameters and the shell constants, this value includes

▶ The shell pages, listed in Table 27.4
▶ The fixed portion of the PHD
▶ The working set list
▶ The process section table (PST)
▶ The PHD page arrays and page table page arrays

As the swapper allocates each physical page, it stores the PFN in its P0PT. The swapper initializes each P0 page table entry (P0PTE) as active and valid, with a protection code of ERKW.

After allocating a balance set slot, the swapper examines PCB$L_WSSWP, the location of the outswapped process. A zero value in this field identifies a newly created process that must be initialized from the shell.

To perform process initialization, the swapper invokes a special routine in the shell called SWP$SHELL_INIT to configure the PHD before completing the final operations of inswap.

SWP$SHELL_INIT copies the shell pages into the swapper's P0 address space. The first six P0PTEs, therefore, map the first six pages of the shell. The remaining P0PTEs map physical pages that the swapper has allocated for the new process but has not yet initialized.

27.3.3   Configuration of the Process Header

When the executive image SHELLxK is linked, the shell pages within it are constructed to resemble an outswapped process. However, a PHD cannot be entirely configured without taking into account several SYSGEN parameters, so part of the PHD configuration must occur dynamically (see Chapter 16).

To complete the configuration of the PHD, the swapper invokes the routine SWP$SHELL_INIT, in module SHELLxK.

Running in kernel mode in the swapper's process context, SWP$SHELL_INIT performs the following actions:

1. SWP$SHELL_INIT has access to the swapper's virtual address space and page table. Starting with the fixed portion of the PHD, SWP$SHELL_INIT copies information from the shell pages into the beginning of the swapper's P0 space, zeroing the pages as necessary:

   a. It copies the fixed portion of the PHD to the first P0 page and zeros any remaining locations in the page.

   b. It zeros areas in P0 space for the working set list and the PST for the process.

   c. It zeros the process-private level 2 page table (L2PT) page.

   d. It copies the initialized part of the kernel stack from the shell template.

   e. If SYSGEN parameter KSTACKPAGES is more than 1, SWP$SHELL_INIT reserves extra kernel stack pages.

   f. SWP$SHELL_INIT computes the sum of kernel stack pages and PHD P1 window pages and verifies that there are enough free PTEs in the shell's level 3 P1 page table (P1PT) to map those pages.

   g. It copies the P1 pointer area from the shell template to the next available swapper P0 page and zeros the remainder of the page.

   h. It copies the Record Management Services (RMS) data area from the shell template to the next available swapper P0 page and zeros the remainder of the page.

   i. If extra kernel stack pages were requested, SWP$SHELL_INIT reserves P1PTEs for the extra pages after zeroing the unused part of the next available swapper P0 page. It then copies the initialized part of the P1PT page from the shell template.

2. SWP$SHELL_INIT calculates the address of the SPTE that maps the start of the balance set slot. It copies the first entry in the swapper's P0PT into this SPTE, thereby initializing it with the PFN of the first page read from the shell.

   It initializes subsequent SPTEs, mapping the working set list and PST from the swapper's P0PTEs that map pages zeroed in step 1.

3. SWP$SHELL_INIT skips the SPTEs that map the empty pages of the PHD (used for working set list expansion), leaving them as no-access pages.

4. It initializes the next SPTEs, which map the PHD page arrays and the L2PT page, from swapper P0PTEs that map pages zeroed in step 1.

5. It invalidates the entire translation buffer.

6. It stores the balance set slot index in the PHD. This value indexes the PHD reference count array and the process index array as well as the balance set slots. Chapter 16 describes these arrays.

7. It stores the SYSGEN parameters that determine the default page fault cluster size and the default page table page fault cluster size in the PHD.

8. It requests the initial page file assignment for the new process and reserves enough pages in the page file for its PHD pages and the shell pages. It stores the page file and reservation count in the PHD.

9. It calculates and stores the pointer to the end of the PST (PHD$L_PST-BASOFF).

10. It calculates and stores PHDL_WSLX, PHDL_BAK, PHD$L_PTWSLE-LCK, and PHD$L_PTWSLEVAL, the pointers to the PHD page arrays and the page table page arrays (see Figure 16.5).

11. SWP$SHELL_INIT initializes the page table page arrays pointed to by PHD$L_PTWSLELCK and PHD$L_PTWSLEVAL. These count the locked and valid PTEs in each page table page. Initializing the entries to –1 indicates that no pages are locked or valid. The next-to-last page table page in P1 space has its entries corrected to reflect the fact that it contains the PTEs for locked pages and valid pages.

12. The fixed portion of the PHD maintains four counters pertaining to page table pages: the number of page table pages with locked pages, the number with valid pages, the number of active page table pages, and the number of page table pages with nonzero entries. SWP$SHELL_INIT initializes the counters to the number of permanent P1PT pages copied from the shell.

13. The PHD page copied from the shell contains initial values for the three working set list longword index values (PHDL_WSLOCK, PHDL_WS-DYN, and PHD$L_WSNEXT). SWP$SHELL_INIT adjusts the indexes to account for any additions to the permanent part of the working set such as extra kernel stack pages.

     After altering the index to the dynamic portion of the working set (PHD$L_WSDYN), SWP$SHELL_INIT moves any dynamic working set list entries from their old location to the new location.

14. If any extra kernel stack pages were allocated, SWP$SHELL_INIT creates working set list entries for them.

15. SWP$SHELL_INIT updates the process working set list with the pages composing the beginning of the PHD (fixed portion, working set list, PST, and page table page arrays). In addition, it updates the PFN database records for the physical pages to indicate that these pages are active modified page table pages. It also records their backing store information, working set list offsets, page file, and PTE back pointers.

16. It initializes the SPTEs for the process P1PT pages as demand zero, no-execute pages with a protection code of ERKW.

17. It copies the swapper P0PTE that maps the L2PT page defined in the shell to an SPTE and zeros that swapper P0PTE, forcing the L2PT to be accessed only through system space.

18. SWP$SHELL_INIT calculates the offsets from the beginning of the PHD to the beginning of the P0PT and the end of the P1PT to reflect the size of the beginning of the PHD (see Chapter 16 and Appendix F). It adjusts the address of the first free virtual address in P1 space (stored in the PHD at offset PHD$L_FREP1VA) and the contents of PHD$L_P1LENGTH to reflect the size of the PHD that is mapped into P1 space.

19. It calculates the address of the P1 window to the PHD and stores it in location CTL$GL_PHD. The swapper can access the P1 address space of the newly created process because its pages are mapped as swapper P0 addresses. CTL$GL_PHD resides in the P1 pointer area copied from the shell. When SWP$SHELL_INIT returns control to the swapper for completion of the inswap, the swapper will complete PTE generation based on the working set list.

20. It initializes the WSEXTENT and WSAUTHEXTENT indexes to reflect the value of the SYSGEN parameter WSMAX, and the WSQUOTA and WSAUTH indexes to reflect the value of WSMAX or 65,536 pages, whichever is smaller. It initializes PHD$L_WSFLUID to the value of the SYSGEN parameter MINWSCNT. The end of the working set list (WSLAST) and the default count (DFWSCNT) initially reflect the value of the SYSGEN parameter PQL_DWSDEFAULT. PHD$L_WSSIZE is initialized to the value of PQL_DWSDEFAULT.

21. SWP$SHELL_INIT marks the PHD resident by setting the bit PCB$V_PHDRES in PCB$L_STS.

22. It adds the PHD's virtual address to the addresses of the L2PT, the P0PT, and the P1PT in the PHD so that they contain the virtual addresses of those page tables.

    SWP$SHELL_INIT returns control to the swapper's main inswap routine, which completes the remaining steps of the inswap operation. As the final step, the swapper invokes the scheduler routine SCH$CHSEP, in module RSE, to change the state of the new process to executable and possibly trigger a rescheduling interrupt. These steps are described in Chapter 20.

27.4 PROCESS CREATION IN THE CONTEXT OF THE NEW PROCESS

The final steps of process creation take place in the context of the newly created process. The process's initial register context is contained within the kernel stack copied from the shell. When it becomes current, the process begins execution at the saved PC in the kernel stack, the address of the routine EXE$PROCSTRT, in module PROCSTRT. The saved PS indicates kernel mode at IPL 2. Thus, the first code that executes in the context of a newly created process is the same for every process in the system.

27.4.1 Operation of EXE$PROCSTRT

When EXE$PROCSTRT begins execution, the PCB and the PHD have been created. In addition, information passed from the creator process has been copied into the PQB by EXE$CREPRC. EXE$PROCSTRT must copy the information from its temporary location in the PQB into the PHD and P1 space (see Figure 27.8). EXE$PROCSTRT then prepares for and activates the image specified by the creator process.

EXE$PROCSTRT begins execution in kernel mode at IPL 2. Later segments of the code execute in executive mode and user mode. Because the PCB$L_PQB field is an overlay of PCB$L_EFWM, the process cannot enter a

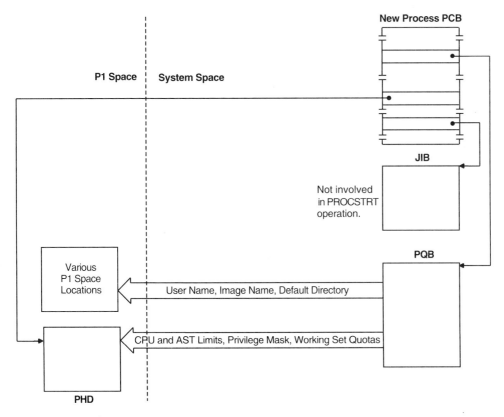

Figure 27.8
Removal of Process Parameters from the Process Quota Block

941

resource or event flag wait state until the PQB address has been copied elsewhere. Since a page fault might cause a process to be placed in a resource wait state, the process cannot page fault until EXE$PROCSTRT has copied the PQB address. Therefore, the first few instructions of EXE$PROCSTRT are located in nonpageable memory. These instructions obtain the address of the process's PCB and copy the PQB address from the PCB to a register. The remainder of EXE$PROCSTRT is pageable.

EXE$PROCSTRT performs the following steps:

1. It obtains the PCB address from CTL$GL_PCB and copies the PQB address from the PCB to a register, as described previously.

2. It stores the address of the RMS dispatcher in the P1 pointer area. It also initializes CTL$GL_CTLBASVA with the value in MMG$GL_CTLBASVA, which represents the initial low-address end of P1 space. The value in CTL$GL_CTLBASVA is updated with each expansion of process-permanent P1 space; it represents the boundary between process-permanent and image-specific P1 space.

3. EXE$PROCSTRT initializes the P1 space locations CTL$GL_USRUNDWN and CTL$GL_USRUNDWN_EXEC with the addresses of the tables within the activated privileged library dispatch vector for kernel and executive mode image rundown routines. It also initializes CTL$GL_GETMSG with the address of the start of the message vector, also in the activated privileged library dispatch vector. Chapter 28 contains details about the dispatch vector and rundown routines, and Chapter 39, about the dispatch vector and the message vector.

4. If the creator process requested an image dump, EXE$PROCSTRT propagates that flag to the PHD.

5. EXE$PROCSTRT initializes the kernel request packet (KRP) lookaside list (see Chapter 21), forming the space into KRPs and inserting them on the list.

6. It moves the CPU time limit and the AST limit from the PQB to the PHD (see Table 27.3).

7. EXE$PROCSTRT initializes the working set list pointers in the PHD to reflect the quotas passed from the creator. It minimizes the SYSGEN parameter WSMAX, the maximum working set size, with the number of potentially available physical pages. It then enforces the following restrictions on quotas:

   - Working set quota must be less than or equal to 64K, the maximum size of a swap slot.
   - Working set extent must be less than or equal to the maximum physical pages.
   - Working set quota must be less than or equal to working set extent.
   - Working set default must be less than or equal to working set quota.

8. EXE$PROCSTRT copies the process's base priority to PHD$L_AUTHPRI

and PCB$L_AUTHPRI. Saving the base priority enables a process without ALTPRI privilege to lower its base priority and later raise it as high as the original base priority.

9. It copies the process privilege mask from the PQB to the first quadword of the PHD (PHD$Q_PRIVMSK), the permanent privilege mask (CTL$GQ_PROCPRIV in the P1 pointer area), and the authorized privilege mask (PHD$Q_AUTHPRIV). Chapter 28 describes the use of each of these privilege masks.

10. It copies the default message flags to P1 space.

11. It saves the login time in CTL$GQ_LOGIN and CTL$GQ_PSTART.

12. EXE$PROCSTRT copies the minimum and maximum authorized security clearance records from the PQB to the PHD.

13. It initializes the following listheads as empty:

   - The objects rights block (ORB) lock database
   - The Declared Resource Manager queue, used by the Digital Distributed Transaction Manager (DECdtm)
   - The three image activator listheads: image control blocks (IMCBs) representing activated images; IMCBs representing work in progress; and the IMCB lookaside list (see Chapter 28)
   - The clusterwide process service (CWPS) queue in the PCB
     Processes are visible and can be manipulated clusterwide. CWPS supports system services in implementing this feature (see Chapter 14).
   - The process scan queue in the PHD
     The $PROCESS_SCAN system service uses this queue to maintain its search context (see Chapter 14).

14. EXE$PROCSTRT creates P1 virtual address space for the channel control block table and the process allocation region. It then calls RM$INIT, in module RMSRESET, to create and initialize the process and image I/O segments.

   Appendix F describes these areas and the SYSGEN parameters that affect their size. EXE$PROCSTRT records the address of each portion and updates the process-permanent boundary address in CTL$GL_CTL-BASVA with the new, lower address.

15. It allocates and initializes space from the P1 allocation region for the process logical name hash table. It computes the size of the table based on the number of hash table entries, but in no case does it allow the size of the hash table to exceed half the size of the P1 allocation region. EXE$PROCSTRT also allocates space for the process-private logical names and tables that it will create. Chapter 38 describes the logical name data structures and their use.

16. EXE$PROCSTRT then allocates space from the P1 allocation region for the process-private logical name table cache. It formats the space into a lookaside list of logical name cache entries.

17. It initializes the process directory logical name table, LNM$PROCESS_ DIRECTORY, and the process logical name table and inserts them into the hash table.

18. It creates the logical name table logical names LNM$PROCESS, LNM$GROUP, and LNM$JOB. It inserts them into the hash table and into LNM$PROCESS_DIRECTORY.

19. Using the equivalence strings and logical name attributes from the PQB, EXE$PROCSTRT creates the logical names SYS$INPUT, SYS$OUTPUT, SYS$ERROR, TT, and SYS$DISK.

20. If the process is not a subprocess, EXE$PROCSTRT creates the job and group logical name tables. (If the process is a subprocess, then the tables already exist.) Because multiple processes access the tables, they must be in system space. EXE$PROCSTRT allocates space for the tables from paged pool. It locks the logical name table mutex for write access and holds it while accessing the shareable logical name hash table. Chapter 9 describes mutexes.

    EXE$PROCSTRT initializes the two tables and inserts the job table into the shareable logical name hash table. It attempts to do the same with the group table. However, the group table may have already been created by some other process with the same UIC group number. If this is the case, the new table is unnecessary and EXE$PROCSTRT deallocates it back to paged pool. Otherwise, EXE$PROCSTRT inserts the group table into the shareable logical name hash table. In either case, it unlocks the logical name table mutex.

21. EXE$PROCSTRT copies the image name from the PQB to the image header buffer for subsequent use by the image activator.

22. EXE$PROCSTRT copies the default directory string, if one exists, from the PQB to P1 space. It also copies the two sets of names for the CLI and the command table, one for this process and another for its subprocesses, from the PQB to P1 space.

23. It copies the $CREPRC flags, user authorization file (UAF) flags, and debug flags from the PQB to P1 space flags.

24. It copies the user name from the JIB and the account name from the PQB into the P1 pointer area.

25. EXE$PROCSTRT deallocates the PQB by inserting it on the PQB looka-side list (see Chapter 21).

26. It invokes MMG$IMGRESET, which resets PHD$L_WSLAST, the pointer to the end of the working set list. MMG$IMGRESET also lowers IPL to 0, making it possible for the process to be deleted.

    Another, more philosophical, interpretation is that at this point in the creation of a process, something exists that is capable of being deleted, a full-fledged process.

27. EXE$PROCSTRT initializes the shareable image list for the Address

Relocation Fixup ($IMGFIX) system service to point to a dummy element. This system service is described in Chapter 28.

28. EXE$PROCSTRT dispatches to F11X$INIT_XQP, in module [F11X]INIFCP, initialization code within the XQP image. The initialization code requests the Expand Program/Control Region ($EXPREG) system service to create a process-private copy of the XQP impure area and space for the XQP's private kernel stack. The code then updates CTL$GL_CTLBASVA. After performing other Files-11 initialization, it returns to EXE$PROCSTRT.

29. EXE$PROCSTRT changes access mode to executive by calling EXE$REI_INIT_STACK, in module REI.

   At this point, EXE$PROCSTRT has moved all the information from the creator to the context of the new process and is now ready to activate the image that will execute in the context of the new process. It must change mode to executive to request the image activator, which is an executive mode system service.

30. Running in executive mode, EXE$PROCSTRT requests the image activator to set up the page tables and perform the other steps necessary to activate the image. Image activation is described in Chapter 28.

31. EXE$PROCSTRT declares an executive mode termination handler, EXE$RMSEXH. This handler will be called when the Exit ($EXIT) system service is requested from executive mode, which usually happens when the process is deleted. When called, it calls SYS$RMSRUNDWN for each open file.

32. EXE$PROCSTRT stores the procedure value of a dummy CLI call back routine in location CTL$AL_CLICALBK. If an image that was activated from EXE$PROCSTRT attempts to communicate with a nonexistent CLI, the dummy CLI call back routine will return the error status CLI$_INVREQTYP.

33. EXE$PROCSTRT changes access mode to user by calling EXE$REI_INIT_STACK.

34. It clears the frame pointer (R29), guaranteeing that the search of the user mode stack for a condition handler by the exception dispatcher will terminate (see Chapter 6).

35. EXE$PROCSTRT sets up an initial stack frame on the user mode stack by calling an inline procedure:

```
        CALLS   #0, 260$
        HALT
260$:  .CALL_ENTRY INPUT=<R8,R9,R10>
        MOVAB   R9, (FP)
    :
    :

            ;Procedure code
```

945

36. EXE$PROCSTRT establishes EXE$CATCH_ALL, the catch-all condition handler, as the condition handler for this stack frame and also as the last chance condition handler for user mode. The purpose and action of this handler are discussed in the next section.

37. EXE$PROCSTRT requests the $IMGFIX system service to perform address relocation for the image.

38. An argument list that is nearly identical to the one used by a CLI (see Chapter 30) is built on the stack. This argument list allows an image to execute in the same manner regardless of whether it was activated from EXE$PROCSTRT or from a CLI.

39. EXE$PROCSTRT determines whether the process was created with the hibernate STSFLG argument. If the PCB$V_HIBER bit in PCB$L_STS is set, it requests the Hibernate ($HIBER) system service. EXE$PROCSTRT will continue when the process is awakened.

40. It calls the image at its initial transfer address. Unless the image requests the $EXIT system service directly, control returns to EXE$PROCSTRT, which places the process back into hibernation if the process was created with the hibernate STSFLG argument. When the process is awakened, EXE$PROCSTRT calls the image again. An effect of this implementation is that the image is not exited and no exit handlers (user-declared or system-declared, such as EXE$RMSEXH) are called.

    If the process was not created with the hibernate flag, EXE$PROC-STRT requests the $EXIT system service itself. In general, there is no difference between an image terminating by returning to EXE$PROCSTRT or by requesting the $EXIT system service. If the process was initially created with the hibernate flag, there is a difference. If a process is to be put into hibernation for future awakenings, it must return to EXE$PROCSTRT rather than terminating by requesting the $EXIT system service.

27.4.2   Catch-All Condition Handler

EXE$PROCSTRT and a CLI establish EXE$CATCH_ALL in module PROC-STRT, the catch-all condition handler, in the outermost stack frame before calling an image. EXE$PROCSTRT also establishes it as the last chance condition handler for user mode through the Set Exception Vector ($SETEXV) system service. Any condition that is resignaled or improperly handled by other handlers (or unfielded because no other handlers have been established) is eventually passed to this handler. The handler outputs a message using the Put Message ($PUTMSG) system service. Depending on the severity level of the condition, it may force image exit.

EXE$CATCH_ALL's arguments are the addresses of the signal and mechanism arrays. It performs the following actions.

1. It calls EXE$CATCHALL_EXTENSION, also in module PROCSTRT. New for OpenVMS AXP, this procedure is called with the same arguments as EXE$CATCH_ALL. It processes user-defined extensions to the catch-all condition handler.

   If the mechanism array's depth argument indicates that EXE$CATCH_ALL was called as the last chance handler, EXE$CATCHALL_EXTENSION returns the status SS$_RESIGNAL to EXE$CATCH_ALL, which proceeds to step 2. Otherwise, EXE$CATCHALL_EXTENSION attempts to call user-defined catch-all condition handlers, (see in Chapter 6).

2. EXE$CATCH_ALL tests the condition in the signal array. If the condition is a system service failure, SS$_SSFAIL, EXE$CATCH_ALL disables system service failure mode to avoid an infinite loop.

3. If the condition is a software condition, that is, if a call to LIB$SIGNAL generated the condition, EXE$CATCH_ALL removes the PC and PS that LIB$SIGNAL fabricated from the signal array, leaving only those arguments passed to LIB$SIGNAL (see Chapter 6).

4. Unless system services are inhibited for this process, EXE$CATCH_ALL requests the $PUTMSG system service to write an error message to SYS$OUTPUT (and to SYS$ERROR if different from SYS$OUTPUT). The $PUTMSG system service is discussed in Chapter 39.

5. If EXE$CATCH_ALL was called as a last chance handler or if the error level is severe or greater (and if system services are not inhibited for this process), it calls SYS$EXCMSG to write an exception summary to SYS$OUTPUT. Chapter 39 describes SYS$EXCMSG.

   EXE$CATCH_ALL then dispatches to EXE$IMGDMP_MERGE, described in Section 27.4.3, to write the process address space to a file for later analysis. When it returns, EXE$CATCH_ALL requests the $EXIT system service.

6. If it was not called as a last chance handler and if the error level is less than severe, EXE$CATCH_ALL returns the status SS$_CONTINUE to the exception dispatcher, which returns to the image.

27.4.3   Image Dump Facility

EXE$IMGDMP_MERGE, in module PROCSTRT, provides the capability to write a dump file of the process's address space in a format that can be mapped later for analysis by the debugger. It is invoked when the image terminates as the result of an exception that it cannot handle. EXE$IMGDMP_MERGE is normally invoked by the condition handler established by the Image Startup system service (see Chapter 28), but it can also be invoked from the last chance handler, EXE$CATCH_ALL.

If the exception occurred in a mode more privileged than user, then no dump may be taken and EXE$IMGDMP_MERGE returns to its invoker. If the exception occurred in user mode, the procedure requests the $GETJPI system service to obtain process privileges, installed image privileges, and the PHD flags. EXE$IMGDMP_MERGE tests whether the PHD$V_IMGDMP flag is set. If it is clear, the process has not requested image dump and EXE$IMGDMP_MERGE returns. This flag can be specified as part of the $CREPRC STSFLG argument and with the DCL commands RUN/DUMP and SET PROCESS/DUMP.

If the flag is set, EXE$IMGDMP_MERGE checks whether the image was installed with more privileges than the process has. If this is so, and the process has neither CMKRNL nor SETPRV privilege, no dump can be taken and EXE$IMGDMP_MERGE returns. Otherwise, it requests the $IMGACT and $IMGFIX system services to activate SYS$LIBRARY:IMGDMP.EXE and transfers control to the image.

27.5   **RELEVANT SOURCE MODULES**

Source modules described in this chapter include

[LIB]JIBDEF.SDL
[LIB]PCBDEF.SDL
[LIB]PHDDEF.SDL
[LIB]PQBDEF.SDL
[SYS]PROCSTRT.MAR
[SYS]SHELL.MAR
[SYS]SYSCREPRC.MAR

28   Image Activation and Exit

I would have you imagine, then, that there exists in the mind of
man a block of wax . . . and that we remember and know what
is imprinted as long as the image lasts; but when the image is
effaced, or cannot be taken, then we forget or do not know.

Plato, *Dialogs, Theaetetus* 191

The images executed in the context of a process are called programs. Before
an image can execute, the OpenVMS AXP executive must locate the image
file, open and read it, map the image into address space, and resolve address references in the image. Image activation is the combination of these
steps.

At image exit the executive must call exit handlers declared by itself or by
the image. In a process with a command language interpreter (CLI), multiple
images can execute one after another. When one image exits, the executive
must eliminate all its traces so that the next image can begin execution with
no side effects from the execution of the previous image. This is referred to
as image rundown.

This chapter details these activities and also describes the initialization
and use of the various privilege masks maintained for each process. It describes the following system services related to image activation and exit:

▶ Image Activate ($IMGACT)
▶ Address Relocation Fixup ($IMGFIX)
▶ Image Startup ($IMGSTA)
▶ Declare Exit Handler ($DCLEXH)
▶ Exit ($EXIT)
▶ Rundown ($RUNDWN)

Use of the $IMGACT, $IMGFIX, $IMGSTA, and RUNDWN system services
is reserved to Digital. Any other use is unsupported.

28.1   IMAGES

An image is a file that contains binary code and data and that can be executed on an OpenVMS AXP system. The linker processes one or more object
modules produced by a language processor such as a compiler and builds an
image.

This section describes the structure of an image and the various types of
image. It summarizes the mapping of image sections into virtual address
space.

949

28.1.1   **Image Structure**

An image consists of several variable-sized pieces, the first of which is the image header. The image header contains information about the virtual address space requirements of each section in the image.

The image header is followed by the image body, the actual program code and data; by a fixup section; and, optionally, by symbol table information. Figure 28.1 shows the organization of an image.

An image can refer to locations within itself or within another image, generating addresses that require adjustment based on the address space assigned by the image activator. The fixup section describes the locations in the image that contain addresses that must be adjusted after all the image sections have been assigned starting addresses. The adjustment to an intra-image address reference is called a relocation. The adjustment to a reference from one image to another, an inter-image reference, is called a fixup. Strictly speaking, the fixup section is part of the image body.

The image body is made up of image sections of varying characteristics. Each image section represents a portion of the virtual memory of any image. As the linker processes the object modules included in the link operation, it combines program sections (PSECTs) with similar attributes to create image sections. The *OpenVMS Linker Utility Manual* details the linker's criteria for combining PSECTs.

Image section attributes include characteristics such as the following:

▶ Writability—Whether the section is read-only or read/write

▶ Shareability—Whether the section can be shared among multiple processes if its image has been installed /SHARED

▶ Executability—Whether the section contains code or data (EXE or NOEXE)

The page size the linker uses in creating an image is another significant characteristic. In particular, it affects the address boundary on which each image section begins. The linker qualifier /BPAGE specifies the page size, also known as the grain, whose default value represents a page size of 64 KB. Although all current AXP CPUs support a page size of 8 KB, an image linked to a 64 KB grain could execute on any future AXP CPU with a page size larger than 8 KB. An image linked to an 8 KB grain has image sections beginning at

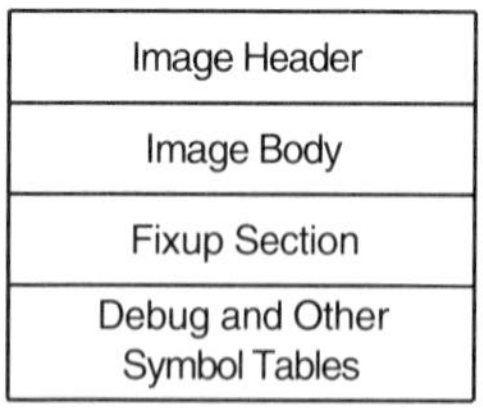

| Image Header |
| Image Body |
| Fixup Section |
| Debug and Other Symbol Tables |

Figure 28.1
Organization of an Image

8 KB boundaries and thus may not be able to run on a CPU with a larger page size without relinking. The only disadvantage to linking with a 64 KB grain is the likelihood of empty page table entries (PTEs) between image sections.

Chapter 29 describes the organization of a translated image.

28.1.2   **Image Characteristics**

An image can be categorized by whether it is

- ▶ Executable or shareable
- ▶ Made known to the system (installed)
- ▶ Protected
- ▶ Installed resident

An executable image has a unique entry point called a transfer address and can be run in response to a Digital command language (DCL) RUN command. A shareable image is a collection of procedures that can be called by code in an executable image or in another shareable image. A shareable image has no transfer address and thus is not directly executable. It must be linked with object modules or other shareable images to produce a main image. An executable image can be linked with multiple shareable images, which themselves can be linked with other shareable images. One special kind of shareable image is an executive image, described in detail in Chapter 32.

In this chapter, the term *main image* refers to the primary controlling executable image invoked by a user through the RUN command. Activating a main image results in activating any shareable images with which it was linked and any with which they were linked. Furthermore, after a main image has begun to execute, code within it or one of its shareable images can call the Run-Time Library procedure LIB$FIND_IMAGE_SYMBOL, a jacket for the $IMGACT system service, to activate another shareable image.

A known image is one identified to the system through the Install utility. Known images have special properties that affect their activation. For example, an executable image that requires enhanced privileges but that must execute in nonprivileged process context (such as SET or SHOW) can be installed with the /PRIVILEGED qualifier. When such an image is activated, the process gains enhanced privileges temporarily. All shareable images activated with the privileged image must have been installed. The enhanced privileges are removed when the image is run down.

The Install utility can also identify images to be shared by multiple processes. Several different types of image can be installed with the /SHARED qualifier:

- ▶ A shareable or executable image whose shareable image sections are to be mapped as global sections into the process-private address space of multiple processes

▶ A shareable image containing code that executes in an inner mode, such as a user-written system service or rundown routine

A protected image contains one or more image sections to be mapped into pages whose protection prohibits user and supervisor mode write. If all image sections are to be protected, the image is linked with the qualifier /PROTECT. Alternatively, a subset of image sections can be specified with the PROTECT link option. To be activated, a protected image must have been installed /PROTECTED. A completely protected image may not make calls to routines in shareable images other than system services or executive routines. One common type of protected image is a privileged shareable image, which typically contains user-written system services or inner mode rundown routines.

The Install utility can also load the shared image sections of specific shareable or executable images into a granularity hint region (also known as a huge page). An executable or shareable image can be installed into a granularity hint region with the /RESIDENT qualifier. Such an image must have been linked with the /SECTION_BINDING qualifier. Its EXE image sections are made permanently resident. References to addresses within these sections are likely to be quicker as a result of reduced translation buffer overhead (see Chapter 15).

An installed image is opened by its file ID rather than its file name, saving the overhead of a file lookup. Image activation can be further shortened if the image is installed /OPEN so that its file remains open. In this case, the image activator's Record Management Services (RMS) $OPEN request is essentially a null operation. If such an image is installed /HEADER_RESIDENT, its image header is stored in paged pool. Keeping the header resident saves the additional read operations otherwise required to read it into memory every time the image is activated.

The Install utility creates and manages the known image database (also called the known file database) to describe images that have been installed. RMS scans the known image database whenever a file is opened with the known file option.

The *OpenVMS System Management Utilities Reference Manual: A-L* describes the Install utility.

28.1.3 Image Mapping

How the image activator maps the sections of an image into virtual address space depends upon their characteristics. The System Dump Analyzer's executable image, SDA.EXE, is used here as an example to illustrate some of the basic concepts of image mapping. Figure 28.2 shows SDA.EXE and some of the shareable images with which it is linked mapped into a process's virtual address space.

Because the SDA.EXE executable image is linked with a default /BPAGE

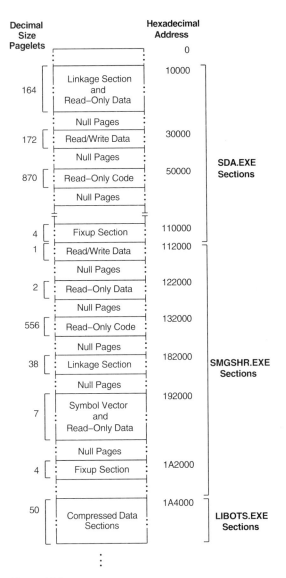

Figure 28.2
Mapping of an Executable Image with Shareable Images

qualifier value, each of its image sections begins on a 64 KB (10000_{16} byte) boundary. The image is activated in the address range at which it was linked, and no address relocations are necessary. By default virtual page 0 is no-access. Thus, SDA's first image section is mapped beginning at 10000_{16}. On current AXP systems, which have an 8 KB page size, that section of 164 pagelets occupies 11 virtual pages (equivalent to 176 pagelets). The last virtual page is only partially backed by its image file (see Chapter 17).

A number of P0 page table entries (P0PTEs) map null pages between the end of the first section and the beginning of the second, which also begins on a 64 KB boundary. There are null pages, or holes, between the end of most sections and the beginning of the next on current AXP CPUs. The linker creates SDA.EXE's fixup section at the high-address end of the image, beginning on a 64 KB boundary.

SDA.EXE in this example has been linked with several shareable images, not all shown in Figure 28.2. On the system from which the example was taken, the shareable image SMGSHR.EXE was installed /SHARED to create a global section from each of its shareable sections. When SMGSHR.EXE is activated, its global sections are mapped into P0 space and process-private P0 sections are created to map its copy-on-reference nonshareable sections. The shaded areas in Figure 28.2 represent global sections.

Note that the linkage and fixup sections are not shareable: each contains addresses that are a function of the address space assigned to the image in this activation in this process; activated in another process, the image is likely to be assigned to a different address range. Any image section in a shareable image with relocated or fixed up data is not shareable. For example, a symbol vector, which consists entirely of relocated data, cannot be shared. An image section that contains a symbol vector is copy-on-reference.

Although SMGSHR.EXE was linked with a grain of 64 KB, the image activator maps it beginning at the next available page, whether or not that address is a 64 KB boundary. This avoids one hole in the virtual address space, decreasing the number of null P0PTEs. The individual image sections of SMGSHR.EXE must maintain their relative position to one another, however, and holes between its sections still exist.

As a shareable image, SMGSHR.EXE contains relocation information in its fixup section that enables the image activator to adjust its intra-image references to reflect its assigned address space. SDA.EXE's fixup section contains information that enables its references to SMGSHR.EXE to be fixed up to reflect the address space assigned to SMGSHR.EXE's sections.

SDA.EXE is also linked with the shareable image LIBOTS.EXE, which in this example has been installed /RESIDENT. The Install utility mapped LIBOTS.EXE's EXE section into a system space granularity hint region and created a global section for its other shareable section. When LIBOTS.EXE is activated, the image activator creates process-private sections for each of its copy-on-reference sections. The combined actions of the Install utility and the image activator result in image sections that are not in the same locations relative to each other as they were in the linked image. Figure 28.3 contrasts the relative positions of LIBOTS.EXE's sections in the linked image and in the activated image. The shaded areas in the figure represent shared sections.

An image installed /RESIDENT must have been linked with the /SECTION_BINDING=CODE qualifier to prevent linker optimization from introducing dependencies in the code sections on their relative positions. The

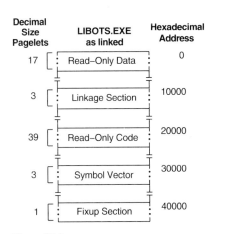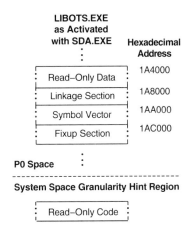

Figure 28.3
Mapping of an Image Installed Resident

image can also be linked /SECTION_BINDING=DATA, which requests the linker to check for dependencies in the nonshareable sections on their relative locations. (Consult the *OpenVMS Linker Utility Manual* for more information.) If there are no dependencies, when the image is activated, its nonshareable sections can be mapped into P0 space, as they have been in this example, to reduce holes in the address space resulting from the absence of the EXE sections and from the 64 KB grain.

The resulting elimination of address space holes is called compression. The term *compressed data sections* describes the newly adjacent sections. Note that the data is intact; it is the virtual holes that have been compressed. When LIBOTS.EXE's intra-image references are relocated and its inter-image references fixed up and when references to it from other images are fixed up, the discontinuity and compression of the image must be accounted for.

28.1.4   Image Header

The image header itself consists of a number of variable-sized pieces. At the beginning is the fixed portion of the header, which contains some standard information about the image and pointers to the other parts of the header. Figure 28.4 shows the organization of the header and the layout of its fixed part.

The acronym for the fixed part of the header is EIHD. The E distinguishes it from IHD, the acronym for the comparable OpenVMS VAX data structure. Definitions for AXP and VAX structures must coexist on the same system to support cross-linking. Similarly, all acronyms for AXP image header structures and their field names begin with E. The macro $EIHDDEF defines symbolic offsets for the fixed part. Offsets for the other parts are defined by the macros shown in Figure 28.4.

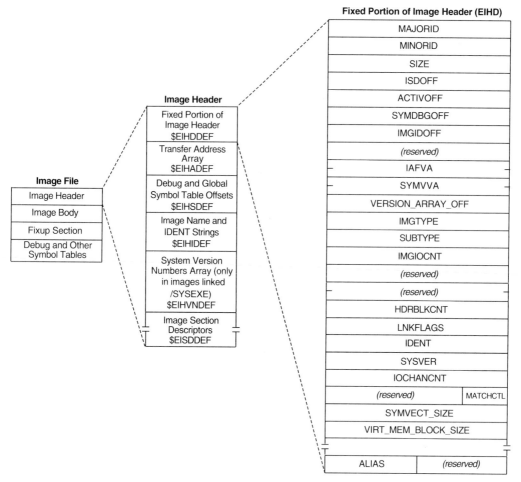

Fixed Portion of Image Header (EIHD)

MAJORID
MINORID
SIZE
ISDOFF
ACTIVOFF
SYMDBGOFF
IMGIDOFF
(reserved)
IAFVA
SYMVVA
VERSION_ARRAY_OFF
IMGTYPE
SUBTYPE
IMGIOCNT
(reserved)
(reserved)
HDRBLKCNT
LNKFLAGS
IDENT
SYSVER
IOCHANCNT

(reserved)	MATCHCTL

SYMVECT_SIZE
VIRT_MEM_BLOCK_SIZE

ALIAS	(reserved)

Image Header

Fixed Portion of Image Header $EIHDDEF
Transfer Address Array $EIHADEF
Debug and Global Symbol Table Offsets $EIHSDEF
Image Name and IDENT Strings $EIHIDEF
System Version Numbers Array (only in images linked /SYSEXE) $EIHVNDEF
Image Section Descriptors $EISDDEF

Image File

Image Header
Image Body
Fixup Section
Debug and Other Symbol Tables

Figure 28.4
Contents of an Image and Layout of an Image Header

Section 28.1.4.1 describes the fixed part of the image header. Section 28.5.1 describes the transfer address array portion of the image header. The details of the debug and other symbol tables are beyond the scope of this book. Section 28.1.4.2 describes the image ident area; Chapter 32, the use of the system version numbers array; and Section 28.1.4.3, image section descriptors.

28.1.4.1   **Fixed Part of the Image Header (EIHD).** EIHD$L_MAJORID and EIHD$L_MINORID contain the major and minor IDs associated with the structure of the image file. For OpenVMS AXP Version 1.5, the major ID is 3 and the minor ID is 0.

EIHD$L_SIZE contains the size of the entire image header in bytes, and EIHD$L_HDRBLKCNT, its size in blocks. EIHD$L_ISDOFF, EIHD$L_

ACTIVOFF, EIHD$L_SYMDBGOFF, EIHD$L_IMGIDOFF, and EIHD$L_
VERSION_ARRAY_OFF contain byte offsets to the variable-length areas of
the image header.

EIHD$Q_IAFVA contains the unrelocated virtual address in the image of
its fixup section. For a shareable image, EIHD$Q_SYMVVA contains the
unrelocated virtual address in the image of the symbol vector, and EIHD$L_
SYMVECT_SIZE, its size in bytes.

EIHD$L_IMGTYPE specifies whether the image is an executable or share-
able image. EIHD$L_SUBTYPE contains 0 except for an image identified as
a CLI through the undocumented linker option IMAGE_TYPE; a CLI has a
subtype value of 1.

EIHD$L_IMGIOCNT contains the number of pagelets of image I/O seg-
ment requested through the IOSEGMENT option when the image was
linked. If the option is not specified, the field contains zero, and the image activator will create a segment whose size is based on the SYSGEN parameter
IMGIOCNT.

EIHD$L_LNKFLAGS contains flags that describe the image and the way in
which it was linked:

- EIHD$V_LNKDEBUG, when set, means the image has been linked with
  the qualifier /DEBUG.
- EIHD$V_LNKNOTFR, when set, means the image has no transfer
  address.
- EIHD$V_NOP0BUFS, when set, means the image was linked with the link
  option IOSEGMENT=n,NOP0BUFS. This value for the option prevents additional image I/O segment pages from being allocated in P0 space. Typically, an image is linked in this way for greater control over the layout and
  allocation of P0 space.
- EIHD$V_P0IMAGE, when set, means the image has been linked with the
  qualifier /P0IMAGE to ensure that its stack and image I/O segment will be
  allocated in P0 space. Typically, an image is linked in this way to enable it
  to allocate P1 space for uses that outlive its activation.
- EIHD$V_DBGDMT, when set, means the image's header contains a debug
  module table for possible use by traceback or a debugger.
- EIHD$V_INISHR, when set, means that this is a shareable image with an
  initialization routine.
- EIHD$V_XLATED, when set, means the image was translated from an
  OpenVMS VAX image by the VAX Environment Software Translator
  (VEST) utility.
- EIHD$V_BIND_CODE_SEC, when set, means that the image has been
  linked in such a way that its code sections can be installed resident in
  system space.
- EIHD$V_BIND_DATA_SEC, when set, means its nonshared data sections
  can be compressed.

For an executable image, EIHD$L_IDENT and EIHD$B_MATCHCTL are not meaningful. For a shareable image, EIHD$L_IDENT contains the global section major and minor IDs specified with the GSMATCH link option. EIHD$B_MATCHCTL, specified with the GSMATCH link option, contains the match algorithm used to determine whether an image linked with another version of the shareable image must be relinked before being activated with this version. It is used in conjunction with the major and minor IDs of the shareable image.

For an image linked with the qualifier /SYSEXE, EIHD$L_SYSVER contains the constant SYS$K_VERSION, the system version number associated with the running system at the time of the link. Otherwise, it contains zero.

EIHD$L_VIRT_MEM_BLOCK_SIZE represents the grain size for image sections in this image. Its value is a power of 2 based on the /BPAGE qualifier with which the image was linked. Each image section begins on a boundary that is a multiple of the grain size.

EIHD$W_ALIAS is reserved for use by the DECnet Maintenance Operations Module, the MOM utility, which enables systems to boot from a network device.

28.1.4.2   **Image Ident Area of the Image Header.** Figure 28.5 shows the layout of the image ident area of the header. EIHI$L_MAJORID and EIHI$L_MINORID contain the major and minor IDs associated with the structure of this section of the header. For OpenVMS AXP Version 1.5, they contain a value of 1. EIHI$Q_LINKTIME contains the system time at which the image was linked.

EIHI$T_IMGNAM is a counted ASCII string containing the name of the image. The linker takes its value from the first of the following that specifies a name:

▸ The link option NAME, if present
▸ The name specified with the /EXE or /SHARE qualifier
▸ The name of the first object module on the link command line

If none specifies a name, the name is blank (the name length is zero).

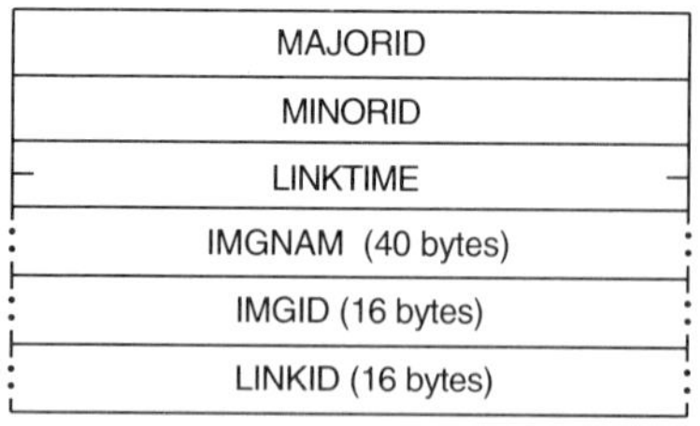

MAJORID
MINORID
LINKTIME
IMGNAM (40 bytes)
IMGID (16 bytes)
LINKID (16 bytes)

Figure 28.5
Layout of Image Ident Area (EIHI)

EIHI$L_IMGID contains the image identification. In an executable image the identification comes from the ID of an object module containing a transfer address. The link option IDENTIFICATION overrides the default. A shareable image does not normally have a transfer address, so either the ID of the first object module or the IDENTIFICATION value is used. EIHI$L_LINKID contains the linker's own identification. Its contents are a function of the version of the linker that built the image.

28.1.4.3   **Image Section Descriptors (EISDs).** The image header contains one image section descriptor (EISD) for each section in the image. Each EISD describes a portion of the image and its location in an image file and in virtual address space. Figure 28.6 shows the layout of the EISD.

The image activator processes EISDs based largely on flags in the field EISD$L_FLAGS and, to a lesser extent, on the contents of the field EISD$B_TYPE:

▶ Demand zero EISD. Identified by the flag EISD$V_DZRO, a demand zero EISD describes a range of virtual addresses that begin as zero-filled pages. The range will be mapped beginning at the virtual address in EISD$L_VIRT_ADDR unless field EISD$B_TYPE identifies the EISD as the one that describes the user access mode stack. The user mode stack is created at the low-address end of P1 space. EISD$L_SECSIZE contains the length of the demand zero section in bytes.

▶ EISD for a section. A section EISD describes a range of virtual addresses initially filled with code or data from the image file. The image section begins in the image file at the virtual block number in the field EISD$L_VBN; its length in bytes is in EISD$L_SECSIZE.

EISD$B_PFC, the pagelet fault cluster factor for the section, will be converted to pages and propagated to the process section table entry built to describe the section in the activated image. Its value is based on the pagelet parameter to the linker CLUSTER option and defaults to the SYSGEN

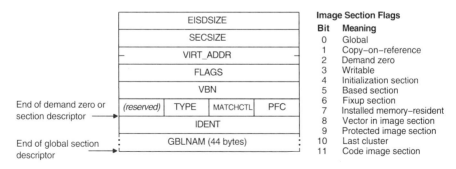

Figure 28.6
Layout of an Image Section Descriptor (EISD)

959

parameter PFCDEFAULT. The image section will be faulted into virtual address space beginning at the virtual address in EISD$L_VIRT_ADDR.

▶ Global EISD. Identified by the flag EISD$V_GBL, a global EISD identifies a shareable image. The global section name is stored as a counted string in the field EISD$T_GBLNAM. The name is based on one of the following:

- The file name part of the file specification supplied on the link option line that includes the shareable image
- The module name for a shareable image taken from a shareable image library

The string _001 is appended to that name, matching the algorithm used by the Install utility to create global section names from an image installed /SHARED.

EISD$L_IDENT and EISD$B_MATCHCTL are taken from the version identification and match control of the shareable image with which this image was linked. EISD$L_VIRT_ADDR contains zero.

A main image linked without any shareable images contains only the first two types of EISD.

A main image linked with a shareable image contains the shareable image's first EISD, primarily to identify the shareable image. The shareable image contains its own image header and EISDs to describe its virtual address space. Address space for the shareable image is not assigned when the main image is linked but when the shareable image is activated. Thus, the size of the shareable image can change without requiring the main image to be relinked.

A shareable image linked with a second shareable image contains a global EISD to identify the second shareable image. If a main image refers only to symbols in the first shareable image but not the second, it does not contain a global EISD for the second shareable image. In this regard, AXP images differ from VAX images. The entire collection of shareable images implied by a main image is not determined until image activation. Thus, a shareable image can be relinked to reference additional shareable images without requiring the relink of the main image linked with it.

The use of these types of EISD is discussed in greater detail in later sections.

28.2   IMAGE-RELATED DATA STRUCTURES

The image activator initializes an image control block (IMCB) to describe each image being activated in a process. The Install utility builds the known file database to describe those images that have been identified for special processing. Section 28.2.1 discusses IMCBs, and Section 28.2.2, the known file database.

28.2.1   Image Control Block

Figure 28.7 shows the layout of an IMCB. IMCBs are initially allocated from the P1 allocation region (see Chapter 21) but are deallocated to an IMCB lookaside list for faster subsequent allocation.

The image activator keeps two queues of IMCBs—one for images already activated and one for images yet to be activated. The listheads for these queues begin at the following P1 space locations:

▸ IAC$GL_IMAGE_LIST—Activated images (known as the done list)
▸ IAC$GL_WORK_LIST—Images to be activated (known as the work list)
▸ IAC$GL_ICBFL—Lookaside list of IMCBs

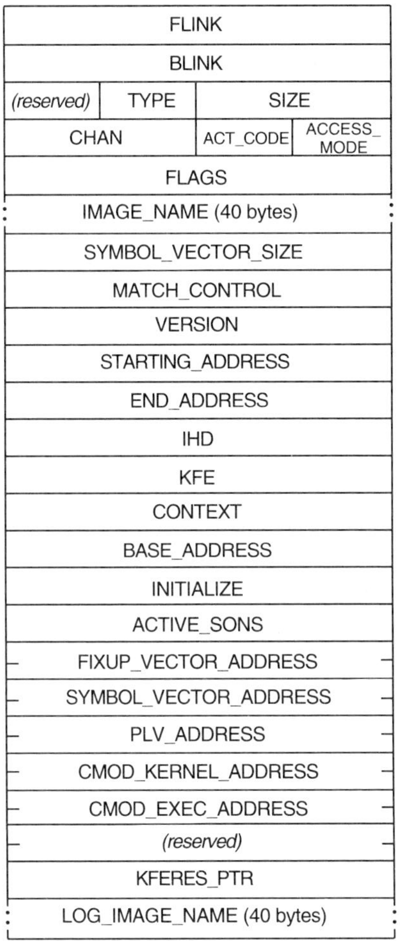

FLINK
BLINK
(reserved) / TYPE / SIZE
CHAN / ACT_CODE / ACCESS_MODE
FLAGS
IMAGE_NAME (40 bytes)
SYMBOL_VECTOR_SIZE
MATCH_CONTROL
VERSION
STARTING_ADDRESS
END_ADDRESS
IHD
KFE
CONTEXT
BASE_ADDRESS
INITIALIZE
ACTIVE_SONS
FIXUP_VECTOR_ADDRESS
SYMBOL_VECTOR_ADDRESS
PLV_ADDRESS
CMOD_KERNEL_ADDRESS
CMOD_EXEC_ADDRESS
(reserved)
KFERES_PTR
LOG_IMAGE_NAME (40 bytes)

Image Flags

Bit	Meaning
0	Mapped at end of address space
1	Installed /SHARED
2	Has writable sections
3	Header already decoded
4	Load from sequential device
5	Contains initialization code
6	Completely activated
7	Linked /SYSEXE
8	Involved in circularity
9	Mapped in address space
10	Installed /PROTECTED
11	Parent image installed /PROTECTED
12	Change mode transfer routines mapped
13	Translated VAX image
14	Contains protected sections
15	Contains no protected sections
16	Installed /RESIDENT
17	Allows POSIX fork
18	Data sections compressed

Figure 28.7
Layout of an Image Control Block (IMCB)

IMCB$B_ACT_CODE describes the manner in which the image was activated—as a main image, as a merged image, or as a shareable image section. IMCB$B_ACCESS_MODE contains the access mode specified in the $IMGACT request, maximized with the requestor's access mode. The image file is opened on a channel assigned in this access mode, and the pages that are mapped are owned by this mode. IMCB$W_CHAN holds the channel number on which the image file is opened.

The image's fully resolved file name is stored as a counted string in the field IMCB$T_IMAGE_NAME. Saving the complete name rather than a logical name prevents problems when a shareable image is referenced by both a native and a translated image. Under these circumstances, multiple activations of the same image would otherwise be possible. (Chapter 29 contains more information on the mechanisms that enable native and translated images to interoperate.) IMCB$T_LOG_IMAGE_NAME contains the global section name of a shareable image, which can be a logical name.

The address range into which the image was mapped is stored in IMCB$L_STARTING_ADDRESS and IMCB$L_END_ADDRESS. For an image installed /RESIDENT, these addresses represent only the sections mapped in process-private address space. IMCB$L_IHD points to the image header, IMCB$L_KFE locates the known file entry associated with the image (if any), and IMCB$L_CONTEXT points to the image activator local context block, a temporary structure that points to image activator buffers.

For an image installed /PROTECTED, IMCB$PS_FIXUP_VECTOR_ADDRESS contains the address of its fixup section in the image. Nonzero contents in this field alert the image activator to perform relocations and fixups while in executive access mode.

For a shareable image, IMCB$PS_SYMBOL_VECTOR_ADDRESS and IMCB$L_SYMBOL_VECTOR_SIZE contain the address and size in bytes of the image's symbol vector. IMCB$L_INITIALIZE contains the unrelocated procedure value of the image's initialization routine, taken from EIHA$L_INISHR (see Section 28.5.1).

For a privileged shareable image, IMCB$PS_PLV_ADDRESS contains the address of the image's privileged library vector. IMCB$PS_CMOD_KERNEL_ADDRESS and IMCB$PS_CMOD_EXEC_ADDRESS contain the beginning addresses of the sets of kernel and executive mode transfer routines created by the image activator.

For an image installed /RESIDENT, IMCB$L_KFERES_PTR contains the address of a user-readable P1 space copy of the system space data structure that describes the resident sections.

28.2.2   Known File Database

A number of data structures describe known images. These data structures are all allocated from paged pool.

▶ Known file entry (KFE)—One for each known image

▶ Known file resident image header (KFRH)—One for each image installed /HEADER_RESIDENT

▶ Known file directory (KFD)—One for each unique combination of mass storage device and directory from which known images are installed

▶ Resident section descriptor (KFERES)—One for each image installed /RESIDENT

▶ One hash table to locate all KFEs

▶ One known file pointer block (KFPB) to locate the KFD list and KFE hash table

The Install utility allocates a KFE when a known image is installed. A KFE contains information used by the image activator to locate and map the image. Figure 28.8 shows the layout of a KFE.

KFE$L_FID and KFE$L_WCB are different symbolic names for the same location in the KFE. If the image header is not memory-resident, three words beginning at KFE$L_FID contain the full file ID of the image, thus locating the file header on the disk.

Otherwise, if the file header is already in memory, KFE$L_WCB contains the address of the file's window control block (WCB), which describes the

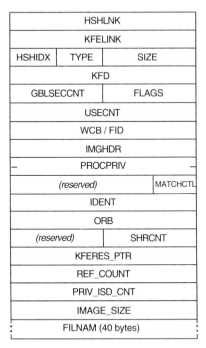

KFE Flags

Bit	Meaning
0	Installed /PROTECTED
1	Shareable image
2	Installed /PRIVILEGED
3	Installed /OPEN
4	Image header resident
5	Shared image
6	*(reserved)*
7	*(reserved)*
8	Installed /NOPURGE
9	Image accounting enabled
10	Has writable sections
11	Execute access only
12	Installed /RESIDENT
13	Delete pending

Figure 28.8
Layout of a Known File Entry (KFE)

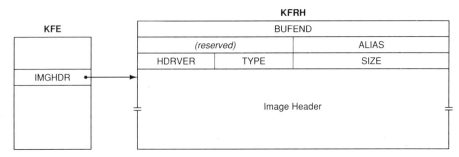

Figure 28.9
Layout of a Known File Resident Image Header (KFRH)

disk location of the blocks of an open file. KFE$L_IMGHDR contains the address of the resident image header.

The field KFE$W_FLAGS contains flag bits indicating the manner in which the image was installed—for example, if KFE$V_PROTECT is set, the image was installed /PROTECTED. An image installed with privileges has its privilege mask recorded in KFE$Q_PROCPRIV.

When an image is installed with the /SHARED qualifier, the number of global sections it consists of is stored in KFE$W_GBLSECCNT. Its global section identifier is at KFE$L_IDENT, and the match control information supplied when the image was linked is stored in KFE$B_MATCHCTL. The image activator maintains a count of the number of processes that have activated the image at KFE$L_USECNT. KFE$L_REF_COUNT contains the number of processes currently accessing an image installed /RESIDENT.

KFE$L_IMAGE_SIZE contains the size in bytes of an installed image.

For an image installed /SHARED or /RESIDENT, KFE$L_PRIV_ISD_CNT contains the number of private, or nonshareable, image sections. It is the number of process-private sections that will have to be created when the image is activated, not counting a stack.

For an image installed /RESIDENT, KFE$L_KFERES_PTR contains the address of the data structure that describes the resident sections.

A data structure called a known file resident image header (KFRH) exists for each known image installed /HEADER_RESIDENT. The KFRH immediately precedes the image header, and space for the image header is allocated with the KFRH. Figure 28.9 shows the layout of a KFRH.

Figure 28.10 shows the layout of a KFD.

The full device and directory names associated with an installed image are stored in the KFD field KFD$T_DDTSTR rather than in the KFE. Typically, multiple known images are installed from the same device and directory combination and thus share the same KFD. Keeping the device and directory information in the KFD rather than in each KFE saves paged pool. The number of KFEs sharing a KFD is found in KFD$W_REFCNT. The KFEs

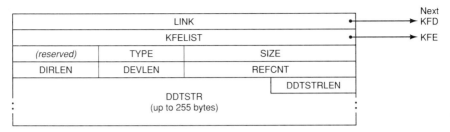

Figure 28.10
Layout of a Known File Directory (KFD)

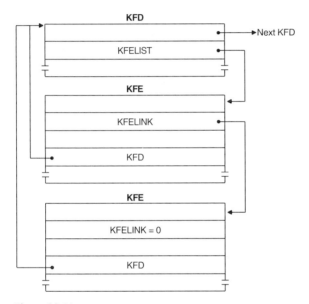

Figure 28.11
Known File Directory (KFD) and Known File Entries
(KFEs)

themselves are linked at KFD$L_KFELIST. Figure 28.11 shows a KFD and its list of KFEs.

A KFE hash table locates all the KFEs. A known image name is hashed to a number between 0 and 127, which is an index into the 128-entry hash table. If the table entry contains a zero, no KFE is associated with that hash index. Otherwise, the table entry is the address of a KFE. As a confirmation, the KFE contains its own hash index value at KFE$B_HSHIDX. KFEs with the same hash index are linked together through the field KFE$L_HSHLNK. The end of the list is a forward link of zero. Figure 28.12 shows the hash table and several KFEs linked to it.

The KFPB contains the hash table address at KFPB$L_KFEHSHTAB and

965

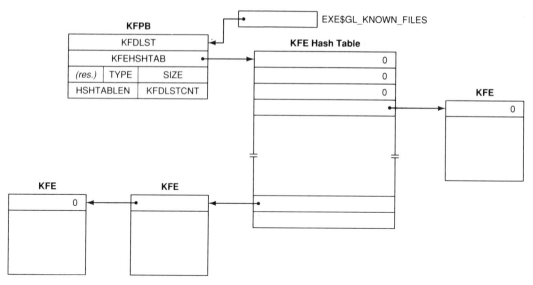

Figure 28.12
Layout of a Known File Pointer Block (KFPB) and a KFE
Hash Table

the number of hash table entries at KFPB$W_HSHTABLEN. It also holds the head of the KFD list at KFPB$L_KFDLST and the KFD count at KFPB$W_KFDLSTCNT. Figure 28.12 shows the layout of the KFPB and its relation to other known image data structures.

For each image installed /RESIDENT, a KFERES structure is built in paged pool to describe it. Figure 28.13 shows the layout of this structure. As such an image is activated, a P1 copy of the structure is built in the process allocation region. The P1 copy of the structure serves the following purposes:

▶ User-readable, it can be accessed by the $IMGFIX system service, a mode of caller service.

▶ Unique to a particular process, it can describe the nonshareable sections of the image, which are allocated in process-private address space.

KFERES$L_KFE contains the address of the KFE that describes the image. KFERES$L_COUNT contains the number of resident sections in the image, and KFERES$L_DATA_COUNT, the number of these that are data sections.

KFERES$W_SIZE, KFERES$B_TYPE, and KFERES$B_SUBTYPE are the standard dynamic data structure fields.

A set of substructures begins at offset KFERES$T_SECTIONS. A paged pool KFERES has one substructure for each resident section. The P1 copy may have additional substructures to describe compressed data sections. KFERES$L_VA contains the starting virtual address of the section, and KFERES$L_LENGTH its length in bytes. KFERES$L_VBN has the starting virtual block number of the section in the image file, and KFERES$L_

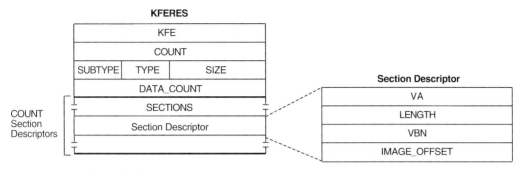

Figure 28.13
Layout of a Known File Entry Resident Section Descriptor
(KFERES)

IMAGE_OFFSET, the starting address of the section in the image as it was linked.

28.3 IMAGE ACTIVATOR

When a user initiates image execution, for example, as part of process creation or through a DCL command in an interactive or batch job, the $IMGACT system service is requested.

The image activator calls RMS to open the main image file, which enables the system to perform all its file protection checks. Then the image activator reads the image and requests a memory management system service to map each image section within it. The memory management system services initialize the process-private page tables to map the pages in the image file. (The image activator does not load the image into memory; instead, pages of the image will be read into memory by the OpenVMS paging mechanism as they are referenced during image execution.) The image activator takes similar steps for shareable images with which the main image was linked. It makes other necessary preparations, such as creating address space for the user stack.

Before control is transferred to the image, the $IMGFIX system service relocates intra-image references that require relocation and fixes up inter-image references. These resolutions are performed at activation time rather than at link time because they depend upon the addresses into which the images are mapped.

Control is transferred to the image as described in Section 28.5.

The next two sections cover the more common types of image activation in detail:

▶ Activation of a simple main image, one linked with no shareable images. This is an artificial separation from the next case, simply to illustrate the difference in the image activator's actions.

▸ Activation of an image linked with one or more shareable images. Because most language processors generate calls to library routines implemented as shareable images, this case includes most images.

Certain types of image are made known to the system through the Install utility, to speed up their activation, to associate special properties with them, or both. Section 28.3.6 briefly describes the activation of various types of known image, including resident images and privileged shareable images. It also summarizes considerations for translated images.

Table 28.1 shows the arguments to the $IMGACT system service.

Direct requests to this system service are reserved for the OpenVMS AXP operating system. Direct requests by users are unsupported. Instead, users can request the image activator indirectly through any CLI command that runs an image and through the Run-Time Library procedure LIB$FIND_IMAGE_SYMBOL.

28.3.1 Activation of a Simple Main Image

Most of the common operations performed by the image activator occur during the activation of a simple main image, one linked with no shareable images. This section therefore follows the general flow through the image activator for simple main images, including those installed /HEADER_RESIDENT or /SHARED. Note that the concept of a main image linked with no shareable images is a simplification, since any image that requests system services is linked with SYS$PUBLIC_VECTORS.EXE to resolve its system service names.

The $IMGACT system service procedure, EXE$IMGACT, runs primarily in executive mode with some kernel mode subroutines. EXE$IMGACT is in module SYSIMGACT; some of the procedures it calls are in modules IMGMAPISD, IMGDECODE, and SYSIMGFIX. EXE$IMGACT and the procedures it calls are known as the image activator.

To activate a simple main image, the image activator takes the following steps:

1. It initializes its P1 space scratch area and various P1 cells.
2. It checks the accessibility of the system service argument list and its arguments and copies them for later use.
3. It resets the activated privileged library dispatch vector (see Chapter 7) to indicate no activated user-written system services or rundown routines.
4. It invokes RMS$RESET, in module RMSRESET, to initialize the image I/O segment.
5. It allocates and zeros an IMCB. If an error occurs later in activation, it deallocates the IMCB before returning.
6. It locks the known file database by requesting the Enqueue Lock Request and Wait ($ENQW) system service. It locks the systemwide resource

Table 28.1   Arguments to the $IMGACT System Service

Argument Name	*Meaning*
NAME	Descriptor of image name to be activated.
DFLNAM	Descriptor of default file name.
HDRBUF	Address of 512-byte buffer in which the EIHD and image file descriptor are returned. The first two longwords in the buffer are the addresses within the buffer of the EIHD and the image file descriptor.
IMGCTL	Image activation control flags:

Flag	*Meaning*
IAC$V_ MERGE	If set, the image activator is directed to merge an image into the address space of an already activated image, ignoring the user stack and the image I/O segment. This flag must be set if the service is requested from user mode.
IAC$V_ EXPREG	If set, the INADR argument does not give an actual address range but merely indicates P0 address space, which is expanded as required. This flag is used only during a merged image activation for a P0 image.
IAC$V_ SETVECTOR	If set, the image activator initializes only the P1 vectors that dispatch to user-written system services, rundown routines, and message sections.
IAC$V_ P1MERGE	If set, the image activator is directed to merge an executable image into P1 space. It first merges it into P0 space to determine its size and thus the correct starting address in P1 space and then maps it into P1 space.
IAC$V_ P1DIRECT	If set, the image activator activates an image directly into P1 space. This flag is intended solely for DCL.EXE's activation.
IAC$V_ PROTECTED	If set, the image activator requires the image and any activated with it to have been installed /PROTECTED. Logical name translations use inner mode logical names and tables.
IAC$V_ PARANOID	If set, the image activator requires the image and any activated with it to have been installed. Logical name translations use inner mode logical names and tables.

INADR	Address of a two-longword array containing the virtual address range into which the image is to be mapped. This argument is usually omitted, in which case the address ranges designated by the EISDs in the EIHD are used or the image is mapped at the next available location.
RETADR	Address of a two-longword array to receive the starting and ending addresses into which the image was actually mapped.
IDENT	Address of a quadword containing the version number and matching criteria for a shareable image.
ACMODE	Access mode for page ownership and image channel assignment. It defaults to user mode. If present, it is maximized with the requestor's mode.

INSTALL$KNOWN FILE for protected read. This blocks any attempt at concurrent changes to the known file database by the Install utility. If an error occurs later in activation, the image activator dequeues the lock before returning.

7. The image activator requests RMS to open the image for execute access, specifying the user-open, process-permanent file, sequential-only, and known file database search options. It specifies that the WCB is to contain complete mapping information for the file, thus avoiding later window turns.

   When activating one of the following image types, the image activator specifies that RMS use only executive or kernel mode logical names to translate the image name and its descendants' image names:

   - A main image installed /PRIVILEGED
   - A main image installed /EXECUTE_ONLY and activated from user mode
   - A main image invoked by a process with execute access but not read access to the image file
   - An image installed /PROTECTED or having an ancestor installed /PROTECTED
   - An image activated with the IAC$V_PARANOID flag specified in the FLAGS argument

8. The image activator then stores the translated image name and channel number in the IMCB. If RMS found the image in the known file database, it returned the address of the KFE in the CTX field of the file access block (FAB); the image activator stores the KFE address in the IMCB and notes whether the image was installed with the /PRIVILEGED, /ACCOUNT, /PROTECTED, /EXECUTE_ONLY, or /SHARED qualifiers.

9. If either IAC$V_PARANOID or IAC$V_PROTECTED was specified in the FLAGS argument, the image activator checks that the image was installed and, if not, returns the error status SS$_PRIVINSTALL to its requestor. If IAC$V_PROTECTED was specified, the image must also have been installed /PROTECTED. If the image passes these checks, the image activator sets IMCB$V_PARENT_PROT, which is propagated to shareable images activated subsequently to ensure that similar checks are made for them.

10. The image activator tests whether the image header is resident. A known image with its header resident in memory can be activated quickly because a header read operation is avoided. If the header is resident, the image activator sets IMCB$V_RES_HEADER and skips to step 12.

11. Otherwise, in routine IMG$DECODE_IHD, in module IMGDECODE, it reads the first block of the image file and examines the first longword in that block to determine if the image is an OpenVMS AXP image. If the value in the longword is out of range, the image activator returns the

error status IMG$_NOTNATIVE to its requestor. If the value is within range, it performs several consistency checks to determine the validity of the header and image.

12. It invokes EXE$CHECK_VERSION, in module CHECK_VERSION, which checks whether an image linked against SYS$BASE_IMAGE.EXE is compatible with the versions of those symbols in the running system. Chapter 32 describes the compatibility check in detail. If the versions are incompatible, the image activator aborts the activation and returns the fatal error status SS$_SYSVERDIF.

   Since the Install utility performs this check as well, the image activator skips the check if the image header is resident.

13. It tests whether the image is an ordinary OpenVMS AXP image or a CLI by examining the contents of EIHD$L_SUBTYPE. If the field contains EIHD$C_CLI, then the image is a CLI and the image activator instead activates LOGINOUT. Section 28.3.6 contains further details about the activation of a CLI.

14. The image activator copies information from the system service argument list into the IMCB and inserts the IMCB at the tail of its work list, which was previously empty. It determines such things as IMCB$L_STARTING_ADDRESS and IMCB$L_END_ADDRESS. It stores the constant IMCB$K_MAIN_PROGRAM in IMCB$B_ACT_CODE to indicate that this is the main image.

15. The image activator enters its main loop, IMG$DO_WORK_LIST, in module IMGMAPISD. It begins processing the work list by removing an IMCB from the head of the list. The first IMCB removed from the work list is the IMCB describing the main image, which was inserted in step 14.

16. The image activator processes the EISDs in the image header. Its main task is setting up the process page tables to reflect the address space produced by the linker. It reads each EISD in the image header (see Figure 28.6) and determines the type of section described: private or demand zero for the simple main image in this example; private, demand zero, or global for a main image linked with shareable images. It then requests the appropriate memory management system service to perform the actual mapping.

   • The most common form of EISD describes a private section. A private section is either read-only or read/write, depending on the attributes of the PSECTs that compose the image section. Initial page faults for all pages in a private section are satisfied from the appropriate blocks in the image file.

     To map a private section into process address space, the image activator normally requests the Create and Map Section ($CRMPSC) system service, using the contents of the EISD as input arguments. It always specifies the NO_OVERMAP flag, so that if pages exist in the desired virtual address range, they are not deleted. If the section is a protected image section or if IAC$V_PARANOID was set in the image activator FLAGS argument and the section is a fixup section, it also specifies the $CRMPSC PROTECT flag and a section owner of executive access mode.

The result is a process section table entry (PSTE) and a series of level 3 page table entries (L3PTEs) containing process section table indexes. If a new L3PT is created, a level 2 PTE is initialized to map it.

Figure 28.14 shows the relations among the L3PTEs, the PSTE, and the EISD. The shaded bits in the L3PTE are either reserved or bits whose contents are irrelevant for that form of PTE. (Because the section in this example is a P0 space section, the L3PTEs are P0 space L3PTEs, also known as P0 page table entries, P0PTEs.) The number of L3PTEs is equal to the section's size in bytes rounded up to an integral number of pages. The first L3PTE maps the page whose virtual address corresponds to the section's base virtual address. All the L3PTEs index the same process section.

• When an image is installed /SHARED, however, the Install utility processes its EISDs and creates global sections wherever image section characteristics allow. When a process activates such an image, the image activator maps those existing global sections into process address space using the Map Global Section ($MGBLSC) system service and creates private sections for those EISDs that describe nonshareable sections.

If the section is read-only and the image was installed /SHARED, the image activator requests the $MGBLSC system service. The result is a series of L3PTEs that contain consecutive global page table indexes. Figure 28.15 shows the L3PTEs, global page table, and EISD. The shaded bits in the L3PTE are either reserved or bits whose contents are irrelevant for that form of PTE. The number of L3PTEs is equal to the section's size in bytes rounded up to an integral number of pages. The first L3PTE maps the page whose virtual address corresponds to the base P0 virtual address at which the global section is mapped.

If the section is writable and the image was installed /SHARED and /WRITE, the image activator requests the $MGBLSC system service.

If the section is writable and copy-on-reference but not installed /SHARED, it requests the $CRMPSC system service to create a private copy of the section.

If the section is writable but not copy-on-reference and not installed /SHARED, it returns the error status SS$_NOTINSTALL to its requestor.

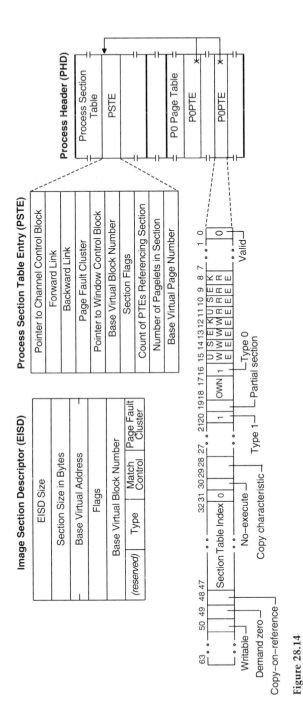

Figure 28.14
EISD and Page Table Entries for Process-Private Section

973

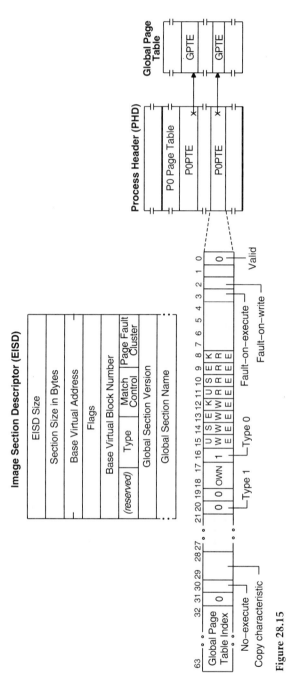

Figure 28.15
EISD and Page Table Entries for Global Section

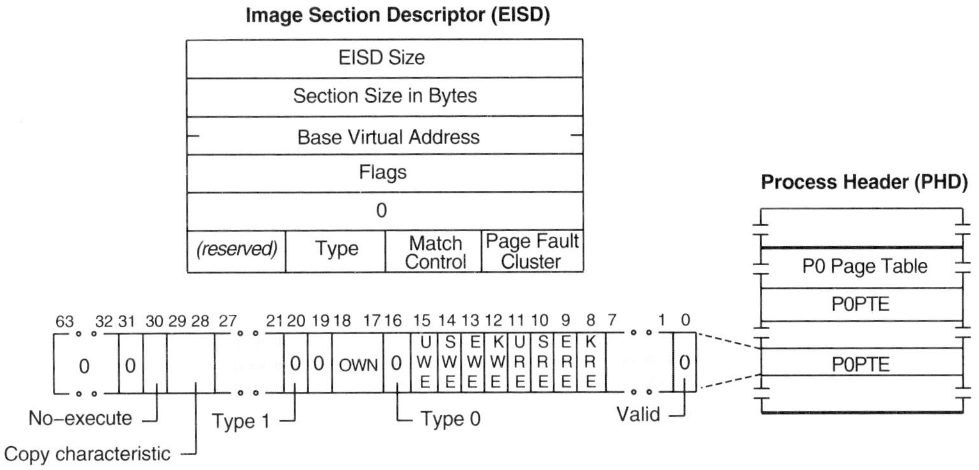

Image Section Descriptor (EISD)

EISD Size
Section Size in Bytes
— Base Virtual Address —
Flags
0

(reserved)	Type	Match Control	Page Fault Cluster

Process Header (PHD)

P0 Page Table
P0PTE

P0PTE

```
63    32 31  30 29 28 27    21 20 19 18  17 16  15 14 13 12 11 10  9  8  7      1  0
 ┌──────┬──┬──────────┬──────┬──┬──┬───┬───────────────────────┬────┬──────┬──┐
 │  0   │0 │          │ 0  0 │OWN│ 0 │U S E K U S E K│          │ 0  │
 │      │  │          │      │   │   │W W W W R R R R│          │    │
 │      │  │          │      │   │   │E E E E E E E E│          │    │
 └──────┴──┴──────────┴──────┴───┴───┴───────────────┴──────────┴────┘
```

No–execute ⌐   Type 1 ⌐   └ Type 0   Valid ⌐

Copy characteristic ⌐

Figure 28.16
EISD and Page Table Entries for Demand Zero Section

If the section is read-only but not installed /SHARED, it requests the $CRMPSC system service.

One special kind of private section is a fixup section. When the image activator encounters an EISD describing a fixup section, it stores the address of the IMCB into EIAF$L_BASE_VA in the fixup section and links it through EIAF$L_FIXUPLNK to the list of fixup sections to be processed later by the $IMGFIX system service (see Section 28.4).

- Another form of EISD is a demand zero section. The linker produces such a section from uninitialized copy-on-reference pages in the image file. The image file does not contain demand zero section pages but merely an indication in the EISD that a certain range of virtual address space contains all zeros.

The image activator uses the contents of this type of EISD as input arguments to an internal interface to the Create Virtual Address Space ($CRETVA) system service. The $CRETVA system service creates new demand zero pages in the specified range of virtual addresses. By default, if it discovers any pages that already exist in the range, they are deleted. The internal interface allows the image activator to specify the NO_OVERMAP flag, overriding this default. The result is a series of demand zero page L3PTEs. The number of L3PTEs is equal to the section's size in bytes rounded up to the next page boundary. Figure 28.16 shows the EISD and PTEs for a demand zero section.

Note that one such section is the area in P1 space that contains the user stack. The linker distinguishes this special demand zero section from others by a special code byte in the type designator in the EISD.

The image activator copies the size from the EISD and delays mapping the user stack until later in the activation.

- The third type of EISD, which would not be found in the simple main image of this example, is a global EISD. A global EISD indicates that the image activator must activate a shareable image. When it encounters a global EISD, it builds an IMCB to describe the shareable image, copying match control, version information, and global section name from the EISD. It inserts the IMCB at the tail of its work list. Section 28.3.2 describes the activation of a shareable image.

17. In this example of a simple main image (with no references to shareable images and thus no global EISDs), the only IMCB on the work list has now been processed. The image activator continues with its end processing, described in Section 28.3.3.

In the case of an image linked with shareable images, the image activator would have found global EISDs while processing the main image IMCB. Thus, additional IMCBs would have been added to the work list. The image activator would process them as described in the following section.

28.3.2   Activation of Shareable Images

Image activation is iterative. When the image activator activates an image linked with shareable images, it potentially adds an IMCB for each shareable image to the tail of its work list. As it activates each of those shareable images, it may find more global EISDs in the shareable image's header and create more work list IMCBs.

Commonly referenced shareable images, such as LIBRTL, can appear in the work list multiple times. Activating an image linked with several shareable images, each linked with LIBRTL, causes multiple insertions of LIBRTL into the work list. No matter how many times a shareable image appears in the work list, it is activated only once. As it activates an image, the image activator moves the image's IMCB from the work list to the done list. Once the IMCB is on the done list, the image activator adds no further IMCBs for that image to the work list.

This section describes the activation of a shareable image. The activation could be the result of activating a main image linked with shareable images. Alternatively, the activation could be a merged image activation, for example, one requested through LIB$FIND_IMAGE_SYMBOL, after the main image and its shareable images have all been activated.

The image activator takes the following steps to activate a shareable image:

1. In routine IMG$DO_WORK_LIST the image activator attempts to remove an IMCB from the head of its work list. If there is none, activation

is complete and the image activator proceeds with its end processing, described in Section 28.3.3.

2. It checks the done list for an IMCB containing the same image name as that in the IMCB removed from the work list. The existence of such an IMCB would indicate that the image named in the work list IMCB had already been activated.

   If there is such an image, the image activator must still ensure that the earlier activation matches current protection requirements. If an image is installed /PROTECTED, all shareable images with which it was linked must be installed. (If several shareable images were linked with the same shareable image X, and only one of those shareable images is installed /PROTECTED, image X might possibly be activated before the /PROTECTED image, that is, before the image activator detects that image X must be an installed image.) The image activator checks for this condition and returns the error status SS$_PRIVINSTALL if the image is not installed. Otherwise, it deallocates the IMCB and goes back to step 1 to process the next IMCB on the work list.

3. If the image has not already been activated, the image activator inserts the IMCB at the top of a stack pointer maintained in the done list. This mechanism ensures that IMCBs appear in the list in the proper order for image initialization (see Section 28.3.4). If an error occurs later in the activation, the image activator removes the IMCB from the done list.

4. If the image is one of the system base images (SYS$BASE_IMAGE.EXE or SYS$PUBLIC_VECTORS.EXE), the image activator copies the starting and ending system space addresses of the corresponding symbol vector to the IMCB. Otherwise, the image activator requests RMS to open the image named by the IMCB. It specifies a default file type of EXE and directory of SYS$SHARE, with file open options of user-open, process-permanent file, sequential-only, and known file database search. The image activator requests a WCB containing complete mapping information for the file, thus avoiding later window turns. If the global EISD specified a writable global section, the image activator requests shared write access. Otherwise, it requests execute access.

   To locate the file, RMS attempts logical name translation of the file name part of the image name. Under the circumstances described in step 7 of Section 28.3.1, it uses only executive or kernel mode logical names to translate the image name.

5. Under those circumstances, the image activator makes the checks in step 9 of Section 28.3.1 and confirms that the image returned by RMS is a known image. If not, the activation is aborted and the image activator returns the error status SS$_PRIVINSTALL.

   In addition, if a shareable image is not installed /EXECUTE_ONLY, and the process does not have both read and execute access to it, the activation is aborted and the image activator returns the error status SS$_ACCONFLICT.

6. If the image is a known image with its header resident, the image activator skips to the next step. Otherwise, it reads in the image's header (see step 11 in Section 28.3.1).

It then invokes EXE$CHECK_VERSION, in module CHECK_VERSION, which checks whether an image linked against SYS$BASE_IMAGE.EXE is compatible with the versions of those symbols in the running system. Chapter 32 describes the compatibility check in detail. If the versions are incompatible, the image activator aborts the activation and returns the fatal error status SS$_SYSVERDIF.

Since the Install utility performs this check as well, the image activator skips the check if the image header is resident.

7. It copies the symbol vector size and address from the image header to the IMCB.

8. The image activator checks that the match control information in the image header is consistent with the match requested in the global EISD whose presence caused the activation of this shareable image. If there is a mismatch, the image activator aborts the activation and returns the error status SS$_SHRIDMISMAT.

9. If the image header indicates that the shareable image has an initialization section, the image activator sets the IMCB$V_INITIALIZE flag and records the address of the initialization section in IMCB$L_INITIALIZE.

10. If the image header is resident, the image activator sets IMCB$V_RES_HEADER.

11. The image activator processes the EISDs for each section in the shareable image.

   • If the EISD is a global EISD, representing a different shareable image, the image activator compares the portion of its name designating the image (that is, without the trailing *nnn*) to the name of the IMCB most recently added to the work list. If the names are the same, the image activator does not add an IMCB to the work list. The comparison prevents some IMCB redundancy in the work list.

   If the names are different, the image activator creates an IMCB to describe the image. Before adding it to the work list, the image activator examines all existing work list entries for an entry whose name matches. If there is no match, the current IMCB is inserted at the head of the work list. Otherwise, the IMCB is inserted in place of the matching IMCB, and the matching IMCB is moved to the head of the work list.

   • If the EISD is not a global EISD, the image activator maps the section into process address space. Step 16 in Section 28.3.1 describes the processing of section EISDs and demand zero EISDs.

If a private section contains a privileged library vector that describes inner mode system services and rundown routines in the image, the image activator checks that the image has been installed /PROTECTED and /SHARED and, if not, returns the error status SS$_PROTINSTALL. It records the address of the vector in IMCB$PS_PLV_ADDRESS.

12. When all EISDs are disposed of, processing for the IMCB is complete. If activating this image has added more IMCBs to the work list, this IMCB becomes the top of the stack maintained in the done list. The image activator goes to step 1 to process the next IMCB in its work list.

After the last IMCB has been processed, the image activator performs the end processing described in Section 28.3.3.

28.3.3   Image Activator End Processing

If a main image was activated, the image activator performs the complete end processing described in this section. For a merged activation, it performs only steps 3, 4, 9, and 10.

The image activator's end processing consists of the following steps:

1. The image activator tests whether the image was linked with an image I/O segment larger than the standard space allocated during process creation. The standard size is determined by the SYSGEN parameter IMGIOCNT, whose default value is 64 pagelets. The default can be overridden at link time with the following line in the linker options file:

   ```
   IOSEGMENT = n
   ```

   If an image I/O segment larger than the default value is requested, the image activator requests the $CRETVA system service to create a replacement image I/O segment.

   If a P0-only image is being activated, the image activator creates the image I/O segment at the high-address end of P0 space.

   It calls RM$SET, in module RMSRESET, to initialize the image I/O segment.

2. The address space for the user stack is created with the Expand Region ($EXPREG) system service. The usual location of the user stack is at the low-address end of P1 space, where the automatic stack expansion can add user stack space as needed. The location of the user stack in P0-only images is at the high-address end of the P0 image.

   The default size of the user stack is 20 pagelets. The following line in the linker options file can override this value:

   ```
   STACK = n
   ```

The image activator creates a user stack with two extra pagelets for system use during exception processing in the event that the user stack is corrupted.

3. If the argument HDRBUF was specified, the image activator copies information from the image header to the user-supplied buffer.

4. If the argument RETADR was specified, it stores the beginning and end of the address range into which the image and any associated shareable images were mapped.

5. Running in kernel mode, the image activator stores the address of the high end of the user stack in the CTL$AL_STACK array. Reserving space for system use during exception processing, the image activator loads an address two pagelets below the high end of the stack into the user mode stack pointer (USP) processor register. This is the value loaded into the stack pointer (SP) register when a CALL_PAL REI instruction returns the process to user mode, which usually occurs following the return from the image activator.

6. The privileges that will be in effect while this image is executing are calculated. The process header (PHD) field PHD$Q_IMAGEPRIV is initialized to zero or the contents of KFE$Q_PROCPRIV, depending on whether an image installed with privileges is being activated. PHD$Q_IMAGEPRIV is ORed with the process-permanent privilege mask at location CTL$GQ_PROCPRIV.

   The result is stored in the process privilege mask in the access rights block (ARB) at offset ARB$Q_PRIV (also known as PCB$Q_PRIV) and in PHD$Q_PRIVMSK. The uses of the various privilege masks are described in Section 28.8.1.

7. The image activator stores the address of the image header buffer in the global location CTL$GL_IMGHDRBF.

8. It checks whether image accounting was requested for this particular image or enabled for the system as a whole. If so, the image activator records various statistics, such as current CPU time, in their P1 locations.

9. If a known image is being activated, its use count (KFE$L_USECNT) is incremented. If the image was installed /OPEN, the share count in its WCB is incremented. If the image was installed /RESIDENT, the image activator also increments KFE$L_REF_COUNT. The image activator then sets the done bit in the IMCB to indicate that it has been activated. The actions in this step are done for each image being activated.

10. At this point, the image activator has finished its work. It releases its lock on the known file list, loads a final status into R0, and returns to its requestor. The requestor (EXE$PROCSTRT, LIB$FIND_IMAGE_SYMBOL, or a CLI) requests the $IMGFIX system service to perform address relocation and fixup. Section 28.4 describes $IMGFIX. When

$IMGFIX returns, the requestor transfers control to the image as described in Section 28.5.

28.3.4   **Computing the Proper Order of Image Initialization**

As a by-product of its normal work, the image activator computes the order of initialization for multiple shareable images activated by a main image. The basic rule for image initialization is that if shareable image A calls shareable image B, then the initialization routine for image B must be called before the initialization routine for image A. This rule enables image A to call any routine in image B (or in any image that B calls) during A's own initialization.

The initialization routine for each activated image is called as part of image fixup (see Section 28.4.9). $IMGFIX first calls the initialization routine specified by the IMCB that is at the tail of the done list. It proceeds toward the head of the done list. The image activator must create the correct order of IMCBs in the done list by careful placement of IMCBs on both the work and done lists.

If code in image A calls code in image B, then at some point during the activation of image A, the image activator encounters a global EISD that references image B. The image activator builds an IMCB to insert at the head of the work list. Inserting these IMCBs at the head of the list ensures that these called, or son, images will be activated after the calling, or parent, image and generally before any siblings of the parent.

Before actually inserting the IMCB into the work list, the image activator examines existing work list entries. If it finds an entry whose name matches that of the IMCB to be added, it inserts the IMCB after the matching IMCB and then moves the matching IMCB to the head of the work list. Since an image is only activated once no matter how many times it is referenced, this ensures that its mapping is controlled by the top-level accessor. Otherwise, the current IMCB is inserted at the head of the work list. This list generates a walk of the image call graph known as a preorder traversal.

A stack, implemented at the tail of the done list, is used to convert the preorder traversal for image activation into a postorder traversal for image initialization. Basically, a parent node remains on the stack until its last son is activated. A stack pointer points to the top of this stack in the done list. (Initially, the stack pointer points to the back link in the queue header.) Figure 28.17 shows how the IMCBs at the head of the done list form this stack.

To pop this stack, the stack pointer is simply moved to the left. The next IMCB from the work list is always inserted to the right of the top of the stack. It becomes the new top of the stack if it has any sons. IMCBs to the right of the top of the stack are always in the proper initialization order. IMCBs at and to the left of the stack pointer are parent IMCBs that still have descendants that have not been activated.

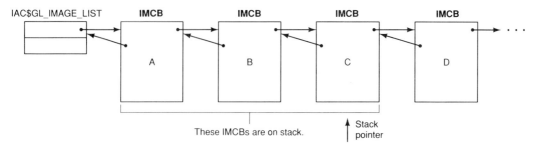

Figure 28.17
IMCB Stack in the Done List

The stack is built to ensure that the sons and descendants of an image are always placed into the done list to the right of the IMCB of the parent. Since the done list is processed in reverse order during initialization, this placement ensures that all images called directly or indirectly by some image are initialized before that image itself.

The manipulation of the work and done lists is controlled by the IMCB$L_ACTIVE_SONS count in each IMCB. This field specifies how many of the image's sons have not yet been activated (their IMCBs are still in the work list) and how many have been activated but still have active sons of their own (these IMCBs are on the stack in the done list). The IMCBs to the right of the stack pointer in the done list have no active sons.

The following steps describe the image activator's manipulation of IMCBs in the work and done lists to generate the proper initialization order. The details of image activation are described in Sections 28.3.1 and 28.3.2 and are not repeated here. These steps are in routines IMG$DO_WORK_LIST and PROCESS_ISD_LIST, in module IMGMAPISD.

1. The image activator attempts to remove an IMCB from the front of the work list. If there is none, it goes on to end processing (see Section 28.3.3).
2. If this image has already been activated (the image is in the done list) and it still has active sons, then the image activator has detected a circularity. (The image is one of its own descendants, so no initialization order is possible.) In this rare case, all the images in the done list that are involved in the circularity must be marked. An error will be reported if a subsequent attempt is made to initialize one of those images. The images involved in the circularity are those IMCBs on the stack from the top of the stack down to and including the previously activated image.

   Regardless of whether there is a circularity, if the image was previously activated, the image activator deallocates the IMCB and continues at step 6.
3. Otherwise, this is a new image needing activation. The image activator

inserts its IMCB just to the right of the top of the stack in the done list and zeros its IMCB$L_ACTIVE_SONS count.

It then performs the detailed work of activation for this image (steps 3 through 11 in Section 28.3.2). During those steps, each time the image activator creates a new global IMCB (son), it places the new IMCB at the front of the work list and increments IMCB$L_ACTIVE_SONS in its parent's IMCB. After the parent image is activated but before its sons have been, this field contains the total number of shareable images referenced by the image.

4. If the field IMCB$L_ACTIVE_SONS in the IMCB to the right of the top of the stack is nonzero after the image has been activated, the image activator makes that IMCB the top of the stack and continues with step 1. This new parent remains on the stack until all its sons, which are located at the front of the work list, are activated and no longer have active sons of their own.

5. Otherwise, the field IMCB$L_ACTIVE_SONS in the IMCB to the right of the top of the stack is zero, and the image activator continues with step 6.

6. This step is called a "decrement parent" operation. IMCB$L_ACTIVE_SONS in the parent IMCB at the top of the stack must be decremented to indicate that one of its sons has been activated. If its count becomes zero, this same step must be repeated for its parent, and so on.

If the stack is empty, there is no parent to decrement. The image activator continues with end processing (see Section 28.3.3). Otherwise, it decrements IMCB$L_ACTIVE_SONS in the IMCB at the top of the stack.

7. If the count is still positive (the image still has active sons), the IMCB remains at the top of the stack and the image activator continues with step 1. Otherwise, if IMCB$L_ACTIVE_SONS is now zero, the image activator must decrement the IMCB$L_ACTIVE_SONS field in the parent of the IMCB.

8. When it reaches the IMCB at the top of the stack (the IMCB that initiated the activations and therefore has no parent), the image activator proceeds to its end processing. Otherwise, the image activator pops the stack by moving the stack pointer to the left in the done list and repeats step 6.

28.3.5   Example of Activation

The details of activating an image linked with several shareable images can be illustrated with an example. The example main image references the shareable images A and LIBRTL, image A references the shareable images B and LIBRTL, and image B references LIBRTL.

At the beginning of the activation, an IMCB representing the main image is placed into the work list. This first IMCB is moved from the work list to the done list. As its EISDs are processed, work list items are added for A and LIBRTL as the result of references in the main image.

Work List	Done List	Stack Top
LIBRTL (main image)	Main image (2 sons)	←
A (main image)		

After mapping the sections of the main image, the image activator removes the IMCB for LIBRTL from its work list. The EISD is processed and the main image's son count is decremented. Since LIBRTL has no sons, the main image remains at the top of the stack.

Work List	Done List	Stack Top
A (main image)	Main image (1 son)	←
	LIBRTL	

The image activator removes the IMCB for image A from its work list. In processing A, work list items are added for B and LIBRTL. Since A has sons, it becomes the new stack top.

Work List	Done List	Stack Top
LIBRTL (A)	Main image (1 son)	
B (A)	A (2 sons)	←
	LIBRTL	

The image activator removes the IMCB for LIBRTL from the work list, discovers the duplication, and discards the entry, decrementing A's son count.

Work List	Done List	Stack Top
B (A)	Main image (1 son)	
	A (1 son)	←
	LIBRTL	

The image activator removes the IMCB for image B from its work list. In processing B, a work list item is added for LIBRTL. Since B has a son, it becomes the new stack top.

Work List	Done List	Stack Top
LIBRTL (B)	Main image (1 son)	
	A (1 son)	
	B (1 son)	←
	LIBRTL	

The image activator removes the IMCB for LIBRTL from the work list, discovers the duplication, and discards the entry, decrementing B's son count. Since this brings B's count to zero, A (B's parent) becomes the stack top and its son count is decremented, again to zero. Thus the main image becomes the stack top, its count is decremented to zero, and the image activator performs its end processing. The done list is left in the correct order for image initialization.

Work List	Done List	Stack Top
	Main image	⟵
	A	
	B	
	LIBRTL	

28.3.6   Special Cases of Image Activation

There are several other special cases for which the image activator must check:

▸ Image activation at system initialization time. During initialization of the system, image files must be opened without the support of either RMS or the file system. The image activator calls special executive code that performs the simpler file system operations in the absence of a file system. These routines are briefly described with system initialization in Chapters 33 and 34.

▸ Merged image activation. A merged image activation occurs subsequent to the activation and transfer of control to a main image. This can be used for mapping a debugger, the Image Dump utility, the traceback handler, a message file, or a CLI into an unused area of P0 or P1 space. It is also used to activate a shareable image when an already activated image calls the Run-Time Library procedure LIB$FIND_IMAGE_SYMBOL.

Rather than using the virtual address descriptors found in the merged image, the image activator simply uses the next available portion of P0 or P1 space. The user stack and image I/O segment are not mapped for a merged image. The RMS initialization routines are not called either, because an image is already executing and has RMS context that cannot be destroyed.

▸ Message sections. These sections add per-process or image-specific entries to the message facility.

▸ P0-only images. The linker can produce images that map all temporary structures, including the user stack and the image I/O segment, in P0 space. The image activator must recognize this type of image and correctly map these two structures, usually located in the lowest address portion of P1 space.

A P0-only image executes when the permanent part of the low-address end of P1 space must be extended without overwriting image structures. For example, the SET MESSAGE command causes a P0-only image called SETP0.EXE to execute. This image maps the indicated message section into the low-address end of P1 space and alters location CTL$GL_CTL-BASVA to reflect the new boundary between the temporary and permanent parts of P1 space. This last step is critical if the message section is to remain mapped when later images terminate.

► Activation of a known image. When the image activator opens a known image, RMS places the address of the KFE in the CTX field of the FAB.

The activation of a known image proceeds in the same way as that of a regular image, although some of the work that the image activator must perform in the regular case is avoided. In particular, a known image with a resident header is activated more quickly, because the header read operation is avoided.

In any case, the EISDs must still be processed and the PTEs set up so that the image can execute. In addition, the image activator must update the usage statistics for this known image.

► Activation of a CLI. When the image activator determines that it is attempting to activate a CLI as a main image, it activates instead the image LOGINOUT. First, the image activator closes the CLI image file, because LOGINOUT performs its own file open. It clears IMCB$L_FLAGS and IMCB$L_IHD. Then it activates LOGINOUT and transfers control to it. LOGINOUT maps the CLI into P1 space and transfers control to it. Chapter 30 describes this flow.

► Images that do not reside on a random access mass storage device. The image activator can activate images from sequential devices (certain magnetic tape devices) and images located on another node of a network. An address space large enough to contain the entire image body is first created. The pages of the image body that are not demand zero are then copied into this address space, thus requiring all image body pages, including read-only pages, to be set up as writable.

► Activation of an image resident in a granularity hint region. The EXE sections of such an image have already been activated in a system space granularity hint region. Global sections have been created for its shareable NOEXE sections. The image activator must map the nonshareable image sections in process-private space.

When the image activator discovers that such an image is being activated, it sets IMCB$V_DISCONTIGUOUS and, if the image has been linked /SECTION_BINDING=(DATA,CODE), sets IMCB$V_COMPRESS_DATASEC as well to indicate that the process-private data sections should be compressed. It copies the KFERES to space allocated in the P1 allocation region. If data sections are to be compressed, it allocates a KFERES large enough to describe each of the process-private image sections that will be created.

As the image activator processes the image's EISDs, if it encounters an EXE section, it confirms that the section has been mapped in system space already. When it encounters a shareable NOEXE section, it requests the

$MGBLSC system service to map the global section. The image activator processes the other types of EISD as described in step 16 of Section 28.3.1. If data sections are being compressed, it bases each data section at the next available page and records information about the section in the corresponding KFERES substructure.

After all the image sections have been activated, the address references in the process-private image sections are relocated and fixed up.

▶ Privileged shareable images. User-written system services and rundown routines are implemented as privileged shareable images. System service procedures that are not part of an executive image (for example, $MOUNT and $DISMOU) are implemented as privileged shareable images. A privileged shareable image contains a privileged library vector (PLV). The PLV for a privileged shareable image with user-written system services or rundown routines lists the kernel and executive mode system services and routines in the privileged shareable image. Figures 7.7 and 7.8 illustrate the layout of the PLV and the organization of a privileged shareable image.

After processing all the EISDs in a privileged shareable image, the image activator calls the routine IMG$PRVSHRIMG, in module SYSIMGFIX, to generate procedure descriptors and transfer routines for the services. If the image is completely protected, the routine checks that no shareable images other than SYS$PUBLIC_VECTORS and SYS$BASE_IMAGE have been linked with it; if any has, it returns the error status SS$_NOSHRIMG.

IMG$PRVSHRIMG relocates intra-image references in the image, in particular, those in the PLV. It creates enough virtual address space to contain system service transfer routines and their procedure descriptors. It processes the PLV as described in Chapter 7 and then does fixups and protection changes as described in Section 28.4. If the image has an initialization procedure, IMG$PRVSHRIMG calls it.

▶ Activation of interoperable images. The OpenVMS AXP system supports the execution of translated OpenVMS VAX images through a run-time environment called the Translated Image Environment (TIE). Moreover, it allows a combination of native and translated images to be activated together. Procedure calls between the two types of image require additional support because the OpenVMS AXP and OpenVMS VAX calling standards differ. An automatic jacketing mechanism detects cross-architecture calls and makes the conversions between the two calling standards. This mechanism is implemented partly by the image activator.

After processing the entire work list, the image activator checks whether any translated images were activated. If so, it must create virtual address space for the structures used in transforming calls from native images to procedures in translated images. It scans the fixup section list for images whose fixup sections include any records for linkage pairs with procedure signature blocks. These represent potential calls from a native image to a

987

translated shareable image. For such fixup that represents a call to a procedure in a translated image, it calculates the amount of virtual address space
required to create a bound procedure descriptor and, optionally, a nondefault procedure signature block. It requests the $CRETVA system service
to create that address space and records its starting address in CTL$GL_
BPD_PTR. The structures are built during image fixup processing, as described in Section 28.4.7.

Chapter 29 describes the jacketing mechanism and the environment for
translated images.

28.4 ADDRESS RELOCATIONS AND FIXUPS

Although the linker typically determines the address range into which an executable image is activated, it does not assign address space for any shareable
images. The linker, the $IMGACT system service, and the $IMGFIX system
service cooperate to postpone shareable image address assignment from link
time to image activation. Delaying address assignment increases the lifetime
of an image by partly decoupling it from the shareable images with which it
is linked. For example, a newer version of a shareable image can grow, shrink,
or even refer to additional shareable images without requiring the relinking
of an image that linked with it.

An image can refer to locations within itself or within another image,
generating addresses that require adjustment based on the address space assigned. The linker creates an image section called a fixup section in each
image. The fixup section describes the locations in the image that contain
addresses that must be adjusted after address assignment. The adjustment to
an intra-image address reference is called a relocation. The location to be adjusted can be a quadword or a longword. The adjustment to a reference from
one image to another, an inter-image reference, is called a fixup.

The types of reference that can require adjustment are as follows:

► Quadword and longword address references. The MACRO .ADDRESS directive (or its high-level language equivalent) references a fixed address in
virtual memory. Resolution of a .ADDRESS reference to a location in a
shareable image is deferred so that the shareable image need not be loaded
at a fixed base address. .ADDRESS references are fixed up when the image is activated, after the starting addresses of its image sections have been
determined.

The MACRO .ASCID directive (or its high-level language equivalent)
builds an ASCII string and a descriptor for it. It incorporates the equivalent of a .ADDRESS directive referencing the string. .ASCID directives
within a shareable image are relocated after the base address of the shareable image has been determined. In the following sections, text references
to .ADDRESS directives include those generated by .ASCID directives.

► Code address references. A code address directive references the entry point of a procedure rather than its procedure descriptor. Most code address directives are contained within procedure descriptors.

▶ Linkage pairs. A language compiler represents a linkage to an external procedure as a two-quadword data structure called a linkage pair. By the time a call using a linkage pair is executed, the first quadword of the linkage pair must contain the external procedure's code entry address, and the second quadword must contain the address of its procedure descriptor. When the linker links an object module containing a call with the object module containing the called procedure, the linker fills in the linkage pair in the calling object module.

▶ Linkage pairs with procedure signature blocks. A compiler can generate a data structure called a procedure signature block to describe a call from a native module. The procedure signature block details the arguments passed to the target procedure. For an image linked with the qualifier /NONATIVE_ONLY, the linker builds the procedure signature blocks in the fixup section. Each is processed during image fixup if its target procedure is in a translated image.

Because the linker assigns the address space for an executable image, it can calculate correct values for intra-image references, and a typical executable image requires no relocations. (However, an executable image linked /SECTION_BINDING to enable it to be installed /RESIDENT does contain relocation records.) If an executable image references any shareable images, it requires fixups. Its fixup section describes the shareable images with which it was linked and lists the locations that must be adjusted after the shareable image address space is assigned.

Because the address space for a shareable image is not assigned until the image is activated, all intra-image address references within a shareable image must be relocated. If the shareable image is linked with other shareable images, its references to addresses in them must be fixed up. Its fixup section describes those shareable images and lists the locations requiring relocation or fixup.

When the $IMGACT system service encounters an EISD describing a fixup section, it stores the base address of the image being processed in the fixup section at EIAF$L_BASE_VA and inserts the section at the head of the list pointed to by CTL$GL_FIXUPLNK. After the main image and its tree of shareable images have been activated, the $IMGFIX system service performs relocations and fixups, using the list of fixup sections. Relocations for all images are performed first, before any fixups; the relocations adjust addresses within symbol vectors that are used in fixups.

Image sections that contain relocated or fixed up addresses must be writable during image activation so that the modifications can be made. If such a section is made up of NOWRT PSECTs, the protection on its pages must be altered after the modifications are made. The linker describes these and other protection changes in the fixup section as well.

The sections that follow describe the fixup section and its use by the $IMGFIX system service.

28.4.1 Fixup Section

A fixup section describes all relocations and fixups to be made to the image and a list of the shareable images referenced by the image. Figure 28.18 shows the organization of an image and the layout of the fixup section within it.

The fixup section is made up of a fixed area and a number of variable-length areas. The following fields in the fixed area contain the byte offset relative to the start of the fixup section of each variable-length area:

- ▸ EIAF$L_QRELFIXOFF—Offset to the quadword relocation records
- ▸ EIAF$L_LRELFIXOFF—Offset to the longword relocation records
- ▸ EIAF$L_QDOTADROFF—Offset to the quadword address fixup records
- ▸ EIAF$L_LDOTADROFF—Offset to the longword address fixup records
- ▸ EIAF$L_CODEADROFF—Offset to the code address fixup records
- ▸ EIAF$L_LPFIXOFF—Offset to the linkage pair fixup records
- ▸ EIAF$L_CHGPRTOFF—Offset to the protection change fixup records
- ▸ EIAF$L_SHLSTOFF—Offset to the shareable image list entries

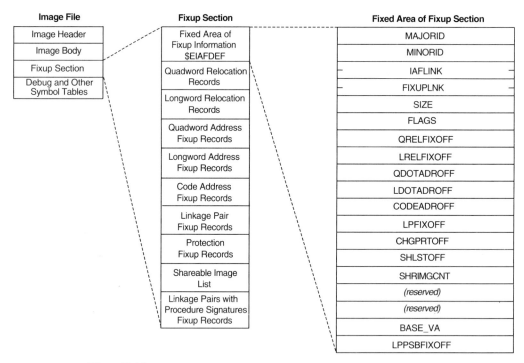

Figure 28.18
Image with Fixup Section Layout

▸ EIAF$L_LPPSBFIXOFF—Offset to the fixup records for linkage pairs with signature blocks

An offset value of zero means the corresponding relocations or fixups are not present in the image and thus the corresponding variable-length area is not present in the fixup section.

EIAF$L_MAJORID and EIAF$L_MINORID describe the version of the fixup section.

EIAF$L_FLAGS contains one defined flag, which, when set, identifies the image as a shareable image.

EIAF$L_SHRIMGCNT contains the number of shareable images with which the image has been linked, actually the number of entries in the shareable image list. In an OpenVMS VAX image, this count includes the image itself; in an OpenVMS AXP image, the count typically does not. If, however, an image has defined universal symbols with alias names, the count includes the image itself.

The fields that follow have meaning only for an in-memory copy of a fixup section in an image being activated.

The two longwords at EIAF$L_IAFLINK link the fixup section into a list of fixup sections from all activated images.

EIAF$L_FIXUPLNK links the fixup section into a list of fixup sections yet to be processed. The listhead is at CTL$GL_FIXUPLNK.

EIAF$L_BASE_VA contains the address of the IMCB describing the image containing this section until the relocations and fixups have been done for the image. Then it contains the base address at which the image was activated.

28.4.2   Shareable Image List

EIAF$L_SHLSTOFF contains the offset to the shareable image list entries (SHLs) in the fixup section, and EIAF$L_SHRIMGCNT contains the number of SHLs. Each SHL identifies a shareable image referenced by the image. Moreover, each shareable image has its own fixup section and SHL list.

An SHL can also represent one of the system base images: an image that requests system services has an SHL representing SYS$PUBLIC_VECTORS.EXE; an image linked /SYSEXE to resolve executive universal symbols has an SHL representing SYS$BASE_IMAGE.EXE.

Although the linker builds the shareable image list, it initializes only the fields SHL$T_IMGNAM and SHL$B_SHL_SIZE.

Figure 28.19 shows the layout of an SHL and SHLs within a fixup section.

Each SHL contains the name of the shareable image it represents at SHL$T_IMGNAM. EXE$IMGFIX uses this name to match the SHL with an IMCB in the done list. It copies the virtual address of the shareable image's symbol vector from the IMCB into SHL$L_BASE_VA. If the SHL represents

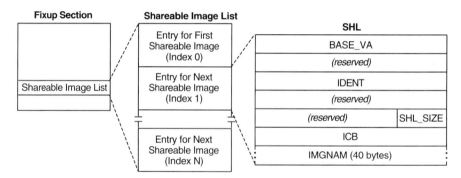

Figure 28.19
Shareable Image List

one of the system base images, EXE$IMGFIX copies the address of its symbol vector from the appropriate system cell instead.

SHL$B_SHL_SIZE contains the size of the SHL, 64 bytes.

SHL$L_IDENT contains the GSMATCH information from the version of the shareable image with which the image was linked. Its contents are copied from the match control information in the global EISD identifying the shareable image.

SHL$L_ICB contains the address of the IMCB that this SHL represents.

28.4.3 Relocation Records

An example of a location in a shareable image that needs relocation is a procedure descriptor, which contains the address of the code entry point for that procedure. After linking, such a location contains an image-relative offset. After the image is assigned address space, the base address of the image must be added to the offset. The fixup section contains relocation records that identify the locations in the image requiring that type of adjustment.

The linkage section and symbol vector contain many of the locations in an image that require relocation. Note that an image section containing relocatable addresses cannot be shared among processes, since the resolutions of those addresses are specific to the virtual address space in each process. Consequently, linkage sections and symbol vectors are not shareable.

Each image section that contains locations with relocatable addresses is represented by one or more relocation records. A relocation record specifies the base address in the image of a range of addresses, some of whose contents need relocation. Each relocation record contains a bitmap with one bit for each location in the address range. When set, a bit indicates that the corresponding location's contents need relocation. The bitmap length is rounded up to an integral number of quadwords. The linker generates enough relocation records so that the bitmaps do not contain large numbers of adjacent

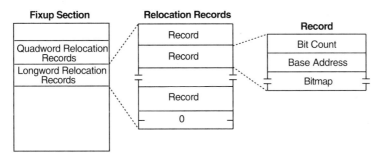

Figure 28.20
Relocation Records

zeros; if a particular record does contain too many adjacent zeros, the linker breaks it into multiple records.

Figure 28.20 shows the layout of relocation records within a fixup section. In a quadword relocation record each bit represents a quadword, and in a longword relocation record each bit represents a longword. Each of the two sets of relocation records ends with a quadword of zero.

To perform the relocations in one record, EXE$IMGFIX adds the base address of the image to the image offset and scans the bitmap for set bits. For each set bit, it calculates the corresponding address whose contents require relocation and adds the base address of the image.

For an image installed /RESIDENT, EXE$IMGFIX first determines whether a range of addresses requiring relocations is within a resident section or a compressed data section and calculates the activated address requiring relocation based on the contents of the KFERES. If an address is within a resident or compressed data section, the new contents will be the old contents minus the image offset of that image section plus the address of the resident section.

28.4.4 Longword and Quadword Address Fixups

A longword address record or quadword address record (or both) exists for each shareable image that is the target of .ADDRESS or .ASCID directives. A longword address record records the locations of longwords in the image being fixed up, and a quadword address record, the locations of quadwords. Each record consists of an entry count; the index of the SHL associated with the shareable image, which contains the referenced data; and a series of fixups. Figure 28.21 shows the layout of longword and quadword address fixup information within a fixup section.

Each fixup is a pair of longwords. The first contains the symbol vector offset of the target symbol, and the second, the offset into the image being fixed up of the longword or quadword. At the specified offset in the image

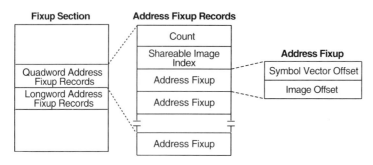

Figure 28.21
Longword and Quadword Address Fixups

is a longword or quadword containing zero or a constant to be added to the fixed-up address.

For each record, EXE$IMGFIX typically performs fixups as follows:

1. It uses the index into the shareable image list to locate the SHL associated with the shareable image.
2. From the SHL, it obtains the address of the shareable image's symbol vector.
3. For each address fixup, it adds the image offset to the base address of the image being fixed up to get the address of the longword or quadword to be fixed up. To the contents of that longword or quadword, it adds the contents of the address portion of the symbol vector linkage pair at the specified offset in the shareable image symbol vector.

For an image installed /RESIDENT, EXE$IMGFIX first determines whether an address requiring a fixup is within a resident section or a compressed data section and, if so, calculates the activated address requiring fixup based on the contents of the KFERES.

28.4.5 Code Address Fixups

There is a code address fixup record for each shareable image that is the target of code address directives. Each record consists of an entry count, the index of the SHL associated with the shareable image, and a series of offsets into the image being fixed up. Figure 28.22 shows the layout of code address fixup information within a fixup section.

At the specified offset in the image is a quadword containing the symbol vector offset of the symbol referenced. To perform each fixup, EXE$IMGFIX calculates the address of the location in the image being fixed up and examines the quadword at that address to get the symbol vector offset of the target address. It stores the code address portion of that symbol vector linkage pair in the specified quadword.

For an image installed /RESIDENT, EXE$IMGFIX first determines whether

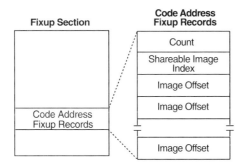

Figure 28.22
Code Address Fixups

an address requiring a fixup is within a resident section or a compressed data section and, if so, calculates the activated address requiring fixup based on the contents of the KFERES.

28.4.6   Linkage Pair Fixups

A linkage pair fixup record exists for each shareable image that is the target of linkage pairs in the image being fixed up. Each record consists of an entry count, the index of the SHL associated with the shareable image, and a series of offsets into the image being fixed up. Figure 28.23 shows the layout of the linkage pair fixup area within a fixup section.

At the specified offset in the image is a linkage pair, the first quadword of which contains the symbol vector offset of the target symbol. To perform each fixup, EXE$IMGFIX calculates the address of the location in the image being fixed up and examines the quadword at that address to get the symbol vector offset of the target address. It stores the linkage pair at that symbol vector entry in the specified linkage pair.

For an image installed /RESIDENT, EXE$IMGFIX first determines whether

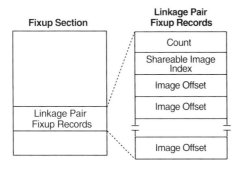

Figure 28.23
Linkage Pair Fixups

an address requiring a fixup is within a resident section or a compressed data section and, if so, calculates the activated address requiring fixup based on the contents of the KFERES.

28.4.7 Fixups for Linkage Pairs with Procedure Signature Blocks

When the modules of a native image are compiled /TIE and the image is linked /NONATIVE_ONLY, code in that image can call procedures in both native and translated images. A call to a translated image has an associated procedure signature block and goes through a jacket procedure. The jacket procedure uses the signature block (see Chapter 29) to transform the native arguments into arguments appropriate for the translated image.

There is a fixup record for linkage pairs with procedure signature blocks for each shareable image that is the target of linkage pairs in the image being fixed up. Each record consists of an entry count, the index of the SHL associated with the shareable image, a series of entries, and a series of procedure signature blocks. Each entry contains an offset into the image being fixed up and the unrelocated address of the corresponding procedure signature block if there is one. If there is not, that is, if the procedure signature is the default one, the entry contains zero instead.

Figure 28.24 shows the layout of the fixup records for linkage pairs with procedure signature blocks.

At the specified offset in the image is a linkage pair, the first quadword of which contains the symbol vector offset of the target symbol. In processing each record, EXE$IMGFIX first determines whether the shareable image is

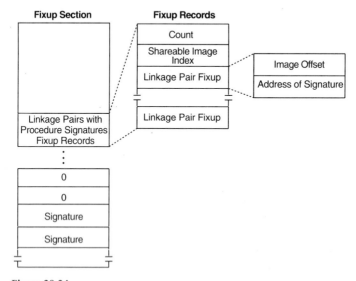

Figure 28.24
Fixups for Linkage Pairs with Procedure Signature Blocks

native or translated. If native, it essentially performs a simple linkage pair fixup as described in the previous section.

If the shareable image is translated, for each fixup EXE$IMGFIX calculates the address of the location in the image being fixed up and saves the contents of the quadword at that address, the symbol vector offset of the target procedure in the translated image.

In the virtual address space the image activator created for bound procedure descriptors and procedure signature addresses (see Section 28.3.6), EXE$IMGFIX builds a bound procedure descriptor to represent a transfer to EXE$NATIVE_TO_TRANSLATED_BP, in module SYSJACKET. The target procedure value is the code entry point of the target translated procedure. If there is a nondefault procedure signature block, EXE$IMGFIX copies it immediately after the bound procedure descriptor and stores its offset in the bound procedure descriptor.

It stores the bound procedure descriptor address and the code entry address of the procedure EXE$NATIVE_TO_TRANSLATED_BP in the linkage pair of the image being fixed up. Later, when the image calls this procedure, control is transferred to the $NATIVE_TO_TRANSLATED system service, which uses the procedure signature block to build arguments for the translated image's procedure and then transfer to the translated procedure.

28.4.8   Page Protection Fixup

After address fixup is complete, EXE$IMGFIX adjusts page protection as specified in the page protection data area of the fixup section. For EXE$IMG-FIX to relocate or fix up a location requires that the page containing the location be writable. A read-only image section containing such a location is originally mapped as writable. The linker creates an entry in the page protection data area for each section of this type, specifying a new page protection of UR. After address fixup, EXE$IMGFIX requests the Set Protection on Pages ($SETPRT) system service for each entry in the page protection data area.

An image that contains a protected section, for example, a privileged shareable image containing user-written system services, has a page protection entry that alters the protection of that section to UREW.

In an image linked with any shareable images, a final page protection entry alters the protection of the fixup section itself to UREW. The fixup section pages are protected from user mode modification so that the SHL entries remain unmodified. Figure 28.25 shows the layout of the page protection area.

28.4.9   Operation of EXE$IMGFIX

The $IMGFIX system service procedure, EXE$IMGFIX in module SYSIMG-FIX, runs in the access mode from which it is requested so that it can perform relocations and fixups and call initialization procedures. Because relocations

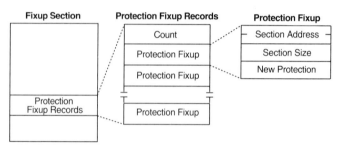

Figure 28.25
Page Protection Area

and fixups modify locations within images, they must be performed in the same access mode at which the main image will be entered. The exceptions are fixups for privileged shareable images, which are performed from executive mode.

EXE$IMGFIX processes entries from the fixup section list created by EXE$IMGACT. It first scans the SHL list in each fixup section and confirms that each shareable image referenced by a fixup section has been activated, returning the error status IMG$_IMAGE_NOT_FOUND if not. It records the address of the image's symbol vector in SHL$L_BASE_VA and its IMCB address in SHL$L_ICB. It then processes the entire fixup section list, first performing all relocations from all sections, then all fixups, and then all protection changes.

In the case of an image installed /RESIDENT with compressed data sections, EXE$IMGFIX and the procedures it calls must tranform image offsets into their equivalent virtual addresses using the KFERES structure.

Following address fixup and page protection modification, EXE$IMGFIX tests whether any privileged shareable images have been activated. If so, it requests the $IMGACT system service, specifying the IAC$V_SETVECTOR flag. Running in executive mode, the image activator initializes the P1 space dispatch vectors for user-written system services, rundown routines, and message sections.

If any shareable image specified an initialization routine, EXE$IMGFIX scans the done list, IMCBs representing activated images, from back to front. Running in user mode, EXE$IMGFIX calls the initialization routine of each shareable image that specified one.

28.5   IMAGE STARTUP

EXE$PROCSTRT or a CLI can request image activation and fixup, as described in Chapter 30. After successful image activation and fixup, the image is called at its transfer address. Depending on how the image was linked, the initial transfer of control may be to a debugger, a user-supplied initialization procedure, or the executable image itself.

28.5.1   Transfer Address Array

In addition to the EISDs previously discussed, the linker includes in the image header a data structure called a transfer address array. This array contains the user-supplied transfer address. It also provides the means for including a debugger or traceback handler in the user image and for specifying that the image contains initialization code.

The layout of the transfer address array is pictured in Figure 28.26, along with several examples of its contents.

EIHA$L_SIZE contains the size of the array, always 48 bytes. For a main image the array can potentially contain three transfer addresses:

▶ Typically, the first address represents the Image Startup ($IMGSTA) system service, sometimes called the debugger bootstrap. Unless the

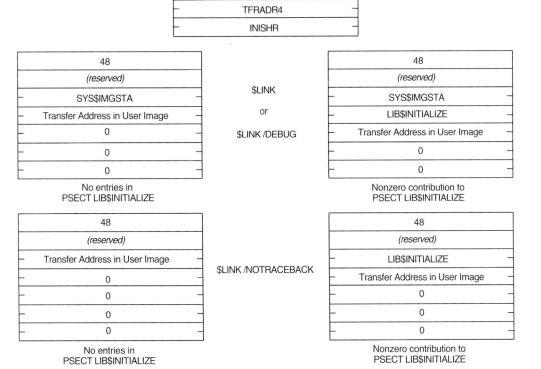

Figure 28.26
Layout of a Main Image Transfer Address Array

image has been linked /NOTRACEBACK or /DEBUG=*file-spec*, the high-order longword of the first transfer address contains –1, and the low-order longword contains the offset of SYS$IMGSTA in the SYS$PUBLIC_VECTORS symbol vector. The –1 identifies this address as SYS$IMGSTA to EXE$IMGFIX, which performs the necessary fixup.

▶ The address LIB$INITIALIZE occurs next for a main image that contains initialization procedures. This address in the image file is image-relative and is relocated by EXE$IMGFIX when the image is activated.

▶ The next transfer address is the one associated with the user image, either the argument of a .END directive for a MACRO-32 or MACRO-64 program or the first statement of a main program written in a high-level language. This address in the image file is image-relative and is relocated by EXE$IMGFIX when the image is activated.

▶ A final entry containing zero is the end-of-list indication, no matter what options were passed to the linker.

Each module that is part of a main image and that contains an initialization procedure contributes a table entry with the procedure value to a PSECT called LIB$INITIALIZE. One or more modules in the main image must declare as external the symbol LIB$INITIALIZE. The presence of that declaration results in the linker's adding to the image a STARLET.OLB object module that contains the procedure LIB$INITIALIZE. The initialization transfer procedure LIB$INITIALIZE and the LIB$INITIALIZE PSECT are described further in the *OpenVMS Programming Concepts* manual.

If the DCL command LINK/DEBUG=*file-spec* is used to link an image, the explicit file specification is the name of a particular debugger object module to be linked with the image. The linker places the transfer address found in the specified debugger file into the first element in the transfer address array rather than the quadword representing SYS$IMGSTA. It puts the image transfer address into the second element of the array. The debugger object module must perform SYS$IMGSTA's role in transferring control to the image.

If the /NOTRACEBACK qualifier is included (and not overridden implicitly by including an explicit /DEBUG qualifier), then there is no debug transfer address. In all other cases (including the DCL command LINK/DEBUG, which does not specify an explicit debugger module), the linker places the address of SYS$IMGSTA in the first element of the transfer address array.

For a shareable image, the last element in the array, at offset EIHA$L_INISHR, contains the procedure value of an initialization routine if one exists.

28.5.2 $IMGSTA System Service

Except for an image linked with the /NOTRACEBACK or the /DEBUG=*file-spec* qualifier, every main native image executes the $IMGSTA system service. The system service procedure, EXE$IMGSTA in module SYSIMGSTA, runs in user mode. This procedure examines link and CLI flags to determine whether to start the image directly or to map the debugger into P0 space and transfer control to it.

EXE$IMGSTA first tests whether it should map a debugger into P0 space. The mapping is done if either of the following conditions is true:

▶ If the program was linked with the DCL command LINK/DEBUG and simply run (that is, not run with a RUN/NODEBUG command)

▶ If the program was run with the DCL command RUN/DEBUG, independent of whether the debugger was requested at link time

The debugger is not mapped if the image was run with a RUN/NODEBUG command or if the /DEBUG qualifier was omitted from both the LINK command and the RUN command.

If a debugger is to be mapped, EXE$IMGSTA requests the Translate Logical Name ($TRNLOG) system service to translate the logical name LIB$DEBUG. If there is no translation, EXE$IMGSTA uses the string DEBUG as the debugger name. EXE$IMGSTA then requests the $IMGACT system service to activate the debugger image from the default device and directory SYS$LIBRARY. It specifies flags for a merged activation in P0 space, so that the debugger will be mapped at addresses just higher than the main image and its shareable images. EXE$IMGSTA then requests the $IMGFIX system service and finally transfers control to the debugger image through the third quadword from the beginning of the debugger image, which contains the procedure value of the debug entry point. The debugger initializes itself, establishes a breakpoint at the beginning of the image, and returns to EXE$IMGSTA.

If no debugger is mapped, EXE$IMGSTA establishes a condition handler for the current call frame. This condition handler, BOOT_HANDLER, gains control on signals that the image does not handle directly. After gaining control, the condition handler invokes the debugger, invokes the traceback handler, or resignals.

Whether or not a debugger is mapped, EXE$IMGSTA alters the arguments with which it was called to point to the next address in the transfer vector array and passes control to the next transfer address. This is either the Run-Time Library procedure LIB$INITIALIZE or the transfer address of the user image.

28.5.3   Exception Handler for Traceback

BOOT_HANDLER, the condition handler established by EXE$IMGSTA before the image was called, has two main functions:

▶ It invokes a debugger if a DEBUG command is typed after an image is interrupted with a CTRL/Y.

▶ If an unfielded condition occurs, it causes an image dump, if one was requested, and invokes the traceback handler to produce a symbolic stack dump.

However the handler is entered, it first calls EXE$CATCHALL_EXTENSION, in module PROCSTRT, which calls any catch-all condition handler extensions declared by the image (see Chapter 6).

If a user interrupts execution of a nonprivileged image by typing CTRL/Y and DEBUG, the DCL CLI generates the signal SS$_DEBUG. (Privileged images are simply run down in response to this command sequence.) If all handlers established by the image resignal the SS$_DEBUG exception, the debugger boot handler eventually gains control.

The handler's response to an SS$_DEBUG signal is to map the debugger (if it is not already mapped) and transfer control to it. Note that an image that was neither linked nor run with the debugger can still be debugged, albeit without a debug symbol table, if the image reaches some undesirable state, such as an infinite loop.

Another function of the condition handler is to field any error conditions (where the severity level is WARNING, ERROR, or SEVERE) and pass them on to the traceback facility. If an image dump was requested, the handler dispatches to EXE$IMGDMP_MERGE (see Chapter 27) to create an image dump. When EXE$IMGDMP_MERGE returns, the handler maps the traceback facility, denoted by the logical name LIB$TRACE, into P0 space. If the condition has a severity level of either SUCCESS or INFO, the handler merely resignals it. The condition is then handled by the catch-all condition handler established by either EXE$PROCSTRT or the CLI that called the image.

28.6 IMAGE EXIT

When an image has completed its work, it passes control back to the executive, either by requesting the $EXIT system service or by returning to its caller, which requests the $EXIT system service. $EXIT calls whatever exit handlers have been declared by the image and then requests the Delete Process ($DELPRC) system service.

28.6.1 Exit Handlers and Related System Services

An exit handler is an optional, user-declared procedure that performs image cleanup. To use this option, an image builds a data structure called an exit control block and passes its address to the $DCLEXH system service. The access mode from which the service is requested is the mode in which the exit handler is to execute. Exit handlers can be declared for user, supervisor, and executive access modes.

An exit control block contains the procedure value of the exit handler and its arguments. The exit handler's first argument is the address of a longword

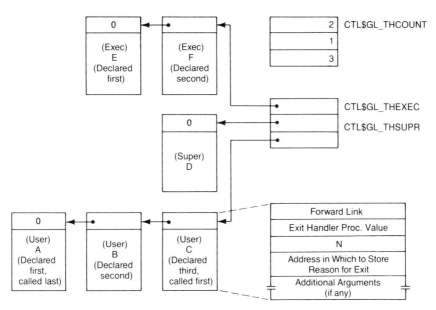

Figure 28.27
Sample Exit Handler Lists

to receive the final image status. The declarer of the exit handler defines any additional arguments and their use. An exit control block also contains a forward link field. This field contains the address of the next exit control block or, if there is none, zero. The $DCLEXH system service links all the exit control blocks for an access mode. Each list is ordered with the most recently declared exit handlers' control blocks first.

The exit handler listheads are in a three-longword array. Another three-longword array contains the number of exit control blocks in each list. Each array is indexed by access mode. Figure 28.27 shows these arrays and exit control blocks.

Both arrays are in P1 space and modifiable only from kernel mode. Exit control blocks, however, are defined by the image in the process-private address space that it controls. Therefore, the system services that access these lists must exercise particular care. An exit control block corrupted through program error could destroy the integrity of its list.

When inserting or removing an exit control block, for example, each system service must test the accessibility of affected forward links. The count array is used to prevent infinite loops that might otherwise result from multiple declarations of the same exit control block.

Two system services other than $DCLEXH access exit control blocks: Cancel Exit Handler ($CANEXH) and $EXIT (see Section 28.6.2). An image requests the $CANEXH system service to delete a particular exit control block or all those for one access mode.

The $DCLEXH and $CANEXH system service procedures are EXE$DCL-EXH and EXE$CANEXH, both in module SYSDCLEXH. Both execute in kernel mode.

28.6.2   **Flow of the $EXIT System Service**

The $EXIT system service procedure, EXE$EXIT in module SYSEXIT, runs initially in kernel mode. It also executes in outer modes, calling exit handlers.

EXE$EXIT is called with a single argument, the final status of the image. It stores the status in CTL$GL_FINALSTS, from which it can be copied for image or process accounting. EXE$EXIT clears the force exit pending flag, PCB$V_FORCPEN in PCB$L_STS.

If EXE$EXIT was called from kernel mode, it requests the $DELPRC system service, and the process is deleted. If EXE$EXIT was called from any other access mode, it examines the exit handler listheads (see Figure 28.27). It begins with the one for the mode from which it was called and proceeds to those of inner (more privileged) access modes.

If EXE$EXIT finds a nonzero listhead, it saves the listhead contents and the number of exit control blocks in the list, and clears both the listhead and the count longwords. EXE$EXIT then restores the integer registers saved at entry to itself and calls EXE$REI_INIT_STACK_ALT, in module REI_INIT_STACK, to clean up the kernel stack, return to the outer access mode from which the service was requested, and enter EXIT_CALLBACK, a routine local to SYSEXIT.

Running in the outer mode, EXIT_CALLBACK removes the first exit control block from the list and saves the address of the next handler, final image status, and count of remaining handlers on the stack. It writes the final image status to the address specified in the exit control block and calls the exit handler. When (if) that handler returns, EXIT_CALLBACK calls the next handler in the list. This continues until the list is exhausted or until EXIT_CALL-BACK has exhausted the count of exit handlers.

Once all the exit handlers for a given access mode have been called, EXIT_CALLBACK must return to a more privileged access mode. It clears the frame pointer (FP) register to terminate the call chain for that access mode. It changes access mode by requesting the $EXIT system service. If none of the exit handlers in the list just processed has done anything extraordinary (such as declaring another exit handler), then the list for that mode is still empty and EXE$EXIT proceeds to the next inner access mode in its search for more exit handlers.

When EXE$EXIT reaches the executive mode exit handler list, if the list is empty, EXE$EXIT tests whether deletion of this process is already in progress (PCB$V_DELPEN set in PCB$L_STS). If not, it requests the $DELPRC system service.

Otherwise, it makes several checks to determine whether, even in the absence of executive mode exit handlers, it should enter executive mode:

1. It tests and sets bit PCB$V_ERDACT in PCB$L_STS to see whether executive mode rundown routines have already been called.

2. If they have not, it tests whether any permanent executive mode rundown routines have been established, either by the process or the system. (A process-permanent executive mode rundown routine is established through calling IMG$ADD_PRIVILEGED_VECTOR_ENTRY, in module IMGMAPISD. Use of this mechanism is reserved to Digital. In contrast, image-temporary rundown routines are defined within a privileged shareable image.)

3. If no rundown routines have been established, it also checks whether any executive mode process event handler has been declared to enable a subsystem, for example, the POSIX subsystem, to receive notification of image rundown.

If there is no reason to enter executive mode, EXE$EXIT requests the $DELPRC system service. Otherwise, it enters executive mode as previously described so that it can call rundown routines, a process event handler, or both, from executive mode. EXIT_CALLBACK runs.

After calling executive mode exit handlers, if any, EXIT_CALLBACK tests whether any permanent executive mode rundown routines have been established, either by the process or the system. If so, it calls each of them.

EXIT_CALLBACK then calls EXE$PRCEVT_DISPATCHER, in module LAYERED_SYSTEM_ROUTINES, to notify any subsystem that requested notification of image rundown. EXIT_CALLBACK then requests the $EXIT system service.

When EXE$EXIT reaches kernel mode, that is, when it has called all existing handlers, it requests $DELPRC to delete the process.

28.6.3 Example of Exit Handler List Processing

To illustrate the processing of exit handlers, suppose that a process has its exit handler lists set up as shown in Figure 28.27. When the image requests the $EXIT system service from user mode, EXE$EXIT takes the following steps:

1. EXE$EXIT finds a nonzero listhead for user mode exit control blocks. The listhead points to the exit control block for procedure C, the most recently declared user mode exit handler.

2. EXE$EXIT stores this address in R0 and clears the listhead. It returns to user access mode and enters EXIT_CALLBACK, which calls procedure C. When C returns, EXIT_CALLBACK calls procedure B and finally procedure A. When A returns, EXIT_CALLBACK determines that the user mode list is exhausted (because the forward pointer in the last exit

handler is zero). EXIT_CALLBACK, running in user mode, requests the $EXIT system service.

3. As in step 1, the search for exit handlers begins with user mode, but this list is now empty. EXE$EXIT continues with the supervisor mode list, which has the single exit control block for handler D. The supervisor listhead is cleared, access mode is changed to supervisor, and EXIT_CALLBACK calls procedure D. When D returns, EXIT_CALL-BACK again requests the $EXIT system service, this time from supervisor mode.

4. Now the search for exit handlers begins with supervisor mode, whose list is empty. The list for executive mode contains two exit handlers, F and E, which are called from executive mode. When they return, the $EXIT system service is again requested, this time from executive access mode. The search that now begins with the executive mode listhead fails and the process is deleted.

The logic illustrated here shows how a process can prevent image exit through the use of exit handlers. Suppose EXE$EXIT called a supervisor mode handler that redeclared itself. When EXIT_CALLBACK exhausted the exit handler list and requested the $EXIT system service again, the handler would be back on the supervisor mode exit handler list and would be reentered to redeclare itself again.

In fact, this use of exit handlers is just the mechanism employed by the DCL CLI to allow multiple images to execute, one after another, in the same process. This mechanism is discussed in more detail in Chapter 30.

Note that an exit handler that is declared later (which implies that it will be called earlier) can prevent previously declared handlers for the same access mode from even being called by simply requesting the $EXIT system service. In the previous example, procedure C could prevent exit handlers B and A from being called by requesting $EXIT itself.

28.7 IMAGE AND PROCESS RUNDOWN

In a process with a CLI, multiple images can execute one after another. Several steps must be taken to prevent a later image from inheriting either enhancements (such as elevated privileges) or degradations (such as a reduced working set) from a previous image. In addition, when a process is deleted, all traces of it must be eliminated from the system data structures and all reusable resources returned to the system.

The $RUNDWN system service serves both those needs. $RUNDWN is called with one argument, access mode. This argument enables $RUNDWN to distinguish between image rundown and process rundown. The service is requested with an argument of user mode by the DCL CLI to clean up between image executions. $RUNDWN is also requested from the $DELPRC system service (see Chapter 31) with an argument of kernel mode to remove traces of a process being deleted.

The $RUNDWN system service performs much of its work by requesting other system services. It first maximizes its access mode argument with the access mode of its caller. It passes the maximized access mode argument to these services to allow them to determine how much work to do. For example, the Dequeue Lock Request ($DEQ) system service (see Chapter 11) can be requested with an access mode argument to release all locks for that access mode and all outer modes. If $RUNDWN is requested with an argument of user mode, its $DEQ request cancels only user mode locks. If $RUNDWN is requested with an argument of kernel mode, then all process locks are dequeued. In this section, the phrase "based on access mode" means "perform this operation for this access mode and all outer (less privileged) access modes."

Although most rundown actions require kernel mode, executive mode rundown routines can only be called from executive mode. Therefore, the $RUNDWN system service is actually a composite mode of caller service that can request first an executive mode form of the rundown service ($ERNDWN) and then a kernel mode form ($KRNDWN).

The $RUNDWN system service procedure, EXE$RUNDWN in module SYSRUNDWN, tests whether it has been entered in kernel mode. If not, it requests the $ERNDWN service, passing it the access mode argument. In either case, it then requests the $KRNDWN service, passing it the access mode argument.

The $ERNDWN service procedure, EXE$ERNDWN in module SYSRUN-DWN, takes the following steps:

1. It maximizes the previous mode with its access mode argument, as previously described.
2. It tests whether executive mode rundown routines have already been called (bit PCB$V_ERDACT set in PCB$L_STS) and, if so, returns to EXE$RUNDWN. This test prevents infinite loops triggered by errors in executive mode rundown routines.
3. It requests the Set Resource Wait Mode ($SETRWM) system service, enabling resource wait mode to ensure that image rundown completes successfully.
4. It requests the Change to Kernel Mode ($CMKRNL) system service to call a kernel mode procedure to set PCB$V_ERDACT (which is in a page whose protection prohibits executive mode write access).
5. It tests CTL$GL_USRUNDWN_EXEC to see whether any process-permanent executive mode rundown routines have been established. It calls each that has, passing it the access mode argument.

    It tests EXE$GL_USRUNDWN_EXEC to see if any systemwide

routines have been established and, if so, calls each with the access mode argument.

6. It then calls EXE$PRCEVT_DISPATCHER, in module LAYERED_ SYSTEM_ROUTINES, to notify any subsystem that requested notice of image rundown.

7. It requests the $SETRWM service to restore the previous setting and returns to its requestor, EXE$RUNDWN.

The $KRNDWN service procedure, EXE$KRNDWN in module SYSRUN-DWN, takes the following steps:

1. It maximizes the previous mode with its access mode argument.

2. It clears any previously requested powerfail asynchronous system trap (AST) and returns AST quota to the process.

3. It requests the $SETRWM system service, enabling resource wait mode.

4. EXE$KRNDWN invokes any per-process or systemwide kernel mode rundown routines. Such a routine might perform cleanup for user-written system services.

5. It then calls EXE$PRCEVT_DISPATCHER, in module LAYERED_SYS-TEM_ROUTINES, to notify any subsystem that requested notification of image rundown.

6. It invokes the License Management Facility rundown routine to release any license units granted to the exiting image or process.

7. It resets the process's current CPU capability and affinity requirements to their permanent values. Chapter 13 explains these requirements.

8. If image accounting is enabled, an image deletion message is written to the accounting log file. It clears CTL$GQ_ISTART to indicate no image is active.

9. EXE$KRNDWN increments the image counter, PHD$L_IMGCNT. Use of this counter can prevent the delivery of ASTs to an image that has exited. The use of this synchronization technique in the operation of the Get Job/Process Information ($GETJPI) system service is described in Chapter 14.

10. It resets the activated privileged library dispatch vector (see Chapter 7) to remove image-temporary user-written system services or rundown routines.

11. It clears PCB$V_ERDACT in PCB$L_STS to indicate executive mode rundown routines are no longer active.

12. Unless process-specific user mode alignment trap reporting has been enabled (see Chapter 39), it disables alignment trap reporting.

13. It calls EXE$WRITE_THREAD_UNQ, in module SYSRUNDWN, to clear thread-unique context.

14. EXE$KRNDWN requests the Set Page Fault Monitoring ($SETPFM) system service to disable any monitoring of process page faults.

15. EXE$KRNDWN searches the channel control block table for channels to

deassign. It compares the access mode of each assigned channel to that of the rundown. For each channel assigned in the same or an outer mode, EXE$KRNDWN requests the Deassign Channel ($DASSGN) system service. The deassign completes unless the channel has an open file. The access mode comparison prevents process-permanent files from being closed when an image is being run down ($RUNDWN from user mode). Other channels that are not deassigned at this stage of image rundown include the image file and any other file that is mapped to a range of virtual addresses.

If the channel's assigned mode is more privileged, EXE$KRNDWN makes an additional check of the flag CCB$V_IMGTMP to see whether the channel is associated with the Breakthrough ($BRKTHRU) system service. If it is, EXE$KRNDWN deassigns the channel so that broadcast operations are aborted at image exit.

16. The rights database identifier table is deallocated to the P1 process allocation region.

17. EXE$KRNDWN requests the Cancel Timer ($CANTIM) and the Cancel Wakeup ($CANWAK) system services to cancel any requests made from this and outer access modes.

18. It requests the $DEQ service to release all locks for this and outer access modes.

19. EXE$KRNDWN invokes MMG$IMGRESET, in module PHDUTL, to reset the image pages. MMG$IMGRESET performs the image cleanup associated with memory management:

   a. MMG$IMGRESET invokes RM$RESET, in module RMSRESET, to reset the image I/O segment.

   b. It invokes EXE$PSCAN_IMGRESET, in module PROCESS_SCAN, to remove and deallocate process scan blocks, restoring the context of the Process Scan ($PROCESS_SCAN) system service.

   c. It returns memory management working set peak checking to its previous state.

   d. At IPL 2, it calls MMG$DELETE_BUFOBJ, in module SYSLKWSET, to delete any buffer objects still allocated by the process.

   e. It releases all IMCBs that describe currently mapped images and places them into the IMCB lookaside list. Each IMCB that describes an image installed /RESIDENT also has an associated KFE and KFE-RES. MMG$IMGRESET deallocates the KFERES and decrements the reference count in the associated KFE. If the count goes to zero and deletion is pending for the KFE, MMG$IMGRESET deallocates the huge page slice that had been occupied by the image and deallocates the KFE and, if necessary, the KFERES.

   If any IMCBs remain in the work list, MMG$IMGRESET places them into the IMCB lookaside list as well.

   f. All of P0 space is deleted. This frees the main image file and any other

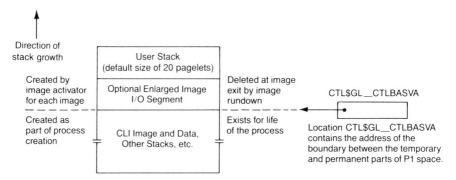

Figure 28.28
Low-Address End of P1 Space That Is Deleted at Image
Exit

image file currently mapped. Physical pages are released, and blocks
in the page files assigned to the process are deallocated.

g. The nonpermanent parts of P1 space are deleted. These are the user
stack and an optional enlarged image I/O segment (see Figure 28.28).
Any expansions to P1 space (at smaller virtual addresses than the user
stack) are also deleted, as well as DEBUG dynamic memory.

h. The working set list is reset to its default value, undoing any previous
expansion or contraction performed by the Adjust Working Set Limit
($ADJWSL) system service. Working set size changes are described in
Chapter 19.

i. At IPL 2, MMG$IMGRESET invokes MMG$SECTBLRST, which
compresses the process section table.

j. The process privilege masks in the PHD and the process control block
(PCB) are reset to their permanent value, found at location CTL$GQ_
PROCPRIV. This step eliminates any privilege enhancements to the
process resulting from the execution of an image installed with privilege. Section 28.8 describes the various privilege masks.

k. The global location CTL$GL_IMGHDRBF is cleared to indicate that
no image is active.

l. If the process was the last accessor of a global section, releasing the
process address space may make the global section deletable. If so, the
global sections are deleted under the protection of the global section
mutex. The associated WCB is released as well.

m. The pointer to the end of the active working set list, PHD$L_WSLAST,
is reset to the end of the minimum working set list.

20. The channel deassignment loop performed in step 15 is executed again.
However, because the image file and other mapped files have now been
dissociated from virtual address space, the channels associated with
those files will also be deassigned. As in step 15, this deassignment is

based on access mode, so that process-permanent files are unaffected by image rundown.

21. EXE$KRNDWN requests the Deallocate Device ($DALLOC) system service to deallocate devices allocated from this and outer access modes.

22. It requests the Disassociate Common Event Flag Cluster ($DACEFC) system service to dissociate clusters 2 and 3.

23. EXE$KRNDWN acquires the SCHED spinlock, elevating IPL to IPL$_SCHED.

24. It checks the system error log mailbox queue EXE$AQ_ERLMBX, and it deassigns each error log mailbox belonging to this process (see Chapter 35).

25. It removes all pending AST control blocks (ACBs) from the queues in the PCB, based on access mode. If the rundown access mode is kernel, it also removes any queued special kernel mode ASTs. If user AST quota was charged for the AST, it returns the quota and deallocates the ACB to nonpaged pool unless its ACB$V_NODELETE or ACB$V_PKAST bit is set. If the ACB describes a piggyback special kernel mode AST, EXE$KRNDWN releases the SCHED spinlock, invokes the AST routine, and reacquires the spinlock to continue scanning the queues. It clears the bit corresponding to the access modes of each emptied queue in PCB$L_AST_PENDING.

    It scans any inner mode queues that were not emptied for ACBs whose AST procedure is in P0 space, which has already been deleted. It removes any such ACB and processes it as the others: possibly returning AST quota, invoking a piggyback kernel AST routine, and deallocating the ACB.

26. If the rundown mode is user mode, EXE$KRNDWN removes any declaration of a user change mode handler and zeros the catch-all extension handler list (see Chapter 6).

27. Any exit handlers for this access mode are canceled.

28. Condition handlers declared as the primary, secondary, and last chance are eliminated for this and outer access modes.

29. The AST active bits for this and outer access modes are cleared. The AST enable bits for this and outer access modes are set.

30. System service failure exceptions are disabled for this and outer access modes.

31. It invokes SCH$RESET_AST, in module ASTDEL, to calculate a new value for the process's AST summary register to reflect the change in the AST queue resulting from step 25.

32. The force exit pending (PCB$V_FORCPEN) and wake pending (PCB$V_WAKEPEN) flags in the PCB are cleared. After clearing these flags, EXE$KRNDWN releases the SCHED spinlock, lowering IPL to 0.

33. EXE$KRNDWN deletes all process logical names based on access mode.

At image exit, all user mode logical names are deleted. At process deletion, all process logical names are deleted.

34. EXE$KRNDWN resets any P0 extension made to the process allocation region (see Chapter 21).

35. Resource wait mode is returned to its previous state, normal completion status is set, and control is returned to its requestor, EXE$RUNDWN.

28.8 PROCESS PRIVILEGES

The executive prevents unauthorized use of the system through process privileges. One or more of these privileges are required to perform particular system services, execute certain commands, or use privileged utilities.

28.8.1 Process Privilege Masks

A process has three sets of privileges available to it: privileges available while executing a particular image, privileges available to the current process context, and privileges from which the process can selectively alter its current context. Each set of privileges is represented by a quadword bit mask. A set bit means the process has the privilege corresponding to that bit.

The executive maintains a number of privilege masks for processes and images. Table 28.2 summarizes the use of the masks.

PCB$Q_PRIV exists in the access rights block, which is a part of the PCB. It is also referenced by the symbol ARB$Q_PRIV. PCB$Q_PRIV contains the working privilege mask, sometimes called an image-specific privilege mask. This mask is checked by most system services that require privilege, and by the file system. At image activation, the mask is initialized to the combination of the privileges of the image and the privileges of the current process context. It can be altered by the Set Privileges ($SETPRV) system service, either during image execution or from DCL level. It is reset at image rundown to the current process privileges.

The other image-specific privilege mask is PHD$Q_PRIVMSK in the process header. It is a duplicate of the privilege mask in the ARB and is altered in the same manner. Some older system services reference this mask rather than ARB$Q_PRIV.

Current process privileges (also called process-permanent privileges) are stored in the P1 pointer area at global location CTL$GQ_PROCPRIV. This mask is initialized at process creation from the user authorization file (UAF) default privilege mask; from the privilege mask argument passed to the Create Process ($CREPRC) system service; or, for a subprocess, from the creator's current privilege mask. It can be altered by the $SETPRV system service, either during image execution or from DCL level. Its contents are copied to the working privilege mask at image rundown.

The authorized privilege mask, PHD$Q_AUTHPRIV, does not change over

Table 28.2   Process Privilege Masks

Symbolic Name	Use of This Mask	Modified by	Referenced by
PCB$Q_PRIV ARB$Q_PRIV	Working privilege mask	EXE$PROCSTRT, LOGINOUT, $SETPRV, Image activator, MMG$IMGRESET	Device drivers, XQP, ACPs, System services requiring privilege
PHD$Q_ PRIVMSK	Duplicate of ARB mask	Same as PCB$Q_ PRIV	Some system services requiring privilege
CTL$GQ_ PROCPRIV	Records permanently enabled privileges	EXE$PROCSTRT, LOGINOUT, $SETPRV	Image activator, SET/SHOW commands, MMG$IMGRESET
PHD$Q_ AUTHPRIV	Records privileges from authorization file	EXE$PROCSTRT, LOGINOUT	$SETPRV, $GETJPI
PHD$Q_ IMAGPRIV	Records privileges of installed image	Image activator	$SETPRV, LOGINOUT, $GETJPI
UAF$Q_PRIV	Records privileges in authorization file	AUTHORIZE	LOGINOUT
UAF$Q_DEF_ PRIV	Records default privileges in authorization file	AUTHORIZE	LOGINOUT
KFE$Q_ PROCPRIV	Records privileges with which an image is installed	Install utility	Image activator

the life of the process. It allows a process to remove a privilege from its current privilege mask with the $SETPRV system service and to later regain that privilege. The authorized privilege mask is initialized at process creation from the UAF privilege mask; from the privilege mask argument passed to the $CREPRC system service; or, for a subprocess, from the creator's current privilege mask.

Each UAF record contains two privilege masks: UAF$Q_DEF_PRIV and UAF$Q_PRIV. UAF$Q_DEF_PRIV contains the default privileges that LOGINOUT copies to CTL$GQ_PROCPRIV, PCB$Q_PRIV, and PHD$Q_PRIV-MSK when an interactive user logs in. UAF$Q_PRIV contains the authorized privileges that LOGINOUT copies to PHD$Q_AUTHPRIV.

KFE$Q_PROCPRIV records the privileges with which a known executable image has been installed. When a process runs such an image, those privileges are temporarily granted to the process as part of the working privilege mask.

PHD$Q_IMAGPRIV contains a copy of the privileged known image's KFE$Q_PROCPRIV mask while that image is executing in the process context. This mask is used by the $SETPRV system service to allow an image installed with privilege to invoke the $SETPRV service without losing privileges.

28.8.2 **$SETPRV System Service**

The $SETPRV system service enables a process to alter its image-specific (PCB$Q_PRIV and PHD$Q_PRIVMSK) privilege masks or its image-specific and process-permanent (CTL$GQ_PROCPRIV) privilege masks, gaining or losing privileges as a result. In addition, the service can return the previous settings of either the image-specific or process-permanent privileges, if requested.

The $SETPRV system service procedure, EXE$SETPRV in module SYSSETPRV, runs in kernel mode.

The path through EXE$SETPRV that disables privileges requires no special privilege and clears the requested privilege bits in the image-specific and, optionally, the process-permanent privilege masks.

The code path that enables privileges requires the requested privilege to be already included in the mask of privileges authorized for this process, PHD$Q_AUTHPRIV. If a process tries to acquire a privilege that is not in its authorized mask, the requested privilege is still granted if any one of the following three conditions holds:

▶ The process has SETPRV privilege in its authorized mask. A process with this privilege can acquire any other privilege with either the $SETPRV system service or the DCL command SET PROCESS/PRIVILEGES (which requests the $SETPRV system service).

▶ The system service was requested from executive or kernel mode. This condition allows code running in either access mode, including user-written system services, to acquire whatever privileges it needs without regard for whether the current process has SETPRV privilege. Such procedures must disable privileges granted in this fashion as part of their return path.

▶ The privilege is being acquired temporarily (enabled in the two image-specific privilege masks) and is included in the mask of privileges authorized for the image, PHD$Q_IMAGPRIV, or the SETPRV privilege is included in this mask. This allows an image to acquire a privilege without permanently granting the new privilege to the process. When the image exits, image rundown copies the process-permanent mask to the image-specific masks, removing privileges acquired temporarily.

Note that the implementation of the $SETPRV system service does not return an error if a nonprivileged process attempts to add unauthorized privileges. In such a case, the service clears all unauthorized bits in the requested privilege mask, loads the modified privilege mask, and returns the alternative success status SS$_NOTALLPRIV.

28.9   RELEVANT SOURCE MODULES

Source modules described in this chapter include

[LIB]EIAFDEF.SDL
[LIB]EICPDEF.SDL
[LIB]EIHADEF.SDL
[LIB]EIHDDEF.SDL
[LIB]EIHIDEF.SDL
[LIB]EISDDEF.SDL
[LIB]IMCBDEF.SDL
[LIB]KFDDEF.SDL
[LIB]KFEDEF.SDL
[LIB]KFERESDEF.SDL
[LIB]KFPBDEF.SDL
[LIB]KFRHDEF.SDL
[LIB]SHLDEF.SDL
[STARLET]IACDEF.SDL
[SYS]IMGDECODE.B32
[SYS]IMGMAPISD.B32
[SYS]PHDUTL.MAR
[SYS]RELOCATE_AND_FIXUP.B64
[SYS]SYSDCLEXH.MAR
[SYS]SYSEXIT.MAR
[SYS]SYSIMGACT.B32
[SYS]SYSIMGFIX.B64
[SYS]SYSIMGSTA.MAR
[SYS]SYSRUNDWN.MAR
[SYS]SYSSETPRV.MAR

29 Translated Image Environment

Untwisting all the chains that tie
The hidden soul of harmony.
Milton, *L'Allegro*

DECmigrate for OpenVMS AXP Systems is a collection of tools that eases the migration of OpenVMS VAX applications to OpenVMS AXP systems. The DECmigrate product provides the VAX Environment Software Translator (VEST) utility, which translates an OpenVMS VAX image to an OpenVMS AXP image. This chapter briefly describes the VEST utility. Its main focus is the run-time environment in which a translated image executes and OpenVMS AXP support of that environment.

29.1 OVERVIEW

During the design of the Alpha AXP architecture, Digital considered the challenges involved in migrating existing OpenVMS VAX applications to AXP processors. Recompiling and relinking the modules of a single image to take advantage of AXP performance is straightforward if the modules are written in a language for which an AXP compiler is available. Migrating a complex application consisting of many executable and shareable images is a more difficult undertaking, however, particularly if not all the sources are available or if they are written in a language for which no AXP compiler is currently available.

To facilitate more difficult migrations, Digital provides software that can translate an OpenVMS VAX image binary file into one that can run on an AXP system. A translated VAX image contains AXP instructions that reproduce the behavior of the VAX image, including simulated compliance with implicit machine state, instruction side effects, and the VAX calling standard. The article "Binary Translation" in *Communications of the ACM* 36 (February 1993) or in *Digital Technical Journal* 4, no. 4 (1992) describes the advantages of binary translation over interpretation and emulation, and explains the design of the binary translator.

One design goal for the binary translator was that it perform automatic open-ended translation of almost all user mode images. (Section 29.3.3 describes image characteristics that prevent successful translation.) In open-ended translation, not all instructions are necessarily found and translated during one translation; some may be discovered, modified, or created during image execution. By default, during image execution, a feedback file is generated, which identifies newly found entry points and code, and which can be input to a later translation.

Another critical design goal for the binary translator was optional exact emulation of VAX architecture details such as precise arithmetic traps and certain atomic memory accesses.

The result of this design is the VEST utility, the major part of the DECmigrate product. The VEST utility translates OpenVMS VAX executable and shareable images into OpenVMS AXP images.

Once translated, an image requires run-time support to make transparent the differences in system environment between OpenVMS VAX and Open-VMS AXP systems, for example, differences in calling standards, architectural features, and exception handling. Run-time support for translated images is bundled with the OpenVMS AXP system. In addition to support within the executive, it consists of the following components:

▸ The jacket system services, $NATIVE_TO_TRANSLATED and $TRANS-LATED_TO_NATIVE, which enable calls between native and translated images (see Section 29.4)

▸ TIE$SHARE.EXE, the shareable image that manages the emulated VAX state required by the translated image, interprets VAX code that was not translated, and emulates D floating-point and H floating-point instructions and certain other frequently used untranslatable instructions such as REI, RET, and MOVC3.

▸ TIE$EMULAT_TV.EXE, a shareable image created by translating existing VAX emulation routines, with procedures for emulating less frequently used complex VAX instructions such as POLYD

▸ Translated versions of various run-time libraries (RTLs) shipped with the OpenVMS VAX system

A translated image consists of the original VAX image, native instructions generated by translating VAX instructions, calls to procedures in TIE$SHARE, and if necessary, calls to procedures in TIE$EMULAT_TV.

A translated image runs in an OpenVMS AXP environment. Its code can call native procedures and request native services. Native images can call procedures in translated shareable images, and the executive can call translated procedures, for example, to deliver an asynchronous system trap (AST). Jacketing routines provided by the executive facilitate cross-architecture calls. Native and translated code share the same stack, with VAX call frames and native procedure frames interleaved by TIE$SHARE. In this chapter, *native* means native within the AXP environment.

29.2   EMULATING THE VAX ENVIRONMENT

The environment in which user mode instructions execute on a VAX consists of the following:

▸ Memory
▸ General registers

▶ Condition codes
▶ Stack
▶ Program counter (PC)

The VEST utility and the OpenVMS AXP system cooperate to emulate a VAX environment for the execution of translated VAX images. A translated image contains a copy of the VAX image with instructions and data at the same locations as in the VAX image. The native instructions generated in translation by VEST reference statically allocated data at the same locations as the VAX instructions do.

Transforming VAX register use into Alpha AXP register use is straightforward, because there are more Alpha AXP registers than VAX registers. VAX register contents are sign-extended to 64 bits. Table 29.1 shows how VAX register use is translated.

Execution of any VAX instruction potentially affects four condition codes, which can be tested by a subsequent branch instruction. To improve performance, translated code calculates condition codes only when necessary. When emulated, all four condition codes are recorded in R22. To facilitate testing whether results are negative, zero, or positive, the N and Z condition codes are recorded in R23. If the N condition code is set, the result is neg-

Table 29.1 Register Use in a Translated Image

VAX Register	Use	AXP Register
R0–R14	Integer arithmetic, address calculation	R0–R14
R0–R12	Floating-point arithmetic	F0–F12
R12	VAX argument pointer	R12
R13	VAX frame pointer	R13
R14	VAX stack pointer	R14
R15	VAX PC-relative addressing	R15
n/a	AXP procedure calls; temporary register	R16–R21
Processor status	Condition codes and exception enable bits	R22
N and Z condition codes		R23
n/a	AXP scratch	R24
n/a	AXP procedure calls; temporary register	R25
n/a	AXP procedure calls	R26, R27
n/a	AXP scratch	R28
n/a	AXP frame pointer	R29
n/a	AXP stack pointer	R30
n/a	AXP sink and zero source	R31

ative. If the Z condition code is set, the result is zero. If both are clear, the result is positive.

Translated VAX code and the native routines that support it share the user mode stack. Translated code refers to the stack using R14, the VAX stack pointer (SP), and R13, the VAX frame pointer (FP). Section 29.6 provides more information on how frames interleave.

The VAX PC is a general register that can be used in operand addressing in addition to identifying the instruction being executed. Translated code emulates PC-relative addressing using R15. When used in this way, R15 typically contains the sum of the base address of the translated image plus 8000_{16} rather than the base address. This extends the range within the image that a signed displacement from R15 can reach by enabling a negative displacement.

The VAX architecture includes several features not present in the Alpha AXP architecture. Correct execution of some translated images depends on the presence of these features. The VEST utility and TIE$SHARE must therefore emulate them.

The sections that follow describe the problematical VAX architectural features, AXP PALcode support for VAX environment emulation, and VEST and TIE$SHARE support.

29.2.1   Significant VAX and Alpha AXP Architectural Differences

The VAX architecture differs in several ways from the Alpha AXP architecture. Areas of difference of particular significance for translation and execution of VAX images are

- ▶ D floating-point precision
- ▶ H floating-point format
- ▶ Precise arithmetic exceptions
- ▶ Form of floating-point zeros
- ▶ Access to unaligned data
- ▶ Byte granularity of memory access
- ▶ Atomic read-modify-write operations
- ▶ Ordered reads and writes to memory
- ▶ Instruction atomicity

By default VEST generates special code sequences that reproduce VAX behavior in some of these regards. For images that depend on other aspects of VAX behavior, VEST optionally generates special code sequences that reproduce it. Some sequences require TIE$SHARE support as well.

Because of limited D floating-point hardware support, by default VEST converts any D floating-point operands to G floating-point operands and generates G floating-point instructions. This conversion loses three bits of precision in the fractional part of the number and trades that precision for improved performance. The VEST qualifier /FLOAT=D56_FLOAT overrides the default. In response to that qualifier, VEST generates calls to TIE$SHARE software emulation routines for the D floating-point operations. Use of this qualifier trades performance for arithmetic precision.

The Alpha AXP architecture does not support H floating-point arithmetic. When VEST detects its use in an image being translated, it generates calls to TIE$SHARE software emulation routines.

The VAX architecture requires that exceptions be precise; that is, if execution of an instruction triggers an exception, no instructions in the stream following the one incurring the exception may be executed. The exception PC precisely identifies the instruction that incurred the exception. In contrast, the Alpha AXP architecture permits imprecise arithmetic exceptions. Under normal operation, a pipelined AXP processor can be executing several instructions in various stages at any given instant; one or more of these can trigger an arithmetic trap. The exception PC does not precisely identify the instruction that incurred the exception. Moreover, an exception can represent more than one error. Exception summary information passed from PALcode identifies which errors occurred.

By default VEST rearranges instructions so as to promote multiple-instruction issue. A VAX image that requires precise exceptions must be translated with the qualifier /PRESERVE=(FLOAT_EXCEPTIONS,INTEGER_EX-CEPTIONS). In response to that qualifier, VEST does not rearrange generated code except within the set of instructions generated for one VAX instruction, and it generates TRAPB instructions after each floating-point operation and after any integer operation that could incur an integer overflow. The TRAPB instruction allows software to guarantee that previously issued arithmetic instructions complete and trigger any pending exceptions before any instructions following the TRAPB are issued. Use of this qualifier trades performance for precision of exception information and an ability to fix up memory operands that cause floating-point overflows or underflows.

A VAX CPU interprets as zero a floating-point pattern with a zero exponent, zero sign bit, and nonzero fraction. Such a pattern is referred to as a dirty zero. In contrast, use of a dirty zero in most AXP floating-point instructions results in an invalid-operation arithmetic exception. When such an error is reported by itself in an arithmetic exception, TIE$SHARE fixes up the operand to create a true zero (64 bits of zero) and repeats the floating-point instruction.

As described in Chapter 9, AXP memory references are more restricted than VAX memory references. One distinction is that AXP memory references are limited to accessing one aligned longword or quadword. By default, in translating a VAX image, VEST assumes that longwords, quadwords, and words whose alignment it cannot determine are naturally aligned. When an instruction references unaligned data, the hardware traps to a PALcode routine that emulates the reference, breaking it into multiple aligned loads or stores. Trapping in this way decreases performance. A VAX image known to have unaligned data can be translated with the VEST qualifier /OPTI-MIZE=NOALIGN. In response to that qualifier, VEST generates multiple instructions to load or store the data. Executing those instructions in-line is faster than trapping to a PALcode routine and having it execute them.

A VAX CPU is required to read or write certain memory operands in a single operation that appears indivisible from the viewpoint of any other thread of execution on a symmetric multiprocessing (SMP) system. These operands include a byte, aligned word, and aligned longword. Certain other types of memory access must appear indivisible from the viewpoint of any other thread of execution on the same CPU. Moreover, a VAX CPU can execute an interlocked instruction to effect a read-modify-write sequence that appears atomic from the viewpoint of any other thread of execution.

The Alpha AXP architecture has no one instruction that both reads and writes memory. It provides only that an aligned longword or aligned quad-word can be read or written atomically with respect to other threads on any CPU of an SMP system. Writing a byte, word, or unaligned longword within one quadword requires a sequence of instructions. The load-locked/store-conditional mechanism, described in Chapter 9, can be used to implement atomic reads or writes to a byte, word, or longword within a quadword. This mechanism can also be used to implement read-modify-write sequences that are atomic from the viewpoint of any other thread of execution.

The atomic move PALcode routine AMOVRM, described in Section 29.2.2, uses the load-locked/store-conditional mechanism to implement writes to multiple quadwords that are atomic from the viewpoint of other threads on the same CPU but not from the viewpoint of threads on other CPUs. This level of atomicity, however, duplicates that of the VAX architecture. The AMOVRM routine can be used, for example, to write atomically an unaligned word or longword that crosses a quadword boundary.

A program that shares memory data with another thread of execution may need to be translated with the VEST qualifier /PRESERVE=MEMORY_ATOMICITY regardless of whether the other thread is an AST, a condition handler, or a program running in another process. If the data is shared explicitly and only accessed with interlocked VAX instructions (for example, ADAWI or INSQTI), the qualifier is not needed for the VEST utility to generate atomic accesses. If the data is shared implicitly and consists of other than aligned longwords and quadwords, use of the qualifier is necessary for atomic accesses. (Chapter 9 explains how two fields in the same quadword accessed by different threads of execution are implicitly shared.) In response to this qualifier, VEST generates code to access VAX instruction memory operands (other than aligned longwords and quadwords) using the load-locked/store-conditional mechanism or the AMOVRM PALcode routine.

The VAX architecture requires that in a multiprocessor system one CPU's reads from memory appear ordered from the viewpoint of another CPU and that one CPU's writes to memory appear ordered from the viewpoint of another CPU. In contrast, the Alpha AXP architecture provides no implicit ordering. Any software that relies on read/write ordering must explicitly order the reads or writes. The fundamental ordering mechanism is the memory barrier (MB) instruction, described in Chapter 9. By default VEST provides no ordering. A program that is part of a multiprocess application intended for an SMP system can be translated with the VEST qualifier /PRESERVE=READ_WRITE_ORDERING. In response to that qualifier, VEST limits its instruction scheduling and generates MB instructions and CALL_PAL AMOVRM to access VAX instructions' memory operands.

Section 29.2.3 discusses VAX instruction atomicity and the ways in which that aspect of VAX behavior is reproduced for translated images.

29.2.2 Alpha AXP Architectural Support for Translated Images

The Alpha AXP architecture provides the following features specifically in support of the translated image environment:

▶ Read and set (RS) instruction
▶ Read and clear (RC) instruction
▶ Atomic move PALcode routines AMOVRR and AMOVRM

These features are provided only for support of translated code. Any other use is unsupported.

When translating an image with the qualifier /PRESERVE=INSTRUC-TION_ATOMICITY, VEST generates code that uses the RS instruction and CALL_PAL AMOVRM to preserve VAX-style instruction atomicity (see Section 29.2.3). Several PALcode routines, including those for AMOVRR and AMOVRM, contain the RC instruction. Currently, the AMOVRR PALcode routine is not used.

Bracketing an instruction sequence with the RS instruction and either CALL_PAL AMOVRM or the RC instruction makes it possible to determine whether a sequence of instructions executed without incurring an exception or being interrupted.

Executing the RS instruction sets a per-processor state bit called intr_flag and returns its previous state in the instruction's register operand. The intr_flag state bit is cleared by the PALcode REI routine. Executing the RC instruction clears the intr_flag state bit and returns its previous state in the instruction's register operand. If the bit was already clear, an interrupt or exception occurred during the execution of the bracketed code sequence. The intr_flag state bit is also tested and cleared during the execution of the atomic move PALcode routines.

The atomic move PALcode routines enable multiple memory stores to be made atomically: all stores happen, or none does. Each routine supports a set of stores to multiple memory locations that is atomic with respect to threads of execution running on the same CPU.

The instruction CALL_PAL AMOVRR invokes the AMOVRR PALcode routine, whose function is to store the contents of its two source registers (R16 and R19) at two arbitrary memory addresses. The data stored from each register can be its low byte, word, longword, or the entire quadword. No alignment constraints are placed on the two addresses. R17 and R20 specify the destination addresses. The low-order two bits of R18 and R21 specify whether a byte, a word, a longword, or a quadword of each source register should be stored.

The instruction CALL_PAL AMOVRM invokes the AMOVRM PALcode routine. It stores the low byte, word, longword, or the entire quadword of its one source register, R16, at the address specified by R17. R18 specifies how much data is stored. In addition, the routine copies 0 to 63 aligned longwords from the memory location specified by R19 to the location specified by R20. R21 specifies the number of longwords to be copied. Either the store and the copy are both done, or neither is done. R18 is set to 1 if both are done, and to 0 otherwise.

Each of the atomic move PALcode routines first tests the intr_flag state bit. If the intr_state flag is clear, the routine clears R18 and exits, without doing any stores. If the intr_state flag is set, the routine clears it and then checks whether any memory access would cause a page fault, fault-on-write, fault-on-read, or access violation. If so, it performs no store and generates the corresponding fault. If the memory accesses can be completed without faulting, the routine attempts the stores using load-locked/store-conditional sequences. If all sequences store successfully with no interruption, the routine completes with R18 set to 1. If not, the routine completes with R18 set to 0.

A typical code sequence using either of these routines begins with an RS instruction, followed by initialization of the source and destination address registers, a CALL_PAL AMOVRM instruction, and a branch to reexecute the sequence if the stores were not successful.

The TIE$SHARE code that interprets untranslated VAX instructions maintains a VAX state save area. After interpreting each VAX instruction, the interpreter executes the CALL_PAL AMOVRM instruction to write the instruction result and update the VAX state save area atomically.

29.2.3 VAX Instruction Atomicity

As described in Chapter 9, the VAX architecture guarantees that, once started, certain instructions execute without interruption. If such an instruction incurs a fault, any side effects are rolled back so that the instruction can be restarted from the beginning after the fault is handled.

Most VAX instructions are translated into a sequence of AXP instructions. Although each AXP instruction is noninterruptible and restartable after a fault, a sequence of instructions is not. The VEST utility and TIE$SHARE cooperate to emulate this aspect of VAX instruction execution.

A VAX program that requires instruction atomicity must be translated with the VEST qualifier /PRESERVE=INSTRUCTION_ATOMICITY. In response to this qualifier, the VEST utility translates code as though the qualifier /OPTIMIZE=NOSCHEDULE were present and does not rearrange generated code to improve performance. Moreover, where necessary, it inserts an RS instruction at the beginning of a sequence of AXP instructions that modifies a VAX memory operand and performs the memory update with the AMOVRM PALcode routine. If an interrupt or exception occurs during the sequence, the memory modification is not made and the sequence is restarted.

In response to the qualifier /PRESERVE=INSTRUCTION_ATOMICITY, the VEST utility also creates an instruction granularity bitmap. Each bit in the instruction granularity bitmap represents one AXP instruction in the translated part of the image. Bit 0 represents the instruction at offset 0 in the translated part of the image; bit 1 represents the instruction at offset 4; and so on. A set bit means that the corresponding AXP instruction is the first instruction in a set of instructions that emulates a given VAX instruction. Each image translated with that qualifier has its own bitmap. Given a PC within the translated part of the image, TIE$SHARE can determine the boundaries of the set of instructions that contains it. Section 29.6.7 describes the use of the instruction granularity bitmap in dealing with delivery of a translated AST during execution of a set of AXP instructions emulating a single VAX instruction.

29.3 TRANSLATING AN IMAGE

The manual *DECmigrate for OpenVMS AXP Systems Translating Images* describes the use of the VEST utility in detail. The sections that follow summarize VEST's actions and describe its output.

29.3.1 Translation Process

The VEST utility processes an OpenVMS VAX image in several main phases:

1. It analyzes the image file to find entry points and distinguish code from data. It determines entry points from global and debug symbol tables in the image and the image's transfer address as well as from optional input files created by the user or TIE$SHARE during a previous execution of the image. Beginning at each entry point it disassembles the image, recursively tracing the program flow. It breaks the flow into sequences of instructions called basic blocks and records information such as condition code use, register use, and stack depth within each block.

2. If VEST encounters a CALL, JSB, or JMP destination that is computed at run time or that is unknown, it generates a call to TIE$SHARE to identify the destination at run time (see Section 29.6.1).

To deal with destinations in shareable images, VEST parses the VAX image's fixup vector table and transforms VAX-style transfers through fixup vector Gˆ and .ADDRESS entries to transfers using linkage pairs. It creates the associated fixup records so that linkage pair contents will be replaced with symbol vector entry contents from shareable images during image activation.

Resolving destinations in shareable images at run time allows a shareable image to be replaced with an upwardly compatible one and also enables the determination of whether the shareable image is translated or native to be postponed until run time.

Destinations that correspond neither to found entry points nor to shareable image entry points can represent system service requests or transfers of control to VAX code that may require interpretation at run time.

3. VEST generates AXP code equivalent to the VAX code, optimizing wherever possible. For example, although executing each VAX instruction sets condition codes that can be tested, VEST does not generate an emulation of a condition code that is not used by the code being translated.

4. VEST generates calls to procedures in TIE$SHARE to control image execution and to emulate complex VAX instructions.

VEST builds an image containing both the original code and the generated code. Such an image is referred to as a translated image.

29.3.2   The Translated Image

A translated image contains the original VAX code and data, and the translated code, as well as data structures built by VEST for use during execution. A translated image undergoes image activation just as a native image does. VEST encapsulates the image body from a VAX image in a file that resembles a native image built by the OpenVMS AXP linker. The encapsulated image body includes the fixup section but not the debug and other symbol tables. Chapter 28 discusses in detail the organization of a native image and structures within it.

The virtual address grain of a translated image is always 64 KB; that is, each image section begins on a 10000_{16} byte boundary. Although all current AXP CPUs support a page size of 8 KB, a translated image with a grain of 64 KB could execute on any future AXP CPU with a page size larger than 8 KB.

VEST merges image sections from the VAX image to the extent possible. For example, if a read-only image section and a writable image section are within the same grain, VEST makes the corresponding image section in the translated image writable. It cannot merge VAX image sections with incompatible attributes such as copy-on-reference and shareable. Successful translation may require a VAX image to be relinked with the linker qualifier /BPAGE=16.

VEST generates one or more image sections that contain all the image sections from the VAX image, one image section that contains the translated code, and one that contains linkage and data for use by the translated code and TIE$SHARE during image execution. Data cells and areas statically declared within the VAX image retain their original addresses. The original VAX instructions may be necessary for run-time interpretation.

A translated image can be distinguished from a native image by a bit in the image header (EIHD$V_XLATED in EIHD$L_LNKFLAGS). Also, the default file name of a translated image has the string _TV appended to it, for example, MONITOR_TV.EXE. (TV stands for Translated from VAX.) Another typical difference is that a translated image begins at virtual address 0, whereas native images by default begin at 64 KB, or 10000_{16}, rather than at virtual page 0. (Recall that the page size on current AXP processors is 8 KB. Leaving virtual page 0 as a no-access page would make it impossible to map a translated image at the same address range on an AXP processor as on a VAX processor.)

Figure 29.1 shows the structure of a translated executable image file, and Figure 29.2, that of a translated shareable image file. (Not all parts of these images are mapped into memory when the images are activated.) Every translated image includes TIE$SHARE in its shareable image list (see Chapter 28).

A translated shareable image includes a symbol vector and a global symbol table built by the VEST utility. The first entry in the symbol table is always reserved for nonstandard interimage references, for example, through a VAX JSB instruction. After relocation the entry contains the base address of the shareable image. When a translated shareable image is replaced by a native shareable image, the first symbol vector entry in the native shareable image must be reserved for upward compatibility. It can be reserved

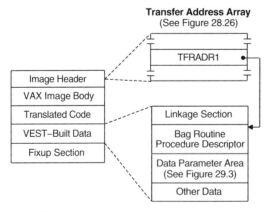

Figure 29.1
Organization of a Translated Executable Image

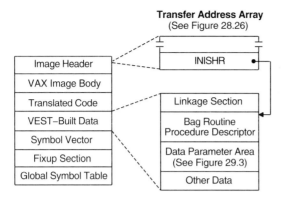

Figure 29.2
Organization of a Translated Shareable Image

through the SPARE keyword on the SYMBOL_VECTOR clause in the linker options.

A translated image also includes a native routine called the bag that VEST defines to be the first code executed within the image (see Section 29.5).

Data structures built by VEST include the following:

► A VAX-to-AXP instruction map for lookups of computed destinations, for example, JSB (R5), and of other destinations where VEST did not find the original VAX code

► Optionally, an instruction granularity bitmap, described in Section 29.2.3

► A data parameter area that describes the image

Figure 29.3 shows the layout of the data parameter area. Its fields are defined in [TIE]TIE.R64 and begin with the string TIE$.

TIE$A_IMAGE_BASE contains the base virtual address of the translated image. TIE$L_ALPHA_START contains the offset in the image of the start of the translated code within the image, and TIE$L_ALPHA_END contains the image offset of its end.

TIE$L_VIA_MAP contains the image offset of the VAX-to-AXP instruction map. TIE$L_BOUNDARY_MAP contains the offset to the instruction granularity bitmap, if present. Otherwise, it contains the value 80000000_{16}.

For an executable image, TIE$A_ROUTINE contains the image offset of the entry point in the translated code.

The fields that contain image offsets are relocated at image activation and thus contain virtual addresses at run time.

TIE$T_VEST_ID is a counted ASCII string identifying the VEST utility version that translated the image. TIE$T_VEST_DATE_TIME is a counted ASCII string of the date and time when the image was translated.

TIE$T_IMAGE_NAME is a counted ASCII string containing the name of the original VAX image. TIE$T_IMAGE_IDENT is a counted ASCII string

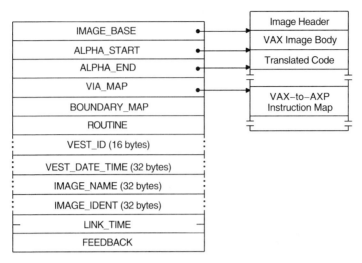

Figure 29.3
Layout of the Translated Image Data Parameter Area

identifying the version of the image. TIE$Q_LINK_TIME contains the time in system time format when the image was linked.

The low bit of TIE$L_FEEDBACK, when clear, indicates the image was translated with the /FEEDBACK qualifier.

29.3.3 Constraints on Candidate Images

Designed for user mode images, the VEST utility does not translate an image that contains user-written system services, or references to system space or P1 space addresses other than OpenVMS VAX system service vector addresses. VEST cannot translate based shareable images or any image that makes an absolute reference to a P0 space address not within it.

VEST will not translate images linked on VAX/VMS versions prior to Version 4.0.

VEST does translate an image that contains VAX instructions requiring kernel mode, for example, MTPR; the bugcheck instructions (BUGW and BUGL); and VAX vector instructions. A run-time error will result, however, if an attempt is made to execute any of them.

It cannot translate images with source modules written in VAX Ada because VAX Ada programs perform certain stack manipulations as part of thread multitasking that are unsupported by the translated image run-time environment.

29.4 CALLING STANDARDS AND JACKETING

The OpenVMS VAX and AXP calling standards differ significantly. While transparent to a high-level language programmer, these differences make it difficult simply to translate between VAX calls and AXP calls. Differences include

▸ Form of procedure frames
▸ Definition of a procedure value
▸ Method of passing arguments

A VAX procedure or call frame is built on the stack and may include the procedure's arguments, depending on the form of the call. When a procedure is entered, the FP register points to its call frame, built by a CALLG or CALLS instruction. Optionally, the call frame can specify the address of a condition handler specific to that procedure invocation. A routine entered with a JSB instruction has no stack frame and, indeed, is not a procedure.

In contrast, there are three types of AXP procedure, distinguished by the existence and form of their procedure frames: stack frame, register frame, and null frame. Compiler-generated code at the beginning of the first two types of procedure builds a procedure frame. (A null frame procedure implements JSB-type transfers and has no frame.)

The procedure value of a VAX procedure is the address of its entry mask, which specifies registers to be saved. The procedure value of an AXP procedure is the address of its procedure descriptor, a data structure that identifies the procedure type, describes its register and stack use, and identifies its code entry point.

Arguments to a VAX procedure are passed in a memory list built by the caller. The list may be on the stack as part of the call frame. The call stores the address of the argument list in the argument pointer (AP) register, which the procedure uses as a pointer to the list.

In contrast, the first six arguments to an AXP procedure are passed in registers, and any others are passed in stack locations. The argument information (AI) register specifies the number of arguments and identifies the types of the first six. Integers in the first six arguments are passed in integer registers, and floating-point numbers in floating-point registers.

Chapter 1 introduces procedure types and other OpenVMS AXP calling standard conventions. The *OpenVMS Calling Standard* manual provides a more complete description.

Despite the calling standard differences, translated and native images that follow their respective calling standards can interoperate transparently. Code in a translated image can call native procedures as well as translated procedures; code in a native image can call native and translated procedures. A shareable translated image can be replaced with a native shareable image without the need to relink or retranslate any of its callers (assuming the order of entries in the native symbol vector matches that of the translated symbol vector). Similarly, a shareable native image can be replaced with a translated shareable image.

Translated and native images that do not follow their respective calling standards may still be able to interoperate. Jacketing images may need to be interposed between them.

The sections that follow briefly describe support for interoperability.

29.4.1 Relevant OpenVMS AXP Calling Standard Features

The OpenVMS AXP calling standard provides the following features to support interoperability:

- ▸ A way to determine whether a given procedure value represents a native or translated procedure
- ▸ A way to determine whether a given procedure frame encapsulates translated frames
- ▸ A mechanism to describe all the arguments input to a procedure and the form and location of the value returned by the procedure
- ▸ A mechanism to enable calling a procedure through an intermediary or bridge procedure

The procedure value of a native procedure is the address of its procedure descriptor, which begins with a word of flags. The calling standard specifies that bit 12 (PDSC$V_NATIVE) of the flags must be set to 1 for native compiled code. The procedure value of a translated procedure is the address of its entry mask. The VAX architecture specifies that bit 12 in that mask must be 0. Thus, testing bit 12 at the address specified by the procedure value distinguishes the two types of procedures: when set, the procedure is native; when clear, it is translated.

Another procedure descriptor flag bit (PDSC$V_TIE_FRAME) is set to indicate a TIE$SHARE procedure frame that encapsulates one or more translated frames (see Section 29.6.2).

The OpenVMS AXP calling standard defines an optional extension to the procedure descriptor called procedure signature information. The additional description specifies the number, type, and location of arguments, and the form and location of the value returned by the procedure. A procedure descriptor includes a field for the offset to its procedure signature information, if any. The value 0 in this field indicates no signature. The value 1 indicates the procedure has a default signature. The signature information enables software to transform a VAX-style argument list into the arguments expected by a native procedure, and any returned function value into the form expected by the translated caller, or to translate native arguments into VAX argument format.

A default signature for a native procedure called by a translated procedure has the following meaning:

- ▸ The count in the VAX argument list is the number of input arguments. The count is copied to the AI register.
- ▸ All arguments, if any, are 32-bit sign-extended integers.
- ▸ The function result, if any, is a 32-bit sign-extended integer.

The OpenVMS AXP calling standard provides bound procedures and bound procedure descriptors, partly to enable a target procedure to be called through an intermediary or bridge procedure. A bound procedure descriptor has a different format from a normal procedure descriptor. The bridge procedure it describes must be simple with no frame or arguments of its own. A bound procedure descriptor includes a field to point to the descriptor of the target procedure. The address of a bound procedure is bound at link time, but the address of the target procedure descriptor is not bound until image activation; the binding may even be dynamically calculated at run time. Bound procedure descriptors interpose jacketing procedures between native and translated procedures.

The bridge procedure code is entered like any other procedure with the address of its procedure descriptor in R27. Like any other procedure descriptor, a bound procedure descriptor can contain the offset of a procedure signature. This makes it possible to connect procedure signature information from the calling procedure with the target procedure. The bridge procedure makes it possible to transform the format of the caller's arguments to the format expected by the target procedure.

A default signature associated with a call from a native procedure through a bound procedure descriptor to a translated procedure has the following meaning:

- The AI register contains the number of input arguments, which is copied to the VAX argument list count.
- The register arguments, if any, are described by the AI register.
- All memory arguments, if any, are 32-bit sign-extended integers.
- The function result, if any, is a 32-bit sign-extended integer.

29.4.2   Automatic Jacketing

A jacket procedure is interposed between caller and target procedures when one is native and the other translated. The jacket procedure transforms the input arguments and, if necessary, the returned function value from one architecture to another. How and when the jacket is interposed depends on the nature of the image containing the caller procedure.

The modules of a native image that call translated procedures or that are called from translated code must be compiled with the /TIE qualifier. In response to that qualifier, the compiler generates procedure signature information for each native procedure. The procedure signature information will be used in any inbound call from a translated procedure to transform its VAX-style argument list to the form expected by the native procedure.

The compiler also compiles outbound calls differently. In particular, it creates a signature for each outbound call and generates an object language record associating the signature with the linkage pair describing the target procedure. When such a native image is linked with the /NONATIVE_ONLY qualifier, the linker creates a special fixup record for each outbound call. The fixup record is called a fixup for a linkage pair with a procedure signature block (see Chapter 28).

When such an image is activated along with one or more translated images, the image activator processes those fixup records and creates virtual address space for bound procedure descriptors and procedure signature blocks. Before the image and all associated shareable images are activated, it is not possible to determine whether the target of the outbound call is native or translated. After all images have been activated, the fixup records are processed. For each fixup record whose target procedure is in a native image, a standard linkage pair fixup is done so that the native image caller will call the target native procedure directly.

For each fixup record whose target procedure is in a translated image, a bound procedure descriptor is built and, optionally, a procedure signature block. The bound procedure descriptor represents a request of the $NATIVE_ TO_TRANSLATED system service. The procedure bound to it is the target translated procedure. The linkage pair is fixed up to point to the bound procedure descriptor. At run time, the native caller will request the system service in order to call the target translated procedure.

Figure 29.4 illustrates the connections among the procedures.

The mechanism just described serves to jacket each call that meets all the following criteria:

▶ Its target procedure is known at link time.
▶ The number of arguments is fixed.
▶ It does not require CALLG emulation.

For calls that do not meet those restrictions, compilers generate calls to intermediate procedures.

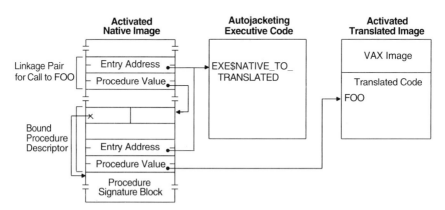

Figure 29.4
Jacketing from a Native Procedure to a Translated
Procedure

Whether or not a module is compiled with the /TIE qualifier, a compiler generates a call to OTS$CALL_PROC, passing it the target procedure value, whenever a call meets all the following criteria:

▸ Its target procedure destination is not known at compile and link time; for example, it is a computed destination.
▸ The number of arguments is fixed.
▸ It does not require CALLG emulation.

If such a module is compiled /TIE, the compiler generates procedure signature information associated with the linkage pair for OTS$CALL_PROC. If the image is then linked /NONATIVE_ONLY, the linker generates a linkage pair fixup with procedure signature information. Because OTS$CALL_PROC is in a native image, at image activation a standard linkage pair fixup is done. Therefore, at run time the caller calls OTS$CALL_PROC directly.

At run time, OTS$CALL_PROC, in module [LIBOTS]OTS$CALL_PROC_ALPHA, checks whether the target procedure is a native or a translated one. If native, it calls the procedure. If translated, it requests the $NATIVE_TO_TRANSLATED system service to call the procedure.

For a call that has a variable number of arguments or that requires CALLG emulation, a different intermediate procedure is used. The procedure is language-specific. The MACRO-32 compiler generates a call to AMAC$EMUL_CALL; the BLISS-32 compiler generates a call to BLI$CALLG; other compilers use equivalent language-specific procedures. Whatever the procedure, it is passed the target procedure value. If the module containing the call is compiled /TIE, the compiler also generates procedure signature information associated with the linkage pair for AMAC$EMUL_CALL or its equivalent. If the image is linked /NONATIVE_ONLY, the linker generates a linkage pair fixup with procedure signature information. Because AMAC$EMUL_CALL and its equivalents are in native images, at image activation a standard linkage pair fixup is done. At run time the caller calls AMAC$EMUL_CALL or its equivalent directly, whether or not the target procedure is translated.

The module containing AMAC$EMUL_CALL itself is compiled /TIE and contains a computed call to the target procedure whose address is passed. The call is thus compiled as a call to OTS$CALL_PROC. When AMAC$EMUL_CALL is called, it forms the argument list, performs whatever call emulation is required, and calls OTS$CALL_PROC. OTS$CALL_PROC tests whether the target procedure is native or translated and, if translated, requests the $NATIVE_TO_TRANSLATED service to call the procedure. Similar considerations apply to the other language-specific procedures equivalent to AMAC$EMUL_CALL.

Section 29.4.3 describes how the executive calls translated procedures.

All external calls made by a translated image are processed by TIE$SHARE.

It checks whether the target procedure is translated or native. If native, it requests the $TRANSLATED_TO_NATIVE system service to call the native procedure (see Section 29.4.5).

29.4.3 Jacketing Initiated by the Executive

Several executive routines call procedures specified by user images. These routines check whether the procedure is native or translated and, if translated, call the procedure through the $NATIVE_TO_TRANSLATED system service.

When delivering an AST to an outer mode (that is, not kernel), the AST delivery interrupt service routine tests bit 12 at the procedure value address. If the bit is set, the AST procedure is a native one and is called in the usual way (see Chapter 8). If the bit is clear, the AST procedure is a translated one. The interrupt service routine executes a CALL_PAL REI instruction to return to the outer mode, specifying the code entry point of the $NATIVE_TO_TRANSLATED service as the return address. The interrupt service routine passes the target AST procedure value and the value 1 to indicate a default procedure signature block. The $NATIVE_TO_TRANSLATED service calls the translated AST procedure.

The AST interrupt service routine is unusual in that it is coded in MACRO-64 assembly language. Other executive and RTL routines that call user-specified procedures are written in MACRO-32 or higher level languages and are compiled with the /TIE qualifier. As a result, their calls to user-specified procedures are done through OTS$CALL_PROC or procedures such as AMAC$EMUL_CALL and BLI$CALLG.

29.4.4 Jacketing Prohibited by the Executive

To help enforce the constraint that translated code must not execute in inner modes, the $CMEXEC and $CMKRNL system services specifically check that the descriptor of the target procedure has PDSC$V_NATIVE set and PDSC$V_TIE_FRAME clear. If either test fails, the service returns the error status SS$_BADPARAM. These tests ensure that the procedure to be entered in inner mode is native and not a procedure that encapsulates a translated procedure.

The Set Exception Vector ($SETEXV) system service confirms that the procedure being established as a primary, secondary, or last chance handler is a native procedure. If not, the service returns the error status SS$_IVSSRQ.

29.4.5 Automatic Jacket System Services

The jacket system services are mode of caller services in module SYS-JACKET.

The $NATIVE_TO_TRANSLATED service is requested with the arguments for the translated procedure in the standard native form (the argument count in AI, the first six arguments in R16 through R21, and arguments beyond six on the stack). In addition, at entry to the service, R23 contains the address of the translated entry point and R24 identifies the signature associated with this call.

EXE$NATIVE_TO_TRANSLATED, the system service procedure for the $NATIVE_TO_TRANSLATED service, takes the following steps:

1. It executes a TRAPB instruction so that any pending exceptions will be delivered in the procedure context of the service's requestor.
2. It builds its own stack frame and establishes itself as the current procedure.
3. It determines the current access mode. If the current mode is executive, it generates the nonfatal bugcheck NOCALLTRANS and requests the $EXIT system service, which will delete the process. If the current mode is kernel, it generates the fatal bugcheck NOCALLTRANS. These tests help enforce the constraint that translated code must not execute in inner modes.

   If the current mode is supervisor or user, it continues.
4. It checks that either a default signature was specified or a procedure signature block is present, signaling the error SS$_NOCALLTRANS if not. This error typically occurs under two circumstances:

   • The source module containing the service's requestor was not compiled with the /TIE qualifier.
   • The image containing that module was linked with the qualifier /NATIVE_ONLY rather than /NONATIVE_ONLY.

5. It analyzes the procedure signature, if one is present, determining the number and types of arguments. It allocates stack space for a VAX-style argument list with one longword for each argument and one for the argument count. If more than six arguments were passed from the native caller, the additional arguments are on the stack, at addresses older than the stack frame built in step 2. In the case of a target procedure that returns a double-complex function value, it reserves 16 bytes for the returned data and passes the address of the 16 bytes as the first argument.

   EXE$NATIVE_TO_TRANSLATED copies the low-order longword of each additional argument to the allocated stack space. It copies the arguments passed in registers to the allocated stack space, for example, storing the low-order longword of an integer argument. It stores the argument count in the first longword of the list.
6. It aligns the stack to an octaword boundary preparatory to a call, loads the address of the argument list into R16, loads the address of the translated entry point into R17, and calls the procedure whose value is in

CTL$GL_NATIVE_TO_TIE, namely, TIE$NATIVE_TO_TIE, which is a TIE$SHARE procedure in module [TIE]TIELOOKU.

TIE$NATIVE_TO_TIE builds a procedure frame to encapsulate the VAX procedure frame, saves its caller's registers, establishes a VAX environment for the translated procedure, and transfers control to it (see Section 29.6). The translated procedure returns to TIE$NATIVE_TO_TIE, which restores saved registers and returns.

7. When TIE$NATIVE_TO_TIE returns, if a nondefault procedure signature block was present, EXE$NATIVE_TO_TRANSLATED checks whether a function value is being returned and, if so, takes the necessary steps to load it from the stack into R0 or F0.

8. EXE$NATIVE_TO_TRANSLATED cleans up the stack, restoring saved registers from the stack frame, and returns to its requestor. If more than six arguments were passed, the requestor is responsible for removing those on the stack.

The $TRANSLATED_TO_NATIVE system service is only requested by the TIE$SHARE procedure TIE$$OUTBOUND_JACKET, in module [TIE]TIE-EXC. The service is requested with two arguments: the address of a VAX-style argument list and the procedure value of the target procedure.

EXE$TRANSLATED_TO_NATIVE, the system service procedure for the $TRANSLATED_TO_NATIVE service, takes the following steps:

1. It executes a TRAPB instruction so that any pending exceptions will be delivered in the procedure context of the service's requestor.

2. It builds its own stack frame and establishes itself as the current procedure.

3. It checks that the target procedure has a default signature or an associated procedure signature block, signaling the error SS$_TRANSCALLER if not. This error typically occurs when the source module containing the target procedure was not compiled with the /TIE qualifier.

4. If the signature is a default one, it loads as many integer argument registers as there are arguments and copies the argument count to the AI register, zeroing the rest of it to indicate integer arguments.

    If the VAX-style argument list contains more than six arguments, it allocates the stack space for them, ensuring the stack remains octaword-aligned. It copies the seventh and succeeding arguments to the stack, sign-extending each longword argument to a quadword.

5. If the signature is a nondefault one, EXE$TRANSLATED_TO_NATIVE analyzes the procedure signature, determining the type and size of each argument. If the target procedure returns a double-complex function value, EXE$TRANSLATED_TO_NATIVE saves the first argument, which is the address of 16 bytes in which the data is to be returned, and decrements the argument count. In the case of an integer quadword input argument or a D or G floating-point argument, it forms one quadword argument from two longwords in the argument list.

It loads the first six arguments into integer or floating-point argument registers as appropriate and stores the others as quadwords in allocated stack space.

If the caller passed more arguments than specified in the procedure signature block, EXE$TRANSLATED_TO_NATIVE treats them as longword integers.

It initializes the AI register with the number of arguments actually present and the type (floating or integer) of the first six.

6. It calls the specified native procedure.
7. When the native procedure returns, EXE$TRANSLATED_TO_NATIVE cleans up the stack, restoring saved registers from the stack frame.
8. If the target procedure has a nondefault signature, EXE$TRANSLATED_TO_NATIVE performs any necessary processing on the function value returned, if present.
9. It returns to its requestor. (Actually, because of the manner in which TIE$$OUTBOUND_JACKET calls the service, it returns to the caller of TIE$$OUTBOUND_JACKET.)

29.5   TRANSLATED IMAGE INITIATION

TIE$SHARE specifies the routine TIE$SHARE_INIT, in module [TIE]TIE, as its initialization procedure. Thus, whenever a set of activated images includes one or more translated images and thus TIE$SHARE, TIE$SHARE_I-NIT executes. Its major function is to record the procedure value of TIE$NA-TIVE_TO_TIE in the cell CTL$GL_NATIVE_TO_TIE for subsequent use by the $NATIVE_TO_TRANSLATED system service.

29.5.1   Translated Executable Image Initiation

When a translated executable image is activated and then invoked, several routines execute before any translated code:

1. The bag routine specified by the transfer address in the image's header
2. TIE$SETUP_IMAGE, in module [TIE]TIEIMG
3. TIE$$SETUP_IMAGE, in module [TIE]TIE
4. The jacketing system service $NATIVE_TO_TRANSLATED
5. TIE$NATIVE_TO_TIE

Like most procedures, the bag routine is entered with its procedure value in R27. It is a null frame procedure and is called by the Digital command language (DCL) interpreter responding to a RUN command or by EXE$PROCSTRT (see Chapter 27). In either case, it is called with the arguments described in Chapter 30.

The data parameter area, shown in Figure 29.3, immediately follows the bag routine's procedure descriptor. The bag routine consists of several instructions that make a nonstandard call to TIE$SETUP_IMAGE, part of

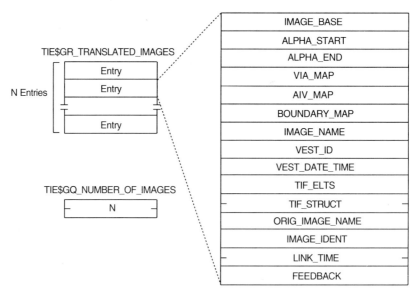

TIE$GR_TRANSLATED_IMAGES

N Entries
Entry
Entry
Entry

TIE$GQ_NUMBER_OF_IMAGES
N

IMAGE_BASE
ALPHA_START
ALPHA_END
VIA_MAP
AIV_MAP
BOUNDARY_MAP
IMAGE_NAME
VEST_ID
VEST_DATE_TIME
TIF_ELTS
TIF_STRUCT
ORIG_IMAGE_NAME
IMAGE_IDENT
LINK_TIME
FEEDBACK

Figure 29.5
Layout of a Translated Image Descriptor Entry

TIE$SHARE, passing it the arguments with which the bag routine was entered. The nonstandard call preserves the contents of R27 for TIE$SETUP_IMAGE's use as a pointer to the parameter area.

TIE$SETUP_IMAGE builds a stack frame, saving in it the bag routine's procedure value and arguments. Dealing with the nonstandard call and building the stack frame in a particular way requires MACRO-64 code. TIE$SETUP_IMAGE calls TIE$$SETUP_IMAGE to do the image-specific initialization that does not require MACRO-64 code.

TIE$$SETUP_IMAGE creates the first entry in an in-memory table to describe the image. It requests the Set Fault ($SETFLT) system service to make every page in the VAX portion of the image a fault-on-execute page. Any subsequent attempt to execute code in such a page will cause an exception that will be dispatched to a condition handler in TIE$SHARE (see Section 29.6.6). TIE$$SETUP_IMAGE returns to TIE$SETUP_IMAGE.

Figure 29.5 shows the layout of the entry built by TIE$$SETUP_IMAGE to describe the image.

Its fields are defined in [TIE]TIE.R64 and have no facility prefix. The entry consists largely of data copied from the image's data parameter area, described in Section 29.3.2, and pointers to fields in the data parameter area. For example, VEST_DATE_TIME contains the address of the VEST date and time stamp in the parameter area, and VEST_ID, the address of the ID of the VEST image used to translate this image.

ORIG_IMAGE_NAME contains the address of the original VAX image name in the parameter area.

AIV_MAP contains the address of the AXP-to-VAX instruction map, an inverted form of the VAX-to-AXP instruction map.

IMAGE_NAME contains the address of this image's name in the image control block that describes it (see Chapter 28).

TIF_ELTS contains the maximum number of elements in the tree. TIF_ STRUCT is the listhead for entries that contain feedback information generated during translated image execution. Each entry identifies untranslated VAX code found at execution and the type of transfer made to the code, for example, call or jump. At image rundown, the feedback information is written to a file that can be input to a subsequent translation for improved performance.

TIE$SETUP_IMAGE examines TIE$A_ROUTINE in the translated image data area to get the address of the routine to call in the translated image. The address corresponds to the routine specified by the image transfer address in the original VAX image. It restores the argument registers and copies the transfer vector array (see Figure 28.26) to its own stack frame so that the translated image's procedure can reference them as an array of longwords. It requests the $NATIVE_TO_TRANSLATED service, passing it the addresses of a default procedure signature block and the translated image's entry point.

As described in Section 29.4.5, the $NATIVE_TO_TRANSLATED system service calls TIE$NATIVE_TO_TIE with the address of the translated routine's entry point. TIE$NATIVE_TO_TIE, described in Section 29.6.2, transfers control to the translated code.

29.5.2   Translated Shareable Image Initiation

A shareable translated image goes through the same first three steps as an executable translated image. During image activation, after an executable image and all related shareable images have been mapped and address relocations and fixups done, shareable image initialization procedures are called. A translated shareable image specifies the bag routine as its initialization procedure. The bag routine calls TIE$SETUP_IMAGE, which calls TIE$$SETUP_IMAGE. TIE$$SETUP_IMAGE adds an entry for the shareable image to the in-memory table that describes activated translated images.

A shareable image has no transfer routine, and control returns from these procedures to image activator code.

29.6   EXECUTION WITHIN THE TRANSLATED ENVIRONMENT

A translated executable image has one entry point, namely, its transfer routine. During its execution it can declare procedures within itself as callable in response to events such as ASTs and exceptions.

A translated shareable image has multiple entry points defined within a symbol vector and global symbol table. It can also declare procedures within itself as callable in response to ASTs and exceptions.

Either type of translated image includes executable code sequences and transfers of various kinds. These transfers include the following:

▸ Transfers from native to translated images, including the initial entry
▸ Transfers within and among translated images
▸ Transfers from translated to native images
▸ Transfers from a translated image to OpenVMS system services

Native and translated codes share the same stack, with VAX call frames and native procedure frames interleaved by TIE$SHARE.

The sections that follow describe how transfer destinations are located and the various kinds of transfers.

29.6.1 Locating Transfer Destinations

VEST generates a call to one of several TIE$SHARE lookup routines for any transfer of control from a translated image to an unknown destination. These include TIEJMP_LOOKUP, TIEJSB_LOOKUP, and TIE$CALLX_LOOKUP, all in module [TIE]TIELOOKU. TIE$NATIVE_TO_TIE calls TIE$CALLX_LOOKUP in transferring from native to translated code.

All the lookup routines can be used for transfers among routines in translated images. TIE$CALLX_LOOKUP, however, is the only routine that can transfer from one domain to another, that is, from translated code to native code, or vice versa. In other words, the only supported way to transfer control between domains is through a procedure call.

Each lookup routine first examines a 1,024-entry lookup cache of frequently referenced destinations. If the destination is not in the cache, each routine calls TIE$XXXX_LOOKUP, in module [TIE]TIE, to perform the actual lookup of the destination.

TIE$XXXX_LOOKUP first uses the translated image table (see Figure 29.5) to determine in which image, if any, the destination lies. The possible outcomes include the following:

▸ The destination is within a translated image but not within the translated part of that image. It is the address of a VAX instruction, possibly generated by some form of computed transfer in the image. In any case, it represents an entry point not found during translation.
▸ The destination is within the translated part of a translated image, and TIE$XXXX_LOOKUP looks up the address in the VAX-to-AXP instruction map for that image. The instruction map table entry contains the corresponding translated code address.
▸ The destination is within TIE$SHARE.
▸ The destination is an address within the range of OpenVMS VAX system

service vectors, and TIE$XXXX_LOOKUP transforms the address as de-
scribed in Section 29.6.5.

▸ The destination is within a native shareable image.

After locating the destination, TIE$XXXX_LOOKUP updates the cache and
returns to its caller with the translated address, if appropriate, and a status
specifying whether the destination is translated, VAX code, or outside any
translated images.

29.6.2   Transfers from Native to Translated Images

As previously described, when control is first transferred to an activated executable translated image, the $NATIVE_TO_TRANSLATED system service
calls TIE$NATIVE_TO_TIE in order to enter the translated code. Most other
transitions from native code to translated code follow the same sequence.
The only other path for a transition from native to translated is described
later in this section.

TIE$NATIVE_TO_TIE is written in MACRO-64 code so that it can control
stack layout and register use. The descriptor for this procedure identifies
it as a PDSC$V_NATIVE frame and as a PDSC$V_TIE_FRAME, one that
encapsulates translated frames.

TIE$NATIVE_TO_TIE creates a special stack frame for saving registers and
exception context. Definitions in module [TIE]TIE.PREFIX specify the layout
of this area, shown in Figure 29.6.

Most of the fields in the frame are for saving registers. TIE_PDV contains
the procedure value of the TIE$SHARE procedure that built the frame. TIE_
TRN_0 to TIE_TRN_7 are scratch locations for use by translated code. The
other fields are used in condition handling.

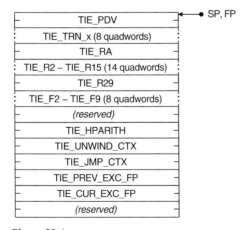

Figure 29.6
Layout of the TIE Frame Register Save Area

TIE$NATIVE_TO_TIE is called with the addresses of the VAX argument list and the translated procedure to be called.

It takes the following steps:

1. It builds the register save area on the stack and records its address in the FP.
2. It calls TIE$$ALIGN_VAX_STATE, in module [TIE]TIESTATE, to initialize R12 and R13, the VAX AP and FP, from the register save area of the TIE frame containing the most recent VAX procedure. When translated code is first entered, there is no earlier VAX procedure, and R12 and R13 are simply cleared.
3. TIE$NATIVE_TO_TIE clears R22 and sets R23 to 1 to initialize the emulated VAX condition codes.
4. It copies the SP to R14, the VAX SP.
5. It calls TIE$CALLX_LOOKUP, in module [TIE]TIELOOKU, to transform the address of the VAX procedure to the address of its translated code and to enter the translated code or to transfer control to the interpreter if the lookup fails.

TIE$CALLX_LOOKUP calls TIE$XXXX_LOOKUP, described in Section 29.6.1. When TIE$XXXX_LOOKUP returns, TIE$CALLX_LOOKUP has two paths into a translated image, depending on what the destination address represents. In either case, it reserves space on the stack for a maximum-size VAX call frame and adjusts the SP to an octaword boundary. (This is somewhat simplified; if the AXP SP is advanced enough beyond the VAX SP so that there is room for the VAX call frame, no adjustment is made to the AXP SP.) If the address is within translated code, TIE$CALLX_LOOKUP transfers control to the translated code, which contains VEST-generated instructions to build a VAX call frame in the allocated space.

If the VAX procedure address is in VAX code, it presumably represents an entry point not found during translation. TIE$CALLX_LOOKUP evaluates the word at that address as a VAX procedure entry mask. It aligns R14, the VAX SP, to a longword boundary and builds a call frame, starting at R14 and saving the specified registers. It then looks up that address plus 2 as a branch destination in case the VAX code has been translated but not identified as a procedure entry point. If the lookup fails, it calls TIE$$INTERPRET_VAX, in module [TIE]TIELOOKU, which performs stack setup for interpretation and then calls the interpreter, TIE$$VAX_INTERPRETER, in module [TIE]VAX_INTERPRETER.

The only other transition from native to translated image code is through TIE$$N_TO_T_CH, in module [TIE]TIEEXC, which dispatches into a translated image condition handler following an exception. TIE$NATIVE_TO_TIE's procedure descriptor identifies procedure TIE$$N_TO_T_CH as its frame-based condition handler. If an exception occurs while translated code is executing, the OpenVMS condition handling dispatcher dispatches to TIE$$N_TO_T_CH.

The descriptor for this procedure identifies it as a PDSC$V_NATIVE frame and as a PDSC$V_TIE_FRAME, one that encapsulates translated frames. TIE$$N_TO_T_CH creates the same special stack frame as TIE $NATIVE_TO_TIE (see Figure 29.6).

TIE$$N_TO_T_CH first checks whether the exception was caused by an attempt to access code in a fault-on-execute page (see Section 29.6.6). If not, it then must find the most recent VAX frame encapsulated within the TIE$NATIVE_TO_TIE frame that established TIE$$N_TO_T_CH as condition handler. If the condition is not handled by a translated code primary or secondary condition handler, TIE$$N_TO_T_CH must scan back through any encapsulated VAX call frames in that TIE$NATIVE_TO_TIE frame for a nonzero FP value.

29.6.3 Encapsulated VAX Call Frames

When one translated procedure calls another, VEST code generated by the caller builds a VAX call frame, and VEST code generated by the called procedure emulates the VAX RET instruction. As one translated procedure calls another and it calls another, nested VAX call frames build up on the stack. These VAX call frames are encapsulated within a native stack procedure frame; that is, from the viewpoint of the rest of the system, the current procedure context is that of TIE$NATIVE_TO_TIE. The VAX call frames are not a visible part of the procedure call chain.

Figure 29.7 shows an example stack with three VAX call frames encapsulated within TIE$NATIVE_TO_TIE's frame. The saved FP in the most recent VAX call frame, VAX Call Frame 0, points to VAX Call Frame 1, and its saved FP points to VAX Call Frame 2.

29.6.4 Transfers from Translated to Native Images

As previously described, TIE$CALLX_LOOKUP is called by VEST-generated code to deal with any transfers of control whose destination is not within the same translated image. It calls TIE$XXXX_LOOKUP, described in Section 29.6.1, to locate the destination.

If the destination is within TIE$SHARE, TIE$CALLX_LOOKUP simply treats it as another translated procedure. It builds a VAX call frame and transfers control, as described in Section 29.6.2.

If the destination is an address within the range of OpenVMS VAX system service vectors, TIE$CALLX_LOOKUP takes the actions described in Section 29.6.5.

If the destination is neither of these special cases, it examines bits 12 and 13 at that address. If either is set, the address is a native procedure value.

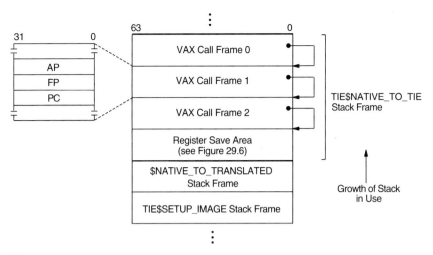

Figure 29.7
Translated Image Frames

TIE$CALLX_LOOKUP builds a VAX call frame, aligns the stack to an octa-word boundary, and requests the $TRANSLATED_TO_NATIVE system service. When it returns, TIE$CALLX_LOOKUP emulates a VAX RET to return to its caller in translated code.

29.6.5   System Service Requests

In general, a system service request from a translated image takes the form of a call to an address that TIE$SHARE must transform. By default VAX system service requests are resolved to P1 space system service vectors. When the call destination is in this range, TIE$XXXX_LOOKUP indexes a table to transform the P1 space system service vector offset into the address of the equivalent OpenVMS AXP system service. Actually, it transforms it into the procedure value of the equivalent system service transfer routine (see Chapter 7). TIE$SHARE then requests the $TRANSLATED_TO_NATIVE system service, specifying that procedure value and the address of the associated argument list.

That sequence works because the OpenVMS AXP executive provides functionally equivalent system services and a system service interface that is upwardly compatible with the OpenVMS VAX interface. OpenVMS AXP system services all have default procedure signatures. Nonetheless, several system service requests require explicit intervention:

▶ Change to Executive Mode ($CMEXEC)
▶ Change to Kernel Mode ($CMKRNL)
▶ Declare Change Mode or Compatibility Mode Handler ($DCLCMH)
▶ Set Exception Vector ($SETEXV)
▶ Unwind Call Stack ($UNWIND)

TIE$SHARE transforms requests for each of these to a procedure value of a procedure in TIE$SHARE whose name has the form TIE$*service-name*. It transfers control to any of these procedures through the $TRANSLATED_ TO_NATIVE service.

TIE$CMEXEC and TIE$CMKRNL, in module [TIE]TIESYS, simply check whether the target inner mode procedure is an OpenVMS VAX system service vector (for example, SYS$ENQ). If so, the TIE procedure transforms it to the address of its counterpart OpenVMS AXP transfer routine. Each then requests either the $CMEXEC or the $CMKRNL service.

Each of these system services explicitly checks if the target procedure is translated and if its descriptor has the bit PDSC$V_TIE_FRAME set. If either condition is true, it returns the error status SS$_BADPARAM. This means that a translated image can request these system services, but the target inner mode procedure must be a native procedure.

TIE$DCLCMH, in module [TIE]TIESYS, intercepts $DCLCMH requests. First, it makes two sanity checks on the request, returning the error status SS$_IVSSRQ if either fails:

▶ That the request is not intended to establish a compatibility mode handler
▶ That the handler being declared is a translated procedure

It then requests the $DCLCMH service, specifying its own procedure as the CHMU or CHMS handler. If the specified change mode exception occurs subsequently, its own handler will be entered and will transform the exception information and environment into what an OpenVMS VAX handler would expect, namely, a stack containing the sign-extended change mode operand, a PC, and a processor status longword (PSL). It will dispatch to the translated handler. When the translated handler is done, it can pop the change mode operand from the emulated VAX stack frame and execute the translated instructions generated for a VAX REI.

TIE$SETEXV, in module [TIE]TIESYS, intercepts $SETEXV requests so that it can ensure a TIE$SHARE condition handler is entered to build the condition handler argument list in the form expected by a translated handler. If the request is to establish a handler rather than to remove one, TIE$SETEXV determines whether the handler is native or translated. If native, TIE$SETEXV requests the $SETEXV service, passing it the original arguments. If translated, TIE$SETEXV requests the $SETEXV service, passing it the address of its own handler, either TIE$PRIMARY_HANDLER, TIE$SECONDARY_HANDLER, or TIE$LAST_CHANCE_HANDLER, depending on the system service argument VECTOR. It saves the address of the translated vectored handler in its own data area to call whenever its own handler is called.

Chapter 6 describes condition handling and vectored handlers.

TIE$UNWIND, in module [TIE]TIESTATE, requests the native system service, passing it the arguments supplied by the translated caller, presumably a condition handler. If the service returns successfully, TIE$UNWIND determines whether the original request came from a translated condition handler. If so, TIE$UNWIND locates that condition handler's call frame and replaces the return PC in it. TIE$SHARE must emulate OpenVMS VAX $UNWIND, which replaces the condition handler call frame return PC with the address of a routine to initiate unwinding. Without this change, the condition handler would return to TIE condition handler search code, which would incorrectly look for another condition handler.

29.6.6   Fault-on-Execute and Interpretation of VAX Code

In addition to run-time support, TIE$SHARE provides a fallback interpreter of VAX code that was not found during translation and a feedback mechanism to provide input for a subsequent translation. The goal is that by using the feedback information to retranslate the image, interpretation will only be required for dynamically created VAX code.

As described in Section 29.5.1, when a translated image is activated, the pages containing the copy of the VAX image are modified to be fault-on-execute. Any subsequent attempt to transfer control to a location in them results in an exception. The OpenVMS fault-on-execute exception service routine signals an access violation with bit 17 set in the signal array reason mask to identify this exception. If any translated code procedures are active, they are preceded by a TIE$NATIVE_TO_TIE frame that established TIE$$N_TO_T_CH as its condition handler.

TIE$$N_TO_T_CH confirms that the exception occurred during the execution of translated code, making the following sanity checks:

▶ The depth in the mechanism array must be 0, indicating that the exception occurred in the same native procedure context that established it as condition handler.

▶ The establisher's procedure value must be that of TIE$NATIVE_TO_TIE or TIE$$N_TO_T_CH.

▶ The faulting virtual address must correspond to the contents of R19 at the time of the exception, indicating that the exception occurred within a translated context.

▶ R17 at the time of the exception must contain 0, 1, 2, or 3, namely, a valid value identifying the type of transfer.

If any check fails, TIE$$N_TO_T_CH resignals the condition.

If they all pass, it alters the signal array faulting PC and the mechanism array's saved R27 to describe the lookup routine in [TIE]TIELOOKU corresponding to the transfer type (TIE$CALLX_LOOKUP or TIE$JSB_LOOKUP, for example). It then returns the status SS$_CONTINUE, as a result of which control is transferred to that lookup routine with all other registers restored to their values at the time of the exception. The lookup routine transfers to translated code if the lookup succeeds or dispatches to the interpreter, as described in Section 29.6.2.

Chapter 6 describes condition handling in detail.

29.6.7   **Achieving Instruction Atomicity**

In an image translated with the qualifier /PRESERVE=INSTRUCTION_ ATOMICITY, some instruction atomicity is achieved because the generated code uses the intr_flag state bit, described in Section 29.2.2. Use of this flag enables detection of an interrupt or exception that has occurred in the middle of a set of native instructions emulating a single VAX instruction.

The TIE$SHARE procedure TIE$$IGC, in module TIESTATE, uses the instruction granularity bitmap to help enforce instruction atomicity. It is called when control is transferred to a translated procedure through TIE$NATIVE_TO_TIE. In its attempt to locate the most recent VAX call frame, TIE$NATIVE_TO_TIE calls TIE$$ALIGN_VAX_STATE. If it finds a VAX call frame representing delivery of a translated AST that has interrupted execution of instructions within the translated part of the image, TIE$$ALIGN_VAX_STATE calls TIE$$IGC.

TIE$$IGC takes the following steps:

1. It identifies which translated image contains the interrupted PC. (A process may have several translated images activated at once.) TIE$$IGC determines whether that image has an instruction granularity bitmap. If not, it returns. The AST procedure can execute immediately, but atomicity is unenforceable.

2. If there is a map, it locates and tests the bit corresponding to the interrupted PC. If the bit is set, execution of that set of instructions has not yet begun, and the AST procedure can execute without further ado. TIE$$IGC returns.

3. If the bit is clear, TIE$$IGC must ensure that the set of instructions complete or appear not to have started before it allows the AST procedure to execute. It scans forward in the bitmap until it reaches a set bit representing the first instruction of the next set.

   During the scan it examines each instruction to determine whether the instruction can be interpreted safely. If the instruction, for example, modifies emulated VAX state, accesses memory other than the current call frame, is a CALL_PAL instruction, or is part of a load-locked/store-conditional sequence, the instruction cannot be interpreted safely.

   At the end of the scan, if all instructions can be interpreted safely, TIE$$IGC interprets them, advances to the next set of instructions, and then allows the AST procedure to execute.

4. If one or more instructions cannot be interpreted safely, TIE$$IGC scans backward in the bitmap until it reaches a set bit representing the first

instruction of the current set. During the scan it examines each instruction to determine whether it destroyed VAX state or whether it could be safely reexecuted.

At the end of the scan, if all instructions can be safely reexecuted, TIE$$IGC resets the interrupted PC to the beginning of that set and allows the AST procedure to execute. (The reset is possible because at the beginning of a set of instructions emulating a VAX instruction all VAX state is recorded in a save area from which it is retrieved.)

If all instructions cannot be safely reexecuted, TIE$$IGC signals the error TIE$_IGCNOTDONE.

29.7   RELEVANT SOURCE MODULES

Source modules described in this chapter include

[LIBOTS]OTS$CALL_PROC_ALPHA.M64
[STARLET]PSIGDEF.SDL
[STARLETOLB]AMAC_CALL.MAR
[SYS]ASTDEL_STACK.M64
[SYS]SYSCHGMOD.MAR
[SYS]SYSJACKET.M64
[TIE]TIE.B64
[TIE]TIE.PREFIX
[TIE]TIE.R64
[TIE]TIEEXC.M64
[TIE]TIEIMG.M64
[TIE]TIELOOKU.M64
[TIE]TIESTATE.B64
[TIE]TIESYS.M64
[TIE]TIESYSVECTOR.M64

30 Process Dynamics

In my end is my beginning.
Motto of Mary, Queen of Scots

Other chapters in Part VII, Life of a Process, describe process creation, image activation, and process deletion. This chapter describes the manner in which OpenVMS components create processes on a user's behalf. It examines the circumstances in which the various components are invoked and the resulting process types.

In addition, this chapter describes the mechanisms supporting the most common situation, a process that executes several images consecutively. Because this mode of operation occurs in all interactive and batch processes, these two process types are discussed in detail.

30.1 PROCESS CLASSIFICATION

A process can be classified by several characteristics:

▶ It is either a subprocess and part of its creator's job tree, sharing its job information block (JIB), or it is detached from its creator, a top-level process with an independent job tree of its own.
▶ It either interacts with a user and receives input from a terminal, or it is noninteractive and receives input from a file or device.
▶ It includes a command language interpreter (CLI) and can make the transition from one image to another, or it executes only one image and exits when the image does.

30.2 THE ROLE OF OPENVMS COMPONENTS

Various OpenVMS components initiate process creation by requesting the Create Process ($CREPRC) system service. They include

▶ The job controller for interactive and batch processes
▶ The Digital command language (DCL) CLI for subprocesses and noninteractive processes
▶ NETACP for network processes

Arguments to the $CREPRC system service determine process characteristics, particularly the arguments UIC, STSFLG, INPUT, and IMAGE. Chapter 27 discusses this system service and its arguments in detail. Tables 30.1 and 30.2 provide examples of arguments passed to the $CREPRC system service by OpenVMS components.

Some components that implement portions of process startup execute in the context of the new process. When the process is created, the creator specifies an image later activated by EXE$PROCSTRT, as described in Chapter 27. This is generally the LOGINOUT image. One of LOGINOUT's functions is to map a CLI into the process's P1 space. The CLI enables the process to execute successive images, accomplishing the transition from one image to the next. This mode of operation occurs in all interactive and batch processes, and is optional but common for detached and network processes. Sections 30.5 and 30.6 provide more information on LOGINOUT and CLIs. A complete description of CLI operation, however, is beyond the scope of this chapter.

Although OpenVMS AXP Version 1.5 supplies only the DCL CLI, the operating system can deal with multiple CLIs and the description in this chapter is based on that capability.

30.3   THE JOB CONTROLLER AND PROCESS CREATION

The job controller process manages the creation of nearly all interactive and batch processes. It creates an interactive process in response to unsolicited terminal input and a batch process as a result of the CLI response to the SUBMIT command.

The job controller is notified by the terminal class driver of unsolicited input via the job controller mailbox. The job controller is requested by the queue manager to create a batch process. In response to each of these, the job controller creates an appropriate process.

The process created by the job controller executes the image LOGINOUT. The actions that LOGINOUT takes, especially mapping a CLI into P1 space, differentiate processes that can execute multiple images in succession, such as interactive and batch processes, from processes that exit after the execution of a single image.

30.3.1   Unsolicited Terminal Input

The term *unsolicited terminal input* refers to characters entered on a device that has no outstanding read request. The common terminal driver character-processing routine, TTY$PUTNEXTCHAR, in module [TTDRVR] TTYCHARI, takes special action for unsolicited terminal input:

- If the terminal has the characteristic NO_TYPEAHEAD, the driver ignores the unsolicited input and dismisses the interrupt.
- If the terminal is owned, the driver inserts the character into the type-ahead buffer. If the owner process had requested notification of unsolicited input, the driver notifies the owner process.
- If the terminal is unowned and has the AUTOBAUD characteristic, the driver tests the incoming character. It senses the baud rate and sets it as appropriate.
- If the terminal is unowned and has the SECURE characteristic, it is attached to a secure server, and the driver merely inserts the character into the type-ahead buffer and echoes the character.

Table 30.1   Arguments Resulting in Interactive
Process Creation

Argument Passed to $CREPRC	*Value*
Process name	_ttcu:
UIC	[1,4]
Image name	SYS$SYSTEM:LOGINOUT.EXE
SYS$INPUT	*ttcu:*
SYS$OUTPUT	*ttcu:*
SYS$ERROR	*ttcu:*
Base priority	DEFPRI (SYSGEN parameter)
Privilege mask	TMPMBX, NETMBX, SETPRV
Status flags	PRC$V_INTER

▶ If the terminal does not have the SECURE characteristic, if logins on it are allowed, and if the character is a standard terminator recognized by the driver, the driver sends a message to the job controller mailbox, notifying the job controller that an unowned terminal has received an unsolicited interrupt. Typically, under these circumstances, the terminal has no type-ahead buffer.

In a sense, the job controller is the default owner of all otherwise un-claimed terminals.

If the type-ahead buffer does not exist when the driver attempts to insert a character, the driver initiates a fork thread to create the buffer. The current character, however, is discarded.

The job controller routine that responds to unsolicited terminal input, UNSOLICITED_INPUT in module [JOBCTL]UNSOLICIT, simply requests the $CREPRC system service. Table 30.1 shows the arguments it passes to the system service.

The string *ttcu:* indicates the controller and unit of the terminal where the unsolicited input was typed. The terminal device type can be an actual physical device; an LT device, if the terminal is connected through a DECserver; an RT device, if the terminal is remote; a VT device, if virtual terminal support is enabled; or an FT device for DECwindows.

The job controller creates each interactive process with a process name indicating its input device and LOGINOUT as the image to be executed. The creation of an interactive process is shown in Figure 30.1.

30.3.2   SUBMIT Command

When the SUBMIT command is entered, DCL activates the SUBMIT.EXE image. SUBMIT sends a message to the queue manager by requesting the Send to Job Controller and Wait ($SNDJBCW) system service, which uses the interprocess communication ancillary control process.

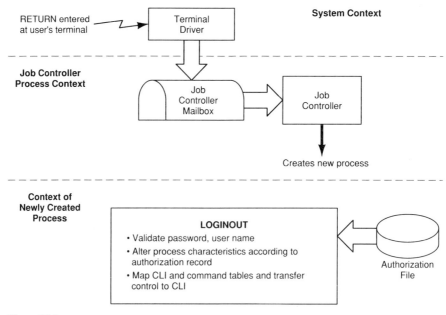

Figure 30.1
Creation of an Interactive Process

The queue manager receives the message and creates a job record in its in-memory database. It inserts the job record into an internal list of pending requests for the desired batch execution queue or generic queue. When the number of active jobs in a batch execution queue drops below the maximum value, the queue manager selects the queue's highest priority pending request. It sends an interprocess communication (IPC) message to the job controller.

The job controller receives the IPC message and requests the $CREPRC system service to create a process for that request, specifying LOGINOUT as the image to be executed. The job controller specifies _NLA0: as the SYS$OUTPUT and SYS$ERROR value, and the string BATCH_*queue-entry-number* as the process name. It specifies SYS$INPUT as the concatenation of the following:

▸ The string QMAN
▸ Eight-digit queue entry number
▸ Eight-digit incarnation number of the queue manager
▸ The string SYS$QUEUE_MANAGER

LOGINOUT requests the $SNDJBCW system service to get more information about the batch process, for example, the name of its CLI, its priority, and its working set list quotas. LOGINOUT redefines SYS$INPUT to be the name of the batch command procedure, and SYS$OUTPUT and SYS$ERROR to be the names of a log file in an appropriate directory. Because LOGINOUT

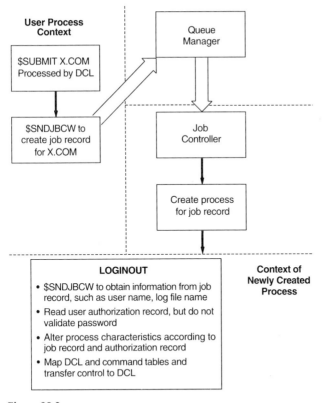

Figure 30.2
Creation of a Batch Process

maps the appropriate CLI into the process's P1 space, the batch input file can contain a series of command language statements. Figure 30.2 shows the processing of the SUBMIT command. Table 30.2 shows the arguments that the job controller passes to $CREPRC for a batch process.

30.4   SPAWN AND ATTACH

DCL provides two commands to create and connect with interactive subprocesses. The DCL command SPAWN creates interactive subprocesses. The ATTACH command transfers terminal control from one process to another within the same job. The module [DCL]SPAWN contains the code for both commands. The Run-Time Library procedures LIB$SPAWN and LIB$ATTACH make the SPAWN and ATTACH functions available to an image by passing the request back to the DCL CLI. The major difference between the two ways of requesting the functions is the method of passing parameters. From DCL level, the command line is parsed to obtain the parameters. The Run-Time Library procedures use an argument list.

Table 30.2   Arguments Resulting in Batch Process
Creation

Argument Passed to $CREPRC	Value
Process name	BATCH_*nnn*
UIC	[1,4]
Image name	SYS$SYSTEM:LOGINOUT.EXE
SYS$INPUT	QMAN*xxxxxxxxxyyyyyyyy*SYS$QUEUE_MANAGER
SYS$OUTPUT	_NLA0:
SYS$ERROR	_NLA0:
Base priority	DEFPRI (SYSGEN parameter)
Privilege mask	All
Status flags	PRC$V_BATCH

30.4.1   SPAWN

Spawning a subprocess primarily involves copying process context information from the creating process to the subprocess. This information includes the process CLI symbols, process-private logical names, current privileges, out-of-band asynchronous system trap (AST) settings, verify flag settings, prompt string, default disk and directory, keypad definitions and states, and the command line that was passed to SPAWN (if one exists).

In response to a SPAWN request, the DCL routine DCL$SPAWN, in module [DCL]SPAWN, performs the following operations:

1. It parses the command line to determine what qualifiers are present. It validates the qualifiers and copies them to a temporary data structure.
2. It temporarily disables the current process's out-of-band ASTs, blocking CTRL/Y ASTs during a critical section of code.
3. It creates or locates a termination mailbox and requests an attention AST if a message is written to the mailbox.

   Termination information from the subprocess is written to the termination mailbox when the subprocess is eventually deleted. The attention AST is delivered to the subprocess's creator at that time. Because four spawned subprocesses can share the same termination mailbox, DCL checks for an available one that the new subprocess can share before creating a new mailbox.
4. DCL records the name of the subprocess's CLI and command table files in P1 space locations CTL$GT_SPAWNCLI and CTL$GT_SPAWN-TABLE. The $CREPRC system service later copies them to the process quota block (PQB). When LOGINOUT eventually runs in the context of the new subprocess, this is the CLI that it will invoke. The default, if no CLI is specified, is the creator's CLI.
5. For CLIs supplied by Digital, DCL creates a second mailbox, called the

communication mailbox, through which further context information is transferred to the spawned subprocess, as described in step 10.

6. DCL creates an attach request mailbox for the current process with a jobwide logical name of the form DCL$ATTACH_*pid*, where *pid* is the extended process ID. Other processes in the job tree can attach to this process by writing attach requests to this mailbox.

7. DCL requests the Get Job/Process Information ($GETJPI) system service to determine the current process's nondeductible quotas, base priority, and current image count. From these quotas, it builds a quota list to be used in the creation of the spawned subprocess.

8. If the process name was not specified in the command line or argument list, DCL creates one by appending _*n* to the user name string, where *n* is a value from 1 to 255. If the new name is a duplicate, DCL increments *n* and tries again.

9. DCL requests the $CREPRC system service to create the subprocess. It specifies LOGINOUT as the IMAGE argument and the name of the communication mailbox from step 5 as the ERROR argument. If the creating process does not specify input and output files to the SPAWN command, DCL uses the creating process's SYS$INPUT and SYS$OUTPUT file specifications as the INPUT and OUTPUT arguments. It specifies the termination mailbox from step 3 to the $CREPRC service to receive a process deletion message from the subprocess. Because the request does not include a privilege mask for the subprocess, the $CREPRC system service creates the subprocess with the current privileges of the current process (see Chapter 27).

10. When LOGINOUT runs in the context of the newly spawned subprocess, it maps the specified CLI, DCL in this example, and passes control to it. DCL determines that it is running in the context of a subprocess and translates the logical name SYS$ERROR. If there is a supervisor mode translation with a mailbox name as the equivalence string, DCL recognizes that a SPAWN operation is in progress and that it must read context information from the creating process.

At this point, both the creating process and the spawned subprocess are executing DCL routines. The creating process passes context information to the spawned subprocess in the following manner:

a. The spawned subprocess assigns a channel to the communication mailbox and issues read requests to it.

b. The creating process writes context information to the mailbox, one record at a time. Each record has a type code identifying its contents. When the subprocess receives the information, it adds the information to its context.

c. The first transferred record contains the permanently enabled privilege mask (CTL$GQ_PROCPRIV), verify and other flag settings, out-of-band AST mask, and prompt string.

1055

The spawned subprocess reads the record and initializes the process accordingly. It requests the Set Privilege ($SETPRV) system service to disable all privileges, then resets the process privileges from those transferred in the record. Thus, the working, permanently enabled (current), and authorized privilege masks of the subprocess contain the privileges its creator possessed when the spawn occurred. This enables a privileged image to tailor the environment in a spawned subprocess.

d. Next, the creating process transfers the SPAWN command string (if one was specified).

e. Unless the SPAWN command specified that logical names should not be copied, the creating process scans the process logical name directory, which contains a list of process logical name table names. It copies all table names that were defined in user or supervisor mode and that do not have the CONFINE attribute. It copies all the logical names defined in those tables. The spawned subprocess creates the corresponding logical name tables and their logical names.

f. Unless the SPAWN command specified that symbols should not be copied, the creating process transfers the contents of the symbol table, one symbol at a time. The spawned subprocess receives each symbol and places it into the subprocess's symbol table. Unless the SPAWN command specified that keypad definitions should not be copied, the creating process transfers terminal keypad definitions. Note that the creating process's potentially modified DCL command tables are not transferred to the subprocess.

11. Once it has transferred all information to the subprocess, the creating process deassigns the channel to the communication mailbox. It tests whether it should wait for the subprocess. If so, it requests a write attention AST on the attach request mailbox and hibernates. Otherwise it restores out-of-band ASTs and resumes normal processing.

12. The spawned subprocess deassigns the channel to the communication mailbox. It deletes the supervisor mode logical name SYS$ERROR, leaving the executive mode logical name. It restores out-of-band ASTs and, if the subprocess is interactive, issues a special I/O request to the terminal driver to declare the subprocess the terminal owner. It then continues normal DCL processing.

When a subprocess created by the SPAWN command is deleted, a termination message is written to its creator's termination mailbox. As a result, a write attention AST is queued to the creator. The AST procedure simply performs cleanup work pertaining to the deleted subprocess. It deassigns the channels to the attach and termination mailboxes and deletes the mailboxes. If the subprocess was created by a call to LIB$SPAWN and if an event flag or AST procedure was specified in the call, and the creating process's image count is the same as when the subprocess was spawned, the event flag is set or the AST is delivered.

30.4.2   ATTACH

The DCL ATTACH request transfers terminal control from the process that issues the command to a target process. The operation of the DCL ATTACH routine, DCL$ATTACH in module [DCL]SPAWN, is as follows:

1. From the context of the issuing process, DCL first obtains the name or process identification (PID) of the target process. It disables out-of-band ASTs, blocking delivery of CTRL/Y ASTs. It then verifies that the target process is not itself and that it is a process in the same job tree.

2. DCL creates an attach request mailbox and logical name for the issuing process. Since interactive input will be detached from the issuing process and attached to the target process, the issuing process must have an attach mailbox to accept attach requests later. Otherwise, the terminal cannot be reattached to it.

3. DCL locates the target process's attach mailbox and writes the name of the current output stream (usually the equivalence name of SYS$INPUT) to the mailbox. Since the target process had declared a write attention AST on its attach mailbox, it is notified of the message placed in the mailbox. The original process then issues a read request on the target process's attach mailbox in anticipation of a message from the target.

4. The target process wakes in response to the write attention AST. The AST procedure determines whether the target process is already attached to a terminal. If not, it writes an affirmative response (a longword with a value of 1) to the attach mailbox. Otherwise, it writes a zero longword to refuse the attach request and reenables the write attention AST for the attach mailbox.

5. Once it receives the affirmation, DCL in the issuing process deassigns its channel to the target process's attach mailbox. It requests a write attention AST for its own attach mailbox so it can be notified of any incoming attach requests. It then hibernates.

6. The AST procedure in the target process issues a wake request to return control to the target process.

30.5   THE LOGINOUT IMAGE

The LOGINOUT image provides three major functions:

1. It validates a user's access to the system, checking password information in the authorization file.

2. It adjusts various process quotas and defaults based on information from the authorization file or from the job controller.

3. It maps a CLI into P1 space.

LOGINOUT need not perform all these functions for every process. Its actions are based on the original arguments passed to the $CREPRC system service, stored in the process control block (PCB), process header (PHD), and P1 space. For example, it does not perform password validation if the $CREPRC STSFLG argument PRC$V_NOUAF was specified.

The LOGINOUT image is installed with privileges, which it enables and disables based on the current function. The image executes primarily in user mode, with some executive and kernel mode procedures.

Normally, the $CREPRC IMAGE argument specifies LOGINOUT and the image is activated by EXE$PROCSTRT. However, under certain conditions, the image activator independently invokes LOGINOUT (see Chapter 28).

OpenVMS AXP Version 1.5 LOGINOUT includes the capability to call site-specific routines (LOGINOUT callout routines). These routines support customer login security programs such as smart card programs, pocket authenticator programs, and other alternative identification and authentication programs. They enable sites to combine portions of LOGINOUT's security policy functions with site security login functions to establish a customized login security environment.

A positive value for the SYSGEN parameter LGI_CALLOUTS enables LOGINOUT installation callouts. The value defines the number of site-specific shareable images that contain LOGINOUT callout routines. The system manager defines the executive mode logical name LGI$LOGINOUT_CALLOUTS in the system table with equivalence names that identify these shareable images. Each shareable image defines the universal symbol LGI$LOGIN_CALLOUTS as the name associated with a table of callout routines. When LOGINOUT runs, it activates each such shareable image and records the value of LGI$LOGIN_CALLOUTS within that image. At particular points in LOGINOUT's execution, it calls the corresponding callout routine in each of these shareable images. If one of these routines returns an error status, LOGINOUT aborts.

The *OpenVMS Utility Routines Manual* provides details on the creation of LOGINOUT callout images and the interfaces to callout routines.

30.5.1 LOGINOUT and Interactive Processes

When the LOGINOUT image executes in an interactive process created in response to unsolicited terminal input, it must verify that the user has access to the system before proceeding with the rest of its operations. Beginning at routine START, in module [LOGIN]LOGIN, it performs the following steps:

1. It establishes a user mode call frame condition handler to service any exceptions or software conditions that occur while LOGINOUT is executing. Should this handler be called, it first requests the Put Message ($PUTMSG) system service to write an error message. It then checks the type and severity of the condition. If the status code has not already been

stored in P1 space, the handler stores it in preparation for writing the code to the termination mailbox.

If the condition is a severe error, the handler calls any LGI$ICR_FIN-ISH LOGINOUT callout routines and requests the Exit ($EXIT) system service from executive mode, causing the process to be deleted. Otherwise, it returns, and LOGINOUT continues execution.

LOGINOUT declares this same condition handler for many of its executive mode procedures.

2. LOGINOUT requests the $GETJPIW system service to obtain the user name, process status flags, job type, and process owner.

3. LOGINOUT requests the Get Device Information and Wait ($GET-DVIW) system service to obtain the name and the characteristics of SYS$INPUT.

4. If LOGINOUT callouts are enabled on this system, LOGINOUT tries to translate LGI$LOGINOUT_CALLOUTS as an executive mode logical name in the system logical name table. There must be a definition with LGI_CALLOUTS equivalence names. It activates an image for each equivalence name and records the address of LGI$LOGIN_CALLOUTS within the image.

5. Continuing in routine LOGIN, in module [LOGIN]LOGIN, LOGINOUT requests the Set Privileges ($SETPRV) system service to acquire necessary privileges temporarily.

6. It temporarily changes the protection of the process-permanent data (PPD) region in P1 space to make it writable from user mode. This enables much of LOGINOUT to execute in user mode. This region is shared by LOGINOUT and the CLI it maps.

7. LOGINOUT translates the logical names SYS$INPUT, SYS$OUTPUT, and SYS$ERROR in the LNM$PROCESS table and saves the resultant strings for later use.

8. LOGINOUT initializes the PPD region in P1 space.

9. It initializes the argument vector for LOGINOUT callout routines and calls each image's LGI$ICR_INIT routine.

10. LOGINOUT classifies the process as one of the following five mutually exclusive types and performs type-specific initialization:

   - Batch—The batch bit is set in CTL$GL_CREPRC_FLAGS, a copy of the flags specified to the $CREPRC system service.
   - Network—The network bit is set in CTL$GL_CREPRC_FLAGS.
   - Subprocess—The parent PID is nonzero.
   - Interactive—The interactive bit is set and the no-password bit is clear in CTL$GL_CREPRC_FLAGS.

     A DECwindows process is an interactive process whose input device type is DC$_WORKSTATION.
   - Detached—Anything not covered by the previous types.

11. For an interactive process, typically one created in response to unsolicited input from a terminal, LOGINOUT does the following in routines INIT_INTERACTIVE and INTERACTIVE_VALIDATION, both
in module [LOGIN]INTERACT, and SET_TERM_NAME in [LOGIN]
INITUSER:

a. It initializes the user name and account name fields in the JIB and P1
space to the string <login>.

b. It creates process-permanent files for the input and output devices
through calls to Record Management Services (RMS). LOGINOUT
redefines the logical names SYS$INPUT and SYS$OUTPUT in the
LNM$PROCESS table. It defines the logical names SYS$ERROR and
SYS$COMMAND with the same equivalence strings as SYS$OUT-
PUT and SYS$INPUT. It prefixes the equivalence names for these log-
ical names by four bytes: an escape ($1B_{16}$), a null character (00_{16}), and
the two-byte internal file identifier (IFI) returned by RMS. When RMS
receives such a string as a result of logical name translation, it uses the
IFI as an index into one of its internal tables. Accessing by IFI allows
fast access to these commonly used files.

c. In the case of an interactive login, the input device must be a terminal
device. Otherwise, LOGINOUT exits with the error message "invalid
SYS$INPUT for interactive login".

d. If the terminal line has modem control enabled, LOGINOUT requires
the TT$V_REMOTE bit to be set. This bit notifies the driver that
the process must be logged off or disconnected if the modem signals
disappear.

e. LOGINOUT determines whether the job type is local, dialup, or remote, based on the characteristics of the SYS$INPUT terminal.

It marks an interactive DECwindows process as local but does not
store a terminal name for it.

f. If LOGINOUT callouts are enabled, it initializes callout variables specific to interactive jobs and calls each image's LGI$ICR_IACT_START
routine.

g. LOGINOUT determines whether there is a system password and
whether it applies to this terminal. If there is, it issues a timed, no-
echo read to the terminal and checks the password entered by the
user.

h. It then translates the logical name SYS$ANNOUNCE and writes the
announcement message defined by the system manager.

i. If LOGINOUT callouts are enabled, it calls each image's LGI$ICR_
IDENTIFY routine.

j. LOGINOUT checks whether autologins are enabled for the terminal that is logging in. If they are, LOGINOUT looks up the terminal
name in SYS$SYSTEM:SYSALF.DAT to determine the user name as-

sociated with the terminal. It then reads the user authorization file (UAF) record associated with the user and stores the user name in the JIB and in CTL$T_USERNAME in P1 space.

k. If autologins are not enabled for the SYS$INPUT terminal, LOG-INOUT prompts on it for the user name. It reads and parses the input, noting the presence of qualifiers, such as /CONNECT and /CLI. It opens the system authorization file and reads the record associated with that user, if any.

l. If LOGINOUT callouts are enabled, it calls each image's LGI$ICR_AUTHENTICATE routine.

m. Whether the desired UAF record exists or not, LOGINOUT always prompts for the password. It reads and verifies the password and, if there is a secondary password for the account, prompts for, reads, and verifies that as well.

n. LOGINOUT stores the user name in the JIB and in CTL$T_USER-NAME.

o. If the account is captive or restricted, LOGINOUT checks that the user did not include login qualifiers to change aspects of the process environment fixed for that account.

p. LOGINOUT then performs a scan of the intrusion database in non-paged pool. The type of scan performed depends on the success of user validation.

If a user validation error (such as invalid user name or password) has occurred, a suspect scan is performed. If evasion is in effect, the user name is set and a break-in audit is performed. Otherwise, the failed password count is incremented in the user's UAF record, and a corresponding intrusion record is either created or updated.

If the login was valid, an intruder scan is performed. If the user is found to be an intruder, a break-in audit is performed and the login terminates.

12. LOGINOUT resets some of the process attributes extracted from the authorization file, overriding the attributes established when the process was created:

- Logical name SYS$DISK
- Default directory string through the Set Default Directory (SYS$SETD-DIR) system service
- Base scheduling priority through the Set Priority ($SETPRI) system service
- User name
- User identification code (UIC)

13. After the process's correct UIC has been set, LOGINOUT recreates the job logical name table and, possibly, the group logical name table.

14. LOGINOUT attempts to change the process name from _ttcu: to the user name. This attempt can fail if another process in the same group already has the same name. (A common cause of user name duplication is a user logged in at more than one terminal.) In the case of failure, the process retains its name (_ttcu:), guaranteed to be unique for a given system.

15. LOGINOUT completes the local rights list entries based on the process characteristics and the identifiers associated with the UIC.

16. It stores the job type in the JIB, at offset JIB$L_JOBTYPE.

17. LOGINOUT copies the remaining attributes extracted from the authorization file to their proper places.

   - It copies information about primary and secondary day restrictions.
   - It moves process quotas and limits, testing as appropriate to ensure that they are within system bounds.
   - It copies the default privilege mask from the UAF record into PHD$Q_AUTHPRIV and CTL$GQ_PROCPRIV.
   - It initializes ARB$Q_PRIV and PHD$Q_PRIVMSK as the default privilege mask ORed with the image privilege mask.

18. It copies the terminal name to PCB$T_TERMINAL.

19. If LOGINOUT callouts are enabled, it calls each image's LGI$ICR_CHKRESTRICT routine.

20. LOGINOUT checks a number of other fields in the authorization file record. These include the user or account job limit, the primary and secondary password expiration flags, the DISUSER flag, the account expiration time, and the account hourly restrictions. These checks are waived in the case of the SYSTEM account logging in on the console terminal.

21. If SYS$INPUT is not a remote terminal and reconnection is allowed for the account, LOGINOUT then checks whether the user has disconnected from a process that still exists. It performs a wildcard $GETJPI, looking for a process with the same user name and UIC and a disconnected terminal. It displays any matches and asks the user to which process, if any, the terminal should be connected. It records the answer for later use.

22. If the user does not have OPER privilege, LOGINOUT checks that the interactive process count would not be exceeded by the logging in of this process, and that logins are not currently disabled.

23. If there is a limit to the number of processes that can log in with the user name or account name associated with this process, LOGINOUT scans the PCB vector, counting the number of top-level processes whose JIB user name or account name matches that of this process. It checks that the maximum would not be exceeded by the logging in of this process.

24. LOGINOUT begins initialization for a CLI. It creates user mode logical names PROC0 through PROC9, each equated to the file specification of a command procedure (or indirect command file) to be executed before the

CLI enters its input loop. Currently, only PROC0 and PROC1 are used. PROC0 is equated to the system name table translation of the logical name SYS$SYLOGIN.

PROC1 is equated to the file specified by the LGICMD field of the user's UAF record or the file specified by the login qualifier /COMMAND at login time (by an authorized user). If the contents of the LGICMD field are null and no /COMMAND qualifier was present on the login command, PROC1 is equated to the string LOGIN. The LGICMD field should indicate the null device (using the string NL:) to provide a default of no login command file.

When the CLI later executes its initialization code, it will translate these logical names and execute the command procedures (or indirect command files).

25. LOGINOUT requests a merged image activation of the selected CLI to map the CLI into the low-address end of P1 space (see Figure 1.7). Except in the case of DCL, LIB$P1_MERGE, in module [VMSLIB]LIBMERGE, first merges the CLI into P0 space to determine its size, deletes the P0 space, and maps the correct amount of P1 space. Next, LOGINOUT requests a merged image activation of the CLI's command table. Because of the way DCL and its table are built and installed, the image activator can determine their size without having to map them.

   Network and DECwindows processes always use DCL and DCL-TABLES as the CLI name and command table name. A restricted user receives the CLI name and command table name specified in the UAF record. However, an unrestricted interactive user can specify /CLI and /TABLE on the login command line to choose a particular CLI and command table. If the login command line does not contain a /CLI qualifier, LOGINOUT assigns the first nonzero CLI name in the following list to an unrestricted user:

   - CTL$GT_CLI_NAMESTRING, the CLI name specified by the image activator
   - CTL$GT_SPAWNCLI, the CLI name specified by a parent process for a spawned subprocess
   - The default CLI specified in the UAF record
   - CTL$GT_CLINAME, the CLI name of the parent process
   - DCL and DCLTABLES

26. LOGINOUT calls a kernel mode procedure to change the owner and protection of the CLI and command table pages. It changes the owner access mode for each page to supervisor and alters the protection on all writable pages to prevent writes from user mode.

27. To accommodate the CLI symbol table, LOGINOUT requests the Expand Process/Control Region ($EXPREG) system service to expand P1 space by a number of pagelets equal to the SYSGEN parameter CLISYM

TBL. It updates the global location CTL$GL_CTLBASVA to reflect the new low-address end of P1 space.

28. It opens SYS$INPUT and SYS$OUTPUT.

29. It records the user's account name in CTL$T_ACCOUNT and in the JIB.

30. If the DISWELCOME flag is clear in the UAF record, LOGINOUT writes to SYS$OUTPUT, announcing successful login. It first translates the logical name SYS$WELCOME and writes the welcome message defined by the system manager. If SYS$WELCOME is not defined, LOGINOUT writes the following message, obtaining the version number from the global location SYS$GQ_VERSION and the node name by translating the logical name SYS$NODE:

```
Welcome to OpenVMS AXP (TM) Operating System, Version V1.5
   on node FOOBAR
```

31. If the DISREPORT flag is clear in the UAF record, LOGINOUT also writes the dates of the last interactive and noninteractive logins and the number of login failures since the last successful login. If the DISNEW-MAIL flag is clear, it writes the number of new mail messages for the user.

32. LOGINOUT creates the logical names SYS$LOGIN, SYS$LOGIN_DEVICE, and SYS$SCRATCH in the process's job logical name table. The equivalence name for these logical names is the default disk and directory specified by the user's UAF record. (To override the default disk, follow the user name portion of the login sequence with the qualifier /DISK=ddcu:.)

    For a DECwindows terminal emulation window, LOGINOUT creates the logical name DECW$DISPLAY, with the workstation device name as the equivalence name. For a remote login, it creates the logical name SYS$REM_NODE, the remote node's name or address, and SYS$REM_ID, the remote user name.

33. LOGINOUT checks whether the primary or secondary password lifetime has ended. If so, it marks the password as expired in the UAF record. If the DISFORCE flag is clear in the UAF record or if the user specified the /NEW_PASSWORD qualifier on the login command line, LOGINOUT forces the user to set a new password before continuing. If the DISFORCE flag is set, LOGINOUT informs the user that the password has expired but allows the login to continue.

    If the lifetime of either the primary or secondary password has not ended but is due to expire within five days, LOGINOUT warns the user of that fact.

34. LOGINOUT records the login time in the UAF record and in CTL$GQ_LASTLOGIN. It updates CTL$GL_LOGFAILS and CTL$GL_LOGIN_FLAGS.

35. It notifies the security audit subsystem of the login.

36. If LOGINOUT callouts are enabled, it calls each image's LGI$ICR_FIN-ISH routine.

37. At this point, LOGINOUT has finished its work and must pass control to the CLI. To pass control to the CLI, LOGINOUT calls an executive mode routine that performs the following actions:

    a. It changes the protection on pages in the PPD region so that the pages can only be accessed from supervisor and inner access modes.

    b. It calls EXE$REI_INIT_STACK, in module REI, passing it the procedure value of the CLI from CTL$AG_CLIMAGE and an access mode of supervisor. EXE$REI_INIT_STACK reinitializes the executive mode stack to empty, creates an exception stack frame with a saved program counter (PC) and processor status (PS) reflecting its arguments, and executes a CALL_PAL REI instruction. This returns the process to supervisor mode with the PC pointing to the first instruction in the CLI, its initialization routine.

30.5.2   LOGINOUT and Batch Processes

Many of the operations performed by LOGINOUT for an interactive process are also necessary for a batch process. For example, LOGINOUT must open the input and output streams and map the CLI. However, LOGINOUT does not perform password verification—either the input symbiont has already checked it or, in the case of a SUBMIT command, it is not necessary.

Rather than describing the steps performed by LOGINOUT again, the following list simply specifies those that are different for a batch process:

1. When the batch flag is set in CTL$GL_CREPRC_FLAGS, a copy of the flags originally specified to the $CREPRC system service, LOGINOUT takes actions to create a batch process.

2. It initializes the account name fields in the JIB and P1 space to the string <batch>.

3. In routine INIT_BATCH, in module [LOGIN]DETACHED, LOGINOUT requests the $SNDJBCW system service to obtain information about the batch process, for example, its user name, process priority, and working set information.

   The prompted reads of user name and password, and the system announcements that occur in the login of an interactive process, are unnecessary for a batch process.

4. If LOGINOUT callouts are enabled, it initializes callout variables specific to batch processes and calls each image's LGI$ICR_IDENTIFY routine.

5. LOGINOUT establishes the file name to correspond to SYS$INPUT and SYS$COMMAND by concatenating the file IFI (returned by RMS) and the batch input file name. For the file name to correspond to SYS$OUTPUT and SYS$ERROR, it concatenates the file IFI (returned

by RMS) with the batch log file name. The files are opened subsequently by code common to batch and interactive processes.

6. LOGINOUT reads the authorization file record for this user. It obtains process attributes to supplement information specified during batch queue creation and job submission. These values from the authorization file are minimized with the values returned by the job controller.

7. The job parameters, P1 through P8, if present, are defined as user mode logical names, which the CLI later translates.

8. If LOGINOUT callouts are enabled, it calls each image's LGI$ICR_JOB-STEP routine.

The procedures of mapping the CLI and transferring control are exactly the same as if the process were interactive. In both cases, if SYS$SYLOGIN is defined as a system logical name, the first commands that execute are the commands in the site-specific login command file. If the UAF does not specify a user login command file, the command file SYS$LOGIN:LOGIN.COM is executed next.

LOGINOUT regains control at the beginning of each job step. Section 30.7 summarizes its job step initialization.

30.5.3 LOGINOUT and Network Processes

The NETACP image requests the $CREPRC system service to create a network process. Many of the operations performed by LOGINOUT for a network process are similar to those for an interactive process. The major difference is that LOGINOUT does not necessarily map a CLI for a network process.

NETACP specifies the $CREPRC input, output, and error arguments as follows:

▶ The input argument is the name of a command procedure or executable image to be invoked by LOGINOUT.

▶ The output argument is a flag indicating whether a proxy login is allowed, followed by access control information.

▶ The error argument is the address of a network control block (NCB) for the connection.

In routine INIT_NETWORK, in module [LOGIN]DETACHED, LOGINOUT obtains the network logical link number from the NCB and stores the remote node name, address, and ID in P1 space. It checks to see whether the network process should use proxy login or the user name and password supplied in the access control information. In the latter case, it reads the system authorization file and, if LOGINOUT callouts are enabled, calls each image's LGI$ICR_AUTHENTICATE and LGI$ICR_IDENTIFY routines. It creates an executive mode logical name SYS$NET, which locates the NCB.

LOGINOUT activates DCL to execute the file's commands and creates a log file.

30.6   CLIS AND IMAGE PROCESSING

Digital provides for the possibility of multiple CLIs, although only DCL is supplied with the OpenVMS software. This section describes various features of DCL, in particular, those that are typical of a CLI.

After the DCL CLI gains control and performs some initialization, it reads and processes successive records from SYS$INPUT. This section describes those operations that result in image execution, to contrast interactive and batch processes with processes that do not map a CLI.

One important step performed by a CLI is to request the Declare Exit Handler ($DCLEXH) system service to declare the routine DCL$EXITHAND in module [DCL]IMAGEXECT, as a supervisor mode exit handler. It is this handler that prevents process deletion following image exit and allows the successive execution of multiple images within the same process.

Figure 30.3 shows the flow of control in a process that does not map a CLI and thus executes only one image. Figure 30.4 shows the flow of control in a process that maps a CLI and thus can execute multiple images.

30.6.1   CLI Initialization

The DCL CLI's initialization code is the routine DCL$STARTUP in module [DCL]INITIAL. Running in supervisor mode, the initialization code performs the following steps before entering the main command processing loop:

1. Entered in supervisor mode, DCL resets the supervisor mode stack pointer (SP) to its base and then calls DCL$STARTUP, creating an initial

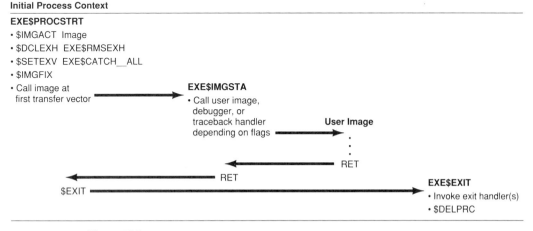

Figure 30.3
Process That Executes a Single Image

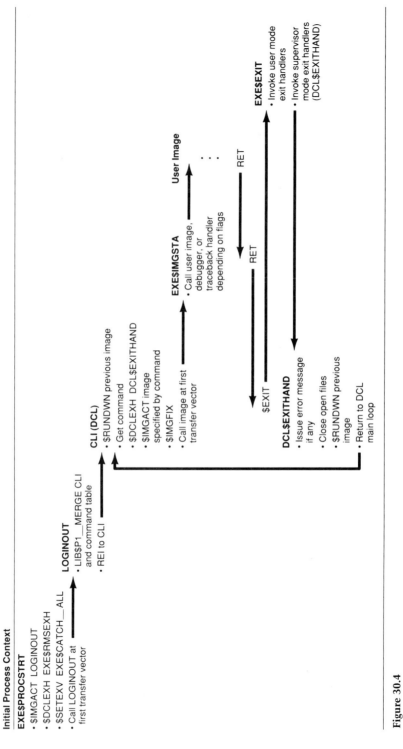

Figure 30.4

Process That Executes Multiple Images

call frame on the supervisor mode stack. This initial call frame contains zero in its saved frame pointer (FP), terminating the call frame chain. DCL calls itself again and establishes a call frame condition handler.

2. DCL writes the address of its CLI callback service routine in the global location CTL$AL_CLICALBK. Callback is a mechanism an image uses to obtain services from the CLI, such as symbol creation and lookup.

3. DCL initializes its work area from internal variables transferred by LOGINOUT to the PPD region, pointed to by CTL$AG_CLIDATA. It initializes the CLI symbol table data structures and defines the reserved symbols $STATUS, $SEVERITY, and $RESTART.

4. For a batch process, DCL translates the logical names for BATCH$RE-START and parameters P1 through P8. It creates symbols whose values are the equivalence names.

5. It initializes RMS data structures to describe the process-permanent files SYS$INPUT and SYS$OUTPUT.

6. It examines CTL$GL_UAF_FLAGS and notes whether the account is captive or restricted.

7. It defines the logical name SYS$OUTPUT.

8. DCL translates PROC0 through PROC9 and saves their equivalence names to identify the command procedures it must execute.

9. It calls SYS$RMSRUNDWN to close the files opened by LOGINOUT.

10. DCL requests the Rundown ($RUNDWN) system service with an argument of user mode to run down the LOGINOUT image.

11. DCL validates the structure of its command table.

12. It issues a special I/O request to the terminal driver, naming the process as the terminal owner.

13. DCL enables CTRL/Y and out-of-band ASTs on the terminal. (CTRL/Y ASTs are not enabled if the UAF record had the DISCTLY flag set.)

14. DCL requests the Declare Change Mode Handler ($DCLCMH) system service to establish a change-mode-to-supervisor handler. This handler allows the CLI to enter supervisor mode from user mode when it needs to access write-protected data structures. One instance where this is required is in symbol definition, because CLI symbol tables are protected from write access by user mode.

15. Finally, DCL branches to the first instruction of the main command processing loop, routine DCL$RESTART in module [DCL]COMMAND.

30.6.2 Command Processing Loop

In its main command processing loop, a CLI reads a record from SYS$INPUT and takes whatever action is dictated by the command. DCL can perform some actions directly. Others require the execution of a separate image. Table 30.3 lists the general operations performed by DCL and indicates those actions that require an external image.

Table 30.3   General Actions Performed by the DCL CLI

General CLI Operations	*Sample Commands*
Commands that the CLI can execute internally (see Table 30.4)	EXAMINE, SET DEFAULT
Commands that require external images	COPY, LINK, some SET commands, some SHOW commands
Commands that require internal processing and an external image	LOGOUT, MCR, RUN
Foreign command definition	*command-string* :== $*image-file-spec*
Other operations that destroy an image	STOP, EXIT
Invoking a command procedure	@*command-file-spec*
Other CLI operations	Symbol definition, expression evaluation

A simplified flow of control through the DCL CLI is pictured in Figure 30.5.

After a CLI reads a record from the input stream and recognizes a command, it either performs the requested action itself or activates an external image. DCL can execute some commands without destroying a currently executing image (see Table 30.4). Any other command either requires an image to execute (such as COPY or LINK) or directly affects the currently executing image (such as STOP).

30.6.3   Image Initiation by a CLI

When a CLI determines that an external image is required, it first performs some command-specific steps. It then enters a common routine to activate and call the image. DCL's common routine is DCL$EXTIMAGE, in module [DCL]IMAGEXECT. The steps it takes are nearly identical to the steps performed by EXE$PROCSTRT, described in Chapter 27:

1. If an image is active, DCL enters user mode and requests the $EXIT system service, which first calls any user mode exit handlers and then supervisor mode exit handlers. Control returns to DCL's previously declared supervisor mode exit handler. DCL calls SYS$RMSRUNDWN to close any files opened by the image. It requests the $RUNDWN system service with an argument of user mode to remove any traces of the previously executing image. If the previous image terminated normally, these actions are unnecessary. However, if the user typed CTRL/Y followed by an external command, the normal image termination path is bypassed; DCL must perform this extra step to ensure that the previous image is eliminated before another is activated.

2. DCL redeclares a supervisor mode exit handler to regain control when

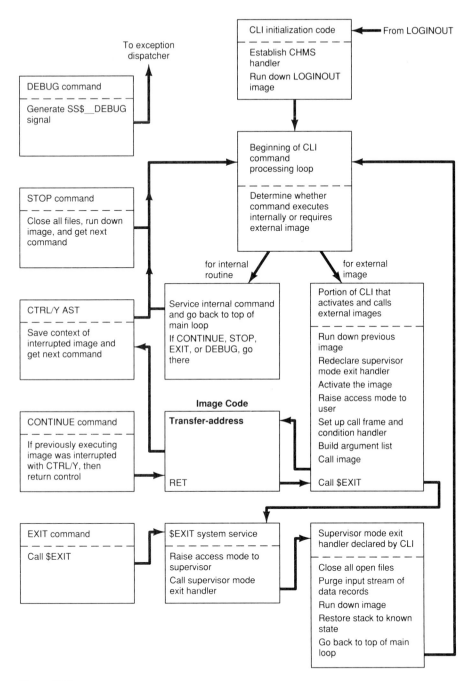

Figure 30.5
Simplified Control Flow Through the DCL Command
Language Interpreter

Table 30.4   Commands Handled by CLI Internal Procedures

Command	Description
@	Execute a command procedure
=	Create/modify a symbol
ALLOCATE	Allocate a device
ASSIGN	Create a logical name
ATTACH	Transfer control to another process in job
CALL	Transfer control to a labeled subroutine in a command procedure
CANCEL	Cancel scheduled wakeups for a process
CLOSE	Close a process-permanent file
CONNECT	Connect the physical terminal to a virtual terminal of another process
CONTINUE	Resume interrupted image
CREATE/NAME_TABLE	Create a new logical name table
DEALLOCATE	Deallocate a device
DEASSIGN	Delete a logical name
DEBUG	Invoke the symbolic debugger
DECK	Delimit the beginning of an input stream
DEFINE	Create a logical name
DEFINE/KEY	Associate a character string and attributes with a terminal key
DELETE/KEY	Delete a key definition
DELETE/SYMBOL	Delete a symbol definition
DEPOSIT	Modify a memory location
DISCONNECT	Disconnect a physical terminal from a virtual terminal
ENDSUBROUTINE	Label the end of a called subroutine in a command procedure
EOD	Delimit the end of an input stream
EOJ	End a batch job or log out an interactive process
EXAMINE	Examine a memory location
EXIT	Exit a command procedure, Run down an image after invoking exit handlers
GOSUB	Transfer control to a labeled subroutine in a command procedure
GOTO	Transfer control within a command procedure
IF/THEN/ELSE/ENDIF	Conditional command execution
INQUIRE	Interactively assign a value to a symbol
ON	Define conditional action
OPEN	Open a process-permanent file
READ	Read a record into a symbol
RECALL	Display previously entered commands for possible reissue
RETURN	Terminate a GOSUB subroutine procedure
SET CONTROL	Determine responses to CTRL/C, CTRL/Y, and CTRL/T
SET DEFAULT	Define default directory string
SET KEY	Change current terminal key definition state
SET [NO]ON	Determine error processing

Table 30.4   Commands Handled by CLI Internal Procedures *(continued)*

Command	*Description*
SET OUTPUT_RATE	Set rate at which output is written to a batch job log file
SET PREFIX	Set a prefix control string for verified command lines
SET PROMPT	Change the CLI's prompt string
SET PROTECTION	Define default file protection
SET SYMBOL	Alter scope of a symbol
SET UIC	Change process UIC and default directory string
SET [NO]VERIFY	Determine echoing of command procedure commands
SHOW DEFAULT	Display default directory string
SHOW KEY	Display terminal key definitions
SHOW PROTECTION	Display default file protection
SHOW QUOTA	Display current disk file usage
SHOW STATUS	Display status of currently executing image
SHOW SYMBOL	Display value of symbol(s)
SHOW TIME	Display current time
SHOW TRANSLATION	Show translation of single logical name
SUBROUTINE	Label beginning of called subroutine in a command procedure
SPAWN	Create a subprocess and transfer control to it
STOP	Run down an image, bypassing exit handlers
WAIT	Wait for specified interval to elapse
WRITE	Write the value of a symbol to a file

the image exits. Recall from Chapter 28 that an exit handler must be redeclared after each use.

3. To activate the image, DCL requests the Image Activate ($IMGACT) system service, described in Chapter 28.

4. If the activation succeeds, DCL enters user mode and calls a DCL procedure to create an initial call frame on the user mode stack. This initial call frame contains zero in its saved FP, terminating the call frame chain.

5. DCL establishes EXE$CATCH_ALL, in module PROCSTRT, as the procedure frame condition handler and as the last chance exception handler.

6. It requests the Address Relocation Fixup ($IMGFIX) system service to perform address relocations and fixups.

7. DCL builds an argument list to pass to the image and to any intervening procedures such as SYS$IMGSTA. The list consists of the following arguments:

    a. Address of image transfer address array

    b. Address of CLI utility routine dispatcher

    c. Address of image header

    d. Address of image file descriptor

    e. Link flags taken from the image header

    f. CLI flags

8. DCL calls the image at the first address in the transfer address array, described in Chapter 28. Unless the image was linked with the /NO-TRACEBACK qualifier, the first transfer address entry is the address of the Image Startup ($IMGSTA) system service. This service establishes the traceback exception handler and maps the debugger, if requested.

9. Later, the image terminates itself by returning to its caller or by requesting the $EXIT system service. Since DCL requests the $EXIT system service anyway, the termination method chosen by the image is generally irrelevant. However, for an image that might be called as a procedure from another image, returning is the preferred method of image termination.

30.6.4   Normal Image Termination

When an image in a process with a CLI terminates normally, the $EXIT system service eventually calls the supervisor mode exit handler established by the CLI before it called the image. DCL's exit handler, DCL$EXITHAND in module [DCL]IMAGEXECT, performs several cleanup steps:

1. If the image exited with an error status in R0, the handler stores the error in the symbol $STATUS. It then writes the corresponding error message.

2. It calls SYS$RMSRUNDWN, closing any files left open by the image and the image file itself, leaving process-permanent files open.

3. It discards any data records in the input stream (records that do not begin with a dollar sign for DCL) and issues a warning message.

4. It runs down the terminated image by requesting the $RUNDWN system service with an argument of user mode.

5. Finally, it transfers control to the beginning of the main command loop so that the CLI can read and process the next command.

30.6.5   Abnormal Image Termination

A user can interrupt an image by typing CTRL/Y or CTRL/C; an image can interrupt itself through the pause capability supplied by the Run-Time Library procedure LIB$PAUSE. Further execution of the image depends on the sequence of commands issued while the image is interrupted.

30.6.5.1   CTRL/Y Processing.

When CTRL/Y is typed at the terminal, the terminal driver transfers control to the AST procedure established by DCL during its initialization. The AST procedure first reestablishes itself, enabling future CTRL/Ys to be passed to the same AST procedure. It then checks whether the process has disabled CTRL/Ys through the SET NOCONTROL=Y command. If so, the AST procedure returns, dismissing the CTRL/Y. Otherwise, its actions depend on the access mode interrupted by the CTRL/Y.

If the previous mode was supervisor, the AST procedure actions depend on whether an ON CONTROL_Y command was issued previously, specifying a particular command to be executed in response. If so, the AST procedure sets a flag to request that the command be executed and returns. If not, DCL is restored to its initial state (with no nesting of indirect levels) and control transfers to the beginning of the main command loop.

If the previous mode was user, the CTRL/Y interrupted an image. If the image was installed with enhanced privileges, DCL saves those privileges and resets the process privileges to those in use before the image was activated. After setting a flag, DCL returns to command processing. If, at this point, the user enters the DCL commands ATTACH, CONTINUE, or SPAWN, the appropriate action is taken and the image is not run down. Any other command causes DCL to run down a privileged image before executing the command; a nonprivileged image may continue (see Section 30.6.5.3). Issuing a STOP command for a nonprivileged image causes DCL to terminate the image without calling user mode exit handlers (see Section 30.6.5.7). However, because a privileged image is run down before the STOP command is processed, its exit handlers are called.

30.6.5.2   **Pause Capability.** The Run-Time Library procedure LIB$PAUSE provides the capability to interrupt an image under program control. An image executing in the context of an interactive process can invoke LIB$PAUSE to interrupt itself and transfer control to the CLI at the beginning of its main command loop.

30.6.5.3   **State of Interrupted Images.** When a nonprivileged image is interrupted, the image context is saved and control is transferred to the beginning of DCL's main command loop, allowing the user to execute commands. If the command is one that DCL can perform internally (see Table 30.4), the image context is not destroyed and the image can be continued.

However, execution of any command that requires an external image destroys the context of the interrupted image. In addition, executing an indirect command file destroys an interrupted image, even if the commands in the indirect command file can be performed internally by DCL.

Six commands that the user can enter when an image has been interrupted by CTRL/Y have special importance. These commands are ATTACH, CONTINUE, DEBUG, EXIT, SPAWN, and STOP. ATTACH and SPAWN are described in Section 30.4. The other commands are described in the following sections.

30.6.5.4   **CONTINUE Command.** If a CONTINUE command is typed and the previous mode was user, DCL tests whether the image being executed is one installed with enhanced privileges. If so, it restores those privileges, dismisses the AST, and returns control to the image at the point where it was interrupted.

30.6.5.5 **DEBUG Command.** If a DEBUG command is typed and the previous mode was user, DCL generates a user mode SS$_DEBUG signal, as described in Chapter 28. The signal is handled by the condition handler established by the $IMGACT system service. (If the image was linked with the /NOTRACE-BACK qualifier, the handler was never established and the image exits.) This handler responds to the SS$_DEBUG signal by mapping the debugger (if it is not already mapped) and transferring control to it. This technique enables the debugger to be used even if the image was not linked with the /DEBUG qualifier.

30.6.5.6 **EXIT Command.** In response to an EXIT command, DCL disables CTRL/Y ASTs and tests whether a CTRL/Y or CTRL/C was just entered. If so, it tests whether the previous mode was user. If it was, DCL restores any enhanced privileges the image had. It enters user mode and requests the $EXIT system service (see Chapter 28), which calls exit handlers and runs down the image.

30.6.5.7 **STOP Command.** In response to a STOP command, DCL first determines whether an image or a process is being stopped. (The various STOP commands are described in the *OpenVMS DCL Dictionary*.)

If an image is being stopped, it tests whether the process is interactive. If so, DCL closes all open image files by calling SYS$RMSRUNDWN. It then requests the $RUNDWN system service with an argument of user mode. Finally, it transfers control to the beginning of the main command loop.

Note that STOP performs nearly identical operations to the exit handler called as a result of an $EXIT system service request or an EXIT command. The only difference between the EXIT sequences and the STOP command is that user mode exit handlers are not called when an image terminates with a CTRL/Y STOP sequence. Thus, in most cases, the STOP and EXIT commands are interchangeable. One useful aspect of the STOP command is that it can eliminate an image containing a user mode exit handler that is preventing completion of image deletion either intentionally or as the result of an error.

30.7 **LOGOUT OPERATION**

LOGINOUT, the image that performs the initialization of an interactive or batch process, also executes to delete such a process. When LOGINOUT executes, it performs login, logout, or batch job step initialization. (When a batch process is submitted with more than one command procedure specified, each procedure is handled as a separate batch job step.) LOGINOUT determines whether the process is logged in already by the existence of the PPD region, used to communicate between LOGINOUT and the CLI.

If the PPD region exists, LOGINOUT's actions depend on whether the process is interactive or batch. For an interactive process, routine LOGOUT, in module [LOGIN]LOGIN, performs the following steps:

1. It enters supervisor mode to cancel any supervisor mode exit handlers declared by the CLI. As a result, if LOGINOUT aborts or is forcibly exited, the process will be deleted anyway. From supervisor mode, it requests the $CANCEL system service to cancel any outstanding I/O requests on SYS$INPUT, in particular requests for attention or out of band ASTs.

2. It enters executive mode to change the protection on the PPD region so that it can write to it from user mode.

3. LOGINOUT copies the IFIs for SYS$INPUT and SYS$OUTPUT from PPD locations into RMS data structures. This restores definitions of SYS$INPUT and SYS$OUTPUT made at login.

4. LOGINOUT notifies the security audit subsystem of the logout.

5. If the user specified the /[NO]HANGUP qualifier on the LOGOUT command, LOGINOUT checks whether it is appropriate to change the terminal characteristics. If the process is interactive and not a subprocess, and the terminal is local, LOGINOUT reads the current terminal characteristics and resets them, altering the hangup bit.

6. LOGINOUT writes the logout message to the restored SYS$OUTPUT. (Thus, it cannot be redirected via a logical name definition.) If the user asked for a full logout message, LOGINOUT requests the $GETJPI system service to get information, such as CPU time, number of page faults, and number of I/O requests.

7. If LOGINOUT callouts are enabled, it calls each image's LGI$ICR_ LOGOUT routine.

8. It closes SYS$INPUT and SYS$OUTPUT.

9. Finally, LOGINOUT requests the $EXIT system service from executive mode. As described in Chapter 28, this limits the search for exit handlers to the executive mode list, bypassing the supervisor mode exit handler established by the CLI to prevent process deletion following image exit.

10. After any executive mode exit handlers have performed their work, the $EXIT system service requests the $DELPRC system service, which removes the logged out process from the system.

If the process is a batch process, LOGINOUT, in routine INIT_BATCH, in module [LOGIN]DETACHED, first closes SYS$INPUT. It requests the $SNDJBCW system service again to determine if there is another job step. If the batch process was submitted with multiple command procedures specified, LOGINOUT opens the new SYS$INPUT and reinitializes the batch process environment. If LOGINOUT callouts are enabled, it calls each image's LGI$ICR_JOBSTEP routine. It reenters the CLI.

If the previous batch job step failed, or the message that is returned from the job controller indicates that the process should be terminated, LOGINOUT terminates it through the following steps:

1. It writes a logout message to the log file.
2. It closes the log file.
3. If the log file is to be printed, then LOGINOUT requests the $SNDJBCW system service again, this time to queue the file to a print queue.
4. It then requests the $EXIT system service from executive mode. After any executive mode exit handlers have performed their work, the $EXIT system service requests the $DELPRC system service, which removes the process from the system.

30.8 RELEVANT SOURCE MODULES

Source modules described in this chapter include

```
[CLIUTL]SUBMIT.B32
[DCL]COMMAND.MAR
[DCL]EXIT.MAR
[DCL]IMAGECTRL.MAR
[DCL]IMAGEXECT.MAR
[DCL]INITIAL.MAR
[DCL]SPAWN.MAR
[JOBCTL]UTILITY.B32
[JOBCTL]UNSOLICIT.B32
[LOGIN]DETACHED.B32
[LOGIN]INTERACT.B32
[LOGIN]INITUSER.B32
[LOGIN]LOGIN.B32
[TTDRVR]TTYCHARI.MAR
```

31 Process Deletion

> . . . for dust you are and unto dust you shall return.
>
> *Genesis* 3:19

A process can delete itself or any other process in a VMScluster system that it has the privilege to affect. For a process to be deleted, a number of cleanup actions are necessary:

- ▶ All resources allocated to the process must be returned to the system.
- ▶ Accounting information must be sent to the job controller.
- ▶ Any subprocesses of the process being deleted must be deleted.
- ▶ If the process being deleted is a subprocess, all quotas and limits taken from its parent (owner) process must be returned.
- ▶ If the owner requested notification of the subprocess's deletion through a termination mailbox, the deletion message must be sent.
- ▶ Finally, all traces of the process must be removed from the system.

Process deletion occurs in three stages: first, in the context of the process requesting the deletion; second, in the context of the process being deleted; and finally, in system context.

31.1 PROCESS DELETION IN CONTEXT OF CALLER

Process deletion is implemented by the Delete Process ($DELPRC) system service. Its initial operation occurs in the context of the process requesting the system service. This part of the operation performs a simple set of privilege checks and then queues a kernel mode asynchronous system trap (AST) that will cause the deletion to continue in the context of the process being deleted. Chapter 8 describes the queuing and delivery of ASTs.

The $DELPRC system service procedure, EXE$DELPRC in module SYSDELPRC, runs in kernel mode. If the requesting process is the process to be deleted, no arguments are required; otherwise, the requesting process can specify either the process name or the extended process ID (EPID) of the process to be deleted.

EXE$DELPRC performs the following steps:

1. It immediately invokes EXE$NAM_TO_PCB, in module SYSPCNTRL, to locate the process control block (PCB) of the process to be deleted.

   EXE$NAM_TO_PCB determines whether the input arguments specify a target process on this VMScluster node or on another node. In the former case, EXE$NAM_TO_PCB confirms the existence of the target process and the ability of the current process to delete it. Chapter 14 describes the possible relation between the two processes and the privileges required in each case. If the process is identified as one on another VMScluster node, EXE$NAM_TO_PCB cannot make those checks; it can only confirm that the VMScluster node identification is valid.

If further action is possible, EXE$NAM_TO_PCB returns at IPL$_SCHED with the SCHED spinlock held; otherwise it returns at IPL 0. In either case, it returns an appropriate status.

2. If the status SS$_REMOTE_PROC is returned by EXE$NAM_TO_PCB, which indicates that the process may exist on another VMScluster node, EXE$DELPRC invokes the clusterwide process service (CWPS) routine CWPS$P_CNTRL, in module SYSPCNTRL. CWPS$P_CNTRL transmits the deletion request to the appropriate VMScluster node and places the process into a wait state. A cooperating CWPS routine on the other node processes the request and transmits status back to this node. Through mechanisms described in Chapter 14, control returns to a CWPS routine running in the context of the $DELPRC requestor. This routine exits from the $DELPRC system service, returning the status transmitted from the other node.

3. If EXE$NAM_TO_PCB returns an error status, EXE$DELPRC simply returns the error status to its requestor.

4. If EXE$NAM_TO_PCB returns a status indicating that the target process exists on this node and that the requesting process may affect it, EXE$DELPRC continues.

5. EXE$DELPRC tests the flag PCB$V_NODELET in PCB$L_STS. The executive uses this flag to prevent deletion of system processes such as the swapper and NETACP. If the flag is set, EXE$DELPRC does not delete the process but instead releases the SCHED spinlock, lowers IPL, and returns the error status SS$_NODELETE. Use of the PCB$V_NODELET flag is reserved to Digital. Any other use is completely unsupported.

6. EXE$DELPRC prepares to queue a kernel mode AST to the target process. It allocates and initializes an AST control block (ACB) to describe the kernel mode AST.

7. It marks the target process for deletion by setting the flag PCB$V_DELPEN in PCB$L_STS. If the bit is found already set, deletion is underway for the target process. In that event, EXE$DELPRC tests whether it is running in the context of the target process. If not, it releases the SCHED spinlock, lowers IPL, deallocates the ACB, and returns the success status SS$_NORMAL.

If EXE$DELPRC is running in the context of the target process, it tests the PCB$V_ERDACT bit in PCB$L_STS to determine whether it was requested from an executive mode rundown procedure. If so, EXE$DELPRC proceeds to the next step as though the process were not marked for deletion. This ensures that process deletion will complete even if the $EXIT system service or the $DELPRC system service is rerequested in the context of a process's executive mode rundown procedure.

If PCB$V_ERDACT is clear, EXE$DELPRC releases the SCHED spinlock, lowers IPL, deallocates the ACB, and returns the success status SS$_NORMAL.

8. EXE$DELPRC sets the target process's PCB$V_RESPEN bit and reports a resume event for the process. This event is significant only for a process in scheduling state SUSP or SUSPO and causes such a process to be resumed. This mechanism is necessary because no ASTs can be delivered to a process suspended in kernel mode, including the delete process kernel mode AST.

9. EXE$DELPRC initializes the ACB with the process ID (PID) of the target process and the procedure value of the kernel mode AST procedure that performs the actual process deletion, procedure DELETE in module SYSDELPRC.

10. Running in kernel or executive mode, EXE$DELPRC sets the PCB$V_ ERDACT bit in PCB$L_STS to indicate that executive mode rundown is active.

11. If the target process requires any current capabilities, EXE$DELPRC calls SCH$RELEASE_CAPABILITY, in module CAPABILITY, to release them; otherwise, the target process may not be able to receive the process deletion AST. Chapter 13 describes process capability requirements.

12. It queues a kernel mode AST to the target process, with a potential boost of PRI$_RESAVL to that process's software priority.

Queuing the AST to the target process makes it computable. Eventually, the scheduler selects that process for execution.

31.2 PROCESS DELETION IN CONTEXT OF PROCESS BEING DELETED

Most of process deletion occurs in the context of the process being deleted. If the process has no pending special kernel mode or other kernel mode ASTs, the process deletion AST procedure executes immediately. Note that a process executing or waiting at IPL 2 or above cannot be deleted because ASTs cannot be delivered.

Deleting a process in its own context means that its address space and process header are readily accessible. The DELETE AST procedure is therefore able to request standard system services, such as Delete Virtual Address Space ($DELTVA) and Deassign I/O Channel ($DASSGN). Special cases, such as the deletion of a process that is outswapped, are avoided by ensuring that the process is first made resident.

31.2.1 DELETE Kernel Mode AST

The DELETE AST procedure performs the following steps:

1. DELETE first enables resource wait mode by clearing PCB$V_SSRWAIT in PCB$L_STS.

2. It then searches for process-private or systemwide executive mode rundown routines to perform image-specific cleanup. Use of executive mode rundown routines is reserved to Digital. Any other use is completely unsupported.

   If executive mode rundown is not already active and executive mode rundown routines exist, DELETE sets PCB$V_ERDACT in PCB$L_STS, indicating that executive mode rundown is active, and queues an executive mode AST to the process, specifying EXEC_RUNDOWN_AST, in module SYSDELPRC, as the AST procedure. DELETE then exits, allowing the executive mode AST to be delivered.

   EXEC_RUNDOWN_AST invokes the process-private executive mode rundown routines and the systemwide executive mode rundown routines if any exist. It then requests the Change to Kernel Mode ($CMKRNL) system service to resume processing in the original DELETE code path at step 4, in kernel mode.

3. If no executive mode rundown routines need to be invoked, DELETE clears the appropriate PCB$L_ASTACT bit to indicate that no kernel mode AST is active. It invokes SCH$RESET_ASTSR, in module ASTDEL, to reset the AST summary register. Taking these steps enables another kernel mode AST to interrupt the DELETE AST. Although interruption of an AST by another at the same mode is usually prohibited, it may be necessary before process deletion can complete.

4. DELETE checks whether the process has a Files-11 operation in progress. This must complete before DELETE can proceed. If PCB$L_DPC is nonzero, indicating this condition, DELETE places the process into a resource wait state for resource RSN$_ASTWAIT. When the queuing and delivery of a kernel mode AST ends the resource wait, DELETE repeats its check. When PCB$L_DPC is zero, the DELETE procedure can continue. Chapter 8 documents the field PCB$L_DPC and its use in stalling process deletion.

5. If process-private or systemwide user-specified kernel mode rundown routines exist, they are called to perform image-specific cleanup.

6. DELETE then zeros each of the activated privileged library dispatch vectors that control dispatching to inner-mode routines in privileged shareable images and user-specified kernel and executive mode rundown routines. This ensures that if DELETE executes again in the context of the same process, the rundown routines will not be called again.

7. It calls SYS$RMSRUNDWN to perform Record Management Services (RMS) rundown. The service routine, RMS$RMSRUNDWN in module [RMS]RMS0RNDWN, aborts RMS I/O for the process. RMS$RMSRUNDWN transfers control to the routine RM$LAST_CHANCE, in module [RMS]RMS0LSTCH, to perform the actual rundown.

   RM$LAST_CHANCE scans the process's open disk files and detaches any file that uses global buffers from the global buffer pool. No further rundown is performed on files that are journaled.

For a sequential file, RM$LAST_CHANCE writes the current buffer operated on by the process to disk if the buffer has been modified. This attempt to preserve the last data records written to the file may help a subsequent attempt to analyze process action prior to deletion. This feature is intended for problem analysis rather than for minimizing data loss.

RM$LAST_CHANCE closes any file open for exclusive access to update the RMS record attributes in its file header, particularly the end-of-file pointer.

During RMS rundown no attempt is made to write all modified data buffers to disk. User applications not using journaling must be able to handle potential data loss resulting from forced process deletion.

8. If the process has any subprocesses (if its PCB$L_PRCCNT field is nonzero), they must be deleted before deletion of the owner process can continue. Section 31.4 contains an example of deleting a process with subprocesses.

   The following steps are performed to delete the subprocesses:

   a. DELETE scans the PCB vector for all PCBs whose PCB$L_OWNER field specifies the PID of the process being deleted. DELETE requests the $DELPRC system service to delete each of these subprocesses.

   b. DELETE again checks the subprocess count PCB$L_PRCCNT. If it is greater than zero, the process is placed into a resource wait state (MWAIT) for resource RSN$_ASTWAIT. This parent process becomes computable again when the RETQUOTA special kernel mode AST returns CPU time quota from one of the subprocesses (see step 18) and control returns to DELETE. DELETE repeats this step until the subprocess count is zero. At that point, all subprocesses have been deleted and the DELETE procedure can continue.

9. DELETE requests the $RUNDWN system service to run down the process from kernel mode and perform an image reset (see Chapter 28).

10. For each section still mapped to the process virtual address space, DELETE requests the $DELTVA system service to delete those virtual pages. The process section table entry is checked before the deletion. If the SEC$V_INPROG flag is set in the process section table entry, the section was being created when the delete process AST was delivered. In this case, DELETE invokes MMG$DECSECREFL to correct the section reference count.

    If any pages are actually deleted, the $RUNDWN system service is requested once again to complete the deassignment of open channels.

11. DELETE calls IOC$SCAN_CCB, in module IOCHANUTILS, to scan the

process's channel control blocks (CCBs) to ensure that all channels have been deassigned. If any channel is still assigned, DELETE generates a fatal FILCNTNONZ bugcheck.

12. If the current process is not a subprocess (if the PCB$L_OWNER field is zero), DELETE dismounts each jobwide mounted volume.

    If the current process is a subprocess, DELETE reassigns any volumes allocated by the subprocess to the owner process. DELETE stores the owner process's PID in UCB$L_PID and sets the UCB$V_DEADMO bit in UCB$L_STS to ensure that the volume will be deallocated when it is eventually dismounted by the owner process.

13. DELETE requests the Deallocate Device ($DALLOC) system service to deallocate all devices allocated by the process.

14. DELETE compares PCB$L_DIOLM to PCB$L_DIOCNT and PCB$L_BIOLM to PCB$L_BIOCNT. The difference between the first two fields is the number of outstanding direct I/O requests; the difference between the latter two is the number of outstanding buffered I/O requests.

    DELETE waits until PCB$L_DIOCNT equals PCB$L_DIOLM and PCB$L_BIOCNT equals PCB$L_BIOLM to ensure that all outstanding process I/O requests have completed. I/O postprocessing code for completed, aborted, and canceled I/O requests is responsible for returning the PCB$L_DIOCNT and PCB$L_BIOCNT quotas to the process (see Chapter 23).

15. If the current process is not a subprocess, DELETE decrements one of two systemwide process counts. If the process is interactive (if PCB$V_INTER in PCB$L_STS is set), DELETE decrements the number of interactive jobs, SYS$GL_IJOBCNT. If the process is a batch job (if PCB$V_BATCH in PCB$L_STS is set), DELETE decrements the number of batch jobs, SYS$GL_BJOBCNT.

16. If the current process is not a subprocess or a Portable Operating System Interface (POSIX) process, DELETE deletes the jobwide logical name table.

17. DELETE resets the process name string in the PCB by zeroing the count byte.

18. If the current process is a subprocess, any remaining deductible quotas must be returned to the owner process. The following steps are taken:

    a. An I/O request packet (IRP) is allocated for use as an ACB.

    b. The procedure value of the return quota special kernel mode AST (routine RETQUOTA in module SYSDELPRC) and the PID of the owner process are stored in the ACB.

    c. The only quota that must be returned to the owner process, unused CPU time, is stored in the portion of the IRP immediately following the ACB. All other quotas are either pooled or nondeductible (see Chapter 27).

    d. Finally, the special kernel mode AST is queued to the owner process, giving it a priority boost of PRI$_RESAVL.

19. If the current process is a subprocess and the owner process requested a termination mailbox message, a termination message is constructed on the stack. DELETE requests the Queue I/O Request ($QIO) system service to send the termination message to the mailbox unit specified by PCB$L_TMBU. The message contents are listed in Table 31.1. The message size is specified by ACC$C_TERMLEN.

20. EXE$PRCDELMSG, in module ACCOUNT, is invoked to send an accounting message to the job controller. It sends the message unless accounting is inhibited for this process (the NOACNT flag was specified at process creation) or process termination accounting is disabled for the entire system. The contents of this message are used to fill in all relevant fields of the accounting identification and resource packets. The data structures used by the Accounting utility are described in the *OpenVMS System Manager's Manual*.

21. After IPL is raised to 2 to prevent AST delivery, most of the remainder of P1 space is deleted. However, the P1 pages permanently locked into the working set list, the kernel stack, for example, are not deleted. Some of P1 space, including the user stack, may have already been deleted as a result of the image reset done in step 9.

22. DELETE acquires the MMG and SCHED spinlocks to synchronize access to the memory management and scheduler databases. It releases all process page table pages, except those with entries for pages permanently locked into the working set, to the head of the free page list and deallocates the associated page file space. The page table pages with entries for pages that are permanently locked into the working set will eventually be released by the swapper.

23. DELETE calls SCH$DELETE_CALLBACK, in module SCHEDULER.
    SCH$DELETE_CALLBACK executes a `CALL_PAL SWPCTX` instruction, leaving the context of the current process (the process being deleted) and entering system context. In system context, SCH$DELETE_CALLBACK calls DELETE_IN_SYS_CONTEXT, in module SYSDELPRC.

31.3   **PROCESS DELETION IN SYSTEM CONTEXT**

Process deletion completes in system context. DELETE_IN_SYS_CONTEXT takes the following steps:

1. If the capability mask of the process being deleted indicates explicit affinity for a particular CPU, DELETE_IN_SYS_CONTEXT decrements that CPU's explicit affinity count and clears PCB$L_CAPABILITY, removing explicit affinity from the process.

2. DELETE_IN_SYS_CONTEXT stores the address of the null PCB in the

Table 31.1   Contents of the Termination Mailbox
Message Sent to the Owner Process

Field in Message Block	*Source of Information*
Message type	MSG$_DELPROC [1]
Final exit status	CTL$GL_FINALSTS
Process ID	PCB$L_EPID
Job ID	Not currently used
Logout time	EXE$GQ_SYSTIME
Account name	CTL$T_ACCOUNT
User name	CTL$T_USERNAME
CPU time	PHD$L_CPUTIM
Number of page faults	PHD$L_PAGEFLTS
Peak paging file usage	Not currently used
Peak working set size	CTL$GL_WSPEAK
Buffered I/O count	PHD$L_BIOCNT
Direct I/O count	PHD$L_DIOCNT
Count of mounted volumes	CTL$GL_VOLUMES
Login time	CTL$GQ_LOGIN
EPID of owner	PCB$L_EOWNER

[1] MSG$_DELPROC is a constant indicating that this is a process termination message.

per-CPU database field CPU$L_CURPCB and in the PCB vector slot formerly occupied by the process being deleted, thus freeing the slot for future use.

3. The pages in process space that were permanently locked into the working set, for example, the kernel stack and the P1 pointer area, are deleted and placed at the head of the free page list. The process header pages that are a permanent part of the working set will be deleted by the swapper when the process header is deleted.

4. Each remaining ACB is removed from each of the five ACB queues in the PCB and deallocated to nonpaged pool unless its ACB$V_NODELETE bit is set. If the ACB$V_NODELETE bit is set, the ACB is assumed to be part of another data structure whose deletion is not allowed.

5. DELETE_IN_SYS_CONTEXT removes any pending CWPS structures from the PCB$Q_CWPSSRV_QUEUE queue of the process being deleted. It inserts them on the swapper's PCB$Q_CWPSSRV_QUEUE queue.

   These structures cannot be deleted until the stalled fork thread that expects to access them is resumed by the arrival of a response from another VMScluster node. When the response arrives, the fork thread determines that the requestor process was deleted and deallocates the structures.

6. If the process had an extended rights list, it is deallocated to nonpaged pool.

7. The process count field in the job information block (JIB) is decremented in an interlocked manner. If the process being deleted is a detached process (the PID of the process being deleted is equal to the master PID field in the JIB), the JIB is deallocated.

8. If the process being deleted is a subprocess, its owner's subprocess count, PCB$L_PRCCNT, is decremented. If the owner process is also being deleted, the owner is currently in a wait state, waiting for the contents of this field to become zero. DELETE_IN_SYS_CONTEXT makes the owner process computable so that it can check the value of PCB$L_PRC-CNT. If the value is now zero, the owner can continue with its own deletion.

9. DELETE_IN_SYS_CONTEXT deallocates the PCB to nonpaged pool.

10. It decrements SWP$GW_BALCNT, the number of processes in the balance set.

11. It invokes SCH$SWPWAKE to awaken the swapper because there is a process header to be removed from the balance set slot area (see Chapter 20).

12. DELETE_IN_SYS_CONTEXT stores the value –1 into the process index array entry for the process header of the process being deleted and increments SCH$GW_DELPHDCT. As a result of these actions, the swapper, when it next executes, will delete the process header.

13. It decrements SCH$GW_PROCCNT, the systemwide process count.

14. Finally, DELETE_IN_SYS_CONTEXT releases the MMG spinlock and returns to SCH$DELETE_CALLBACK, which, while still holding the SCHED spinlock, proceeds to select the next process to run (see Chapter 13).

31.4   DELETION OF A PROCESS THAT OWNS SUBPROCESSES

In early versions of VAX VMS prior to the existence of the JIB and its job-wide pooled quotas (see Chapter 27), several quotas were charged against a process when it created a subprocess. At deletion of the subprocess, the subprocess returned those quotas. All the quotas treated in this way are now pooled except for CPU time limit, which is the only quota returned at subprocess deletion. To ensure that any quotas taken from an owner process are returned, the deletion of an owner process must be delayed until all its subprocesses are deleted.

During the execution of the DELETE AST procedure, a check is made to see if the process being deleted owns any subprocesses. If it does, these processes must be located and deleted.

As Figure 31.1 shows, there are no forward pointers in the JIB or PCB of an owner process to indicate which subprocesses it has created. The only indication that a process has created subprocesses is a nonzero value in PCB$L_PRCCNT. The process's subprocesses can only be located by scanning all the

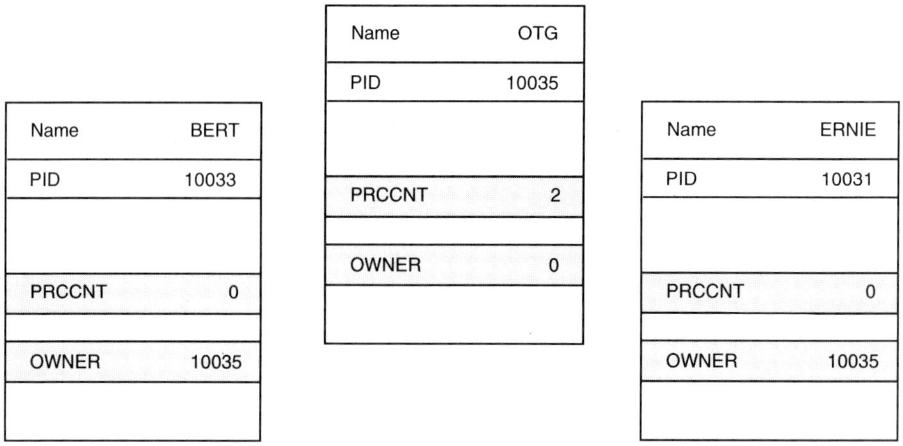

Name	OTG
PID	10035
PRCCNT	2
OWNER	0

Name	BERT
PID	10033
PRCCNT	0
OWNER	10035

Name	ERNIE
PID	10031
PRCCNT	0
OWNER	10035

Figure 31.1
Sample Job to Illustrate Process Deletion with
Subprocesses

PCBs in the system until each PCB is located whose owner field contains the PID of interest.

The details of this situation can best be illustrated with an example. Figure 31.1 shows a process whose process ID equals 10035 and whose name is OTG. The process OTG owns two subprocesses: the first has a process ID of 10033 and the name BERT; the second has a process ID of 10031 and the name ERNIE.

Neither of these subprocesses owns any further subprocesses. The following steps occur as a result of the process OTG being deleted. Assume that the priorities are such that the processes execute in the order OTG, BERT, and ERNIE.

1. The deletion of process OTG proceeds normally until it is determined that this process has created two subprocesses. The PCB vector is scanned until the two PCBs containing 10035 in the PCB$L_OWNER field are located. These two processes are marked for deletion. This means that the DELETE kernel mode AST is queued to the two subprocesses and they are made computable. Process OTG is placed into a wait state because its count of owned subprocesses is nonzero (actually 2, at this point).

2. The previous assumption about priorities implies that process BERT executes next. Its deletion proceeds past the point where process OTG stopped because it owns no subprocesses. However, the next step in the DELETE AST procedure determines that process BERT is a subprocess and must return quotas to its owner. The return of quotas is accomplished by queuing a special kernel mode AST (RETQUOTA) to

process OTG, changing its state back to computable. When the system context portion of the deletion of BERT has finished with all actions that require the presence of the JIB, it decrements the process count in OTG's PCB$L_PRCCNT and declares a resource availability event, which awakens OTG. However, the count of owned subprocesses is still not zero (down to 1 now), so process OTG is put back into the resource wait state. The deletion of process BERT continues until BERT is entirely deleted.

3. Process ERNIE now begins execution of the DELETE AST procedure. Again, the check for owned subprocesses indicates none, but the check for being a subprocess is positive. A RETQUOTA AST is again queued to process OTG and the count of owned subprocesses decremented (finally to zero).

4. Now process OTG resumes execution as a result of the delivery of the RETQUOTA AST and subsequently finds that the count of owned subprocesses has gone to zero. In fact, process OTG continues to be deleted at this point, even though process ERNIE has not been entirely deleted. This overlapping is simply a result of the timing in this example. Process ERNIE is well on the way to being deleted and is no longer of any concern to process OTG. The important point is that the quotas given to process ERNIE have been returned to OTG. Once OTG's PCB$L_PRC-CNT is equal to zero, it is irrelevant which process executes next. Because ERNIE and BERT have finished work that depended on the presence of the JIB, OTG and the JIB can be deleted totally.

In the general case of a series of subprocesses arranged in a tree structure, the deletion of some arbitrary process requires that each subprocess further down in the tree must execute the process deletion step, which returns quotas to its owner.

31.5   RELEVANT SOURCE MODULE

The source module described in this chapter is

[SYS]SYSDELPRC.MAR

PART VIII / Life of the System

32 The Modular Executive

Non sunt multiplicanda entia praeter necessitatem.
[Entities should not be multiplied beyond necessity.]
William of Occam

The OpenVMS AXP executive consists of two base images and a number of separately loadable executive images. Some of these images are loaded on all systems, while others support features unique to particular system configurations.

SYS$PUBLIC_VECTORS.EXE and SYS$BASE_IMAGE.EXE, the base images, connect requests for system services and other system functions with the routines that provide them. These routines are located in separately loadable executive images.

This chapter describes the organization of executive images and the connections among them. It also discusses how executive images are loaded and initialized.

32.1 OVERVIEW

The organization of the OpenVMS AXP executive is based upon that of the OpenVMS VAX executive. In early VAX/VMS versions, much of the executive was in SYS.EXE, the system image, and RMS.EXE, the image containing Record Management Services. Features not common to all system configurations were supported in separate images, such as device drivers and the SYS-LOA*xxx*.EXE images. With this relatively monolithic design, changing the executive often meant applying complex patches to SYS.EXE or rebuilding it. Rebuilding had the undesirable side effect of requiring subsequent relinking of all images, both VMS- and user-supplied, that linked against SYS.STB to resolve SYS.EXE references.

In VAX VMS Version 5, the executive was further partitioned to simplify subsequent changes to it and to reduce the number of system-dependent images that would require relinking when the executive changed. This partitioned executive came to be known as the modular executive.

The concept underlying the OpenVMS VAX modular executive is similar to that of a shareable image, which contains transfer vectors and routines. The system image is split into a base image named SYS.EXE and a number of other images called executive images. Unlike transfer vectors for a standard shareable image, which are in the same image as the routines, all the transfer vectors of executive images are collected in SYS.EXE. SYS.EXE also contains systemwide data cells that are referenced from multiple executive images and pointers to data cells in executive images that are referenced from other executive images. The executive images contain the routines to which the transfer vectors dispatch as well as data cells primarily referenced from within the image.

Like the VAX VMS executive, the OpenVMS AXP executive is modular. The concept underlying its organization is also that of a shareable image, although AXP shareable images differ somewhat from VAX shareable images. An AXP shareable image contains a global symbol table and a symbol vector. The global symbol table lists the name of each universal symbol in the image along with the offset of its corresponding entry in the symbol vector. Although part of the image file, the global symbol table is not loaded into memory. The linker uses it to resolve symbolic references when another image links to the shareable image.

The symbol vector contains an entry for each universal symbol. For a universal symbol that is the name of a data cell, the symbol vector entry contains the address of the data cell. For a universal symbol that is the name of a procedure, the symbol vector entry contains a pair of addresses: the address of the procedure's code entry point and the address of its procedure descriptor. As long as the universal symbol's offset in the symbol vector remains constant across shareable image rebuilds, images referencing the symbol do not need to be rebuilt. When the shareable image is activated, the symbol vector is loaded into memory and the addresses in its entries relocated to point to the actual locations of the loaded code and data. When another image is activated that references universal symbols in the shareable image, its references are fixed up with the contents of the symbol vector entries for those symbols.

Section 32.4.2 describes extensions to the implementation of shareable images required for executive images.

The OpenVMS AXP executive is implemented in the form of two base images, SYS$PUBLIC_VECTORS.EXE and SYS$BASE_IMAGE.EXE, and a number of separately loadable executive images. These images are loaded during system initialization: SYS$PUBLIC_VECTORS.EXE from directory SYS$LIBRARY and the others from directory SYS$LOADABLE_IMAGES. Most are permanently mapped, although a particular image can be identified at load time as removable and later unloaded.

The base images contain the symbol vectors against which images invoking executive routines, requesting system services, and referencing system data cells link.

An executive routine executes in the mode from which it is invoked, typically executive or kernel mode. Executive images and inner access mode procedures that execute in privileged processes invoke executive routines to perform various functions, for example, to allocate nonpaged pool.

The executive images that contain the executive routines and system service procedures have no symbol vectors. Instead, their universal symbols are represented in the symbol vector in the base image SYS$BASE_IMAGE.EXE.

SYS$BASE_IMAGE.EXE also contains data, pointers to data in executive images, and some primitive routines used by most executive images. Section 32.2 describes SYS$BASE_IMAGE.EXE in more detail.

SYS$PUBLIC_VECTORS.EXE is the pathway to system services. A system service is an executive procedure that performs a service for a process. Generally, the service is requested from an outer access mode, although the procedure that performs the service executes in an inner mode. The symbol vector in SYS$PUBLIC_VECTORS.EXE contains entries for the universally available symbols that represent system service names. These symbols typically are the names of transfer routines, minimal procedures in SYS$PUBLIC_VECTORS.EXE that change access mode and dispatch to the actual service procedures in executive images. Section 32.3 presents an overview of SYS$PUBLIC_VECTORS.EXE.

In general, neither base image needs to be rebuilt when corrections or changes are made to executive images. It is possible to replace an executive image with a corrected or enhanced one without any impact on SYS$BASE_ IMAGE.EXE. However, if universally available entry points or data cells are removed or added, the base image whose symbol vector contains the affected entry points may need to be rebuilt. Note that removals and additions should be made so as not to change the symbol vector offsets of valid symbols.

The modular organization of the executive also makes it possible to have alternative versions of an executive image and to select the one to be loaded at system initialization. For example, there are three versions of the system synchronization image; during system initialization the version appropriate to the configuration is selected and loaded.

Executive images are loaded much like user images. During system operation a user image is mapped into address space by the Image Activate ($IMGACT) system service, commonly known as the image activator. The image's references to addresses within and outside itself are relocated and fixed up by the Address Relocation Fixup ($IMGFIX) system service. The term *relocation* means the adjustment of address references in an image to locations in itself. An image's address references cannot be relocated before the image's sections have been mapped. The term *fixup* means the adjustment of references in an image to locations in another image. An image's references to locations in another image cannot be fixed up until the other image's sections have been mapped and the addresses in its symbol vector entries relocated.

After these two system services, whose operations are described in Chapter 28, prepare an image to execute, the image initialization procedure, if any, is called. As the image executes, its pages are read into memory in response to page faults.

Similar steps are required to prepare an executive image to execute. There are, however, several key differences.

▸ Executive images are mapped into system space.

▸ Although the pageable pages of an executive image are read into memory in response to page faults, the nonpageable pages are read into memory as part of the loading process.

▸ Like address references in any image, those in an executive image must be relocated and fixed up. Many executive images are loaded during a stage of system initialization when no page faults are allowed. Nonpageable sections' references are relocated and fixed up when the image is loaded; relocation and fixup of references within a pageable section may have to be deferred until paging is possible.

▸ The contents of SYS$BASE_IMAGE.EXE symbol vector entries that represent universal symbols in the executive image must be replaced by addresses within the executive image.

▸ An executive image's initialization procedure may require that other executive images' initialization procedures have executed or that a particular stage of system initialization has been reached. When an initialization procedure is called, it checks whether the environment is suitable for its execution and, if not, returns a status indicating that it must be called again at a later stage.

These steps are described throughout the rest of this chapter.

32.2 THE BASE IMAGE SYS$BASE_IMAGE.EXE

SYS$BASE_IMAGE.EXE is loaded by SYSBOOT, the secondary bootstrap program (see Chapter 33). Most important, SYS$BASE_IMAGE.EXE contains a symbol vector whose entries represent universally available routines and data in other executive images and in itself. It contains data accessed by many other executive images and a small amount of executable code: several small routines and some library procedures used by most executive images.

SYS$BASE_IMAGE.EXE is the pathway to routines and data in other executive images. All images that refer to executive universal symbols link with SYS$BASE_IMAGE.EXE. For example, each executive image is linked with it to resolve references to routines and data in other executive images and in SYS$BASE_IMAGE.EXE. The OpenVMS VAX and OpenVMS AXP operating systems differ in this regard: an OpenVMS VAX image links with SYS.STB to resolve SYS.EXE references.

The offsets of entries in SYS$BASE_IMAGE.EXE's symbol vector are guaranteed to remain the same in subsequent OpenVMS AXP versions. It is thus possible that an image linked with SYS$BASE_IMAGE.EXE can continue to execute on a later version than the one with which it linked. Whenever algorithmic or data structure changes in an executive subsystem might prevent correct execution of an image that referenced the earlier version, the version category associated with that subsystem is updated. An image linked with

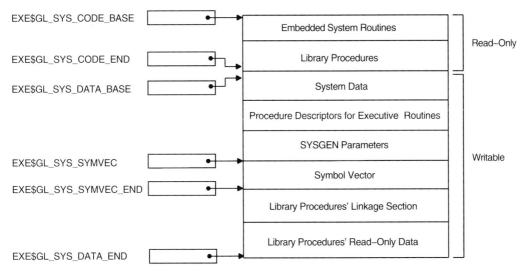

Figure 32.1
Layout of SYS$BASE_IMAGE.EXE

an earlier version of that subsystem cannot then be activated on a system running the updated version (see Section 32.8).

Figure 32.1 shows the organization of SYS$BASE_IMAGE.EXE, which is defined at link time. Entirely nonpageable, SYS$BASE_IMAGE.EXE consists of a single read-only image section and a single writable image section. As shown in the figure, data cells within it (in module SYSTEM_DATA_CELLS) are initialized at load time to point to the loaded base and end of some of its areas.

Its image sections are made up of the following areas:

▶ Several small system routines, here labeled embedded system routines
▶ Library procedures and their associated read-only data and linkage section
▶ Commonly accessed writable data and pointers to data structures in executive images
▶ Procedure descriptors for universally available routines in executive images and for the embedded system routines
▶ SYSGEN parameters
▶ A symbol vector with entries for the data, parameter, routine, and procedure names to be universally available through SYS$BASE_IMAGE.EXE

32.2.1   Embedded System Routines

Several small routines are defined in SYSTEM_ROUTINES and included in SYS$BASE_IMAGE.EXE. Most are routines to which procedure descriptors for executive image routines are initially bound, for example, EXE$LOAD_

1097

ERROR and EXE_RSB. If an attempt is made to call an executive image procedure prior to the loading of the image that contains it, control is transferred to one of these routines instead.

Others include the last chance condition handlers for unexpected executive and kernel mode exceptions and the XDELTA-related routines INI$BRK and INI$MASTERWAKE.

32.2.2 Library Procedures

SYS$BASE_IMAGE.EXE includes a number of procedures that implement low-level operations like division, character string operations, and field operations. Most calls to these procedures are compiler-generated.

Although a typical image's references to these procedures would be resolved through the Run-Time Library shareable image LIBOTS.EXE, an executive image cannot be linked this way. One alternative is for each executive image to link with an object library containing the procedures the image needs. A simpler and more efficient alternative is to build the executive with only a single copy of each procedure.

Several areas in SYS$BASE_IMAGE.EXE are related to these procedures: one for their code, another for read-only data, and another for their linkage section.

32.2.3 Procedure Descriptors for Executive Image Routines

A universally available procedure or routine in an executive image is represented by both a procedure descriptor in the executive image and a bound procedure descriptor in SYS$BASE_IMAGE.EXE. A bound procedure descriptor contains the address of a second procedure descriptor to which the first is initially bound. The code entry point specified by the bound procedure descriptor is the address of a minimal routine that calls the second procedure. This provides a mechanism by which the target of a procedure call can be resolved at run time. Section 32.2.6 and Figure 32.2 show an example of this mechanism.

The bound executive image procedure descriptors found in SYS$BASE_IMAGE.EXE are defined in module SYSTEM_ROUTINES, usually through its macro DEFINE_ROUTINE and, less commonly, through the macros DEFINE_ROUTINE_INTERRUPT and DEFINE_ROUTINE_EXCEPTION. The MACRO-64 assembler generates a bound procedure descriptor for each invocation of one of these macros. The difference among the macros is the procedure to which the generated procedure descriptor is initially bound: a procedure descriptor defined through DEFINE_ROUTINE is bound to EXE$LOAD_ERROR; one defined through either of the other two macros is bound to EXE$HALT. Example 32.1 shows two such macro invocations. Section 32.8 describes the use of the VERSION_MASK keyword.

Example 32.1
Definition of Executive Image Procedure Descriptors

```
; Procedure descriptors from SYSTEM_ROUTINES

        DEFINE_ROUTINE -
                EXE$ALLOCIRP,-
                VERSION_MASK=<MEMORY_MANAGEMENT>
;
        DEFINE_ROUTINE_EXCEPTION -
                EXE$FRKIPL8DSP,-
                VERSION_MASK=<IO>
```

When an executive image is loaded into system space, its SYS$BASE_IM-AGE.EXE procedure descriptors are reinitialized to point to the corresponding procedure descriptors in the loaded executive image. If the image is permanently loaded, its SYS$BASE_IMAGE.EXE symbol vector entries are also reinitialized to point to addresses in the loaded executive image. (As a result, any references to those procedures that are fixed up through the updated symbol vector entries do not reference the bound procedure descriptors in SYS$BASE_IMAGE.EXE.) If the image is removable, its symbol vector entries are not modified; they continue to point to the bound procedure descriptors and associated transfer routines.

32.2.4   System Data

Module SYSTEM_DATA_CELLS contains data accessed by multiple executive images and by other images that link with SYS$BASE_IMAGE.EXE. Data cells accessed by only a limited set of routines typically reside in the same executive image as the routines.

A data cell located in one executive image and referenced by another is represented by a pointer in SYS$BASE_IMAGE.EXE, although if the data cell is small, the cell itself resides in SYS$BASE_IMAGE.EXE to minimize overhead. If the data cell is represented by a pointer, the pointer is modified when the image is loaded to contain the loaded address of the data. Its symbol name has the type AR to indicate that it contains the address of a record or a structure. For example, LNM$AR_SYSTEM_DIRECTORY contains the address of the logical name table system directory, part of LOGICAL_NAMES.EXE.

The local macro DEFINE_DATA_CELL is invoked for each data cell or structure, along with a MACRO-32 directive to allocate and possibly initialize storage for the cell or structure. Example 32.2 illustrates the use of this macro to define cells within SYS$BASE_IMAGE.EXE and to define a pointer to data in another executive image.

There is one difference in the macro invocations for these two kinds of definition. The nondefault value for the POINTER keyword argument prevents a cell that contains a pointer from being defined as a data structure offset.

Example 32.2
Definition of Executive Data Cells

```
; Head of PFN lists
        DEFINE_DATA_CELL -
                PFN$AL_HEAD,-
                VERSION_MASK=<MEMORY_MANAGEMENT>
        .LONG   0,0,0

; Pointer to system logical name table directory
        DEFINE_DATA_CELL -
                LNM$AR_SYSTEM_DIRECTORY,-
                VERSION_MASK=<LOGICAL_NAMES>,-
                POINTER=YES
        .LONG 0
```

By default global cells in SYSTEM_DATA_CELLS are defined both as relocatable symbols and as offsets into a data structure based at EXE$GR_SYSTEM_DATA_CELLS. MACRO-32 executive modules are built to transform their references to such cells into offsets from EXE$GR_SYSTEM_DATA_CELLS for improved performance. The transformation of such a reference to a pointer cell would not work. Appendix B provides more information.

When an executive image is mapped and loaded into system space, its data cell pointers in SYS$BASE_IMAGE.EXE are reinitialized to point to their corresponding data structures in the loaded executive image.

Section 32.4.1 describes other criteria for choosing whether to locate a system data cell or structure in SYS$BASE_IMAGE.EXE or in a particular executive image.

32.2.5 SYSGEN Parameters

The SYSGEN parameters area is defined in module SYSPARAM. This area contains all the SYSGEN parameters. For coordination with SYSBOOT, which copies the current parameters to this area during system boot, all SYSGEN parameters are virtually contiguous. Chapter 34 describes this in more detail.

SYSGEN parameters are part of SYS$BASE_IMAGE.EXE rather than of a particular executive image so that they can be referenced directly. No one executive image references them most often; they are widely referenced from many executive images and from other images linked with SYS$BASE_IMAGE.EXE.

32.2.6 Symbol Vector

A symbol in a shareable image that is to be externally available to other images, such as the name of a data structure or a procedure, must be a universal symbol. A universal symbol must have been defined as a global symbol when the module that contains it was compiled, and it must be declared in a SYMBOL_VECTOR option statement when the image that contains it is linked.

To describe the universal symbols, the linker creates two structures in the shareable image file: a global symbol table and an image section called a symbol vector. Each global symbol has an entry in the global symbol table containing the name of the symbol and the offset of the symbol's entry in the symbol vector. The global symbol table is not loaded into memory with the rest of the image. It is used only during linking as an index into the symbol vector. The symbol vector is loaded into memory as part of the image and is used during image activation and fixup. Each symbol vector entry contains the offset in the image of the location that the symbol names.

SYS$BASE_IMAGE.EXE's global symbol table and symbol vector have entries for all the externally visible executive routines and data that make up the executive. Some of the routines and data are within SYS$BASE_IMAGE.EXE itself, for example, the library procedures, described in Section 32.2.2, and SYSGEN parameters. Many entries in its symbol vector, however, represent global symbols in executive images. Example 32.3 shows the definition of a number of SYS$BASE_IMAGE.EXE symbol vector entries; definitions of some of these universal symbols are shown in the previous examples.

Each such symbol is defined as a global symbol at compile time in one of the modules that compose SYS$BASE_IMAGE.EXE and is declared in SYS$BASE_IMAGE.EXE's SYMBOL_VECTOR link option. The symbol vector entry points to the SYS$BASE_IMAGE.EXE location named by the symbol. Each such symbol is also defined as a global symbol in an executive image. The executive image is linked with a VECTOR_TABLE option statement that identifies SYS$BASE_IMAGE.EXE as containing its symbol vector. After processing the modules that make up an executive image, the linker searches the specified symbol vector. For each symbol in the symbol vector that is defined as a global symbol in a module of the executive image, the linker creates a vectored universal symbol in the executive image's global symbol table. A vectored universal symbol has two values: the address of the location it names in the executive image and the offset of its entry in the SYS$BASE_IMAGE.EXE symbol vector.

When a nonexecutive image is linked with SYS$BASE_IMAGE.EXE, the linker searches SYS$BASE_IMAGE.EXE's global symbol table for each universal SYS$BASE_IMAGE.EXE symbol referenced to get the offset of its associated symbol vector entry. At link time, SYS$BASE_IMAGE.EXE's symbol vector entries contain the following:

▸ Relative addresses of data cells within it
▸ Relative addresses of cells that will eventually point to data cells in executive images
▸ Relative code entry and procedure descriptor addresses, both those that will eventually point to routines in executive images and those that will point to routines in SYS$BASE_IMAGE.EXE

When SYSBOOT loads SYS$BASE_IMAGE.EXE into memory, it relocates

Example 32.3
Definition of SYS$BASE_IMAGE.EXE Universal Symbols

```
! Following are excerpts from [SYS.COM]SYSLNK.OPT, the option file
! for linking SYS$BASE_IMAGE.EXE.

        .
        .
        .
SYMBOL_VECTOR = (-                      !Vectors from SYSPARAM
        .
        .
        .
    SGN$GL_NPAGEDYN     = DATA, -
    SGN$GL_NPAGEVIR     = DATA, -
    SGN$GL_PAGEDYN      = DATA, -
        .
        .
        .
    SGN$GL_DNVOST1      = DATA)
!
SYMBOL_VECTOR = (-                      !Vectors from SYSTEM_ROUTINES
    ACP$ACCESS          = PROCEDURE, -
        .
        .
        .
    EXE$ALLOCIRP        = PROCEDURE, -
    EXE$ALLOCJIB        = PROCEDURE, -
        .
        .
        .
    EXE$SAVE_ALIGN_FAULT_DATA = PROCEDURE)
!
SYMBOL_VECTOR = (-                      !Vectors from SYSTEM_DATA_CELLS
        .
        .
        .
    PFN$AL_HEAD         = DATA, - !Head of PFN lists
    PFN$AL_TAIL         = DATA, - !Tail of PFN lists
        .
        .
        .
    EXE$AR_DECPS_VECTORS = DATA)    !Address of DECps vectors
```

the addresses in the loaded symbol vector entries to reflect the address at which SYS$BASE_IMAGE.EXE was loaded. It also records the starting and ending addresses of the symbol vector within the loaded SYS$BASE_IM-AGE.EXE in the cells EXE$GL_SYS_SYMVEC and EXE$GL_SYS_SYMVEC_END.

As an executive image is loaded, the symbol vector entries in SYS$BASE_IMAGE.EXE that should point to data cells in that image are updated. Whether the image is permanent or removable, its SYS$BASE_IMAGE.EXE procedure descriptors are rebound to the actual procedures in the loaded executive image. If the image is permanent, the symbol vector entries in SYS$BASE_IMAGE.EXE that had pointed to the bound SYS$BASE_IM-AGE.EXE procedure descriptors are updated to point directly to the procedures in the loaded image. If the image is removable, the symbol vector entries are left pointing to the bound SYS$BASE_IMAGE.EXE procedure descriptors to facilitate removal. This change happens as part of executive image loading. Figure 32.2 illustrates the changes in an example SYS$BASE_IMAGE.EXE symbol vector entry and bound procedure descriptor.

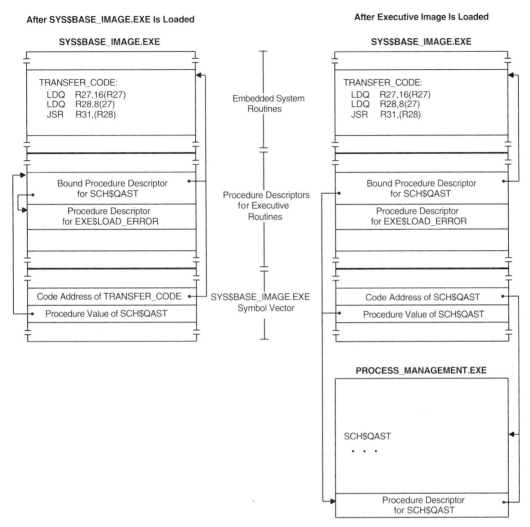

Figure 32.2
SYS$BASE_IMAGE.EXE Symbol Vector Entry and Bound
Procedure Descriptor

When an image linked with SYS$BASE_IMAGE.EXE is activated, its references to SYS$BASE_IMAGE.EXE symbols are fixed up with the current contents of the corresponding symbol vector entries in the loaded SYS$BASE_IMAGE.EXE.

32.3   THE BASE IMAGE SYS$PUBLIC_VECTORS.EXE

SYS$PUBLIC_VECTORS.EXE contains a symbol vector whose entries represent all the universally available names for system services provided by executive images. An image requests a particular system service by calling

SYS$*service,* the universally available system service name. The linker resolves system service names using global definitions from SYS$LIBRARY: SYS$PUBLIC_VECTORS.EXE, which it searches by default.

The offsets of entries in SYS$PUBLIC_VECTORS.EXE's symbol vector are guaranteed to remain the same in subsequent OpenVMS AXP versions. This ensures that an image linked with SYS$PUBLIC_VECTORS.EXE can execute on a later version than the one with which it linked.

The base image cells EXE$GL_PUBLIC_VECTOR_SYMVEC and EXE$GL_PUBLIC_VECTOR_SYMVEC_END contain the starting address and ending address of the symbol vector in the loaded SYS$PUBLIC_VECTORS.EXE.

Built from the module SYSTEM_SERVICES, SYS$PUBLIC_VECTORS.EXE contains procedure descriptors for system service transfer routines and the system service transfer routines themselves. It also contains several universally available data cells holding system addresses that must be accessible to images that do not link with SYS$BASE_IMAGE.EXE. An example is the address of SYS$CALL_HANDL's procedure descriptor. Chapter 6 describes this procedure and its purpose.

A system service transfer routine is a minimal procedure that executes in the mode of the caller and that serves as a bridge to the actual procedure implementing the service request. The actual procedures are within executive images and typically execute in an inner access mode.

When an executive image is loaded, each system service in it that executes in an inner access mode is assigned a unique change mode number. Its system service transfer routine is overwritten to contain an instruction that loads this change mode number into R0 and executes a CALL_PAL CHMx instruction.

When an image requesting a system service calls its transfer routine, the transfer routine executes these instructions, resulting in an exception. The change mode exception service routine uses the change mode number to index a table that contains the addresses of the actual system service procedure descriptor and its code entry point. It then calls the actual procedure.

When a permanent executive image is loaded that contains a mode of caller system service, the contents of the SYS$PUBLIC_VECTORS.EXE symbol vector entry for that universal system service name are updated to point to the executive image. When a removable executive image is loaded that contains a mode of caller system service, the symbol vector entry contents are left pointing to the SYS$PUBLIC_VECTORS.EXE bound procedure descriptor to facilitate removal. In either case, as described in Section 32.6.1, the procedure descriptor in SYS$PUBLIC_VECTORS.EXE is bound to the procedure in the executive image.

Chapter 7 contains further information about system service transfer routines, change mode dispatching, and synchronous system services. Section 32.7.5 describes the initialization of system service transfer routines.

32.4   **EXECUTIVE IMAGES**

The two base images contain relatively little executable code. Their executive image procedure descriptors generally cause dispatch to routines in loaded executive images.

Each executive image consists of data, routines, and initialization code specific to the image's functions and features. In most cases, to simplify maintenance and enhancement, routines supporting related functions and features are collected into the same image. In some cases, routines used early in system initialization are combined into an executive image, such as EXEC_INIT.EXE. Table 33.1 lists the executive images and summarizes their contents.

The OpenVMS AXP executive differs from the OpenVMS VAX executive in that all images loaded into system space other than the two base images are executive images. That is, device drivers and images containing, for example, CPU-specific support, are implemented as executive images.

Although maintainability considerations might lead to more specialized executive images and thus more executive images, several AXP hardware and software considerations make decreasing the number of executive images desirable:

▶ The larger physical page size increases the average unused physical memory for an image section that is not an integral number of pages.

▶ Branch destination hint optimizations can be effective only within an image. With the branch destination hint mechanism the CPU uses the otherwise unused displacement bits in a JSR or JMP instruction to calculate the low-order bits of the destination's address. The CPU performs an early instruction cache lookup of the likely destination address. If the hint bits are correct, the instruction at the destination address can be fetched more quickly. OpenVMS software only calculates branch destination hints when the branch and its target are in the same image.

▶ Calls within an image can be made more efficiently than calls between two images. OpenVMS AXP compilers generate object language records that enable the linker to replace intra-image call sequences with BSR instructions.

32.4.1   **Data in an Executive Image**

A data cell private to routines in an executive image resides in that image. A data cell accessed by routines in multiple executive images can be placed in SYS$BASE_IMAGE.EXE or in one of the executive images. If the data itself is not in SYS$BASE_IMAGE.EXE, SYS$BASE_IMAGE.EXE contains a pointer to it for use by the other executive images. That is, a routine in one executive image does not directly reference data in another but instead makes an indirect reference through a SYS$BASE_IMAGE.EXE pointer.

A data structure whose size is likely to vary from version to version is traditionally stored in an executive image. A cell in SYS$BASE_IMAGE.EXE points to the structure if it is referenced from other executive images.

Certain data cells reside in executive images even though they are small and unlikely to change size. A data cell that is referenced primarily by routines within the image is typically in the image itself, to reduce the access overhead for the most frequent references.

Writable data cells referenced by commonly executed code paths are stored in the image with the most time-critical accesses.

32.4.2 Structure of a Linked Executive Image

An executive image is implemented as a form of shareable image. Like any shareable image, it has a global symbol table, image section descriptors, and an image activator fixup section. Unlike other types of shareable image, an executive image does not contain a symbol vector. Instead, its universally available procedures and data cells are reached through entries in the loaded SYS$BASE_IMAGE.EXE and SYS$PUBLIC_VECTORS.EXE symbol vectors.

The internal structure of an executive image is more constrained than that of a typical shareable image. An executive image is allowed at most one image section of each of the following types and no others:

▸ Nonpageable read-only, for code
▸ Nonpageable writable, for both read-only and writable data, locations containing addresses that must be relocated at image activation, and the linkage section for nonpageable or pageable code
▸ Pageable read-only, for code
▸ Pageable writable, for both read-only and writable data, locations containing addresses that must be relocated at image activation, and the linkage section for pageable code
▸ Initialization section, for initialization procedures and their associated data and linkage section
▸ Image activator fixup section

The first five of these image sections are defined as program sections (PSECTs) within the modules of an executive image. An executive image is linked so as to place the initialization routine section after the others. The linker creates the image activator fixup section as the last image section. The initialization routine and image activator fixup section are last because their address space is deallocated after initialization and fixups are done.

The image activator fixup section (see Chapter 28) contains information needed to relocate address references from the loaded image to locations within itself and to fixup references to locations in the base images. These references are found in procedure descriptors and linkage pairs and also generated by the MACRO-32 directives .ADDRESS and .ASCID and their high-level language equivalents.

The first four sections allow for the combinations of pageability and protection required for executive code and data. Because they have different virtual memory characteristics, each must begin at a page boundary. (Protection and pageability requirements could be met by placing read-only data with the code in the appropriate image section, as they are in an OpenVMS VAX executive image. However, an AXP processor typically has both a data translation buffer and an instruction translation buffer, as described in Chapter 15. Mixing data and code in the same page could result in two translation buffer entries mapping the same physical page, an inefficient use of a relatively scarce resource that could reduce overall performance.) That each section begins on a page boundary can result in unused disk and address space at the end of each image section. An executive image on disk may have on average half a disk block unused at the end of each image section. Section 32.4.3 discusses how the image sections of an executive image are mapped into virtual address space and what unused space might result.

Constraining the number of image sections may limit the potential unused space; it also simplifies the loading mechanism.

Most modules invoke the DECLARE_PSECT macro to define standard executive PSECT names and attributes. Each image is built with a linker options file that collects and orders the image sections. Table 32.1 lists the clusters and PSECTs that make up a typical executive image. It shows some of the modules that make contributions to the PSECTs. This information is extracted from the image map of SYS$VM.EXE.

An executive image is further constrained in that it must be linked with the /NATIVE_ONLY qualifier and must not call routines in translated images. To be loaded sliced (see Section 32.4.3), the image must also be linked with the qualifier /SECTION_BINDING=(CODE,DATA) and contain no relative references from one image section to another.

OpenVMS AXP supports executive images through several shareable image mechanisms, some of them unique to executive images:

► The linker SYMBOL_VECTOR option identifies the symbols in a shareable image that are to be universal. For an OpenVMS executive image, the symbol vector entries are in SYS$BASE_IMAGE.EXE rather than in each executive image.

► A vectored universal symbol has two values: the relative address of the symbol in the executive image, and the offset of the symbol's entry in the SYS$BASE_IMAGE.EXE symbol vector.

► The image header contains space for an array of version numbers, described in Section 32.8.

► The linker COLLECT qualifier /ATTRIBUTES identifies special characteristics of a particular image section. The possible values for the qualifier

Table 32.1   Organization of SYS$VM.EXE, a Typical Executive Image

PSECT Name	Object Module Name
NONPAGED_READONLY_PSECTS CLUSTER	
EXEC$HI_USE_PAGEABLE_CODE [1]	SYSCREDEL
	. . .
EXEC$NONPAGED_CODE	SYSCLONEVA
	. . .
NONPAGED_READWRITE_PSECTS CLUSTER	
EXEC$HI_USE_PAGEABLE_DATA [1]	SYSCREDEL
	. . .
EXEC$HI_USE_PAGEABLE_LINKAGE [1]	SYSCREDEL
	. . .
EXEC$NONPAGED_DATA	OSWPSCHED
	. . .
EXEC$NONPAGED_LINKAGE	SYSCLONEVA
	. . .
PAGED_READONLY_PSECTS CLUSTER	
EXEC$PAGED_CODE	SYSCLONEVA
	. . .
PAGED_READWRITE_PSECTS CLUSTER	
EXEC$PAGED_DATA	GSD_ROUTINES
	. . .
EXEC$PAGED_LINKAGE	SYSCLONEVA
	. . .
INITIALIZATION_PSECTS CLUSTER	
EXEC$INIT_000	SYS$DOINIT
EXEC$INIT_001	SYS$DOINIT
	. . .
EXEC$INIT_002	SYS$DOINIT
EXEC$INIT_CODE	SYS$DOINIT
	SYSCLONEVA
	. . .
EXEC$INIT_LINKAGE	SYS$DOINIT
	SYSCLONEVA
	. . .
EXEC$INIT_SSTBL_000	SYS$DOINIT
EXEC$INIT_SSTBL_001	SYS$DOINIT
	SYSCLONEVA
	. . .
EXEC$INIT_SSTBL_002	SYS$DOINIT
IMAGE ACTIVATOR FIXUP SECTION	
	(Built by the linker)

[1] This PSECT represents code or data that could be paged but that has been placed in a nonpageable image section to improve performance.

are RESIDENT, to designate a nonpageable image section, and INITIAL-IZATION_CODE, to designate the initialization image section. These values initialize the image section descriptor flags EISD$V_RESIDENT and EISD$V_INITIALCODE.

32.4.3   **Mapping an Executive Image**

An executive image can be mapped into system space in one of two ways:

▶ In contiguous virtual pages with the virtual layout created by the linker
▶ With some of its sections in granularity hint regions and thus in discontiguous virtual addresses

By default the OpenVMS operating system allocates one or more granularity hint regions at the low-address end of system space for each of the following purposes:

▶ Base and executive images' nonpageable code
▶ Base and executive images' nonpageable read-only and writable data
▶ Nonpageable system data, such as the PFN database

The granularity hint region or regions associated with each of these uses is commonly referred to as a huge page.

By default most executive images are mapped with sections in granularity hint regions. This option provides better performance. Chapter 15 introduces granularity hint regions and explains their performance advantage.

Because all pages in a granularity hint region must be in physically contiguous pages, OpenVMS does not page the virtual pages occupying a huge page; they must all be resident. If the SYSGEN parameter S0_PAGING is nonzero to disable paging of executive images, their usually pageable image sections occupy the same huge pages as the nonpageable sections.

If any executable or shareable images are installed /RESIDENT, their code also occupies the first huge page (see Chapter 28).

The effect of loading an executive image's nonpageable image sections into huge pages is that the image does not retain the virtual layout created by the linker. The nonpageable read-only section of the image (which contains only code) is loaded into one huge page; its nonpageable writable section is loaded into another; and its pageable sections are in yet a third part of system virtual address space. When resident, the image's pageable sections occupy ordinary physical pages.

The memory represented by a huge page is allocated to an image section in a unit called a slice. Different huge pages can have different slice sizes. An integral number of slices is allocated for each image section. For example, the nonpageable read-only section of one executive image occupies one or more

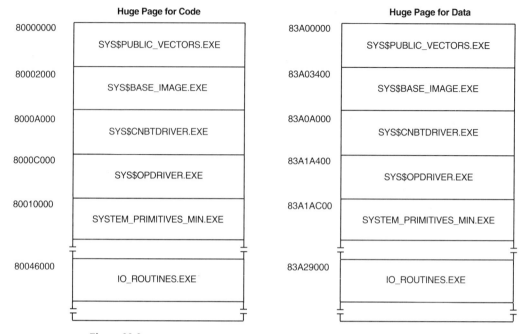

Figure 32.3
Executive Images Loaded Sliced

contiguous slices that are immediately adjacent to those of the previous and next images. An image mapped into a huge page is said to be sliced. Chapter 16 discusses the SYSGEN parameters that affect granularity hint regions and the data structures that describe them.

Figure 32.3 shows an example extract from the first two huge pages of a system whose executive images have been loaded sliced. The code page slice size is 8 KB, and the data page slice size is 512 bytes.

It is possible to specify that a particular executive image not be loaded into a huge page, even if slicing is enabled, through a flag passed as an argument to the procedure that loads executive images. This flag is set, for example, so that the image EXEC_INIT.EXE, which is deallocated at the end of system initialization, is not loaded into a huge page.

Loading the different sections of an executive image into different virtual addresses adds some complexity to relocating absolute addresses and fixing up references to external addresses. It also requires that the data structure that describes a loaded executive image specify the location and length of each image section (see Section 32.5).

When an executive image is not mapped into a huge page, a different issue can affect its mapping. The Alpha AXP architecture allows for several different page sizes. Any particular CPU type has a given page size of 8, 16, 32, or 64 KB. To run on a CPU with a particular page size, an image must have

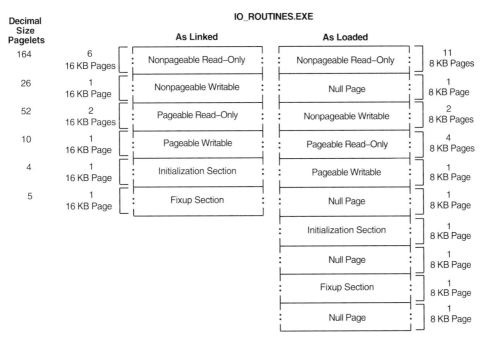

IO_ROUTINES.EXE

Decimal Size Pagelets		As Linked	As Loaded	
164	6 16 KB Pages	Nonpageable Read–Only	Nonpageable Read–Only	11 8 KB Pages
26	1 16 KB Page	Nonpageable Writable	Null Page	1 8 KB Page
52	2 16 KB Pages	Pageable Read–Only	Nonpageable Writable	2 8 KB Pages
10	1 16 KB Page	Pageable Writable	Pageable Read–Only	4 8 KB Pages
4	1 16 KB Page	Initialization Section	Pageable Writable	1 8 KB Page
5	1 16 KB Page	Fixup Section	Null Page	1 8 KB Page
			Initialization Section	1 8 KB Page
			Null Page	1 8 KB Page
			Fixup Section	1 8 KB Page
			Null Page	1 8 KB Page

Figure 32.4
An Executive Image Loaded Nonsliced

been linked to that page size or a larger one. (An image linked to a smaller page size might have an image section that must begin at an address that is a multiple of the smaller page size but not of the larger.)

When an image is loaded on a CPU with a smaller page size than the one to which the image was linked, each of the image sections can begin on a page boundary and be mapped with appropriate pageability and protection. However, if an image section ends with unused address space that is one or more of the smaller pages in length, the unused space is mapped with one or more null pages, that is, no-access PTEs. Figure 32.4 shows an executive image linked to a 16 KB page size and mapped on a CPU with an 8 KB page size.

32.4.4   Symbol Resolution and Executive Images

In general, an OpenVMS AXP image can refer to symbols and addresses within itself and in shareable images with which it is linked. An executive image is more constrained in that it may only be linked with the base images SYS$BASE_IMAGE.EXE and SYS$PUBLIC_VECTORS.EXE and thus can only refer to its own symbols or symbols in one of the base images. Some symbolic references are self-relative and can be fully resolved at compile time. Most symbolic references in an executive image, however, cannot be resolved before address space is assigned to the image and the base images.

The base images are loaded first, followed by executive images. As each image is loaded, address references are resolved:

▶ References from an image to locations within itself are relocated. These are found in procedure descriptors and linkage pairs and also generated by MACRO-32 directives such as .ADDRESS and .ASCID or by their high-level language equivalents. LDR$RELOCATE_IMAGE, in module LDR_RELOCATE_FIXUP, relocates such address references in a base or executive image. Chapter 28 provides a more detailed description of address relocations.

▶ References from an executive image to universal symbols defined in SYS$BASE_IMAGE.EXE or SYS$PUBLIC_VECTORS.EXE are fixed up. These are found in procedure descriptors and linkage pairs and also generated by MACRO-32 directives such as .ADDRESS and .ASCID or by their high-level language equivalents. They derive from system service requests, accesses to systemwide data or data pointers in SYS$BASE_IMAGE.EXE, and invocations of routines defined in SYS$BASE_IMAGE.EXE's symbol vector.

In a fixup, one or two addresses from a previously relocated symbol vector entry replace a reference in an image. LDR$FIXUP_IMAGE, in module LDR_RELOCATE_FIXUP, fixes up address references in executive images using the already relocated contents of SYS$BASE_IMAGE.EXE and SYS$PUBLIC_VECTORS.EXE symbol vector entries. Chapter 28 gives a more detailed description of fixups.

As described in Section 32.2.3, one executive image calls a routine in another executive image through a SYS$BASE_IMAGE.EXE universal symbol. The relocated value of the universal symbol is initially a procedure descriptor in SYS$BASE_IMAGE.EXE bound to an error-handling routine. If image A, loaded first, calls routine Y in image B, which is not yet loaded, then A's reference to Y is fixed up as the address of the relocated bound procedure descriptor. The relocated procedure descriptor is still bound to an error routine.

When image B is loaded, the procedure descriptor is rebound to routine Y in image B. If code in image A then called routine Y, control would be transferred to the SYS$BASE_IMAGE.EXE procedure, which transfers control to routine Y. To avoid the indirection, after all executive images are loaded, second-pass fixups of references to permanently loaded images are performed so that interimage calls can be direct regardless of the order in which the executive images were loaded.

Figure 32.5 shows a simple example of one executive image referencing the external routines SCH$QAST and COM$POST.

Both routines are defined in SYS$BASE_IMAGE.EXE's symbol vector. After the example executive image is linked, its linkage pairs contain the symbol vector offsets of these symbols. After the executive images that define SCH$QAST and COM$POST are loaded, SYS$BASE_IMAGE.EXE's symbol

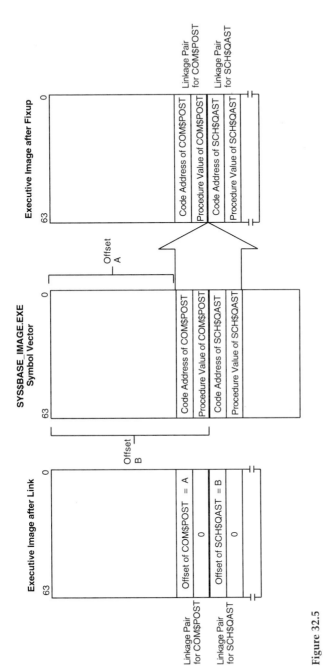

Figure 32.5
Symbol Resolution Through SYS$BASE_IMAGE.EXE

1113

vector entries are updated with actual addresses of the procedure descriptors and their code entry points. After the example executive image is loaded, its linkage pairs are fixed up to contain the contents of the loaded symbol vector entries.

32.5 LOADABLE IMAGE DATA STRUCTURES

Each loaded base and executive image is described by a nonpaged pool data structure called a loader image data block (LDRIMG).

The LDRIMGs are linked together through LDRIMG$L_FLINK and LDR-IMG$L_BLINK in a doubly linked list whose head is at LDR$GQ_IMAGE_LIST. The list is searched before an executive image is loaded to ensure that the image has not already been loaded. XDELTA, DELTA, and the System Dump Analyzer scan the list to determine where executive images have been loaded. Figure 32.6 shows the layout of an LDRIMG. Access to the LDRIMG list is synchronized through the base image mutex, EXE$GQ_BASIMGMTX.

LDRIMG$W_SIZE contains the size in bytes of the structure. LDRIMG$B_TYPE contains the constant DYN$C_LOADCODE. LDRIMG$B_IMGNAM-LEN is the start of a counted ASCII string containing the name of the executive image.

LDRIMG$L_FLAGS describes the state of the loaded image and the manner in which it was loaded. Figure 32.6 lists the flag names, omitting the prefix LDRIMG$V_, and their meanings.

For an image whose sections are loaded into contiguous address space, LDRIMG$L_BASE contains its starting virtual address; for an image loaded sliced, it contains zero. LDRIMG$L_PAGE_COUNT represents the length in pages from the start of the loaded image to the end of its highest image section. The page size is that of the CPU on which the image is loaded.

In LDRIMG$Q_LINKTIME is the system time at which the image was linked. LDRIMG$L_ECO_LEVEL contains revision data. Both fields are copied from the image's image header.

There are five LDRIMG fields for each of the six types of image section. Each field has a unique name, as shown in Figure 32.6. Additionally, the following symbols represent offsets from the beginning of the set of fields for each image section:

► LDRIMG$L_ISD_BASE—Base virtual address at which this image section has been loaded
► LDRIMG$L_ISD_LEN—Size in bytes of this image section
► LDRIMG$L_ISD_VBN—Virtual block number (VBN) in the image file at which this section begins
► LDRIMG$L_ISD_OFFSET—Virtual offset in the image at which this section begins
► LDRIMG$L_ISD_END—Virtual offset in the image at which this section ends

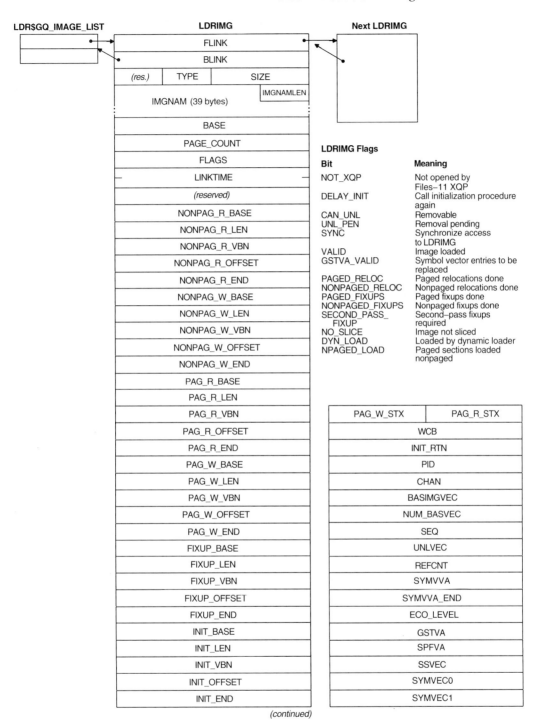

Figure 32.6
Layout of a Loader Image Data Block (LDRIMG)

If an executive image lacks a particular type of image section, most of the fields that represent that section contain 0. After the fixup and initialization sections are deallocated, their fields are cleared. (The LDRIMG$L_ISD_OFF-SET and LDRIMG$L_ISD_LEN fields of an image loaded sliced are initialized to –1 and do not change.)

LDRIMG$W_PAG_W_STX and LDRIMG$W_PAG_R_STX contain the global section table indexes of the pageable sections, if they exist.

LDRIMG$L_WCB contains the address of the window control block (WCB) that describes the image file on disk.

If the image defines an initialization procedure, LDRIMG$L_INIT_RTN contains the loaded virtual address of its procedure descriptor. After the initialization procedure is done and the initialization section deallocated, this field is cleared.

While an image is being loaded by LDR$LOAD_IMAGE, in module SYS-LDR_DYN, LDRIMG$L_PID and LDRIMG$L_CHAN describe the process ID in whose context the image file has been opened and the channel on which it has been opened. After loading is complete, these two fields are cleared.

LDRIMG$L_BASIMGVEC points to a nonpaged pool structure that contains information necessary to restore SYS$BASE_IMAGE.EXE symbol vector entries to their original contents after they have been modified to point into this executive image. LDRIMG$L_NUM_BASVEC contains the number of such entries in the structure. These fields are meaningful only for a removable image or one loaded dynamically.

LDRIMG$L_SEQ contains a sequence number taken from the contents of EXE$GL_LDR_SEQ at the time the image was loaded. The sequence number uniquely identifies the combination of an executive image and a process attempting to load or unload it. The combination of this field, LDRIMG$L_REFCNT, and the flags LDRIMG$V_SYNC, LDRIMG$V_VALID, and LDR-IMG$V_UNL_PEN enables the executive to synchronize attempts to load and unload the same executive image as well as to synchronize concurrent accesses to the image. XDELTA can identify a particular loaded executive image through its sequence number.

If the image defines one or more procedures to be called when the image is unloaded, LDRIMG$L_UNLVEC contains the address of a table within the image that lists those procedures.

For an image that can be removed from memory, LDRIMG$L_REFCNT counts the number of current references made to the image.

When the reference count is nonzero, the image may not be unloaded.

LDRIMG$L_SYMVVA and LDRIMG$L_SYMVVA_END delimit a symbol vector within a loaded base image.

LDRIMG$L_GSTVA, when flag LDRIMG$V_GSTVA_VALID is set, points to a nonpaged pool structure containing entries from the image's global symbol table that cannot be processed until paging is possible. After the entries are processed, the pool is deallocated, and both the flag and field are cleared.

LDRIMG$L_SPFVA, when flag LDRIMG$V_SECOND_PASS_FIXUP is set, points to a nonpaged pool structure containing entries that represent external fixups to SYS$BASE_IMAGE.EXE procedures that need to be redone after the executive image containing the target procedure is loaded. After the entries are processed, the pool is deallocated, and both the flag and field are cleared.

LDRIMG$L_SSVEC contains the address of a nonpaged pool data structure that summarizes the inner mode system services in an executive image (see Section 32.7.5).

LDRIMG$L_SYMVEC0 and LDRIMG$L_SYMVEC1 contain the addresses of up to two symbol vectors in which the executive image's universal symbols are defined, namely, the contents of EXE$GL_SYS_SYMVEC, the contents of EXE$GL_PUBLIC_VECTOR_SYMVEC, neither, or both.

32.6   EXECUTIVE IMAGE LOADING

Executive images are loaded and initialized at several stages in system initialization. An image is initially loaded at one particular stage. However, if the image contains pageable sections and is loaded before paging is possible, relocations and fixups in its pageable sections must be deferred to a later stage of system initialization. An image's initialization procedure can potentially be executed when the image is loaded and again at any of several succeeding stages of initialization. In general, loading of executive images is deferred to the later stages of system initialization, if possible, for simplicity.

The major stages of system initialization at which images are loaded, initialized, or fixed up are as follows:

1. SYSBOOT.EXE, the secondary bootstrap program, which initializes system space and loads the base images and executive images needed during the early stages of system initialization
2. EXEC_INIT.EXE (routine EXE$INIT), the executive image that performs initialization of system data and that loads most of the other executive images
3. The swapper process, the first process to execute
4. The SYSINIT process, which loads a few executive images
5. The startup process, in whose context the routine LDR$RELEASE_MEM, in module LDR_MEM_ALLOC, is invoked to complete fixup of executive images

Chapter 33 lists the images loaded at each stage of system initialization. That chapter and Chapter 34 describe these and other stages of system initialization in detail. This section is concerned only with their role in the loading and initialization of executive images.

Table 32.2   Boot Stages and Conditions (EXE$GL_STATE Bits)

Bit Name	Set by	Meaning
SYSBOOT	SYSBOOT	SYSBOOT has begun
EXEC_SLICING [1]	LDR$INIT_MEM	Executive images should be sliced
POOL_INIT	SYSBOOT	Nonpaged pool allocation is possible
INIT	EXE$INIT	EXE$INIT has begun
CONSOLE	EXE$INIT	Console I/O routines are available
NORDONLY [1]	EXE$INIT	Executive images should not be set read-only
PFN_INIT	EXE$INIT	Page frame number (PFN) database is initialized
SPNLCK_AVAIL	SYNCH$INIT_ONCE	Spinlock database is available
SWAPPER	EXE$SWAPINIT	Swapper process has begun, and paging is possible
SYSINIT	SYSINIT	SYSINIT process has begun
RMS	SYSINIT	RMS has been loaded
XQP	SYSINIT	File system has been loaded
STARTUP	SYSINIT	Startup process has been created

[1] This bit represents a condition rather than a substage of booting.

The stages of system initialization are divided into substages, primarily to control loading and initialization of executive images. The system global EXE$GL_STATE describes these substages with a bit set to represent each substage that has been reached. The macro $BOOSTATEDEF defines symbolic values for these bits. Table 32.2 lists the symbols in the order in which their bits are set. For simplicity, it omits the prefix BOOSTATE$V_.

Executive images are loaded during system initialization by two versions of LDR$LOAD_IMAGE. The first, in module SYSLDR, which is sometimes referred to as the boot loader, is linked with SYSBOOT.EXE and EXEC_INIT.EXE. The other version, in module SYSLDR_DYN, which is sometimes referred to as the dynamic loader, is part of the executive image SYSLDR_DYN.EXE. Routines used by both versions of LDR$LOAD_IMAGE are in module SYSLDR_COMMON.

The loading and initialization of executive images are described in the sections that follow.

32.6.1   Actions of LDR$LOAD_IMAGE

LDR$LOAD_IMAGE must effectively activate an executive image and establish connections between the symbol vector entries and pointers in SYS$BASE_IMAGE.EXE and SYS$PUBLIC_VECTORS.EXE and their targets in the loaded image. This section describes the basic operations of

LDR$LOAD_IMAGE, with some details of the differences that arise from its execution in different initialization stages.

LDR$LOAD_IMAGE is called with the name of an executive image and a set of flags to control its actions. The symbolic values of these flags, which are defined by the macro $LDRDEF, and their meanings are as follows:

▸ LDR$V_PAG—When set, indicates that the image should be loaded with its pageable sections resident. The flag is generally based on the value of bit S0PAGING$V_EXEC (bit 0) of the SYSGEN parameter S0_PAGING.

▸ LDR$V_UNL—When set, indicates that the image may be removed from memory.

▸ LDR$V_OVR—When set, indicates that the image's read-only sections should not be overwritten during bugcheck processing. This flag is currently not used but is provided for compatibility with OpenVMS VAX load requests.

▸ LDR$V_USER_BUF—When set, indicates that the caller has passed the address of a buffer that should be passed on to the image's initialization procedure.

▸ LDR$V_NO_SLICE—When set, indicates the image's sections should not be loaded into a huge page.

LDR$LOAD_IMAGE takes the following steps:

1. It opens the image file using whatever mechanism is available at this stage, either minimal file system routines or the full file system. A WCB is created for a file opened with the minimal file system routines. Later, after SYSINIT has loaded the file system and RMS, SYSINIT opens the file and leaves it open so that, for example, normal file system checks will prevent the file's deletion.

   Running in process context and after system initialization is complete, LDR$LOAD_IMAGE in module SYSLDR_DYN is entered in executive mode and uses RMS to open the image. It then requests the Change to Kernel Mode ($CMKRNL) system service and performs the rest of its processing in kernel mode.

2. LDR$LOAD_IMAGE reads the image header of the file.

3. Unless the image is SYS$BASE_IMAGE.EXE, LDR$LOAD_IMAGE verifies that the executive versions with which the image was linked are compatible with those specified in the loaded SYS$BASE_IMAGE.EXE.

   If the versions are incompatible, LDR$LOAD_IMAGE does not load the executive image and returns the severe error status SS$_SYSVERDIF.

4. If the versions are compatible, LDR$LOAD_IMAGE allocates an LDR-IMG and initializes it, copying information from its arguments and the image header, such as the procedure value of the initialization procedure and link time.

Depending on the boot stage, it performs one of the following:

- If LDR$LOAD_IMAGE is running as part of SYSBOOT.EXE before non-paged pool allocation is possible, it builds the LDRIMG in local storage and places it on a local list. Called after nonpaged pool initialization is complete, LDR$LOAD_IMAGE copies each local LDRIMG to nonpaged pool and inserts the nonpaged pool copy at the front of the systemwide LDRIMG list. For each such local LDRIMG, it increments EXE$GL_LDR_CNT, copies the contents of EXE$GL_LDR_SEQ to LDRIMG$L_SEQ as that image's sequence number, and adds the value 2 to EXE$GL_LDR_SEQ.
- If LDR$LOAD_IMAGE is running after pool allocation is possible but not as part of SYSLDR_DYN.EXE, it allocates an LDRIMG from nonpaged pool and inserts it at the front of the systemwide LDRIMG list. It increments EXE$GL_LDR_CNT, copies the contents of EXE$GL_LDR_SEQ to LDRIMG$L_SEQ as the image's sequence number, and adds the value 2 to EXE$GL_LDR_SEQ.
- If LDR$LOAD_IMAGE is running as part of SYSLDR_DYN.EXE, it allocates an LDRIMG from nonpaged pool and locks the base image mutex, EXE$GQ_BASIMGMTX, for write access. It searches the LDRIMG list to see if an executive image with the same name has already been loaded or is being loaded. If one exists and its flags indicate that it is valid, being unloaded, or being loaded by another process, LDR$LOAD_IMAGE deallocates the LDRIMG, unlocks the mutex, and returns the error status SS$_DUPLNAM to its caller. If one does not, LDR$LOAD_IMAGE sets bit LDRIMG$V_SYNC to indicate that image loading is not complete, inserts the LDRIMG at the front of the LDRIMG list, and unlocks the mutex.

5. It tests BOOSTATE$V_EXEC_SLICING and its argument flags to determine whether the executive image should be loaded sliced and, if not, sets LDRIMG$V_NO_SLICE in LDRIMG$L_FLAGS.

   If executive image slicing is enabled and has not been disabled for this particular image, it checks that the image has been linked with the qualifier /SECTION_BINDING=(CODE,DATA). If not, LDR$LOAD_IMAGE sets LDRIMG$V_NO_SLICE. By default most executive images loaded prior to the end of system initialization are loaded sliced.

6. It initializes various other bits in LDRIMG$L_FLAGS based on argument flags.

7. LDR$LOAD_IMAGE tests LDRIMG$V_NO_SLICE to see whether the image is to be loaded sliced. If so, it proceeds with step 8.

   Otherwise, scanning the image section descriptors in the image header, LDR$LOAD_IMAGE initializes the appropriate LDRIMG fields to describe each section: its size in bytes, starting VBN within the image file, and starting and ending virtual offsets of the section within the image file. For example, it initializes the fields LDRIMG$L_NONPAG_W_LEN, LDRIMG$L_NONPAG_W_VBN, LDRIMG$L_NONPAG_W_OFFSET, and LDRIMG$L_NONPAG_W_END to describe the resident writable section.

It calculates the number of pages of address space required to map the image and stores the number in LDRIMG$L_PAGE_COUNT.

LDR$LOAD_IMAGE allocates contiguous system page table entries (SPTEs) for the pages of all the image sections (see Section 32.9.1). It computes the system address represented by the lowest SPTE as the base address of the image, stores it in LDRIMG$L_BASE, relocates the virtual offset of each section by the base address of the image, and updates the corresponding LDRIMG fields. It proceeds with step 9.

8. For an image that is to be loaded sliced, LDR$LOAD_IMAGE scans the image section descriptors in the image header to initialize LDRIMG fields. It allocates address space for the sections as follows:

   - For the nonpageable read-only and writable sections, it allocates slices from either the code or data huge page. If the allocation fails for lack of room, the boot loader simply returns the error status to its caller. The dynamic loader disables further sliced loading by clearing BOO-STATE$V_EXEC_SLICING, returns whatever resources were allocated, and processes the image as described in step 7.
   - If the flag LDRIMG$V_NPAGED_LOAD is clear (its default state), LDR$LOAD_IMAGE allocates SPTEs for each pageable section. If the flag is set (typically because SYSGEN parameter S0_PAGING is nonzero), it allocates slices from the code or data huge page.
   - For both the initialization and fixup sections, it allocates SPTEs.

   LDR$LOAD_IMAGE records the base virtual address of each image section in the LDRIMG.

9. If the image is either of the two base images, LDR$LOAD_IMAGE stores the relocated starting and ending virtual addresses of its symbol vector in LDRIMG$L_SYMVVA and LDRIMG$L_SYMVVA_END.

10. It relocates the address of the initialization routine.

11. Depending on whether the image is being loaded sliced, LDR$LOAD_IMAGE invokes LDR$LOAD_NONPAGED or LDR$LOAD_SLICE, in module SYSLDR_COMMON. It invokes the routine twice—once to map and load the nonpageable read-only code section and once to map and load the nonpageable writable section. Section 32.6.2 describes LDR$LOAD_NONPAGED, and Section 32.6.3, LDR$LOAD_SLICE.

12. It tests whether the pageable image sections are to be loaded as non-pageable. If the LDRIMG$V_NPAGED_LOAD flag is clear, LDR$LOAD_IMAGE invokes LOAD_PAGED, in module SYSLDR_COMMON, once to map the pageable read-only section and once to map the pageable writable section. If the flag is set, LDR$LOAD_IMAGE instead invokes

either LDR$LOAD_NONPAGED or LDR$LOAD_SLICE. Section 32.6.4 describes LOAD_PAGED.

13. LDR$LOAD_IMAGE invokes LDR$LOAD_NONPAGED to map and load the fixup section and again to map and load the initialization section. (Even if the image is being loaded sliced, these transient sections are not loaded into a huge page.)

14. LDR$LOAD_IMAGE performs relocations and fixups on references within the loaded image:

   a. It checks that the image was linked /NATIVE_ONLY, returning the error status LOADER$_PSB_FIXUPS if it was not.

   b. It calls LDR$RELOCATE_IMAGE, in module LDR_RELOCATE_FIX-UP, to relocate the image's intra-image references so that they reflect the addresses of the locations in the loaded image. LDR$RELOCATE_IMAGE relocates references within nonpageable sections and, if paging is possible, within the pageable writable section as well. It sets bit LDRIMG$V_NONPAGED_RELOC in LDRIMG$L_FLAGS. If paging is possible and it can relocate references to pageable sections, or if there are no such references, it sets bit LDRIMG$V_PAGED_RELOC as well.

   c. In the probable event that the image itself references SYS$BASE_IMAGE.EXE symbols or contains resolutions for any SYS$BASE_IMAGE.EXE vectored universal symbols, the image's fixup section contains a shareable image list entry for SYS$BASE_IMAGE.EXE. If the image requests system services or contains resolutions for any SYS$PUBLIC_VECTORS.EXE vectored universal symbols, its fixup section also contains a shareable image list entry for SYS$PUBLIC_VECTORS.EXE. These entries are built by the linker and must be updated to reflect addresses at which the base images were loaded. LDR$LOAD_IMAGE updates the address of the loaded symbol vector corresponding to each shareable image list entry.

   d. LDR$LOAD_IMAGE calls LDR$FIXUP_IMAGE, in module LDR_RE-LOCATE_FIXUP, to perform fixups, that is, to store correct values in the image's locations that reference external addresses, namely, references to locations in SYS$BASE_IMAGE.EXE and SYS$PUBLIC_VECTORS.EXE. LDR$FIXUP_IMAGE fixes up references within nonpageable sections and, if paging is possible, within the pageable writable section as well. It sets bit LDRIMG$V_NONPAGED_FIX-UPS in LDRIMG$L_FLAGS to indicate that those fixups have been done. If paging is possible, it sets bit LDRIMG$V_PAGED_FIXUPS as well.

   When fixing up references for a permanent image, LDR$FIXUP_IMAGE checks whether a second-pass fixup is necessary for each SYS$BASE_IMAGE.EXE or SYS$PUBLIC_VECTORS.EXE reference being fixed up. If the reference is to a procedure that is still bound to EXE$LOAD_ERROR, LDR$FIXUP_IMAGE records information about the symbol and reference in a nonpaged pool structure pointed to by LDRIMG$L_SPFVA. Section 32.7.2 describes second-pass fixups.

e. LDR$LOAD_IMAGE then scans the executive image's global symbol table, looking for vectored universal symbols. As previously described, a vectored universal symbol has two values: the offset of its entry in a base image (either SYS$BASE_IMAGE.EXE or SYS$PUBLIC_VEC-TORS.EXE) symbol vector and its relative offset within the executive image. For each vectored universal symbol, LDR$LOAD_IMAGE calculates both its address in the loaded base image symbol vector and its address based on its offset within the loaded image.

For a vectored universal data cell, LDR$LOAD_IMAGE updates the data cell pointer in SYS$BASE_IMAGE.EXE to point into the loaded executive image.

For a vectored universal procedure, LDR$LOAD_IMAGE must update the entry in the base image symbol vector and the base image bound procedure descriptor. LDR$LOAD_IMAGE first determines whether it can access the executive image's procedure descriptor corresponding to the universal symbol. If the procedure descriptor is in a pageable section but paging is not yet possible, LDR$LOAD_IMAGE defers the update. Instead, it stores the information in a piece of nonpaged pool pointed to by LDRIMG$L_GSTVA.

If the procedure descriptor can be accessed and if the executive image, once loaded, may not be removed, then for each vectored universal procedure or routine, LDR$LOAD_IMAGE updates the base image symbol vector and binds the base image procedure descriptor to the one in the executive image. If the image may be removed, LDR$LOAD_IMAGE merely binds the base image procedure descriptor to the one in the executive image.

If the vectored universal symbol is the name of a system service transfer routine (that is, if its bound procedure descriptor is within SYS$PUBLIC_VECTORS.EXE), LDR$LOAD_IMAGE initializes the procedure descriptor in the cxccutive image to specify a default procedure signature, thereby enabling a translated image to request system services.

f. LDR$LOAD_IMAGE executes an instruction memory barrier instruction (see Chapter 9) to flush any prefetched instructions and to ensure that the symbol vector is rewritten before any subsequent writes to memory.

15. LDR$LOAD_IMAGE tests whether the fixup data can be deallocated, that is, whether all needed paged relocations and fixups have been done. If not, it proceeds with the next step. Otherwise, it also tests whether

the PFN database has been initialized and, if not, proceeds with the next step. If the PFN database has been initialized, the routine processes the SPTEs that map the fixup section. It deallocates the physical page, if any, associated with each SPTE; it updates the PFN database accordingly; it increments PFN$GL_PHYPGCNT to indicate one more available page of memory; and it clears the SPTE.

LDR$LOAD_IMAGE triggers invalidation of its own processor's TB and that of any other SMP members. It clears the fields in the LDRIMG that describe the fixup section, subtracts its pages from LDRIMG$L_PAGE_COUNT, and invokes LDR$DEALLOC_PT (see Section 32.9.2) to deallocate the SPTEs.

16. If LDR$LOAD_IMAGE is running as part of SYSBOOT.EXE and there is an initialization procedure, it sets the flag LDRIMG$V_DELAY_INIT in LDRIMG$L_FLAGS so that the procedure will be called at a later stage of initialization. If it is not running as part of SYSBOOT.EXE and the image has an initialization procedure, LDR$LOAD_IMAGE invokes LDR$INIT_SINGLE to call the procedure (see Section 32.7.1).

17. If it is not running as part of SYSLDR_DYN.EXE, it sets LDRIMG$V_VALID to indicate that loading is complete.

If LDR$LOAD_IMAGE is running after system initialization is complete, as part of SYSLDR_DYN.EXE, it locks the base image mutex and clears LDRIMG$V_SYNC and sets LDRIMG$V_VALID to indicate that loading is complete. It also increments EXE$GL_LDR_CNT, copies the contents of EXE$GL_LDR_SEQ to LDRIMG$L_SEQ as the image's sequence number, and adds the value 2 to EXE$GL_LDR_SEQ. It unlocks the base image mutex and returns from the kernel mode procedure.

18. LDR$LOAD_IMAGE returns to its caller.

32.6.2   Actions of LDR$LOAD_NONPAGED

LDR$LOAD_IMAGE invokes LDR$LOAD_NONPAGED to map and load nonpageable executive image sections. Its arguments specify the address of the LDRIMG; base, length, and virtual block number of the section; and protection for the section's pages.

LDR$LOAD_NONPAGED performs the following steps:

1. It calculates the number of pages in the section and the address of the SPTE that maps the first page of the section.

2. If the spinlock database has been initialized, LDR$LOAD_NONPAGED acquires the MMG spinlock.

3. For each page of the section, it does the following:

   a. It allocates a page of physical memory.

   b. It initializes the SPTE for that section page with the allocated PFN, owner mode of kernel, valid and address space match bits set, and a protection permitting kernel mode writes. The page must be writable so that it can be overwritten with the contents of the image file. Its protection is changed later.

   c. If the PFN database has been initialized, LDR$LOAD_NONPAGED updates its information about the page, recording information such as the address of the SPTE that contains it, and its state and type. It decrements PFN$GL_PHYPGCNT, the number of physical pages available.

     If the PFN database has not been initialized, recording this information is deferred until EXE$INIT executes.

4. If LDR$LOAD_NONPAGED has acquired the MMG spinlock, it releases the spinlock.

5. It reads the image section into the allocated space. If there are any errors reading the section, it returns to its invoker. If the last page of the section is only partially backed by section file, it zeros the unused part of the page.

6. If LDR$LOAD_IMAGE is running at a stage before the swapper process, LDR$LOAD_NONPAGED returns to its invoker. Otherwise, it acquires the MMG spinlock and changes the protection in the section's SPTEs to the protection specified by LDR$LOAD_IMAGE. Its value depends on whether the section is writable:

- Read-only section pages have a protection of UR.
- Writable section pages have a protection of URKW.

LDR$LOAD_NONPAGED triggers invalidation of its own processor's TB and that of any other active SMP members. It releases the MMG spinlock.

7. It returns to its invoker.

32.6.3   Actions of LDR$LOAD_SLICE

LDR$LOAD_SLICE is invoked with the same arguments as LDR$LOAD_NONPAGED. One key difference between the two routines is that memory has already been allocated in the case of a sliced section. Another key difference is that if the granularity hint region has already been set read-only, the pages that make up the slice must first be double-mapped temporarily. The pages are double-mapped by SPTEs that permit write accesses to enable the section to be loaded into memory.

   LDR$LOAD_SLICE performs the following steps:

1. It checks whether it is running at a boot stage before the swapper process. If not, LDR$LOAD_SLICE is running at a boot stage where the code page is still writable and no double mapping is required. LDR$LOAD_SLICE continues with step 3.

2. If double mapping is required, LDR$LOAD_SLICE acquires the MMG spinlock and gets the starting physical address of the slice allocated to this section. It allocates enough available SPTEs to map the section and

initializes them with appropriate PFNs and a protection of KW. It saves the contents of LDRIMG$L_ISD_BASE and replaces them with the system virtual address corresponding to the temporary mapping. It releases the MMG spinlock.

3. It reads the section into the address space specified by LDRIMG$L_ISD_BASE. LDRIMG$L_ISD_LEN contains the length in bytes of the section. The pages that map the section have been initialized with a protection of KW so that they can be overwritten with the contents of the image file.

4. If the section was doubly mapped, it deletes the double mapping, restores the former contents of LDRIMG$L_ISD_BASE, and releases the spinlock.

5. It returns to its invoker.

32.6.4   **Actions of LOAD_PAGED**

LOAD_PAGED is invoked with the same arguments as LDR$LOAD_NON-PAGED. It performs the following steps:

1. LOAD_PAGED checks that the BOOSTATE$V_INIT stage of bootstrap has been reached and returns immediately if not. As a result, no image containing pageable sections can be loaded by SYSBOOT.

2. Next it forms prototype PTE contents suitable for mapping each page of the section. The protection, passed as an argument, is either UR for a read-only or URKW for a writable section. The page owner is kernel mode. The type bits in the PTE are set to indicate that the page is part of a section and currently in the image file. If the section is writable, its PTEs also have the copy-on-reference bit set to ensure that page file backing store is allocated for the modified pages.

3. LOAD_PAGED tests and sets the shared bit in the image's WCB. If the bit was clear (if the file had been opened with primitive file routines), LOAD_PAGED initializes its reference count to 2. These steps make the WCB look like any other WCB describing a section file, even if it had been created by primitive file routines, and ensure that the file is permanently open.

4. LOAD_PAGED, running as part of SYSLDR_DYN.EXE, locks the global section mutex for write access.

5. It allocates and initializes a section table entry from the system header (see Chapter 16).

6. LOAD_PAGED, running as part of SYSLDR_DYN.EXE, unlocks the global section mutex.

7. LOAD_PAGED stores the index number of the section table entry in the prototype PTE contents. It records information such as the WCB address, number of pagelets, section base system virtual page number, and a flag indicating whether the section is writable.

8. It records the number of section pages in SEC$L_REFCNT and charges them against the system header's PHD$L_PPGFLVA.

9. LOAD_PAGED writes the prototype PTE to each of the SPTEs previously allocated for the section by LDR$LOAD_IMAGE. If the section does not contain an integral number of AXP pages, LOAD_PAGED sets the partial section bit in the PTE that maps the last page. The section's pages will be read in later from the executive image in response to page faults, possibly during image initialization when address fixups are done or later during image execution.

10. It returns to LDR$LOAD_IMAGE.

32.6.5   Loading of Optional Images

If the value of bit 0 (SGN$V_LOAD_SYS_IMAGES) of the SYSGEN parameter LOAD_SYS_IMAGES is 1, its default, the loading of optional images is enabled. The images to be loaded are listed in the file SYS$LOADABLE_IMAGES:VMS$SYSTEM_IMAGES.DATA. Each entry specifies the name of an executive image and in which phase, EXE$INIT or SYSINIT, the image should be loaded.

This mechanism provides for the loading of

▶ Optional OpenVMS-supplied executive images
▶ Executive images that are part of optional software products

Both EXE$INIT and SYSINIT call LDR$ALTERNATE_LOAD, in module ALTERNATE_LOAD. LDR$ALTERNATE_LOAD takes the following steps:

1. It tests bit 0 of LOAD_SYS_IMAGES. If the value is zero, the procedure returns.

2. Otherwise, it opens and reads SYS$LOADABLE_IMAGES:VMS$SYSTEM_IMAGES.DATA.

3. For each record in the file, LDR$ALTERNATE_LOAD tests whether it is running during the specified initialization phase. If it is not, LDR$ALTERNATE_LOAD reads the next record.

4. If the current initialization phase matches that in the record, LDR$ALTERNATE_LOAD opens the specified image and reads its image header. It then calls LDR$LOAD_IMAGE to map the image.

5. When LDR$ALTERNATE_LOAD reaches the end of the file, it closes the file and returns to its caller.

32.7   INITIALIZATION OF AN EXECUTIVE IMAGE

Executive image initialization procedures perform a variety of functions, some specific to the features and functions supported by the image, and others required by many executive images.

An initialization procedure may need to execute in an environment that does not exist when the procedure's executive image is first loaded. The initialization mechanism therefore provides for delayed and multiple invocations of initialization procedures. An initialization procedure can be called again, for example, so that it can execute after the PFN database has been created or once paging is possible. The space occupied by these procedures is deallocated when initialization is complete.

Initialization procedures are described by an initialization table within each executive image. Each table entry is a quadword. The first longword contains the procedure value of an initialization procedure. The second longword contains flags that describe the initialization procedure and its state.

Each executive image that requires execution of initialization procedures is linked with either the module DOINIT or the module DOINIT_UNL. DOINIT_UNL has all the functionality of DOINIT but also provides for procedures to be called if the image is removed from memory.

Each module defines a number of PSECTs, all of which are clustered into the initialization image section. Three of the PSECTs build the initialization table: EXEC$INIT_000 defines its start and names it INI$A_VECTOR_ TABLE; EXEC$INIT_001 defines its body; and EXEC$INIT_002 defines its end with an entry of zero.

Modules in an executive image, including DOINIT or DOINIT_UNL itself, make entries in the body of the initialization table by invoking the macro INITIALIZATION_ROUTINE. An entry for a procedure that should be called before others is made with the macro argument PRIORITY specified as 1. As a result, the entry goes into PSECT EXEC$INIT_000. Otherwise, by default, the entry goes into PSECT EXEC$INIT_001. The other PSECTs and their uses are described in Section 32.7.5.

DOINIT and DOINIT_UNL also include the initialization procedure dispatcher, INI$DOINIT. Each image linked with DOINIT or DOINIT_UNL specifies this dispatcher as its transfer address. LDR$LOAD_IMAGE copies the transfer address from the image header and stores its relocated value in the field LDRIMG$L_INIT_RTN.

INI$DOINIT is called multiple times during system initialization. It scans the initialization table and calls the specified procedures. Each procedure can examine the flags in EXE$GL_STATE to identify the current phase of system initialization and determine whether its execution is appropriate.

DOINIT and DOINIT_UNL each invoke INITIALIZATION_ROUTINE to create a table entry for one common initialization procedure used by most executive images: INI$SYSTEM_SERVICE, which performs initialization for any system services in the image. Section 32.7.5 describes initialization procedures.

The macro $INIRTNDEF defines symbolic values for the flags in the initialization table. The flag INIRTN$V_CALLED, when set, means that INI$DOINIT has called the initialization routine. The flag INIRTN$V_NO_ RECALL, when set, means that the initialization routine should not be called again. The use of these flags is described in Section 32.7.4.

32.7.1   Initialization Sequence

LDR$INIT_SINGLE and LDR$INIT_ALL are the routines that trigger executive image initialization. LDR$INIT_SINGLE initializes a single executive image. LDR$INIT_ALL scans the LDRIMG list, which contains image data blocks for the images loaded thus far, and invokes LDR$INIT_SINGLE for each of them. Both these routines are in module SYSLDR_COMMON and linked with SYSBOOT.EXE, EXEC_INIT.EXE, and SYSLDR_DYN.EXE.

These routines are entered multiple times during system initialization:

1. In the case of each image loaded by SYSBOOT, LDR$LOAD_IMAGE sets the flag LDRIMG$V_DELAY_INIT so that the executive image will be initialized at a later stage.

2. Before switching to the standard system control block (SCB), EXE$INIT calls LDR$INIT_ALL to perform initialization of the images loaded by SYSBOOT, in particular, the image SYSTEM_DEBUG.EXE, if it is resident.

3. After the PFN database is initialized, EXE$INIT sets a flag in EXE$GL_STATE to indicate its initialization and calls LDR$INIT_ALL again to perform further initialization of the images loaded by SYSBOOT.

4. EXE$INIT loads the set of executive images listed in Table 33.1 by repeatedly calling LDR$LOAD_IMAGE, which invokes LDR$INIT_SINGLE.

5. EXE$INIT then calls LDR$INIT_ALL to perform further initialization of all the images loaded thus far. This additional initialization is done in case actions in one image's initialization routine depend on actions taken in another image's initialization routine.

6. The swapper process sets a flag in EXE$GL_STATE to indicate that it is running and that paging is possible. It initializes paged pool and calls LDR$INIT_ALL. Now that paging is possible, address relocations and external fixups in pageable sections of executive images can be done and system services can be connected.

7. The SYSINIT process loads each of several executive images by calling LDR$LOAD_IMAGE, which invokes LDR$INIT_SINGLE.

In addition, LDR$INIT_SINGLE is invoked to initialize an executive image loaded dynamically after system initialization is complete.

32.7.2   Actions of LDR$INIT_ALL

LDR$INIT_ALL scans the LDRIMG list from the end of the list to the beginning. This ensures that initialization procedures are called in the order in which their images were loaded.

For each LDRIMG, it performs any relocations and fixups that can be done and then calls the initialization procedure through the following steps.

1. It tests whether the image has a fixup section and, if not, proceeds to step 4. If there is one, it represents relocations and fixups in pageable sections. LDR$INIT_ALL tests whether paging is possible and, if not, defers the relocations and fixups and proceeds to step 3.

2. If the image has a fixup section and paging is possible, LDR$INIT_ALL takes the following steps to perform relocation and fixup:

   a. If intra-image references from pageable sections of the image have not been relocated, LDR$INIT_ALL calls LDR$RELOCATE_IMAGE, in module LDR_RELOCATE_FIXUP, to relocate them so that they reflect the addresses of the locations in the loaded image.

   b. If references to other images from pageable sections of this one remain to be fixed up, LDR$INIT_ALL calls LDR$FIXUP_IMAGE, in module LDR_RELOCATE_FIXUP.

   c. If SYS$BASE_IMAGE.EXE or SYS$PUBLIC_VECTORS.EXE symbol vector entries still need to be replaced, LDR$INIT_ALL processes each entry in the nonpaged pool structure whose address is in LDRIMG$L_GSTVA. Each entry represents a vectored universal symbol that is the name of a procedure or routine whose procedure descriptor is pageable and thus inaccessible in early stages of system initialization. Each entry contains the address of its corresponding symbol vector entry and the address of its executive image procedure descriptor.

      LDR$INIT_ALL examines the contents of the symbol vector entry to get the address of the bound procedure descriptor for that vectored universal symbol and binds it to the procedure descriptor in the executive image.

      If the vectored universal symbol is the name of a system service transfer routine (that is, if its bound procedure descriptor is within SYS$PUBLIC_VECTORS.EXE), LDR$INIT_ALL initializes the procedure descriptor in the executive image to specify a default procedure signature, thereby enabling a translated image to request system services.

      Unless the executive image is removable, LDR$INIT_ALL replaces the symbol vector entry contents with the addresses of the procedure and its code entry point.

      After it has processed all entries, LDR$INIT_ALL deallocates the nonpaged pool structure, clears LDRIMG$L_GSTVA, and clears LDRIMG$V_GSTVA_VALID.

3. LDR$INIT_ALL tests whether the fixup data can be deallocated, that is, whether all needed pageable relocations and fixups have been done. If not, it proceeds with the next step. Otherwise, it also tests whether the PFN database has been initialized and, if not, proceeds with the next step.

If the PFN database has been initialized, the routine processes the SPTEs that map the fixup section. For each such page, it acquires the MMG spinlock. It determines the PFN occupied by the virtual page and changes its PFN database to reflect its new unused status. It increments PFN$GL_PHYPGCNT to show one more page of available memory, invokes MMG$DALLOC_PFN to release the page, clears the SPTE, and releases the MMG spinlock.

If the executive image containing the invalidate code has been loaded (if BOOSTATE$V_SWAPPER in EXE$GL_STATE is set), LDR$INIT_ALL triggers invalidation of its own processor's TB and that of any other SMP members.

It clears the fields in the LDRIMG that describe the fixup section, subtracts its pages from LDRIMG$L_PAGE_COUNT, and invokes LDR$DE-ALLOC_PT (see Section 32.9.2) to deallocate the SPTEs.

4. LDR$INIT_ALL tests whether the initialization procedure should be called again. If so, LDR$INIT_ALL invokes LDR$INIT_SINGLE (see Section 32.7.3) to call the initialization procedure and possibly release the pages of the section that contain it. If not, it releases the pages of the initialization section, as described in Section 32.7.3.

After processing the entire list, LDR$INIT_ALL performs second-pass fixups. It scans the LDRIMG list. For each image, it takes the following steps:

1. It tests whether any second-pass fixups need to be performed for this image. If not, it proceeds to the next image.

   If second-pass fixups need to be done, LDRIMG$L_SPFVA points to a nonpaged pool structure that contains a list of fixup entries. Each entry in the structure represents a linkage pair, procedure descriptor address, or code entry address. Each entry contains an identifying type, the address in the executive image to be fixed up, and the address of the corresponding SYS$BASE_IMAGE.EXE or SYS$PUBLIC_VECTORS.EXE symbol vector entry.

2. For each entry in the nonpaged pool structure, LDR$INIT_ALL examines the corresponding symbol vector entry to determine whether it still contains the address of a bound procedure descriptor in the specified base image. If not, LDR$INIT_ALL performs the fixup, replacing the reference in the executive image with the appropriate address or addresses in the other executive image.

3. For each fixup performed, LDR$INIT_ALL decrements the number of entries left in the nonpaged pool structure. If none is left, it deallocates the structure and clears LDRIMG$L_SPFVA and LDRIMG$V_SECOND_PASS_FIXUP.

LDR$INIT_ALL returns to its caller.

32.7.3   **Actions of LDR$INIT_SINGLE**

LDR$INIT_SINGLE performs the following steps:

1. It tests whether the value of LDRIMG$L_INIT_RTN is zero. If so, the routine proceeds to step 4.

2. Otherwise, it calls the routine whose procedure value is in LDRIMG$L_INIT_RTN. Although this mechanism allows for other possibilities, LDRIMG$L_INIT_RTN currently always contains the procedure value of INI$DOINIT. LDR$INIT_SINGLE passes two arguments, the address of the LDRIMG and possibly the address of a buffer. If the caller of LDR$LOAD_IMAGE specified the address of a user-defined buffer, its address has been passed to LDR$INIT_SINGLE, which passes it to the initialization procedure.

3. If INI$DOINIT returns an error status, LDR$INIT_SINGLE returns to its invoker.

4. LDR$INIT_SINGLE tests the flag LDRIMG$V_DELAY_INIT, which is set by INI$DOINIT when an initialization routine specifies that it must be reinvoked. If the flag is clear, LDR$INIT_SINGLE tests whether the PFN database has been initialized and, if not, returns to its invoker.

5. If the PFN database has been initialized, LDR$INIT_SINGLE tests if the virtual address space occupied by the initialization section has already been deallocated. If so, it returns to its invoker.

6. Otherwise, it calculates the number of pages of initialization routine and the first SPTE that maps these pages from the fields in the LDRIMG that describe the initialization routine section.

7. For each such page, LDR$INIT_SINGLE acquires the MMG spinlock. It determines the PFN occupied by the virtual page, if any, and the state of the virtual page. In the case of a transition page, it releases the MMG spinlock, accesses the page to trigger a page fault so that the page will be made valid, and reacquires the spinlock.

   It changes the PFN database to reflect the physical page's new unused status. It increments PFN$GL_PHYPGCNT to show one more page of available memory, invokes MMG$DALLOC_PFN to release the page, clears the SPTE, and releases the MMG spinlock.

8. LDR$INIT_SINGLE triggers invalidation of its own processor's TB and that of any other active SMP members.

9. It clears the fields in the LDRIMG that describe the deallocated initialization section except for LDRIMG$L_OFFSET and LDRIMG$L_END, whose contents are used during relocation and fixup. It tests whether the section is at the end of the loaded image. If so, it updates LDRIMG$L_PAGE_COUNT to reflect the deallocation of that address space and invokes LDR$DEALLOC_PT to insert the SPTEs that map the deallocated section into the free SPTE list. Section 32.9.2 describes the deallocation of system space.

10. It returns to its invoker.

32.7.4 **Actions of INI$DOINIT**

INI$DOINIT is the initialization procedure dispatcher. It performs the following steps:

1. It clears the flag LDRIMG$V_DELAY_INIT to implement its default of not scanning the initialization table again.
2. It scans the table.
3. For each entry, it tests and sets the INIRTN$V_NO_RECALL flag to implement its default of calling an initialization procedure only once. If the flag was already set, it goes on to the next entry.
4. If the flag was clear, INI$DOINIT calls the initialization procedure.

    If the initialization procedure determines that it should be reentered at a later stage of system initialization, it clears the INIRTN$V_NO_RECALL flag.
5. When the routine returns, INI$DOINIT sets flag INIRTN$V_CALLED to record that the procedure was called and tests INIRTN$V_NO_RECALL. If the flag is clear, INI$DOINIT sets LDRIMG$V_DELAY_INIT to ensure that LDR$INIT_SINGLE does not deallocate the initialization section and that INI$DOINIT will be recalled at a later stage of system initialization.

32.7.5 **Initialization Procedures**

An image-specific initialization procedure might do a number of things, including, but not limited to, the following:

▶ Initialize an SCB entry to describe an interrupt or exception service routine
▶ Initialize SYS$BASE_IMAGE.EXE globals
▶ Initialize data in the executive image
▶ Allocate pool for a data structure

Chapter 34 summarizes the actions of the initialization procedures for various executive images. One common initialization procedure, INI$SYSTEM_SERVICE, is part of many executive images.

INI$SYSTEM_SERVICE connects any inner mode system services in the executive image to the system service transfer routines and procedure descriptors in the loaded SYS$PUBLIC_VECTORS.EXE and assigns change mode numbers. Chapter 7 describes in detail the relations among SYS$PUBLIC_VECTORS.EXE's symbol vector, system service transfer routines, their procedure descriptors, and loaded services in executive images. (Connection of a mode of caller service to its transfer routine and procedure descriptor is done by LDR$LOAD_IMAGE.)

INI$SYSTEM_SERVICE is table-driven, using INI$A_BUILD_TABLE, a table of system service descriptor blocks within the image. The module DOINIT defines three PSECTs that build the table: EXEC$INIT_SSTBL_000 defines its start; EXEC$INIT_SSTBL_001 defines its body; and EXEC$INIT_SSTBL_002 defines its end with an entry of zero. Modules in an executive

1133

VECTOR_ADDRESS			
ENTRY_ADDRESS			
MODE	INHIBIT_MASK	FLAGS	*(reserved)*

Figure 32.7
Layout of a System Service Descriptor Block

image make entries in the body of its table by invoking the macro SYSTEM_ SERVICE. The macro initializes the fields in a system service descriptor block (see Figure 32.7) for each inner mode service.

Each system service descriptor block contains the following fields:

▸ SSDESCRDEF_A_VECTOR_ADDRESS—The address of the system service transfer routine's procedure descriptor within SYS$PUBLIC_VECTORS.EXE

▸ SSDESCRDEF_A_ENTRY_ADDRESS—The address of the procedure descriptor for the system service-specific procedure within the executive image

▸ SSDESCRDEF_B_FLAGS—Flags indicating, for example, whether the service can return the status SS$_WAIT_CALLERS_MODE and whether the scratch registers should be cleared after the service exits

▸ SSDESCRDEF_B_INHIBIT_MASK—The system service filter group

▸ SSDESCRDEF_B_MODE—A value indicating the access mode in which the system service procedure executes

The macro $SSDESCRDEF defines symbolic offsets for these fields, and Chapter 7 explains the significance of their contents.

INI$SYSTEM_SERVICE takes the following steps:

1. Because INI$SYSTEM_SERVICE requires process context to execute, it first tests a flag in EXE$GL_STATE to determine whether the swapper process has begun to execute. If not, the procedure clears INIRTN$V_ NO_RECALL so that the routine will be entered in process context, when paging is possible, and returns.

   If the swapper process has begun to execute, INI$SYSTEM_SERVICE proceeds.

2. It scans the system service descriptor block table. For each block it finds, it calls EXE$CONNECT_SERVICES, in module SYSTEM_SERVICE_LOADER, passing it the addresses of the system service descriptor block and the LDRIMG.

3. When INI$SYSTEM_SERVICE reaches the end of the table, it returns.

EXE$CONNECT_SERVICES takes the following steps:

1. It first gets the code entry point addresses of the system service transfer routine and the system service-specific procedure from their procedure descriptors.

2. It converts the virtual address of the system service transfer routine to a physical address. Rather than alter protection of the pages containing the transfer routines, it will access them using CALL_PAL LDQP and CALL_PAL STQP instructions.

3. It determines whether the service is kernel mode or executive mode.

4. It acquires write ownership of a mutex referred to as the change mode mutex, which prevents multiple processes from adding system services concurrently.

5. It examines the transfer routine to see whether this system service has previously been loaded. If so, it continues with step 15.

6. It performs several sanity checks on the system service transfer routine and, if they fail, generates the fatal bugcheck BADVECTOR.

7. If they are correct, EXE$CONNECT_SERVICES gets the change mode number to be assigned to this system service (from CMOD$GL_CHMK_LIMIT for kernel mode, CMOD$GL_CHME_LIMIT for executive mode) and tests that the number is less than or equal to 255, the maximum number. If it is not, EXE$CONNECT_SERVICES generates the fatal bugcheck SSVECFULL.

8. If the change mode number is less than or equal to 255, EXE$CON-NECT_SERVICES overwrites the system service transfer routine with an instruction to save the stack pointer (SP), an instruction to load the change mode number into R0, the appropriate change mode instruction, and a RET.

9. It executes an instruction memory barrier instruction (see Chapter 9) to flush any prefetched instructions in case any of those just rewritten had been prefetched and to ensure that the transfer routine is rewritten before subsequent writes to memory.

10. EXE$CONNECT_SERVICES records information from the system service descriptor block in arrays used by the change mode dispatchers. One set of arrays describes kernel mode system services; another set describes executive mode services. Each array is indexed by the change mode number of the service. Chapter 7 describes these arrays and their uses.

11. EXE$CONNECT_SERVICES increments CMODGL_CHMx$_LIMIT. (The change mode dispatcher compares the contents of that cell against the number associated with a change mode instruction to test whether it is within an executive image, as described in Chapter 7.)

12. If the executive image is either removable or is being loaded by the dynamic loader, EXE$CONNECT_SERVICES allocates nonpaged pool to record enough information about the inner mode services in the image so that they can be disconnected if the image is unloaded. It stores the address of the allocated pool in LDRIMG$L_SSVEC and initializes the pool with a longword containing the number of entries and one longword entry per service. Each entry contains the access mode in the low-order word and the assigned change mode number in the high-order word.

13. It releases the change mode mutex.

14. It returns to its caller.

15. For a service being reloaded, EXE$CONNECT_SERVICES makes additional sanity checks, generating the fatal bugcheck BADVECTOR if they fail. It extracts the assigned change mode number from the existing transfer routine and updates the arrays described in step 10 with information from the new image. It executes an instruction memory barrier instruction, releases the change mode mutex, and returns to its caller.

32.7.6   Actions of LDR$RELEASE_MEM

LDR$RELEASE_MEM, in module LDR_MEM_ALLOC, is called by image LDR$WRAP.EXE, which runs at the end of system initialization after sliced loading of executive images and installed resident images is complete.

It releases unused memory from huge pages, if appropriate, and completes executive image loading by performing second-pass fixups. It can also be invoked with its input argument set to the value 1 to force release of all unused memory in huge pages.

LDR$RELEASE_MEM takes the following steps:

1. It locks the base image mutex.

2. If the input argument is set, LDR$RELEASE_MEM releases all unused pages in the code huge page to the free page list.

3. LDR$RELEASE_MEM determines which types of huge page have been created. For each huge page created, it examines field LDR$Q_START-UP_PAGES in the loader huge page descriptor (LDRHP) for that huge page (see Figure 16.16). If the field contains zero, LDR$RELEASE_MEM records in it the number of pages used by slices allocated from the huge page. This information is normally recorded at the end of system initialization for use by the AUTOGEN utility. It releases unused portions of huge pages, if possible.

   - It tests SYSGEN parameter ITB_ENTRIES to determine whether a code huge page has been created. If so, it optionally reserves an unused portion for later installation of resident images, depending on SYSGEN parameter GH_RSRVPGCNT. The parameter specifies the number of pages to be reserved for later use. If the parameter is nonzero, LDR$RELEASE_MEM reserves a slice large enough for the larger of the unused portion and the value of the parameter. It deallocates to the free page list any physical pages that were not allocated or reserved and clears their bitmap entries in the LDRHP. It clears the SPTEs that mapped them and triggers invalidation of its own processor's TB and that of any other SMP members.

     A subsequent attempt to access these unused virtual pages will be translated, even though those pages are invalid, if any TB entry maps a valid page within the huge page. However, the protection on the valid pages in the region will result in faults for any access but attempted execution from such a page through the system virtual address that would have mapped it.

- If executive image slicing has been enabled, LDR$RELEASE_MEM examines the bitmap in the data huge page LDRHP. If space is left unused in the data huge page, it shrinks the huge page to a multiple of eight-page regions, deallocating the associated physical pages and SPTEs, as described for the code huge page.

  Unused physical pages within a data page granularity hint region, part of which is in use, cannot simply be deallocated. If they were deallocated and then reallocated for another use, the protection on the SPTEs that map the used pages could enable undesired read or write access to the reallocated pages. Instead, LDR$RELEASE_MEM transforms the two 64-page granularity hint regions that made up that huge page into a set of granularity hint regions, possibly one each of 64 pages, 32 pages, 16 pages, and 8 pages, in order to cover all the eight-page regions. It rewrites the SPTEs for the pages in use, modifying the granularity hint region bits as appropriate.

- It releases no pages from the huge page for systemwide data. That page is sized during system initialization for the areas it is to contain.

Chapter 15 describes the implications for address translation of releasing pages from a granularity hint region.

4. LDR$RELEASE_MEM performs any remaining possible second-pass fixups and deallocates all nonpaged pool structures pointed to by any executive image's LDRIMG$L_SPFVA field.
5. It releases the base image mutex.
6. It returns to its caller.

32.8 VERSION NUMBERS

The intent of dividing the executive into two base images and a number of executive images is to minimize the frequency with which images linked with SYS$BASE_IMAGE.EXE must relink. A change to an executive image does not alter the offsets of its vectored universal symbols in SYS$BASE_IMAGE.EXE's symbol vector. However, data structure and routine interface changes within an executive image may require algorithmic changes and reassembly of any images using its routines and data.

The operating system implements a form of internal system version identifier that can denote data structure and routine interface changes. This number is independent of the external OpenVMS version number. Because the executive organization does not tie a routine to a particular executive image, a version number for each executive image is not a good solution. Instead, the executive is divided into conceptual categories, such as I/O or memory management, each with its own version number. Table 32.3 lists these conceptual categories, each of which is identified by a number. The $SYS-VERSIONDEF macro defines symbols for these numbers.

Each SYS$BASE_IMAGE.EXE global symbol specifies the conceptual categories with which it is associated, through the VERSION_MASK keyword in the macro that defines the global symbol. Each bit in the mask corresponds to the number of a conceptual category. The macros that define SYS$BASE_IMAGE.EXE data cell and routine name symbols can be compiled to generate a mask global for each global.

For example, the routine EXE$ALLOCIRP, invoked to allocate an IRP, is associated with the category MEMORY_MANAGEMENT. The symbol PFN$AL_HEAD is also associated with that category. Extracts from SYSTEM_ROUTINES and SYSTEM_DATA_CELLS that define those symbols and their masks are shown in Examples 32.1 and 32.2.

Each category version number is a longword, with major ID in the high-order word and minor ID in the low-order word. Each is defined by a symbol named SYS$K_*category-name*. The category version numbers are defined in SYS$BASE_IMAGE.EXE.

The version number for a category changes when an interface in that category changes. The minor ID changes for an upwardly compatible change; the major ID changes for an incompatible change. For example, if a routine's input arguments or a data structure's fields are redefined, then images referencing that routine or data structure will not execute properly unless they are changed. In this case, the major ID is incremented. Examples of an upwardly compatible change are the addition of optional arguments to a routine and the use of data structure fields previously defined as spare.

Four of the modules that make up SYS$BASE_IMAGE.EXE are conditionally assembled to generate mask globals:

► SYSTEM_ROUTINES
► SYSTEM_DATA_CELLS
► SYSPARAM
► SHELL

The resulting object modules are concatenated to form a module called BASE_IMAGE.MASK. When SYS$BASE_IMAGE.EXE is linked, BASE_IMAGE.MASK is specified in the option statement MASK_TABLE. The linker checks whether each SYS$BASE_IMAGE.EXE global symbol is also defined in BASE_IMAGE.MASK. If it is, the linker creates another definition of the global symbol that is its mask value. The mask values are used when some other image links with SYS$BASE_IMAGE.EXE.

An image header includes space for an array of category version numbers. The first longword of the array contains a mask identifying which categories are relevant to the image. The image header field EIHD$L_SYSVER contains the overall system version number, with the major version number in the high-order byte and the minor version number in the low-order three bytes. When an image referencing a SYS$BASE_IMAGE.EXE masked global symbol is linked, the linker ORs the value of the corresponding mask global into

Table 32.3   Executive Version Categories

Category Name	Number	Description
BASE_IMAGE	0	Base image
MEMORY_MANAGEMENT	1	Memory management and dynamic pools
IO	2	I/O data structures and routines
FILES_VOLUMES	3	RMS and file system
PROCESS_SCHED	4	Process control, scheduling, and structure; layout of P1 space; timer events, ASTs, and event flags
SYSGEN	5	SYSGEN parameters
CLUSTERS_LOCKMGR	6	VMScluster connection manager, lock manager, and other clusterwide facilities
LOGICAL_NAMES	7	Logical names
SECURITY	8	Security subsystem
IMAGE_ACTIVATOR	9	Image activation and image file interpretation
NETWORKS	10	DECnet and support for datalink drivers
COUNTERS	11	Cells that are interpreted as counts
STABLE	12	Routines and data structures expected to be stable
MISC	13	Miscellaneous
CPU	14	CPU-specific support
VOLATILE	15	Routines and data structures expected to change in the next release
SHELL	16	Layout of the SHELL module and P1 space
POSIX	17	Data cells related to OpenVMS support of the Portable Operating System Interface (POSIX)
MULTI_PROCESSING	18	Routines and data structures related to symmetric multiprocessing support

the image's category mask longword. After all globals have been resolved, the mask has a bit set for each conceptual category relevant to the image. Starting from bit 0, the linker stores the relevant category version number constants from SYS$BASE_IMAGE.EXE's symbol vector into the subsequent longwords of the version array. There are no entries in the version array for categories not relevant to that image.

Example 32.4 shows an extract from the output of the DCL command ANALYZE/IMAGE SDA.EXE.

The BASE_IMAGE category describes the SYS$BASE_IMAGE.EXE layout

1139

Example 32.4
Extract from Output of ANALYZE/IMAGE SDA.EXE
Command

```
   .
   .
   .

SDA.EXE;1
ANALYZ A05-15


This is an OpenVMS Alpha image file

IMAGE HEADER


Fixed Header Information


  image format major id: 3, minor id: 0
  header block count: 3
  image type: executable (EIHD$K_EXE)
  I/O channel count: default
  I/O pagelet count: default
  Symbol Vector Virtual Address: %X'00000000'
  Symbol Vector Size: 0 bytes
  Virtual Memory Block Size: 65536 (BPAGE = 16)
  Fixup Section Virtual Address: %X'00110000'
  linker flags:
   (0)  EIHD$V_LNKDEBUG  0
   (1)  EIHD$V_LNKNOTFR  0
   (2)  EIHD$V_NOPOBUFS  0
   (3)  EIHD$V_PICIMG    1
   (4)  EIHD$V_POIMAGE   0
   (5)  EIHD$V_DBGDMT    1
   (6)  EIHD$V_INISHR    0
   (7)  EIHD$V_XLATED    0
   (8)  EIHD$V_BIND_CODE 0
   (9)  EIHD$V_BIND_DATA 0
  system version (major/minor): 3.0
  system version array information: (Image / Current System)
   SYS$K_MEMORY_MANAGEMENT : (1.64 / 1.64)
   SYS$K_PROCESS_SCHED     : (1.64 / 1.64)
   SYS$K_SYSGEN            : (1.64 / 1.64)
   SYS$K_STABLE            : (1.64 / 1.64)
   SYS$K_VOLATILE          : (1.64 / 1.64)
   SYS$K_MULTI_PROCESSING  : (1.0 / 1.0)
   .
   .
   .
```

rather than any particular conceptual category. The BASE_IMAGE minor ID is altered when a new universal procedure or data cell is added, so that an image using the new symbol cannot run on an older version. An alteration to the BASE_IMAGE major ID forces all images linked with SYS$BASE_IMAGE.EXE to be relinked before they can be activated. Required when the layout of SYS$BASE_IMAGE.EXE changes, this is expected to be rare.

The overall system version, SYS$K_VERSION, has for its major ID the major ID of the BASE_IMAGE category. Its minor ID represents the particular release or build; its use is reserved to the OpenVMS operating system.

SYS$BASE_IMAGE.EXE global SYS$GL_VERSION begins a 32-longword array of version numbers generated from the assembly of module VERSION_ NUMBERS. When an image linked with SYS$BASE_IMAGE.EXE is activated, the routine EXE$CHECK_VERSION, in module CHECK_VERSION, is invoked to compare the array of version numbers in its image header with the versions of the running executive. All of the following must be true:

▶ The major ID of the image must match the major ID of the running system.

▶ The minor ID must be less than or equal to that of the running system.

▶ The first longword of the EIHD version array contains a mask of conceptual executive categories relevant to the image. For each bit set in the mask, the major ID of the executive category at the time the image was linked must be equal to that of the category in the running system. The minor ID must be less than or equal to that of the category in the running system.

If the versions are incompatible, the image activator aborts the activation and returns the fatal error status SS$_SYSVERDIF.

32.9   DYNAMIC ALLOCATION AND DEALLOCATION OF SPTES

The executive implements dynamic allocation and deallocation of SPTEs. This enables more flexible allocation of system virtual address space than would be possible if all system virtual address space were assigned during system initialization. Instead, for example, virtual address space can be allocated for an executive image when it is loaded, and the space occupied by its initialization and fixup sections can be deallocated after they are no longer needed. (Even if the image is loaded sliced, its initialization and fixup sections are not loaded into a huge page.) The freed address space can be reused.

As described in Chapter 33 and Appendix F, SYSBOOT defines the initial size and layout of system space, based largely on SYSGEN parameter values. If there is insufficient system space, it can be expanded toward higher addresses during normal system operation.

Two routines in module PTALLOC maintain a list of available system pages:

▶ LDR$ALLOC_PT, which allocates SPTEs
▶ LDR$DEALLOC_PT, which deallocates SPTEs

Their actions are described in Sections 32.9.1 and 32.9.2.

The list of available pages of system space is kept within the available SPTEs themselves. Its listhead is at global cell LDR$GL_FREE_PT, which points to the first element on the list. Figure 32.8 shows the form of the list, with free SPTEs shaded.

Each element on the list represents a group of adjacent available SPTEs. The smallest group is one SPTE. A single available SPTE contains, in bits ⟨63 : 32⟩, a pointer to the next group. Bit 31 is set to identify the SPTE as the sole member of its group.

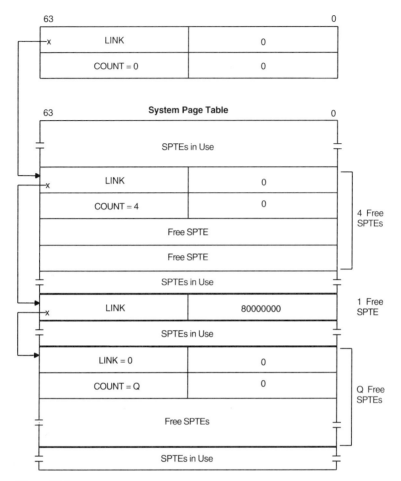

Figure 32.8
List of Available SPTEs

Two SPTEs are required to describe an element consisting of a group of two or more adjacent available SPTEs. The first SPTE points to the next group of free SPTEs; the second contains the number of SPTEs in this group.

The low-order 16 bits of each free SPTE, which include protection code bits and the valid bit, must be zero so that the SPTE appears to map an invalid page with all access prohibited.

A group of free SPTEs is identified by its quadword index from the beginning of the system page table (SPT), that is, by the virtual page number corresponding to the first free SPTE in that group. The quadword index of the next element is stored in bits $\langle 63 : 32 \rangle$ of the SPTE. (Each SPTE is a quadword.) For example, if LDR\$GL_FREE_PT + 4 contains 100_{16}, the first SPTE available for allocation is at offset $(100_{16} * 8)$ from the base of the SPT. The number of SPTEs in that group is at offset $(100_{16} * 8) + C_{16}$.

The SPTE allocation algorithm is first-fit and takes the lower end of a group of SPTEs if the group is larger than needed. The SPTE deallocation algorithm orders the list from smaller virtual page number to larger.

Much SPTE allocation occurs during system initialization, in SYSBOOT and EXE$INIT. These execute on the primary CPU of an SMP system at interrupt priority level (IPL) 31. When LDR$ALLOC_PT and LDR$DEALLOC_PT are invoked at later stages of initialization, they synchronize their accesses to the SPTE list by acquiring the MMG spinlock.

32.9.1   **Actions of LDR$ALLOC_PT**

LDR$ALLOC_PT is invoked with the number of SPTEs to be allocated. It takes the following steps:

1. If it is running after the swapper process has begun, it acquires the MMG spinlock, raising IPL to IPL$_MMG.
2. It scans the list of available SPTEs, starting with the group whose offset is stored in LDR$GL_FREE_PT + 4, looking for a large enough group.
3. If LDR$ALLOC_PT finds a group exactly the right size, it removes that group from the list by changing the forward pointer of the predecessor group to point to the next group.
4. If it finds a group larger than needed, it subtracts the number of SPTEs needed from the count longword. If the count is reduced to 1, LDR$ALLOC_PT sets bit 31 in the single available SPTE. It allocates the SPTEs at the low end of the group. It copies the pointer and count from the current beginning of the group to the longwords at the new beginning of the group and alters the longword pointing to the beginning of the group.
5. It zeros the allocated SPTEs and returns to its invoker the address of the lowest SPTE in the allocated group and a status of SS$_NORMAL.
6. If it cannot make the allocation, either because there are no free SPTEs or no group large enough, LDR$ALLOC_PT attempts to expand the SPT. An OpenVMS AXP SPT can be expanded to map higher addresses, as long as there is an unused level 2 PTE (L2PTE) to map a new page of the SPT. LDR$ALLOC_PT first calculates the L2PTE index corresponding to the highest system virtual address currently defined (the contents of PHD$L_FREP0VA, in the system header).
7. It calculates the number of SPTEs to be added, based on the request size and the number of any contiguous free SPTEs at the end of existing system space. If there are not enough L2PTEs to create that much system space, it returns the error status SS$_INSFSPTS to its invoker, releasing the MMG spinlock and lowering IPL if appropriate.

   The minimum number of SPTEs added at once is the number of SPTEs in a page of a level 3 page table (L3PT).
8. For each page of SPT to be added, LDR$ALLOC_PT allocates a physical page of memory. If it is unable to allocate a page of memory, it returns

the error status SS$_INSFSPTS to its invoker, releasing the MMG spin-lock and lowering IPL if appropriate.

If allocation was successful, LDR$ALLOC_PT updates the PFN database for that page to reflect its new status as an active system page. LDR$ALLOC_PT decrements PFN$GL_PHYPGCNT, the number of fluid physical pages. It initializes the L2PTE with the PFN of the physical page just allocated; a protection permitting kernel reads and writes; and valid, address space match, and fault-on-execute bits set. Chapter 16 describes the PFN database and the address translation algorithm.

9. It clears the newly allocated SPTEs, forms them into a group, and inserts the group into the free SPTE list. If the new SPTEs are adjacent to the last group on the list, LDR$ALLOC_PT merges them into that group.
10. LDR$ALLOC_PT allocates the requested SPTEs.
11. It updates PHD$L_FREP0VA and MMG$GL_FRESVA to reflect the new high end of system space and PHD$L_P0LENGTH, the new length in bytes of the SPT.
12. It releases the MMG spinlock, if it has been acquired, lowering IPL.

32.9.2 Actions of LDR$DEALLOC_PT

LDR$DEALLOC_PT is invoked with the address of the lowest SPTE in the group to be deallocated and the number of SPTEs in the group. The invoker must have already deallocated any physical memory associated with the SPTEs, invalidated cached TB entries, and zeroed the SPTEs.

LDR$DEALLOC_PT takes the following steps:

1. If it is running after the swapper process has begun, it acquires the MMG spinlock, raising IPL to IPL$_MMG.
2. It first checks that the SPTEs all contain zero. If they do not, it releases the spinlock, lowering IPL, and returns the error status LOADER$_PTE_NOT_EMPTY to its invoker.
3. Otherwise, it scans the list of available SPTEs, looking for the first group whose address is higher than that of the group being deallocated.
4. It inserts the group being deallocated at that point and checks if it can be merged with the group on either side of it. It makes whatever merges are possible, altering pointers and count longwords as appropriate.
5. It releases the spinlock, if it has been acquired, lowering IPL, and returns the status SS$_NORMAL to its invoker.

32.10 RELEVANT SOURCE MODULES

Source modules described in this chapter include

[LIB]BOOSTATEDEF.SDL
[LIB]EXEC_REORG_MACROS.MAR

[LIB]INIRTNDEF.SDL
[LIB]LDRDEF.SDL
[LIB]LDRIMGDEF.SDL
[LIB]VECTORS.SDL
[SYS]ALTERNATE_LOAD.MAR
[SYS]DOINIT.MAR
[SYS]LDR_MEM_ALLOC.B64
[SYS]LDR_MEM_INIT.B64
[SYS]LDR_RELOCATE_FIXUP.B64
[SYS]PTALLOC.MAR
[SYS]SYSLDR.MAR
[SYS]SYSLDR_COMMON.MAR
[SYS]SYSLDR_DYN.MAR
[SYS]SYSTEM_SERVICE_LOADER.MAR

33 Bootstrap Processing

Ante mare et terras et quod tegit omnia caelum unus erat toto
naturae vultus in orbe, quem dixere chaos: rudis indigestaque
moles.
[Before the sea was, and the lands, and the sky that hangs over
all, the face of Nature showed all alike, which state has been
called chaos: a rough unordered mass of things.]

Ovid, *Metamorphoses* I, 5–7

The process by which the OpenVMS AXP operating system assumes control
of a system is called system initialization. System initialization occurs in
two phases. In the first phase, a series of stand-alone programs (often called
bootstrap programs) initialize system hardware blocks and load part of the
executive into memory. In the second phase, the rest of the executive is
loaded and initialized.

This chapter describes the first phase of system initialization, Chapter 34
describes the next phase, and Chapter 37 describes the portions of system
initialization specific to a symmetric multiprocessing (SMP) system.

33.1 OVERVIEW OF SYSTEM INITIALIZATION

System initialization requires a number of programs. Some of them run prior
to the establishment of an operating system environment; others execute in
system context; and others, in process context. In general, the executive post-
pones each initialization task to as late a stage of initialization as possible
because initialization is progressively easier as more of the operating system
becomes available.

The sequence of operations that occurs during system initialization is
shown in Figure 33.1 and outlined in the following list:

1. The console subsystem initializes the processors; locates enough good
   memory for APB, the AXP primary bootstrap program; sets up APB's initial environment; loads privileged architecture library code (PALcode);
   loads APB; and transfers control to it. Section 33.2 summarizes the console's role in system initialization.
2. APB runs stand-alone at interrupt priority level (IPL) 31. In an SMP system, APB runs on the processor selected to be the primary by the console
   subsystem. It loads the secondary bootstrap program and transfers control to it. Section 33.3 describes APB.
3. SYSBOOT, the AXP secondary bootstrap program, also runs stand-alone
   at IPL 31. Based on parameters from the System Generation (SYSGEN)

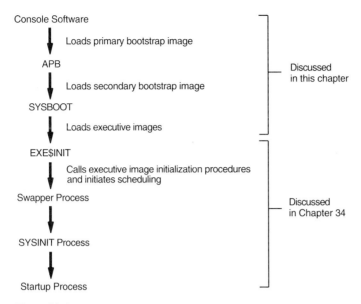

Figure 33.1
System Initialization Overview

utility parameter file and the console operator, it creates the system page table (SPT) and maps system virtual address space. It loads into memory the system base images and several executive images.

SYSBOOT then transfers control to EXE$INIT, the executive initialization procedure. Section 33.4 describes SYSBOOT.

4. Running at IPL 31, EXE$INIT, in the executive image EXEC_INIT, loads many of the remaining executive images and calls each loaded executive image's initialization procedure. The executive images initialize the scheduler, memory management, spinlock, and I/O databases, and perform other operations.

EXE$INIT then configures and starts secondary CPUs (see Chapter 37) and calls SCH$INIT, the scheduler routine that lowers IPL from 31 to IPL$_RESCHED and initiates scheduling. SCH$INIT places the swapper process into execution (see Chapter 34).

5. Initialization code that runs in the context of the swapper process performs the minimum processing that must complete in process context before any other processes can be created. Its tasks include initializing paged pool and the pageable logical name database, and invoking executive image initialization routines that require process context to execute. The swapper creates the SYSINIT process.

6. The SYSINIT process performs initialization tasks that must be done in process context and that do not lend themselves to Digital command

language (DCL) commands. These include opening the swap and page files, initializing VMScluster software, and creating the startup process.

7. The startup process maps DCL and can thus execute a series of DCL commands. It executes the command procedure SYS$SYSTEM:START-UP.COM, which processes other command procedures and data files in the SYS$STARTUP directory. The various command procedures create system processes, such as OPCOM and JOB_CONTROL. They create systemwide logical names, use the System Management (SYSMAN) utility to autoconfigure the I/O database, and install images specified by the VMSIMAGES.DAT data file. The startup process executes a series of site-specific command procedures and finally enables interactive login.

From SYSBOOT onward, the files and programs used in bootstrap operations are primarily independent of processor type. Table 33.1 lists bootstrap programs and processes used during system initialization, the files they process, and the function of each file.

In theory, most operations performed by APB, SYSBOOT, and EXEC_INIT could potentially be performed by a single bootstrap program. However, they have been left as distinct entities for the following reasons:

▶ For facilitating the porting of VAX VMS.
▶ If there should ever be a need to load a secondary bootstrap program other than SYSBOOT, the separation between APB and SYSBOOT would be convenient.
▶ Certain pieces of initialization cannot be done by SYSBOOT because they would affect the execution of SYSBOOT itself; hence they must be done by another piece of initialization code such as EXE$INIT. For example, modification of the boot hardware privileged context block (HWPCB) cannot be done within SYSBOOT.

33.2 CONSOLE SUBSYSTEM

The preliminary steps in the initialization of the system depend on the particular AXP system being booted. The console subsystem, or simply, the console, is the part of the system that assumes control when the system is powered on. It performs the following tasks:

▶ It initializes, tests, and prepares the system for system software.
▶ It loads system software into memory and transfers control to it.
▶ It provides services to system software that simplify control of and access to the system hardware.
▶ It provides a means for an operator to monitor and control the system hardware.
▶ It controls and monitors the state and state transitions of each processor in an SMP system.

Table 33.1   Files and Programs Used During System Initialization

Files Accessed	*Function of File*
	SYSBOOT
ALPHAVMSSYS.PAR and other parameter files	System configuration parameters
ERRORLOG.EXE	Error logging routines and system services
EXEC_INIT.EXE	Next image in bootstrap sequence
PAGEFILE.SYS	Primary page file, located and sized if dump file not found
SYS$BASE_IMAGE.EXE	System base image
SYSDUMP.DMP	System dump file, located and sized for later use
SYSTEM_DEBUG.EXE	System debugger (XDELTA), conditionally loaded
SYSTEM_PRIMITIVES_ xxx.EXE	Basic system support routines (one of two—see Chapter 21)
SYSTEM_SYNCHRONIZA- TION_xxx.EXE	SMP synchronization image (one of three—see Chapter 9)
SYS$CPU_ROUTINES_ xxyy.EXE	CPU-specific routines
SYS$OPDRIVER.EXE	Console terminal port driver
SYS$PUBLIC_VECTORS.EXE	System service vector base image
SYS$xxBTDRIVER.EXE	One or more system device boot drivers
	EXEC_INIT
CPULOA.EXE	Tables of CPU data
EXCEPTION.EXE	Exception service routines and system services, bugcheck routines
F11BXQP.EXE	File system support
IMAGE_MANAGE- MENT.EXE	Image activation services and routines
IO_ROUTINES.EXE	I/O-related routines and system services
LMF$GROUP_TABLE.EXE	Tables of license data
LOCKING.EXE	Lock management routines and system services
LOGICAL_NAMES.EXE	Logical name routines and system services
MESSAGE_ROUTINES.EXE	Message routines and system services
MSCP.EXE	Mass storage control protocol (MSCP) server
PROCESS_MANAGE- MENT.EXE	Scheduling routines, process creation and control system services
SECURITY.EXE	Security-related routines and system services
SHELLxxK.EXE	Process shell, where xx is 8, 16, 32, or 64
SYS$CLUSTER.EXE	VMScluster support, conditionally loaded
SYS$NETWORK_ SERVICES.EXE	DECnet support
SYS$SCS.EXE	System communication services, conditionally loaded
SYS$TRANSACTION_ SERVICES.EXE	Digital Distributed Transaction Management (DECdtm) support
SYS$TTDRIVER.EXE	Terminal class driver

(continued)

Table 33.1   Files and Programs Used During System Initialization *(continued)*

Files Accessed	*Function of File*
	EXEC_INIT
SYS$UTC_SERVICES.EXE	Universal time coordinates-related system services
SYS$VCC.EXE	Virtual I/O cache support routines
SYS$VM.EXE	Page fault service and related routines, virtual address space system service routines, swapper and supporting routines, and related system services
SYS$xxDRIVER.EXE	One or more run-time drivers for the system device
SYSDEVICE.EXE	Pseudo device drivers and mailbox system services
SYSGETSYI.EXE	$GETSYI system service
SYSLICENSE.EXE	$LICENSE system service
SYSLDR_DYN.EXE	Dynamic executive image loader
	SYSINIT PROCESS
DDIF$RMS_EXTEN-SION.EXE	Support for Digital Document Interchange Format (DDIF) file operations
PAGEFILE.SYS	System page file
QUORUM.DAT	VMScluster system quorum file
RECOVERY_UNIT_SERVICES.EXE	Record Management Services (RMS) recovery services
RMS.EXE	RMS
SYS$INCARNATION.DAT	VMScluster system incarnation file
SYSMSG.EXE	System message file
SWAPFILE.SYS	System swap file
	STARTUP PROCESS
DCL.EXE	CLI, mapped into P1 space to interpret and execute commands
DCLTABLES.EXE	Command tables, mapped into P1 space and used by DCL.EXE
LOGINOUT.EXE	First image that runs in startup process
STARTUP.COM	SYS$INPUT for startup process
SATELLITE_PAGE.COM	VMScluster satellite page file installation
SYCONFIG.COM	Site-specific device configuration command procedure
SYLOGICALS.COM	Site-specific logical names
SYPAGSWPFILES.COM	Site-specific page and swap files
SYSTARTUP_V5.COM	Site-specific startup command procedure
VMS$LAYERED.DAT	Procedure definition data file for layered products
VMS$PHASES.DAT	Startup phase definition data file
VMS$VMS.DAT	Procedure definition data file the operating system
Various	Procedures and images defined by previous two data files

Table 33.1   Files and Programs Used During System Initialization *(continued)*

Files Accessed	*Function of File*
INSTALL UTILITY, IN CONTEXT OF STARTUP PROCESS	
VMSIMAGES.DAT	List of images to be installed
All installed images	Set up as known images
SYSGEN UTILITY, IN CONTEXT OF STARTUP PROCESS	
ALPHAVMSSYS.PAR	SYSGEN parameters
SYSMAN UTILITY, IN CONTEXT OF STARTUP PROCESS	
Various device drivers	I/O database and device initialization

This section describes aspects of the console that are relevant to a basic understanding of AXP system initialization. For other information about the console, see the *Alpha AXP Architecture Reference Manual* and the installation and technical guides for a particular Alpha system.

The basic elements of an AXP console subsystem include a processor, software to run on it, storage for the software, and a terminal. Storage can be on a primary medium, such as nonvolatile read-only memory (NVROM), or on a secondary medium, such as disk or tape. (No current AXP system provides secondary storage for console software.)

The console processor runs console software to implement console functionality. There is no requirement that this be a separate and distinct processor. In fact, on all current AXP systems the console processor is also the AXP processor.

Console software gives the console operator access to all required console functionality at all times, even when console software runs on a console processor that is also the AXP processor.

An SMP system has only one primary processor and one or more secondary processors. Any processor that can access the console terminal, console I/O devices, and the system's battery-backed watch is capable of being the primary processor.

The mechanism by which the primary processor is chosen depends on the implementation. Only the primary processor can be the console processor. Secondary processors communicate with the console terminal through the primary processor.

Console storage is an area from which console software is loaded. Typically, it is nonvolatile read-only memory. Unlike many VAX consoles, AXP consoles do not generally have secondary storage such as disk or tape. For this reason, AXP consoles do not generally support console command procedures. (Note that remote software that behaves like a console operator by connecting to the console terminal can execute a series of console commands to achieve the effect of a console command procedure.)

The console operator is a human operator or remote software that can monitor and control the console's actions through the console terminal. Console software displays messages to and accepts commands from the console operator through the console terminal. The operating system uses the console terminal to display messages during system initialization, during a crash, and at other times, for example, to print security, error logging, and operator request messages. Section 33.2.5.3 provides information on console terminal routines through which the executive accesses the console terminal.

The interaction of console software with the operating system is through the following:

► Environment variables, a few of which allow the console operator to control some of the console's actions and communicate information about the booting environment to the operating system (see Section 33.2.3)

► Console callback routines, which allow the operating system to access console functionality directly (see Section 33.2.4)

► The hardware restart parameter block (HWRPB), which contains information shared between console software and the operating system (see Section 33.2.5)

PALcode, briefly described in Chapter 1, is part of console software. Console software typically loads PALcode from console storage into system memory prior to system bootstrap, as outlined in Section 33.2.2.

Upon power up, console software locates and initializes system hardware blocks. Next, it examines the environment variable AUTO_ACTION (see Section 33.2.3). If AUTO_ACTION is set to BOOT or RESTART, console software initiates a cold bootstrap sequence, described in Section 33.2.2. If AUTO_ACTION is set to HALT, console software enters the Halted state, displaying the following prompt at the console terminal and awaiting commands from the console operator: >>>.

In response to a BOOT command, described in Section 33.2.1, console software initiates a bootstrap.

33.2.1   BOOT Console Command

Console software attempts to locate, load and transfer the primary bootstrap program from the boot devices specified in the BOOT console command, which has the following form:

```
>>>BOOT [-FLAGS SYSTEM_ROOT,BOOT_FLAGS] [DEVICE_LIST] [-FILE FILE_NAME]
```

The qualifier –FLAGS indicates that the next two comma-separated strings are the parameters SYSTEM_ROOT and BOOT_FLAGS. Console software passes both parameters to APB without interpretation as an ASCII string such as 0,0 in the environment variable BOOTED_OSFLAGS. The qualifier –FILE specifies the name of the primary bootstrap program file for network initial system load (ISL) bootstrap.

The parameter SYSTEM_ROOT specifies the hexadecimal number of the root directory on the system disk device in which the bootstrap files and programs listed in Table 33.1 reside. A root directory is a top-level directory whose name is of the form SYS*nn*, where *nn* is the number specified by SYSTEM_ROOT.

The parameter BOOT_FLAGS specifies the hexadecimal representation of the sum of the desired boot flags. Table 33.2 lists possible boot flags and their values. The operating system defines names for these flags in the $SWRPBDEF macro. For simplicity, the names are shown in the table without the prefix SWRPB_BOOT_FLAGS$V_.

The parameter DEVICE_LIST is a list of device names, delimited by commas, from which the console must attempt to boot. A device name in DEVICE_LIST does not necessarily correspond to the OpenVMS device name for a given device. In fact, console software translates the device name to an internal path name before it attempts bootstrap. The internal path name enables the console to locate the boot device through intervening adapters, buses, and widgets. The internal path name specification and the algorithm that translates the device name to an internal path name are system-specific.

The BOOT_DEV environment variable contains the device list used by the most recent or currently in-progress bootstrap attempt. Console software modifies BOOT_DEV at console initialization and when a BOOT console command is issued. BOOT_DEV is initialized from the DEVICE_LIST argument or, if the argument is not specified, from the BOOTDEF_DEV environment variable (see Section 33.2.3).

In response to the BOOT console command, console software attempts to load the primary bootstrap program from devices in the boot device list, starting with the first one. As it attempts to load from a specific device, console software initializes the BOOTED_DEV environment variable with the path name of that device. If an attempt to load the primary bootstrap program from a specific device fails, console software attempts to load it from the next device in the list. If all attempts fail, console software prints an error message on the console and enters the Halted state to await operator action. Section 33.2.6 outlines the steps involved in primary bootstrap program loading.

Later, APB uses the value in BOOTED_DEV to determine the boot device.

33.2.2 Initialization Performed by Console Software

Before transferring control to the primary bootstrap program, console software performs either a cold or a warm bootstrap, depending on whether the

Table 33.2   Boot Flags

Hexadecimal Value	Name	Meaning if Set
1	CONV	Bootstrap conversationally, that is, allow the console operator to modify SYSGEN parameters in SYSBOOT
2	DEBUG	Map XDELTA to running system
4	INIBPT	Stop at initial system breakpoint
8	DIAG	Perform diagnostic bootstrap
10	BOOBPT	Stop at bootstrap breakpoints
20	NOHEADER	Secondary bootstrap image contains no header
40	NOTEST	Inhibit memory test
80	SOLICIT	Prompt for the name of the secondary bootstrap file
100	HALT	Halt before secondary bootstrap
200	SHADOW	Reserved
400	ISL	Unused, reserved
800	PALCHECK	Disable PALcode revision check halt
1000	DEBUG_BOOT	Reserved
2000	CRDFAIL	Mark corrected read data error pages bad
4000	ALIGN_FAULTS	Report bootstrap unaligned data traps
8000	BIT15	Reserved
10000	DBG_INIT	Enable verbose mode [1] in APB, SYSBOOT, EXEC_INIT, SWAPPER, and SYSINIT
20000	USER_MSGS	Enable a subset of verbose mode [1] messages

[1] Verbose mode enables a number of console messages to be printed that would normally be suppressed; these messages are useful when the executive is being debugged and to determine the point of failure during system initialization if the system will not boot.

system must be fully or partly initialized. Typically, console software does this in response to a BOOT console command, an operating system reboot request, or an error halt that occurs when the AUTO_ACTION environment variable has been set to BOOT.

By default console software always attempts a warm bootstrap unless a cold bootstrap is implicitly (through the BOOT_RESET environment variable) or explicitly requested. A warm bootstrap is possible only if a previous cold bootstrap has already initialized the hardware blocks and the console software data structures, in particular, the HWRPB. Console software verifies this by checking the consistency of the HWRPB. Performing a warm bootstrap is faster and more efficient because console software can skip certain initial steps, such as initializing hardware blocks and building console software data structures, that it must perform during a cold bootstrap.

Console software always performs a cold bootstrap in response to the following:

▶ The first BOOT command after the system is powered up
▶ The INITIALIZE console command when the AUTO_ACTION environment variable has been set to BOOT (see Section 33.2.3)
▶ The BOOT console command or an error halt condition when the BOOT_RESET environment variable has been set to ON and the AUTO_ACTION environment variable is not set to RESTART (see Section 33.2.3)
▶ A request from the executive to perform a cold reboot

The following list summarizes console actions for a cold bootstrap. All console implementations do not necessarily perform the steps in this order.

1. It selects the primary processor. The bootstrap sequence executes in a uniprocessor environment; secondary processors are not activated until executive initialization occurs.
2. Console software locates and initializes CPU, memory, and I/O modules.
3. It determines the amount of physical memory available on the system and tests a sufficient amount for the following components:
   • PALcode memory and scratch areas
   • Console software data structures and routines that are shared by the operating system
   • Page tables for bootstrap virtual address space
   • The primary bootstrap program
   • The initial boot stack
4. It builds the HWRPB and its associated substructures, as described in Section 33.2.5.
5. Console software loads PALcode from console storage into memory. It records the physical addresses and sizes of the PALcode memory and scratch areas in the appropriate per-CPU slot (SLOT) of the HWRPB (see Section 33.2.5.1). It initializes SLOT$IQ_STATE to indicate that PALcode memory is valid and that PALcode is loaded and valid (see Table 33.7).
6. It creates level 1, 2, and 3 page tables, shown in Figure 33.2, for bootstrap virtual address space. The layout of bootstrap virtual address space at the time the primary bootstrap program gains control is shown in Figure 33.3. Chapter 15 describes page tables and memory management.
7. It maps the HWRPB and console callback routines into bootstrap address space beginning at virtual address 10000000_{16}.
8. It locates and loads APB, as described in Section 33.2.6.
9. Console software builds a HWPCB in the per-CPU slot for the primary processor (see Section 33.2.5.2). It initializes HWPCB$IQ_KSP with the high-end address of the bootstrap stack and HWPCB$IQ_PTBR with the page frame number (PFN) of the L1PT. It then sets SLOT$V_CV in SLOT$IQ_STATE to indicate that the HWPCB is valid.

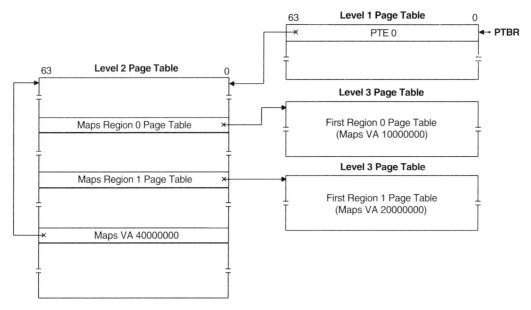

Figure 33.2
Bootstrap Page Tables

10. It initializes every processor to the state shown in Table 33.3.
11. It transfers control to the first longword of APB in kernel mode at IPL 31 with memory management enabled.

33.2.3 Environment Variables

The console subsystem communicates information through environment variables to the console operator and the operating system. Also, a console operator or the operating system can control some of the console's actions by setting certain environment variables. A console operator accesses environment variables through console commands; the operating system accesses environment variables through console callback routines (see Section 33.2.5.4).

An environment variable consists of an identifier and an associated ASCII string. The identifier is a numeric value between 0 and FF_{16}. The Alpha AXP architecture divides environment variables into three categories based on identifier value, as shown in Table 33.4.

Table 33.5 summarizes environment variables common to all system implementations. A console operator identifies an environment variable by its name. The operating system uses the numeric identifiers to access environment variables. The $HWRPBDEF macro defines symbolic values for the environment variables with names as listed in Table 33.5 and the prefix HWRPB_CRB$K_.

Two undocumented system services, Get Environment Variable ($GET-

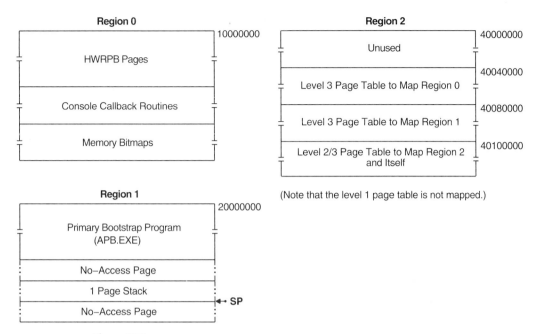

Figure 33.3
Bootstrap Virtual Address Space after APB Is Loaded

ENV) and Set Environment Variable ($SETENV), allow read and write access to console environment variables through an appropriate console callback routine. The undocumented DCL lexical function F$GETENV can be used to retrieve the value of a console environment variable. Use of either system service and the lexical function F$GETENV is reserved to Digital; any other use is unsupported. Chapter 39 contains more information about these system services.

33.2.4 Console Callback Routines

The term *callback routine* describes a routine in console software that the operating system can call. Console software provides the operating system with a set of callback routines to perform I/O operations to console subsystem devices, to access environment variables, and to perform address fixups (see Section 33.2.5.5) within the callback routines if they need to be remapped in system virtual address space. Console callback routines are in bootstrap address space. After the operating system creates system virtual address space, it deletes bootstrap address space. To continue to use console callback routines, the operating system must call the address fixup callback routine to remap them into system address space before it deletes bootstrap address space.

A console callback routine can be called only in kernel mode and only with the HWRPB and all console callback routines virtually mapped. Table 33.6

Table 33.3   Processor State Immediately Prior to Primary Bootstrap

Processor Register	Initialized State
Address space number (ASN)	0
AST enable (ASTEN)	0 (all disabled)
AST summary (ASTSR)	0
Floating enable (FEN)	0 (disabled)
Interrupt priority level (IPL)	31
Machine check error summary (MCES)	8
Privileged context block base (PCBB)	Virtual address of processor's HWPCB
Processor status (PS)	IPL 31, all else is 0
Page table base (PTBR)	PFN of level 1 page table (L1PT)
Software interrupt summary (SISR)	0
Who am I (WHAMI)	Processor number
System cycle counter (SCC)	0
Process cycle counter (PCC)	0
Stack pointer (SP)	20000000_{16} + (size of APB.EXE) + 2 $*$ (page size)—see Figure 33.3
Kernel stack pointer (KSP)	Same as SP
Other internal processor registers	Unpredictable
Other integer registers	Unknown
Floating-point registers	Unknown

Table 33.4   Numerical Ranges for Environment Variables

Range	Description
$0–3F_{16}$	Common to all system implementations
$40_{16}–7F_{16}$	Specific to a system implementation
$80_{16}–FF_{16}$	Specific to system software

lists common console callback routines. The $HWRPBDEF macro defines symbolic values for the console callback routines with names as shown in the table and the prefix HWRPB_CRB$K_.

Some console callback routines modify their operating context and can be called only during system bootstrap or crash, when the operating system is not fully functional.

Other console callback routines do not modify their operating context and can be called in any environment.

The executive performs all console terminal I/O through the console terminal callback routines. All console callback routines except FIXUP are indirectly entered through the DISPATCH callback routine. Section 33.2.5.4 describes how the operating system locates and calls console callback routines.

33.2.5   **Hardware Restart Parameter Block**

The HWRPB contains information that is shared between the console and the operating system. Console software creates the HWRPB in physically contiguous memory during console initialization and uses it during and after bootstrap. Before passing control to APB, console software maps the HWRPB in bootstrap space at virtual address 10000000_{16}. During system initialization SYSBOOT remaps the HWRPB into system virtual address space and records its address in global location EXE\$GPQ_HWRPB.

Figure 33.4 shows the HWRPB. Significant fields of the HWRPB are briefly

Table 33.5   Standard Environment Variables

ID	Symbol	Key[2]	Description
1	AUTO_ACTION [1]	NV, W	Console action following power on or an error halt. Set to BOOT, HALT, or RESTART.
2	BOOT_DEV	W	Device list used by the most recent or in-progress bootstrap attempt. The console derives the value from BOOTDEF_DEV at console initialization.
3	BOOTDEF_DEV [1]	NV, W	Default bootstrap device list for BOOT command.
4	BOOTED_DEV	RO	Specific device used by the most recent or in-progress bootstrap attempt (see BOOT_DEV).
5	BOOT_FILE [1]	NV, W	Default bootstrap file name.
6	BOOTED_FILE [1]	RO	Bootstrap file name used by the most recent or in-progress bootstrap attempt.
7	BOOT_OSFLAGS	NV, W	Default value for the –FLAGS BOOT command qualifier to be passed to APB.
8	BOOTED_OSFLAGS	RO	Value of the –FLAGS BOOT command qualifier during the most recent or in-progress bootstrap attempt.
9	BOOT_RESET [1]	NV, W	When set to ON, indicates a cold bootstrap must be performed in response to an error halt or BOOT command.

(continued)

Table 33.5 Standard Environment Variables *(continued)*

ID	Symbol	Key[2]	Description
A_{16}	DUMP_DEV[1]	NV, W	Crash dump device.
B_{16}	ENABLE_AUDIT[1]	NV, W	When set to ON, enables display of audit trail messages during bootstrap.
C_{16}			Reserved.
D_{16}	CHAR_SET[1]	NV, W	Current console terminal character-set encoding.
E_{16}	LANGUAGE[1]	NV, W	Current console terminal language.
F_{16}	TTY_DEV	NV, W, RO	Current console terminal unit.

[1] Although console software uses these variables, the operating system does not currently access them. Note that the operating system does provide system services to access environment variables.

[2] NV—Nonvolatile. The last value saved by system software or set by console commands is preserved across system initializations, cold bootstraps, and long power outages.

W—Warm nonvolatile. The last value set by system software is preserved across warm bootstraps and restarts.

RO—Read-only. The variable cannot be modified by system software or console commands.

described here. The HWRPB has a number of substructures, which are described in subsequent sections.

HWRPB$PQ_BASE contains the physical address of the HWRPB, and HWRPB$IQ_IDENT contains the null-terminated ASCII string HWRPB. Both fields are used by the console to validate the HWRPB. HWRPB$IQ_REVISION identifies the format of the HWRPB. HWRPB$IQ_SIZE contains the size in bytes of the HWRPB.

HWRPB$IQ_PRIMARY contains the processor ID of the primary processor in an SMP system.

HWRPB$IQ_PAGESIZE contains the number of bytes within a page for this processor. HWRPB$IQ_PA_SIZE contains the number of bits needed to represent the highest physical address for the system. The Alpha AXP architecture restricts this number to 48 or less. HWRPB$IQ_ASN_MAX contains the maximum address space number value allowed by this processor. Chapter 15 describes AXP physical and virtual address representations.

Information on the state of a processor is maintained in the per-CPU slot of the HWRPB (see Section 33.2.5.1). Information in HWRPB$IQ_PAGESIZE, HWRPB$IQ_PA_SIZE, and HWRPB$IQ_ASN_MAX is common to all processors. For an SMP system, this implies that all processors on the system must implement the same page size, the same number of physical address bits, and the same ASN scheme.

HWRPB$B_SYS_SERIALNUM contains a ten-byte ASCII serial number stored in the system at the time of manufacture. HWRPB$IQ_SYSTYPE

Table 33.6   Common Console Callback Routines

Value	Name	Description
		CONSOLE TERMINAL ROUTINES
1	GETC	Get character from console terminal
2	PUTS	Put byte stream to console terminal
3	RESET_TERM	Reset console terminal to default
4	SET_TERM_INTR	Enable or disable console terminal interrupts
5	SET_TERM_CTL	Enable or disable console terminal controls
6	PROCESS_KEYCODE [1]	Process and translate keycode
7–F_{16}		Reserved
		CONSOLE GENERIC DEVICE I/O ROUTINES
10_{16}	OPEN	Open I/O device for access
11_{16}	CLOSE	Close I/O device for access
12_{16}	IOCTL	Perform I/O device-specific operation
13_{16}	READ	Read I/O device
14_{16}	WRITE	Write I/O device
15_{16}–$1F_{16}$		Reserved
		CONSOLE ENVIRONMENT VARIABLE ROUTINES
20_{16}	SET_ENV	Write an environment variable
21_{16}	RESET_ENV	Reset an environment variable to its default
22_{16}	GET_ENV	Read an environment variable
23_{16}	SAVE_ENV [2]	Save current environment variable
		CONSOLE MISCELLANEOUS ROUTINES
30_{16}	PSWITCH	Switch primary processor
None	FIXUP	Remap console callback routines
None	DISPATCH	Dispatch to console callback routine

[1] Some console implementations may not provide this routine.
[2] Most console implementations do not provide this routine.

contains the system type. HWRPB$IQ_SYSVAR contains system variation information, for example, whether the system is multiprocessor capable, or whether it has an embedded graphics controller. HWRPB$IQ_SYSREV contains a four-byte ASCII string that indicates system revision information.

HWRPB$IQ_CLOCK_INT_FREQ contains 4,096 times the number of interval timer interrupts per second. HWRPB$IQ_CYCLE_COUNT_FREQ contains the number of times per second the system cycle counter and process cycle counter are updated. Chapter 12 describes interval timer interrupts and these counters.

HWRPB$IQ_CRB_OFFSET contains the byte offset to the HWRPB_CRB, the console routine block (see Section 33.2.5.4); and HWRPB$IQ_MEM_OFF-

Figure 33.4
Hardware Restart Parameter Block (HWRPB)

SET contains the byte offset to the HWRPB_PMD, the physical memory descriptor table (see Section 33.2.5.5).

After system initialization HWRPB$IQ_RESTART will contain the virtual address of the code entry point of EXE$RESTART, the processor restart routine. HWRPB$IQ_RESTART_PD will contain the virtual address of its procedure descriptor. Together, these two fields form a linkage pair. Chapter 36 describes EXE$RESTART and the circumstances under which it is entered.

HWRPB$PQ_SWRPB contains the physical address of the software restart parameter block (SWRPB), described in Section 33.3.1.

HWRPB$IQ_CHKSUM contains the checksum of all quadwords from the beginning of the HWRPB up to and including the quadword at HWRPB$IQ_HARDWARE1. The checksum is computed as a 64-bit 2's complement sum ignoring overflows. It is used to validate the HWRPB during warm bootstraps and restarts. It is set during console initialization and recomputed each time the console or the operating system modifies any field in the HWRPB within the region for which the checksum is computed.

33.2.5.1 **Per-CPU Slot.** Information about the state of a processor is contained in the SLOT for that processor.

The HWRPB has an array of n SLOTs, where n is the number of processors and $n - 1$ is the highest possible processor ID for the system implementation. HWRPB$IQ_SLOT_OFFSET contains the byte offset from the beginning of the HWRPB to the base of this array. HWRPB$IQ_NPROC contains the number of SLOTs present in the HWRPB. HWRPB$IQ_SLOT_SIZE contains the size in bytes of each SLOT rounded up to the next multiple of 128. The $HWRPBDEF macro defines offsets within the SLOT structure prefixed with SLOT$. The starting virtual address of a processor's SLOT is determined using the following formula:

SLOT virtual address = Virtual address of HWRPB base

+ Processor ID

∗ Contents of HWRPB$IQ_SLOT_SIZE

+ Contents of HWRPB$IQ_SLOT_OFFSET

Each SLOT contains a HWPCB substructure for that processor. Figure 33.5 shows a SLOT, and Figure 13.6, a HWPCB. Console software initializes the primary processor's HWPCB with the limited context of the bootstrap HWPCB. Section 33.2.5.2 discusses the bootstrap and other HWPCBs.

In addition, a SLOT contains the following:

▸ Processor state flags in SLOT$IQ_STATE, listed in Table 33.7.
▸ Processor halt action mask, also in SLOT$IQ_STATE, whose possible values are listed in Table 33.8. Prior to requesting a halt, the operating system records one of these values in SLOT$IQ_STATE. Console software examines this location and takes appropriate action.
▸ Processor halt reason code, in SLOT$IQ_HALTCODE, whose possible values are listed in Table 33.9. Console software initializes this field when it halts the processor.
▸ Fields that describe PALcode memory space, scratch space, and revision.
▸ Processor type, variation, revision, and serial number.
▸ The values of various processor registers at the last time the processor was halted.

33.2.5.2 **Hardware Privileged Context Block.** A process's hardware context includes, among others, the following registers: the kernel, executive, supervisor, and user mode stack pointer registers, the PTBR, the ASN register, the AST summary and AST enable registers, the FEN register, and the PCC register.

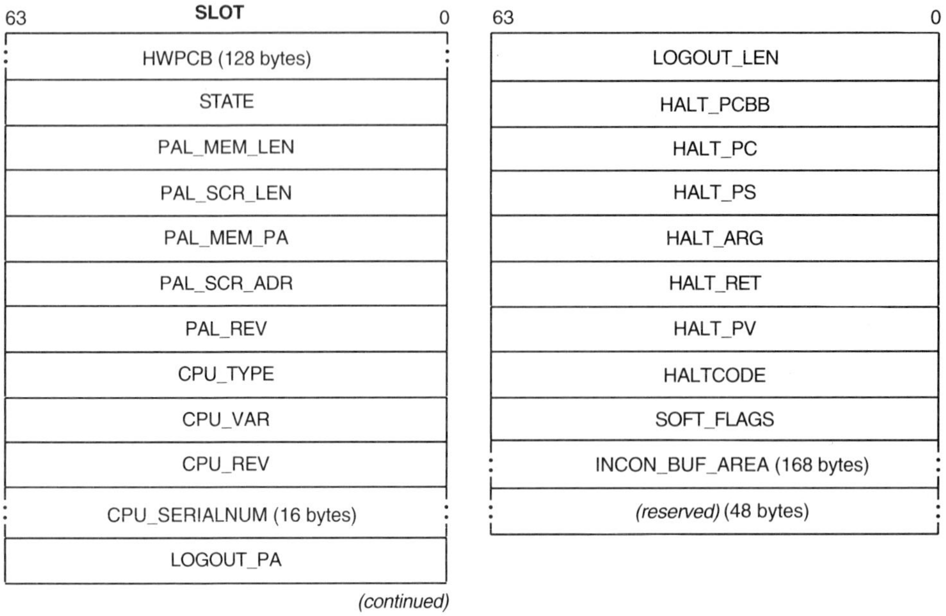

63	SLOT	0
	HWPCB (128 bytes)	
	STATE	
	PAL_MEM_LEN	
	PAL_SCR_LEN	
	PAL_MEM_PA	
	PAL_SCR_ADR	
	PAL_REV	
	CPU_TYPE	
	CPU_VAR	
	CPU_REV	
	CPU_SERIALNUM (16 bytes)	
	LOGOUT_PA	

63		0
	LOGOUT_LEN	
	HALT_PCBB	
	HALT_PC	
	HALT_PS	
	HALT_ARG	
	HALT_RET	
	HALT_PV	
	HALTCODE	
	SOFT_FLAGS	
	INCON_BUF_AREA (168 bytes)	
	(reserved) (48 bytes)	

(continued)

Figure 33.5
Per-CPU Slot

A noncurrent process's hardware privileged context is stored in the process's HWPCB.

The Alpha AXP architecture requires that there always be a valid HWPCB to define a context for CPU execution, minimally to specify the address of a kernel stack and the PFN of the L1PT. During bootstrap the console subsystem builds a HWPCB in the per-CPU slot in the HWRPB. APB and SYSBOOT run in the context of that HWPCB. After a power failure recovery or error halt, the console subsystem transfers control to the operating system restart code in the context of that HWPCB.

During system initialization the executive builds a HWPCB and allocates a kernel stack to define a context in which the system can run when there is no computable process to be placed into execution.

The executive builds another HWPCB that defines a context to which the system can switch in the final stages of saving state during a power failure. The executive also runs in that context after having been restarted. (After restart, it switches context from the boot HWPCB as soon as possible so that the console can perform another restart if necessary.)

The HWPCB built by the console subsystem is often called the boot process, and the two HWPCBs built by the OpenVMS AXP executive are often called the system process and the termination process. None, however, represents a process that can be scheduled; each merely provides a limited environment for the execution of kernel mode code in system space at ele-

Table 33.7   Processor State Flags

Bit	Meaning if Set
SLOT$V_BIP	Bootstrap in progress
SLOT$V_RC	Processor is restart capable
SLOT$V_PA	Processor is available
SLOT$V_PP	Processor is present
SLOT$V_OH	Processor has been halted by explicit operator action
SLOT$V_CV	Processor's HWPCB is valid
SLOT$V_PV	PALcode is valid
SLOT$V_PMV	PALcode memory is valid
SLOT$V_PL	PALcode has been loaded

Table 33.8   Processor Halt Action Mask

Mask	Action Taken when Processor Halts
SLOT$M_NOACTION	None
SLOT$M_SAVE_RESTORE_TERM	Save or restore console terminal
SLOT$M_COLD_REBOOT	Initiate cold bootstrap
SLOT$M_WARM_REBOOT	Initiate warm bootstrap
SLOT$M_REMAIN_HALTED	Do not attempt restart

Table 33.9   Reasons for Processor Halt

Halt Code	Meaning
SLOT$M_RESTART	Bootstrap, processor start, or power failure
SLOT$M_CRASH_CMD	CRASH console command
SLOT$M_KSP_NOT_VALID	Kernel stack not valid
SLOT$M_INVALID_SCBB	Invalid SCB base register
SLOT$M_INVALID_PTBR	Invalid PTBR
SLOT$M_CALL_PAL_HALT	CALL_PAL HALT executed in kernel mode
SLOT$M_DOUBLE_ERROR	Double error abort

vated IPL. To avoid confusion of these contexts with normal processes, this book refers to them as the boot HWPCB, system HWPCB, and termination HWPCB.

33.2.5.3   **Console Terminal Block.** A console terminal block (HWRPB_CTB) describes a terminal device connected to the console. There can be one or more such devices; however, only one of them is designated the console terminal. Console software communicates information about console terminal I/O

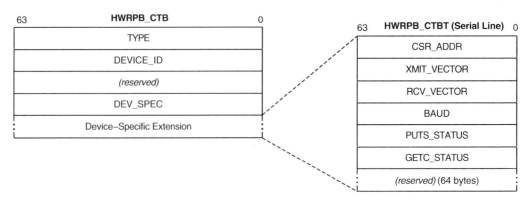

Figure 33.6
Console Terminal Block (HWRPB_CTB)

and interrupts to the console terminal driver (SYS$OPDRIVER) through the HWRPB_CTB.

The HWRPB contains a table of HWRPB_CTBs (see Figure 33.4). HWRPB$IQ_CTB_QUANTITY contains the number of HWRPB_CTBs in the table. HWRPB$IQ_CTB_SIZE contains the size of the largest HWRPB_CTB in the table. HWRPB$IQ_CTB_OFFSET contains the byte offset to the table from the HWRPB base. The index of a HWRPB_CTB in the table is the unit number of the associated terminal device.

A HWRPB_CTB consists of a device-independent portion and a device-specific portion. Figure 33.6 shows a HWRPB_CTB and the device-specific extension (HWRPB_CTBT) for a serial line interface. The $HWRPBDEF macro defines symbolic offsets for HWRPB_CTB, HWRPB_CTBT, and also the following other device-specific extensions: an integrated workstation (HWRPB_CTBWS) extension and a graphics processor (HWRPB_CTBG) extension. Each HWRPB_CTB contains its own length in HWRPB_CTB$IQ_DEV_SPEC.

During console initialization the console creates HWRPB_CTBs for all terminal devices attached to the console, records their default states in the respective HWRPB_CTBs, and stores the unit number of the designated console terminal in the environment variable TTY_DEV.

33.2.5.4   **Console Routine Block.** The HWRPB_CRB, shown in Figure 33.7, enables the operating system to locate the DISPATCH and FIXUP routines. Additionally, it contains information for mapping console callback routines and I/O space locations that they reference into virtual address space. If the executive remaps console callback routines, the I/O space locations that they reference, or the HWRPB, it must call FIXUP to adjust virtual address references in the console callback routines.

To call a particular console callback routine, the executive calls DIS-

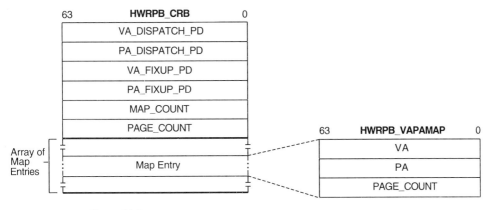

Figure 33.7
Console Routine Block (HWRPB_CRB)

PATCH, passing as its first argument the corresponding numeric value listed in Table 33.6. The executive defines symbolic names for these numeric values in the $HWRPBDEF macro. The remaining arguments to DISPATCH depend on the function requested. The following BLISS code fragment illustrates how the DISPATCH routine is called to get the value of an environment variable:

```
!Get address of DISPATCH routine from console routine block
!
BIND ROUTINE DISPATCH = .crb[hwrpb_crb$iq_va_dispatch_pd];
status = DISPATCH(hwrpb_crb$k_getenv,     !Get environment variable
                  hwrpb_crb$k_booted_dev, !BOOTED_DEV
                  devnambuf,              !Buffer to get value in
                  16);                    !Length of buffer
```

33.2.5.5   **Physical Memory Descriptor Table.** During cold bootstrap, the console sizes physical memory on the system. Typically, it permanently reserves some memory for its own use and to load PALcode. It builds a table, the HWRPB_ PMD, to describe memory and identify the reserved pages. The operating system uses this table to determine what memory is available for its own use. Both console software and the operating system use the table to record information about which pages of memory are unavailable either because they have not yet been tested or because they failed the test.

The HWRPB_PMD has a fixed part, which describes the structure as a whole, and a variable part. The variable part is an array of physical memory region descriptors (HWRPB_PMRs). Figure 33.8 shows a HWRPB_PMD and HWRPB_PMR. The $HWRPBDEF macro defines offsets for the HWRPB_ PMD and HWRPB_PMR.

In the fixed part, HWRPB_PMD$IQ_CHKSUM is the checksum of all the remaining quadwords in the HWRPB_PMD. HWRPB_PMD$IQ_OPT_DATA

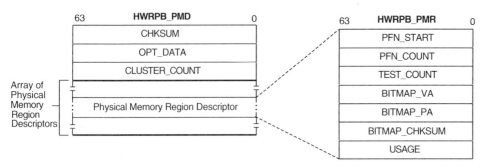

Figure 33.8
Physical Memory Descriptor Table (HWRPB_PMD)

is the physical address of system-specific data; if no such data exists, the console zeros this field. HWRPB_PMD$IQ_CLUSTER_COUNT contains the number of HWRPB_PMRs that immediately follow.

Each HWRPB_PMR describes a memory cluster, a series of physically contiguous pages of memory. If the flag HWRPB_PMR$V_CONSOLE in HWRPB_PMR$IQ_USAGE is clear, the descriptor and the memory cluster it describes are available to system software; otherwise, they are in use by console software.

HWRPB_PMR$IQ_PFN_START contains the PFN of the first physical page of memory in the cluster. HWRPB_PMR$IQ_PFN_COUNT contains the number of physical pages in the cluster. HWRPB_PMR$IQ_TEST_COUNT contains the number of pages in the cluster that have already been tested.

HWRPB_PMR$IQ_BITMAP_VA and HWRPB_PMR$IQ_BITMAP_PA contain the starting virtual and physical addresses of the cluster's memory testing bitmap in bootstrap address space. (Note that SYSBOOT remaps the bitmap into system space.) If the cluster is untested, or used by the console, these fields may be zero. HWRPB_PMR$IQ_BITMAP_CHKSUM contains the checksum of the cluster's memory testing bitmap. In the memory testing bitmap, each bit represents a page of memory. If the bit is set, the page is available for use; otherwise it is not. If the bit is not set, either the page may not have been tested or it may be bad.

A typical console implementation creates two HWRPB_PMRs in the HWRPB: one that describes memory used by the console (including memory used by and for PALcode), and one that describes memory used by the operating system.

33.2.6   APB Loading

How APB is located and loaded depends on the type of bootstrap device, which can be one of the following: a local Files-11 On-Disk Structure Level 2 (ODS-2) disk or a network device. If the bootstrap device is a network device, two styles of network booting are possible: booting from an ISL server,

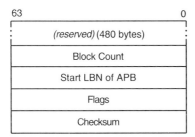

Figure 33.9
Disk Boot Block (LBN 0)

or booting from an OpenVMS system on the network using the network interconnect system control architecture (NISCA) protocol. A system can be bootstrapped either as a stand-alone system or as a node in a VMScluster system.

33.2.6.1   **Disk Bootstrap.** When bootstrapping from an ODS-2 disk, console software reads logical block number (LBN) 0 of the disk. LBN 0 of a bootable disk contains the boot block, shown in Figure 33.9. The first 480 bytes of the boot block typically contain a VAX boot block. This allows a disk to be bootable from either a VAX system or an AXP system, provided that images required for both the OpenVMS VAX and OpenVMS AXP operating systems are present on the disk. (This feature is not currently supported.)

Console software on an AXP system attempts to load APB using two pieces of information in the boot block: the block count and starting LBN of APB. This implies that APB must be present on contiguous disk blocks. Console software has no knowledge of the file system on the disk.

Console software loads APB into bootstrap virtual address space at address 20000000_{16}.

33.2.6.2   **Network Bootstrap.** When booting from a network device, console software issues a Digital Network Architecture Maintenance Operations Protocol (MOP) request over the network:

▸ If a file name is specified through the –FILE BOOT console command qualifier, console software sends a file load MOP request, which is serviced typically by an InfoServer ISL server.
▸ If the file name is not specified, console software sends a bootstrap MOP request, which is serviced typically by the boot node of a VMScluster of which the booting node is a member. This is also called an NISCA bootstrap.

The physical ID of the network device is sent as part of the bootstrap request and plays an important role in whether and by which server or node the MOP request is serviced. In either case, the end result of the MOP operation is that APB is loaded and console software transfers control to it.

The *OpenVMS AXP Version 1.5 Upgrade and Installation Manual* contains more information about the two styles of network bootstrap.

33.3 PRIMARY BOOTSTRAP PROGRAM (APB)

APB is the AXP primary bootstrap program. Running in kernel mode at IPL 31 in the context of the boot HWPCB, it locates a secondary bootstrap program, loads it into memory, and transfers control to it. By default APB loads SYSBOOT. APB can also load other secondary bootstrap programs in response to certain boot flags, as described in Section 33.3.1.

APB and SYSBOOT are conceptually one program. The VAX-11/780 system, on which VAX/VMS Version 1.0 was implemented, required that the initial bootstrap program reside on the console floppy diskette, whose capacity of 512 blocks was also used for microcode, console software, and console command procedures. Rather than impose artificial restrictions on the size of the bootstrap program, the designers divided the program into two pieces:

▶ A primary piece that resides in console storage, one of whose major purposes is to locate the secondary piece

▶ A secondary piece that resides on the system device (with no real limits on its size) that performs the bulk of the bootstrap operation

Once this division was achieved, VMB, the VAX/VMS primary bootstrap program, became a more flexible tool that could load programs other than VAX/VMS. To preserve this flexibility, the division of the bootstrap into primary and secondary pieces was continued in subsequent versions of VAX/VMS.

OpenVMS AXP preserves the separation of APB and SYSBOOT, although the original reasons for such separation no longer apply. Unlike VMB, APB does not load bootstrap programs for other operating systems, although it is sometimes used to load firmware update utilities and at other times to load a secondary bootstrap program for debugging purposes. The Alpha AXP console architecture allows console software to locate the primary bootstrap program for any operating system.

33.3.1 APB Flow

APB runs in kernel mode at IPL 31. Among other things, this blocks interrupts until the mechanisms for handling them are in place. APB performs the following steps:

1. It records the system type from HWRPB$IQ_SYSTYPE and the processor type from the per-CPU slot of the primary CPU at offset SLOT$IQ_SYSTYPE. It then records the index of the CPU table entry in the CPU

Table 33.10   Bootstrap Argument List

Field	Description
ARG_REVISION	Argument list revision
BOOT_REVISION	Primary bootstrap revision
HWRPB	Virtual address of the HWRPB
DISPATCH_VECTOR	Reserved
FILE_CACHE	File cache directory
FILE_CACHE_SIZE	Size of file cache directory
LOW_PFN	Lowest tested PFN
HIGH_PFN	Highest tested PFN
MAX_PFN	Highest available PFN
NEXT_PFN	Next available PFN
PFN_MAP	Address of allocation bitmap
NEXT_VA	Next available virtual address
BOOT_STYLE	Style of booting (disk, tape, or network)
IO_CHAN	Boot driver selector
CPU_CHAN	CPU selector
IOVEC	List of boot drivers needed
SYSBOOT_IMAGE_HDR	Virtual address of SYSBOOT's image header
IO_CHAN_MASK	I/O channel mask
IOVEC_SIZE	Size of each entry in IOVEC
IOVEC_CNT	Number of boot drivers needed
FIXUP_BLOCK	Virtual address of fixup block

dispatch table (see Section 33.3.2.1) that matches the system's and processor's type. APB subsequently uses this index to locate the system-specific routine for a given operation.

2. APB initializes a number of cells that are used by the boot time memory management code, based primarily on the system page size in HWRPB$IQ_PAGESIZE. In addition, APB builds the memory allocation bitmap through which the allocation of bootstrap virtual address space is managed.

3. APB initializes the primitive console terminal driver that is linked into APB and its associated data structures. Because APB and SYSBOOT run at IPL 31 they must perform polled, rather than interrupt-driven, I/O to the console terminal. APB disables console terminal interrupts.

4. It allocates and initializes the bootstrap argument list (ARG) structure, defined in [APB]BOODEF. APB passes information to the secondary bootstrap program in the ARG. Table 33.10 provides a summary of information in the argument list. For simplicity, the table omits the prefix ARG$IL_ from the byte offset names for the cells.

5. APB allocates and initializes the SWRPB, shown in Figure 33.10. The SWRPB contains booting-related information that enables the executive to restart the system if necessary. SYSBOOT later copies this structure

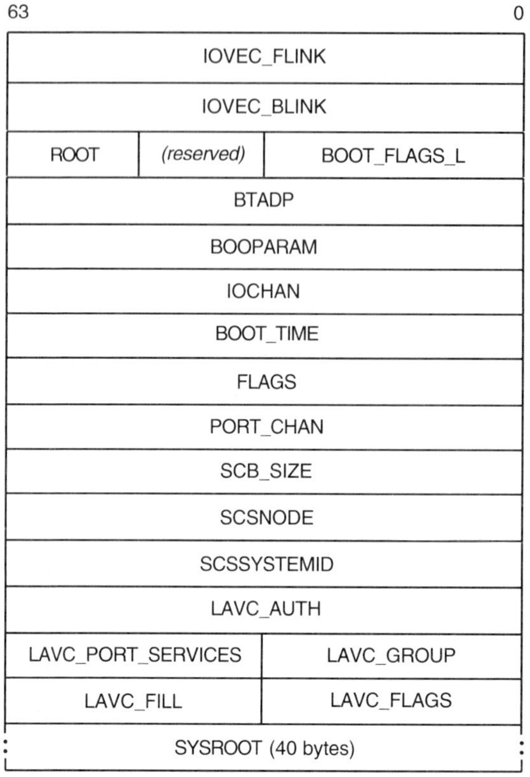

63   0

IOVEC_FLINK		
IOVEC_BLINK		
ROOT	*(reserved)*	BOOT_FLAGS_L
BTADP		
BOOPARAM		
IOCHAN		
BOOT_TIME		
FLAGS		
PORT_CHAN		
SCB_SIZE		
SCSNODE		
SCSSYSTEMID		
LAVC_AUTH		
LAVC_PORT_SERVICES		LAVC_GROUP
LAVC_FILL		LAVC_FLAGS
SYSROOT (40 bytes)		

Figure 33.10
Software Restart Parameter Block (SWRPB)

into nonpaged pool and records its address in EXE$GPQ_SWRPB. The $SWRPBDEF macro defines offsets into this structure.

6. APB allocates a page of physical memory for the system control block (SCB) and maps the page into bootstrap address space. This is a temporary SCB, used only by APB. The run-time SCB is built by SYSBOOT (see Section 33.4) after it creates the SPT. APB initializes all entries in the temporary SCB. In each entry, it initializes the SCB vector with the address of a common dispatcher; it initializes the SCB parameter with its own offset from the SCB base. APB then records the physical address of the SCB in the SCB base (SCBB) register.

Chapter 3 gives more information on SCB entries.

7. APB locates the DISPATCH console callback routine through the HW-RPB_CRB and calls it to get the value of the BOOTED_OSFLAGS environment variable. APB parses BOOTED_OSFLAGS, which contains the ASCII representation of the boot flags, and records the binary representation in SWRPB$IQ_BOOT_FLAGS.

Table 33.2 describes the bits in SWRPB$IQ_BOOT_FLAGS. For simplicity, this chapter omits the prefix SWRPB_BOOT_FLAGS$V_ from their names.

8. APB calls BOO$INIT_XDELTA, in module [APB]EXCEPTION, to initialize the XDELTA debugger. BOO$INIT_XDELTA calls XDT$INIT, in module [DELTA]XDELTA, to set up an SCB entry for the breakpoint fault (BPT) exception and to perform other initialization of the debugging environment.

9. If the BOOBPT boot flag is set, APB executes a CALL_PAL BPT instruction at a location known to XDELTA. As a result of the exception, control transfers to XDELTA. Through XDELTA commands, a console operator can examine and modify locations in APB data structures and set breakpoints in APB to troubleshoot problems that prevent a system from being booted.

10. APB calls the CPU-specific routine to validate PALcode revision information (see Section 33.3.2.1).

11. APB allocates virtual memory for a boot time equivalent of nonpaged pool. This pool will disappear when bootstrap space is later deleted.

12. It calls EXE$INI_TIMWAIT, in module [SYSLOA]TIMEDWAIT, to perform system-specific setup of certain constants required for the proper operation of the TIMEDWAIT macro (see Chapter 12).

13. APB determines the boot device type from the BOOTED_DEV environment variable. The returned value corresponds to one of the values defined in module [APB]BDTDEF.

14. It calls BOO$CREATE_IOVEC, in module [APB]CPU_VECTOR, to create the boot device I/O vector (IOVEC) data structure, discussed in Section 33.3.2.2.

15. It selects one or more boot drivers for the boot device and calls the unit initialization routine in each selected driver (see Section 33.3.2.2).

16. If this is a network bootstrap, it calls BOO$LAN_PARSE_NISCA_PA-RAMETERS, in module [APB]LAN_BOOT, to validate and parse the BOOT console command parameters.

17. APB selects the secondary bootstrap file, which must reside on an ODS-2 Files-11 volume, as follows:

- By default it uses the name [SYSEXE]SYSBOOT.EXE.
- If the SOLICIT boot flag has been set, it prompts the console operator for the file name of a secondary bootstrap program. Digital uses this flag to debug the secondary bootstrap program and to load firmware and diagnostic utilities.
- If the DEBUG_BOOT boot flag is set, it uses the name [SYSEXE]DE-BUG_APB.EXE. Digital uses this flag to debug the primary bootstrap program; any other use is unsupported.
- If this is a network bootstrap, it uses the name [SYSEXE]NISCS_LOAD.EXE.

18. APB mounts the system device and opens the file selected in step 17 as the secondary bootstrap program. It loads the secondary bootstrap program into bootstrap address space, starting at virtual address 0.

19. As its final step, APB transfers control to the secondary bootstrap program. For a secondary bootstrap program like SYSBOOT that contains a standard OpenVMS AXP image header, APB obtains the transfer address from the image header and calls it at its transfer address. APB calls a secondary bootstrap program without a standard image header at virtual address 0.

33.3.2 Structure of APB.EXE

Most modules that make up APB.EXE are from the [APB] and |BOOT-DRIVER] facilities. APB procedures are structured so that APB can be easily extended to support any one of multiple processor types, system types, or boot devices. The XDELTA debugger is linked into APB.EXE. The main components of the APB.EXE image are described in the following sections.

33.3.2.1

CPU Dispatch Table and CPU-Specific Code. For each combination of system and processor type supported by OpenVMS AXP, the system-specific module |APB|CPU*xxyy* provides a set of routines that APB uses. *xx* is the system type designator, and *yy* is the processor type designator.

Each system-specific module uses the $CPU macro, which is defined in [APB]BOOT_MACROS.REQ, to declare its system-specific routines, as in this BLISS code fragment from module [APB]CPU0401:

```
$CPU (
    SYS_TYPE = HWRPB_SYSTYPE$K_FLAMINGO,   !System type
    CPU_TYPE = (HWRPB_CPU_TYPE$K_EV3,
               HWRPB_CPU_TYPE$K_EV4),      !CPU type
    GET_BOOT_DEVTYPE =
                GET_BOOT_DEVTYPE_0401,      !Determine boot device
                                            ! type routine
    MEM_TEST = MEM_TEST_0401,              !Memory test routine
    MCHECK   = MCHECK_0401,                !Machine check routine
    BOOT_CRAM_IO = BOOT_CRAM_IO_0401,      !CRAM I/O routine
    REV_CHECKS = REVISION_CHECKS_0401,     !Revision check routine
    CREATE_IOVEC =
                CREATE_IOVEC_0401);        !Get boot device list
```

Each invocation of the $CPU macro creates a CPU table (CPUTAB) structure and an entry in the CPU dispatch table (CPU_TABLE). CPU_TABLE and two CPUTAB structures are shown in Figure 33.11. Each entry in CPU_TABLE points to a CPUTAB structure in a system-specific module. Each CPUTAB structure contains procedure values for the system-specific routines in the module that invoked the $CPU macro.

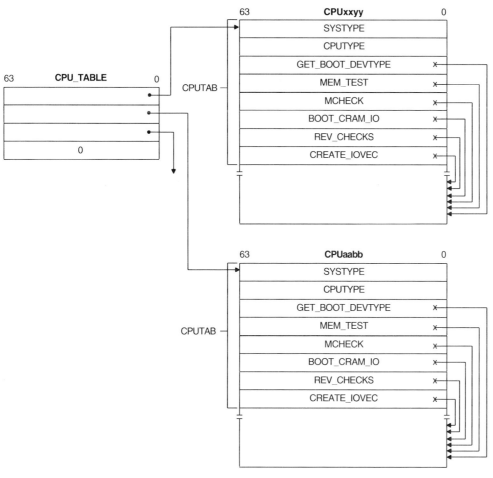

Figure 33.11
CPU Dispatch Table and CPUTAB Structures

APB's first action is to determine the system and processor types for the system being booted. Based on this information, it selects the appropriate system-specific module for use (see Section 33.3.1).

33.3.2.2 **Boot Drivers and the Boot Driver Table.** A boot driver is a skeleton device driver that is used only while the system is booting or crashing; it implements the minimum functionality required in such an environment. It performs polled, rather than interrupt-driven, I/O. It bears little resemblance to a fully functional run-time OpenVMS AXP device driver such as one described in Chapter 22. The only OpenVMS AXP components that use boot drivers are APB, SYSBOOT, EXE$INIT, and bugcheck processing code. Chapter 35 contains more information on bugcheck processing.

Every OpenVMS AXP boot driver is built in two ways:

► It is linked into APB.EXE.
► It is also linked into a separate executive image, SYS$*xx*BTDRIVER.EXE, where *xx* is the device name designator.

APB and SYSBOOT use the boot drivers built into APB.EXE, which operate in bootstrap virtual address space. EXE$INIT and bugcheck processing code use the boot driver executive images, which operate in system space. After SYSBOOT creates system virtual address space, it loads executive images for the selected boot drivers.

A boot driver interface consists of three procedures: a unit initialization procedure, a queue I/O request (QIO) procedure, and a unit disconnect procedure. Prior to initial use of the boot driver, the executive calls the unit initialization procedure to establish a logical link to the device. To perform read or write operations to the device, the executive uses the QIO procedure. After it has completed all I/O operations to the device, the executive calls the unit disconnect procedure.

APB is built with a set of boot drivers for all devices from which bootstrapping is supported. Each boot driver invokes the $BOOT_DRIVER macro as shown in the following BLISS code fragment from [BOOTDRIVER]DKBT-DRIVER:

```
$BOOT_DRIVER (
BOOT_DEVICE = BDT$K_DK,                    !Boot device type
CPU_LIST = (EV3, EV4),                     !CPUs supported by this driver
UNIT_INIT = DK_INIT,                       !Unit init procedure
QIO = DK_QIO,                              !QIO procedure
UNIT_DISC = DK_DISC,                       !Unit disconnect procedure
DRIVER_LIST = (
     ((SYS_DEV, DEF_PREFIX, HW_CTRL_LTR, CREATE_DEV),
      'DK',                                !System device name
      'SYS$DKDRIVER.EXE')),                !System device driver name
BT_DRIVER_NAME = 'SYS$DKBTDRIVER.EXE',     !Boot driver executive
                                           ! image name
DEVICE_CLASS = DC$_DISK,                    !Device class
BTADP_SIZE = BTADP$C_LENGTH);              !Size of BTADP structure
```

Each invocation of the $BOOT_DRIVER macro creates a boot driver table (BDTAB) structure, shown in Figure 33.12, and an entry in BOOT_DRIVER_TABLE, an array of pointers to BDTABs for all boot drivers in APB.EXE. Figure 33.13 shows the relation between BOOT_DRIVER_TABLE and two BDTAB structures.

The CREATE_IOVEC argument of the $CPU macro (see Section 33.3.2.1) specifies the system-specific routine that creates the IOVEC data structure. The IOVEC structure is an array of IOVEC entries. APB parses the BOOT console command parameters to determine the bootstrap device types. Then it loops through the IOVEC structure to select the appropriate boot drivers for the bootstrap device.

```
63                                              0
┌───────────────────────────────────────────────┐
│                BOOT_DEVICE                      │
├───────────────────────────────────────────────┤
│               DRIVER_NAMTBL                     │
├───────────────────────────────────────────────┤
│                  CPU_LIST                       │
├───────────────────────────────────────────────┤
│                    QIO                          │
├───────────────────────────────────────────────┤
│                 UNIT_INIT                       │
├───────────────────────────────────────────────┤
│                 UNIT_DISC                       │
├───────────────────────────────────────────────┤
│              BT_DRIVER_NAME                      │
├───────────────────────────────────────────────┤
│               DEVICE_CLASS                      │
├───────────────────────────────────────────────┤
│                BTADP_SIZE                       │
├───────────────────────────────────────────────┤
│               CLASS_DRIVER                      │
├────────────────────────┬──────────────────────┤
│    INIT_ADAPTER         │    REINIT_ADAPTER     │
├────────────────────────┼──────────────────────┤
│    XMT_INITIATE         │     INIT_POLL         │
├────────────────────────┼──────────────────────┤
│     RCV_POLL            │     XMT_POLL          │
├────────────────────────┼──────────────────────┤
│    LAN_HDR_SIZE         │  RCV_RELEASE_BUFFER   │
├────────────────────────┼──────────────────────┤
│    MAX_XMT_SIZE         │    MIN_XMT_SIZE       │
├────────────────────────┼──────────────────────┤
│  INITIALIZATION_TIME    │ DMA_MAP_REGS_NEEDED   │
└────────────────────────┴──────────────────────┘
```

Figure 33.12
BDTAB Structure

Some bootstrap drivers, like their run-time counterparts, use a layered class/port approach to simplify the implementation of support for a new bootstrap device. For example, NISCA_BOOTDRIVER is a class driver that supports NISCA network boots. NISCA_BOOTDRIVER uses port-specific routines in a port boot driver, such as EZBTDRIVER or FCBTDRIVER, specific to the network device over which the bootstrap occurs. When APB selects a boot driver such as NISCA_BOOTDRIVER, APB must also connect to the appropriate port boot driver. APB uses the IOVEC structure for this purpose.

33.3.2.3 **File System Access Routines.** Booting from a local disk, the primary and secondary bootstrap programs must locate files before the file system itself is in full operation. Many files must be looked up before the Files-11 Extended QIO Processor (XQP) has been loaded into memory and initialized by EXE$INIT. Module [APB]F11_FILEREAD exists for this purpose. This module is linked into the APB, SYSBOOT, and NISCS_LOAD images as well as the executive images EXEC_INIT and SYSLDR_DYN.

The routines in module [APB]F11_FILEREAD support primitive file operations for Files-11 ODS-2 files on a supported disk device. These routines

1177

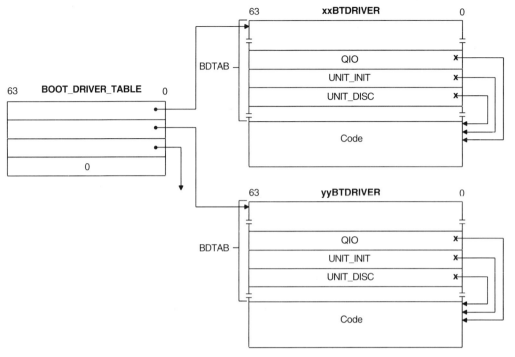

Figure 33.13
BOOT_DRIVER_TABLE and BDTAB Structures

allow APB to mount the volume that contains the secondary bootstrap program, open the file that contains the image, load the file into memory, close the file, and dismount the volume.

APB and SYSBOOT call the procedure F11FR$OPEN_BOOTFILE, in module [APB]F11_FILEREAD, to locate and read files such as SYS$BASE_IMAGE.EXE. The procedure F11FR$OPEN_BOOTFILE calls F11FR$FIND_FILE, in the same module, to look up the file.

To improve performance, F11FR$FIND_FILE caches information about directories used in the file lookup. For example, locating SYS$BASE_IMAGE.EXE might require looking up and reading the master file directory, SYS*n*.DIR, SYSCOMMON.DIR, and SYS$LDR.DIR. To avoid repeated lookups and directory and subdirectory reads, F11FR$FIND_FILE caches blocks from directory files in a primitive file cache. SYSBOOT remaps this primitive file cache to system space for use by EXE$INIT and the SYSINIT process until the XQP is operational.

33.4 SECONDARY BOOTSTRAP PROGRAM (SYSBOOT)

SYSBOOT, the AXP secondary bootstrap program, performs the following major functions.

1. It configures the system by loading a set of adjustable SYSGEN parameters, by default it uses the parameters stored in the file [SYS*n*.SYSEXE] ALPHAVMSSYS.PAR.

   If a conversational bootstrap was requested, SYSBOOT allows the console operator to change the value of specific SYSGEN parameters, select a whole different set of parameters from a different parameter file, or use a set of default values built into SYSBOOT. SYSBOOT calculates other system parameters whose values depend on the values of the adjustable parameters.

2. SYSBOOT sets up the SPT to map system virtual address space. The sizes of many pieces of system address space depend on the values of one or more SYSGEN parameters. The calculations that SYSBOOT performs and the results of these calculations are detailed in Appendix F.

3. After it has established system virtual address space, SYSBOOT calls LDR$LOAD_IMAGE, in module SYSLDR, to load the following images into memory:

   • SYS$PUBLIC_VECTORS.EXE and SYS$BASE_IMAGE.EXE, the system base images
   • The system-specific image SYS$CPU_ROUTINES_*xxyy*, where *xx* is the system type designator and *yy* is the processor type designator
     Note that the image SYS$CPU_ROUTINES_*xxyy* is functionally equivalent to the OpenVMS VAX image SYSLOA*xxx*.
   • The executive images that contain the boot drivers for the system device
   • A number of executive images common to all systems (see Table 33.1)

SYSBOOT is initiated and runs in kernel mode at IPL 31 in bootstrap space in the boot HWPCB's context. APB loads SYSBOOT into region 3 of bootstrap space, which starts at virtual address 0. Figure 33.14 shows bootstrap virtual address space after SYSBOOT is loaded.

SYSBOOT is built from a number of modules in facilities [SYSBOOT], [APB], and [SYS]. SYSBOOT has its own copies of APB's CPU-specific routines, primitive file system routines, primitive exception handling code, and memory allocation routines. SYSBOOT is linked with XDELTA.

Note that SYSBOOT uses APB's boot drivers to load executive images.

APB calls SYSBOOT's main procedure, BOO$EVMS_SYSBOOT in module [SYSBOOT]SYSBOOT, passing it a single argument, the address of the argument list described in Table 33.10.

BOO$EVMS_SYSBOOT performs the following steps:

1. It sets the BOOSTATE$V_SYSBOOT flag in EXE$GL_STATE to indicate that secondary bootstrap is in progress.

2. It copies a number of cells from the argument list to locations within the SYSBOOT image that are referenced by SYSBOOT's own memory management routines.

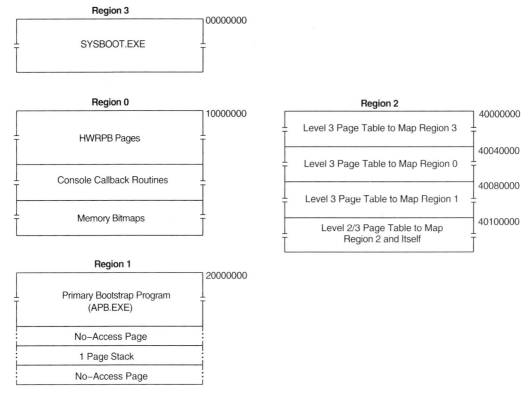

Figure 33.14
Bootstrap Virtual Address Space after SYSBOOT Is Loaded

3. APB operates in region 0 of bootstrap virtual address space, whereas SYSBOOT operates in region 3. However, SYSBOOT uses a number of APB routines. To establish an environment for these routines in region 3 of bootstrap virtual address space, SYSBOOT repeats steps 2, 3, 6, 8, and 9 in Section 33.3.1.

4. It sets SWRPB_BOOT_FLAGS$V_NOHEADER in the SWRPB to indicate that LDR$LOAD_IMAGE must read executive image headers.

5. It loads the SYSGEN parameter file, ALPHAVMSSYS.PAR. Chapter 34 describes in detail the movement of parameter information during the initialization sequence.

6. Many OpenVMS AXP SYSGEN parameters are specified in units of VAX pages, or pagelets. A pagelet is 512 bytes in size. The size of an AXP page is processor-dependent and can be 8 KB, 16 KB, 32 KB, or 64 KB. On all current AXP processors the page size is 8 KB. SYSBOOT converts parameters that are specified in pagelets into units of AXP pages.

7. If a conversational bootstrap was requested (the CONV boot flag is set), SYSBOOT calls BOO$GETPARAM, in module [SYSBOOT]SYSBOO-CMD. BOO$GETPARAM allows the console operator to examine and

modify SYSGEN parameters interactively. As a result of this step, SYS-BOOT might have to convert parameters from pagelets to AXP pages once more.

8. It allocates a page of physical memory and records its PFN in the last page table entry (PTE) of the L1PT for bootstrap virtual address space. It then makes that PTE valid. This makes the newly allocated page the level 2 page table (L2PT) of system virtual address space.

   At this point, system virtual address space comes into existence. Until the PTEs in the L2PT are filled in later by SYSBOOT, however, all pages in system virtual address space are invalid.

9. SYSBOOT calls LDR$INIT_MEM, in module LDR_MEM_INIT. If the SYSGEN parameter LOAD_SYS_IMAGES indicates that executive image slicing is enabled, or if images installed /RESIDENT are enabled, LDR$INIT_MEM reserves two physically and virtually contiguous regions of address space (huge pages) for later loading of executive images.

   Regardless of the value of LOAD_SYS_IMAGES, LDR$INIT_MEM reserves one huge page for nonpageable system data such as the PFN database. Use of such regions improves performance by reducing translation buffer misses. Chapter 32 contains more information.

10. It loads the base system images, SYS$PUBLIC_VECTORS.EXE and SYS$BASE_IMAGE.EXE, into memory and initializes the following:

    • EXE$GL_SYS_SYMVEC—Base of SYS$BASE_IMAGE.EXE's symbol vector

    • EXE$GL_SYS_SYMVEC_END—End of SYS$BASE_IMAGE.EXE's symbol vector

    • EXE$GL_SYS_CODE_BASE—Base of SYS$BASE_IMAGE.EXE's code area

    • EXE$GL_SYS_CODE_END—End of SYS$BASE_IMAGE.EXE's code area

    • EXE$GL_SYS_DATA_BASE—Base of SYS$BASE_IMAGE.EXE's data area

    • EXE$GL_SYS_DATA_END—End of SYS$BASE_IMAGE.EXE's data area

    • EXE$GL_PUBLIC_VECTOR_SYMVEC—Base of SYS$PUBLIC_VEC-TORS's symbol vector

    • EXE$GL_PUBLIC_VECTOR_SYMVEC_END—End of SYS$PUBLIC_VECTORS's symbol vector

11. Once the base system images have been loaded, SYSBOOT fixes up its own references to locations in them. To do so, it calls UPDATE_SHL_SYSBOOT, in module SYSLDR_COMMON, and FIXUP_IMAGE, in module RELOCATE_AND_FIXUP.

    After the SYSBOOT image is fixed up, its image header is no longer required; SYSBOOT deallocates it.

12. It initializes miscellaneous data cells used for memory management and executive image loading.

13. It sizes and allocates system virtual memory for the balance set slots. No physical memory is allocated. Appendix F contains more details on the sizing of balance set slots.

14. SYSBOOT allocates system virtual memory for the global page table (GPT). No physical memory is allocated. Chapter 16 provides more information on the GPT.

15. It allocates and initializes a piece of the nonpageable system data huge page, called a slice (see Chapter 32), for the system header. This step is analogous to the process header configuration performed by code in the shell as a part of process creation (see Chapter 27).

16. It sizes, allocates, and initializes a slice of the nonpageable system data huge page for the PFN database. Appendix F contains detailed information about the calculations.

17. It allocates and initializes a slice of the nonpageable system data huge page for error log buffers.

18. It allocates and initializes a slice of the nonpageable system data huge page for the nonpaged pool allocation region. If the SYSGEN parameter POOLPAGING is set to zero, it allocates and initializes virtual and physical memory for the paged pool allocation region also. Otherwise, it simply allocates address space for the paged pool allocation region.

19. SYSBOOT allocates a page of virtual and physical memory for the SCB, records the SCB starting virtual address in EXE$GL_SCB, and copies the SCB template at location SCB$A_BASE, in module SCBVECTOR, to the newly allocated SCB.

20. It allocates the processor's per-CPU database from nonpaged pool, clears it, and records its address in the processor base register (PRBR). Chapter 37 describes the per-CPU database in detail.

21. It remaps the primitive file cache created by APB into system space.

22. It calls the boot drivers' unit disconnect routines in preparation for remapping data structures used by boot drivers into system space.

23. SYSBOOT remaps the HWRPB from bootstrap space into system space and records its address in EXE$GPQ_HWRPB. It copies the SWRPB from bootstrap space into nonpaged pool and records its address in EXE$GPQ_SWRPB. It remaps console callback routines into system space and records their new addresses in the HWRPB_CRB.

24. SYSBOOT remaps the IOVEC and associated data structures from bootstrap space into system space.

25. SYSBOOT remaps the tested physical memory bitmaps from bootstrap space into system space.

26. It calls the boot drivers' unit initialization routines so that each boot driver can access data structures such as the HWRPB and the SWRPB from system space.

27. It initializes the primary processor's per-CPU database by performing the following steps:

    a. It saves the virtual address of the primary processor's per-CPU slot in the per-CPU database.

    b. It records the PFN of the L1PT in the system HWPCB's HWPCB$IQ_PTBR. It maps the L1PT into system space and records the L1PT's self-mapped virtual address in MMG$GQ_PT_VA.

    c. It allocates virtual memory for the kernel stack and two guard pages, one on each side of the kernel stack. SYSGEN parameter KSTACK-PAGES specifies the number of pages required for the kernel stack. SYSBOOT allocates physical memory for all kernel stack pages but not for the guard pages. It records the high-end address of the kernel stack in the kernel stack pointer register in the system HWPCB in the per-CPU database (see Chapter 37). It also initializes the executive, supervisor, and user mode stack pointer registers in the system HWPCB to point to one of the guard pages.

28. It allocates the boot control block (BOOTCB), shown in Figure 33.15, from nonpaged pool and initializes it. It records the address of the BOOTCB in EXE$GL_BOOTCB.

    a. If the system device is a disk, SYSBOOT opens and maps the system dump file, [SYS*n*.SYSEXE]SYSDUMP.DMP, and records the file's mapping information for use in the event of a bugcheck.

    b. If SYSBOOT does not find the dump file, it opens and maps the primary page file, [SYS*n*.SYSEXE]PAGEFILE.SYS, and sets the flag EXE$V_PAGFILDMP in EXE$GL_DEFFLAGS. The first blocks of the page file, if one exists, are used as an alternative dump file when the system bugchecks. When the SYSINIT process runs (see Chapter 34), it will look in the page file instead of the dump file for saved error log messages to restore.

    c. SYSBOOT records the LBN of the block in SYS$BASE_IMAGE.EXE that contains the cell EXE$GQ_TODCBASE.

29. SYSBOOT loads one or more executive images for boot drivers selected by APB. The boot drivers built into APB.EXE operate in bootstrap space and are used only by APB and SYSBOOT. The ones loaded in this step operate in system space and are used by EXE$INIT and bugcheck processing code.

30. It selects executive images to be loaded in the next step and adds a file statistics block pointer to the array BOO$IMAGE_BLOCK for each one. Table 33.1 lists the executive images that SYSBOOT loads.

31. SYSBOOT loops through BOO$IMAGE_BLOCK, calling LDR$LOAD_IMAGE to load each executive image selected in step 30.

32. It calls LDR$COPY_HPDESC, in module LDR_MEM_INIT, to copy the huge page descriptors to nonpaged pool.

CHECKSUM		
TIMELBN		
SUBTYP	TYPE	SIZE
DMP_VBN		
DMP_SIZE		
DMP_MAP		
BUG_WCB		
BUG_IMAGE_VA		
BUG_PTE_ADDR		
SCB_LBN		

Figure 33.15
Boot Control Block (BOOTCB)

63	0
ARG_REVISION	
PFN_MAP	
STATE	
VA_TO_VPN	
VPN_TO_VA	
BWP_MASK	
FILE_CACHE	
CACHE_SIZE	
SPTBASE	
SCB	
HPDESC	
XDTSCB	

Figure 33.16
Boot Parameter Argument List

33. It initializes the boot parameter argument list (BOOPAR), shown in Figure 33.16. This is the argument list that SYSBOOT passes to EXE$INIT.
34. It initializes the listhead of available system page table entries (SPTEs) for use by the dynamic SPTE allocation and deallocation routines (see Chapter 32).

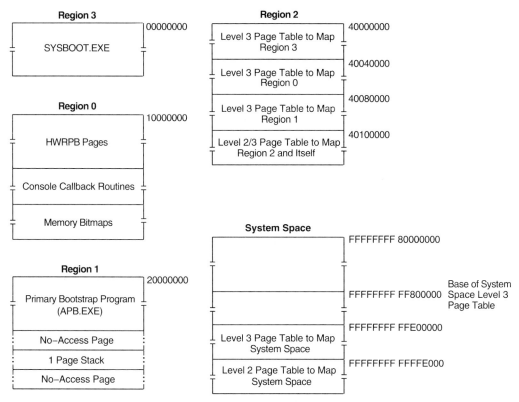

Figure 33.17
Virtual Address Space at the End of SYSBOOT

35. It calls the boot drivers' unit disconnect routines because there is no longer any use for boot drivers linked into APB. EXE$INIT will perform the initialization necessary for the system device's boot driver executive image.

36. SYSBOOT copies its system parameter area to SYS$BASE_IMAGE.EXE's parameter area to record any parameter changes that occurred during conversational bootstrap.

37. If the BOOBPT boot flag is set, SYSBOOT executes a CALL_PAL BPT instruction at a location known to XDELTA. As a result of the exception, control transfers to XDELTA.

38. If SYSTEM_DEBUG.EXE has been loaded, SYSBOOT calls XDT$SYS-DBG_INIT, in module [DELTA]XDELTA. This informs XDELTA that INI$BRK, in module SYSTEM_ROUTINES, and not BOO$BRK, is to be the permanent XDELTA breakpoint.

39. It executes the CALL_PAL SWPCTX instruction to swap from the bootstrap HWPCB to the system HWPCB. At this point, virtual address space is laid out as shown in Figure 33.17.

40. As its final step, SYSBOOT calls EXE$INIT, in module INIT, to begin initialization of the executive. Early in the execution of EXE$INIT, the physical memory occupied by regions 0 through 3 is freed up and the virtual address space occupied by these regions is deleted; only system space remains.

33.5   RELEVANT SOURCE MODULES

Source modules described in this chapter include

    [APB]BDTAB.SDL
    [APB]BDTDEF.SDL
    [APB]BDVDEF.SDL
    [APB]BOODEF.SDL
    [APB]BOOLIB.BLI
    [APB]BOOT_FLAGS.BLI
    [APB]CPU_VECTOR.BLI
    [APB]FILE_SYSTEM.BLI
    [APB]LAN_BOOT.BLI
    [APB]MAIN.BLI
    [BOOTDRIVER]BTDRIVER_INIT.BLI
    [BOOTDRIVER]BTDRIVER_SUPPORT.BLI
    [BOOTDRIVER]DKBTDRIVER.BLI
    [LIB]BOODEF.SDL
    [LIB]BOOPARDEF.SDL
    [LIB]HWRPBDEF.SDL
    [LIB]SWRPBDEF.SDL
    [SYSBOOT]SYSBOOCMD.MAR
    [SYSBOOT]SYSBOOT.BLI
    [SYSBOOT]SYSBOOT64.B64

34 Operating System Initialization and Shutdown

Had I been present at the creation, I would have given some
useful hints for the better ordering of the universe.

Alfonso the Wise

Chapter 33 provides an overview of the two phases of system initialization
and describes the first phase, in which APB, the primary bootstrap program,
and SYSBOOT, the secondary bootstrap program, execute. This chapter describes the second phase of system initialization.

This chapter also outlines the role of the System Generation (SYSGEN)
utility in system initialization, and the operations of the system shutdown
DCL command procedure, SHUTDOWN.COM, and the system crash image,
OPCCRASH.EXE.

34.1 OVERVIEW

These components take part in the second phase of system initialization:

- ▶ Procedure EXE$INIT, in the EXEC_INIT executive image, called by SYS-
  BOOT. EXE$INIT loads all remaining required executive images, config-
  ures I/O subsystem hardware, and initializes a number of system data
  structures.
- ▶ Initialization procedures of loaded executive images, called at various
  points during the execution of EXE$INIT. An initialization procedure per-
  forms initialization that relates to the function of its associated image.
  Because it may need to execute in more than one stage of system initialization, it can be called more than once based on its own request, passed
  via a flag to its caller (see Chapter 32).
- ▶ Initialization code that runs in the swapper process's context when the
  swapper process begins execution.
- ▶ SYSINIT, a process created by the swapper's initialization code to complete
  process-based system initialization. SYSINIT opens system files, creates
  system processes, loads the Record Management Services (RMS) and system message executive images, and creates a process to execute the startup
  command procedure.
- ▶ STARTUP, the first process that is able to execute Digital command language (DCL) commands, created by SYSINIT. STARTUP runs the DCL

command procedure SYS$SYSTEM:STARTUP.COM, which in turn invokes a number of DCL command procedures, including system-specific ones.

34.2 LOADING AND INITIALIZATION OF THE EXECUTIVE

Chapter 33 describes the first phase of bootstrap processing, ending with a description of SYSBOOT. As its final action, SYSBOOT calls EXE$INIT, in module INIT.

In an OpenVMS VAX system, the primary and secondary bootstrap programs execute before memory management is enabled; EXE$INIT's first action is to enable memory management. In an OpenVMS AXP system, console software enables memory management before transferring control to APB.

EXE$INIT begins execution in system virtual address space at interrupt priority level (IPL) 31 in the context of the system hardware privileged context block (HWPCB). It runs on a uniprocessor or on the primary processor of a symmetric multiprocessing (SMP) system. Its actions depend on parameters passed to it by SYSBOOT in the software restart parameter block (SWRPB), which contains information about the boot device and boot flags requested by the console operator (see Chapter 33). SYSBOOT passes additional parameters in the boot parameter argument list.

EXE$INIT copies relevant information from bootstrap virtual address space to system virtual address space, releases physical pages mapped to bootstrap virtual address space, deletes bootstrap virtual address space, and populates the page frame number (PFN) database for pages mapped to system space. It loads several executive images and calls their initialization procedures. It calls a system-specific procedure to initialize the I/O subsystem and its associated data structures. As its final step, EXE$INIT calls SCH$INIT to begin process scheduling.

Detailed operation of EXE$INIT is as follows:

1. EXE$INIT takes note of the settings of the USER_MSGS and DBG_INIT boot flags. All messages from module INIT are displayed if either boot flag is set. Certain elaborate debugging messages from module INIT_IO are displayed only if the DBG_INIT boot flag is set.
2. EXE$INIT sets the BOOSTATE$V_INIT flag in EXE$GL_STATE, indicating that EXE$INIT is running.
3. EXE$INIT copies the boot parameters from bootstrap virtual address space to global locations in system virtual address space. Table 34.1 lists these parameters.
4. It calls the console terminal initialization procedure to initialize the environment for console polled I/O routines and sets the BOOSTATE$V_CONSOLE flag in EXE$GL_STATE.
5. It copies the system type from the hardware restart parameter block (HWRPB) to EXE$GQ_SYSTYPE. The MACRO-32 macro SYSDISP depends on this value's having been correctly initialized.

Table 34.1   SYSBOOT Parameters That Are Copied to System Space

Bootstrap Virtual Address Location	*System Virtual Address Location*	*Description*
BOOPAR$L_STATE	EXE$GL_STATE	System state flags
BOOPAR$L_VA_TO_VPN	MMG$GL_VA_TO_VPN	Number of bits to shift right to derive a virtual page number (VPN) from a virtual address
BOOPAR$L_VPN_TO_VA	MMG$GL_VPN_TO_VA	Number of bits to shift left to derive a virtual address from a VPN
BOOPAR$L_BWP_MASK	MMG$GL_BWP_MASK	Byte offset within page mask
BOOPAR$L_CACHE_SIZE	FIL$GQ_CACHE	Size of primitive file system cache
BOOPAR$L_FILE_CACHE	FIL$GQ_CACHE + 4	Address of primitive file system cache
BOOPAR$L_SCB	EXE$GL_SCB	Address of the run-time system control block (SCB)
BOOPAR$L_SPTBASE	MMG$GL_SPTBASE	Address of the system page table
BOOPAR$L_HPDESC	LDR$GQ_HPDESC	Address of the huge page descriptor area
BOOPAR$L_XDTSCB	XDT$GL_SCB	Address of XDELTA's private SCB

6. Using the instruction CALL_PAL MFPR_WHAMI, EXE$INIT gets the processor ID and records it in SMP$GL_PRIMID. It records the processor's physical ID in the per-CPU database at CPU$L_PHY_CPUID. Note that these two values are the same and range from 0 through 31.

7. It copies SLOT$IQ_CPU_TYPE from the per-CPU slot in the HWRPB to EXE$GQ_CPUTYPE.

8. It initializes the per-CPU database (see Chapter 37).

9. EXE$INIT calls LDR$INIT_ALL, in module SYSLDR_COMMON, to call the initialization procedures for the executive images loaded by SYSBOOT. The initialization procedures for SYSTEM_PRIMITIVES, SYSTEM_SYNCHRONIZATION, ERRORLOG, and if requested, SYSTEM_DEBUG execute (see Section 34.3).

10. EXE$INIT loads the SCB base (SCBB) register with the PFN of the SCB to be used during normal system operations.

11. EXE$INIT prints an announcement message of the following form:

```
OpenVMS AXP (TM) Operating System Version 1.5
```

This important milestone, while not very far into EXE$INIT, indicates that bootstrap processing has completed and that the base images and several executive images have been read into memory.

12. The SWRPB, located through EXE$GPQ_SWRPB (see Chapter 33), contains the boot flags passed to APB through the BOOTED_OSFLAGS console environment variable. If the DEBUG boot flag was specified, SYSBOOT loaded the optional executive image SYSTEM_DEBUG, the XDELTA debugger. If the initial breakpoint flag, INIBPT, was specified,

EXE$INIT invokes INI$BRK, a routine that causes entry into XDELTA by executing a CALL_PAL BPT instruction.

XDELTA prompts on the console terminal and responds to any commands entered. In response to a proceed command, it returns to the INI$BRK routine, which returns to EXE$INIT.

EXE$INIT also copies the SYSGEN parameter BREAKPOINT to the global location EXE$GL_BRKMSK. This parameter controls other breakpoints later in EXE$INIT.

If the DEBUG boot flag was not specified, EXE$INIT replaces the CALL_PAL BPT instruction at INI$BRK with a BIS R31, R31, R31 instruction, which is effectively equivalent to the VAX NOP instruction.

13. EXE$INIT limits the maximum number of processes on the system to the value of the SYSGEN parameter MAXPROCESSCNT by initializing the system cell SCH$GW_PROCLIM.

14. It sets the values for the high and low thresholds of the modified page list using the SYSGEN parameters MPW_HILIMIT and MPW_LOLIMIT.

15. EXE$INIT prepares to delete bootstrap space by first releasing all the physical pages allocated to bootstrap space to the free page list. Next, it goes through the system page table, initializing the PFN database entries for those pages that are already mapped in system space. SYS-BOOT's memory allocation routines that performed the mapping could not initialize the entries because the PFN database had not yet been created.

EXE$INIT locates the physical memory descriptor table (HWRPB_PMD) in the HWRPB (see Chapter 33). Recall that all physical pages usable by the running system are described by the collection of physical memory region descriptors (HWRPB_PMRs) that console software built before transferring control to APB. For every HWRPB_PMR, EXE$INIT checks the HWRPB_PMR$IQ_USAGE field:

- If the whole memory region is in use by console software, EXE$INIT marks all the entries in the PFN database for PFNs in this region that fall within the usable memory region (any whose PFN is less than the contents of MMG$GL_MAXMEM) active, unavailable, and unknown.
- If a physical page from the memory region is marked available, and it was tested at some point and found to be good, EXE$INIT releases the page to the free page list and initializes its PFN database entry accordingly.
- If a physical page is available but tested bad, EXE$INIT puts the page on the bad page list and initializes its PFN database entry accordingly.

After it has processed all the HWRPB_PMRs, EXE$INIT sets the BOO-STATE$V_PFN_INIT flag in EXE$GL_STATE, indicating that the PFN database has been initialized. EXE$INIT deletes bootstrap virtual address space by clearing the level 1 page table entry that maps it. It then flushes the entire translation buffer to ensure that any further references to boot-strap space will be invalid.

16. Now that the PFN database has been initialized, EXE$INIT once again calls the initialization procedures of the executive images loaded by SYS-BOOT.

17. EXE$INIT allocates memory for a kernel stack page flanked on each side by a guard page. It maps these pages in system virtual address space and records the virtual address of the high-address end of the kernel stack in the boot HWPCB at HWPCB$IQ_KSP. It then copies the boot HWPCB to the termination HWPCB (see Chapter 37) in the per-CPU database. It also records the physical address of the termination HWPCB in the per-CPU database. Note that the boot HWPCB is reused as the restart HWPCB.

18. EXE$INIT initializes the permanent local system block. The SYSGEN parameters SCSSYSTEMID, SCSSYSTEMIDH, and SCSNODE deter-mine the system ID and VMScluster system node name.

19. If the system is a VMScluster node and requested a remote bootstrap over its network device, SCS$GB_NODENAME contains the node name of the remote system serving the system disk. EXE$INIT creates a system block for this node.

20. EXE$INIT allocates the following lock management data structures from nonpaged pool: the lock ID table and the resource hash table. Chapter 11 describes these structures.

21. EXE$INIT constructs the name of the executive image SHELL*xx*.EXE, where *xx* is 8, 16, 32, or 64, based on the size of a page of memory on the system.

22. EXE$INIT calls BOO$INIT, in module [BOOTDRIVER]BTDRIVER_SUP-PORT, which in turn locates and calls the initialization procedure for the system device's boot driver. The boot driver's initialization proce-dure was called once before by APB and by SYSBOOT; however, it was operating in bootstrap space at that time. By calling it here, EXE$INIT makes the boot driver operational in system space.

23. EXE$INIT inhibits the loading of the following:

- SYS$SCS.EXE, if the system does not have a computer interconnect (CI) widget or system communication services (SCS) type of system device
- SYS$CLUSTER.EXE, if the system is not to participate in a VMScluster system
- SYS$VCC.EXE, if the setting of the SYSGEN parameter VCC_FLAGS inhibits the operation of the virtual I/O cache (see Chapter 26), or if the system is a VMScluster node

24. For each executive image in its list whose loading is not inhibited, EXE$INIT calls LDR$LOAD_IMAGE, in module SYSLDR, to load the

image into memory and call its initialization procedure. If the value of SYSGEN parameter S0_PAGING disables paging of executive images, LDR$LOAD_IMAGE maps all image sections as nonpageable. Chapter 32 describes its actions in detail.

25. EXE$INIT calls LDR$ALTERNATE_LOAD, described in Chapter 32, to load optional images.

   LDR$ALTERNATE_LOAD opens [SYS*x*.SYS$LDR]VMS$SYSTEM_IMAGES.DATA and loads any images flagged for the current boot phase. LDR$ALTERNATE_LOAD also executes later, in the SYSINIT phase.

26. EXE$INIT calls INI$IOMAP, in the system-specific executive image SYS$CPU_ROUTINES_*xxyy*, where *xx* is the system type designator and *yy* is the processor type designator as described in Appendix G. INI$IOMAP, in module [CPU*xxyy*]IO_SUPPORT_*xxyy*, is a system-specific procedure that performs the following operations:

   a. It calls MAP_LOCAL_IO_SPACE, in module [SYSLOA]MAP_LO-CAL_IO_SPACE, passing it a system-specific table that describes local I/O space. The routine maps local I/O space, that is, I/O space locations directly accessible on the processor-memory interconnect (see Chapter 2), into system virtual address space.

   b. INI$IOMAP probes all tightly coupled interconnects on the system, looking for I/O adapters and I/O widgets. For every I/O adapter or multichannel I/O widget it finds, it allocates and initializes an adapter control block (ADP). INI$IOMAP links ADPs into a hierarchical list, described in Chapter 22. The ADP list is used later by autoconfiguration code to determine which drivers to load.

   c. INI$IOMAP also initializes various hardware interface registers for the adapters and multichannel I/O widgets it recognizes.

27. SYSBOOT allocated physical memory for the maximum possible size of 32 KB for the SCB. EXE$INIT now deallocates the unused portion of physical memory, if any, based on the actual size of the SCB, which is contained in SWRPB$IL_SCB_SIZE_L.

28. EXE$INIT calls INIT_IO_DB, in module INIT_IO_DB, which performs the following operations:

   a. It calls the disconnect procedure for the system device's bootstrap space boot drivers (see Chapter 33).

   b. It loads SYS$TTDRIVER.EXE, the terminal class driver executive image, and binds SYS$OPDRIVER, the console terminal port driver, to SYS$TTDRIVER through the console terminal unit control block (UCB).

   c. SYSBOOT parsed the DEVICE_LIST argument to the BOOT console command and constructed the boot device I/O vector (IOVEC) list describing all potential boot devices. For each device in the IOVEC list,

INIT_IO_DB loads the normal driver executive image and creates the I/O database data structures (see Chapter 22).

From this point onward, I/O requests to the system device are serviced by its normal driver.

d. INIT_IO_DB copies the address of the system device's UCB into the window control blocks (WCBs) for all the loaded executive images.

29. EXE$INIT invokes the CPU-specific routine SMP$SETUP_SMP, described in Chapter 37, to initialize the multiprocessing environment if the configuration is a suitable one.

30. EXE$INIT allocates the process bitmap, which has one bit for every possible process, from nonpaged pool. The lock manager uses the process bitmap, whose beginning virtual address is contained in LCK$GL_PRCMAP, for deadlock detection.

31. It allocates the process control block (PCB) and sequence number vectors from nonpaged pool. Chapter 27 describes these structures.

The initialization procedure (see Section 34.3) for the PROCESS_MANAGEMENT executive image, in module SYSTEM_PCBS_AND_PHDS, initialized three PCBs: a system PCB used by the page fault handler to read faulted pages into the system working set, the swapper PCB for the swapper process, and the null process PCB.

EXE$INIT stores the address of the swapper PCB in the second slot of the PCB vector. It initializes all other PCB vector slots to contain the address of the PCB for the null process. The PCB vector has one extra entry, where EXE$INIT stores the address of the system PCB. It initializes all entries in the sequence number vector to zero.

32. EXE$INIT calculates an extended process ID (EPID) for the swapper process and the null PCB and then invokes SCH$CHSE, in module RSE (see Chapter 13), to make the swapper process computable.

33. From nonpaged pool, it allocates the process header (PHD) vectors, two arrays that describe the balance set slots: the reference count array and the process index array. Chapter 16 describes these arrays.

Each element in the reference count array is initialized to –1.

Process index zero is reserved to identify the null PCB, which does not represent a schedulable process that occupies a balance set slot. An index of zero can thus be used for another purpose, namely, to indicate a free balance set slot. Thus, to indicate free balance set slots, EXE$INIT zeros the process index array.

34. EXE$INIT allocates a WCB from nonpaged pool and initializes its header. Despite its name, NET$AR_WCB, the structure serves as a header for a kernel mode work queue used by the network logging monitor.

35. Based on the maximum possible number of page and swap files on the system, EXE$INIT sizes, allocates from nonpaged pool, and initializes

the page-and-swap-file vector. Each array element is the address of a page file control block (PFL) for a page or swap file recognized by the system. It initializes each array element with the address of the null page file block.

36. EXE$INIT sets the process index of the system PCB as the value of the SYSGEN parameter MAXPROCESSCNT.

37. EXE$INIT calls LDR$INIT_ALL to call any remaining executive image initialization procedures.

38. From nonpaged pool, EXE$INIT allocates the Create Logical Name ($CRELNM) system service argument lists for SYS$DISK and SYS$SYS-DEVICE. The swapper process accesses this area in nonpaged pool and creates the logical names after it initializes paged pool and the logical name database.

39. Once the system device name is determined, the equivalence names for SYS$DISK and SYS$SYSDEVICE are stored in the $CRELNM argument lists for later use by the swapper process.

40. EXE$INIT allocates two system page table entries (SPTEs) for tape mount verification and stores the virtual address of the first SPTE at EXE$GL_TMV_SVAPTE.

41. It allocates a page of physical memory and an SPTE to map it for disk mount verification and stores the virtual address of the SPTE in EXE$GL_SVAPTE.

42. It allocates an SPTE, computes the associated system virtual address, and stores that address in MMG$GL_DZRO_VA. This is used to optimize global demand zero page deletion.

43. It allocates two pages of physical memory and two SPTEs to map them. These become the system erase pattern buffer and a pseudo page table mapping the buffer. The virtual addresses are stored in EXE$GL_ERASEPB and EXE$GL_ERASEPPT. These optimize erasure of disk blocks during the deletion of an erase-on-delete file.

44. It allocates a page of physical memory and an SPTE to map it. It zeros the page, marks its protection user read, executive write, and stores its address in EXE$AR_EWDATA. RMS uses this page.

45. EXE$INIT adjusts the maximum allowable working set (if necessary) to reflect the amount of available physical memory. It subtracts the number of physical pages used by the executive from the amount of available physical memory.

46. It clears the bootstrap-in-progress flag (SLOT$V_BIP) in the per-CPU slot to indicate that bootstrap is complete. It sets the restart-capable flag (SLOT$V_RC) in the per-CPU slot to enable warm restarts. Both these flags are used by the restart mechanism, described in Chapter 36.

47. If the BPT$V_INITEND flag in EXE$GL_BRKMSK is set, EXE$INIT invokes INI$BRK, causing the end-of-INIT XDELTA breakpoint to be

taken. XDELTA prompts on the console terminal and responds to any commands entered. In response to a proceed command, XDELTA returns to EXE$INIT.

48. EXE$INIT invokes INI$RDONLY, in module INIRDWRT, to set the protection for executive image code pages to read-only. This step is necessary because LDR$LOAD_IMAGE, for reasons described in Chapter 32, kept the pages writable.

49. EXE$INIT removes the CPU on which it is running, the primary CPU, from the override set and determines SMP status (enabled or disabled) from the SYSGEN parameter MULTIPROCESSING. If SMP is enabled and more than one functional CPU exists, EXE$INIT sets the go bit in SMP$GL_FLAGS, indicating that secondary CPU initialization may proceed. Chapter 37 describes these flags and SMP initialization.

50. EXE$INIT executes the CALL_PAL MFPR_MCES and CALL_PAL MTPR_MCES instructions to set the appropriate bits in the machine check error summary register to enable memory corrected error interrupts.

51. Finally, EXE$INIT calls SCH$INIT, in module SCHEDULER, which lowers IPL to IPL$_SCHED and initiates scheduling for this processor. There is only one schedulable process at this point—the swapper, made computable by EXE$INIT in an earlier step. The initial actions of the swapper are described in Section 34.4.1.

34.3   EXECUTIVE IMAGE INITIALIZATION PROCEDURES

Chapter 32 describes the general mechanism by which executive image initialization procedures are called. The actions of these procedures are constrained by the current stage of system initialization, represented by the flags in EXE$GL_STATE. For instance, a procedure that needs to allocate paged pool cannot do so before the swapper sets the BOOSTATE$V_SWAPPER flag. An initialization procedure unable to perform its tasks in the current stage returns a status to its invoker indicating that it should be reinvoked at a later stage. When the initialization procedure completes all its tasks, it is deallocated. Several modules can contribute to a single initialization procedure.

Each initialization procedure performs initialization that logically relates to the function of its associated image. For instance, the SYSTEM_PRIMITIVES image contains the interrupt service routines (ISRs) that handle fork dispatching. The SYSTEM_PRIMITIVES initialization procedure stores the code addresses and procedure values of these ISRs in the appropriate SCB entries. Chapter 3 describes the format of an SCB entry.

The following paragraphs summarize the actions of some executive image initialization procedures called from EXE$INIT, the swapper process, and the SYSINIT process. These can be called multiple times and thus may not perform all listed functions in the same system initialization stage.

The SYSTEM_PRIMITIVES initialization procedure initializes the I/O database structures for the system, console, and mailbox devices and initializes the SCB entries for the fork interrupts. It queues three permanent system timer queue entries into the timer queue and initializes the SCB entries for the interval timer interrupt and the software timer interrupt. It initializes data cells used for accurate update of the system clock based on the interval timer interrupt frequency in the HWRPB (see Chapter 12). It also initializes the SCB entry for the data alignment trap handler.

The SYSTEM_DEBUG initialization procedure stores the procedure value and code address of the XDELTA ISR in its SCB entry.

The SYSTEM_SYNCHRONIZATION initialization procedure initializes the static spinlock vector area. It initializes spinwait timeout values; assigns device spinlocks to the null device, console device, and permanent mailbox devices; and initializes the buffer pool used by SMP$FORK_TO_PRIMARY. It also sets the BOOSTATE$V_SPNLCK_AVAIL flag in EXE$GL_STATE to indicate that spinlock-based synchronization is available.

The ERRORLOG initialization procedure initializes error log allocation buffers that SYSBOOT earlier allocated. It stores the procedure value and code address of ERL$UNEXP, in module ERRORLOG, in every uninitialized SCB entry, that is, every SCB entry that still has the procedure value and code address of EXE$HALT, the default SCB service routine.

The PROCESS_MANAGEMENT initialization procedure initializes the swapper PCB and PHD, the system PCB, and the null PCB. It initializes some scheduler and memory management data structures. It stores the address of the system logical name table in the group and job templates used for process creation. It initializes a number of SCB entries, including those for the rescheduling (IPL 3) interrupt, translation-not-valid fault, floating-point fault, fault-on-execute, fault-on-read, and the kernel, executive, supervisor, and user mode asynchronous system trap (AST) interrupts.

The IO_ROUTINES initialization procedure initializes the IPL 4 software interrupt SCB entry with the code address and procedure value of IOC$IOPOST. It stores the code address of the common I/O interrupt dispatcher (see Chapter 24) at the global location IOC$INTDISP. It stores the procedure value and code address of EXE$RESTART, the system restart procedure, in the HWRPB at HWRPB$IQ_RESTART and HWRPB$IQ_RESTART_PD, thus enabling system restart. It initializes the powerfail SCB entry with the procedure value and code address of EXE$POWERFAIL, the powerfail ISR.

The SYS$VM initialization procedure creates the swapper process's P0 page table. It ensures that modified page writer SYSGEN parameters are sensible; for instance, it checks that MPW_WAITLIMIT is not less than MPW_HILIMIT and adjusts it if necessary. MPW_IOLIMIT specifies the number of concurrent I/O operations that the modified page writer can have in progress. The initialization procedure allocates that many I/O request packets (IRPs) for the modified page writer and inserts them into a private lookaside list. It also allocates and associates a kernel process block for each IRP. The SYS$VM initialization procedure initializes the SCB entry for the fault-on-write handler.

The EXCEPTION initialization procedure initializes SCB entries for many exceptions and interrupts, including the access violation fault, the arithmetic fault, the reserved operand fault, the change mode exceptions, the IPL 14 software interrupt, and the bugcheck exception. It also saves, among other things, the address of the EXCEPTION image's loader image data block (LDRIMG) and WCB in the boot control block for use during system shutdown or crash.

The IMAGE_MANAGEMENT initialization procedure stores the length and address of the known file entry resource name string and its size in the global descriptor EXE$GQ_KFE_LCKNAM.

The SHELL*xx*K initialization procedure initializes various cells with values that depend on the system page size and the kernel stack size. It copies the code address and procedure value of EXE$PROCSTRT to the kernel stack template in the SHELL*xx*K image (see Chapter 27).

34.4   INITIALIZATION IN PROCESS CONTEXT

The remaining steps in system initialization must be performed by a process. For instance, system services can only be called from process context, and a command language interpreter (CLI) can only be mapped into P1 space by code executing in process context.

The process stage of system initialization is divided into several parts: initialization code that runs only once, when the swapper process begins execution, in the swapper process's context; the SYSINIT process; and the startup process.

34.4.1   Swapper Process

EXE$INIT transfers control to SCH$SCHED, in module SCHED, which selects the highest priority computable process for execution. Since only one process is computable at this time, thc choice is easy: the scheduler selects the swapper process.

Several procedures have cooperated to initialize the swapper's process context. An initialization procedure in the PROCESS_MANAGEMENT executive image initialized the swapper PCB, PHD, and kernel stack. An initialization procedure in the SYS$VM executive image allocated memory for the swapper's P0 page table, described in Chapter 16. (The page table's address is stored in the global location SWP$GL_MAP, and pages mapped in the swapper map are accessible as P0 virtual pages when the swapper is the current process.) EXE$INIT allocated a P1 page table page and the P1 pointer page.

When the swapper process is first entered, it executes one-time initialization code that is part of the routine SWP$MAIN_LOOP, in module SWAP-PER. This initialization code is the first piece of pageable code that executes. It performs the following actions:

1. It sets the BOOSTATE$V_SWAPPER flag in EXE$GL_STATE to indicate that paging is possible.
2. If the USER_MSGS or DBG_INIT boot flag is set, it sets a local flag, enabling various debug messages.
3. It initializes paged pool.
4. It calls LDR$INIT_ALL to enable any executive image initialization procedures that require a pageable system to execute.
5. It invokes EXE$PAGED_SYSTEM_INIT, in module PAGED_SYSTEM_INIT, to initialize the logical name database and create the SYSINIT process.
6. It executes the swapper's main loop, described in Chapter 20.

EXE$PAGED_SYSTEM_INIT performs the following steps to initialize the logical name database, described in Chapter 38:

1. It allocates paged pool for the shareable logical name hash table.
2. It zeros the allocated area, initializes its header, and stores its address in the longword pointed to by LNM$AL_HASHTBL.
3. It initializes the logical name table header (LNMTH) of the system directory. It records the hash table address in the LNMTH. It then hashes the system directory name and inserts it into the appropriate hash chain of the shareable hash table.
4. It initializes the system logical name table, recording the hash table address in its LNMTH. It invokes LNM$INSLOGTAB, in module LNM-SUB, to insert the system table into the database.
5. EXE$PAGED_SYSTEM_INIT requests the $CRELNM system service to create the following logical names:
   - LNM$DIRECTORIES, whose equivalence names are the shareable and process-private shareable directories
   - The executive mode table name LNM$FILE_DEV
   - The supervisor mode table name LNM$FILE_DEV
   - The table names that provide upward compatibility from VAX/VMS Version 3: LOG$PROCESS, LOG$GROUP, LOG$SYSTEM, TRN-LOG$_GROUP_SYSTEM, TRNLOG$_PROCESS_GROUP, TRNLOG$_PROCESS_SYSTEM, and TRNLOG$_PROCESS_GROUP_SYSTEM
   - The table names LNM$PERMANENT_MAILBOX and LNM$TEMPO-RARY_MAILBOX
   - The table name LNM$SYSTEM
   - The executive mode names SYS$DISK and SYS$SYSDEVICE in the LNM$SYSTEM table

6. EXE$PAGED_SYSTEM_INIT deallocates the nonpaged pool used by EXE$INIT to pass information needed for the creation of SYS$DISK and SYS$SYSDEVICE.

EXE$PAGED_SYSTEM_INIT creates the SYSINIT process, which does more system initialization requiring process context. EXE$PAGED_SYS-TEM_INIT returns to SWP$MAIN_LOOP, which begins executing the swapper's main loop.

34.4.2   SYSINIT Process

In one sense, SYSINIT is an extension of the swapper process. However, the initialization code is isolated to prevent encumbering the swapper with more code that only executes once during the life of a system. This isolation is one of several techniques used during system initialization and process creation to cause seldom-used code to disappear after it executes. A list of such techniques appears in Appendix B.

SYSINIT performs the following major functions:

▸ It loads RMS and other executive images.
▸ It initializes VMScluster software for a VMScluster node.
▸ It opens the swap and page files and records their extents.
▸ It initializes the Files-11 extended QIO processor (XQP).
▸ It loads the system message file.
▸ It creates the startup process.

34.4.2.1   Pool Allocation by SYSINIT.
SYSINIT, like SYSBOOT, allocates nonpaged pool. It also allocates some paged pool. Structures that are allocated from nonpaged pool as a result of the execution of SYSINIT include the following:

▸ Four security audit structures
▸ PFL structures and bitmaps for the page and swap files
▸ Lock and resource blocks
▸ File control blocks (FCBs) and WCBs for all opened files
▸ Space to copy the contents of the error log allocation buffers from the crash dump file

34.4.2.2   Detailed Operation of SYSINIT.
SYSINIT is a normal process, scheduled and placed into execution in the ordinary way. Its main module is [SYSINI]SYS-INIT. SYSINIT begins execution in user mode but performs much of its work in kernel and executive modes.

SYSINIT takes the following steps:

1. It changes mode to kernel and sets the BOOSTATE$V_SYSINIT flag within EXE$GL_STATE to indicate that the SYSINIT process context is available.
2. It calls LDR$UNLOAD_IMAGE, in module SYSLDR_DYN, to release the physical pages and address space occupied by EXE$INIT.

3. SYSINIT allocates four security audit vectors from nonpaged pool. It initializes the structure headers and the pointers to the structures: NSAAR_ALARM_VECTOR, NSAAR_AUDIT_VECTOR, NSA$AR_ALARM_FAILURE, and NSA$AR_AUDIT_FAILURE.

4. SYSINIT calls LDR$LOAD_IMAGE, in module SYSLDR_DYN, to load the executive images RMS.EXE, RECOVERY_UNIT_SERVICES.EXE, D-DIF$RMS_EXTENSION.EXE, and SYSMSG.EXE and execute their initialization procedures.

    SYSINIT sets the BOOSTATE$V_RMS flag in EXE$GL_STATE to indicate that RMS is loaded. RMS cannot be used, however, until the XQP is initialized later by SYSINIT.

5. From user mode, SYSINIT calls LDR$ALTERNATE_LOAD to load optional images. The latter opens the file [SYSx.SYS$LDR]VMS$SYSTEM_IMAGES.DATA and loads those images that must be loaded during the current boot stage.

6. SYSINIT changes mode to kernel to create a system-specific root resource. It requests the Enqueue Lock Request ($ENQ) system service to create an executive mode system resource and acquire an exclusive lock on it. The resource name is the string SYS$SYS_ID concatenated with the system's SCS system ID (SYSGEN parameters SCSSYSTEMID and SCSSYSTEMIDH). The name is therefore unique within the VMScluster system.

    SYSINIT locks the root resource with a system-owned lock so that the lock will survive the deletion of SYSINIT. SYSINIT stores the lock ID in EXE$GL_SYSID_LOCK. The lock is always mastered on the local VMScluster system, since each VMScluster node locks its own unique name. Any sublocks of this lock are guaranteed to be mastered locally. Appendix H provides more information on the system ID lock, and Chapter 11 describes lock management in general.

7. SYSINIT changes mode to kernel to set the system time. It calls the procedure EXE$INIT_HWCLOCK, in module [SYSLOA]TIMROUT. This procedure verifies that the system time, maintained in the time-of-year clock, is correct. If not, it prompts the console operator to enter the date and time. Chapter 12 describes EXE$INIT_HWCLOCK and altering the system time.

8. SYSINIT changes mode to kernel to perform the following steps:

   a. If this system is not a VMScluster member, SYSINIT zeros the global location LCK$GB_STALLREQS and proceeds with step 9. This action allows the lock manager to perform locking operations efficiently on a stand-alone system.

   b. SYSINIT opens the incarnation file, SYS$SYSTEM:SYS$INCARNATION.DAT, reads the first block, and stores the WCB address and the data in the cluster incarnation block (CLUICB).

c. SYSINIT creates the stand-alone configure process, STACONFIG, to autoconfigure disks and SCS communication ports. STACONFIG is required early in the operation of the system potentially to locate an SCS system disk.

d. If the SYSGEN parameter DISK_QUORUM indicates there is to be a quorum disk, STACONFIG starts SCS polling to discover remote mass storage control protocol (MSCP) disk servers. Connection to the quorum disk may be necessary for the node to join the VMScluster system.

e. SYSINIT sets a flag to tell the VMScluster connection manager to proceed with cluster formation and prints the following message on the console terminal:

```
waiting to form or join a VMScluster system
```

It waits for 100 milliseconds, during which time the STACONFIG process and the VMScluster connection manager run, and then tests whether the quorum disk has been found.

If it has, SYSINIT assigns a channel to it, opens the quorum file, and starts the quorum disk polling routine to run at an interval of SYSGEN parameter QDISKINTERVAL seconds. It then checks whether the system is a node of a VMScluster system yet. If not, SYSINIT waits again.

When the system is a VMScluster node, SYSINIT takes out a concurrent read lock on the system device and resets the time to correspond to the clusterwide time.

9. It forces the STACONFIG process to exit. The function of STACONFIG, to establish SCS connections with any SCS disks or tapes that become available, will be performed by the CONFIGURE process later. STACONFIG and CONFIGURE differ in file system use: the former uses the primitive file system for its operations, and the latter, the normal file system.

10. SYSINIT calls LOCKDOWN, in module [SYSINI]LOCKDN, to lock pages in its working set that will be accessed at elevated IPL.

11. Back in user mode, SYSINIT redefines executive mode logical names for SYS$SYSDEVICE and SYS$DISK in the system logical name table. In the case of an MSCP system disk, their equivalence names are not quite right. When EXE$INIT created them, the allocation class of the system disk was not yet known. When SYSINIT runs, the MSCP server for the system disk has communicated its allocation class and SYSINIT can form an equivalence name that contains the allocation class.

SYSINIT also defines the following logical names:

SYS$SYSROOT
SYS$COMMON

SYS$SHARE
SYS$MESSAGE
SYS$SYSTEM
SYS$LOADABLE_IMAGES

These names are defined now because they will be needed to create the startup process. STARTUP initially executes the image SYS$SYSTEM:LOGINOUT, and SYS$SYSTEM is defined in terms of SYS$SYSROOT and SYS$COMMON. LOGINOUT performs a merged image activation of the DCL CLI and its command tables. It specifies logical name SYS$SYSTEM to locate the CLI and SYS$SHARE to locate the tables.

12. If the SYSGEN parameter UAFALTERNATE is set, SYSINIT creates the executive mode logical name SYSUAF in the system table with equivalence name SYS$SYSTEM:SYSUAFALT.DAT. This feature allows an alternative authorization file to be used. If the alternative authorization file does not exist, logins will be possible only from the console terminal.

13. In kernel mode, SYSINIT uses the primitive file I/O routines to open the following files on the system disk:

   • [SYSn.SYSEXE]PAGEFILE.SYS, if not already opened by SYSBOOT as the dump file (see Chapter 33)
   • [SYSn.SYSEXE]SYSDUMP.DMP, if it exists and has not been opened by SYSBOOT
   • [SYSn.SYSEXE]SWAPFILE.SYS, if the SYSGEN parameter SWPFILCNT is nonzero

   It ensures that the file highwater mark is set to the end of each of these files. The file system uses a highwater mark to prevent access to file blocks that are allocated but not yet written. These blocks may have previously belonged to another file, now deleted, and may still contain data from the other file.

   Executive code, however, neither tests nor adjusts the highwater mark when accessing any of these special-purpose files. To permit a suitably privileged process to access any part of one of these files through the file system, SYSINIT adjusts each of their highwater marks to the end of the file.

14. It calls a kernel mode procedure that performs the following functions:

   a. It initializes the global page table entry (GPTE) list.
   b. It checks the sizes of the page file, dump file, and swap file. If any file is found to have no disk space allocated, the kernel mode procedure inhibits the file's use by the system.
   c. The dump file (or the page file if no dump file exists) contains the contents of the error log allocation buffers at the time of the crash

or shutdown. These buffers were written by the bugcheck code, de-scribed in Chapter 35, so their contents would not be lost.

SYSINIT multiplies the number of buffers by the number of pagelets per buffer, adds sufficient space for a header and an extra buffer for the bugcheck error log entry, and allocates this amount of nonpaged pool. It stores the address of this area in EXE$GL_SAVED_EMBS. It copies the error log buffers and bugcheck error log entry from the dump or page file to the area and records the number of buffers copied in EXE$GW_SAVED_EMBS_COUNT. Eventually, the messages will be written to SYS$ERRORLOG:ERRLOG.SYS.

d. The kernel mode procedure initializes the page file data structures. It allocates a PFL and a bitmap from nonpaged pool to describe the page file and the availability of each block in the file. The bitmap is initialized to all 1's to indicate that all blocks are available. If the page file contains a valid dump and the SYSGEN parameter SAVEDUMP is set to 1, the routine marks unavailable the blocks in the page file that contain the dump. Otherwise, the blocks are made available for paging. The address of the page file WCB, the page file size, the bitmap address, the free page count, and other items are stored in the PFL, whose address is then stored in the page-and-swap-file vector.

Page file blocks marked unavailable because they contain a crash dump may be reclaimed by copying them to another file using the System Dump Analyzer (SDA) command COPY, or released with the command ANALYZE/CRASH_DUMP/RELEASE. However, releasing the blocks deletes the crash dump.

e. If present, the swap file is initialized. The routine allocates a PFL and a bitmap from nonpaged pool to describe the swap file and the availability of each block in the file. It initializes the bitmap to all 1's, indicating that all blocks are available. The address of the swap file WCB, the swap file size, the bitmap address, the free page count, and other items are stored in the PFL, whose address is then stored in the page-and-swap-file vector.

Chapter 16 describes the page-and-swap-file vector.

At this stage in system initialization no more than one page file and one swap file have been installed. Later, the STARTUP process ex-ecutes the DCL command procedure SYS$MANAGER:SYPAGSWP-FILES.COM to install any secondary page and swap files.

f. SYSINIT logs a cold start in the system error log. In this context a cold start implies operating system startup rather than an error halt restart (see Chapter 36), and not a cold bootstrap (see Chapter 33).

15. In kernel mode, SYSINIT calls F11X$INIT_XQP, in module [F11X]INI-FCP. This procedure initializes the XQP's environment for the process in whose context it is called. The first time this procedure is called (which

is here), it sets the EXE$V_INIT flag in the EXE$GL_FLAGS longword and performs once-only XQP initialization. Once EXE$V_INIT is set, EXE$PROCSTRT, the process initialization procedure that runs during the creation of every process, will call F11X$INIT_XQP to initialize the XQP's environment for the process in whose context it is executing.

Note that EXE$V_INIT is not to be confused with the similarly named BOOSTATE$V_INIT flag in EXE$GL_STATE; the latter, when set, indicates that EXE$INIT has begun executing.

Upon return from F11X$INIT_XQP, SYSINIT sets the BOOSTATE$V_XQP flag in EXE$GL_STATE to indicate that the normal file system is operational.

16. In user mode, SYSINIT assigns a channel to the system disk. In executive mode, it calls MOUNT_SYSTEM, in module [SYSINI]SYSMOU, which mounts the system disk.

17. SYSINIT requests the Set Time ($SETIME) system service to record the system time in the SYS$BASE_IMAGE.EXE base image.

18. SYSINIT disables the primitive file system cache and deallocates its pages.

19. It creates the logical name SYS$TOPSYS, the top-level system directory, for example, SYS0.

20. From executive mode, SYSINIT permanently opens the page file, swap file, dump file, and all executive image files. From kernel mode, it converts each WCB into a shared window by clearing the WCB$L_PID field, setting the WCB$V_SHRWCB flag, and incrementing its reference count to 2. Thus, any subsequent attempt to delete one of these open files will only mark the file for deletion.

21. Finally, SYSINIT creates the startup process, specifying that it execute the LOGINOUT image, which maps the DCL CLI into P1 space. Chapter 30 describes LOGINOUT.

34.4.3   Startup Process

The startup process created by SYSINIT (referred to here as STARTUP) completes system initialization. This process is the first in the system to include a CLI. The inclusion of DCL allows this process to execute a DCL command procedure, SYS$SYSTEM:STARTUP.COM.

34.4.3.1   STARTUP.COM.

The STARTUP command procedure directs the execution of other command procedures that perform the actual work, using input from three data files in the SYS$STARTUP directory.

▶ VMS$PHASES lists eight startup phases from INITIAL to END. It sequences the invocation of the command procedures and executable images defined in the other two data files.

▶ VMS$VMS is reserved for use by the operating system. Each record contains the name of an OpenVMS-supplied command procedure or executable image, the startup phase in which it executes, a flag through which execution is enabled or disabled, and a mode field defining the manner in which the file executes (for instance, mode b signifies that the file should be submitted as a batch job).

By convention, the file name in each VMS$VMS record begins with the string VMS$ followed by the name of the phase in which the image or procedure executes. For instance, the command procedure VMS$INITIAL-050_VMS.COM executes in the INITIAL phase.

▶ VMS$LAYERED is reserved for the use of customers and layered products. A customer or layered product installation procedure uses the System Management (SYSMAN) utility to insert the name of the layered product startup file, its execution phase, and the flag, mode, and other fields, as in VMS$VMS, into a VMS$LAYERED record. STARTUP executes the command procedure in the specified phase and manner.

VMSVMS, VMSLAYERED, and all files that they specify reside in the SYS$STARTUP directory. STARTUP processes them as follows:

1. It reads the first phase defined in VMS$PHASES and stores it as the current phase.
2. For records in VMS$VMS whose phase matches the current phase, STARTUP executes the associated image or command procedure if it is enabled.

   When no more records in VMS$VMS match the current phase, STARTUP executes each image or command procedure defined in VMS$LAYERED whose phase matches the current phase.
3. STARTUP waits for all batch processes and subprocesses to complete.
4. When no more records exist for the current phase, STARTUP reads the next phase from VMS$PHASES and processes records from VMS$VMS and VMS$LAYERED that match the new phase.
5. Finally, when no more phases remain, STARTUP exits.

Some of the more important files executed and their actions follow. Note that this section describes the full set of STARTUP actions, some of which are disabled when the SYSGEN parameter STARTUP_P1 has the value MIN.

VMS$INITIAL-050_VMS.COM, the first command procedure invoked by STARTUP, performs these actions:

1. It creates the following system logical names:

   SYS$SPECIFIC
   SYS$SYSDISK
   SYS$ERRORLOG
   SYS$EXAMPLES
   SYS$HELP

> SYS$INSTRUCTION
> SYS$LIBRARY
> SYS$MAINTENANCE
> SYS$MANAGER
> SYS$UPDATE
> SYS$TEST
> ALPHA$LIBRARY
> ALPHA$LOADABLE_IMAGES
> SDA$READ_DIR

In addition, it defines a number of logical names for shareable image libraries.

2. It preserves SYSGEN parameters. If the SYSGEN parameter WRITESYS-PARAMS is set, it runs SYSGEN to execute WRITE CURRENT, which records the parameters in SYS$SYSTEM:ALPHAVMSSYS.PAR.

3. It makes privileged and shareable images known to the system by running the Install utility with input taken from the file SYS$MANAGER: VMSIMAGES.DAT.

VMS$INITIAL-050_LIB.COM defines logical names and name tables for the Text Processing utility (TPU), the debugger (DBG), and RMS. It also invokes SYLOGICALS.COM for site-specific logical name creation.

VMS$CONFIG-050_ERRFMT.COM creates the error logger (ERRFMT) process.

VMS$CONFIG-050_CACHE_SERVER.COM creates the Files-11 XQP cache server (CACHE_SERVER) process for VMScluster nodes.

VMS$CONFIG-050_CSP.COM creates the cluster server (CLUSTER_SER-VER) process for VMScluster nodes.

VMS$CONFIG-050_OPCOM.COM creates the operator communication (OPCOM) process.

VMS$CONFIG-050_AUDIT_SERVER.COM executes the site-specific security procedure, SYS$MANAGER:SYSECURITY.COM, if it exists. It then creates the audit server (AUDIT_SERVER) process.

VMS$CONFIG-050_JOBCTL.COM creates the job controller (JOB_CON-TROL) process.

VMS$CONFIG-050_LMF.COM loads software licenses from the license database.

VMS$DEVICE_STARTUP.COM directs device configuration:

1. VMS$DEVICE_STARTUP.COM executes the site-specific command procedure, SYS$MANAGER:SYCONFIG.COM, if it exists. This procedure can disable autoconfiguration by clearing the DCL symbol START-UP$AUTOCONFIGURE.

2. Unless disabled by the SYSGEN parameter NOAUTOCONFIG or the STARTUP$AUTOCONFIGURE symbol, the command procedure runs the SYSMAN utility to configure external I/O devices.

3. If the file SYS$SYSTEM:SWAPFILE1.SYS exists, then the command procedure invokes SYSGEN to install it as a secondary swap file.

4. Unless disabled by the SYSGEN parameter NOAUTOCONFIG or the STARTUP$AUTOCONFIGURE symbol, the command procedure invokes VMS$INITIAL-050_CONFIGURE.COM to create the CONFIGURE process if the system is a VMScluster node so that page and swap files on disks other than the system disk can be located and installed.

5. It executes SYS$MANAGER:SYLOGICALS.COM, if the file exists, to define any system-specific logical names.

6. For a satellite VMScluster node, it executes SYS$SPECIFIC:[SYSEXE] SATELLITE_PAGE.COM, if the file exists, to install the page and swap files.

7. It executes SYS$MANAGER:SYPAGSWPFILES.COM, if the file exists, to install any secondary page and swap files, if they exist.

VMS$BASEENVIRON-050_VMS.COM configures the operator's console as appropriate for the system and determines the message classes that will be logged to the console and the operator log file.

VMS$BASEENVIRON-050_SMISERVER.COM creates the system management server (SMISERVER) process for VMScluster nodes and larger standalone systems.

VMS$LPBEGIN-050_STARTUP.COM performs miscellaneous tasks:

1. It invokes SYS$MANAGER:SYSTARTUP_VMS.COM, the site-specific startup command procedure, if it exists.

2. It invokes the DECwindows startup procedure, which starts the windowing software.

3. If the SCSNODE SYSGEN parameter is not blank and the rights database is in use, the command procedure creates the node-specific identifier (the string SYS$NODE_ concatenated with the node name).

4. It enables interactive logins.

LDR$WRAPUP.EXE, executed in the END phase, releases unused portions of the huge pages if the SGN$V_RELEASE_PFNS flag (bit 2) is set in the SYSGEN parameter LOAD_SYS_IMAGES. It also returns the nonpaged pool allocated for second-pass fixups (see Chapter 32).

34.4.3.2   **Site-Specific Startup Command Procedure.** The site-specific startup command procedure, SYS$MANAGER:SYSTARTUP_VMS.COM, is typically edited by the system manager to do the following:

▸ Start batch and print queues
▸ Set terminal speeds and other device characteristics
▸ Create site-specific system logical names
▸ Install additional privileged and shareable images
▸ Mount volumes other than the system disk

> ▸ Start DECnet, if present on the system
> ▸ Produce an error log report
> ▸ Announce system availability

34.5 SYSGEN

SYSGEN and SYSBOOT both use the SYS$SYSTEM:ALPHAVMSSYS.PAR parameter file. SYSGEN typically sets or modifies values of various system parameters; SYSBOOT configures a system using these parameters. SYS-BOOT can also modify system parameters. Table 34.2 briefly compares the operations that SYSGEN and SYSBOOT perform on parameter files.

In an OpenVMS VAX system, SYSGEN also provides device driver loading, device database creation, and device autoconfiguration support. In an Open-VMS AXP system, this functionality has been removed from SYSGEN; the SYSMAN utility provides it.

34.5.1 SYSGEN Parameters

SYSGEN parameters are defined in the source module SYSPARAM.MAR. Through different settings of conditional assembly parameters, this source module produces two object modules: PARAMETER and SYSPARAM. Both of these link into SYSGEN, SYSBOOT, and SYSMAN, and SYSPARAM links into SYS$BASE_IMAGE.EXE as well.

The SYSPARAM source module invokes a macro named PARAMETER to define each adjustable system parameter.

Note that all SYSGEN system parameters are adjustable. The SYSPARAM module also defines a number of system parameters that are not directly adjustable: their values are either static or depend on the values of one or more SYSGEN parameters. The macro $PRMDEF defines the fields of the data structures created by PARAMETER. Table 34.3 lists these fields and flags. For each parameter, the macro also creates a Get System Information ($GET-SYI) item code in the form SYI$_ followed by parameter name. The following code demonstrates the PARAMETER macro invocation that defines the SYS-GEN parameter GBLPAGES:

```
PARAMETER      ADDRESS=SGN$GL_MAXGPGCT_PAGELETS,-
               INTERNAL_VALUE_ADDRESS=SGN$GL_MAXGPGCT_PAGES,-
               DEFAULT=20000,-
               MIN=10240,-
               INTERNAL_MIN=640,-
               NAME=GBLPAGES,-
               SIZE=LONG,-
               TYPE=<SYSGEN,SYS,MAJOR,CONVERT_PAGE>,-
               UNIT=Pagelets,-
               VERSION_MASK=<SYSGEN>
```

In an initialized system, each parameter occupies a cell in a table of active values stored within the address space reserved for the system base image, SYS$BASE_IMAGE.EXE.

Table 34.2 Comparison of SYSGEN and SYSBOOT

SYSGEN	*SYSBOOT*
PURPOSE	
SYSGEN has three unrelated purposes: ▸ It creates parameter files for use in future bootstrap operations. ▸ It modifies dynamic parameters in the running system with the WRITE ACTIVE command. ▸ It creates and installs additional page and swap files.	SYSBOOT configures the system using parameters from ALPHAVMSSYS.PAR or another parameter file.
USE IN SYSTEM INITIALIZATION	
During initialization SYSGEN can be run to record the current SYSGEN parameters.	SYSBOOT is the secondary bootstrap program that executes after APB and before control is passed to the executive.
ENVIRONMENT	
SYSGEN executes in the normal environment of a utility program. The swap/page function requires CMKRNL privilege. A WRITE ACTIVE command also requires CMKRNL privilege. The parameter file operations are protected through the file system.	SYSBOOT runs in a stand-alone environment.
VALID COMMANDS	
USE	USE
USE *file-spec*	USE *file-spec*
USE CURRENT	USE CURRENT
USE DEFAULT	USE DEFAULT
USE ACTIVE	No equivalent command
SET	SET
SHOW	SHOW
EXIT	EXIT (CONTINUE)
WRITE	No equivalent command
Commands associated with additional page and swap files	No equivalent commands
INITIAL CONDITIONS	
Implied USE ACTIVE	Implied USE CURRENT

When SYSBOOT or SYSGEN executes, it maintains a private table of working parameters. It is manipulated by the following SYSGEN and SYS-BOOT commands:

▸ Displayed by SHOW *parameter-name* commands
▸ Altered by SET *parameter-name value* commands

Table 34.3   Information Stored for Each Adjustable Parameter by SYSGEN, SYSBOOT, and SYSMAN

Item	Size of Item
Parameter address in SYS$BASE_IMAGE.EXE [1]	Longword
Parameter default value	Longword
Minimum value that the parameter can assume	Longword
Maximum value that the parameter can assume	Longword
Parameter type flags	Longword

Parameter Type	Display Command
DYNAMIC	SHOW /DYN
STATIC	
SYSGEN	SHOW /GEN
ACP	SHOW /ACP
JBC	SHOW /JOB
RMS	SHOW /RMS
SYS	SHOW /SYS
SPECIAL	SHOW /SPECIAL
DISPLAY	
CONTROL	
MAJOR	SHOW /MAJOR
PQL	SHOW /PQL
NEG	
TTY	SHOW /TTY
SCS	SHOW /SCS
CLUSTER	SHOW /CLUSTER
ASCII	
LGI	SHOW /LGI
CONVERT_PAGE	
MULTIPROCESSING	SHOW /MULTIPROCESSING

Parameter size	Longword
Bit position (if parameter is a flag)	Longword
Parameter's SYSGEN name (counted ASCII string)	16 bytes
Units of allocation (counted ASCII string)	12 bytes

[1] The working value of each parameter is found not only in internal tables in SYSBOOT and SYSGEN but also in the executive itself. In fact, the parameter address (first item) stored for each parameter locates the working value of each parameter in memory within the loaded SYS$BASE_IMAGE.EXE base image.

▶ Overwritten in memory by a USE command
▶ Written to the file ALPHAVMSSYS.PAR by the SYSGEN WRITE CURRENT command
▶ Written to a selected file by the SYSGEN WRITE *file-spec* command
▶ Dynamic parameters are written to SYS$BASE_IMAGE.EXE's memory image by the SYSGEN WRITE ACTIVE command

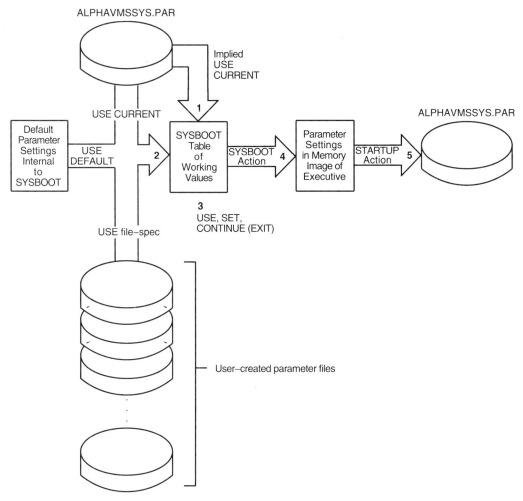

Figure 34.1
Movement of Parameter Data by SYSBOOT and
STARTUP

34.5.2   Use of Parameter Files by SYSBOOT

Figure 34.1 shows the flow of parameter value data during a bootstrap operation. The numbers in the figure correspond to the following steps:

① SYSBOOT first locates the file [SYSEXE]ALPHAVMSSYS.PAR in the SYS$SYSROOT directory and reads its parameter settings into SYSBOOT's working table. In the language of SYSGEN and SYSBOOT commands, this step is an implied command:

```
USE CURRENT
```

This initializes the system with the parameter settings that were saved in ALPHAVMSSYS.PAR through the AUTOGEN command procedure, through the explicit SYSGEN command WRITE CURRENT, or through the setting of the SYSGEN parameter WRITESYSPARAMS during the last boot of the system, as described in step 5. The SYS$UPDATE:AUTO-GEN.COM command procedure (often simply called AUTOGEN) is a system management tool that automatically sets the values of system parameters, the sizes of the page, swap, and dump files, and the contents of the default installed image list. The *OpenVMS System Manager's Manual* gives more information on AUTOGEN.

Each node of a VMScluster system has its own version of ALPHAVMS-SYS.PAR.

② When a conversational bootstrap is selected (that is, the CONV boot flag is requested), SYSBOOT prompts for commands to alter current parameter settings. A USE command at the SYSBOOT prompt results in the working table's being overwritten with an entire set of parameter values. There are three possible sources of these values:

- USE *file-spec* directs SYSBOOT to the indicated parameter file for a new set of values.
- USE DEFAULT causes the working table in SYSBOOT to be filled with the default values for each parameter.
- USE CURRENT causes the parameter values in ALPHAVMSSYS.PAR to be loaded into SYSBOOT's working table. A USE CURRENT command is redundant if it is the first command issued to SYSBOOT.

③ Once the initial conditions are established, individual parameters can be altered with SET commands. The conversational phase of SYSBOOT ends with a CONTINUE (or EXIT) command.

④ Before SYSBOOT transfers control to EXE$INIT, it copies the contents of its working table to the corresponding table in the memory image of the executive.

⑤ One of the steps performed by the startup process copies the parameter table from the memory image of the executive to SYS$SYSTEM:ALPHA-VMSSYS.PAR if the WRITESYSPARAMS parameter is set. SYSBOOT sets this parameter automatically when another parameter is altered in a conversational boot. Since SYSBOOT always uses ALPHAVMSSYS.PAR unless directed otherwise, subsequent bootstraps will use the latest parameter settings even if no conversational bootstrap is selected.

34.5.3   Use of Parameter Files by SYSGEN

SYSGEN's actions, pictured in Figure 34.2, closely correspond to those of SYSBOOT. The numbers in the figure correspond to the following steps:

① The initial contents of SYSGEN's working table are the values taken from the memory image of the executive. The data movement pictured in

Figure 34.2 is a movement from one memory area to another rather than the result of an I/O operation. In any event, SYSGEN begins its execution with an implied command:

```
USE ACTIVE
```

This copies the parameter table from the memory image of the executive into SYSGEN's working table.

    The ACTIVE parameters in the base image in memory are not different from the CURRENT parameters in ALPHAVMSSYS.PAR on disk unless SYSGEN is run and parameters are written to either ACTIVE (memory) or CURRENT (ALPHAVMSSYS.PAR).

② Alternatively, SYSGEN can load its working table from the same sources available to SYSBOOT.

③ SET commands alter individual parameter values. SET only alters the parameter in SYSGEN's working table; the setting disappears on exit from SYSGEN unless preserved with a WRITE command.

④ The WRITE command preserves the contents of SYSGEN's working table in the following way:

- WRITE *file-spec* creates a new parameter file that contains the contents of SYSGEN's working table.
- WRITE CURRENT changes the copy of SYS$SYSTEM:ALPHAVMS-SYS.PAR. The next bootstrap operation will use the updated values automatically.
- Several parameters determine the size of portions of system address space. Other parameters determine the size of blocks of pool space allocated by EXE$INIT. These parameters cannot be changed in a running system. However, many parameters are not used in configuring the system. These parameters are designated DYNAMIC, as discussed in Table 34.3.

    A WRITE ACTIVE command to SYSGEN alters the settings only of dynamic parameters, and only in the memory image of the executive.

    A word of caution is in order here. Before experimenting with a new configuration, save the parameters from a working system in a parameter file. If the new configuration creates an unusable system, the system can be restored to its previous state by rebooting with the saved parameters.

34.6   SYSTEM SHUTDOWN

The operating system provides two mechanisms to shut down a system in a controlled fashion. The preferred method, running SYS$SYSTEM:SHUT-DOWN.COM, provides a warning of the shutdown to system users and performs extensive housekeeping. The alternative method, SYS$SYSTEM:OPC-CRASH.EXE, performs minimal cleanup.

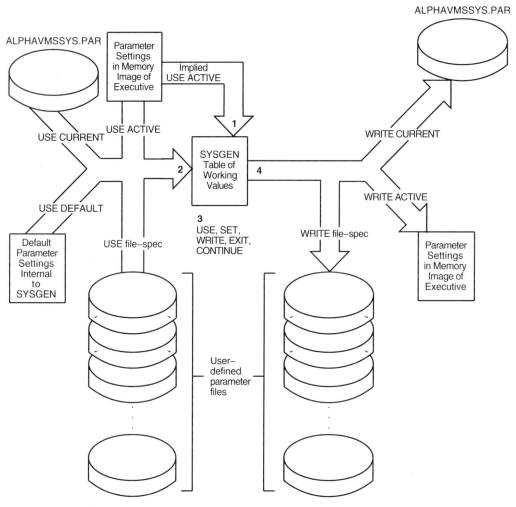

Figure 34.2
Movement of Parameter Data by SYSGEN

34.6.1 SHUTDOWN.COM

SHUTDOWN.COM is an OpenVMS-supplied command procedure that performs extensive cleanup and shuts down a system in a controlled fashion. It requires the privileges CMKRNL, EXQUOTA, LOG_IO, NETMBX, OPER, SECURITY, SYSNAM, SYSPRV, TMPMBX, and WORLD to execute successfully, and will enable them automatically for a user with the SETPRV privilege. SHUTDOWN is typically run from the SYSTEM account or one similarly privileged. SHUTDOWN's tasks include the following:

▸ Optionally saving AUTOGEN feedback information to the file SYS$SYS-TEM:AGEN$FEEDBACK.DAT

- Disabling interactive logins
- Shutting down DECnet
- Stopping queue operations and terminating the queue manager if it is running on this system
- Stopping user processes
- Dismounting mounted volumes
- Stopping secondary processors on an SMP system
- Removing installed images
- Invoking the site-specific shutdown procedure SYSHUTDWN.COM
- Closing the operator's log file
- Stopping the AUDIT_SERVER and ERRFMT processes
- Resetting the battery-backed watch and the time field in the base image based on the current system time

If a shutdown is requested in an AUTOGEN command procedure parameter, AUTOGEN defines the logical name SHUTDOWN$AUTOGEN_SHUT-DOWN before executing the SHUTDOWN command procedure. This notifies SHUTDOWN that the shutdown is coordinated from AUTOGEN and the standard shutdown questions need not be asked.

In addition, SHUTDOWN allows a reboot consistency check to be performed without actually shutting down the system. If a translation exists for the logical name SHUTDOWN$LOG_REBOOT_CHECK, SHUTDOWN creates the file REBOOT_CHECK_*nodename*.LOG, where *nodename* is the name of the system on which SHUTDOWN is executing. The following factors determine the files required to reboot:

- VMScluster membership
- MSCP requirements
- Processor type
- An SMP versus a uniprocessor system
- System boot device (remote boot over the network)

SHUTDOWN's reboot consistency check verifies the existence of files required to reboot. Defining SHUTDOWN$LOG_REBOOT_CHECK causes SHUTDOWN to write the verified file names to the log file and discontinue the shutdown.

SHUTDOWN runs the OPCCRASH program to actually shut down the system. It passes parameters to OPCCRASH via logical names.

The *OpenVMS System Manager's Manual* describes other actions of the SHUTDOWN procedure and its use of the following logical names:

```
SHUTDOWN$MINIMUM_MINUTES
SHUTDOWN$TIME
SHUTDOWN$INFORM_NODES
```

34.6.2   OPCCRASH

OPCCRASH.EXE, built from module [OPCOM]OPCCRASH.MAR, performs the minimal tasks required to shut down a system. Typically it is executed as the final step of the SHUTDOWN.COM procedure, but it can be executed directly in an emergency.

OPCCRASH performs the following:

1. It flushes the file system caches for the system disk (or multiple disks for a volume set) by marking the UCB for dismount and requesting a dismount Queue I/O ($QIO) system service. If the logical name OPC$UNLOAD evaluates as true, OPCCRASH also marks the UCB for unload. When OPCCRASH is executed from SHUTDOWN, SHUTDOWN defines this logical name based on the user's answer to the question, Do you want to spin down the disk volumes?

2. If the logical name OPC$REBOOT does not exist, or if it does not have an equivalence name that begins with Y, y, T, t, or 1, OPCCRASH proceeds to the next step. Otherwise, OPCCRASH sets the EXE$V_REBOOT flag in EXE$GL_FLAGS. This determines whether EXE$BUGCHECKHANDLER, in module BUGCHECK, halts the system or invokes a processor-dependent routine that directs the console to attempt a reboot. When OPCCRASH is executed from SHUTDOWN, SHUTDOWN defines this logical name based on the user's answer to the question, Should an automatic system reboot be performed?

3. If the logical name OPC$NODUMP does not exist, or if it does not have an equivalence name that begins with Y, y, T, t, or 1, OPCCRASH proceeds to the next step. Otherwise, OPCCRASH sets the low-order bit in EXE$GL_DUMPMASK. This determines whether EXE$BUGCHECK writes the contents of memory to the dump file. When OPCCRASH is executed from SHUTDOWN, SHUTDOWN defines the logical name as true. Thus, although EXE$BUGCHECK writes the error log buffers and dump header, no memory dump occurs for an operator-requested shutdown.

4. OPCCRASH acquires the MMG and SCHED spinlocks, forces the modified page list to be written, and releases the MMG spinlock. It places the process into the resource wait state RSN$_MPLEMPTY, where it remains until the modified page list is completely empty. When the process is taken out of the wait state, it resumes execution at IPL 0 with no spinlocks held.

5. If the system is a VMScluster node, OPCCRASH translates the logical name OPC$CLUSTER_SHUTDOWN. If the logical name does not exist, or if it does not have an equivalence name that begins with Y, y, T, t, or 1, OPCCRASH proceeds to the next step. Otherwise, OPCCRASH raises IPL to IPL$_SCS, acquires the SCS spinlock, and invokes the connection manager routine CNX$SHUTDOWN, in module [SYSLOA]CONMAN.

This routine coordinates a clusterwide shutdown. OPCCRASH lowers IPL to 0 and hibernates; the connection manager ultimately crashes the system with a bugcheck. When OPCCRASH is executed from SHUT-DOWN, SHUTDOWN sets this parameter based on the shutdown option CLUSTER_SHUTDOWN.

6. If the system is a VMScluster node, OPCCRASH translates the logical name OPC$REMOVE_NODE. If the logical name does not exist, or if it does not have an equivalence name that begins with Y, y, T, t, or 1, OPC-CRASH proceeds to the next step. Otherwise, OPCCRASH raises IPL to IPL$_SCS, acquires the SCS spinlock, and invokes CNX$SHUTDOWN to communicate the shutdown to the VMScluster connection manager on this and the other nodes. It computes a new value for expected votes by subtracting this node's votes from the current expected votes and invokes the connection manager routine CNX$ADJ_EXPT_VOTES, in module [SYSLOA]CONMAN, to communicate the new value to the remaining VMScluster nodes. It releases the SCS spinlock and waits until quorum is adjusted. When OPCCRASH is executed from SHUTDOWN, SHUTDOWN sets this parameter based on the shutdown option RE-MOVE_NODE.

7. Finally, OPCCRASH crashes the system by generating a fatal OPER-ATOR bugcheck. Chapter 35 describes the bugcheck macro, bugcheck processing, and the actions of EXE$BUGCHECK.

34.7   RELEVANT SOURCE MODULES

Source modules described in this chapter include

[OPCOM]OPCCRASH.MAR
[SYS]ALIGN_FAULT_INIT.MAR
[SYS]ASTDEL.MAR
[SYS]BUGCHECK.B32
[SYS]ERRORLOG.MAR
[SYS]EXCEPTION_INIT.MAR
[SYS]EXCEPTION_ROUTINES.MAR
[SYS]FORKCNTRL.MAR
[SYS]IMAGE_MANAGEMENT_INIT.MAR
[SYS]INIT.MAR
[SYS]IOCINTDISP.M64
[SYS]IOCIOPOST.MAR
[SYS]LOCK_SYSTEM_PAGES.MAR
[SYS]MEMORYALC_DYN.B32
[SYS]MEMORYALC.MAR
[SYS]MODIFY_FAULT.MAR
[SYS]PAGED_SYSTEM_INIT.MAR
[SYS]PAGEFAULT.MAR

[SYS]PERMANENT_DEVICE_DATABASE.MAR
[SYS]POWERFAIL_CONTINUE.MAR
[SYS]PTALLOC.MAR
[SYS]SCHED_ROUTINES.MAR
[SYS]SHELL8K.MAR
[SYS]SMPROUT.MAR
[SYS]SWAPPER.MAR
[SYS]SWAPPER_INIT.MAR
[SYS]SYSCLONEVA.MAR
[SYS]SYSINIT.MAR
[SYS]SYSSETPRT.MAR
[SYS]SYSTEM_PCBS_AND_PHDS.MAR
[SYS]TIMESCHDL.MAR
[SYS]WRTMFYPAG.MAR

35 Error Handling

There is always something to upset the most careful of human calculations.

Ihara Saikaku, *The Japanese Family Storehouse*

This chapter discusses OpenVMS mechanisms used for reporting system-wide errors. Process-specific and image-specific errors are handled by the exception mechanism described in Chapter 6.

Systemwide error-reporting mechanisms include

- The error logging subsystem, by which device drivers and other system components record errors and other events for later inclusion in an error log report
- The bugcheck mechanism, by which the executive shuts down the system and records its state when internal inconsistencies or other unrecoverable errors are detected

35.1 ERROR LOGGING

The error logging subsystem records device errors, CPU-detected errors, and other noteworthy events, such as volume mounts, system startups, system shutdowns, and bugchecks.

35.1.1 Overview of the Error Logging Subsystem

During system initialization a set of fixed-length buffers called error log allocation buffers is created. To log an error, a thread of execution reserves a variable-length portion of an error log allocation buffer, sometimes called an error message buffer, into which an error message can be written. Logging an error occurs in the following steps:

1. A thread of execution, such as a device driver, invokes an executive routine to reserve space for an error message in the current error log allocation buffer.
2. The thread of execution writes an error message into the reserved space and then invokes another executive routine to indicate that the error message is complete.
3. When appropriate, the ERRFMT process is awakened to copy completed error messages to the error log file, SYS$ERRORLOG:ERRLOG.SYS.

Subsequently, the system manager can run the Error Log utility to analyze the contents of the error log file and produce a formatted report.

If the system is shut down or crashes, the error log allocation buffers are copied to the dump file to prevent the loss of valid error messages that have not yet been copied to ERRLOG.SYS. If the system crashes, an error log message is formed and also saved in the dump file. On the next system boot, the SYSINIT process copies the error log allocation buffers and the crash error log message that had been saved in the dump file to a piece of nonpaged pool. When ERRFMT runs, it scans the nonpaged pool copies for valid messages to write to the error log file. In this way, no error log information is lost across a system crash or shutdown.

35.1.2   Error Log Data Structures

During system initialization a set of error log allocation buffers is created in contiguous nonpageable system address space. The number of buffers created is specified by the SYSGEN parameter ERRORLOGBUFFERS, whose default value is 4. The starting address of the set of buffers is recorded in global location EXE$AL_ERLBUFADR.

The size of each error log allocation buffer in 512-byte units, or pagelets, is specified by the SYSGEN parameter ERLBUFFERPAGES, whose default value is 2.

The set of allocation buffers is treated as a ring. Initially, space for error messages is reserved in the first allocation buffer. When it fills, space for error messages is reserved in the second allocation buffer. After an allocation buffer fills, the ERRFMT process is awakened to copy its contents to the error log file so that it can be reused. By the time the last allocation buffer becomes full, the first allocation buffer should be reusable.

The global location EXE$GW_ERLBUFTAIL contains the number of the allocation buffer in which space for error messages is currently being reserved. EXE$GW_ERLBUFHEAD contains the number of the allocation buffer whose contents should be written to the error log file next.

The address of a particular error log allocation buffer is computed as follows:

$$offset = @EXE\$GB\_ERLBUFPAGELETS * 512 * buffer\text{-}number$$
$$address = @EXE\$AL\_ERLBUFADR + offset$$

A header in each error log allocation buffer describes its state. The macro $ERLDEF defines symbolic names for fields in the header. The following fields are of particular interest:

▶ ERL$B_BUSY contains the number of pending error messages in the allocation buffer, messages for which space has been reserved but which have not been completely written.

▶ ERL$B_MSGCNT contains the number of completed messages.

▶ ERL$B_FLAGS has one defined flag, ERL$V_LOCK, which is set to inhibit further reservations in the allocation buffer while ERRFMT is copying its contents.

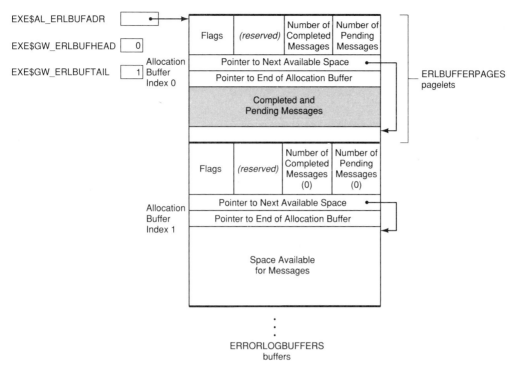

Figure 35.1
Error Log Allocation Buffers

▶ ERL$L_NEXT points to the first available space in the allocation buffer.
▶ ERL$L_END points to the first byte past the end of the allocation buffer and is used to test if it is full.

Figure 35.1 shows these data structures and globals. In this figure, allocation buffer 0 has been filled. Space for error messages will be allocated from allocation buffer 1 next.

The format and length of an error message vary with its type. Each error message has a header that contains type identification and information common to all types of message. The macro $EMBHDDEF defines fields in the header. The macro $EMBETDEF defines the error message types. Most of the common information in the header is written by the routine that reserves space for the error message. Information specific to the error type is written by the component logging the error.

Each message is uniquely identified by a systemwide error sequence number, the contents of global location ERL$GL_SEQUENCE. The number is incremented on each successful attempt to reserve space for an error message. Sequence number gaps in an error log file may indicate lost error messages but most likely indicate deleted time stamp messages (see Section 35.1.6).

35.1.3   **Operation of the Error Logger Routines**

The routines that manage the error log allocation buffers are

- ERL$ALLOCEMB—Reserve space for an error message
- ERL$RELEASEMB—Mark an error message complete

Both are in module ERRORLOG.

ERL$ALLOCEMB is invoked with the size of the error message to be reserved. It takes the following steps.

1. It acquires the EMB spinlock, raising interrupt priority level (IPL) to 31, to synchronize access to the allocation buffer data structures.
2. It tests whether the requested size is larger than an empty allocation buffer and, if so, returns an error status.
3. ERL$ALLOCEMB calculates the address of the allocation buffer indicated by EXE$GW_ERLBUFTAIL.
4. It tests whether the lock flag of that allocation buffer is clear (the usual state). If it is, ERL$ALLOCEMB tests whether the requested space can be reserved within the unused space in the allocation buffer.
5. If the lock flag is set or if the requested space is not available, ERL$ALLOCEMB forces a wakeup of the ERRFMT process. It switches to the next allocation buffer, incrementing EXE$GW_ERLBUFTAIL.

   If the next available allocation buffer is still full of error messages not yet written to the error log file, ERL$ALLOCEMB advances to the next allocation buffer, wrapping back to the beginning of the buffer ring if necessary.

   If it fails to find the requested space, ERL$ALLOCEMB continues in this way until it is successful or reaches its starting point, the allocation buffer whose number is in EXE$GW_ERLBUFHEAD. If unsuccessful, ERL$ALLOCEMB then increments ERL$GL_ALLOCFAILS; releases the EMB spinlock, restoring IPL; and returns an error status. Incrementing ERL$GL_ALLOCFAILS for each unsuccessful attempt to log an error makes it possible to detect messages lost to insufficient allocation buffer capacity.
6. If the requested space is available in an allocation buffer, ERL$ALLOCEMB reserves space for an error message of the requested size, advances the ERL$L_NEXT pointer, and increments the pending message count.

   It fills in certain fields of the message, such as CPU ID, system communication services (SCS) node name, size of the message, number of its allocation buffer, contents of ERL$GL_SEQUENCE, and system time. It then increments the sequence number; releases the EMB spinlock, restoring IPL; and returns a success status, the error sequence number, and the address of the space reserved for the message.

When the component logging the error has written its information in the message buffer, it invokes ERL$RELEASEMB.

ERL$RELEASEMB takes the following steps.

1. It acquires the EMB spinlock, raising IPL to 31, to synchronize access to the allocation buffer data structures.
2. It sets a flag in the error message to indicate that this message is now complete.
3. It extracts the number of the allocation buffer containing the message and computes its address.
4. It subtracts 1 from the allocation buffer pending message count and adds 1 to the completed message count.
5. If the ERRFMT process is hibernating and there are ten or more completed messages in the allocation buffer, ERL$RELEASEMB forces a wakeup of the ERRFMT process.
6. It releases the EMB spinlock, restoring the previous IPL, and returns.

The routine ERL$WAKE, in module ERRORLOG, is invoked to wake the ERRFMT process. It is invoked once a second from EXE$TIMEOUT (see Chapter 12). ERL$WAKE does not necessarily wake the ERRFMT process. Rather, it decrements a counter at global location ERL$GB_BUFTIM and only wakes ERRFMT when the counter reaches zero.

When the counter reaches zero, it is reset to its starting value of 30. (This value is a compile-time parameter, not a SYSGEN parameter.) Thus, a maximum of 30 seconds can elapse before ERRFMT is awakened. This ensures that error messages are written to the error log file at reasonable intervals, even on systems with very few errors.

Both ERL$ALLOCEMB and ERL$RELEASEMB exploit this timing mechanism to force a wakeup of ERRFMT. These routines simply set ERL$GB_BUFTIM to 1 so that the next invocation of ERL$WAKE will wake ERRFMT. ERL$WAKE must acquire the SCHED spinlock to synchronize access to the scheduler database (see Chapters 9 and 13). Thus, it cannot be invoked with a higher ranking spinlock held or from an IPL higher than IPL$_SCHED. ERL$ALLOCEMB and ERL$RELEASEMB run at higher IPLs, holding the EMB spinlock, and are thus unable to invoke ERL$WAKE directly.

ERL$ALLOCEMB forces a wakeup whenever the current error log allocation buffer fills and it must switch to the next one. ERL$RELEASEMB forces a wakeup if the current allocation buffer contains ten or more messages.

If the ERRFMT process is not running, there is no way for messages to be written to the error log file. Initially, attempts to log errors by reserving space for them would be successful. However, once the error log allocation buffers were filled, any subsequent attempt to reserve space would fail. System operation would otherwise be normal.

35.1.4   Device Driver Error Logging

It is not mandatory for device drivers to log errors, although, under most circumstances, it is good practice. To facilitate driver error logging, the executive provides several routines in module ERRORLOG that a driver can invoke to log errors.

Two commonly used routines are ERL$DEVICERR and ERL$DEVIC-TMO. Each of these logs an error associated with a particular I/O request. A driver invokes ERL$DEVICERR to report a device-specific error, and it invokes ERL$DEVICTMO to report a device timeout.

Each routine executes the following sequence:

1. The routine determines whether an error should be logged by testing that error logging is enabled on the device (bit DEV$V_ELG set in unit control block field UCB$L_DEVCHAR) and that error logging is not inhibited for this I/O request (bit IO$V_INHERLOG clear in UCB$L_FUNC). If either of these tests fails, the routine returns.

2. The routine increments UCB$L_ERRCNT, the cumulative number of errors that have occurred on the unit.

3. The routine then tests whether an error log message is already in progress on the device (bit UCB$V_ERLOGIP set in UCB$L_STS) and returns if one is.

4. The routine invokes ERL$ALLOCEMB to reserve space for an error message. The size of the message is defined in the driver dispatch table field DDT$W_ERRORBUF as the sum of the device error message header size and space for device-specific information. If the reservation fails, the routine returns. Otherwise, it records the address of the reserved space in UCB$L_EMB and sets bit UCB$V_ERLOGIP to indicate that an error log message is in progress.

5. In the error message, the routine records information common to all devices, for example, unit number, device name, count of completed operations, error count, and I/O function.

6. The routine then invokes the device driver's register dump routine to record device-specific information in the error message. Typically, this information consists of device register contents at the time of the error.

7. When the driver register dump routine returns, the error logging routine returns control to the device driver. When the device driver finishes processing the I/O request, it invokes IOC$REQCOM, in module IOSUBN-PAG.

8. IOC$REQCOM, finding that there is an error log message in progress, records the final I/O request status, device status, and error retry counters in the error message. It then invokes ERL$RELEASEMB to indicate that the error message has been completely written.

Some device drivers report conditions that are not associated with a particular I/O request; such conditions are called device attention errors. To log this kind of an error, a driver invokes ERL$DEVICEATTN. This routine is similar to ERL$DEVICERR and ERL$DEVICTMO in that it reserves space for and fills in an error message. However, the routine itself, rather than IOC$REQCOM, invokes ERL$RELEASEMB to indicate that the message is completely written.

In addition to ERL$DEVICEATTN, the SCS port and class drivers use several other error log routines:

▶ ERL$LOGSTATUS—Used by the disk and tape class drivers to log an error status code returned in a mass storage control protocol (MSCP) end packet. The end packet itself is written to the error log file with ERL$LOGMESSAGE.

▶ ERL$LOGMESSAGE—Used by the port and class drivers to log an error condition associated with a command packet, for example, a packet that contains invalid data.

▶ ERL$LOG_DMSCP—Used by the disk class driver (DUDRIVER) to log controller errors and resets.

▶ ERL$LOG_TMSCP—Similar to ERL$LOG_DMSCP, this is used by the tape class driver (TUDRIVER) to log controller errors and resets.

35.1.5   Other Error Log Messages

The OpenVMS operating system uses the error log subsystem to record events other than device errors. Other kinds of entries written to the error log include the following:

▶ "Warm start," a successful restart after a power failure
▶ "Cold start," a successful system bootstrap (either a cold or warm boot)
▶ Fatal and nonfatal bugchecks (see Section 35.2)
▶ Machine check
▶ Memory and other CPU-specific errors
▶ Volume mount and dismount
▶ A user-requested message written by the Send Message to Error Logger ($SNDERR) system service (see Chapter 39)
▶ Time stamp (see Section 35.1.6)

35.1.6   The ERRFMT Process

During system initialization the detached ERRFMT process is created with user identification code [1,6] and several privileges, including CMKRNL. ERRFMT runs partly in kernel mode and partly in user mode. In kernel mode, it can access the error log allocation buffers and copy their contents to its own process space. In user mode, it scans the copied allocation buffer contents for valid messages and writes the messages to the error log file SYS$ERRORLOG:ERRLOG.SYS.

When ERRFMT is first started, it enters kernel mode, using the Change to Kernel Mode ($CMKRNL) system service. It tests whether there are any error log allocation buffers restored from the dump file to be processed. (During system initialization SYSINIT copied them and, if appropriate, the error log entry in the dump header to nonpaged pool and stored the address of the nonpaged pool in global location EXE$GL_SAVED_EMBS.) If EXE$GL_SAVED_

EMBS has nonzero contents, ERRFMT initializes several variables to indicate that some saved error log allocation buffers require processing in a later step.

ERRFMT requests the Set Timer ($SETIMR) system service to request an asynchronous system trap (AST) notification in ten minutes. When the time expires, its AST procedure executes and invokes ERL$ALLOCEMB, writes a time stamp message containing the time of day, invokes ERL$RELEASEMB, and requests the $SETIMR system service again. Thus, every ten minutes, ERRFMT's kernel mode AST procedure logs a time stamp to indicate that ERRFMT is executing and that the system is operational.

After kernel mode initialization is complete, ERRFMT returns to user mode and executes the following loop to process an error log allocation buffer:

1. In a kernel mode procedure, ERRFMT tries to select an error log allocation buffer to process:

   a. If there are multiple allocation buffers restored from the dump file to be processed, it selects the first one in the buffer ring, advances the ring pointer, copies the buffer contents to P0 space, decrements the count of restored unprocessed allocation buffers, and returns.

   b. If there is only one restored allocation buffer left to be processed, ERRFMT copies its contents, deallocates the nonpaged pool occupied by the restored buffers, clears EXE$GL_SAVED_EMBS, and returns.

   c. If there are no restored allocation buffers to be processed, ERRFMT acquires the EMB spinlock, raising IPL to 31. It determines the next ordinary error log allocation buffer to be processed and sets the lock flag in it to prevent any further reservations.

   d. It tests the pending error message counter in the allocation buffer to determine whether there are error messages for which space has been reserved and not yet released.

   If there are pending messages, ERRFMT releases the EMB spinlock, lowering IPL to 0. It sets a timer and waits for half a second before testing the counter again. ERRFMT repeats its wait-and-test sequence until there are no more pending messages or until it has waited 255 times. It then reacquires the EMB spinlock.

   e. ERRFMT then copies the error log allocation buffer contents to its own P0 space and compares the copy to the original to detect any changes that might have occurred during the copy. If the two are not equal, ERRFMT repeats the copy, trying to get a consistent copy of the buffer contents. If necessary, it repeats the copy-and-compare sequence 255 times. This sequence is an alternative to copying the buffer contents with the EMB spinlock held and at IPL 31. If 255 attempts fail to get a consistent copy, ERRFMT uses the copy it has.

   f. Once ERRFMT has copied the allocation buffer contents, it reacquires the EMB spinlock, clears the pending and completed message counts in the copied buffer, resets ERL$L_NEXT to point to the space just after the buffer header, and clears its lock flag. It updates EXE$GW_ERLBUFHEAD to point to the next allocation buffer, advancing it to the beginning of the ring if necessary. It releases the EMB spinlock, restoring the previous IPL.

   g. ERRFMT then returns to user mode with a status indicating whether there are any completed messages in the copied allocation buffer.

2. In user mode, ERRFMT checks whether any completed messages require processing. If not, ERRFMT hibernates until it is awakened through ERL$WAKE and then returns to the first step to select an error log allocation buffer.

3. If there are completed messages in the buffer, ERRFMT processes them and writes the valid ones to the error log file. Whenever ERRFMT finds one of its time stamp messages, it checks whether the previous message written to the error log file is also a time stamp. If so, ERRFMT updates the record containing the older time stamp with the newer one. This avoids filling the error log file with time stamps and ensures that the newest time stamp is recorded. Note, however, that this can cause a sequence number gap in the error log file messages.

4. If ERRFMT detects a volume mounted or dismounted message in the error log allocation buffer, it checks the SYSGEN parameter MOUNTMSG or DISMOUMSG. If the appropriate parameter is set, ERRFMT sends a volume mounted or dismounted message to terminals enabled as disk or tape operators. By default the SYSGEN parameters are zero, disabling the sending of these messages to operator terminals.

5. If any process has declared an error log mailbox (see Section 35.1.7), ERRFMT writes every message in the error log allocation buffer to that mailbox.

6. ERRFMT proceeds to the first step to select another error log allocation buffer.

35.1.7   Error Log Mailbox

The error logging subsystem provides the capability for up to five processes to monitor error logging activity as it happens rather than wait for offline processing with the Error Log utility. This capability is provided through the undocumented Declare Error Log Mailbox ($DERLMB) system service. This system service is provided for use by Digital's software only and is unsupported for any other use.

To assign an error log mailbox, a process with DIAGNOSE privilege requests the $DERLMB system service with the unit number of a mailbox to receive error log messages. A process requests this service with a unit number of zero to cancel its use of an error log mailbox.

The $DERLMB system service procedure, EXE$DERLMB in module SYS-DERLMB, runs in kernel mode. It first tests whether the process has DIAGNOSE privilege; if it does not, the system service returns the error status SS$_NOPRIV. If it does, EXE$DERLMB scans the array of error log mailbox descriptors, which begins at EXE$AQ_ERLMBX. It synchronizes access to the array by acquiring the SCHED spinlock, raising IPL to IPL$_SCHED.

If the process is trying to assign an error log mailbox, EXE$DERLMB tries to find a free descriptor. If it finds one, it stores the unit number in the first word of the mailbox descriptor and the internal process ID (IPID) of the requesting process in the second longword. It releases the SCHED spinlock and returns the status SS$_NORMAL. Otherwise, if no descriptor is free, EXE$DERLMB releases the SCHED spinlock and returns the error status SS$_DEVALLOC.

If the process is trying to cancel use of an error log mailbox, EXE$DERLMB scans the descriptor array for the one associated with this process's IPID. If it finds one, it clears it. The Image Rundown ($RUNDWN) system service (see Chapter 28) performs a similar scan to ensure that error log mailbox use is canceled at image rundown.

35.2 BUGCHECKS

When OpenVMS code detects an internal inconsistency, such as a corrupted data structure or an unexpected exception, it generates a bugcheck. If the inconsistency is not severe enough to prevent continued system operation, the bugcheck generated is nonfatal and merely results in an error log entry.

If the error is serious enough to jeopardize system operation and data integrity, OpenVMS code generates a fatal bugcheck. This generally results in aborting normal system operation, recording the contents of memory to a dump file for later analysis, and rebooting the system.

35.2.1 Bugcheck Mechanism

The Alpha AXP architecture defines the basic bugcheck mechanism: the unprivileged CALL_PAL BUGCHK instruction, which generates a bugcheck exception. As a result of the exception, access mode is changed to kernel, an exception frame (see Chapter 3) is built on the kernel stack, and control is transferred to the service routine specified in the system control block entry for bugcheck exceptions.

When entered, the OpenVMS bugcheck exception service routine expects R16 to contain a value identifying the bugcheck.

MACRO-32 source code generates a bugcheck by invoking the BUG_CHECK macro. The macro has one required argument, a name representing the bugcheck, and two optional arguments:

▶ The TYPE argument specifies whether the system should continue after processing the bugcheck (a value of CONT) or crash (a value of FATAL). Its default value is CONT.

▶ The REBOOT argument specifies whether a crash should be followed by a warm bootstrap (a value of WARM_BOOT) or a cold bootstrap (a value of COLD_BOOT). Its default value is WARM_BOOT. Chapter 33 describes the distinction between these types of bootstrap.

The BUG_CHECK macro constructs a value to load into R16 based on its arguments.

It prefaces the bugcheck name with the string BUG$_ to generate a symbolic bugcheck name. Constant values for all the bugcheck names are defined in module BUGCHECK_CODES, which is part of the object module library SYS$LIBRARY:VMS$VOLATILE_PRIVATE_INTERFACES.OLB. Some bugcheck names represent unique problems and are used in only one BUG_CHECK invocation; other bugcheck names represent more common problems and have multiple uses throughout the executive.

Each value is a multiple of 8 so that the low-order three bits can represent the bugcheck severity. The BUG_CHECK macro ORs bits representing the other two arguments into the bugcheck value. If TYPE is FATAL, bit 2 of the value is 1; otherwise, it is 0. If TYPE is FATAL and REBOOT is COLD_BOOT, bit 0 of the value is 1; otherwise, it is 0. Bit 1 is not used and is always 0.

This fatal bugcheck MACRO-32 example is extracted from SCH$FIND_NEXT_PROC, in module SCHED_ROUTINES:

```
QEMPTY:   BUG_CHECK   INCON_SCHED,FATAL
```

Its invocation generates the following MACRO-32 code:

```
        EVAX_STQ    R16,-(SP)
        EVAX_BUGCHK #<BUG$_INCON_SCHED!4>
        HALT
```

The EVAX_BUGCHK built-in generates a load into R16 of the value BUG$_INCON_SCHED ORed with 4 and a CALL_PAL BUGCHK instruction. After a fatal bugcheck, control never returns from the bugcheck exception service routine, and the HALT instruction is not executed. It must, however, be there for the compiler to analyze the code flow correctly.

This example of a fatal bugcheck is extracted from EXE$ALONONPAGED_INT, in the BLISS module MEMORYALC_DYN_MON:

```
        $BUG_CHECK (BADALORQSZ,FATAL);
```

Its invocation generates the following AXP instructions:

```
        LDQ       R1, 16(R4)
        BIS       R1, 4, R1
        SEXTL     R1, R16
        CALL_PAL  129
        HALT
```

This nonfatal bugcheck MACRO-32 example is extracted from module SYSQIOREQ.

```
BUG_CHECK   NONEXSTACP
```

Its invocation generates the following MACRO-32 code:

```
EVAX_STQ    R16,-(SP)
EVAX_BUGCHK #<BUG$_NONEXSTACP>
EVAX_LDQ    (SP)+,R16
```

When the bugcheck exception service routine is entered, the stack contains an exception stack frame and may contain contents of R16 saved prior to the load of the bugcheck value. The program counter (PC) in the exception stack frame is the address of the instruction following the CALL_PAL BUGCHK. As a result, the bugcheck PC shown in a dump is an address four bytes past the actual bugcheck.

The OpenVMS bugcheck exception service routine is implemented in two parts. Initially, the exception is dispatched to routine EXE$BUGCHECK, in module BUGCHECK_SAVE. Written in Alpha AXP assembly language, EXE$BUGCHECK can control the order in which the registers are saved.

EXE$BUGCHECK first saves all the integer registers on the stack except those already saved in the exception frame (R2–R7). It saves all the processor registers, and if the process is performing floating-point calculations, it saves all the floating-point registers on the stack.

It then calls EXE$BUGCHECKHANDLER, in module BUGCHECK, which performs most of the processing associated with both fatal and nonfatal bugchecks. The actions of EXE$BUGCHECKHANDLER vary, depending on the access mode in which the bugcheck occurred and the severity of the bugcheck. The sections that follow describe its actions.

35.2.2   Bugchecks from User and Supervisor Modes

The OpenVMS operating system itself generates few bugchecks from user or supervisor mode. It provides the mechanism for use by other software.

When a bugcheck is generated from user or supervisor mode code running in a process with BUGCHK privilege, EXE$BUGCHECKHANDLER writes an error log message, invoking ERL$ALLOCEMB and ERL$RELEASEMB (see Section 35.1.3). The error message resembles that shown in Table 35.1 but has an entry type of user-generated bugcheck and lacks the contents of CPU-specific registers.

EXE$BUGCHECKHANDLER returns to EXE$BUGCHECK with a value indicating whether the bugcheck is fatal. If it is fatal, EXE$BUGCHECK executes an REI instruction to return to the access mode of the bugcheck and requests the Exit ($EXIT) system service. It specifies the value SS$_BUGCHECK as the final image status. What happens as a result of this service request depends on whether the process is executing a single image (without a command language interpreter, CLI, to establish a supervisor mode exit handler) or is an interactive or batch job.

Table 35.1   Contents of Error Log Message for Fatal Bugcheck (CRASH CPU)

Description	Size
Error message header	12 bytes
▸ Size in bytes of message	Word
▸ Allocation buffer number	Word
▸ Reserved	Longword
▸ Error message valid indicator	Byte
▸ Reserved	3 bytes
System ID of CRASH CPU	Longword
Error message header revision level (contains $FFFB_{16}$)	Word
Extended system ID information from CRASH CPU	Longword
CPU ID of CRASH CPU	Longword
Device class (unused)	Byte
Device type (unused)	Byte
SCS node name	16 bytes
Flags	Word
Operating system type	Byte
Header size	Byte
Entry type (contains EMB$K_CR = 25_{16})	Word
System time when crash occurred (from EXE$GQ_SYSTIME)	Quadword
Error log sequence number (low-order word of ERL$GL_SEQUENCE)	Word
Software version	Quadword
Error type mask	Longword
System absolute time in seconds (from EXE$GL_ABSTIM)	Longword
Contents of KSP, ESP, SSP, USP, from CRASH CPU	4 quadwords
Contents of R0–R28, FP, SP, PC, PS from CRASH CPU	33 quadwords
Contents of PTBR, PCBB, PRBR, VPTB, SCBB, SISR, ASN, ASTSR and ASTEN, FEN, IPL, MCES from CRASH CPU	11 quadwords
Contents of CPU-specific registers from CRASH CPU	24 longwords
Bugcheck value on CRASH CPU	Longword
ID of process current on CRASH CPU	Longword
Name of process current on CRASH CPU	16 bytes

▸ If the process is executing a single image, a fatal bugcheck from user or supervisor mode typically results in process deletion.

▸ If the process has a CLI, a fatal bugcheck generated from an interactive or batch job typically causes the currently executing image to exit and control to be passed to the CLI through its supervisor mode exit handler. The CLI prompts for the next command.

In either case, the only difference between fatal user and supervisor mode bugchecks is that user mode exit handlers are not called when a fatal bugcheck is generated from supervisor mode.

If the bugcheck is not fatal, EXE$BUGCHECK restores the scratch registers from the stack (any nonscratch registers used by EXE$BUGCHECK-

HANDLER were saved and restored by compiler-generated code) and dismisses the exception. Execution continues with the instruction following the CALL_PAL BUGCHK instruction.

The SYSGEN parameter BUGCHECKFATAL has no effect on bugchecks generated from user or supervisor mode. Only bit 2 of the bugcheck value determines whether a given bugcheck is fatal. Fatal user and supervisor mode bugchecks affect only the current process.

35.2.3   Bugchecks from Executive and Kernel Modes

Various OpenVMS components generate bugchecks from executive and kernel modes.

If an executive or kernel mode bugcheck value is not fatal and the SYSGEN parameter BUGCHECKFATAL is zero, EXE$BUGCHECKHANDLER proceeds as it does for nonfatal bugchecks for the outer two access modes. It writes an error log message, as described in Section 35.2.2, and returns to EXE$BUGCHECK. EXE$BUGCHECK restores the scratch registers from the stack and dismisses the exception, passing control back to the instruction following the CALL_PAL BUGCHK instruction. (In contrast, after a fatal bugcheck, control never returns from the bugcheck exception service routine.)

Typically, execution continues with no further effects. However, the routine that detected the error and generated the bugcheck can take further action. One example of such a routine is the last chance handler for executive mode exceptions. It generates the nonfatal bugcheck SSRVEXCEPT (unexpected system service exception). On the presumption that process data structures are inconsistent, it then requests the $EXIT system service. Exiting from executive mode results in process deletion. Another example is the Record Management Services (RMS) routine that generates the nonfatal bugcheck RMSBUG. On the presumption that process RMS data structures are inconsistent, it deletes the process by requesting the Delete Process ($DELPRC) system service.

In the case of a fatal bugcheck, EXE$BUGCHECKHANDLER's most important function is to record the contents of the error log allocation buffers and memory in the dump file. After the system reboots, during system initialization, error log allocation buffers in the dump file are copied to nonpaged pool for processing by the ERRFMT process. The dump file can be examined subsequently with the System Dump Analyzer (SDA) to determine the cause of the crash. EXE$BUGCHECKHANDLER also halts the system to prevent any further system operations in case they might lead to data corruption.

If BUGCHECKFATAL is 1, any executive or kernel mode bugcheck is treated as fatal, independent of bit 2 of the bugcheck value. By default BUGCHECKFATAL is 0, which means that a nonfatal inner access mode bugcheck does not cause the system to crash. If either BUGCHECKFATAL is 1 or the bugcheck is fatal, EXE$BUGCHECKHANDLER performs fatal bugcheck processing.

Section 35.2.4 describes the contents of the dump file, and Section 35.2.5 provides details about fatal bugcheck processing.

35.2.4   System Dump File

System initialization code locates and opens the dump file. The dump file must be in directory SYS$SPECIFIC:[SYSEXE] on the system disk. Members of a VMScluster system can share a dump file: each must have a synonym directory entry for the shared file in its own root. By default the dump file is SYSDUMP.DMP. In its absence, the executive instead writes a dump to PAGEFILE.SYS, if it exists. (Subsequent analysis of a dump written to the page file requires that the SYSGEN parameter SAVEDUMP be 1.)

The dump file is divided into several pieces:

1. The first two blocks of the file, virtual block numbers (VBN) 1 and 2, contain the dump header. The dump header includes information that enables SDA to determine the state of the dump file and locate key information in it. The contents of the dump header are shown in Table 35.2. Symbolic offsets for its field names are defined by the macro $DMPDEF. The field names are displayed in the table without the prefix DMP$x_.

2. The next blocks contain the error log allocation buffers. The SYSGEN parameter ERLBUFFERPAGES specifies the number of pagelets or blocks in each buffer. The SYSGEN parameter ERRORLOGBUFFERS specifies how many allocation buffers there are. The dump header fields DMP$B_ERLBUFPAGES and DMP$W_ERLBUFCNT contain copies of this information.

3. The rest of the dump file is filled with memory contents.

Note that the dump header includes an error log message. The message associated with a fatal bugcheck, shown in Table 35.1, is recorded in the header to avoid loss of information in case the error log allocation buffers are full when the bugcheck occurs. The macros $EMBHDDEF and $EMBCRDEF define symbolic offsets for fields in this error log message.

After the system reboots, SYSINIT (see Chapter 34) copies the fatal bugcheck error log message to nonpaged pool, along with the error log allocation buffers saved in the dump file. It stores their starting address in global location EXE$GL_SAVED_EMBS. Later, as described in Section 35.1.6, the ERRFMT process will record them in the error log file.

There are two types of dump: a dump of physical memory and a dump of selected virtual addresses.

A physical dump generally requires that all physical memory be written to the dump file to ensure the presence of all the page table pages required for

SDA to emulate translation of system virtual addresses. These include the level 1 page table of the current process, the shared level 2 page table that maps the system page table, and the level 3 page table pages that compose the system page table. To ensure the presence of all the necessary page table pages, a dump file for a physical memory dump should be large enough for a complete dump. The required file size is the sum of two blocks for the header; ERRORLOGBUFFERS times ERLBUFFERPAGES blocks for the error log allocation buffers; and as many blocks as required for the physical pages of memory in use by the executive. Note that one page of memory on an AXP system with a page size of 8 KB will occupy 16 disk blocks.

A dump of selected virtual address spaces makes possible a dump of a system with more physical memory than dump file space. In a selective dump, related pages of virtual address space are written to the dump file as a unit called a logical memory block (LMB). For example, one LMB consists of the system page table; another is the address space of a particular process. Those LMBs likely to be most useful in crash dump analysis are written first. Section 35.2.5.2 describes LMBs in more detail.

A value of 1 or 3 for the SYSGEN parameter DUMPSTYLE specifies a selective crash dump. The parameter's default value specifies a physical dump. Its default after the AUTOGEN utility has been run is 1, specifying a selective dump.

35.2.5 Fatal Bugcheck Processing

In an OpenVMS VAX system, the code that performs fatal bugcheck processing and its data are not referenced during normal system operation. When needed, they are read into memory, overlaying nonpaged read-only executive code. This implementation saves memory during normal operations but results in added complexity when a fatal bugcheck occurs.

In contrast, all OpenVMS AXP fatal bugcheck code and most of the associated data are permanently resident. As a result of the Alpha AXP instruction set and addressing modes, moving a piece of code to a different virtual address requires that its address references be relocated. Rather than overlay other code with the fatal bugcheck code and then have to relocate the fatal bugcheck code, OpenVMS AXP makes the code and data resident, except for the ASCII bugcheck messages.

A unique ASCII message describes each bugcheck value. The text messages and a table identifying the location of each are built as part of the BUGCHECK module. The table is resident, but the text messages are in a pageable image section. When a fatal bugcheck occurs, the block containing its message is read into memory. No message can span two blocks.

EXE$BUGCHECKHANDLER does not use standard I/O mechanisms to read the bugcheck messages or write the dump because they may be affected by the system inconsistency that triggered the fatal bugcheck. Instead, it performs I/O through the bootstrap system device driver, the one used during system initialization (see Chapter 33). Furthermore, EXE$BUGCHECKHAN-DLER does not request the file system to look up the image containing the bugcheck messages or the dump file. Instead, it uses information about their locations that was recorded and checksummed at system initialization.

In processing a fatal bugcheck, EXE$BUGCHECKHANDLER takes the following steps:

1. It raises IPL to 31. It copies the saved register contents from the stack to the per-CPU database (see Chapter 37). It also stores the bugcheck value in the per-CPU database. (Information about the bugcheck cannot be saved in the per-CPU database until IPL has been raised to block process context switching and other threads of execution.)

2. It invokes EXE$SAVE_CONTEXT, in module [CPU*xxyy*]CRD_ROU-TINES_*xxyy*, to save processor-specific registers. For example, if running on the primary, EXE$SAVE_CONTEXT for the DEC 7000 Model 600 series CPUs records information about correctable memory errors in the error log allocation buffers and returns.

3. In an SMP system, the first CPU to execute EXE$BUGCHECKHAN-DLER is called the CRASH CPU. It informs the other CPUs that a fatal bugcheck is in progress and takes a number of steps to ensure that a consistent system state can be saved. After these steps, the primary CPU in the system completes fatal bugcheck processing. Chapter 37 contains further details on fatal bugcheck processing in an SMP system.

4. EXE$BUGCHECKHANDLER joins the override set (see Chapter 37) and sets bit SMP$V_ENABLED in SMP$GL_FLAGS to prevent spinlock acquisition and release routines from altering IPL.

5. EXE$BUGCHECKHANDLER invokes SCS$SHUTDOWN, in module [CLUSTER]SYS$SCS, to shut down any SCS circuits.

6. It invokes EXE$SHUTDWNADP, in module [SYSLOA]MISC_SUPPORT, to shut down all adapters and invokes EXE$INIBOOTADP, in module [CPU*xxyy*]MISC_SUPPORT, to initialize the adapter that connects the system device. Appendix G explains the meaning of *xxyy* in the directory name.

7. It validates the checksum of the boot control block, the data structure containing the locations of the bugcheck messages and dump file. If the boot control block checksum is no longer valid, EXE$BUGCHECKHAN-DLER clears a flag tested in a later step.

8. If the boot control block checksum is valid, EXE$BUGCHECKHAN-DLER calls the device initialization routine in the bootstrap system device driver.

9. If this is an operator-requested shutdown bugcheck, it skips to step 11. If this is any other type of bugcheck and the boot control block checksum is valid, it determines the block number in EXCEPTION.EXE that contains the bugcheck message associated with the bugcheck type and reads that block.

Table 35.2 Contents of the Dump Header

Field Name	Description		Size
ERRSEQ	Next error log sequence number		Longword
FLAGS	Dump file flags		Word
		Bit	
	Meaning if Set	*Position*	
	Dump file has been analyzed	0	
	Dump has no valid data	1	
	Error occurred writing header	2	
	Error occurred writing error log allocation buffers	3	
	Error occurred writing memory	4	
	Error occurred writing system page table	5	
	Dump completely written	6	
	Header and error log allocation buffers completely written	7	
	Dump style	8–11	
	0 = full physical memory dump		
	1 = selective memory dump		
	Unused	12–15	
	Unused		Byte
ERLBUFPAGES	Number of pagelets in each error log allocation buffer		Byte
PTBR, *x*SP	Contents of PTBR, KSP, ESP, SSP, USP		5 quadwords
PALREV	PALcode revision level		Longword
MEMPAG	Size of a page of memory, in bytes		Longword
PAGEBITS	Left-shift factor to convert page number to address		Longword
PAGEMASK	Mask for converting address to byte within page offset		Longword
SYMVECT_VA	Virtual address of SYS$BASE_ IMAGE.EXE symbol vector		Longword
SYSVER	System version number		Longword
CHECK	1's complement of previous longword		Longword
DUMPVER	Dump file version (0536$_{16}$ for OpenVMS AXP Version 1.5)		Word
ERLBUFCNT	Number of error log allocation buffers		Word
ERLBUFHEAD	Index of error log allocation buffer ring head		Word
ERLBUFTAIL	Index of error log allocation buffer ring tail		Word
ERRSTATUS	Last I/O status from writing the dump		Longword
DUMPERRS	Number of errors that occurred writing the dump		Longword
DUMPBLOCKCNT	Actual number of dump blocks written		Longword

Table 35.2   Contents of the Dump Header *(continued)*

Field Name	Description	Size
NEEDBLOCKCNT	Number of blocks required for complete dump	Longword
SAVPRCCNT	Number of processes written in selective dump	Longword
SYSIDENT	System version number in ASCII	Quadword
HWRPB_VBN	Virtual block number in dump of hardware restart parameter block	Longword
TRAP_VALID	Low bit set if an exception occurred during the writing of a selective dump	Longword
TRAP_R*n*	Contents of R2–R7 at time of exception	6 quadwords
TRAP_PC	Contents of PC at time of exception	Quadword
TRAP_PS	Contents of PS at time of exception	Quadword
TRAP_VA	Faulting virtual address at time of exception	Quadword
TRAP_MMF	Memory management flags describing the exception	Quadword
EXTRA_SPACE	Unused	64 bytes
CRASHERL	Error log message for fatal bugcheck (see Table 35.1)	158 longwords

10. EXE$BUGCHECKHANDLER writes information about the bugcheck to the console terminal. This information can include the bugcheck message, addresses of loaded executive images, current process name, contents of integer and processor registers, and contents of stacks relevant to the crash. In an SMP system, EXE$BUGCHECKHANDLER writes additional information, such as which CPUs are active and which CPU incurred the fatal bugcheck. How much is written depends on the value of the SYSGEN parameter DUMPSTYLE. A value of 0 or 1 inhibits most output. The default value of this parameter specifies brief rather than verbose output.

    The console output is written before the dump file and should not be interrupted by halting the processor from the console terminal. Such an interruption prevents the dump file from being written.

11. If the SYSGEN parameter BUGREBOOT is zero and if XDELTA has been loaded, EXE$BUGCHECKHANDLER executes a CALL_PAL BPT instruction to transfer control to XDELTA. This enables a human operator to examine the state of the operating system through XDELTA commands.

12. Based on the value of the BUGREBOOT parameter and bit 0 of the bugcheck value, EXE$BUGCHECKHANDLER selects one of the following halt action values: perform a cold bootstrap, perform a warm bootstrap, or remain halted. It stores the value in the hardware restart parameter block (HWRPB) per-CPU slot.

13. EXE$BUGCHECKHANDLER determines whether a dump is to be written and, if so, what kind of dump:

    - If the SYSGEN parameter DUMPBUG is 0, no dump is written. (Its default value is 1.)
    - If the boot control block was found to be invalid, no dump is written.
    - If neither SYS$SPECIFIC:[SYSEXE]SYSDUMP.DMP nor PAGEFILE.SYS existed at boot time, no dump is written.
    - If, during system initialization, system page table entries (SPTEs) could not be allocated for EXE$BUGCHECKHANDLER's use in I/O requests, no dump can be written. INIT_BUGCHECK, in module BUGCHECK, an executive image initialization routine, attempts to allocate enough SPTEs to be able to write 128 blocks at once. On an AXP CPU with a page size of 8 KB, it tries to allocate eight SPTEs.
    - If this is an operator-requested shutdown generated through the system shutdown command procedure, only the dump header and error log allocation buffers are written to the dump file.
    - If the parameter DUMPSTYLE is 1 or 3, memory is dumped selectively; otherwise, a physical memory dump is written. (The default value of this parameter specifies a physical dump.)

14. If no dump is to be written, EXE$BUGCHECKHANDLER concludes with the steps described in Section 35.2.5.3.

15. If any type of dump is to be written, EXE$BUGCHECKHANDLER next builds the dump header and its error log message. It writes the dump header and the contents of the error log allocation buffers to the dump file. Then it rewrites the dump header with a status indicating that the dump contains the error log allocation buffers.

16. If this is an operator-requested shutdown and no further dump is necessary, EXE$BUGCHECKHANDLER concludes with the steps described in Section 35.2.5.3. Otherwise, it determines whether a physical or selective dump is to be written. The next two sections describe its actions in writing these different types of memory dumps.

35.2.5.1 **Physical Memory Dump.** EXE$BUGCHECKHANDLER uses the memory descriptors in the HWRPB constructed by the console subsystem (see Chapter 33) to provide an accurate description of physical address space. It uses the contents of the global cell MMG$GL_MAXMEM as the largest page frame number (PFN) that should be written to the dump file. This cell is initialized as the highest page in use by the operating system. If the SYSGEN parameter PHYSICAL_MEMORY has been set to less memory than is available, the executive only uses the lowest PHYSICAL_MEMORY megabytes of memory.

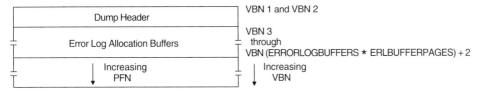

Figure 35.2
Layout of a Physical Memory Dump

Writing a maximum of 128 blocks at a time, EXE$BUGCHECKHANDLER writes memory contents to the dump file. It begins writing to the block following the error log allocation buffers and continues until it gets to the end of the dump file or until it has written all the physical memory in use by the operating system. If EXE$BUGCHECKHANDLER encounters a page on the bad page list, it does not write it to the dump file and instead skips over the number of disk blocks the page would have occupied. Figure 35.2 shows the layout of a physical memory dump.

35.2.5.2 **Selective Memory Dump.** In a selective dump, related pages of virtual address space are written to the dump file as an LMB. A list in EXE$BUG-CHECKHANDLER explicitly specifies the order in which LMBs are written to the dump file, as follows:

1. The system page table.
2. System space. This excludes the system page table but includes the global page table. It includes any system transition pages, pages that are invalid but on the free or modified page list.
3. Global pages in use at the time of the crash.
4. The process-private address space of the process current at the time of the crash, excluding global pages and including any of its pages on the free and modified page lists. In an SMP system, the address space of the process current on the CRASH CPU is written in this step.
5. The process-private address spaces of the following processes, in the specified order:
   a. MSCPmount
   b. NETACP
   c. REMACP
   d. LES$ACP
   e. In an SMP system, processes current on other active CPUs
   f. Other resident processes, in order by process index

Following the dump header and error log allocation buffers, EXE$BUG-CHECKHANDLER writes LMBs to the dump file until it is full or the end of the list is reached.

Each LMB in a dump begins with a descriptor that identifies the block and gives its size. The range of addresses to be included in a block is determined by the particular address space being dumped.

Not all virtual addresses in the range spanned by an LMB are necessarily included in it. Because nonresident pages (those not currently in memory) are not dumpable, a nonresident page is a hole in the address space. In the case of a process LMB, a global page is also a hole, because global pages are all dumped together in the global page LMB.

An LMB with holes in its address space contains a hole table, which lists the pages of address space not present in the dump. The rest of the block consists of pages of address space in order by ascending address. Figure 35.3 shows the organization of an LMB and the layout of a typical selective dump.

EXE$BUGCHECKHANDLER's general sequence in writing an LMB is the following:

1. It writes an LMB descriptor in the next block of the dump.
2. It scans the page tables that describe the address space to be dumped, looking for invalid pages that are not transition pages. It writes an entry in a hole table for each such sequence of pages found. It writes the hole table to the next block (or blocks) of the dump. Chapter 16 describes the different page table entry (PTE) forms.
3. EXE$BUGCHECKHANDLER scans the page tables again, filling in its allocated SPTEs with information from each valid or transition PTE found. That is, it double-maps those pages so that it can write virtually noncontiguous pages in one I/O request. On an AXP CPU with a page size of 8 KB, it writes eight pages in one I/O request.
4. When EXE$BUGCHECKHANDLER has written all the valid and transition pages in a particular LMB to the dump file, it rewrites the block containing the descriptor with correct information about the number of holes in the address space and the number of data blocks (valid and transition pages) in the LMB.

Generally, EXE$BUGCHECKHANDLER reaches the end of a file sized for selective dumps before it reaches the end of the LMB list. When it does, it rewrites the descriptor of the current LMB with the hole count and actual number of data blocks written. It then rewrites the dump header, filling in status information such as number of I/O errors encountered writing the dump file, whether the SPT was dumped, how many process LMBs were written, and so on.

In writing a selective dump, EXE$BUGCHECKHANDLER must defend against the possibility that whatever error led to the bugcheck corrupted the data structures necessary to write virtual address space. It replaces the page fault and access violation exception service routines with its own routines to prevent recursive bugchecks if either of those errors occur. It also performs consistency checks on certain key data structures. For example, it checks that an address presumed to be that of a process header is "syntactically" cor-

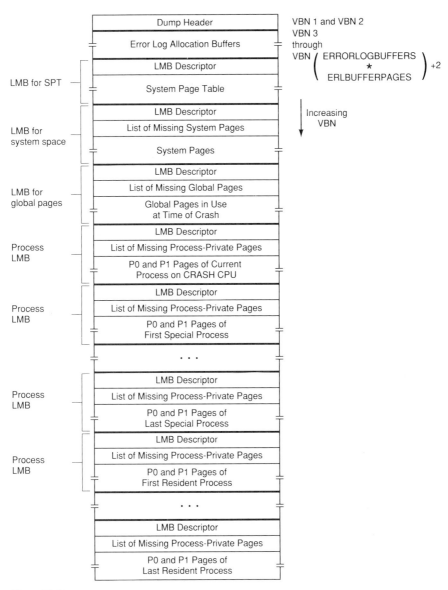

Figure 35.3
Layout of a Selective Memory Dump

rect; that is, it must be within known address boundaries and at an integral number of process headers from the beginning of the address range.

35.2.5.3 **Final Fatal Bugcheck Processing.** If a dump was written, EXE$BUGCHECK-HANDLER rewrites the dump header again, so that information such as the error count and number of blocks of memory in the dump reflect what was actually written to the dump file. It then calls the disconnect routine in the bootstrap system device driver.

As a last step, EXE$BUGCHECKHANDLER either loops or halts the system. If the SYSGEN parameter BUGREBOOT is 0, EXE$BUGCHECKHANDLER writes a message on the console terminal and loops at IPL 31, waiting for a command to be entered at the console terminal.

If BUGREBOOT is 1, its default value, EXE$BUGCHECKHANDLER halts. When the HALT instruction is executed, the console subsystem gains control and acts on the halt action value stored in the per-CPU slot of the HWRPB. Typically, it performs a warm bootstrap.

35.3 RELEVANT SOURCE MODULES

Source modules described in this chapter include

[ERRFMT]ERRFMT.MAR
[LIB]DMPDEF.SDL
[LIB]EMBCRDEF.SDL
[LIB]EMBHDDEF.SDL
[LIB]ERLDEF.SDL
[SYS]BUGCHECK.B32
[SYS]BUGCHECK_SAVE.M64
[SYS]ERRORLOG.MAR
[SYS]SYSDERLMB.MAR

36   Error Halt Processing

For there are moments when one can neither think nor feel. And
if one can neither think nor feel, she thought, where is one?

Virginia Woolf, *To the Lighthouse*

This chapter describes the processing performed by the OpenVMS AXP operating system when a processor halts because of an error condition.

36.1   PROCESSOR STATES

The console subsystem defines five major states for an Alpha AXP processor:

- ► Off—System is powered off.
- ► Halted—Operating system software execution is suspended.
- ► Booting—An attempt is being made to load and start execution of operating system software.
- ► Running—Operating system software is executing.
- ► Restarting—A restart of operating system software is being attempted.

Figure 36.1 shows these major states and the conditions that trigger processor state transitions. As shown in the figure, a number of elements govern processor state transitions, among them the following:

- ► The power ON/OFF switch, which supplies or cuts off electricity to the system unit.
- ► The implementation-specific method of forcing a processor to enter console mode, that is, a state where it is capable of accepting console commands. Most systems provide a halt button for this purpose; others respond to a CTRL/P keystroke or the combination of a CTRL/P keystroke and the HALT console command.
- ► The value of the AUTO_ACTION console environment variable, which can be set to BOOT, HALT, or RESTART (see Chapter 33). This variable determines the action console software performs any time the system is powered on or is halted because of an error. Pressing the halt button always halts the primary (or only) CPU in the system regardless of the AUTO_ACTION environment variable setting. The factory setting for this environment variable is typically BOOT. The console operator can change its setting using the SET console command.
- ► The setting of the console lock, which is a physical lock on the system. Of the systems supported by OpenVMS AXP Version 1.5, only the DEC 7000 and DEC 10000 systems have console locks. The settings of the console lock can be changed using a key in the console operator's possession.

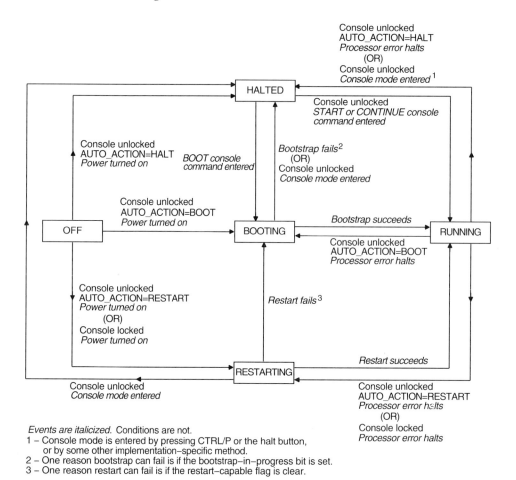

Figure 36.1
Processor State Transitions

► The settings of the processor's bootstrap-in-progress and restart-capable software flags, located in the per-CPU slot area of the hardware restart parameter block (HWRPB). These flags prevent infinite loops during bootstraps and restarts, as described in Section 36.4. Console software's power-on initialization code clears these flags for each processor.

A number of serious error conditions can cause a processor to halt, for example, an invalid kernel stack, a double error abort, or the execution of the CALL_PAL HALT instruction in kernel mode. As shown in Figure 36.1, a processor transitions from Running to the Halted, Booting, or Restarting state when an error halt occurs.

In a symmetric multiprocessing (SMP) system an error halt directly affects only the processor that incurred it. Multiple processors can simultaneously and coincidentally incur their own error halt conditions. If restarts are enabled, console software independently restarts each error-halted processor in an order that may be different from the order of failure. If any processor requests a bootstrap, pending or in-progress restarts are canceled.

36.2   CONSOLE SOFTWARE'S ACTIONS

When an error halt occurs, the console software saves the following state information:

▶ The current hardware privileged context in the hardware privileged context block (HWPCB) pointed to by the privileged context block base (PCBB) register

▶ The current processor status (PS), program counter (PC), R25, R26, R27, and PCBB register contents in the processor's per-CPU slot area (see Chapter 33) of the HWRPB

▶ The reason for halting in the per-CPU slot at SLOT$IQ_HALTCODE

Table 33.9 lists the possible halt reason codes. After saving the state information, console software either halts execution or attempts a boot or a restart, depending on the state of the console lock and the contents of the AUTO_ACTION environment variable (see Figure 36.1). Console software attempts a restart in either of the following cases:

▶ The console is locked when the error halt occurs.

▶ The console is unlocked and the AUTO_ACTION environment variable is set to RESTART when the error halt occurs.

Console software begins a processor restart sequence by first locating and validating the HWRPB (see Chapter 33):

1. The first quadword of the HWRPB must contain the HWRPB's physical address.

2. The second quadword must contain the ASCII string HWRPB padded with zeros.

3. The quadword HWRPB$IQ_CHECKSUM must contain the checksum of all quadwords from the beginning of the HWRPB up to and including the quadword HWRPB$IQ_HARDWARE1. The checksum is computed as the 64-bit 2's complement sum ignoring overflows.

4. The first quadword of the physical memory descriptor table (HWRPB_PMD) must contain the checksum of all remaining quadwords of the HWRPB_PMD.

5. The first quadword of the console configuration table, if one exists, must contain the checksum of all remaining quadwords of the configuration table. Of the systems supported by OpenVMS AXP Version 1.5, only DEC 4000 series systems provide a console configuration table.

If the HWRPB is valid, console software locates the processor's per-CPU slot and examines the following flags in SLOT$IQ_STATE.

▸ SLOT$V_PV (PALcode valid)—If clear, restart fails and the processor transitions to Booting.

▸ SLOT$V_CV (processor context valid)—If clear, restart fails and the processor transitions to Booting.

▸ SLOT$V_RC (restart-capable)—If clear, restart fails and the processor transitions to Booting.

▸ SLOT$V_BIP (bootstrap-in-progress)—If set, restart fails and the processor transitions to Halted.

Console software checks SLOT$V_BIP only if SLOT$V_RC is clear.

If the flags all permit restart, console software loads the hardware privileged context from the HWPCB in the per-CPU slot. It then loads the procedure value of EXE$RESTART from HWRPB$IQ_RESTART into R27, clears R26 (return address) and R25 (argument information), loads the virtual page table base (VPTB) register from the HWRPB (decimal offset 120), and transfers control to EXE$RESTART.

36.3 EXE$RESTART'S ACTIONS

EXE$RESTART, in module POWERFAIL, is the OpenVMS AXP operating system halt-restart procedure. It can be called for two reasons: to perform error halt processing, or to boot a secondary CPU in an SMP system. EXE$RESTART can also be called to recover from a power failure, although at present no system supported by OpenVMS AXP Version 1.5 has implemented powerfail recovery. (The Alpha AXP architecture does provide mechanisms for powerfail recovery.)

Running at interrupt priority level (IPL) 31 in kernel mode in the context of its boot HWPCB, EXE$RESTART performs the following actions:

1. EXE$RESTART determines the current processor's CPU ID by reading the who am I (WHAMI) register and, through SMP$GL_CPUDATA, the address of its per-CPU database.

2. EXE$RESTART determines the state of the current CPU from the per-CPU database. If it is not RUN, this is a boot of a secondary processor rather than a restart. EXE$RESTART calls SMP$START_SECONDARY, in module SMPINITIAL (see Chapter 37).

   If the CPU's state is RUN, this is a processor restart. If so, EXE$RESTART examines SLOT$IQ_HALTCODE to see what caused the halt that led to this restart. The architecturally defined possibilities are powerfail recovery or various other error halt conditions. Because current systems do not implement powerfail recovery, EXE$RESTART should see only the error halt codes (see Table 33.9).

   EXE$RESTART generates one of the following fatal bugchecks based on the error halt code.

- UNKRSTRT—Unknown restart
- OPERCRASH—Operator-forced crash
- KRNLSTAKNV—Kernel stack invalid
- INVSCBB—Invalid system control block base (SCBB) register
- INVPTBR—Invalid page table base register (PTBR)
- HALT—Halt instruction executed
- DBLERR—Double error halt

36.4   PREVENTION OF INFINITE RESTART LOOPS

The restart-capable (SLOT$V_RC) and bootstrap-in-progress (SLOT$V_BIP) flags prevent infinite loops such as the following from occurring:

1. An error halt condition occurs.
2. The console subsystem locates the HWRPB and transfers control to EXE$RESTART.
3. Prior to crashing the system, EXE$RESTART incurs an error halt condition.
4. The console subsystem locates the HWRPB and transfers control to EXE$RESTART.
5. EXE$RESTART incurs the same error halt condition. . . .

The operating system sets or clears these flags to indicate to console software whether the system can be bootstrapped or restarted. During console power-up initialization (that is, during a cold bootstrap), both flags are cleared. Just prior to transferring control to the operating system, console software sets the bootstrap-in-progress flag and clears the restart-capable flag.

After enough of the operating system has been loaded to make a restart possible, the operating system sets the restart-capable flag. Console software will abort any restart attempt if the restart-capable flag is clear.

The operating system clears the bootstrap-in-progress flag to indicate to console software that a bootstrap operation is complete. Console software will abort any bootstrap attempt if the bootstrap-in-progress flag is set.

EXE$INIT, the system initialization procedure in module INIT, clears SLOT$V_BIP and sets SLOT$V_RC during system initialization. The secondary processor bootstrap procedure, SMP$START_SECONDARY, in module SMPINITIAL, also uses these flags, as described in Chapter 37.

36.5   RELEVANT SOURCE MODULE

The source module described in this chapter is

[SYS]POWERFAIL.M64

37 Symmetric Multiprocessing

Virtue can only flourish amongst equals.

Mary Wollstonecraft, *A Vindication of the Rights of Men*

OpenVMS AXP Version 1.5 supports tightly coupled symmetric multiprocessing (SMP). This chapter describes

- Communication and cooperation among the members of an SMP system
- Initialization of the SMP environment
- Addition and removal of a member

37.1 OVERVIEW

A multiprocessing system consists of two or more CPUs that address common memory and that can execute instructions simultaneously. If all CPUs in the system execute the same copy of the operating system, the multiprocessing system is said to be tightly coupled. If all CPUs have equal access to memory, interrupts, and I/O devices, the system is said to be symmetric.

In most respects the members of an OpenVMS SMP system are symmetric. Each member can perform the following tasks:

- Initiate an I/O request
- Service exceptions
- Service software interrupts
- Service hardware interrupts, such as interprocessor and interval timer interrupts
- Execute process context code in any access mode

One CPU can be executing process context code while another services a software interrupt. Section 37.4 describes how this concurrency is implemented.

The members of an SMP system are characterized in several ways. One important characteristic is that of primary CPU. During system operation the primary CPU has several unique responsibilities for system timekeeping, writing messages to the console terminal, and accessing any other I/O devices that are not accessible to all members. Although the hardware and software permit device interrupts to be serviced by any processor, in practice all device interrupts are serviced on the primary CPU. Section 37.6.2 describes this division of labor. An SMP configuration may include some devices that are not accessible from all SMP members. The console terminal, for example, is accessible only from the primary processor. Section 37.6.3 describes a mechanism called device affinity by which such devices are supported.

Booting the system is initiated on a CPU with full access to the console subsystem and terminal, called the BOOT CPU. The BOOT CPU controls the bootstrap sequence and boots the other available CPUs. In OpenVMS AXP Version 1.5, the BOOT CPU and the primary CPU are always the same; the others are called secondary processors.

(The terms *CPU* and *processor* are used interchangeably in this chapter and throughout the book.)

The booted primary and all currently booted secondary processors are called members of the active set. These processors actively participate in system operations and respond to interprocessor interrupts, which coordinate systemwide events. Section 37.5.2 contains more information on the use of interprocessor interrupts.

The operating system imposes little binding between a process and a particular CPU. That is, in general, each CPU is equally able to execute any process. However, a process may need capabilities possessed only by certain CPUs or may have populated the memory and translation buffer caches of a specific CPU. For those cases, a mechanism reserved to Digital exists by which a process may be bound to one or more CPUs. Chapter 13 describes the implementation of process affinity and processor capabilities.

As described in Chapter 5, the executive performs many key system functions through software interrupts. In an SMP system, each processor services its own software interrupt requests, of which the most significant are the following:

▶ When a process receives an asynchronous system trap (AST) delivery interrupt at interrupt priority level (IPL) 2, the AST delivery interrupt service routine runs on the same processor as the process. Chapter 8 describes IPL 2 interrupts and their servicing.

▶ When a current process is preempted by a higher priority computable resident process, the IPL 3 rescheduling interrupt service routine, running on that processor, takes the current process out of execution and switches to the higher priority process. Chapter 13 describes scheduling in more detail as well as the circumstances under which the rescheduling interrupt is requested.

▶ When a device driver completes an I/O request, an IPL 4 I/O postprocessing interrupt is requested: some completed requests are queued to a CPU-specific postprocessing queue and are serviced on that CPU; others are queued to a systemwide queue and serviced on the primary CPU. Section 37.6.4 describes the different postprocessing queues and their uses. Chapter 23 describes the I/O postprocessing interrupt service routine.

▶ When the current process has used its quantum of CPU time, the IPL 7 software timer interrupt service routine, running on that CPU, performs quantum-end processing. Chapter 12 describes software timer interrupts and their servicing.

▶ Software interrupts at IPLs 6 and 8 through 11 are requested to execute fork processes. Each processor services its own set of fork queues. A fork process generally executes on the same CPU from which it was requested. However, since many fork processes are requested from device interrupt service routines, which currently execute only on the primary CPU, more fork processes execute on the primary than on other processors. Chapter 5 describes fork interrupts and their servicing.

SMP support has the following goals:

▶ One version of the operating system. As part of the standard OpenVMS AXP product, SMP support does not require its own version. The same OpenVMS version runs on all AXP processors. The synchronization methodology and the interface to synchronization routines are the same on all systems. However, as described in Chapter 9, there are different versions of the synchronization routines themselves in different versions of the executive image that implements synchronization. Partly for that reason, SMP support imposes relatively little additional overhead on a uniprocessor system.

▶ Parallelism in kernel mode. SMP support might have been implemented such that any single processor, but not more than one at a time, could execute kernel mode code. However, more parallelism was required for a solution that would support configurations with more CPUs. The members of an SMP system can be executing different portions of the executive concurrently. The executive has been divided into different critical regions, each with its own lock, called a spinlock.

▶ Flexibility in the granularity of the locking mechanisms. The spinlock mechanism allows for the creation of additional static spinlocks in future versions of the operating system. The IOLOCK8 spinlock, for example, could be subdivided to allow increased parallelism.

37.2 SMP HARDWARE CONFIGURATIONS

The executive is currently configured to support a CPU name space of CPU IDs ranging from 0 to 31. For any particular processor type, the actual maximum configuration is likely to be smaller. The CPU ID is taken from the who am I (WHAMI) processor register.

OpenVMS SMP requires a hardware configuration of multiple CPUs of the same model type. Each processor can execute an instruction stream independently of the others. An interprocessor interrupt mechanism enables kernel mode software running on one processor to interrupt one or more of the others.

The CPUs access common physical memory through the same physical addresses. The CPUs' memory caches are invalidated as needed by the hardware without software involvement. This feature is called cache coherency. As required for any AXP processor, the memory supports the load-locked/store-conditional mechanism, described in Chapter 9. This mechanism enables a processor to update a memory location atomically. The processor loads a register with the location's contents using a load-locked instruction, updates the register, and stores the new contents using a store-conditional instruction. If a second processor has modified the location between the load-locked and the attempted store, the store-conditional fails. The first processor repeats the entire sequence, loading the latest contents of the memory location.

In addition, the CPUs must be at the same hardware and compatible privileged architecture library (PALcode) revision levels. These requirements exist because a process running on one CPU can be taken out of execution in the middle of a set of instructions and resumed on another processor.

The primary processor must be able to access all I/O peripherals. All CPUs must be able to access most I/O peripherals. The console terminal, however, is accessible only to the primary processor.

37.3   DATA STRUCTURES RELATED TO SMP SUPPORT

Two longwords, SMP$GL_FLAGS and EXE$GL_TIME_CONTROL, contain flags controlling SMP operations. These flags are modified only with the load-locked/store-conditional mechanism. Symbolic names for the bits in SMP$GL_FLAGS are defined by the $SPLCODDEF macro:

- ▶ SMP$V_ENABLED—When set, indicates that SMP operation is enabled
- ▶ SMP$V_START_CPU—When set, indicates that the primary CPU has finished initialization
- ▶ SMP$V_CRASH_CPU—When set, indicates that a member has initiated a fatal bugcheck
- ▶ SMP$V_TODR—When set, indicates that SMP$GQ_PROPOSED_HW-CLOCK, described in Section 37.5.2, is in use
- ▶ SMP$V_TODR_ACK—When set, indicates that the primary CPU has completed its part in an SMP time-of-year clock access
- ▶ SMP$V_BENIGN—When set, indicates that a benign state, described in Section 37.5.4, has been requested

Symbolic names for the bits in EXE$GL_TIME_CONTROL are defined by the macro $SYSPARDEF. Those relevant for SMP are

- ▶ EXE$V_NOSMPSANITY—When set, disables SMP sanity timeouts
- ▶ EXE$V_NOSPINWAIT—When set, disables SMP spinwait timeouts

SMP supports a maximum of 32 CPUs, each having a unique ID from 0 to 31. Kernel mode code running at an IPL above 2 can identify the CPU on which it is executing by examining its per-CPU database, described later in this section.

The global cell SMP$GL_PRIMID contains the ID of the primary processor. When the system crashes, the ID of the CPU that initiates the bugcheck, the CRASH CPU, is recorded in the global cell SMP$GL_BUGCHKCP.

A number of global cells describe the members of an SMP system. Each is a longword with one bit for each CPU; when set, bit 0, for example, indicates that the CPU whose ID is 0 has the characteristic described by the cell.

▶ SMP$GL_CPUCONF identifies the available set, those physically present processors that have passed the power-on hardware diagnostics and are available for booting into the SMP system.

▶ SMP$GL_ACTIVE_CPUS identifies the active set, those CPUs that are participating in the SMP system and responding to interprocessor interrupt requests.

▶ Generally, SCH$GL_IDLE_CPUS identifies the idle set, those CPUs without a process to execute. However, whenever a resident computable process becomes available, the bits representing idle CPUs on which the process can run are cleared as a signal that those CPUs should reschedule.

▶ XDT$GL_BENIGN_CPUS identifies those CPUs in the benign state, described in Section 37.5.4.

▶ SMP$GL_OVERRIDE marks the override set, described in Section 37.5.5.

▶ EXE$GL_AFFINITY contains the default device affinity mask, which is normally all 1's to specify that a device can be accessed from all SMP members. This mask is copied to the unit control block field UCB$L_AFFINITY of each device unit when it is created.

▶ SMP$GL_BUG_DONE identifies those CPUs that have completed fatal bugcheck processing, described in Section 37.9.

The spinlock-related data structures are described in Chapter 9. The CPU mutex is described in Section 37.5.

XDT$GL_INTERLOCK and XDT$GL_OWNER_ID, cells related to the use of XDELTA, are described in Section 37.5.4.

The use of cell SMP$GQ_INVALID is related to invalidation of a single translation buffer entry, described in Section 37.5.3.

Each member of an SMP system has memory for data that describes the state of that CPU. CPU-specific data is maintained within both a per-CPU area (called a CPU slot) in the hardware restart parameter block (HWRPB) and a nonpaged pool data structure called the per-CPU database. The HWRPB, described in Chapter 33, contains CPU-specific data that is architecturally defined. The per-CPU database contains software-defined data specific to one CPU. The MACRO-32 $CPUDEF macro defines symbolic names for its fields. Leaving software-defined CPU-specific data in one data structure simplified the porting of OpenVMS from the VAX to the Alpha AXP architecture and the addition of SMP support.

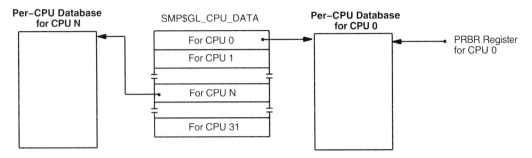

Figure 37.1
CPU Data Vector and Per-CPU Databases

37.3.1   Locating Per-CPU Data

The Alpha AXP architecture defines the processor base register to contain CPU-specific data. The OpenVMS operating system loads the virtual address of the per-CPU database into the PRBR. Code running in kernel mode can read the register by executing the CALL_PAL MFPR_PRBR instruction or by invoking a language-specific FIND_CPU_DATA macro.

An example of a MACRO-32 FIND_CPU_DATA macro invocation and its expansion follows:

```
; Macro invocation
;
        FIND_CPU_DATA R4              ;Get per-CPU database address in R4
;
; Macro expansion
;
        $PRDEF                       ;Define processor register numbers
        MFPR      #PR$_PRBR,R4
        .SET_REGISTERS ALIGNED=R4    ;Tell MACRO-32 that R4 contents
                                     ; are longword-aligned
```

Note that use of this macro or instruction is restricted to code that executes in kernel mode. Also, the code must run at an IPL above 2 before getting and while using the address of the per-CPU database. Code running at IPL 2 or below is subject to rescheduling and subsequent execution on another processor whose per-CPU data area is at a different address.

In an SMP configuration, an array called the CPU data vector contains the addresses of the per-CPU databases of the individual members. The 32-longword array begins at global cell SMP$GL_CPU_DATA. It is indexed by CPU ID number to get the address of the database for a particular processor. Figure 37.1 shows the relation between the per-CPU databases and the CPU data vector.

37.3.2 Per-CPU Stack

The Alpha AXP architecture defines a per-process stack for each of the four access modes in which the CPU can execute but, unlike the VAX architecture, does not include an interrupt stack. Executing in process context, a processor runs on an access mode stack private to that process. Executing in the context of a system or termination hardware privileged context block (HWPCB), a processor executes on the kernel stack specified by that HWPCB. In an SMP system, multiple processors can each execute in its own system or termination context at the same time.

Simultaneous use of the same stack or HWPCB by more than one processor is not viable. The console subsystem therefore provides a boot HWPCB for each processor in an area of the HWRPB called a per-CPU slot; OpenVMS AXP provides a system HWPCB and a termination HWPCB for exclusive use by each processor. Currently, the termination HWPCB is unused. Figure 37.2 shows the relations among the per-CPU database, the per-CPU slot, and the per-CPU HWPCBs and their associated stacks. Chapter 33 contains more information on the HWRPB and per-CPU slot.

37.3.3 Per-CPU Database

The per-CPU database contains information for each processor such as the process control block (PCB) address and priority of its current process, its CPU ID, and its fork queues. Figure 37.3 shows the per-CPU database.

The per-CPU database can be extended to include data specific to a particular processor type. By default there is no extension. If the structure were extended, CPU$L_VARIABLE_OFFSET would contain the offset from the beginning of the structure to the CPU-type-specific data, and CPU$L_VARIABLE_LENGTH would contain the size in bytes of the extension. Currently, no CPU requires use of this extension, and these two fields contain zero.

CPU$L_CURPCB contains the PCB address of the process currently executing on this processor. CPU$B_CUR_PRI contains the process's current priority. (This field has been expanded to a longword and is also called CPU$L_CUR_PRI.) When the CPU is idle, CPU$L_CURPCB contains the address of the null PCB, and CPU$B_CUR_PRI contains –1.

CPU$L_SLOT_VA contains the virtual address of the per-CPU slot in the HWRPB.

CPUW_SIZE, CPUB_TYPE, and CPU$B_SUBTYPE contain the standard dynamic data structure header fields. CPU$W_SIZE contains the length in bytes of only the standard part of the structure, which does not include the length of any processor-type-specific extension.

CPU$L_STATE identifies the processor's current state, for example, CPU$C_BOOTED. Section 37.7 describes the different states and the transitions among them.

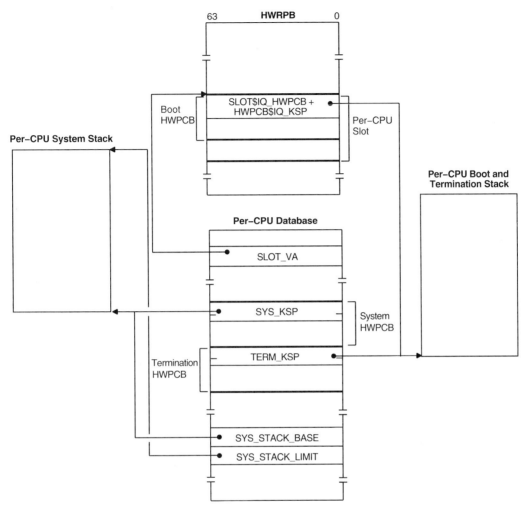

Figure 37.2
Per-CPU Contexts and Stacks

CPU$L_CPUMTX is the number of times the CPU mutex has been acquired by the processor; the CPU mutex can be acquired multiple times by nested routines.

CPU$L_WORK_REQ is a bit mask describing outstanding work requests made by other processors of this processor. Section 37.5.2 describes these requests and their handling.

CPU$L_PHY_CPUID contains the ID of the processor, the same value as that in its WHAMI processor register. CPU$L_CPUID_MASK is a mask of 31 zeros with a single bit set in the bit position corresponding to the CPU ID number.

CURPCB			⊢ BC_SCBB ⊣		
SLOT_VA			⊢ BC_SISR ⊣		
SUBTYPE	TYPE	SIZE	⊢ BC_FPCR ⊣		
STATE			BUGCODE		
CPUMTX			CAPABILITY		
CUR_PRI			⊢ BOOT_TIME ⊣		
WORK_REQ			⊢ ASN ⊣		
PHY_CPUID			ASNSEQ		
CPUID_MASK			⫶ KERNEL (5 quadwords) ⫶		
BUSYWAIT			⊢ MPSYNCH ⊣		
⫶ SWIQFL (6 quadwords) ⫶			⊢ NULLCPU ⊣		
PSFL			HARDAFF		
PSBL			RANK_VEC		
⊢ WORK_FQFL ⊣			IPL_VEC		
ZEROED_PAGE_SPTE			⫶ IPL_ARRAY (32 longwords) ⫶		
ZEROED_PAGE_VA			TPOINTER		
ZEROED_PAGE_STATE			SANITY_TIMER		
(reserved)			SANITY_TICKS		
⊢ PHY_SYS_HWPCB ⊣			FLAGS		
⫶ SYS_HWPCB (16 quadwords) ⫶			INTFLAGS		
⫶ TERM_HWPCB (16 quadwords) ⫶			SYS_STACK_BASE		
⊢ PHY_TERM_HWPCB ⊣			SYS_STACK_LIMIT		
⊢ SAVED_PCBB ⊣			VARIABLE_OFFSET		
⊢ SCBB ⊣			VARIABLE_LENGTH		
⊢ *(reserved)* ⊣			MCHK_MASK		
⫶ BC_KSP (16 quadwords) ⫶			MCHK_SP		
⫶ BC_R0 – BC_R29 (30 quadwords) ⫶			⊢ MCHK_CRASH_AREA_VA ⊣		
⊢ BC_PC ⊣			*(reserved)*		
⊢ BC_PS ⊣			*(reserved)*		
⫶ BC_F0 – BC_F30 (31 quadwords) ⫶			⊢ LOGOUT_AREA_VA ⊣		
⊢ BC_IPL ⊣			SOFT_TICK		
⊢ BC_MCES ⊣			TIME_DEVIATION		
⊢ BC_PCBB ⊣			PCSAMPLE_BUFFER		
⊢ BC_PRBR ⊣			PCSAMPLE_FLAGS		
⊢ BC_VPTB ⊣					

(continued)

Figure 37.3
Per-CPU Database

A processor's fork dispatching queues begin at CPU$Q_SWIQFL. Chapter 5 describes fork dispatching and the use of fork queues. The per-processor I/O postprocessing queue is at CPU$L_PSFL and CPU$L_PSBL. Section 37.6.4 describes its use.

CPU$Q_WORK_FQFL is a work queue for switching fork processes from other processors to this one. Section 37.5.2 describes the use of this field.

During system initialization the scheduling initialization routine allocates an SPTE and stores its virtual address in CPU$L_ZEROED_PAGE_SPTE. It stores the system virtual address the SPTE maps in CPU$L_ZEROED_PAGE_VA. During normal system operation, when there is no computable process to execute, the scheduler idle loop routine clears unused pages of memory for future allocation. Clearing them in the idle loop minimizes the time required for a process to allocate a demand zero page.

The idle loop code maps a free physical page to be cleared with the SPTE in CPU$L_ZEROED_PAGE_SPTE and accesses it through the virtual address in CPU$L_ZEROED_PAGE_VA. Whenever a process becomes computable, the idle loop code discontinues zeroing and records how many 32-byte chunks in the page have not yet been zeroed in CPU$L_ZEROED_PAGE_STATE. In an SMP system, multiple processors can execute the idle loop, concurrently zeroing pages, and thus each needs its own SPTE and place to record its progress. Chapter 18 describes this mechanism in more detail.

The per-CPU database contains two HWPCBs: the system HWPCB begins at field CPU$Q_SYS_HWPCB, and the termination HWPCB, at field CPU$Q_TERM_HWPCB. CPU$Q_PHY_SYS_HWPCB and CPU$Q_PHY_TERM_HWPCB contain their physical addresses. The layout of the HWPCB is shown in Figure 13.6.

CPU$Q_SCBB contains the physical address of the system control block (SCB).

When a powerfail occurs on a system that implements powerfail recovery, the current contents of various volatile registers are stored in the per-CPU database so that they can be restored during restart. (At present, no system supported by OpenVMS AXP Version 1.5 has implemented powerfail recovery.) During fatal bugcheck processing, the current contents of the volatile registers are stored in the per-CPU database so that they can be examined during crash dump analysis. Chapter 35 describes bugcheck processing and the use of these fields.

Generally, bugcheck processing and powerfail save the same set of registers in the same per-CPU database fields. These per-CPU database fields and their contents are as follows:

▶ CPU$Q_SAVED_PCBB—Physical address of the current process's HWPCB at the time of a powerfail

▶ CPU$Q_BC_KSP and the next 15 quadwords—Contents of the registers whose save area is in the HWPCB at the time of a bugcheck

- CPU$Q_BC_R*x*, where *x* is a number from 0 to 29—Contents of the integer registers at the time of a powerfail or bugcheck
- CPU$Q_BC_PC and CPU$Q_BC_PS—Contents of the program counter (PC) and processor status (PS) at the time of a powerfail or bugcheck
- CPU$Q_BC_F*x*, where *x* is a number from 0 to 30—Contents of the floating-point registers at the time of a powerfail or bugcheck (if the current process is using floating-point)
- CPU$Q_BC_PCBB—Physical address of the current process's hardware PCB at the time of a bugcheck
- CPUQ_BC_IPL, CPUQ_BC_MCES, CPU$Q_BC_SCBB, and CPU$Q_BC_VPTB—Contents of these processor registers (IPL, machine check error summary, system control block base, and virtual page table base) at the time of a bugcheck
- CPUQ_BC_SISR, CPUQ_BC_FPCR, and CPU$Q_BC_PRBR—Contents of these processor registers (software interrupt summary register, floating-point control register, and processor base register) at the time of a powerfail or bugcheck

CPU$L_BUGCODE contains the bugcheck code for a CPU that is crashing.

CPU$L_CAPABILITY is a bit mask with bits set to represent the capabilities of this processor. The low bit, when set, means that this CPU is the primary processor. The macro $CPBDEF defines symbolic values for the bits in this field. CPU$L_HARDAFF is the number of processes that have explicit affinity for this CPU. Chapter 13 describes processor capabilities and process affinity.

CPU$Q_BOOT_TIME contains the system time at which the CPU was booted.

To enable per-process address translations to remain cached in the translation buffer when process context is switched, the Alpha AXP architecture supports the association of a process address space number with each per-process translation. CPU$Q_ASN and CPU$Q_ASNSEQ describe the address space number associated with the current process or, if there is none, the most recent one. On a CPU that does not implement address space numbers, when process context is switched, per-process virtual address translations that are cached in the translation buffer must be flushed to preclude stale translations in the context of the next process. Chapter 16 describes translation buffer invalidation and address space numbers in more detail.

Beginning at field CPU$Q_KERNEL is a five-quadword array that records the amount of time the processor executes in each access mode; the first four elements are for process context time in each mode, and the fifth is for time in system context. Two additional fields record execution time:

- CPU$Q_KERNEL does not contain time spent in a spinwait: CPU$Q_MPSYNCH records the amount of time the processor spins waiting to acquire a spinlock from a process context kernel mode thread of execution.

▶ CPU$Q_NULLCPU records the amount of time spent in the scheduler idle loop. These counts are maintained by the interval timer interrupt service routine, described in Chapter 12.

Each bit, excluding bit 31, set in the field CPU$L_RANK_VEC corresponds to a static spinlock held by the processor; its bit position identifies the spinlock rank. Each bit set in the field CPU$L_IPL_VEC corresponds to an IPL at which the processor holds one or more spinlocks. The IPL representation is inverted. When a processor acquires a spinlock, the IPL of the spinlock is subtracted from 31. The bit in CPU$L_IPL_VEC corresponding to that number is set. The field thus represents the current set of (inverted) spinlock IPLs active on the processor. The inverted number is also used as an index into the 32-longword array at CPU$L_IPL_ARRAY, which records the number of different spinlocks held at each IPL. These fields are used only with the full-checking version of the spinlock routines, described in Chapter 9.

The fields CPU$L_TPOINTER, CPU$L_SANITY_TIMER, and CPU$L_SANITY_TICKS are part of the SMP sanity timer mechanism, described in Section 37.5.7.

CPU$L_FLAGS and CPU$L_INTFLAGS contain various flags such as CPU$V_STOPPING, which, when set, means that the processor is stopping. The flags in CPU$L_INTFLAGS are set and cleared with MACRO-32 interlocked statements.

CPU$L_SYS_STACK_BASE and CPU$L_SYS_STACK_LIMIT contain the high and low addresses of the kernel stack on which the processor runs during normal operations when there is no current process to execute. It is the kernel stack identified by the system HWPCB.

CPU$L_MCHK_MASK and CPU$L_MCHK_SP are related to the machine check protection mechanism, which inhibits the executive's default reaction to a nonexistent memory machine check. Autoconfiguration code enables this mechanism while probing I/O space to determine which devices are present.

CPU$PQ_LOGOUT_AREA_VA is the system virtual address at which the machine check logout area is mapped. The machine check logout area is an area of physical memory for logging error- and machine-specific information for corrected error interrupts and machine checks. Before dispatching to a corrected error or machine check service routine, PALcode records in R4 the offset from the base of the logout area to the logout frame that describes that error. For an error severe enough to warrant generating a fatal bugcheck, the service routine calculates the corresponding virtual address and records it in CPU$PQ_MCHK_CRASH_AREA_VA to facilitate the System Dump Analyzer (SDA) SHOW MACHINE_CHECK command.

CPU$L_SOFT_TICK and CPU$L_TIME_DEVIATION are part of the implementation of soft 10-millisecond ticks. Because the interval timer interrupts at a CPU-specific frequency that is not necessarily an integral factor of 10 milliseconds, the OpenVMS AXP executive simulates a 10-millisecond interval to provide compatibility with OpenVMS VAX. In CPU$L_SOFT_TICK, the OpenVMS AXP executive maintains the number of timer interrupts left until the current calculated 10-millisecond interval is over. When the interval is over, the executive checks how close the approximation is to true time. CPU$L_TIME_DEVIATION is a running count used to determine whether an additional tick is necessary to average out the length of the simulated intervals. Chapter 12 contains further information.

CPU$L_BUSYWAIT is nonzero while the processor is spinning, trying to acquire a spinlock, as described in Chapter 9. While this field is nonzero, the interval timer interrupt service routine does not charge a timer tick against the quantum of the current process (see Chapter 12). It also uses this field to determine whether to record a process context kernel mode tick in CPU$Q_KERNEL or CPU$Q_MPSYNCH.

CPU$L_PCSAMPLE_BUFFER and CPU$L_PCSAMPLE_FLAGS support PC sampling, a mechanism for monitoring performance. CPU$L_PCSAMPLE_BUFFER, when nonzero, contains the address of a nonpaged pool data structure in which regularly sampled PC values are stored. A monitoring process periodically collects the PC samples. A bit in CPU$L_PCSAMPLE_FLAGS indicates whether a PC sample is being stored. The bit is cleared to indicate that the data structure is in a stable state from which PC samples can be retrieved.

37.4   IMPLICATIONS OF SHARING MEMORY

All memory is physically accessible to all members of an SMP system. Because a process executes on only CPU at a time, its per-process address space is mapped only on that CPU and is not accessed concurrently from multiple processors. Thus, SMP support generally requires no additional synchronization of access to per-process address space. (Note, however, that multiprocessing applications sharing a writable global section must synchronize possible concurrent accesses to the global section from processes running on different processors.)

However, all processors use the same system page table (SPT) and thus share system address space. This has several important implications for system operation. First, because multiple processors can execute kernel mode threads and make concurrent access to system space data, SMP requires additional synchronization beyond that required for a uniprocessor system. This section summarizes these effects.

Second, if code running on one processor changes a valid system page table entry (SPTE), it must inform all the other active SMP members, so that they will flush the cached contents of that SPTE, now stale, from their translation buffers. This mechanism is described in more detail in Section 37.5.3.

Third, multiple processors concurrently accessing pageable system space affect the movement of pages into and out of the system working set list. Chapter 19 describes techniques by which a page can be forced into the system working set list.

Prior to the implementation of SMP, the VAX/VMS executive, on which the OpenVMS AXP executive is based, used two different synchronization methods: IPL and mutual exclusion (mutex) semaphores. Since many important system functions are performed by software interrupt service routines, it was possible to synchronize access to shared system data by raising IPL to block the highest priority interrupt whose service routine accessed that data. In cases where raising IPL would be inappropriate (for example, access to pageable shared data), the need to acquire a mutex prevented access by more than one process at a time. No synchronization was required for shared system data accessed only by single uninterruptible instructions. For example, a processor executing an `CALL_PAL INSQUE` instruction to insert an element at the tail of a lookaside list makes the multiple memory references required without allowing interrupts.

In an SMP system, processors execute concurrently; raising IPL on one processor blocks interrupts only on that processor and has no effect on the others. At an architectural or hardware level, the basic multiprocessing synchronization primitive is based on atomic updates to shared data. The Alpha AXP architecture provides the load-locked/store-conditional mechanism, described in Chapter 9, to serve this need. Using this primitive, the OpenVMS executive has implemented spinlocks, an extension to IPL-based synchronization. In its simplest form, a spinlock is a bit that describes the state of a set of shared data; the bit is set to indicate that a processor is accessing the data and is clear to indicate no processor is accessing the data. The state of the bit is tested and changed with the load-locked/store-conditional mechanism.

Shared system data is divided into a number of subsets, each with an associated IPL and spinlock. To access one of these subsets, a thread of execution raises IPL to the associated level and acquires the spinlock. The acquired spinlock synchronizes access from threads of execution on other processors. It could also synchronize the access of other threads of execution on the same processor, except that the executive allows any processor to reacquire a spinlock that it already holds. For that reason, elevated IPL is used to synchronize the access of threads of execution on the same processor. When done, the thread of execution releases the spinlock and typically restores the previous IPL.

SMP support requires identification of each shared piece of data or resource needing synchronization and determination of an appropriate synchronization method.

▸ Certain synchronization IPLs have a corresponding spinlock; for example, use of IPL 6 now also requires that the QUEUEAST spinlock be owned. In contrast, the use of IPL$_SYNCH is subdivided into six different spinlocks, increasing the amount of parallelism possible.

▸ A simple update to a single shared piece of data is done with the load-locked/store-conditional mechanism. A more complex update to a shared database is done with the protection of a spinlock. While a processor owns a spinlock, it can make multiple modifications to the database protected by the spinlock.

▸ A shared queue can be either an interlocked (self-relative) queue or accessed with the protection of a spinlock. Accesses to the head or tail of a shared queue can be synchronized with interlocked queue operations, which are implemented through PALcode routines that synchronize access to the queue head through the load-locked/store-conditional mechanism. A spinlock is required to synchronize access to a queue whose elements can be inserted or removed anywhere in the queue. A spinlock is also required to synchronize access to a shared absolute (noninterlocked) queue.

Some queues, such as fork queues, are local to a CPU and accessed only by threads of execution running on that CPU. For these, synchronization is achieved by accessing the head or tail of the queue with noninterlocked queue instructions or raising IPL to scan the queue.

Chapter 9 describes the use and implementation of synchronization mechanisms in more detail.

37.5 INTERPROCESSOR COOPERATION

The members of an SMP system that are participating in system operation make up the active set. The global cell SMP$GL_ACTIVE_CPUS identifies these members with a bit set corresponding to the CPU ID of each. The primary, by definition, is always a member of the active set. A secondary processor becomes a member during its initialization (see Section 37.8.4) and leaves when it is shut down (see Section 37.8.5).

A semaphore called the CPU mutex controls additions to the active set. Despite its name, the CPU mutex is a simplified form of spinlock, not an ordinary OpenVMS mutex. An executive routine acquires and releases the CPU mutex semaphore using the LOCK and UNLOCK macros, as it would a spinlock.

A member of the active set must be responsive to interprocessor interrupts. The executive may interrupt a particular CPU to request a specific task, or it may interrupt all active set members to coordinate a systemwide action that requires all active set members to cooperate. The following sections describe the interprocessor interrupt mechanism and the different work requests and their handling.

Some of the work requests do not require immediate action and are not acknowledged, for example, reschedule and I/O postprocessing work requests.

A member typically responds to them by requesting a software interrupt at a priority lower than that of the interprocessor interrupt.

Several work requests, however, require acknowledgment for the requestor to proceed. These are a request to enter the benign state, a request to bugcheck, a request to invalidate a single translation buffer entry, and a request for the primary to access its battery-backed watch chip. Some of these requests require a timed interprocessor dialogue to complete. Some require all members to respond. A processor executing for an extended period at an IPL at or above that of the interprocessor interrupt must check for and service certain of the requests.

A member of the active set must also release held spinlocks in a timely fashion. When a processor loops as described in Section 37.5.6, to wait for a spinlock to be released, it waits a finite amount of time. Typically, the wait is based on one of the SYSGEN parameters SMP_SPINWAIT or SMP_LNGSPINWAIT. If the wait time elapses before the other member releases the spinlock, the waiting processor may presume the other member is hung and crash the system.

Sanity, spinlock wait, and busy wait timeouts exist to prevent the entire system, and the VMScluster system of which it may be a part, from hanging when one member of the active set becomes unresponsive. Section 37.5.7 describes the sanity timer mechanism. Section 37.5.6 describes the need for processor responsiveness to certain interprocessor interrupt requests.

37.5.1   Requesting Interprocessor Interrupts

Several MACRO-32 macros request an interprocessor interrupt. The most commonly used are

▸ IPINT_ALL, to interrupt all other members of the active set
▸ IPINT_CPU, to interrupt a particular CPU

Each of these macros is typically invoked with an argument identifying the reason for the interrupt request. The macro generates code that sets the corresponding bit in CPU$L_WORK_REQ in the per-CPU databases of the processors to be interrupted. A work request bit is set, tested, and cleared with a load-locked/store-conditional sequence that includes one or more memory barriers to synchronize access to it. Some interprocessor interrupt requests, however, are identified by means other than a work request bit.

Table 37.1 lists the possible work request bits. Prefaced by CPU$V_ or CPU$M_, these symbols are defined by the macro $CPUDEF. The functioning of these bits is discussed in further detail in the following sections. In addition, four bits are reserved for processor-type-specific requests. No use is made of these bits currently.

The following is an example of the invocation and expansion of the IPINT_CPU MACRO-32 macro.

Table 37.1   Interrupt Work Request Bits

Name	Meaning
INV_TBS	Invalidate a specific translation buffer (TB) entry
INV_TBA	Invalidate all TB entries
BUGCHK	Generate a fatal bugcheck
BUGCHKACK	Unused
RECALSCHD	Unused
UPDASTSR	Update current process's ASTSR
UPDATE_HWCLOCK	Access the battery-backed up watch chip
WORK_FQP	Service requests on the interprocessor fork queue
QLOST	Unused
RESCHED	Request an IPL 3 reschedule interrupt
VIRTCONS	Unused
IOPOST	Request an IPL 4 I/O postprocessing interrupt
INV_ISTREAM	Invalidate prefetched instruction stream
INV_TBSD	Invalidate a specific data TB entry
INV_TBS_MMG	Invalidate a specific TB entry while holding MMG spinlock
INV_TBSD_MMG	Invalidate a specific data TB while entry holding MMG spinlock

```
; Macro invocation
;
      IPINT_CPU    IOPOST,SMP$GL_PRIMID ;Tell primary to request an
                                        ; I/O post software interrupt
;
; Macro expansion
;
      $PUSH64 R0                        ;Save all 64 bits of R0
      MOVL    SMP$GL_PRIMID,R0
      $PUSH64 R1
      MOVAL   G^SMP$GL_CPU_DATA,R1
      MOVL    (R1)[R0],R1
      BBSSI   S^#CPU$V_IOPOST,CPU$L_WORK_REQ(R1),30010$
30010$:
      $POP64  R1
      JSB     G^SMP$INTPROC
      $POP64  R0                        ;Restore all 64 bits of R0
```

The generated statements invoke routine SMP$INTPROC, in module SMP-INT_COMMON.

SMP$INTPROC executes a memory barrier instruction to ensure systemwide data updates are visible prior to the interrupt. To request an interprocessor interrupt on the CPU whose ID is in R0, it executes a CALL_PAL MTPR_IPIR instruction, which copies R0 to the interprocessor interrupt register (IPIR). SMP$INTPROC then returns.

There are actually four slightly different routines, all in module SMPINT_

COMMON, for requesting interprocessor interrupts of all active set members. The IPINT_ALL macro selects one of the following routines based on its arguments:

▶ SMP$INTALL—Interrupt each other active set member.

▶ SMP$INTALL_BIT—Set the specified work request bit in each other active set member's per-CPU database and interrupt it.

▶ SMP$INTALL_ACQ—Acquire the CPU mutex, interrupt all other active set members, and release the CPU mutex.

▶ SMP$INTALL_BIT_ACQ (the default)—Acquire the CPU mutex, set the specified work request bit in each other active set member's per-CPU database and interrupt it, and release the CPU mutex.

37.5.2 Servicing Interprocessor Interrupts and Work Requests

SMP$INTSR, in module SMPINT_COMMON, is the interprocessor interrupt service routine. It runs at IPL 22.

After executing a memory barrier instruction, SMP$INTSR tests system global cells and the processor's work request bits to determine what actions are appropriate responses to the interrupt request. Note that the service routine may have to respond to multiple requests. It tests and clears each work request bit with a BBCCI MACRO-32 statement, which is implemented with the load-locked/store-conditional mechanism.

SMP$INTSR checks whether it is running on the primary. If so, it tests HWRPB$IL_TXRDY_L to see whether any secondaries' console subsystems have sent a message to the primary processor. A console sends a message by setting the bit corresponding to the CPU ID in HWRPB$IL_TXRDY_L, writing the message in the CPU's HWRPB slot, beginning at SLOT$B_TXBUFFER, and requesting an interprocessor interrupt. If any bit is set, SMP$INTSR invokes SMP$SEC_MESSAGE, in module SMPROUT, passing it the lowest CPU ID that has a waiting message.

SMP$SEC_MESSAGE processes the message for that CPU. It first copies the message and clears the CPU's HWRPB$IL_TXRDY_L bit. If the message is the string ?STARTREQ?, indicating that the CPU has just come on line, SMP$SEC_MESSAGE sets the corresponding bit in SMP$GL_CPUCONF. SMP$SEC_MESSAGE outputs any other message to the console terminal. It then returns to SMP$INTSR.

SMP$INTSR tests XDT$GL_OWNER_ID to see whether a processor executing XDELTA has requested the other processors to stall. If so, it raises IPL to 31 and enters a benign state, as described in Section 37.5.4. Entry into the benign state is not requested through a work request bit. It is a request for the processor to continue to perform an action until told to stop. The signal to stop is a change in value in the relevant system global cell. When the benign state ends, SMP$INTSR restores the previous IPL, that of the interprocessor interrupt, and continues.

SMP$INTSR tests CPU$L_WORK_REQ to see if another processor has incurred a fatal bugcheck and is requesting this processor to bugcheck. If so, it generates the fatal bugcheck CPUEXIT. Section 37.9 describes how fatal bugchecks are processed on an SMP system.

SMP$INTSR tests whether any translation buffer invalidations are required:

▶ For a single translation buffer entry invalidation, it invokes SMP$IN-VALID_SINGLE, in module SMPINT_COMMON.

▶ For a single data translation buffer invalidation, it invokes SMP$IN-VALID_SINGLE_DATA, in module SMPINT_COMMON.

▶ For a single translation buffer invalidation request made from a CPU holding the MMG spinlock, it invokes INVALID_SINGLE_MMG, in module SMPINT_COMMON.

▶ For a single data translation buffer invalidation request made from a CPU holding the MMG spinlock, it invokes INVALID_SINGLE_DATA_MMG, in module SMPINT_COMMON.

Section 37.5.3 describes these routines and their requests in more detail.

If an I/O postprocessing interrupt was requested, SMP$INTSR requests an IPL 4 software interrupt. Executive code running on a secondary that queues an I/O request packet to the systemwide I/O postprocessing queue makes this work request of the primary. Later, when IPL drops, IOC$IOPOST, running on the primary processor, will service the systemwide queue. Section 37.6.4 discusses the need for systemwide and per-CPU I/O postprocessing queues.

If a work request was made to invalidate the entire translation buffer, SMP$INTSR takes that action by writing to the TBIA processor register. The work request is typically made through the MACRO-32 TBI_ALL macro. This macro is invoked, for example, when the swapper process deletes or fills a process header slot.

A work request to update the AST summary register (ASTSR) for this processor's current process is made when SCH$QAST, in module ASTDEL, running on another processor, queues an AST to a process current on this processor. SCH$QAST has no direct way to update another processor's ASTSR register. Furthermore, the architecture does not permit software to modify the HWPCB of a current process. While holding the SCHED spinlock to ensure that the process remains current on the other processor, SCH$QAST requests the interprocessor interrupt. It busy waits until the interrupted processor clears SMP$GL_ASTSR_ACK as a signal that the ASTSR has been modified.

In response to an update ASTSR work request, SMP$INTSR writes the contents of SMP$GL_ASTSR_ACK to the ASTSR. If the ASTSR bit is set to indicate a kernel mode AST is pending, SMP$INTSR enables delivery to kernel mode in case a special kernel AST has been queued but the process had disabled delivery of normal kernel mode ASTs. If delivery had been disabled, it sets the low-order bit of PCB$L_AST_BLOCKED in the process's PCB. It executes a memory barrier instruction and then clears SMP$GL_ASTSR_ ACK as a signal to the processor that made this work request.

If there is a work request indicating a fork process to be moved from another processor to this one, SMP$INTSR executes a CALL_PAL REMQHI instruction to remove the first fork block from the queue at CPU$Q_ WORK_FQFL. It invokes EXE$QUEUE_FORK, in module FORKCNTRL. EXE$QUEUE_FORK inserts the fork block in the fork queue on this processor corresponding to the appropriate IPL. (FKB$B_FLCK contains the index of a spinlock from which the IPL is taken.) SMP$INTSR repeats this for each fork block in the queue at CPU$Q_WORK_FQFL. If SMP$INTSR is running on the primary, it processes each fork block on the queue at SMP$GQ_PRI-MARY_WORKQ in the same manner.

Two routines in module SMPROUT make interprocessor fork work requests: SMP$FORK_TO_PRIMARY_CPU and SMP$CPU_SWITCH. The first is typically invoked from SMP$WRITE_OPA0, in module SMPROUT, running on a secondary processor, to broadcast a message to the console terminal. The second is invoked to queue an I/O request to a device with affinity for a CPU other than the current processor. Section 37.6.3 describes device affinity.

If a work request was made to access the battery-backed watch chip, SMP$INTSR checks whether it is running on the primary. If not, it ignores the request. As the only processor allowed to access the watch chip, the primary has the role of timekeeper. The value in the watch chip is the basis for initializing system time after a boot or power failure.

Associated with this work request are two bits in SMP$GL_FLAGS:

▶ SMP$V_TODR, which a secondary tests and sets to ensure that only one secondary at a time engages in this dialogue
▶ SMP$V_TODR_ACK, for whose setting a secondary waits as a signal that the cell SMP$GQ_NEW_HWCLOCK contains valid data

SMP$GQ_PROPOSED_HWCLOCK describes the type of watch chip access desired:

▶ In response to a value of zero, the primary reads the time of year from the watch chip.
▶ In response to any other value, the primary writes this value to the watch chip and then reads the watch chip.

The primary writes the new value of the watch chip into SMP$GQ_NEW_HWCLOCK.

The software interrupt request to access the watch chip is made from a secondary executing one of the following routines:

▶ EXE$INIT_HWCLOCK, in module [SYSLOA]TIMROUT, which is invoked by the SYSINIT process

1267

▶ EXE$READ_HWCLOCK or EXE$WRITE_HWCLOCK, both in module [SYSLOA]TIMROUT

Accessing the primary's watch chip from a secondary processor requires an interprocessor dialogue, whose general sequence is as follows:

1. Prior to requesting the interprocessor interrupt, each of the previously listed routines tests and sets bit SMP$V_TODR. If the bit was clear, it writes SMP$GQ_PROPOSED_HWCLOCK, requests an interprocessor interrupt of the primary, and waits for bit SMP$V_TODR_ACK to be set.
2. Running on the primary, SMP$INTSR examines SMP$GQ_PROPOSED_HWCLOCK. If that cell contains a nonzero value, SMP$INTSR invokes EXE$WRITE_LOCAL_HWCLOCK in module [SYSLOA]TIMROUT, to write that value to the watch chip.
3. SMP$INTSR then invokes EXE$READ_HWCLOCK to read the time value and record it in SMP$GQ_NEW_HWCLOCK. It sets SMP$V_TODR_ACK.
4. Once bit SMP$V_TODR_ACK has been set, the requesting secondary clears it, copies the time from SMP$GQ_NEW_HWCLOCK, and clears bit SMP$V_TODR.

Chapter 12 gives further information on timekeeping and the role of the watch chip.

If there is a work request for a rescheduling interrupt, SMP$INTSR requests an IPL 3 interrupt. Chapter 13 describes the circumstances under which this interrupt is requested. Briefly, they are

▶ When a resident process becomes computable whose priority allows it to preempt a process current on another CPU
▶ When a current process's priority is changed by a thread of execution running on a different CPU and there is a computable resident process of higher priority
▶ When a current process acquires explicit affinity for a different CPU
▶ When a capability has been removed from a CPU that is needed by its current process

If there is a work request to flush instruction prefetch, SMP$INTSR executes an instruction memory barrier (IMB). This work can be requested by the MACRO-32 INSTRUCTION_MB macro. It is also requested by XDELTA after it makes nonwritable executive pages system-writable to force the other members into the benign state and then at its end to flush instruction prefetch. This prevents other members from executing stale instructions or accessing stale data changed as the result of XDELTA commands. In particular, the XDELTA user may have added a breakpoint, replacing an existing instruction; removed a breakpoint, restoring an instruction; or simply deposited new data and instructions over existing data and instructions.

When no more work request bits are set, SMP$INTSR dismisses the interrupt.

37.5.3   Translation Buffer Invalidation

As described in Chapter 15, a translation buffer (TB) is a CPU component that caches the result of recent successful virtual address translations of valid pages. Some CPUs have both an instruction stream TB (ITB) and a data stream TB (DTB). The executive ensures the consistency of the TB by invalidating the TB entry corresponding to a valid PTE that it is changing, for example, during virtual address space deletion. Kernel mode software can invalidate either a single TB entry or all entries.

In an SMP system, each processor has its own TB, which is filled with entries as the result of instruction stream execution on that processor. Since all members share the SPT, when one member changes a valid SPTE, it must ensure that all other members invalidate their TB entries for it. To meet this requirement, an active set member changing a valid SPTE requests interprocessor interrupts of the others. The possibility also exists that at the time of the interprocessor interrupt request a member might be executing a relatively lengthy sequence, at an IPL higher than that of the interprocessor interrupt. Consequently, there is a timed multistep interprocessor dialogue for invalidating SPTEs.

A MACRO-32 kernel mode routine can invalidate the entire TB with the TBI_ALL macro. It can invalidate a single PTE with a macro such as TBI_SINGLE, TBI_SINGLE_64, or TBI_DATA_64, one of whose arguments is the address mapped by the PTE. TBI_SINGLE's argument is a 32-bit address; the others' arguments are 64-bit addresses. Another argument to these macros identifies the scope of the invalidation—whether it is local to the processor or systemwide.

A systemwide invocation of the TBI_ALL macro generates code to call MMG$TBI_ALL, in module PAGEFAULT. MMG$TBI_ALL requests an interprocessor interrupt of each other active set member (see Section 37.5.2) to flush the entire TB. It executes a `CALL_PAL MTPR_TBIA` to flush its own TB. Flushing the entire translation buffer is a preferred alternative to flushing a number of pages within a loop that includes the interprocessor dialogue described in the following paragraphs.

The actions that result from use of the TBI_SINGLE macro are similar to those of TBI_SINGLE_64 or TBI_DATA_64. A systemwide invocation of the TBI_SINGLE macro generates code to call MMG$TBI_SINGLE, in module PAGEFAULT, with the address argument from the macro. MMG$TBI_SINGLE tests in which address space the address argument lies. In the case of a process space address, it executes a `CALL_PAL MTPR_TBIS` instruction and returns. Since the same per-process space is not accessed concurrently by multiple processors, nothing further is necessary. In the case of a

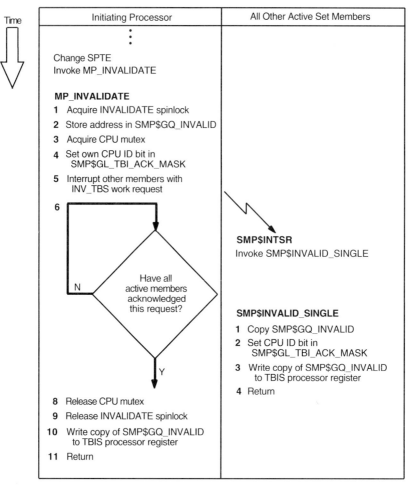

Figure 37.4
Invalidation of a Single TB Entry

system space address, MMG$TBI_SINGLE calls MP_INVALIDATE, in module PAGEFAULT, to implement the TB invalidation.

The following steps describe the sequence of a system space TB invalidation requested through TBI_SINGLE as it might occur concurrently on the CPU requesting the invalidation and the active set members. The numbers in Figure 37.4 correspond to the following steps, not all of which are represented in the figure.

The sequence begins with MP_INVALIDATE, in module PAGEFAULT, which runs on the processor changing the SPTE:

① It acquires the INVALIDATE spinlock, raising IPL to 1 less than the interprocessor interrupt IPL.

② It stores the address to be invalidated in SMP$GQ_INVALID.

③ It acquires the CPU mutex to block entry of new members into the active set.

④ It stores a mask with only its CPU ID bit set in SMP$GL_TBI_ACK_MASK.

⑤ It requests an interprocessor interrupt of all other active set members with a work request type of INV_TBS. In response, each member should copy SMP$GQ_INVALID, invalidate the appropriate TB entry, and set its own CPU ID bit in SMP$GL_TBI_ACK_MASK.

⑥ Within a busy wait loop like that described in Section 37.5.6, MP_INVALIDATE compares SMP$GL_TBI_ACK_MASK to the active set mask. When all active set members have responded, it goes on to step 8.

⑦ If the busy wait time elapses before all members have responded, MP_INVALIDATE invokes SMP$TIMEOUT, described in Section 37.5.6, to determine whether the lack of response is serious enough to warrant crashing the system. If that routine returns, MP_INVALIDATE resets the wait time and continues with step 6.

⑧ It releases the CPU mutex.

⑨ It releases the INVALIDATE spinlock, restoring the previous IPL.

⑩ MP_INVALIDATE executes a `CALL_PAL MTPR_TBIS` to invalidate the TB entry on this processor.

⑪ It returns to its invoker.

In response to the INV_TBS interprocessor interrupt described in step 5, the routine SMP$INTSR runs on each other active set member and invokes the routine SMP$INVALID_SINGLE, in module SMPINT_COMMON. SMP$INVALID_SINGLE takes the following steps:

① It copies SMP$GQ_INVALID.

② It sets the processor's CPU ID bit in SMP$GL_TBI_ACK_MASK.

③ It uses the copy of SMP$GQ_INVALID as the source in a `CALL_PAL MTPR_TBIS` instruction.

④ It returns to SMP$INTSR, which checks for other work requests and finally dismisses the interrupt.

37.5.4 Benign State and XDELTA

When one member of the active set requires that all other members temporarily cease their normal operations, it initiates the benign state. All the other members are quiescent until the initiating member terminates the benign state. While in a benign state, a processor loops at IPL 31, checking whether the state has been terminated. The benign state is currently used only when one processor executes XDELTA code. The other CPUs effectively pause rather than continue with operations that might disrupt or confuse the debugging session.

When a processor enters XDELTA, through a breakpoint exception, the processor executes code within XDELTA that makes it the sole user of XDELTA:

1. It raises IPL to 31.
2. It tests and sets the low bit of XDT$GL_INTERLOCK, the XDELTA interlock bit. If the bit was clear, the processor's exclusive access to the XDELTA owner cell, XDT$GL_OWNER_ID, is now guaranteed.
3. It tests the high bit of that cell to see whether any processor owns XDELTA.
   - If the bit is set, this processor writes its own CPU ID into the cell, clears the interlock bit, and proceeds with XDELTA.
   - If the bit is clear, indicating that some processor owns XDELTA, and the owner ID is that of this processor, it clears the interlock bit and proceeds with XDELTA.
   - If the bit is clear and the owner ID is that of another processor, the processor clears the interlock bit and invokes the benign state routine.

     When the benign state ends, the processor backs up the PC in the exception stack frame and executes a CALL_PAL REI instruction in order to reexecute the instruction at that address. Reexecuting it allows for the possibility that it was altered as a result of XDELTA commands. If the instruction is still a CALL_PAL BPT, this sequence will be repeated from step 1.
4. Proceeding with XDELTA, the processor requests an interprocessor interrupt of all the other members of the active set with a work request to invalidate instruction prefetch (see Section 37.5.2). As they execute SMP$INTSR, each finds XDELTA owned and enters the benign state by invoking the benign state routine.
5. When XDELTA is done, before the processor restores the thread of execution that incurred the exception, it acquires the XDELTA owner interlock bit, writes −1 to XDT$GL_OWNER_ID, and releases the owner interlock bit.

The benign state routine, XDT$CPU_WAIT in module [DELTA]XDELTA, takes the following steps:

1. To record its entry into the benign state, the processor sets the bit corresponding to its ID in XDT$GL_BENIGN_CPUS.
2. The processor tests whether it is the primary processor.
3. If it is not the primary processor, it continually tests the high bit of XDT$GL_OWNER_ID, waiting for the bit to be clear. When the bit is clear, the processor clears its bit in XDT$GL_BENIGN_CPUS. It invalidates the entire TB and also any instruction prefetch, flushing any prefetch of instructions that might have been altered by XDELTA commands or actions.
4. The primary processor is responsible for performing XDELTA console

terminal I/O on behalf of a secondary processor. The primary communicates to the secondary processor through memory locations that are treated like simple terminal interface registers by the secondary. The primary serves the console by relaying data between the real console driver and the virtual terminal interface registers. The primary processor leaves the benign state in the same manner as the other processors.

There is provision for an alternative entry into and exit from the benign state, through routines SMP$INITIATE_BENIGN and SMP$TERMINATE_BENIGN, in module SMPROUT. SMP$INTSR tests for this form of the benign state and loops, checking for concurrent bugcheck and translation buffer invalidate requests. No current use is made of this form of benign state.

37.5.5   Override Set

The override set consists of all processors currently in the override state. The override state allows a thread of execution to inhibit any IPL change or checks associated with spinlock acquisition or release. Such changes or checks would be awkward for the thread of execution, which may be executing a code sequence beyond question, such as initialization code, or code that confirms that local synchronization is not at issue.

A processor enters the override set when it must perform a synchronization operation that otherwise might be considered illegal. It sets its CPU ID bit in SMP$GL_OVERRIDE and leaves the override set when it clears the bit. While in the override set, a processor's IPL is not changed when the processor acquires a spinlock. Furthermore, the spinlock acquisitions and releases of a member of the override set are not subject to the IPL checks in the full-checking SMP synchronization image, which test that local CPU synchronization is not being violated.

Some examples of circumstances under which a processor joins the override set are

▶ During bootstrap and initialization, while the processor is executing at IPL 31
▶ During fatal bugcheck processing

Note that widespread use of this mechanism is not supported or recommended. In many cases where it might seem like a good solution, a better structured alternative usually exists, for example, creating a lower IPL fork process.

37.5.6   Spinwaits and Busy Waits

The spinwait code sequence and BUSYWAIT macro enable a processor to wait a finite length of time for another processor to take some action. Both generate waits of a maximum duration based on spinlock timeout count. The spinwait code sequence generates a test for the availability of a spinlock within the code sequence, while the BUSYWAIT macro allows the user to specify the test to be made. If the wait time is exhausted before the test succeeds, each mechanism invokes SMP$TIMEOUT to determine whether the system should be crashed.

The spinwait code sequences are defined in the SPINLOCKS module within the routines that acquire a spinlock. The sequence depends upon the IPL at entry to the routines. The sequence for IPLs below 22, the interprocessor interrupt IPL, is as follows:

1. Increment CPU$L_BUSYWAIT so that time spent spinwaiting is accounted for in CPU time statistics as MPSYNCH time rather than charged to the current process.
2. Establish a wait time roughly equivalent to the spinlock's timeout count converted to nanoseconds.
3. Invoke EXE$TIMEDWAIT_SETUP, in module TIMEDWAIT.
4. Test whether the spinlock is available. If so, leave this loop.
5. If EXE$V_NOSPINWAIT in EXE$GL_TIME_CONTROL is set, go to step 3.
6. Invoke EXE$TIMEDWAIT_COMPLETE, in module TIMEDWAIT, to see if the wait time has elapsed. If it has not, go to step 4.
7. If the spinlock does not become available within the wait time and the spinlock owner has not changed, invoke SMP$TIMEOUT to determine whether to generate a CPUSPINWAIT fatal bugcheck.
8. If SMP$TIMEOUT returns, continue with step 3.

Even while spinwaiting, a processor must be responsive to certain interprocessor work requests to prevent deadlocks. If the processor is looping at an IPL below that of the interprocessor interrupt, its loop can be interrupted to service a work request. However, if it is looping at a higher IPL, it cannot be interrupted and must minimally check for work requests to bugcheck, to enter the benign state, or to access the watch chip.

An incomplete dump or deadlock would result if such a spinwaiting processor were unresponsive to a bugcheck request and if, when its spinwait count was exhausted, SMP$TIMEOUT returned rather than crashing. If a fatal bugcheck were initiated in these circumstances, regardless of which active set member owned the spinlock of interest, it is likely that the spinlock would not be released and that the spinwaiting processor would simply continue to spinwait and fail to save its context in the dump. If the spinwaiting processor were the primary processor and failed to respond to the bugcheck request, the system would hang, deadlocked. Section 37.9 describes how fatal bugchecks are handled in an SMP system.

A deadlock could result if a primary processor spinwaiting at an IPL equal to or above that of the interprocessor interrupt were unresponsive to a request to enter the benign state. Once the benign state is initiated, whether the initiator or a processor already in the benign state owns the spinlock, it is likely that the spinlock would not be released and that the spinwait would continue. (Because the system has been booted with XDELTA, a spinwait crash would not result at the end of the spinwait loop.) The system would deadlock as soon as the benign state initiator required the primary processor to service secondary processor console I/O. Section 37.5.4 describes the benign state in more detail.

A processor that spinwaits at an IPL above that of the interprocessor interrupt and that is not in the override set cannot be trying to acquire the INVALIDATE spinlock, whose IPL is defined to be 1 less than that of the interprocessor interrupt. Thus, for example, even if there is an active set member initiating an interprocessor dialogue for translation buffer invalidation, that processor cannot also be holding the higher ranked spinlock that the spinwaiting processor is trying to acquire. Thus there can be no deadlock between that processor and the spinwaiting one.

If, on the other hand, the spinwaiting processor is in the override set, the value of its IPL is not necessarily the IPL of the spinlock for which it is waiting. The spinwait sequence, therefore, also generates explicit tests for whether a processor in the override set should service requests to invalidate a single translation buffer entry or, as the primary, to access the watch chip.

The spinwait code sequence for IPLs 22 and above is as follows:

1. Increment CPU$L_BUSYWAIT so that time spent spinwaiting is accounted for in CPU time statistics as MPSYNCH time rather than charged to the current process.
2. Establish a wait time roughly equivalent to the spinlock's timeout count converted to nanoseconds.
3. Invoke EXE$TIMEDWAIT_SETUP, in module TIMEDWAIT.
4. Test whether the spinlock is available. If so, leave this loop.
5. If another processor has begun to execute XDELTA (if the high bit of XDT$GL_OWNER_ID is zero), invoke XDT$CPU_WAIT to enter the benign state, as described in Section 37.5.4.
6. If a bugcheck work request has been made, generate a fatal CPUEXIT bugcheck.
7. If the processor is not a member of the override set (described in Section 37.5.5), go to step 11.
8. If a work request to invalidate a single translation buffer entry has been made, invoke SMP$INVALID_SINGLE.
9. If a work request to invalidate a single data translation buffer entry has been made, invoke SMP$INVALID_SINGLE_DATA.
10. If a work request to access the watch chip has been made, examine SMP$GQ_PROPOSED_HWCLOCK to determine whether a read or write is requested and perform the requested access. Store the time in SMP$GQ_NEW_HWCLOCK and set SMP$V_TODR_ACK in SMP$GL_FLAGS.

11. If EXE$V_NOSPINWAIT in EXE$GL_TIME_CONTROL is set, go to step 3.
12. Invoke EXE$TIMEWAIT_COMPLETE, in module TIMEDWAIT, to see if the wait time has elapsed. If it has not, go to step 4.
13. If the spinlock does not become available within the wait time and the spinlock owner has not changed, invoke SMP$TIMEOUT to determine whether to generate a CPUSPINWAIT fatal bugcheck.
14. If SMP$TIMEOUT returns, continue with step 4.

SMP$TIMEOUT, in module SMPROUT, invokes SMP$CONTROLP_ CPUS, described in Section 37.5.7, to determine if any active set member has been halted through the console. If an active set member is halted, SMP$TIMEOUT returns. If no active set member is halted, SMP$TIMEOUT tests bit EXE$V_NOSPINWAIT in EXE$GL_TIME_CONTROL. This bit is set on a system booted with XDELTA and during the execution of the IPL 12 interrupt service routine. If the bit is clear, SMP$TIMEOUT generates the fatal bugcheck CPUSPINWAIT. If the bit is set, SMP$TIMEOUT returns.

By default the BUSYWAIT macro does not generate any tests for outstanding work requests that should be serviced. Any code that invokes the BUSY-WAIT macro from IPLs at or above that of the interprocessor interrupt service routine should include the same tests as the SPINWAIT macro.

The BUSYWAIT macro generates the following sequence:

1. Establish a wait time roughly equivalent to the spinlock's timeout count converted to nanoseconds.
2. Invoke EXE$TIMEDWAIT_SETUP, in module TIMEDWAIT.
3. Execute the test instructions specified with macro invocation. If the test is satisfied, leave this loop.
4. If a bugcheck work request has been made, generate a fatal CPUEXIT bugcheck.
5. If EXE$V_NOSPINWAIT in EXE$GL_TIME_CONTROL is set, go to step 2.
6. Invoke EXE$TIMEDWAIT_COMPLETE to see if the wait time has elapsed. If it has not, go to step 3.
7. If the test is not satisfied within the wait time, invoke SMP$TIMEOUT to determine whether to generate a CPUSPINWAIT fatal bugcheck.
8. If SMP$TIMEOUT returns, continue with step 3.

37.5.7 Sanity Timer Mechanism

The sanity timer mechanism enables detection of a member of the SMP system that is hung or otherwise nonfunctional. It acts as a check that each member is responding to interval timer interrupts. Each of the members of the active set monitors one other member, creating a sanity timer chain. A member monitors the one with the next lower ID than its own. The CPU with the lowest ID monitors the one with the highest ID, forming a circular list. When a CPU is booted and joins the active set, it inserts itself into the sanity timer chain.

The following fields in the per-CPU database are related to the sanity timer mechanism:

▸ CPU$L_SANITY_TIMER, initialized to the value of the SYSGEN parameter SMP_SANITY_CNT, is the number of soft ticks until this CPU times out. Its default value is 300.

▸ CPU$L_SANITY_TICKS, initialized to the value of the SYSGEN parameter SMP_TICK_CNT, is the number of interval timer ticks until the next time the processor monitors its neighbor in the sanity timer chain. Its default value is 30.

▸ CPU$L_TPOINTER contains the address of CPU$L_SANITY_TIMER in the per-CPU database of the active set member that is being monitored by this CPU.

The sanity timer mechanism is implemented as part of the interval timer interrupt service routine. At the end of each soft tick, each processor resets its own sanity timer and monitors one other member's sanity timer, periodically decrementing it. If a processor decrements the watched CPU's sanity timer to zero, that means the watched CPU has not reset its sanity timer.

The interval timer interrupt service routine, EXE$HWCLKINT in module TIMESCHDL, running on each member of an SMP system, takes the following steps to implement the sanity timer mechanism:

1. It tests the low bit of SMP$GL_FLAGS to determine whether the system is multiprocessing. If the bit is clear, EXE$HWCLKINT bypasses all the sanity timer related code.

2. It resets the current processor's sanity timer.

3. It decrements CPU$L_SANITY_TICKS, the number of ticks until the next time it should check its neighbor's sanity timer. If the number has reached zero, it resets CPU$L_SANITY_TICKS from SMP_TICK_CNT and, with the load-locked/store-conditional mechanism, subtracts the value of that SYSGEN parameter from its neighbor's sanity timer.

    Note that EXE$HWCLKINT resets its own sanity timer at each interval timer interrupt but decrements its neighbor's sanity timer less frequently, giving its neighbor ample opportunity to reset its own sanity timer.

4. If its neighbor's timer is now less than or equal to zero, the routine makes several tests to determine how serious the situation is:

    • If bit EXE$V_NOSMPSANITY in EXE$GL_TIME_CONTROL is set to indicate that sanity timeout is disabled, then the routine merely resets its neighbor's sanity timer and continues.

    On a system booted with XDELTA, sanity timeouts are disabled in this way. During extended execution at high IPL in the IPL 12 (IPC) interrupt service routine (see Chapter 5), the service routine sets EXE$V_NOSMPSANITY and then clears it when done.

- It checks the timer again and if the timer is now positive, indicating that its neighbor has resumed normal operations, it continues.
- It invokes SMP$CONTROLP_CPUS, in module SMPROUT, to see whether any active set members are at present halted via the console. SMP$CONTROLP_CPUS examines the HWRPB slot of each active set member. Bit SLOT$V_OH in SLOT$IL_STATE is set when the CPU is halted through operator action. SMP$CONTROLP_CPUS returns a mask with a bit set for each such CPU.

  If it returns any nonzero value, EXE$HWCLKINT merely resets its neighbor's sanity timer and continues, since the halted CPU could have triggered the timeout. For example, if the halted CPU holds a high-IPL spinlock for which another CPU is spinwaiting at an IPL high enough to block interval timer interrupts, the first CPU's being halted too long can trigger sanity timeout of the second CPU. EXE$HWCLKINT therefore resets the sanity timer. If the second CPU's timeout was merely coincident with the first CPU's halt, the second CPU is likely to time out again after the halted CPU continues.

5. If all the tests fail, EXE$HWCLKINT generates the fatal bugcheck CPU-SANITY.

37.6 I/O CONSIDERATIONS

A number of issues specific to I/O support arise under SMP, some of them software and some hardware:

- ▶ Synchronizing access to the device controller and device data structures from the asynchronous threads of execution that make up a device driver
- ▶ Impact of devices' interrupting all SMP members
- ▶ Access to a device by a subset of SMP members
- ▶ Order in which I/O requests complete

37.6.1 Synchronizing Driver Routines

The various routines that compose a driver are essentially independently activated threads of execution:

- ▶ Function decision table (FDT) action routines and cancel routines are entered in response to processes' system service requests.
- ▶ Some routines trigger others; for example, an FDT routine that jumps to EXE$QIODRVPKT eventually causes entry to the driver's start I/O routine.
- ▶ Device interrupt service routines are entered in response to device interrupts.

▶ Some routines are entered by the executive in response to events such as powerfail recovery and expected interrupt timeout.

On a uniprocessor system, some of these routines can interrupt others. The device unit control block (UCB) has state bits that specify, for example, whether a fork process is active on that device unit (UCB$V_BSY in UCB$L_STS), whether an interrupt is expected (UCB$V_INT in UCB$L_STS), and whether there is a time limit for the interrupt's arrival (UCB$V_TIM in UCB$L_STS). The state bits help control the activation of driver threads. An important additional synchronization technique is raising IPL to block interrupts, either to fork level (the IPL specified through the contents of UCB$B_FLCK) or to device level (UCB$B_DIPL). These techniques are not sufficient for the concurrency possible on an SMP system and are augmented by spinlocks.

Each device controller has its own dynamic spinlock, called a device lock, that synchronizes access to the controller's registers and extends the concept of raising IPL to UCB$B_DIPL. Each device UCB identifies a static spinlock, called a fork lock, that synchronizes access to the UCB and extends the synchronization formerly achieved by raising IPL to fork level. The executive enters a driver's start I/O and cancel I/O routines with the appropriate fork lock held. It enters the timeout routine holding both the fork lock and the device lock. The start I/O routine acquires the device lock as necessary. The interrupt service routine, to which the hardware may dispatch directly, must acquire the device lock immediately. (Chapter 9 provides a detailed description of spinlocks, and the manual *OpenVMS AXP Device Support: Developer's Guide* explains when each is used.) In an SMP system, multiple processes can be executing FDT action routines or canceling I/O requests concurrently with interrupt service routine and fork process execution.

37.6.2 Device Interrupts

The executive and current processors that support SMP have mechanisms to pass device interrupts on to every system member. If these mechanisms were enabled, the first member to respond to the interrupt would service it, and the others would dismiss the interrupt. Currently, however, interrupts are not distributed; device interrupts are delivered to and serviced only by the primary processor.

Performance studies have shown no improvement from distributing interrupts and, in some cases, significantly increased overhead, as a result of several factors. If interrupt requests are distributed, on some current processor types each member must interrupt what it is currently doing and perform bus transactions to determine the source of the interrupt. The first member to respond to the device would continue with interrupt processing; the others would receive passive releases and dismiss their interrupts. In some systems, the superfluous bus transactions would make a noticeable difference in bus throughput. In all such systems, all but the first member would have interrupted what they were doing to execute an unproductive thread of execution, with potential losses from their memory caches and TBs.

A further issue is that a typical device interrupt service routine requests a fork interrupt on the current processor. Distributing device interrupts thus requires distributing fork interrupts and fork processing. Time spent in the device interrupt service routine is small compared to fork processing time. Although a number of spinlocks are used as fork locks, the IOLOCK8 spinlock is used more heavily and would become a bottleneck if fork interrupts were distributed as a result of distributing device interrupts. As a result, processors that could otherwise have executed applications while the primary processor serviced device and fork interrupts would spend time spinwaiting for IOLOCK8.

While splitting IOLOCK8 into several spinlocks to enable more parallelism is possible in a future release of the operating system, thus far the current scheme has not been a problem.

37.6.3 Device Affinity

Many devices can be accessed equally by every processor of an SMP system, but some can be accessed by only a subset of the processors. The SMP design for device support must take that into account.

▸ The console terminal is typically accessible only from the primary.
▸ An application design might require that a particular device be accessed from a subset of available processors.

Software-implemented device affinity supports these hardware limitations by providing a mechanism to restrict device access to a subset of the system's processors.

Each device UCB has a longword mask in field UCB$L_AFFINITY that specifies a device affinity set, those processors from which its device registers may be accessed. By default the mask is all 1's, enabling access from all processors. For console devices, the mask is zero, a value that means only the primary processor can access the device registers. In theory, the device affinity mask can express the idea that access from the primary is prohibited. However, in practice, under the current OpenVMS version, the primary processor is always presumed to be a member of every device's affinity set.

Before the executive enters any driver routine, it must ensure that the routine will run on a processor that is part of the device's affinity set. The major driver entry points are

▸ FDT action routines
▸ Start I/O and alternate start I/O routines
▸ Interrupt service routine
▸ Register dumping routine
▸ Device timeout routine

- Unit and controller initialization routines
- Cancel I/O routine

FDT action routines preprocess an I/O request and are expected not to access device registers. Thus, they can execute on any processor regardless of device affinity.

Before entering a device driver at either its start I/O or alternate start I/O routine, the executive tests whether it is running on a processor for which the device has affinity. If not, the executive invokes routine SMP$CPU_ SWITCH, in module SMPROUT, which stores fork process context in reserved fields in the I/O request packet (IRP). It identifies the processor with the lowest CPU ID for which the device has affinity, queues the IRP to that processor's per-CPU database, and requests an interprocessor interrupt of work request type WORK_FQP (see Sections 37.5.1 and 37.5.2). The interprocessor interrupt service routine queues the IRP/fork block to the appropriate fork queue and requests a fork interrupt. When the fork interrupt is granted, the fork dispatcher acquires the appropriate fork lock and then enters the driver start I/O or alternate start I/O routine.

As previously described, device interrupt service routines always run on the primary processor. After the interrupt service routine forks, the fork process (generally, the reentered start I/O routine) executes on the primary processor. At that point, to run on a different processor in its affinity set, the fork process could itself invoke SMP$CPU_SWITCH.

A register dumping routine is entered indirectly by the start I/O routine when it invokes IOC$DIAGBUFILL or logs an error and thus runs on the same processor as the start I/O routine.

A device timeout routine is entered at device IPL from EXE$TIMEOUT, which runs on the primary as an IPL$_TIMER fork process. To run on another processor in its affinity set, the timeout routine must invoke SMP$CPU_SWITCH.

Unit and controller initialization routines run when a device is configured by the System Management (SYSMAN) utility. Running in process context in kernel mode, SYSMAN calls SCH$REQUIRE_CAPABILITY, in module CAPABILITY, to ensure that SYSMAN executes only on the primary processor during device configuration and similar operations. Power recovery code executes on the primary processor as part of system restart following system powerfail and recovery or as part of an adapter interrupt service routine following adapter powerfail and recovery.

A driver's cancel I/O routine is entered from process context code, either EXE$CANCEL in module SYSCANCEL, which is the Cancel I/O on Channel ($CANCEL) system service procedure, or IOC$LAST_CHAN, in module IOSUBNPAG. Both check whether the device's affinity mask is the same as the default mask. If not, these routines call SCH$REQUIRE_CAPABILITY to ensure execution on the primary before invoking the cancel routine.

37.6.4   I/O Postprocessing

An SMP system has one systemwide I/O postprocessing queue and one in each CPU's per-CPU database. Most IRPs are queued to the systemwide queue. Since only the primary processor services this queue, the sequence in which requests complete is preserved, even if they complete on different processors, and a process receives AST notification of I/O completion in the order in which the requests complete.

Without the systemwide queue, AST notifications of the completion of asynchronous I/O requests could occur out of order. This might happen to requests made of a driver able to complete I/O requests on a secondary. To complete an I/O request on a secondary processor, a driver would need to have unrestricted device affinity and be able to complete a request in the start I/O routine without the need for a device interrupt. Synchronous I/O requests, made through the Queue I/O Request and Wait ($QIOW) system service, are processed one at a time and cannot complete out of order.

With multiple processor-specific I/O postprocessing queues rather than a single systemwide one, problems such as the following can occur. A process requests several small asynchronous reads to a communications driver. The first read causes a device operation, whose interrupt service routine runs on the primary. The driver, in fact, receives a large transmission of data, sufficient to satisfy several small reads. The IRP of the first read is queued to the primary's I/O postprocessing queue. Before IPL drops low enough on the primary for the I/O postprocessing interrupt to be granted, several subsequent read requests from the process could complete on a secondary and their IRPs could be queued to its own I/O postprocessing queue. If the secondary's I/O postprocessing interrupt is serviced first, the process receives AST notification of the later requests before the first one.

Several routines that are commonly invoked from device drivers can queue an IRP to the systemwide queue. If the routine is running on the primary, it requests an I/O postprocessing interrupt. Otherwise, it sets the primary's I/O postprocessing work bit and requests an interprocessor interrupt. These routines are

▸ COM$POST and COM$POST_NCNT, in module COMDRVSUB, for completed and canceled requests
▸ IOC$REQCOM, in module IOSUBNPAG, for completed requests

EXE$ABORTIO and EXE$FINISHIO[C] are routines invoked from device driver FDT action routines to complete an I/O request at FDT level. Each queues the IRP to the per-CPU I/O postprocessing queue and, running at IPL 2, requests an I/O postprocessing interrupt, which typically is granted immediately. Postprocessing such a request on the same processor enables it to complete immediately, synchronously with the system service.

Table 37.2   Processor States

Name	Meaning
INIT	CPU is initializing
RUN	CPU is running
BOOTED	CPU is booted and waiting for go bit
STOPPED	CPU has stopped
TIMOUT	CPU has timed out during boot
BOOT_REJECTED	CPU was booted but refused to join the active set

37.7   PROCESSOR STATES

A secondary SMP member can be characterized by its state, stored in the per-CPU database field CPU$L_STATE. Prefaced by CPU$C_, the state symbols are defined by the macro $CPUDEF. These states are defined by the executive and should not be confused with the console processor states described in Chapter 36. Table 37.2 lists the possible state values and a brief description of each.

After system initialization the primary processor itself is always in the RUN state. A secondary processor participating in the SMP system is in the RUN state. Most of the other states are stages through which a secondary passes on its way to or from the RUN state. Members of the active set are always in the RUN state. Figure 37.5 shows the transitions among them. These are summarized here and described in detail in subsequent sections.

When SMP$SETUP_CPU, described in Section 37.8.3, first initializes the environment for each secondary processor, it sets each CPU's state to INIT. SMP$SETUP_CPU makes three attempts to boot a secondary by sending

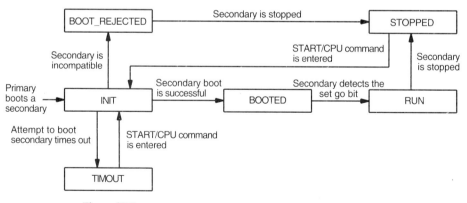

Figure 37.5
State Transitions of a Secondary Processor

a message to the console subsystem. If all fail, it sets the CPU's state to TIMOUT.

Routine SMP$START_SECONDARY, described in Section 37.8.4, running on each secondary, makes the other transitions from the INIT state:

▶ It changes the CPU's state to BOOT_REJECTED if the CPU's revision or type is inconsistent with those of the BOOT CPU.

▶ It changes the CPU's state to BOOTED when it begins to loop, waiting for the BOOT CPU to set the go bit. Once the go bit is set, it changes the CPU's state to RUN.

SMP$SHUTDOWN_CPU, described in Section 37.8.5, makes the transitions to the STOPPED state.

37.8   INITIALIZATION

At system cold start, the console subsystems identify the primary CPU, also called the BOOT CPU. Once it is selected, the secondary CPUs' console subsystems do not access memory and take no further action until notified by the primary CPU. The primary's console builds the HWRPB and any console-internal structures for the secondaries. It initializes the HWRPB:

▶ It stores the primary's CPU ID in HWRPB$IQ_PRIMARY.

▶ It clears HWRPB$IQ_TXRDY and HWRPB$IQ_RXRDY, which are used for communication among the processors.

▶ In each per-CPU slot field SLOT$IQ_STATE, the primary's console clears the SLOT$V_BIP, SLOT$V_RC, SLOT$V_OH, and SLOT$V_CV bits and, if appropriate, sets SLOT$V_PP, SLOT$V_PA, SLOT$V_PMV, SLOT$V_PL, and SLOT$V_PV (see Table 33.7).

▶ It sets SLOT$V_BIP in the primary's SLOT$IQ_STATE.

▶ It clears each per-CPU slot field SLOT$IQ_HALTCODE.

The BOOT CPU does most of the work of system initialization, loading the executive into memory and performing the tasks involved in bootstrapping a single-processor system.

SMP-related initialization is performed in several phases of bootstrap:

1. SYSBOOT, the secondary bootstrap, runs on the BOOT CPU. It allocates and initializes the per-CPU database for the BOOT CPU.

2. EXE$INIT, running on the BOOT CPU, performs some SMP initialization.

3. Routines SMP$SETUP_SMP and SMP$SETUP_CPU run on the BOOT CPU to perform further SMP initialization and boot the secondary processors.

4. Bootstrap code, running on each secondary, adds the processor to the active set.

Chapter 33 provides a detailed description of CPU initialization, loading and execution of APB, and SYSBOOT. Chapter 34 describes EXE$INIT and further steps in system initialization.

The following sections describe those parts of each bootstrap phase specifically related to SMP and the operations of the Digital command language (DCL) commands START/CPU and STOP/CPU. Figure 37.6 shows the major steps in these phases.

37.8.1   Initialization by SYSBOOT

SYSBOOT runs on the BOOT CPU in kernel mode at IPL 31 in the context of the boot HWPCB.

SYSBOOT allocates the primary's per-CPU database from nonpaged pool and stores its address in the PRBR register. It initializes the system HWPCB and allocates a kernel stack for it.

SYSBOOT determines which version to load of the executive image that supports synchronization by testing the SYSGEN parameter MULTIPROCESSING in combination with the number of CPUs present in the configuration. Chapter 9 describes SYSBOOT's criteria.

It maps the HWRPB into system space and copies the SWRPB from console address space into allocated nonpaged pool.

It initializes many of the fields in the primary's per-CPU database.

It swaps to the context of the system HWPCB and calls EXE$INIT.

37.8.2   Initialization by EXE$INIT

This section describes SMP-related initialization in EXE$INIT, which takes place on each CPU type unless otherwise noted. EXE$INIT runs on the BOOT CPU in kernel mode at IPL 31.

1. EXE$INIT stores the CPU ID of the current processor in SMP$GL_PRIMID.
2. It initializes the BOOT CPU's per-CPU data base:
   a. It zeros the per-CPU database.
   b. It stores the CPU ID in CPU$L_PHY_CPUID.
   c. It stores the address of the per-CPU data base in the CPU data vector entry for this CPU.
   d. It stores a mask with a single bit set to represent this CPU in CPU$L_CPUID_MASK.
   e. It stores the value BUG$_CPUCEASED in CPU$L_BUGCODE.
   f. It initializes the per-CPU I/O postprocessing queue and fork queues as empty lists.
   g. It clears CPU$L_HARDAFF to indicate no processes with explicit affinity to this CPU.
   h. It sets the processor's CPU$L_STATE field to RUN.

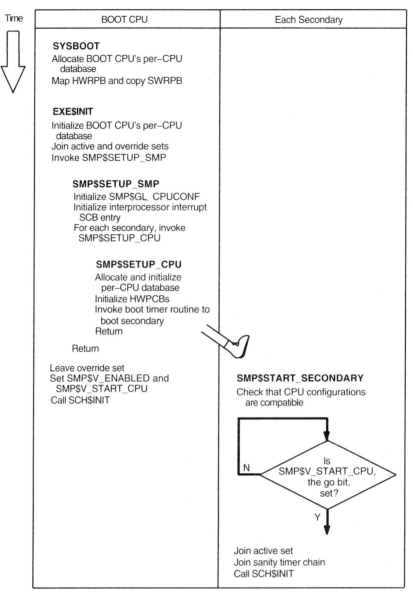

Figure 37.6
Major Steps in SMP Bootstrap

i. It copies the SYSGEN parameter SMP_SANITY_CNT, the number of interval timer ticks until SMP sanity timeout, to CPU$L_SANITY_TIMER, the BOOT CPU's sanity timer. It stores the address of the BOOT CPU's sanity timer in CPU$L_TPOINTER. When a secondary processor boots and inserts itself into the sanity timer chain, the BOOT CPU's CPU$L_TPOINTER will be altered to point to the secondary's sanity timer. Section 37.5.7 describes the sanity timer mechanism.

3. EXE$INIT initializes the available set mask to the contents of CPU$L_ CPUID_MASK, that is, a configuration with the BOOT CPU available, and copies it to the active, idle, and override set masks.

4. It initializes EXE$GL_AFFINITY, the default device affinity mask, to all 1's, so that, by default, device access is not limited to a subset of the SMP members.

5. It allocates three SPTEs to map a system space kernel stack and a guard page on each side for use when the CPU is running in the context of the boot HWPCB. It allocates a physical page of memory for the stack and initializes its PFN database entry. It initializes the guard SPTEs as no-access and the stack page to be owned by kernel mode, writable from kernel mode. It sets the address space match bit as well. It stores the address of the high-address end of the stack in HWPCB$IQ_KSP of the boot HWPCB.

6. EXE$INIT copies the boot HWPCB to the termination HWPCB and records the physical address of the termination HWPCB in CPU$Q_ PHY_TERM_HWPCB.

7. It sets the BOOT CPU's capabilities to the capability PRIMARY plus the default ones in SCH$GL_DEFAULT_CPU_CAP: RUN and QUORUM.

8. It initializes CPU$L_CURPCB to the address of the null PCB.

9. EXE$INIT invokes SMP$SETUP_SMP, in module SMPSTART_COM-MON (see Section 37.8.3).

10. It clears SLOT$V_BIP and sets SLOT$V_RC in its own SLOT$IQ_STATE field.

11. It clears the BOOT CPU ID bit in SMP$GL_OVERRIDE, leaving the override set. After this, to acquire a spinlock, the processor must first lower IPL.

12. EXE$INIT tests a combination of the SYSGEN parameter MULTIPRO-CESSING, whose default value is 3, and bit ARC$V_LOAD_SMP in EXE$GL_ARCHFLAG (initialized within SMP$SETUP_SMP) to determine whether to enable multiprocessing. If either of the following is true, EXE$INIT does not enable multiprocessing:

   • MULTIPROCESSING has the value 0.
   • MULTIPROCESSING has the value 1 or 3 and ARC$V_LOAD_SMP is clear to indicate no other CPUs are present or this is not a multiprocessing CPU type.

13. If ARC$V_LOAD_SMP is set, or if MULTIPROCESSING has the value 2 or 4, EXE$INIT sets SMP$V_ENABLED and SMP$V_START_CPU in SMP$GL_FLAGS. The latter is known as the go bit, for whose setting the secondary processors wait, as described in Section 37.8.4.

37.8.3   Initialization by SMP-Specific Routines

SMP$SETUP_SMP, in module SMPINITIAL, runs on the BOOT CPU in kernel mode at IPL 31 in the context of the system HWPCB. It takes the following steps to initialize the SMP environment:

1. It first establishes device affinity to the primary for the console terminal by clearing its unit control block field UCB$L_AFFINITY.
2. It initializes the interprocessor interrupt entry in the SCB with the procedure value and code entry address of the routine SMP$INTSR, in module SMPINT_COMMON.
3. It stores the address of the BOOT CPU's per-CPU database in the appropriate element of the CPU data vector.
4. SMP$SETUP_SMP then checks whether to establish an SMP environment. If the BOOT CPU is not a type capable of multiprocessing, or if the SYSGEN parameter MULTIPROCESSING is zero, the routine returns.
5. To establish an SMP environment, the routine first initializes the global cell SMP$GL_CPUCONF, the CPU configuration bit mask, by testing the SLOT$V_PP and SLOT$V_PA bits in each processor's HWRPB SLOT$IQ_STATE to see what CPUs are actually present and available.
6. Systemwide SMP initialization is now complete. SMP$SETUP_SMP compares the available set mask and the SYSGEN parameter SMP_CPUS to determine which CPUs are to be booted immediately. The default value of the parameter is –1, a mask with all bits set, indicating that all available CPUs should be booted. It can be modified to block the automatic booting of particular CPUs. An available CPU not booted automatically can be brought on line later with the DCL command START/CPU.

   For each secondary processor in the available set whose bit in SMP_CPUS is set, SMP$SETUP_SMP invokes SMP$SETUP_CPU to perform CPU-specific initialization. It then returns to its invoker.

SMP$SETUP_CPU, in module SMPINITIAL, is invoked with a register argument containing the CPU ID of the processor to be booted. Typically, it is invoked from SMP$SETUP_SMP but can also be invoked through the DCL START/CPU command. It performs the following steps:

1. It confirms that the specified CPU is in the available set, returning the status SS$_BADPARAM immediately if not.
2. It acquires the MMG spinlock. (This step is not necessary in the environment in which EXE$INIT runs, that of a uniprocessor, but is needed when SMP$SETUP_CPU is invoked in response to a later START/CPU command.)
3. It tests whether a per-CPU database already exists for this processor. If this routine is running as part of EXE$INIT, there is none, and control proceeds to step 4.

If this routine is running later, it is possible that the CPU has been booted once and is being restarted or that there are multiple concurrent attempts to start it. If the processor has a per-CPU database and is in the INIT state, SMP$SETUP_CPU clears the processor's bug done bit in SMP$GL_BUG_DONE and transfers control to step 12.

Otherwise, the processor is being started by another process. The routine releases the MMG spinlock and returns to its invoker.

4. It invokes EXE$INIT_HWPCB, in module SMPINITIAL, to initialize the boot HWPCB in the specified CPU's slot in the HWRPB. It takes the following steps:

   a. It allocates three SPTEs to map a kernel stack and a guard page on each side for use when the secondary CPU is running in the context of the boot HWPCB. It allocates a physical page of memory for the stack and initializes its PFN database entry. It initializes the guard SPTEs as no-access and the stack page to be writable from kernel mode and readable from executive mode. It sets the address space match and modify bits as well. It stores the address of the high-address end of the stack in HWPCB$IQ_KSP of the secondary's boot HWPCB.
   b. It copies the physical address of the level 1 page table (L1PT) from the primary processor's system HWPCB to the specified CPU's HWPCB.
   c. It clears the PALcode scratch area in the HWPCB.

5. SMP$SETUP_CPU sets bit SLOT$V_CV in that CPU's SLOT$IQ_STATE slot field to indicate its boot HWPCB context is now valid.
6. It allocates a piece of nonpaged pool aligned on a 128-byte boundary for use as per-CPU database for that CPU and zeros the pool.
7. It records the virtual address of the CPU's slot in CPU$L_SLOT_VA.
8. It initializes the termination HWPCB, copying stack pointer and L1PT values from the boot HWPCB.
9. SMP$SETUP_CPU stores the physical addresses of the boot and system HWPCBs in CPU$Q_PHY_TERM_HWPCB and CPU$Q_PHY_SYS_HW-PCB.
10. It invokes EXE$INIT_HWPCB to initialize the system HWPCB and allocate a kernel stack of SYSGEN parameter KSTACKPAGES for use in that context.
11. It invokes EXE$INIT_CPUDB, in module SMPINITIAL, to initialize the rest of the specified CPU's per-CPU database. EXE$INIT_CPUDB takes the following steps:

    a. It initializes many of the per-CPU database fields (see Section 37.8.2).
    b. It initializes the processor's state to INIT.
    c. It stores the physical address of the SCB in CPU$Q_SCBB.
    d. It initializes CPU$L_SYS_STACK_BASE, CPU$L_SYS_STACK_LIMIT, and CPU$L_SYS_KSP to describe the system HWPCB's kernel stack.

e. It copies EXE$GL_SOFT_TICK and EXE$GL_TIME_DEVIATION to CPU$L_SOFT_TICK and CPU$L_TIME_DEVIATION in order to initialize this processor's soft tick information.

f. It allocates an SPTE for the scheduler idle loop's use in zeroing free pages and initializes CPU$L_ZEROED_PAGE_SPTE and CPU$L_ZEROED_PAGE_VA accordingly.

g. It allocates SPTEs to map the machine check logout area for this processor, calculating the number based on the length in SLOT$IQ_LOGOUT_LEN and the page offset from SLOT$IQ_LOGOUT_PA. It initializes the SPTEs and stores the virtual address of the logout area in CPU$Q_LOGOUT_AREA_VA.

h. It stores the virtual address of the per-CPU data area in the CPU data vector.

12. SMP$SETUP_CPU invokes the local routine START_WITH_TIMER, in module SMPINITIAL. START_WITH_TIMER invokes local routine TRY_BOOT to send a command to the console subsystem to boot a particular secondary CPU. The effect of the command is that the console subsystem initializes the CPU and passes control to the procedure identified by HWRPB$IQ_RESTART and HWRPB$IQ_RESTART_PD, EXE$RESTART in module POWERFAIL.

13. SMP$SETUP_CPU releases the MMG spinlock and returns to its invoker.

Booting a secondary CPU is not instantaneous and may not be successful the first time. To permit a retry, START_WITH_TIMER initializes a timer queue entry (TQE) specific to that secondary CPU to describe a system subroutine with a due time of 30 seconds from the current time. Because the routine is running with a higher ranking spinlock than the TIMER spinlock and at too high an IPL, it first forks, using the TQE as a fork block and the TIMER spinlock as fork lock. The fork routine queues the TQE. Chapter 12 describes TQEs and timer system subroutines.

When the TQE comes due, its system subroutine, the routine TIMER_WAKE, in module SMPINITIAL, checks whether that secondary is still in the INIT state. If not, it exits on the assumption that the secondary has successfully booted. If it is, the routine invokes TRY_BOOT again. If, after three attempts, the secondary has failed to boot, its state is changed to TIMOUT and a failure message is written to the console terminal.

37.8.4   Secondary Bootstrap Code

Each secondary processor begins executing in kernel mode at IPL 31 in the context of its boot HWPCB. A secondary processor begins executing at EXE$RESTART, in module POWERFAIL, the OpenVMS AXP halt-restart procedure.

1. EXE$RESTART first determines its own CPU ID by reading the WHAMI register and, through SMP$GL_CPUDATA, the address of its per-CPU database.
2. It initializes CPU$Q_TERM_KSP to the value of the kernel stack pointer at entry and CPU$Q_TERM_PTBR to the contents of the PTBR.
3. If the CPU's state is RUN, this is a restart rather than a boot. EXE$RESTART examines SLOT$IQ_HALTCODE to see what caused the halt that led to this restart. The architecturally defined possibilities are a powerfail recovery and various kinds of error halts. Because current systems do not implement powerfail recovery, EXE$RESTART should see only error halt codes (see Table 33.9). As described in Chapter 36, it generates a bugcheck whose type is based on the error halt code.
4. If the CPU's state is not RUN, this is a boot. EXE$RESTART calls SMP$START_SECONDARY, in module SMPINITIAL.

SMP$START_SECONDARY is typically entered from EXE$RESTART but can also be entered from SMP$HALT_CPU, described in Section 37.8.5, when a shutdown CPU is started with a START/CPU command. It takes the following steps:

1. It invalidates its translation buffer.
2. It determines its own CPU ID by reading the WHAMI register and, through SMP$GL_CPUDATA, the address of its per-CPU database.
3. It stores that address in its PRBR.
4. SMP$START_SECONDARY initializes its SCBB register from the contents of CPU$Q_SCBB.
5. It joins the override set by setting its CPU bit in SMP$GL_OVERRIDE.
6. SMP$START_SECONDARY calls SMP$VALIDATE_HW_CONFIGURATION, in module [SYSLOA]SMPSTART, to validate the system. It checks that the CPU type is the same as that of the boot CPU and that the PALcode revision levels of the two CPUs are the same.
7. If any check fails, SMP$START_SECONDARY writes an error message on the console terminal and changes the CPU state to BOOT_REJECTED. It leaves the override set and loops.
8. If the checks pass, it records the current system time in CPU$Q_BOOT_TIME.
9. It sets bit SLOT$V_RC in SLOT$IQ_STATE to indicate the CPU can be restarted.
10. It sets the CPU's state to BOOTED.
11. It then loops, testing the go bit, SMP$V_START_CPU in SMP$GL_FLAGS, set by the primary at the end of EXE$INIT.
12. When it sees that the bit is set, it invokes SMP$WRITE_OPA0 to write a message to the console terminal indicating that it has joined the primary in multiprocessor operation.
13. SMP$START_SECONDARY resets its SP to the high-address end of the

termination HWPCB kernel stack and swaps context to the system HW-PCB.

14. Running in the system HWPCB, it acquires the CPU mutex.

15. It changes the processor's state to RUN and sets the bit corresponding to its ID in SMP$GL_ACTIVE_CPUS, joining the active set.

16. It clears bit SLOT$V_BIP in its SLOT$IQ_STATE to indicate bootstrap is done.

17. It invokes SMP$INIT_SANITY, in module SMPROUT, to join the sanity timer chain and initialize the processor's sanity timer. Section 37.5.7 describes the sanity timer mechanism.

18. It releases the CPU mutex.

19. It executes an IMB instruction and tests whether it should enter the benign state (see Section 37.5.4).

20. SMP$START_SECONDARY acquires the SCHED spinlock and calls SCH$ADD_CPU_CAP, in module CAPABILITY, to initialize the processor's entry in the capabilities array; and releases the SCHED spinlock.

21. Clearing its CPU ID bit in SMP$GL_OVERRIDE, it leaves the override set.

22. It sets its CPU ID bit in SCH$GL_IDLE_CPUS to indicate that the processor is idle.

23. It removes the boot TQE from the TQE list and clears bit TQE$V_BOOT_TQEACT.

24. It calls SCH$INIT to select a process to run.

37.8.5   Operation of START/CPU and STOP/CPU Commands

Several DCL commands support SMP:

▸ START/CPU [/ALL] [*cpu-id,...*]
▸ STOP/CPU [/ALL/OVERRIDE_CHECKS] [*cpu-id,...*]
▸ SHOW CPU [/ALL] [*cpu-id,...*]

For a complete description of the commands and their qualifiers, not all of which are listed here, see the *OpenVMS DCL Dictionary*. All three commands are implemented by the single-module image [MP]SMPUTIL. This section describes the implementation of the first two commands.

In response to a START/CPU command, the SMPUTIL image determines what CPUs have been specified. For each specified CPU, the image checks that the specified CPU is available and not already a member of the active set. It then checks the CPU's state to see if it can be started: the CPU must have never been started or it must be in either the TIMOUT or STOPPED state.

Running in kernel mode, the image confirms that SMP is enabled, exiting if not. If a CPU has been started and thus has a per-CPU database, the image changes the CPU's state to INIT. It calls SCH$REQUIRE_CAPABILITY, in module SCHED, to ensure that the process in which it is running is executing on the primary processor. As a result, the process may be taken out of execution and then rescheduled on the primary. Running in kernel mode on the primary, it invokes SMP$SETUP_CPU, described in Section 37.8.3, to create the per-CPU database and set the CPU's state to INIT, if necessary, and to initialize the specified secondary CPU. If the initialization is successful, the SMPUTIL image then calls SCH$RELEASE_CAPABILITY to remove the requirement that the process execute on the primary, and returns.

In response to a STOP/CPU command, the SMPUTIL image checks that each specified CPU is available and a member of the active set. Running in kernel mode, it invokes SMP$REQUEST_SHUTDOWN_CPU, in module SMPROUT, once for each specified CPU.

SMP$REQUEST_SHUTDOWN_CPU takes the following steps:

1. It acquires the CPU mutex to prevent additions to the active set.
2. It checks the CPU state:

   - If the CPU has just been put into the STOPPED state, it simply returns.
   - If the CPU is in the BOOT_REJECTED state, the routine changes its state to STOPPED.
   - If the CPU is in any other state than RUN, or if it is in RUN but not a member of the active set (a pathological combination that should not occur), SMP$REQUEST_SHUTDOWN_CPU returns to its invoker with the error status SS$_DEVOFFLINE; only a running active set member can be stopped.

3. If there are no other CPUs in the active set, the routine unlocks the CPU mutex and returns.
4. It sets bit CPU$V_STOPPING in CPU$L_INTFLAGS and, if the STOP /CPU command included the qualifier /FOREVER, sets bit CPU$V_FOREVER in CPU$L_FLAGS.
5. It unlocks the CPU mutex.
6. It acquires the SCHED spinlock to serialize access to the data structures describing processor capabilities and process affinities.
7. If affinity checks are required (that is, if they are not to be overridden), SMP$REQUEST_SHUTDOWN_CPU checks whether any process has explicit affinity for this processor. If any does, it cannot continue the shutdown. Instead, it releases the SCHED spinlock, clears CPU$V_FOREVER and CPU$V_STOPPING, and returns an error status to its invoker.
8. If affinity checks are overridden or if no process has explicit affinity, it calls SCH$REMOVE_CPU_CAP, in module SCHED, to remove the CPU's capability to RUN.
9. It releases the SCHED spinlock and returns to its invoker.

As a result of losing the RUN capability, the CPU being stopped eventually becomes idle. Executing the scheduler idle loop, SCH$IDLE in module

SCHED_ROUTINES, the CPU determines that it no longer has the RUN capability. It invokes SMP$SHUTDOWN_CPU, in module SMPROUT.

SMP$SHUTDOWN_CPU takes the following steps:

1. It invokes SMP$WRITE_OPA0, in module SMPROUT, to create a fork process to execute on the primary processor and write to the console terminal a message about this CPU's being shut down.
2. It raises IPL to 31.
3. It clears its CPU ID bit in SMP$GL_ACTIVE_CPUS, leaving the active set.
4. If it is being stopped forever, it clears its bit in SMP$GL_CPUCONF, the available set.
5. It acquires the CPU mutex, removes itself from the sanity timer chain, and sets the CPU state to STOPPED.
6. SMP$SHUTDOWN_CPU releases the CPU mutex.
7. It invokes the routine SMP$HALT_CPU, in module [SYSLOA]SMP-START.
8. SMP$HALT_CPU resets the stack pointer to the high end of the system HWPCB stack. It also resets the termination HWPCB kernel stack pointer to its high end.
9. It swaps to the context of the termination HWPCB.
10. It sets bit SLOT$V_BIP and clears SLOT$V_RC in SLOT$IL_STATE to indicate to the console subsystem that a bootstrap is in progress and the CPU has not reached a point where it can be restarted. These values prevent the CPU from restarting or rebooting if a machine check occurs.
11. SMP$HALT_CPU cannot execute a HALT instruction, since that would trigger halt-restart processing and a system crash. Instead, it loops at IPL 31, continually testing whether CPU$L_STATE has changed to the INIT state as the result of the DCL command START/CPU.

    If the state changes to INIT, SMP$HALT_CPU transfers control to SMP$START_SECONDARY, described in Section 37.8.4, to effect a reboot.

37.9   FATAL BUGCHECK PROCESSING

When one member of an SMP system incurs a fatal bugcheck, all members crash; the executive takes the conservative approach that an inconsistency severe enough that operations on one CPU should cease is likely to be systemwide. All members of the active set participate in fatal bugcheck processing.

The CRASH CPU, the CPU that first incurs a fatal bugcheck, drives the crash, informing the other active CPUs that a bugcheck sequence has been initiated. In response, the other active CPUs crash with the fatal bugcheck CPUEXIT. The primary CPU performs most of the rest of fatal bugcheck processing.

Chapter 35 describes in detail the uniprocessor bugcheck sequence; this

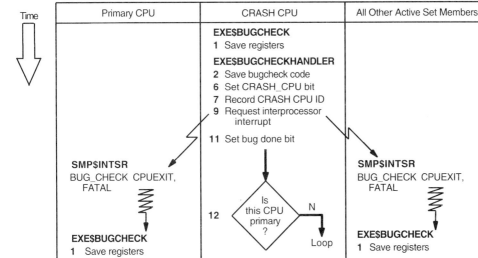

Figure 37.7
Fatal Bugcheck Processing on an SMP System

section describes the steps in fatal bugcheck processing specific to an SMP system.

Figure 37.7 shows the sequence of some of the steps in fatal bugcheck processing as they might occur concurrently on the CRASH CPU, which as pictured is not the primary processor; the primary processor; and the other active set members. Note that steps shown in different columns but on the same line do not necessarily execute at the same time on all CPUs. The numbers in the figure correspond to the following steps, not all of which are represented in the figure.

①   EXE$BUGCHECK, in module BUGCHECK_SAVE, initially runs on the CRASH CPU and subsequently on the other SMP members. As described in Chapter 35, it saves the integer registers and processor registers on the current stack and, optionally, the floating-point registers on the current stack. It then calls EXE$BUGCHECKHANDLER, in module BUGCHECK.

②   EXE$BUGCHECKHANDLER also initially runs on the CRASH CPU and subsequently on other SMP members. It determines whether the bugcheck is fatal. For a fatal bugcheck, it performs several sanity checks to confirm that fatal bugcheck processing is possible. It raises IPL to 31 and stores the bugcheck code in the per-CPU database field CPU$L_BUG-CODE.

③   If it is not running on the primary, it copies integer, processor, and, optionally, floating-point registers from the current stack to the per-CPU database.

④   It invokes EXE$SAVE_CONTEXT, in module [CPU*xxyy*]CRD_ROU-TINES_*xxyy*, to save processor-specific registers. For example, if running on the primary, EXE$SAVE_CONTEXT for the DEC 7000 Model 600 series system records information about correctable memory errors in the error log allocation buffers and returns.

⑤   EXE$BUGCHECKHANDLER tests whether it is running on a member of the active set. If not (a pathological and unlikely case), it proceeds to step 10 rather than taking any steps that might interfere with SMP operations.

⑥   If it is running on a member of the active set, it tests and sets the bit SMP$V_CRASH_CPU in SMP$GL_FLAGS. Only the first CPU to crash actually sets this bit and thus becomes the CRASH CPU.

   If the bit is already set, EXE$BUGCHECKHANDLER continues with step 10. Use of the bit prevents confusion during concurrent independent crashes.

⑦   It records its own ID in SMP$GL_BUGCHKCP as the CRASH CPU.

⑧   It acquires the CPU mutex to prevent any other processors from joining the active set.

⑨   EXE$BUGCHECKHANDLER requests an interprocessor interrupt of each member of the active set, specifying bugcheck as the work request type (see Section 37.5.2).

⑩   If it owns the XDELTA lock (if its ID is in XDT$GL_OWNER_ID), it breaks the lock, releasing other active set members from the benign state so that each can respond to the interprocessor interrupt and save its own context. Section 37.5.4 describes XDELTA processing and the benign state.

⑪   It then sets its CPU ID bit in SMP$GL_BUG_DONE to indicate that it has saved its context.

⑫   It compares its CPU ID to that in SMP$GL_PRIMID to determine if it is executing on the primary. If it is not, it loops, awaiting a later reboot. All members of the active set except the primary should eventually execute this loop. A crashing CPU that is not a member of the active set also executes this loop.

⑬ This and later steps execute only on the primary processor because it is the only member guaranteed access to the console terminal.

EXE$BUGCHECKHANDLER sets its CPU ID in SMP$GL_OVERRIDE, adding itself to the override set. As a member of the override set, its spinlock acquisitions and releases are not subject to the normal IPL checks. Moreover, executing the bugcheck sequence on the primary processor, it has the ability arbitrarily to break existing ownership of a spinlock it needs during bugcheck processing. The spinlock acquire routines specifically check for this combination of circumstances when a spinlock acquisition would otherwise fail.

⑭ EXE$BUGCHECKHANDLER waits, up to a maximum of 60 seconds, for all active members to save their context. Under normal circumstances, much of this wait does not occur. However, if one member is restarting following a halt, it could take the member a significant time to complete that and respond to the interprocessor interrupt requesting bugcheck processing. If the time passes before all are done, EXE$BUGCHECKHANDLER proceeds.

It continues with steps common to fatal bugcheck processing on a uniprocessor system.

⑮ Still running on the primary, EXE$BUGCHECKHANDLER tests whether the CRASH CPU has saved its register context. If not, it uses its own per-CPU database in the steps that follow.

⑯ It uses the bugcheck code in the CRASH CPU's per-CPU database to select the bugcheck message text. This field is initialized to BUG$_CPUCEASED, in case a problem on the CRASH CPU prevents it from recording the real bugcheck code.

It writes bugcheck information from the CRASH CPU's per-CPU database to the console terminal.

Running on the primary, EXE$BUGCHECKHANDLER continues with steps common to fatal bugcheck processing on a uniprocessor.

37.10   RELEVANT SOURCE MODULES

Source modules described in this chapter include

[DELTA]XDELTA.BLI
[DELTA]XDELTA_ISRS.M64
[LIB]CPUDEF.SDL
[LIB]SPLCODDEF.SDL
[LIB]SYSMAR.MAR

[LIB]SYSPARDEF.SDL
[MP]CLIUTL.MAR
[SYS]BUGCHECK.BLI
[SYS]BUGCHECK_SAVE.M64
[SYS]INIT.MAR
[SYS]PAGEFAULT.M64
[SYS]POWERFAIL.M64
[SYS]SMPINITIAL.MAR
[SYS]SMPINT_COMMON.MAR
[SYS]SMPROUT.MAR
[SYSLOA]SMPSTART.MAR
[SYSLOA]TIMROUT.MAR

PART IX / Miscellaneous Topics

38 Logical Names

Call things by their right names. . . . Glass of brandy and water!
That is the current but not the appropriate name: ask for a glass
of liquid fire and distilled damnation.

Robert Hall, *Olinthus Gregory, Brief Memoir of the Life of Hall*

A logical name definition is a mapping of a string to zero or more replacement strings. A replacement string is called an equivalence name. A logical name can represent a node name, file specification, device name, application-specific information, or another logical name. Replacing an occurrence of the logical name with an equivalence string is called logical name translation.

The OpenVMS operating system provides automatic logical name translation for a name used in a file specification or a device name. A logical name that refers to a device or file enables transparent device independence and I/O redirection. For example, a program or command procedure can refer to a disk volume by logical name rather than by the name of the specific drive on which the disk volume is mounted.

A user can define a logical name as a shorthand way to refer to a file or directory that is referenced frequently.

This chapter first summarizes the characteristics of logical names. It then describes the data structures that implement logical names and the internal operation of the system services related to logical names:

▶ Create Logical Name ($CRELNM)
▶ Create Logical Name Table ($CRELNT)
▶ Delete Logical Name ($DELLNM)
▶ Translate Logical Name ($TRNLNM)

Logical name concepts are described in the *OpenVMS User's Manual* and the *OpenVMS Programming Concepts* manual. The *OpenVMS System Services Reference Manual* documents the use of the logical name system services.

38.1 GOALS OF LOGICAL NAME SUPPORT

The goals of OpenVMS support for logical names are as follows:

▶ Independent name spaces for logical names. A logical name of a given access mode must be unique in any given table. Creation of an arbitrarily large number of logical name tables is allowed, reducing the likelihood of logical name collisions.
▶ User control over the order in which logical name tables are searched. Each request to translate a logical name can determine which tables are to be

searched by specifying a logical name whose multiple translations are the tables to be searched.

▶ Provision of a basis for Record Management Services (RMS) search lists. A multivalued logical name enables an ordered list of equivalence names to be associated with a single logical name. An RMS search list is a multivalued logical name, supplied as part or all of a file specification. Through its multiple equivalence names, a logical name can refer to multiple file specifications.

▶ Control over sharing of logical names. A number of possibilities are provided, ranging from no sharing to sharing based on access control lists (ACLs). Degree of shareability is specified when a shareable table is created. A process can control its sharing by partitioning its logical names into different tables.

▶ Upward compatibility for VAX/VMS Version 3 and earlier logical names and their system services. The superseded system services are provided as jacket routines for calls to the newer services. The executive automatically defines system, group, and process logical name tables whose properties are similar to those of older tables.

38.2   CHARACTERISTICS OF LOGICAL NAMES

A logical name is uniquely identified by the combination of the logical name string, the logical name table that contains its definition, and its access mode. That is, two otherwise identical name strings that have different access modes or that are defined in different logical name tables are different logical names.

A logical name string is from 1 to 255 bytes long.

The scope of a logical name varies. A logical name definition can be any of the following:

▶ Private to one process
▶ Handed down from a process to its spawned subprocesses
▶ Shared among a detached process and all its subprocesses (job tree)
▶ Shared among all the processes with the same user identification code (UIC) group code
▶ Shared among all the processes on the system
▶ Shared among a subset of processes on the system as specified by an ACL

A logical name definition cannot be shared among processes on different nodes of a VMScluster system.

The scope of a logical name is determined primarily by the logical name table in which it is defined. By default a name in a shareable table is shareable. A logical name in a process-private table can only be used by the process and, by default handed down to any subprocess it spawns through the Digital command language (DCL). When a subprocess is spawned, each logical name created without the CONFINE attribute is copied to the spawned sub-process. That is, the logical name definitions current at the time of the spawn are copied; any subsequent changes to the definitions are not shared.

The access mode of a logical name can be specified when it is defined. If not specified, access mode defaults to that of the requestor of the $CRELNM system service. If the ACMODE argument is specified and if the process has the privilege SYSNAM, the logical name is created with the specified access mode. If a name of the same mode already exists, it is superseded. Otherwise, if the process lacks the privilege, the argument is maximized with (made no more privileged than) the mode of the system service requestor.

A logical name table can contain multiple definitions of the same logical name with different access modes. These are called aliases. When a request to translate such a logical name specifies the ACMODE argument, any definition made at a less privileged mode is ignored.

The access mode of a logical name specifies an integrity level. Because kernel and executive access mode logical names can only be created by the system manager or someone of equivalent privilege, they are used where the security of the system is at stake. For example, during certain system operations, such as the activation of an image installed with privilege, only executive and kernel mode logical names are used.

A process-private user mode logical name is deleted at the next image rundown. Shareable user mode names, however, survive image exit and process deletion.

A logical name can be created with several attributes:

- The CONFINE attribute indicates that DCL should not propagate the logical name to a spawned subprocess. Logical names of files created with the DCL OPEN command have the CONFINE attribute.
- The NO_ALIAS attribute indicates that the existence of this logical name precludes another definition for that name in the same logical name table and with an outer access mode. When a NO_ALIAS logical name is created, any definition for the name made in an outer mode is deleted, as well as any definition in the same mode.
- The CRELOG attribute indicates that the logical name was defined using the superseded $CRELOG system service. RMS uses this attribute to ensure translation compatible with VAX/VMS Version 3 and earlier versions. Use of this attribute is reserved. Section 38.9 briefly describes support for the superseded logical name system services.

Two other attributes, TABLE and NODELETE, are described in later sections.

A logical name can have more than one equivalence name. In that case, it is called a multivalued logical name, and its equivalence names are treated as an ordered list.

38.3 LOGICAL NAME TABLES

A logical name table is a container for logical names. Each table defines an independent name space. This section describes the characteristics of logical name tables and the tables that the executive creates by default.

38.3.1 Characteristics of Logical Name Tables

A logical name table has the following characteristics:

- ► Scope (whether it is shareable or process-private)
- ► Access mode
- ► Name
- ► Parent logical name table
- ► Access control in the case of a shareable logical name table
- ► Quota to limit the amount of pool occupied by its logical names

During system initialization several shareable logical name tables are created. During the creation of each process several other tables, shareable and process-private, are created. Section 38.3.2 documents these default tables. The $CRELNT system service enables a process to create additional tables at will. Process-private name tables are created in P1 space. Shareable tables are created in system space.

The access mode of a logical name table can be specified when it is created. If not specified, the mode defaults to that of the requestor of the $CRELNT system service. If the ACMODE argument is specified and if the process has the privilege SYSNAM, the logical name table is created with the specified access mode. Otherwise, the argument is maximized with the mode of the system service requestor.

A logical name table can contain logical names of its own and less privileged access modes. A logical name table can be a parent table to another table of the same or a less privileged access mode.

A logical name table is identified by its name, which is itself a logical name. The name of a logical name table has the logical name attribute TABLE. In fact, the name table data structure is a special form of equivalence name. As a logical name, each logical name table name must be contained within a logical name table. Two special logical name tables called directories exist as containers for logical name table names. A logical name that is to translate directly or iteratively to the name of a logical name table must be contained in a directory table. That is, there are only two name spaces for the names of logical name tables.

The system directory, named LNM$SYSTEM_DIRECTORY, contains the names of all shareable tables. The process directory, LNM$PROCESS_DIRECTORY, contains the names of all process-private tables for that process. Each directory contains its own table name. Each directory table name has the logical name attributes TABLE, NO_ALIAS, and NODELETE. The NODELETE attribute prevents the deletion of a directory table name.

The address of either directory table can be determined indirectly through the two-longword array at LNM$AL_DIRTBL. Its first longword points to a longword containing the address of the system directory. Its second longword points to CTL$GL_LNMDIRECT, which contains the address of the process directory. Each process has its own process directory.

Any logical name in a directory table, including a logical name table name, is restricted to a length no longer than 31 characters. It can only consist of the characters $, _, the digits, and uppercase alphabet. The bytes of a logical name string in any other table can have any value.

All logical name tables are in one of two hierarchies. The system directory is the ancestor of the tables in one hierarchy. For each process, its process directory is the ancestor of the other. That is, each logical name table except the directory tables has a parent logical name table. A directory anchors the quota and access hierarchy for its name space. The hierarchical structure enables finer control over quota allocation and access to logical name tables. When a logical name table is deleted, all its descendant tables are deleted.

The parent of a logical name table is not necessarily a directory table. This hierarchical structure is distinct from the location of logical name table names. Consider logical name table A, created by the DCL command

```
$ CREATE/NAME_TABLE/PARENT=LNM$PROCESS A
```

The parent table of logical name table A is the process-private logical name table LNM$PROCESS. A's table name, however, like all table names, is contained in a directory; in this case, it is contained in LNM$PROCESS_DIRECTORY, the same directory that contains the name of its parent table.

There is a quota on how much memory the names in a logical name table may occupy. The quota is managed in a hierarchical fashion; a newly created name table inherits quota through its parent. At the top of the inheritance tree are the two logical name directories. Each of them has "infinite" memory quota, the largest possible positive longword number.

A table that manages or holds its own quota is called a quota holder table. The two directories are the quota holder tables at the top of the hierarchy.

When a new name table is created, its memory quota can be specified as limited or pooled. A nonzero $CRELNT QUOTA value indicates that the quota is limited; a zero value indicates that it is pooled.

When a name table is created with limited quota, it subtracts its quota from the quota of its parent or of the most recent ancestor that is a quota holder table. It then becomes a quota holder table itself.

If the quota is specified as pooled, the name table does not hold its own quota but shares quota with its parent. If its parent was created with pooled quota, the new table and its parent share quota with the grandparent table.

Sharing continues upward in the hierarchy to the most recent ancestor to hold its own quota.

A shareable logical name table has UIC-based protection. Each class of user (system, owner, group, and world) can be granted four types of access:

▶ Read (R) access allows the user to read the contents of the logical name table, that is, to translate logical names.

▶ Write (W) access allows the user to modify the contents of the table, for example, to delete or alter logical name translations. Write access to a directory table enables the user to delete the logical name table names in the directory.

▶ Enable (E) access allows the user to withdraw quota from the table when creating a descendant logical name table.

▶ Delete (D) access allows the user to delete the table itself, including all its logical names and descendant tables and their names. A logical name table is deleted when it or its parent table is deleted.

The default protection mask for a table created through the $CRELNT system service allows RWED access to system and owner users and no access to group or world users.

A logical name table can also be given ACL-based protection. An ACL for a logical name table enables fine-tuning of UIC-based protection. The DCL command SET ACL/OBJECT=LOGICAL_NAME_TABLE creates or modifies access control entries. The *OpenVMS User's Manual* provides further information.

To provide compatibility with earlier versions of the system, a suitably privileged process can read and write certain logical name tables even if UIC- and ACL-based mechanisms would otherwise prohibit access. That is, a process with GRPNAM privilege can access its group table, LNM$GROUP_ *gggggg*, to translate, create, or delete logical names, regardless of UIC- and ACL-based protection. A process with SYSNAM privilege can similarly access the system table, LNM$SYSTEM_TABLE.

38.3.2   Default Logical Name Tables

Table 38.1 lists the default tables created by the executive. All names of logical name tables must be in one of the two directories. A directory table can contain other types of logical names as well.

The system directory and table are created during system initialization by initialization code that runs in the swapper process. The process directory and table are created during process creation by code in EXE$PROCSTRT, in module PROCSTRT. When creating a top-level process, EXE$PROCSTRT invokes EXE$CRE_JGTABLE, also in module PROCSTRT, to create the job table and, if it does not already exist, the group table. LOGINOUT, the first

Table 38.1   Default Logical Name Tables

Table Name	Directory	Use
LNM$PROCESS_ DIRECTORY	Process	Contains definitions of process-private logical name table names and names that translate iteratively to these table names
LNM$PROCESS_ TABLE	Process	Contains process-private logical names, such as SYS$DISK and SYS$INPUT
LNM$SYSTEM_ DIRECTORY	System	Contains definitions of shareable logical name table names and names that translate iteratively to these table names
LNM$SYSTEM_ TABLE	System	Contains names shared by all processes in the system, for example, SYS$LIBRARY and SYS$SYSTEM
LNM$JOB_ *xxxxxxxx* [1]	System	Contains names shared by all processes in the job tree, for example, SYS$LOGIN and SYS$SCRATCH
LNM$GROUP_ *gggggg* [2]	System	Contains names shared by all processes in that UIC group

[1] The string *xxxxxxxx* represents an eight-digit hexadecimal number that is the address of the job information block.

[2] The string *gggggg* represents a six-digit octal number containing the process's UIC group number.

image to run in many processes, also invokes EXE$CRE_JGTABLE so that any changes in the process's UIC are reflected in its tables.

A number of predefined logical names for logical name tables are used in particular contexts for translating and creating logical names. By convention, these names have the prefix LNM$. For example, RMS and other system components specify the table LNM$FILE_DEV for file specification and device name translations. Table 38.2 lists some of the default logical names that translate to table names.

Some of these table names are normally referenced indirectly, through predefined logical names. Typically, for example, LNM$JOB is specified as a logical name for the table rather than the actual name, LNM$JOB_*xxxxxxxx*. The indirection enables a generic and transparent reference to a process's job table rather than to the very specific and transient name LNM$JOB_ *xxxxxxxx*. In addition, indirections make it possible for users to redefine some of the predefined names to modify the search order or the tables to be used. LNM$PROCESS, for example, can be redefined as a multivalued logical name to subsume other tables into the process table.

Some table names exist to allow for user redefinition. For example, the table name LNM$DCL_LOGICAL is used for the SHOW LOGICAL and SHOW TRANSLATION DCL commands and for the logical name lexical functions. By default, as defined in LNM$SYSTEM_DIRECTORY, the name

Table 38.2 Default Logical Names That Translate to Logical Name Table Names

Logical Name	Equivalence Name
LNM$PROCESS	LNM$PROCESS_TABLE
LNM$JOB	LNM$JOB_xxxxxxxx [1]
LNM$GROUP	LNM$GROUP_gggggg [2]
LNM$SYSTEM	LNM$SYSTEM_TABLE
LNM$DCL_LOGICAL	LNM$FILE_DEV
LNM$FILE_DEV (supervisor mode)	LNM$PROCESS, LNM$JOB, LNM$GROUP, LNM$SYSTEM
LNM$FILE_DEV (executive mode)	LNM$SYSTEM
LNM$PERMANENT_MAILBOX	LNM$SYSTEM
LNM$TEMPORARY_MAILBOX	LNM$JOB
LOG$PROCESS [3]	LNM$PROCESS, LNM$JOB
LOG$GROUP [3]	LNM$GROUP
LOG$SYSTEM [3]	LNM$SYSTEM
TRNLOG$_GROUP_SYSTEM [3]	LOG$GROUP, LOG$SYSTEM
TRNLOG$_PROCESS_GROUP [3]	LOG$PROCESS, LOG$GROUP
TRNLOG$_PROCESS_SYSTEM [3]	LOG$PROCESS, LOG$SYSTEM
TRNLOG$_PROCESS_GROUP_SYSTEM [3]	LOG$PROCESS, LOG$GROUP, LOG$SYSTEM

[1] The string *xxxxxxxx* represents an eight-digit hexadecimal number that is the address of the job information block.

[2] The string *gggggg* represents a six-digit octal number containing the process's UIC group number.

[3] This table provides upward compatibility for tables used by the superseded logical name services.

LNM$DCL_LOGICAL translates to LNM$FILE_DEV. However, a user interested in displaying names and translations in the directory tables themselves might define a new translation for this name (see Example 38.1).

Because TRNLOG$_PROCESS_GROUP is defined in LNM$SYSTEM_DIRECTORY, the first SHOW LOGICAL command fails to find it. After the new definition of LNM$DCL_LOGICAL to include both directory tables, SHOW LOGICAL can translate TRNLOG$_PROCESS_GROUP. It can translate iteratively all its equivalence names as well, because they are defined in one of the two directory tables. The *OpenVMS DCL Dictionary* describes the SHOW LOGICAL and DEFINE commands.

Example 38.1
Use of LNM$DCL_LOGICAL Logical Name

```
$ SHOW LOGICAL TRNLOG$_PROCESS_GROUP
%SHOW-S-NOTRAN, no translation for logical name TRNLOG$_PROCESS_GROUP
$ !
$ ! Since LNM$DCL_LOGICAL is to be a name that translates to a
$ ! table name, it must be defined in a directory.
$ !
$ DEFINE/SUPERVISOR/TABLE=LNM$PROCESS_DIRECTORY LNM$DCL_LOGICAL -
_$ LNM$FILE_DEV,LNM$PROCESS_DIRECTORY,LNM$SYSTEM_DIRECTORY
$ !
$ SHOW LOGICAL TRNLOG$_PROCESS_GROUP
   "TRNLOG$_PROCESS_GROUP" = "LOG$PROCESS" (LNM$SYSTEM_DIRECTORY)
        = "LOG$GROUP"
1  "LOG$PROCESS" = "LNM$PROCESS" (LNM$SYSTEM_DIRECTORY)
        = "LNM$JOB"
2  "LNM$PROCESS" = "LNM$PROCESS_TABLE" (LNM$PROCESS_DIRECTORY)
2  "LNM$JOB" = "LNM$JOB_80471670" (LNM$PROCESS_DIRECTORY)
1  "LOG$GROUP" = "LNM$GROUP" (LNM$SYSTEM_DIRECTORY)
2  "LNM$GROUP" = "LNM$GROUP_000100" (LNM$PROCESS_DIRECTORY)
```

38.4   **CHARACTERISTICS OF LOGICAL NAME TRANSLATION**

A logical name with only one equivalence name has only one translation. A multivalued logical name has multiple equivalence names, up to a maximum of 128. An equivalence name is from 1 to 255 bytes long. Each byte can have any value. Each equivalence name is uniquely identified by a number called an index number.

An equivalence name can be defined with several attributes. Each equivalence name of a multivalued logical name can have different attributes.

▶ The CONCEALED attribute means that the equivalence name should not be displayed in system output. Typically, this is used to foster device independence by displaying logical names rather than showing the names of specific devices. It is also used in the creation of logical names for rooted directories.

▶ The TERMINAL attribute means that the equivalence name should not itself be treated as a logical name and translated further.

When a logical name is translated, the translation attribute CASE_BLIND can be specified. This attribute means that the search for that logical name is independent of the case (uppercase or lowercase) in which the logical name was originally defined and the case in which the logical name was specified to the $TRNLNM system service.

When access mode is specified for a logical name translation, it applies to both the translation of the name and of the name tables involved. For example, if executive access mode translation is requested, then all outer mode logical names and table names are ignored.

Logical name translation has two dimensions:

▸ Breadth. A logical name can have multiple equivalence strings.

▸ Depth. One logical name can translate to another logical name, which, in turn, translates to another logical name, and so on.

These dimensions apply to the name of a logical name table as well as to a logical name. To translate a logical name, the executive must also translate the name of the tables in which to look for the logical name. The translation for a logical name table name, done implicitly as part of translating a logical name, is different from that for a logical name.

38.4.1 Dimensions of Logical Name Translation

Logical name translation, as performed by the logical name system services, deals with the breadth of a name but not its depth. That is, if requested by the user, the $TRNLNM system service returns multiple equivalence strings when it translates a logical name. One of the $TRNLNM arguments is an item list through which multiple equivalence names can be returned. For the user to receive multiple equivalence names, the item list must include entries and buffer addresses for them.

However, when the $TRNLNM system service translates a logical name, it does not translate iteratively. That is, it does not check whether an equivalence name is itself a logical name. Further translation must be requested explicitly; the equivalence name returned must be supplied as the logical name argument in another $TRNLNM request. Certain system services, such as Assign Channel ($ASSIGN), make iterative $TRNLNM requests to translate a logical name as deeply as possible, up to a maximum iteration count, typically of nine translations.

RMS has a more complex form of iteration. It parses a file specification and requests the $TRNLNM system service iteratively to translate certain components of it. The *Guide to OpenVMS File Applications* gives more details.

38.4.2 Dimensions of Logical Name Table Name Translation

Each logical name system service must translate a logical name table name to perform its main function. A table name can be one of the following:

▸ A logical name whose single translation is the table data structure itself rather than an equivalence name (see Section 38.5.2)

▸ A name whose equivalence name is itself a logical name that translates to the table data structure after one or more iterations

▸ A multivalued logical name, each of whose equivalence names is a logical name that translates iteratively to a table data structure

Unlike logical name translation, table name translation must deal with both the depth and the breadth of the name. To locate a particular logical name, for example, a table name and all its equivalence names might have to be translated iteratively. In the $TRNLNM system service, and sometimes the $DELLNM system service, translation of a table name continues until one is found that contains the target logical name. In the system services $CRELNT, $CRELNM, and under some circumstances (see Section 38.8.5) $DELLNM, translation of a table name only goes as far as finding the first table.

The table name translation sequence is depth-first. That is, the first equivalence name is translated until it translates to a table data structure or can be translated no further. If the table name found does not contain the logical name of interest, the next equivalence name is translated, and so on. This is a simplified description of the algorithm, which is described in more detail in Section 38.7.

38.5   LOGICAL NAME DATA STRUCTURES

The logical name database consists of the following kinds of structures:

- ► Logical name blocks (LNMBs), describing the logical names that are defined
- ► Logical name translation blocks (LNMXs), which contain equivalence names
- ► Logical name table headers (LNMTHs), which describe logical name tables
- ► Hash tables that locate the LNMBs (LNMHSHs)
- ► Logical name table name cache blocks (LNMCs)

The macro $LNMSTRDEF defines symbolic offsets for all these data structures. The data structures are described in the sections that follow.

38.5.1   Logical Name Blocks and Logical Name Translation Blocks

Each defined logical name is described by an LNMB. LNMB$L_FLINK and LNMB$L_BLINK link an LNMB into a hash chain of LNMBs whose logical names have the same hash value. The field LNMB$L_TABLE specifies the address of the header of the logical name table in which the logical name is defined. The access mode of the name is stored in LNMB$L_ACMODE and its attributes in LNMB$L_FLAGS.

An LNMB contains the exact length of the logical name in LNMB$L_NAMELEN and the logical name string itself at LNMB$T_NAME. (The name string is a simple character string, not a counted ASCII string.) Extra space is allocated at the end of the string, if necessary, so that the name takes up an integral number of quadwords.

An LNMB is typically followed by at least one LNMX, whose address is stored in the field LNMB$L_LNMX. An LNMX contains flags for the equivalence name attributes in field LNMX$L_FLAGS, an index identifying the equivalence name in field LNMX$L_INDEX, and the equivalence name string beginning at LNMX$T_XLATION with its length in LNMX$L_

XLEN. (The name string is a simple character string, not a counted ASCII string.) Extra space is allocated at the end of the string, if necessary, so that the equivalence name takes up an integral number of quadwords. The field LNMX$L_HASH contains the result of hashing the logical name. It is used only for table names.

There is one LNMX for each equivalence name defined for the logical name. A multivalued logical name is described by an LNMB immediately followed by several adjacent LNMXs. The address of one LNMX could be calculated using the address and equivalence name length of its predecessor LNMX. For improved performance, however, LNMX$L_NEXT contains the address of the next LNMX, or zero if there is none.

Figure 38.1 shows the layouts of the LNMB and LNMX data structures. The field LNMB$W_SIZE contains the size of the LNMB, including the sizes of the LNMXs that follow it. Before the memory for the LNMB and the LNMXs is allocated, the size required for each structure is rounded up to the next quadword. As a result, although the name strings in an LNMB and its LNMXs are of variable length, the substructures and the combined data structures are always an integral number of quadwords.

Translation to a particular equivalence name can be requested by specifying its index. The index of an equivalence name is a one-byte signed number. By default the first equivalence name is assigned an index value of 0, the second a value of 1, and so forth.

The positive values 0 to 127 are available for users. The negative values –1 to –128 are reserved for system use. Currently, the executive uses two special index values. The value 82_{16}, or –126, indicates that the equivalence string

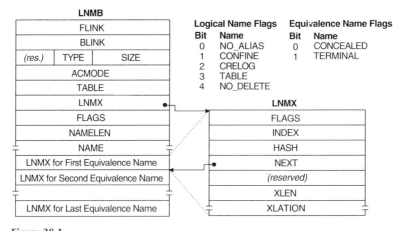

Figure 38.1
Layouts of Logical Name Block (LNMB) and Logical Name Translation Block (LNMX)

is a logical name table header. The value 81_{16}, or -127, indicates that the equivalence string is a back pointer, the address of another data structure. A back pointer can be used to link a mailbox unit control block (UCB) with the LNMB that contains its logical name. It can also be used to connect a mounted volume list entry and its LNMB. Only shareable logical names can have back pointers.

It is possible for the creator of a logical name explicitly to assign an index value to each equivalence name. Translation indexes can be sparse. For example, a particular logical name might have translations 1, 3, 5, and 10. The executive uses this feature itself to create back pointer logical names. Any general use of this feature is discouraged, however, because RMS and other system components assume that equivalence names have dense ascending indexes.

A process-private LNMB is allocated from the process allocation region. An LNMB for a shareable logical name must be accessible by multiple processes and is allocated from paged pool.

38.5.2   Logical Name Table Headers

The data structure describing a logical name table is an LNMB whose single LNMX has the index value 82_{16} to indicate that it contains an LNMTH instead of an equivalence name.

An LNMTH describes a logical name table. Figure 38.2 shows its layout. The field LNMTH$L_HASH contains the address of either the shareable hash table or the process-private hash table, depending on whether the logical name table is shareable or process-private. Section 38.5.3 describes the use of logical name hash tables.

For a shareable table, LNMTH$L_ORB contains the address of the object rights block (ORB) associated with the table. The ORB defines the protection information for the logical name table: its system-owner-group-world

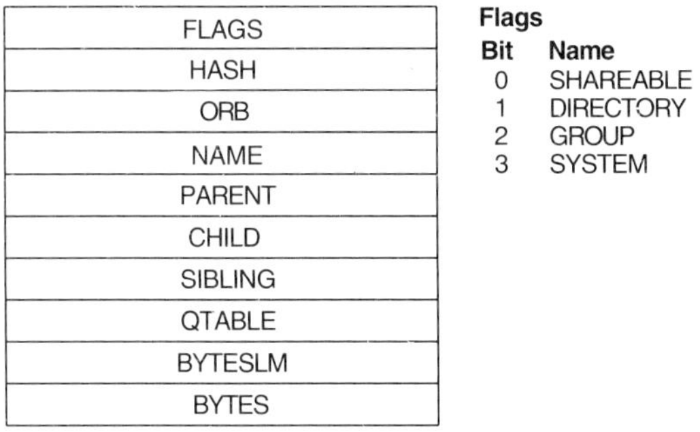

FLAGS
HASH
ORB
NAME
PARENT
CHILD
SIBLING
QTABLE
BYTESLM
BYTES

Flags

Bit	Name
0	SHAREABLE
1	DIRECTORY
2	GROUP
3	SYSTEM

Figure 38.2
Layout of Logical Name Table Header (LNMTH)

protection mask and any access control entries that have been defined. For a process-private table, the field is unused. LNMTH$L_NAME contains the address of the beginning of the LNMB that contains this header; that is, it points back to the beginning of the data structure, an address impossible to compute from the LNMTH address, given the counted logical name string between them.

The fields LNMTH$L_PARENT, LNMTH$L_CHILD, and LNMTH$L_SIB-LING contain addresses of other LNMTHs and link logical name tables into a quota and access hierarchy. The hierarchy consists of singly linked lists. A zero value in a pointer indicates the end of the list.

Figure 38.3 shows the hierarchical relations between several logical name tables: tables A and B are siblings whose parent is table R; R's parent is LNM$PROCESS_TABLE. For simplicity, the figure shows only LNMTHs and omits LNMBs. LNMTH$L_CHILD in table R contains the address of table A's header. Table A's LNMTH$L_PARENT field contains the address of table R's LNMTH. Because table R has another child table, A's field LNMTH$L_SIBLING contains the address of R's next child, table B.

LNMTH$L_QTABLE contains the LNMTH address of the table's quota holder table. In the case of a table with limited quota, the table is its own quota holder, and the field contains the address of the start of the table's own header. For a table with limited quota, LNMTH$L_BYTESLM and LNMTH$L_BYTES contain the initial quota given to the table at its creation and the amount left. These fields are unused for a table whose quota is pooled. Figure 38.3 shows table R as its own quota holder and also the holder for tables A and B.

Note that an LNMTH contains no listhead for LNMBs. The intuitive view of the relation between a logical name and its containing table is different from the implementation. A logical name table contains logical names in an abstract sense, but it is not possible to examine a table header to locate logical names in that table. The only connection between a logical name and its containing table is from the LNMB to the table header; the field LNMB$L_TABLE contains the address of the LNMTH. Every LNMB of the appropriate hash table must be examined to determine which ones are in the table of interest.

A logical name directory is described by an LNMTH whose LNMTH$V_DIRECTORY flag is set and whose LNMTH$L_PARENT field is zero.

In a logical name table name, the field LNMB$L_TABLE always contains the address of its directory table's LNMTH. The directory's LNMB$L_TABLE also points to the directory's LNMTH.

Figure 38.4 shows the relation between the process directory; a particular logical name table, LNM$PROCESS_TABLE; and a particular logical name, SYS$LOGIN. For simplicity, Figure 38.4 omits hash table links, which are pictured in Figure 38.5.

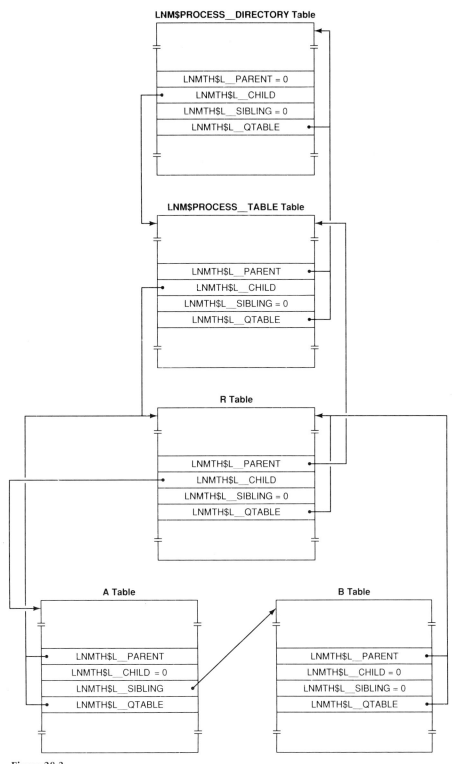

Figure 38.3
Hierarchical Relations Between Logical Name Tables

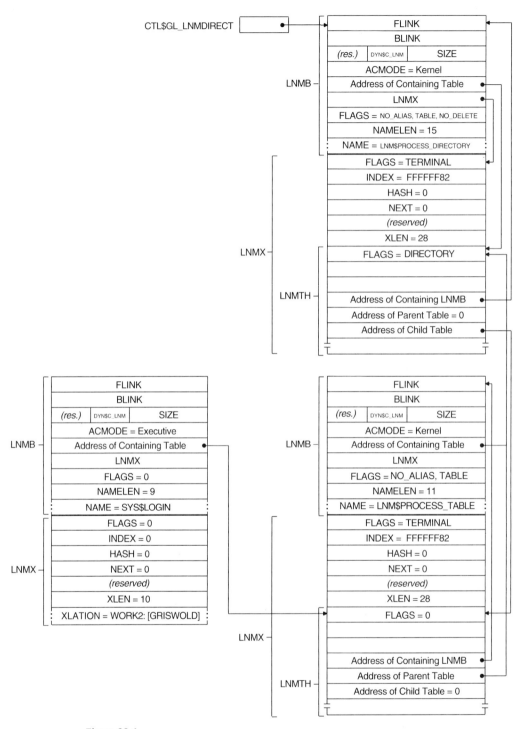

Figure 38.4
Relation Between Logical Name Table and Directory
Table

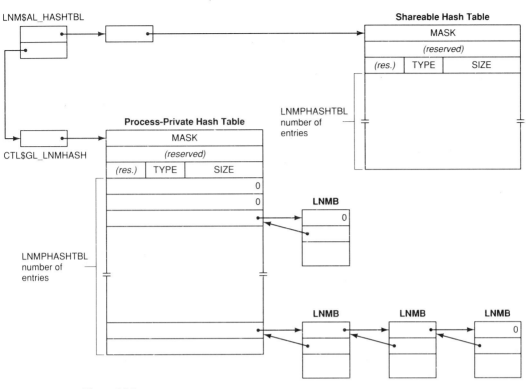

Figure 38.5
Logical Name Hash Tables and Logical Name Blocks

38.5.3   **Logical Name Hash Tables**

Locating a translation for a particular logical name requires first hashing the logical name in the appropriate hash table and then determining whether the name found matches the name of interest.

Each process has its own hash table to locate all process-private logical names. All shareable logical names are hashed in the shareable hash table.

A hash table consists of a 12-byte header and a number of longword entries. Each entry in the hash table is either zero or a pointer to a hash chain of LNMBs with the same hash value. The chain is doubly linked through the fields LNMB$L_FLINK and LNMB$L_BLINK. The last LNMB in a chain has a forward pointer of zero.

The order of LNMBs in a hash chain is determined by the following criteria:

1. Length of the logical name, with shorter strings first
2. Alphabetical order, according to the ASCII collating sequence, of the logical name string for LNMBs that have logical names of the same length
3. Address of the containing table address, with lowest address first, for LNMBs with the same logical name

1317

4. Access mode of the logical name, with outermost access mode first, for LNMBs with the same logical name string in the same table

Recall that a logical name can be defined in different name tables and at different access modes. Translating a logical name means locating the first definition that satisfies containing table and access mode constraints. The last criterion supplies the mechanism by which an outer mode definition for a name can override an inner mode definition.

The SYSGEN parameter LNMPHASHTBL specifies the number of long-word entries in the process-private hash table. During process creation, EXE$PROCSTRT allocates it from the process allocation region and initializes its header. Because the process allocation region consists of demand zero pages, the table's longword entries are zeroed as a side effect of allocating space from the region for the first time.

The SYSGEN parameter LNMSHASHTBL specifies the number of long-word entries in the shareable hash table. The shareable hash table is allocated from paged pool, its header built, and longword entries cleared by the swapper process during system initialization.

The address of either hash table can be determined indirectly through the two-longword array at global location LNM$AL_HASHTBL. Its first long-word points to a longword containing the address of the shareable hash table. Its second longword points to CTL$GL_LNMHASH, which contains the address of the process hash table. The field LNMTH$L_HASH in each logical name table contains the address of the hash table for its logical names.

Figure 38.5 shows this array, the two hash tables, and two hash chains.

The algorithm used to hash the logical names was chosen to be relatively fast and provide a good distribution within the hash table. It is implemented by the routine LNM$HASH, in module LNMSUB.

The hashing algorithm is as follows:

1. The size of the logical name string is moved to a longword. This is the base hash value.
2. Starting at the beginning of the string, LNM$HASH clears bit 5 in each of the four bytes, effectively converting alphabetic characters to upper-case. It XORs the result into the hash longword. The hash is then rotated by nine bits to the left.
3. Step 2 is repeated with the next four bytes until there are fewer than four bytes remaining in the string.
4. One byte at a time, it clears bit 5 in each of the remaining bytes, XORs the result into the hash longword, and rotates the hash longword left by 13 bits.
5. The hash longword is then multiplied by an eight-digit hexadecimal number (71279461_{16}).
6. It rotates the hash longword left by 13 bits.

Logical name routines that invoke LNM$HASH to calculate the hash long-word clear a number of high-order bytes in the resulting hash longword against the mask in LNMHSH$L_MASK. The result is a number no larger than the number of entries in the hash table minus 1. It is used as a long-word index into the hash table. The hash value for a logical name table name is stored in its field LNMX$L_HASH and is used to speed up translation of table names.

38.5.4   Logical Name Table Name Cache Blocks

To speed up logical name translation, information about logical name tables is cached. Every logical name translation entails translating a table name. If the table name translates to another logical name or is a multivalued logical name, iterative translation of multiple names may be required, as described in Section 38.7.

A cache block records the result of a particular table name translation for subsequent use. Figure 38.6 shows the layout of the logical name table name cache block.

A cache block contains the address of the LNMB of the table name in field LNMC$L_TBLADDR and addresses of up to 24 LNMTHs obtained from translating that table name. As a fixed-size data structure, a cache block can hold the addresses of only 24 LNMTHs. A table name that resolves to more than 24 table headers cannot be cached. As a table name is translated, table header addresses are stored in its cache block. LNMC$B_TYPE records the access mode associated with the translation whose results are recorded. For the cached translation to be used in a subsequent translation, its access mode must match the one recorded.

If a particular logical name is located in a table whose name requires iterative translation and the name's table is found before the table name is

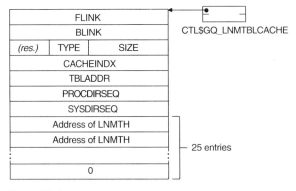

Figure 38.6
Layout of Logical Name Table Name Cache Block (LNMC)

exhaustively translated, the cache block contains valid but incomplete data. The valid entries are followed by a zero longword. If the cache block describes the complete translation of the table name, the valid entries are followed by a longword containing –1. An incomplete list of table headers can be extended during later resolutions of the logical table name that require more translations. LNMC$L_CACHEINDX contains the index of the current entry, the one most recently entered or examined.

Each time the contents of a logical name table directory change, the sequence number associated with it is incremented. For example, when a process-private logical name table is created or deleted, global location CTL$GL_LNMDIRSEQ is incremented. It is also incremented if a logical name in the process directory is changed, for example, through the definition of an outer mode alias or the definition of a name that supersedes the old one. The sequence number for the shareable directory, LNM$GL_SYSDIRSEQ, is similarly incremented whenever the system directory is altered.

The cache block fields LNMC$L_PROCDIRSEQ and LNMC$L_SYSDIR-SEQ record the sequence numbers of the process and system directories current when a table name translation is cached. The fields are used as a validity check on the cached LNMTH addresses. During translation of that table name, the cached sequence numbers are checked against the current ones. The data cached in the block is valid only if both its sequence numbers are current. If one of the sequence numbers is out-of-date, it is possible that there have been changes in the directory contents that affect the cached translations.

Each process has its own cache with blocks for the most recently referenced logical name table names. During process startup, EXE$PROCSTRT, in module PROCSTRT, allocates cache blocks from the process allocation region. It initializes and inserts them in a doubly linked list whose head is at CTL$GQ_LNMTBLCACHE. The amount of space used for cache blocks is approximately twice that used for the process hash table. Each cache block is 128 bytes. The number of cache blocks is related to the SYSGEN parameter LNMPHASHTBL in the following way:

```
number_of_cache_blocks = (LNMPHASHTBL * 8)/128
```

38.5.5 Synchronization of Access to the Logical Name Database

A single mutex named LNM$AQ_MUTEX provides synchronization to the shareable logical name database. Chapter 9 describes the use of mutexes.

The $TRNLNM system service locks the mutex for read access. Multiple processes can lock the mutex for concurrent read access and logical name translation. The other logical name system services all modify the database and therefore lock the mutex for write access, blocking any concurrent access by another process.

SEARCHING FOR A LOGICAL NAME

To search for a logical name, the $TRNLNM and $DELLNM logical name
system services invoke the routine LNM$SEARCHLOG, in module LNM-
SUB. LNM$SEARCHLOG's input arguments include a flag specifying
whether the match is case-blind. The $TRNLNM service sets the flag if
the translation attribute CASE_BLIND was specified when the service was
requested. The $DELLNM service clears the flag, specifying that searches
should be case-sensitive. LNM$SEARCHLOG invokes a number of other
routines, some of which are invoked directly from the $CRELNM system
service.

LNM$SEARCHLOG must first hash the name in both logical name hash
tables to find out whether it exists. These hashes are independent of the containing table and are performed to find out whether the logical name has
been defined at all. Because many file specifications are translated to check
whether they are logical names, attempted logical name translation is most
frequent. That is, most translations fail. The data structures and search algorithm were designed to optimize the determination that a particular string is
not a logical name.

If LNM$SEARCHLOG determines that one or more names with a match-
ing logical name string exist, it must locate the first one whose containing
table and access mode match the routine's input arguments. This requires
that LNM$SEARCHLOG translate its input table name to one or more name
table header addresses.

LNM$SEARCHLOG takes the following steps:

1. It initializes a stack local data structure called a name translation block
   (NT) to describe the state of the name translation.
2. It then invokes LNM$PRESEARCH, in module LNMSUB, with the ad-
   dress of the process-private hash table. If the current process is the swapper, which has no process-private logical names, LNM$SEARCHLOG
   begins with the shareable logical name hash table.

   LNM$PRESEARCH and its associated routines, all in module LNM-
   SUB, take the following steps:

   a. LNM$PRESEARCH invokes LNM$HASH to hash the logical name.
      The resulting value is used as an index into the hash table. The hash
      table entry located by the index is a listhead of LNMBs with that hash
      value, a hash chain.
   b. LNM$PRESEARCH invokes LNM$CONTSEARCH to search the
      hash chain for one with a matching logical name.
   c. Beginning with the first LNMB in the chain, LNM$CONTSEARCH
      compares the length of the logical name with the length of the tar-
      get logical name. Comparing logical name lengths eliminates the
      overhead of a string comparison instruction that is bound to fail

if the lengths differ. If the logical name in the LNMB is shorter, LNM$CONTSEARCH skips that LNMB and goes on to the next. If the name in the LNMB is longer, the search has passed the possible LNMBs, and the routine returns the error status SS$_NOLOGNAM. If the names are the same length, the routine compares them.

d. If the names are identical, LNM$CONTSEARCH returns a success status and the address of the LNMB with the matching name.

e. If the names differ, but the search is case-blind, one in which the uppercase versions of both names must be compared, LNM$CONT-SEARCH converts the names one character at a time and compares them. It continues converting and comparing until it reaches the end of the names or a character comparison fails.

If it reaches the end of the names, the names are identical. It returns a success status and the address of the LNMB with the matching name.

f. If the search is not case-blind or the converted names differ, it tests whether the name in the LNMB is alphabetically lower than the target logical name. If it is higher, the search has passed the last possible LNMB. LNM$CONTSEARCH returns the error status SS$_NOLOG-NAM to its invoker.

g. If the name is alphabetically lower, the routine continues the search until it reaches the end of the hash chain, an LNMB containing a name of a different length, an LNMB containing a name higher in the sort sequence, or an LNMB with a matching name. In the first three circumstances, LNM$CONTSEARCH returns the error status SS$_NOLOGNAM to its invoker.

3. Regardless of the outcome, LNM$SEARCHLOG initializes a second data structure and invokes LNM$PRESEARCH again, this time with the address of the shareable hash table.

4. If there was no match in either hash table, LNM$SEARCHLOG returns the error status SS$_NOLOGNAM to its invoker.

5. If at least one logical name matched in either of the hash tables, LNM$SEARCHLOG must check whether the containing table and access mode also match.

LNM$SEARCHLOG invokes LNM$SETUP to confirm that the target logical name's table name exists and to initialize logical name table processing. Section 38.7 describes table name resolution in detail.

- If the table name does not exist, LNM$SETUP returns the error status SS$_NOLOGNAM, which LNM$SEARCHLOG returns to its invoker.

- If the table name does exist, LNM$SETUP returns the address of the first LNMTH to which the table name resolves. Recall that a table name can be a multivalued logical name with equivalence names that are themselves logical names.

6. LNM$SEARCHLOG invokes LNM$CONTSEARCH, this time with the address of the containing table header.

7. Beginning at a point determined by the previous searches, LNM$CONT-SEARCH scans the hash chain for a matching logical name. If the table is shareable, LNM$CONTSEARCH looks in the shareable hash table chain; otherwise, it checks the process-private one.

   This time, however, when it finds a match, it also compares containing table name addresses.

   - If the LNMTH address in the hash chain LNMB is higher, the search has failed, since LNMBs with the same logical name are ordered by LNMTH address.

   - If the LNMTH address is lower, LNM$CONTSEARCH goes on to the next LNMB.

   - If the LNMTH addresses match, the routine must also check the access mode. If the LNMB access mode is greater (less privileged) than the requested mode, it goes on to the next LNMB. If the LNMB mode is equal to or less than the requested mode, the LNMB matches, and LNM$CONTSEARCH returns a success status and the address of the LNMB to LNM$SEARCHLOG.

8. If a logical name matches, LNM$SEARCHLOG returns the success status SS$_NORMAL and the address of the target LNMB.

9. If there is no matching name in the first table, the next table to which the table name resolves must be checked. LNM$SEARCHLOG invokes LNM$TABLE to continue the table processing begun with the invocation of LNM$SETUP. LNM$TABLE returns the address of the next LNMTH. LNM$SEARCHLOG invokes LNM$CONTSEARCH again, as in step 6, with that address.

   This sequence continues until the first matching logical name is found or there are no more tables to check. If no match is found in any table, LNM$SEARCHLOG returns the failure status SS$_NOLOGNAM to its invoker.

System services other than logical name services, such as the $ASSIGN system service, invoke the routine LNM$SEARCH_ONE. LNM$SEARCH_ONE locks the logical name database mutex for read access. It invokes LNM$SEARCHLOG to find the LNMB and extracts the translation with index zero. It unlocks the mutex and returns to its invoker.

The SHOW LOGICAL utility builds an NT structure and invokes the routines LNM$PRESEARCH and LNM$CONTSEARCH directly. In contrast to the use of LNM$SEARCHLOG, where locating the first matching logical name is sufficient, the utility must be able to generate every possible match.

38.7   **LOGICAL NAME TABLE NAME RESOLUTION**

To resolve a logical name table name, the logical name system services and routines and the DCL SHOW LOGICAL utility invoke either the routine LNM$FIRSTTAB or the combination of LNM$SETUP and LNM$TABLE. These three routines are all in module LNMSUB.

LNM$FIRSTTAB is called to return only the first table in the translation of a table name. A typical use of it is to identify the table in which to create a new logical name. LNM$FIRSTTAB itself invokes LNM$SETUP.

LNM$SETUP and LNM$TABLE perform iterative and potentially exhaustive translations of a table name. LNM$SETUP is invoked first to initialize the search context and return the address of the first table header. Subsequently, LNM$TABLE is invoked again and again, to return the next table header address, potentially until the table name has been exhaustively translated in a depth-first sequence.

When LNM$SETUP is entered, its invoker has allocated and partially initialized a stack local data structure called a recursive table translation block (RT). Its fields include recursion depth, recursion tries, access mode of the request, address of the associated table name cache block, and ten longwords in which to maintain search context. The recursion depth is an index into these ten longwords.

LNM$SETUP takes the following steps:

1. It initializes the recursion depth to zero and the number of remaining recursion tries to 255.
2. It invokes LNM$LOOKUP to confirm that the table exists.

    Invoking LNM$PRESEARCH, LNM$LOOKUP checks the process directory and, if that fails, the system directory for the starting table name. Recall that all logical names involved in the translation of table names must be contained in one of the two directories.

    • If the table name does not exist, LNM$LOOKUP returns the error status SS$_NOLOGNAM, which LNM$SETUP then returns to its own invoker.

    • If the table name exists, LNM$LOOKUP returns the address of the LNMB that defines it.

3. If the name exists, LNM$SETUP saves the address of its LNMB$L_ NAME field in the RT's top search context longword as the starting point of the translation.
4. It then scans for a valid table name cache block describing this table name.

    • If one is found whose access mode matches that of the current translation, its cache entries contain the addresses of some (possibly all) of the table headers to which the table name resolves.

- If a valid table name cache block is not found, the least recently used one is selected for reuse and initialized. Its first cache entry is cleared to indicate that it contains no valid entries.

5. LNM$SETUP saves the address of the cache block in the RT structure. It initializes the cache block index to –1 to indicate no cache entries have been examined yet and enters the routine LNM$TABLE.

Each time LNM$TABLE is entered to resolve the table name, it increments the cache index. It then checks whether the index selects a valid entry, one whose value is nonzero.

► If the longword is nonzero, LNM$TABLE returns it as the address of the next table header to its invoker.

► If the longword is zero, the valid cached data has been exhausted. In this case, LNM$TABLE invokes LNM$TABLE_SRCH to expand the resolution of the table name and add entries to the end of the cache block.

The fundamental recursion loop in resolving a table name is within LNM$TABLE_SRCH. LNM$TABLE_SRCH uses the RT data structure to keep track of the breadth and depth of its position in resolving the table name.

At the beginning of the loop, it decrements the number of remaining recursion tries. If none is left, LNM$TABLE_SRCH returns the error status SS$_TOOMANYLNAM to its invoker. This check prevents the code, for example, from looping endlessly trying to resolve a circular logical name table definition.

LNM$TABLE_SRCH examines the next equivalence name at the current recursion depth to determine what to do. There are several possibilities:

a. If the equivalence name is an ordinary string, LNM$TABLE_SRCH updates the contents in the stack longword to point to the equivalence name following it.

b. It tests that the maximum recursion depth (10) has not been exceeded. If the depth has been exceeded, LNM$TABLE_SRCH returns the error SS$_TOOMANYLNAM.

   Otherwise, LNM$TABLE_SRCH increments the recursion depth and invokes LNM$LOOKUP to find the LNMB associated with the string. It positions to the name string in the LNMX and examines its equivalence name, beginning the loop again.

c. If there are no more equivalence names, LNM$TABLE_SRCH decrements the recursion depth and selects the corresponding RT search longword. It begins the loop again.

d. If the equivalence name is a table header, which is the desired result, LNM$TABLE_SRCH decrements the recursion depth and returns the address of the table header to its invoker.

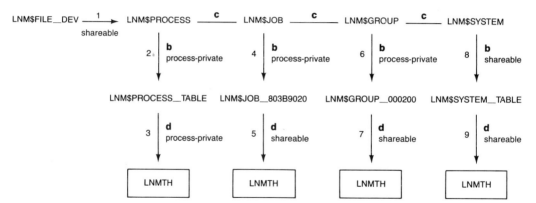

Figure 38.7
Example Resolution of a Logical Name Table Name

Figure 38.7 is an example showing complete resolution of the logical name LNM$FILE_DEV. The first step is translating LNM$FILE_DEV, a shareable name found in the system directory with four equivalence names. The second step is translating the "leftmost" equivalence name, LNM$PROCESS. It is a process-private name whose equivalence name is LNM$PROCESS_TABLE. The third step translates LNM$PROCESS_TABLE to its equivalence name, the first table header for LNM$FILE_DEV.

In the figure, the numbers indicate the sequence of translations. The letters on each step correspond to the possible actions in the recursion loop previously listed.

In this example, each equivalence name of LNM$FILE_DEV is translated as deeply as required to reach a table header. In practice, during logical name translation or deletion, table name resolution stops as soon as the first table that contains the logical name is found. During logical name creation, table resolution stops with the first table, in this example, LNM$PROCESS_TABLE.

38.8 LOGICAL NAME SYSTEM SERVICES

The logical name system service procedures all run in kernel mode. The procedures themselves are in the module SYSLNM. Logical name subroutines that they use are in module LNMSUB.

Before describing the specific system service procedures, this section describes some checks common to the services.

38.8.1 Privilege and Protection Checks

Each system service has an access mode argument. If the requestor explicitly specifies it and has the privilege SYSNAM, the desired access mode is used with no further check. If the requestor specifies it but does not have the privilege, the access mode is maximized with the mode from which the system service was requested. That is, the less privileged of the two is used.

Any string argument passed to the services must be probed to test accessibility from the mode of the system service requestor. An input string is tested for read accessibility and an output string for write accessibility. An item list must be probed for read accessibility and each buffer in it must also be probed.

The logical name system services must check a process's access to a shareable table. (A process always has access to a process-private table, although it may be constrained by access mode considerations.) The system services use standard OpenVMS protection checks. That is, they invoke the routine LNM$CHECK_PROT, which calls an internal entry point of the Check Access Protection ($CHKPRO) system service.

The $CHKPRO system service determines whether the process, given its rights and privileges, can access the table. The system service's checks encompass the process UIC, the protection mask of the table, any ACLs defined for the table, and whether the process has any of the following privileges:

SYSPRV
GRPPRV
BYPASS
READALL

If the $CHKPRO system service returns a failure status, LNM$CHECK_PROT makes two checks of its own to provide compatibility with earlier versions of the system. If the intended access is read or write, LNM$CHECK_PROT tests whether the table of interest is either a group table or the system table. If this is the group table corresponding to the group code in the process's UIC and the process has the privilege GRPNAM, its access is allowed. If this is the system table and the process has the privilege SYSNAM, its access is allowed.

38.8.2   Logical Name Translation

The $TRNLNM system service procedure, EXE$TRNLNM, takes the following steps to translate a logical name:

1. It first confirms the presence and accessibility of its required arguments: descriptors for the logical name string and the name of its containing table.
2. It locks the logical name database mutex for read access.
3. It invokes LNM$SEARCHLOG to locate the first logical name that meets the table name and access mode constraints, as described in Section 38.6.

    If LNM$SEARCHLOG returns the error status SS$_NOLOGNAM, indicating that the logical name does not exist, EXE$TRNLNM unlocks the logical name database mutex and passes the error status back to its requestor.

4. If the logical name exists, LNM$SEARCHLOG returns the address of the LNMB of the first matching logical name. EXE$TRNLNM examines the address to determine whether it is a process-private or a shareable name.

5. If the name is shareable (a system space LNMB), EXE$TRNLNM invokes LNM$CHECK_PROT to determine whether the process has read access to the containing table. If the process does not have access, EXE$TRNLNM unlocks the logical name database mutex and returns the error status SS$_NOPRIV.

6. If the name is a process-private one or a shareable one to whose table the process has access, it processes the item list, which contains the list of specific information to be returned. It probes any specified output buffers for write access and copies information from the LNMB, its LNMXs, and the LNMTH of its containing table, as requested.

7. It then unlocks the logical name database mutex and returns.

   If there was insufficient space in the output buffers for all requested information, it returns the success status SS$_BUFFEROVF. Otherwise, it returns the success status SS$_NORMAL.

38.8.3 Logical Name Creation

The $CRELNM system service procedure, EXE$CRELNM, takes the following steps to create a logical name:

1. It confirms the presence and accessibility of its required arguments: the descriptors for the logical name string and the name of its containing table. It checks the accessibility of any optional arguments specified.

2. If the requestor specified the address of an item list containing equivalence strings and their attributes, EXE$CRELNM scans the list to determine their cumulative size. The item list is not a required argument, but there is little purpose served in creating a logical name with no translations, other than perhaps the creation of a logical name whose existence or nonexistence serves as an on-off flag.

3. EXE$CRELNM then locks the logical name database mutex for write access and invokes LNM$FIRSTTAB (see Section 38.7) to translate the name of the containing logical name table. A new logical name is always created in the first table of a table name search list.

   If LNM$FIRSTTAB returns the error status SS$_NOLOGTAB to indicate that the containing table name did not translate to any existing table, EXE$CRELNM unlocks the logical name database mutex and returns the error status to its requestor.

4. If the search is successful, LNM$FIRSTTAB returns the address of the containing table's LNMTH. EXE$CRELNM examines a flag in the LNMTH to determine whether it is a shareable table.

- If the table is process-private, EXE$CRELNM allocates enough pool for the LNMB and all its LNMXs from the process allocation region. If there is insufficient process allocation region, it unlocks the mutex and returns the error status SS$_INSFMEM.
- If the table is shareable, it invokes LNM$CHECK_PROT to determine whether the process has write access to the containing table (see Section 38.3). If the process does not have access, EXE$CRELNM unlocks the mutex and returns the error status SS$_NOPRIV.

  If the process does have access, it allocates enough paged pool for the LNMB and all its LNMXs. If there is insufficient paged pool, EXE$CRELNM returns the error status SS$_INSFMEM to its caller.

5. If the table is process-private or a shareable one to which the process has access, EXE$CRELNM then checks that there is sufficient quota for the LNMB in the table that holds the quota for the containing table (LNMTH$L_QTABLE). If there is not, it deallocates the pool, unlocks the mutex, and returns the error status SS$_EXLNMQUOTA.

6. It begins to fill in the LNMB. If the containing table is one of the directories, it tests that the length of the logical name string is less than 32 characters and that it contains no characters other than those allowed for logical names contained in a directory. (Note that if a logical name is being created that is not a table name but whose containing table is one of the directories, it must meet those same requirements.) If the logical name string does not meet those requirements, it deallocates the pool, unlocks the mutex, and returns the error status SS$_IVLOGNAM.

7. It copies the logical name string to the LNMB. It then begins processing the item list, building LNMXs as specified by the requestor.

8. It invokes LNM$INSLOGTAB to insert the LNMB into the logical name database.

   LNM$INSLOGTAB scans any LNMBs with the same name and containing table until there are no more or it encounters one with a more privileged access mode. It compares their access modes to that of the logical name being created and examines the NO_ALIAS attribute of the new name to determine what to do:

   - If there is an LNMB with the same access mode, the old LNMB is deleted and superseded by the new one.
   - If there is one with a more privileged mode and the NO_ALIAS attribute, the new logical name cannot be inserted. The routine returns the error status SS$_DUPLNAM to EXE$CRELNM. EXE$CRELNM deallocates the LNMB to pool, unlocks the mutex, and returns the error status to its requestor.
   - If there is one with a more privileged mode and without the NO_ALIAS attribute, the new logical name can be created.
   - If one is found with a less privileged mode and the new name has the NO_ALIAS attribute, the outer mode logical names are deleted and the

new one is inserted. Section 38.8.5 describes the possible side effects of logical name deletion.

LNM$INSLOGTAB charges the size of the LNMB against the containing table's quota holder. If the containing table is a directory, it increments the appropriate directory sequence number as part of the cache invalidation mechanism. Section 38.5.4 describes the use of logical name caches.

9. If the containing table is a directory, EXE$CRELNM computes and stores a hash value for each of the equivalence names of the newly created logical name. The assumption behind this is that the logical name translates to one or more name table names, whose hash values will be needed whenever a table search involving this name is performed.

10. It unlocks the mutex and returns.

38.8.4 Logical Name Table Creation

The $CRELNT system service procedure, EXE$CRELNT, takes the following steps to create a logical name table:

1. It confirms the presence and accessibility of the descriptor for the name of the parent table, its one required argument. It checks the accessibility of any optional arguments specified.

2. If the requestor omits the name of the table to be created, EXE$CRELNT supplies a default name of the form LNM$xxxxxxxxeeeeeeee, where xxxxxxxx is the address of the LNMB of the table and eeeeeeee is the process's extended process ID (EPID). Using a default table name ensures that the name of a table does not conflict with any other defined table.

3. EXE$CRELNT locks the logical name database for write access and invokes LNM$FIRSTTAB (see Section 38.7) to translate the name of the parent logical name table. If the parent table is a table name search list, its first table name becomes the parent of the new table.

   If LNM$FIRSTTAB returns the error status SS$_NOLOGTAB to indicate that the parent table name does not translate to any existing table, EXE$CRELNT unlocks the logical name database mutex and returns the error status to its requestor.

4. If the parent table name does translate, LNM$FIRSTTAB returns the address of the parent table's LNMTH.

   - If the parent table is process-private, EXE$CRELNT allocates enough space from the process allocation region for the LNMB, its single LNMX and LNMTH, and an ORB.
   - If the parent table is shareable, EXE$CRELNT calls LNM$CHECK_PROT to determine whether the process has enable access to the parent table and can thus withdraw quota from it. If the process does not have

access, EXE$CRELNT unlocks the mutex and returns the error status SS$_NOPRIV.

If the parent table is shareable and the process specified the name of the table to be created, EXE$CRELNT checks whether the process has write access to the system directory. If a default table name was constructed, the process does not need write access to the system directory. On error, EXE$CRELNT unlocks the mutex and returns the error status SS$_NOPRIV.

If the process has the necessary access, it allocates enough paged pool for the LNMB, its single LNMX and LNMTH, and an ORB.

5. It checks that there is sufficient quota for the table name (its LNMB, LNMX, and LNMTH) in the directory table. If a quota for the new table was specified, then it also checks that the parent table's quota holder has sufficient quota for the names that will be contained in the new table. If it does not, EXE$CRELNT deallocates the pool, unlocks the mutex, and returns the error status SS$_EXLNMQUOTA.

6. If there is sufficient quota, it fills in the LNMB and translation blocks. If the requestor specified the name of the table to be created, EXE$CRE-LNT tests that it is a legal table name. If the table is also shareable, EXE$CRELNT initializes its ORB.

7. EXE$CRELNT then invokes LNM$INSLOGTAB to insert the LNMB into the logical name database.

LNM$INSLOGTAB scans all LNMBs with the same name and containing table until there are no more or it encounters one with a more privileged access mode. Its actions depend on the NO_ALIAS attribute of the new name and any old ones, the access modes of the new and old names, and the presence or absence of the CREATE_IF ATTR argument. The CREATE_IF attribute means that the table should be created only if there is not already one with the same name and access mode.

- If there is an LNMB with the same access mode and CREATE_IF was not specified, the old LNMB is deleted and superseded by the new one. Deleting an LNMB whose equivalence name is an LNMTH means that all the logical names contained in that table must be deleted. Any descendant tables and their logical names must also be deleted.
- If there is an LNMB with the same access mode and CREATE_IF was specified, LNM$INSLOGTAB returns the status SS$_NORMAL and the address of the old LNMB. EXE$CRELNT deallocates the new LNMB to pool.
- If there is an LNMB with a more privileged mode and the NO_ALIAS attribute, the new LNMB cannot be inserted. LNM$INSLOGTAB returns the error status SS$_DUPLNAM to EXE$CRELNT, which deallocates the new LNMB to pool.
- If there is an LNMB with a more privileged mode and without the

NO_ALIAS attribute, LNM$INSLOGTAB can insert the new LNMB. It returns the status SS$_LNMCREATED.

- If one or more LNMBs are found with a less privileged mode and the new name has the NO_ALIAS attribute, the outer mode LNMBs are deleted. The new LNMB is inserted. LNM$INSLOGTAB returns the status SS$_SUPERSEDE.

To insert the new LNMB (and its table), LNM$INSLOGTAB inserts the LNMB into the hash chain and the LNMTH into the name table hierarchy as the first child of its parent table. If there already was a child, LNM$INSLOGTAB stores the address of its LNMTH in the new table's LNMTH$L_SIBLING. If this table is to be its own quota holder, quota is withdrawn from the parent's quota holder and allocated to the new table. Otherwise, the table's LNMTH$L_QTABLE is set to the same value as that of its parent table. Quota for the table's LNMB is withdrawn from the appropriate directory table. LNM$INSLOGTAB increments the appropriate directory sequence number.

8. EXE$CRELNT unlocks the logical name database mutex and returns, passing back the status from LNM$INSLOGTAB and, if requested, the name of the newly created table.

38.8.5 Logical Name Deletion

The $DELLNM system service procedure, EXE$DELLNM, takes the following steps to delete a logical name:

1. It confirms the presence of the descriptor for the name of the table containing the names to be deleted, its one required argument.

   The LOGNAM argument is the logical name to be deleted; it can be a logical name table name. The absence of the logical name argument is a request to delete all the table's logical names with access mode equally or less privileged than that of the request.

2. EXE$DELLNM locks the logical name database mutex for write access.

3. If deletion of a particular logical name was requested, EXE$DELLNM invokes LNM$SEARCHLOG, described in Section 38.6, to determine whether the name exists. If the name is not found or if its access mode is more privileged than that of the service request, EXE$DELLNM unlocks the mutex and returns the error status SS$_NOLOGNAM to its requestor.

4. If the name found is shareable, EXE$DELLNM invokes LNM$CHECK_PROT to ensure that the requestor has write access to the containing logical name table. If the requestor does not, but the name being deleted is a table name, delete access to the table being deleted is sufficient.

   If the requestor does not have access, EXE$DELLNM unlocks the mutex and returns the error status SS$_NOPRIV.

5. EXE$DELLNM invokes LNM$DELETE_LNMB to remove the logical

name and any of its outer access mode aliases from the database. If the name is not the name of a table, deleting it is straightforward and consists of the following steps for each alias:

a. Remove the LNMB and those of any outer mode aliases from the hash chain.
b. Return the quota charged for them.
c. Deallocate them to the process allocation region or paged pool.

If, however, the LNMB is a table name, deleting it also requires deleting each LNMB contained within it, and any descendant tables and their logical names. LNM$DELETE_LNMB removes the LNMB from its hash chain and inserts it into a holding list. It then invokes a routine called DELETE_TABLE to delete the table.

DELETE_TABLE examines the table header to determine whether this table has any descendants. If it does, DELETE_TABLE finds the first one, removes it from its hash chain, inserts it into the holding list, and branches back to itself. DELETE_TABLE is now one level lower in the logical name table hierarchy. It continues recursively, until it reaches a childless level.

It then invokes DELETE_NAMES to delete all the logical names in that table. This requires scanning the appropriate hash table and examining each LNMB to see whether it is contained within the table. Each such LNMB is removed from its hash chain and deallocated to its pool, with quota returned to the containing table. If the table is shareable, the LNMB is deallocated to paged pool. Otherwise, it is deallocated to the process allocation region. DELETE_NAMES checks that the NODELETE flag is clear in each LNMB before deleting it, to ensure that it does not delete either directory table.

After all its names are deleted, the table is then removed from the table hierarchy, its table quota is returned to its quota holder, and the LNMB quota is returned to the appropriate directory. The appropriate directory sequence number is incremented and the LNMB deallocated to its pool.

DELETE_TABLE then processes the first LNMB in the holding list, the parent of the one just deleted. DELETE_TABLE examines the table header of that LNMB to see whether it still has descendants. If it does not, then all the logical names in that table and the table itself are deleted. If it still has descendants, DELETE_TABLE places the LNMB for the first child into the holding list and branches back to itself. Eventually, DELETE_TABLE empties the holding list and returns.

6. EXE$DELLNM unlocks the mutex and returns.

If EXE$DELLNM is called without the logical name argument, it invokes LNM$FIRSTTAB to find the first table header to which the table name resolves. If the table is shareable, it invokes LNM$CHECK_PROT to confirm that the process has delete access to the table or write access to the directory. DELETE_NAMES is invoked to delete all the names in that table.

As described previously, it scans the appropriate hash table, looking for LNMBs with a matching table header address and an access mode equally or less privileged than that of the delete request. Each such LNMB is removed from the hash chain, its quota is returned, and it is deallocated to pool.

When all the names of suitable access mode in that table are deleted, EXE$DELLNM unlocks the mutex and returns to its requestor.

When an image exits, the Rundown Image ($RUNDWN) system service must delete all process-private logical names with an access mode less or equally privileged to the exit mode.

The $RUNDWN system service invokes the routine LNM$DELETE_ HASH, specifying the exit access mode and the address of the process-private hash table. LNM$DELETE_HASH locks the logical name table mutex and invokes DELETE_NAMES with the address of the hash table. Many of its logical names, of course, are names of tables. Deleting each of them requires the steps previously described to delete a table, its descendant tables, and its logical names. When all the names are deleted, LNM$DELETE_HASH unlocks the mutex and returns to the $RUNDWN system service, described in detail in Chapter 28.

38.9 SUPERSEDED LOGICAL NAME SYSTEM SERVICES

The current logical name system services supersede several system services from VAX/VMS Version 3 and earlier versions:

- ▶ Create logical name ($CRELOG)
- ▶ Delete logical name ($DELLOG)
- ▶ Translate logical name ($TRNLOG)

These services are still supported to provide upward compatibility for software written for earlier versions. Table 38.3 shows the correspondence between the table numbers used in early VAX/VMS versions and the table names that currently implement them as well as the access mode associated with each table. Table 38.2 shows the translation of those table names.

Table 38.3 Correspondence Between Table Numbers and Logical Name Table Names

Table Number	Table Name	Access Mode
0	LOG$SYSTEM	Executive
1	LOG$GROUP	User
2	LOG$PROCESS	Mode of caller

It is possible for users of the superseded logical name system services to make some use of current features without reprogramming. By defining aliases to the table names used by these system services, a process can access tables other than the standard process, group, and system logical name tables. In fact, the executive defines the name LOG$PROCESS to equate to both the process and jobwide logical name tables. This enables translation of logical names within the jobwide logical name table by default.

The superseded system service procedures are in module SYSLOGNAM and are mode of caller services. Each service confirms that the minimum number of arguments expected is present and that the argument list is accessible. Each service then transforms its argument list and invokes the equivalent replacement system service.

The arguments for each superseded service include access mode and table number. Each service checks that its table number argument is valid and converts it to the corresponding logical name table name.

For the process table, any access mode specified by the requestor is used. If the argument is omitted, the requestor's access mode is used. The access mode is passed as an argument to the replacement logical name system service, which checks that the process has suitable privileges.

The following paragraphs supply a few specific additional details about the implementation of the $CRELOG and $TRNLOG system services.

A name created with the $CRELOG system service has only one translation, the equivalence name supplied to $CRELOG. The logical name has the CRELOG attribute. The equivalence name is assigned translation index 0. If the equivalence name begins with a leading underscore, the underscore is removed and the equivalence name has the TERMINAL attribute.

The $TRNLOG system service returns translation number 0 of the specified logical name. If the translation has the TERMINAL attribute, $TRNLOG prefixes an underscore to the equivalence name. This manipulation enables most logical names, including file names, to be created and used through either the old or new system services.

Two arguments to the $TRNLOG system service control its actions: the TABLE and DSBMSK arguments. The TABLE argument is the address to receive the translation table number. The DSBMSK argument specifies which subset of the process, group, and system tables is to be searched. (The mask is a disable mask; by identifying which tables to omit, it indirectly identifies those to be searched.)

If the TABLE argument is zero, EXE$TRNLOG transforms the DSBMSK argument into a table name search list with the names of the tables to be searched. It selects one of the logical name table names whose name begins with the string TRNLOG$. It requests the $TRNLNM system service and transforms its return arguments into forms compatible with the VAX/VMS Version 3 interface.

A nonzero TABLE argument means that EXE$TRNLOG must return the number of the containing table. To determine the containing table, it requests the $TRNLNM system service once for each table to be searched, until the logical name is found or the end of the table subset is reached.

38.10   RELEVANT SOURCE MODULES

Source modules described in this chapter include

[LIB]LNMSTRDEF.SDL
[SYS]LNMSUB.MAR
[SYS]PROCSTRT.MAR
[SYS]SYSLNM.MAR
[SYS]SYSLOGNAM.MAR

39 Miscellaneous System Services

> . . . Of shoes—and ships—and sealing wax—
> Of cabbages—and kings—
> And why the sea is boiling hot—
> And whether pigs have wings.
>
> Lewis Carroll, *Through the Looking Glass*

This chapter briefly describes a number of system services not covered in other chapters. The *OpenVMS System Services Reference Manual* contains detailed descriptions of most of these services and their arguments, return status codes, required process privileges, and options.

39.1 COMMUNICATION WITH SYSTEM PROCESSES

The executive performs some operations often associated with an operating system from independent processes rather than from code in executive images. Examples of this type of system activity include the following:

- ▶ Managing print and batch jobs and queues
- ▶ Gathering accounting information about utilization of system resources
- ▶ Communicating with one or more system operators
- ▶ Reporting device errors

39.1.1 Services Supported by the Job Controller and the Queue Manager

The job controller is a system process named JOB_CONTROL, which runs the image JBC$JOB_CONTROL.EXE. In earlier versions, the job controller had a number of roles, including creation of batch and interactive processes, creation and management of batch and print queues, and process accounting. In OpenVMS AXP Version 1.5, the role of creation and management of batch and print queues is assumed by a new queue manager process. The job controller and the queue manager cooperate closely.

The job controller performs the following functions:

- ▶ As the job manager, the job controller creates interactive, batch, and symbiont processes.
  - In response to unsolicited terminal input, it creates an interactive process.
  - In response to a request from the queue manager process, the job controller creates a batch or symbiont process.

  Chapter 30 describes the job controller's actions as the job manager.
- ▶ The job controller creates the queue manager process in response to the Digital command language (DCL) command START/QUEUE/MANAGER.

▶ As the system accounting manager, the job controller records the use of system resources in the file SYS$MANAGER:ACCOUNTNG.DAT. On a VMScluster system, each node has its own job controller process, which accesses a node-specific accounting file.

The queue manager is the system process named QUEUE_MANAGER, which runs the image QMAN$QUEUE_MANAGER.EXE. It performs the following functions:

▶ As the manager of the batch/print subsystem, the queue manager is responsible for all transactions to and from the queue files: SYS$QUEUE_MANAGER.QMAN$QUEUES and SYS$QUEUE_MANAGER.QMAN$JOURNAL, in the SYS$SYSTEM directory. These transactions include the creation and deletion of queues, and the creation, modification, and dispatching of batch and print jobs.

▶ The queue manager requests the job controller to create a batch process when a process issues the DCL command SUBMIT or requests an equivalent Send Message to Job Controller ($SNDJBC) system service function.

▶ It requests the job controller to create a symbiont process when a process issues the DCL command INITIALIZE/QUEUE to create a print queue or requests an equivalent $SNDJBC system service function. A print symbiont process executes a standard image supplied with the operating system, such as PRTSMB.EXE or LATSMB.EXE, an image supplied with a layered product, or a user-written image that links with SYS$SHARE:SMBSRVSHR.EXE.

▶ The queue manager creates and dispatches a print job when a process issues the DCL command PRINT or requests an equivalent $SNDJBC system service function.

▶ It notifies a requesting process when a batch or print job that the process created completes.

The $SNDJBC system service and the Get Queue Information ($GETQUI) system service, which are described in subsequent sections, enable processes to communicate with the job controller and the queue manager. For a valid request, the $SNDJBC system service procedure sends a message either to the job controller or to the queue manager. For a valid request, the $GETQUI system service procedure sends a message to the queue manager. A message to the job controller is sent through the mailbox driver. A message to the queue manager is sent through a set of private, undocumented, system services for interprocess communication.

39.1.1.1 **$SNDJBC System Service.** A process can request the $SNDJBC system service to direct the actions of the job controller or the queue manager.

A user typically requests the $SNDJBC system service indirectly through a DCL command such as PRINT, SUBMIT, START/QUEUE, INITIAL-IZE/QUEUE, STOP/QUEUE, or DELETE/QUEUE. In response to such a request, the $SNDJBC system service procedure sends a message to the job controller or to the queue manager, whichever is appropriate. The queue manager services all requests relating to queues, batch jobs, and print jobs; the job controller services the rest.

Some functions previously handled by the job controller are now handled by the queue manager. The $SNDJBC system service automatically dispatches such functions to the queue manager. The name and user interface of the system service were retained for compatibility with older software.

Arguments to the $SNDJBC system service include the following:

- ► The event flag number to set upon request completion
- ► The function code
- ► A place-holding null argument
- ► The address of an item list, each entry of which includes an item code corresponding to the function code, the size and address of an associated buffer, and a location to store the size of information returned
- ► A status block (IOSB) to receive final status information
- ► The procedure value and parameter for an asynchronous system trap (AST) procedure to call when the request completes

The $SNDJBC system service procedure, EXE$SNDJBC in module SYS-SNDJBC, runs in executive mode. It takes the following steps:

1. If the null argument is not null, or the function code is invalid, it returns the error status SS$_BADPARAM.
2. If the IOSB is not write-accessible, it returns the error status SS$_ACCVIO.
3. It clears the event flag specified with the request.
4. EXE$SNDJBC calls BUILD_MESSAGE, in module SYSSNDJBC, to validate each item in the item list and to allocate and build a message to send to the job controller or to the queue manager.

   BUILD_MESSAGE invokes EXE$ALOP1PROC, in module MEMO-RYALC, to allocate a message buffer from the process allocation region. For each item, it checks that the item code is valid; that the buffer descriptor and buffer are accessible; and that if a file is specified, it is accessible to the requesting process. BUILD_MESSAGE copies the following into the message buffer:

   - Items in the item list
   - Function code
   - Procedure value of the AST procedure and address of AST parameter
   - IOSB address
   - Event flag number
   - Access rights block (ARB)

- Process user name (CTL$T_USERNAME) and account name (CTL$T_ACCOUNT)
- Process base priority (PCB$L_PRIB)
- Access mode of system service requestor
- Extended process ID (PCB$L_EPID)
- Process status longword (PCB$L_STS)
- Extended owner process ID (PCB$L_EOWNER)
- Terminal name of the requesting process (PCB$L_TERMINAL)
- System time quadword (EXE$GQ_SYSTIME)
- Image count (PHD$L_IMGCNT)
- Message type, in this case MSG$_SNDJBC

5. EXE$SNDJBC requests the Change to Kernel Mode ($CMKRNL) system service to call one of two procedures in kernel mode:

   - If the $SNDJBC function request is one that is serviced by the job controller, EXE$SNDJBC calls SEND_TO_JOBCTL_KERNEL, in module SYSSNDJBC.
   - Otherwise, it calls EXE$SEND_TO_QMAN_KERNEL, in module SYSSNDJBC.

6. EXE$SNDJBC returns to the system service requestor.

Section 39.1.1.2 describes the manner in which the $SNDJBC system service request completes.

SEND_TO_JOBCTL_KERNEL performs the following steps:

1. It checks and charges the process's AST quota if AST notification is requested. If the AST quota is insufficient, it returns the error status SS$_EXASTLM.
2. After raising interrupt priority level (IPL) to 2, the procedure invokes EXE$COPY_ARB, in module IMPERSONATE, to copy the ARB into the message buffer.
3. It invokes EXE$SENDMSG, in module SYSSNDMSG, which writes the message buffer to the job controller's mailbox, whose address is in SYS$AR_JOBCTLMB.

   Many system services that communicate with system processes invoke EXE$SENDMSG. EXE$SENDMSG verifies that the target mailbox has a process reading messages written to the mailbox. It invokes EXE$WRTMAILBOX, in module MBDRIVER, to perform the I/O operation. Chapter 25 describes the operation of EXE$WRTMAILBOX.
4. SEND_TO_JOBCTL_KERNEL restores IPL to 0.

EXE$SEND_TO_QMAN_KERNEL sends the message to the queue manager rather than to the job controller.

The description of EXE$SEND_TO_QMAN_KERNEL is outside the scope of this book.

39.1.1.2 **$SNDJBC Special Kernel Mode AST.** When a $SNDJBC request completes, the job controller queues a special kernel mode AST to the requesting process. An extended AST control block (ACB) describes the AST. The ACB contains any data requested by the process, plus information about the amount of data to return and where to store the data. The special kernel mode AST routine, EXE$JBCRSP in module SYSSNDJBC_RESPONSE, uses this information to return status and any requested data from the $SNDJBC service to the process. Chapter 8 describes the implementation of special kernel mode ASTs.

EXE$JBCRSP first tests that the process is still executing the image that requested the system service. It compares the process's current PHD$L_IMGCNT against its value at the time of the service request. PHD$L_IMGCNT is incremented at each image rundown, as described in Chapter 28. If the two values are different, the process is executing a different image. Thus, an address from the previous image, such as that of the IOSB, is no longer valid. In this case, EXE$JBCRSP deallocates the extended ACB, returning AST quota to the process if appropriate, and returns.

If the process is still executing the image that requested the system service, EXE$JBCRSP completes the request through the following actions:

1. It stores data in any output buffer items from the original request.
2. It stores a status value in the IOSB if specified.
3. It sets the specified event flag by invoking routine SCH$POSTEF with a null priority class increment (see Chapters 13 and 14).
4. If the user requested AST notification, EXE$JBCRSP invokes the routine SCH$QAST to queue the ACB as a completion AST and returns.
5. If the user did not request AST notification, EXE$JBCRSP deallocates the ACB and returns.

39.1.1.3 **$GETQUI System Service.** The $GETQUI system service obtains information about the queues and jobs initiated and managed by the queue manager. The $GETQUI system service shares common code with the $SNDJBC system service, described in Section 39.1.1.1, and thus performs the same operations. One minor difference is that $GETQUI messages have a message type of MSG$_GETQUI. DCL, in response to commands such as SHOW QUEUE and SHOW ENTRY, requests the $GETQUI service to obtain information for the user.

When the information for a $GETQUI request is ready, the queue manager causes an interprocess communication request completion AST to execute in the context of the requesting process. This AST completes the $GETQUI request in the same manner in which EXE$JBCRSP completes a $SNDJBC request. EXE$JBCRSP's actions are described in Section 39.1.1.2.

39.1.1.4 **$GETQUI Wildcard Support.** A $GETQUI request causes the system service procedure to create a $GETQUI context block (GQC), in which it stores the requestor's context information. The system service procedure maintains a linked list of GQCs in the requestor's process space. If the $GETQUI request specifies wildcard mode, the system service procedure allows the GQC to remain on the linked list; otherwise, it deallocates the GQC when the service completes. A GQC on the linked list describes the process's current $GETQUI wildcard context. The system service procedure locates a process's GQC by an offset containing the requestor process ID (PID). The *Open-VMS System Services Reference Manual* describes wildcard mode and its use.

39.1.2   Operator Communications

The system process OPCOM handles operator communications. OPCOM executes the image OPCOM.EXE, and performs the following functions:

- It selects the terminals used as operator terminals and the class of activity, such as disk or tape operations, for which the operator terminals receive messages.
- It replies to or cancels a user request to an operator.
- It manages the operator log file.

The Send Message to Operator ($SNDOPR) system service sends a request to OPCOM through OPCOM's mailbox. A user requests the $SNDOPR service to request actions normally available through the DCL command REQUEST and the operator command REPLY.

The $SNDOPR system service requires that a user have the OPER privilege to enable a terminal as an operator's terminal, reply to or cancel a user's request, or initialize the operator log file.

The $SNDOPR system service uses the mailbox whose address is in SYS$AR_OPRMBX and the message type MSG$_OPRQST.

Chapter 25 describes the OPCOM mailbox.

39.1.3   Error Logger

As described in Chapter 35, the error logging subsystem contains three pieces:

- The executive contains routines that maintain a set of error message buffers. These routines are called by device drivers and other components that log errors so that error messages can be written to some available space in one of these buffers.
- The error formatting process, process ERRFMT running image ERRFMT. EXE, is awakened to copy the contents of these error message buffers to the error log file for subsequent analysis.
- The Error Log utility reads the error messages in the error log file and produces an error log report, based on the contents of the error log file and the options selected when the utility executes.

A user can request the Send Message to Error Logger ($SNDERR) system service to send messages to the error logger (put messages into error message buffers for later transmission to the error log file). Using this system service requires the BUGCHK privilege.

Unlike the $SNDJBC and $SNDOPR system services, the $SNDERR system service has the following characteristics:

▸ It executes entirely in kernel mode rather than in executive and kernel modes.

▸ It writes a message to an error message buffer rather than sending a mailbox message.

The $SNDERR system service procedure, EXE$SNDERR in module SYS-SNDMSG, performs the following actions:

1. It checks the request for access and privilege violations.
2. It invokes ERL$ALLOCEMB, in module ERRORLOG, to allocate an error message buffer.
3. It fills the message buffer with the message type (EMB$C_SS), the message size, and the message text. An error log sequence number and the current time are also a part of every error message.
4. It invokes ERL$RELEASEMB, also in module ERRORLOG, to release the buffer to the error logging routines for subsequent output to the error log file.

Chapter 35 contains a discussion of the error log routines and a brief description of the ERRFMT process.

39.2   SYSTEM MESSAGE FILE SERVICES

The executive provides three levels of message file capability: image-specific message files, a process-permanent message file, and a system message file.

The creation and declaration of image-specific and process-permanent message files is discussed in the *OpenVMS Command Definition, Librarian, and Message Utilities Manual* and the *OpenVMS DCL Dictionary*. The following list provides a brief overview:

▸ The Message utility compiles a message source file, producing an object file that can be linked with a main program. When the resulting executable image is activated, the image activator maps the image-specific message file, which remains available until image rundown.

▸ In response to the command SET MESSAGE, DCL maps a process-specific message file, available for the life of the process or until the command is reissued specifying a different message file name.

▸ During system initialization SYSINIT loads the system message file, the executive image SYS$MESSAGE:SYSMSG.EXE. Chapter 34 describes SYSINIT's actions.

Two system services allow a user to locate and display messages from the various message files:

▶ The Get Message ($GETMSG) system service searches for a message text corresponding to a given message code.

▶ The Put Message ($PUTMSG) system service writes one or more message texts to SYS$OUTPUT.

The executive uses procedure EXE$EXCMSG, in module EXCEPTMSG, as part of condition handling. EXE$EXCMSG does not use the various message files but formats and displays a process's exception arguments and general registers.

39.2.1 Data Structures Related to Message Files

When it compiles a message file, the Message utility produces an object module that contains a message section header and as many message sections as necessary.

The macro $PLVDEF defines a message section header. The Message utility creates a message section header for the message file and sets its type code to PLV$C_TYP_MSG. At the offset PLV$L_MSGDSP + 6, it stores the binary code corresponding to the VAX instruction JSB (R5). The instruction merely identifies the section header; it is never executed. It exists for compatibility with translated VAX images. The offset to the first message section follows this instruction, then offsets to other message sections, if any. A longword of zero ends the message section offsets.

The $MSCDEF macro defines a message section. The first byte of this structure, MSC$B_TYPE, contains either a 0, indicating a normal message section, or a 1, indicating an indirect message section.

Linking a normal message file, which includes text, with user object modules generates a normal message section within the executable image.

In a normal message section, the field MSC$L_INDEX_OFF contains an offset to an index structure defined by the $MIDXDEF macro, and MSC$L_FAC_OFF is an offset to the table of facility codes.

Rather than incorporate a message file within an executable image, an image can establish a pointer to a nonexecutable message file. The message file can then be changed without recompiling and relinking the image. Compiling an indirect message file with the Message utility produces a pointer object module to link with user modules and a nonexecutable message file that contains the message data.

In an indirect message section, the MSC$B_TYPE field contains a 1. The field MSC$T_INDNAME contains the name of the associated message file, for example, PRGDEVMSG. At run time the $GETMSG system service uses the flag MSC$V_MAPPED to indicate whether the message file has been mapped into virtual memory. The *OpenVMS Command Definition, Librar-*

ian, and Message Utilities Manual describes normal and indirect message files.

Three global symbols locate message section headers:

► CTL$A_DISPVEC locates image-specific message section headers.
► CTL$GL_PPMSG locates process-permanent message section headers.
► EXE$GL_MSGVEC locates system message section headers.

CTL$A_DISPVEC contains the address of a compound data structure called the activated privileged library dispatch vector, offsets to which are defined by the macro $APLDDEF. Chapter 7 describes the structure. APLD$L_MESSAGE_VECTOR in this structure is the base of the dispatch vector, an array of up to 128 message vectors. APLD$L_MESSAGE_COUNT contains the number of valid entries in the dispatch vector. When the image activator activates an image that includes a message section, it loads the next available entry into the dispatch vector with the address of an offset in the message section header.

CTL$GL_PPMSG contains the address of a message section header, or zero if no process-permanent message section is defined.

EXE$GL_MSGVEC contains the address of the system activated privileged library dispatch vector, which is similar to the structure pointed to by CTL$A_DISPVEC.

Figure 39.1 shows how the dispatch vector, message section headers, and message sections are linked.

39.2.2 **$GETMSG System Service**

The $GETMSG system service procedure, EXE$GETMSG in module SYSGETMSG, executes in its requestor's access mode.

It is requested with the following arguments:

► The numeric identification of the desired message, called the message code
► A location in which EXE$GETMSG stores the length of the returned message
► A buffer in which EXE$GETMSG stores the returned message
► A FLAGS argument defining the message components to return
► An optional array containing, among other items, the Formatted ASCII Output ($FAO) argument count for the returned message

EXE$GETMSG searches each message section until it locates one containing a matching message code, at which point its search terminates, or until it processes all message sections. It begins with image-specific message sections, then process-permanent message sections, and finally system message sections.

The following list describes EXE$GETMSG's message search. If a matching message is found at any time, this search terminates.

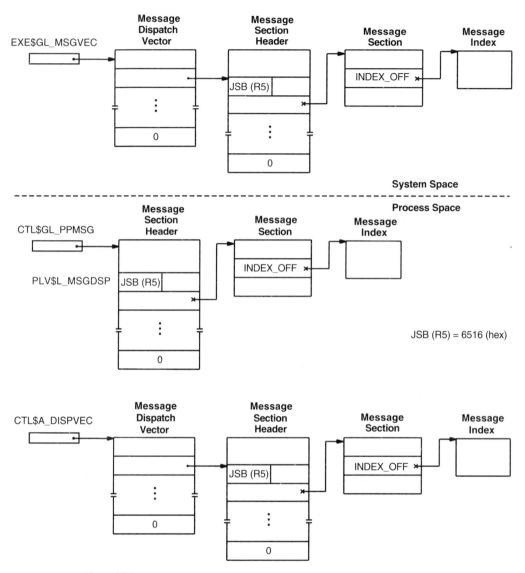

Figure 39.1
Message Dispatch Vector, Section Headers, and Sections

1. From the process's message dispatch vector, whose address is in CTL$A_DISPVEC, EXE$GETMSG obtains the first entry, the address of an image-specific message section header.
2. The message section header contains a list of message sections, and EXE$GETMSG searches each section in order until it either encounters a matching message or processes all sections.

For each normal message section, EXE$GETMSG calculates the starting address and length of the message section index. It then performs a binary search of the message section index to determine if it contains the specified message code.

For an indirect message section, one with the MSC$B_TYPE field containing a 1, EXE$GETMSG tests the flag MSC$V_MAPPED. If the flag is clear, the file is not yet mapped. EXE$GETMSG sets the flag and invokes the image activator to perform a merged activation of the indirect message section.

The image activator maps the nonexecutable image named in the file specification into the user's virtual address space. It adds the address of the new message section header to the end of the message dispatch vector; thus, all sections located by the message section header are processed later in the search. The search for the message code continues normally.

3. If no matching message is encountered, EXE$GETMSG locates the next image-specific message section header from the next entry in the process's message dispatch vector and searches its message sections as in step 2.

4. When all image-specific message section headers in the message dispatch vector have been processed and the search has not been successful, EXE$GETMSG proceeds to the process-permanent message section header. If one exists, CTL$GL_PPMSG contains its address; otherwise, CTL$GL_PPMSG contains zero.

5. EXE$GETMSG searches each process-permanent message section located by the message section header until it finds a matching message or has no more process-permanent message sections.

6. If the search is not successful, EXE$GETMSG proceeds to the system message dispatch vector, pointed to by EXE$GL_MSGVEC. Each entry in the system message dispatch vector points to a message section header.

7. EXE$GETMSG searches each system message section located by the message section header until it finds a matching message or has no more system message sections. EXE$GETMSG gets each successive entry in the system message dispatch vector and performs the same search until there are no more entries.

8. If no message section exists or no matching message code is found, the service returns the status SS$_MSGNOTFND and a message declaring that the message file does not contain the desired code.

Otherwise, if it discovers a matching message code, EXE$GETMSG copies selected information into the user-defined buffer.

- If the FLAGS argument is not specified, EXE$GETMSG uses the process default message flags (CTL$GB_MSGMASK) to select the information.
- If the combine bit is set in the FLAGS argument (bit 4), EXE$GETMSG returns only the information selected by both the FLAGS argument and by CTL$GB_MSGMASK.

• Otherwise, EXE$GETMSG returns the information selected by the FLAGS argument.

9. EXE$GETMSG returns to the system service requestor.

39.2.3 $PUTMSG System Service

The $PUTMSG system service provides the ability to write one or more error messages to SYS$ERROR (and SYS$OUTPUT if it is different from SYS$ERROR). It executes in the access mode of its requestor and requests the $GETMSG system service to retrieve the associated text for a particular message code.

The $PUTMSG system service is requested with the following four arguments:

▶ A message argument vector describing the messages in terms of message codes, message field selection flag bits, and $FAO arguments (see Section 39.4.2).

▶ Procedure value of an optional action routine to call before writing the message texts.

▶ An optional facility name to associate with the first message written. If not specified, the $PUTMSG system service uses the default facility name associated with the message.

▶ An optional parameter to pass to the requestor's action routine. If not specified, it defaults to zero.

The *OpenVMS System Services Reference Manual* discusses the construction of the message argument vector. The *OpenVMS RTL Library (LIB$) Manual* describes other uses of the $PUTMSG service.

The $PUTMSG system service procedure, EXE$PUTMSG in module SYS-PUTMSG, processes each argument of the message argument vector as follows:

1. It determines whether the facility code of the request is a system, Record Management Services (RMS), or standard facility code. Standard facility codes can require $FAO arguments. System messages (facility code 0) and RMS messages (facility code 1) do not use associated $FAO arguments in the message argument vector. System exception messages require $FAO arguments to follow immediately after the message identification in the message vector.

2. It requests the $GETMSG system service with the message code and field selections based upon the selection bits and $FAO arguments.

3. If the message flags indicate at least one $FAO argument, EXE$PUTMSG requests the $FAOL system service (see Section 39.4.2) to assemble all the portions of the message (supplied facility code, optionally specified delimiters, output from $GETMSG).

4. EXE$PUTMSG calls the user's action routine, if one was specified.

5. If the action routine returns an error status, EXE$PUTMSG does not write the message. Otherwise, it uses an RMS $PUT request to write the formatted message to SYS$OUTPUT, if it is informational, or to SYS$ERROR, if it is an error. In the latter case, it also writes the formatted error message to SYS$OUTPUT if SYS$ERROR is different from SYS$OUTPUT.

When all the arguments in the message argument vector have been processed, the $PUTMSG system service returns to its requestor.

39.2.4 Procedure EXE$EXCMSG

The catch-all condition handler calls EXE$EXCMSG, in module EXCEPT-MSG, to report a condition that has not been properly handled by any condition handlers further up the call chain. EXE$EXCEPTION also calls EXE$EXCMSG to write the contents of the general registers to SYS$OUTPUT if a condition is not handled in any other way. Chapter 6 contains information on condition handling.

EXE$EXCMSG requires two input arguments: the address of an ASCII string, and the address of a VAX-style argument list with two arguments, the addresses of the signal array and the mechanism array.

The procedure writes a formatted dump of the integer registers, signal array, and stack, as well as the caller's message text, to SYS$OUTPUT (and to SYS$ERROR if different from SYS$OUTPUT). Chapter 6 contains a sample message printed by EXE$EXCMSG. This message appears for all fatal errors that occur in images that were linked without the traceback handler. Note that most images shipped with the operating system are linked without the traceback handler.

Although it is not documented as a system service, EXE$EXCMSG has an associated system service transfer routine.

39.3 SYSTEM INFORMATION SYSTEM SERVICES

The Get System Information ($GETSYI) system service provides selected information about the running system or about a target node in the VMScluster system. Although the operating system provides synchronous and asynchronous forms of the service, both forms complete synchronously. Currently, the only information available about other VMScluster nodes is the information that already resides in the nonpaged pool data structures on the local system.

$GETSYI arguments include the following:

▶ An event flag to set when the request completes
▶ The address of the cluster system identification (CSID) of the target system
▶ The node name of the target system
▶ The address of an item list that includes (for each requested item) the type

of information to return (item code), the size and address of a buffer to hold the information, and a location to receive the actual size of the returned information

▶ The address of an IOSB to receive the final request status

▶ The procedure value and parameter for an AST procedure to call when the request completes

39.3.1 Operation of the $GETSYI System Service

The $GETSYI system service procedure, EXE$GETSYI in module SYSGET-SYI, executes in kernel mode and performs the following actions:

1. It invokes its local routine NAMCSID to validate the node name/CSID pair. NAMCSID tests CLU$GL_CLUB to determine whether the running system is a VMScluster node.

   • If the system is a VMScluster node, NAMCSID (after resolving a wild-card reference) invokes another local routine, EXE$NAMCSID, to obtain the address of the cluster system block (CSB) specified by CSID or node name. EXE$NAMCSID returns the address of the CSB or, if no CSB is located, the error status SS$_NOSUCHNODE. EXE$GETSYI returns this status to its requestor.

   • If the system is not a VMScluster node and the user specified a CSID, NAMCSID returns the error SS$_NOMORENODE, which EXE$GET-SYI returns as system service status.

   • If the system is not a VMScluster node and the user specified a node name, NAMCSID checks that the node name is that of the running system. If it is, NAMCSID returns successfully with the address of the system block (SB). If the node name is not that of the running system, NAMCSID returns the error status SS$_NOSUCHNODE, which EXE$GETSYI returns as system service status.

2. If an IOSB is specified, EXE$GETSYI checks it for write access and clears it.

3. It clears the event flag.

4. If AST notification is requested, EXE$GETSYI checks that the process has sufficient AST quota and charges the quota.

5. EXE$GETSYI checks each item in the list for the following conditions:

   • The buffer descriptor is readable and the buffer writable.

   • The requested item is a recognized one.

6. If these conditions are met, EXE$GETSYI retrieves the requested information and copies it to the user-defined buffer. All available information can be obtained immediately in the context of the requesting process. If the target is not the local system, EXE$GETSYI only returns information contained in the CSB or SB for that target. For the local system,

EXE$GETSYI obtains additional information from various system global locations.

7. When no information remains to be gathered, the system service returns to its requestor after performing the following actions:

    a. Setting the specified event flag

    b. Queuing requested AST notification to the process

    c. Writing status information to an IOSB, if one was specified

39.3.2 $GETSYI Wildcard Support

The $GETSYI system service provides the ability to obtain information about all nodes in a VMScluster system, that is, to perform a wildcard search of the cluster vector table. The cluster vector table is a table of CSB addresses, indexed by the low word of the CSID. The global location CLU$GL_CLUSVEC contains its address.

A negative CSID argument to the $GETSYI system service indicates a wildcard request. EXE$GETSYI recognizes a wildcard request and passes information back to the requestor about the first system described in the cluster vector table.

In addition, it alters the cluster system identification field of the requestor's CSID argument to contain the target system's node index. When the service requestor requests $GETSYI again, the negative sequence number (in the high-order word of the CSID) indicates that a wildcard operation is in progress. The positive node index (in the low-order word of the CSID) indicates the cluster vector table offset where the search resumes. Note that the user program will not work correctly if it alters the value of the CSID argument between requests to $GETSYI.

The user program repeatedly requests the $GETSYI system service until it receives the status SS$_NOMORENODE, indicating that the cluster vector table has been completely searched.

39.4   FORMATTING SUPPORT

This section describes services that support time format conversion and formatted ASCII output.

39.4.1   Time Conversion Services

Module SYSCVRTIM contains the time conversion system services. The Convert Binary Time to Numeric Time ($NUMTIM) system service executes in executive mode and converts a binary quadword time value in system time format (described in Chapter 12) into the following seven numerical word-length fields: year, month, day, hour, minute, second, and hundredths of seconds.

The $NUMTIM system service converts a positive time argument into the corresponding absolute system time. It interprets a negative time argument as a delta time, the current system time plus a time interval. A zero-valued time argument requests the conversion of the current system time.

The Convert Binary Time to ASCII String ($ASCTIM) system service executes in the access mode of its requestor. It converts a system time format quadword into an ASCII character string. It passes the input binary time argument to the $NUMTIM system service and converts the seven fields returned into ASCII character fields. The input time format (absolute or delta) and the conversion flag determine the field selection. The conversion flag can be set to request conversion of day and time or only the time portion.

The $ASCTIM system service uses the $FAO system service (described in Section 39.4.2) to concatenate and format the string components before returning the string to the requestor.

The Convert ASCII String to Binary Time ($BINTIM) system service executes in the access mode of its requestor. It converts an ASCII time string into a quadword absolute or delta time. If the input string expresses an absolute time, the service requests the $NUMTIM system service to convert the current system time to supply any fields omitted in the ASCII string. The $BINTIM system service converts each ASCII field to numerical values and stores the values in the seven-word $NUMTIM format. It then combines the seven word fields into a binary quadword value. It negates the resulting value if the ASCII string specifies a delta time.

39.4.2   Formatted ASCII Output System Services

The $FAO and $FAOL system services format and convert binary and ASCII input parameters into a single ASCII output string. The two system services, in module SYSFAO, execute in the access mode of the requestor and use common code. The only difference between them is whether the parameters are passed individually ($FAO) or as the address of the first parameter in a list ($FAOL).

The common routine, FAO, parses the control string character by character. It copies information not preceded by the control character ! into the output string without further action. When it encounters a control character and operation code in the control string, it executes the appropriate conversion routine to process zero, one, or two of the system service input parameters. When the control string is completely and correctly parsed, the service returns to the requestor with a normal status code. It returns a buffer overflow error if the output string length is exceeded.

The *OpenVMS System Services Reference Manual* describes the proper manner in which to specify $FAO requests.

39.5   ALIGNMENT TRAP REPORTING SERVICES

An Alpha AXP processor provides fastest access to naturally aligned data. To be naturally aligned, a longword datum must be on a longword boundary and a quadword datum must be on a quadword boundary. When an attempt is made to load or store a quadword or longword to or from a memory location that does not have a naturally aligned address, the processor transfers control to privileged architecture library code (PALcode). PALcode executes a series of instructions that perform the desired access.

Performing unaligned access is significantly slower than performing aligned access. To assist software writers in detecting unaligned data access, the OpenVMS AXP system provides a number of system services, outlined in the following sections. The executive supports these system services through the alignment trap exception processing mechanism, described in Section 39.5.3.

The executive provides two sets of services for alignment trap reporting: systemwide alignment trap reporting services and user mode alignment trap reporting services. Systemwide alignment trap reporting services can be used to collect information about all alignment traps occurring on the system, regardless of mode, IPL, or current process. User mode alignment trap reporting services can be used to detect alignment traps occurring within a single process. Information can be collected about each detected alignment trap, or the trap can be reported as an SS$_ALIGN exception to the process.

Alignment traps in operating system code or in privileged application software can occur in any mode, typically with the trap virtual address (VA), trap program counter (PC), or both, in system space. Using the systemwide alignment trap reporting services outlined in Section 39.5.2, a process with the CMKRNL privilege can collect information about some or all data alignment traps occurring on the system. The requesting process can restrict the types of alignment traps for which information is collected by specifying a match table when it initiates systemwide alignment trap reporting. When systemwide alignment trap reporting is enabled, data is recorded about each alignment trap on the system that matches the criteria specified in the match table.

Alignment traps in nonprivileged application software occur in user mode, usually with the trap PC and trap VA both in process-private space. A user can use the Performance Coverage Analyzer (PCA) utility or the debugger command SET BREAK/UNALIGNED_DATA to detect these traps. Alternatively, if these methods are inadequate, the user can write a program requesting the user mode alignment trap reporting services outlined in Section 39.5.1. A sample program is shown in the *OpenVMS System Services Reference Manual*.

When process-specific reporting is enabled, all user mode traps with the trap PC or trap VA in process-private space are reported for every image that a process runs. When image-specific reporting is enabled, all user mode traps with the trap PC or trap VA in process-private space are reported for the specific image that requested image-specific reporting.

When enabling image-specific reporting, the system service requestor can choose one of two methods of reporting: exception or buffered. In the exception method, the executive generates an SS$_ALIGN exception for each user mode trap that occurs when executing in or accessing process space. In the buffered method, the executive records the trap PC and trap VA in an associated user alignment trap reporting buffer. Image-specific alignment trap reporting is disabled during image rundown.

For process-specific reporting, the executive uses only the exception method. Once enabled, process-specific alignment trap reporting remains enabled until it is explicitly disabled or the process is deleted. When both image- and process-specific reporting are enabled, the executive chooses the buffered method of reporting over the exception method, if buffered reporting was requested.

Central to the executive's ability to report alignment traps is the data alignment trap (DAT) bit in each process's hardware privileged context block (HWPCB). After PALcode has performed an unaligned data access, it examines the DAT bit of the current HWPCB. If the bit is clear, PALcode generates an alignment trap. Otherwise, it resumes normal processing at the instruction following the one that accessed unaligned data. The executive executes the privileged PALcode instruction CALL_PAL MTPR_DATFX to initialize the DAT bit. By default the DAT bit is set, disabling data alignment traps.

When a request is made to enable image- or process-specific alignment trap reporting, the executive sets, among other bits, the AFR$V_ENABLED bit of the P1 space location CTL$GL_REPORT_USER_FAULTS. The executive also clears the DAT bit of the requesting process. When a request is made to enable systemwide alignment trap reporting, the executive sets, among other bits, the AFR$V_ENABLED bit of global location EXE$GL_REPORT_SYS_FAULTS. The executive also clears the DAT bit of the requesting process.

Table 39.1 explains the meaning of each bit in CTL$GL_REPORT_USER_FAULTS and EXE$GL_REPORT_SYS_FAULTS. The function of the low (AFR$V_ENABLED) bit in each of these longwords is to allow reporting to be temporarily disabled. Image-specific and systemwide reporting must be temporarily disabled when there is no more room in the associated buffer. User mode alignment trap reporting must be temporarily disabled when the debugger is active. The debugger requests the undocumented Toggle Alignment Fault Reporting ($TOGGLE_ALIGN_FAULT_REPORT) system service for this purpose.

To support systemwide alignment trap reporting, the executive must clear the DAT bit for every process on the system. The quantum-end processing routine, SCH$QEND in module RSE, which executes whenever a current process reaches quantum end, does this. When the low bit of EXE$GL_REPORT_SYS_FAULTS is set, SCH$QEND clears the current process's DAT bit.

Table 39.1   Bits in CTL$GL_REPORT_USER_FAULTS and
EXE$GL_REPORT_SYS_FAULTS

Bit	*Meaning if Set*
CTL$GL_REPORT_USER_FAULTS BITS	
AFR$V_ENABLED	Enable user alignment trap reporting
AFR$V_TEMP_ENABLED	Report image-specific alignment traps
AFR$V_PERM_ENABLED	Report process-specific alignment traps
EXE$GL_REPORT_SYS_FAULTS BITS	
AFR$V_ENABLED	Enable systemwide alignment trap reporting
AFR$V_TEMP_ENABLED	Report systemwide alignment traps
AFR$V_USER_INFO	Record user name and image name of current process, if valid

39.5.1   User Mode Alignment Trap Reporting

An image can request one of the following system services for user mode alignment trap reporting:

▸ The Start Alignment Fault Reporting ($START_ALIGN_FAULT_REPORT) system service, which enables image-specific reporting

▸ The Stop Alignment Fault Reporting ($STOP_ALIGN_FAULT_REPORT) system service, which disables image-specific reporting

▸ The Get Alignment Fault Data ($GET_ALIGN_FAULT_DATA) system service, which gets the alignment trap data buffer

▸ The Report Alignment Fault ($PERM_REPORT_ALIGN_FAULT) system service, which enables process-specific reporting

▸ The Disable Alignment Fault Reporting ($PERM_DIS_ALIGN_FAULT_ REPORT) system service, which disables process-specific reporting

(Originally, an unaligned data access was reported as a fault rather than as a trap. The names of the system services reflect the original design.)

The *OpenVMS System Services Reference Manual* describes the use and arguments of these system services. A full description of each system service procedure is outside the scope of this book. The following description of the $START_ALIGN_FAULT_REPORT system service procedure is provided as an example of the steps involved.

EXE$START_ALIGN_FAULT_REPORT, the system service procedure, executes in kernel mode and takes the following steps:

1. If image-specific alignment trap reporting is already enabled, it returns the error status SS$_AFR_ENABLED.

2. If any of its arguments is invalid, it returns the error status SS$_BAD-PARAM.

3. If the specified reporting buffer is not quadword-aligned, it returns the error status SS$_ALIGN. If the buffer is inaccessible in the requestor's access mode, it returns the error status SS$_ACCVIO. Otherwise, EXE$START_ALIGN_FAULT_REPORT initializes the buffer and records its address in CTL$GL_REPORT_BUFFER.

4. It records the reporting method in CTL$GL_REPORT_METHOD.

5. If processwide alignment trap reporting has not been enabled, it executes the instruction CALL_PAL MTPR_DATFX to initialize the process's DAT bit in the HWPCB.

6. It sets the AFR$V_ENABLED and AFR$V_TEMP_ENABLED bits in CTL$GL_REPORT_USER_FAULTS.

7. It returns to the system service requestor.

39.5.2   **Systemwide Alignment Trap Reporting**

An image can request one of the following services for systemwide alignment trap reporting:

▶ The Start System Alignment Fault Reporting ($INIT_SYS_ALIGN_FAULT_REPORT) system service, which enables systemwide alignment trap reporting

▶ The Stop System Alignment Fault Reporting ($STOP_SYS_ALIGN_FAULT_REPORT) system service, which disables systemwide alignment trap reporting

▶ The Get System Alignment Fault Data ($GET_SYS_ALIGN_FAULT_DATA) system service, which gets the system alignment trap data

The *OpenVMS System Services Reference Manual* describes the use and arguments of these services. They are intended for use by a privileged process to collect systemwide alignment trap data.

The steps involved in systemwide alignment trap reporting are similar to the ones in image-specific alignment trap reporting, with the following exceptions:

▶ A process that requests systemwide reporting must have the CMKRNL privilege.

▶ An argument to the $INIT_SYS_ALIGN_FAULT_REPORT system service is a match table, which is used by the alignment trap exception service routine to determine whether to report a trap. The match table, which is allocated out of nonpaged pool, is an array of longwords, with the first longword containing a count of entries in the table. Each entry in the match table is a bit mask that indicates a specific type of alignment trap, for example, kernel mode trap with the PC in system space, or executive mode trap with the VA in P0 space. The form of a match table entry is shown in Figure 39.2. Section 39.5.3 describes how this table is used.

▶ In the buffered method, the buffer for image-specific reporting is in P0

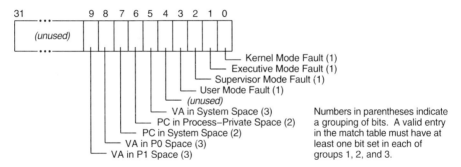

Figure 39.2
Match Table Entry

space, whereas the buffer for systemwide reporting is allocated from non-paged pool.

▶ To ensure that the nonpaged pool allocated for the match table and the alignment trap reporting buffer is deallocated even if the image requesting the $INIT_SYS_ALIGN_FAULT_REPORT system service terminates abnormally, the system service procedure establishes an image rundown handler, SHUTDOWN_SYS_ALIGN_FAULT_REPORT, in module ALIGN_SERV, by calling IMG$ADD_PRIVILEGED_VECTOR_ENTRY, in module IMGMAPISD.

39.5.3   Alignment Trap Exception Processing

After PALcode has performed an unaligned data access, it examines the DAT bit in the HWPCB. If the bit is clear, PALcode generates an alignment trap. EXE$REPORT_ALIGN_FAULT, in module ALIGN, handles this trap. Executing in the access mode of the exception, it performs the following steps:

1. It builds a bit mask whose form is similar to that of a match table entry (see Figure 39.2), based on the PC, the VA of the unaligned data, and the mode in which the unaligned access occurred.

2. If system trap reporting is disabled, EXE$REPORT_ALIGN_FAULT proceeds to step 3. Otherwise, it saves the trap data by requesting the $SAVE_SYS_ALIGN_FAULT_DATA system service. If the exception occurred in kernel mode, EXE$REPORT_ALIGN_FAULT calls EXE$SAVE_SYS_ALIGN_FAULT_DATA, the system service procedure, directly rather than through the system service dispatcher.

   EXE$SAVE_SYS_ALIGN_FAULT_DATA compares the bit mask to each entry in the match table. If no match is found, it simply returns. If a match is found, the procedure allocates an entry in the system trap reporting buffer and fills that entry with the trap information: the PC, the VA, and if requested and accessible, the user name and the image name of the associated process. If the system HWPCB is current, or if the IPL is above 0, the user name and image name are considered inaccessible. EXE$SAVE_SYS_ALIGN_FAULT_DATA temporarily disables system trap reporting if there is no more space in the system trap reporting buffer. When the $GET_SYS_ALIGN_FAULT_DATA system service is next requested, system alignment trap reporting is reenabled.

3. If the exception PC and VA are not both in process-private space, or if the exception mode is not user, EXE$REPORT_ALIGN_FAULT dismisses the exception. Otherwise, if image-specific or process-specific reporting is enabled, the procedure examines CTL$GL_REPORT_METHOD to determine the reporting method:

- If an exception is to be reported, EXE$REPORT_ALIGN_FAULT invokes EXE$ALIGN, in module EXCEPTION, to report the SS$_ALIGN exception, as described in Chapter 6.
- If information about the unaligned data is to be buffered instead, EXE$REPORT_ALIGN_FAULT requests the $SAVE_ALIGN_FAULT_DATA system service.

    EXE$SAVE_ALIGN_FAULT_DATA, the $SAVE_ALIGN_FAULT_DATA system service procedure, allocates an entry in the process-private trap reporting buffer and fills that entry with the trap information: the trap PC and VA. EXE$SAVE_ALIGN_FAULT_DATA disables process-specific reporting if there is no more room in the process-private trap reporting buffer.

4. EXE$REPORT_ALIGN_FAULT dismisses the alignment trap.

Note that it is possible for an alignment trap to be reported both as a systemwide trap and as a process- or image-specific trap.

When the system trap reporting buffer is created, it is initialized as a doubly linked list of entries, each of which has the layout shown in Figure 39.3. The CALL_PAL INSQHIL and CALL_PAL REMQTIL instructions are used to insert and remove entries from the list. Such synchronization is needed because EXE$REPORT_ALIGN_FAULT can allocate entries from any access mode and any IPL while running concurrently on one or more processors in a symmetric multiprocessing system.

39.6 CONSOLE ENVIRONMENT VARIABLE ACCESS SERVICES

Two undocumented system services, the Get Environment Variable ($GETENV) system service and the Set Environment Variable ($SETENV) system service, allow read and write access to console environment variables through an appropriate console callback routine. Console environment variables and console callback routines are described in Chapter 33. The undocumented DCL lexical function F$GETENV can be used to retrieve the value of a console environment variable. Use of either system service and the lexical function F$GETENV is reserved to Digital; any other use is unsupported.

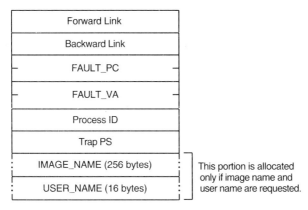

Figure 39.3
Layout of System Trap Reporting Buffer Entry

Each system service takes a single argument, the address of a standard item list. Each item in the list specifies the name of an environment variable and a buffer for the environment variable's value. The STARLET macro $ST-ENVDEF defines offsets into the item list and code names for the environment variables. Each system service probes for accessibility of the item list in the requestor's access mode before performing other actions and can return either of the following error statuses:

▸ SS$_BADPARAM if the item list is unspecified or has an incorrect form
▸ SS$_ACCVIO if the item list or a specified buffer is inaccessible in the requestor's access mode

EXE$GETENV, in module GETENV_ROUTINES, is the $GETENV system service procedure. It runs in kernel mode and performs the following steps:

1. It calls SCH$REQUIRE_CAPABILITY, in module CAPABILITY, to acquire affinity to the primary CPU. Chapter 13 describes process affinity.
2. EXE$GETENV gets the value of each environment variable specified in the request by invoking the get-environment-variable console callback routine, which it locates through the hardware restart parameter block (HWRPB). Chapter 33 describes the HWRPB.
3. It calls SCH$RELEASE_CAPABILITY, in module CAPABILITY, to release affinity to the primary CPU.
4. It returns to the system service requestor.

EXE$SETENV, in module SETENV_ROUTINES, is the $SETENV system service procedure. Currently, it allows a requestor to update only the BOOT_OSFLAGS environment variable. This system service is functional only for certain platforms, for example, the DEC 7000 AXP and the DEC 10000 AXP systems, in OpenVMS AXP Version 1.5.

39.7   **RELEVANT SOURCE MODULES**

Source modules described in this chapter include

[LIB]APLDDEF.SDL
[LIB]PLVDEF.SDL
[STARLET]MSGSTRUCT.SDL
[SYS]ALIGN.M64
[SYS]ALIGN_SERV.B32
[SYS]ALIGN_FAULT_INIT.MAR
[SYS]ENV_ROUTINES.B64
[SYS]ERRORLOG.MAR
[SYS]EXCEPTMSG.MAR
[SYS]GETENV_ROUTINES.B64
[SYS]IOSUBNPAG.MAR
[SYS]IOSUBPAGD.MAR
[SYS]SYSCVRTIM.MAR
[SYS]SYSFAO.MAR
[SYS]SYSGETDVI.MAR
[SYS]SYSGETMSG.MAR
[SYS]SYSGETSYI.MAR
[SYS]SYSPUTMSG.MAR
[SYS]SYSSNDJBC.B32
[SYS]SYSSNDMSG.MAR
[SYSLOA]BOOTFLAG_ROUTINES.B64

PART X / Appendixes

A   System Processes and Privileged Images

Table A.1   System Processes

Image Name	Linked /SYSEXE	Description
AUDIT_SERVER.EXE	Yes	Security audit server process (AUDIT_SERVER)
CONFIGURE.EXE	Yes	VMScluster device configuration process (CONFIGURE)
CSP.EXE	Yes	VMScluster server process (CLUSTER_SERVER)[1]
ERRFMT.EXE	Yes	Error logger format process (ERRFMT)
EVL.EXE	No	Network event logger (EVL)
F11CACP.EXE	Yes	Files-11 ancillary control process (ACP) for compact disk read-only memory (CD-ROM)[2]
F11DACP.EXE	Yes	Files-11 ACP for CD-ROM in High Sierra on-disk format[2]
FILESERV.EXE	Yes	VMScluster Files-11 XQP cache server process (CACHE_SERVER)[1]
IPCACP.EXE	Yes	Interprocess communication ACP (IPCACP)
JBC$JOB_CONTROL.EXE	Yes	Job controller (JOB_CONTROL)
LATACP.EXE	Yes	Local area transport ACP (LATACP)
MTAAACP.EXE	Yes	Magnetic tape ACP[2]
NETACP.EXE	Yes	Network ACP (NETACP)
OPCOM.EXE	Yes	Operator communication facility (OPCOM)
PRTSMB.EXE	No	Print symbiont (SYMBIONT_n)
QMAN$QUEUE_MANAGER.EXE	Yes	Queue manager (QUEUE_MANAGER)
REMACP.EXE	Yes	Remote terminal ACP (REMACP)
SHADOW_SERVER.EXE	Yes	Host-based shadowing copy and merge support (SHADOW_SERVER)
SMISERVER.EXE	Yes	System management utility process (SMISERVER)
TPSERV.EXE	Yes	DECdtm services process (TP_SERVER)

[1] This process runs only on a system that is a VMScluster node.
[2] The name of this process is a function of the device name and unit number of the associated mounted volume.

Table A.2   Images Installed with Privilege on a Standard OpenVMS System

Image Name	Linked /SYSEXE	Description
ANALIMDMP.EXE	Yes	Image Dump Analyzer utility
AUTHORIZE.EXE [1]	Yes	Authorize utility
CDU.EXE	Yes	Command Definition utility
INSTALL.EXE	Yes	Known Image Installation utility
LOGINOUT.EXE	Yes	Login/logout image
LTPAD.EXE	No	Local area transport terminal emulation
MAIL_SERVER.EXE	No	Network Mail utility server
PHONE.EXE	No	Phone utility
REQUEST.EXE	No	Operator request facility
RTPAD.EXE [1]	No	Remote Terminal utility
SET.EXE [1]	Yes	SET command processor
SETAUDIT.EXE [1]	Yes	SET AUDIT command processor
SETP0.EXE	Yes	SET command processor
SETRIGHTS.EXE	No	SET RIGHTS_LIST command processor
SHOW.EXE [1]	Yes	SHOW command processor
SHWCLSTR.EXE	Yes	SHOW CLUSTER command processor
SUBMIT.EXE	No	Batch and print job submission facility
SYSMAN.EXE [1]	Yes	System management facility command interface
VPM.EXE	Yes	Remote performance data collector server

[1] Although this image is installed with privilege, successful use may require additional privileges of the user.

Table A.3   Images Requiring Privilege That Are Typically Not Installed

Image Name	Linked /SYSEXE	Description
CIA.EXE	Yes	Show Intrusion utility
INSTALL.EXE	Yes	Install Image utility
LATCP.EXE	Yes	Local area transport control program
MAIL.EXE	No	Mail utility
NCP.EXE	No	Network control program
OPCCRASH.EXE	Yes	System shutdown facility
QUEMAN.EXE	Yes	Queue manipulation command processor
REPLY.EXE	No	OPCOM message-handling facility
RUNDET.EXE	No	RUN [process] command processor
SDA.EXE	Yes	System Dump Analyzer utility
SETSHOACL.EXE	No	SET and SHOW ACL command processor
SETUSR.EXE	Yes	SET UIC command processor
SMPUTIL.EXE	Yes	Multiprocessing utility
STOPREM.EXE	Yes	Stop REMACP Process utility
SYSGEN.EXE	Yes	System Generation and Configuration utility

Table A.4   Images Whose Operations Are Protected by User Identification Code or Volume Ownership

Image Name	Linked /SYSEXE	Description
AUTHORIZE.EXE	Yes	Authorize utility
BACKUP.EXE	Yes	Backup utility
BADBLOCK.EXE	Yes	Bad block locator
DISKQUOTA.EXE	Yes	Disk Quota utility
DISMOUNT.EXE	No	Volume Dismount utility
ERF*.EXE	No	Error Log Formatting utility and CPU-specific extensions
INIT.EXE	No	Volume Initialization utility
VERIFY.EXE	No	File Structure Verification utility
VMOUNT.EXE	No	Volume Mount utility

Table A.5   Miscellaneous Other Images Linked /SYSEXE

Image Name [1]	Description
AGEN$FEEDBACK.EXE	AUTOGEN feedback data reader
ANALIMDMP.EXE	ANALYZE/PROCESS_DUMP command processor
ANALIMDMPSHR.EXE	ANALYZE/PROCESS_DUMP shareable image
ANALYZOBJ.EXE	Analyze Object Module utility
DEBUG.EXE	Debugger utility
DECW$TRANSPORT_ LAT.EXE	DECwindows local area transport privileged shareable image
DECW$DWT_ DECNET.EXE	DECwindows terminal DECnet access image
DECW$DWT_ STARTXTDRIVER.EXE	DECwindows terminal support enviroment
DECW$DWT_FONT_ DAEMON.EXE	DECwindows terminal font support
DCL.EXE	Digital command language interpreter
DELTA.EXE	Executive debugger
DISMNTSHR.EXE	Dismount system service privileged shareable image
DISMOUNT.EXE	Dismount command processor
DTI$SHARE.EXE	DECdtm system services privileged shareable image
DUMP.EXE	File Dump utility
ESS$LADCP	Local area disk control program
ESS$LASTCP	Local area system transport control program
HSCPAD.EXE	SET HOST/DUP command processor
IMGDMP.EXE	Write Image Dump utility shareable image
INIT$SHR.EXE	Volume Initialization utility privileged shareable image
IOGEN$*.EXE	IOGEN shareable images
LMCP.EXE	DECdtm transaction log manager control program
MAILSHR.EXE	Callable Mail utility shareable image
MAILSHRP.EXE	Callable Mail utility privileged shareable image
MOM.EXE	Network management maintenance operations image
MOUNTSHR.EXE	Mount system service privileged shareable image
MSCP.EXE	Mass Storage Control Protocol server
NISCS_LAA.EXE	Local area VMScluster system downline load assist agent
NISCS_LOAD.EXE	Local area VMScluster downline load secondary bootstrap
PTD$SERVICES_ SHR.EXE	Pseudo terminal system services privileged shareable image
RECOVER.EXE	RECOVER/RMS_FILE command processor
SECURESHR.EXE	Security system services shareable image
SECURESHRP.EXE	Security system services privileged shareable image
SERVER_STAT.EXE	Audit server statistics display utility
SMBSRVSHR.EXE	Print symbiont shareable image
SMISHR.EXE	SYSMAN privileged shareable image
SMIOBJSHR.EXE	SYSMAN privileged shareable image

Table A.5   Miscellaneous Other Images Linked /SYSEXE *(continued)*

Image Name [1]	Description
SPISHR.EXE	Get System Performance Information system service (undocumented) privileged shareable image; used by MONITOR
SYS$ICBM_*.EXE	IOGEN shareable images
TFFSHR.EXE	Terminal fallback facility shareable image
TFU.EXE	Terminal fallback utility
TIE$SHARE.EXE	Translated image environment shareable image
TRACE.EXE	Traceback shareable image

[1] Executive images are also linked /SYSEXE but are not listed in this table. They are described in Chapter 32.

B   Use of Listing and Map Files

This book presents a detailed overview of the OpenVMS executive. The ultimate authority on how the executive or any other component of the system works, however, is the source code for that component. This appendix shows how you can use the listing and map files produced by the language processors and the linker with other tools to investigate further how a given component works. The appendix assumes that you are familiar with the AXP instruction set, the MACRO-32 compiler, and the linker.

B.1   READING THE EXECUTIVE LISTINGS

Digital provides listing kits on compact disk read-only memory (CD-ROM) to customers who purchase and sign a source license agreement. The listing kit includes listings and maps for most components but excludes certain proprietary modules, such as the License Management Facility. The listings also include a few source files:

- Macro and constant definition files written in MACRO-32, MACRO-64, BLISS-32, and BLISS-64
- Command definition language (CLD) files
- Structure definition language (SDL) files

Most modules described in this book are written in MACRO-32 and BLISS-32. Some are also written in MACRO-64 assembler and BLISS-64. This appendix provides some tips on how to read and use these modules for system programming and debugging purposes.

B.1.1   OpenVMS Listing Structure

A directory structure divides and organizes the more than 4,800 OpenVMS modules into more than 150 facilities. A facility consists of related modules and has a directory. Examples of facility directories include [SYS], [RMS], [JOBCTL], [DCL], and [COPY]. Each directory consists of a set of subdirectories, most of which are used only when an OpenVMS system is built from source.

The system build procedure places the listing and map files into the appropriate [*facility*.LIS] subdirectory of the result disk volume. The result disk is often referenced by a logical name such as RESD. The listing kit contains a subset of files from the result disk.

B.1.1.1   Online Listing Structure. The build procedures that assemble, compile, and link the OpenVMS source modules produce the listing and map files found

on the listing CD-ROM. Starting with OpenVMS AXP Version 1.5, the listing CD-ROM has a volume label of the form OVMSAXPLS*vn*, where *v* is the OpenVMS AXP version number and *n* is the volume number. For example, the OpenVMS AXP Version 1.5 CD-ROM listing kit contains two compact disks labeled OVMSAXPLS151 and OVMSAXPLS152. Each compact disk has two top-level directories: [V*v*] and [V*v*_DECW]. For example, the OpenVMS AXP Version 1.5 CD-ROM listing kit has [V15], which contains the Open-VMS source listings, and [V15_DECW], which contains the DECwindows source listings.

The second volume of the listing kit contains listings for facilities that did not fit into the first volume. This means that if you intend to search all the facilities in the listing kit, you must make sure that your search procedure will span both volumes. The examples in this appendix assume that all facilities reside on one volume represented by the logical name RESD.

B.1.1.2   **Locating a Listing File.** Locating an address or symbol involves identifying both the facility and the file name. First, you must narrow the search to one or a few facilities. Next, since each facility contains a small number of map files, you can search each map file for the address or global symbol of interest. Once you find the address or symbol in a map file, you can see which module defines it and read the corresponding listing file.

You should become somewhat familiar with the facilities that contain the listings read most often. The [SYS] facility contains the system services and most of the other executive routines described in this book. Most of the system service listing file names are of the form SYS*servicename*.LIS. The [DRIVER] facility contains class and port drivers for many disk and tape drives.

Many utilities have their own facilities, such as [MOUNT] and [OPCOM]. Some facility names are abbreviations of their associated facilities, such as [F11X] for the Files-11 Extended $QIO Processor (XQP) and [PRTSMB] for the print symbiont.

OpenVMS utilities can help locate the facilities and modules of interest. For example, to search for a particular module without knowing the facility or exact file name, use wildcard directory searches. The following Digital command language (DCL) command helps locate event-flag-related files:

```
$ DIRECTORY RESD:[V15.*.LIS]*EVENT*.*,*EVT*.*
```

You might find it convenient to have a separate file containing a complete directory listing of all facilities in both volumes of the listing kit. Searching such a file would be quicker than performing the DCL command DIRECTORY as shown.

Use the DCL SEARCH command to search several listing or map files for a particular routine, data cell, or comment. The following example locates the modules that reference the global data cell MMG$GL_GPTBASE.

```
$ SEARCH RESD:[V15.SYS.LIS]*.LIS MMG$GL_GPTBASE
```

Based on the search results, you can determine the names of the source modules that reference the symbol. For example, MMG$GL_GPTBASE, is referenced by the PAGEFAULT module, among others. Use an editor to peruse the file:

```
$ EDIT/READ_ONLY RESD:[V15.SYS.LIS]PAGEFAULT.LIS
```

You can also search all the map files in the same directory for occurrences of MMG$GL_GPTBASE, although such a search will yield only a small number of modules in comparison to a search of all the listing files. The OpenVMS AXP executive differs significantly from the OpenVMS VAX executive in the way it references global cells. The OpenVMS AXP executive accesses most global cells as offsets in a data structure, whereas the OpenVMS VAX executive references them using absolute or relocatable system virtual addresses. For this reason, all references to global cells on an OpenVMS VAX system can be traced through the map files, whereas those on an OpenVMS AXP system cannot. To locate all instances of an executive global cell on an OpenVMS AXP system, you must search all the listing files in the appropriate facility. Section B.2.1 contains more details.

B.1.1.3   **Locating a DCL Command Routine.** Some DCL commands are implemented by routines within DCL, and others are implemented by external images or routines. When you need to identify the module that implements a particular DCL command, first determine whether it is an internal routine (sometimes also called an internal image) by examining the second and third tables built by the INTIMAGES macro in [DCL]COMMAND.LIS. The first table contains the first eight characters of each command. The second table is a CASE table, and the third is a list of the internal routine names. Internal routines have names of the form DCL$*command*. Examine [DCL]DCL.MAP to identify the module that contains the internal routine of interest.

If the command is not implemented within DCL itself, find the command definition file that defines the command. Many command definition file listings are combined in [CLD]DCLTABLEx.LIS; others reside in the same facility as their related listings and maps. A command definition file associates one or more commands with either the image or the routine that implements each command. Locate the DEFINE VERB or DEFINE SYNTAX statement for the command of interest.

A command definition file either modifies the system or process command table or is linked with a related program. The presence of a ROUTINE statement indicates that the file is linked with a related program. The MODULE statement assigns a name to the object module that contains the command table, and the ROUTINE statement specifies the routine in the related program that implements the command. The following example from [IN-STAL]INSCMD.LIS defines two of the commands for the Install utility:

```
module INSCMD
    .
    .
    .
define verb CREATE
        routine INS$CREATE_VERB
    .
    .
    .
define verb LIST
        routine INS$LIST_VERB
```

Look for a map file that contains the object module named by the MODULE statement, and in it find the module that defines the symbol named by the ROUTINE statement. Read the routine in the module's listing. The following example is part of [INSTAL]INSTALL.MAP:

```
               +------------------------+
               ! Object Module Synopsis !
               +------------------------+


Module Name     Ident       Creator
-----------     -----       -------
INSMAIN         X-5    ...  BLISS-32E T1.0-020
    .
    .
INSCMD          0-0    ...  VMS Command Definition Utility
    .
    .

               +------------------------+
               ! Symbol Cross Reference !
               +------------------------+


Symbol           Value       Defined By    Referenced By ...
------           -----       ----------    -----------------
    .
    .
INS$CREATE_VERB  00010560-R  INSMAIN       INSCMD
    .
    .
INS$LIST_VERB    000103B0-R  INSMAIN       INSCMD
```

If a command definition file does not contain a ROUTINE statement, then it modifies a command table and uses the IMAGE statement to specify the name of the image that implements the command. (Most command definition files explicitly specify the image name. If it is missing, it defaults to the command verb.) Look in the image's map file to identify the modules to read. The following example from [CLD]DCLTABLE1.LIS defines three of the DCL ANALYZE commands:

```
define syntax ANALYZE_CRASH_DUMP
  image SDA
```

```
        qualifier CRASH_DUMP,default
        qualifier RELEASE
          .
          .
          .
  define syntax ANALYZE_DISK_STRUCTURE
    image VERIFY
    qualifier CONFIRM
    qualifier DISK_STRUCTURE,default
          .
          .
          .
  define verb ANALYZE
    image ANALYZOBJ
    qualifier CRASH_DUMP,nonnegatable,syntax=ANALYZE_CRASH_DUMP
    qualifier DISK_STRUCTURE,nonnegatable,syntax=ANALYZE_DISK_STRUCTURE
    qualifier OBJECT,default,nonnegatable
```

The *OpenVMS Command Definition, Librarian, and Message Utilities Manual* gives more information on command definition files.

B.1.2   Data Structure Offset, Constant, and Macro Definitions

Some data structure offset, constant, and macro definitions are contained in facility source modules. Others reside in several libraries in the directory SYS$LIBRARY. Some of these libraries are supplied as part of the OpenVMS binary distribution and are used by the operating system as well as privileged and nonprivileged applications. There are separate MACRO-32, MACRO-64, BLISS-32, and BLISS-64 libraries. Various SDL source files contribute definitions to each library file. This section discusses these and other libraries and the source files that contribute to them.

On an OpenVMS AXP system, the logical name SYS$LIBRARY is equivalent to the logical name ALPHA$LIBRARY. On an OpenVMS VAX system that supports cross-development for OpenVMS AXP, the logical name SYS$LIBRARY points to a directory that contains VAX-specific files, and the logical name ALPHA$LIBRARY points to a directory that contains AXP-specific files. (The same distinction holds for the logical names SYS$LOADABLE_IMAGES and ALPHA$LOADABLE_IMAGES.) This appendix assumes that SYS$LIBRARY is equivalent to ALPHA$LIBRARY.

ALPHA$LIBRARY:STARLET.MLB, the default macro library that is automatically searched by the MACRO-32 compiler, defines offsets, constants, and macros that are used in system services and other public interfaces. The STARLET definitions are primarily intended for use in nonprivileged applications.

Most of the offsets, constants, and macros used by the executive are not public; that is, they are subject to change. These are defined in a special library called ALPHA$LIBRARY:LIB.MLB. Applications such as user-written system services using this library must be reassembled or recompiled with each new release of LIB, which usually occurs with each major release of the operating system.

The STARLET.MLB and LIB.MLB files contain libraries of MACRO-32 macros. Counterparts of these libraries exist in BLISS-32 (.L32 extension) and BLISS-64 (.L64 extension). Subsets of the definitions contained in these libraries also exist for MACRO-64 in the files STARLET.PREFIX and LIB.PREFIX in the ALPHA$LIBRARY directory.

B.1.2.1   **Locating Data Structure Offset and Constant Definitions.** One set of SDL files contributes data structure offset and constant definitions to the STARLET libraries. These files are in the [STARLET] facility and have names of the form *xyz*DEF.SDL, where *xyz* represents the data structure whose offsets are defined. Another set of similarly named SDL files in the [LIB] facility contributes to the LIB libraries. In addition, various MACRO-32 source files contribute definitions to these libraries. An SDL source file, when processed by the SDL utility, can yield definitions in one of a few programming languages including MACRO-32 and BLISS. A BLISS file generated by the SDL utility has the .REQ extension and is called a REQUIRE file.

Section B.4 briefly discusses SDL files. Appendix E lists many of the data structures described in this book.

Since the BLISS-32 versions of the LIB and STARLET REQUIRE files retain the comments, they are particularly helpful. Even readers unfamiliar with BLISS-32 can read the comments about the data structures, fields, and constants. Use of an editor facilitates searching for the section of interest:

```
$ EDIT/READ_ONLY ALPHA$LIBRARY:LIB.REQ
```

The OpenVMS Librarian utility can extract modules from ALPHA$LIBRARY:STARLET.MLB or ALPHA$LIBRARY:LIB.MLB but not from the BLISS-32 REQUIRE files. An editor or the BLISS-32 compiler can extract modules from the BLISS-32 REQUIRE files. The following example illustrates how to extract the macro that defines the unit control block (UCB) offset definitions from LIB.MLB:

```
$ LIBRARY/MACRO/EXTRACT=$UCBDEF/OUTPUT=SYS$OUTPUT: -
_$ ALPHA$LIBRARY:LIB.MLB
```

B.1.2.2   **The $*xyz*DEF Macros.** Most MACRO-32 and MACRO-64 executive modules begin by invoking a series of macros that define symbolic offsets into data structures referenced by the module. The general form of these macros is $*xyz*DEF, where *xyz* represents the data structure whose offsets are required.

For example, a module that deals with the I/O subsystem probably invokes the $IRPDEF and $UCBDEF macros to define offsets into I/O request packets (IRPs) and UCBs. Some of the $*xyz*DEF macros, such as $SSDEF (system service status returns), and $IODEF (I/O function codes and modifiers), define constants rather than offsets into data structures.

The following sequence of DCL commands on an OpenVMS AXP system produces a list of symbols:

```
$ CREATE xyzDEF.MAR
    .       TITLE xyzDEF
    $       xyzDEF GLOBAL
    .       END
^Z
$ MACRO/MIGRATION ALPHA$LIBRARY:LIB.MLB/LIBRARY+xyzDEF.MAR
$ LINK/NOEXECUTABLE/MAP/FULL xyzDEF
$ PRINT xyzDEF.MAP
```

Note that the qualifier /MIGRATION invokes the MACRO-32 compiler. This command sequence produces a single object module that contains all the symbols produced by the $xyzDEF macro. The argument GLOBAL makes all the symbols produced by the macro global. (This argument must appear in uppercase to be properly interpreted by the MACRO-32 compiler's macro processor.) That is, the MACRO-32 compiler passes the symbol names and values to the linker so that they appear in whatever map the linker produces. The full map contains two lists of symbol definitions, one in alphabetical order and one in numeric order.

The System Dump Analyzer (SDA) utility can read the resulting object file to add symbols to its symbol table.

B.1.2.3 **Data Structure References.** Data structure references are usually made using displacement mode addressing. For example, the following MACRO-32 instruction stores the contents of R3 (presumably the address of an IRP) into the IRP pointer field (a longword) in a UCB pointed to by R5:

```
MOVL    R3,UCB$L_IRP(R5)
```

Such references are practically self-documenting. You do not need to know the overall arrangement of data in a particular structure to understand them.

B.1.2.4 **Locating Macro Definitions.** Commonly used instruction and code sequences are often coded as macros. Other instruction sequences, particularly those that read or write internal processor registers, are more readable if hidden in a macro. Because macros are rarely expanded as a part of the compiler listing, you must sometimes be able to locate the macro definitions to understand the invoking code. Macros fall into the following classes:

▸ Macros that are local to a module are defined in the module. Such macros are often used to generate data tables used by a single module. For example, the GENTAB macro in module SYSGETDVI.MAR builds an item code table.

▸ Macros that are part of a specific facility are defined in a separate file and appear with the listings for that facility. For example, the DCL listings include the macros that are used to assemble the DCL images in

[DCL]CLIMAC.MAR. Sometimes related facilities, such as [CLIUTL], contain related listings and macro definitions.

► Macros that are used by many components of the operating system are defined in the LIB or STARLET libraries.

Many MACRO-32 macro definition files reside in the [LIB], [STARLET], and [VMSLIB] facilities. For example, the [LIB] facility contains EXEC_REORG_MACROS.MAR, LOADER_MACROS.MAR, and SYSMAR.MAR, among others. SYSMAR.MAR defines macros for many common instruction sequences that appear in several components. [STARLET]UTLDEFM.MAR defines macros commonly used in structure and constant definitions. [STARLET]STARMISC.MAR defines macros for common instruction sequences. Other facilities also contain macro source definition files.

Use the techniques described in Section B.1.2.1 to search for a particular macro.

B.1.2.5   **The MACRO-32 Macro ASSUME and the BLISS Macro $ASSUME.** The MACRO-32 macro ASSUME and its BLISS equivalent, $ASSUME, both check an assumed relation and issue an error during compilation if the assumption is not true. These macros produce no executable code. Since they perform their checks during compilation, there is no execution performance penalty for using them.

Mostly, assumptions are made about the relative location of fields within a data structure:

► A single MACRO-32 statement could move two or more adjacent fields. For example, a single MOVQ MACRO-32 statement could move two adjacent longword fields.

► MACRO-32 autoincrement or autodecrement addressing could be used to traverse a structure.

Changes in the data structure could cause these statements to fail. For example, module ASTDEL uses MACRO-32 displacement mode addressing to get the address of one of four asynchronous system trap (AST) queues using the following sequence of MACRO-32 statements:

```
GET_NEXT_ASTQ:
        ASSUME      PCB$L_ASTQFL_E EQ PCB$L_ASTQFL_K+8
        ASSUME      PCB$L_ASTQFL_S EQ PCB$L_ASTQFL_K+16
        ASSUME      PCB$L_ASTQFL_U EQ PCB$L_ASTQFL_K+24
        ;
        MOVAQ       PCB$L_ASTQFL_K(R4)[R6],R7
                    ;Get address of PCB AST queue
```

In executive code, you can find an occasional use of the ASSUME macro to test for relations between two constants that are not data structure offsets. For example, the Process Scan ($PROCESS_SCAN) system service procedure assumes that the constant that indicates an interactive process is 1 higher than that which indicates a dialup process:

```
ASSUME  JPI$K_DIALUP EQ JPI$K_INTERACTIVE+1
```

ALPHA$LIBRARY:STARLET.MLB defines the ASSUME macro; its source, including comments, is in [STARLET]UTLDEFM.MAR. Examine the definition of the ASSUME macro to determine what options are available. The BLISS macro $ASSUME is defined in ALPHA$LIBRARY:STARLET.L32 and ALPHA$LIBRARY:STARLET.L64.

B.1.3 Executive Listings

The *VAX MACRO and Instruction Set Reference Manual* describes the general format of a MACRO-32 listing file. The *MACRO-64 Assembler for OpenVMS AXP Systems Reference Manual* describes the MACRO-64 assembler language and the format of a MACRO-64 listing file. This section should aid you in reading executive MACRO-32 listings and, to a limited extent, MACRO-64 listings. (In some respects, executive listings for AXP systems are significantly different than for VAX systems.) If you are porting VAX code to AXP systems, please refer to the manual *Migrating to an OpenVMS AXP System: Porting VAX MACRO Code* rather than relying on information from this section.

B.1.3.1 Compiler-Generated Code.

This section provides a brief look at the correspondence between generated code and a MACRO-32 source file. The following example shows an excerpt from the listing file produced by the MACRO-32 compiler for a simple program. Two PSECTs, named DATA and CODE, are defined in the program. The leftmost column shows the hexadecimal value of the offset within the current PSECT that corresponds to the MACRO-32 statement on the same line. As described in Section B.2.2.1, this offset is meaningless for a code PSECT on an OpenVMS AXP system, as it represents the offset for MACRO-32 instructions, not AXP assembly code. Note that the offset is meaningful for a data PSECT, however.

```
00000000     1
00000000     2           .PSECT   DATA, rd, nowrt, noexe
00000000     3 msg:      .ASCID   "Hello, World!"
00000015     4
00000015     5           .PSECT   CODE, rd, exe, nowrt
00000000     6           .ENTRY   MAIN, ^M<>
00000002     7           pushab   msg
00000008     8           calls    #1, lib$put_output
0000000F     9           ret
00000010    10           .END     MAIN
```

A careful examination of the rest of the listing file can be educational. The .ENTRY directive, for example, results in the generation of the following code.

```
               0000   MAIN::                              ;000006 ①
43C4153E ②     0000   SUBQ   SP, 32, SP       ;SP, 32, SP
B77E0000       0004 ③ STQ    R27, (SP)        ;R27, (SP)
B75E0008       0008   STQ    R26, 8(SP)       ;R26, 8(SP)
B5BE0010       000C   STQ    R13, 16(SP)      ;R13, 16(SP)
B7BE0018       0010   STQ    FP, 24(SP)       ;FP, 24(SP)
47FB040D       0014   MOV    R27, R13         ;R27, R13
47FE041D       0018   MOV    SP, FP           ;SP, FP
```

① The ;000006 following MAIN:: is the line number in the listing file to which the generated code corresponds. A single MACRO-32 statement can generate a number of AXP instructions, not all of which are adjacent to each other. As explained later in this section, instructions generated by one statement can be interleaved with instructions generated by other statements. The general rule that the MACRO-32 compiler uses to display line numbers is as follows: until another line number is shown, the instructions that follow correspond to the current line number.

② Each hexadecimal number displayed in the leftmost column represents the corresponding instruction's opcode and operands.

③ The hexadecimal numbers in the second column are offsets into the current PSECT.

The few lines of code following the MAIN:: symbol constitute the prologue code. (Chapter 1 discusses prologue code, epilogue code, linkage sections, procedure descriptors, and other elements described in the *OpenVMS Calling Standard* manual.) For a compiled language, prologue code is generated by the compiler.

MAIN:: is a stack frame procedure. Prologue code for a stack frame procedure typically performs the following operations. It allocates space for the stack frame; saves the contents of R27, the procedure value register, R26, the return address register, the frame pointer (FP) register, and the called procedure's scratch registers; and records the new frame's address in the FP register. Typically, prologue code for a called procedure saves the calling procedure's state.

Prologue code can also contain other compiler-specific code. For example, the MACRO-32 compiler copies R27 to R13 in the prologue code; it normally uses R13 as the linkage pointer register. Another compiler might use a different register for this purpose. Prologue code for a null frame procedure or a register frame procedure performs many of the same operations.

Lines 7 and 8, which are the MACRO-32 statements PUSHAB MSG and CALLS #1, LIB$PUT_OUTPUT, are compiled into the following sequence of AXP instructions:

```
               001C   $L1:
A78D0040       001C   LDQ   R28, 64(R13)     ;R28, 64(R13)  ;000007 ④
47E03419       0020   BIS   R31, 1, R25      ;R31, 1, R25   ;000008
A74D0030       0024   LDQ   R26, 48(R13)     ;R26, 48(R13)
```

```
A76D0038      0028      LDQ   R27, 56(R13)      ;R27, 56(R13)
47FC0410      002C      MOV   R28, R16          ;R28, R16          ;000007 ⑤
6B5A4000      0030      JSR   R26, R26          ;R26, R26          ;000008
```

R13 contains the address of the linkage section.

④ The instruction at offset $1C_{16}$ loads the address of the data area that contains the ASCII descriptor MSG.

⑤ The instruction at offset $2C_{16}$ copies this address to R16, the first argument register.

Note that code generated by line 7 is interleaved with code generated by line 8. Code generated by line 8 would look as follows were it not for instruction reordering by the compiler (comments have been added for clarity):

```
BIS   R31, 1, R25    ;Set argument count register to 1
LDQ   R26, 48(R13)   ;Load code address into return
                     ; address register
LDQ   R27, 56(R13)   ;Load procedure descriptor address into
                     ; procedure value register
JSR   R26, R26       ;Transfer control
```

Section B.1.3.4 briefly describes the reasons for instruction reordering.

Finally, the RET MACRO-32 statement, line 9, generates the following instruction sequence, which is the epilogue code for the MAIN procedure:

```
              0034   $L2:                              ;000009
47FD041E      0034      MOV   FP, SP          ;FP, SP
A79E0008      0038      LDQ   R28, 8(SP)      ;R28, 8(SP)
A5BE0010      003C      LDQ   R13, 16(SP)     ;R13, 16(SP)
A7BE0018      0040      LDQ   FP, 24(SP)      ;FP, 24(SP)
43C4141E      0044      ADDQ  SP, 32, SP      ;SP, 32, SP
6BFC8001      0048      RET   R28             ;R28
```

This epilogue code restores the return address, linkage pointer, saved scratch registers, and previous FP from the frame, restores stack space, and returns to the caller. Like prologue code, epilogue code is generated by the compiler and can contain other compiler-specific code. Typically, epilogue code restores the state saved by the prologue code.

B.1.3.2   **Register Conventions.** The OpenVMS AXP calling standard provides a convention for register use, as described in the *OpenVMS Calling Standard* manual. This convention must be strictly followed regardless of application or programming language.

In addition, each major subsystem of the executive uses a set of register conventions in its main routines. That is, the same registers are used to hold the same contents from routine to routine. Some of the more common conventions used by parts of the executive written in the MACRO-32 language are listed here. To a certain extent, these conventions are followed by executive code written in BLISS-32 also.

Note that this section is a reading aid for executive listings, not a programmer's aid for writing MACRO-32 programs. Use of MACRO-32 is strongly discouraged for new programs.

- ▶ R4 usually contains the address of the process control block (PCB) of the current process. Nearly all system service procedures and scheduling routines use this convention. In fact, the change-mode-to-kernel system service dispatcher loads the address of the PCB of the current process into R4 before passing control to the service-specific procedure.
- ▶ When it is necessary to refer to the process header (PHD), R5 is usually chosen and contains the address of the P1 window to the PHD. However, during the execution of the swapper and certain memory management code that executes holding the MMG spinlock, R5 contains the system space address of the PHD.
- ▶ The memory management subsystem uses R2 to contain the virtual address of an invalid page and R3 to contain the system virtual address of the page table entry (SVAPTE) that maps the page, although this convention is not strictly observed. After a physical page is associated with the page, its page frame number (PFN) is stored in R0 and the virtual address of the corresponding PFN database record is stored in R15.
- ▶ The I/O subsystem uses two nearly identical conventions, depending on whether it is executing in process context (in the Queue I/O Request ($QIO) system service and in device driver function decision table (FDT) routines) or in response to an interrupt. The most common register contents are the current IRP address stored in R3 and the UCB address in R5. In process context, R4 contains the address of the PCB of the requesting process.
- ▶ The synchronization routines generally store a spinlock structure address or a spinlock index in R0. Many invocations of these routines are enveloped in macros, some of which set up R0 before passing control to the synchronization routine. For the convenience of the invoking code, these macros optionally preserve and restore the previous value of R0 with the PRESERVE= argument.

B.1.3.3   **System- and CPU-Dependent Code.** The executive uses two different methods for incorporating system- and CPU-dependent code.

When there are only a few instructions or data references that depend on a specific system or CPU type, the code includes the instruction or data sequences for all systems or CPUs. The SYSDISP macro uses the contents of global location EXE$GQ_SYSTYPE to select the appropriate instructions or data, and the CPUDISP macro uses the contents of global location EXE$GQ_

CPUTYPE. Procedure EXE$INIT, in the EXEC_INIT executive image, initializes these global locations. The $HWRPBDEF macro defines constants of the form HWRPB_SYSTYPE$K_*system-type* and HWRPB_CPU_TYPE$K_*CPU-type* to identify system and CPU types. The SYSDISP and CPUDISP macros are defined in [LIB]SYSMAR.MAR.

When many instructions or data references depend on the specific CPU type, they are linked together into a set of CPU-dependent images (see Section B.2.4).

B.1.3.4   **Techniques for Increasing Execution Speed.** This section lists some of the techniques that the executive employs to increase execution speed. The list is not exhaustive. Although some of the techniques used by executive code that are described here have a direct impact on the generated code on VAX systems, this is not the case on AXP systems. The MACRO-32 and BLISS-32 compilers, like other AXP compilers, apply most of these techniques in their generated code even if the source programs are not written with these techniques in mind. Even the MACRO-64 assembler can, in certain instances, rearrange instructions to take advantage of certain architectural features. Understanding these techniques will help you better understand the generated code.

The AXP architecture provides fastest access to naturally aligned longwords and quadwords. Aligning data on "natural" boundaries is the most universally applied technique to reduce access time and improve execution speed. Naturally aligned data begins at certain address boundaries, for example, aligned longwords begin at addresses that are multiples of 4. An AXP processor can perform only aligned longword and quadword memory accesses. When a compiler recognizes an unaligned data reference, or any reference to a byte or a word, it generates a sequence of instructions that perform the equivalent access using aligned longword or quadword accesses. This can involve, for example, reading a longword or quadword memory location into a register and using a byte-mask instruction such as ZAP or ZAPNOT to extract the desired byte, word, or part of an unaligned longword or quadword into a register.

Several techniques are used to align data and thus avoid the performance penalty of unaligned access:

▸ The MACRO-32 .PSECT directive and the DECLARE_PSECT macro, the MACRO-64 DECLARE_PSECT_ASM macro, and the BLISS-32 PSECT statement specify code and data program section (PSECT) alignments. EXEC_REORG_MACROS.MAR defines the DECLARE_PSECT and DECLARE_PSECT_ASM macros.
▸ The MACRO-32 .ALIGN directive aligns data.
▸ The MACRO-32 .SYMBOL_ALIGNMENT directive associates either a longword or a quadword alignment with a MACRO-32 symbol like ACB$L_ASTQFL.

Without such an association, the MACRO-32 compiler would generate code to access such an offset using the best alignment information it could compute for the base register. This may result in generation of more code than necessary and reduce performance if the compiler assumes that the alignment is weaker than that which exists.

► Fields within data structures are ordered so that they begin on natural boundaries. Every structure allocated from pool is at least octaword-aligned. Sometimes unused dummy fields are included to force subsequent fields to natural boundaries.

► In the executive, most byte and word fields in data structures have been promoted to longword fields.

► The OpenVMS AXP operating system offers several system services that enable detection and reporting of unaligned references, allowing a programmer an opportunity to correct such references where possible. Chapter 39 describes these services.

An instruction that performs memory read or write access is slower than one that does not. Compilers can exploit this fact and rearrange instructions so that instructions that perform memory access are interleaved with ones that do not. Compilers can also try to minimize memory references by, for example, fetching two adjacent longwords with one quadword instruction.

A processor often has multiple instructions at varying stages of completion at any point in time in the pipeline. The overlapped instruction execution provides improved performance.

► A compiler inserts unrelated instructions between two instructions if the second instruction depends on the result of the first. If the first instruction has not completed, the dependent instruction stalls. Inserting unrelated instructions allows the first instruction to complete before the dependent instruction begins.

► The most common code path is in line. A compiler arranges code to minimize branching and maximize falling through to the next instruction or routine. Linear code executes faster than branching code because after a branch the pipe might be empty, causing the advantages of pipelined execution to be lost. In addition, linear code also results in better cache behavior, which also improves performance.

When it is necessary to include a test-and-branch operation, a programmer must decide which sense of the test to branch on and which sense to allow to continue in line. One basis for this decision is to allow the common (usually error-free) case to continue in line, only requiring the (slower) branch operation in unusual cases. An AXP processor assumes that a backward conditional branch will be taken, whereas a forward conditional branch will not.

By default the MACRO-32 compiler generates code on the assumption that a conditional branch is not taken. Where a conditional branch is likely to be taken, the programmer directs the MACRO-32 compiler otherwise, using the .BRANCH_LIKELY directive. An example of this, taken from module ALLOCPFN, follows:

```
       ⋮
MOVL  R1,PFN$L_FLINK(R23)   ;FLINK(PREV) = NEXT
.BRANCH_LIKELY              ;Assume not tail
BNEQ  15$                   ;Branch if not tail
       ⋮
```

The MACRO-32 compiler also supports a .BRANCH_UNLIKELY directive. Use of the .BRANCH_LIKELY and .BRANCH_UNLIKELY directives should be made after careful consideration, because unwise use of these directives could lead to performance loss. The *Migrating to an OpenVMS AXP System: Porting VAX MACRO Code* manual contains more details.

A number of compiler optimization techniques can result in instruction rearrangement, causing the generated code to appear in an order that seemingly has no correspondence to the MACRO-32 code. Some of these techniques are listed here:

▶ The compiler recognizes multiple references to the same addresses and data locations and loads these only once.
▶ Using a technique called peephole optimization, the compiler replaces certain long instruction sequences with equivalent short instruction sequences.
▶ The AXP architecture provides for the ability of processor implementations to allow multiple instruction issue. Using a technique called instruction scheduling, the compiler can optimize code for this feature. Note that instruction scheduling does not affect the correctness of a program; it only increases the performance on a processor that can take advantage of it. For example, code that is optimized for a quad-issue processor will still run correctly on a processor that does not support quad-issue.

Under certain circumstances, you may notice a discrepancy between the generated code in the listings and code in an image, for example, when you are performing crash dump analysis using SDA. The linker optimizes certain instructions in a standard call sequence by replacing them with different instructions. Specifically, if certain criteria are met, the linker replaces a code sequence like

```
MOV   R27, R3
LDQ   R26, X(R3)
LDQ   R27, X+8(R3)
JSR   R26, R26
```

with a code sequence of the following type.

```
MOV    R27, R3
BIS    R31, R31, R31
LDA    R27, offset1(R3)
BSR    R26, offset2
```

The crux of this optimization is the replacement of the JSR instruction with the BSR instruction. This can be done if the value of offset1 in the example can be expressed as a 21-bit signed integer and the routine about to be invoked is in the same image as the invoking routine. This optimization eliminates a memory reference. The *OpenVMS Linker Utility Manual* contains more details.

B.1.3.5   **CALL_PAL REI Instruction Use.** The CALL_PAL REI privileged architecture library code (PALcode) instruction dismisses an interrupt or exception at the end of an interrupt or exception service routine. It is also the only means of reaching a less privileged access mode from a more privileged mode.

The OpenVMS AXP executive rarely executes the CALL_PAL REI instruction to transfer directly to a less privileged mode. Rather, it uses the following routines that execute the instruction in a controlled way: EXE$REI_TO_AST, in module ASTDEL_STACK, used by AST delivery code to deliver an AST to a less privileged mode, and EXE$REI_INIT_STACK and EXE$REI_INIT_STACK_ALT, in module REI, used by most executive routines to transfer control to a less privileged mode. Chapter 8 describes EXE$REI_TO_AST, and Chapter 6, the other two routines.

The most general technique for going to a less privileged access mode alters the flow of execution at the same time. The following code sequence, taken from module PROCSTRT, transfers control to routine EXEC_MODE while changing access mode from kernel to executive:

```
PUSHAL  EXEC_MODE              ;Callback routine
PUSHL   #PSL$C_EXEC
CALLS   #2,EXE$REI_INIT_STACK  ;Change mode to executive
HALT                          ;Never returns here
```

Note that the protection checks built into the CALL_PAL REI instruction (see Chapter 3) prevent the CALL_PAL REI instruction from being used by a non-privileged user to get into a more privileged access mode or to elevate IPL, two operations that would allow such a user to damage the system.

B.1.4   **Elimination of Seldom-Used Code**

Several different techniques are used to eliminate code and data that are not used very often. For example, none of the programs used during the initialization of an OpenVMS system remains after its work is accomplished. The executive allows these routines to do their work as efficiently as possible and then eliminates them.

B.1.4.1   **Bootstrap Programs.** The following are some techniques used to remove system initialization code from memory after it has done its work:

▸ Both the AXP primary bootstrap program (APB) and the secondary bootstrap program (SYSBOOT) execute in physical pages whose use is not recorded anywhere. When module EXEC_INIT places all physical pages except those occupied by the permanently resident executive on the free page list, it includes the pages used by APB and SYSBOOT. Their contents are overwritten the first time each physical page is used.

▸ After the initialization of an executive image is complete, the address space occupied by its fixup and initialization sections is deallocated.

▸ The SYSINIT process deallocates to the free page list the physical pages occupied by EXEC_INIT (see Chapter 34).

▸ Part of system initialization takes place in process context. The swapper creates the SYSINIT process, which in turn creates the startup process. Because SYSINIT and startup are separate processes, they disappear after they have completed their work.

B.1.4.2   **Seldom-Used System Routines.** The simplest and most common technique used to prevent seldom-used code and data from permanently occupying memory is to put them into one of the pageable image sections of an executive image. Chapter 32 describes executive images, their image sections, and their loading. The normal operation of system working set replacement eventually forces infrequently referenced pages out of the system working set.

This technique is defeated if the system is made nonpageable through the use of the SYSGEN parameter S0_PAGING.

B.1.4.3   **Alternative Versions of Modules and Images.** Some executive modules and images have alternative versions. An alternative version might contain code used only for debugging, performance-monitoring, or field-testing purposes. For example, module MEMORYALC_DYN is conditionally compiled to produce two object modules: MEMORYALC_DYN_MIN and MEMORYALC_DYN_MON. A few other modules in the [SYS] facility are conditionally compiled in a similar manner to produce two versions, one with the _MIN suffix, the other with the _MON suffix. The object file with the _MON suffix contains additional debugging and performance-monitoring code that is not present in the _MIN version.

MEMORYALC_DYN_MON is linked into the executive image SYSTEM_PRIMITIVES.EXE, and MEMORYALC_DYN_MIN is linked into the executive image SYSTEM_PRIMITIVES_MIN.EXE. When alternative executive images exist, the value of a SYSGEN parameter typically determines which one is loaded. For example, if the SYSGEN parameter POOLCHECK is nonzero, SYSBOOT loads SYSTEM_PRIMITIVES.EXE; otherwise, it loads SYSTEM_PRIMITIVES_MIN.EXE.

B.1.5   **Locking Code or Data into Memory**

While infrequent use may lead to a routine's being placed in a pageable image section, other considerations may require that the code be nonpageable. For example, the page fault handler assumes that page faults do not occur above IPL 2; it enforces this assumption by generating a fatal bugcheck if it is violated.

Several infrequently used and thus pageable system services (including $CREPRC, the Create Process system service) elevate IPL to IPL$_SCHED (for example, as a result of acquiring a spinlock while synchronizing access to the scheduler database) and thus need to lock some code pages into memory.

Several different techniques are used to lock pages into memory. One that the executive commonly uses is placing code in the nonpageable image sections. Code and data in the executive images reside in pageable and nonpageable image sections. The minimum amount possible is placed into the PSECTs that comprise the nonpageable image sections. A subroutine call transfers control from the paged to the nonpaged code. The following variation on a routine within the Get Job/Process Information ($GETJPI) system service illustrates the technique. The entire routine cannot exist in a pageable image section because the routine EXE$NAM_TO_PCB returns at IPL$_SCHED and thus may not incur a page fault.

```
        DECLARE_PSECT  EXEC$PAGED_CODE ;Pageable code
        .
        .
        CALLS       #3,GONAMTOPCB        ;Get into nonpageable code
        MOVL        R1,R11               ;Save PID
        .
        .
        .SAVE_PSECT                      ;Save current .PSECT context
        DECLARE_PSECT  EXEC$NONPAGED_CODE
                                         ;EXE$NAM_TO_PCB returns at
                                         ; IPL$_SCHED
GONAMTOPCB:
        .CALL_ENTRY INPUT=<R4>,-
        .
        .
        JSB         EXE$NAM_TO_PCB       ;Get PCB address and check
                                         ; privileges
        BLBC        R0,20$               ;Branch if error, SCHED
                                         ; not locked
        .
        .
        RET                              ;Go back to pageable code
        .RESTORE_PSECT                   ;Get pageable .PSECT context back
```

The technique described here is useful when a small amount of code needs to be placed into the nonpaged executive. When much more code needs to be locked into memory, the executive might use another technique. Chapter 19 describes some techniques that the executive uses to lock pages into the system or process working set list.

B.2 **EXECUTIVE IMAGE MAP FILES**

The map files produced when an OpenVMS system is built from source are indispensable to readers of listing files. The listing kit contains map files for many images of interest, including the base images, executive images, device drivers, and utilities. (Chapter 32 describes the base images and executive images.) Most map files reside in the same facility as their related listing files. For example, the map files for the base images and most executive images reside in the [SYS] facility. Table B.1 lists some of the facilities in the listing kit.

It is often necessary to identify which module defines a given symbol. Because of the modular construction of OpenVMS, many symbols referenced by one routine are defined in some other module. Many images are built from a large number of modules, so the map file alphabetical cross-reference listing is particularly valuable. It identifies the modules that define and reference each global symbol.

A map file lists the value of each global and universal symbol. A global symbol in an executive image is one whose scope extends to the entire image. A global symbol can represent the procedure value of a routine, a constant value, or the address of a data cell. A global symbol can be relative or absolute. The value of a relative, or relocatable, global symbol is its offset from the beginning of the image.

Symbols for constants like data structure offsets, interrupt priority levels (IPLs), and the sizes of preallocated buffers are not affected by the ultimate location of an executive image. They are therefore not relocatable, as seen in the following fragment of an executive image map file:

```
Symbol            Value       Defined By    Referenced By ...
------            -----       ----------    -----------------
PQL$C_SYSPQLLEN   00000046    SWAPPER
```

A universal symbol in an executive image is a global symbol that is made visible to the executive loader through the linker option VECTOR_TABLE. The linker creates a global symbol table entry for each symbol in the image that matches a name in the vector table.

For an ordinary shareable image, a section of the image called the symbol vector contains all the symbol vector entries. The structure of an executive image is somewhat different from that of an ordinary shareable image: an executive image does not have a symbol vector; rather it uses the symbol vector of one of two base images, SYS$BASE_IMAGE.EXE and SYS$PUBLIC_VECTORS.EXE. Chapter 32 describes the structure of the base images and executive images.

A symbol whose value must be adjusted to account for an image's base address is identified as a relocatable symbol in a map file, indicated by R after the symbol's value.

Table B.1   Selected List of Facilities

Directory	Facility Name
[ACC]	Accounting utility
[AMATHRTL]	AXP Mathematics Run-Time Library
[APB]	Primary bootstrap program
[BOOTDRIVER]	Bootstrap device drivers
[CLD]	Command definition language files
[CLIUTL]	DCL utility routines
[CLUSTER]	VMScluster-related images
[CPU0202]	Code specific to DEC 4000 systems
[CPU0302]	Code specific to DEC 7000 and DEC 10000 systems
[CPU0402]	Code specific to DEC 3000 Models 400 and 500 series systems
[CPU0702]	Code specific to DEC 3000 Model 300 series systems
[DCL]	DCL command language interpreter
[DELTA]	DELTA/XDELTA system debugger code
[DRIVER]	Device drivers
[ERF]	Error Log Formatting utility
[ERRFMT]	Error logger format process
[F11X]	Files-11 extended QIO processor
[INIT]	Volume Initialization utility
[INSTAL]	Install utility
[IOGEN]	SYSMAN I/O command support
[JOBCTL]	Job controller
[LAN]	Local area network drivers
[LIB]	Private interface library
[LIBOTS]	General purpose Run-Time Library
[LIBRTL]	Run-Time Library
[LINKER]	Linker utility
[LOADSS]	System services in privileged shareable images
[LOGIN]	LOGINOUT image
[MOUNT]	Mount utility
[NETACP]	Network driver and network ancillary control process
[OPCOM]	OPCOM process
[OPDRIVER]	Console terminal driver
[PPLRTL]	Parallel Processing Run-Time Library
[PRTSMB]	Print symbiont
[QMAN]	Queue manager
[RMS]	Record Management Services utility
[SDA]	System Dump Analyzer utility
[SHRLIB]	Shareable image library
[STARLET]	Public interface library
[SYS]	Most executive code, including system services
[SYSBOOT]	Secondary bootstrap program
[SYSGEN]	System Generation utility
[SYSINI]	System initialization process
[SYSLOA]	Code shared across platforms
[TIE]	Translated Image Environment (TIE) facility
[TTDRVR]	Terminal class and port drivers
[UTIL32]	Command language utilities
[VMSLIB]	Item code definitions for some system services

```
                    +------------------------+
                    ! Symbol Cross Reference !
                    +------------------------+

    Symbol          Value         Defined By        Referenced By ...
    ------          -----         ----------        -----------------
     .
     .
     .
    CHECK_PACKET    00019C58-R    MEMORYALC_MON     MEMORYALC_DYN_MON
     .
     .
     .
    Key for special characters above:
        +--------------------+
        ! *  - Undefined     !
        ! A  - Alias Name    !
        ! I  - Internal Name !
        ! U  - Universal     !
        ! R  - Relocatable   !
        ! X  - External      !
        ! WK - Weak          !
        ! V  - Vectored      !
        ! M  - Mask value    !
        +--------------------+
```

Executive code refers to routines and data cells in other executive images through universal symbols in a base image. A symbol vector entry in a base image is filled in with the correct address when its corresponding executive image is loaded. A map file identifies the symbols for these routines and data cells as vectored universal symbols, indicated by V after the symbol's value.

Vectored universal symbols appear twice in a map file. In the first occurrence, usually indicated by the RV suffix, the symbol's value is its offset from the beginning of the image that defines the symbol. The linker creates a second map file entry, indicated by (V) after the symbol's name in the map file. The second symbol's value equals the symbol vector entry's offset from the base of the symbol vector in the appropriate base image.

For example, the routine EXE$DEANONPAGED resides in module MEMORYALC_DYN, part of the executive image SYSTEM_PRIMITIVES.EXE. (Module EXSUBROUT invokes this routine directly, since EXSUBROUT is also part of SYSTEM_PRIMITIVES.EXE.) The following fragment is from SYSTEM_PRIMITIVES.MAP:

```
    Symbol              Value          Defined By        Referenced By ...
    ------              -----          ----------        -----------------
    EXE$DEANONPAGED     0001A0A0-RV    MEMORYALC_        ALLOC_CNT_RES
                                       DYN_MON           EXSUBROUT
                                                         KERNEL_PROCESS_MON
                                                         TIMESCHDL
    EXE$DEANONPAGED (V) 00002A10
```

Each executive image is linked with the base images SYS$BASE_IM-AGE.EXE and SYS$PUBLIC_VECTORS.EXE to resolve references to externally defined vectored universal symbols, such as routines in other images and system services.

To continue the previous example, module ACCOUNT (part of the executive image PROCESS_MANAGEMENT.EXE) invokes EXE$DEANON-PAGED. The following fragment is from PROCESS_MANAGEMENT.MAP:

```
Symbol              Value           Defined By      Referenced By ...
------              -----           ----------      -----------------

EXE$DEANONPAGED     00002A10-RX     SYS$BASE_IMAGE  ACCOUNT
  .
  .
00002A10     RX-EXE$DEANONPAGED
```

A relocatable symbol referenced by other executive images is generally a vectored universal symbol. Relocatable symbols that are referenced only by modules within the same executive image are not vectored universal symbols. The X in the RX following EXE$DEANONPAGED's value indicates that the symbol is external to the PROCESS_MANAGEMENT executive image, the image whose map file is examined here.

Some base image global symbols have an associated version mask. The map file identifies these mask value symbols with M after the symbol values. The map file lists the symbol values, not the mask values:

```
Symbol              Value           Defined By      Referenced By ...
------              -----           ----------      -----------------

ACP$ACCESS          0000A0C0-RM     SYSTEM_ROUTINES SYSTEM_ROUTINES_MASK
BOO$C_SYSPARSZ      00000960-M      SYSPARAM        SYSPARAM_MASK
```

The DCL command ANALYZE/IMAGE, when executed on a shareable image that was linked with the linker option /SYSEXE, displays the array of category version numbers that the linker creates based on the mask values shown. Chapter 32 and the *OpenVMS Linker Utility Manual* contain more details.

Alias name and internal name symbols are not used by the executive.

B.2.1   Locating All Instances of an Executive Global Symbol

To locate all references to an executive global symbol, it is not sufficient to search only the executive map files. Rather, all executive listing files should be searched. A map file does not record the name of a global cell resolved as an offset from a base register. For example, a search of all listing files in the [SYS] facility reveals that the modules RSE, SCHEDULER, and SCHED_ROUTINES reference the global location SCH$GQ_ACTIVE_PRIORITY. However, a search of all map files in the [SYS] facility reveals only the reference in module SCHEDULER.

The reason for this apparent discrepancy is the restructuring of the SYS-TEM_DATA_CELLS, PARAMETER, and SHELL*xx*K modules in the Open-VMS AXP executive. These modules define global cells.

On an OpenVMS VAX system, a global cell is usually defined as a relocatable symbol whose value corresponds to the offset from the beginning of the image. On an OpenVMS AXP system, a global cell can be defined in two different ways: as a relocatable symbol and also as an offset into a global data structure. Many, but not all, OpenVMS AXP global cells are defined in both ways.

For example, the OpenVMS AXP module SYSTEM_DATA_CELLS defines the global cell SCH$GQ_ACTIVE_PRIORITY as a relocatable symbol whose value corresponds to an offset in the base image SYS$BASE_IMAGE.EXE. The same module, when compiled with a special prefix file called SYSTEM_DATA_PREFIX, defines the same cell as an offset into the global data structure pointed to by the universal symbol EXE$GR_SYSTEM_DATA_CELLS. That is, SCH$GQ_ACTIVE_PRIORITY is defined as EXE$GR_SYSTEM_DATA_CELLS+*x*, where *x* is an appropriate offset.

Defining a global cell as an offset into a global data structure allows the MACRO-32 compiler to avoid loading the linkage section pointer every time the contents of a global cell need to be accessed. Instead, the compiler can use a common base register for several references based on the same global symbol (EXE$GR_SYSTEM_DATA_CELLS, in this case). This improves performance by allowing the compiler to eliminate several memory references.

A side effect of this performance optimization is that the map file for an image that refers to a global cell defined as an offset into a global structure will instead list the global structure. For example, the map file for an executive image in the [SYS] facility that references SCH$GQ_ACTIVE_PRIORITY will instead list EXE$GR_SYSTEM_DATA_CELLS.

Most references to global cells in the [SYS] facility have been converted to take advantage of this optimization. The other method of referencing global cells still works. For example, the primary and secondary bootstrap programs and the executive loader still reference global cells as global symbols.

B.2.2 Locating an Executive Image Address in the Listings

You need an executive map file to correlate a system virtual address within a loaded executive image to its location in a listing file. For example, when the system crashes, the addresses reported on either the console terminal or in the system dump file must be related to actual routines and data cells in system address space. The procedure to do this, described in Section B.2.2.1, can be tedious. Fortunately, the SDA command MAP simplifies the procedure by performing a number of these steps. The DELTA/XDELTA commands ;W and ;L can also help simplify the procedure during debugging.

Executive slicing, a technique introduced in OpenVMS AXP to take advantage of an AXP architectural feature called granularity hint regions, is described in Chapter 32. By default a system is bootstrapped with executive slicing enabled. If bit 1 of the SYSGEN parameter LOAD_SYS_IMAGES is clear, executive slicing is not performed. There are some differences in the way an executive image address is correlated to its listing location depending on whether executive slicing is enabled or disabled. The following sections show an example of a system that is not sliced and point out the differences on a system that is sliced.

B.2.2.1   **Nonsliced Executive Example.** The list of executive images and their addresses reported on the console terminal and in the system dump file help identify which executive image contains the reference of interest. Compare the address in question with the base and end addresses for each executive image to find the correct range. Subtract the image's base address from the address in question to get its offset within the executive image.

In the following example, output from the System Dump Analyzer, the location 81858500_{16}, is in the executive image PROCESS_MANAGEMENT. EXE:

```
SDA>EXAMINE 81858500
SCH$GL_NULLPCB+00008:   00000000 000C0260    "'......."

SDA>SHOW EXECUTIVE
Image                       Base     End      Length   SymVec
    .
    .
    .
      Paged read/write      818AE000 818AF400 00001400
PROCESS_MANAGEMENT          81844000 81878000 00034000
      Nonpaged read only    81844000 81857A00 00013A00
      Nonpaged read/write   81858000 8185C400 00004400
      Paged read only       81860000 8186D000 0000D000
      Paged read/write      81870000 81872800 00002800
    .
    .
    .
SYS$BASE_IMAGE              80A9A000 80ABA000 00020000 80AABF60
      Nonpaged read only    80A9A000 80AA1000 00007000
      Nonpaged read/write   80AA2000 80AB8C00 00016C00
SYS$PUBLIC_VECTORS          80A90000 80A98000 00008000 80A95DD8
      Nonpaged read only    80A90000 80A91E00 00001E00
      Nonpaged read/write   80A94000 80A97400 00003400
```

Calculate the offset of the location in question:

```
 81858500   Location in question
-81844000   Base address of executive image PROCESS_MANAGEMENT
    14500   Location's offset within the executive image PROCESS_
            MANAGEMENT
```

The identified image's map file then helps translate the offset within the image to an offset within a PSECT. An executive image's base address is not determined until the image is loaded, so the addresses within the map file are offsets from the beginning of the image.

The SDA command MAP can help you directly get a location's offset from the base of an executive image, as shown in the following example:

```
SDA>MAP 81858500
Image                            Base      End       Image Offset
PROCESS_MANAGEMENT               81844000  81878000  00014500
```

Compare the image offset with each PSECT address range until you find the PSECT that contains the offset. Note the PSECT's name, since it is required later. From the following fragment of PROCESS_MANAGE-MENT.MAP, one sees that offset 14500_{16} is in PSECT EXEC$NONPAGED_DATA:

```
                    +--------------------------+
                    ! Program Section Synopsis !
                    +--------------------------+


Psect Name       Module Name      Base      End       Length
----------       -----------      ----      ---       ------
EXEC$NONPAGED_DATA                00014200  00015497  00001298...
                 SYSTEM_PCBS_AND_PHDS
                                  00014200  000150C7  00000EC8...
                 SCHED_ROUTINES   000150E0  000153EF  00000310...
                 RSE              00015400  00015443  00000044...
                 PROC_READ_WRITE  00015460  00015467  00000008...
```

Often, several modules contribute to a given PSECT. The map file's program section synopsis lists the beginning and ending address of each module's contribution to the PSECT. Compare the offset in question with each module's contribution to the identified PSECT to find the module that defines the location. In this example, the module SYSTEM_PCBS_AND_PHDS contributes offset 14500_{16}.

Subtract the beginning address of the identified module's contribution to the PSECT from the offset of interest to produce an offset into the correct module and PSECT:

```
 14500     Location's offset within PROCESS_MANAGEMENT
-14200     Base of EXEC$NONPAGED_DATA in PROCESS_MANAGEMENT
   300     PSECT offset within module SYSTEM_PCBS_AND_PHDS
```

This is the offset of the location in question within module SYSTEM_PCBS_AND_PHDS's contribution to PSECT EXEC$NONPAGED_DATA. You must ensure that you locate the correct PSECT within the listing, since there may be several PSECTs. The following MACRO-32 code fragment is from SYSTEM_PCBS_AND_PHDS.LIS.

```
    .
    .
    .
00000000    10396    DECLARE_PSECT    EXEC$NONPAGED_DATA,ALIGNMENT=PAGE
    .
    .
    .
000002F8    10403 ;
000002F8    10404 ;PROCESS CONTROL BLOCK FOR NULL PROCESS
000002F8    10405 ;
000002F8    10406    GENPCB       SCH$GL_NULLPCB,PHD=NULPHD,PID=NULPIX,-
00000558    10407                 PRIORITY=NULL_EXT_PRIO,PNAME=NULL
    .
    .
    .
```

You can confirm that you have located the correct location in the listing file by the fact that SDA symbolizes the address 81858500_{16} as SCH$GL_NULLPCB+8 (equivalent to the image offset $2F8_{16}+8$). In general, you can apply this technique of transforming an address into an offset within a module's contribution to a PSECT to any type of image.

Note that for a data PSECT, the numbers in the leftmost column of the source listing section of the MACRO-32 compiler listing file are meaningful offsets. In fact, they provide the only way to locate the source line corresponding to an offset within a data PSECT, because the MACRO-32 compiler does not print the source line number corresponding to a data declaration in the machine code listing section. For a code PSECT, the numbers in the leftmost column of the source listing section of the MACRO-32 compiler listing file are meaningless, as they correspond to MACRO-32 offsets.

B.2.2.2   **Sliced Executive Example.** When the executive is loaded sliced, the image sections within each executive image are not loaded at consecutive system virtual addresses. Rather, image sections with similar attributes from multiple images are clustered. The SDA command SHOW EXECUTIVE shows the system virtual address range for each image section of an executive image. When the same system used in the previous section is bootstrapped with executive slicing enabled, the SDA output is as follows:

```
SDA>SHOW EXECUTIVE
Image                        Base     End      Length    SymVec
    .
    .
    Paged read/write         81862000 81863400 00001400
PROCESS_MANAGEMENT
    Nonpaged read only       80060000 80073A00 00013A00
    Nonpaged read/write      8042CE00 80431200 00004400
    Paged read only          81840000 8184D000 0000D000
    Paged read/write         8184E000 81850800 00002800
    .
    .
SYS$BASE_IMAGE                                            8040D360
    Nonpaged read only       80002000 80009000 00007000
    Nonpaged read/write      80403400 8041A000 00016C00
```

1393

```
SYS$PUBLIC_VECTORS                                        80401DD8
    Nonpaged read only       80000000 80001E00 00001E00
    Nonpaged read/write      80400000 80403400 00003400
```

For the sake of comparison with the nonsliced example, start with the address corresponding to SCH$GL_NULLPCB+8, $8042D300_{16}$, as displayed by the SDA command EVALUATE on the sliced system. From the SHOW EXECUTIVE display, you can determine that this address is in the nonpaged read/write section of the PROCESS_MANAGEMENT executive image. To calculate the image offset, first calculate the image section offset as follows:

```
 8042D300    Location's offset within PROCESS_MANAGEMENT
-8042CE00    Base of nonpaged read/write section
      500    Image section offset
```

From the image section synopsis in the map file, you can determine that the nonpaged read/write image section begins at a relative address of 14000_{16}:

```
        +------------------------+
        ! Image Section Synopsis !
        +------------------------+

Cluster       Type Pglts   Base Addr    Disk VBN PFC Protection ...
-------       ---- -----   ---------    -------- --- ----------
    .
    .
    .
NONPAGED_READONLY_PSECTS
              4    157     00000000-R   3        0   READ ONLY ...
NONPAGED_READWRITE_PSECTS
              4    34      00014000-R   160      0   READ WRITE...
PAGED_READONLY_PSECTS
              4    104     0001C0000-R  194      0   READ ONLY ...
    .
    .
    .
```

Add the relative address of the nonpaged read/write image section to the image section offset to get the image offset of the address in question:

```
  14000    Relative address of nonpaged read/write image section
+  500    Base of nonpaged read/write section
  14500    Image offset of address in question
```

You can use the SDA command MAP instead of the steps outlined to get the image offset. The remaining steps are identical to the nonsliced case.

B.2.3   DCL.MAP

A command language interpreter (CLI) is mapped into a virtual address range that is not known until the mapping occurs. The first longword at global location CTL$AG_CLIMAGE in the P1 pointer area contains the base address of any CLI. Because a CLI is linked with a base address of zero, the contents of this location can be used to relate an address extracted from the map with a virtual address in a running system. DCL is currently the only supported CLI.

For example, if the location of interest is $7FED8ECC_{16}$ in P1 space and the contents of the first longword at CTL$AG_CLIMAGE is $7FED8000_{16}$, then the difference between these two numbers equals the offset into the DCL image. Obviously, if this difference is larger than the size of the DCL image, then the address is not in DCL:

```
 7FED8ECC   Location of interest
-7FED8000   Base address of DCL
      ECC   Location's offset within DCL image
```

Compare the location's offset within DCL to the address ranges listed in [DCL]DCL.MAP to determine which PSECT and module contain the location of interest. Subtract the beginning address of the identified module's contribution to the PSECT from the offset within DCL to produce an offset into the correct module and PSECT. This offset then locates in the listing file the routine or data cell of interest.

To calculate the P1 space address of a data cell or instruction in a DCL module, start with the location as shown in the module's listing. Add to it the base address of the module's contribution to the correct PSECT (taken from [DCL]DCL.MAP) to form the offset into the DCL image. Add this sum to the contents of global location CTL$AG_CLIMAGE to form the P1 address of the location in question.

B.2.4   CPU-Dependent Routines

Entire routines or modules that are CPU-dependent, such as the machine check service routine, are linked into a set of CPU-dependent images. The images have names of the form SYS$CPU_ROUTINES_*xxyy*.EXE, where *xx* identifies the system type and *yy* the CPU type (see Appendix G). SYSBOOT uses the system type and CPU type to determine which SYS$CPU_ROUTINES_*xxyy* image to load. Segregating CPU-dependent routines into separate images minimizes the number of CPU-dependent decisions that are made at execution time and reduces the size of the executive.

The map files for the CPU-dependent images have names of the form [CPU*xxyy*]SYS$CPU_ROUTINES_*xxyy*.MAP. Perform address calculations using the techniques described in Section B.2.2.1.

B.2.5   Other Map Files

You can use other map files for the cross-reference capabilities already mentioned. In addition, many other components of the operating system execute as normal images, so no base addresses have to be used to locate addresses in virtual address space. The addresses on the map correspond to the virtual addresses that are used for an executable image, albeit with some exceptions.

1395

The map file does not include the base address of shareable images; their base addresses are determined at image activation time. Also, the addresses in the map file for an OpenVMS AXP executable image installed resident (using the Install utility's /RESIDENT qualifier) may not correspond to the virtual addresses on the running system. This is because the image section containing code in such an image may be loaded into a granularity hint region while at the same time the other image sections of that image are relocated to adjust for this change.

As the image activator processes an image and its references to other images, the image activator builds image control blocks (IMCBs) (see Chapter 28). An IMCB includes the image name and the starting and ending addresses of the image. The IMCBs for activated images form a doubly linked list starting at the listhead IAC$GL_IMAGE_LIST. The listhead and the IMCBs are pageable, so they may not be present in a system dump file. The SDA command SHOW PROCESS/IMAGE traverses this list, if it is resident, to display the names of images mapped into P0 and P1 space. The IMCB for an image that has been installed resident includes relocation data for the image sections that constitute the image.

B.3   SYSTEM DUMP ANALYZER

SDA allows you to analyze a running system or examine the contents of a dump file. Map files can supply only addresses of static data storage areas in the system, not their contents. In addition, many data structures are dynamically allocated. With SDA you can examine these data structures, other memory locations, and the hardware context of each processor.

The *OpenVMS AXP System Dump Analyzer Utility Manual* describes how to use SDA. This section mentions several of the many SDA commands that are especially useful when studying how the operating system works.

SDA maintains a symbol table that it uses to interpret memory addresses and contents. SDA reads certain symbols, including those from SDA$READ_DIR:SYS$BASE_IMAGE.EXE and SDA$READ_DIR:REQSYSDEF.STB into its symbol table when it first executes. You can add symbols to SDA's table with the DEFINE and READ commands. Since SYSDEF.STB contains many common data structure definitions, reading it into SDA's symbol table is frequently useful. Use the following command:

```
SDA> READ SDA$READ_DIR:SYSDEF.STB
```

Many dynamic data structures are located through global pointers in the base image. These static locations are loaded when these structures are created or modified, either as a part of system initialization or some other loading mechanism.

The SDA command SHOW SYMBOL/ALL is one way to display these global pointers. It shows both the addresses and the contents of all locations for which SDA has symbols in its symbol table. This list, together with the map files, enables you to locate any data structure in system address space if you know the global name that locates the structure. Alternatively, use the EXAMINE command to determine the contents of particular global pointers. The SHOW SYMBOL/ALL command produces a very long list. The SHOW SYMBOL/ALL *xyz* command lists only those symbols that begin with *xyz*.

A universal symbol defined by an executive image has a corresponding symbol vector entry in the image SDA$READ_DIR:SYS$BASE_IMAGE.EXE. For each such symbol that identifies a procedure within an executive image, SDA creates a new symbol (suffixed with _C) for the code address corresponding to that procedure value:

```
SDA> SHOW SYMBOL EXE$ALLOCIRP
EXE$ALLOCIRP = 804209D8 :   00003008
SDA> EXAMINE/INSTRUCTION EXE$ALLOCIRP
EXE$ALLOCIRP_C:          SUBQ            SP,#X10,SP
```

A global symbol within an executive image is not visible in SDA until that executive image's symbol table is read. You can find OpenVMS AXP executive image symbol tables in the SDA$READ_DIR directory. The SDA command READ/EXECUTIVE can read the symbol table of a specific executive image or all of them. By default, when no argument is passed to the SDA command READ/EXECUTIVE, SDA searches the SDA$READ_DIR directory for the symbol tables for all known executive images:

```
SDA> READ/EXECUTIVE
%SDA-I-READSYM, 329 symbols read from
            SYS$COMMON:[SYS$LDR]SYSLICENSE.STB;1
%SDA-I-READSYM, 768 symbols read from SYS$COMMON:[SYS$LDR]F11BXQP.STB;1
    :
    :
%SDA-I-READSYM, 2957 symbols read from
            SYS$COMMON:[SYS$LDR]SYS$BASE_IMAGE.EXE;1
%SDA-I-READSYM, 331 symbols read from
            SYS$COMMON:[SYSLIB]SYS$PUBLIC_VECTORS.EXE
```

The SDA command SHOW EXECUTIVE produces a list of the executive images, their starting and ending addresses, and their sizes. Section B.2.2.1 describes the use of this list in conjunction with the executive map files. For each sliced executive image, SDA defines symbols for the base addresses of the different image sections. For example, SDA defines the symbols SYSVM_NPRO, SYSVM_NPRW, SYS$VM_PRO, and SYS$VM_PRW, for the nonpaged read-only, nonpaged read/write, paged read-only, and paged read/write image sections of the SYS$VM executive image. For a nonsliced executive image, SDA defines a symbol of the same name as the image, for example SYS$VM, whose value corresponds to the base address of the image.

Section B.1.2.2 describes a technique for adding data structure offset and other symbols to SDA's symbol table. This technique can be used if the symbol table for an executive image does not contain the desired symbols.

The OpenVMS AXP Version 1.5 distribution kit CD-ROM contains a directory called [SYMBOL_TABLES], which contains the symbol tables for all drivers from the [DRIVER], [TTDRVR], and [LAN] facilities.

B.4   **INTERPRETING SDL FILES**

Most data structures and other systemwide constants used by the executive and other system components are defined with SDL files. SDL enables data structures to be defined in a language-independent way. SDL can generate language-specific versions of the same structure in any of several languages.

When an OpenVMS system is built from source, the SDL preprocessor reads and processes system data structure definitions written in SDL. It produces a set of macro definitions for use by the MACRO-32 compiler and another set for the BLISS-32 compiler.

In particular, there are SDL files that generate the macros that define data structures and constants in the libraries ALPHA$LIBRARY:LIB.* and AL-PHA$LIBRARY:STARLET.*. The OpenVMS listing kit includes these SDL files. The SDL definition of a data structure typically includes comments describing the fields of the structure. The SDL definition can thus be a source of information about the meaning of system data structure fields. These comments are not propagated to LIB.MLB and STARLET.MLB, although they do appear in LIB.R32, LIB.R64, STARLET.R32, and STARLET.R64, the BLISS-32 and BLISS-64 versions.

This section shows how the SDL description of a data structure relates to both the resulting MACRO-32 definition and a picture of the structure. Its sole purpose is to assist in the interpretation of SDL files supplied with the OpenVMS listing kit. Note that SDL is an internal Digital tool. Any other use is completely unsupported.

B.4.1   **A Sample Structure Definition**

To see how a structure is defined, look at the symbol definitions and compare the SDL definition of a given structure with the resulting MACRO-32 or BLISS-32 symbols. Any listing that uses the structure in question includes these symbols. Alternatively, use the command procedure described in Section B.1.2.2.

Many SDL files begin and end with the following sequence of directives:

```
     .
     .
     .

IFLANGUAGE MACRO;
LITERAL;
     .SYMBOL_ALIGNMENT     LONG
END_LITERAL;
END_IFLANGUAGE MACRO;
```

```
    .
    .
    .
;definitions included here
    .
    .
    .
IFLANGUAGE MACRO;
LITERAL;
      .SYMBOL_ALIGNMENT    NONE
END_LITERAL;
END_IFLANGUAGE MACRO;
```

The SDL directive IFLANGUAGE MACRO tests whether the SDL file is being processed to create equivalent MACRO-32 definitions. If true, this enables all SDL directives before the SDL directive END_IFLANGUAGE MACRO to be processed. The directive LITERAL directs SDL to output whatever follows until the directive END_LITERAL is encountered. The net result of the directives in this example is that when the SDL file is being processed for MACRO-32, the following MACRO-32 directives are entered into the output stream: .SYMBOL_ALIGNMENT LONG and .SYMBOL_ALIGN- MENT NONE. The purpose of the .SYMBOL_ALIGNMENT directive is explained in Section B.1.3.4.

Example B.1 shows the SDL definition of the AST control block (ACB) and the comments that accompany each field definition. Figure 8.1 shows the layout of an ACB. Table B.2 lists each SDL directive in the ACB definition, its meaning, the symbol it creates, and the value of that symbol. The following sections briefly describe the individual SDL directives.

B.4.2   Commonly Used SDL Statements

An SDL statement consists of SDL keywords, user-specified names, and expressions. A semicolon terminates an SDL statement. It can be followed by a comment to be included in the output macro. The comment must begin with the character pair /*.

Valid SDL expressions can contain any of the following:

► Numeric constants
► Local symbols
► Special offset location symbols: period (.), colon (:), and circumflex (^)
► Arithmetic, shift, and logical operators
► Parentheses to define the order of evaluation

The next sections describe the SDL statements commonly employed to define structures used by OpenVMS. They emphasize the SDL files used to build the system. A complete syntax of each statement is not given.

B.4.2.1   MODULE Statement.
A MODULE statement groups related symbols and data structures. It defines a collection of SDL statements to be processed. Typically, each OpenVMS data structure is defined within its own module.

Table B.2   SDL Directives and Resulting MACRO-32 Symbol Definitions for AST Control Block

SDL Directive	Directive Meaning	Resulting Symbol	Symbol Value
module $ACBDEF	Begin $ACBDEF macro		
aggregate ACBDEF structure prefix ACB$	Begin ACB structure		
ASTQFL longword unsigned	Longword field	ACB$L_ASTQFL	0
ASTQBL longword unsigned	Longword field	ACB$L_ASTQBL	4
SIZE word unsigned	Word field	ACB$W_SIZE	8
TYPE byte unsigned	Byte field	ACB$B_TYPE	10
RMOD_OVERLAY union fill	Begin overlay structure		
RMOD byte unsigned	Byte field	ACB$B_RMOD	11
RMOD_BITS structure fill	Begin RMOD_BITS structure		
MODE bitfield length 2	Bit field of length 2	ACB$V_MODE ACB$S_MODE	0 2
FILL_1 bitfield fill prefix ACBDEF tag $$	Skip one spare bit		
POSIX_ACB bitfield mask	Single bit field	ACB$V_POSIX_ACB ACB$M_POSIX_ACB	3 8_{16}
PKAST bitfield mask	Single bit field	ACB$V_PKAST ACB$M_PKAST	4 10_{16}
NODELETE bitfield mask	Single bit field	ACB$V_NODELETE ACB$M_NODELETE	5 20_{16}
QUOTA bitfield mask	Single bit field	ACB$V_QUOTA ACB$M_QUOTA	6 40_{16}
KAST bitfield mask	Single bit field	ACB$V_KAST ACB$M_KAST	7 80_{16}
end RMOD_BITS	End RMOD_BITS structure		
end RMOD_OVERLAY	End overlay structure		
PID longword unsigned	Longword field	ACB$L_PID	12
AST longword unsigned	Longword field	ACB$L_AST	16
ASTPRM longword unsigned	Longword field	ACB$L_ASTPRM	20
FKB_FILL longword dimension 2 fill	2-longword field	ACB$L_FKB_FILL	24
KAST longword unsigned	Longword field	ACB$L_KAST	32
constant "LENGTH" equals . prefix ACB$ tag K	Define a constant	ACB$K_LENGTH	36
constant "LENGTH" equals . prefix ACB$ tag C	Define a constant	ACB$C_LENGTH	36
end ACBDEF	End ACB structure		
end_module $ACBDEF	End $ACBDEF macro		

Example B.1
SDL Definition of AST Control Block

```
module $ACBDEF;
/*+
/* AST CONTROL BLOCK DEFINITIONS
/*
/* AST CONTROL BLOCKS EXIST AS SEPARATE STRUCTURES AND AS SUBSTRUCTURES
/* WITHIN LARGER CONTROL BLOCKS SUCH AS I/O REQUEST PACKETS AND TIMER
/* QUEUE ENTRIES.
/*
/*-
    .
    .
    .
aggregate ACBDEF structure prefix ACB$;
    ASTQFL longword unsigned;                /*AST QUEUE FORWARD LINK
    ASTQBL longword unsigned;                /*AST QUEUE BACKWARD LINK
    SIZE word unsigned;                      /*STRUCTURE SIZE IN BYTES
    TYPE byte unsigned;                      /*STRUCTURE TYPE CODE
    RMOD_OVERLAY union fill;
        RMOD byte unsigned;                  /*REQUEST ACCESS MODE
        RMOD_BITS structure fill;
            MODE bitfield length 2;          /*MODE FOR FINAL DELIVERY
            FILL_1      bitfield fill prefix ACBDEF tag $$;      /* SPARE
            POSIX_ACB   bitfield mask;       /*USED FOR DELIVERING SIGNALS/EVENTS
            PKAST bitfield mask;             /*PIGGYBACK SPECIAL KERNEL AST
            NODELETE bitfield mask;          /*DON'T DELETE ACB ON DELIVERY
            QUOTA bitfield mask;             /*ACCOUNT FOR QUOTA
            KAST bitfield mask;              /*SPECIAL KERNEL AST
        end RMOD_BITS;
    end RMOD_OVERLAY;
    PID longword unsigned;                   /*PROCESS ID OF REQUEST
    AST longword unsigned;                   /*AST ROUTINE ADDRESS
    ASTPRM longword unsigned;                /*AST PARAMETER
    FKB_FILL longword dimension 2 fill;      /*FILL TO ALLOW OVERLAY OF FORK BLOCK
    KAST longword unsigned;                  /*INTERNAL KERNEL MODE XFER ADDRESS
    constant "LENGTH" equals . prefix ACB$ tag K;      /* Length of block
    constant "LENGTH" equals . prefix ACB$ tag C;      /* Length of block

end ACBDEF;
    .
    .
    .
end_module $ACBDEF;
```

The name of the module is the name of the generated macro. For example, the following statement from Example B.1 defines the beginning of the module that defines the ACB data structure:

```
module   $ACBDEF;
```

B.4.2.2   **AGGREGATE Statement.** An AGGREGATE declaration defines a single data structure within a module. There are two types of AGGREGATE declaration:

- ▸ STRUCTURE
- ▸ UNION

1401

The fields in a STRUCTURE occupy consecutive storage locations; the fields in a UNION reuse the same storage location.

The period character symbolizes the current byte offset within an AGGRE-GATE declaration.

Each OpenVMS data structure definition begins with an AGGREGATE STRUCTURE statement. This statement includes a PREFIX keyword that specifies the prefix characters in each symbol definition. For example, the following statement from Example B.1 defines the beginning of the ACB structure, each of whose symbol definitions begins with the characters ACB$:

```
aggregate ACBDEF structure prefix ACB$;
```

B.4.2.3   **Data Structure Fields.** Each field in a data structure is defined in a statement consisting of a name and one or more keywords. A keyword can identify the type of data or its size. For example, the keywords BYTE, WORD, LONG-WORD, QUADWORD, and OCTAWORD specify integer fields of those sizes. A keyword can specify some attribute of a field. For example, the keyword SIGNED specifies that an integer field is signed. The default is un-signed. Many other keywords are used to define OpenVMS data structures. Examples are F_FLOATING, BITFIELD, and CHARACTER.

The value of the symbol name is set equal to the current value of an internal offset counter. In general, as each field definition is processed, the internal counter value is increased by the size of the field (1, 2, 4, or 8).

B.4.2.4   **Symbol Names.** The naming conventions that apply to OpenVMS symbols defined through SDL are listed in Appendix D. In general, a data structure symbol has the form *structure$type_field-name*. *Structure* identifies its data structure. *Type* identifies the type of data. *Field-name* names the field.

A data structure symbol name is formed from a combination of the follow-ing elements:

► PREFIX keyword value, which includes a dollar sign ($) to indicate a Digital-defined symbol
► Letter indicating type. Data type keywords of BYTE, WORD, LONG-WORD, QUADWORD, or OCTAWORD generate characters B, W, L, Q, or O. A CONSTANT statement usually specifies a TAG value of C or K.
► Underscore (_)
► Field name from the data type statement

B.4.2.5   **Symbol Values.** It is possible for the user to assign values directly to a symbol defined as part of an SDL structure (for example, with the DEFAULT key-word). Normally, however, SDL assumes that a symbol will be used as an offset from the beginning of its data structure. SDL keeps track of the current offset from the start of the structure, and SDL assigns that value to the symbol.

B.4.2.6 **UNION Statement.** It is often desirable to give a field multiple names. In addition, subfields within a field often exist. The UNION statement defines the beginning of a substructure whose members reuse the same storage locations. The following extract from Example B.1 shows a UNION substructure:

```
RMOD_OVERLAY union fill;
  RMOD byte unsigned;
  RMOD_BITS structure fill;
    .
    .
    .
  end RMOD_BITS;
end RMOD_OVERLAY;
```

This extract defines both the symbol ACB$B_RMOD and the structure ACB$R_RMOD_BITS to be the value of the current byte offset.

The FILL qualifier indicates that no symbol is to be generated in the MACRO-32 and BLISS-32 expansions of the structure definition.

B.4.2.7 **CONSTANT Statement.** The CONSTANT statement defines a constant. Depending on what TAG argument is supplied, the CONSTANT statement produces symbols of the form *xyz$C_name*, *xyz$K_name*, or *xyz$_name*. By convention, symbols with C in the type field of the symbol name define ASCII character constants, while symbols with K in the type field define other constants. Early versions of VMS used only the C type for both character and other constants, and these symbols are still in use.

Table B.2 illustrates the use of the CONSTANT statement:

```
constant "LENGTH" equals . prefix ACB$ tag K;
```

This statement defines the symbol ACB$K_LENGTH equal to the value of the period character, the current byte offset in the ACB structure.

There are several other examples of constant definitions in both the SYSDEF and STARDEF SDL files. The definitions of the DYN$ symbols describe dynamically allocated structures. The JPI$ symbols describe an information list to the $GETJPI system service.

B.4.2.8 **BITFIELD Statement.** Bit fields require two numbers to completely describe them, a bit position and a size. SDL always defines a bit position (indicated by V in the type field of the symbol name). The bit position is specified by the current bit offset. The circumflex character (^) symbolizes the current bit offset within the current subaggregate.

The size of a field (indicated by S in the type field of the symbol name) is defined when the field size is specified explicitly with the LENGTH keyword. It is often useful to define a mask symbol (indicated by M in the type field of the symbol name) that has 1's in each bit position defined by the bit field and 0's elsewhere. SDL defines such a symbol if the MASK keyword is present in the BITFIELD statement.

Because this section merely tries to show what symbols result from a given SDL definition, the simplest way to describe the bit field syntax is with some examples. Table B.2 includes SDL BITFIELD statements extracted from the definition of the ACB.

B.4.2.9   **END and END_MODULE Statements.** The structure definition is terminated with an END statement. The module is terminated with an END_MODULE statement.

B.5   **RELEVANT SOURCE MODULES**

Source modules described in this appendix include

[CLD]DCLTABLE1.CLD
[DCL]COMMAND.BLI
[LIB]ACBDEF.SDL
[SYS]ASTDEL.MAR

C   SYSGEN Parameters and Their Locations

The following table lists the SYSGEN parameters alphabetically and indicates the names of the cells where the parameters are stored.

SYSGEN Parameter	Cell Name
ACP_BASEPRIO	ACP$GB_BASEPRIO
ACP_DATACHECK	ACP$GB_DATACHK
ACP_DINDXCACHE	ACP$GW_DINDXCACHE
ACP_DIRCACHE	ACP$GW_DIRCACHE
ACP_EXTCACHE	ACP$GW_EXTCACHE
ACP_EXTLIMIT	ACP$GW_EXTLIMIT
ACP_FIDCACHE	ACP$GW_FIDCACHE
ACP_HDRCACHE	ACP$GW_HDRCACHE
ACP_MAPCACHE	ACP$GW_MAPCACHE
ACP_MAXREAD	ACP$GB_MAXREAD
ACP_MULTIPLE	EXE$V_MULTACP (EXE$GL_DEFFLAGS)
ACP_QUOCACHE	ACP$GW_QUOCACHE
ACP_REBLDSYSD	EXE$V_REBLDSYSD (EXE$GL_STATIC_FLAGS)
ACP_SHARE	EXE$V_SHRF11ACP (EXE$GL_DEFFLAGS)
ACP_SWAPFLGS	ACP$GB_SWAPFLGS
ACP_SYSACC	ACP$GW_SYSACC
ACP_WINDOW	ACP$GB_WINDOW
ACP_WORKSET	ACP$GW_WORKSET
ACP_WRITEBACK	ACP$GB_WRITBACK
ACP_XQP_RES	EXE$V_XQP_RESIDENT (EXE$GL_STATIC_FLAGS)
AFFINITY_SKIP	SCH$GL_AFFINITY_SKIP
AFFINITY_TIME	SCH$GL_AFFINITY_TIME
ALLOCLASS	CLU$GL_ALLOCLS
AWSMIN	SCH$GL_AWSMIN_PAGELETS
AWSTIME	SCH$GL_AWSTIME
BALSETCNT	SGN$GL_BALSETCT
BJOBLIM	SYS$GW_BJOBLIM

SYSGEN Parameter	Cell Name
BOOT_STYLE	EXE$GL_BOOT_STYLE
BORROWLIM	SCH$GL_BORROWLIM
BREAKPOINTS	SGN$GL_BRKMSK
BUGCHECKFATAL	EXE$V_FATAL_BUG (EXE$GL_DEFFLAGS)
BUGREBOOT	EXE$V_BUGREBOOT (EXE$GL_DEFFLAGS)
CHANNELCNT	SGN$GW_PCHANCNT
CLASS_PROT	EXE$V_CLASS_PROT (EXE$GL_DYNAMIC_FLAGS)
CLISYMTBL	EXE$GL_CLITABL
CLOCK_INTERVAL	EXE$GW_CLKINT
CONCEAL_DEVICES	EXE$V_CONCEALED (EXE$GL_DEFFLAGS)
CRDENABLE	EXE$V_CRDENABL (EXE$GL_DEFFLAGS)
CRD_CONTROL	EXE$GB_CRD_CONTROL
CTLIMGLIM	SGN$GW_CTLIMGLIM
CTLPAGES	SGN$GW_CTLPAGELETS
DEADLOCK_WAIT	LCK$GL_WAITTIME
DEFMBXBUFQUO	IOC$GW_MBXBFQUO
DEFMBXMXMSG	IOC$GW_MBXMXMSG
DEFPRI	SYS$GB_DEFPRI
DEFQUEPRI	SYS$GB_DEFQUEPRI
DISK_QUORUM	CLU$GB_QDISK
DISMOUMSG	EXE$V_DISMOUMSG (EXE$GL_MSGFLAGS)
DLCKEXTRASTK	LCK$GL_EXTRASTK
DNVOSI1	SGN$GL_DNVOSI1
DORMANTWAIT	SCH$GW_DORMANTWAIT
DUMPBUG	EXE$V_BUGDUMP (EXE$GL_DEFFLAGS)
DUMPSTYLE	SGN$GL_DUMP_STYLE
ERLBUFFERPAGES	EXE$GB_ERLBUFPAGELETS
ERRORLOGBUFFERS	SGN$GW_ERLBUFCNT
EXPECTED_VOTES	CLU$GW_EXP_VOTES
EXTRACPU	SGN$GL_EXTRACPU
EXUSRSTK	SGN$GL_EXUSRSTK
FREEGOAL	SGN$GL_FREEGOAL
FREELIM	SGN$GL_FREELIM
GBLPAGES	SGN$GL_MAXGPGCT_PAGELETS
GBLPAGFIL	SGN$GL_GBLPAGFIL
GBLSECTIONS	SGN$GW_GBLSECNT
GH_RSRVPGCNT	EXE$GL_GH_RSRVPGCNT

SYSGEN Parameter	*Cell Name*
GROWLIM	SCH$GL_GROWLIM
IEEE_ADDRESS	UID$GL_IEEE_ADDRESS
IEEE_ADDRESSH	UID$GW_IEEE_ADDRESSH
IJOBLIM	SYS$GW_IJOBLIM
IMGIOCNT	SGN$GW_IMGIOCNT
IOTA	SCH$GW_IOTA
ITB_ENTRIES	EXE$GL_ITB_ENTRIES
JOBCTLD	SGN$GL_JOBCTLD
KSTACKPAGES	SGN$GL_KSTACKPAG
LAMAPREGS	IOC$GW_LAMAPREG
LGI_BRK_DISUSER	EXE$V_BRK_DISUSER (EXE$GL_DYNAMIC_FLAGS)
LGI_BRK_LIM	SYS$GB_BRK_LIM
LGI_BRK_TERM	EXE$V_BRK_TERM (EXE$GL_DYNAMIC_FLAGS)
LGI_BRK_TMO	SYS$GL_BRK_TMO
LGI_CALLOUTS	SYS$GB_CALLOUTS
LGI_HID_TIM	SYS$GL_HID_TIM
LGI_PWD_TMO	SYS$GB_PWD_TMO
LGI_RETRY_LIM	SYS$GB_RETRY_LIM
LGI_RETRY_TMO	SYS$GB_RETRY_TMO
LNMPHASHTBL	LNM$GL_HTBLSIZP
LNMSHASHTBL	LNM$GL_HTBLSIZS
LOAD_PWD_POLICY	EXE$V_LOAD_PWD_POLICY (EXE$GL_DYNAMIC_FLAGS)
LOAD_SYS_IMAGES	SGN$GL_LOADFLAGS
LOCKDIRWT	CLU$GW_LCKDIRWT
LOCKIDTBL	LCK$GL_IDTBLSIZ
LOCKIDTBL_MAX	LCK$GL_IDTBLMAX
LOCKRETRY	EXE$GL_LOCKRTRY
LONGWAIT	SCH$GW_LONGWAIT
MAXBUF	IOC$GW_MAXBUF
MAXCLASSPRI	SCH$GB_MAXCLASSPRI
MAXPROCESSCNT	SGN$GW_MAXPRCCT
MAXQUEPRI	SYS$GB_MAXQUEPRI
MAXSYSGROUP	EXE$GL_SYSUIC
MINCLASSPRI	SCH$GB_MINCLASSPRI
MINPRPRI	SCH$GB_MINPRPRI
MINWSCNT	SGN$GL_MINWSCNT
MMG_CTLFLAGS	MMG$GB_CTLFLAGS

SYSGEN Parameters and Their Locations

SYSGEN Parameter	Cell Name
MOUNTMSG	EXE$V_MOUNTMSG (EXE$GL_MSGFLAGS)
MPW_HILIMIT	MPW$GW_HILIM
MPW_IOLIMIT	MPW$GB_IOLIM
MPW_LOLIMIT	MPW$GW_LOLIM
MPW_LOWAITLIMIT	MPW$GL_LOWAITLIM
MPW_PRIO	MPW$GB_PRIO
MPW_THRESH	MPW$GL_THRESH
MPW_WAITLIMIT	MPW$GL_WAITLIM
MPW_WRTCLUSTER	MPW$GW_MPWPFC
MSCP_BUFFER	CLU$GL_MSCP_BUFFER
MSCP_CREDITS	CLU$GL_MSCP_CREDITS
MSCP_LOAD	CLU$GL_MSCP_LOAD
MSCP_SERVE_ALL	CLU$GL_MSCP_SERVE_ALL
MULTIPROCESSING	SGN$GB_MULTIPROCESSING
MVTIMEOUT	IOC$GW_MVTIMEOUT
NET_CALLOUTS	SYS$GB_NET_CALLOUTS
NISCS_CONV_BOOT	CLU$V_NISCS_CONV_BOOT (CLU$GL_SGN_FLAGS)
NISCS_LAN_OVRHD	CLU$GL_NISCS_LAN_OVRHD
NISCS_LOAD_PEA0	CLU$V_NISCS_LOAD_PEA0 (CLU$GL_SGN_FLAGS)
NISCS_MAX_PKTSZ	CLU$GL_NISCS_MAX_PKTSZ
NISCS_PORT_SERV	CLU$GL_NISCS_PORT_SERV
NJOBLIM	SYS$GW_NJOBLIM
NOAUTOCONFIG	EXE$V_NOAUTOCNF (EXE$GL_DEFFLAGS)
NOCLUSTER	EXE$V_NOCLUSTER (EXE$GL_DEFFLAGS)
NOPGFLSWP	EXE$V_NOPGFLSWP (EXE$GL_DYNAMIC_FLAGS)
NPAGEDYN	SGN$GL_NPAGEDYN
NPAGEVIR	SGN$GL_NPAGEVIR
PAGEDYN	SGN$GL_PAGEDYN
PAGFILCNT	SGN$GW_PAGFILCT
PAGTBLPFC	SGN$GB_PGTBPFC_PAGELETS
PAMAXPORT	SCS$GB_PAMXPORT
PANOPOLL	SCS$GB_PANOPOLL
PANUMPOLL	SCS$GB_PANPOLL
PAPOLLINTERVAL	SCS$GW_PAPOLINT
PAPOOLINTERVAL	SCS$GW_PAPOOLIN
PASANITY	SCS$GB_PASANITY
PASTDGBUF	SCS$GW_PAPPDDG

SYSGEN Parameter	*Cell Name*
PASTIMOUT	SCS$GW_PASTMOUT
PE1	SGN$GL_PE1
PE2	SGN$GL_PE2
PE3	SGN$GL_PE3
PE4	SGN$GL_PE4
PE5	SGN$GL_PE5
PE6	SGN$GL_PE6
PFCDEFAULT	SGN$GW_DFPFC_PAGELETS
PFRATH	SCH$GL_PFRATH
PFRATL	SCH$GL_PFRATL
PHYSICAL_MEMORY	MMG$GL_PHYMEM
PIOPAGES	SGN$GW_PIOPAGELETS
PIXSCAN	SGN$GW_PIXSCAN
POOLCHECK	EXE$GL_POOLCHECK
POOLPAGING	EXE$V_POOLPGING (EXE$GL_DEFFLAGS)
PRCPOLINTERVAL	SCS$GW_PRCPOLINT
PRIORITY_OFFSET	SCH$GB_PRIORITY_OFFSET
PROCSECTCNT	SGN$GW_MAXPSTCT
PSEUDOLOA	SGN$GL_PSEUDOLOA
PU_OPTIONS	SGN$GL_PU_OPTIONS
QBUS_MULT_INTR	SGN$GB_QBUS_MULT_INTR
QDSKINTERVAL	CLU$GW_QDSKINTERVAL
QDSKVOTES	CLU$GW_QDSKVOTES
QUANTUM	SCH$GW_QUAN
RECNXINTERVAL	CLU$GW_RECNXINT
RESALLOC	EXE$V_RESALLOC (EXE$GL_DEFFLAGS)
RESHASHTBL	LCK$GL_HTBLSIZ
RJOBLIM	SYS$GW_RJOBLIM
RMS_DFMBC	SYS$GB_DFMBC
RMS_DFMBFHSH	SYS$GB_DFMBFHSH
RMS_DFMBFIDX	SYS$GB_DFMBFIDX
RMS_DFMBFREL	SYS$GB_DFMBFREL
RMS_DFMBFSDK	SYS$GB_DFMBFSDK
RMS_DFMBFSMT	SYS$GB_DFMBFSMT
RMS_DFMBFSUR	SYS$GB_DFMBFSUR
RMS_DFNBC	SYS$GB_DFNBC
RMS_GBLBUFQUO	SYS$GW_GBLBUFQUO

SYSGEN Parameter	*Cell Name*
RSRVPAGCNT	MMG$GL_RSRVPAGCNT
S0_PAGING	EXE$GL_S0_PAGING
SAVEDUMP	EXE$V_SAVEDUMP (EXE$GL_DEFFLAGS)
SA_APP	EXE$V_SA_APP (EXE$GL_STATIC_FLAGS)
SBIERRENABLE	EXE$V_SBIERR (EXE$GL_DEFFLAGS)
SCH_CTLFLAGS	SCH$GL_CTLFLAGS
SCSBUFFCNT	SCS$GW_BDTCNT
SCSCONNCNT	SCS$GW_CDTCNT
SCSFLOWCUSH	SCS$GW_FLOWCUSH
SCSMAXDG	SCS$GW_MAXDG
SCSMAXMSG	SCS$GW_MAXMSG
SCSNODE	SCS$GB_NODENAME
SCSRESPCNT	SCS$GW_RDTCNT
SCSSYSTEMID	SCS$GB_SYSTEMID
SCSSYSTEMIDH	SCS$GB_SYSTEMIDH
SETTIME	EXE$V_SETTIME (EXE$GL_DEFFLAGS)
SHADOWING	EXE$GL_SHADOWING
SHADOW_MAX_COPY	EXE$GL_SHADOW_MAX_COPY
SHADOW_MBR_TMO	EXE$GL_SHADOW_MBR_TIMEOUT
SHADOW_SYS_DISK	EXE$GL_SHADOW_SYS_DISK
SHADOW_SYS_UNIT	EXE$GL_SHADOW_SYS_UNIT
SMP_CPUS	SGN$GL_SMP_CPUS
SMP_CPUSH	SGN$GL_SMP_CPUSH
SMP_LNGSPINWAIT	SGN$GL_SMP_LNGSPINWAIT
SMP_SANITY_CNT	SGN$GL_SMP_SANITY_CNT
SMP_SPINWAIT	SGN$GL_SMP_SPINWAIT
SMP_TICK_CNT	SGN$GL_SMP_TICK_CNT
SSINHIBIT	EXE$V_SSINHIBIT (EXE$GL_DEFFLAGS)
STARTUP_P1	SGN$GB_STARTUP_P1
STARTUP_P2	SGN$GB_STARTUP_P2
STARTUP_P3	SGN$GB_STARTUP_P3
STARTUP_P4	SGN$GB_STARTUP_P4
STARTUP_P5	SGN$GB_STARTUP_P5
STARTUP_P6	SGN$GB_STARTUP_P6
STARTUP_P7	SGN$GB_STARTUP_P7
STARTUP_P8	SGN$GB_STARTUP_P8
SWPALLOCINC	SWP$GW_SWPINC

SYSGEN Parameter	*Cell Name*
SWPFAIL	SCH$GW_SWPFAIL
SWPFILCNT	SGN$GW_SWPFILES
SWPOUTPGCNT	SWP$GL_SWPPGCNT_PAGELETS
SWPRATE	SCH$GL_SWPRATE
SWP_PRIO	SWP$GB_PRIO
SYSMWCNT	SGN$GL_SYSDWSCT_PAGELETS
SYSPFC	SGN$GB_SYSPFC_PAGELETS
TAILORED	SGN$GB_TAILORED
TAPE_ALLOCLASS	CLU$GL_TAPE_ALLOCLS
TAPE_MVTIMEOUT	IOC$GW_TAPE_MVTIMEOUT
TBSKIPWSL	SGN$GW_WSLMXSKP
TIMEPROMPTWAIT	SGN$GW_TPWAIT
TIME_CONTROL	EXE$GL_TIME_CONTROL
TIMVCFAIL	SCS$GW_TIMVCFAIL
TMSCP_LOAD	CLU$GL_TMSCP_LOAD
TTY_ALTALARM	TTY$GW_ALTALARM
TTY_ALTYPAHD	TTY$GW_ALTYPAHD
TTY_AUTOCHAR	TTY$GB_AUTOCHAR
TTY_BUF	TTY$GW_DEFBUF
TTY_CLASSNAME	TTY$GW_CLASSNAM
TTY_DEFCHAR	TTY$GL_DEFCHAR
TTY_DEFCHAR2	TTY$GL_DEFCHAR2
TTY_DEFPORT	TTY$GL_DEFPORT
TTY_DIALTYPE	TTY$GB_DIALTYP
TTY_DMASIZE	TTY$GW_DMASIZE
TTY_OWNER	TTY$GL_OWNUIC
TTY_PARITY	TTY$GB_PARITY
TTY_PROT	TTY$GW_PROT
TTY_RSPEED	TTY$GB_RSPEED
TTY_SCANDELTA	TTY$GL_DELTA
TTY_SILOTIME	TTY$GB_SILOTIME
TTY_SPEED	TTY$GB_DEFSPEED
TTY_TIMEOUT	TTY$GL_TIMEOUT
TTY_TYPAHDSZ	TTY$GW_TYPAHDSZ
UAFALTERNATE	EXE$V_SYSUAFALT (EXE$GL_DEFFLAGS)
UDABURSTRATE	SCS$GB_UDABURST
USER3	SGN$GL_USER3

SYSGEN Parameter	Cell Name
USER4	SGN$GL_USER4
USERD1	SGN$GL_USERD1
USERD2	SGN$GL_USERD2
VAXCLUSTER	CLU$GB_VAXCLUSTER
VCC_FLAGS	CACHE$GL_FLAGS
VCC_MAXSIZE	CACHE$GL_BLOCKCNTMAX
VECTOR_MARGIN	EXE$GL_VP_MARGIN
VECTOR_PROC	EXE$GB_VP_LOAD
VIRTUALPAGECNT	SGN$GL_MAXVPGCT_PAGELETS
VMS5	SGN$GL_VMS5
VMS6	SGN$GL_VMS6
VMS7	SGN$GL_VMS7
VMS8	SGN$GL_VMS8
VMSD1	SGN$GL_VMSD1
VMSD2	SGN$GL_VMSD2
VMSD3	SGN$GL_VMSD3
VMSD4	SGN$GL_VMSD4
VOTES	CLU$GW_VOTES
WINDOW_SYSTEM	EXE$GL_WINDOW_SYSTEM
WPRE_SIZE	SGN$GW_WPRE_SIZE
WPTTE_SIZE	SGN$GL_WPTTE_SIZE
WRITABLESYS	EXE$V_SYSWRTABL (EXE$GL_DEFFLAGS)
WRITESYSPARAMS	EXE$V_WRITESYSPARAMS (EXE$GL_DYNAMIC_FLAGS)
WSDEC	SCH$GL_WSDEC_PAGELETS
WSINC	SCH$GL_WSINC_PAGELETS
WSMAX	SGN$GL_MAXWSCNT_PAGELETS
XFMAXRATE	IOC$GW_XFMXRATE
XQP_ALLOC_BLKS	XQP$GL_ALLOC_BLOCKS
ZERO_LIST_HI	MMG$GL_ZERO_LIST_HI_LIM

D Naming Conventions

The conventions described in this appendix were adopted to aid implementors in producing meaningful public names. Public names are names that are global (known to the linker) or that appear in parameter or macro definition files. Public names follow these conventions for the following reasons:

- Using reserved names ensures that customer-written software will not be invalidated by subsequent releases of Digital products that add new symbols.
- Using definite patterns for different uses tells someone reading the source code what type of object is being referenced. For example, the form of a macro name is different from that of an offset, which is different from that of a status code.
- Using length codes within a pattern associates the size of an object with its name, increasing the likelihood that reference to this object will use the correct MACRO-32 statements.

    As the use of MACRO-32 decreases, it is expected that the use of length codes will decline. Software writers are encouraged not to explicitly specify the data size of a variable unless the situation demands it (see Section D.1).

- Using a facility code in symbol definitions gives the reader an indication of where the symbol is defined. Separate groups of implementors choose facility code names that will not conflict with one another.

To fully conform with these standards, local synonyms should never be defined for public symbols. The full public symbol should be used in every reference to give maximum clarity to the reader.

D.1 PUBLIC SYMBOL PATTERNS

All Digital symbols contain a dollar sign. Thus, customers and applications developers are strongly advised to use underscores instead of dollar signs to avoid potential conflicts.

Public symbols should be constructed to convey as much information as possible about the entities they name. Frequently, private names follow a similar convention. The private name convention is then the same as the public one, with the underscore replacing the dollar sign in symbol names. Private names are used both within a module and globally between modules of a facility that is never in a library. All names that might ever be bound into a user's program must follow the rules for public names. In the case of internal names, a double dollar sign convention can be used, as shown in item 4 in the following list of formats.

1. System service and Record Management Services (RMS) MACRO-32 names are of the form

   $*service-name*

   In a system service MACRO-32 name, a trailing _S or _G distinguishes the stack form from the separate argument list form. Details about the names of system service macros can be found in the *OpenVMS Programming Concepts* manual.

   These names appear in the system macro library STARLET.MLB and represent a call to one of the OpenVMS system services or RMS services. The following examples show this form of symbol name:

$ASCEFC_S	Associate common event flag cluster
$CLOSE	Close a file
$TRNLNM_G	Translate logical name

2. Facility-specific public macro names are of the form

   $*facility_macro-name*

   The executive does not use any symbol names of this form.

3. System macros using local symbols or macros always use names of the form

   $*facility*$*macro-name*

   This is the form to be used both for symbols generated by a macro and included in calls to it, and for internal macros that are not documented. The executive does not use any symbol names of this form.

4. Global entry point names are of the form

   facility$*entry-name*

   The following examples show this form of symbol name:

EXE$ALOPAGED	Allocate paged pool
IOC$KP_WFIKPCH	Wait for interrupt and keep channel
MMG$PAGEFAULT	Page fault handler

   Global entry point names that are intended for use only within a set of related procedures but not by any calling programs outside the set are of the form

   facility$$*entry-name*

   The executive contains few symbol names of this form. However, the Run-Time Library contains several examples of symbol names that follow this convention, for example:

BAS$$STOP	Signal a BASIC fatal error
FOR$$SIGNAL_STO	Signal a FORTRAN error and call LIB$STOP
OTS$$CLOSE_FILE	Internal routine to close file

5. Global entry point names that have nonstandard invocations (MACRO-32 JSB entry point names) are of the following form, where _R*n* indicates that R0 through R*n* are not preserved by the routine:

> *facility*$*entry-name*_R*n*

In OpenVMS VAX, the invoker of such an entry point must include at least registers R2 through R*n* in its own entry mask so that all registers used can be restored properly. In OpenVMS AXP, these routines are no longer supported. Users of a Run-Time Library routine of this form must call the corresponding routine whose name is derived by dropping the suffix _R*n*. Until code changes are actually made, routines in VAX Run-Time Libraries translated by the VAX environment software translator (VEST) utility can be used. Translated Run-Time Libraries contain examples of such routines:

LIB$ANALYZE_ SDESC_R2	Analyze string descriptor
OTS$MOVE3_R5	Copy string without any fill characters
STR$COPY_DX_R8	JSB entry to general string-copying routine

6. Status codes and condition values are of the form

> *facility*$_*status*

The following examples show this form of symbol name:

RMS$_FNF	File not found
SS$_ILLEFC	Illegal event flag cluster
SS$_WASCLR	Flag was previously clear

7. Global variable names are of the form

> *facility*$G*t*_*variable-name*

The letter G indicates a global variable. The letter *t* represents the type of variable (see Section D.2). The following examples show this form of symbol name:

CTL$GQ_PROCPRIV	Process privilege mask
EXE$GQ_SYSTIME	System date and time
SCH$GL_FREECNT	Number of pages on the free page list

8. Addressable global arrays use the letter A (instead of the letter G) and are of the form

> *facility*$A*t*_*array-name*

The letter A indicates a global array. The letter *t* indicates the type of array element (see Section D.2). In some uses, the symbol's value is the address of the beginning of the array; in other uses, the symbol is the name of a variable that contains the address of the beginning of the array.

The following examples show both uses of this form of symbol name:

CTL$AQ_EXCVEC	Array of primary and secondary exception vectors
CTL$AL_STACK	Array of stack limits
EXE$AL_ERLBUFADR	Address of array of error log allocation buffers

9. The letter A, along with the letter R, indicates a vectored universal symbol in the SYS$BASE_IMAGE.EXE base image that contains the address of an executive image data structure. Chapter 32 describes the modular organization of the executive in detail. The following examples show this form of symbol name:

EXE$AR_NPOOL_DATA	Address of data related to nonpaged pool allocation
SMP$AR_SPNLKVEC	Address of table of spinlock control blocks
SYS$AR_JOBCTLMB	Address of job controller's mailbox unit control block

10. New for OpenVMS AXP, pointer variables are of the form

    structure$P*x_variable-name*

    where *x* stands for S, H, L, or Q. For most variables, *x* stands for S or H, the software-defined or hardware-defined default pointer size. In such a form, the software writer makes no assumption about pointer size. This is the preferred form of pointer definition for new data structures. Where the size of a pointer must be explicitly specified as a longword or quadword, *x* stands for L or Q. This form of variable has been useful for porting OpenVMS VAX.

    In OpenVMS AXP Version 1.5, the size of a software-defined pointer is a longword and that of a hardware-defined pointer a quadword. The structure definition language (SDL) keyword POINTER defines a longword pointer in OpenVMS AXP Version 1.5. The SDL keywords POINTER_LONG and POINTER_QUAD allow the explicit specification of pointer size. When loading a longword quantity into a quadword register, an OpenVMS AXP compiler uses an instruction that sign-extends the longword quantity.

    To facilitate development of OpenVMS AXP, many pointer variables have been allowed to remain as they are rather than being changed to conform to this convention.

    The following examples show this form of symbol name.

ADP$PS_MBPR   Address of mailbox pointer register (in
                          adapter control block)

ICB$PH_PROGRAM_   Address of the program counter (in
  COUNTER   the invocation context block of the
                          translated image environment)

SYSG$PQ_CTB_PTR   Address of console terminal block (in the
                          SYSGEN utility data block)

SYSG$PL_CTB_PTR_L   Low-order longword of the console
                          terminal block address

Note that SYSG$PQ_CTB_PTR and SYSG$PL_CTB_PTR_L address the same offset in the SYSGEN data block, although the latter addresses only the low-order longword. This convention of suffixing a variable name with an _L to address the low-order longword part of a larger structure is widely used in OpenVMS AXP. Similarly, the suffix _H is used to address the high-order longword.

11. New for OpenVMS AXP, integer variables and public structure offset names for integer data are of the form

    structure$I*x*_*variable-name*

    where *x* is the same as *t* for standard-sized variables (B, W, L, or Q) and *x* stands for S or H for integers whose size is the software-defined or hardware-defined default. Unless an integer variable must be of a specific size, it is defined using the S or H form. In OpenVMS AXP Version 1.5, the size of a software-defined integer is a longword and that of a hardware-defined integer a quadword.

    The following examples show this form of the symbol name:

    KPB$IS_STACK_SIZE   Stack size (in the kernel process block)

    CHF$IH_MCH_SAVR0   Register R0 save area (in the mechanism
                            array)

    HWPCB$IQ_KSP   Kernel stack pointer (in the hardware
                            privileged context block)

    DDB$IL_ALLOCLS   Device allocation class (in the device data
                            block)

    DPT$IW_INAME_LEN   Length of driver's image name (in the
                            driver prologue table)

    KPB$IB_TYPE   Data structure type (in the kernel process
                            block)

    Most offset names that have been modified to adhere to the new convention have also retained their old names as synonyms for ease of porting OpenVMS VAX code. For example, DDB$L_ALLOCLS is a synonym for DDB$IL_ALLOCLS.

12. New for OpenVMS AXP, floating-point variables and public structure offset names for floating-point data are of the form

    structure$FH_*variable-name*

    The following example shows this form of symbol name:

    CHF$FH_MCH_SAVF29   Save area for floating-point register F29 (in mechanism array)

    The size of a floating-point datum is a quadword.

13. Public structure definition macro names are of the form

    $*facility_structure*DEF

    Invoking this macro defines all symbols of the form *structure*$*xxxxxx*.

    Most of the public structure definitions used by the operating system do not include the string *facility_* in the macros that define structure offsets. Rather, macros of the following form are used to define *structure*$*xxxxxx* symbols:

    $*structure*DEF

    The following examples show the $*structure*DEF form of the macro:

    $ACBDEF   Offsets into asynchronous system trap (AST) control block

    $PCBDEF   Offsets into software process control block

    $PHDDEF   Offsets into process header

    Many of the macros of this form are contained in the macro libraries LIB.MLB or STARLET.MLB. These macros are initially defined in a language-independent structure definition language, as described in Appendix B.

14. Public structure offset names are of the form

    structure$*t_field-name*

    The letter *t* indicates the data type of the field (see Section D.2). The value of the public symbol is the byte offset to the start of the data element in the structure. The following examples show this form of symbol name:

    CEB$L_EFC   Event flag cluster (in common event block)

    GSD$W_SIZE   Size of global section descriptor in bytes

    PCB$B_PGFLINDEX   Process page file index (in software process control block)

15. MACRO-32 public structure bit field offsets and single bit names are of the form

    structure$V_*field-name*

    The value of the public symbol is the bit offset from the start of the field that contains the data, not from the start of the control block. The following examples show this form of symbol name:

ACB$V_QUOTA	Charge AST to process AST quota
CRB$V_BSY	Controller is busy (in controller request block)
UCB$V_CANCEL	Cancel I/O on this unit

16. MACRO-32 public structure bit field size names are of the form

    structure$S_*field-name*

    The value of the public symbol is the number of bits in the field. The following examples show this form of symbol name:

ACB$S_MODE	Length of requestor's access mode field (2 bits)
VA$S_BYTES_PER_ PAGELET	Length of bytes per pagelet field (9 bits)
PTE$S_PROT	Length of memory protection field (4 bits)

17. For BLISS, the functions of the symbols in the previous three items are combined into a single name used to reference an arbitrary datum. Names are of the following form, where x is the same as t for standard-sized data (B, W, L, and Q) and x stands for V for arbitrary and bit fields:

    structure$x_*field-name*

    The macro includes the offset, position, size, and sign extension suitable for use in a BLISS field selector. Most typically, this name is defined by the following BLISS statement:

```
    MACRO
  structure$V_field-name=
        structure$t_field-name,
        structure$V_field-name,        !MACRO-32 V
                                       ! bit field definition
        structure$S_field-name,
        <sign extension> %;
```

18. Public structure mask names are of the form

    structure$M_*field-name*

    The value of the public symbol is a mask with bits set for each bit in the field. This mask is not right-justified. Rather, it has *structure*$V_*field-name* zero bits on the right. The following examples show this form of symbol name.

PCB$M_RES	Mask of process residency field
VA$M_BYTES_PER_ PAGELET	Mask of bytes within pagelet field
PTE$M_PROT	Mask of memory protection field

19. Public structure constant names are of the form

    structure$K_*constant-name*

    The following examples show this form of symbol name:

PCB$K_LENGTH	Length (in bytes) of software process control block
EIHD$K_EXE	Image is executable (in image header)

    For historical reasons, many of the constants used by the executive have the letter C instead of K to indicate that the object data type is a constant. Examples of this form of symbol name are

DYN$C_PCB	Structure type is software process control block
EXE$C_SYSEFN	Common system event flag
PRT$C_URKW	Protection code of user read, kernel write

20. PSECT names are of the form

    facility$*mnemonic*

    When these names are put into a library, they have the form

    _*facility*$*mnemonic*

    The following examples show symbols of the form *facility*$*mnemonic*:

COPY$COPY_FILE	File copying main routine program section
DCL$ZCODE	Program section that contains most code for the Digital command language interpreter
DBG$CODE	Program section containing debugger routines

    This convention is not adhered to as strictly as the other naming conventions because PSECT names control the way that the linker allocates virtual address space. Names are often chosen to affect the relative locations of routines and the data they reference.

    Some sample PSECT names from the Run-Time Library show examples of the form _*facility*$*mnemonic*:

_LIB$CODE	General library (read-only) code section
_STR$DATA	Data section in the string manipulation library
_OTS$CODE	Code portion of language-independent support library

D.2   OBJECT DATA TYPES

Table D.1 shows some of the letters used to indicate data types or reserved for various other purposes. N, P, and T strings are typically variable-length.

Table D.1 Letters and the Data Types They Indicate

Letter	Data Type or Use
A	Address
B	Byte integer
C	Character[1]
D	Double precision floating
E	Reserved to Digital
F	Single precision floating
G	G floating-point values
H	H floating-point values
I	Reserved for integer extensions
J	Reserved to customers for escape to other codes
K	Constant
L	Longword integer
M	Field mask
N	Numeric string (all byte forms)
O	Octaword
P	Packed string
Q	Quadword integer
R	Reserved for records (structure)
S	Field size
T	Text (character) string
U	Smallest unit of addressable storage
V	Field position (MACRO-32)
	Field reference (BLISS)
W	Word integer
X	Context-dependent (generic)
Y	Context-dependent (generic)
Z	Unspecified or nonstandard

[1] In many symbols used by OpenVMS AXP, C is used as a synonym for K. Although K is the preferred indicator for constants, many constants used by OpenVMS AXP are indicated by a C in their name. Some constants, such as lengths of data structures, have both a C form and a K form.

In structures or I/O records, they frequently contain a byte-sized digit or character count preceding the string. If so, the location or offset is to the count. Counted strings cannot be passed in procedure calls. Instead, a string descriptor must be generated.

D.3   FACILITY PREFIX TABLE

Table D.2 lists some of the facility prefixes used by Digital-supplied software. This list is not inclusive and is intended to show examples of several facility prefixes. Each facility name has a unique facility code.

Note that bit ⟨27⟩, the customer facility bit, is clear in all the facility codes listed here. Customers are free to use any of the facility codes listed here,

Table D.2   Facility Names and Their Prefixes

Prefix	Description	Condition ⟨27 : 16⟩
	EXECUTIVE AND SYSTEM PROCESSES	
SS	System service status codes	0
CLI	Command language interpreters	3
JBC	Job controller	4
OPC	Operator communication	5
ERF	Error Log Formatting utility	8
	RUN-TIME LIBRARY COMPONENTS	
SMG	Screen management routines	18
LIB	General-Purpose Library	21
MTH	Mathematics Library	22
OTS	Language-independent object time system	23
FOR	FORTRAN Run-Time Library	24
SORT	SORT procedures	28
STR	String manipulation procedures	36
	UTILITIES AND COMPILERS	
DBG	Symbolic debugger	2
LIN	OpenVMS Linker	100
DIF	File Differences utility	108
PAT	Image File Patch utility	109
LAT	Local area transport	374

provided that they set bit ⟨27⟩. The default action of the message compiler is to set this bit.

The location of the facility code within a status code and the meaning of the other fields in the status code are described in the *OpenVMS Utility Routines Manual.*

Individual products such as compilers also have unique facility codes formed from the product name.

Structure name prefixes are typically local to a facility. Refer to the individual facility documentation for its structure name prefixes. Individual facility structure names do not cause problems, because these names are not global and are therefore not known to the linker. They become known at assembly or compile time only by explicit invocation of the macro defining the facility structure.

For example, the macro $FORDEF defines all the status codes that can be returned from the FORTRAN support library. The facility code of 24 is included in the upper 16 bits of each of the status codes defined with this macro.

Digital provides a registration service for customer facility names. For information on this service, write to the following address.

Product Registrar—ZKO1-1/E33
Digital Equipment Corporation
110 Spitbrook Road
Nashua, NH 03062-2698

The Digital Guide to Software Development gives further information about the topics discussed in this chapter.

E   Data Structure Definitions

This book has described the OpenVMS AXP operating system in terms of the data structures used by various components of the executive. This appendix summarizes those data structures.

E.1   LOCATION OF DATA STRUCTURE DEFINITIONS

The data structures used by OpenVMS AXP are defined in a language called structure definition language (SDL), which is briefly described in Appendix B. Two facilities contain most SDL definitions: [LIB] and [STARLET].

Most structure and constant definitions used internally by the OpenVMS AXP executive are in the [LIB] facility. These files have names of the form [LIB]*xyz*DEF.SDL, where *xyz* typically represents the name of a data structure or constant, for example, PCB (for process control block) or DYN (for data structure type constants). The MACRO-32 and MACRO-64 definitions based on these files are stored in the files LIB.MLB and LIB.PREFIX. The BLISS-32 and BLISS-64 definitions based on these files are stored in the files LIB.REQ, LIB.L32, LIB.R64, and LIB.L64. Many OpenVMS AXP components are built with the definitions in these files. They are also available to users for special applications such as user-written device drivers and system services.

Most structure and constant definitions available for general applications, such as system service requests, are in the [STARLET] facility. These files have names of the form [STARLET]*xyz*DEF.SDL. The definitions based on these files are stored in the files STARLET.MLB, STARLET.PREFIX, STARLET.REQ, and STARLET.R64.

The distinction between the SDL files in [LIB] and in [STARLET] is that a structure or constant defined in [STARLET] is considered an external interface and does not change from release to release. A structure or constant defined in [LIB] is considered an internal interface and is subject to change. Consequently, programs that use definitions based on [LIB] modules must be recompiled (or reassembled) and relinked with each major release of the OpenVMS AXP operating system.

E.2   OVERVIEW

Table E.1 lists the data structures and constants summarized in this appendix. The majority of them are defined in the [LIB] facility. The following classes of structures are in the table.

Table E.1   Summary of Data Structures in Appendix E

SYSTEMWIDE DATA STRUCTURES

ACB	GSD	LDRIMG	PFLMAP
ACL	GSTE	LKB	PHD
Activated privileged library dispatch vector	HWPCB	LNMB	PLV
ARB	HWRPB	LNMC	PQB
BDTAB	IMCB	LNMHSH	PSCANCTX
BOD	JIB	LNMTH	PSTE
BOOTCB	KFD	LNMX	RSB
CEB	KFE	MPW IRP	SCB
CPU	KFERES	MTX	SPL
CPUTAB	KFPB	MUTEX	SWRPB
EIHD	KFRH	ORB	TQE
EISD	KPB	PCB	
FKB	LDRHP	PFL	

STRUCTURES USED BY THE I/O AND FILE SUBSYSTEMS

ADP	CDRP	FCB	VCB
AQB	CRAM	FDT	VEC
BRK	CRB	IDB	VLE
BUSARRAY	DDB	IRP	WCB
CCB	DDT	TAST	
CDDB	DPT	UCB	

SYMBOLIC CONSTANTS

BDT	IO*xxyy*	NDT	SPL
DYN	IPL	PR	

[1] This structure is defined in the [STARLET] facility.

- ► Data structures used by memory management, the scheduler, and other executive components. At least one figure or table in this book describes each of these structures.
- ► Data structures used by the I/O and file subsystems.
- ► Constants such as data structure types, interrupt priority levels (IPLs), and local I/O space definitions.

E.3   EXECUTIVE DATA STRUCTURES

This section contains a brief summary of each of the data structures described in this book. Three data structures, the process control block (PCB), the process header (PHD), and the job information block (JIB), are partly described in several places throughout the book. They are illustrated here in their entirety, with references to other partial descriptions.

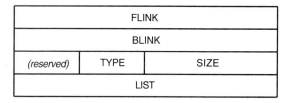

Figure E.1
Layout of an Access Control List (ACL)

E.3.1 ACB—Asynchronous System Trap (AST) Control Block

Purpose	Describes a pending AST for a process.
Usual location	AST queues with listheads in PCB.
Allocated from	Nonpaged pool.
Reference	Figure 8.1.
Special notes	ACBs are usually a part of a larger structure, such as an I/O request packet (IRP) or timer queue entry (TQE).

E.3.2 ACL—Access Control List

Purpose	List of entries that grant or deny access to a particular system resource.
Usual location	ACL queue with listhead in resource's object rights block (ORB$L_ACLFL).
Allocated from	Paged pool.
Reference	Figure E.1.
Special notes	An ACL contains access control entries beginning at offset ACL$L_LIST.

E.3.3 ADP—Adapter Control Block

Purpose	Defines characteristics and current state of the processor-memory interconnect (PMI) or a tightly coupled I/O interconnect.
Usual location	Linked into listhead IOC$GL_ADPLIST.
Allocated from	Nonpaged pool.
Reference	Figure 22.12.
Special notes	The operating system creates an ADP for the PMI, each tightly coupled I/O interconnect, and each multichannel I/O widget (see Chapter 2). The hierarchy of tightly coupled I/O interconnects on a system is represented by the interconnections between ADPs in the ADP list.

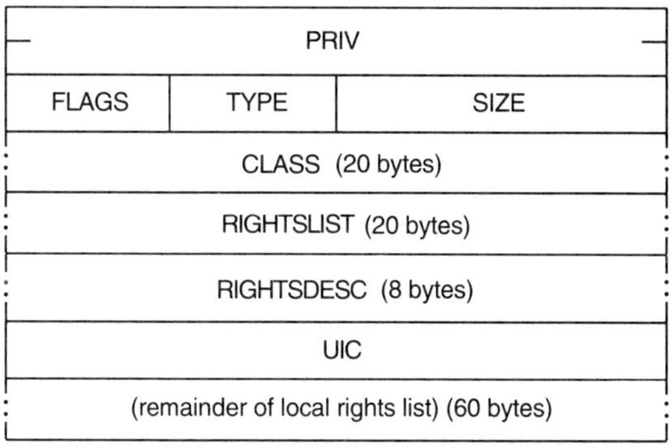

Figure E.2
Layout of an Access Rights Block (ARB)

E.3.4   **Activated Privileged Library Dispatch Vector**

Purpose	Contains information about the privileged shareable images in a given process.
Usual location	P1 space location CTL$A_DISPVEC.
Reference	Figure 7.9.

E.3.5   **AQB—Ancillary Control Process (ACP) Queue Block**

Purpose	Contains information specific to an ACP.
Usual location	Linked into listhead IOC$GL_AQBLIST.
Allocated from	Nonpaged pool.
Reference	Figure 22.20.

E.3.6   **ARB—Access Rights Block**

The ARB is currently a part of the PCB. The ARB pointer (PCB$L_ARB) points to this overlaid data structure. Program references that use the ARB pointer in the PCB to locate the ARB or any fields within the ARB (such as the privilege mask) will continue to work without modification should the ARB become an independent data structure in a future release of the OpenVMS AXP operating system.

Purpose	Defines process access rights and privileges.
Usual location	Currently a part of the PCB.
References	Table 28.2, Figure E.2.

E.3.7   **BDTAB—Boot Driver Table Structure**

Purpose	Locates standard boot driver routines in a boot driver. Created by the invocation of $BOOT_DRIVER macro.

Usual location	Part of the boot driver image linked into APB.EXE and pointed to by the BOOT_DRIVER_TABLE array within APB.
Reference	Figure 33.12.

E.3.8 BOD—Buffer Object Descriptor

Purpose	Describes a process's buffer object.
Usual location	Listhead in PCB$Q_BUFOBJ_LIST.
Allocated from	Nonpaged pool.
Reference	Figure 16.17.

E.3.9 BOOTCB—Boot Control Block

Purpose	Contains information used in booting and crashing the operating system.
Usual location	Pointed to by EXE$GL_BOOTCB.
Allocated from	Nonpaged pool.
Reference	Figure 33.15.

E.3.10 BRK—Breakthrough Message Descriptor Block

Purpose	Used to send asynchronous messages to one or more terminals.
Usual location	P1 space.
Allocated from	Process allocation region.
Reference	Figure 26.6.

E.3.11 BUSARRAY—Adapter Bus Array

Purpose	Supplements the ADP with information about nodes on the PMI or tightly coupled I/O interconnect.
Usual location	Pointed to by ADP$PS_BUS_ARRAY.
Allocated from	Nonpaged pool.
Reference	Figure 22.14.

E.3.12 CCB—Channel Control Block

Purpose	Describes the logical path between the process and the UCB of the specific device.
Usual location	In P1 space table; pointed to by CTL$GA_CCB_TABLE.
Allocated from	P1 space.
Reference	Figure 23.3.

E.3.13   **CDDB—Class Driver Data Block**

Purpose   Auxiliary data structure for each system communi-
                          cation services (SCS) connection between a disk or
                          tape class driver and a remote Mass Storage Control
                          Protocol (MSCP) server.

Usual location   Pointed to by CRB$L_AUXSTRUC.

Allocated from   Nonpaged pool.

Reference   Figure E.3.

Special notes   There is one CDDB per MSCP controller.

E.3.14   **CDRP—Class Driver Request Packet**

Purpose   Data structure used to communicate between SCS and
                          a class driver.

Usual location   Part of an IRP; linked into listhead CDDB$L_
                          CDRPQFL.

Allocated from   Nonpaged pool.

References   Figures 22.16, 26.2.

Special notes   Contains within it, at negative offsets, a full IRP.

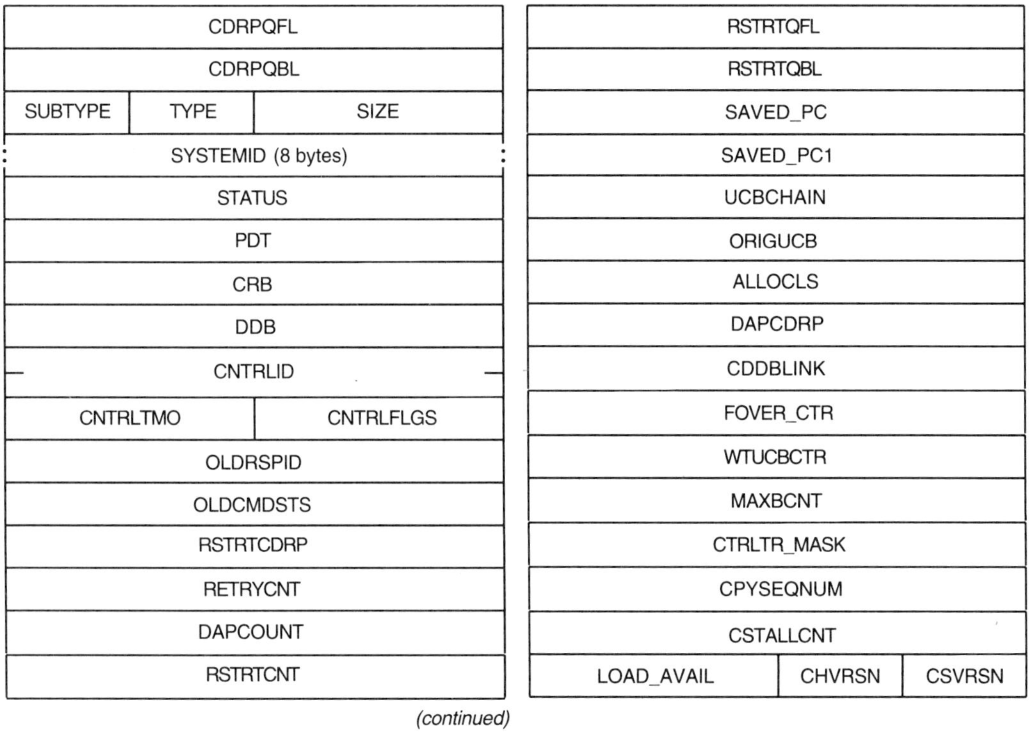

CDRPQFL				RSTRTQFL		
CDRPQBL				RSTRTQBL		
SUBTYPE	TYPE	SIZE		SAVED_PC		
SYSTEMID (8 bytes)				SAVED_PC1		
STATUS				UCBCHAIN		
PDT				ORIGUCB		
CRB				ALLOCLS		
DDB				DAPCDRP		
CNTRLID				CDDBLINK		
CNTRLTMO		CNTRLFLGS		FOVER_CTR		
OLDRSPID				WTUCBCTR		
OLDCMDSTS				MAXBCNT		
RSTRTCDRP				CTRLTR_MASK		
RETRYCNT				CPYSEQNUM		
DAPCOUNT				CSTALLCNT		
RSTRTCNT				LOAD_AVAIL	CHVRSN	CSVRSN

(continued)

Figure E.3
Layout of a Class Driver Data Block (CDDB)

E.3.15   CEB—Common Event Block

Purpose	Describes and synchronizes access to a common event flag cluster.
Usual location	In list with listhead at SCH$GQ_CEBHD.
Allocated from	Nonpaged pool.
Reference	Figure 10.1.

E.3.16   CPU—Per-CPU Database

Purpose	Records processor-specific information. There is one CPU structure for each CPU in the system.
Usual location	Pointed to by CPU data vector array entry and PRBR processor register.
Allocated from	Nonpaged pool.
References	Figures 37.1, 37.3.

E.3.17   CPUTAB—CPU Table Structure

Purpose	Contains procedure values for system-specific routines within APB.EXE.
Usual location	Pointed to by entries in the CPU dispatch table (CPU_TABLE).
Reference	Figure 33.11.

E.3.18   CRAM—Controller Register Access Mailbox

Purpose	Describes a hardware interface register access transaction. The access can be direct or through a hardware mailbox.
Usual location	Pointed to by IDB$PS_CRAM or UCB$PS_CRAM.
Allocated from	Nonpaged pool.
Reference	Figure 22.11.

E.3.19   CRB—Controller Request Block

Purpose	Describes and synchronizes access to an I/O controller.
Usual location	Pointed to by UCB$L_CRB.
Allocated from	Nonpaged pool.
Reference	Figure 22.7.

E.3.20   **DDB—Device Data Block**

Purpose	Contains information for all devices of the same type connected to a controller. There is at least one DDB for each controller in a system.
Usual location	Linked into listhead IOC$GL_DEVLIST.
Allocated from	Nonpaged pool.
Reference	Figure 22.4.

E.3.21   **DDT—Driver Dispatch Table**

Purpose	Locates standard device driver entry points, such as the start I/O routine or the unit initialization routine.
Usual location	Pointed to by DDB$L_DDT and UCB$L_DDT.
Allocated from	Nonpaged pool.
Reference	Figure 22.18.

E.3.22   **DPT—Driver Prologue Table**

Purpose	Identifies and describes a driver to the system driver-loading procedure.
Usual location	Beginning of the driver image; pointed to by the driver global symbol EVMS$DRIVER_DPT. All DPTs on the system are linked in a list with listhead at IOC$GL_DPTLIST.
Reference	Figure 22.17.

E.3.23   **EIHD—OpenVMS AXP Image Header**

Purpose	Describes an image.
Usual location	Image file.
References	Figures 28.1, 28.4.

E.3.24   **EISD—Image Section Descriptor**

Purpose	Describes virtual address range and corresponding information (virtual block range, global section name) to the image activator.
Usual location	Image header.
References	Figures 28.6, 28.14, 28.15, 28.16.

| FCBFL |
| FCBBL |

| ACCLKMODE | TYPE | SIZE |

| EXFCB |
| WLFL |
| WLBL |

ACNT	REFCNT
LCNT	WCNT
STATUS	TCNT

| FID |

| SEGN |

| STVBN |
| STLBN |
| HDLBN |
| FILESIZE |
| EFBLK |

| DIRSEQ | VERSIONS |

| DIRINDX |
| ACCLKID |
| LOCKBASIS |
| TRUNCVBN/NUMEXTENT |

| CACHELKID |
| HIGHWATER |
| NEWHIGHWATER |

| HWM_ERASE | HWM_UPDATE |
| REVISION | HWM_PARTIAL |

| HWMQHD/LIMBOQHD |
| FILEOWNER |
| *(reserved)* (12 bytes) |
| ACMODE |
| SYS_PROT |
| OWN_PROT |
| GRP_PROT |
| WOR_PROT |
| ACLFL |
| ACLBL |
| MIN_CLASS_PROT (20 bytes) |
| MAX_CLASS_PROT (20 bytes) |
| *(reserved)* (76 bytes) |
| ORB |
| CFCB |
| PRIMFCB |

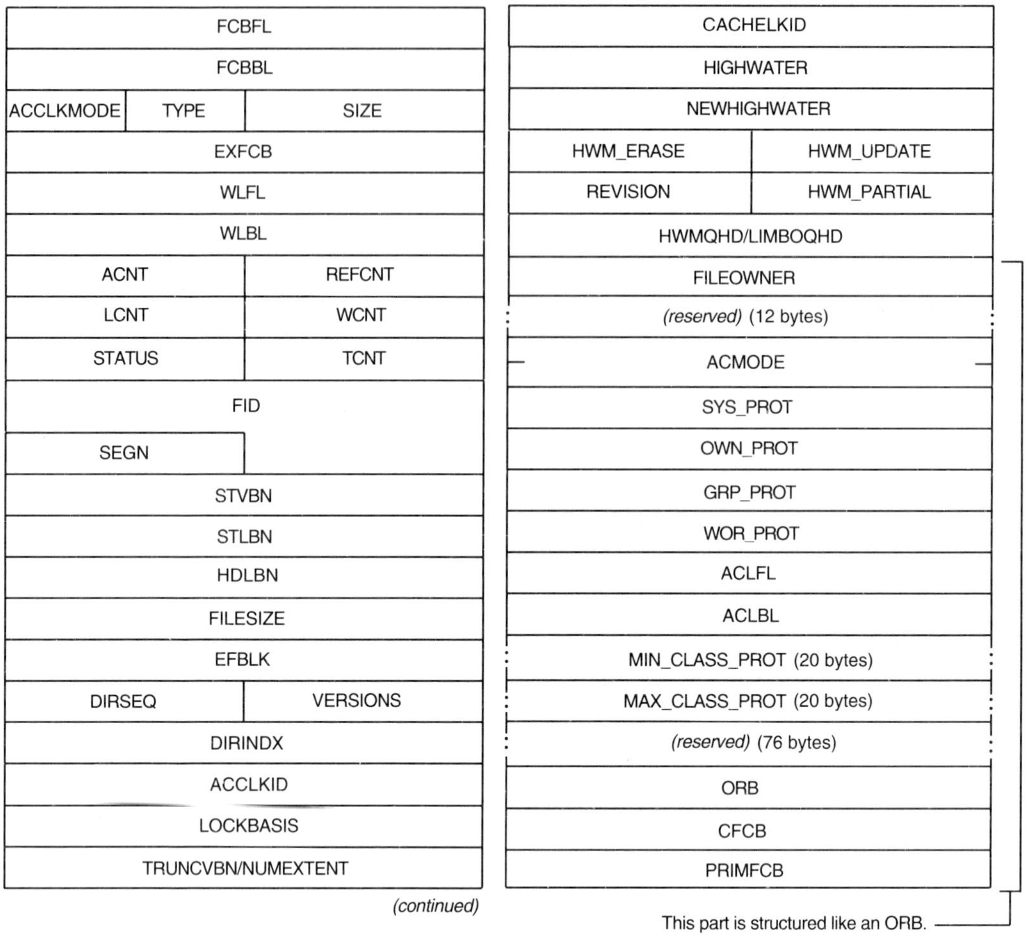

(continued)

This part is structured like an ORB.

Figure E.4
Layout of a File Control Block (FCB)

E.3.25 FCB—File Control Block

Purpose	Describes a uniquely accessed file on a volume; provides a means for controlling shared access to a file.
Usual location	Linked into listhead VCB$L_FCBFL.
Allocated from	Nonpaged pool.
Reference	Figure E.4.

E.3.26 FDT—Function Decision Table

Purpose	Associates a device's valid I/O function codes with FDT routines, specific I/O preprocessing routines.
Usual location	In driver image.
Reference	Figure 22.19.

E.3.27   **FKB—Fork Block**

Purpose	Stores minimum context for a fork process.
Usual location	Unit control block fork block (UCB$L_FQFL), linked into the fork queue in the per-CPU database (CPU$Q_SWIQFL).
Allocated from	Nonpaged pool.
Reference	Figure 5.1.
Special notes	FKBs are usually a part of a larger structure like a UCB or a CDRP.

E.3.28   **GSD—Global Section Descriptor**

Purpose	Contains identifying information about a global section.
Usual location	Group or system GSD list.
Allocated from	Paged pool.
Reference	Figure 16.18.
Special notes	There are two types of GSD: a normal GSD and a GSD for a page frame number (PFN) mapped section.

E.3.29   **GSTE—Global Section Table Entry**

Purpose	Describes the association between a contiguous set of global pages and the contiguous portion of a file.
Usual location	System header.
References	Figures 16.4, 16.13.

E.3.30   **HWPCB—Hardware Privileged Context Block**

Purpose	Defines a process's hardware privileged context.
Usual location	Process header.
References	Figures 13.6, 13.7.

E.3.31   **HWRPB—Hardware Restart Parameter Block**

Purpose	Contains information shared between the console and the operating system.
Usual location	At global location EXE$GPQ_HWRPB.
References	Figures 33.4, 33.6, 33.7, 33.8.

E.3.32 IDB—Interrupt Dispatch Block

Purpose	Contains information for a controller-specific interrupt dispatcher to dispatch an interrupt to the appropriate driver for that device unit.
Usual location	Pointed to by CRB$L_INTD + VEC$L_IDB.
Allocated from	Nonpaged pool.
Reference	Figure 22.9.

E.3.33 IMCB—Image Control Block

Purpose	Describes an image being activated by the image activator.
Usual location	In a list of activated images (IAC$GL_IMAGE_LIST), in the image activator's work list (IAC$GL_WORK_LIST), or in a lookaside list (IAC$GL_ICBFL).
Allocated from	Process allocation region.
Reference	Figure 28.7.

E.3.34 IRP—I/O Request Packet

Purpose	Constructed by the Queue I/O Request ($QIO) system service to describe an I/O function to be performed on a device unit.
Usual location	All IRPs pending for a particular device unit are linked, typically at UCB$L_IOQFL.
Allocated from	Nonpaged pool.
Reference	Figure 22.16.

E.3.35 JIB—Job Information Block

The JIB appears in several figures in this book. Figure E.5 shows all the fields currently defined in this structure.

Purpose	Contains quotas pooled by all processes in the same job.
Usual location	Pointed to by PCB$L_JIB field of all PCBs in the same job.
Allocated from	Nonpaged pool.
Reference	Figure E.5.

E.3.36 KFD—Known File Directory

Purpose	Contains the file device and directory names associated with an installed image. Multiple known images share the same KFD.
Usual location	Pointed to by KFPB$L_KFDLST.

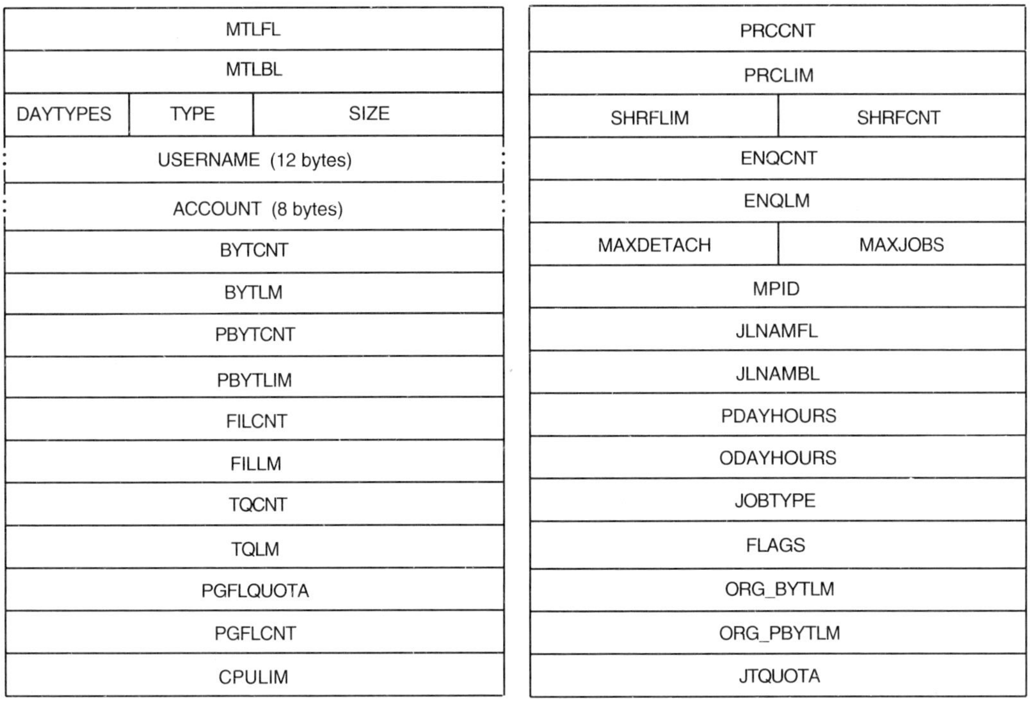

MTLFL		
MTLBL		
DAYTYPES	TYPE	SIZE
USERNAME (12 bytes)		
ACCOUNT (8 bytes)		
BYTCNT		
BYTLM		
PBYTCNT		
PBYTLIM		
FILCNT		
FILLM		
TQCNT		
TQLM		
PGFLQUOTA		
PGFLCNT		
CPULIM		

PRCCNT	
PRCLIM	
SHRFLIM	SHRFCNT
ENQCNT	
ENQLM	
MAXDETACH	MAXJOBS
MPID	
JLNAMFL	
JLNAMBL	
PDAYHOURS	
ODAYHOURS	
JOBTYPE	
FLAGS	
ORG_BYTLM	
ORG_PBYTLM	
JTQUOTA	

(continued)

Figure E.5
Layout of a Job Information Block (JIB)

Allocated from	Paged pool.
Reference	Figure 28.10.

E.3.37   KFE—Known File Entry

Purpose	Identifies the file name of an installed image and its properties.
Usual location	Pointed to by the KFE hash table, whose address is contained in KFPB$L_KFEHSHTAB.
Allocated from	Paged pool.
References	Figures 28.8, 28.11.

E.3.38   KFERES—Known File Entry Resident Section Descriptor

Purpose	Describes the sections of an image installed /RESIDENT.
Usual location	Pointed to by KFE$L_KFERES and IMCB$L_KFERES_PTR.
Allocated from	Paged pool; process allocation region.
Reference	Figure 28.13.

1435

E.3.39   **KFPB—Known File Pointer Block**

Purpose	Contains the address of the KFE hash table and the listhead for the KFDs.
Usual location	Pointed to by EXE$GL_KNOWN_FILES.
Allocated from	Paged pool.
Reference	Figure 28.12.

E.3.40   **KFRH—Known File Resident Image Header**

Purpose	Exists for each known image installed /HEADER_RESIDENT.
Usual location	Immediately precedes the EIHD and specifies its size and version number.
Allocated from	Paged pool.
Reference	Figure 28.9.

E.3.41   **KPB—Kernel Process Block**

Purpose	Describes a kernel process.
Usual location	Pointed to by IRP$PS_KPB or in the KPB lookaside list with listhead at IOC$GQ_KPBLAL.
Allocated from	Nonpaged pool.
Reference	Figure 5.4.

E.3.42   **LDRHP—Loader Huge Page Descriptor**

Purpose	Describes a huge page allocated during system initialization.
Usual location	Pointed to by LDR$GQ_HPDESC.
Allocated from	Nonpaged pool.
Reference	Figure 16.16.

E.3.43   **LDRIMG—Loader Image Data Block**

Purpose	Describes each loaded base and executive image.
Usual location	In a doubly linked list with listhead at LDR$GQ_IMAGE_LIST.
Allocated from	Nonpaged pool.
Reference	Figure 32.6.

E.3.44   **LKB—Lock Block**

Purpose	Contains information about a request to the Enqueue Lock ($ENQ) system service.

Usual location	Locatable through the lock ID table, whose address is in global location LCK$GL_IDTBL.
Allocated from	Nonpaged pool.
Reference	Figure 11.4.

E.3.45   LNMB—Logical Name Block

Purpose	Contains the logical name string, its access mode, and attributes.
Usual location	Chained from the shared logical name hash table or a process-private hash table.
Allocated from	Paged pool for shared logical names; process allocation region for process logical names.
References	Figures 38.1, 38.5.

E.3.46   LNMC—Logical Name Table Name Cache Block

Purpose	Facilitates logical name translation.
Usual location	Doubly linked from P1 space listhead CTL$GQ_LNMTBLCACHE.
Allocated from	Process allocation region.
Reference	Figure 38.6.

E.3.47   LNMHSH—Logical Name Hash Table

Purpose	Locates all logical names.
Usual location	Indirectly pointed to by the array of addresses at LNM$AL_HASHTBL.
Allocated from	Paged pool; process allocation region.
Reference	Figure 38.5.

E.3.48   LNMTH—Logical Name Table Header

Purpose	Describes a logical name table.
Usual location	Part of a logical name translation block (LNMX).
Allocated from	Paged pool for the shared table; process allocation region for process tables.
Reference	Figure 38.2.

E.3.49   LNMX—Logical Name Translation Block

Purpose	Describes an equivalence name for a logical name.
Usual location	Follows an LNMB.

Allocated from	Paged pool for shared names; process allocation region for process names.
Reference	Figure 38.1.

E.3.50   MPW IRP—Modified Page Writer I/O Request Packet

Purpose	Describes an I/O request to write a cluster of modified pages.
Usual location	Pointed to by MPW$GL_IRPFL.
Allocated from	Nonpaged pool.
Reference	Figure 18.10.

E.3.51   MTX—Longword Mutex (Mutual Exclusion Semaphore)

Purpose	Controls process access to systemwide data.
Usual location	Typically part of a data structure, for example, an ORB; otherwise, a statically allocated longword in system space.
Reference	Figure 9.9.

E.3.52   MUTEX—Quadword Mutex (Mutual Exclusion Semaphore)

Purpose	Controls process access to systemwide data.
Usual location	Statically allocated quadwords in system space.
Reference	Figure 9.9.

E.3.53   ORB—Object Rights Block

Purpose	Defines the protection information for objects in the system.
Usual location	Linked to a data structure like a UCB via offset *xxx*$L_ORB.
Allocated from	Paged pool.
Reference	Figure E.6.

E.3.54   PCB—Process Control Block

Purpose	Contains the permanently resident information about a process.
Usual location	Linked into a scheduling state queue; also pointed to by one of the PCB vector elements.
Allocated from	Nonpaged pool.
References	Figures 8.2, 10.3, 13.1, 16.1, 27.4, E.7.

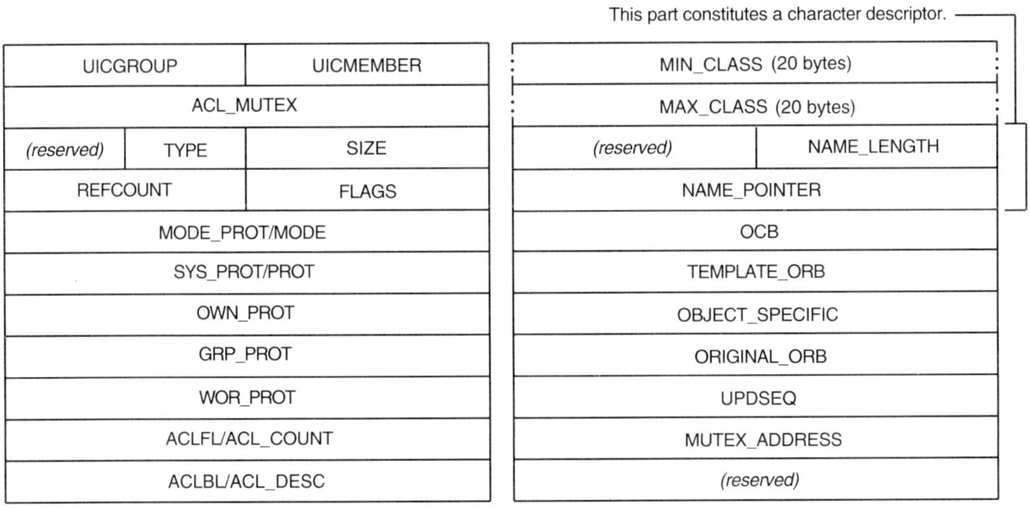

This part constitutes a character descriptor. ⎯⎯⎯

UICGROUP	UICMEMBER
ACL_MUTEX	
(reserved)	TYPE	SIZE
REFCOUNT	FLAGS
MODE_PROT/MODE	
SYS_PROT/PROT	
OWN_PROT	
GRP_PROT	
WOR_PROT	
ACLFL/ACL_COUNT	
ACLBL/ACL_DESC	

MIN_CLASS (20 bytes)
MAX_CLASS (20 bytes)
(reserved)	NAME_LENGTH
NAME_POINTER
OCB
TEMPLATE_ORB
OBJECT_SPECIFIC
ORIGINAL_ORB
UPDSEQ
MUTEX_ADDRESS
(reserved)

(continued)

Figure E.6
Layout of an Object Rights Block (ORB)

E.3.55   PFL—Page File Control Block

Purpose	Describes a page or swap file in use.
Usual location	Pointed to by elements in the page-and-swap-file vector.
Allocated from	Nonpaged pool.
Reference	Figure 16.24.

E.3.56   PFLMAP—Page File Map

Purpose	Describes the discontiguous extents of one process's outswap space.
Usual location	Pointed to by PCB$L_WSSWP.
Allocated from	Nonpaged pool.
Reference	Figure 20.1.

E.3.57   PHD—Process Header

Purpose	Contains process context data that must reside in system space but can be outswapped.
Usual location	Balance set slot area in system space. PHD pages that are not page table pages are double-mapped by a range of P1 space addresses.
References	Figures 13.4, 16.2, 16.3, 16.5, 16.6, 16.22, E.8.

1439

Special notes   The process's HWPCB is contained in the PHD, beginning at field PHD$L_HWPCB.

E.3.58   PLV—Privileged Library Vector

Purpose   Contains user-specified fields that describe system services or rundown routines in a privileged shareable image.

Usual location   In the image.

Reference   Figure 7.7.

E.3.59   PQB—Process Quota Block

Purpose   Used during process creation to store new process parameters that are copied to the PHD and P1 space after those areas are accessible.

Usual location   Pointed to by PCB$L_EFWM.

Allocated from   Paged pool.

Reference   Table 27.1.

E.3.60   PSCANCTX—$PROCESS_SCAN Context Block

Purpose   Created by the $PROCESS_SCAN system service to store the process filter and associated comparison data.

Usual location   Listhead at PHD$L_PSCANCTX_QUEUE.

Allocated from   Process allocation region.

Reference   Figure 14.2.

E.3.61   PSTE—Process Section Table Entry

Purpose   Describes the association between a contiguous portion of virtual address space and the contiguous portion of a file.

Usual location   In the PHD.

References   Figures 16.3, 16.4.

E.3.62   RSB—Resource Block

Purpose   Contains information about a resource defined to the lock management system services.

Usual location   Locatable through the resource hash table, pointed to by LCK$GL_HASHTBL.

Allocated from   Nonpaged pool.

Reference   Figure 11.1.

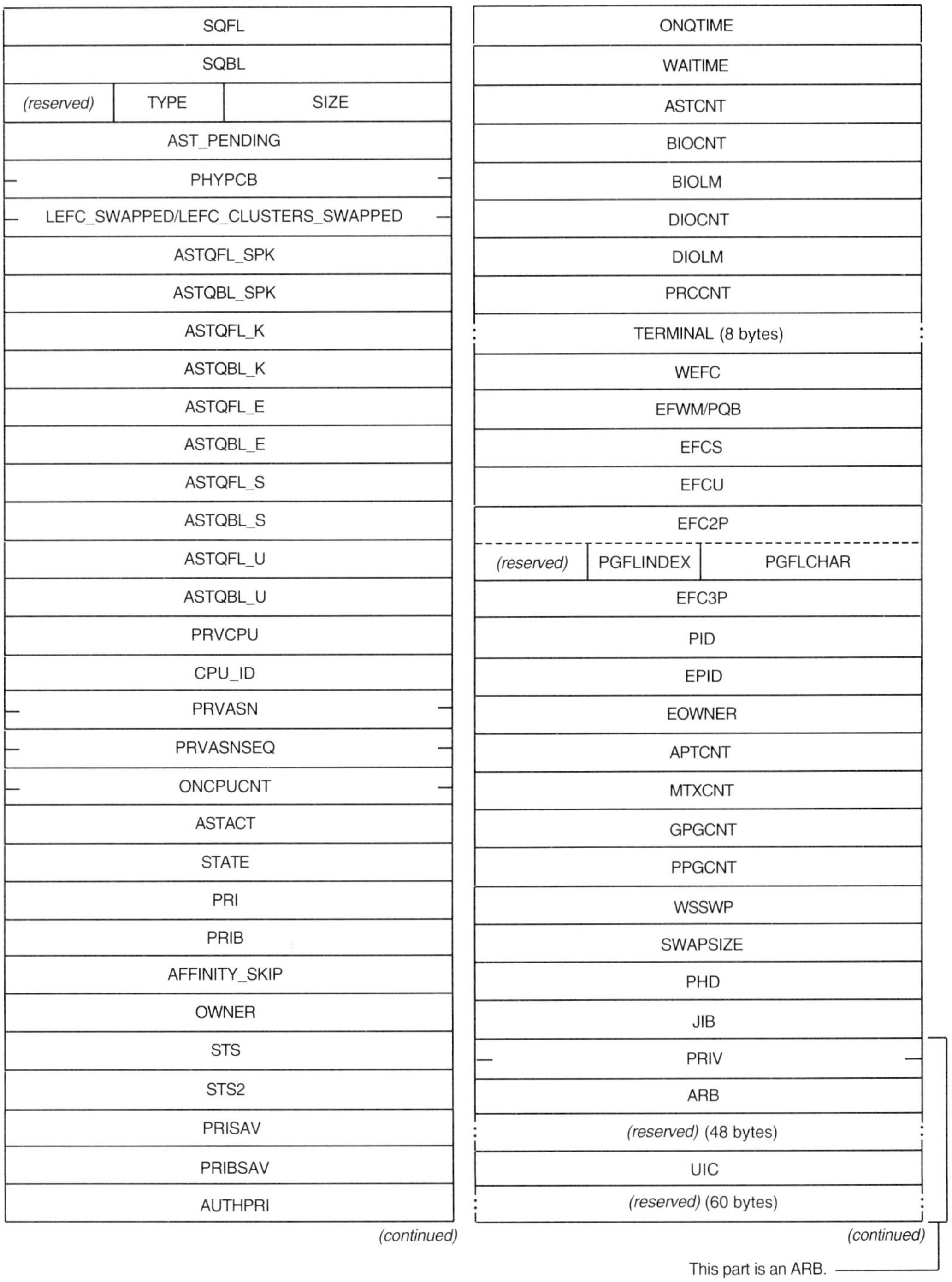

SQFL

SQBL

(reserved)	TYPE	SIZE

AST_PENDING

PHYPCB

LEFC_SWAPPED/LEFC_CLUSTERS_SWAPPED

ASTQFL_SPK

ASTQBL_SPK

ASTQFL_K

ASTQBL_K

ASTQFL_E

ASTQBL_E

ASTQFL_S

ASTQBL_S

ASTQFL_U

ASTQBL_U

PRVCPU

CPU_ID

PRVASN

PRVASNSEQ

ONCPUCNT

ASTACT

STATE

PRI

PRIB

AFFINITY_SKIP

OWNER

STS

STS2

PRISAV

PRIBSAV

AUTHPRI

(continued)

ONQTIME

WAITIME

ASTCNT

BIOCNT

BIOLM

DIOCNT

DIOLM

PRCCNT

TERMINAL (8 bytes)

WEFC

EFWM/PQB

EFCS

EFCU

EFC2P

(reserved)	PGFLINDEX	PGFLCHAR

EFC3P

PID

EPID

EOWNER

APTCNT

MTXCNT

GPGCNT

PPGCNT

WSSWP

SWAPSIZE

PHD

JIB

PRIV

ARB

(reserved) (48 bytes)

UIC

(reserved) (60 bytes)

(continued)

This part is an ARB. ————

Figure E.7
Layout of a Process Control Block (PCB)

1441

ORB
TMBU
LOCKQFL
LOCKQBL
DLCKPRI
DEFPROT
PMB
AFFINITY
CAPABILITY
CPUTIM
LNAME (16 bytes)
PRCPDB
PIXHIST
AFFINITY_CALLBACK
PERMANENT_CAPABILITY
PERMANENT_CPU_AFFINITY
— CWPSSRV_QUEUE —
CURRENT_AFFINITY
CAPABILITY_SEQ
— BUFOBJ_LIST —
AST_BLOCKED
ADB_LINK
TOTAL_EVTAST
CURRENT_TX

CURRENT_CD
CURRENT_VERTEX
— XSCB_QUE —
— RMCB_QUE —
— CD_QUE —
DPC
CPUTIME_REF
ACC_WAITIME
PRCSTR
XPCB
PSX_FORK_STATUS
PSX_FLAGS
PSX_SPARE_L1
PSX_ACTRTN
PSX_ACTPRM
KERNEL_COUNTER
EXEC_COUNTER
SUPER_COUNTER
USER_COUNTER
SCHED_POLICY
FREWSLE_CALLOUT
FREWSLE_PARAM
— RDPB_QUE —
SOURCE_EPID

(continued)

Figure E.7 *(continued)*
Layout of a Process Control Block (PCB)

E.3.63   SCB—System Control Block

Purpose	Determines where control is transferred in the event of an interrupt or exception.
Usual location	Pointed to by EXE$GL_SCB and the SCB base register (SCBB).
References	Figures 3.1, 3.2.

E.3.64   SPL—Spinlock Control Block

Purpose	Synchronization tool for multiprocessing.

PRIVMSK		
(reserved)	TYPE	SIZE
WSLIST		
WSLOCK		
WSDYN		
WSNEXT		
WSLAST		
WSEXTENT		
WSQUOTA		
DFWSCNT		
CPULIM		
PSTBASOFF		
PSTLAST		
PSTFREE		
P0LENGTH		
P1LENGTH		
FREP0VA		
FREPTECNT		
FREP1VA		
DFPFC		
PGTBPFC		
QUANT		
ASTLM		
WSLX		
BAK/PSTBASMAX		
WSSIZE		
DIOCNT		
BIOCNT		
PHVINDEX		
PAGFIL		
HWPCB/KSP		
ESP		

(continued)

SSP
USP
PTBR
ASN
ASTSR_ASTEN
FEN_DATFX
CC
UNQ
PAL_RSVD (48 bytes)
FPR (256 bytes)
ASNSEQ
LEFC
L2PT_VA
L3PT_VA
L3PT_VA_P1
PAGEFLTS
FOW_FLTS
FOR_FLTS
FOE_FLTS
CPUTIM
CPUMODE
AWSMODE
PRCPAGFIL
PGFLCNT
PTWSLELCK
PTWSLEVAL
PTCNTLCK
PTCNTVAL
PTCNTACT
PTCNTMAX
WSFLUID
EMPTPG

(continued)

Figure E.8
Layout of a Process Header (PHD)

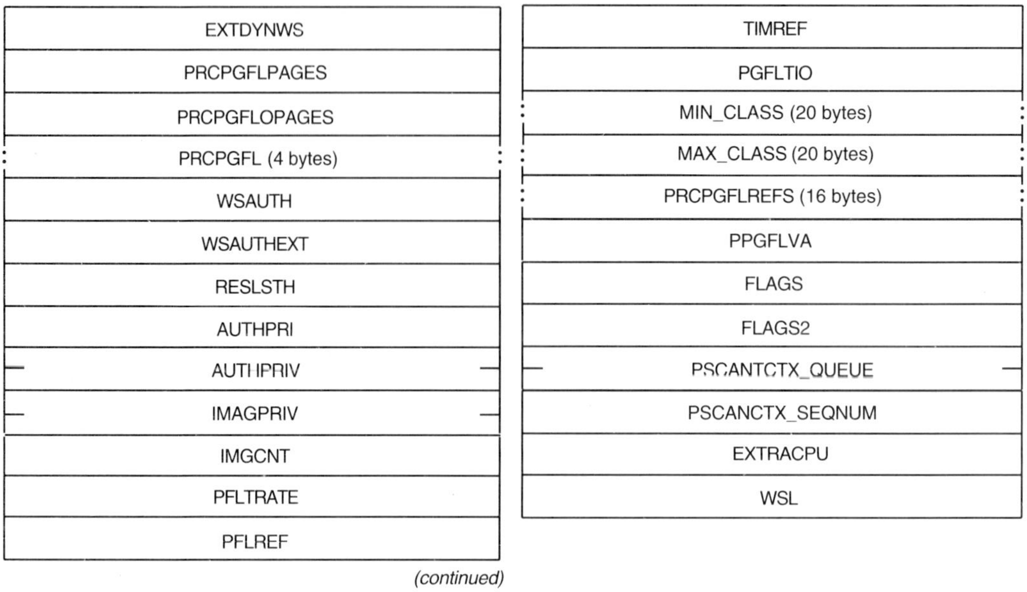

EXTDYNWS
PRCPGFLPAGES
PRCPGFLOPAGES
PRCPGFL (4 bytes)
WSAUTH
WSAUTHEXT
RESLSTH
AUTHPRI
AUTHPRIV
IMAGPRIV
IMGCNT
PFLTRATE
PFLREF

TIMREF
PGFLTIO
MIN_CLASS (20 bytes)
MAX_CLASS (20 bytes)
PRCPGFLREFS (16 bytes)
PPGFLVA
FLAGS
FLAGS2
PSCANTCTX_QUEUE
PSCANCTX_SEQNUM
EXTRACPU
WSL

(continued)

Figure E.8 *(continued)*
Layout of a Process Header (PHD)

Usual location	A static spinlock is identified by the position of its address in SMP$AR_SPNLKVEC, a table of static spinlock addresses.
	A dynamic (device) spinlock is pointed to by the field CRB$L_DLCK in the CRB that describes the device's controller, and by the field UCB$L_DLCK in the device's UCB.
Allocated from	Static spinlocks are in nonpageable system space. Dynamic spinlocks are allocated from nonpaged pool.
Reference	Figure 9.7.

E.3.65   SWRPB—Software Restart Parameter Block

Purpose	Contains booting-related information that allows OpenVMS AXP to restart the system if necessary.
Usual location	Pointed to by EXE$GPQ_SWRPB and HWRPB$PQ_SWRPB.
Allocated from	Nonpaged pool.
Reference	Figure 33.10.

E.3.66   **TAST—Terminal AST Block**

Purpose   Contains information for delivery of out-of-band
                 character ASTs.

Usual location   Linked to a terminal UCB listhead at UCB$L_TL_
                 BANDQUE.

Allocated from   Nonpaged pool.

References   Figures 8.5, 8.6, 8.7.

E.3.67   **TQE—Timer Queue Entry**

Purpose   Describes pending timer or scheduled wakeup request.

Usual location   Linked to the timer queue at EXE$GL_TQFL.

Allocated from   Nonpaged pool.

Reference   Figure 12.1.

E.3.68   **UCB—Unit Control Block**

Purpose   Describes the status, characteristics, and current state
                 of a device unit.

Usual location   Linked from DDB$L_UCB.

Allocated from   Nonpaged pool.

References   Figures 22.3, 25.3.

Special notes   Figure 22.3 shows the part of the UCB common to all
                 device units. Figure 25.3 shows the UCB fields used
                 by mailboxes. The manual *OpenVMS AXP Device
                 Support: Creating a Step 1 Driver from an OpenVMS
                 VAX Device Driver* gives information on extensions
                 to the UCB's common part.

E.3.69   **VCB—Volume Control Block**

Purpose   Describes a mounted device volume.

Usual location   Pointed to by UCB$L_VCB.

Allocated from   Nonpaged pool.

Reference   Figure 22.22.

E.3.70   **VEC—Interrupt Transfer Vector**

Purpose   Used by the common I/O interrupt dispatcher to
                 transfer control to a device-specific interrupt service
                 routine.

Usual location   In the CRB at offset CRB$L_INTD.

Allocated from   Nonpaged pool.

References   Figures 22.8, 22.12.

E.3.71   VLE—Vector List Extension

Purpose   Lists vector offset (into the SCB or ADP) associated
                 with each interrupt for an I/O controller with
                 multiple interrupts.

Usual location   Pointed to by IDB$L_VECTOR.

Allocated from   Nonpaged pool.

Reference   Figure 22.10.

E.3.72   WCB—Window Control Block

Purpose   Describes the virtual-to-logical correspondence for the
                 blocks of a file.

Usual location   Linked to an FCB listhead at FCB$L_WLFL.

Allocated from   Nonpaged pool.

Reference   Figure 23.8.

E.4   SYMBOLIC CONSTANTS

The SDL files in facilities [LIB] and [STARLET] define many systemwide
symbolic codes that identify structures, resources, quotas, priorities, and so
on. Many of these constants are listed in the *OpenVMS System Services
Reference Manual* and the *OpenVMS I/O User's Reference Manual*. Those
that are most closely tied to the material in this book but not listed in those
manuals are listed here.

E.4.1   BDT—Bootstrap Device Codes

The bootstrap device codes are used by APB, the primary bootstrap program,
and by SYSBOOT, the secondary bootstrap program, to determine the boot
device. Bootstrap device codes are defined in module [APB]BDTDEF.

E.4.2   DYN—Data Structure Type Definitions

Most structures allocated from nonpaged and paged pool have a unique code
in the type field, at offset *xxx*$B_TYPE (see Table E.2). The System Dump
Analyzer (SDA) uses the contents of this field when formatting dumps of
pool and in automatic formatting of a data structure with the FORMAT
command.

   Codes that have numeric values greater than or equal to DYN$C_SUB-
TYPE are subtypable codes. Each subtypable code refers to a generic function.
Different data structures related to the same generic function have the same
value in the type field but different values in the subtype field. The subtype
field is at offset *xxx*$B_SUBTYPE within a subtypable data structure. For ex-
ample, the system block (SB) and the path block (PB) are data structures used

Table E.2   Data Structure Type Definitions

Symbolic Name	Code	Structure Type
DYN$C_ADP	1	Adapter control block
DYN$C_ACB	2	AST control block
DYN$C_AQB	3	ACP queue block
DYN$C_CEB	4	Common event block
DYN$C_CRB	5	Controller request block
DYN$C_DDB	6	Device data block
DYN$C_FCB	7	File control block
DYN$C_FRK	8	Fork block
DYN$C_IDB	9	Interrupt dispatch block
DYN$C_IRP	10	I/O request packet
DYN$C_LOG	11	Reserved
DYN$C_PCB	12	Process control block
DYN$C_PQB	13	Process quota block
DYN$C_RVT	14	Relative volume table
DYN$C_TQE	15	Timer queue entry
DYN$C_UCB	16	Unit control block
DYN$C_VCB	17	Volume control block
DYN$C_WCB	18	Window control block
DYN$C_BUFIO	19	Buffered I/O buffer
DYN$C_TYPAHD	20	Terminal type-ahead buffer
DYN$C_GSD	21	Global section descriptor
DYN$C_MVL	22	Magnetic tape volume list
DYN$C_NET	23	Network message block
DYN$C_KFE	24	Known file entry
DYN$C_MTL	25	Mounted volume list entry
DYN$C_BRDCST	26	Broadcast message block
DYN$C_CXB	27	Complex chained buffer
DYN$C_NDB	28	Network node descriptor block
DYN$C_SSB	29	Logical link subchannel status block
DYN$C_DPT	30	Driver prologue table
DYN$C_JPB	31	Job parameter block
DYN$C_PBH	32	Performance buffer header
DYN$C_PDB	33	Performance data block
DYN$C_PIB	34	Performance information block
DYN$C_PFL	35	Page file control block
DYN$C_PFLMAP	36	Page file mapping window
DYN$C_PTR	37	Pointer control block
DYN$C_KFRH	38	Known file image header
DYN$C_DCCB	39	Data cache control block
DYN$C_EXTGSD	40	Extended global section descriptor
DYN$C_SHMGSD	41	Reserved
DYN$C_SHB	42	Reserved
DYN$C_MBX	43	Mailbox control block
DYN$C_IRPE	44	Reserved
DYN$C_SLAVCEB	45	Reserved
DYN$C_SHMCEB	46	Reserved
DYN$C_JIB	47	Job information block

(continued)

Table E.2   Data Structure Type Definitions *(continued)*

Symbolic Name	Code	Structure Type
DYN$C_TWP	48	Terminal driver write packet ($TTYDEF)
DYN$C_RBM	49	Reserved
DYN$C_VCA	50	Disk volume cache block
DYN$C_CDB	51	X25 low-end system (LES) channel data block
DYN$C_LPD	52	X25 LES process descriptor
DYN$C_LKB	53	Lock block
DYN$C_RSB	54	Resource block
DYN$C_LKID	55	Lock ID table
DYN$C_RSHT	56	Resource hash table
DYN$C_CDRP	57	Class driver request packet
DYN$C_ERP	58	Error log packet
DYN$C_CIDG	59	CI datagram buffer
DYN$C_CIMSG	60	CI message buffer
DYN$C_XWB	61	DECnet logical link context block
DYN$C_WQE	62	DECnet work queue block
DYN$C_ACL	63	Access control list queue entry
DYN$C_LNM	64	Logical name block
DYN$C_FLK	65	Fork lock request block
DYN$C_RIGHTSLIST	66	Rights list
DYN$C_KFD	67	Known file directory
DYN$C_KFPB	68	Known file pointer block
DYN$C_CIA	69	Compound intrusion analysis block
DYN$C_PMB	70	Page fault monitor control block
DYN$C_PFB	71	Page fault monitor buffer
DYN$C_CHIP	72	Internal check protection block
DYN$C_ORB	73	Object rights block
DYN$C_QVAST	74	Reserved
DYN$C_MVWB	75	Mount verification work buffer
DYN$C_UNC	76	Universal context block
DYN$C_DCB	77	DECnet control block for chained I/O
DYN$C_DLL	78	General DECnet datalink block
DYN$C_SPL	79	Spinlock control block
DYN$C_ARB	80	Access rights block
DYN$C_SUBTYPE	96	Beginning of subtypable codes
DYN$C_SCS	96	SCS control block
DYN$C_CI	97	CI port structure
DYN$C_LOADCODE	98	Reserved
DYN$C_INIT	99	Structure set up by INIT
DYN$C_CLASSDRV	100	Class driver structure
DYN$C_CLU	101	VMScluster structure
DYN$C_PGD	102	Paged pool structure
DYN$C_DECW	103	DECwindows structure
DYN$C_VWS	104	Reserved
DYN$C_DSRV	105	Disk server structure
DYN$C_MP	106	Multiprocessing-related structure
DYN$C_NSA	107	Nondiscretionary security audit structure
DYN$C_CWPS	108	Clusterwide process services

Table E.2   Data Structure Type Definitions *(continued)*

Symbolic Name	Code	Structure Type
DYN$C_VCC	111	Virtual I/O cache structure
DYN$C_SMI	114	System management integrator structure
DYN$C_TSRV	115	Tape server structure
DYN$C_LAVC	116	VMScluster structure
DYN$C_DECNET	117	DECnet structure
DYN$C_PSX	118	Portable Operating System Interface (POSIX) structure
DYN$C_QMAN	119	Queue manager structure
DYN$C_SM	120	Storage manager structure
DYN$C_MISC	121	Miscellaneous type
DYN$C_RC	122	Redundant array of inexpensive disks (RAID) structure
DYN$C_IPC	123	Reserved
DYN$C_SPECIAL	128	Code that defines beginning of special dynamic memory types

by SCS. Both structures have the value DYN$C_SCS in their type field; the SB has the value DYN$C_SCS_SB in its subtype field, whereas the PB has the value DYN$C_SCS_PB in its subtype field. SDA can interpret the subtype fields of standard system data structures.

E.4.3   IOxxyy—I/O Address Space Definitions

The [LIB] macros $IOxxyyDEF define the layout of local I/O space for each CPU. Appendix G lists the values of xxyy.

E.4.4   IPL—Interrupt Priority Level Definitions

IPLs that are used by OpenVMS AXP for synchronization and other purposes are given the symbolic names listed in Tables 4.1 and 5.1.

E.4.5   NDT—Nexus Device Type

Each I/O adapter has an associated code that is used by APB and INIT to determine which adapter-specific action should be taken to initialize each adapter. These codes are defined by the $NDTDEF macro.

E.4.6   PR—Processor Register Definitions

The macro $PRDEF, in STARLET.MLB, defines symbolic names for the processor registers that are common to all types of AXP processor.

E.4.7   SPL—Static Spinlock Definitions

Symbolic names such as SPL$C_SCHED for the static spinlocks used by OpenVMS AXP are listed in Table 9.2.

F System and P1 Virtual Address Spaces

The layout of system virtual address space is determined during system initialization. The location and composition of the images that make up the executive are determined when they are loaded. Many OpenVMS data structures are created dynamically when the system is bootstrapped so that their sizes can be determined from SYSGEN parameters.

Although some of the layout of P1 space is determined when the executive is built, the sizes of other parts vary.

This appendix describes the relations among the parameters that affect data areas and image loading, and the resulting use of virtual address space.

F.1   INTRODUCTION

In the examples in this appendix, two features are common. One is converting an input parameter expressed as a number of bytes, such as the SYSGEN parameter NPAGEDYN, into a page count. The conversion is performed as an arithmetic shift, although for simplicity it is shown here as a division. The Alpha AXP architecture supports a page size of 8 KB, 16 KB, 32 KB, or 64 KB, but each system supported by OpenVMS AXP Version 1.5 has a page size of 8 KB.

Adding the page size minus 1 to a byte expression before converting it to pages rounds up to the next highest page boundary. MMG$GL_PAGE_SIZE contains the size of a page in bytes, and MMG$GL_BWP_MASK, page size minus 1. In the examples, Page_Size represents the contents of global cell MMG$GL_PAGE_SIZE, and Page_Size − 1 represents the contents of MMG$GL_BWP_MASK.

The other common feature is the number of page table entries (PTEs) in a page. This number appears in expressions that convert a page count into the number of page table pages required to map that page count. Since a PTE is eight bytes long, each page table page on the systems supported by this release contains 1,024 PTEs, mapping 1,024 pages. In the examples, PTEs_Per_Page represents this number. Division by this number, actually an arithmetic shift, converts an input parameter expressed as a number of pages (and therefore the same number of PTEs) into a count of page table pages. In these divisions, the rounding factor is the number of PTEs minus 1.

The calculations related to the process header (PHD) are described first, to introduce the methods used and because PHD size affects both system space and P1 space. Subsequent sections describe the organization and components of system and P1 virtual address spaces.

F.2   **PROCESS HEADER**

During system initialization SYSBOOT reads SYSGEN parameters and sizes various portions of address space. In an early calculation of this type, it sizes the PHD based on specific SYSGEN parameters. The following segments make up the PHD:

- ▸ Fixed portion, which contains offsets to the other segments
- ▸ Working set list (WSL)
- ▸ Process section table (PST)
- ▸ Empty pages reserved for working set list expansion
- ▸ Two PHD page arrays and two page table page arrays
- ▸ The level 2 page table (L2PT) that maps the level 3 process-private page tables (L3PTs)
- ▸ The L3PTs that make up the P0 and P1 page tables

Most examples in this appendix treat the fixed portion, WSL, and PST as a unit.

Table F.1 lists the PHD segments, the global locations where segment sizes are stored, and the SYSGEN parameters that affect segment sizes. The table also introduces the notation used to describe the segments of the PHD. Figure F.1 shows the layout of the PHD and the relation among the segments described in Table F.1.

Table F.1   Discrete Portions of the Process Header

PHD Segment	Symbolic Name Used in Examples	Location of Segment Size	Parameters That Affect Size
Fixed portion, WSL, PST	PHD(Fixed, WSL, PST)	SWP$GW_WSLPTE	PHD$C_LENGTH, PROCSECTCNT, PQL_DWSDEFAULT
Empty pages for working set list expansion	PHD(Expansion_Pages)	SWP$GW_EMPTPTE	WSMAX, PQL_DWSDEFAULT
PHD and page table page arrays	PHD(Page_Arrays)	SWP$GW_BAKPTE	Number of PHD pages and L3PTs
L2PT		MMG$GL_PAGE_SIZE	CPU page size
P0 and P1 page tables	PHD(Page_Tables)	SGN$GL_PTPAGCNT	VIRTUALPAGECNT

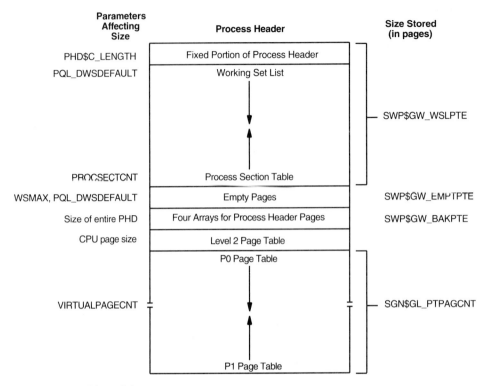

Figure F.1
Process Header and SYSGEN Parameters

The following global locations contain the sums of various segments listed in Table F.1:

$$\text{SGN\$GL\_PHDAPCNT} = \text{PHD(Fixed, WSL, PST)} + \text{PHD(Page\_Arrays)}$$

$$\text{SGN\$GL\_PHDRESPAG} = \text{PHD(Fixed, WSL, PST)} + \text{PHD(Expansion\_Pages)} + \text{PHD(Page\_Arrays)} + 1$$

$$\text{SWP\$GL\_BSLOTSZ} = \text{PHD(Fixed, WSL, PST)} + \text{PHD(Expansion\_Pages)} + \text{PHD(Page\_Arrays)} + \text{PHD(Page\_Tables)} + 1$$

F.2.1 Process Page Tables

The P0 and P1 page tables compose a large portion of the PHD. The total number of pages allocated for the process-private page tables depends on the parameter VIRTUALPAGECNT, expressed in pages (see Eq. F1). One extra page is added to account for the fact that the P0 and P1 page tables must be disjoint and cannot occupy the same page of memory.

$$\text{PHD(Page\_Tables)} = \frac{\text{VIRTUALPAGECNT\_Pages} + (\text{PTEs\_Per\_Page} - 1)}{\text{PTEs\_Per\_Page}} + 1 \qquad (F1)$$

1452

F.2.2 Working Set List and Process Section Table

The fixed portion of the PHD is first. Immediately following it are the working set list and the PST, which grow toward each other. The SYSGEN parameter PROCSECTCNT determines the PST size. The working set list size depends on the value of the WSMAX parameter, expressed in pages. In most systems, however, the working set of an average process is much smaller than the allowed maximum. Therefore, the parameter PQL_DWSDEFAULT, expressed in pages, determines the initial working set list size, and the difference between WSMAX and PQL_DWSDEFAULT is reserved for working set list expansion.

To calculate the initial size of the PHD fixed portion, WSL, and PST (see Eq. F2), SYSBOOT first uses WSMAX to establish the maximum number of pages for that area. Next, it determines the extra space reserved for working set list expansion, and finally it uses the difference between the two numbers as the number of pages initially required for the fixed portion, WSL, and PST. In the following calculation, 4 is the size in bytes of a working set list entry, and 40 is the size in bytes of a process section table entry. WSMAX_Pages and PQL_DWSDEFAULT_Pages refer to the converted values of the parameters.

$$\text{Temp} = \frac{\text{PHD\$C\_LENGTH} + (4 * \text{WSMAX\_Pages}) + (40 * \text{PROCSECTCNT}) + (\text{Page\_Size} - 1)}{\text{Page\_Size}}$$

$$\text{PHD(Expansion\_Pages)} = \frac{(\text{WSMAX\_Pages} - \text{PQL\_DWSDEFAULT\_Pages}) * 4}{\text{Page\_Size}} \tag{F2}$$

$$\text{PHD(Fixed, WSL, PST)} = \text{Temp} - \text{PHD(Expansion\_Pages)}$$

F.2.3 Process Header and Page Table Page Arrays

The PHD contains two PHD page arrays: the working set list index (WSLX) array, and the backing store (BAK) array. The swapper stores information about PHD pages in these arrays while the header is outswapped. The BAK array entries are quadwords. The WSLX array entries are longwords. The PHD also contains two arrays of longword entries that describe each L3PT.

Thus, each page of the PHD requires an entry in each of two parallel arrays, and most pages require an entry in each of the other two arrays. This requires 12 bytes of memory per PHD page plus eight additional bytes for the pages that are L3PTs.

Because the page arrays are in the PHD, their size must be included in the PHD page count. Thus, the space allocated for this area depends on its own size. SYSBOOT's calculation of this portion of the PHD proceeds iteratively.

1. SYSBOOT computes the size of the PHD in pages, excluding the page arrays.
2. It calculates the size of the page arrays necessary to describe the result of step 1.
3. It converts the bytes into an integral number of pages, rounding up.
4. It calculates the number of additional bytes required for entries to describe the page array pages themselves, namely 12 bytes times the number of page array pages.
5. It recalculates the number of page array pages required as the sum of steps 2 and 4, converted to pages.
6. It repeats steps 2–5 until the difference between two successive iterations is zero pages.

F.3   **SYSTEM VIRTUAL ADDRESS SPACE**

System virtual address space contains executive images, systemwide data, and optionally, shareable and executable images installed resident. During system initialization the images that make up the executive are loaded into system space: the system base images, system device boot driver, device driver images, an image containing CPU-specific support, and executive images, such as SYS$VM.EXE, IO_ROUTINES.EXE, and RMS.EXE.

Many areas of system space vary in size depending on one or more SYS-GEN parameters, on CPU configuration, or on image size. Most areas of system space do not have a fixed location.

The only area of system space whose location is constant across all currently supported systems is the system page table (SPT). (Its location is actually a function of page size, but all systems supported by OpenVMS AXP Version 1.5 have a page size of 8 KB.) To enable the executive to access the SPT virtually, the SPT maps itself. Virtually, it is at the high-address end of system space. Its beginning address, $FFE00000_{16}$, is a function of the space required for the number of L3PTs to map a fully populated system space.

The Alpha AXP architecture does not require a set of L3PTs to be physically contiguous, and it permits sparse mapping. As a result, the SPT can be physically discontiguous and expanded during normal operation; there is no need to calculate the maximum size of system space and allocate all the L3PTs to map that space.

A major influence on the organization of system space is whether the relevant SYSGEN parameters specify the creation of granularity hint regions for executive code and data. A granularity hint region, more commonly known as a huge page, is a group of virtual pages that can be described by one translation buffer (TB) entry. The group must consist of physically and virtually contiguous pages based at naturally aligned physical and virtual addresses.

The required alignment is a function of the group size. This feature is described in more detail in Chapter 15.

If the code and data huge pages exist, the nonpageable code and data sections of executive images are loaded into them. This form of loading is known as slicing of executive images. If they do not exist, executive images are loaded into available address space, described in Section F.3.4.

Figure F.2 shows how SYSBOOT organizes system virtual address space on a system with code and data huge pages. In the figure, a symbol name with an arrow leading from it represents the name of a global cell containing a pointer to the area.

On a system with executive image slicing disabled, the system data huge page begins at 80000000_{16}, and both nonpageable and pageable sections of executive images are allocated from the area labeled Available System Pages.

Table F.2 lists each area of system virtual address space mapped by SYSBOOT, the factors that affect its size, its protection, and its pageability. The owner access mode of all system space pages is kernel.

F.3.1   **Code and Data Huge Pages**

If executive image slicing is enabled and the parameter ITB_ENTRIES is nonzero, as they are by default, SYSBOOT creates code and data huge pages. ITB_ENTRIES is the number of 512-page granularity hint regions it creates for loading executive image code sections. The huge page for data sections is always created as 128 pages.

SYSBOOT always allocates physical memory and system space for the code huge page first, because it is the largest and has the most stringent alignment constraints. As a result, if the code huge page exists, it begins at the base of system space, 80000000_{16}. The data huge page begins at the next available address.

SYSBOOT loads the nonpaged code sections of several executive images into the code huge page, as described in Chapter 16. It loads nonpageable data from those images into the data huge page. It allocates available address space (see Section F.3.4) for their pageable, fixup, and initialization sections. The structure of executive images is described in Chapter 32.

Table 33.1 lists the executive images loaded by SYSBOOT as well as those loaded at later stages of bootstrap. SYSBOOT loads SYS$PUBLIC_VECTORS.EXE as the first image and SYS$BASE_IMAGE.EXE next.

When the STARTUP process runs, it loads into the code huge page the code sections of shareable and executable images that are being installed resident.

At the end of system initialization, routine LDR$RELEASE_MEM, in module LDR_MEM_ALLOC, releases to the free page list unused pages from the

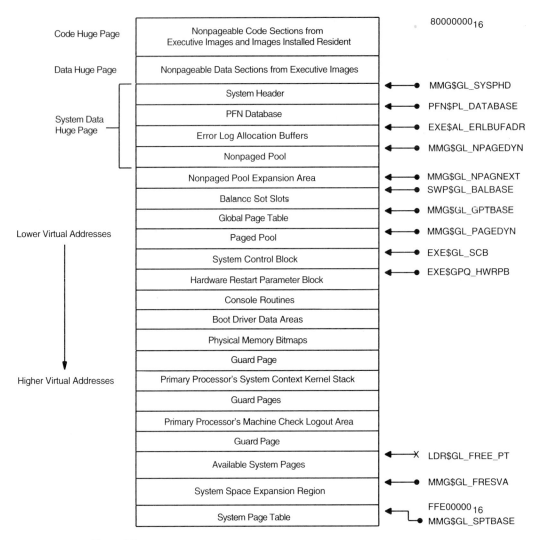

Figure F.2
Initial Layout of System Virtual Address Space

data huge page. Unless the SYSGEN parameter GH_RSRVPGCNT specifies otherwise, LDR$RELEASE_MEM releases unused pages from the code huge page also. Chapter 32 describes the loading of executive images and the operations of LDR$RELEASE_MEM.

The System Dump Analyzer (SDA) command SHOW EXECUTIVE displays the location and size of every image currently loaded and thus provides a fairly complete picture of these huge pages.

Table F.2   Areas of System Virtual Address Space Mapped by SYSBOOT

Item	Factors Affecting Size	Protection	Pageable
Code huge page	ITB_ENTRIES	UR	No
Data huge page	128 pages maximum	URKW	No
System PHD	SYSMWCNT, GBLSECTIONS	ERKW	No
PFN database	Amount of physical memory	ERKW	No
Error log allocation buffers	ERLBUFFERPAGES, ERRORLOGBUFFERS	ERKW	No
Nonpaged pool	NPAGEDYN, NPAGEVIR	ERKW	No
Balance set slot area	BALSETCNT, size of a PHD	ERKW	Yes, no [1]
Global page table	GBLPAGES	URKW	Yes [2]
Paged pool	PAGEDYN	ERKW	Yes
System control block	Maximum of 8000_{16} bytes	ERKW	No
Hardware restart parameter block	System-specific	URKW	No
Console routines	System-specific	URKW	No
Boot driver data	System-specific	URKW	No
Physical memory bitmaps	System-specific	KW	No
Guard page for system context stack	1 page		No
Kernel stack for system context	KSTACKPAGES	ERKW	No
Guard pages for system context stack	1 page		No
Machine check logout area for primary CPU	System-specific	ERKW	No
Available system virtual address space [3]	Various		
System space expansion region	Amount of system space used		n/a
System page table	Amount of system space	ERKW	No

[1] Each PHD in the balance set slot area is part of a process working set. Some portions of the PHD do not page, but those physical pages are accounted for in a process working set and do not count toward the executive's use of memory.

[2] Global page table pages are initially configured as demand zero pages and are pageable. However, every global page table page containing at least one global PTE representing a global section page is locked into the system working set.

[3] The pageable sections of all executive images reside in this area.

F.3.2   **System Data Huge Page**

Whether or not huge pages for executive image code and data are created, SYSBOOT always allocates a huge page for system data. It contains the system header, the PFN database, the error log allocation buffers, nonpaged pool, and if pool paging is disabled (see Chapter 21), paged pool as well. Except for the pools, SYSBOOT calculates the size of each area by rounding up to the next largest 8,192-byte unit, the size of an allocation slice from a huge page.

The system header size calculation (see Eq. F3) is similar to the calculation of PHD size. However, since the size of the system working set list should not vary dramatically, the optimization technique for empty working set expansion pages is not used. Also, since the system header will never swap, it need not contain page arrays. The system header contains only the fixed portion, WSL, and PST. Its section table is actually the system global section table. Two SYSGEN parameters, SYSMWCNT and GBLSECTIONS, control the size of these areas.

In the following calculation, 4 is the size in bytes of a working set list entry, and 40 is the size in bytes of a section table entry. SYSMWCNT_Pages is the SYSGEN parameter expressed in units of pages.

$$\text{SYSPHD\_Size} = (\text{PHD\$C\_LENGTH} + (4 * \text{SYSMWCNT\_Pages})$$
$$+ (40 * \text{GBLSECTIONS}) + 1\text{FFF}_{16}) \qquad \text{(F3)}$$
$$\text{AND FFFFE000}_{16}$$

The page frame number (PFN) database describes each page of physical memory on the system except for memory beyond the limit specified by SYSGEN parameter PHYSICAL_MEMORY. The PFN database consists of a 32-byte record for each page of physical memory. (Its extent differs from that in OpenVMS VAX Version 5.5 systems, in which physical pages that permanently retain the same virtual contents are not represented in the PFN database.) Chapter 16 describes the PFN database and the fields within each record. In Eq. F4, PFN_Entry_Size represents the number 32. Available_Pages represents the lesser of actual physical memory and the SYSGEN parameter PHYSICAL_MEMORY, expressed in pages.

$$\text{PFN\_DB\_Size} = ((\text{PFN\_Entry\_Size} * \text{Available\_Pages}) + 1\text{FFF}_{16}$$
$$\text{AND FFFFE000}_{16} \qquad \text{(F4)}$$

The error log allocation buffers, described in Chapter 35, hold error log messages not yet written to the error log file. In Eq. F5, SYSGEN parameter ERRORLOGBUFFERS specifies the number of buffers, and parameter ERLBUFFERPAGES, the size of each in pagelets.

$$\text{Erl\_Buf\_Size} = ((\text{ERLBUFFERPAGES} * 512 * \text{ERRORLOGBUFFERS})$$
$$+ 1\text{FFF}_{16}) \text{ AND FFFFE000}_{16} \qquad \text{(F5)}$$

Two SYSGEN parameters describe nonpaged pool: NPAGEDYN defines its initial size in bytes, and NPAGEVIR defines the maximum size in bytes to which it can expand. SYSBOOT rounds both down to represent an integral number of pages. Later, SYSBOOT will allocate memory at the high-address end of the system data huge page for the initial size and reserve enough adjacent system space for nonpaged pool to expand into contiguous virtual addresses. The expanded region will not be within the huge page.

To calculate the total space required for the system data huge page, SYSBOOT sums the sizes of the four areas (five, if pool paging is disabled) and rounds the sum up so that it represents an integral multiple of eight pages.

F.3.3   Other System Space Areas

The sizes of many areas of system space listed in Table F.2 are simply based on one or two SYSGEN parameters. SYSBOOT computes their sizes in a straightforward manner.

It determines the size of the area devoted to balance set slots by multiplying the size of a PHD in pages, described in Section F.2, by the SYSGEN parameter BALSETCNT. The area devoted to balance set slots constitutes a considerable portion of system space in a typical configuration.

SYSBOOT calculates the amount of system space to reserve for the global page table based on the SYSGEN parameter GBLPAGES (see Eq. F6). In the following calculation, 8 is the size in bytes of a PTE.

$$\text{Global\_Page\_Table} = \frac{(\text{GBLPAGES} * 8) + (\text{Page\_Size} - 1)}{\text{Page\_Size}} \tag{F6}$$

The SYSGEN parameter PAGEDYN is the number of bytes reserved for paged pool. SYSBOOT rounds PAGEDYN down to represent the number of bytes in an integral number of pages.

The size of the system control block (SCB) is CPU-dependent. All processors have at least a one-page architecturally defined SCB, but the bus and device configuration of a particular processor may require more SCB pages. SYSBOOT allocates physical memory and system space for a maximum-size SCB of 8000_{16} bytes. In a later stage of system initialization any unnecessary pages of it are deallocated.

SYSBOOT allocates system space to map the hardware restart parameter block (HWRPB), console routines, and physical memory bitmaps. As described in Chapter 33, the console subsystem allocates physical memory for these structures and initializes them and their substructures. The HWRPB contains a substructure for each of these areas that specifies its size and starting virtual and physical addresses. Figures 33.4 through 33.8 illustrate the HWRPB and the substructures.

SYSBOOT also maps the primary processor's machine check logout area, which is in physical memory allocated by the console subsystem. The per-CPU database field CPU$PQ_LOGOUT_AREA_VA contains the system virtual address of this area. In any per-CPU slot in the HWRPB, the field SLOT$IL_LOGOUT_LEN_L contains the length in bytes of this area.

SYSBOOT allocates a kernel stack for the primary processor's system context (system hardware privileged context block). The stack consists of SYSGEN parameter KSTACKPAGES pages, with a guard page on each side.

The page protection code of guard pages is set to permit no access. These pages cause a kernel-stack-not-valid processor halt on either stack overflow or stack underflow.

The SPT contains a system page table entry (SPTE) for each page of created system virtual address space, including the pages of L3PT that make up the SPT. L3PTs can be added to the SPT dynamically to map a system space of almost 2 GB (see Figure 16.15).

There is therefore no need to calculate and allocate a maximum-size SPT at system initialization.

F.3.4 Available System Pages

The section labeled Available System Pages in Figure F.2 represents areas of system space that can be created by initializing SPTEs.

The global location LDR$GL_FREE_PT contains the offset from the base of the SPT to the first available SPTE in this address range; the actual contents are system-dependent. The routine LDR$ALLOC_PT, described in Chapter 32, allocates SPTEs that map pieces of this virtual address space.

In this area SYSBOOT, EXE$INIT, and SYSINIT map I/O space, load non-sliced executive images, and load the pageable, fixup, and initialization sections of sliced executive images. They and other components use the space to map various other data structures.

This address space is reusable. For instance, SYSBOOT maps the executive image containing EXE$INIT into this region. When EXE$INIT completes, its address space is deallocated and becomes available to the next invoker of LDR$ALLOC_PT. The contents as well as the size of this area are system-dependent. The allocator of this address space determines the protection and pageability of particular pages. The owner access mode of all such pages is kernel.

The SDA command SHOW EXECUTIVE displays the location and size of every image currently loaded and thus provides a fairly complete picture of executive images loaded nonsliced and of sliced executive images' pageable sections. Table F.3 lists other allocations made from this area by EXE$INIT and their protections.

Table F.3   Areas of Available System Virtual Address Space Mapped by EXE$INIT

Item	*Location* [1]	*Protection*
Buffers for forking from secondary processor to primary (1 page)	@SMP$GL_PFORK_POOL	ERKW
Lock ID table (function of SYSGEN parameter LOCKIDTBL_MAX)	@LCK$GL_IDTBL	KW
Machine check logout area for secondary CPUs (system-specific size)	CPU$PQ_LOGOUT_AREA_VA	ERKW
Per-CPU termination context stack and guard pages	CPU$Q_TERM_HWPCB + HWPCB$IQ_KSP	KW
Secondary CPUs' system context kernel stacks and guard pages	CPU$Q_SYS_KSP	KW
Mapping of memory to be written to dump file	@EXE$AR_DUMP_PTES [2]	
Mapping for idle loop's zeroing pages	CPU$L_ZEROED_PAGE_VA	KW
Swapper process kernel stack	@SWP$AL_SWAPPER_STACK	KW
Mapping for zeroing partial section pages (1 page)	@ZERO_SVA [3]	KW
Swapper level 2 and 3 page tables (function of WSMAX)	(@@SWP$GL_MAP) − 2000_{16}	ERKW
Mapping for a level 1 page table for process creation (1 page)	@SWP$GL_L1PT_VA	
Mapping for parent's page during POSIX address space cloning	@MMG$GL_RESERVED_SVA	
Mapping for child's page during POSIX address space cloning	@MMG$GL_RESERVED_SVA2	
Executive mode data page (1 page)	@EXE$AR_EWDATA	UREW
Erase pattern page table page (1 page)	@EXE$GL_ERASEPPT	URKW
Erase pattern buffer page (1 page)	@EXE$GL_ERASEPB	URKW
Demand zero optimization page (1 page)	@MMG$GL_DZRO_VA	KW
Mount verification buffer (1 page)	@EXE$GL_SVAPTE [2]	KW
Tape mount verification buffer (2 pages)	@EXE$GL_TMV_SVABUF	KR
Mapping for caching file I/O blocks (function of VCC_MAXSIZE)		KW
Mapping for caching paging I/O blocks (2 pages)	@CACHE$GL_PAGEIO_VA	KW

[1] If the symbol @ precedes the location name, the global location contains the address of the area. If not, the name's value is a data structure field offset.

[2] This location contains the system virtual address of an SPTE, not a system virtual address.

[3] This local symbol is in module PAGEFAULT.

F.4   PHYSICAL MEMORY REQUIREMENTS

The number of pages of physical memory required by the operating system, that is, the number of pages not available for user processes, is the sum of the nonpaged areas, the system working set, the low-limit thresholds for the

˙free and modified page lists, and the working sets of memory-resident system processes:

$$\text{System\_Memory} = \text{Nonpaged} + \text{SYSMWCNT\_Pages} + \text{FREELIM}$$
$$+ \text{MPW\_LOLIMIT} + \text{System\_Processes}$$
$$\text{Available\_Memory} = \text{Total\_Physical\_Memory} - \text{System\_Memory}$$
$$- \text{BALSETCNT} - \text{Console\_Memory}$$

(F7)

Each process has one page of memory for its level 1 page table (L1PT). This page is not mapped virtually and is thus not described in a process's working set list. In Eq. F7, BALSETCNT pages are subtracted to account for these L1PTs.

In addition, the console subsystem reserves physical memory for its own code, privileged architecture library (PALcode) routines, and data areas shared with the operating system, such as the HWRPB and machine check logout area.

F.4.1 Executive Memory Requirements

The nonpaged areas on a given system include the physical pages permanently occupied by areas such as the system header and nonpaged pool, the permanently mapped pages for mount verification and similar items, and the nonpageable image sections of loaded executive images and shareable and executable images that have been installed resident.

As shown in this appendix, SYSGEN parameters determine the size of many executive data areas and whether the normally pageable portions of the executive are made nonpageable. They influence which executive images are loaded, and consequently, they affect both paged and nonpaged memory use.

Table F.4 categorizes the executive structures mentioned in this appendix as paged or nonpaged. Where possible, the table includes either the size in pages or a reference to the description in this appendix of how the size is determined. The table does not include the sizes of executive image sections. As explained in Chapter 32, an executive image is allowed two pageable and two nonpageable image sections in addition to initialization and fixup sections, which are deallocated before the end of system initialization. Also, each of the two base images contains a symbol vector.

The amount of physical memory used by an executive image is the sum of the sizes of its two nonpageable image sections. The Analyze/Image utility can be used to display the characteristics and size of each executive image section.

Paged pool, the paged portions of executive images, and the global page table pages also require physical memory. However, it is reasonable to

Table F.4   Division of System Virtual Address Space into Nonpaged and Paged Sections

Item	*Size*
Nonpageable system space.	
Code huge page	Section F.3.1
Data huge page	Section F.3.1
System header	Eq. F3
PFN database	Eq. F4
Error log allocation buffers	Eq. F5
Nonpaged pool	Section F.3.2
Per-CPU system context kernel stack	KSTACKPAGES per CPU
Per-CPU termination context stack	1 page per CPU
System control block	Maximum of 8000_{16} bytes
System page table	Amount of system space
Nonpageable image sections in executive images loaded nonsliced	Size displayed by SDA command SHOW EXECUTIVE
Buffers for forking from secondary processor to primary	1 page
Lock ID table	Function of LOCKIDTBL_MAX
Executive mode data page	1 page
Erase pattern buffer page	1 page
Erase pattern page table page	1 page
Mount verification buffer	1 page
Swapper process kernel stack	KSTACKPAGES
Swapper level 2 and 3 page tables	Function of WSMAX
Pages for caching file I/O blocks	Function of VCC_MAXSIZE
Pages for caching paging I/O blocks	2 pages

This system space is pageable and can occupy no more pages at once than the SYSGEN parameter SYSMWENT, expressed in pages.

Pageable image sections of loaded executive images	
Paged executive data	1 page
Paged pool	Section F.3.3
Global page table pages	Eq. F6

This system space does not affect executive memory requirements.

Hardware restart parameter block	Console memory area
Console routine block	Console memory area
Physical memory bitmaps	Console memory area
Machine check logout area	Console memory area
I/O space mapping	I/O addresses
Balance set slot area	PHD pages and page table pages charged to process working sets

assume that the system working set is full at all times, so the physical memory requirements of the paged portions are simply the number of pages represented by SYSMWCNT.

The SYSGEN parameters FREELIM and MPW_LOLIMIT affect how many physical pages are used by the executive. These parameters set low-limit thresholds on the number of pages on the free and modified page lists.

F.4.2 Console Subsystem Memory Requirements

After sizing memory, the console subsystem builds descriptors of physical memory in the HWRPB. One such descriptor specifies the amount and starting page frame number of the memory the console subsystem has reserved for console code, PALcode routines, and data structures shared with the operating system.

To determine the amount of memory reserved by the console subsystem, examine the HWRPB to locate the memory descriptors. Any memory descriptor whose HWRPB_PMR$IQ_USAGE field contains 1 represents memory reserved by the console subsystem. Figures 33.4 and 33.8 illustrate the HWRPB and memory descriptors.

F.4.3 System Processes

The working sets of memory-resident system processes should also be included in total OpenVMS memory requirements. Table A.1 lists the processes considered to be part of an OpenVMS system. Not all are required on each system; however, all are considered to be system processes.

The Digital command language (DCL) command SHOW SYSTEM lists the pages of physical memory in use by each of those processes at a given time. However, the amount of memory varies over time for these reasons:

▶ The memory the process consumes is its working set. Automatic working set limit adjustment changes the size of the process working set over time. (This assumes that the process reaches its working set limit, a reasonable assumption for a system process.)

▶ A system process can be outswapped, temporarily reducing its physical memory requirement to zero.

Because many system processes are optional and their physical memory requirements vary over time, this appendix cannot describe their memory use. Use the Monitor utility and the DCL command SHOW SYSTEM to obtain the process working set size and other characteristics. Use the DCL command SHOW MEMORY/PHYSICAL to obtain the number of pages permanently allocated for system use.

F.5 SIZE OF P1 SPACE

P1 space includes both fixed and dynamically configured areas. The fixed-size area is defined by the SHELLxK module, where *x* is 8, 16, 32, or 64, the system's page size in kilobytes. The dynamic areas are configured by other modules based on SYSGEN parameters, image sizes, and other variables. Figure F.3 shows these areas and the global symbols that delimit them. A symbol name with an arrow leading from it represents the name of a global cell containing a pointer to the area. A symbol name without an arrow is one whose value is the address of the area. Upper-case names in parentheses indicate SYSGEN parameters that control size.

The fixed-size area defined in SHELLxK is arranged so that data areas with identical owner access mode and protection are adjacent in a region. Because the unit of protection is the page, each area or region with a different protection or page ownership must begin at a page boundary. To accommodate a possible range of system page sizes from 8 to 64 KB, many such regions begin on 64 KB boundaries. These are regions containing areas whose beginning addresses have traditionally been identified by name. Beginning the region at the maximum page size boundary enables such symbols to have the same value no matter which SHELL module defines them. A region whose beginning address is stored in a pointer cell (whose location is at a fixed address) can begin at a page boundary.

Table F.5 describes the areas of P1 space, beginning at the low-address end of P1 space. The process's PHD field PHD$L_FREP1VA contains the lowest defined P1 space address. The highest P1 address range is the fixed-size portion defined in SHELLxK—the initial P1 mapping for every process.

F.5.1   P1 Space Creation

The P1 space for a particular process is built by a number of components:

1. The SHELLxK module initially defines P1 space. It constructs a skeleton P1 page table, mapping a predetermined virtual address range, which includes the inner mode stacks.

   CTL$AL_STACK is the name of a four-longword array whose elements contain the initial values of the four per-process stack pointers. An array element is indexed by access mode. A similar array, CTL$AL_STACK-LIM, contains the lowest limit of each stack.

   The SHELLxK module also creates the P1 window to the PHD, which maps all PHD virtual pages except the page table pages. Section F.2 discusses each segment of the PHD and the SYSGEN parameter that controls its size.

   The global location MMG$GL_CTLBASVA contains the next available P1 space virtual address below the P1 window to the PHD.

2. Following SHELLxK, EXE$PROCSTRT dynamically configures more of P1 space, primarily determining the sizes from SYSGEN parameters. It calls initialization code within the file system, which creates P1 space for the file system impure area and the private kernel stack. The space added is the sum of the impure area size, the SYSGEN parameter KSTACKPAGES, and two guard pages for the kernel stack.

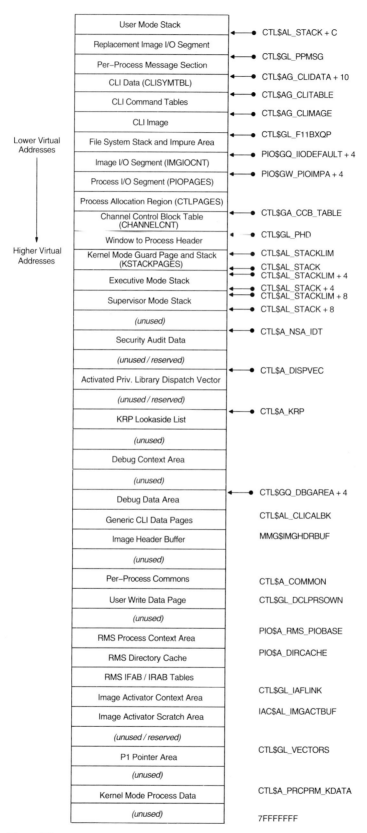

User Mode Stack	← CTL$AL_STACK + C
Replacement Image I/O Segment	
Per–Process Message Section	← CTL$GL_PPMSG
CLI Data (CLISYMTBL)	← CTL$AG_CLIDATA + 10
CLI Command Tables	← CTL$AG_CLITABLE
CLI Image	← CTL$AG_CLIMAGE
File System Stack and Impure Area	← CTL$GL_F11BXQP
Image I/O Segment (IMGIOCNT)	← PIO$GQ_IIODEFAULT + 4
Process I/O Segment (PIOPAGES)	← PIO$GW_PIOIMPA + 4
Process Allocation Region (CTLPAGES)	
Channel Control Block Table (CHANNELCNT)	← CTL$GA_CCB_TABLE
Window to Process Header	← CTL$GL_PHD
Kernel Mode Guard Page and Stack (KSTACKPAGES)	← CTL$AL_STACKLIM / ← CTL$AL_STACK / ← CTL$AL_STACKLIM + 4
Executive Mode Stack	← CTL$AL_STACK + 4 / ← CTL$AL_STACKLIM + 8
Supervisor Mode Stack	← CTL$AL_STACK + 8
(unused)	
Security Audit Data	← CTL$A_NSA_IDT
(unused / reserved)	
Activated Priv. Library Dispatch Vector	← CTL$A_DISPVEC
(unused / reserved)	
KRP Lookaside List	← CTL$A_KRP
(unused)	
Debug Context Area	
(unused)	
Debug Data Area	← CTL$GQ_DBGAREA + 4
Generic CLI Data Pages	CTL$AL_CLICALBK
Image Header Buffer	MMG$IMGHDRBUF
(unused)	
Per–Process Commons	CTL$A_COMMON
User Write Data Page	CTL$GL_DCLPRSOWN
(unused)	
RMS Process Context Area	PIO$A_RMS_PIOBASE
RMS Directory Cache	PIO$A_DIRCACHE
RMS IFAB / IRAB Tables	
Image Activator Context Area	CTL$GL_IAFLINK
Image Activator Scratch Area	IAC$AL_IMGACTBUF
(unused / reserved)	
P1 Pointer Area	CTL$GL_VECTORS
(unused)	
Kernel Mode Process Data	CTL$A_PRCPRM_KDATA
(unused)	7FFFFFFF

Lower Virtual Addresses → Higher Virtual Addresses

Figure F.3
Layout of P1 Space

Table F.5   Areas of P1 Space

Item	Factors That Affect Size [1]	Protec-tion	Owner	Page-able
MAPPED BY THE IMAGE ACTIVATOR				
User mode stack	20 pagelets by default	UW	U	Yes
Extra user mode stack pages	2 pagelets	UW	U	Yes
Replacement image I/O segment	IOSEGMENT link option	UREW	E	Yes
MAPPED IN RESPONSE TO THE DCL COMMAND SET MESSAGE				
Per-process message section	Size of section	UR	E	Yes
MAPPED BY LOGINOUT				
CLI symbol table	CLISYMTBL	SW	S	Yes
CLI command tables	Size of command tables	UR	S	Yes
CLI image	Size of CLI image	UR	S	Yes
MAPPED BY EXE$PROCSTRT				
File system data and stack		KW	K	Yes, no [2]
Image I/O segment	IMGIOCNT	UREW	K	Yes
Process I/O segment	PIOPAGES	UREW	K	Yes
Process allocation region	CTLPAGES	UREW	K	Yes
Channel control block table	CHANNELCNT	UREW	K	Yes
FIXED-SIZE PORTION—DEFINED IN SHELLxK				
P1 window to PHD	Size of PHD	URKW, ERWK	K	No
Kernel mode stack guard page	1 page			
Kernel mode stack	KSTACKPAGES	SRKW	K	No
Executive mode stack	16 KB	SREW	E	Yes
Supervisor mode stack	32 KB	URSW	S	Yes
Security audit data pages	5,120 bytes	KW	K	Yes

(continued)

Table F.5   Areas of P1 Space *(continued)*

Item	Factors That Affect Size [1]	Protec- tion	Owner	Page- able
FIXED-SIZE PORTION—DEFINED IN SHELL*x*K				
Vectors for user- written system services and messages	APLD$C_VECTOR_ LENGTH bytes	UREW	K	Yes
Kernel request packet look- aside list	4 KB	URKW	K	Yes
Debug context pages	2 KB	UW	U	Yes
Debug dynamic memory	64 KB	UW	U	Yes
Generic CLI data pages	6 KB	URSW	S	Yes
Image header buffer	512 bytes	URSW	E	Yes
Per-process common for users	2 KB	UW	K	Yes
Per-process common for Digital	2 KB	UW	K	Yes
User write data page	512 bytes	UW	K	Yes
RMS process context area	1 KB	UREW	E	Yes
RMS directory cache	2 KB	UREW	E	Yes
RMS internal structures	512 bytes	UREW	E	Yes
Image activator context area	512 bytes	UREW	E	Yes
Image activator scratch area	4 KB	UREW	E	Yes
P1 pointer area	1 KB	UREW	K	No
Kernel mode data area	1 KB	UREW	K	No

[1] These sizes are decimal.

[2] The file system stack and some data pages are accessed at elevated interrupt priority levels (IPLs). Therefore, they are locked into the process's working set list and are not pageable.

3. A process typically executes LOGINOUT next. LOGINOUT maps a selected command language interpreter (CLI), expanding P1 space to include the CLI, CLI command tables, and CLI symbol table. The size of these images and the SYSGEN parameter CLISYMTBL determine these P1 virtual address space requirements.

4. The DCL command SET MESSAGE maps a message file into P1 space as a process-permanent message section.

5. The mapping and configuration of the remaining P1 space are altered by the activation of each new image. This area is bounded by the contents of PHD$L_FREP1VA, the next available P1 space virtual address, and CTL$GL_CTLBASVA, which divides the area from permanently allocated P1 space. Image sizes and link options determine the size of this area.

   CTL$GL_CTLBASVA contains the address of the boundary between the process-permanent portion of P1 space and the image-specific portion of P1 space (deleted at image exit by routine MMG$IMGRESET). Each time the process-permanent portion of P1 space expands, for example, to map a process-permanent message section, CTL$GL_CTLBASVA is updated.

Chapter 27 describes the actions of the SHELLxK module and EXE$PROCSTRT; Chapter 30, LOGINOUT's actions; and Chapter 28, image activation.

F.5.2 Selected Dynamic P1 Areas

This section provides some details on several dynamic portions of P1 space.

The channel control block (CCB) table contains SYSGEN parameter CHANNELCNT elements, each 32 bytes long. CTL$GA_CCB_TABLE points to the beginning of the table.

The process allocation region is a P1 space dynamic memory pool (see Chapter 21). The SYSGEN parameter CTLPAGES specifies its size in pagelets.

The process I/O segment contains Record Management Services (RMS) data structures describing process-permanent files, those that can and usually do remain open across image activations. The SYSGEN parameter PIOPAGES specifies its size in pagelets.

The SYSGEN parameter IMGIOCNT specifies the default number of pagelets created by EXE$PROCSTRT for the image I/O segment, the RMS impure area for files opened during the execution of a specific image.

The following line in a link option file for a specific image overrides the default number of image I/O segment pagelets when the image is activated:

```
IOSEGMENT = n
```

If the IOSEGMENT option specifies more pagelets than the IMGIOCNT parameter, the image activator allocates a replacement image I/O segment of size IOSEGMENT.

The image activator allocates two extra pagelets adjacent to the user stack. These pagelets allow the operating system to recover if the user stack is corrupted.

The default user mode stack size is 20 pagelets. The following line in the link option file overrides the default user mode stack size when the image is activated:

STACK = *n*

Because the system's access violation handler automatically expands the user stack on overflow, the link option is generally unnecessary. One possible exception might be an image that requires a large amount of stack space but cannot afford the overhead required for automatic run-time stack expansion.

F.6   RELEVANT SOURCE MODULES

Source modules described in this chapter include

> [SYS]INIT.MAR
> [SYS]LDR_INIT_MEM.B64
> [SYS]SHELL.MAR
> [SYSBOOT]SYSBOOT.BLI

G Summary of AXP Systems

This appendix provides a summary of AXP systems—system and processor designations, system configuration, physical address space layout, and system control block (SCB) vectors for each AXP system type. Chapter 2 defines much of the terminology used here.

Each section describes a class of system, for example, the DEC 3000 class, rather than a specific model, such as DEC 3000 Model 400. The description presents a broad idea of how a certain class of system is constructed rather than specific model information. For model-specific variations, consult the appropriate hardware manual.

The *OpenVMS AXP Operating System, Version 1.5 Software Product Description* (SPD 41.87.01) contains information on supported configurations of AXP systems.

G.1 AXP SYSTEM DESIGNATIONS

Most parts of the OpenVMS AXP operating system are independent of AXP system type. However, certain components, such as the modules that support I/O hardware interface register addressing, machine check logging, and memory error correction and logging, are system-specific. The names of these components contain system and processor designations in the positions shown as *xxyy*, where *xx* is the system type and *yy* is the processor type. For all AXP systems supported by OpenVMS AXP Version 1.5, the processor type (*yy*) is 02, which represents the DECchip 21064 microprocessor. Table G.1 lists the system designations for AXP systems.

System-specific OpenVMS AXP components include the following:

▶ The set of macros \$IO*xxyy*DEF, which define the physical addresses in local I/O space for the hardware interface registers of CPU, memory, and I/O modules of system *xxyy*

▶ The set of macros \$KA*xxyy*DEF, which define the layout in virtual address space of hardware interface registers for CPU, memory, and I/O modules of system *xxyy*

Table G.1 AXP System Designations

xxyy	*System Type*
0202	DEC 4000 Model 600 series
0302	DEC 7000 Model 600 series, DEC 10000 Model 600 series
0402	DEC 3000 Models 400, 400S, 500, 500S, and 500X
0702	DEC 3000 Models 300 and 300L

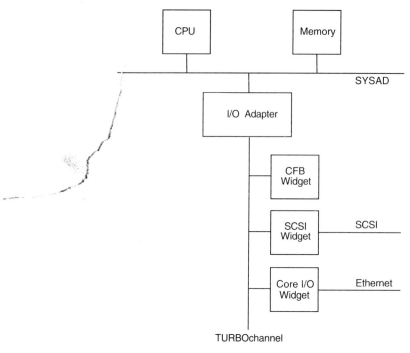

Figure G.1
DEC 3000 System Configuration

▶ Modules in [CPU*xxyy*], which provide system-specific support functions

▶ Modules [APB]CPU*xxyy*, described in Chapter 33, which are linked into APB.EXE, the primary bootstrap program

▶ Modules [IOGEN]SYS$ICBM_*xx*, used to create SYS$ICBM_*xx*.EXE images, which provide system-specific autoconfiguration support

▶ Module [CPULOA]CPUDATA, which contains a table defining VAX and AXP system types and model names, built with the help of symbols defined by the STARLET macros $ALPHADEF and $VAXDEF

▶ Module [SDA]CPUDATA, which contains the same information as module [CPULOA]CPUDATA

G.2 DEC 3000 SYSTEM

G.2.1 System Description

Figure G.1 shows a functional block diagram of the DEC 3000 system.

The CPU, memory, and I/O adapter communicate with each other through the SYSAD, an internal interconnect. The I/O adapter, also known as the TURBOchannel interface, connects a tightly coupled I/O interconnect called the TURBOchannel to the SYSAD. Some slots on the TURBOchannel are reserved for user options.

The remaining slots can be occupied by the following modules:

- A color frame buffer (CFB) widget, also called the CXTurbo, with console read-only memory (ROM)
- A Small Computer System Interface (SCSI) widget for up to two SCSI interconnects
- A core I/O interface (CII) widget, which provides an Ethernet interface; two serial line interfaces, each supporting up to two serial lines; a time-of-year (TOY) clock; and console ROM

G.2.2   Address Space

Memory space spans the lowest 4 GB of the DEC 3000 processor's physical address space; I/O space spans the next 4 GB locations. The maximum amount of physical memory supported on a DEC 3000 system is 128 MB or 256 MB, depending on the model.

The DEC 3000 system does not implement hardware mailbox access for interface registers in remote I/O space. It maps all interface registers into the I/O space, as shown in Figure G.2. Note that the mapping may be somewhat different for a specific model.

Each TURBOchannel node's node space is mapped into two different areas of I/O space: dense space and sparse space. Longword and quadword reads and writes of interface registers (using load or store instructions) will work in either space. However, byte and word operations on interface registers can only be performed through sparse space. The appropriate hardware manual gives more details.

G.2.3   SCB Vectors

The first I/O interrupt vector in the SCB, at offset 800_{16}, is reserved for the TURBOchannel interface. Its interrupt service routine determines the interrupting device and dispatches to the appropriate interrupt service routine.

G.3   DEC 4000 SYSTEM

G.3.1   System Description

Figure G.3 shows a functional block diagram of a DEC 4000 system. The DEC 4000 system's processor-memory interconnect (PMI) is called the C-bus. Up to two CPU modules, four memory modules, and one I/O module can be connected to the C-bus. The I/O module connects two different tightly coupled I/O interconnects to the C-bus: the DEC 4000 system local I/O bus (L-bus) and the Futurebus+.

The L-bus connects four SCSI/DSSI (Digital Storage Systems Interconnect) widgets, one SCSI-only widget, two network interconnect (NI) widgets, a console widget, a serial line widget, a TOY clock, and console ROM to the C-bus. Each SCSI/DSSI widget can be configured either as a SCSI widget

1473

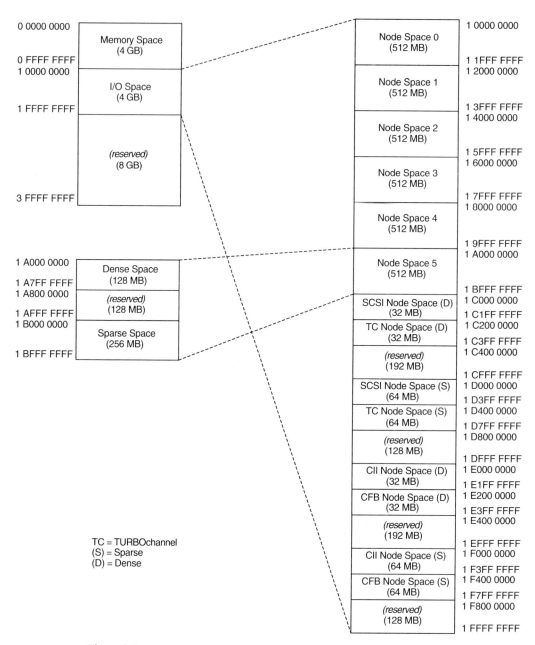

Figure G.2
Physical Address Space of a DEC 3000 Processor

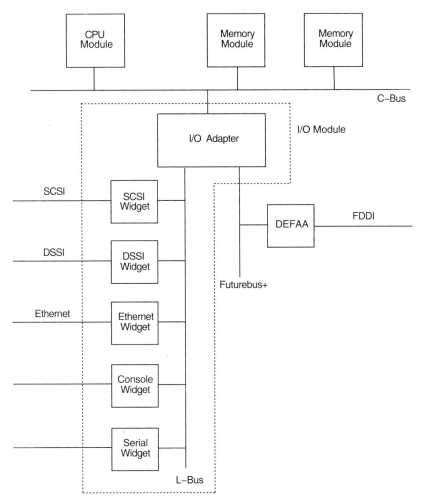

Figure G.3
DEC 4000 System Configuration

or a DSSI widget. The L-bus and its concomitant widgets reside within the I/O module, as shown by the dotted lines in Figure G.3. The Futurebus+ to Fiber Distributed Data Interconnect (FDDI) widget (DEFAA) option can be connected to the Futurebus+.

G.3.2   Address Space

Figure G.4 shows the physical address space of a DEC 4000 processor.

Up to 2 GB of physical memory can be directly addressed in the lowest physical address range. Interface registers for the CPU modules, the I/O module, and all memory modules can be accessed through the I/O space as shown.

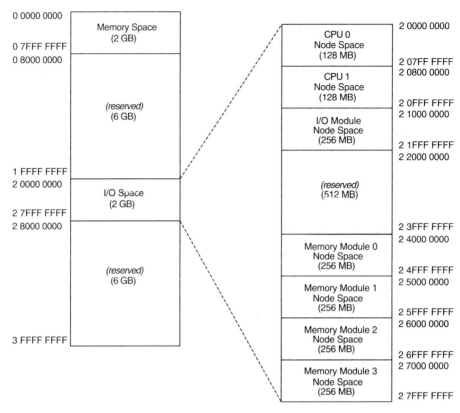

Figure G.4
Physical Address Space of a DEC 4000 Processor

G.3.3   **SCB Vectors**

The first nine I/O interrupt vectors in the SCB, starting at offset 800_{16}, are reserved for the following devices:

- Four SCSI/DSSI widgets
- One SCSI-only widget
- One console serial line widget
- Up to two Ethernet widgets
- One serial bus widget

All other SCB vectors are assigned by software, as discussed in Chapter 4.

G.4   **DEC 7000 AND DEC 10000 SYSTEMS**

G.4.1   **System Description**

Figure G.5 shows a functional block diagram of a DEC 7000 system. A DEC 10000 system is a performance-enhanced version of the DEC 7000 system; the description in this section applies equally to DEC 10000 systems. The

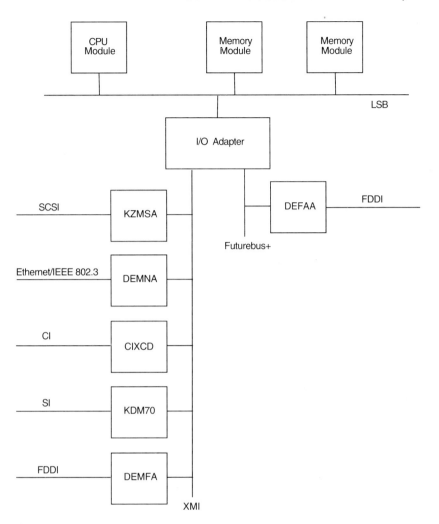

Figure G.5
DEC 7000 System Configuration

PMI for a DEC 7000 system is called the DEC 7000 system bus (LSB). A total of nine nodes can be connected to the LSB. One of the nine slots is reserved for an I/O module. Up to four CPU modules, up to seven memory modules, and one I/O module can be configured on the LSB.

The I/O adapter in Figure G.5 is a logical block composed of a number of different hardware blocks, as shown in Figure G.6. The I/O module, also called the IOP on a DEC 7000 system, implements the function of the local side of an I/O adapter that supports up to four hoses. Each hose can be attached to a remote side such as the extended memory interconnect (XMI) remote side (DWLMA) or the Futurebus+ remote side (DWLAA).

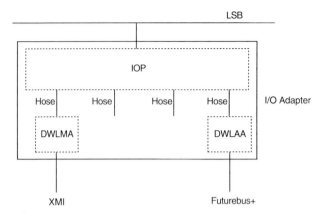

Figure G.6
Components of the Local I/O Adapter on a DEC 7000
System

G.4.2   Address Space

Figure G.7 shows the physical address space of a DEC 7000 processor.

The memory region spans 15.75 GB of the lowest physical address range; the I/O space spans the remaining 256 MB. The low portion of I/O space, referred to as node private space, is used privately by the processor. Each LSB node implements its own copy of node private space. The region referred to as broadcast space is common to all LSB nodes.

G.4.3   SCB Vectors

The first I/O interrupt vector in the SCB, at offset 800_{16}, is reserved for the I/O module. All other SCB vectors are assigned by software, as discussed in Chapter 4.

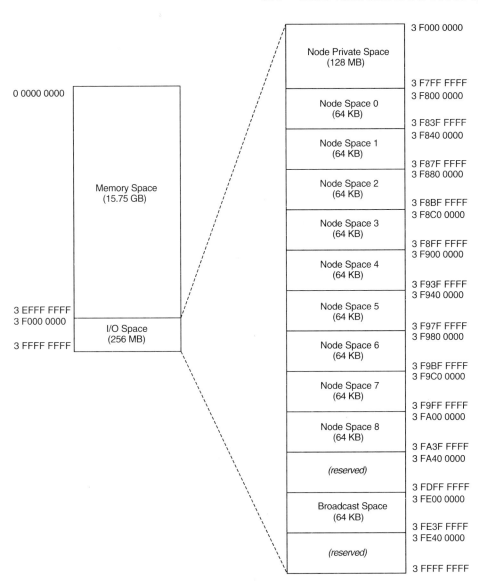

Figure G.7
Physical Address Space of a DEC 7000 Processor

H Lock and Resource Use by OpenVMS Components

Many OpenVMS facilities use lock management system services to coordinate their own activities, both locally and within a VMScluster system. This appendix examines a number of those facilities and describes their lock use. The aim is to demonstrate a variety of locking techniques and to provide examples of situations where specific techniques are beneficial.

This appendix is by no means a complete description of OpenVMS lock use or of the various facilities mentioned. It assumes that the reader is familiar with Chapter 11 of this book and with the description of the OpenVMS lock management system services found in the *OpenVMS System Services Reference Manual*.

H.1 ASPECTS OF RESOURCE AND LOCK USE

The data structure that represents the entity being locked is a resource block, commonly referred to as a resource. A resource is uniquely identified by the combination of its resource name string, scope, access mode, and parent resource, if any.

A lock on a resource is characterized by its lock mode, the extent to which it allows shared access with other locks on the same resource. Chapter 11 lists the different lock modes: concurrent read/write (CR, CW), protected read/write (PR, PW), null (NL), and exclusive (EX). The context of a lock is also relevant: locks on some resources are owned by the system rather than by a particular process. For convenience in describing resources and their associated locks, the discussion often mentions only the lock; in these cases, the resource is implied.

The resource name string of a resource created by OpenVMS for its own use typically begins with a facility code. The remainder of the string further identifies the specific resource, for example, SCSNODE, device name, or file ID.

Table H.1 lists some OpenVMS facilities, their associated facility codes, and the sections in this appendix that further describe the facility's lock use.

The scope of a resource, and of its locks, is the extent to which the resource name is available to processes sharing the resource. By default, OpenVMS includes as part of a resource name the user identification code (UIC) group of the process creating the resource. Processes belonging to other UIC groups cannot share such a resource.

To share resources throughout a VMScluster system independent of UIC, many OpenVMS facilities specify the Enqueue Lock Request ($ENQ) system

Table H.1   OpenVMS Facility Codes

Facility	*Code*	*Section*
OpenVMS executive	SYS$	Section H.2
$MOUNT system service	MOU$	Section H.3
$DISMOU system service	DMT$	Section H.4
File system (Files-11 XQP)	F11B$	Section H.5
Record Management Services (RMS)	RMS$	Section H.6
Image activator and Install utility	INSTALL$	Section H.7
DECnet – VMScluster alias	CLU$	Section H.8.1
DECnet – proxy	NET$	Section H.8.2
Job controller	JBC$	Section H.9
Queue manager	QMAN$	Section H.9
System Management (SYSMAN) utility	SMISERVER$	Section H.10

service flag LCK$V_SYSTEM. (A process not in kernel or executive mode requires the SYSLCK privilege to specify this flag.) The flag causes OpenVMS to omit the UIC group from the resource name. Thus, a process belonging to any UIC group can share the resource if it specifies the LCK$V_SYSTEM flag in its lock request. Such a resource is usually characterized as being systemwide. To avoid confusion with the characteristic system-owned, this chapter refers to the scope of these resources and locks as UIC-independent.

Other OpenVMS facilities, such as the job controller, require a process on each VMScluster node. The processes are created in a controlled fashion and belong to the same UIC group. Each process synchronizes access to private structures and files using a protocol shared by its counterparts on other nodes. These processes do not use the LCK$V_SYSTEM flag in their lock requests; thus, their resources and locks are available only to members of the same UIC group. This chapter refers to the scope of these resources and locks as UIC-specific.

The lock manager deallocates a resource block (RSB) when its last lock is dequeued. Locks are dequeued and lock blocks deallocated when their creating process is deleted. To guarantee the survival of an important lock so that its resource block and especially its value block remain available, an OpenVMS facility enqueuing a lock can declare its context to be system-owned rather than process-owned. The use of system-owned locks is reserved to Digital. Any other use is strongly discouraged by Digital and completely unsupported.

A parent resource is used to create a logical lock grouping or, in the case of the System ID lock, to restrict resource mastership to a particular node (see Section H.2.1).

Other significant aspects of OpenVMS lock use include a lock's value block; the presence or absence of a blocking asynchronous system trap (AST) and the trigger for delivery of a blocking AST; and the name of any symbol used to locate the lock or define the resource name. Blocking ASTs are described in Chapter 11.

Every lock description in this appendix begins with a table of the lock's significant attributes.

H.2   EXECUTIVE LOCK USE
H.2.1   System ID Lock

Resource name string	"SYS$SYS_ID" + SCSSYSTEMID
Symbol	EXE$GL_SYSID_LOCK
Mode of acquisition	EX
Scope	UIC-independent
Access mode	Executive
Parent	None
Value block	None
Blocking AST	None
Context	System-owned

The System ID lock guarantees a unique identity for each VMScluster node by enforcing the requirement that the SYSGEN parameter SCSSYSTEMID be unique within the VMScluster system.

During system initialization every OpenVMS system requests an EX lock on a resource whose name is based on its own SCSSYSTEMID. Since SCSSYSTEMID is required to be unique in a VMScluster system, the lock should be granted immediately. If the lock request is successful, the numeric lock ID is stored in the cell EXE$GL_SYSID_LOCK. If the lock request fails, an identical SCSSYSTEMID exists in the VMScluster system. An error message is generated and further system initialization is prevented.

Since each VMScluster node builds and locks a unique resource, the System ID lock is always mastered on the local system. Therefore, any sublock of the System ID lock is mastered on the local system. Many OpenVMS facilities take advantage of this feature and use the lock ID in EXE$GL_SYSID_LOCK as a parent for locks to be mastered locally and for locks whose range is limited to a specific VMScluster node rather than to the entire VMScluster system.

H.2.2   Set Time Lock

Resource name string	"SYS$CWSETIME"
Symbol	None
Mode of acquisition	EX
Scope	UIC-independent
Access mode	Kernel

Parent	None
Value block	None
Blocking AST	None
Context	Process-owned

The Set Time lock serializes concurrent SET TIME/CLUSTER operations. The image that runs in response to this undocumented Digital command language (DCL) command acquires an EX mode lock on the resource SYS$CWSETIME. Even if more than one process enters the SET TIME/CLUSTER command simultaneously, only one process acquires the lock while the others wait. Therefore, the same time value is broadcast to all VMScluster nodes during this interval. When the owning process releases the lock, a waiting process may acquire it and broadcast its own time value. This mechanism ensures that time is broadcast consistently across all VMScluster nodes.

H.2.3   Device Lock

Resource name string	"SYS$" + allocation class device name
Symbol	UCB$L_LOCKID
Modes of acquisition	CR, PW, EX
Scope	UIC-independent
Access mode	Kernel
Parent	None
Value block	Yes
Blocking AST	None
Context	System-owned

Device locks propagate the standard OpenVMS properties for device allocation throughout a VMScluster system. They manage the availability of devices visible clusterwide. The Deallocate Device ($DALLOC), Assign I/O Channel ($ASSIGN), Mount Volume ($MOUNT), Dismount Volume ($DISMOU), and Deassign I/O Channel ($DASSGN) system services, among others, acquire and release Device locks either directly or using the routines IOC$LOCK_DEV and IOC$UNLOCK_DEV in module IOSUBPAGD.

A VMScluster node actually has at most one Device lock enqueued per device, with a resource name based on the allocation class device name as returned by the Get Device/Volume Information ($GETDVI) system service argument DVI$_ALLDEVNAM. Its lock ID is stored in the device's unit control block (UCB) at UCB$L_LOCKID.

A Device lock is enqueued or converted for a device visible to the VMScluster system when the device is explicitly allocated, when the $MOUNT system service implicitly allocates the device for a private mount request, when the $MOUNT system service must ensure that the device is available and not allocated for a shareable request, when the $ASSIGN system service creates the first channel to a device that is available cluster-wide, and through other code paths as well.

The lock mode varies depending on the operation and its arguments:

▸ At device allocation, an EX mode lock is requested.

▸ For a private mount, the $MOUNT system service requests an EX mode lock.

▸ For a system or group mount, the $MOUNT system service initially requests a PW mode lock with the LCK$V_NOQUEUE flag. If the device is already allocated or mounted privately, an EX mode lock exists, the PW request fails, and the $MOUNT system service returns an error. If the device is already mounted in a shareable fashion by any other VMScluster nodes, only CR mode locks exist. The PW mode lock is granted and eventually converted to CR mode.

▸ The $ASSIGN system service requests a CR mode lock.

The value block of a Device lock contains such information as a device's mount state, protection, ownership, and write lock state. It coordinates these attributes across the cluster.

System services like $DALLOC, $DASSGN, and $DISMOU invoke the routine IOC$UNLOCK_DEV to dispose of the Device lock correctly:

▸ If the device remains allocated by a process, the lock is not dequeued until device deallocation.

▸ If channels remain open to a dismounted device, the lock is converted to CR mode and eventually dequeued during the closing of the last channel.

▸ Otherwise, the lock is dequeued.

H.3 $MOUNT LOCK USE

The $MOUNT system service establishes a lock to guard against concurrent mount requests for a particular device or volume from the local node or from other VMScluster nodes. In addition, it acquires the system-owned Device lock (see Section H.2.3) to synchronize clusterwide device access with the $DISMOU, $DALLOC, and $ASSIGN system services, among others. The $MOUNT system service uses the file system's Volume Allocation lock (see Section H.5.1) to synchronize its accesses to mounted volumes with those of the file system. It compares the mount context information in the value blocks of the Device lock and the Volume Allocation lock to ensure that volume labels are unique within a VMScluster system.

H.3.1   Label Lock

Resource name string	"MOU$" + CSID or zero + volume label as specified in $MOUNT argument
Symbol	None

Mode of acquisition	EX
Scope	UIC-independent
Access mode	Executive
Parent	None
Value block	None
Blocking AST	None
Context	Process-owned

The Label lock serializes shareable mount requests for the same volume from multiple processes on the same system. In response to a request to mount a volume to be shared, for example, among all UIC-group members, the $MOUNT system service requests this lock in EX mode. It includes the VMScluster system ID (CSID) to make the Label lock node-specific. If the system is not a VMScluster node, a CSID of zero is used.

For a shareable mount request, the $MOUNT system service searches the local I/O database to ensure that no other volume has been mounted with the same volume label and shareability. It holds the Label lock for the duration of local mount processing to prevent other processes running on the same node from trying to mount the same volume on other devices.

The $MOUNT system service cannot use either of the other two locks involved in mount processing to accomplish that purpose. The Mount Device lock (see Section H.3.2) is based on device name, not volume label, so its use would not detect simultaneous attempts to mount a volume with the same label on different devices. Neither would the use of the system-owned Device lock, which is only acquired for devices available clusterwide.

The $MOUNT system service does not acquire the Label lock for a private mount request, because process-private use of a particular volume name cannot conflict with that of any other use.

H.3.2   Mount Device Lock

Resource name string	"MOU$" + allocation class device name
Symbol	None
Mode of acquisition	· EX
Scope	UIC-independent
Access mode	Executive
Parent	None
Value block	None
Blocking AST	None
Context	Process-owned

The Mount Device lock synchronizes simultaneous mount requests for the same device. The $MOUNT system service first locates the device to be mounted and reserves it with the system-owned Device lock. It then attempts to acquire the Mount Device lock in EX mode. If the Mount Device lock cannot be immediately acquired because another $MOUNT request is proceeding concurrently on the same device, the $MOUNT system service releases the system-owned Device lock and queues for the Mount Device lock in EX mode. When the Mount Device lock is granted, the $MOUNT system service releases it and repeats its attempt to acquire the system-owned Device lock.

Thus, mount attempts in a VMScluster wait for the Mount Device lock rather than the system-owned Device lock when the system-owned Device lock is not immediately available. A process cannot wait for a system-owned lock.

The Mount Device lock's resource name is based on the allocation class device name as returned in the $GETDVI system service argument DVI$_ALLDEVNAM.

H.4 $DISMOU LOCK USE

H.4.1 Dismount Lock

Resource name string	"DMT$" + allocation class device name
Symbol	None
Mode of acquisition	EX
Scope	UIC-independent
Access mode	Executive
Parent	None
Value block	None
Blocking AST	None
Context	Process-owned

The $DISMOU system service acquires an EX mode Dismount lock to synchronize simultaneous dismount requests for the same volume from processes on the local system and on other VMScluster nodes. The Dismount lock's resource name is based on the allocation class device name returned in the $GETDVI system service argument DVI$_ALLDEVNAM.

In addition to the Dismount lock, the $DISMOU system service acquires, converts, and releases the system Device lock to update the value block. The $DISMOU system service also dequeues file system locks for Files-11 volumes.

H.5 FILE SYSTEM LOCK USE

The file system uses locks to arbitrate access to volumes and files as well as access to local cache structures and their contents. In a VMScluster system, all locks described in this section are necessary for proper synchronization.

In a stand-alone system, the volume locks and File Serialization lock are required for synchronization of local processes, but the File Access Arbitration and Cache locks are unnecessary and unused.

H.5.1   Volume Allocation Lock

Resource name string	"F11B$v" + VCB$T_VOLCKNAM or RVT$T_VLSLCKNAM
Symbol	VCB$L_VOLLKID or RVT$L_STRUCLKID
Modes of acquisition	CR, PW
Scope	UIC-independent
Access mode	Kernel
Parent	EXE$GL_SYSID_LOCK if private mount
Value block	Yes
Blocking AST	Yes
Context	System-owned

The Volume Allocation lock synchronizes volume space allocation by coordinating access to the storage and file header bitmaps. Each volume has a unique volume allocation resource name. Every VMScluster node acquires a PW mode lock on that resource when it mounts the volume through the $MOUNT system service. The resource name string is based on the contents of VCB$T_VOLCKNAM or, for volume sets, the volume set name contained in relative volume table (RVT) field RVT$T_VLSLCKNAM:

▶ For a privately mounted volume, the resource name string is based on the name of the system issuing the $MOUNT request and that system's UCB address for the device. The Volume Allocation lock is a sublock of the lock ID stored in EXE$GL_SYSID_LOCK.

▶ For a shareable native volume, the resource name string is based on the volume label.

▶ For a shareable native volume set, the resource name string is the volume set name.

The naming convention for shareable volumes guarantees that volume labels are unique in a VMScluster system.

The Volume Allocation lock is converted to CR mode by each VMScluster node when the $MOUNT system service completes. The lock ID is stored in VCB$L_VOLLKID (or, for volume sets, RVT$L_STRUCLKID). This lock is held in CR mode for as long as the volume remains mounted. The $DISMOU system service dequeues it. In addition, any code path that allocates or deallocates space on the volume (that is, accesses the index file bitmap or the storage bitmap) acquires an additional lock in PW mode. This is compatible with the CR mode locks but would block another PW mode lock; thus, it allows multiple readers but only one writer.

H.5.2   **Volume Blocking Lock**

Resource name string	"F11B$b" + VCB$T_VOLCKNAM or RVT$T_ VLSLCKNAM
Symbol	VCB$L_BLOCKID or RVT$L_BLOCKID
Modes of acquisition	CR, PW, EX
Scope	UIC-independent
Access mode	Kernel
Parent	None
Value block	None
Blocking AST	Yes
Context	System-owned and process-owned

The Volume Blocking lock enables exclusive access to a volume by utilities such as the Analyze/Disk Structure utility. Its lock ID is stored in VCB$L_BLOCKID or RVT$L_BLOCKID as appropriate.

The Volume Blocking lock is normally held by all nodes in CR mode. To lock the volume, a utility requests an EX mode process-owned lock on the resource. This causes a blocking AST to be delivered to each VMScluster node holding a Volume Blocking lock, including the node on which the utility is executing. The lock manager dispatches to the blocking AST procedure at IPL$_SCS while holding the SCS spinlock.

The blocking AST procedure clears VCB$L_BLOCKID. The field VCB$L_ACTIVITY reflects the state of the Volume Blocking lock. The field is initialized to 1, and the volume remains usable as long as the field is odd. Normal file system activity on the volume increments the VCB$L_ACTIVITY count by 2 and decrements it by 2 on completion. The blocking AST procedure decrements VCB$L_ACTIVITY by 1, making its value even, and thus blocks further file system requests for the volume. If this decrement of VCB$L_AC-TIVITY brings its value to zero, the routine requests a kernel mode AST to dequeue the Volume Blocking lock from the context of the swapper process. Otherwise, as each outstanding file system request completes, it decrements VCB$L_ACTIVITY by 2. When VCB$L_ACTIVITY eventually falls to zero, the completing file system request dequeues the CR mode lock. This allows the EX mode lock to be granted so that the operation requiring exclusive access can proceed.

After the EX mode lock is released, the next file system request reacquires the Volume Blocking lock before accessing the volume.

H.5.3   **File Access Arbitration Lock**

Resource name string	"F11B$a" + volume lock name + FCB$L_ LOCKBASIS

Symbol	FCB$L_ACCLKID
Modes of acquisition	All
Scope	UIC-independent
Access mode	Kernel
Parent	None
Value block	Yes
Blocking AST	Yes
Context	System-owned

The file system provides access arbitration for files; that is, users can open files for read or write operations and specify whether other users may open the file concurrently. The Access Arbitration lock extends the scope of file arbitration to be clusterwide. Its resource name string uniquely identifies a particular file by including the volume lock name from VCB$T_VOLCK-NAM or RVT$T_VLSLCKNAM, and the file's ID number and relative volume number from the file control block (FCB) field FCB$L_LOCKBASIS. Each VMScluster node on which at least one process has that file open holds one system-owned Access Arbitration lock. Each lock represents the state of all accesses to the file from a given node. Thus, a VMScluster node acquires the lock in the most restrictive mode in which any of its local processes have opened the file.

The Access Arbitration lock's blocking AST synchronizes access to its associated FCB, which contains information from the file header, such as protection and size. Each VMScluster node accessing the file has an FCB and an Access Arbitration lock for the file. When a node alters an FCB in its memory, it also requests an EX mode Access Arbitration lock. This causes execution of the blocking AST procedure on every node accessing the file, causing each to mark its FCB as stale. Each node rebuilds its FCB on the next local access.

H.5.4   File Serialization Lock

Resource name string	"F11B$s" + FCB$L_LOCKBASIS
Symbol	None
Modes of acquisition	NL, PW
Scope	UIC-independent
Access mode	Kernel
Parent	VCB$L_VOLLKID or RVT$L_STRUCLKID
Value block	Yes
Blocking AST	None
Context	System-owned when NL, process-owned when PW

A File Serialization lock synchronizes access to a file on a particular volume. The file's ID number and relative volume number from FCB$L_LOCKBASIS make up the resource name string; its parent is a Volume Allocation lock. The file system, running in local process context, requests a File Serialization lock in PW mode for the duration of a single file operation, such as create, extend, or truncate. A process must hold the lock before accessing a file header or associated data in a file system cache. The lock value block contains two sequence numbers, one for the file header and one for associated data.

Upon completion of the file operation, the file system converts the lock to a NL mode system-owned lock, rewrites the sequence numbers into the value block, and records them in a cache descriptor. The system-owned lock is maintained until the cache entry is removed from cache or reused as described in the following paragraph.

If a process on this VMScluster node requests a subsequent access to the file, the file system acquires the File Serialization lock in PW mode and obtains the sequence numbers in its value block. It compares the sequence numbers to the stored values in the cache descriptor. If the values match, the cached information is still accurate. Otherwise, another VMScluster node acquired a PW mode lock while this node held a NL mode lock, and performed a file operation that updated a sequence number. The information in the local cache is no longer accurate and must be reread.

H.5.5 Cache Locks

Cache locks synchronize access to the per-volume caches that exist on each VMScluster node for each mounted volume: the file ID cache, extent cache, and disk quota cache. This section describes the general mechanism used to cause each VMScluster node in turn to flush a particular cache's contents to disk. Sections H.5.5.1, H.5.5.2, and H.5.5.3 describe the individual locks. The file system flushes all per-volume caches when a volume is dismounted. It flushes an individual cache when the cache becomes full, when a privileged user attempts to access the associated cache disk file directly, when one VMScluster node's cache is empty, and on similar occasions.

Each cache type has a defined cache flush resource name. Each VMScluster node that mounts a volume acquires a lock on each of the three cache flush resources for the volume. These locks are normally system-owned and held in PR mode.

To flush cache entries back to disk, a VMScluster node writes its own cache back under the protection of a PW mode Volume Allocation lock. It then marks the particular cache invalid, lowers the system-owned PR mode Cache lock to NL mode, and lowers the Volume Allocation lock back to CR mode, rewriting the value block. The node then requests an additional process-owned CW mode lock on the cache flush resource.

This causes blocking AST delivery to all other VMScluster nodes holding

PR mode Cache locks. Since these are system-owned locks, the lock manager dispatches to the blocking AST routine at IPL$_SCS while holding the SCS spinlock. The AST parameter identifies which volume and cache to flush. Each blocking AST routine uses an AST control block (ACB) built into the cache data structure to deliver an AST to the CACHE_SERVER process. The CACHE_SERVER process requests the Queue I/O ($QIO) system service with the function code IO$_ACPCONTROL and a parameter identifying the device and cache.

The file system, running in the context of the CACHE_SERVER process, requests a PW mode Volume Allocation lock on the appropriate volume. Only one VMScluster node's request for this lock is granted; the other nodes wait. The node that successfully acquires the Volume Allocation lock flushes its cache, marks the cache invalid, and lowers its PR mode Cache lock to NL mode. Next it converts the Volume Allocation lock back to CR mode, rewriting the value block. One waiting Volume Allocation lock request from another node is granted, and that node flushes its cache. This sequence is repeated until each node in turn has flushed its cache.

While the cache flush is in progress, the cache is marked invalid. If the file system accesses it and finds it invalid, the file system requests conversion of the NL mode Cache lock back to PR mode.

When the last VMScluster node completes and converts its PR mode Cache lock to NL mode, the original CW mode request is granted and immediately dequeued, and the cache flush is complete.

H.5.5.1   File ID Cache Lock

Resource name string	"F11B$c" + lock basis of INDEXF.SYS
Symbol	VCA$L_FIDCLKID
Modes of acquisition	NL, CW, PR
Scope	UIC-independent
Access mode	Kernel
Parent	VCB$L_VOLLKID or RVT$L_STRUCLKID
Value block	Yes
Blocking AST	Yes
Context	System-owned

Each VMScluster node maintains its own cache of available file headers for each mounted volume. This cache is filled primarily by file deletion on the local node. Any file identification numbers (FIDs) held in the cache are still marked "in-use" in the disk file number bitmap. A cache flush requires each VMScluster node to write all entries in its local cache back to the file number bitmap on disk. The File ID Cache lock arbitrates this cache flush across the VMScluster system, as described in Section H.5.5.

H.5.5.2   Extent Cache Lock

Resource name string	"F11B$c" + lock basis of BITMAP.SYS
Symbol	VCA$L_EXTCLKID
Modes of acquisition	NL, CW, PR
Scope	UIC-independent
Access mode	Kernel
Parent	VCB$L_VOLLKID or RVT$L_STRUCLKID
Value block	Yes
Blocking AST	Yes
Context	System-owned

Each VMScluster node maintains its own cache of available disk space for each mounted volume. Any disk blocks held in this cache are still marked "in-use" in the disk storage allocation bitmap. A cache flush requires each VMScluster node to write all entries in its local cache back to the storage allocation bitmap on disk. The Extent Cache lock arbitrates this cache flush across the VMScluster system, as described in Section H.5.5.

H.5.5.3   Disk Quota Cache Lock

Resource name string	"F11B$c" + lock basis of QUOTA.SYS
Symbol	VCA$L_QUOCLKID
Modes of acquisition	NL, CW, PR
Scope	UIC-independent
Access mode	Kernel
Parent	VCB$L_VOLLKID or RVT$L_STRUCLKID
Value block	Yes
Blocking AST	Yes
Context	System-owned

If disk quotas are enabled for a volume, a disk quota cache and Disk Quota Cache lock are created when the volume is mounted.

Each VMScluster node maintains its own cache of quota entries. It must sometimes flush all valid entries back to disk, for example, before dismounting the device. The Disk Quota Cache lock arbitrates this cache flush across the VMScluster system, as described in Section H.5.5.

H.5.5.4   Quota Cache Entry Lock

Resource name string	"F11B$q" + VCB$T_VOLCKNAM or RVT$T_VLSLCKNAM + quota record UIC
Symbol	VCA$L_QUOLKID
Modes of acquisition	CR, PW, EX

Scope	UIC-independent
Access mode	Kernel
Parent	None
Value block	Yes
Blocking AST	Yes
Context	System-owned

To acquire a user's quota information, a VMScluster node enqueues a PW mode system-owned Quota Cache Entry lock. On the first access to a specific quota cache entry, the user's quota information is read from disk into a cache block. The dynamic portion of the user's quota information is shared among VMScluster nodes through the value blocks of the Quota Cache Entry locks for that user.

When another VMScluster node needs the same user's quota information, it requests its own PW mode system-owned Quota Cache Entry lock. This request causes a blocking AST to be delivered to the original lock owner. The blocking AST procedure, running in the swapper's process context, marks the local cache entry invalid. It converts the PW mode lock to CR mode, updating the value block with the shared quota information. The other node's PW mode lock request is granted, and it receives this quota information from the value block.

An EX mode lock on a quota cache entry causes VMScluster nodes to remove the entry from the quota cache. This is used when a quota record is deleted.

H.6   RMS LOCK USE

RMS uses lock management system services to protect files and records. When a file is accessed in a shareable fashion with write access allowed, RMS uses locks to coordinate the actions of the file sharers. The locks that it requests depend on a file's organization, the presence of global buffers, and numerous file-sharing and record-locking options specified by the user application. This section describes some of the more common RMS locks, sometimes in a simplified manner. It does not include locks used for RMS journaling.

RMS runs in a process's context and maintains private data structures in process space. It requires a file access block (FAB) for each initial access (open) of a file and a record access block (RAB) for each stream connected to a FAB. It creates internal copies of FABs and RABs called IFABs and IRABs (in data structures named IFB$ and IRB$) as well as many internal structures mentioned briefly in this appendix.

A process can optionally open a file multiple times (with multiple FABs). The term *accessor*, as used in this appendix, indicates an entity in process context that has opened the file; for example, a file opened twice by process A and once by process B would have three accessors. Additionally, each accessor can optionally connect multiple record streams to the file (multiple RABs to each FAB). RMS therefore must synchronize file access among accessors and record streams from the same process through a variety of mechanisms. The focus of this appendix, however, is primarily on the synchronization that RMS provides among independent processes sharing a file on a local system or in a VMScluster.

RMS transfers a bucket of data on a process's behalf from a file into a buffer in memory. An RMS local buffer is mapped in process space and is available to only one process. A global buffer is mapped in system space within an OpenVMS global section and can be shared by any process on the system. Global buffers, however, cannot be shared by processes on different VMScluster nodes.

RMS performs some functions that affect the internal file structure, such as altering the end-of-file marker; some functions that affect internal bucket or buffer structure or contents; and some functions that affect only record contents. It uses locks of different scope to protect these different functions. RMS enforces a strict hierarchy in the acquisition of locks to ensure that deadlocks do not occur. Thus, for locks other than Record locks, RMS can safely specify the LCK$V_NODLCKWT and LCK$V_NODLCKBLK flags in its $ENQ system service requests. Chapter 11 gives more information on these flags.

A user application has no direct control over most RMS locks. However, it can directly control record locking. Therefore, RMS does not use these $ENQ flags when requesting Record locks.

With the exception of Record locks, RMS holds locks in restrictive lock modes only for the duration of an RMS service request. To operate more efficiently and to preserve lock value block information, especially the sequence number, RMS typically converts a lock to NL mode rather than releasing it altogether.

H.6.1   File Lock

Resource name string	"RMS$" + file ID + device name
Symbol	SFSBL_LOCK_ID, IFBL_PAR_LOCK_ID
Modes of acquisition	NL, PW
Scope	UIC-independent
Access mode	Executive
Parent	None
Value block	Yes
Blocking AST	Yes
Context	Process-owned

A File lock's resource name identifies one specific file. Locks on that resource serialize access to the file – clusterwide, interprocess, and intraprocess. When an accessor opens a file, it tells RMS how it wishes to access the file and the type of access that it will allow to other accessors. RMS creates a File lock for a file opened in a shareable fashion where the opener either specifies write access for itself or allows write access from others.

The File lock provides a consistent view of the file through the information in its value block, which includes the current end-of-file marker and the length of the longest record. RMS always uses the File lock as the parent lock of a file's Record locks (see Section H.6.4). It stores the lock ID of the File lock in IFB$L_PAR_LOCK_ID when global buffers are not present, so the File lock sometimes serves as the parent lock of Bucket locks as well (see Section H.6.2).

RMS builds the File lock resource name string from the six-byte file identifier plus the device identifier returned in the $GETDVI system service argument DVI$_DEVLOCKNAM. The device identifier is normally the mount type code followed by the volume name from VCB$T_VOLCKNAM or RVT$T_VLSLCKNAM. The mount type code is 1 for a privately mounted device or 2 for a device mounted in a shareable fashion.

When an accessor uses RMS to open a shareable, writable file, RMS acquires a File lock in PW mode and declares an RMS procedure as the associated blocking AST procedure. The accessor retains the lock in PW mode until another accessor requires an RMS file-level service on the same file and requests the File lock in PW mode.

The lock request causes the blocking AST to be delivered to the accessor holding the PW mode lock. The blocking AST procedure converts the PW mode File lock to NL mode. This allows RMS to acquire the lock in PW mode for the new accessor, again declaring an RMS procedure as the associated blocking AST procedure.

Therefore, only one accessor of the file holds the File lock in PW mode. Every other accessor either holds a NL mode File lock, is waiting for a new PW mode lock, or is waiting for its NL mode lock to be converted to PW mode.

When a file accessor requests the File lock in PW mode and cannot obtain it immediately, it stalls. When an accessor closes a file, RMS dequeues its File lock.

RMS creates a shared file synchronization block (SFSB) in process space for each accessor using a File lock. The SFSB describes the accessor's File lock: its resource name, lock ID, lock value block contents, and other items. An SFSB also contains three status bits identifying the lock state:

Bit Field Name	*Meaning if Set*
SFSB$V_TAKEN	File lock is held in PW mode
SFSB$V_INUSE	File lock is currently in use by a record stream
SFSB$V_WANTED	File lock is wanted by another accessor

RMS uses these status bits to support file sharing by multiple record streams associated with one accessor (when multistreaming is selected) as well as among multiple accessors.

For example, when RMS acquires the File lock in PW mode for a record stream, it sets the SFSB$V_TAKEN and SFSB$V_INUSE bits in the process's SFSB. When the record stream finishes the operation requiring the File lock, RMS clears the SFSB$V_INUSE bit. The accessor still holds the File lock in PW mode.

If a record stream from a different accessor now requires the PW mode lock, RMS requests the $ENQ system service and stalls the stream awaiting $ENQ completion.

The accessor holding the PW mode lock must lower the lock to NL mode before the stalled stream can proceed. It receives blocking AST notification that another accessor has requested the lock. The blocking AST procedure tests the SFSB$V_INUSE bit. If the File lock is not in use, it lowers the lock to NL mode and clears the SFSB$V_TAKEN bit.

Otherwise, the blocking AST procedure sets the SFSB$V_WANTED bit and exits. When the current operation completes, RMS will discover that the SFSB$V_WANTED bit is set, convert the File lock to NL mode, and clear the SFSB$V_TAKEN bit.

In either case, the lock is eventually converted to NL mode and the stalled stream's outstanding PW mode request is granted. RMS now sets the SFSB$V_TAKEN and SFSB$V_INUSE bits in this accessor's SFSB.

When the RMS multistreaming option is selected, there may be more than one record stream for a given file access (an accessor may have multiple RABs for one FAB). If a record stream needs a File lock that is already held by another record stream sharing its FAB, the requesting stream stalls by inserting its context on a wait queue without requesting the $ENQ system service. When the other record stream finishes with the File lock, it checks this wait queue and resumes the stalled stream through the Declare AST ($DCLAST) system service. There is no need to convert the File lock unless a record stream from a different FAB requests it.

H.6.2   Bucket Lock

Resource name string	Bucket virtual block number
Symbol	BLB$L_LOCK_ID
Modes of acquisition	NL, PW, EX
Scope	UIC-independent
Access mode	Executive
Parent	IFB$L_PAR_LOCK_ID
Value block	Yes
Blocking AST	Sometimes
Context	System-owned, process-owned

RMS Bucket locks ensure the integrity of buckets held in local or global buffers. The resource name string of the Bucket lock identifies the first virtual block number of the bucket data within the file. Because RMS must acquire an EX mode process-owned Bucket lock for an accessor before it can read or write the bucket, it can maintain a consistent picture of the bucket contents clusterwide.

RMS reads a bucket into either an I/O buffer in a process's address space or an RMS global I/O buffer in an OpenVMS global section in system space. It protects buckets in both locations through Bucket locks. One difference between Bucket locks for buckets in local and in global buffers is the parent lock. The IFB$L_PAR_LOCK_ID cell identifies the Bucket lock's parent: the File lock for a local buffer, or the Global Buffer Master lock (see Section H.6.3.1) if global buffers are being used.

RMS I/O buffers are a limited commodity; both local and global buffers are used and reused under the control of an RMS cache replacement algorithm. RMS maintains information about local buffer entries that are in use through buffer descriptor blocks (BDBs) and buffer lock blocks (BLBs). Before a process fills a local buffer from a bucket, it obtains a BDB and, if RMS locking is being performed, a BLB. It then acquires an EX mode, process-owned Bucket lock.

RMS stores information regarding the Bucket lock in the BLB, including the lock ID, an identifier for the record stream that owns the lock, the lock status block, the lock value block, the lock resource name, and the associated BDB address. The BDB contains, among other items, the actual address of the buffer and a saved clusterwide sequence number for the bucket that currently resides in the buffer.

The Bucket lock value block contains a sequence number for the bucket. A process must own the Bucket lock in EX mode before modifying the bucket so that it can increment the sequence number in the lock. This invalidates any buffer containing an earlier version of the bucket. For example, an accessor might have a version (possibly an outdated version) of a bucket in a local buffer, with an associated NL mode Bucket lock, BLB, and BDB. To reaccess the bucket, RMS converts the NL mode Bucket lock to EX mode, rereading the value block. RMS compares the new sequence number from the lock value block with the buffer's saved sequence number, stored in the BDB. If the sequence numbers do not match, this buffer contains an outdated copy of the bucket and RMS rereads the bucket from disk. If the accessor subsequently modifies the bucket, it increments the sequence number. When it completes its bucket access, it converts the lock from EX to NL mode, rewriting the value block with the updated sequence number.

RMS maintains a NL mode Bucket lock on a bucket as long as that bucket is in a local or global buffer cache. This preserves the bucket's lock value block and thus its sequence number. One NL mode lock is required per copy of the bucket. Thus, each process that has a copy of a bucket in a local RMS

I/O buffer maintains its own NL mode Bucket lock until it reuses that local buffer for a different bucket. For a bucket in a global buffer, however, one copy of the bucket in memory is shared by any interested process on the system. In this case, only one NL mode lock is required per VMScluster node to preserve the bucket's sequence number.

The first accessor of a bucket in a global buffer converts its Bucket lock to a NL mode system-owned Global Buffer Backing lock (see Section H.6.3.3) when it completes its operation on the bucket. Subsequent accessors merely dequeue their Bucket locks.

An exception to this local conversion to NL mode is the case of a deferred write of modified buckets. For a deferred write, RMS converts the lock to a PW mode lock with an associated blocking AST. When another accessor of the file wants to use the modified bucket, its lock request triggers the execution of the blocking AST procedure, which writes the modified bucket. If no other accessor requests the modified bucket, RMS eventually writes the bucket and dequeues the Bucket lock when cache replacement dictates that the buffer should be reused for another bucket.

H.6.3 Locks Associated with Global Buffers

To minimize I/O operations, RMS can share buffers among multiple accessors of the same file. It maintains these global buffers in system space, within an OpenVMS global section. A file using global buffers has one such global section on each VMScluster node from which a process accesses the file. When the first process on a VMScluster node opens a file that uses global buffers, RMS creates the file's global section in that node's memory.

RMS constructs the name of the file's global section by appending the hexadecimal address of the file's FCB to the string RMS$. Any accessor subsequently opening the file in the same memory space shares the same FCB and thus constructs the same global section name and maps to the existing global section.

Each global buffer global section contains a global buffer header (GBH), a global buffer descriptor (GBD) for each global I/O buffer within the section, and the global buffers themselves. The actual data resides in buckets within the global buffers.

The GBH describes the global section and its locks. It contains the size of the global section, the access count, and the Global Buffer Master lock ID at offset GBH$L_LOCK_ID, among other information.

One GBD exists for each global buffer in the global section. A global buffer's GBD contains the lock ID of the buffer's Global Buffer Backing lock in the field GBD$L_LOCK_ID, the lock sequence number, the offset to the buffer within the global section, and similar information.

RMS maintains a section's GBDs in an interlocked queue ordered by the virtual block number (VBN) of the bucket currently residing in the GBD's associated buffer. The head of the GBD queue is in the GBH, at offset GBH$L_GBD_FLINK.

The Global Buffer Section (GBS) lock serializes access to the global buffer header and thus to the GBD queue and the global buffer pool (see Section H.6.3.2).

RMS deletes a file's global section when the last accessor of the file on a VMScluster node closes the file.

H.6.3.1   Global Buffer Master Lock

Resource name string	"RMS$" + file ID + device name
Symbol	GBHL_LOCK_ID, IFBL_PAR_LOCK_ID
Mode of acquisition	NL
Scope	UIC-independent
Access mode	Executive
Parent	None
Value block	None
Blocking AST	None
Context	System-owned

RMS creates a Global Buffer Master lock only for a file that uses global buffers. The Global Buffer Master lock is a system-owned NL mode version of the File lock (see Section H.6.1).

When an accessor requests shareable write access to a file, RMS creates a File lock. If the file uses global buffers, RMS converts that File lock to a system-owned NL mode Global Buffer Master lock on the connect of the first record stream. It copies the lock ID of the Global Buffer Master lock to IFB$L_PAR_LOCK_ID, overriding the accessor's File lock as parent of its Bucket locks. RMS then creates a new File lock.

The Global Buffer Master lock's sole purpose is to serve as the parent lock for an accessor's Bucket locks on global buffers. Since a global buffer survives the deletion of processes that use it, the Bucket lock on a global buffer must be backed up with a system-owned lock so that the value block, which maintains the integrity of the bucket, survives. Since a system-owned lock cannot be a sublock of a process-owned lock such as the File lock, a Bucket lock needs a system-owned version of the File lock to act as parent.

RMS dequeues the Global Buffer Master lock when it deletes the global section.

H.6.3.2   Global Buffer Section Lock

Resource name string	"RMS$" + file ID + device name
Symbol	GBSB$L_LOCK_ID

Modes of acquisition	NL, EX
Scope	UIC-independent
Access mode	Executive
Parent	EXE$GL_SYSID_LOCK
Value block	Yes
Blocking AST	Yes
Context	Process-owned

The Global Buffer Section (GBS) lock synchronizes access to a file's global buffer header, the global buffer descriptor queue in the GBH, and thus the global buffer pool. Each VMScluster node accessing the file has a separate global buffer global section for the file. Therefore, a lock guaranteed to be mastered on the local VMScluster node is a more efficient way to serialize global section access, so RMS creates the GBS lock as a sublock of EXE$GL_SYSID_LOCK.

The GBS lock resource name string matches that of the file's corresponding File lock, thus uniquely identifying a device and file in a VMScluster system (see Section H.6.1).

When an accessor connects a record stream to a file that uses global buffers, RMS requests an EX mode GBS lock. The GBS lock remains in EX mode until another accessor sharing the file on the same VMScluster node requests a GBS lock in EX mode, to search the GBD list, for example.

The request triggers blocking AST notification, and the lock holder converts the initial GBS lock to NL mode, allowing the requestor to acquire its own lock.

Before the original lock holder accesses the global section again, it requests the conversion of its NL mode lock back to EX mode.

Therefore, the accessor that most recently examined the global buffer header or searched the global buffer descriptor queue holds the only granted EX mode lock. Every other accessor sharing the globally buffered file on this VMScluster node holds a NL mode lock or is waiting for a new or converted EX mode lock.

When an accessor closes the file, RMS dequeues its GBS lock.

RMS creates a global buffer synchronization block (GBSB) in the P1 space of each accessor holding a NL mode or EX mode GBS lock. The GBSB is similar to the SFSB for the File lock. It maintains information about the lock and the associated global section, including the lock ID at GBSB$L_LOCK_ID. The GBSB also contains the lock value block, the resource name copied from the SFSB, and three status bits:

Bit Field Name	Meaning if Set
GBSB$V_TAKEN	GBS lock is held in EX mode
GBSB$V_INUSE	GBS lock is in use by a record stream
GBSB$V_WANTED	GBS lock is wanted by another accessor

These status bits describe the state of the GBS lock and are treated like the corresponding status bits in the SFSB (see Section H.6.1).

H.6.3.3   Global Buffer Backing Lock

Resource name string	Bucket virtual block number
Symbol	GBD$L_LOCK_ID
Mode of acquisition	NL
Scope	UIC-independent
Access mode	Executive
Parent	IFB$L_PAR_LOCK_ID
Value block	Yes
Blocking AST	None
Context	System-owned

The Global Buffer Backing lock ensures the integrity of buckets contained in global buffers. To guard the integrity of a bucket, its sequence number must be preserved in the lock value block of a Bucket lock. However, a global buffer can contain a bucket that no longer has any current accessors and therefore would have no Bucket locks. Therefore, a system-owned lock must be used to prevent the loss of the bucket's sequence number.

Before reading a bucket from a file into a buffer, an accessor acquires a process-owned Bucket lock. For each global buffer within the global section, the original accessor that stores a bucket in a global buffer converts its process-owned Bucket lock to a NL mode system-owned Global Buffer Backing lock when it completes its access to the bucket. It saves the lock ID in the buffer's GBD at the offset GBD$L_LOCK_ID.

A subsequent accessor of the bucket in this global buffer acquires its own Bucket lock. When it completes its access, it can safely dequeue its Bucket lock, since a Global Buffer Backing lock already exists for the bucket.

RMS also stores the sequence number of a bucket in a global buffer in the buffer's associated GBD. RMS copies the sequence number from the Bucket lock value block of the first accessor of the bucket and updates it for each subsequent accessor. When each accessor obtains its Bucket lock, RMS compares the sequence number in the Bucket lock value block with the saved sequence number in the GBD. If they do not match, RMS rereads the bucket from disk into the global buffer.

RMS dequeues the Global Buffer Backing lock when cache replacement policy dictates that the global buffer should be reused for another bucket or when the global section is deleted.

Since the Global Buffer Backing lock must be system-owned, and system-owned locks cannot be sublocks of process-owned locks, the Global Buffer Master lock was instituted (see Section H.6.3.1).

H.6.4   Record Lock

Resource name string	Record file address
Symbol	RLB$L_LOCK_ID
Modes of acquisition	CR, PR, PW, EX
Scope	UIC-independent
Access mode	Executive
Parent	SFSB$L_LOCK_ID
Value block	None
Blocking AST	None
Context	Process-owned

A Record lock coordinates access to a record in a bucket. It is always process-owned and always a sublock of the File lock. RMS builds the Record lock resource name string from the three-word record file address (RFA), which locates the record within the file. The resource name string consists of RFA4, the last of the three words, followed by two bytes of zeros, followed by RFA0, the first word (see the *OpenVMS Record Management Services Reference Manual*).

If a file is opened in a shareable manner with record locking enabled, the following locking options in the user-specified RAB at field RAB$L_ROP determine the RMS lock mode:

Bit Field State	Lock Mode
RAB$V_REA clear and RAB$V_RLK clear	EX
RAB$V_RLK set	PW
RAB$V_REA set and RAB$V_RLK clear	PR
RAB$V_NLK set	CR

- ► EX mode is the default.
- ► PW mode locks the record for write access, allowing readers at CR mode but no other writers.
- ► PR mode locks the record for read access, allowing other readers at CR or PR mode but no writers.
- ► The RAB$V_NLK option temporarily takes a CR mode lock to verify that the record is not locked against reading (in EX mode). These CR mode locks are never returned to the application.

A record stream associates each of its Record locks with a record lock block (RLB). An RLB contains the resource name, an identifier for the owning stream, and the lock status block, including the lock ID. RLBs are linked to the stream's IRAB at the IRBL_RLB_FLINK/IRBL_RLB_BLINK queue.

Application record deadlocks are possible because of the control that an application has over its record locking, especially when it selects the manual unlocking (RAB$V_ULK) option.

H.7   IMAGE ACTIVATOR AND INSTALL UTILITY LOCK USE

H.7.1   KFE Lock

Resource name string	"INSTALL$KNOWN FILE"
Symbol	EXE$GQ_KFE_LCKNAM
Modes of acquisition	PR, EX
Scope	UIC-independent
Access mode	Executive
Parent	EXE$GL_SYSID_LOCK
Value block	None
Blocking AST	None
Context	Process-owned

Section H.7.2 describes the use of the KFE lock.

H.7.2   Install Lock

Resource name string	"INSTALL$INSLOCK"
Symbol	None
Mode of acquisition	EX
Scope	UIC-independent
Access mode	Executive
Parent	EXE$GL_SYSID_LOCK
Value block	None
Blocking AST	None
Context	Process-owned

The Install utility manages the known file entry (KFE) list and requires read and write access to it. The image activator system service requires protected read access to the KFE list before opening images. The Install utility and the image activator coordinate access to the KFE list through the KFE lock and use the Install lock to provide priority access to image activation.

Each VMScluster node maintains a private KFE list. KFE locks are requested as sublocks of the lock ID stored in EXE$GL_SYSID_LOCK to guarantee that they will be unique to the local node and mastered there. The resource is declared to be systemwide because the activation of images and use of the Install utility is not restricted to a single UIC group. Multiple processes running from different UIC groups are synchronized.

All code paths in the image activator and the Install utility that read the KFE list acquire PR mode locks on the KFE resource. In addition, the Install utility ensures that readers of the KFE list (particularly the image activator) are not blocked too long by multiple writers of the KFE (for example, several INSTALL ADD commands). Code paths that write the KFE must acquire the

Install lock in PW mode before acquiring the KFE lock in EX mode. Since only one writer at a time can acquire the Install lock, other writers queue for the Install lock rather than for the KFE lock.

When a writing process completes, it first converts the EX mode lock on the KFE to a PR mode lock. The only possible waiting requests are PR mode requests, and these are granted. The writer next dequeues the Install lock, allowing another writer to acquire it. This new writer requests an EX mode lock on the KFE. The request is granted when the readers complete and release their PR mode locks.

The combination of these two locks guarantees that writers cannot block readers for extended time periods.

H.8 DECNET LOCK USE

In VMScluster configurations, NETACP, the network ancillary control process, uses two categories of locks: locks to implement VMScluster alias functions and locks to implement network proxy access functions.

H.8.1 VMScluster Alias Locks

H.8.1.1 Master Registration Lock

Resource name string	"CLU$NETACP_" + alias node address
Symbol	None
Modes of acquisition	NL, CR, PW, EX
Scope	UIC-specific
Access mode	Kernel
Parent	None
Value block	Yes
Blocking AST	Yes
Context	Owned by NETACP process

The NETACP process on each VMScluster node that participates in the Alias Node service enqueues a lock on a resource whose name contains the alias node address. This lock is called the Master Registration lock (MRL) and is normally held at CR mode. The MRL is used as the parent lock for all other VMScluster alias locks.

The value block in the MRL contains a quadword bit mask, with a bit set for each VMScluster node participating in the VMScluster alias. A new node enqueues the MRL in PW mode, uses the value block to determine the first free alias index number from this bit mask, allocates that index number for its own use, updates the value block, and stores its alias index at NET$GW_CLUSTER_INDEX. The MRL is then converted to a NL mode lock, updating the value block. The new participant next converts the lock to EX mode. This forces delivery of blocking ASTs to the current members, notifying them of the new VMScluster alias member.

H.8.1.2   Individual Index Lock

Resource name string	"IXL_" + alias index number
Symbol	None
Modes of acquisition	NL, EX
Scope	UIC-specific
Access mode	Kernel
Parent	Master Registration lock
Value block	Yes
Blocking AST	None
Context	Owned by NETACP process

Each participant in the VMScluster alias scheme requires an Individual Index lock (IXL). An IXL is a sublock of the MRL and has a resource name formed from the string IXL_ + alias index number. Its value block contains registration data for the participating member, such as DECnet node address, alias maximum links, and routing/nonrouting status. Each new member enqueues an EX mode lock on its own IXL resource name. The member updates the value block with information about itself by lowering the lock to NL mode. Other participating members cycle through a set of lock states to allow each member to read the updated value block.

H.8.1.3   Individual Departure Lock

Resource name string	"IDL_" + alias index number
Symbol	None
Modes of acquisition	CR, EX
Scope	UIC-specific
Access mode	Kernel
Parent	Master Registration lock
Value block	None
Blocking AST	None
Context	Owned by NETACP process

Each participating VMScluster member enqueues an EX mode lock on its own Individual Departure lock (IDL) resource. All other members request a CR mode lock on that resource, with deadlock search disabled. If a CR request is ever granted, the other member knows that the original member that held the EX mode lock is no longer participating.

H.8.1.4   **Individual Link Registration Lock**

Resource name string	"ILR_" + alias index number
Symbol	None
Modes of acquisition	NL, CR, EX, PW
Scope	UIC-specific
Access mode	Kernel
Parent	Master Registration lock
Value block	Yes
Blocking AST	Yes
Context	Owned by NETACP process

An Individual Link Registration (ILR) lock is a sublock of the MRL. Each alias member has an associated resource, whose name is the string ILR_ concatenated with the alias index number. A member always holds an ILR lock for itself in NL mode. In addition, a member that is a router holds a CR mode lock for itself and every other member. Each CR mode lock has an associated blocking AST.

An ILR lock is used for flow control between a participating alias node and one or more alias routers. When an alias member needs to communicate to each alias router that it can or cannot accept any more links, it converts its NL mode lock to PW mode. (Converting to PW mode instead of EX mode prevents premature triggering of the CR mode lock blocking AST on a router.) The PW mode lock is then converted to NL. As a result, the value block is updated with information about the current and maximum links for this member. Next, the NL mode lock is converted to EX mode to trigger the blocking AST on each router's CR mode lock for that member. Finally, the lock is converted back to NL mode.

When the blocking AST for the CR mode lock is triggered on each router, the CR mode lock is immediately converted to NL mode. Then each alias router requests an EX mode lock to read the value block. One of the routers will be granted the EX mode lock when all the routers have transitioned the lock from CR mode to NL mode. The router acquiring the EX mode lock then updates its tables based on the new value block, converts the lock to NL to allow another router to obtain the lock in EX mode, and finally converts the lock back to CR mode.

H.8.2   **Network Proxy Access Locks**

The NETACP process uses standard RMS locks to synchronize access to the proxy file, NETPROXY.DAT. In addition, it uses the following locks to propagate the volatile proxy database changes to other VMScluster nodes.

H.8.2.1   Modified Proxy Lock

Resource name string	"NET$NETPROXY_MODIFIED"
Symbol	None
Modes of acquisition	PR, PW
Scope	UIC-independent
Access mode	Kernel
Parent	None
Value block	None
Blocking AST	Yes
Context	Owned by NETACP process

This is the main proxy lock, typically granted to all VMScluster nodes in PR mode with an associated blocking AST. If proxy information is modified on a participating node, the Authorize utility or the network management listener (NML) requests that NETACP obtain a new lock on this resource in PW mode. This triggers blocking AST delivery to the NETACP process on all VMScluster nodes, including the one that queues the PW lock, as notice of proxy modification.

H.8.2.2   Proxy Function Lock

Resource name string	"NET$NETPROXY_FNCT"
Symbol	None
Modes of acquisition	NL, EX
Scope	UIC-independent
Access mode	Kernel
Parent	None
Value block	Yes
Blocking AST	None
Context	Owned by NETACP process

The Proxy Function lock is used to transmit the function to be performed on the NETPROXY.DAT file, for example, Rebuild_Proxy, Add_Proxy, and Delete_Proxy. The function code is transmitted in the value block. Holding this lock in EX mode also serializes NETACP's use of the Proxy Key locks.

H.8.2.3   Proxy Key Locks

Resource name string	"NET$NETPROXY_KEY" + key number
Symbol	None
Modes of acquisition	NL, EX

Scope	UIC-independent
Access mode	Kernel
Parent	None
Value block	Yes
Blocking AST	None
Context	Owned by NETACP process

NETACP uses these locks to determine whether a record with a specified key exists in the NETPROXY.DAT database used by the local node. The value blocks of these four key locks pass the RMS key values desired for the NETPROXY.DAT indexed file.

The four key numbers allow a total of 64 bytes of key information:

- NET$NETPROXY_KEY1 : first 16 bytes of the key
- NET$NETPROXY_KEY2 : second 16 bytes of the key
- NET$NETPROXY_KEY3 : third 16 bytes of the key
- NET$NETPROXY_KEY4 : fourth 16 bytes of the key

H.9   JOB CONTROLLER AND QUEUE MANAGER LOCK USE

In OpenVMS AXP Version 1.5, queue manager functions were separated from job controller functions. A new process called the queue manager performs the queue management functions previously performed by the job controller.

The job controller processes running on multiple VMScluster nodes and the queue manager process use a variety of locks to synchronize their activities. Many of these locks coordinate access to the queue file and the master file. Since the queue file and master file are accessed through RMS, standard RMS locking activity occurs as well (see Section H.6). This, however, is transparent to the job controller.

H.9.1   Job Controller Upgrade Lock

Resource name string	"JBC$UPGRADE"
Symbol	None
Modes of acquisition	PR, EX
Scope	UIC-independent
Access mode	User
Parent	None
Value block	None
Blocking AST	Yes
Context	Owned by job controller process

The Job Controller Upgrade lock is used to force the transition from the old-style job controller (the OpenVMS AXP Version 1.0 job controller) to the new-style job controller.

Each old-style job controller process requests the Job Controller Upgrade lock in PR mode during startup. When a new-style job controller is started up during the upgrade process, the new job controller requests the lock in EX mode, triggering blocking ASTs on all other nodes. The blocking ASTs force the creation of new-style job controllers and the termination of old-style job controllers.

H.9.2   New Master File Lock

Resource name string	"QMAN$NEW_MASTER"
Symbol	None
Modes of acquisition	PR, EX
Scope	UIC-independent
Access mode	User
Parent	None
Value block	None
Blocking AST	Yes
Context	Owned by job controller process

The New Master File lock is used to signal job controllers on other nodes of a VMScluster system that a new queue manager master file, QMAN$MAS-TER.DAT, has been created. A new master file is created in response to the DCL command START /QUEUE /MANAGER /NEW.

During startup each job controller in a VMScluster system requests a PR mode lock on the New Master File resource. To signal job controllers on other nodes of a VMScluster system that it has created a new master file, the job controller that created the new file requests the same lock in EX mode, triggering blocking ASTs on all other nodes. Upon receiving the blocking AST, each job controller opens the new master file. The signaling job controller dequeues the lock and requests it in PR mode, so that the blocking AST mechanism is rearmed.

H.9.3   Master File Access Lock

Resource name string	"QMAN$MSR_" + device name + file ID
Symbol	None
Modes of acquisition	NL, PR, PW
Scope	UIC-independent
Access mode	User
Parent	None
Value block	None

Blocking AST	None
Context	Requested by job controller and queue manager processes

The Master File Access lock synchronizes access to the queue manager master file. The queue manager process and all job controller processes in a VMS-cluster system request this lock in NL mode when they are started. Before reading the master file, the queue manager or job controller process requests a lock conversion to PR mode. Similarly, before writing to the master file, the queue manager or job controller process requests a lock conversion to PW mode.

This lock serves as the parent lock to many other job controller and queue manager locks.

H.9.4   **Master File Check Lock**

Resource name string	"JBC$_CHECK_DB"
Symbol	None
Modes of acquisition	PR, EX
Scope	UIC-independent
Access mode	User
Parent	Master File Access lock
Value block	None
Blocking AST	Yes
Context	Requested by job controller and queue manager processes

This lock is used to request job controllers to check the queue manager master file when a change is made to it. Each job controller process normally holds a PR mode lock on the Master File Check resource.

When a job controller makes a change to the master file, it requests the lock in EX mode, triggering blocking ASTs on all other job controllers. The blocking AST causes each job controller to examine the master file records and take appropriate actions if necessary. Possible actions include starting the queue manager, stopping the queue manager, or notifying waiting processes of the queue manager's termination.

After recording its startup status in the master file, the queue manager requests the lock in EX mode to force all job controllers to check the master file.

H.9.5   **New Job Controller Lock**

Resource name string	"QMAN$NEW_JOBCTL"
Symbol	None

Modes of acquisition	PR, EX
Scope	UIC-independent
Access mode	User
Parent	Master File Access lock
Value block	None
Blocking AST	Yes
Context	Owned by job controller process

The New Job Controller lock helps the queue manager establish a link with each job controller in a VMScluster system. During its startup the queue manager requests a PR mode lock on this resource. When a node is added to the VMScluster, its job controller reads the master file's queue manager information, creates a queue manager data block for the node, and requests an EX mode lock on the New Job Controller resource. This triggers a blocking AST on the queue manager, which establishes a communication link with the new node. Any process on the new node can then communicate with the queue manager using this communication link.

H.9.6   **Queue Manager Alive Lock**

Resource name string	"QMAN$JBC_ALIVE_" + queue manager ID
Symbol	None
Modes of acquisition	CR, PR, EX
Scope	UIC-independent
Access mode	User
Parent	Master File Access lock
Value block	None
Blocking AST	Yes
Context	Owned by job controller process

During startup, a job controller process requests a PR mode lock on the Queue Manager Alive resource using the LCK$V_NOQUEUE flag. If the request is not granted, the queue manager process has already been started (by another job controller in the VMScluster system); the job controller continues with other processing.

If the PR mode request is granted, the queue manager has not been started. Running on a VMScluster system, the job controller determines whether its node is the best candidate to run the queue manager process. If so, the job controller converts the PR mode lock to an EX mode lock and starts up the queue manager process. Otherwise, the job controller arms a timer, which upon expiration triggers it to attempt startup of the queue manager process anyway.

During its startup the queue manager process queues a request for the Queue Manager Alive lock in CR mode. Since the job controller already holds the lock in EX mode, the request will be queued. If the CR mode request is ever satisfied, the queue manager process will exit. The queue manager's CR mode lock is granted only when the job controller releases the EX mode lock, which happens only when the job controller decides to terminate the queue manager or the job controller itself terminates.

H.9.7   Queue Definition and Journal Files Lock

Resource name string	"QMAN$OWNER_" + queue manager ID
Symbol	None
Mode of acquisition	EX
Scope	UIC-independent
Access mode	User
Parent	Master File Access lock
Value block	None
Blocking AST	None
Context	Owned by queue manager process

When the queue manager starts, it requests an EX mode lock on the Queue Definition and Journal Files resource. If the request is denied, indicating that another queue manager process has already started, the second queue manager process exits. Only one queue manager can exist on a VMScluster system running OpenVMS AXP Version 1.5.

H.9.8   Queue ORB Lock

Resource name string	"ORB$JBC_" + queue ID
Symbol	None
Mode of acquisition	PW
Scope	UIC-independent
Access mode	User
Parent	None
Value block	None
Blocking AST	None
Context	Owned by process changing access control on the queue

When the access control list on a queue is being modified, for example, with the DCL command EDIT/ACL, a PW mode lock on the Queue ORB resource is requested on behalf of the process modifying the list. This lock ensures that the queue manager or any other process does not modify the ORB for a queue while the queue's access control list is being changed by another process.

H.10 SYSMAN LOCK USE

H.10.1 Driver-Loading and Autoconfiguration Lock

Resource name string	CSID + "IOGEN$LOCK"
Symbol	None
Mode of acquisition	EX
Scope	UIC-independent
Access mode	User
Parent	None
Value block	None
Blocking AST	None
Context	Owned by driver-loading process

The SYSMAN IO commands LOAD, RELOAD, AUTOCONFIGURE, and CONNECT require exclusive access to a system's SYSMAN I/O database. SYSMAN protects its database from concurrent access by SYSMAN executing in multiple processes simultaneously through an EX mode lock on the Driver-Loading and Autoconfiguration resource.

H.10.2 SMISERVER Main Lock

Resource name string	"SMISERVER$" + SCSNODE
Symbol	None
Mode of acquisition	EX
Scope	UIC-independent
Access mode	Executive
Parent	None
Value block	None
Blocking AST	None
Context	Owned by SMISERVER process

The SMISERVER process uses the Main lock to ensure that only one SMISERVER process at a time exists on a system. It requests an EX mode lock on the resource using the LCK$V_NOQUEUE flag. If the request is not granted immediately, another SMISERVER process is already running; the current one is redundant and deletes itself.

When SMISERVER performs a clusterwide Set Time ($SETIME) system service, it synchronizes using the Set Time lock (see Section H.2.2).

H.10.3   **Parameter Lock**

Resource name string	"SYSPARMS_LOCK"
Symbol	None
Modes of acquisition	NL, PR, EX
Scope	UIC-independent
Access mode	Executive
Parent	EXE$GL_SYSID_LOCK
Value block	Yes
Blocking AST	None
Context	Process-owned

SYSMAN uses the Parameter lock to synchronize access to the current and active SYSGEN parameters on a system. It obtains the Parameter lock in PR mode before reading the current or active SYSGEN parameters. When the read completes, it converts the lock to NL mode. SYSMAN enqueues the Parameter lock in EX mode before writing the current or active SYSGEN parameters. When the write completes, it again converts the lock to NL mode. The Parameter lock is dequeued when this SYSMAN session completes.

Selected Acronyms

These acronyms are selected from those that appear in this book. This list is not exhaustive; for instance, acronyms for facilities, programs, and instructions are not included.

Acronym	Meaning
ACB	AST control block
ACL	access control list
ACP	ancillary control process
ADP	adapter control block
AI	argument information (register)
AIB	ACP I/O buffer
APLD	activated privileged library dispatch vector entry
AQB	ACP queue block
ARB	access rights block
ARG	bootstrap argument list
ASCII	American Standard Code for Information Interchange
ASN	address space number
AST	asynchronous system trap
ASTEN	AST enable (register)
ASTSR	AST summary register
BDTAB	boot driver table structure
BOD	buffer object descriptor
BOOPAR	boot parameter argument list
BOOTCB	boot control block
BRK	breakthrough message descriptor block
BUSARRAY	adapter bus array
CCB	channel control block
CD-ROM	compact disk read-only memory
CDDB	class driver data block
CDRP	class driver request packet
CEB	common event block
CEF	common event flag wait (scheduling state)
CFCB	cache file control block
CI	computer interconnect

Acronym	*Meaning*
CLI	command language interpreter
CMDTABLE	adapter command table
COLPG	collided page wait (scheduling state)
COM	computable (scheduling state)
COMO	computable outswapped (scheduling state)
CPU	central processing unit
CPUTAB	CPU table structure
CRAB	counted resource allocation block
CRAM	controller register access mailbox
CRB	controller request block
CRCTX	counted resource context block
CRD	corrected read data
CSB	cluster system block
CSID	cluster system ID
CSR	control/status register
CUR	currently executing (scheduling state)
CWPS	clusterwide process service
DAT	data alignment trap
DATFX	data alignment trap fixup (register)
DCL	Digital command language
DDB	device data block
DDIF	Digital Document Interchange Format
DDT	driver dispatch table
DMA	direct memory access
DPT	driver prologue table
DSSI	Digital Storage Systems Interconnect
DTB	data stream translation buffer
ECC	error correction code
EIHD	OpenVMS AXP image header
EIHI	image ident area
EISD	image section descriptor
EPID	extended process ID
ER	executive read (protection)
ERKW	executive read, kernel write (protection)
ESP	executive mode stack pointer (register)

Acronym	*Meaning*
ESR	exception service routine
EW	executive write (protection)
FAB	file access block
FCB	file control block
FDDI	Fiber Distributed Data Interconnect
FDT	function decision table
FEN	floating-point enable (register)
FIFO	first-in/first-out
FKB	fork block
FP	frame pointer (register)
FPCR	floating-point control register
FPG	free page wait (scheduling state)
GB	gigabyte
GPT	global page table
GPTE	global page table entry
GPTX	global page table index
GQC	Get Queue Information system service context block
GSD	global section descriptor
GST	global section table
GSTE	global section table entry
GSTX	global section table index
HIB	hibernate wait (scheduling state)
HIBO	hibernate wait outswapped (scheduling state)
HWPCB	hardware privileged context block
HWRPB	hardware restart parameter block
HWRPB_CRB	console routine block
HWRPB_CTB	console terminal block
HWRPB_PMD	physical memory descriptor
HWRPB_PMR	physical memory region descriptor
I/O	input/output
ID	identification
IDB	interrupt dispatch block
IHD	OpenVMS VAX image header

Acronym	Meaning
IMCB	image control block
IOSB	I/O status block
IOVEC	boot device I/O vector
IPID	internal process ID
IPIR	interprocessor interrupt request (register)
IPL	interrupt priority level
IRP	I/O request packet
IRPE	IRP extension
ISR	interrupt service routine
ITB	instruction stream translation buffer
JIB	job information block
KB	kilobyte
KFD	known file directory
KFE	known file entry
KFERES	known file entry resident section descriptor
KFPB	known file pointer block
KFRH	known file resident image header
KPB	kernel process block
KR	kernel read (protection)
KRP	kernel request packet
KSP	kernel mode stack pointer (register)
KW	kernel write (protection)
L1PT	level 1 page table
L1PTE	level 1 page table entry
L2PT	level 2 page table
L2PTE	level 2 page table entry
L3PT	level 3 page table
L3PTE	level 3 page table entry
LAT	local area transport
LBN	logical block number
LDRHP	loader huge page descriptor
LDRIMG	loader image data block
LEF	local event flag wait (scheduling state)
LEFO	local event flag wait outswapped (scheduling state)

Acronym	Meaning
LIFO	last-in/first-out
LKB	lock block
LKSB	lock status block
LMB	logical memory block
LNMB	logical name block
LNMC	logical name table name cache block
LNMHSH	logical name hash table
LNMTH	logical name table header
LNMX	logical name translation block
MB	megabyte
MBPR	mailbox pointer register
MCES	machine check error summary (register)
MSCP	Mass Storage Control Protocol
MWAIT	miscellaneous wait (scheduling state)
NA	no access (protection)
NI	network interconnect
ODS-2	On-Disk Structure Level 2
ORB	object rights block
P0PT	P0 page table
P0PTE	P0 page table entry
P1PT	P1 page table
P1PTE	P1 page table entry
PA	physical address
PALcode	privileged architecture library code
PC	program counter (register)
PCB	process control block
PCBB	privileged context block base (register)
PCC	process cycle counter
PDT	port descriptor table
PFL	page file control block
PFLMAP	page/swap file mapping window block
PFN	page frame number
PFW	page fault wait (scheduling state)

Acronym	Meaning
PHD	process header
PID	process ID
PLV	privileged library vector
PME	performance monitoring enable (register)
PMI	processor-memory interconnect
POSIX	Portable Operating System Interface
PQB	process quota block
PRBR	processor base register
PS	processor status (register)
PSCANCTX	$PROCESS_SCAN context block
PSECT	program section
PST	process section table
PSTE	process section table entry
PSTX	process section table index
PSXFR	resource wait—POSIX fork creation (scheduling state)
PTBR	page table base register
PTE	page table entry
PV	procedure value (register)
RA	return address (register)
RAB	record access block
RAM	random access memory
RCB	routing control block
RISC	reduced instruction set computer
RMS	Record Management Services
RSB	resource block
RWAST	resource wait—AST (scheduling state)
RWCAP	resource wait—CPU capability (scheduling state)
RWCLU	resource wait—VMScluster transition (scheduling state)
RWCSV	resource wait—VMScluster server (scheduling state)
RWMBX	resource wait—mailbox full (scheduling state)
RWMPB	resource wait—modified page writer busy (scheduling state)
RWMPE	resource wait—modified page list empty (scheduling state)
RWNPG	resource wait—nonpaged dynamic memory (scheduling state)
RWPAG	resource wait—paged dynamic memory (scheduling state)
RWPFF	resource wait—page file full (scheduling state)

Acronym	Meaning
RWSCS	resource wait—distributed lock manager (scheduling state)
SB	system block
SCB	system control block
SCBB	system control block base (register)
SCC	system cycle counter
SCS	system communication services
SCSI	Small Computer System Interconnect
SHL	shareable image list entry
SI	storage interconnect
SIRR	software interrupt request register
SISR	software interrupt summary register
SLOT	per-CPU slot
SMP	symmetric multiprocessing
SP	stack pointer (register)
SPL	spinlock control block
SPT	system page table
SPTE	system page table entry
SR	supervisor read (protection)
SREW	supervisor read, executive write (protection)
SRKW	supervisor read, kernel write (protection)
SSP	supervisor mode stack pointer (register)
SUSP	suspend wait (scheduling state)
SUSPO	suspend wait outswapped (scheduling state)
SW	supervisor write (protection)
SWRPB	software restart parameter block
SYSAP	system application
TAST	terminal AST block
TB	terabyte, translation buffer
TBCHK	translation buffer check (register)
TMSCP	tape MSCP
TQE	timer queue entry
UAF	user authorization file
UCB	unit control block

Acronym	Meaning
UIC	user identification code
UR	user read (protection)
UREW	user read, executive write (protection)
URKW	user read, kernel write (protection)
URSW	user read, supervisor write (protection)
USP	user mode stack pointer (register)
UW	user write (protection)
VA	virtual address
VBN	virtual block number
VCB	volume control block
VEC	interrupt transfer vector
VLE	vector list extension
VMS	virtual memory system
VPN	virtual page number
VPTB	virtual page table base (register)
WCB	window control block
WHAMI	who am I (register)
WSLE	working set list entry
WSLX	working set list index
XMI	Extended Memory Interconnect
XQP	Extended QIO Processor

Trademarks

Windows NT is a trademark of Microsoft Corporation. Motif is a registered trademark of the Open Software Foundation, Inc. UNIX is a registered trademark of UNIX System Laboratories, Inc. Futurebus+ and Portable Operating System Interface (POSIX) are IEEE Standards. Alpha AXP, AXP, CI, DDIF, DEC, DECdtm, DECmigrate, DECnet, DECthreads, DECwindows, Digital, MSCP, OpenVMS, PALcode, PATHworks for VMS, TMSCP, TURBOchannel, VAX, VAX/VMS, VAXcluster, VMS, VMS RMS and VMScluster are trademarks of the Digital Equipment Corporation. TeX is a trademark of the American Mathematical Society.

Index

Index

Index

Index